Football Outsiders Almanac 2015

THE ESSENTIAL GUIDE TO THE 2015 NFL AND COLLEGE FOOTBALL SEASONS

Edited by Aaron Schatz

With Bill Connelly, Cian Fahey, Brian Fremeau, Tom Gower,

Andrew Healy, Scott Kacsmar, Rivers McCown, Chad Peltier,

Christopher Price, Mike Tanier, Robert Weintraub, Vincent Verhei, and Sterling Xie

Copyright 2015 Football Outsiders, Inc.

ISBN-10: 1515363082

ISBN-13: 978-1515363088

D1335624

Table of Contents

Player Comments

College Football

Further Research

Introduction

The best plays have a sample size of one.

When you try to do statistical analysis of sports, you always have to worry about sample size. Are there really enough games here that these numbers are meaningful? Are there really enough plays, enough shots or at bats or pass attempts?

When Bill James first popularized statistical analysis of baseball, broadcasters tended to completely misunderstand the whole concept. They just thought the point was to introduce as many numbers as possible, leading to your local radio guy pointing out that Eddie Smith was hitting .354 in Thursday afternoon games. Of which the entire season contained, oh, let's say eight.

We run into this problem with our football analysis too. We often have to ask ourselves whether we've found a split that really means something, or just some funky numbers that are interesting but not really predictive. Sometimes, we tell our readers about an interesting split and try to really underline that the stat in question isn't tremendously prophetic, but just neat to know about. Sometimes we're not even sure which it is.

Do you know which plays are not very predictive? Plays with a sample size of one.

But the entire 2014 NFL season came down to an incredible play with a sample size of one. The two best teams of the 2014 season made it to the final game, Super Bowl XLIX. Before the game, it looked like the closest matchup in Super Bowl history. The game itself, broken down to the play-by-play, was essentially a tie. New England and Seattle pretty much played each other to a standoff. It all came down to one play. The probability that play would work out in New England's favor was very low. It did anyway.

And that wasn't even the only time that Seattle's season came down to a single play. Two weeks before, the Seahawks lined up for an onside kick with 2:13 left, down by five points. In must-have situations like this, the odds say a team will recover the onside kick less than 20 percent of the time. The Seahawks recovered. Win probability models showed that even after they recovered the kick, the Seahawks had a less than 20 percent probability of winning the game. They won anyway.

The best plays have a sample size of one. If you are a Patriots fan, like a couple of the authors of this book, the best play of 2014-2015 was the Immaculate Interception. If you are a Seahawks fan, like one of the other authors of this book, the best play of 2014-2015 was the Chris Matthews onside kick recovery. If you are a fan of one of the other teams, the best play of 2014-2015 was some other play that was exciting and exhilarating and not necessarily predicted by statistical analysis.

Are you all picturing the Odell Beckham catch against Dallas in your minds right now?

I write all this to once again remind readers of our book that at Football Outsiders, we don't love numbers. We love football. There's a lot more to our analysis than numbers, and you're going to find a lot of scouting knowledge in this book as well. There's a rumor that stat analysts don't watch game tape. In reality, stat analysts watch more tape than most beat writers or national Internet columnists, and *a lot* more tape than the average fan. We take everything we learn off the tape, synthesize it with the statistics, and deliver it to you. Occasionally, there are also jokes.

At its heart, the football analytics revolution is about learning more about the intricacies of the game instead of just accepting the boilerplate storylines produced by color commentators, lazy beat reporters, and crotchety old players from the past. It's about not accepting the idea that some guy "just wins." It's about understanding that the "skill players" aren't the only guys on the team with skills. It's about gaining insight into the complexity behind the modern offense, and that you don't just shove the ball into the line hoping to gain yardage. It's about understanding the dramatic way that strength of schedule affects the way we see a team's performance, especially at the college level. It's about figuring out which player skills translate from college to the pros, and which skills just produce meaningless scoutspeak. And it's about accepting that the pass dominates the run in the National Football League, and that it's been that way for 30 years.

Everybody who writes about football uses both statistics (whether they be basic yardage totals or more advanced stats like ours) and scouting (whether scouting reports by professionals or just their own eyes). The same goes for us, except that the statistics portion of our analysis is far more accurate than what you normally see from football coverage. Those numbers are based on two ideas:

1) **Conventional football statistics are heavily dependent on context.** If you want to see which teams are good and which are bad, which strategies work and which do not, you first need to filter out that context. Down and distance, field position, the current score, time left on the clock, the quality of the opponent—all of these elements influence the objective of the play and/or its outcome. Yet, the official NFL stats add together all yardage gained by a specific team or player without considering the impact of that particular yardage on wins and losses.

A close football game can turn on a single bounce of the ball. In a season of only 16 games, those effects can have a huge impact on a team's win-loss record, thus obscuring the team's true talent level. If we can filter out these bits of luck and random chance, we can figure out which teams are really more likely to play better for the rest of the season, or even in the following season.

2) **On any one play, the majority of the important action is not tracked by the conventional NFL play-by-play.** That's why we started the Football Outsiders game charting project in 2005. A cadre of football-obsessed volunteers watches every single game and adds new detail to our record of each play. We know how many pass rushers teams send on each pass, how often teams go three-wide or use two tight

ends, how often teams use a play-fake or a zone blitz, and which defensive backs are in coverage, even when they don't get a tackle in the standard play-by-play.

There's also a third important precept that governs the work we do at Football Outsiders, although it's more about how to interpret numbers and not the numbers themselves. **A player's production in one year does not necessarily equal his production the next year.** This also applies to teams, of course. Even when stats are accurate, they're often extremely variable from year to year and subject to heavy forces of regression to the mean. Field-goal percentage, red-zone performance, third-down performance on defense, interceptions and fumble recoveries—these are but a few examples. In addition, the age curves for football players are much steeper than in other sports. Old players break down faster, and young players often improve faster. A number of football analysts concentrate on looking at what players did last year. We'll talk about that as well, but we're more interested in what players are going to do *this* year. Which performances from a year ago are flukes, and which ones represent long-term improvement or decline? What will one more year of experience do to this player's production? And how will a player's role change this year, and what does it mean for the team?

As with past books, *Football Outsiders Almanac 2015* starts off with "Pregame Show" (reviewing the most important research we've done in past books) and "Statistical Toolbox" (explaining all our stats). Once again, we preserve the ridiculousness of the football season for posterity with another version of "The Year in Quotes" and we introduce you to some of the more promising (and lesser-known) young bench players with our seventh annual list of Top 25 Prospects chosen in the third round or later.

Each NFL team gets a full chapter covering what happened in 2014 and our projections for the upcoming season. Are there reasons to believe that the team was actually better or worse than its record last year? What did the team do in the offseason, and what does that mean for the team's chances to win in 2015? Each chapter also includes all kinds of advanced statistics covering 2014 performance and strategic tendencies, plus detailed commentary on each of the major units of the team: offensive line, defensive front seven, defensive secondary, special teams, and coaching staff.

"Skill players" (by which we mean "players who get counted in fantasy football") get their own section in the back of the book. We list the major players at each position alphabetically, along with commentary and a 2015 KUBIAK projection that will help you win your fantasy football league. We also have the most accurate projections anywhere for two fantasy football positions that people wrongly consider impossible to predict: kickers and team defense.

Next comes our preview of the college football season. This year, we've done something different. Instead of spending time on the teams at the bottom of the big conferences, we're going deeper with the top 50 teams in the nation. Just like with our NFL coverage, the goal of our college previews is to focus as much as possible on "why" and how," not just "which team is better." We're not just here to rank the Football Bowl Subdivision teams from 1 to 128. We break things down to offense and defense, pass and run, and clutch situations compared to all plays.

We hope our book helps you raise your level of football expertise, win arguments with your friends, and win your fantasy football league—even if this year it is helping you do those things a couple weeks later than usual.

Aaron Schatz
Framingham, MA
August 1, 2015

Pregame Show

It has now been a dozen years since we launched Football Outsiders. In that time, we've done a lot of primary research on the National Football League, and we reference that research in many of the articles and comments in *Football Outsiders Almanac 2015*. New readers may come across an offhand comment in a team chapter about, for example, the idea that fumble recovery is not a skill, and wonder what in the heck we are talking about. We can't repeat all our research in every new edition of *Football Outsiders Almanac*, so we start each year with a basic look at some of the most important precepts that have emerged from Football Outsiders research. You will see these issues come up again and again throughout the book.

You can also find this introduction online at http://www.footballoutsiders.com/info/FO-basics, along with links to the original research in the cases in which that research appeared online instead of (or as well as) in print.

Our various methods for projecting NFL success for college prospects are not listed below, but are referenced at times during the book. Those methods are detailed in an essay on page 478.

You run when you win, not win when you run.

If we could only share one piece of anti-conventional wisdom with you before you read the rest of our book, this would be it. The first article ever written for Football Outsiders was devoted to debunking the myth of "establishing the run." There is no correlation whatsoever between giving your running backs a lot of carries early in the game and winning the game. Just running the ball is not going to help a team score; it has to run successfully.

There are two reasons why nearly every beat writer and television analyst still repeats the tired old school mantra that "establishing the run" is the secret to winning football games. The first problem is confusing cause and effect. There are exceptions, but for the most part, winning teams have a lot of carries because their running backs are running out the clock at the end of wins, not because they are running wild early in games.

The second problem is history. Most of the current crop of NFL analysts came of age or actually played the game during the 1970s. They believe that the run-heavy game of that decade is how football is meant to be, and today's pass-first game is an aberration. As we addressed in an essay in *Pro Football Prospectus 2006* on the history of NFL stats, it was actually the game of the 1970s that was the aberration. The seventies were far more slanted towards the run than any era since the arrival of Paul Brown, Otto Graham, and the Cleveland Browns in 1946. Optimal strategies from 1974 are not optimal strategies for 2012.

A sister statement to "you have to establish the run" is "team X is 5-1 when running back John Doe runs for at least 100 yards." Unless John Doe is possessed by otherworldly spirits the way Adrian Peterson was a couple years ago, the team isn't winning because of his 100-yard games. He's putting up 100-yard games because his team is winning.

A great defense against the run is nothing without a good pass defense.

This is a corollary to the absurdity of "establish the run." With rare exceptions, teams win or lose with the passing game more than the running game—and by stopping the passing game more than the running game. Ron Jaworski puts it best: "The pass gives you the lead, and the run solidifies it." The reason why teams need a strong run defense in the playoffs is not to shut the run down early; it's to keep the other team from icing the clock if they get a lead. You can't mount a comeback if you can't stop the run.

Note that "good pass defense" may mean "good pass rush" rather than "good defensive backs."

Running on third-and-short is more likely to convert than passing on third-and-short.

On average, passing will always gain more yardage than running, with one very important exception: when a team is just one or two yards away from a new set of downs or the goal line. On third-and-1, a run will convert for a new set of downs 36 percent more often than a pass. Expand that to all third or fourth downs with 1-2 yards to go, and the run is successful 40 percent more often. With these percentages, the possibility of a long gain with a pass is not worth the tradeoff of an incomplete that kills a drive.

This is one reason why teams have to be able to both run and pass. The offense also has to keep some semblance of balance so they can use their play-action fakes, and so the defense doesn't just run their nickel and dime packages all game. Balance also means that teams do need to pass occasionally in short-yardage situations; they just need to do it less than they do now. Teams pass roughly 60 percent of the time on third-and-2 even though runs in that situation convert 20 percent more often than passes. They pass 68 percent of the time on fourth-and-2 even though runs in that situation convert twice as often as passes.

Standard team rankings based on total yardage are inherently flawed.

Check out the schedule page on NFL.com, and you will find that each game is listed with league rankings based on total yardage. That is still how the NFL "officially" ranks teams, but these rankings rarely match up with common sense. That is because total team yardage may be the most context-dependent number in football.

It starts with the basic concept that rate stats are generally more valuable than cumulative stats. Yards per carry says more about a running back's quality than total yardage, completion percentage says more than just a quarterback's total number of completions. The same thing is true for teams; in fact, it is even more important because of the way football strategy influences the number of runs and passes in the game plan. Poor teams will give up fewer passing yards and more rushing yards because opponents will stop passing once they have a late-game lead and will run out the clock instead. For winning teams, the opposite is true. For example, which team had a better pass defense last year: San Diego or Denver? The answer is obviously Denver, yet according to the official NFL rankings, San Diego (3,427 net yards allowed on 550 pass attempts, 6.2 net yards per pass) was a better pass defense than Denver (3,607 net yards allowed on 682 pass attempts, 5.3 net yards per pass).

Total yardage rankings are also skewed because some teams play at a faster pace than other teams. For example, in 2013 Buffalo (5,410) had roughly the same number of yards as Pittsburgh (5,400). However, the Steelers were the superior offense and much more efficient; they gained those yards on only 183 drives while the Bills needed 207 drives.

A team will score more when playing a bad defense, and will give up more points when playing a good offense.

This sounds absurdly basic, but when people consider team and player stats without looking at strength of schedule, they are ignoring this. In 2004, Carson Palmer and Byron Leftwich had very similar numbers, but Palmer faced a much tougher schedule than Leftwich did. Palmer was better that year, and better in the long run. A similar comparison can be made between Russell Wilson and Robert Griffin III in their rookie years: Wilson had a higher DVOA rating because he faced a more difficult schedule, even though Griffin had slightly better standard stats.

If their overall yards per carry are equal, a running back who consistently gains yardage on every play is more valuable than a boom-and-bust running back who is frequently stuffed at the line but occasionally breaks a long highlight-worthy run.

Our brethren at Baseball Prospectus believe that the most precious commodity in baseball is outs. Teams only get 27 of them per game, and you can't afford to give one up for very little return. So imagine if there was a new rule in baseball that gave a team a way to earn another three outs in the middle of the inning. That would be pretty useful, right?

That's the way football works. You may start a drive 80 yards away from scoring, but as long as you can earn 10 yards in four chances, you get another four chances. Long gains have plenty of value, but if those long gains are mixed with a lot of short gains, you are going to put the quarterback in a lot of difficult third-and-long situations. That means more punts and more giving the ball back to the other team rather than moving the chains and giving the offense four more plays to work with.

The running back who gains consistent yardage is also going to do a lot more for you late in the game, when the goal of running the ball is not just to gain yardage but to eat clock time. If you are a Colts fan watching your team with a late lead, you don't want to see three straight Trent Richardson stuffs at the line followed by a punt. You want to see a game-icing first down.

A common historical misconception is that our preference for consistent running backs means that "Football Outsiders believes that Barry Sanders was overrated." Sanders wasn't just any boom-and-bust running back, though; he was the greatest boom-and-bust runner of all time, with bigger booms and fewer busts. Sanders ranked in the top five in DYAR five times (third in 1989, first in 1990, and second in 1994, 1996, and 1997).

Rushing is more dependent on the offensive line than people realize, but pass protection is more dependent on the quarterback himself than people realize.

Some readers complain that this idea contradicts the previous one. Aren't those consistent running backs just the product of good offensive lines? The truth is somewhere in between. There are certainly good running backs who suffer because their offensive lines cannot create consistent holes, but most boom-and-bust running backs contribute to their own problems by hesitating behind the line whenever the hole is unclear, looking for the home run instead of charging forward for the four-yard gain that keeps the offense moving.

As for pass protection, some quarterbacks have better instincts for the rush than others, and are thus better at getting out of trouble by moving around in the pocket or throwing the ball away. Others will hesitate, hold onto the ball too long, and lose yardage over and over.

Note that "moving around in the pocket" does not necessarily mean "scrambling." In fact, a scrambling quarterback will often take more sacks than a pocket quarterback, because while he's running around trying to make something happen, a defensive lineman will catch up with him.

Shotgun formations are generally more efficient than formations with the quarterback under center.

Over the past five seasons, offenses have averaged roughly 5.9 yards per play from Shotgun (or Pistol), but just 5.1 yards per play with the quarterback under center. This wide split exists even if you analyze the data to try to weed out biases like teams using Shotgun more often on third-and-long, or against prevent defenses in the fourth quarter. Shotgun offense is more efficient if you only look at the first half, on every down, and even if you only look at running back carries rather than passes and scrambles.

It's hard to think of a Football Outsiders axiom that has been better assimilated by the people running NFL teams since we started doing this a decade ago. In 2001, NFL teams only used Shotgun on 14 percent of plays. Five years later, in 2006, that had increased slightly, to 20 percent of plays. By 2012, Shotgun was used on a 47.5 percent of plays (including the Pistol, but not counting the Wildcat or other direct snaps to non-quarterbacks). Last year, the league as a whole was up to an average of 60.9 percent of plays from Shotgun or Pistol. Remember, before 2007, no team had ever used Shotgun on more than half its offensive plays. Now, the league *averages* over 60 percent. At some point, defenses will adapt and the benefit of the formation will become less pronounced, but it doesn't look like it is happening yet. Success on Shotgun plays dropped slightly last year, but so did success on non-Shotgun plays.

A running back with 370 or more carries during the regular season will usually suffer either a major injury or a loss of effectiveness the following year, unless he is named Eric Dickerson.

Terrell Davis, Jamal Anderson, and Edgerrin James all blew out their knees. Larry Johnson broke his foot. Earl Campbell and Eddie George went from legendary powerhouses to plodding, replacement-level players. Shaun Alexander broke his foot *and* became a plodding, replacement-level player. This is what happens when a running back is overworked to the point of having at least 370 carries during the regular season.

The "Curse of 370" was expanded in our book *Pro Football Prospectus 2005*, and now includes seasons with 390 or more carries in the regular season and postseason combined. Research also shows that receptions don't cause a problem, only workload on the ground.

Plenty of running backs get injured without hitting 370 carries in a season, but there is a clear difference. On average, running backs with 300 to 369 carries and no postseason appearance will see their total rushing yardage decline by 15 percent the following year and their yards per carry decline by two percent. The average running back with 370 or more regular-season carries, or 390 including the postseason, will see their rushing yardage decline by 35 percent, and their yards per carry decline by eight percent. However, the Curse of 370 is not a hard and fast line where running backs suddenly become injury risks. It is more of a concept where 370 carries is roughly the point at which additional carries start to become more and more of a problem.

Wide receivers must be judged on both complete and incomplete passes.

Last year, for example, Miles Austin had 568 receiving yards for Cleveland while Cecil Shorts had 557 receiving yards for Jacksonville. Both played for teams with poor quarterback situations, and both ran their average route roughly 8.3 yards downfield. But there was a big difference between them: Austin caught 65 percent of intended passes, while Shorts caught 48 percent.

Some work has been done on splitting responsibility for incomplete passes between quarterbacks and receivers, but not enough that we can incorporate this into our advanced stats at this time. We know that wide receiver catch rates are almost as consistent from year to year as quarterback completion percentages, but it is also important to look at catch rate in the context of the types of routes each receiver runs. Four years ago, we expanded on this idea with a new plus-minus metric, which is explained in the introduction to the chapter on wide receivers and tight ends.

The total quality of an NFL team is four parts offense, three parts defense, and one part special teams.

There are three units on a football team, but they are not of equal importance. For a long time, the saying from Football Outsiders was that the total quality of an NFL team is three parts offense, three parts defense, and one part special teams.

Further recent research suggests that offense is even more important than we originally believed. Recent work by Chase Stuart, Neil Paine, and Brian Burke suggests a split between offense and defense of roughly 58-42, without considering special teams. Our research suggests that special teams contributes about 13 percent to total performance; if you measure the remaining 87 percent with a 58-42 ratio, you get roughly 4:3:1. When we compare the range of offense, defense, and special teams DVOA ratings, we get the same results, with the best and worst offenses roughly 130 percent stronger than the best and worst defenses, and roughly four times stronger than the best and worst special teams.

Offense is more consistent from year to year than defense, and offensive performance is easier to project than defensive performance. Special teams is less consistent than either.

Nobody in the NFL understood this concept better than former Indianapolis Colts general manager Bill Polian. Both the Super Bowl champion Colts and the four-time AFC champion Buffalo Bills of the early 1990s were built around the idea that if you put together an offense that can dominate the league year after year, eventually you will luck into a year where good health and a few smart decisions will give you a defense good enough to win a championship. (As the Colts learned in 2006, you don't even need a year, just four weeks.) Even the New England Patriots, who are led by a defense-first head coach in Bill Belichick, have been more consistent on offense than on defense since they began their run of success in 2001.

Field goal percentage is almost entirely random from season to season, while kickoff distance is one of the most consistent statistics in football.

This theory, which originally appeared in the *New York Times* in October 2006, is one of our most controversial, but it is hard to argue against the evidence. Measuring every kicker from 1999 to 2006 who had at least ten field goal attempts in each of two consecutive years, the year-to-year correlation coefficient for field goal percentage was an insignificant .05. Mike Vanderjagt didn't miss a single field goal in 2003, but his percentage was a below-average 74 percent the year before and 80 percent the year after. Adam Vinatieri has long been considered the best kicker in the game. But even he had never enjoyed two straight seasons with accuracy better than the NFL average of 85 percent until 2010 and 2011.

On the other hand, the year-to-year correlation coefficient for kickoff distance, over the same period as our measurement of field-goal percentage and with the same minimum of ten kicks per year, is .61. The same players consistently lead the league in kickoff distance. In recent years, that group includes Steven Hauschka, Graham Gano, Stephen Gostkowski, Pat McAfee, and Thomas Morstead.

Teams with more offensive penalties generally lose more games, but there is no correlation between defensive penalties and losses.

Specific defensive penalties of course lose games; we've all sworn at the television when the cornerback on our favorite team gets flagged for a 50-yard pass interference penalty. Yet overall, there is no correlation between losses and the total of defensive penalties or even the total yardage on defensive penalties. One reason is that defensive penalties often represent *good* play, not bad. Cornerbacks who play tight coverage may be just on the edge of a penalty on most plays, only occasionally earning a flag. Defensive ends who get a good jump on rushing the passer will gladly trade an encroachment penalty or two for ten snaps where they get off the blocks a split-second before the linemen trying to block them.

In addition, offensive penalties have a higher correlation from year to year than defensive penalties. The penalty that correlates highest with losses is the false start, and the penalty that teams will have called most consistently from year to year is also the false start.

Recovery of a fumble, despite being the product of hard work, is almost entirely random.

Stripping the ball is a skill. Holding onto the ball is a skill. Pouncing on the ball as it is bouncing all over the place is not a skill. There is no correlation whatsoever between the percentage of fumbles recovered by a team in one year and the percentage they recover in the next year. The odds of recovery are based solely on the type of play involved, not the teams or any of their players.

Fans like to insist that specific coaches can teach their teams to recover more fumbles by swarming to the ball. Chicago's Lovie Smith, in particular, is supposed to have this ability. However, in Smith's first three seasons as head coach of the Bears, their rate of fumble recovery on defense went from a league-best 76 percent in 2004 to a league-worst 33 percent in 2005, then back to 67 percent in 2006.

Fumble recovery is equally erratic on offense. In 2013, the Dallas Cowboys fumbled 15 times on offense and recovered 9 of them. Last year, the Cowboys fumbled 17 times on offense and only recovered 5.

Fumble recovery is a major reason why the general public overestimates or underestimates certain teams. Fumbles are huge, turning-point plays that dramatically impact wins and losses in the past, while fumble recovery percentage says absolutely nothing about a team's chances of winning games in the future. With this in mind, Football Outsiders stats treat all fumbles as equal, penalizing them based on the likelihood of each type of fumble (run, pass, sack, etc.) being recovered by the defense.

Other plays that qualify as "non-predictive events" include two-point conversions, blocked kicks, and touchdowns during turnover returns. These plays are not "lucky," per se, but they have no value whatsoever for predicting future performance.

Field position is fluid.

As discussed in the Statistical Toolbox, every yard line on the field has a value based on how likely a team is to score from that location on the field as opposed to from a yard further back. The change in value from one yard to the next is the same whether the team has the ball or not. The goal of a defense is not just to prevent scoring, but to hold the opposition so that the offense can get the ball back in the best possible field position. A bad offense will score as many points as a good offense if it starts each drive five yards closer to the goal line.

A corollary to this precept: The most underrated aspect of an NFL team's performance is the field position gained or lost on kickoffs and punts. This is part of why players like Devin Hester and Cordarrelle Patterson can have such an impact on the game, even when they aren't taking a kickoff or punt all the way back for a touchdown.

The red zone is the most important place on the field to play well, but performance in the red zone from year to year is much less consistent than overall performance.

Although play in the red zone has a disproportionately high importance to the outcome of games relative to plays on the rest of the field, NFL teams do not exhibit a level of performance in the red zone that is consistently better or worse than their performance elsewhere, year after year. The simplest explanation why is a small(er) sample size and the inherent variance of football, with contributing factors like injuries and changes in personnel.

Defenses which are strong on first and second down, but weak on third down, will tend to improve the following year. Defenses which are weak on first and second down, but strong on third down, will tend to decline the following year. This trend also applied to offenses through 2005, but may or may not still apply today.

We discovered this when creating our first team projection system in 2004. It said that the lowly San Diego Chargers would have one of the best offenses in the league, which seemed a little ridiculous. But looking closer, our projection system treated the previous year's performance on different downs as different variables, and the 2003 Chargers were actually good on first and second down, but terrible on third.

Teams get fewer opportunities on third down, so third-down performance is more volatile—but it's also is a bigger part of a team's overall performance than first or second down, because the result is usually either very good (four more downs) or very bad (losing the ball to the other team with a punt). Over time, a team will play as well in those situations as it does in other situations, which will bring the overall offense or defense in line with the offense and defense on first and second down.

This trend is even stronger between seasons. Struggles on third down are a pretty obvious problem, and teams will generally target their off-season moves at improving their third-down performance ... which often leads to an improvement in third-down performance.

However, we have discovered something surprising over the past few years: The third-down rebound effect seems to have disappeared on offense, as we explained in the Philadelphia chapter of *Football Outsiders Almanac 2010*. We hope to do some additional research on this in the coming months to look at whether the third-down effect still exists, and how strong it is on offense and/or defense.

Injuries regress to the mean on the seasonal level, and teams that avoid injuries in a given season tend to win more games.

There are no doubt teams with streaks of good or bad health over multiple years. However, teams who were especially healthy or especially unhealthy, as measured by our adjusted games lost (AGL) metric, almost always head towards league average in the subsequent season. Furthermore, injury—or the absence thereof—has a huge correlation with wins, and a significant impact on a team's success. There's no doubt that a few high-profile teams have resisted this trend in recent years. The Patriots seem to overcome injuries every year, and a number of recent Super Bowl champions such as the 2010 Packers and 2011 Giants have overcome a number of injuries to win the championship. Nonetheless, the overall rule still applies. Last year, six of the seven teams with the lowest AGL won at least 10 games (the Jets were the exception).

In the past, we have written that teams with a high number of injuries are a good bet to improve the following season. However, work we did on this year's new team projection system suggests this may not actually be the case. AGL totals correlate strongly with how well a team plays in that year, but not necessarily with improvement or decline the following season. We will be writing about this issue more on our website in the coming months.

By and large, a team built on depth is better than a team built on stars and scrubs.

Connected to the previous statement, because teams need to go into the season expecting that they will suffer an average number of injuries no matter how healthy they were the previous year. You cannot concentrate your salaries on a handful of star players because there is no such thing as avoiding injuries in the NFL. The game is too fast and the players too strong to build a team based around the idea that "if we can avoid all injuries this year, we'll win."

Running backs usually decline after age 28, tight ends after age 29, wide receivers after age 30, and quarterbacks after age 32.

This research was originally done by Doug Drinen (editor of pro-football-reference.com) in 2000. In recent years, a few players have had huge seasons above these general age limits (most notably Tony Gonzalez), but the peak ages Drinen found a few years ago still apply to the majority of players.

As for "non-skill players," research we did in 2007 for *ESPN The Magazine* suggested that defensive ends and defensive backs generally begin to decline after age 29, linebackers and offensive linemen after age 30, and defensive tackles after age 31. However, because we still have so few statistics to use to study linemen and defensive players, this research should not be considered definitive.

The strongest indicator of how a college football team will perform in the upcoming season is their performance in recent seasons.

It may seem strange because graduation enforces constant player turnover, but college football teams are actually much more consistent from year to year than NFL teams. Thanks in large part to consistency in recruiting, teams can be expected to play within a reasonable range of their baseline program expectations each season. Our Program F/+ ratings, which represent a rolling five-year period of play-by-play and drive efficiency data, have an extremely strong (.76) correlation with the next year's F/+ rating.

Championship teams are generally defined by their ability to dominate inferior opponents, not their ability to win close games.

Football games are often decided by just one or two plays: a missed field goal, a bouncing fumble, the subjective spot of an official on fourth-and-1. One missed assignment by a cornerback or one slightly askew pass that bounces off a receiver's hands and into those of a defensive back five yards away and the game could be over. In a blowout, however, one lucky bounce isn't going to change things. Championship teams—in both professional and college football—typically beat their good opponents convincingly and destroy the cupcakes on the schedule.

Aaron Schatz

Statistical Toolbox

After a dozen years of Football Outsiders, some of our readers are as comfortable with DVOA and ALY as they are with touchdowns and tackles. Yet to most fans, including our newer readers, it still looks like a lot of alphabet soup. That's what this chapter is for. The next few pages define and explain all of all the unique NFL statistics you'll find in this book: how we calculate them, what the numbers mean, and what they tell us about why teams win or lose football games. We'll go through the information in each of the tables that appear in each team chapter, pointing out whether those stats come from advanced mathematical manipulation of the standard play-by-play or simple counting of what we see on television with the Football Outsiders game charting project. This chapter covers NFL statistics only. College metrics such as Adjusted POE and F/+ are explained in the introduction to the college football section on page 408.

We've done our best to present these numbers in a way that makes them easy to understand. This explanation is long, so feel free to read some of it, flip around the rest of the book, and then come back. It will still be here.

Defense-Adjusted Value Over Average (DVOA)

One running back runs for three yards. Another running back runs for three yards. Which is the better run?

This sounds like a stupid question, but it isn't. In fact, this question is at the heart of nearly all of the analysis in this book.

Several factors can differentiate one three-yard run from another. What is the down and distance? Is it third-and-2, or second-and-15? Where on the field is the ball? Does the player get only three yards because he hits the goal line and scores? Is the player's team up by two touchdowns in the fourth quarter and thus running out the clock, or down by two touchdowns and thus facing a defense that is playing purely against the pass? Is the running back playing against the porous defense of the Raiders, or the stalwart defense of the Bears?

Conventional NFL statistics value plays based solely on their net yardage. The NFL determines the best players by adding up all their yards no matter what situations they came in or how many plays it took to get them. Now, why would they do that? Football has one objective—to get to the end zone—and two ways to achieve that, by gaining yards and achieving first downs. These two goals need to be balanced to determine a player's value or a team's performance. All the yards in the world won't help a team win if they all come in six-yard chunks on third-and-10.

The popularity of fantasy football only exacerbates the problem. Fans have gotten used to judging players based on how much they help fantasy teams win and lose, not how much they help *real* teams win and lose. Typical fantasy scoring further skews things by counting the yard between the one and the goal line as 61 times more important than all the other yards on the field (each yard worth 0.1 points, a touchdown worth 6.0). Let's say Odell Beckham catches a pass on third-and-15 and goes 50 yards but gets tackled two yards from the goal line, and then Andre Williams takes the ball on first-and-goal from the two-yard line and plunges in for the score. Has Williams done something special? Not really. When an offense gets the ball on first-and-goal at the two-yard line, they are going to score a touchdown five out of six times. Williams is getting credit for the work done by the passing game.

Doing a better job of distributing credit for scoring points and winning games is the goal of **DVOA**, or Defense-adjusted Value Over Average. DVOA breaks down every single play of the NFL season, assigning each play a value based on both total yards and yards towards a first down, based on work done by Pete Palmer, Bob Carroll, and John Thorn in their seminal book, *The Hidden Game of Football*. On first down, a play is considered a success if it gains 45 percent of needed yards; on second down, a play needs to gain 60 percent of needed yards; on third or fourth down, only gaining a new first down is considered success.

We then expand upon that basic idea with a more complicated system of "success points," improved over the past four years with a lot of mathematics and a bit of trial and error. A successful play is worth one point, an unsuccessful play zero points, with fractional points in between (for example, eight yards on third-and-10 is worth 0.54 "success points"). Extra points are awarded for big plays, gradually increasing to three points for 10 yards (assuming those yards result in a first down), four points for 20 yards, and five points for 40 yards or more. Losing three or more yards is -1 point. Interceptions average -6 points, with an adjustment for the length of the pass and the location of the interception (since an interception tipped at the line is more likely to produce a long return than an interception on a 40-yard pass). A fumble is worth anywhere from -1.7 to -4.0 points depending on how often a fumble in that situation is lost to the defense—no matter who actually recovers the fumble. Red zone plays get a bonus: 20 percent for team offense, five percent for team defense, and 10 percent for individual players. There is a bonus given for a touchdown that acknowledges that the goal line is significantly more difficult to cross than the previous 99 yards (although this bonus is nowhere near as large as the one used in fantasy football).

(Our system is a bit more complex than the one in *Hidden Game* thanks to our subsequent research, which added larger penalty for turnovers, the fractional points, and a slightly higher baseline for success on first down. The reason why all fumbles are counted, no matter whether they are recovered by the offense or defense, is explained in the essay "Pregame Show.")

Every single play run in the NFL gets a "success value" based on this system, and then that number gets compared to the average success values of plays in similar situations for all players, adjusted for a number of variables. These include down and distance, field location, time remaining in game, and the team's lead or deficit in the game score. Teams are always compared to the overall offensive average, as the team made its own choice whether to pass or rush. When it comes to individual players, however, rushing plays are compared to other rushing plays, passing plays to other passing plays, tight ends to tight ends, wideouts to wideouts, and so on.

Going back to our example of the three-yard rush, if Player A gains three yards under a set of circumstances in which the average NFL running back gains only one yard, then Player A has a certain amount of value above others at his position. Likewise, if Player B gains three yards on a play on which, under similar circumstances, an average NFL back gains four yards, that Player B has negative value relative to others at his position. Once we make all our adjustments, we can evaluate the difference between this player's rate of success and the expected success rate of an average running back in the same situation (or between the opposing defense and the average defense in the same situation, etc.). Add up every play by a certain team or player, divide by the total of the various baselines for success in all those situations, and you get VOA, or Value Over Average.

Of course, the biggest variable in football is the fact that each team plays a different schedule against teams of disparate quality. By adjusting each play based on the opposing defense's average success in stopping that type of play over the course of a season, we get DVOA, or Defense-adjusted Value Over Average. Rushing and passing plays are adjusted based on down and location on the field; passing plays are also adjusted based on how the defense performs against passes to running backs, tight ends, or wide receivers. Defenses are adjusted based on the average success of the *offenses* they are facing. (Yes, technically the defensive stats are actually "offense-adjusted." If it seems weird, think of the "D" in "DVOA" as standing for "opponent-Dependent" or something.)

The biggest advantage of DVOA is the ability to break teams and players down to find strengths and weaknesses in a variety of situations. In the aggregate, DVOA may not be quite as accurate as some of the other, similar "power ratings" formulas based on comparing drives rather than individual plays, but, unlike those other ratings, DVOA can be separated not only by player, but also by down, or by week, or by distance needed for a first down. This can give us a better idea of not just which team is better, but why, and what a team has to do in order to improve itself in the future. You will find DVOA used in this book in a lot of different ways—because it takes every single play into account, it can be used to measure a player or a team's performance in any situation. All Pittsburgh third downs can be compared to how an average team does on third down. Brian Hoyer and Ryan Mallett can each be compared to how an average quarterback performs in the red zone, or with a lead, or in the second half of the game.

Since it compares each play only to plays with similar circumstances, it gives a more accurate picture of how much better a team really is compared to the league as a whole. The list of top DVOA offenses on third down, for example, is more accurate than the conventional NFL conversion statistic because it takes into account that converting third-and-long is more difficult than converting third-and-short, and that a turnover is worse than an incomplete pass because it eliminates the opportunity to move the other team back with a punt on fourth down.

One of the hardest parts of understanding a new statistic is interpreting its scale, or what numbers represent good performance or bad performance. We've made that easy with DVOA. For each season, ratings are normalized so that 0% represents league average. A positive DVOA represents a situation that favors the offense, while a negative DVOA represents a situation that favors the defense. This is why the best offenses have positive DVOA ratings (last year, Green Bay led the league at 24.7%) and the best defenses have negative DVOA ratings (with Seattle on top at -16.8%).

The scale of offensive ratings is wider than the scale of defensive ratings. In most years, the best and worst offenses tend to rate around +/- 30%, while the best and worst defenses tend to rate around +/- 20%. (In 2014, both offense and defense were packed closer together than usual.) For starting players, the scale tends to reach roughly +/-40% for passing and receiving, and +/- 30% for rushing. As you might imagine, some players with fewer attempts will surpass both extremes.

Team DVOA totals combine offense and defense by subtracting the latter from the former because the better defenses will have negative DVOA ratings. (Special-teams performance is also added, as described later in this essay.) Certain plays are counted in DVOA for offense and not for defense, leading to separate baselines on each side of the ball. In addition, although the league ratings for offense and defense are always 0%, the league averages for passing and rushing separately are *not* 0%. Because passing is more efficient than rushing, the average for team passing is almost always positive and the average for team rushing is almost always negative. However, ratings for individual players only compare passes to other passes and runs to other runs, so the league average for individual passing is 0%, as are the league averages for rushing and the three separate league averages for receiving by wide receivers, tight ends, and running backs.

Some other important notes about DVOA:

• Only four penalties are included in DVOA. Two penalties count as pass plays on both sides of the ball: intentional grounding and defensive pass interference. The other two penalties are included for offense only: false starts and delay of game. Because the inclusion of these penalties means a group of negative plays that don't count as either passes or runs, the league averages for pass offense and run offense are higher than the league averages for pass defense and run defense.

• Aborted snaps and incomplete backwards lateral passes are only penalized on offense, not rewarded on defense.

• Adjustments for playing from behind or with a lead in

Table 1. Correlation of Various Stats to Wins, 2002-2014

Stat	Offense	Defense	Total
Points Scored/Allowed	.755	-.676	.920
DVOA	.708	-.490	.859
Yards Gained/Allowed	.546	-.371	.681
Yards Gained/Allowed per Play	.546	-.339	.725

Table 2. Correlation of Various Stats to Wins Following Year, 2002-2014

Stat	Correlation	Stat	Correlation
DVOA	.370	Yards per Play Differential	.316
Point Differential	.353	Wins	.307
Pythagorean Wins	.347	Yardage Differential	.298

the fourth quarter are different for offense and defense, as are adjustments for the final two minutes of the first half when the offense is not near field-goal range.

• Offense gets a slight penalty and defense gets a slight bonus for games indoors.

How well does DVOA work? Using correlation coefficients, we can show that only actual points scored are better than DVOA at indicating how many games a team has won (Table 1) and DVOA does a better job of predicting wins in the coming season than either wins or points scored in the previous season (Table 2).

(Correlation coefficient is a statistical tool that measures how two variables are related by using a number between 1 and -1. The closer to -1 or 1, the stronger the relationship, but the closer to 0, the weaker the relationship.)

Special Teams

The problem with a system based on measuring both yardage and yardage towards a first down is what to do with plays that don't have the possibility of a first down. Special teams are an important part of football and we needed a way to add that performance to the team DVOA rankings. Our special-teams metric includes five separate measurements: field goals and extra points, net punting, punt returns, net kickoffs, and kick returns.

The foundation of most of these special-teams ratings is the concept that each yard line has a different value based on the likelihood of scoring from that position on the field. In *Hidden Game*, the authors suggested that each additional yard for the offense had equal value, with a team's own goal line being worth -2 points, the 50-yard line 2 points, and the opposing goal line 6 points. (-2 points is not only the value of a safety, but also reflects the fact that when a team is backed up in its own territory, it is likely that its drive will stall, forcing a punt that will give the ball to the other team in good field position. Thus, the negative point value reflects the fact that the defense is more likely to score next.) Our studies have updated this concept to reflect the actual likelihood that the offense or defense will have the next score from a given position on the field based on actual results from the past few seasons. The line that represents the value of field position is not straight, but curved, with the value of each yard increasing as teams approach either goal line.

Our special-teams ratings compare each kick or punt to league average based on the point value of the position of the kick, catch, and return. We've determined a league average

for how far a kick goes based on the line of scrimmage for each kick (almost always the 35-yard line for kickoffs, variable for punts) and a league average for how far a return goes based on both the yard line where the ball is caught and the distance that it traveled in the air.

The kicking or punting team is rated based on net points compared to average, taking into account both the kick and the return if there is one. Because the average return is always positive, punts that are not returnable (touchbacks, out of bounds, fair catches, and punts downed by the coverage unit) will rate higher than punts of the same distance which are returnable. (This is also true of touchbacks on kickoffs.) There are also separate individual ratings for kickers and punters that are based on distance and whether the kick is returnable, assuming an average return in order to judge the kicker separate from the coverage.

For the return team, the rating is based on how many points the return is worth compared to average, based on the location of the catch and the distance the ball traveled in the air. Return teams are not judged on the distance of kicks, nor are they judged on kicks that cannot be returned. As explained below, blocked kicks are so rare as to be statistically insignificant as predictors for future performance and are thus ignored. For the kicking team they simply count as missed field goals, for the defense they are gathered with their opponents' other missed field goals in Hidden value (also explained below).

Field goal kicking is measured differently. Measuring kickers by field goal percentage is a bit absurd, as it assumes that all field goals are of equal difficulty. In our metric, each field goal is compared to the average number of points scored on all field goal attempts from that distance over the past 16 years. The value of a field goal increases as distance from the goal line increases. Kickoffs, punts, and field goals are then adjusted based on weather and altitude. It will surprise no one to learn that it is easier to kick the ball in Denver or a dome than it is to kick the ball in Buffalo in December. Because we do not yet have enough data to tailor our adjustments specifically to each stadium, each one is assigned to one of four categories: Cold, Warm, Dome, and Denver. There is also an additional adjustment dropping the value of field goals in Florida (because the warm temperatures allow the ball to carry better).

The baselines for special teams are adjusted in each year for rule changes such as the introduction of the special-teams-only "k-ball" in 1999 as well as the move of the kickoff line from the 35 to the 30 in 1994 and then back to the 35 in 2011. Baselines have also been adjusted each year to make up for the gradual improvement of kickers over the last two decades.

Once we've totaled how many points above or below average can be attributed to special teams, we translate those points into DVOA so the ratings can be added to offense and defense to get total team DVOA.

There are three aspects of special teams that have an impact on wins and losses, but don't show up in the standard special-teams rating because a team has little or no influence on them. The first is the length of kickoffs by the opposing team, with an asterisk. Obviously, there are no defenders standing on the 35-yard line, ready to block a kickoff after the whistle blows. However, over the past few years, some teams have deliberately kicked short in order to avoid certain top return men, such as Devin Hester and Cordarrelle Patterson. The special-teams formula now includes adjustments to give teams extra credit for field position on kick returns if kickers are deliberately trying to avoid a return.

The other two items that special teams have little control over are field goals against your team, and punt distance against your team. Research shows no indication that teams can influence the accuracy or strength of field goal kickers and punters, except for blocks. As mentioned above, although blocked field goals and punts are definitely skillful plays, they are so rare that they have no correlation to how well teams have played in the past or will play in the future, thus they are included here as if they were any other missed field goal or botched punt, giving the defense no additional credit for their efforts. The value of these three elements is listed separately as "Hidden" value.

Special-teams ratings also do not include two-point conversions or onside kick attempts, both of which, like blocks, are so infrequent as to be statistically insignificant in judging future performance.

Defense-Adjusted Yards Above Replacement (DYAR)

DVOA is a good stat, but of course it is not a perfect one. One problem is that DVOA, by virtue of being a percentage or rate statistic, doesn't take into account the cumulative value of having a player producing at a league-average level over the course of an above-average number of plays. By definition, an average level of performance is better than that provided by half of the league and the ability to maintain that level of performance while carrying a heavy workload is very valuable indeed. In addition, a player who is involved in a high number of plays can draw the defense's attention away from other parts of the offense, and, if that player is a running back, he can take time off the clock with repeated runs.

Let's say you have a running back who carries the ball 300 times in a season. What would happen if you were to remove this player from his team's offense? What would happen to those 300 plays? Those plays don't disappear with the player, though some might be lost to the defense because of the associated loss of first downs. Rather those plays would have to be distributed among the remaining players in the offense, with the bulk of them being given to a replacement running back. This is where we arrive at the concept of replacement level, borrowed from our friends at Baseball Prospectus. When a player is removed from an offense, he is usually not replaced by a player of similar ability. Nearly every starting player in the NFL is a starter because he is better than the alternative. Those 300 plays will typically be given to a significantly worse player, someone who is the backup because he doesn't have as much experience and/or talent. A player's true value can then be measured by the level of performance he provides above that replacement level baseline, totaled over all of his run or pass attempts.

Of course, the *real* replacement player is different for each team in the NFL. Last year, the player who originally was the third-string running back in Denver (C.J. Anderson) ended up as the starter with a much higher DVOA than either Montee Ball or Ronnie Hillman. Sometimes a player such as Ryan Grant or Danny Woodhead will be cut by one team and turn into a star for another. On other teams, the drop from the starter to the backup can be even greater than the general drop to replacement level. The 2011 Indianapolis Colts will now be the hallmark example of this until the end of time. The choice to start an inferior player or to employ a sub-replacement level backup, however, falls to the team, not the starter being evaluated. Thus we generalize replacement level for the league as a whole as the ultimate goal is to evaluate players independent of the quality of their teammates.

Our estimates of replacement level are computed differently for each position. For quarterbacks, we analyzed situations where two or more quarterbacks had played meaningful snaps for a team in the same season, then compared the overall DVOA of the original starters to the overall DVOA of the replacements. We did not include situations where the backup was actually a top prospect waiting his turn on the bench, since a first-round pick is by no means a "replacement-level" player.

At other positions, there is no easy way to separate players into "starters" and "replacements," since unlike at quarterback, being the starter doesn't make you the only guy who gets in the game. Instead, we used a simpler method, ranking players at each position in each season by attempts. The players who made up the final 10 percent of passes or runs were split out as "replacement players" and then compared to the players making up the other 90 percent of plays at that position. This took care of the fact that not every non-starter is a freely available talent. (Think of Donte Moncrief or Ladarius Green, for example.)

As noted earlier, the challenge of any new stat is to present it on a scale that's meaningful to those attempting to use it. Saying that Tony Romo's passes were worth 236 success value points over replacement in 2011 has very little value without a context to tell us if 236 is good total or a bad one. Therefore, we translate these success values into a number called "Defense-adjusted Yards Above Replacement, or DYAR. Thus, Romo was fifth among quarterbacks with 1,187 passing DYAR. It is our estimate that a generic replacement-level quarterback, throwing in the same situations as Romo, would have been worth 1,187 fewer yards. Note that this doesn't mean the replacement level quarterback would have gained exactly 1,187 fewer yards. First downs, touchdowns, and turnovers all have an estimated yardage value in this system, so what we are saying is that a generic replacement-level quarterback would have fewer yards and touchdowns (and more turnovers) that would total up to be equivalent to the value of 1,187 yards.

Problems with DVOA and DYAR

Football is a game in which nearly every action requires the work of two or more teammates—in fact, usually 11 teammates all working in unison. Unfortunately, when it comes to individual player ratings, we are still far from the point at which we can determine the value of a player independent from the performance of his teammates. That means that when we say, "In 2014, Le'Veon Bell had a DVOA of 8.6%," what we really are saying is, "In 2014, Le'Veon Bell, playing in Todd Haley's offensive system with the Pittsburgh offensive line blocking for him and Ben Roethlisberger selling the fake when necessary, had a DVOA of 8.6%."

DVOA is limited by what's included in the official NFL play-by-play or tracked by the Football Outsiders game charting project (introduced below). Because we need to have the entire play-by-play of a season in order to compute DVOA and DYAR, these metrics are not yet ready to compare players of today to players throughout the league's history. As of this writing, we have processed 26 seasons, 1989 through 2014, and we add seasons at a rate of roughly two per year (the most recent season, plus one season back into history.) We're close to finishing up with 1986-1988 and will unveiling those numbers on our website in the next few months.

Pythagorean Projection

The Pythagorean projection is an approximation of each team's wins based solely on their points scored and allowed. This basic concept was introduced by baseball analyst Bill James, who discovered that the record of a baseball team could be very closely approximated by taking the square of team runs scored and dividing it by the sum of the squares of team runs scored and allowed. Statistician Daryl Morey, now general manager of the Houston Rockets, later extended this theorem to professional football, refining the exponent to 2.37 rather than 2.

The problem with that exponent is the same problem we've had with DVOA in recent years: the changing offensive levels in the NFL. 2.37 worked great based on the league 20 years ago, but in the current NFL it ends up slightly underprojecting teams that play high-scoring games. The most accurate method is actually to adjust the exponent based on the scoring environment of each individual team. Saints games have a lot of points. Jaguars games feature fewer points.

This became known as Pythagenport when Clay Davenport of Baseball Prospectus started doing it with baseball teams. In the middle of the 2011 season, we switched our measurement of Pythagorean wins to a Pythagenport-style equation, modified for the NFL[1]. The improvement is slight, but noticeable due to the high-scoring teams that have dominated the last few years.

For a long time, Pythagorean projections did a remarkable job of predicting Super Bowl champions. From 1984 through 2004, 10 of 21 Super Bowls were won by the team that led the NFL in Pythagorean wins. Seven other Super Bowls during that time were won by the team that finished second. Super Bowl champions that led the league in Pythagorean wins but not actual wins include the 2004 Patriots, 2000 Ravens, 1999 Rams, and 1997 Broncos.

Super Bowl champions have been much less predictable over the last few seasons. As of 2004, the 1980 Oakland Raiders held the mark for the fewest Pythagorean wins by a Super Bowl champion, 9.7. In the past nine seasons, four different teams have won the Super Bowl with a lower Pythagorean win total: the 2006 Colts (9.6), the 2012 Ravens (9.4), the 2007 Giants (8.6), and the 2011 Giants (7.9), the first team in the 90-year history of the National Football League to ever be outscored during the regular season and still go on to win the championship. The last two years, we've returned to more standard playoff results, and both Super Bowl XLVIII and Super Bowl XLIX matched the top two teams in Pythagorean wins from the regular season.

Pythagorean wins are also useful as a predictor of year-to-year improvement. Teams that win a minimum of one full game more than their Pythagorean projection tend to regress the following year; teams that win a minimum of one full game less than their Pythagorean projection tend to improve the following year, particularly if they were at or above .500 despite their underachieving. The Kansas City Chiefs are the team favored by this trend in 2015; they went 9-7 last year despite 10.1 Pythagorean wins.

Adjusted Line Yards

One of the most difficult goals of statistical analysis in football is isolating the degree to which each of the 22 men on the field is responsible for the result of a given play. Nowhere is this as significant as the running game, in which one player runs while up to nine other players—including not just linemen but also wideouts and tight ends—block in different directions. None of the statistics we use for measuring rushing—yards, touchdowns, yards per carry—differentiate between the contribution of the running back and the contribution of the offensive line. Neither do our advanced metrics DVOA and DYAR.

---

[1] The equation, for those curious, is 1.5 x log ((PF+PA)/G).

We do, however, have enough play-by-play data amassed that we can try to separate the effect that the running back has on a particular play from the effects of the offensive line (and other offensive blockers) and the opposing defense. A team might have two running backs in its stable: RB A, who averages 3.0 yards per carry, and RB B, who averages 3.5 yards per carry. Who is the better back? Imagine that RB A doesn't just average 3.0 yards per carry, but gets exactly 3 yards on every single carry, while RB B has a highly variable yardage output: sometimes 5 yards, sometimes -2 yards, sometimes 20 yards. The difference in variability between the runners can be exploited not only to determine the difference between the runners, but the effect the offensive line has on every running play.

At some point in every long running play, the running back passes all of his offensive line blocks as well as additional blocking backs or receivers. From there on, the rest of the play is dependent on the runner's own speed and elusiveness and the speed and tackling ability of the opposing defense. If Frank Gore breaks through the line for 50 yards, avoiding tacklers all the way to the goal line, his offensive line has done a great job—but they aren't responsible for the majority of the yards gained. The trick is figuring out exactly how much they *are* responsible for.

For each running back carry, we calculated the probability that the back involved would run for the specific yardage on that play based on that back's average yardage per carry and the variability of their yardage from play to play. We also calculated the probability that the offense would get the yardage based on the team's rushing average and variability using all backs *other* than the one involved in the given play, and the probability that the defense would give up the specific amount of yardage based on its average rushing yards allowed per carry and variability.

A regression analysis breaks the value for rushing yardage into the following categories: losses, 0-to-4 yards, 5-to-10 yards, and 11-plus yards. In general, the offensive line is 20 percent more responsible for lost yardage than it is for positive gains up to four yards, but 50 percent less responsible for additional yardage gained between five and ten yards, and not at all responsible for additional yardage past ten yards.

By applying those percentages to every running back carry, we were able to create **Adjusted Line Yards**, a statistic that measured offensive line performance. (We don't include carries by receivers, which are usually based on deception rather than straight blocking, or carries by quarterbacks, although we may need to reconsider that given the recent use of the read option in the NFL.) Those numbers are then adjusted based on down, distance, situation, opponent and whether or not a team is in the shotgun. (Because defenses are generally playing pass when the quarterback is in shotgun, the average running back carry from shotgun last year gained 4.54 yards, compared to just 3.95 yards on other carries.) The adjusted numbers are then normalized so that the league average for Adjusted Line Yards per carry is the same as the league average for RB yards per carry. (Historically, this is roughly 4.25 yards. Last year, it was only 4.14 yards; if lower numbers continue, we'll need to look at adjusting the way we normalize Adjusted Line Yards to account for this.)

The NFL distinguishes between runs made to seven different locations on the line: left/right end, left/right tackle, left/right guard, and middle. Further research showed no statistically significant difference between how well a team performed on runs listed as having gone up the middle or past a guard, so we separated runs into just five different directions (left/right end, left/right tackle, and middle). Note that there may not be a statistically significant difference between right tackle and middle/guard either, but pending further research (and for the sake of symmetry) we still list runs behind the right tackle separately. These splits allow us to evaluate subsections of a team's offensive line, but not necessarily individual linemen, as we can't account for blocking assignments or guards who pull towards the opposite side of the line after the snap.

Success Rate

Success rate is a statistic for running backs that measures how consistently they achieve the yardage necessary for a play to be deemed successful. Some running backs will mix a few long runs with a lot of failed runs of one or two yards, while others with similar yards-per-carry averages will consistently gain five yards on first down, or as many yards as necessary on third down. This statistic helps us differentiate between the two.

Since Success Rate compares rush attempts to other rush attempts, without consideration of passing, the standard for success on first down is slightly lower than those described above for DVOA. In addition, the standard for success changes slightly in the fourth quarter when running backs are used to run out the clock. A team with the lead is satisfied with a shorter run as long as it stays in bounds. Conversely, for a team down by a couple of touchdowns in the fourth quarter, four yards on first down isn't going to be a big help.

The formula for Success Rate is as follows:

- A successful play must gain 40 percent of needed yards on first down, 60 percent of needed yards on second down, and 100 percent of needed yards on third or fourth down.
- If the offense is behind by more than a touchdown in the fourth quarter, the benchmarks switch to 50 percent, 65 percent, and 100 percent.
- If the offense is ahead by any amount in the fourth quarter, the benchmarks switch to 30 percent, 50 percent, and 100 percent.

The league-average Success Rate in 2014 was 46.4 percent. Success Rate is not adjusted based on defenses faced, and is not calculated for quarterbacks and wide receivers who occasionally carry the ball.

Similarity Scores

Similarity scores were first introduced by Bill James to compare baseball players to other baseball players from the past. It was only natural that the idea would spread to other sports as statistical analysis spread to other sports. NBA analyst John Hollinger has created his own version to compare basketball players, and we have created our own version to compare football players.

Similarity scores have a lot of uses, and we aren't the only football analysts who use them. Doug Drinen of the website Footballguys.com has his own system that is specific to comparing fantasy football performances. The major goal of our similarity scores is to compare career progressions to try to determine when players have a higher chance of a breakout, a decline, or—due to age or usage—an injury (much like Baseball Prospectus's PECOTA player projection system). Therefore we not only compare numbers such as attempts, yards, and touchdowns, but also age and experience. We often are looking not for players who had similar seasons, but for players who had similar two- or three-year spans in their careers.

Similarity scores have some important weaknesses. The database for player comparison begins in 1978, the year the 16-game season began and passing rules were liberalized (a reasonable starting point to measure the "modern" NFL), thus the method only compares standard statistics such as yards and attempts, which are of course subject to all kinds of biases from strength of schedule to quality of receiver corps. For our comparisons, we project full-season statistics for the strike years of 1982 and 1987, although we cannot correct for players who crossed the 1987 picket line to play more than 12 games.

In addition to our similarity scores for skill players, we also have a similarity score system for defensive players based on FO's advanced statistics going back to 1997. It measures things like average distance on run tackles or pass tackles, as well as Stops and Defeats. It does not account for game-charting stats like hurries or Success Rate in coverage.

If you are interested in the specific computations behind our similarity scores system, we have listed the standards for each skill position online at http://www.footballoutsiders.com/stats/similarity. (The defensive system is not yet listed.) In addition, as part of our online premium package, all player pages for current players—both offensive and defensive—list the top ten similar players over one-, two-, and three-year spans.

KUBIAK Projection System

Most "skill position" players whom we expect to play a role this season receive a projection of their standard 2015 NFL statistics using the KUBIAK projection system. KUBIAK takes into account a number of different factors including expected role, performance over the past two seasons, age, height, weight, historical comparables, and projected team performance on offense and defense. When we named our system KUBIAK, it was a play on the PECOTA system used by our partners at Baseball Prospectus—if they were going to name their system after a long-time eighties backup, we would name our system after a long-time eighties backup. Little did we know that Gary Kubiak would finally get a head coaching job the very next season. After some debate, we de-

cided to keep the name, although discussing projections for Denver players can be a bit awkward.

To clear up a common misconception among our readers, KUBIAK projects individual player performances only, not teams.

2015 Win Projection System

In this book, each of the 32 NFL teams receives a **2015 Mean Projection** at the beginning of its chapter. These projections stem from three equations that forecast 2015 DVOA for offense, defense, and special teams based on a number of different factors. This offseason, we overhauled and improved the team projection system for the first time in a few years. The new system starts by considering the team's DVOA over the past three seasons and, on offense, a separate projection for the starting quarterback. The new system also does a much better job of measuring the value of offseason personnel changes by incorporating a measure that's based on the net personnel change in DYAR among non-quarterbacks (for offense) and the net change in Pro Football Reference's Approximate Value stat above replacement level (for defense). Other factors include coaching experience, recent draft history, certain players returning from injury, and combined tenure on the offensive line.

These three equations produce precise numbers representing the most likely outcome, but also produce a range of possibilities, used to determine the probability of each possible offensive, defensive, and special teams DVOA for each team. This is particularly important when projecting football teams, because with only 16 games in a season, a team's performance may vary wildly from its actual talent level due to a couple of random bounces of the ball or badly timed injuries. In addition, the economic structure of the NFL allows teams to make sudden jumps or drops in overall ability more often than in other sports.

From 2003-2014, the mean DVOA forecast by the new projection system had a correlation coefficient of .539 with actual wins and a correlation coefficient of .642 with actual DVOA.

The next step in our forecast involves simulating the season one million times. We use the projected range of DVOA possibilities to produce 1,000 different simulated seasons with 32 sets of DVOA ratings. We then plug those season-long DVOA ratings into the same equation we use during the season to determine each team's likely remaining wins for our Playoff Odds Report. The simulation takes each season game-by-game, determining the home or road team's chance of winning each game based on the DVOA ratings of each team as well as home-field advantage. A random number between 0 and 100 determines whether the home or road team has won that game. We ran 1,000 simulations with each of the 1,000 sets of DVOA ratings, creating a million different simulations. The simulation was programmed by Mike Harris.

This year, for the first time, we used what we're calling a "dynamic simulation" to better approximate the true distribution of wins in the NFL. When simulating the season, each team had 2.0% DVOA added or subtracted after a win or loss, reflecting the fact that a win or loss tends to tell us whether a team is truly better or worse than whatever their mean projection had been before the season. Using this method, a team projected with 20.0% DVOA which goes 13-3 will have a 40.0% DVOA entering the playoffs, which is much more realistic. This change gave us more projected seasons at the margins, with fewer seasons at 8-8 and more seasons at 14-2 or 2-14. The dynamic simulation also meant a slight increase in projected wins for the best teams, and a slight decrease for the worst teams. However, the conservative nature of our projection system still means the distribution of mean projected wins has a much smaller spread than the actual win-loss records we will see by the end of December. We will continue to experiment with changes to the simulation in order to produce the most accurate possible forecast of the NFL season in future years.

In addition, this year's simulation was programmed to deal with a number of injuries and suspensions. The most important of those is the four-game suspension given to New England quarterback Tom Brady. In 75 percent of simulations, the Patriots were given a much lower DVOA rating in their first four games. In 25 percent of simulations, the Patriots had the same DVOA rating for the entire season, reflecting the possibility of a federal court injunction that will allow Brady to start in Week 1. The simulation was also programmed to give Pittsburgh a lower rating in Weeks 1-2 and to give San Diego, Dallas, and the New York Jets a lower rating in Weeks 1-4. Finally, the simulation made the New York Giants slightly better in the second half of the season, due to the expectation that William Beatty and Jason Pierre-Paul will be able to return from injury sometime around midseason.

Football Outsiders Game Charting Project

Each of the formulas listed above relies primarily on the play-by-play data published by the NFL. When we began to analyze the NFL, this was all that we had to work with. Just as a television broadcast has a color commentator who gives more detail to the facts related by the play-by-play announcer, so too do we need some color commentary to provide contextual information that breathes life into these plain lines of numbers and text. The Football Outsiders Game Charting Project is our attempt to provide color for the simple play-by-play.

Providing color to 512 hours of football is a daunting task. To put it into perspective, there were more than 54,000 lines of play-by-play information in the 2014 NFL season and our goal is to add several layers of detail to nearly all of them. We recruited more than 50 volunteers to collectively chart each week's NFL games, and we've charted data on nearly every play since 2005. Through trial-and-error, we have gradually narrowed our focus to charting things both traceable and definitive. Charting a game, and rewinding to make sure mistakes are minimized, can take two to three hours. More than a couple of these per week can be hazardous to

one's marriage. Our goal was to provide comprehensive information while understanding that our charters were doing this on a volunteer basis.

The project is helped significantly now that the NFL makes coaches' film available publicly through their NFL Game Rewind project. That tape includes a sideline and end zone perspectives for each play, and shows all 22 players at all times, making it easier to see the cause-and-effect of certain actions taken on the field. Nonetheless, our charting is still imperfect. You often cannot tell which players did their jobs particularly well or made mistakes without knowing the play call and each player's assignment, particularly when it comes to zone coverage or pass rushers who reach the quarterback without being blocked. Therefore, the goal of Football Outsiders game charting is *not* to "grade" players, but rather to attempt to mark specific events: a pass pressure, a blown block, a dropped interception, and so on.

There are lots of things we would like to do with all-22 film that we simply haven't been able to do yet, such as charting coverage by cornerbacks when they aren't the target of a given pass, or even when pass pressure prevents the pass from getting into the air. Unfortunately, we are still limited by how much time our volunteers can give to the project, and the fact that our financial resources do not match those of our competitors.

The second major change for the game charting project in 2012 was an agreement to link our project up with the game charting done by the ESPN Stats & Information for internal ESPN use. ESPN charts games live on Sundays and our agreement allowed us to get access to their data immediately rather than waiting two to three weeks for our game charters to complete each game. In return, we provided suggestions to correct mistakes in the data—the more eyes we have on data like this, the more accurate it will be—and supplied ESPN with some of our older charting data, which allowed them to produce their new Total QBR metric for the 2006 and 2007 seasons. All data that comes from the ESPN Stats & Information is designated as such in the description of game charting that follows.

We emphasize that all data from the charting project is unofficial. Other sources for football statistics may keep their own measurements of yards after catch or how teams perform against the blitz. Our data will not necessarily match theirs. However, any other group that is publicly tracking this data is also working off the same footage, and thus will run into the same issues of difficulty.

The Football Outsiders game charting project tracks the following information:

Formation/Personnel

For each play, we have the number of running backs, wide receivers, and tight ends on the field courtesy of ESPN Stats & Information. Players were marked based on their designation on the roster, not based on where they lined up on the field. Obviously, this could be difficult with some hybrid players or players changing positions in 2014, but we did our best to keep things as consistent as possible.

Football Outsiders charters then added to ESPN's data by

marking the names of players who were lined up in unexpected positions. This included marking tight ends or wide receivers in the backfield, and running backs or tight ends who were lined up either wide or in the slot (often referred to as "flexing" a tight end). Football Outsiders charters also marked when a fullback or tight end was actually a sixth (or sometimes even seventh) offensive lineman, and they marked the backfield formation as empty back, single back, I formation, offset I, split backs, full house, or "other." These notations of backfield formation were recorded directly before the snap and do not account for positions before pre-snap motion.

We also ask game charters to mark defensive formations by listing the number of linemen, linebackers, and defensive backs. There will be mistakes—a box safety may occasionally be confused for a linebacker, for example—but for the most part the data for defensive backs will be accurate. Figuring out how to mark whether a player is a defensive end or a linebacker can be a different story. The rise of hybrid defenses has led to a lot of confusion. Edge rushers in a 4-3 defense may play standing up because they used to play for a 3-4 defense and that's what they are used to. A player who is usually considered an outside linebacker for a 3-4 defense may put his hand on the ground on third down (thus looking like a 4-3 defensive end), but the tackle next to him is still two-gapping (which is generally a 3-4 principle). This year, due to time constraints, we are listing defensive formations based solely on ESPN's data, which simplified the process by designating any front seven player in a standing position as a linebacker and designating any front seven player in a crouching position as a defensive lineman.

Rushers and Blockers

ESPN Stats & Information provided us with two data points regarding the pass rush: the number of pass rushers on a given play, and the number defensive backs blitzing on a given play. Football Outsiders charters then added a count of blockers, although this has proved to be an art as much as a science. Offenses base their blocking schemes on how many rushers they expect. A running back or tight end's assignment may depend on how many pass-rushers cross the line at the snap. Therefore, an offensive player was deemed to be a blocker if he engaged in an actual block, or there was some hesitation before running a route. A running back who immediately heads out into the flat is not a blocker, but one who waits to verify that the blocking scheme is working and then goes out to the flat would, in fact, be considered a blocker.

Pass Play Details

ESPN Stats & Information recorded the following data for all pass plays:

• Did the play begin with a play-action fake, including read-option fakes that developed into pass plays instead of being handed to a running back. Football Outsiders charters also added notation of fake end-arounds and flea flickers.
• Was the quarterback in or out of the pocket.
• Was the quarterback under pressure in making his pass.
• Was this a screen pass.

Football Outsiders charters then added to the ESPN data by identifying the defender who caused the pass pressure. Charters were allowed to list two names if necessary, and could also attribute a hurry to "overall pressure." No defender was given a hurry and a sack on the same play, but defenders were given hurries if they helped force a quarterback into a sack that was finished by another player. Football Outsiders charters also identified which defender(s) caused the pass pressure which forced a quarterback to scramble for yardage. If the quarterback wasn't under pressure but ran anyway, the play could be marked either as "coverage scramble" (if the quarterback ran because there were no open receivers) or "hole opens up" (if the quarterback ran because he knew he could gain significant yardage).

For the most part, Football Outsiders defaulted to ESPN's opinion on whether a play counted as pass pressure or not. The exception was for plays where the quarterback ran around solely because nobody was open; even if the quarterback eventually threw a pass, we changed these plays to "coverage scramble" and did not count them when counting up performance under pressure.

Some places in this book, we divide pass yardage into two numbers: distance in the air and yards after catch. This information is tracked by the NFL, but it can be hard to find and the official scorers often make errors, so we corrected the original data based on input from our charters as well as ESPN Stats & Information. Distance in the air is based on the distance from the line of scrimmage to the place where the receiver either caught or was supposed to catch the pass. We do not count how far the quarterback was behind the line or horizontal yardage if the quarterback threw across the field. All touchdowns are counted to the goal line, so that distance in the air added to yards after catch always equals the official yardage total kept by the league.

Incomplete Passes

Quarterbacks are evaluated based on their ability to complete passes. However, not all incompletes should have the same weight. Throwing a ball away to avoid a sack is actually a valuable incomplete, and a receiver dropping an otherwise quality pass is hardly a reflection on the quarterback.

This year, our evaluation of incomplete passes began with ESPN Stats & Information, which marked passes as Overthrown, Underthrown, Thrown Away, Batted Down at the Line, Defensed, or Dropped. Our charters then made changes to reflect a couple of additional categories we have kept in past years for Football Outsiders: Hit in Motion (indicating the quarterback was hit as his arm was coming forward to make a pass), Caught out of Bounds, and Hail Mary.

Our count of passes defensed will be different from the unofficial totals kept by the league, as well as the totals kept by ESPN Stats & Information, for reasons explained below in the section on Defensive Secondary tables.

ESPN Stats & Information also marked when a defender dropped an interception, and Football Outsiders then added the name of the defender responsible. When a play is close, we tend to err on the side of not marking a dropped interception, as we don't want to blame a defender who, for example, jumps high for a ball and has it tip off his fingers. This year for the first time, we also counted a few "defensed" interceptions, when a quarterback threw a pass that would have been picked off if not for the receiver playing defense on the ball. These passes counted as dropped interceptions for quarterbacks but not for the defensive players.

Defenders

The NFL play-by-play lists tackles and, occasionally, tipped balls, but it does not definitively list the defender on the play. Charters were asked to determine which defender was primarily responsible for covering either the receiver at the time of the throw or the location to which the pass was thrown, regardless of whether the pass was complete or not.

Every defense in the league plays zone coverage at times, some more than others, which leaves us with the question of how to handle plays without a clear man assigned to that receiver. We gave charters three alternatives:

• We asked charters to mark passes that found the holes in zone coverage as Hole in Zone, rather than straining to assign that pass to an individual defender. We asked the charter to also note the player who appeared to be responsible for that zone, and these defenders are assigned half credit for those passes. Some holes were so large that no defender could be listed along with the Hole in Zone designation.
• Charters were free to list two defenders instead of one. This could be used for actual double coverage, or for zone coverage in which the receiver was right between two close defenders rather than sitting in a gaping hole. When two defenders are listed, ratings assign each with half credit.
• Screen passes and dumpoffs are marked as Uncovered unless a defender (normally a linebacker) is obviously shadowing that specific receiver on the other side of the line of scrimmage.

Since we began the charting project in 2005, nothing has changed our analysis more than this information on pass coverage. However, even now with the ability to view all-22 film, it can be difficult to identify the responsible defender except when there is strict man-to-man coverage. We continue to hone our craft and do our best. Please note that although the definition of Hole in Zone did not change and most of our charters returned from previous years, the percentage of passes charted as Hole in Zone dropped significantly from past years. Just 5.8 percent of passes were charted as Hole in Zone in 2014, compared to 8.7 percent in 2013 and 8.6 percent in 2012.

Additional Details from ESPN Stats & Information

All draw plays were marked, whether by halfbacks or quarterbacks. Option runs and zone reads were also marked.

ESPN tracked when the formation was pistol as opposed to shotgun; the official play-by-play simply marks these plays all as shotgun.

ESPN also marks the number of defenders in the box for each snap, and tags each play as either "loaded" or "not loaded." A loaded box is when the defense has more players in the box than the offense has available blockers for running plays. Finally, ESPN marks yards after contact for each play.

Additional Details from Football Outsiders Charters

Football Outsiders game charters marked each quarterback sack with one of the following terms: Blown Block, Coverage Sack, QB Fault, or Blitz/Overall Pressure. Blown Blocks were listed with the name of a specific offensive player who allowed the defender to come through. (Some blown block sacks are listed with two blockers, who each get a half-sack. There are also a handful of rare three-man blown blocks.) Coverage Sack denotes when the quarterback has plenty of time to throw but cannot find an open receiver. QB Fault represents "self sacks" listed without a defender, such as when the quarterback drops back, only to find the ball slip out of his hands with no pass-rusher touching him.

Our charters track "broken tackles" on all runs or pass plays. We define a "broken tackle" as one of two events: Either the ballcarrier escapes from the grasp of the defender, or the defender is in good position for a tackle but the ballcarrier jukes him out of his shoes. If the ballcarrier sped by a slow defender who dived and missed, that did not count as a broken tackle. If the defender couldn't bring the ballcarrier down because he is being blocked out of the play by another offensive player, this did not count as a broken tackle. It was possible to mark multiple broken tackles on the same play. Broken tackles are not marked for special teams.

Please note that broken tackle numbers went up substantially in 2014 compared to previous years, because of two changes in our methodology rather than any specific changes on the field. First, this year we decided to track "dragged" broken tackles where defenders were able to bring the ball carrier to the ground, but only after the runner had gained at least 5 yards from the point where the tackle started. This seemed like a reasonable compromise to deal with plays we had struggled with in years past, where what looked like a broken tackle would end up with a defender getting marked with a tackle or assist by the NFL because he was the last player to make contact before a ballcarrier fell down ten yards later. Second, this year we flagged any plays where ESPN Stats & Information marked a minimum of 5 yards after contact and asked game charters to specifically look for broken tackles on those plays. Because of these two changes, the league-wide total of broken tackles went up roughly 25 percent over what it had been between 2009 and 2013.

We track which defensive players draw offensive holding calls; the list of leaders for 2014 can be found in the appendix.

An additional column called Extra Comment allowed the charters to add any description they wanted to the play. These comments might be good blitz pickup by a running back, a missed tackle, a great hit, a description of a pass route, an angry tirade about the poor camera angles of network broadcasts, or a number of other possibilities.

Finally, we asked the game charters to mark when a mistake was made in the official play-by-play. These mistakes include missing quarterback hits, incorrect names on tackles or penalties, missing direction on runs or passes, or the absence of the "scramble" designation when a quarterback ran on a play that began as a pass. Thanks to the diligence of our volunteer game charters and a friendly contact at the league office, the NFL corrected more than 500 mistakes in the official play-by-play based on the data collected by our game charters.

Sack Timing Project

Separate from the regular game charting project is J.J. Cooper's sack timing project, which began as a series of columns for AOL Fanhouse in 2009-2010 and continued with Football Outsiders in 2011. Cooper has timed every sack in the NFL from the time of the snap to the time of initial contact on the sack. The median sack time is roughly 2.8 seconds. The project also assigns blame for blown blocks that lead to sacks or designates a sack as "QB/Play Call," roughly akin to when the regular game charting project designates a sack as "Rusher Untouched" or "QB Fault." We used this data to clean up some mistakes in our original game charting of sacks.

Acknowledgements

None of this would have been possible without the time spent by all the volunteer game charters. There are some specific acknowledgements at the end of the book, but we want to give a general thank you here to everyone who has helped collect data over the last few seasons. Without your unpaid time, the task of gathering all this information would have been too time-consuming to yield anything useful. If you are interested in participating in next year's charting project, please e-mail your contact information to gamecharting@gmail.com with the subject "New Game Charter." Please make sure to mention where you live, what team you follow, and whether or not you have the Sunday Ticket package.

Our thanks to lots of people at ESPN Stats & Information for helping us coordinate our sharing of data, particularly John McTigue, Allison Loucks, and Henry Gargiulo. Additional extra thanks to Peter Koski, who collects and compiles the data from all the other game charters.

How to Read the Team Summary Box

Here is a rundown of all the tables and stats that appear in the 32 team chapters. Each team chapter begins with a box in the upper-right hand corner that gives a summary of our statistics for that team, as follows:

2014 Record gives each team's actual win-loss record. **Pythagorean Wins** gives the approximate number of wins expected last year based on this team's raw totals of points scored and allowed, along with their NFL rank. **Snap-Weighted Age** gives the average age of the team in 2014, weighted based on how many snaps each player was on the field and ranked from oldest (New Orleans, first at 27.3) to youngest (Jacksonville, 32nd at 25.4). **Average Opponent** gives a ranking of last year's schedule strength based on the average DVOA of all 16 opponents faced during the regular season. Teams are ranked from the hardest schedule (Oakland) to the easiest (Houston).

Total DVOA gives the team's total DVOA rating, with rank. **Offense, Defense,** and **Special Teams** list the team's DVOA rating in each category, along with NFL rank. Remember that good offenses and special teams have positive DVOA numbers, while a negative DVOA means better defense, so the lowest defensive DVOA is ranked No. 1 (last year, Seattle).

2015 Mean Projection gives the average number of wins for this team based on the 2015 Win Projection System described earlier in this chapter. Please note that we do not expect any teams to win the exact number of games in their mean projection. First of all, no team can win 0.8 of a game. Second, because these projections represent a whole range of possible values, the averages naturally tend to drift towards 8-8. (This was stronger than usual in 2013, and ended up *even stronger* for 2014, with the exception of Denver and Oakland as outlier teams, one on each end.) If every team were to hit its mean projection, the worst team in the league would finish 5-10-1 and the best team 10-5-1. Obviously, we're not expecting a season where no team goes 4-12 or 12-4. (The changes we're making to address these issues are discussed above in the section on the new team projection system.) For a better way to look at the projections, we offer **Postseason Odds**, which give each team's chance of making the postseason based on our simulation, and **Super Bowl Appearance** odds, which give each team's chance of representing its conference in Super Bowl XLIX. The average team will make the playoffs in 37.5 percent of simulations, and the Super Bowl in 6.3 percent of simulations.

Projected Average Opponent gives the team's strength of schedule for 2015; like the listing for last year's schedule strength in the first column of the box, this number is based not on last year's record but on the mean projected DVOA for each opponent. A positive schedule is harder, a negative schedule easier. Teams are ranked from the hardest projected schedule (Arizona, first) to the easiest (Atlanta, 32nd). This strength of schedule projection does not take into account which games are home or away, or the timing of the bye week. The strength of schedule projections for Pittsburgh, Buffalo, Jacksonville, and Dallas are based on facing the Patriots with Jimmy Garoppolo rather than Tom Brady, and each team's average opponent would go up by roughly 1.0% DVOA if Brady plays.

The final column of the box gives the team's chances of finishing in four different basic categories of success:

- On the Clock (0-4 wins; NFL average 11%)
- Mediocrity (5-7 wins; NFL average 33%)
- Playoff Contender (8-10 wins; NFL average 38%)
- Super Bowl Contender (11-plus wins; NFL average 19%)

The percentage given for each category is dependent not only on how good we project the team to be in 2015, but the level of variation possible in that projection, and the expected performance of the teams on the schedule.

You'll also find a table with the team's 2015 schedule placed within each chapter, along with a graph showing each team's

2014 week-to-week performance by single-game DVOA. The second, dotted line on the graph represents a five-week moving average of each team's performance, in order to show a longer-term view of when they were improving and declining. After the essays come statistical tables and comments related to that team and its specific units.

Weekly Performance

The first table gives a quick look at the team's week-to-week performance in 2014. (Table 3). This includes the playoffs for those teams that made the postseason, with the four weeks of playoffs numbered 18 (wild card) through 21 (Super Bowl). All other tables in the team chapters represent regular-season performance only unless otherwise noted.

Looking at the first week for the Atlanta Falcons in 2014, the first five columns are fairly obvious: the Falcons opened the season with a 37-34 win at home against New Orleans. **YDF** and **YDA** are net yards on offense and net yards against the defense. These numbers do not include penalty yardage or special teams yardage. **TO** represents the turnover margin. Unlike other parts of the book in which we consider all fumbles as equal, this only represents actual turnovers: fumbles lost and interceptions. So, for example, the Panthers had one more turnover than the Falcons in Week 11, but then the Falcons turned the ball over three more times than Carolina in the Week 17 rematch.

Finally, you'll see DVOA ratings for this game: Total **DVOA** first, then offense (**Off**), defense (**Def**), and special teams (**ST**). Note that these are DVOA ratings, adjusted for opponent, so a loss to a good team will often be listed with a higher rating than a close win over a bad team. For example, the Falcons have a positive DVOA for their close Week 14 loss to the Packers but a negative DVOA for their Week 10 win over last-place Tampa Bay.

Table 3: 2014 Falcons Stats by Week

Wk	vs.	W-L	PF	PA	YDF	YDA	TO	Total	Off	Def	ST
1	NO	W	37	34	568	472	1	34%	40%	13%	6%
2	at CIN	L	10	24	309	472	-3	-32%	-8%	25%	1%
3	TB	W	56	14	488	217	1	71%	33%	-23%	14%
4	at MIN	L	28	41	411	558	-2	-8%	42%	47%	-3%
5	at NYG	L	20	30	397	317	1	-15%	0%	17%	2%
6	CHI	L	13	27	287	478	-1	-60%	-37%	32%	9%
7	at BAL	L	7	29	254	371	2	-45%	-25%	11%	-9%
8	vs. DET	L	21	22	291	385	0	12%	18%	11%	6%
9	BYE										
10	at TB	W	27	17	322	373	3	-2%	19%	25%	4%
11	at CAR	W	19	17	346	391	1	12%	8%	-2%	2%
12	CLE	L	24	26	315	475	1	-18%	2%	20%	0%
13	ARI	W	29	18	500	329	2	27%	11%	0%	17%
14	at GB	L	37	43	465	502	-1	7%	40%	31%	-1%
15	PIT	L	20	27	407	398	-1	-22%	6%	25%	-3%
16	at NO	W	30	14	403	328	4	34%	14%	-28%	-8%
17	CAR	L	3	34	288	306	-3	-74%	-54%	30%	10%

Trends and Splits

Next to the week-to-week performance is a table giving DVOA for different portions of a team's performance, on both offense and defense. Each split is listed with the team's rank among the 32 NFL teams. These numbers represent regular season performance only.

Total DVOA gives total offensive, and defensive DVOA in all situations. **Unadjusted VOA** represents the breakdown of play-by-play considering situation but not opponent. A team whose offensive DVOA is higher than its offensive VOA played a harder-than-average schedule of opposing defenses; a team with a lower defensive DVOA than defensive VOA player a harder-than-average schedule of opposing offenses.

Weighted Trend lowers the importance of earlier games to give a better idea of how the team was playing at the end of the regular season. The final four weeks of the season are full strength; moving backwards through the season, each week is given less and less weight until the first three weeks of the season, which are not included at all. **Variance** is the same as noted above, with a higher percentage representing less consistency. This is true for both offense and defense: Houston, for example, was very consistent on offense (3.1%, third) but one of the league's less consistent defenses (7.1%, 22nd). Houston's variance also demonstrates that *consistency* is not the same as *quality*. **Average Opponent** is that the same thing that appears in the box to open each chapter, except split in half: the average DVOA of all opposing defenses (for offense) or the average DVOA of all opposing offenses (for defense).

Passing and **Rushing** are fairly self-explanatory. Note that rushing DVOA includes all rushes, not just those by running backs, including quarterback scrambles that may have began as pass plays.

The next three lines split out DVOA on **First Down**, **Second Down**, and **Third Down**. Third Down here includes fourth downs on which a team runs a regular offensive play instead of punting or attempting a field goal. **First Half** and **Second Half** represent the first two quarters and last two quarters (plus overtime), not the first eight and last eight games of the regular season. Next comes DVOA in the **Red Zone**, which is any offensive play starting from the defense's 20-yard line through the goal line. The final split is **Late and Close**, which includes any play in the second half or overtime when the teams are within eight points of each other in either direction. (Eight points, of course, is the biggest deficit that can be made up with a single score, a touchdown and two-point conversion.)

Five-Year Performance

This table gives each team's performance over the past five seasons (Table 4). It includes win-loss record, Pythagorean Wins, **Estimated Wins**, points scored and allowed, and turnover margin. Estimated wins are based on a formula that estimates how many games a team would have been expected to win based on 2014 performance in specific situations, normalized to eliminate luck (fumble recoveries, opponents' missed field goals, etc.) and assuming average schedule strength. The formula emphasizes consistency and overall DVOA as well as DVOA in a few specifically important situations. The next columns of this table give total DVOA along with DVOA for offense, defense, and special teams, and the rank for each among that season's 32 NFL teams.

The next four columns give the adjusted games lost (AGL) for starters on both offense and defense, along with rank. (Our total for starters here includes players who take over as starters due to another injury, such as Drew Stanton or Chris Borland last year, as well as important situational players who may not necessarily start, such as pass-rush specialists and slot receivers.) Adjusted games lost was introduced in *Pro Football Prospectus 2008*; it gives a weighted estimate of the probability that players would miss games based on how they are listed on the injury report. Unlike a count of "starter games missed," this accounts for the fact that a player listed as questionable who does in fact play is not playing at 100 percent capability. Teams are ranked from the fewest injuries (2014: Pittsburgh on offense, Carolina on defense) to the most (2014: San Diego on offense, Oakland on defense).

Individual Offensive Statistics

Each team chapter contains a table giving passing and receiving numbers for any player who either threw five passes or was thrown five passes, along with rushing numbers for any players who carried the ball at least five times. These numbers also appear in the player comments at the end of the book (except for wide-receiver rushing attempts). By putting them together in the team chapters we hope we make it easier to compare the performances of different players on the same team.

Players who are no longer on the team are marked with an asterisk. New players who were on a different team in 2014 are in italics. Changes should be accurate at least July 15. Rookies are not included.

All players are listed with DYAR and DVOA. Passing statistics (Table 5, next page) then list total pass plays (**Plays**), net yardage (**NtYds**), and net yards per pass (**Avg**). These numbers include not just passes (and the positive yardage from them) but aborted snaps and sacks (and the negative yardage from them). Then comes average yards after catch (**YAC**), as determined by the game charting project. This average is based on charted receptions, not total pass attempts. The final three numbers are completion percentage (**C%**), passing touchdowns (**TD**), and interceptions (**Int**).

It is important to note that the tables in the team chapters contain Football Outsiders stats, while the tables in the player comments later in the book contain official NFL totals, at least when it comes to standard numbers like receptions and yardage. This results in a number of differences between the two:

• Team chapter tables list aborted snaps as passes, not runs, although aborted handoffs are still listed as runs. Net yardage for quarterbacks in the team chapter tables includes the lost yardage from aborted snaps, sacks, and intentional grounding penalties. For official NFL stats, all aborted snaps are listed as runs.
• Football Outsiders stats omit kneeldowns from run totals and clock-stopping spikes from pass totals.
• In the Football Outsiders stats, we have changed a number of lateral passes to count as passes rather than runs, under the theory that a pass play is still a pass play, even if the receiver is standing five inches behind the quarterback. This results in some small differences in totals.
• Players who played for multiple teams in 2014 are only listed in team chapters with stats from that specific team; combined stats are listed in the player comments section.

Rushing statistics (Table 4) start with DYAR and DVOA, then list rushing plays and net yards along with average yards per carry and rushing touchdowns. The final two columns are fumbles (**Fum**)—both those lost to the defense and those recovered by the offense—and Success Rate (**Suc**), explained earlier in this chapter. Fumbles listed in the rushing table include all quarterback fumbles on sacks and aborted snaps, as well as running back fumbles on receptions, but not wide receiver fumbles.

Receiving statistics (Table 5) start with DYAR and DVOA and then list the number of passes thrown to this receiver (**Plays**), the number of passes caught (**Catch**) and the total receiving yards (**Yds**). Yards per catch (**Y/C**) includes total yardage per reception, based on standard play-by-play, while yards after catch (**YAC**) is based on information from our game charting project. Finally we list total receiving touchdowns, and catch percentage (**C%**), which is the percentage of passes intended for this receiver which were caught. Wide receivers, tight ends, and running backs are separated on the table by horizontal lines.

Table 4: Seattle Seahawks' Five-Year Performance

Year	W-L	Pyth W	Est W	PF	PA	TO	Total	Rk	Off	Rk	Def	Rk	ST	Rk	Off AGL	Rk	Def AGL	Rk	Off Age	Rk	Def Age	Rk	ST Age	Rk
2010	7-9	5.4	6.9	310	407	-9	-22.9%	30	-17.3%	29	12.0%	29	6.4%	2	47.1	32	9.7	4	27.8	11	27.6	10	26.4	14
2011	7-9	8.2	8.1	321	315	+8	-1.5%	19	-8.7%	22	-7.1%	10	0.2%	16	66.5	32	43.5	27	25.8	31	26.2	26	26.0	26
2012	11-5	12.5	13.0	412	245	+13	38.7%	1	18.5%	4	-14.5%	2	5.7%	3	28.0	16	8.3	3	25.9	27	25.6	31	26.0	18
2013	13-3	12.8	13.0	417	231	+20	40.0%	1	9.4%	7	-25.9%	1	4.7%	5	26.1	10	21.4	10	25.7	32	26.0	27	26.1	14
2014	12-4	11.9	12.7	394	254	+10	31.9%	1	16.8%	5	-16.8%	1	-1.7%	19	37.6	21	26.5	7	25.3	31	26.3	23	25.8	24

Table 5: Philadelphia Eagles' Passing

Player	DYAR	DVOA	Plays	NtYds	Avg	YAC	C%	TD	Int
M.Sanchez	210	-1.4%	334	2226	6.7	5.7	64.3%	14	11
N.Foles*	264	1.8%	322	2108	6.5	5.3	60.4%	13	10

Table 6: Baltimore Ravens' Rushing

Player	DYAR	DVOA	Plays	Yds	Avg	TD	Fum	Suc
J.Forsett	149	6.7%	234	1267	5.4	8	1	44%
B.Pierce*	-24	-14.8%	93	366	3.9	2	1	42%
L.Taliaferro	4	-7.2%	68	292	4.3	4	1	49%
J.Flacco	-1	-12.9%	24	85	3.5	2	1	-
F.Toussaint	-10	-52.0%	6	12	2.0	0	0	33%

Table 7: Arizona Cardinals' Receiving

Player	DYAR	DVOA	Plays	Ctch	Yds	Y/C	YAC	TD	C%
L.Fitzgerald	54	-5.8%	104	63	785	12.5	5.3	2	61%
Jo.Brown	1	-12.5%	103	48	696	14.5	3.8	5	47%
M.Floyd	81	-1.9%	100	48	846	17.6	2.5	6	48%
Ja.Brown	27	-2.0%	32	22	231	10.5	2.9	2	69%
T.Ginn*	-6	-15.5%	26	14	190	13.6	3.3	0	54%
J.Carlson	-43	-20.0%	55	33	350	10.6	4.3	1	60%
R.Housler*	8	0.2%	17	9	129	14.3	9.3	0	53%
D.Fells	-2	-10.7%	11	5	71	14.2	4.2	0	45%
A.Ellington	44	-2.6%	65	47	389	8.3	7.7	2	72%
S.Taylor	48	41.9%	15	11	79	7.2	5.9	3	73%
R.Hughes	61	66.9%	12	8	140	17.5	13.8	0	67%
M.Grice	-28	-55.0%	12	8	25	3.1	6.0	0	67%
K.Williams	-12	-56.6%	6	2	11	5.5	6.5	0	33%

Performance Based on Personnel

These tables provide a look at performance in 2014 based on personnel packages, as defined above in the section on marking formation/personnel as part of the Football Outsiders game charting project. There are four different tables, representing:

- Offense based on personnel
- Offense based on opponent's defensive personnel
- Defense based on personnel
- Defense based on opponent's offensive personnel

Most of these tables feature the top five personnel groupings for each team. Occasionally, we will list the personnel group which ranks sixth if the sixth group is either particularly interesting or nearly as common as the fifth group. Each personnel group is listed with its frequency among 2014 plays, yards per play, and DVOA. Offensive personnel are also listed with how often the team in question called a running play instead of a pass play from given personnel. (Quarterback scrambles are included as pass plays, not runs.)

Offensive personnel are given in the standard two-digit format where the first digit is running backs and the second digit is tight ends. You can figure out wide receivers by subtracting that total from five, with a couple of exceptions. Plays with six or seven offensive linemen will have a three-digit listing such as "611" or "622." Any play with a direct snap to a non-quarterback, or with a specific running quarterback taking the snap instead of the regular quarterback, was counted as "Wildcat." No team ends up with Wildcat listed among its top five offensive personnel groups.

When defensive players come in to play offense, defensive backs are counted as wide receivers and linebackers as tight ends. Defensive linemen who come in as offensive linemen are counted as offensive linemen; if they come in as blocking fullbacks, we count them as running backs.

This year, we are not giving personnel data based on the number of defensive linemen and linebackers. Part of this is because of the difficulty in separating between the two, especially with ESPN Stats & Information's simplified designation of players as defensive linemen or linebackers based simply on who has a hand on the ground. There are just too many hybrid defensive schemes in today's game: 4-3 schemes where one or both ends rush the passer from a standing position, or hybrid schemes that one-gap on one side of the nose tackle and two-gap on the other. Therefore, defensive personnel is listed in only five categories:

- Base (four defensive backs)
- Nickel (five defensive backs)
- Dime+ (six or more defensive backs)
- Big (either 4-4-3 or 3-5-3)
- Goal Line (all other personnel groups with fewer than four defensive backs)

11, or three-wide personnel, was by far the most common grouping in the NFL last year, used on 54 percent of plays, followed the standard two-tight end set 12 personnel (21 percent of plays) and the more traditional (and slowly dying) 21 personnel (10 percent). Defenses lined up in Base on 38 percent of plays, Nickel on 47 percent of plays, Dime+ on 13 percent of plays, and either Big or Goal Line on 1.6 percent of plays.

Strategic Tendencies

The Strategic Tendencies table (Table 6) presents a mix of information garnered from both the standard play by play and the Football Outsiders game charting project. It gives you an idea of what kind of plays teams run in what situations and with what personnel. Each category is given a league-wide **Rank** from most often (1) to least often (32) except as noted below. The sample table shown here lists the NFL average in each category for 2014.

The first column of strategic tendencies lists how often teams ran in different situations. These ratios are based on the type of play, not the actual result, so quarterback scrambles count as "passes" while quarterback sneaks, draws and option plays count as "runs."

Runs, first half and **Runs, first down** should be self evident. **Runs, second-and-long** is the percentage of runs on second down with seven or more yards to go, giving you an idea of how teams follow up a failed first down. **Runs, power situations** is the percentage of runs on third or fourth down with 1 or 2 yards to go, or at the goal line with 1 or 2 yards to go. **Runs, behind 2H** tells you how often teams ran when they were behind in the second half, generally a passing situation. **Pass, ahead 2H** tells you how often teams passed when they had the lead in the second half, generally a running situation.

In each case, you can determine the percentage of plays that were passes by subtracting the run percentage from 100 (the reverse being true for "Pass, ahead 2H," of course).

The second column gives information about offensive formations and personnel, as tracked by ESPN Stats & Information.

The first two entries detail formation, i.e. where players were lined up on the field. **Form: Single Back** lists how often the team lined up with only one player in the backfield, and **Form: Empty Back** lists how often the team lined up with no players in the backfield.

The next three entries are based on personnel, no matter where players were lined up in the formation. **Pers: 3+ WR** marks how often the team plays with three or more wide receivers. **Pers: 4+ WR** marks how often the team plays with four or more wide receivers. (Although announcers will often refer to a play as "five-wide," formations with five wide receivers are actually quite uncommon.) **Pers: 2+ TE/6+ OL** marks how often the team plays with either more than one tight end or more than five offensive linemen. Finally, we give the percentage of plays where a team used **Shotgun or Pistol** in 2014. This does not count "Wildcat" or direct snap plays involving a non-quarterback.

The third column shows how the defensive **Pass Rush** worked in 2014.

Rush 3/Rush 4/Rush 5/Rush 6+: The percentage of pass plays (including quarterback scrambles) on which our game charters recorded this team rushing the passer with three or fewer defenders, four defenders, five defenders, and six or more defenders. These percentages do not include goal-line plays on the one- or two-yard line.

Sacks by LB/Sacks by DB: The percentage of this team's sacks that came from linebackers and defensive backs. To figure out the percentage of sacks from defensive linemen,

simply subtract the sum of these numbers from 100 percent.

The fourth column has more data on the use of defensive backs.

4 DB/5DB/6+ DB: The percentage of plays where this defense lined up with four, five, and six or more defensive backs.

CB by Sides: One of the most important lessons from game charting is that each team's best cornerback does not necessarily match up against the opponent's best receiver. Most cornerbacks play a particular side of the field and in fact cover a wider range of receivers than we assumed before we saw the charting data. This metric looks at which teams prefer to leave their starting cornerbacks on specific sides of the field. It replaces a metric from previous books called "CB1 on WR1," which looked at the same question but through the lens of how often the top cornerback covered the opponent's top receiver.

To figure CB by Sides, we took the top two cornerbacks from each team and looked at the percentage of passes where that cornerback was in coverage on the left or right side of the field, ignoring passes marked as "middle." For each of the two cornerbacks, we took the higher number, right or left, and then we averaged the two cornerbacks to get the final CB by Sides rating. Teams which prefer to leave their cornerbacks in the same place, such as Detroit, Philadelphia, and Jacksonville, will have high ratings. Teams that do more to move their best cornerback around to cover the opponent's top targets, such as Arizona and New Orleans, will have low ratings.

DB Blitz: We have data on how often the defense used at least one defensive back in the pass rush courtesy of ESPN Stats & Information.

Hole in Zone: The percentage of passes where this defense was listed with "Hole in Zone" in the column for pass coverage. Obviously, it can be hard to determine whether a defense is trying to play a man or zone coverage, so these numbers are imperfect, but we think they provide a general idea of whether a team's defense is more man- or zone-based.

Finally, in the final column, we have some elements of game strategy.

Play action: The percentage of pass plays (including quarterback scrambles) which began with a play-action fake to the running back. This percentage does not include fake end-arounds unless there was also a fake handoff. It does include flea flickers.

Average Box: Another item added to our charting courtesy of ESPN Stats & Information is the number of defenders in the box before the snap. We list the average box faced by each team's offense and the average box used by this team's defense.

Table 8: League Average Strategic Tendencies

Run/Pass		Rk	Formation		Rk	Pass Rush		Rk	Secondary		Rk	Strategy		Rk
Runs, first half	38%	--	Form: Single Back	74%	--	Rush 3	6.6%	--	4 DB	27%	--	Play action	21%	--
Runs, first down	49%	--	Form: Empty Back	6%	--	Rush 4	62.5%	--	5 DB	54%	--	Avg Box (Off)	6.27	--
Runs, second-long	31%	--	Pers: 3+ WR	59%	--	Rush 5	23.1%	--	6+ DB	18%	--	Avg Box (Def)	6.27	--
Runs, power sit.	56%	--	Pers: 4+ WR	3%	--	Rush 6+	7.8%	--	CB by Sides	79%	--	Offensive Pace	30.13	--
Runs, behind 2H	27%	--	Pers: 2+ TE/6+ OL	32%	--	Sacks by LB	37.6%	--	DB Blitz	10%	--	Defensive Pace	30.09	--
Pass, ahead 2H	47%	--	Shotgun/Pistol	61%	--	Sacks by DB	7.4%	--	Hole in Zone	6%	--	Go for it on 4th	0.98	--

Offensive Pace: Situation-neutral pace represents the seconds of game clock per offensive play, with the following restrictions: no drives are included if they start in the fourth quarter or final five minutes of the first half, and drives are only included if the score is within six points or less. Teams are ranked from quickest pace (Philadelphia, the quickest situation-neutral pace we've ever measured at 22.2 seconds) to slowest pace (St. Louis, 33.1 seconds)

Defensive Pace: Situation-neutral pace based on seconds of game clock per defensive play. This is a representation of how a defense was approached by its opponents, not the strategy of the defense itself (an issue discussed in the Indianapolis chapter of *PFP 2006*). Teams are ranked from quickest pace (Houston, 28.0 seconds) to slowest pace (Seattle, 31.8 seconds).

Go for it on fourth: This is the aggressiveness index (AI) introduced by Jim Armstrong in *Pro Football Prospectus 2006*, which measures how often a team goes for a first down in various fourth down situations compared to the league average. A coach over 1.00 is more aggressive, and one below 1.00 is less aggressive. Coaches are ranked from most aggressive to least aggressive. Contrary to popular wisdom, coaches on the whole have actually been less aggressive in recent seasons than they were five or six years ago. The AI for the league in 2013 was only 0.90. Aggressiveness Index has been slightly updated this season to include situations where a head coach chooses to take a Delay of Game penalty to move his punter five yards back on fourth-and-1 at midfield; previously, these plays were not counted for AI because they would be listed in the play-by-play as fourth-and-6.

Following each strategic tendencies table, you'll find a series of comments highlighting interesting data from that team's charting numbers. This includes DVOA ratings split for things like different formations, draw plays, or play-action passing. Please note that all DVOA ratings given in these comments are standard DVOA with no adjustments for the specific situation being analyzed. The average DVOA for a specific situation will not necessarily be 0%, and it won't necessarily be the same for offense and defense. For example, the average offensive DVOA on play-action passes in 2014 was 24.0%, while the average defensive DVOA was 15.9%. The average offensive DVOA when the quarterback was hurried

was -77.0%; if we remove sacks, scrambles, and intentional grounding and only look at actual passes, the average offensive DVOA was -17.0%. On average last year, there was pressure marked on 24.6 percent of pass plays.

Previous books included an item in the Strategic Tendencies table called "max protect." Although we have not included it in the table this year, we do discuss it in some of the Strategic Tendencies comments. Max protect is defined as all passing plays where blockers outnumber pass rushers by at least two, with a minimum of seven blockers.

How to Read the Offensive Line Tables

Game charters mark blown blocks not just on sacks but also on hurries, hits, and runs stuffed at the line. In recent seasons, we have gone back after the season and dedicated time to checking plays with possible blown blocks in order to create more consistency between charters. The result is much more useful numbers for individual linemen.

However, while we have blown blocks to mark bad plays, we still don't have a metric that consistently marks good plays, so blown blocks should not be taken as the end all and be all of judging individual linemen. It's simply one measurement that goes into the conversation.

All offensive linemen who had at least 100 snaps in 2014 (not including special teams) are listed in the offensive line tables along with the position they played most often and their **Age** as of the 2015 season, listed simply as the difference between birth year and 2015. Players born in January and December of the same year will have the same listed age.

Then we list games, games started, snaps, and offensive penalties (**Pen**) for each lineman. Finally, there are three numbers for blown blocks in 2015.

- Blown blocks leading directly to sacks
- All blown blocks on pass plays, not only including those that lead to sacks but also those that lead to hurries, hits, or offensive holding penalties
- All blown blocks on run plays; generally this means plays

Table 9: Denver Broncos' Offensive Line

Player	Pos	Age	GS	Snaps	Pen	Sk	Pass	Run	Player	Pos	Age	GS	Snaps	Pen	Sk	Pass	Run
Manny Ramirez*	C/G	32	16/16	1123	5	1.0	9.0	12.0	Will Montgomery*	C	32	16/8	581	4	0.5	0.5	2.5
Louis Vasquez	G/T	28	16/16	1120	6	3.0	12.0	5.0	Chris Clark	RT	30	13/7	472	7	2.0	5.5	4.5
Orlando Franklin*	LG	28	16/16	1090	10	0.5	7.0	9.5	Paul Cornick	OT	26	12/6	300	4	1.0	4.0	1.0
Ryan Clady	LT	29	16/16	1052	7	2.0	13.5	5.0	Shelley Smith	G	28	11/3	359	3	2.0	7.0	4.0

Year	Yards	ALY	Rk	Power	Rk	Stuff	Rk	2nd Lev	Rk	Open Field	Rk	Sacks	ASR	Rk	Short	Long	F-Start	Cont.
2012	4.07	4.13	12	67%	9	20%	20	1.19	16	0.53	25	21	4.2%	2	10	5	12	29
2013	4.38	4.07	8	64%	17	16%	3	1.30	4	0.63	20	20	3.6%	1	9	6	14	36
2014	4.39	3.98	12	75%	5	18%	9	1.24	10	0.83	7	17	3.7%	1	10	0	18	36

| 2014 ALY by direction: | Left End 3.38 (24) | Left Tackle 2.98 (31) | Mid/Guard 4.27 (4) | Right Tackle 4.12 (12) | Right End 3.54 (18) |

where the running back is tackled for a loss or no gain, but it also includes a handful of plays where the running back would have been tackled for a loss if not for a broken tackle, as well as offensive holding penalties on running plays

Players are given half a blown block when two offensive players are listed with blown blocks on the same play; there are also a few plays where we assigned one-third of a blown block to three different players.

As with all player tables in the team chapters, players who are no longer on the team have an asterisk and those new to the team in 2015 are in italics.

The second offensive line table lists the last three years of our various line stats.

The first column gives standard yards per carry by each team's running backs (**Yards**). The next two columns give adjusted line yards (**ALY**) followed by rank among the 32 teams.

Power gives the percentage of runs in "power situations" that achieved a first down or touchdown. Those situations include any third or fourth down with 1 or 2 yards to go, and any runs in goal-to-go situations from the two-yard line or closer. Unlike the other rushing numbers on the Offensive Line table, Power includes quarterbacks.

Stuff gives the percentage of runs that are stuffed for zero or negative gain. Since being stuffed is bad, teams are ranked from stuffed least often (1) to most often (32).

Second-Level (**2nd Lev**) Yards and **Open Field** Yards represent yardage where the running back has the most power over the amount of the gain. Second-Level Yards represent the number of yards per carry that come 5 to 10 yards past the line of scrimmage. Open-Field Yards represent the number of yards per carry that come 11 or more yards past the line of scrimmage. A team with a low ranking in Adjusted Line Yards but a high ranking in Open-Field Yards is heavily dependent on its running back breaking long runs to make the running game work, and therefore tends to have a less consistent running attack. Second Level Yards fall somewhere in between.

The next five columns give information about pass protection. That starts with total sacks, followed by adjusted sack rate (**ASR**) and its rank among the 32 teams. Some teams allow a lot of sacks because they throw a lot of passes; adjusted sack rate accounts for this by dividing sacks and intentional grounding by total pass plays. It is also adjusted for situation (sacks are much more common on third down, particularly third-and-long) and opponent, all of which makes it a better measurement than raw sacks totals. Remember that quarterbacks share responsibility for sacks, and two different quarterbacks behind the same line can have very different adjusted sack rates. We also give two specific totals that come from J.J. Cooper's sack-timing project. **Short Sacks** are the total of sacks that took shorter than 2.5 seconds; **Long Sacks** are the total of sacks that took longer than 3.0 seconds.

F-Start gives the number of false starts, which is the offensive penalty which best correlates to both wins and wins the following season. This total includes false starts by players other than offensive linemen, but it does not include false starts on special teams. Seattle led the league with 29, Jack-

sonville was last with 8, and the NFL average was 17.0. Finally, Continuity score (**Cont.**) tells you how much continuity each offensive line had from game-to-game in that season. It was introduced in the Cleveland chapter of *Pro Football Prospectus 2007*. Continuity score starts with 48 and then subtracts:

• The number of players over five who started at least one game on the offensive line;
• The number of times the team started at least one different lineman compared to the game before; and
• The difference between 16 and that team's longest streak where the same line started consecutive games.

The perfect Continuity score is 48, which no team achieved last year. Continuity scores in 2014 ranged from 19 (Indianapolis) to 43 (Green Bay).

Finally, underneath the table in italics we give 2014 Adjusted Line Yards in each of the five directions with rank among the 32 teams. As noted earlier, these averages were down from past years. The league average was 3.74 on left end runs (**LE**), 3.97 on left tackle runs (**LT**), 3.93 on runs up the middle (**MID**), 3.98 on right tackle runs (**RT**), and 3.79 on right end runs (**RE**).

How to Read the Defensive Front Seven Tables

Defensive players make plays. Plays aren't just tackles—interceptions and pass deflections change the course of the game, and so does the act of forcing a fumble or beating the offensive players to a fumbled ball. While some plays stop a team on third down and force a punt, others merely stop a receiver after he's caught a 30-yard pass. We still cannot measure each player's opportunities to make a tackle. We can measure opportunities in pass coverage, however, thanks to the Football Outsiders game charting project.

Defensive players are listed in these tables if they made at least 20 plays during the 2014 season, or if they played at least eight games and played 25 percent of defensive snaps in those games.

Defensive Linemen/Edge Rushers

As we've noted earlier in this toolbox: as hybrid defenses become more popular, it becomes more and more difficult to tell the difference between a defensive end and an outside linebacker. What we do know is that there are certain players whose job is to rush the passer, even if they occasionally drop into coverage. We also know that the defensive ends in a two-gapping 3-4 system have a lot more in common with run-stuffing 4-3 tackles than with smaller 4-3 defensive ends.

Therefore, we have separated front seven players into three tables rather than two. All defensive tackles and defensive ends from 3-4 teams are listed as **Defensive Linemen**, and all ranked together. Defensive ends from 4-3 teams and outside linebackers from 3-4 teams are listed as **Edge Rushers**, and all ranked together. All 4-3 linebackers are ranked along with 3-4 inside linebackers, and listed simply as **Linebackers**. For the most part this categorization puts players with similar roles together, although you occasionally get a 4-3 outside linebacker who becomes a pass-rushing specialist on third downs (Von Miller being the best example).

The tables for defensive linemen and edge rushers are the same, although the players are ranked in two separate categories. Players are listed with the following numbers:

Age, position (**Pos**) and the number of defensive **Snaps** played in 2014.

Plays (**Plays**): The total defensive plays including tackles, pass deflections, interceptions, fumbles forced, and fumble recoveries. This number comes from the official NFL gamebooks and therefore does not include plays on which the player is listed by the Football Outsiders game charting project as in coverage, but does not appear in the standard play-by-play. Special-teams tackles are also not included.

Percentage of team plays (**TmPct**): The percentage of total team plays involving this defender. The sum of the percentages of team plays for all defenders on a given team will exceed 100 percent, primarily due to shared tackles. This number is adjusted based on games played, so an injured player may be fifth on his team in plays but third in **TmPct**.

Stops (**Stop**): The total number of plays which prevent a "success" by the offense (45 percent of needed yards on first down, 60 percent on second down, 100 percent on third or fourth down).

Defeats (**Dfts**): The total number of plays which stop the offense from gaining first down yardage on third or fourth down, stop the offense behind the line of scrimmage, or result in a fumble (regardless of which team recovers) or interception.

Broken tackles (**BTkl**): The number of broken tackles recorded by our game charters.

The next five columns represent runs only, starting with the number of plays each player made on Runs. Stop rate (**St%**) gives the percentage of these run plays which were stops. Average yards (**AvYd**) gives the average number of yards gained by the runner when this player is credited with making the play.

Finally, we have pass rush numbers, starting with standard NFL **Sack** totals.

Hit: To qualify as a quarterback hit, the defender must knock the quarterback to the ground in the act of throwing or after the pass is thrown. We have listed hits on all plays, including those cancelled by penalties. (After all, many of the hardest hits come on plays cancelled because the hit itself draws a roughing the passer penalty.)

Hurries (**Hur**): The number of quarterback hurries recorded

Table 10: Detroit Lions' Defensive Front Seven

Defensive Line	Age	Pos	G	Snaps	Plays	TmPct	Rk	Stop	Dfts	BTkl	Runs	St%	Rk	RuYd	Rk	Sack	Hit	Hur	Dsrpt
Ndamukong Suh*	28	DT	16	851	56	7.1%	11	49	26	3	40	85%	22	1.0	8	8.5	11	16.0	3
C.J. Mosley	32	DT	15	490	26	3.5%	74	20	6	1	21	76%	57	3.0	84	2.5	5	8.0	0
Nick Fairley*	27	DT	8	288	14	3.5%	73	11	4	0	12	83%	24	1.6	24	1.0	4	4.0	0
Andre Fluellen	30	DT	8	158	10	2.5%	--	6	5	0	7	43%	--	1.3	--	2.0	2	3.0	0
Haloti Ngata	*31*	*DE*	*12*	*529*	*39*	*6.2%*	*19*	*30*	*12*	*1*	*26*	*77%*	*53*	*3.1*	*86*	*2.0*	*2*	*7.5*	*5*
Tyrunn Walker	*25*	*DE*	*16*	*304*	*18*	*2.2%*	*--*	*15*	*11*	*1*	*11*	*82%*	*--*	*2.2*	*--*	*2.5*	*2*	*4.5*	*0*

Edge Rushers	Age	Pos	G	Snaps	Plays	TmPct	Rk	Stop	Dfts	BTkl	Runs	St%	Rk	RuYd	Rk	Sack	Hit	Hur	Dsrpt
Ezekiel Ansah	26	DE	16	664	47	5.9%	27	38	24	3	30	77%	36	2.0	27	7.5	19	29.5	0
Jason Jones	29	DE	16	645	23	2.9%	82	18	11	2	11	82%	22	4.3	81	5.0	12	14.5	2
George Johnson*	28	DE	16	491	25	3.2%	79	19	13	0	14	71%	57	1.6	17	6.0	6	11.5	1
Darryl Tapp	31	DE	16	283	19	2.4%	--	11	2	0	9	56%	--	2.9	--	0.5	11	9.5	2

Linebackers	Age	Pos	G	Snaps	Plays	TmPct	Rk	Stop	Dfts	BTkl	Sack	Hit	Hur	Runs	St%	Rk	RuYd	Rk	Tgts	Suc%	Rk	AdjYd	Rk	PD	Int
DeAndre Levy	28	OLB	16	1045	155	19.5%	3	87	35	13	2.5	1	6	76	68%	26	3.1	29	58	56%	17	6.2	29	5	1
Tahir Whitehead	25	OLB	16	722	82	10.3%	59	40	10	4	0.0	2	3.5	33	73%	16	3.4	46	35	54%	23	6.4	32	4	2
Josh Bynes	26	OLB	13	209	20	3.1%	--	11	3	1	0.0	1	1	10	70%	--	2.1	--	9	41%	--	6.3	--	1	1
Stephen Tulloch	30	MLB	3	138	20	13.5%	--	14	7	3	2.0	0	0	13	69%	--	2.5	--	4	54%	--	12.6	--	0	0

Year	Yards	ALY	Rk	Power	Rk	Stuff	Rk	2nd Level	Rk	Open Field	Rk	Sacks	ASR	Rk	Short	Long
2012	4.30	3.69	5	72%	28	26%	2	1.33	29	1.03	27	34	5.2%	29	5	20
2013	4.08	3.13	2	50%	3	26%	4	1.13	19	1.07	29	33	5.8%	31	7	14
2014	3.17	2.82	1	63%	15	25%	3	0.86	1	0.50	5	42	6.6%	18	17	10

2014 ALY by direction:	Left End 2.54 (1)	Left Tackle 3.3 (11)	Mid/Guard 2.68 (1)	Right Tackle 2.87 (3)	Right End 2.51 (4)

by the Football Outsiders game charting project. This includes both hurries on standard plays and hurries that force an offensive holding penalty that cancels the play and costs the offense yardage.

Disruptions (**Dsrpt**): This stat combines two different but similar types of plays. First, plays where a pass-rusher forced an incomplete pass or interception by hitting the quarterback as he was throwing the ball. These plays are generally not counted as passes defensed, so we wanted a way to count them. Second, plays where the pass-rusher batted the ball down at the line of scrimmage or tipped it in the air. These plays are usually incomplete, but occasionally they lead to interceptions, and even more rarely they fall into the hands of offensive receivers. As with the "hit in motion" disruptions, some plays counted as tips by Football Outsiders were not counted as passes defensed by the NFL.

Defensive linemen and edge rushers are both ranked by percentage of team plays, run stop rate, and average yards per run tackle. The lowest number of average yards earns the top rank (negative numbers indicate the average play ending behind the line of scrimmage). Defensive linemen and edge rushers are ranked if they played at least 40 percent of defensive snaps in the games they were active. (We made an exception to leave out Scott Solomon, who played for two different teams and barely made the minimum.) There are 93 defensive linemen ranked, and 87 edge rushers.

Linebackers

Most of the stats for linebackers are the same as those for defensive linemen, except that the sections for pass rush and run tackles are reversed.[2] Linebackers are ranked in percentage of team plays, and also in stop rate and average yards for running plays specifically. Linebackers are ranked in these stats if they played at least 40 percent of defensive snaps in the games they were active, though we made an exception and left out Stephen Tulloch because while he hit the minimum of 20 plays, he only played in three games. There are 86 linebackers ranked.

The final six columns in the linebacker stats come from the Football Outsiders game charting project.

Targets (**Tgts**): The number of pass players on which our game charters listed this player in coverage.

Success rate (**Suc%**): The percentage plays of targeting this player on which the offense did not have a successful play. This means not only incomplete passes and interceptions, but also short completions which do not meet our baselines for success (45 percent of needed yards on first down, 60 percent on second down, 100 percent on third or fourth down). Success Rate is adjusted for the quality of the receiver covered.

Adjusted yards per pass (**AdjYd**): The average number of yards gained on plays on which this defender was the listed target, adjusted for the quality of the receiver covered.

Passes defensed (**PD**): Football Outsiders' count of passes defensed. Unlike the official NFL count of passes defensed, this does not include passes batted down or tipped at the line.

These stats, including other differences between the NFL's count of passes defensed and our own, are explained in more detail in the section on secondary tables. Plays listed with two defenders or as "Hole in Zone" with this defender as the closest player count only for half credit in computing both success rate and average yards per pass. Sixty-three linebackers are ranked in the charting stats, with a minimum of 16 charted passes. As a result of the different thresholds, some linebackers are ranked in standard stats but not charting stats.

Further Details

Just as in the offensive tables, players who are no longer on the team are marked with asterisks, and players who were on other teams last year are in italics. Other than the game charting statistics for linebackers, defensive front seven player statistics are not adjusted for opponent.

Numbers for defensive linemen and linebackers unfortunately do not reflect all of the opportunities a player had to make a play, but they do show us which players were most active on the field. A large number of plays could mean a strong defensive performance, or it could mean that the linebacker in question plays behind a poor part of the line. In general, defensive numbers should be taken as information that tells us what happened on the field in 2014, but not as a strict, unassailable judgment of which players are better than others— particularly when the difference between two players is small (for example, players ranked 20th and 30th) instead of large (players ranked 20th and 70th).

After the individual statistics for linemen and linebackers, the Defensive Front Seven section contains a table that looks exactly like the table in the Offensive Line section. The difference is that the numbers here are for all opposing running backs against this team's defensive front. As we're on the opposite side of the ball, teams are now ranked in the opposite order, so the No. 1 defensive front seven is the one that allows the fewest Adjusted Line Yards, the lowest percentage in Power situations, and has the highest Adjusted Sack Rate. Directions for Adjusted Line Yards are given from the offense's perspective, so runs to left end and left tackle are aimed at the right defensive end and (assuming the tight end is on the other side) weakside linebacker.

How to Read the Secondary Tables

The first few columns in the secondary tables are based on standard play-by-play, not game charting, with the exception of broken tackles. Age, total plays, percentage of team plays, stops, and defeats are computed the same way they are for other defensive players, so that the secondary can be compared to the defensive line and linebackers. That means that total plays here includes passes defensed, sacks, tackles after receptions, tipped passes, and interceptions, but not pass

---

2 This is a vestigial remnant of how we built these tables in previous books and we keep forgetting to fix it.

plays on which this player was in coverage but was not given a tackle or passed defense by the NFL's official scorer.

The middle five columns address each defensive back's role in stopping the run. Average yardage and stop rate for running plays is computed in the same manner as for defensive linemen and linebackers.

The third section of statistics represents data from the game charting project. In all game charting coverage stats, passes where two defenders are listed and those listed as "Hole in Zone" with this player as the closest zone defender count for half credit. We do not count pass plays on which this player was in coverage, but the incomplete was listed as Thrown Away, Batted Down, or Hit in Motion. Hail Mary passes are also not included.

Targets (**Tgts**): The number of pass plays on which our game charters listed this player in coverage.

Target percentage (**Tgt%**): The number of plays on which this player was targeted divided by the total number of charted passes against his defense, not including plays listed as Uncovered. Like percentage of team plays, this metric is adjusted based on number of games played.

Distance (**Dist**): The average distance in the air beyond the line of scrimmage of all passes targeted at this defender. It does not include yards after catch, and is useful for seeing which defenders were covering receivers deeper or shorter.

Adjusted Success rate (**Suc%**): The percentage plays of targeting this player on which the offense did not have a successful play. This means not only incomplete passes and interceptions, but also short completions which do not meet our baselines for success (45 percent of needed yards on first down, 60 percent on second down, 100 percent on third or fourth down). Defensive pass interference is counted as a failure for the defensive player similar to a completion of equal yardage (and a new first down). This number is adjusted based on the quality of the receiver covered.

Adjusted Yards per Pass (**AdjYd**): The average number of yards gained on plays on which this defender was the listed target, adjusted for the quality of the receiver covered.

Passes Defensed (**PD**): This is our count of passes defensed, and will differ from the total found in NFL gamebooks. Our count includes:

- All passes listed by our charters as Defensed.
- All interceptions, or tipped passes leading to interceptions.
- Any pass on which the defender is given a pass defensed by the official scorer, and our game charter marked either Miscommunication or Caught Out of Bounds.

Our count of passes defensed does not include passes marked as defensed in the official gamebooks but listed by our charters as Overthrown, Underthrown, or Thrown Away. It also does not include passes tipped in the act of rushing the passer. In addition, we did a lot of work with both the NFL head office and the folks from ESPN Stats & Information to get the most accurate numbers possible for both drops and passes defensed. Official scorers and game charters will sometimes disagree on a drop vs. a pass defensed, or even an overthrown/underthrown ball vs. a pass defensed, and there are a number of passes where the league marked the official stats in one way and ESPN marked their stats the other way. We reviewed all these passes and on each one chose to either go with the NFL's decision or ESPN Stats & Information's decision, so we no longer have passes where we were unsure whether to give a pass defensed (as given by the NFL) or a drop (as given by charters). Each pass is marked as one or the other.

Interceptions (**Int**) represent the standard NFL interception total.

With more and more wide receivers playing, that means more and more cornerbacks are playing, so we've had to increase our minimums so we aren't ranking a zillion cornerbacks. Cornerbacks need 50 charted passes or eight games

Table 11: New England Patriots' Defensive Secondary

Secondary	Age	Pos	G	Snaps	Plays	TmPct	Rk	Stop	Dfts	BTkl	Runs	St%	Rk	RuYd	Rk	Tgts	Tgt%	Rk	Dist	Suc%	Rk	AdjYd	Rk	PD	Int
Darrelle Revis*	30	CB	16	1011	61	7.7%	56	28	15	1	10	40%	38	6.7	40	69	17.0%	3	13.2	62%	2	7.3	25	13	2
Devin McCourty	28	FS	16	998	73	9.2%	48	15	9	3	30	20%	68	11.7	70	19	4.6%	4	15.1	54%	34	7.7	44	5	2
Patrick Chung	28	SS	16	839	92	11.6%	25	47	9	5	52	54%	14	4.5	9	39	11.4%	58	10.8	54%	35	7.4	38	8	1
Brandon Browner*	31	CB	9	580	31	6.9%	67	15	6	4	5	100%	1	2.4	2	53	22.5%	29	14.5	56%	16	7.4	28	9	1
Logan Ryan	24	CB	16	509	41	5.2%	76	15	8	1	8	50%	21	6.3	35	52	25.2%	50	12.7	46%	60	9.4	65	7	2
Kyle Arrington	29	CB	14	439	38	5.5%	--	15	6	2	8	75%	--	4.3	--	39	21.8%	--	11.9	55%	--	6.3	--	4	0
Duron Harmon	24	FS	16	279	12	1.5%	--	1	1	0	4	0%	--	10.0	--	3	2.2%	--	24.8	99%	--	0.8	--	1	1
Tavon Wilson	25	SS	16	183	20	2.5%	--	11	4	1	11	36%	--	6.6	--	9	11.5%	--	10.2	78%	--	7.5	--	2	0
Bradley Fletcher	29	CB	15	1047	80	9.8%	19	34	13	8	19	47%	25	4.5	12	115	29.4%	69	16.6	51%	36	8.9	55	22	1
Tarell Brown	30	CB	14	961	58	8.0%	47	22	7	2	14	50%	21	5.4	26	58	18.3%	7	12.8	52%	31	8.0	42	5	0
Robert McClain	27	CB	16	628	61	7.4%	60	21	5	9	18	44%	29	5.3	21	56	24.4%	45	12.9	45%	62	7.8	39	5	2

Year	Pass D Rank	vs. #1 WR	Rk	vs. #2 WR	Rk	vs. Other WR	Rk	vs. TE	Rk	vs. RB	Rk
2012	23	-5.0%	14	-16.4%	6	27.3%	30	21.3%	29	14.8%	23
2013	14	-1.9%	16	17.9%	29	5.5%	21	-1.1%	13	5.1%	19
2014	12	-14.4%	7	1.8%	17	-13.8%	7	22.0%	30	-4.6%	14

started to be ranked in the defensive stats, with 77 cornerbacks ranked in total. Safeties require 20 charted passes or eight games started, with 71 safeties ranked in total. Strong and free safeties are ranked together. Players listed with two positions, usually safeties who move to slot cornerback in nickel, are ranked at the first positon listed.

Just like the front seven, the secondary has a table of team statistics following the individual numbers. This table gives DVOA figured against different types of receivers. Each offense's wide receivers have had one receiver designated as No. 1, and another as No. 2. (Occasionally this is difficult, due to injury or a situation such as Washington which effectively has "co-No. 1 receivers," but it's usually pretty obvious.) The other receivers form a third category, with tight ends and running backs as fourth and fifth categories. The defense is then judged on the performance of each receiver based on the standard DVOA method, with each rating adjusted based on strength of schedule. (Obviously, it's a lot harder to cover the No. 1 receiver of the Detroit Lions than to cover the No.1 receiver of the Jacksonville Jaguars.) **Pass D Rank** is the total ranking of the pass defense, as seen before in the Trends and Splits table, and combines all five categories plus sacks and passes with no intended target.

The "defense vs. types of receivers" table should be used to analyze the defense as a whole rather than individual players. The ratings against types of receivers are generally based on defensive schemes, not specific cornerbacks, except for certain defenses that really do move one cornerback around to cover the opponent's top weapon (i.e., Arizona). The ratings against tight ends and running backs are in large part due to the performance of linebackers.

How to Read the Special Teams Tables

The special teams tables list the last three years of kick, punt, and return numbers for each team.

The first two columns list total special-teams DVOA and rank among the 32 teams (Table 10). The next two columns list the value in actual points of field goals and extra points (**FG/XP**) when compared to how a league average kicker would do from the same distances, adjusted for weather and altitude, and rank among the 32 teams. Next, we list the estimated value in actual points of field position over or under the league average based on net kickoffs (**Net Kick**), and rank that value among the 32 teams. That is followed by the estimated point values of field position for kick returns (**Kick Ret**), net punting (**Net Punt**), and punt returns (**Punt Ret**) and their respective ranks.

The final two columns represent the value of "**Hidden**" special teams, plays which throughout the past decade have usually

been based on the performance of opponents without this team being able to control the outcome. We combine the opposing team's value on field goals, kickoff distance, and punt distance, adjusted for weather and altitude, and then switch the sign to represent that good special teams by the opponent will cost the listed team points, and bad special teams will effectively hand them points. We have to give the qualifier of "usually" because, as explained above, certain returners such as Devin Hester will affect opposing special teams strategy, and a handful of the missed field goals are blocked. Nonetheless, the "hidden" value is still "hidden" for most teams, and they are ranked from the most hidden value gained (Philadelphia, 23.5 points) to the most value lost (New Orleans, minus-23.1 points).

We also have methods for measuring the gross value of kickoffs and punts. These measures assume that all kickoffs or punts will have average returns unless they are touchbacks or kicked out of bounds, then judge the kicker or punter on the value with those assumed returns. These metrics may be listed in special-teams comments as **KickPts+** and **PuntPts+**. We also count special-teams tackles; these include both tackles and assists, but do not include tackles on two-point conversions, tackles after onside kicks, or tackles of the player who recovers a fumble after the punt or kick returner loses the ball. The best and worst individual values for kickers, punters, returners, and kick gunners (i.e. tackle totals) are listed in the statistical appendix at the end of the book.

Administrative Minutia

Receiving statistics include all passes intended for the receiver in question, including those that are incomplete or intercepted. The word passes refers to both complete and incomplete pass attempts. When rating receivers, interceptions are treated as incomplete passes with no penalty.

For the computation of DVOA and DYAR, passing statistics include sacks as well as fumbles on aborted snaps. We do not include kneeldown plays or spikes for the purpose of stopping the clock. Some interceptions which we have determined to be "Hail Mary" plays that end the first half or game are counted as regular incomplete passes, not turnovers.

All statistics generated by ESPN Stats & Information or the Football Outsiders game charting project may be different from totals compiled by other sources.

Unless we say otherwise, when we refer to third-down performance in this book we are referring to a combination of third down and the handful of rushing and passing plays that take place on fourth down (primarily fourth-and-1).

Aaron Schatz

Table 12: Dallas Cowboys' Special Teams

Year	DVOA	Rank	FG/XP	Rank	Net Kick	Rank	Kick Ret	Rank	Net Punt	Rank	Punt Ret	Rank	Hidden	Rank
2012	0.2%	15	7.8	5	-3.1	24	-10.9	32	-1.4	17	8.4	4	2.5	10
2013	3.4%	8	7.0	5	1.2	14	3.2	7	-1.5	21	7.3	5	0.9	14
2014	0.9%	13	5.3	6	5.0	8	-3.0	23	-0.6	19	-2.5	16	3.1	11

The Year In Quotes

LET'S DO THIS THING!

"Is this thing on? Because it's getting ready to be."

—New Buffalo Bills head coach Rex Ryan, delivering his opening line at his introductory press conference, and nailing it in true Rex fashion. (NJ.com)

TO PARAPHRASE: I HATE YOU

"We're on to Cincinnati."

—New England Patriots head coach Bill Belichick's answer to multiple questions during a press conference, including anything pertaining to football. (Shutdown Corner)

I'M AFRAID TO MAKE A JOKE ABOUT SABAN

"No, I don't realize that. I still feel like I'm a kid from West Virginia. It's hard for me to understand why anyone would be intimidated."

—Alabama head coach Nick Saban, when asked if he realizes how intimidating he is. (Sports Illustrated)

WE ARE THE MUSIC MAKERS AND WE ARE THE DREAMERS OF DREAMS

"It's like playing for Willy Wonka. He's crazy. He wants to be young. He just is one of those guys who's always upbeat, wants to have a good time, and lets you be yourself."

—Seattle Seahawks defensive end Michael Bennett on Seahawks head coach Pete Carroll. (Tacoma News Tribune)

BY THE WAY, EDDIE LACY'S A FREE AGENT IN TWO YEARS

"Congrats, you just cost me a lot of money."

—Seattle Seahawks general manager John Schneider, in a phone call to Ryan Tannehill's agent Pat Dye, regarding keeping quarterback Russell Wilson after Tannehill's $96 million deal drove up the market cost of quarterbacks. (Twitter)

THE BELICHICK FASHION TREE

"Here's the deal. I finally realized why [he does it]. They're sized where the sleeves come up so the sleeves aren't quite long enough and they start [bunching]. I don't have a problem emulating him or what they do."

—New Orleans Saints head coach Sean Payton, explaining why during the Saints-Panthers game he was wearing a Bill Belichick-style team hoodie with cutoff sleeves. (New Orleans Advocate)

NOTHING LIKE THE MONEY IN THE BANK CONTRACT THOUGH

"Well, a lot of us have bonuses in our contracts."

—Green Bay Packers quarterback Aaron Rodgers, explaining why veterans come to voluntary offseason workouts. (SB Nation)

ESPECIALLY WHEN D-BO IS AROUND

"Ain't no reason to go around a block."

—San Diego Chargers draft pick linebacker Denzel Perryman, giving us his philosophy on the art of blocking. (Twitter)

DON'T WORRY, NOBODY EVEN KNOWS THE VETERAN COMBINE EXISTS

"4.91? There you go, there goes my career."

—Veteran NFL running back Michael Bush, after learning he ran a 4.91 40-yard dash at the NFL's inaugural veteran combine. (Sporting News)

DO YOUR JOB

"I made a play to help my team win. I've worked so hard in practice and I just wanted to play so bad and help my team out. I got out there and did exactly what I needed to do to help my team win. I was fired up ready. I was ready to play ... I was on the sidelines waiting to get in and I was ready. I prepared hard this weekend...

"I knew they were going to throw it. Our defensive coordinator is real smart and with a goal-line, three-cornerback formation we knew they were going to throw the ball."

—New England Patriots cornerback Malcolm Butler, following the New England Patriots' 28-24 comeback victory over the Seattle Seahawks in Super Bowl XLIX (Boston.com)

THE BEST EVAH

"You're the best ever. Ever."

"I don't know about that."

"EVAH."

"I love you man."

"Fuck that! EVAH!"

"Thank you."

"You're going to add a couple more to that resume."

—On-field exchange between actor and Southie native Mark Wahlberg and Super Bowl XLIX MVP Tom Brady, following the game. (Eye on Football)

ALSO, DO YOU KNOW WHEN NAP TIME IS?

"I don't answer preschool questions. Improve your line of questioning, then we'll talk."

—Seattle Seahawks cornerback Richard Sherman, after Sherman was asked at Super Bowl Media Day if he's the NFL's best cornerback, and additionally to compare himself to Darrelle Revis. (Instagram)

THE YEAR IN BEAST MODE

"I know I'm gonna get got, but I'm going to get mine more than I get got."

—Seattle Seahawks running back Marshawn Lynch, explaining what "Beast Mode" is. (Eye on Football)

"I done got in a lot of trouble for grabbing my ding-ding."

—Lynch, discussing the repercussions for his crotch-grabbing habit with Conan O'Brien. (Pro Football Talk)

"I'm just here so I don't get fined."

—Lynch, in response to every single question during Super Bowl Media Day. (ESPN)

THAT'S A PRO'S RANT RIGHT THERE'

"A guy like [Eichorst] who has no integrity, he doesn't even understand what a core value is. And he hasn't understood it from the day he got here. I saw it when I first met with the guy. To have core values means you have to be about something, you have to represent something that is important to you. He's a f---ing lawyer who makes policies. That's all he's done since he's been here: hire people and make policies to cover his own ass.

"I didn't really have any relationship with the A.D. The guy, you guys saw him [Sunday], the guy's a total p----. I mean, he is. He's a total c---."

—Youngstown State head coach and recently fired Nebraska head coach Bo Pelini, insulting his former boss, Nebraska athletic director Shawn Eichorst, in an expletive-filled rant to Huskers players, which was recorded and sent to the Omaha World-Herald because it's 2014 and everyone has a microphone. (Omaha World-Herald)

OR JUST CHANGE THE RULEBOOK

"Maybe those guys gotta study the rule book and figure it out. We obviously knew what we were doing and we made some pretty important plays. It was a real good weapon for us. Maybe we'll have something in store next week."

—New England Patriots quarterback Tom Brady, responding to Baltimore Ravens head coach John Harbaugh's comments that Patriots plays using four offensive lineman and an ineligible receiver was something he had never seen before. (For The Win)

WHO DOESN'T LOVE A GOOD BIKE RIDE?

"I was like 'Man, shoot we're going to the Super Bowl again, they're not going to mind if I take the bike. I'm not going to take his gun, but I'm going to take his bike.' So I was just riding around the stadium, I didn't know it was going to get that much exposure. I was just having a good time, popping wheelies, riding around giving the fans high-fives and stuff. I just thought it was a cool thing to do."

—Seattle Seahawks defensive end Michael Bennett, on taking a police officer's bicycle and riding it around following the Seahawks shocking comeback victory over the Packers in the NFC Championship Game. (JimRome.com)

MORE RAPID THAN THE EAGLES'
OFFENSE, HIS COURSERS THEY CAME

"If it kept [Richardson] out of the Pro Bowl because some guy had 'X' amount of sacks, and that guy can't hold his jock as a player, to be honest with you, I think that's kind of strange to me.

"I guess you guys will figure out who I'm talking about."

—New York Jets head coach Rex Ryan, wondering aloud why Jets defensive tackle Sheldon Richardson did not make the Pro Bowl over players who "can't hold his jock"—namely, St. Louis Rams rookie defensive tackle Aaron Donald. (NJ.com)

TAKE OUT HIGH FIVES AND IT SOUNDS
LIKE HE'S DESCRIBING A HORSE

"You've got to—got to—be prepared for his headbutts and high-fives, because they are coming… You've got to brace yourself. It doesn't look like much coming at you but it's intense. If he throws the ball 50 yards and you run 50 yards and score, he's going to run all 50 yards and headbutt the hell out of you."

—New England Patriots wide receiver Brian Tyms, breaking down quarterback Tom Brady's celebration techniques. (Wall Street Journal)

WELL I WOULD THINK NOT

"You'll get a little bit more movement if Manziel's the quarterback, the thing that they did against Buffalo. But other than that, no, it doesn't impact you at all. You've got to go defend the offense, you don't defend the player, particularly a midget."

—Cincinnati Bengals head coach Marvin Lewis, calling this week's opponent, Cleveland Browns quarterback Johnny Manziel a midget. Lewis apologized multiple times for using the slur. (Cleveland Plain Dealer)

YOU AREN'T COACHING THE JAGUARS, MAN

"I don't think our pro offense would work at the college level."

—*Philadelphia Eagles head coach Chip Kelly, cheekily denying that he had any interest in the University of Florida head coaching vacancy, which was filled by Jim McElwain. (Twitter)*

CORTLAND FINNEGAN IS CRAZY

"[Steve Smith] comes over to me, and tells me 'None of that crazy stuff, Finnegan.' I'd never played him before, so I was like, 'Yes sir. Absolutely. Nothing crazy.' Back then, they called me crazy. Midway through the game, [the Panthers] ran a toss sweep, and I had him pinned. I was going to push the running back out of bounds. Next thing I know, he picks me up and he throws me into the water cooler. The very next play, he runs a slant, they run a boot, and I run as fast as I could and went helmet-to-helmet with him. I remember his helmet bouncing on the ground and he bounced up so fast, telling me he was going to kill me. I've enjoyed Steve Smith."

—*Miami Dolphins cornerback Cortland Finnegan, telling a story about the first time he played Baltimore Ravens wide receiver Steve Smith (Miami Herald)*

FAMILY FIRST

"The whole experience… I have been just stunned. It has helped so much. I can't believe that in this sport that has no so-called heart, it's really so full of heart. That's the truth: football is full of heart."

—*Cincinnati Bengals defensive tackle Devon Still, reflecting on the support of the organization after his daughter Leah was diagnosed with terminal cancer. The Bengals cut Still after training camp, but re-signed him to the practice squad to retain health insurance. Still was activated Week 2. (MMQB)*

REAL TALK

"They're the world champs. We're just 9-1. We haven't done shit."

—*Arizona Cardinals head coach Bruce Arians, talking about taking on the Super Bowl Champion Seattle Seahawks. (AZCardinals.com)*

COME ON GUYS, HE RAN 50 FEET

"It was the slowest 17 yards I've ever seen in my life. It's always fun seeing the Clydesdale run."

—*New England Patriots wide receiver Julian Edelman, reflecting on quarterback Tom Brady's 17-yard run against the Dolphins on Sunday. (ESPN)*

YOU COULD BUY AN ISLAND WITH THAT

"A $5 million dollar cashed check. When I got pushed out the door, or shoved out the door, they owed me $5 million dollars and that's what I received. And I'm planning on taking one of those vacations from that money this weekend on our bye week."

—*Baltimore Ravens wide receiver Steve Smith, on what he is doing with his Panthers' salary that they paid him this season. (Eye on Football)*

WELL, FITZPATRICK IS JUST HOLDING A CLIPBOARD NOW

"Man, that was a tough question. You might want to ask that question to Ryan Fitzpatrick or something, man. Harvard graduate. Jesus Christ, this is an interview at my locker."

—*New York Jets quarterback Michael Vick, responding to a long-winded question about his thoughts on fans directing all of the blame for the Jets' poor season on general manager John Idzik. (Twitter)*

THIS IS BRYAN COX'S FAULT SOMEHOW

"It's one of my great regrets in life that I didn't take that part. I know the movie would've had a successful run had I been in it. Had I taken that part instead of Brett, we're talking Academy Awards and all those things."

—*Former New England Patriots quarterback Drew Bledsoe, lamenting the fact that he missed out on Brett Favre's cameo role in There's Something About Mary. Bledsoe had to drop out after an ugly mosh-pit incident at an Everclear concert. Steve Young was the Farrelly Brothers' second choice, with Favre coming in third. (NFL Now)*

THERE'S A TEBOW JOKE IN HERE SOMEWHERE

"Going to play quarterback for the Jets … it's kind of like, you know when they used to take the pretty young virgin up to the edge of the volcano and then just throw them in? That's kind of what it is when you play quarterback for the Jets. It just feels bad."

—*Former NFL quarterback Drew Bledsoe, making an interesting analogy to describe Philadelphia Eagles quarterback Mark Sanchez and his career in New York with the Jets. (Eye on Football)*

THERE'S A 100 PERCENT CHANCE OF BELICHICK BEING GRUMPY

"There was 100 percent chance of rain last week and the only water I saw was on the Gatorade table.

"If I did my job the way they do theirs, I'd be here about a week."

—*New England Patriots head coach Bill Belichick, basically saying that meteorologists suck at their jobs. (Eye on Football)*

IS THAT WHY YOU DROPPED SO MANY PASSES LAST NIGHT AS WELL?

"Because I wanted to play for the Carolina Panthers."

—Carolina Panthers wide receiver Kelvin Benjamin, on why he ran a 4.61 40-yard dash at this year's NFL combine. Benjamin noted that he has been clocked at 4.41 seconds, which would have ranked fifth at the 2014 combine. (ESPN NFL Nation Blog)

THIS SEEMS TOTALLY PLAUSIBLE

"Well, he called me one time (when) we were having a tough time of it. 'Now don't take this wrong. You know how much I respect you.' But he said 'I've got some advice for you.' And I kind of rolled my eyes on the other end of the phone, thought, well here goes. And he said 'Drink a lot.'"

—Dallas Cowboys owner Jerry Jones, telling a story about a time Washington owner Dan Snyder gave him some advice on how to handle losing seasons. (D.C. Sports Blog)

AND GUESS WHAT: THE WORK IS REALLY SHODDY

"I have a really nice condo, and guess what: Jay Cutler built that condo. We're great. We're great."

—Chicago Bears wide receiver Brandon Marshall, on his relationship with Bears quarterback Jay Cutler; it is strong. (Chicago Sun-Times)

PROBABLY SHOULD UPDATE YOUR RESUME

"Contact my boss, John Elway."

—Former Broncos practice squad safety John Boyett, repeatedly, after he was arrested for disorderly public intoxication and resisting arrest. (Shutdown Corner

GARCON, MORE FUEL TO THE FIRE PLEASE

"Pierre [Garçon] doesn't matter in this league. I mean exactly what I said."

—Seattle Seahawks cornerback Richard Sherman, on Washington Redskins wide receiver Pierre Garçon's relevance in the National Football League.

"Yeah. Pierre did a few things. When you can't get open, you got to do whatever you can. The crowd is acting like I'm holding him. Obviously the TV copy you can see what happened."

—Sherman, when asked if Garçon pulled his hair during Monday Night Football. (SB Nation)

HE DID NOT HAVE THE EYE OF THE TIGER

"I did not see her, but I was looking for her. I was hoping I would see her, maybe get a selfie in or two. I didn't see her, but I could definitely tell she had a good time and definitely hope she'll be back after this weekend. We are gonna have a good season so I have a feeling she'll be back"

—Ole Miss tight end Evan Engram, on being disappointed that he did not get to meet singer Katy Perry after Ole Miss defeated Alabama. (Eye on Football)

BIG MAN ON CAMPUS

"That film is a coaching session. I'm 35 years old, and I ran around those boys like they were schoolyard kids."

—Baltimore Ravens wide receiver Steve Smith, assessing his performance in his reunion game against the Carolina Panthers, a 38-10 victory for the Ravens. (Shutdown Corner)

ELI MANNING ADVENTURE TIME!

"It's almost like seeing a UFO or seeing a unicorn or something like that. But it's cool. We will take it. I know Eli will take it."

—New York Giants wide receiver Victor Cruz, laughing as he described quarterback Eli Manning's rushing touchdown in their victory against Washington. (New York Post)

ANYTIME YOU CAN TEAR AN ACL, YOU GOTTA DO IT

"Hell, no. I'd do it again, brother. You do it every time. If it's going to happen, it's going to happen. Just a matter of time."

—Detroit Lions linebacker Stephen Tulloch, on whether he had any regrets after he tore his ACL celebrating a sack of Aaron Rodgers while mimicking the quarterback's "Discount Double Check" move. (Detroit Free Press)

I'D RATHER WIN AT REALITY FOOTBALL

"Would've won if I played me. During the game, I'm like, 'Really?' That's the honest truth."

—New York Giants tight end Larry Donnell, revealing that he lost his fantasy football matchup in Week 4 because he left himself on the bench during his three-touchdown performance. (ESPN New York)

STATE FARM JUST FOUND THEIR NEW SLOGAN

"Five letters here just for everybody out there in Packerland: R-E-L-A-X. Relax. We're going to be OK."

—Green Bay Packers quarterback Aaron Rodgers, giving a positive message to Packers fans. (ESPN)

ISN'T THAT A QUALIFICATION FOR OWNING AN NFL TEAM?

"I don't want to paint all the owners with a broad brush, because I've developed some relationships with some who, I don't think they're, like, a--holes, to put it that way. But I think a lot of them are, honestly."

—Former NFLPA President Domonique Foxworth, in an interview with WNYC saying that a lot of owners are... well, he said it. (Shutdown Corner)

JOSH GORDON LOVES PAPA JOHN'S, BELIEVE IT OR NOT

"I've gotten to know some of the folks here in Colorado. There's some different laws out here in Colorado. Pizza business is pretty good out here, believe it or not, due to some recent law changes."

—Peyton Manning, Denver Broncos quarterback and owner of a number of Papa John's franchises. (The MMQB)

WHAT ABOUT IN THE LOCKER ROOM?

"On the football field, I think that we were a quarterback away from having a team."

—Chicago Bears wide receiver Brandon Marshall, asked what he made of his time in Miami as the Bears prepared to play the Dolphins. (Miami Herald)

AT LEAST YOU ARE NOT IN SUPLEX CITY

"Bruh... Please get all of the punter curb stomps out of your system before we make a visit to the Steel city… #Ruthless"

—Indianapolis Colts punter Pat McAfee, sending a tweet to Pittsburgh Steelers wide receiver Antonio Brown, after Brown hit Cleveland Browns punter Spencer Lanning in the face with his foot. (Twitter)

COME ON GUYS, WHO DOESN'T TAKE LASER TAG WAY TOO SERIOUSLY?

"There's some accuracy there. But it wasn't paintball. It's just another one of those half-truths. Just a half-truth. It was laser tag. That seemed part of the game."

—University of Michigan head coach Jim Harbaugh admitting he destroyed a 10-year-old kid in laser tag at his bachelor party in order to win. (Eye on Football)

THINGS COVERED IN GOLD, I ASSUME

"I Googled 'What do rich people buy?' Because I don't feel like a rich person, and I don't really try to act like a rich person, so I don't know what they buy. I didn't really like the stuff I saw, so I'm gonna stick with my humble lifestyle and just keep working out."

—Houston Texans defensive end J.J. Watt, revealing what he did after signing his massive $100 million contract extension. (Eye on Football)

FANTASY OUTLOOK: OH MY GOD NO

"I think I could play, as far as throwing. Of course, we're not trying to start some he's-coming-out-of-retirement deal. Do I think I could play and lead a team? Look, no. But I could play. I could make all the throws I made before, I just couldn't throw it near as far, but that never matters anyway."

—Retired NFL quarterback Brett Favre, 45, claiming that he is still capable of making of making all the throws the NFL requires. (Sports Illustrated)

THAT'S WHAT SOMEONE WHO DOES DRUGS WOULD SAY

"I wouldn't have any idea where to get a Molly or what a Molly is. That's a joke. I don't do marijuana, I don't do drugs. I don't do any drugs."

—Suspended Denver Broncos wide receiver Wes Welker, in part of an email to the Denver Post after being suspended for the first four games of the season for the use of amphetamines. (Denver Post)

EAST COAST WEST COAST WORLDWIDE

"You got to do a little bit of whatever it takes to win. Whether it is West Coast, East Coast, side coast, north coast, whatever coast. We'll be whatever coast you need us to be to win games. It will be Bengal coast. That's what it is going to be."

—Cincinnati Bengals offensive coordinator Hue Jackson, on what the team's offensive strategy would be going into Week 1. (Cincinnati Enquirer)

I MEAN, YEAH

"About like I expected. Jerry comes across as a rich a--hole."

—Former Dallas Cowboys head coach Jimmy Johnson, when asked how Cowboys owner Jerry Jones comes across in a recent lengthy article written about Jones. (The Port Arthur News)

PLEASE ALLOW ME TO INTRODUCE MYSELF, I'M A MAN OF WEALTH AND TASTE

"Here's what I don't like. I don't like what Roger Goodell is doing. He has so much power that he can almost shut people down. I just don't like him.

"And I don't like that on draft day these kids don't know that they're hugging the devil. I hate to see kids that are lost and then happy but they really don't know that the man they're hugging will rip their throat apart. If he has an opportunity to take money from them, or there's a situation where they're guilty before they go to court, he'll rip them apart. And there's nothing no one can do about it. If the owners are happy with Roger Goodell, the fans, the media, no one can take his job from him. I hate it."

—Former New Orleans Saints wide receiver Joe Horn, when asked for his thoughts on the current state of the NFL. (ESPN)

"You could be the worst bartender at spring break, but you'd still be killing it."

—President of the NFL Players Association, Cincinnati Bengals tackle Eric Winston, letting on that he and other players believe the league has succeeded these past few years in spite of NFL commissioner Roger Goodell, not because of him. (GQ)

"@nflcommish ain't no fun when the rabbit got the gun huh?"

—Recently retired linebacker James Harrison, in a tweet to NFL commissioner Roger Goodell regarding the mishandling of the Ray Rice situation. (Shutdown Corner)

AND FINALLY, THE YEAR IN GRONK

"He's become a sex symbol with some kittens. It's crazy. Whoever thought that some furry little cats would've created a sex symbol? Go figure."

—New England Patriots running back Shane Vereen, needling teammate Rob Gronkowski about a photo Gronk took with some kittens earlier this season. (ESPN Boston)

"She cleans, cooks, makes big cash, stays at home, lets me do whatever I want."

—Gronkowski, describing his ideal wife to Jim Rome on Showtime. (YouTube)

"[Brown] was just yappin' at me the whole time. So I took him and threw him out of the club."

—Gronkowski, explaining the rationale behind a long, extended block on Colts safety Sergio Brown which earned him a 15-yard penalty. (CSN New England)

"There were a lot of hot, sexy Mexican ladies there, but I picked out the largest, healthiest looking one, who had to be 260 pounds, like I was. After 10 seconds of me dancing on top of her in the chair, the collective 520 pounds of the two of us collapsed the fold-up chair. The crowd exploded with laughter. I got up and continued dancing [or twerking] to that Mariachi music. That was the best $30 I ever made!"

—Gronkowski, describing his experience at a bachelor party he recently attended because, well, he's Gronk and you're not. (from the book It's Good to Be Gronk)

Compiled by Rory Hickey

Full 2015 Projections

The following table lists the mean DVOA projections for all 32 NFL teams. We also list the average number of wins for each team in our one million simulations, along with how often each team made the playoffs, reached the Super Bowl, and won the NFL Championship.

Please note that the mean DVOA projections do not incorporate any of the player suspensions which are programmed into this year's simulation. However, the average opponent listed for Buffalo, Dallas, Jacksonville, and Pittsburgh is based on the New England Patriots being led by backup quarterback Jimmy Garoppolo in the first four games of the season.

Full 2015 Projections

Team	Avg Wins	Make Playoffs	Reach Super Bowl	Win Super Bowl	Total DVOA	Rk	Off DVOA	Rk	Def DVOA	Rk	ST DVOA	Rk	Average Opponent	Rk
SEA	10.7	75.0%	25.2%	14.8%	22.2%	1	10.2%	4	-13.4%	1	-1.3%	27	1.2%	14
NE	10.5	71.7%	22.3%	12.4%	18.8%	2	12.7%	2	-0.8%	12	5.4%	1	-2.8%	25
DEN	9.5	59.1%	15.3%	8.3%	14.2%	4	9.0%	5	-7.7%	3	-2.5%	31	2.8%	8
GB	9.7	60.2%	14.6%	8.0%	14.4%	3	18.4%	1	1.9%	21	-2.1%	30	2.5%	10
IND	9.3	61.1%	9.9%	4.6%	4.6%	12	4.6%	10	0.1%	16	0.1%	12	-4.4%	30
STL	8.8	45.6%	7.5%	3.7%	7.3%	5	-1.0%	20	-7.1%	4	1.2%	7	1.1%	15
BAL	8.6	45.6%	7.6%	3.7%	5.6%	7	-1.9%	21	-4.2%	6	3.4%	3	0.9%	16
CIN	8.6	45.3%	7.5%	3.5%	5.1%	11	2.2%	13	-2.9%	7	0.1%	13	1.4%	12
MIN	8.5	41.8%	6.8%	3.4%	6.7%	6	0.7%	15	-1.9%	8	4.1%	2	3.2%	5
PHI	8.8	48.5%	7.1%	3.4%	3.6%	14	2.9%	12	-1.1%	11	-0.4%	15	-2.4%	22
SD	8.5	42.7%	6.9%	3.3%	5.2%	9	9.0%	6	2.9%	23	-0.9%	21	1.2%	13
DAL	8.4	43.8%	6.5%	3.1%	3.6%	13	6.6%	8	2.4%	22	-0.6%	18	-1.1%	19
PIT	8.1	39.5%	6.5%	3.1%	5.4%	8	11.4%	3	4.7%	28	-1.2%	25	2.6%	9
ATL	8.9	49.2%	6.6%	3.0%	1.2%	16	4.8%	9	6.4%	29	2.8%	4	-5.3%	32
NO	8.7	45.3%	6.2%	2.9%	-0.3%	17	7.1%	7	6.5%	31	-0.9%	23	-5.3%	31
DET	8.2	37.5%	5.6%	2.8%	5.1%	10	4.2%	11	-1.5%	10	-0.6%	17	3.8%	3
KC	7.9	34.3%	4.9%	2.2%	2.4%	15	1.3%	14	1.0%	18	2.1%	5	2.0%	11
NYJ	8.2	37.2%	4.5%	2.0%	-1.4%	18	-11.8%	31	-8.4%	2	2.0%	6	-2.7%	24
BUF	8.0	34.3%	4.1%	1.8%	-2.8%	20	-9.4%	27	-6.4%	5	0.2%	11	-1.8%	21
CAR	8.0	35.1%	3.8%	1.7%	-2.8%	19	-0.7%	19	1.4%	20	-0.7%	19	-2.7%	23
NYG	7.7	32.9%	3.2%	1.3%	-4.0%	22	0.5%	16	4.1%	26	-0.5%	16	-1.3%	20
MIA	7.5	27.7%	3.1%	1.3%	-3.8%	21	-0.3%	18	0.9%	17	-2.6%	32	-0.5%	18
HOU	7.3	29.2%	2.4%	0.9%	-9.0%	26	-10.6%	29	-1.7%	9	0.0%	14	-3.4%	27
SF	6.8	19.9%	2.0%	0.9%	-4.9%	23	-4.4%	23	-0.3%	14	-0.8%	20	4.4%	2
ARI	6.7	18.4%	1.8%	0.8%	-5.2%	24	-3.5%	22	-0.2%	15	-1.9%	28	4.8%	1
OAK	6.5	18.1%	1.6%	0.6%	-9.2%	27	-6.8%	24	1.2%	19	-1.2%	24	3.1%	6
CLE	6.4	17.1%	1.5%	0.6%	-9.9%	28	-7.1%	25	3.1%	24	0.3%	10	2.9%	7
CHI	6.5	16.1%	1.3%	0.5%	-8.6%	25	-0.1%	17	6.4%	30	-2.1%	29	3.3%	4
JAC	6.3	18.9%	1.1%	0.4%	-15.1%	29	-11.4%	30	4.2%	27	0.5%	8	-3.5%	28
WAS	6.0	14.5%	0.9%	0.3%	-15.1%	30	-10.2%	28	3.7%	25	-1.2%	26	-0.2%	17
TB	6.4	16.1%	0.9%	0.3%	-16.3%	31	-17.0%	32	-0.4%	13	0.4%	9	-3.4%	26
TEN	6.4	18.1%	0.9%	0.3%	-17.2%	32	-9.4%	26	6.9%	32	-0.9%	22	-4.1%	29

Arizona Cardinals

2014 Record: 11-5	**Total DVOA:** -6.4% (22nd)	**2015 Mean Projection:** 6.7 wins	**On the Clock (0-4):** 21%
Pythagorean Wins: 8.3 (16th)	**Offense:** -9.3% (23rd)	**Postseason Odds:** 18.4%	**Mediocrity (5-7):** 42%
Snap-Weighted Age: 27.1 (4th)	**Defense:** -5.0% (7th)	**Super Bowl Odds:** 1.8%	**Playoff Contender (8-10):** 29%
Average Opponent: 4.6% (2nd)	**Special Teams:** -2.2% (21st)	**Proj. Avg. Opponent:** 4.8% (1st)	**Super Bowl Contender (11+):** 8%

2014: Hey, you try winning a playoff game with a practice squad quarterback.

2015: When your defense leaves town, winning a playoff game with a veteran quarterback can be pretty hard too.

Officially, the Arizona Cardinals' 2014 season ended on January 3, 2015, when they lost to the Carolina Panthers 27-16 in the wild-card round of the playoffs. Realistically, though, their status as a playoff contender ended a month before that when Drew Stanton suffered sprained knee ligaments in St. Louis. And if we're being honest, their Super Bowl chances likely died in November, when Carson Palmer tore his ACL against the Rams. Down to third-string quarterback Ryan Lindley and with injuries devastating his front seven, Bruce Arians won Coach of the Year for guiding the Cardinals to a franchise record 11 wins. Arizona actually held a lead at halftime in a road playoff game before succumbing to the inevitable. It's only natural to assume they'll get better injury luck in 2015, and threaten to knock the Seahawks from their throne atop the division and conference, right?

Well, maybe not. Win-loss record tells us the Cardinals were a very good team over the course of the season, but most other statistics say otherwise. Though specific units were ravaged by injuries last year, overall they weren't any less healthy than an average team. And Palmer, the quarterback they're getting back to lead them to the promised land, isn't likely to be as good in 2015 as he was in 2014—and he wasn't as good in 2014 as you probably think. Between Palmer's advancing age, the lack of a running game, and depth concerns (again) in the front seven, we see Arizona as a long shot to get back to the playoffs.

Let's start by dissecting that 11-5 record. On the surface, it looks like Arizona's win total was boosted by a schedule that only included five games against playoff teams. The Cardinals went 2-3 in those five games, but 9-2 against teams that failed to make the postseason. However, a lot of those non-playoff teams were pretty good clubs, including Kansas City, San Diego, Philadelphia, and San Francisco twice. According to DVOA, Arizona played a tougher schedule than any team last year except Oakland. How can you discount 11 wins against teams like that?

Answer: by looking at the lucky breaks the Cardinals got on the field, rather than the breaks they got from the schedule-makers. The Cardinals had the league's biggest gap between their 11 wins and 8.3 Pythagorean wins. They went 5-1 in games decided by eight points or less and just 6-4 otherwise. It's easy to find one play in each of those games that could have led to a loss rather than a win if it had gone the other way. The Cardinals needed two fourth-quarter touchdowns to beat the Chargers; a 75-yard John Brown score to beat the Eagles; late fourth-and-short stops to beat the Lions and Rams; and a down-by-contact call reversed to a fumble on instant replay to beat the Chiefs. If four plays turn out differently, that 5-1 record turns to 1-5 and the Cardinals are a losing team.

And while it's hard to say that fortune smiled on the Arizona quarterbacks when they kept getting hurt, whichever quarterback was healthy got away with a lot of mistakes. The Cardinals threw only 12 interceptions last year, a lower-than-average number. However, they led the league with 26 adjusted interceptions, which includes passes that should have been intercepted but were dropped by defenders. Four of those dropped interceptions came in the games that the Cardinals won by eight points or less. If Arizona's opponents had simply caught the balls that were right there for the taking, the Cardinals would have missed the playoffs, and Jason Garrett would probably have won Coach of the Year.

Our advanced stats look at that performance and aren't impressed. The Cardinals finished 22nd in DVOA, only the third team in DVOA history to finish in the 20s despite an 11-5 record. (The 2000 Vikings fell to 5-11 and last place in DVOA the next year. The 2012 Colts improved to 13th and went 11-5 again, but we'll get back to them in a few paragraphs.) And those injuries that allegedly shipwrecked Arizona's season? The Cardinals were 17th in AGL last year, almost exactly average and only one rank lower than the 2013 team that went 10-6. If we included suspensions in AGL, then Daryl Washington's punishment would drop them another half-dozen or so spots, but even then we would judge their health as below average, not catastrophic. In fact, overall, their offense was quite healthy last year, ranking eighth in AGL on that side of the ball.

It goes without saying, though, that some injuries hurt a team more than others, and quarterback injuries are the most important of the bunch. Only one team lost more games at quarterback than Arizona last year, and coincidentally, it was the team that caused all of the Cardinals' quarterback woes, the Rams. And the numbers make it clear that it's hard to overcome injuries at the quarterback position. In the past three years, 26 teams have suffered at least 2.0 AGL at quarterback, and only three of those teams made the playoffs: the 2013 Eagles (who saw Nick Foles come off the bench and catch fire), the 2013 Packers (who won a horrible NFC North at

2015 Cardinals Schedule

Week	Opp.	Week	Opp.	Week	Opp.
1	NO	7	BAL (Mon.)	13	at STL
2	at CHI	8	at CLE	14	MIN (Thu.)
3	SF	9	BYE	15	at PHI
4	STL	10	at SEA	16	GB
5	at DET	11	CIN	17	SEA
6	at PIT	12	at SF		

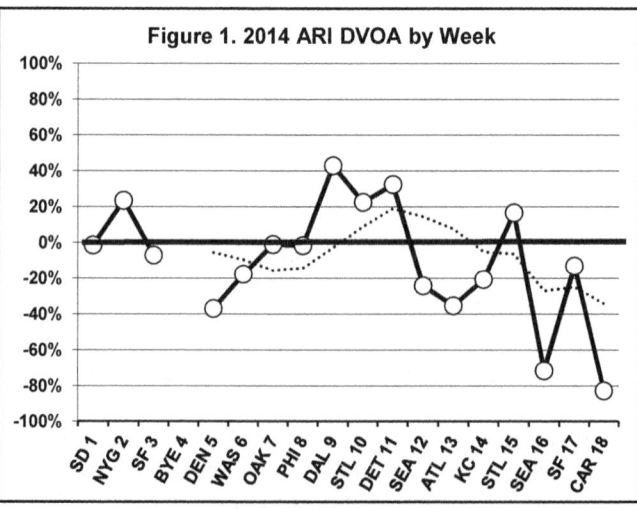

Figure 1. 2014 ARI DVOA by Week

8-7-1), and last year's Cardinals. In those same three seasons, 32 teams put up a perfect 0.0 AGL at quarterback, and 16 of those teams made it to the postseason. Keeping your passer upright and healthy for 16 games looks to be half the battle in making it to January.

It's quite possible, though, that Palmer won't ever play 16 games in a season again. Though he's on pace to recover from his torn ACL and start in Week 1, let's not forget that he also missed a month early in the season with a shoulder injury. In 11 seasons as a starter, Palmer has started 16 games only six times, and only once in the past four years. Palmer turns 36 in December, and quarterbacks of that age have historically gotten more fragile, not less.

It's also questionable whether even a healthy Palmer would be able to get Arizona back to the playoffs. Palmer's base stats last year were nice enough: he completed 62.9 percent of 224 passes for 7.3 yards per pass, with 11 touchdowns and just three interceptions. Those are decent numbers, especially considering Arizona's lack of targets at running back or tight end. (Among quarterbacks with at least 200 dropbacks, only Tony Romo and Aaron Rodgers had better DVOA ratings when throwing to wide receivers than Palmer; on throws to other positions, only Josh McCown was worse.)

Really, though, the only exceptional facet of Palmer's game in 2014 was his ability to avoid interceptions. That's fluky, and not because of the dropped picks that were thrown by his teammates; Palmer only had five adjusted interceptions, compared to 13 for Stanton and eight for Lindley. No, it's fluky because Palmer has not historically been particularly good at ball security. Last season was just the second time in Palmer's career (and first since 2006) that he has finished in the top ten for lowest interception rate. Meanwhile, he has ranked in the top ten for total interceptions five times. In 2013, he was second in the league with 22 picks. Put another way: Palmer threw three interceptions in the six games he played last year, but he threw three interceptions in one game *nine times* between 2010 and 2013. If Palmer's interception rate in 2015 returns to his historical norms, then he'll be close to the average starter he has always been for most of his career; his DVOA last season was his best since 2007. And though an average starting quarterback would be a lot better than what Arizona had for much of last year, it's not the caliber of play that tends to win championships.

We must also note that while Arizona as a team played a very difficult schedule, Palmer was lucky enough to play nothing but subpar secondaries. Palmer's VOA of 16.4% was

sixth-best among qualifiers, but his DVOA of 8.5% was just 12th, and the difference between the two of 7.9% was the biggest in the league. In other words, no starting quarterback in 2014 faced an easier slate of defenses. Palmer avoided not only the Seahawks and 49ers, but also the Broncos and Lions. Every team Palmer faced last year finished 18th or worse in pass defense DVOA; half were in the bottom eight. A full season for Palmer this year would mean eight games against teams that finished 11th or better in pass defense DVOA in 2014, including two games each against Seattle and San Francisco. Palmer's age, health history, prior performance, and future schedule all point to a decline this season.

Though Palmer's injury was the biggest of Arizona's season, he certainly wasn't the only guy on the team to miss time. Darnell Dockett's torn ACL, John Abraham's concussion, and Daryl Washington's suspension cost the Cardinals three defensive starters for all or most of the season. Calais Campbell, Matt Shaughnessy, and Alex Okafor all moved in and out of the lineup with various maladies. When the season was done, Arizona had the fifth-highest AGL among linebackers last year, and the fifth-highest AGL at defensive line as well. That latter number is particularly impressive because the Cardinals were theoretically a 3-4 team. In reality, defensive coordinator Todd Bowles was forced to field a dime defense virtually full-time, with rookie safety Deone Bucannon playing a "dollar" linebacker spot and safeties Tony Jefferson and Tyrann Mathieu often crashing the box.

And yet, despite all those injuries, the Cardinals' defense was seventh in DVOA, 14th against the pass and sixth against the run. Bowles pulled that off by going to an aggressive, blitz-heavy scheme that filled all running lanes and put opposing passers under constant harassment. The run defense was especially impressive, leading the league in short-yardage run defense and finishing second in stuff rate despite the smaller bodies Bowles was forced to put on the field. It helps, obviously, when you have Calais Campbell, who makes more plays against the run than almost any other lineman in the NFL, but Arizona's run defense was a team effort. The Cardinals were one of four teams to field at least 12 players who finished the season with at least three run defeats.

Bowles' success in 2014 led to a promotion, and now he's the head coach of the Jets. He'll be replaced in Arizona by James Bettcher, who has been the Cardinals' outside linebackers coach for the past two years. He's familiar with the team's roster and schemes, and it's likely he'll use the same aggressive philosophy that worked so well for Bowles. Our sidebar lists some of the tenets that Bowles relied on in 2014.

While Arizona's defensive scheme may look the same this fall, the players running that scheme will be vastly different. Between retirements, suspensions, and free agency, the Cardinals have lost eight players who might have been key defenders this season, most of them in the front seven. Some of those players were also injured (or suspended) last year, but that is still an awful lot of turnover for one defense in one season. We discuss these moves in detail later in the chapter, but for now we'll just point out that many of the players expected to fill those holes are either questionable draft picks, or veterans with injury histories of their own.

With a new coordinator trying to line up so many new faces, we're expecting the Cardinals to take a step back on defense. We're also pessimistic that the offense will be able to overcome an aging, damaged Carson Palmer. Where else could the team improve? The Cardinals are still excellent at receiver, but John Carlson's retirement has left them even weaker at tight end. Additions on the offensive line are likely to disappoint: Mike Iupati's performance hasn't lived up to his reputation for years in San Francisco, and first-round pick D.J. Humphries might not earn a starting spot in his first season.

With so many question marks on the field, we'll have to look to the sidelines for Arizona's best hope in 2015. Remember who was in charge of that 2012 Colts team that went 11-5 despite finishing 25th in DVOA? In two seasons as Arizona's

In Todd We Trust

Todd Bowles' defensive game plan in 2014 was a little more complicated than "blitz everyone all the time." Here's a look at where and when Bowles was most likely to use blitzes:

• **Thou shalt blitz a lot of defensive backs.** The Cardinals were just seventh in plays with exactly five rushers, and fifth in big blitzes of six or more, but they led the league by using a defensive back blitz on more than 20 percent of all dropbacks. Arizona had five defensive backs with at least one sack; only Tennessee had more. Tyrann Mathieu, Tony Jefferson, Rashad Johnson, and Jerraud Powers were each among the top 40 defensive backs in the league in both quarterback hits and hurries.

• **Thou shalt be conservative when down by one score.** The Cardinals used a DB blitz about twice as often as the average team when winning, tied, or down by more than eight points. When they were down by one score, though, they DB blitzed less than 10 percent of the time, and no more than the average team. This may be a reflection of Arizona's offense; with Stanton and Lindley at the helm, the Cardinals couldn't risk a close game turning into a blowout. When they were already down by two scores, though, blitzing and forcing a big play was their best bet to get back in the game. It's a similar story for big blitzes, where they were the league's most aggressive team when winning or tied (both at 16 percent or higher), but just sixth when losing at 13 percent. This is unusual, because league-wide big blitz rates actually went up when teams were losing.

• **Thou shalt blitz more in the beginning and end of games than in the middle.** The Cardinals used DB blitzes less than 17 percent of the time in both the second and third quarters, but more than one-fifth of the time in the first quarter and more than one-fourth of the time in the fourth quarter. This pattern was also true for five-man rushes, which went from about 40 percent in the second and third quarters to more than 45 percent in the first and fourth. Big blitzes, though, were more frequent after halftime, going from less than 13 percent in either of the first two quarters to a league-high 20 percent in the third and 18 percent in the fourth.

• **Thou shalt blitz like crazy at crunch time.** In the fourth quarter or overtime when the game was within one score, the Cards led the NFL in DB blitzes (23 percent) and five-man rushes (52 percent), and they were third in big blitzes (22 percent). This strategy was obvious from the first game of the season, when the Cardinals sent heavy pressure over and over while the Chargers inexplicably left Philip Rivers without extra blockers.

• **Thou shalt blitz all over the field—with one notable exception.** In the front zone (the area on the field between the opponents' 20- and 40-yard lines), the Cardinals' used a DB blitz only 16 percent of the time and rushed five 38 percent of the time. They still big-blitzed fairly often, but overall this was where the Cardinals were most conservative. That's somewhat unusual, because this seems like the area where a sack would turn a scoring chance into a punt, but it worked—the Cardinals had the league's best front-zone defensive DVOA.

• **Thou shalt open all barrels when it's time to get off the field.** Regardless of which type of blitz you're looking at, Arizona got significantly more aggressive on later downs. Their DB blitzes went from 10 percent on first down to 14 percent on second down, and then 35 percent on third downs. The splits on five-man rushes (36%/38%/57%) and big blitzes (9%/14%/24%) were similar. When opposing quarterbacks had to pass, the Cardinals would do anything they could to put him on the ground.

That's an awful lot of data to take in, but remember that James Bettcher's Cardinals will probably be just as aggressive as Bowles' teams, so we should see similar patterns in 2015.

head coach and one as the interim boss in Indianapolis, Bruce Arians—let's not sugarcoat this—has absolutely kicked our ass. His teams have won 11, 10, and 11 games (including two wins when Chuck Pagano was still on the sidelines for the Colts) when we gave them mean projections of 6.4, 6.4, and 7.3. And while most teams that win a bunch of close games in one season tend to lose those close games the following year, Arians may be the rare coach who bucks that trend. His 2013 Cardinals went 5-3 in close games, while the 2012 Colts went 8-0 after he took over for Pagano. Prior to his time in Indianapolis, Arians ran the offense for five years in Pittsburgh, and those Steelers teams went 24-18 in one-score games. (Since he left, Pittsburgh's close-game record has slipped to 13-14.) That's eight full NFL seasons for Arians as an offensive coordinator or head coach (or, sometimes, both), and those teams have won nearly twice as many close games as they have lost, going 43-23 in such contests. It's easy to write off six close games in 2014 as a fluke of small sample size, but the 66 games under Arians' belt seem a lot more concrete.

But with less than three years as a head coach, our projection system can't produce a significant variable for the play-calling or witchcraft or whatever it is that has made Arians so effective winning close games. What we do know is that the Cardinals had some bad luck on the medical report last year that offset their good luck on the field. Assuming their luck evens out this fall, we're left to analyze the tangible personnel moves of this offseason, and that analysis tells us the Cardinals are a fringe playoff team at best.

Vincent Verhei

2014 Cardinals Stats by Week

Wk	vs.	W-L	PF	PA	YDF	YDA	TO	Total	Off	Def	ST
1	SD	W	18	17	403	290	-1	-1%	-7%	-24%	-18%
2	at NYG	W	25	14	266	341	4	23%	-17%	-12%	28%
3	SF	W	23	14	338	318	-1	-7%	10%	21%	4%
4	BYE										
5	at DEN	L	20	41	215	568	2	-37%	-18%	8%	-11%
6	WAS	W	30	20	317	407	4	-18%	-27%	-4%	6%
7	at OAK	W	24	13	365	220	-1	-1%	2%	2%	-2%
8	PHI	W	24	20	400	521	2	-2%	-1%	0%	-1%
9	at DAL	W	28	17	339	266	1	43%	-2%	-50%	-5%
10	STL	W	31	14	335	244	2	22%	-17%	-40%	-1%
11	DET	W	14	6	352	262	-1	32%	6%	-29%	-3%
12	at SEA	L	3	19	204	293	-1	-24%	-20%	-16%	-20%
13	at ATL	L	18	29	329	500	-2	-35%	-21%	2%	-12%
14	KC	W	17	14	366	390	2	-21%	-8%	-1%	-13%
15	at STL	W	12	6	274	280	2	17%	-19%	-23%	13%
16	SEA	L	6	35	216	596	-1	-72%	-34%	38%	0%
17	at SF	L	17	20	397	395	-3	-13%	17%	32%	2%
18	at CAR	L	16	27	78	386	0	-83%	-75%	0%	-8%

Trends and Splits

	Offense	Rank	Defense	Rank
Total DVOA	-9.3%	23	-5.0%	7
Unadjusted VOA	-10.4%	25	-3.0%	12
Weighted Trend	-10.5%	24	-5.2%	14
Variance	2.0%	1	5.9%	15
Average Opponent	-2.8%	3	2.0%	6
Passing	7.2%	19	3.8%	14
Rushing	-18.1%	30	-17.3%	6
First Down	-4.4%	20	-6.3%	7
Second Down	-27.6%	32	5.0%	23
Third Down	7.8%	14	-18.4%	6
First Half	-5.5%	20	2.3%	22
Second Half	-13.8%	23	-12.1%	4
Red Zone	-34.8%	30	-9.7%	11
Late and Close	-13.5%	26	-22.2%	3

Five-Year Performance

Year	W-L	Pyth W	Est W	PF	PA	TO	Total	Rk	Off	Rk	Def	Rk	ST	Rk	Off AGL	Rk	Def AGL	Rk	Off Age	Rk	Def Age	Rk	ST Age	Rk
2010	5-11	4.3	3.1	289	434	-5	-37.1%	32	-35.6%	31	5.6%	25	4.2%	9	26.7	17	11.3	8	26.7	23	28.0	8	26.8	11
2011	8-8	6.9	4.9	312	348	-13	-19.7%	28	-18.4%	28	2.4%	20	1.2%	11	46.3	28	40.5	25	27.0	17	27.5	11	27.0	2
2012	5-11	4.8	4.8	250	357	-1	-16.3%	26	-30.9%	32	-13.5%	6	1.1%	11	50.3	28	22.0	12	26.7	18	27.6	8	27.1	4
2013	10-6	9.5	10.4	379	324	-1	10.0%	10	-2.4%	20	-16.4%	2	-4.1%	27	26.8	11	36.1	22	27.9	4	28.0	2	27.0	3
2014	11-5	8.3	7.4	310	299	+8	-6.4%	22	-9.3%	23	-5.0%	7	-2.2%	21	24.0	8	48.8	24	27.3	10	27.1	9	26.4	5

2014 Performance Based on Most Common Personnel Groups

ARI Offense					ARI Offense vs. Opponents					ARI Defense				ARI Defense vs. Opponents			
Pers	Freq	Yds	DVOA	Run%	Pers	Freq	Yds	DVOA	Run%	Pers	Freq	Yds	DVOA	Pers	Freq	Yds	DVOA
11	47%	5.6	-10.6%	30%	Base	39%	4.7	-7.8%	56%	Base	29%	5.3	-1.5%	11	61%	6.3	-7.2%
12	23%	5.4	7.2%	48%	Nickel	42%	5.3	-10.9%	31%	Nickel	4%	5.4	29.7%	12	16%	5.1	-11.5%
10	9%	6.4	-3.6%	12%	Dime+	19%	7.6	25.8%	7%	Dime+	64%	6.4	-7.8%	21	10%	6.1	18.6%
13	5%	4.5	-22.5%	78%	Goal Line	1%	0.8	8.3%	80%	Goal Line	1%	0.5	-40.4%	22	2%	5.7	4.0%
21	5%	4.8	-13.7%	57%	Big	1%	0.7	-51.4%	85%	Big	2%	5.9	-8.7%	10	2%	5.0	13.1%
01	4%	6.8	46.1%	0%													
22	4%	2.3	-42.9%	77%													

Strategic Tendencies

Run/Pass		Rk	Formation		Rk	Pass Rush		Rk	Secondary		Rk	Strategy		Rk
Runs, first half	36%	25	Form: Single Back	74%	15	Rush 3	8.0%	9	4 DB	20%	27	Play action	17%	27
Runs, first down	46%	22	Form: Empty Back	15%	1	Rush 4	47.4%	31	5 DB	4%	32	Avg Box (Off)	6.27	18
Runs, second-long	34%	9	Pers: 3+ WR	62%	16	Rush 5	29.4%	7	6+ DB	74%	1	Avg Box (Def)	6.33	13
Runs, power sit.	51%	25	Pers: 4+ WR	14%	1	Rush 6+	15.2%	5	CB by Sides	69%	28	Offensive Pace	30.01	16
Runs, behind 2H	24%	24	Pers: 2+ TE/6+ OL	33%	11	Sacks by LB	40.0%	16	DB Blitz	20%	1	Defensive Pace	30.27	16
Pass, ahead 2H	48%	16	Shotgun/Pistol	51%	25	Sacks by DB	17.1%	3	Hole in Zone	3%	29	Go for it on 4th	0.60	28

This was the second straight year that the Cardinals led the league in using empty-back sets, and the seventh straight year they ranked either first or second in the percentage of plays with four or more wide receivers. ☜ Arizona's defense had the best DVOA in the league against running back carries out of two-back sets (2.7 yards per carry, -47.6% DVOA) but was only slightly above average against runs from one-back sets (4.5, -17.6% DVOA). ☜ The Cardinals ranked 31st in the league allowing 6.2 average yards after catch. ☜ Arizona benefitted from a league-leading 1,192 yards on opponent penalties, though Washington and San Diego did draw more opponent flags in total.

Passing

Player	DYAR	DVOA	Plays	NtYds	Avg	YAC	C%	TD	Int
D.Stanton	238	4.2%	252	1644	6.5	4.9	55.2%	7	5
C.Palmer	285	8.5%	235	1562	6.6	5.3	63.3%	11	3
R.Lindley*	-32	-16.5%	99	516	5.2	3.4	48.4%	2	4
L.Thomas	-18	-41.4%	11	70	6.4	64.0	11.1%	1	0

Rushing

Player	DYAR	DVOA	Plays	Yds	Avg	TD	Fum	Suc
A.Ellington	-29	-12.3%	200	669	3.3	3	2	39%
S.Taylor	11	-4.4%	63	208	3.3	1	0	41%
K.Williams	23	2.6%	53	246	4.6	0	1	58%
J.Dwyer	-4	-15.9%	16	51	3.2	1	0	25%
M.Grice	7	1.0%	14	45	3.2	1	0	57%
D.Stanton	27	36.2%	13	78	6.0	0	0	-
R.Hughes	-4	-17.3%	7	11	1.6	0	0	43%
C.Palmer	-20	-94.8%	5	28	5.6	0	1	-

Receiving

Player	DYAR	DVOA	Plays	Ctch	Yds	Y/C	YAC	TD	C%
L.Fitzgerald	54	-5.8%	104	63	785	12.5	5.3	2	61%
Jo.Brown	1	-12.5%	103	48	696	14.5	3.8	5	47%
M.Floyd	81	-1.9%	100	48	846	17.6	2.5	6	48%
Ja.Brown	27	-2.0%	32	22	231	10.5	2.9	2	69%
T.Ginn*	-6	-15.5%	26	14	190	13.6	3.3	0	54%
J.Carlson	-43	-20.0%	55	33	350	10.6	4.3	1	60%
R.Housler*	8	0.2%	17	9	129	14.3	9.3	0	53%
D.Fells	-2	-10.7%	11	5	71	14.2	4.2	0	45%
A.Ellington	44	-2.6%	65	47	389	8.3	7.7	2	72%
S.Taylor	48	41.9%	15	11	79	7.2	5.9	3	73%
R.Hughes	61	66.9%	12	8	140	17.5	13.8	0	67%
M.Grice	-28	-55.0%	12	8	25	3.1	6.0	0	67%
K.Williams	-12	-56.6%	6	2	11	5.5	6.5	0	33%

Offensive Line

Player	Pos	Age	GS	Snaps	Pen	Sk	Pass	Run	Player	Pos	Age	GS	Snaps	Pen	Sk	Pass	Run
Bobby Massie	RT	26	16/16	1059	6	6.0	23.0	2.0	Paul Fanaika*	RG	29	14/14	891	7	0.5	12.0	3.0
Lyle Sendlein*	C	31	16/16	1059	3	2.5	12.0	5.0	Jonathan Cooper	G	25	10/2	184	0	0.0	0.5	2.0
Jared Veldheer	LT	28	16/16	1059	7	1.5	17.5	5.5	Mike Iupati	G	28	15/15	944	4	6.0	20.0	5.5
Ted Larsen	LG	28	16/16	1040	11	3.0	20.5	3.5	A.Q. Shipley	C	29	15/5	423	1	0.0	3.8	2.0

Year	Yards	ALY	Rk	Power	Rk	Stuff	Rk	2nd Lev	Rk	Open Field	Rk	Sacks	ASR	Rk	Short	Long	F-Start	Cont.
2012	3.26	2.93	32	48%	31	27%	32	0.85	32	0.66	20	58	8.1%	26	25	16	17	31
2013	3.89	3.84	17	73%	6	19%	16	1.00	24	0.71	15	41	6.8%	13	18	7	19	42
2014	3.47	3.68	24	59%	24	19%	14	0.92	32	0.42	30	28	4.8%	6	14	5	22	42

2014 ALY by direction:	Left End 4.29 (9)	Left Tackle 1.83 (32)	Mid/Guard 3.84 (22)	Right Tackle 4.02 (14)	Right End 3.43 (21)

Give the Cardinals credit: they really tried to get better here in the offseason, signing one of the biggest names available in free agency, and then adding further reinforcements in the first round of the draft. Unfortunately, there's reason to think that neither of those moves will actually help Arizona, at least not in 2015. Left guard Mike Iupati made three Pro Bowls in San Francisco, and his move to the desert was supposed to cripple a key division rival as much as it would help the Cardinals. Iupati's on-field performance, though, has declined severely in recent years. He averaged one blown block every 59.3 snaps in 2012, but that number fell to 36.8 in 2013 and 37.0 last season, among the five worst figures at the position in both years. Between holding penalties and sacks, hits, and hurries allowed, we marked Iupati with 20 blown blocks on pass plays last season. Only one interior lineman had more blown blocks on passes: Ted Larsen, who played left guard for Arizona last year but will now move over to center. That's a bad combination to have side-by-side, especially when you must play Aaron Donald, Brandon Mebane, and ex-teammate Darnell Dockett twice each. Meanwhile, the Cardinals are hopeful that Jonathan Cooper will finally be able to survive an NFL season at right guard. The seventh overall pick in the 2013 draft, Cooper missed his entire rookie season with a broken leg, and started only two games in 2014 due to assorted toe, wrist, and knee injuries.

The Cardinals spent another first-round pick on an offensive lineman this year, taking Florida tackle D.J. Humphries 24th overall, but early reports indicated that Humphries was unlikely to immediately take a starting spot away from either left tackle Jared Veldheer or right tackle Bobby Massie. That's not as bad as it sounds—Veldheer and Massie make for a perfectly adequate tackle combo, better than you'd find on many teams in the league. It does mean, though, that significant improvement from this unit would be a big surprise this fall.

Defensive Front Seven

Defensive Line	Age	Pos	G	Snaps	Plays	TmPct	Overall Rk	Stop	Dfts	BTkl	Runs	St%	vs. Run Rk	RuYd	Rk	Sack	Hit	Pass Rush Hur	Dsrpt
Calais Campbell	29	DE	14	782	60	8.6%	5	51	22	2	48	85%	21	1.6	22	7.0	4	19.0	3
Tommy Kelly	35	DE	16	708	35	4.4%	51	29	8	1	26	81%	30	2.2	46	1.0	8	17.5	2
Frostee Rucker	32	DE	15	475	25	3.4%	75	24	15	3	17	94%	2	0.3	2	5.0	3	15.0	1
Dan Williams*	28	DT	16	412	33	4.2%	--	28	4	3	30	87%	--	1.7	--	1.0	3	2.5	1
Ed Stinson	25	DE	10	203	10	2.0%	--	6	2	0	9	56%	--	4.3	--	0.0	3	4.0	0
Cory Redding	35	DE	16	740	36	4.6%	45	31	7	6	28	86%	17	2.0	39	3.5	12	13.5	1
Corey Peters	27	DT	15	528	24	3.1%	80	18	5	0	19	79%	40	2.4	52	2.0	3	5.5	0

Edge Rushers	Age	Pos	G	Snaps	Plays	TmPct	Overall Rk	Stop	Dfts	BTkl	Runs	St%	vs. Run Rk	RuYd	Rk	Sack	Hit	Pass Rush Hur	Dsrpt
Alex Okafor	24	OLB	13	699	33	5.1%	41	26	13	9	19	68%	67	3.5	72	8.0	5	20.5	2
Sam Acho*	27	OLB	16	469	31	3.9%	65	26	10	3	20	85%	11	1.5	10	1.0	2	11.0	1
Matt Shaughnessy	29	OLB	8	334	17	4.3%	59	12	3	0	15	73%	50	1.7	20	0.0	0	7.0	0

Linebackers	Age	Pos	G	Snaps	Plays	TmPct	Overall Rk	Stop	Dfts	BTkl	Sack	Hit	Pass Rush Hur	Runs	St%	vs. Run Rk	RuYd	Rk	Tgts	Suc%	vs. Pass Rk	AdjYd	Rk	PD	Int
Larry Foote*	35	ILB	15	994	86	11.6%	50	51	17	14	2.0	5	12.5	52	65%	35	3.2	36	32	51%	34	6.7	39	3	1
Kevin Minter	25	ILB	16	317	44	5.5%	--	24	6	4	1.0	2	2.5	35	60%	--	3.7	--	12	47%	--	4.3	--	0	0

Year	Yards	ALY	Rk	Power	Rk	Stuff	Rk	2nd Level	Rk	Open Field	Rk	Sacks	ASR	Rk	Short	Long
2012	4.58	4.49	32	55%	7	17%	25	1.31	28	0.80	17	38	7.2%	7	11	15
2013	3.19	3.09	1	48%	2	28%	1	1.01	8	0.46	7	47	7.2%	12	23	15
2014	4.10	3.50	6	43%	1	26%	2	1.14	16	0.98	28	35	5.3%	28	10	14
2014 ALY by direction:			Left End 3.52 (13)			Left Tackle 3.3 (12)			Mid/Guard 3.36 (5)			Right Tackle 3.62 (10)			Right End 4.33 (25)	

Between the retirement of Larry Foote and the free-agent losses of Dan Williams and Sam Acho, the Cardinals must replace more than 1,800 snaps of front seven football. Only Dallas, Miami, and San Francisco lost more snaps in the front seven this offseason. And even that doesn't fully detail the turnover Arizona is facing here. Darnell Dockett, a three-time Pro Bowler who missed all of 2014 with a torn ACL, signed with San Francisco. John Abraham, second among active players in sacks—just half a sack behind Chicago's Jared Allen—is considering retirement after missing most of last year with a concussion. And veteran Tommy Kelly remained unsigned as of mid-June, though both player and team have left the door open for a return there. In response to those departures, Arizona added a bevy of free agents of their own, signing Corey Peters and Sean Weatherspoon away from Atlanta, LaMarr Woodley from Oakland, Daryl Sharpton from Chicago, and Cory Redding from Indianapolis. They also added three players in the draft. Second-rounder Markus Golden (Missouri) and fifth-rounder Shaquille Riddick (West Virginia) played defensive end in college but will move to outside linebacker in Arizona's 3-4 scheme. Fourth-rounder Rodney Gunter, a 305-pounder out of Delaware State, will be among those fighting for time at nose tackle. That's a lot of new faces, and even the players who are still on the team are switching around—2014 third-rounder Kareem Martin is moving from defensive end to linebacker, while veteran Matt Shaughnessy is going from linebacker to end.

It's difficult to project a starting lineup with that much turnover, and given that Arizona figures to rotate most players on and off the field, it's also somewhat pointless. Still, here's our best guess. The only cinch is that Calais Campbell (top-ten among all defensive linemen last year in run tackles, run stops, and run defeats) will take one of the defensive end spots. Frostee Rucker is most likely to get the other, while Peters handles the bulk of the nose tackle duties. Golden has a horrible SackSEER rating of 10.5 percent and a projection for just 4.3 sacks in his first five seasons. His combine performance showed a lack of athletic explosiveness, and he had just 16.5 sacks in three years at Missouri, though partly because of all the other pass-rushers (Kony Ealy, Shane Ray, Michael Sam) who competed for playing time. The Cardinals believe in Golden's motor, nasty attitude, and ability to set the edge against the run—we are in the NFC West, after all—and he will probably win one outside linebacker job. The other is up in the air between Woodley and Alex Okafor. Woodley missed ten games last year with a torn biceps and has only nine sacks in the past three years. Okafor, a 2013 fourth-rounder, missed most of his rookie year with his own torn biceps. He rebounded as a sophomore, but his future is in doubt following an arrest this March on suspicion of evading police following a disturbance at a Texas nightclub.

The picture at inside linebacker is even murkier. Weatherspoon was available in part because he missed 28 games in Atlanta over the last three years with various injuries; including a torn Achilles that cost him all of 2014. Kevin Minter has yet to justify his second-round selection in 2013, starting only five of his 29 NFL games. The only other active inside linebacker with NFL experience is Sharpton. He was a spot starter for many years in Houston, but he spent most of his only year in Chicago as a healthy inactive on one of the NFL's worst defenses. Finally, there's Daryl Washington, the former Pro Bowler who was suspended for all of 2014 for his second substance abuse violation. The league had not announced his reinstatement as of mid-July, and he could be subject to another suspension concerning an 2013 arrest on domestic violence charges. (Washington pleaded guilty to the charges in March of 2014; he served ten months' probation, which expired in February.) It's a safe bet that Deone Bucannon will spend more time at "dollar" linebacker this year, simply because the other options are so sparse.

Defensive Secondary

Secondary	Age	Pos	G	Snaps	Plays	TmPct	Rk	Stop	Dfts	BTkl	Runs	St%	Rk	RuYd	Rk	Tgts	Tgt%	Rk	Dist	Suc%	Rk	AdjYd	Rk	PD	Int
Rashad Johnson	29	FS	16	1051	97	12.2%	19	30	17	17	33	30%	55	10.8	66	31	7.4%	27	13.7	50%	52	11.6	67	7	4
Antonio Cromartie*	31	CB	16	987	59	7.4%	59	24	13	10	14	43%	33	10.5	67	78	20.0%	15	13.7	49%	46	9.2	60	11	3
Patrick Peterson	25	CB	16	969	57	7.2%	65	19	7	5	7	14%	71	8.9	60	93	24.3%	43	13.5	55%	19	7.1	22	8	3
Jerraud Powers	28	CB	16	745	62	7.8%	50	25	15	8	7	14%	71	9.6	63	76	26.0%	57	9.7	56%	18	7.7	34	8	3
Deone Bucannon	23	SS	16	692	78	9.8%	41	37	13	9	26	65%	3	4.3	8	35	12.7%	63	6.7	34%	69	10.1	63	2	0
Tony Jefferson	23	SS	16	680	77	9.7%	43	29	8	8	38	53%	16	5.1	15	25	9.4%	44	9.1	35%	68	8.1	46	1	0
Tyrann Mathieu	23	FS/CB	13	428	42	6.5%	--	20	11	4	13	46%	--	4.2	--	19	11.0%	--	5.6	72%	--	5.0	--	4	1

Year	Pass D Rank	vs. #1 WR	Rk	vs. #2 WR	Rk	vs. Other WR	Rk	vs. TE	Rk	vs. RB	Rk
2012	2	-7.4%	11	-18.2%	4	-46.0%	1	-2.5%	15	-52.4%	1
2013	5	-27.3%	1	-10.5%	9	-9.3%	10	6.4%	20	-11.3%	8
2014	14	-4.0%	12	2.7%	19	-40.0%	1	16.9%	27	-26.2%	3

The 2014 Cardinals used six or more defensive backs 20 percent more often than any other defense in the four seasons for which we have data, and quite likely in the history of the NFL. As such, they didn't really have a starting four in the defensive backfield, they had a starting six. So it's a good thing that six of their top seven defensive backs from 2014 return. Patrick Peterson is one of the most athletically gifted players in the league, but his charting stats show that as a cornerback, he is merely very good, not great. The Cardinals move him around to cover opponents' top receivers very often, but Peterson is hardly dominant in those battles. He gave up 85 yards to DeSean Jackson in Week 5, 81 yards to Jeremy Maclin in Week 7, and a mammoth 171 yards to Julio Jones in Week 12. Jerraud Powers will return to the first string after Antonio Cromartie's single season on the team. In 2013, Powers started every game for Arizona, finishing 40th among corners in adjusted success rate and 55th in adjusted yards per pass allowed—close to average, considering there were 87 corners ranked that year. In his first season as a full-time starter, free safety Rashad Johnson didn't stand out statistically, except when it came to missed tackles—only three defenders missed more tackles last season than the 2009 third-rounder. Strong safety Tony Jefferson would be the final starter in a more traditional defense; in his second season, the former undrafted free agent's biggest games came in wins against San Francisco (10 tackles) and Philadelphia (12).

That leaves two guys who played hybrid positions last season. Tyrann Mathieu usually played safety when opponents used two or fewer wide receivers, but moved to slot corner against multiple-receiver sets. He made 0.4 run plays per pass play, which would have been one of the ten highest rates among cornerbacks, and one of the ten lowest rates among safeties. Deone Bucannon, last year's first-round pick, will tell you that he's a safety, the position he played at Washington State and where he's listed on the team's media guide. In execution, though, he was almost exclusively a linebacker, albeit one who only saw the field in dime packages. That's why the average pass distance on his targets was so short. Bucannon's charting numbers are undoubtedly ugly, but his average yards allowed per target drops by a yard and a half if you take away one 59-yard gain by Jared Cook.

Special Teams

Year	DVOA	Rank	FG/XP	Rank	Net Kick	Rank	Kick Ret	Rank	Net Punt	Rank	Punt Ret	Rank	Hidden	Rank
2012	1.1%	11	4.4	10	-6.7	27	-2.5	20	19.7	1	-9.3	31	14.4	2
2013	-4.1%	27	-4.9	25	-1.0	18	-6.5	30	3.9	14	-11.8	31	3.4	10
2014	-2.2%	21	0.0	16	2.0	13	-6.2	30	-9.6	30	3.0	11	-0.3	18

Between kickoffs and punts, only Washington and Oakland have worse total value on returns than Arizona over the last three seasons. Ted Ginn handled both duties last year, and he was particularly dreadful. He was last among qualified players in average kickoff return yardage, and more than a quarter of his punt return yardage came on just one play, although that was a nice 71-yard touchdown against the Giants. The Cardinals hope to have solved this perennial issue with the fifth-round selection of J.J. Nelson. The fastest player at the combine this year, Nelson returned five kickoffs and a punt for touchdowns in his career at Alabama-Birmingham.

Dave Zastudil missed 14 games last year with a groin injury, and in his place Drew Butler was next to last in gross punting value. Zastudil was just average in this category in 2013, but ranked third in the NFL in 2012. Butler and Zastudil will battle for the punting job in training camp. Chandler Catanzaro was roughly average in both kickoffs and placekicking as a rookie last year. The Cardinals' coverage teams overall weren't anything special, but reserve cornerback Justin Bethel led the NFL in both special-teams tackles and stops (i.e. tackles that stop a return for a below-average value). That wasn't a fluke, either; he was second in both categories in 2013.

Atlanta Falcons

2014 Record: 6-10   Total DVOA: -5.4% (20th)   2015 Mean Projection: 8.9 wins   On the Clock (0-4): 5%

Pythagorean Wins: 7.1 (22nd)   Offense: 7.2% (10th)   Postseason Odds: 49.2%   Mediocrity (5-7): 25%

Snap-Weighted Age: 26.6 (20th)   Defense: 15.7% (32nd)   Super Bowl Odds: 6.6%   Playoff Contender (8-10): 42%

Average Opponent: -3.1% (27th)   Special Teams: 3.0% (9th)   Proj. Avg. Opponent: -5.3% (32nd)   Super Bowl Contender (11+): 29%

2014: When the division title is on the line in your building, you aren't supposed to lose by 31 points.

2015: Their time in the wilderness is about to end. Thanks, schedule gods!

After a promising start, the Mike Smith Era came up short like so many Matt Ryan fourth-and-1 sneaks. Under Smith, the Falcons broke in Ryan, watched Roddy White blossom with him, and added the crownpiece to the offense by trading up for Julio Jones in 2011. With Tony Gonzalez in town putting up Hall of Fame season after Hall of Fame season in his sleep, the Atlanta offense was poised for success. The Falcons never reached greatness to match the Patriots or Packers, but they fielded an above-average offense in every year of Smith's tenure.

Instead, where Atlanta failed was the area that was supposed to be Smith's strong suit: defense. In the eyes of DVOA, Smith improved the Falcons on defense five seasons in a row, peaking at eighth in 2011. Then, the Falcons saw the other side of the rollercoaster, as they hit freefall by going from 11th in 2012 to 29th in 2013. Smith and general manager Thomas Dimitroff followed this up with a free-agency bender to try to salvage what they could, giving $57 million in theoretical dollars to defensive linemen Paul Soliai and Tyson Jackson. Of course, Soliai and Jackson were non-entities in stopping the pass, which is where Atlanta's defense ranked dead last in 2013, but the hope was probably that better run defense would force Atlanta opponents into more third-and-long situations.

Then, the Falcons finished dead last in defensive DVOA in 2014, and Smith was canned for it.

You can read this collapse in a number of ways, but given what we know about how pass defense works, it's hard to avoid the fact that the Falcons never found a way to replace edge rusher John Abraham. Smith has always been a more cautious defensive game-planner, eschewing blitzes in favor of solid coverage. Sure enough, the Falcons under Smith hadn't had a top-20 adjusted sack rate since 2008, his first season as a head coach (Table 1). When Abraham signed with Arizona two years ago, the little pressure they were getting dried up completely. A dead-cat bounce got them from last in 2013 to 30th in 2014, but Kroy Biermann led the team in sacks with 4.5. To put that into perspective, Rex Ryan once engineered a six-sack season out of complete draft bust Aaron Maybin. The Falcons couldn't even get Aaron Maybin-level pass rush last year.

Atlanta is the victim of bad drafting in the front seven and poor luck. Of the 12 front-seven players that were drafted from 2008-2012, Biermann is the only one left on the roster.

Prince Shembo, the most promising of the recent picks in the front seven, was released after the season upon allegedly killing his girlfriend's dog. The remaining 2013-2014 picks currently on the roster have combined to play just 1,342 snaps so far, with just 11 starts—all by Malliciah Goodman, a defensive end with zero career sacks.

Sean Weatherspoon should have been a correct answer at linebacker, but couldn't stay healthy. Curtis Lofton fled for New Orleans after being deemed a poor fit for Mike Nolan's scheme. Past those two, a look at Atlanta's front-seven draft picks produces nothing but could-have-beens and lengthy sighs for other players that were on the board at that point (Table 2, next page).

Those front-seven players started 150 games and recorded 55.5 sacks. To put that into perspective, Abraham by himself picked up 122 sacks in 161 starts with the Jets and Falcons. And if you look at the amount of AV their off-ball linebackers currently on the roster produced, it is zero.

Obviously this can't all be blamed on Smith. Dimitroff, the general manager, is in theory the one who should be shopping for the groceries. But the fact that Smith couldn't make anything riskier than gazpacho with these ingredients helped speed his demise.

That was the input, and this is the output. So the Falcons made the odd move of having to replace a defense-first coach with … a defense-first coach. By bringing in defensive coordinator Dan Quinn from Seattle, the Falcons are hoping for a repeat of the first few years of the Smith era.

But where they won't repeat the Smith era is in the mistake of not finding worthwhile pass-rushers. Atlanta already

Table 1: Atlanta Defensive DVOA and Adjusted Sack Rate under Mike Smith

Year	Def. DVOA	Rank	ASR	Rank
2008	7.5%	25	6.9%	10
2009	4.1%	22	5.6%	26
2010	-2.1%	14	5.8%	23
2011	-9.1%	8	6.0%	24
2012	-2.9%	12	5.8%	26
2013	13.5%	29	5.3%	32
2014	15.7%	32	4.5%	30

2015 Falcons Schedule

Week	Opp.	Week	Opp.	Week	Opp.
1	PHI (Mon.)	7	at TEN	13	at TB
2	at NYG	8	TB	14	at CAR
3	at DAL	9	at SF	15	at JAC
4	HOU	10	BYE	16	CAR
5	WAS	11	IND	17	NO
6	at NO (Thu.)	12	MIN		

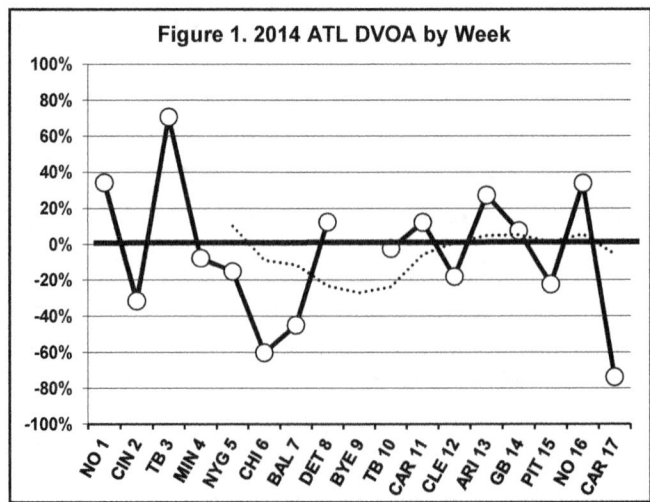

Figure 1. 2014 ATL DVOA by Week

reached out to stock the spot in free agency, bringing in reclamation project Adrian Clayborn and Seattle depth rusher O'Brien Schofield. Then, they found the best fit any team possibly could by stumbling into Clemson edge rusher Vic Beasley with the eighth overall pick.

Based on every available metric the internet draftsphere has created so far—be it Force Players, SPARQ, or our own SackSEER—Beasley is the best bet to be a top-quality edge rusher of anyone in this draft. Nathan Forster, in writing up Beasley for this year's article on SackSEER, noted that he "gives you almost everything you want in an edge rusher prospect." Beasley blew up the NFL combine, and created 32 sacks and nine passes defensed over his four-year career at Clemson. It was ridiculous that he was available at that point, and he should immediately step in as Quinn's Leo, concerns about his run-stopping ability be damned.[1]

Beasley and cornerback Desmond Trufant are two building blocks this defense can begin to work around. Second-round cornerback Jalen Collins and fifth-round defensive tackle Grady Jarrett also have their share of believers. Jarrett should be able to eventually replace Jonathan Babineaux, Abraham's lone pass-rushing sidekick who has grown long in the tooth, as a penetrating three-tech lineman. Collins has every physical attribute Quinn wants from his cornerbacks and not much experience using them, which is why he was around on Day 2.

But we hope by now you understand that this is not a one-

---

1 The entire SackSEER projections table can be found in our Rookie Projections on page 478.

Table 2. Atlanta Front Seven Draft Picks, 2008-2014

Player	Year	Round	Pick	College	Snaps for ATL	G/GS	Sacks
Kroy Biermann*	2008	5	154	Montana	3,809	98/37	21
Peria Jerry	2009	1	24	Mississippi	1,829	63/29	5.5
Lawrence Sidbury	2009	4	125	Richmond	356	48/0	5
Vance Walker	2009	7	210	Georgia Tech	1,436	58/11	5
Corey Peters	2010	3	83	Kentucky	2,814	71/55	11
Jonathan Massaquoi	2012	5	164	Troy	900	39/7	6
Travian Robertson	2012	7	249	South Carolina	126	12/0	0
Malliciah Goodman*	2013	4	127	Clemson	899	30/11	0
Stanley Maponga*	2013	5	153	TCU	219	24/0	1
Ra'Shede Hageman*	2014	2	37	Minnesota	224	16/0	1
Defensive Linemen					**12,612**		**55.5**
Player	Year	Round	Pick	College	Snaps for ATL	G/GS	Sacks
Curtis Lofton	2008	2	37	Oklahoma	3,561	64/63	32
Robert James	2008	5	138	Arizona State	7	18/0	1
Spencer Adkins	2009	6	176	Miami	46	24/1	2
Sean Weatherspoon	2010	1	19	Missouri	2,673	47/41	21
Akeem Dent	2011	3	91	Georgia	883	47/20	10
Prince Shembo	2014	4	139	Notre Dame	347	16/3	2
Marquis Spruill*	2014	5	168	Syracuse	0	0/0	0
Yawin Smallwood	2014	7	253	Connecticut	0	0/0	0
Tyler Starr*	2014	7	255	South Dakota	0	0/0	0
Linebackers					**7,517**		**68**

* currently on the roster

year project. As random as defensive DVOA tends to be as compared to offensive DVOA, the Atlanta defense is shooting for mediocrity, not heading back to the top in their first season under Quinn. The only truly big contract they handed out to a free-agent was a five-year, $22.5 million investment in former Texans edgebacker Brooks Reed, who is more about versatility than impact splash plays.

But even another year of poor defense doesn't mean the Falcons won't be competitive. We have them with the easiest projected schedule in the NFL this year thanks to a dose of AFC South, a sprinkle of NFC East, and two games against the Bucs. And of course, they have a good and consistent offense.

Even with Gonzalez gone, a patchwork offensive line, and White so banged up he's reaching the Larry Fitzgerald stage of his career, Ryan has kept his offense on point. The Falcons have never placed lower than 13th in passing DVOA during Ryan's eight-year career. What they haven't had is a running game to complement their quarterback, as they've finished with a negative rushing DVOA in every season of Ryan's career as well—even when Michael Turner was actually good (Table 3).

New offensive coordinator Kyle Shanahan, who is used to creating running games around bad quarterbacks after the degradation of Robert Griffin and his bit part in a Brian Hoyer/Johnny Manziel joint last year, is doing his part to praise Ryan. He's already called him a good fit for the outside-zone, run-action plays that have been staples of Shanahan's playbook. After working with Hoyer and Manziel last year, Ryan probably looks like Peyton Manning to Shanahan. Shanahan couldn't build much of a running game for the Browns offense, but a couple of nice mid-round running back prospects in Tevin Coleman and Devonta Freeman should have more room to work with in Atlanta than Isaiah Crowell and company had in Cleveland.

As we've established over the course of this chapter, for bet-

Table 3: Atlanta Offensive DVOA, 2008-2014

Year	Pass DVOA	Rank	Run DVOA	Rank
2008	32.3%	4	-0.8%	18
2009	19.0%	13	-1.5%	13
2010	26.5%	7	-8.4%	23
2011	23.2%	8	-7.3%	23
2012	23.6%	10	-17.2%	30
2013	14.7%	11	-7.0%	21
2014	24.5%	8	-9.9%	22

ter or worse, the Falcons have been a stagnant team in many ways since Ryan arrived. They've accumulated some incredibly important assets—building blocks that helped get them to the edge of the Super Bowl—but they failed to address need areas properly for the entire course of the Smith regime.

Atlanta needs to approach these next few seasons with urgency. Ryan and Jones have proven their worth time and time again, but with Ryan heading into his thirties, they can't stay this way forever. In selecting Beasley, the Quinn regime at least showed that they won't stand idly by when the team has an essential need. But they'll have to keep shoveling water out of the defensive boat before the patches can completely hold up.

At least Atlanta fans can take heart that there's short-term hope while Quinn is doing some longer-term building on defense. That creampuff schedule makes Atlanta the favorite to win the NFC South. Provided the Saints can't turn back time and the Panthers don't take any major steps forward, the Falcons should at least get another chance to defeat their reputation as playoff chokers. And hey, if Joe Flacco can get hot at the right time and win a Super Bowl, so can Matt Ryan.

Rivers McCown

2014 Falcons Stats by Week

Wk	vs.	W-L	PF	PA	YDF	YDA	TO	Total	Off	Def	ST
1	NO	W	37	34	568	472	1	34%	40%	13%	6%
2	at CIN	L	10	24	309	472	-3	-32%	-8%	25%	1%
3	TB	W	56	14	488	217	1	71%	33%	-23%	14%
4	at MIN	L	28	41	411	558	-2	-8%	42%	47%	-3%
5	at NYG	L	20	30	397	317	1	-15%	0%	17%	2%
6	CHI	L	13	27	287	478	-1	-60%	-37%	32%	9%
7	at BAL	L	7	29	254	371	2	-45%	-25%	11%	-9%
8	vs. DET	L	21	22	291	385	0	12%	18%	11%	6%
9	BYE										
10	at TB	W	27	17	322	373	3	-2%	19%	25%	4%
11	at CAR	W	19	17	346	391	1	12%	8%	-2%	2%
12	CLE	L	24	26	315	475	1	-18%	2%	20%	0%
13	ARI	W	29	18	500	329	2	27%	11%	0%	17%
14	at GB	L	37	43	465	502	-1	7%	40%	31%	-1%
15	PIT	L	20	27	407	398	-1	-22%	6%	25%	-3%
16	at NO	W	30	14	403	328	4	34%	14%	-28%	-8%
17	CAR	L	3	34	288	306	-3	-74%	-54%	30%	10%

Trends and Splits

	Offense	Rank	Defense	Rank
Total DVOA	7.2%	10	15.7%	32
Unadjusted VOA	8.1%	10	15.0%	32
Weighted Trend	2.1%	12	14.5%	31
Variance	7.7%	17	4.1%	6
Average Opponent	1.7%	25	-1.1%	21
Passing	24.5%	8	26.0%	31
Rushing	-9.9%	22	3.4%	30
First Down	4.5%	13	13.0%	31
Second Down	9.6%	9	16.8%	31
Third Down	8.6%	13	19.3%	26
First Half	7.4%	11	13.9%	30
Second Half	7.1%	8	17.5%	30
Red Zone	9.5%	9	-4.4%	17
Late and Close	2.0%	17	17.2%	30

Five-Year Performance

Year	W-L	Pyth W	Est W	PF	PA	TO	Total	Rk	Off	Rk	Def	Rk	ST	Rk	Off AGL	Rk	Def AGL	Rk	Off Age	Rk	Def Age	Rk	ST Age	Rk
2010	13-3	11.4	11.3	414	288	+14	16.3%	7	8.0%	9	-2.1%	14	6.3%	3	5.2	1	10.7	6	28.6	4	26.6	19	27.1	6
2011	10-6	9.4	10.2	402	350	+8	13.9%	8	6.1%	11	-9.1%	8	-1.3%	22	22.2	11	26.4	16	28.0	4	26.7	20	26.4	12
2012	13-3	11.2	9.1	419	299	+13	9.1%	10	6.1%	12	-2.9%	12	0.1%	16	17.3	7	35.6	21	28.6	1	28.0	3	26.5	9
2013	4-12	5.9	6.5	353	443	-7	-10.4%	25	3.2%	14	13.5%	29	-0.1%	17	53.9	27	36.1	23	27.6	7	26.7	15	25.9	21
2014	6-10	7.1	7.2	381	417	+5	-5.4%	20	7.2%	10	15.7%	32	3.0%	9	60.6	30	33.2	12	26.8	16	26.6	21	26.4	7

2014 Performance Based on Most Common Personnel Groups

ATL Offense					ATL Offense vs. Opponents					ATL Defense					ATL Defense vs. Opponents			
Pers	Freq	Yds	DVOA	Run%	Pers	Freq	Yds	DVOA	Run%	Pers	Freq	Yds	DVOA		Pers	Freq	Yds	DVOA
11	53%	6.0	9.5%	26%	Base	32%	5.4	5.3%	53%	Base	33%	6.2	8.0%		11	54%	6.6	22.9%
21	15%	5.1	0.3%	41%	Nickel	54%	5.9	8.0%	23%	Nickel	38%	5.8	13.0%		12	23%	6.3	9.0%
10	11%	7.9	44.7%	3%	Dime+	11%	8.7	55.7%	21%	Dime+	26%	7.9	36.0%		21	9%	5.0	-1.1%
12	8%	8.1	38.7%	47%	Goal Line	1%	0.1	-10.0%	50%	Goal Line	3%	1.7	-5.7%		22	5%	5.0	-27.8%
611	6%	3.8	-14.5%	67%	Big	1%	0.7	-51.4%	85%						10	2%	8.8	88.6%

Strategic Tendencies

Run/Pass		Rk	Formation		Rk	Pass Rush		Rk	Secondary		Rk	Strategy		Rk
Runs, first half	33%	29	Form: Single Back	78%	9	Rush 3	5.0%	20	4 DB	23%	22	Play action	17%	26
Runs, first down	45%	26	Form: Empty Back	4%	19	Rush 4	65.0%	14	5 DB	36%	26	Avg Box (Off)	6.10	30
Runs, second-long	23%	30	Pers: 3+ WR	65%	10	Rush 5	23.2%	16	6+ DB	40%	6	Avg Box (Def)	6.22	22
Runs, power sit.	40%	30	Pers: 4+ WR	11%	2	Rush 6+	6.7%	17	CB by Sides	79%	18	Offensive Pace	29.00	6
Runs, behind 2H	24%	23	Pers: 2+ TE/6+ OL	20%	30	Sacks by LB	43.2%	15	DB Blitz	9%	17	Defensive Pace	30.03	13
Pass, ahead 2H	47%	20	Shotgun/Pistol	48%	27	Sacks by DB	13.6%	6	Hole in Zone	4%	28	Go for it on 4th	0.21	32

As you might expect after Tony Gonzalez's retirement, the Falcons led the NFL by not having a tight end on the field on 11.9 percent of plays. They averaged 8.2 yards with 54.1% DVOA on these plays, way beyond the NFL averages of 6.1 yards and 18.0% DVOA. ☙ When the tight end went back on the field, a sixth lineman often went on with him. The Falcons used six linemen on 10.0 percent of plays, more than any team except Denver. However, they only averaged 3.0 yards per play and -14.2% DVOA with the extra lineman. Even when using the extra lineman in a non-short yardage situation, they only averaged 3.5 yards per play. ☙ Atlanta had led the league in draws by running backs in 2013, but hardly used the play in 2014; we only have a dozen runs listed as draws. ☙ Last year, the Falcons may have been the first team in NFL history to list their base defense as nickel, but they actually used nickel less than most other teams. That's partly because they were using dime so much. Atlanta had never used dime personnel on more than 5.5 percent of plays since we started tracking defensive personnel in 2011, but shot up to 26 percent last year. ☙ Though the Falcons had the worst defense in the league by DVOA, they were average in the red zone. But the split there is strange: the Falcons ranked third against red zone passes but 30th against red zone runs. ☙ One last word on last year's horrible defense: Atlanta allowed 37.7 yards per drive in 2014, the highest figure in our entire drive database (since 1997).

Passing

Player	DYAR	DVOA	Plays	NtYds	Avg	YAC	C%	TD	Int
M.Ryan	1101	14.9%	654	4491	6.9	5.0	66.6%	28	13

Rushing

Player	DYAR	DVOA	Plays	Yds	Avg	TD	Fum	Suc
S.Jackson*	70	-0.3%	189	708	3.7	6	0	51%
D.Freeman	-38	-22.9%	65	249	3.8	1	1	31%
J.Rodgers	-7	-11.4%	58	217	3.7	1	1	40%
M.Ryan	23	4.8%	25	146	5.8	0	1	-
A.Smith	35	27.3%	23	144	6.3	2	1	57%
D.Hester	20	6.4%	6	36	6.0	1	0	-

Receiving

Player	DYAR	DVOA	Plays	Ctch	Yds	Y/C	YAC	TD	C%
J.Jones	356	16.2%	163	104	1593	15.3	5.2	6	64%
R.White	113	-1.3%	125	80	923	11.5	2.3	7	64%
H.Douglas*	108	5.9%	74	51	556	10.9	4.7	2	69%
D.Hester	38	-4.3%	59	38	504	13.3	6.8	2	64%
E.Weems	50	41.5%	11	10	102	10.2	2.8	2	91%
L.Toilolo	-115	-37.5%	53	31	238	7.7	3.2	2	58%
T.Moeaki	14	9.8%	13	8	134	16.8	9.0	1	62%
J.Rodgers	18	-5.8%	40	29	173	6.0	6.4	1	73%
D.Freeman	33	4.1%	37	30	225	7.5	5.7	1	81%
S.Jackson*	20	-0.2%	27	20	148	7.4	6.1	0	74%
A.Smith	96	91.6%	15	13	222	17.1	17.9	3	87%
P.DiMarco	16	2.4%	14	9	62	6.9	5.0	1	64%

Offensive Line

Player	Pos	Age	GS	Snaps	Pen	Sk	Pass	Run	Player	Pos	Age	GS	Snaps	Pen	Sk	Pass	Run
Justin Blalock*	LG	32	15/15	970	6	3.0	11.5	2.3	Gabe Carimi*	OT	27	16/7	585	7	5.5	18.0	1.0
Jon Asamoah	RG	27	15/15	945	4	1.5	5.5	3.5	Joe Hawley	C	27	4/4	243	2	0.0	1.0	2.0
Jake Matthews	LT	23	15/15	944	11	4.0	21.0	5.8	Lamar Holmes	RT	26	4/4	226	1	0.0	4.5	1.0
James Stone	C	23	12/9	672	2	0.0	4.5	3.0	Peter Konz	C	26	7/3	183	1	0.0	0.0	1.5
Ryan Schraeder	RT	27	13/10	646	4	2.5	7.0	3.0									

Year	Yards	ALY	Rk	Power	Rk	Stuff	Rk	2nd Lev	Rk	Open Field	Rk	Sacks	ASR	Rk	Short	Long	F-Start	Cont.
2012	3.69	3.87	24	39%	32	23%	27	1.03	26	0.66	21	28	5.1%	8	9	9	9	40
2013	3.91	3.74	24	63%	18	21%	25	0.98	25	0.76	14	44	5.9%	7	14	5	18	23
2014	3.93	3.96	14	67%	13	21%	20	1.02	24	0.68	17	31	5.1%	11	16	7	16	27
2014 ALY by direction:		Left End 2.73 (29)			Left Tackle 4.35 (6)			Mid/Guard 4.41 (3)			Right Tackle 4.23 (8)				Right End 3.02 (26)			

This is an area of the team that has caused much consternation over the last couple of seasons, as Matt Ryan keeps hitting the deck more and more. Last year, only Andrew Luck was knocked down more often after a pass attempt. The main problem is tackle, where rookie first-round pick Jake Matthews had a trying first season. Matthews was particularly hapless in Weeks 5-7, where we charted him with nine blown blocks, and over the course of the season he committed seven holding penalties, which tied him for second among offensive linemen. He was a little better late in to his rookie season though, which gives some reason for optimism. Matthews was drafted because 2008 first-rounder Sam Baker was brutal and injury-plagued, and Matthews was forced to move to the blind side earlier than anticipated because Baker tore his patellar tendon before the 2014 season. There was pre-draft talk of moving Baker inside this year, but instead he was released during OTAs. Former UDFA Ryan Schraeder is probably first in line at right tackle after some halfway-decent play down the stretch, with Lamar Holmes, who has looked overmatched in both of the last two seasons, as the swing tackle. Tyler Polumbus was signed to a low-risk deal and could also factor into that equation, which says a lot about the equation.

Long-time guard Justin Blalock was released as a schematic casualty, as he's much more effective running power plays than Kyle Shanahan's preferred zones, and followed that up by retiring. Jon Asamoah came over from the Chiefs in free agency last offseason and was probably the line's most consistent performer. He's certainly the best run blocker they have, whatever faint praise that is to damn someone with. After the draft, the Falcons brought in Chris Chester, a cap casualty in Washington. He's the in-house favorite at the other guard spot, though he's more stopgap than solution. Former second-round pick Peter Konz is the depth at the position, but his next good season will be his first.

Joe Hawley will likely start at center in a contract year. He's coming off a torn ACL in Week 4 last season, but he's a decent fit for the zone scheme. James Stone, yet another undrafted free agent, stood in for Hawley last season and, to his credit, only got Ryan maimed instead of killed.

Defensive Front Seven

Defensive Line	Age	Pos	Overall								vs. Run					Pass Rush			
			G	Snaps	Plays	TmPct	Rk	Stop	Dfts	BTkl	Runs	St%	Rk	RuYd	Rk	Sack	Hit	Hur	Dsrpt
Jonathan Babineaux	34	DE	15	696	32	4.2%	58	25	9	4	23	78%	44	1.9	30	2.0	6	15.5	1
Malliciah Goodman	25	DE	16	582	17	2.1%	92	15	4	1	16	88%	13	2.9	80	0.0	2	5.0	0
Corey Peters*	27	DT	15	528	24	3.1%	80	18	5	0	19	79%	40	2.4	52	2.0	3	5.5	0
Tyson Jackson	29	DE	16	512	24	2.9%	82	20	2	1	20	80%	32	2.9	77	0.0	2	4.5	3
Paul Soliai	32	DT	15	502	30	3.9%	66	23	8	3	25	84%	23	1.1	12	1.0	1	1.0	0
Osi Umenyiora	35	DE	16	338	13	1.6%	--	7	3	1	7	43%	--	3.7	--	2.5	6	14.5	0

Edge Rushers	Age	Pos	Overall								vs. Run					Pass Rush			
			G	Snaps	Plays	TmPct	Rk	Stop	Dfts	BTkl	Runs	St%	Rk	RuYd	Rk	Sack	Hit	Hur	Dsrpt
Kroy Biermann	30	OLB	16	848	77	9.4%	2	60	14	9	58	84%	12	1.7	18	4.5	4	19.5	1
Jonathan Massaquoi*	27	OLB	15	328	23	3.0%	--	11	4	3	14	36%	--	4.3	--	2.0	5	12.0	1
Brooks Reed	28	OLB	16	786	44	5.2%	40	32	15	3	31	74%	43	2.6	49	3.0	9	16.0	1
O'Brien Schofield	28	DE	16	338	15	2.0%	--	9	4	2	10	70%	--	4.0	--	2.0	5	13.5	0

Linebackers	Age	Pos	Overall								Pass Rush			vs. Run					vs. Pass						
			G	Snaps	Plays	TmPct	Rk	Stop	Dfts	BTkl	Sack	Hit	Hur	Runs	St%	Rk	RuYd	Rk	Tgts	Suc%	Rk	AdjYd	Rk	PD	Int
Paul Worrilow	25	ILB	16	1079	145	17.6%	10	86	18	15	2.0	7	7.5	94	73%	15	3.4	43	42	32%	63	9.1	60	2	0
Joplo Bartu	25	ILB	16	486	82	10.0%	60	39	4	4	1.0	0	1	61	56%	69	4.4	75	19	38%	58	7.8	53	0	0
Prince Shembo	24	ILB	16	340	57	6.9%	--	31	9	1	0.0	1	2	43	63%	--	4.0	--	8	42%	--	8.3	--	0	0
Justin Durant	30	OLB	6	324	53	17.8%	8	36	11	4	0.0	0	2.5	28	82%	1	2.2	7	18	44%	48	7.2	46	3	1

Year	Yards	ALY	Rk	Power	Rk	Stuff	Rk	2nd Level	Rk	Open Field	Rk	Sacks	ASR	Rk	Short	Long
2012	4.47	3.81	8	65%	21	20%	11	1.18	14	1.11	29	29	5.8%	26	10	15
2013	4.85	4.30	27	68%	20	16%	25	1.17	23	1.26	31	32	5.3%	32	7	14
2014	4.09	4.16	24	80%	30	15%	30	1.11	12	0.54	6	22	4.5%	30	6	6

2014 ALY by direction:	Left End 4.5 (30)	Left Tackle 3.44 (13)	Mid/Guard 4.32 (27)	Right Tackle 4.07 (18)	Right End 4.05 (18)

We spent a lot of the main essay talking about Atlanta's edge rusher woes and their silly 2014 offseason. Vic Beasley is as terrific a head start on creating a pass rush as Atlanta could have hoped to find in the draft, but depth is still an issue. Atlanta made a couple of interesting low-cost bets in Adrian Clayborn and O'Brien Schofield. You may remember Schofield as the guy who failed his physical with the Giants in 2014, killing a two-year deal. He returned to the depth pool in Seattle and should have a leg up in knowing Dan Quinn's defense, though he doesn't have much experience starting in it. (Only once last year did Schofield play more than 50 percent of defensive snaps in a game.) Clayborn comes over from Tampa Bay, where he only played two full seasons. 2011, his rookie year, was full of pass-rush promise. After tearing his ACL in 2012, he was decidedly less explosive in 2013, then tore his biceps early in 2014. Somewhere between these two additions, the puzzling five-year, $22.5 million deal handed to Brooks Reed, and incumbents Kroy Biermann and Mallicah Goodman, the Falcons need to find credible second and third rushers.

The buzzword for the rest of Atlanta's defensive line is "diet." Tyson Jackson hired a personal chef as he attempts to slide into the Red Bryant role. Ra'Shede Hageman dropped 15 pounds upon reporting to OTAs, and is probably aiming to play three-technique. Jonathan Babineaux turns 34 in the middle of the season, but still works as a situational inside rusher. Paul Soliai, at nose tackle, had little impact on turning around Atlanta's run defense. Without a better 2015 season, he'll likely be let go in 2016.

But Atlanta's clearest flaw, and one that they flailed desperately to try to solve this offseason, is off-the-line linebacker. In theory, Reed has the versatility to play here, but the Texans quickly scuttled the idea of him at middle linebacker. He may be a better fit at Sam, though he's never played there before. Justin Durant, formerly of the Cowboys, has roots as a good run-stuffing linebacker, but spent the last two seasons as an oft-injured bit part on a defense that could've used his calling card. Incumbent middle linebacker Paul Worrilow is the NFL's answer to the TSA, in that his coverage is as ceremonial as taking your shoes off. Joplo Bartu has proven to be much the same when he steps on the field on third down. They both fall into that murky category of "undrafted free agent finds that don't do much but fill space," where it's an interesting debate as to how much they've helped. Either way, Bobby Wagner is not walking through that door.

Defensive Secondary

Secondary	Age	Pos	G	Snaps	Plays	Overall TmPct	Rk	Stop	Dfts	BTkl	vs. Run Runs	St%	Rk	RuYd	Rk	vs. Pass Tgts	Tgt%	Rk	Dist	Suc%	Rk	AdjYd	Rk	PD	Int
Desmond Trufant	25	CB	16	1076	77	9.4%	24	29	15	6	14	29%	53	9.6	63	90	22.9%	34	14.2	47%	53	7.4	30	16	3
Dwight Lowery*	29	FS	16	1029	83	10.1%	38	23	6	6	26	31%	53	10.0	62	48	12.8%	64	11.1	59%	24	7.1	31	4	2
Kemal Ishmael	24	FS/SS	16	806	100	12.2%	20	28	12	7	52	33%	49	6.2	30	27	9.2%	41	16.1	53%	41	11.7	69	6	4
Robert McClain*	27	CB	16	628	61	7.4%	60	21	5	9	18	44%	29	5.3	21	56	24.4%	45	12.9	45%	62	7.8	39	5	2
Robert Alford	27	CB	10	617	41	8.0%	46	14	9	3	8	25%	59	7.9	53	60	26.4%	61	14.9	42%	71	10.9	75	12	3
Josh Wilson*	30	CB	16	445	35	4.3%	--	19	6	5	8	100%	--	2.5	--	30	18.5%	--	9.0	46%	--	8.9	--	7	1
William Moore	30	SS	7	322	25	7.0%	--	5	2	7	15	20%	--	8.5	--	6	4.7%	--	17.1	47%	--	11.5	--	0	0
Dezmen Southward	25	FS	16	251	21	2.6%	--	7	6	3	5	40%	--	7.8	--	11	12.0%	--	13.2	65%	--	8.5	--	2	1
Charles Godfrey	30	CB	12	206	17	2.8%	--	6	1	3	4	75%	--	4.0	--	12	14.8%	--	6.0	36%	--	9.9	--	0	0
Phillip Adams	27	CB	12	306	26	4.5%	--	6	3	4	6	33%	--	15.7	--	38	33.2%	--	16.5	43%	--	11.8	--	4	1

Year	Pass D Rank	vs. #1 WR	Rk	vs. #2 WR	Rk	vs. Other WR	Rk	vs. TE	Rk	vs. RB	Rk
2012	11	-15.2%	7	-28.5%	1	-3.0%	13	3.0%	21	-3.0%	14
2013	32	24.1%	30	18.6%	30	22.5%	30	9.1%	23	-8.8%	12
2014	31	-12.9%	8	28.9%	28	15.7%	27	-8.9%	12	27.4%	30

Desmond Trufant had only pedestrian charting numbers, but his emergence last season was probably the lone bright spot for the depleted Falcons secondary. Trufant played primarily off-coverage in 2014 (117 of 205 qualifying snaps according to the research that Cian Fahey published on Bleacher Report), so it is not completely surprising that he looked mediocre statistically given how many shorter completions he allowed. He's a building block. Everything else in this secondary is completely up in the air. Second-rounder Jalen Collins is the physical ideal of a press-man corner, but he wasn't even a starter at LSU, and missed early team activities while recovering from foot surgery. Collins should be fine for training camp, but it may take him a bit to be up to starting in the NFL. Head coach Dan Quinn talked about moving nominal No. 2 cornerback Robert Alford to safety, but there may not be enough depth to allow that to happen. Robert McClain fled to New England, and ex-Jets corner Phillip Adams is the only experienced depth here, if you count getting torched as experience. Quinn has also talked about trying sophomore Dezmen Southward, who played safety last year, at corner. Southward could barely get on the field for the 2014 Falcons, so it's interesting trying to imagine him doing so for the 2015 squad at a tougher position. Seventh-rounder Akeem King (San Jose State) could not have picked a better depth chart to start his career on.

All this reshuffling of positions is necessary because safety is also an issue for the Falcons. William Moore morphed back into a pumpkin following a Pro Bowl appearance in 2012, which looks especially bad because the Falcons gave him an extension prior to said morphing. After missing most of 2014 with a shoulder injury that required surgery again this offseason, it's clear the 30-year-old Moore shouldn't be in Atlanta's long-term plans. If Moore doesn't come back, it leaves 2013 seventh-rounder Kemal Ishmael, an adequate-at-best box safety, paired with 2014 fifth-rounder Ricardo Allen, a cornerback conversion who spent the entire year on the practice squad and left OTAs on the first team. Former Panthers defensive back Charles Godfrey is also hanging around the depth chart because, best we can tell, Keion Carpenter wouldn't return phone calls. On the optimistic side, uh ... hey, Desmond Trufant is really good!

Special Teams

Year	DVOA	Rank	FG/XP	Rank	Net Kick	Rank	Kick Ret	Rank	Net Punt	Rank	Punt Ret	Rank	Hidden	Rank
2012	0.1%	16	-2.3	20	4.7	7	0.8	13	1.1	14	-3.7	21	-0.6	19
2013	-0.1%	17	0.0	18	-0.4	16	1.2	10	4.8	12	-6.2	25	-6.2	25
2014	3.0%	9	8.8	2	-6.2	26	-0.3	16	5.2	8	7.7	6	-1.2	20

Punter Matt Bosher is in the Pat McAfee mold as a punter who also handles kickoffs. He had a down 2014 season on kickoffs, but has been fairly good, if not McAfeeian, in the past. Kicker Matt Bryant's best season yet came when he was asked to take 10 field goals of 50 yards or longer, and hit seven of them. At 39, he may be winding down, or he may just be entering the beginning of his Morten Andersen phase.

Teams didn't do much punting to the Falcons in 2014, so fans didn't get to enjoy as much Devin Hester as they wanted. By our metrics, Hester was exactly average on kickoffs but was worth 7.7 points worth of field position on just 18 punt returns. Even at 33, he can still change a game. Eric Weems makes a terrific gunner and would probably return if misfortune were to occur to Hester.

Baltimore Ravens

2014 Record: 10-6	**Total DVOA:** 21.9% (5th)	**2015 Mean Projection:** 8.6 wins	**On the Clock (0-4):** 7%
Pythagorean Wins: 10.9 (5th)	**Offense:** 9.4% (9th)	**Postseason Odds:** 45.6%	**Mediocrity (5-7):** 28%
Snap-Weighted Age: 26.8 (17th)	**Defense:** -4.6% (8th)	**Super Bowl Odds:** 7.6%	**Playoff Contender (8-10):** 41%
Average Opponent: -4.9% (30th)	**Special Teams:** 8.0% (2nd)	**Proj. Avg. Opponent:** 0.9% (16th)	**Super Bowl Contender (11+):** 25%

2014: Ozzie Newsome rebuilding the roster: as much a Baltimore tradition as pit beef and Natty Boh.

2015: Poised for another title run, unless the new play-caller has PTSD.

When the 2013 season ended, the Ravens appeared to be, for the first time in recent memory, a franchise in distress. That's a relative term, of course; the team had hardly sunk to the bottom of the Mariana Trench with the likes of Jacksonville. But after five straight postseason appearances, including a Super Bowl championship in 2012, the Ravens went 8-8 in 2013. Still in playoff contention with two games left, they ended the season getting whacked by two rivals they had clearly fallen behind, New England and Cincinnati. Root causes were an aging defense that had lost the immortal Ray Lewis to retirement, an offensive line that had more holes than Dunkin' Donuts, and quarterback Joe Flacco's enormous contract extension, which had apparently robbed the team of its ability to swiftly re-float the sinking vessel.

Baltimore fans didn't panic, though. They kept calm and looked to Ozzie.

Sure enough, Ozzie Newsome, the Ravens' exemplary general manager, delivered. He rebuilt the team on the fly despite injuries, the aforementioned cap crunch, and an offseason incident that only rocked the franchise and changed the course of the NFL (indeed, all sports). The recast Ravens went 10-6 before demolishing the hated Steelers on the road in the wild-card round; they then took a 14-point lead at New England, forcing the Pats to stretch NFL rules and empty their supply of trick plays to eke out a victory. Baltimore improved a remarkable 18 spots in DVOA, the only team to finish in the top ten in all three phases of the game. According to Estimated and Pythagorean Wins, the Ravens even left a couple of victories on the table.

Not since Flacco was drafted in 2008 had the team required such an overhaul. This time, it wasn't the addition of a franchise quarterback, or any single transformative player, that keyed the resurgence. Instead, a flurry of moves combined with the team's proven organizational system and excellence at player development. It may have been Newsome's finest job as shot-caller and culture-creator during his reign in Baltimore. And his work has left the Ravens as a team well-placed to build upon that success in 2015.

Ozzie has been in charge since the franchise broke hearts on Lake Erie and moved to Charm City in 1996. Since 2000, when the Ravens won Super Bowl XXXV behind Ray Lewis and Jonathan Ogden (Newsome's very first two draft choices in 1996), the Ravens have had a losing record just three times. The first came in 2002, when the team crashed hard against the cap and went a desultory 7-9. Newsome and his staff succumbed to a classic temptation: keeping a championship core together for one last run at glory. It didn't work out, and Newsome learned a valuable lesson that he hasn't repeated since. As evidence, a mere six players who started Super Bowl XLVII remain on the team. Baltimore is as unsentimental about personnel as any franchise outside of the Commonwealth of Massachusetts.

This has given Newsome plenty of reps when it comes to adjusting the roster, be it fine-tuning or changing it wholesale. Oz's wizardry is achieved through a variety of methods. Drafting well is crucial, as is canny scouting and signing of undrafted free agents. The scouting department is full of guys who started as starvation-wage interns, sitting at Newsome's knee and learning through endless hours at the video screen what qualities the team prizes in potential players. (*The New York Times* once reported that these lifers are called the "20-20 Club," for their ages and salary.)[1]

But what separates Newsome from other GMs is his multi-faceted approach to team construction, including a willingness to take risks. Newsome specializes in signing veterans to cheap, "please just let me stay in the league and postpone real life a little longer" contracts. From Shannon Sharpe and Tony Siragusa back in 2000 to mid-decade problem-solvers such as Derrick Mason and Trevor Pryce and Willis McGahee through Bernard Pollard and Bryant McKinnie in the recent title run, the Ravens always seem to have a handful of newly-acquired old pros on hand to augment the frisky pups. Baltimore has consistently gotten high-quality work from these last round-ups; the older players often look so natural in purple you could imagine them all as lifetime Ravens.

Entering last season Baltimore was seriously depleted in the pass-catching department, thanks in part to dumping Anquan Boldin's salary on the 49ers in the wake of his 2012 postseason heroics. So Ozzie brought in Steve Smith and Owen Daniels, two very productive players in the decline phases of their careers who had been released by their former teams. Smith even added a "Sr." to his name, as if to emphasize his veteran status. Both were highly motivated and played very well. Daniels is now gone, and Smith will be replaced this year or next by new,

1 http://www.nytimes.com/2009/04/19/sports/football/19ravens.html

2015 Ravens Schedule

Week	Opp.	Week	Opp.	Week	Opp.
1	at DEN	7	at ARI (Mon.)	13	at MIA
2	at OAK	8	SD	14	SEA
3	CIN	9	BYE	15	KC
4	at PIT (Thu.)	10	JAC	16	PIT
5	CLE	11	STL	17	at CIN
6	at SF	12	at CLE (Mon.)		

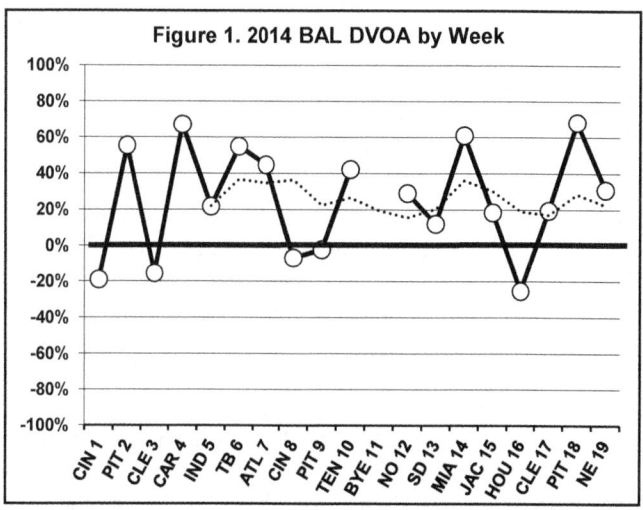

Figure 1. 2014 BAL DVOA by Week

highly drafted talent. Their usefulness as bridges to the next generation has been used up, but thanks in part to their efforts, a supposed "rebuilding season" lasted well into January.

Many of those older players arrived in Baltimore thanks to a key element in Newsome's team-building, one that cuts against the conventional wisdom—trading draft choices in order to fill specific roles. McGahee, for example, cost the Ravens a pair of third-rounders and a seventh. Boldin came from Arizona for picks in the third and fourth rounds. There is always risk involved in this tactic. Moving up in the draft to take Flacco worked brilliantly, but the quarterback he supplanted, Kyle Boller, came at a terrible cost during the 2003 draft. (Newsome gave Bill Belichick his 2004 first-rounder, a move unfathomable today in part because of the history between the two teams.) Lee Evans, acquired in 2011 for a fourth-round pick, was supposed to be the final piece of the passing game. Instead, he caught just four of 26 targets in the regular season, then couldn't keep his hands on the touchdown pass that would have sent the Ravens to Super Bowl XLVI.

It took courage to trade more draft ammo so soon after the Evans failure, and Newsome showed his stones again a year later. Baltimore's offensive line was so bad in 2013 that Newsome couldn't wait for the draft to improve it. Before the season was over, he dealt fourth- and fifth-round picks to Jacksonville for Eugene Monroe, who took over for the increasingly immobile McKinnie at left tackle. In the offseason, Newsome sent a 2015 fifth-rounder to Tampa Bay for center Jeremy Zuttah, a stark improvement over incumbent Geno Gradkowski. The ever-rebuilding Florida teams got some extra draft ammo, and Newsome got forty percent of a new front wall, which quickly developed into one of the best lines in football.

Many of those traded picks were in play due to the Ravens' penchant for annually loading up on compensatory draft picks. Few teams value these as much as Baltimore, and few teams get as many because few teams are raided in free agency with such regularity. According to an MMQB article by Jenny Vrentas, the Ravens front office uses a cost-benefit formula they call the "special sauce."[2] This algorithm assesses the team's willingness to let free agents leave, which is usually high. Few of these players fare better outside of Maryland. Meanwhile, the extra picks allow Newsome to bring in multiple talents each year regardless of position. Sam Koch, Tony Pashos, Le'Ron McClain, and Haruki Nakamura are just some of the compensatory picks that have contributed over the years.

A third starter on last year's stalwart line, right tackle Ricky Wagner, was picked during the compensatory stage of the fifth round in 2013. Two other, lesser contributors, running back Lorenzo Taliaferro and tight end Crockett Gilmore, were extra choices in 2014. Pernell McPhee, who finally broke through as a pass-rushing linebacker last season and was a key element in the team's return to defensive excellence, was a compensatory pick in the fifth round of the 2011 draft. The circle became complete when McPhee was allowed to walk for a rich free-agent contract in March. No doubt the compensatory picks for losing McPhee will be used wisely next spring.

Perhaps the most important move Newsome made last year wasn't adding a player, however. Hiring Gary Kubiak as offensive coordinator reanimated the Baltimore attack. Kubiak's patented zone-running and play-action passing concepts found an eager group of players able to execute them at a high level. Offensive DVOA leapt from 30th to ninth. The running game went from dead last in the NFL in yards per carry (3.1) to seventh (4.5). The offensive line was top-notch (third in adjusted line yards), and journeyman runner Justin Forsett fit perfectly into the system, allowing the team to turn the page on Ray Rice without so much as a "don't let the door coldcock you in an elevator on the way out." Forsett had been released by four different teams before signing with the Ravens, where he rushed for 1,266 yards and 8 touchdowns.

Yet Kubiak's best work was with the oft-inconsistent Flacco. The Delaware Destroyer improved mightily under Kubiak, in part by dumping many of the heave-and-hope bombs that were a mainstay of the Ravens attack. In 2012 and 2013, 24 percent of Flacco's passes went over 15 yards in the air; in 2014, those passes were down to 16 percent, below the NFL average. In their stead were less dramatic but more effective play-action rollouts to tight ends and crossing wideouts, staples of the Kubiak playbook. Flacco's DVOA skyrocketed (and was positive for the first time since 2010), and he set career bests in QBR, yards and touchdown passes.

But just as success frequently leaves Baltimore's roster depleted, so it also goes with the coaching staff. Kubiak has gone home to Denver to work with old buddy John Elway. He is replaced by Marc Trestman, last seen taking his "passing-game guru" status to the 50-yard line at Soldier Field and setting it aflame.

Now, the list of excellent coordinators who failed as head coaches is long and distinguished, and it stands to reason Trestman learned something from the Chicago disaster. Nevertheless, just how closely Trestman hews to the Kubiak model is subject to intense discussion in Baltimore—not since *The Wire* went off the air has there been such fervent fan dissection. Will the new coordinator keep fans partying like McNulty or muttering *"Sheeeeeeeeee-iiiiiiiiiiiiiiitttttttttt"* as the punt team repeatedly jogs on to the field?

Trestman stepped in for Kubiak once before, becoming quarterbacks coach of the 49ers in 1995 when Kubiak left with Mike Shanahan for, coincidentally enough, Denver. Trestman actually replaced both Kubiak and Shanahan, holding the dual title of quarterbacks coach and offensive coordinator, and there were few changes to the Shanahan/Kubiak rocket-paced attack. The 1995 Niners led the league in points scored and passing yards, so something Trestman did worked. Of course, Flacco is no Steve Young, and all the Ravens receivers combined don't equal Jerry Rice. But the important takeaway is that history backs up Trestman's vow not to make substantial changes to Kubiak's offense. That means running the ball far more often than Trestman usually does. (Chicago ran it nearly a hundred fewer times than Baltimore last season, although constantly trailing in games played a large role in that.) More to the point, even if Trestman were tempted to go all Martzy or hallucinate about being back in the CFL, John Harbaugh is there to ensure he keeps his mad scientist tendencies under wraps.

"I'm the one who sets the philosophy as the head coach," Harbaugh told Ravens.com after hiring Trestman. "You decide what the philosophy is going to be and you bring people into your organization who are going to best carry that forward." Harbaugh has precedent on his side. Over the years, the Ravens have lost such supposedly irreplaceable defensive geniuses as Marvin Lewis, Rex Ryan, and Chuck Pagano without missing a beat, leaving the organization confident that success is due to the system, not the individuals running it. On the other hand, the Ravens haven't always been as wedded to the run as they were under Kubiak. Trestman's offensive scheme from Chicago would have looked awfully familiar to Ravens fans two years ago, even though it was extremely different from what Kubiak was doing with the Ravens last season (Table 1).

Just how well Trestman keeps the offense humming should determine the team's ceiling in 2015. We project them to be right there at the top of the AFC, despite a much tougher schedule (replacing the South divisions with the West divisions will do that). There are concerns, however, and the Ravens still have work to do to supplant the Patriots atop the conference and the Steelers and Bengals atop the division. Yes, hard as it may be to recall, the Ravens finished third in the AFC North, and were 15 minutes from not qualifying for the playoffs before slogging past the Browns on the last Sunday of the regular season.

In addition to the versatile McPhee, the defense must re-

Table 1. Is Marc Trestman Actually Jim Caldwell in Disguise?

Metric	2014 Ravens	Rk	2013 Ravens	Rk	2014 Bears	Rk
Runs, first half	41%	10	35%	25	30%	32
Runs, first down	53%	8	50%	13	39%	32
Pass, ahead 2H	37%	32	51%	11	53%	3
Form: Single Back	60%	30	75%	11	81%	7
Pers: 3+ WR	38%	31	76%	2	68%	6
Shotgun/Pistol	24%	32	73%	4	73%	6

place Haloti Ngata, the longtime world destroyer in the middle of the line of scrimmage, who was dealt to the Lions in yet another salary cap-affected move. His replacements, Timmy Jernigan and Brandon Williams, are extremely promising linemen, but there is certain to be at least a small dropoff.

More worrying is the secondary, which was hit by a nasty pandemic of injuries last year. If Newsome's team-wide rework fell short, it was in this unit, which lacked depth and was weak at safety even before ligaments began snapping. Newsome was unable to halt a slow-motion collapse in the defensive backfield, one that inevitably led to the team's defeat in the postseason. The secondary remains far too dependent upon the health of Jimmy Smith's foot.

On offense, the free-agent departure of wideout Torrey Smith was mitigated by the first-round selection of Breshad Perriman from Central Florida. But the receiver corps remains comprised of the aged Steve Smith and a bunch of unproven kids, including second-rounder Maxx (Double-X) Williams, a tight end from Minnesota. The youngsters need to come through, because Flacco's contract strikes again next year, when his cap hit nearly doubles to a terrifying $28.5 million. Regardless of how well Newsome restructures (or tears up and redoes) the deal, he will have to employ more of his magic to keep the offense humming and financially viable at the same time.

Off-field issues also linger. For all of the love we have poured on the front office in this essay, this franchise is still recovering from the massive blow it took to its image during the Rice imbroglio, damage that may take a while to heal. A lesser but still unseemly story broke in May, when it was revealed that the Ravens accepted nearly a million dollars from the Pentagon in return for in-game salutes to veterans (14 teams took Defense Department cash for this deeply cynical tightening of the military-pigskin-industrial complex, but only Atlanta received more than Baltimore). Owner Steve Bisciotti's close friendship with Roger Goodell seemed like a positive not long ago. Now the commish's toxicity has rubbed off on Bisciotti, tainting his reputation.

But whatever problems enmesh the Ravens, they seldom cause long-term harm. That's because Ozzie Newsome is there to ease the pain and keep the franchise in perennial contention. Don't expect that to change in 2015.

Robert Weintraub

2014 Ravens Stats by Week

Wk	vs.	W-L	PF	PA	YDF	YDA	TO	Total	Off	Def	ST
1	CIN	L	16	23	423	423	-2	-19%	9%	9%	-19%
2	PIT	W	26	6	323	323	3	55%	1%	-47%	8%
3	at CLE	W	23	21	377	377	-1	-16%	13%	37%	9%
4	CAR	W	38	10	454	454	1	67%	77%	12%	1%
5	at IND	L	13	20	287	287	1	22%	-3%	-20%	5%
6	at TB	W	48	17	475	475	0	55%	71%	25%	9%
7	ATL	W	29	7	371	371	-2	45%	7%	-30%	8%
8	at CIN	L	24	27	294	294	0	-7%	-26%	-12%	8%
9	at PIT	L	23	43	332	332	-1	-2%	-20%	21%	39%
10	TEN	W	21	7	312	312	2	42%	1%	-28%	13%
11	BYE										
12	at NO	W	34	27	449	449	0	29%	30%	5%	4%
13	SD	L	33	34	350	350	2	12%	19%	23%	16%
14	at MIA	W	28	13	447	447	-1	61%	38%	-20%	3%
15	JAC	W	20	12	314	314	0	18%	9%	-9%	0%
16	at HOU	L	13	25	211	211	-2	-25%	-69%	-29%	15%
17	CLE	W	20	10	419	419	2	19%	3%	-7%	9%
18	at PIT	W	30	17	30	17	2	68%	13%	-49%	5%
19	at NE	L	31	35	31	35	-1	31%	37%	15%	9%

Trends and Splits

	Offense	Rank	Defense	Rank
Total DVOA	9.4%	9	-4.6%	8
Unadjusted VOA	12.1%	7	-6.2%	7
Weighted Trend	5.8%	8	-6.2%	12
Variance	12.2%	31	5.8%	14
Average Opponent	3.1%	31	-1.4%	23
Passing	31.9%	6	5.9%	15
Rushing	-6.0%	18	-19.3%	5
First Down	12.9%	7	-4.7%	12
Second Down	7.6%	11	-7.8%	9
Third Down	5.2%	15	0.4%	16
First Half	-1.0%	16	-11.1%	7
Second Half	19.0%	4	2.4%	19
Red Zone	-15.1%	22	-42.4%	1
Late and Close	21.2%	7	-3.7%	15

Five-Year Performance

Year	W-L	Pyth W	Est W	PF	PA	TO	Total	Rk	Off	Rk	Def	Rk	ST	Rk	Off AGL	Rk	Def AGL	Rk	Off Age	Rk	Def Age	Rk	ST Age	Rk
2010	12-4	10.6	12.1	357	270	+7	21.7%	5	5.4%	12	-10.3%	6	6.0%	4	23.7	15	27.0	19	27.9	9	28.2	6	25.8	23
2011	12-4	11.2	10.6	378	266	+2	14.5%	7	2.9%	13	-17.1%	1	-5.6%	30	8.0	1	10.9	4	27.8	9	28.2	3	26.6	6
2012	10-6	9.4	9.2	398	344	+9	9.8%	8	3.0%	13	2.2%	19	9.0%	1	8.1	2	46.4	25	27.3	10	27.7	7	26.9	7
2013	8-8	7.1	6.8	320	352	-5	-6.7%	23	-21.7%	30	-8.7%	7	6.3%	3	34.0	16	13.4	5	26.6	18	27.5	6	25.9	22
2014	10-6	10.9	11.5	409	302	+2	21.9%	5	9.4%	9	-4.6%	8	8.0%	2	25.0	10	27.6	8	27.4	8	26.8	15	25.4	31

2014 Performance Based on Most Common Personnel Groups

BAL Offense					BAL Offense vs. Opponents					BAL Defense					BAL Defense vs. Opponents			
Pers	Freq	Yds	DVOA	Run%	Pers	Freq	Yds	DVOA	Run%	Pers	Freq	Yds	DVOA	Pers	Freq	Yds	DVOA
21	35%	6.3	15.0%	59%	Base	58%	6.2	16.7%	55%	Base	36%	5.1	-0.9%	11	61%	5.4	-4.1%
11	32%	6.8	24.1%	20%	Nickel	28%	6.4	34.4%	20%	Nickel	61%	5.5	-3.6%	12	22%	6.0	11.0%
12	20%	5.7	8.8%	42%	Dime+	10%	6.0	-17.3%	11%	Dime+	1%	7.0	-80.1%	21	8%	4.5	-16.6%
22	4%	3.9	-19.3%	81%	Goal Line	3%	0.3	-40.7%	71%	Goal Line	1%	0.4	-73.8%	13	3%	3.6	-17.2%
01	3%	3.9	11.5%	0%	Big	1%	1.6	-81.7%	86%	Big	1%	3.0	-33.9%	22	2%	4.1	-3.8%

Strategic Tendencies

Run/Pass		Rk	Formation		Rk	Pass Rush		Rk	Secondary		Rk	Strategy		Rk
Runs, first half	41%	10	Form: Single Back	60%	30	Rush 3	3.3%	27	4 DB	25%	18	Play action	18%	23
Runs, first down	53%	8	Form: Empty Back	10%	5	Rush 4	67.5%	10	5 DB	73%	4	Avg Box (Off)	6.59	1
Runs, second-long	27%	22	Pers: 3+ WR	38%	31	Rush 5	21.6%	21	6+ DB	1%	28	Avg Box (Def)	6.25	17
Runs, power sit.	63%	8	Pers: 4+ WR	4%	8	Rush 6+	7.6%	15	CB by Sides	80%	17	Offensive Pace	28.63	5
Runs, behind 2H	23%	27	Pers: 2+ TE/6+ OL	28%	20	Sacks by LB	82.7%	1	DB Blitz	10%	16	Defensive Pace	31.31	30
Pass, ahead 2H	37%	32	Shotgun/Pistol	24%	32	Sacks by DB	1.0%	30	Hole in Zone	8%	6	Go for it on 4th	1.31	4

We hope Justin Forsett likes catching screen passes, because Marc Trestman's Bears led the league in running back screens last year while the Ravens were near the bottom of the league. ☜ For Joe Flacco, one of the big differences between 2013 and 2014 was how he handled the blitz. With three or four pass rushers, Flacco averaged 6.8 yards per pass two years ago and 6.7 yards per pass last year. But with five or more pass rushers, Flacco went from 4.3 yards per pass two years ago to 7.6 yards per pass last year. Flacco faced a blitz on 38 percent of pass plays; only Tampa Bay's quarterbacks were blitzed more often. ☜ Flacco was even better if the blitz was from a defensive back. He averaged 8.6 yards on DB blitzes, even though Tony Romo was the only quarterback who faced DB blitzes more often. ☜ The Ravens allowed just 4.8 yards per play when they sent a big blitz of six or more, but allowed 9.2 yards per play whenever they rushed at least one defensive back. (They allowed 7.6 yards on plays that qualified for both categories.) ☜ Baltimore opponents only dropped 14 passes by our count, for a league-low 2.5 percent dropped pass rate. ☜ The Ravens ranked fourth in DVOA on short passes (up to 15 yards in the air) but ranked 31st against deep passes (16+ yards in the air).

Passing

Player	DYAR	DVOA	Plays	NtYds	Avg	YAC	C%	TD	Int
J.Flacco	987	15.5%	569	3825	6.7	5.1	63.0%	27	12
M.Schaub	-158	-220.7%	13	28	2.2	4.8	50.0%	0	2

Receiving

Player	DYAR	DVOA	Plays	Ctch	Yds	Y/C	YAC	TD	C%
S.Smith	79	-5.4%	134	79	1068	13.5	4.7	6	59%
T.Smith*	310	26.8%	92	49	767	15.7	3.4	11	53%
K.Aiken	106	29.7%	32	24	267	11.1	2.5	3	75%
M.Brown	61	13.9%	31	24	255	10.6	4.1	0	77%
J.Jones*	11	-4.1%	18	9	131	14.6	9.2	0	50%
M.Campanaro	50	60.5%	9	7	102	14.6	5.0	1	78%
O.Daniels*	49	2.2%	79	48	527	11.0	3.7	4	61%
D.Pitta	5	-3.5%	21	16	125	7.8	3.4	0	76%
C.Gillmore	20	11.2%	15	10	121	12.1	5.9	1	67%
J.Forsett	-64	-33.5%	60	45	262	5.8	7.4	0	75%
K.Juszczyk	11	-6.7%	27	19	182	9.6	8.9	1	70%
L.Taliaferro	33	61.1%	10	8	114	14.3	11.8	0	80%
F.Toussaint	-2	-19.7%	6	3	27	9.0	10.3	0	50%
B.Pierce*	-20	-80.0%	6	2	13	6.5	5.0	0	33%

Rushing

Player	DYAR	DVOA	Plays	Yds	Avg	TD	Fum	Suc
J.Forsett	149	6.7%	234	1267	5.4	8	1	44%
B.Pierce*	-24	-14.8%	93	366	3.9	2	1	42%
L.Taliaferro	4	-7.2%	68	292	4.3	4	1	49%
J.Flacco	-1	-12.9%	24	85	3.5	2	1	-
F.Toussaint	-10	-52.0%	6	12	2.0	0	0	33%

Offensive Line

Player	Pos	Age	GS	Snaps	Pen	Sk	Pass	Run	Player	Pos	Age	GS	Snaps	Pen	Sk	Pass	Run
Jeremy Zuttah	C	29	16/16	1069	6	1.0	5.5	7.5	Eugene Monroe	LT	28	11/11	730	9	3.0	12.0	3.0
Marshal Yanda	RG	31	16/16	1064	5	1.5	8.0	4.0	James Hurst	LT	24	16/5	380	6	2.5	11.5	5.0
Ricky Wagner	RT	26	15/15	971	2	1.0	9.5	8.0	John Urschel	G	24	11/3	223	2	0.0	3.5	1.0
Kelechi Osemele	LG	26	14/14	936	6	2.0	11.0	4.5									

Year	Yards	ALY	Rk	Power	Rk	Stuff	Rk	2nd Lev	Rk	Open Field	Rk	Sacks	ASR	Rk	Short	Long	F-Start	Cont.
2012	4.53	4.33	6	64%	14	16%	4	1.22	14	0.87	11	38	6.1%	13	9	13	23	30
2013	2.95	3.01	32	49%	31	26%	32	0.76	32	0.30	32	48	7.3%	16	14	20	25	37
2014	4.83	4.25	3	55%	28	21%	23	1.36	3	1.30	1	19	4.5%	4	8	8	16	34
2014 ALY by direction:		Left End 4.43 (5)			Left Tackle 3.8 (16)			Mid/Guard 4.11 (9)			Right Tackle 5.07 (1)				Right End 3.59 (17)			

The massive improvement up front was not entirely attributable to Gary Kubiak's zone schemes. Marshal Yanda had a phenomenal rebound season (we marked him with 24 blown blocks in 2013, then just half as many last year) and was one of the best guards in football. Runs off right tackle ranked tops in the league, just one indicator of Yanda and right tackle Ricky Wagner's athleticism and technique. While Yanda's performance was just a great player returning to form, Wagner's was a revelation. Thought to be the line's weak link entering the season, the second-year tackle committed just two penalties and gave up just a single sack. The former walk-on at Wisconsin is clearly used to overcoming low expectations, but that won't be a problem henceforth.

Equally important to the unit's improvement was the signing of dependable Jeremy Zuttah to replace the ineffective Geno Gradkowski at center. Re-signing left tackle Eugene Monroe was also key, even though he missed time to injury. Absence made the heart grow fonder, as rookie James Hurst was up and down when forced to take over. He has the makings of a decent backup, but if the Ravens are to go as far as they can in 2015, they need Monroe in there. Kelechi Osemele is solid next to Monroe at left guard. Seemingly overnight, the purple wall transformed from a glaring weakness to the best position group on the roster.

Now the Ravens must make sure it doesn't transform back after the 2015 season. Both Yanda and Osemele are free agents after the season, and given Baltimore's track record, one will be allowed to walk, most likely the older Yanda. How the angry man who once tasered himself for kicks deals with any perceived disrespect will be an interesting subplot to the Ravens season. Reserve guard John Urschel is being groomed to take over for whomever leaves, but he would be a step down.

Defensive Front Seven

Defensive Line	Age	Pos	G	Snaps	Plays	Overall TmPct	Rk	Stop	Dfts	BTkl	Runs	vs. Run St%	Rk	RuYd	Rk	Sack	Pass Rush Hit	Hur	Dsrpt
Brandon Williams	26	DT	16	550	47	5.6%	30	36	5	1	46	76%	58	2.3	51	0.5	1	6.0	0
Haloti Ngata*	31	DE	12	529	39	6.2%	19	30	12	1	26	77%	53	3.1	86	2.0	2	7.5	5
Chris Canty	33	DE	11	346	35	6.1%	20	28	5	2	31	77%	51	2.5	61	0.5	1	0.0	1
Timmy Jernigan	23	DE	12	302	23	3.6%	--	21	6	0	18	89%	--	2.7	--	4.0	6	5.5	0
DeAngelo Tyson	26	DE	11	275	21	3.6%	--	16	5	1	17	82%	--	2.4	--	1.0	2	2.0	0
Lawrence Guy	25	DE	14	254	17	2.3%	--	14	0	0	16	81%	--	3.1	--	0.0	1	2.0	1

Edge Rushers	Age	Pos	G	Snaps	Plays	Overall TmPct	Rk	Stop	Dfts	BTkl	Runs	vs. Run St%	Rk	RuYd	Rk	Sack	Pass Rush Hit	Hur	Dsrpt
Terrell Suggs	33	OLB	16	850	61	7.3%	16	49	22	2	40	80%	28	1.6	16	12.0	6	14.5	0
Elvis Dumervil	31	OLB	16	603	37	4.4%	57	30	22	1	10	70%	59	6.4	87	17.0	9	13.5	0
Courtney Upshaw	26	OLB	16	524	43	5.1%	42	30	7	4	33	73%	51	2.3	36	0.0	3	6.0	0
Pernell McPhee*	26	OLB	16	515	31	3.7%	67	28	18	5	15	87%	9	1.5	12	7.5	19	22.5	3

Linebackers	Age	Pos	G	Snaps	Plays	Overall TmPct	Rk	Stop	Dfts	BTkl	Sack	Pass Rush Hit	Hur	Runs	vs. Run St%	Rk	RuYd	Rk	Tgts	vs. Pass Suc%	Rk	AdjYd	Rk	PD	Int
C.J. Mosley	23	ILB	16	1065	134	15.9%	17	78	30	6	3.0	9	11	65	66%	33	3.7	58	52	47%	44	5.9	26	6	2
Daryl Smith	33	ILB	16	1042	134	15.9%	17	80	19	6	1.0	2	6	77	69%	24	3.0	23	30	80%	1	3.8	3	6	1

Year	Yards	ALY	Rk	Power	Rk	Stuff	Rk	2nd Level	Rk	Open Field	Rk	Sacks	ASR	Rk	Short	Long
2012	4.10	4.33	28	76%	29	14%	32	1.16	11	0.42	3	37	6.9%	10	11	14
2013	3.92	3.95	19	59%	8	18%	16	1.08	14	0.48	9	40	7.3%	10	16	11
2014	3.53	3.55	7	55%	4	18%	19	0.86	2	0.46	2	49	8.0%	5	23	10
2014 ALY by direction:			Left End 3.7 (18)			Left Tackle 3.91 (20)			Mid/Guard 3.33 (3)			Right Tackle 4.36 (22)			Right End 3.14 (8)	

They may be on the wrong side of 30, but bookend rush linebackers Terrell Suggs and Elvis Dumervil show no signs of decay. T-Sizzle and Tiny E combined for 29 sacks—no other pass rush duo brought enemy quarterbacks down as often—and 43 more hits and hurries. If they were the Splash Brothers, Pernell McPhee played the role of Draymond Green; he was an excellent pass rusher who lined up everywhere and drafted off the attention paid to the edge speedsters, while also stuffing the run. McPhee may not be as valuable in Chicago without all this excellence around him, but his versatility will be missed in the Inner Harbor. Courtney Upshaw was far less effective in the same amount of playing time. It's on him to up his play with fourth-round pick Za'Darius Smith of Kentucky in his rearview mirror. Smith is more of an edge-setter against the run than a pass-rusher, but Upshaw hasn't particularly excelled in either role since the Ravens took him 35th overall in 2012.

In the rush to anoint C.J. Mosley the second coming of Ray Lewis—he's good, but cool your jets, Ravens fans—the continued excellence of fellow inside linebacker Daryl Smith often gets ignored. Smith was particularly effective in defending the pass, an art seldom lauded but much appreciated by defensive coordinator Dean Pees. At 33, Smith makes it happen through smarts more than athleticism, and if he can pass along those diagnostic abilities to Mosley while they remain a duo, the Ravens will have an even bigger treasure. Mosley wore down a bit late in the season, hardly unusual for rookies. But his promise is enormous. The team needs both Smith and Mosley to stay strong, as former second-round pick Arthur Brown has disappointed so far.

The front line will look different with man mountain Haloti Ngata dealt away, but AFC North interior linemen should hold those sighs of relief; Timmy Jernigan is a handful too. The rookie showed extreme agility and quickness in penetrating lines last season, and while not as massive as Ngata, he proved stout against the run thanks to his high-quality movement through traffic. Nose tackle Brandon Williams provides bulk, but look for third-rounder Carl Davis (Iowa) to push for an increased role by late fall. Davis is an exploder off the snap in the Jernigan mold, though questions about his motor and pass-rush ability dropped him out of the first round, where he was originally projected to go. Veteran Chris Canty is usually the third end on the field in run situations; the Ravens cut him after the season but re-signed him at a lower rate, and they'll undoubtedly use one of their 2016 draft picks to snag his replacement.

Defensive Secondary

Secondary	Age	Pos	G	Snaps	Plays	TmPct	Rk	Stop	Dfts	BTkl	Runs	St%	Rk	RuYd	Rk	Tgts	Tgt%	Rk	Dist	Suc%	Rk	AdjYd	Rk	PD	Int
								Overall					vs. Run						vs. Pass						
Lardarius Webb	30	CB	13	772	54	7.9%	48	18	9	3	7	14%	71	13.7	74	72	24.2%	42	12.0	49%	47	9.3	64	8	1
Darian Stewart*	27	FS	16	755	56	6.7%	63	21	4	9	27	52%	19	6.3	33	16	5.3%	11	17.5	61%	14	8.4	51	3	1
Matt Elam	24	SS	16	636	51	6.1%	67	20	4	10	19	47%	25	4.2	6	26	10.4%	50	11.8	36%	65	12.5	70	3	0
Will Hill	25	FS	10	563	44	8.4%	53	21	10	2	20	65%	4	2.8	1	15	6.7%	23	11.5	72%	2	5.2	10	3	1
Jimmy Smith	27	CB	8	459	34	8.1%	44	13	4	3	6	17%	69	8.5	56	37	20.6%	20	12.0	51%	40	6.8	15	6	1
Jeromy Miles*	28	SS	16	326	24	2.9%	--	11	4	1	13	54%	--	4.7	--	10	7.9%	--	11.1	73%	--	3.1	--	1	1
Asa Jackson	26	CB	7	323	30	8.2%	--	11	4	4	4	50%	--	3.3	--	32	25.7%	--	11.1	52%	--	6.9	--	1	0
Danny Gorrer*	29	CB	10	321	24	4.6%	--	9	4	2	0	0%	--	0.0	--	29	22.9%	--	12.6	39%	--	12.1	--	2	1
Terrence Brooks	24	FS	11	232	21	3.6%	--	3	1	1	2	0%	--	8.5	--	9	9.5%	--	18.6	45%	--	14.7	--	2	0
Anthony Levine	28	CB	16	180	26	3.1%	--	8	3	1	6	67%	--	3.2	--	19	27.3%	--	10.5	42%	--	7.9	--	2	0
Kendrick Lewis	27	FS	16	1077	90	10.6%	29	31	14	13	50	28%	57	7.4	48	24	5.3%	10	12.6	67%	5	5.6	16	5	2

Year	Pass D Rank	vs. #1 WR	Rk	vs. #2 WR	Rk	vs. Other WR	Rk	vs. TE	Rk	vs. RB	Rk
2012	13	6.4%	20	21.0%	30	-16.0%	6	-6.8%	9	-20.8%	7
2013	9	-27.2%	2	-1.8%	13	5.9%	22	2.1%	16	-10.6%	9
2014	15	3.4%	18	8.6%	23	11.7%	24	4.8%	21	-13.5%	9

Cornerback depth was an area of concern coming into the season, but over the course of the season it gradually descended into complete catastrophe. Jimmy Smith was playing at a high level when Mr. Lisfranc struck and ended his season halfway through. The other starter, Lardarius Webb, has never seemed to fully recover from 2012's ACL tear, and struggled with a bad back and other nagging injuries last season. He's hardly the player he was before the tendon tear, but the Ravens are relying on him to be in there. The backups went down like duckpins, and four others, including original nickelback Asa Jackson, went on injured reserve. When Tom Brady got a hold of street free agents like Rashaan Melvin, the Achilles heel proved fatal to the Ravens' chances of a Super Bowl run.

Clearly, a full return to health for Smith (not to mention Jackson and Webb) is critical. Depth remains an issue, which is why the team moved quickly to snap up Patriots castoff Kyle Arrington without asking too many questions about why a team that also desperately needs corners would dump him. Fourth-round pick Tray Walker fits the Ravens profile in length (6-foot-2) and pedigree (the team loves small school guys, including Webb and Jackson, and Walker went to Texas Southern). But he has a lot of developing to do before he's ready to play consistently.

The safeties were healthier in 2014, but not a whole lot better. Strong safety Matt Elam, a former first-rounder, continues to struggle mightily, leading the team in missed tackles and badly lacking coverage skills. Troubled but talented former Giant Will Hill played well across the board and is likely to take Elam's job this season, provided he can stay clean. Kendrick Lewis was signed from Houston to replace former starter Darian Stewart, a tough but less than instinctive player who signed with the Broncos in free agency. The Ravens also tried to snag fellow Texans castoff D.J. Swearinger in May, so clearly they remain unsatisfied with the safeties they have.

Special Teams

Year	DVOA	Rank	FG/XP	Rank	Net Kick	Rank	Kick Ret	Rank	Net Punt	Rank	Punt Ret	Rank	Hidden	Rank
2012	9.0%	1	9.4	3	12.4	3	13.3	3	7.4	10	2.5	9	-21.7	32
2013	6.3%	3	11.4	2	-1.4	21	9.2	3	-2.9	24	15.5	2	-1.1	17
2014	8.0%	2	5.3	7	8.3	4	10.2	3	17.9	1	-1.9	14	-3.2	24

A dominant unit in 2014, and a consistent one in recent years: Baltimore has ranked in the top four of special teams DVOA in four of the past five seasons. Punter Sam Koch and kicker Justin Tucker provide the best one-two specialist punch in the NFL, and the coverage teams have been solid. The strong return game was paced by Jacoby Jones, but the Ravens cut him since they were paying him as a wide receiver but using him like a return specialist. It may take a village to replace him. Receiver Michael Campanaro and nickelback Asa Jackson have the early edge, but the job will be wide open. Lardarius Webb was an electrifying returner once upon a time, but is likely too valuable to risk fielding kicks. One dark horse is undrafted free agent wideout DeAndre Carter from Sacramento State, a waterbug with quick feet.

Buffalo Bills

2014 Record: 9-7	**Total DVOA:** 10.5% (9th)	**2015 Mean Projection:** 8.0 wins	**On the Clock (0-4):** 10%
Pythagorean Wins: 9.6 (12th)	**Offense:** -11.2% (26th)	**Postseason Odds:** 34.3%	**Mediocrity (5-7):** 33%
Snap-Weighted Age: 26.3 (26th)	**Defense:** -15.5% (2nd)	**Super Bowl Odds:** 4.1%	**Playoff Contender (8-10):** 39%
Average Opponent: 1.6% (10th)	**Special Teams:** 6.2% (4th)	**Proj. Avg. Opponent:** -1.8% (21st)	**Super Bowl Contender (11+):** 18%

2014: Great, underrated defense plus terrible offense equals mediocrity.

2015: Great, properly rated defense plus terrible offense equals mediocrity.

The 2015 Buffalo Bills are like a TV show with seemingly all the right pieces except one. They have the right supporting actors, the best writers, even the time slot right after *Friends*. But there's no escaping that the headliner is *Garfield: The Movie* lead Breckin Meyer. Everyone around him could be perfect and it just doesn't matter.

The Bills are almost certain to start a Breckin Meyer at quarterback this year. Noise coming from Buffalo's offseason workouts suggests that the EJ Manuel-Matt Cassel-Tyrod Taylor troika has underachieved even the already low expectations. The quarterback vacuum is even more depressing because the Bills are stacked throughout the roster, so stacked that they could drag whichever Breckin Meyer they end up starting to the playoffs. The Bills thus find themselves in a tricky spot. They have a roster ready to win now, but no quarterback to seal the deal. Moreover, the longer-term outlook for the rest of the roster is much less rosy. Poor asset valuation and shortsighted decisions soon will make it hard for the Bills to keep their core together.

Last season, an impressive defense carried the Bills to nine wins, but could not quite end football's longest playoff drought, which now stands at 15 years. (Yes, Frank Wycheck was Music City Miracling the last time Buffalo played past Week 17.) The Bills have had some very good defenses during that stretch. In addition to last year's second-ranked unit, the Bills have ranked in the top ten in defensive DVOA five other times, including first in 2004.

The Bills, however, are still the only team that is 0-for-the-millenium in having a top-ten offense. (Even the Browns cracked the top ten once.) Just once since 2003 has Buffalo ranked higher than 20th. Last year, the Bills ranked 26th, one spot worse than the year before. The great defense-bad offense combination has not worked much better for the rest of the league than it did for the 2014 Bills. Since the NFL expanded to 32 teams in 2002, 19 teams have ranked in the top five in defense and the bottom ten in offense. Just seven of those teams finished over .500, and only six made the playoffs.

Merely competent offense would have been enough to make the playoffs last year with the Bills fielding football's best front four. Tackle Marcell Dareus played at a Suh-like level in 2014. Last year, Dareus led all tackles with ten sacks, despite frequently facing double teams. At the other tackle

spot, Kyle Williams, who would be the best defensive lineman on most teams, continued a vaguely Justin Smith-like trajectory that has seen his career peak late. Helped by the attention paid to Dareus, Williams generated even more pressure, with 31.5 sacks, hits, or hurries (Dareus had 21.5). Running inside against Williams and Dareus was next to impossible, too. The Bills ranked second in adjusted line yards on runs up the middle, second on inside runs to the left, and second on inside runs to the right. The Week 16 game against the Raiders illustrated how crucial the tackles, and Dareus in particular, were to the Bills' defense. After Dareus left the game in the second quarter with a knee injury, the previously impotent Raiders (who entered the game ranked 30th in offensive DVOA) started to gash the Bills on the ground. To that point, Oakland had gained six yards on six carries. From then on, Oakland rolled up 136 yards on 28 attempts, leading to a 26-24 loss that ended Buffalo's playoff hopes.

Dareus was joined as a first-team All-Pro by defensive end Mario Williams, who dominated in all facets. In pass defense, Williams generated 14 sacks. Against the run, Williams finished fourth among defensive ends with a 91 percent stop rate. (The Williams brothers-in-name are in contention for the best last-name-sharing defensive duo ever, although Jack Youngblood may win that without needing much help from non-brother Jim.) Pass-rusher Jerry Hughes (32 hurries, 10 sacks) took advantage of a favorable situation to break out with the Bills after struggling with the Colts.

While the front four drove the NFL's best pass defense, also essential to the Bills' success were their secret studs: linebacker Nigel Bradham and cornerback Corey Graham. If Bradham played more in prime time, the 2012 fourth-round pick could have been the beneficiary of the kind of gushing that Cris Collinsworth heaped on the Patriots' Jamie Collins. Bradham combined remarkable explosion against the run (80 percent stop rate, ranked fourth among linebackers) with sideline-to-sideline range in coverage (60 percent adjusted success rate on 22 targets). As an occasional pass rusher, Bradham disrupted opponents' throws 37 percent of the time that he blitzed (2.5 sacks, 5 hits, and 9.5 hurries on 46 pass rushes).

Just as valuable as Bradham was the similarly underrated Graham. Playing mostly out of the slot, Graham had the best adjusted success rate (71 percent) and allowed the fewest adjusted yards per pass (4.5) of any cornerback with at least 50

2015 Bills Schedule

Week	Opp.	Week	Opp.	Week	Opp.
1	IND	7	at JAC (U.K.)	13	HOU
2	NE	8	BYE	14	at PHI
3	at MIA	9	MIA	15	at WAS
4	NYG	10	at NYJ (Thu.)	16	DAL
5	at TEN	11	at NE (Mon.)	17	NYJ
6	CIN	12	at KC		

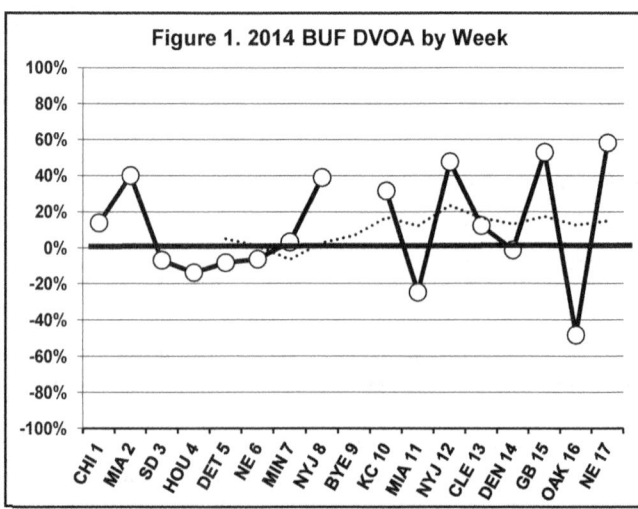

Figure 1. 2014 BUF DVOA by Week

targets. For success rate, the gap between Graham and second-place Darrelle Revis is as big as the gap between Revis and 24th-ranked Keenan Lewis. Graham mostly succeeded against opponents' No. 3 receivers, but he also succeeded in a small sample against opponents' No. 2 wideouts, allowing a 38 percent completion rate on 16 targets. The cornerback charting stats can bounce around like a free-agent Rickey Henderson from year to year, but Graham is anything but a one-year blip. He ranked 15th in adjusted yards per pass in 2013 and fourth in 2014, making Graham the only cornerback to rank in the top 20 in adjusted yards per pass for three straight years. No. 1 corner Stephon Gilmore also charted well, so Graham's stats do not mean he is the Bills' best corner heading into 2015. But his numbers are so good that his likely move to safety (where Graham started in a 37-22 Week 6 loss to the Patriots) could be a mistake even if it is one way to get him on the field more often. Rex Ryan's defense relies on great corner play and the Bills are heading towards not starting one of their two best players at that spot. However, given that Gilmore and No. 2 corner Leodis McKelvin each missed games due to injury in both 2013 and 2014, Graham is likely to end up seeing time at corner regardless of where he starts on opening day.

With secret studs Bradham and Graham joining Gilmore and the front four, Ryan actually has more to work with than he did when the Jets hired him in 2009. There, he took a defense that ranked 14th in defensive DVOA in 2008 and brought them to the top spot in his first year. In Buffalo, Ryan starts with a defense that ranked fourth and second the last two years, and features a contract-motivated Dareus along with a still-improving Gilmore. Ryan's coaching ability will likely counteract the regression towards the mean we would usually expect from the league's No. 2 defense. The Bills are poised to challenge Seattle for the title of the NFL's best defense this year.

Unfortunately, the Bills' new coach has no track record of improving offense, and that's where Buffalo needs much more help. The Jets ranked 18th in offense the year before Ryan took over and then averaged a ranking of 20th in Ryan's first three years, before falling to 28th over his last three years. In Buffalo, Ryan inherits an offense that is much worse than the Jets had when he arrived. The 2014 Bills were a train wreck on offense and the signs are mixed at best as to whether 2015 will be any better.

They are at least likely to turn back the clock strategically. "Are we going to do ground and pound? Yeah, you're darn right we are," said Ryan in his first press conference as Buffalo's head coach. And then the team went about trying to im-

prove its ground game, with a re-working of the offensive line and a trade that brought LeSean McCoy from Philadelphia to be the featured running back.

Last year's offensive line certainly was not going to successfully implement the running-focused offense that Ryan prefers. Buffalo ranked 28th in rushing DVOA and averaged just 3.7 yards per carry. The Bills' primary weakness, moreover, is a poor match for their new running back who likes to run outside. (63 percent of McCoy's runs were to the outside compared to 49 percent for the rest of the league and 50 percent for other Eagles runners.) The Bills ranked dead last on adjusted line yards on outside runs, becoming the first team since 1995 to bat below the Mendoza Line (2.00 adjusted line yards) on both left end runs (1.99 yards) and right end runs (1.65 yards).

For 2015, at most two players (left tackle Cordy Glenn and center Eric Wood) appear likely to return as starters. Rex Ryan happy-talk has applied to both of the likely new starters at guard, veteran Richie Incognito and third-round pick John Miller. Sometimes forgotten amidst Incognito's off-field issues, though, is the decline in his play. In his last full season (2012), Incognito made the Pro Bowl but ranked 25th (out of 38) among left guards with 53 snaps per blown block. Now 32, Incognito is at an age when Bill Belichick might trade a left guard to Tampa. With his leash undoubtedly short, one would hope Incognito will at least be less of a jackass to John Miller than he was towards his last young linemate who had the same initials.

While the line will likely improve by virtue of being different, the quarterback situation heading into 2015 is even worse than it was last year. Kyle Orton (-6.8% DVOA, ranked 26th out of 37 qualifiers) started 12 games a year ago after a horrible September got EJ Manuel benched. Orton provided the kind of below-average competence that has mostly eluded Manuel and Matt Cassel, the main competitors for this year's starting job. The situation is so dire that Bills reporters Vic Carucci and Jay Skursky seemingly cannot go an episode on their weekly podcast without answering fans who want to know if the current quarterback might still come from outside the current roster. The questions might as well be subtitled, "Someone, anyone, just not one of these guys. Please."

Nevertheless, if only because other options appear unavailable, Ryan's statement that there is a 99.9 percent chance the opening day quarterback would come from the current crop seems about right. And that is pretty scary. Only Tyrod Taylor lacks clear on-field evidence strongly suggesting that he is right now likely to be a poor NFL quarterback. That might only be because the long-time Baltimore second-stringer has only thrown 35 more NFL passes than Breckin Meyer. Taylor has generated little buzz thus far in workouts, but the unknown has some appeal given the quality of the competition.

Ryan is more likely to choose either Cassel, a veteran who should be a backup, or Manuel, a third-year player who has shown almost no evidence that he will become a solid NFL starter. In only 71 attempts last season, Cassel posted a DVOA even worse than Manuel's. In contrast to Orton's reliable near-averageness, Cassel has been in the vicinity of average only twice in his last six seasons. In three of his four seasons in Kansas City, Cassel posted a DVOA below -25.0% and ranked 30th or lower among quarterbacks with at least 200 passes. Cassel has Orton's low ceiling, but with a much lower floor.

Meanwhile, Manuel's career seems to be crashing on Cassel's floor, having apparently fallen off the couch. Last year, Manuel started the first four weeks and compiled a -17.1% DVOA, closely matching the -19.9% DVOA from Manuel's rookie season. The reasons underlying Manuel's struggles suggest little reason to expect improvement in 2015. Like the periods from his first name, the ability to throw intermediate routes has been missing from EJ Manuel's game. In 2014, Manuel averaged 5.78 yards per pass when throwing less than ten yards downfield, compared to a league average of 5.79. But when throwing from 10-25 yards through the air, Manuel averaged just 7.68 yards, 2.5 yards less than the league average of 10.18. His completion percentage shows the same pattern. On throws traveling less than ten yards, Manuel completed 73.3 percent of his throws compared to a league average of 72.6 percent. On throws 10-25 yards downfield, Manuel posted a 35.3 percent completion rate, the worst in the league and far below the 54.0 percent league average.

Facing ineptitude at quarterback, the Bills looked for salvation on the ground and made the most notable of their splashy but questionable personnel moves. LeSean McCoy gives the Bills one of the league's best running backs over the last five years. Obviously, in a vacuum, any team in the NFL would choose to add a player such as McCoy. But smart teams are generally not looking to spend $40 million ($26.5 million guaranteed) on a running back, much less give up a young and cheap asset (linebacker Kiko Alonso) for the right to do so. More generally, it is a bit eerie how much Doug Whaley's regime in Buffalo resembles the early days of the Mike Tannenbaum era in New York. As with Tannenbaum, Whaley's moves are easy to get excited about in the short run, but carry a cost that will soon come due.

The list is long. McCoy's unnecessarily reworked contract included a $13.5 million signing bonus that means the Bills likely will be carrying an expensive running back at least through the end of 2017. Charles Clay, while worth having at the right price, is not worth having at $7.6 million per season

with a signing and roster bonus set up so that the tight end is likely to see most of that. Signing fullback Jerome Felton makes some sense with the hiring of Greg Roman as offensive coordinator. Last year, his 49ers offense used two running backs more than twice as frequently as the league average. But, as with Clay, the Bills did not get Felton for the right price. The Bills took a player whom the Vikings only saw fit to play 170 snaps last year and made him the league's second-highest paid fullback. Each of these contracts has little chance of becoming a bargain for the Bills.

The Bills again overpaid when they moved up in the 2014 draft to take Sammy Watkins. The problem isn't that Whaley, who has a good track record of picking players from his time in Pittsburgh, took Watkins (-5.7% DVOA) instead of Odell Beckham (25.8% DVOA). It's easy now to say Beckham was the better choice, but it was not foreseeable at the time. What was foreseeable at the time Whaley made the deal was that it was a bad long-term idea. Dealing next year's first-round pick is almost never wise, particularly for a team in Buffalo's non-contending situation. Furthermore, it was well-known that the 2014 draft was going to be one of the deepest in history at the wide receiver position. A shortsighted GM decides he has to have Watkins, no matter the price. A farsighted GM understands talent evaluation is imperfect and waits to extract a king's ransom from the impatient one. There is a long-term cost to pay in not having the picks the Bills gave up in the Watkins deal. Just as Ryan's Jets started to feel the cost of traded-away draft picks after a few years had passed, his Bills might, too.

The consistent theme in these personnel decisions is that the Bills rarely get good value in either contract signings or trades. Consistently winning teams either have great quarterbacks (e.g. the Colts) or find bargains (e.g. the Ravens) or both. In their most important ongoing negotiation, with Marcell Dareus, the Bills appear to be heading towards a Suh-like contract that Dareus has little hope of outperforming. In the best-case scenario, Dareus plays to his 2014 level and is worth a huge number. The worst-case scenario has Dareus, who reached a new level just last year, either getting complacent with a huge contract or finding more off-field trouble like the substance abuse suspension that will keep him out for the season-opener against Indianapolis. It feels like the Bills have no choice but to keep Dareus and take the chance, but why exactly? If Billy Beane or Daryl Morey were in Whaley's shoes, he might try to trade Dareus now for a high future draft pick, knowing that a contender would put very high value on his elite skills.

The point is not that the 2015 Bills would be better without Dareus. Any team would love to have the great defensive tackle at his fifth-year salary. But the Bills enter 2015 with four of their top five cap hits coming from players in their front four, even with Dareus coming relatively cheap. Over 25 percent of their cap is tied up in those four players. The Bills are already up against the cap for next season, with just $1.4 million in projected cap space according to overthecap.com.

Getting even more invested at that position keeps a great player but leaves the Bills unbalanced with a formula that mostly has not worked. By Pro Football Reference's Approximate Value, the Bills had 44.7 percent of their total roster value coming from their front seven in 2014, the highest share of any team since at least 1970. Of the other 11 teams to top 40 percent, just two made the playoffs. Every dollar the Bills spend up front on defense is one dollar less to fix the offense, just like every high draft pick lost means one less opportunity to find a quarterback.

Nonetheless, right now the Bills have most of the pieces in place for a run. The supporting talent here is top-notch, and the coaches have a strong track record. But with only Breck-in Meyers available at quarterback, it's hard to imagine this show topping the ratings.

Andrew Healy

2014 Bills Stats by Week

Wk	vs.	W-L	PF	PA	YDF	YDA	TO	Total	Off	Def	ST
1	at CHI	W	23	20	360	427	2	14%	13%	12%	13%
2	MIA	W	29	10	315	290	2	40%	6%	-15%	18%
3	SD	L	10	22	292	333	0	-7%	-6%	7%	7%
4	at HOU	L	17	23	316	301	1	-14%	-38%	-26%	-3%
5	at DET	W	17	14	343	273	1	-8%	-38%	-34%	-4%
6	NE	L	22	37	336	396	-3	-6%	7%	14%	0%
7	MIN	W	17	16	373	276	-2	3%	-29%	-33%	-1%
8	at NYJ	W	43	23	280	312	6	39%	0%	-28%	11%
9	BYE										
10	KC	L	13	17	364	278	-2	31%	-2%	-26%	7%
11	at MIA	L	9	22	237	330	2	-25%	-14%	10%	0%
12	NYJ	W	38	3	336	218	1	48%	4%	-38%	5%
13	CLE	W	26	10	287	315	1	12%	-25%	-27%	10%
14	at DEN	L	17	24	415	306	0	-1%	2%	-2%	-5%
15	GB	W	21	13	253	333	1	53%	-31%	-49%	35%
16	at OAK	L	24	26	321	347	-2	-48%	-37%	10%	-2%
17	at NE	W	17	9	268	260	-1	58%	16%	-34%	7%

Trends and Splits

	Offense	Rank	Defense	Rank
Total DVOA	-11.2%	26	-15.5%	2
Unadjusted VOA	-10.6%	26	-15.1%	1
Weighted Trend	-10.7%	25	-19.0%	2
Variance	3.7%	5	4.5%	10
Average Opponent	-0.5%	15	2.1%	5
Passing	0.3%	24	-18.2%	1
Rushing	-16.1%	28	-12.0%	12
First Down	-12.0%	25	-5.3%	9
Second Down	0.6%	14	-18.8%	1
Third Down	-28.1%	28	-31.1%	2
First Half	-17.1%	28	-22.3%	1
Second Half	-4.8%	20	-8.3%	5
Red Zone	-31.9%	29	-4.5%	16
Late and Close	-21.9%	29	-9.7%	7

Five-Year Performance

Year	W-L	Pyth W	Est W	PF	PA	TO	Total	Rk	Off	Rk	Def	Rk	ST	Rk	Off AGL	Rk	Def AGL	Rk	Off Age	Rk	Def Age	Rk	ST Age	Rk
2010	4-12	4.3	5.5	283	425	-17	-21.3%	29	-14.5%	26	6.8%	28	-0.1%	17	10.4	5	31.2	22	26.4	27	27.5	13	27.1	8
2011	6-10	6.4	7.1	372	434	+1	-9.7%	23	0.3%	16	8.3%	24	-1.7%	24	33.8	20	37.1	21	26.3	27	27.4	12	26.7	5
2012	6-10	5.7	6.5	344	435	-13	-12.1%	23	-4.2%	20	10.6%	27	2.7%	9	51.5	29	28.2	16	26.2	25	26.7	18	26.5	10
2013	6-10	6.7	7.1	339	388	+3	-3.3%	18	-11.5%	25	-13.8%	4	-5.6%	30	17.9	6	26.4	12	26.4	24	26.0	26	26.1	12
2014	9-7	9.6	9.0	343	289	+7	10.5%	9	-11.2%	26	-15.5%	2	6.2%	4	27.2	14	31.9	11	26.6	21	26.1	26	26.1	15

2014 Performance Based on Most Common Personnel Groups

BUF Offense					BUF Offense vs. Opponents					BUF Defense					BUF Defense vs. Opponents			
Pers	Freq	Yds	DVOA	Run%	Pers	Freq	Yds	DVOA	Run%	Pers	Freq	Yds	DVOA	Pers	Freq	Yds	DVOA
11	61%	5.5	-6.8%	22%	Base	37%	4.3	-9.1%	59%	Base	34%	5.1	-11.5%	11	56%	5.2	-11.8%
12	21%	5.0	-5.5%	57%	Nickel	45%	5.5	-5.1%	28%	Nickel	52%	5.1	-11.8%	12	20%	5.2	-8.6%
21	10%	3.2	-32.6%	54%	Dime+	16%	5.5	-15.4%	10%	Dime+	11%	5.2	-47.9%	21	7%	5.1	-8.4%
13	5%	5.4	34.9%	77%	Goal Line	1%	0.8	59.2%	75%	Goal Line	1%	2.8	-23.6%	20	4%	5.6	-5.5%
22	2%	1.1	-56.7%	94%	Big	1%	8.0	49.9%	67%	Big	3%	4.7	-35.1%	22	4%	5.2	-52.1%

Strategic Tendencies

Run/Pass		Rk	Formation		Rk	Pass Rush		Rk	Secondary		Rk	Strategy		Rk
Runs, first half	37%	19	Form: Single Back	83%	6	Rush 3	6.4%	14	4 DB	29%	9	Play action	15%	30
Runs, first down	48%	17	Form: Empty Back	3%	28	Rush 4	72.2%	6	5 DB	54%	21	Avg Box (Off)	6.30	14
Runs, second-long	33%	10	Pers: 3+ WR	61%	17	Rush 5	16.2%	30	6+ DB	15%	13	Avg Box (Def)	6.20	24
Runs, power sit.	53%	21	Pers: 4+ WR	0%	29	Rush 6+	5.3%	25	CB by Sides	86%	8	Offensive Pace	29.71	14
Runs, behind 2H	20%	31	Pers: 2+ TE/6+ OL	29%	17	Sacks by LB	9.3%	28	DB Blitz	9%	18	Defensive Pace	29.41	8
Pass, ahead 2H	42%	26	Shotgun/Pistol	68%	11	Sacks by DB	2.8%	24	Hole in Zone	13%	1	Go for it on 4th	0.55	29

The Bills ranked 29th in offensive DVOA through three quarters, but eighth in the fourth quarter or overtime. But this was mostly just catch-up; in fact, the Bills were a dismal 29th in "late and close" offense. ⬡ The Bills tend to use a lot of running back screens, and were much better with them last year (6.3 yards per play, 46.5% DVOA) after struggling in 2013 (5.5 yards per play, -12.9% DVOA). ⬡ Buffalo led the league with 67 defensive penalties and 505 defensive penalty yards. ⬡ As with all Jim Schwartz defenses, the Bills were one of the teams most likely to rush just four men. And as with all Rex Ryan defenses, that's about to change substantially in 2015. ⬡ On third or fourth down, the Bills had the best pass defense in the league, but ranked 23rd against the run.

Passing

Player	DYAR	DVOA	Plays	NtYds	Avg	YAC	C%	TD	Int
K.Orton*	131	-6.8%	478	2808	5.9	5.4	64.8%	18	10
EJ Manuel	-53	-17.1%	136	785	5.8	7.0	58.9%	5	3
M.Cassel	-147	-40.4%	79	351	4.4	7.2	57.7%	4	4
M.Simms	0	-11.1%	8	39	4.9	7.7	37.5%	0	0

Rushing

Player	DYAR	DVOA	Plays	Yds	Avg	TD	Fum	Suc
F.Jackson	23	-4.7%	141	525	3.7	2	0	46%
A.Dixon	4	-7.7%	105	432	4.1	2	1	49%
C.J.Spiller*	-76	-33.2%	78	303	3.9	0	3	40%
B.Brown	-21	-22.9%	36	126	3.5	0	1	50%
EJ Manuel	-10	-26.3%	13	58	4.5	1	0	-
F.Summers*	26	63.0%	6	17	2.8	1	0	100%
K.Orton*	0	-11.2%	6	24	4.0	1	0	-
L.McCoy	87	-1.6%	310	1317	4.2	5	3	45%
P.Harvin	138	34.9%	33	202	6.1	1	0	-

Receiving

Player	DYAR	DVOA	Plays	Ctch	Yds	Y/C	YAC	TD	C%
S.Watkins	71	-5.7%	128	65	982	15.1	5.3	6	51%
R.Woods	11	-11.4%	104	65	699	10.8	3.1	5	63%
C.Hogan	21	-8.1%	61	41	433	10.6	4.6	4	67%
M.Williams*	-26	-30.7%	19	8	142	17.8	4.4	1	42%
M.Goodwin	-58	-95.0%	9	1	42	42.0	6.0	0	11%
P.Harvin	-55	-21.4%	78	51	483	9.5	5.1	1	65%
S.Chandler*	17	-3.6%	70	47	497	10.6	4.1	3	67%
C.Gragg	-1	-8.4%	10	7	48	6.9	3.1	1	70%
M.Gray	40	55.1%	9	8	118	14.8	10.0	0	89%
L.Smith*	-2	-11.3%	8	7	42	6.0	3.4	1	88%
F.Jackson	-38	-21.5%	90	66	501	7.6	8.8	1	73%
B.Brown	55	28.0%	25	16	176	11.0	11.1	0	64%
C.J.Spiller*	28	7.8%	22	19	125	6.6	9.7	1	86%
A.Dixon	8	2.5%	9	8	49	6.1	5.5	0	89%
F.Summers*	-30	-80.0%	8	5	9	1.8	1.4	0	63%
L.McCoy	-9	-18.2%	39	30	160	5.3	6.6	0	77%

Offensive Line

Player	Pos	Age	GS	Snaps	Pen	Sk	Pass	Run	Player	Pos	Age	GS	Snaps	Pen	Sk	Pass	Run
Seantrel Henderson	RT	23	16/16	1062	4	7.5	29.5	6.0	Cordy Glenn	LT	26	16/16	1046	6	8.5	17.0	3.5
Erik Pears*	RG	33	16/16	1062	5	3.0	13.5	3.0	Kraig Urbik	LG	30	16/9	622	3	1.0	6.0	3.0
Eric Wood	C	29	16/16	1059	3	3.5	6.5	4.0	Cyril Richardson	LG	25	12/4	312	4	2.0	10.5	3.0

Year	Yards	ALY	Rk	Power	Rk	Stuff	Rk	2nd Lev	Rk	Open Field	Rk	Sacks	ASR	Rk	Short	Long	F-Start	Cont.
2012	5.15	4.25	7	57%	26	17%	8	1.42	3	1.14	4	30	5.5%	10	11	13	22	27
2013	4.38	3.85	16	65%	14	18%	11	1.14	14	0.96	6	48	8.5%	29	14	22	12	41
2014	3.83	3.62	26	63%	16	17%	7	0.94	30	0.64	20	39	6.9%	20	17	13	19	37
2014 ALY by direction:			Left End 1.99 (32)			Left Tackle 3.82 (15)			Mid/Guard 3.77 (24)			Right Tackle 4.16 (10)			Right End 1.65 (32)			

Directional running stats are by no means a perfect representation of how well an offensive line is blocking, and Buffalo's last-place finish in adjusted line yards (ALY) around both left and right end reflects in part the strengths and weaknesses of running backs Fred Jackson and Boobie Dixon. Still, those ALY figures are so bad that they have to say *something* about the blocking that both tackles, Cordy Glenn and Seantrel Henderson, provided on outside runs. Nevertheless, our charting of blown blocks actually found Glenn performed solidly overall across both pass protection and run blocking. Glenn ranked 11th among left tackles with a rate of 51 snaps per blown block. As a 2014 seventh-round pick, Henderson was a surprising starter at right tackle over second-rounder Cyrus Kouandjio, but Bills GM Doug Whaley has said that the Bills knew Henderson was better at that point in their careers when they drafted him. Five years ago, the Prep Football Report declared Henderson the No. 1 recruit in the 2010 high school class, a bow to the kind of size (6-foot-7, 331 pounds), speed (5.04 seconds in the 40), and athleticism that earned him comparisons to Jonathan Ogden before he played a college snap at Miami. Now that he's a pro, however, Henderson looked mostly like a raw seventh-rounder, faring much worse than Glenn despite Doug Marrone's apparent belief that Henderson performed the best among last year's Buffalo linemen. Henderson ranked 34th out of 39 right tackles with 30 snaps per blown block. Pass protection posed a particular problem for Henderson, and game charters marked him with more blown blocks on passing plays than any lineman in the NFL other than Seattle's Justin Britt.

After the line's struggles in 2014, wholesale changes are coming in 2015. At right tackle, Kouandjio looks poised to take over for Henderson, who has fallen from a potential candidate to start at left tackle to Rex Ryan's doghouse after being the lone player to miss the start of mandatory minicamp. Kouandjio, a major disappointment as a rookie last year, does not have Henderson's speed, but is similarly house-sized (6-foot-7, 322 pounds) with freakishly long arms. Both Henderson and Kouandjio certainly look the part of an NFL tackle, but red flags trail each of them. Henderson dropped to the bottom of the draft in large part due to three marijuana suspensions in college. Kouandjio's on-and-off motor was apparently switched off in 2014. After an offseason training at LeCharles Bentley's lineman training center, Kouandjio impressed at OTAs.

Inside, Eric Wood returns at center but neither starting guard from 2014 will. The underwhelming duo of opening-day starters Chris Williams and Erik Pears will likely be replaced by Richie Incognito and 2015 third-round pick John Miller (Louisville). Williams missed most of the season with a back injury and is likely to be cut, which would open up $2.48 million in 2015 cap space. Pears has already left for Denver in free agency. Improvement is likely this year just by virtue of jettisoning the detritus.

The Bills' offensive line also faces coaching uncertainty as bizarre bullying does not appear to be limited to Incognito. After being arrested for punching a teenager, offensive line coach Aaron Kromer appears likely to be fired and replaced by assistant line coach Kurt Anderson.

Defensive Front Seven

Defensive Line	Age	Pos	G	Snaps	Plays	TmPct	Rk	Stop	Dfts	BTkl	Runs	St%	Rk	RuYd	Rk	Sack	Hit	Hur	Dsrpt
						Overall						vs. Run					Pass Rush		
Kyle Williams	32	DT	15	718	43	5.6%	31	39	22	3	31	90%	7	1.1	13	5.5	9	17.0	2
Marcell Dareus	26	DT	15	678	50	6.5%	18	43	17	3	35	89%	11	1.4	20	10.0	4	7.5	1
Corbin Bryant	27	DT	16	353	15	1.8%	--	11	5	0	11	73%	--	2.3	--	1.5	3	3.5	0
Stefan Charles	27	DT	16	337	23	2.8%	--	16	7	3	18	72%	--	2.5	--	3.0	1	5.5	0

Edge Rushers	Age	Pos	G	Snaps	Plays	TmPct	Rk	Stop	Dfts	BTkl	Runs	St%	Rk	RuYd	Rk	Sack	Hit	Hur	Dsrpt
						Overall						vs. Run					Pass Rush		
Mario Williams	30	DE	16	788	43	5.2%	39	41	25	0	22	91%	4	0.8	3	14.0	4	19.5	3
Jerry Hughes	27	DE	16	782	52	6.3%	23	38	20	6	32	72%	56	1.6	14	10.0	10	32.0	0
Manny Lawson	31	DE	16	340	18	2.2%	--	14	5	1	13	77%	--	2.2	--	1.5	3	4.5	2
Jarius Wynn	29	DE	11	311	19	3.3%	73	14	4	2	13	69%	64	1.8	22	2.0	2	8.5	1

Linebackers	Age	Pos	G	Snaps	Plays	TmPct	Rk	Stop	Dfts	BTkl	Sack	Hit	Hur	Runs	St%	Rk	RuYd	Rk	Tgts	Suc%	Rk	AdjYd	Rk	PD	Int
						Overall						Pass Rush			vs. Run						vs. Pass				
Preston Brown	23	OLB	16	1020	110	13.3%	36	61	21	5	0.0	1	2.5	76	63%	45	3.9	66	35	57%	15	5.0	10	1	1
Nigel Bradham	26	OLB	14	806	105	14.5%	27	70	19	11	2.5	5	9.5	55	80%	4	3.0	24	22	60%	11	3.9	4	4	1
Brandon Spikes	28	MLB	16	504	57	6.9%	78	38	15	5	1.5	0	0	38	76%	9	1.7	2	12	56%	--	4.8	--	3	0

Year	Yards	ALY	Rk	Power	Rk	Stuff	Rk	2nd Level	Rk	Open Field	Rk	Sacks	ASR	Rk	Short	Long
2012	4.77	4.30	24	68%	25	18%	17	1.40	32	1.05	28	36	6.0%	23	8	17
2013	4.54	3.99	20	65%	15	17%	24	1.13	20	1.07	28	57	8.7%	3	19	18
2014	3.99	3.34	4	64%	16	26%	1	1.14	17	0.83	23	54	8.8%	1	16	19
2014 ALY by direction:		Left End 4.41 (27)			Left Tackle 2.83 (2)			Mid/Guard 3.22 (2)			Right Tackle 2.65 (2)			Right End 5.7 (32)		

The Bills' front four seized their positional championship belt in 2014. Regression happens, but the front four is well-positioned to maintain most of its 2014 form in 2015. Wide Williams (tackle Kyle) turns 32 this season, but his productivity in recent seasons suggests he has an aging curve different from the NFL norm. Fellow tackle Marcell Dareus took his game to another level in 2014 and is playing for a new contract. That motivation may mitigate the concern with Dareus' previously inconsistent motor. Tall Williams (defensive end Mario) and edge rusher Jerry Hughes appear to be close to their peaks. Whether each of them is now called a linebacker in Rex Ryan's scheme is irrelevant semantics, since the edge rusher label will still apply. Providing depth at tackle are Corbin Bryant and Stefan Charles. That pair played about the same number of snaps in 2014 with Charles performing better and collecting three sacks in just 337 snaps. Outside, depth comes from Manny Lawson and Jairus Wynn. Last year, Wynn provided more quarterback pressure with fewer snaps and one-third the cost.

At linebacker, Preston Brown got perhaps too much positive press for a good, not great, rookie season, but he also played over 100 snaps more than any other Bills defender and held up well. Nigel Bradham was the standout on the unit. After a marijuana incident during training camp in 2013, Bradham fell out of favor with Marrone and started just two games in his second season. But last year, a rededicated Bradham brought new energy and started to show the talent that made him the top linebacker prospect in the country coming out of high school. The emergence of Bradham and Brown helped make the Bills feel comfortable trading 2013 rookie standout Kiko Alonso, who missed all of last season with a torn ACL. The Bills drafted Clemson's frequently injured Tony Steward in the sixth round to add depth, but undrafted rookie A.J. Tarpley (Stanford) has outshone Steward in offseason workouts.

Defensive Secondary

Secondary	Age	Pos	G	Snaps	Plays	Overall TmPct	Rk	Stop	Dfts	BTkl	vs. Run Runs	St%	Rk	RuYd	Rk	vs. Pass Tgts	Tgt%	Rk	Dist	Suc%	Rk	AdjYd	Rk	PD	Int
Aaron Williams	26	SS	15	903	81	10.5%	35	20	5	10	40	25%	62	8.4	55	25	7.3%	26	14.6	58%	26	8.5	53	4	1
Stephon Gilmore	25	CB	14	838	52	7.2%	64	20	11	2	17	47%	26	8.5	57	63	20.2%	17	14.3	54%	23	7.4	29	7	3
Corey Graham	30	CB	16	778	93	11.3%	3	30	14	4	27	26%	58	7.1	45	58	20.0%	14	15.0	71%	1	4.8	1	17	2
Da'Norris Searcy*	27	SS	15	648	62	8.0%	57	23	9	1	39	46%	29	6.2	29	10	4.2%	2	18.6	61%	19	5.1	7	4	3
Nickell Robey	23	CB	16	640	50	6.1%	--	28	13	11	12	58%	--	5.7	--	38	15.8%	--	10.1	58%	--	10.3	--	8	0
Leodis McKelvin	30	CB	10	534	56	10.9%	10	24	9	3	4	75%	3	6.3	35	64	32.2%	75	13.1	51%	35	9.3	62	7	4
Duke Williams	25	FS	16	528	50	6.1%	68	20	11	3	24	54%	12	7.7	49	22	11.3%	57	11.4	43%	59	9.0	58	3	1
Ron Brooks	27	CB	14	145	24	3.3%	--	12	5	1	7	71%	--	4.6	--	16	28.9%	--	12.5	40%	--	9.5	--	1	0

Year	Pass D Rank	vs. #1 WR	Rk	vs. #2 WR	Rk	vs. Other WR	Rk	vs. TE	Rk	vs. RB	Rk
2012	22	20.7%	26	-2.7%	15	24.2%	29	-24.5%	2	20.1%	26
2013	2	1.9%	20	-45.2%	1	5.2%	20	-27.4%	4	-29.7%	2
2014	1	-22.6%	3	6.6%	22	-5.8%	12	-26.2%	2	-20.0%	5

As with Bradham, the front four blocks out the light that can reach the Bills' underrated cornerbacks. Stephon Gilmore emerged in 2014 as a better-than-average No. 1 corner. Compared to 2013, Gilmore improved both his adjusted success rate (from 51 percent, ranked 55th in 2013) and his adjusted yards per pass (from 7.6, ranked 44th in 2013). While Gilmore owes some of his success in 2014 to the front four, the Bills' pass rush was almost exactly as effective in 2013, so Gilmore's apparent ascending trajectory reflects more on him. The positive trend is also a promising sign for a player who will turn 25 only this September. Gilmore is entering the stage of his career when cornerbacks ordinarily peak, with a new head coach who gets the most out of his defensive talent.

As Gilmore ascends towards the upper echelon of cornerbacks, No. 2 corner Leodis McKelvin is moving in the opposite direction. Before breaking his ankle in Week 10, McKelvin charted as a below-average corner last year. His adjusted success rate dropped four percentage points from 55 percent in 2013, but the bigger fall came in adjusted yards per pass. McKelvin fell 50 spots from 2013, when his 6.4 yards per pass ranked 12th. A healthier McKelvin could rebound this year. Ryan's scheme will be similar to the one Mike Pettine ran in 2013 that produced McKelvin's best season. At the same time, he is also entering his age-30 season and has not played all 16 games since 2011.

The Bills' other corner who will be 30 on opening night, Corey Graham, is one of the most underrated players in the NFL. The current plan to move Graham to safety to take over for the erratic Duke Williams at least keeps Graham on the field for more snaps. Graham likely can handle the increased load, too. While he has not started more than nine games in any season, Graham has played a full slate of 16 games every year since 2008. If Graham moves to safety, the nickel corner role will likely fall to speedster Ronald Darby, Buffalo's second-round pick out of Florida State.

Moving Graham to safety might help keep a below-average player off the field. After losing the underrated Da'Norris Searcy in free agency, the Bills other safety options are 2013 fourth-rounder Duke Williams and 2011 second-rounder Aaron Williams. While that pair would give the Bills an impressive four Williams non-brothers in the defensive starting lineup, there's no doubt that Duke Williams struggled in pass coverage last year, particularly in comparison to Searcy. Ex-corner Aaron Williams is still just 25 and improving as a safety.

Special Teams

Year	DVOA	Rank	FG/XP	Rank	Net Kick	Rank	Kick Ret	Rank	Net Punt	Rank	Punt Ret	Rank	Hidden	Rank
2012	2.7%	9	1.1	15	-5.1	26	13.3	2	-12.3	26	16.2	2	4.0	6
2013	-5.6%	30	5.7	7	-1.5	23	-4.4	25	-15.7	29	-12.1	32	-9.8	29
2014	6.2%	4	8.5	3	7.9	5	5.3	6	2.2	13	7.1	7	1.4	14

The Bills went from 30th to fourth in special-teams DVOA last year, providing one more example of special-teams ratings bouncing around like an overactive bunny. The natural tendency is to assume regression towards the mean this season, but earlier Bills teams showed that consistency on special teams is rare but not impossible. From 2004-2008, the Bills followed up a long run of poor special-teams play with one of the most dominant special-teams stretches ever. The Bills ranked no worse than sixth in that five-year span, finishing No. 1 three times. The constant across that stretch was special-teams coordinator Bobby April, who found a groove in Buffalo.

Rex Ryan has experience with a special-teams coordinator who bucks the trend and leads above-average special teams year after year. When he took over the Jets, Ryan retained coordinator Mike Westhoff, who had run New York's special teams since 2001. Westhoff had the Jets in the DVOA top ten for nine of his first 11 years in New York, including sixth, fifth, and fourth in Ryan's first three seasons. In Buffalo, Ryan is trying the same strategy, retaining 2013-14 coordinator Danny Crossman. In contrast to Westhoff's Jets units, however, Crossman's units have mostly struggled over the last decade. In 2011 and 2012, Crossman's Lions units finished 29th and 30th in special-teams DVOA. Carolina finished 29th (2009) and 30th (2007) in two of Crossman's three seasons there. Crossman has coordinated eight special-teams units and finished in the bottom four in DVOA five times.

Even if Crossman is not the next Mike Westhoff, at least the Bills will not have the disastrous punting and punt return units of 2013. The Bills finally moved on last year from Brian Moorman, whose struggles particularly hurt a team that punted more than most. After ranking no higher than 26th in our net punting metric from 2011-2013, the Bills were slightly above average last year. New punter Colton Schmidt was poor in our measure of gross punting value, worth 7.5 points below average. But the Bills had very effective punt (and kickoff) coverage led once again by Marcus Easley, who led the Bills with 11 special-teams tackles a year after leading the league with 23. On punt returns, the Bills improved from their NFL-worst performance in 2013 in part by Leodis McKelvin regressing towards average (8.7 yards per return after averaging 5.6 in 2013), and in part by having Marcus Thigpen (12.9 yards per return) assume punt return duties when McKelvin went down with an ankle injury. With C.J. Spiller out of town and part-time track star Marquise Goodwin unlikely to make the 53-man roster, Percy Harvin appears in line to pick up kick return duties.

Dan Carpenter, the lone bright spot for Buffalo's special teams in 2013, was even better last year. Kicking in a difficult environment, he has made 17-of-19 from 40-plus yards and 10-of-14 from 50-plus yards over the last two seasons. Last season, he won a Week 5 game against Detroit with a very sweet 58-yard kick. The Bills also utilized kickoff specialist Jordan Gay, but they may not be able to justify spending a roster spot on him this year, especially given that Carpenter's career kickoff stats are reasonable.

We thank Jay Skurski of the Buffalo News for information utilized in the unit comments.

Carolina Panthers

2014 Record: 7-8-1	Total DVOA: -8.5% (24th)	2015 Mean Projection: 8.0 wins	On the Clock (0-4): 10%
Pythagorean Wins: 7.0 (23rd)	Offense: -4.7% (20th)	Postseason Odds: 35.1%	Mediocrity (5-7): 33%
Snap-Weighted Age: 26.7 (19th)	Defense: -1.7% (15th)	Super Bowl Odds: 3.8%	Playoff Contender (8-10): 40%
Average Opponent: 0.8% (14th)	Special Teams: -5.5% (30th)	Proj. Avg. Opponent: -2.7% (23rd)	Super Bowl Contender (11+): 17%

2014: A unique perspective on roster construction brings a unique result, the first 7-8-1 division champion in NFL history.

2015: Did you enjoy our big rookie receiver and questionable offensive line? Let's double down on that.

For all the hand-wringing when the traditional media talks about the NFL's salary cap, it's actually hard to get stuck in salary-cap purgatory for more than a season or two. A team has to both be very intentional about which players get over-paid *and* find itself in a time period where the salary cap isn't climbing. It's like getting stuck in *Monopoly* jail and not having any way out besides rolling doubles.

This is the scenario that Carolina general manager Dave Gettleman inherited from the deposed Marty Hurney. The Panthers had bottomed out far enough to land with quarterback Cam Newton, because not only had Hurney put all of his chips on players like Armanti Edwards, but they also rewarded their veterans rather than cutting bait on them. Linebacker Jon Beason got $20 million in full guarantees on a $50 million extension and played a total of five games over the next two seasons before getting traded. Defensive end Charles Johnson got an insane $30 million signing bonus over a six-year, $72 million deal, a contract that's had to be restructured multiple times to keep Carolina under the cap. DeAngelo Williams, coming off a season-ending injury, was given five years and $43 million.

Those were the headliners, but hardly the only contract issues that Gettleman was forced to deal with upon taking the job. All of Gettleman's 2013 maneuvering to generate the salary-cap space he needed to actually sign rookies and create a roster—trading Beason, releasing players like Charles Anderson, restructuring Jordan Gross and Williams—added $9 million in dead money to a team that already had plenty of it. After lopping off franchise icon Steve Smith in 2014, the Panthers led the NFL in dead cap space at $17.8 million. An optimistic fan might see it as a blessing in disguise, because

had Carolina actually had cap space they may have signed end Greg Hardy to his own bad long-term deal instead of franchising him before his domestic violence court dates. But it's clear that Gettleman was forced to play from behind for the first two years of his tenure.

You probably don't think about Carolina as a bastion of football analytics, Ron Rivera's fourth-down conversion coming-of-age story notwithstanding. But the Panthers were forced to develop some pretty interesting philosophies to compensate for the lack of money. The most impressive story is at defensive back.

Let us bring you back to these times with some quotes from previous *FOA*s. 2013: "Before the draft, our own Andy Benoit dubbed this 'the worst secondary in football.' Since the Panthers selected no defensive backs on draft day, it's safe to say the gap between them and the rest of the league has grown since then." 2014: "Speaking of coming to pass, that's what visiting teams in Carolina will do if the Panthers' changes in the secondary don't work out. Four of the top five defensive backs in snaps played—Captain Munnerlyn, Mike Mitchell, Quintin Mikell, and Drayton Florence—are no longer on the roster." In fact, of the four cornerbacks and three safeties with the most snaps in 2013, only Melvin White would repeat on the list in 2014.

Of course, if you actually read *FOA 2014*'s treatise on the Panthers defense, you're ahead of the game. The long story short is that because Carolina plays more deep-zone and off-man coverage than most teams, their system is actually extremely forgiving to defensive backs. Thus, the Panthers have been able to keep their acquisition costs on this position low and still turn out solid success rates. Not a single defensive

Table 1. Carolina Secondary Changes, 2013-2014

	2013 Player	Snaps	How Acquired	2014 Player	Snaps	How Acquired
CB	Captain Munnerlyn	992	2009 (Round 7)	Antoine Cason	690	FA, one-year deal
CB	Melvin White	697	2013 UDFA	Josh Norman	647	2012 (Round 5)
CB	Drayton Florence	600	FA, one-year deal	Melvin White	522	2013 UDFA
CB	Josh Thomas	271	Waiver claim	Bene Benwikere	459	2014 (Round 5)
S	Mike Mitchell	920	FA, one-year deal	Roman Harper	949	FA, two-year deal
S	Quintin Mikell	688	FA, one-year deal	Thomas DeCoud	683	FA, two-year deal
S	Robert Lester	301	2013 UDFA	Tre Boston	369	2014 (Round 4)
Pass D DVOA (Rk)	**-15.6% (3rd)**			**0.0% (9th)**		

2015 Panthers Schedule

Week	Opp.	Week	Opp.	Week	Opp.
1	at JAC	7	PHI	13	at NO
2	HOU	8	IND (Mon.)	14	ATL
3	NO	9	GB	15	at NYG
4	at TB	10	at TEN	16	at ATL
5	BYE	11	WAS	17	TB
6	at SEA	12	at DAL (Thu.)		

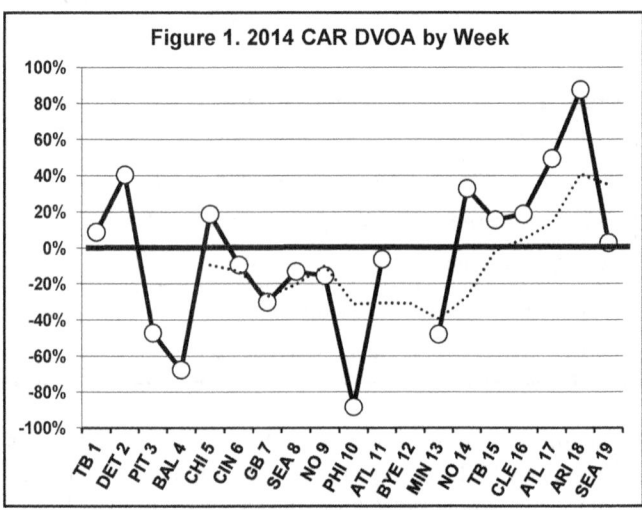

Figure 1. 2014 CAR DVOA by Week

back on this roster has been acquired on Day 1 or 2 of the NFL draft under Gettleman (Table 1).

The turnover here is not a one-year trend. Antoine Cason was cut before last season even ended, and Thomas DeCoud was let go this offseason. Instead, veteran free agents Chris Houston and Peanut Tillman are set to compete for spots at corner along with Kurt Coleman at safety. If your favorite defensive back has officially reached "journeyman" status, he'll wind up on the Panthers roster one of these seasons.

Of course, a key reason Carolina is able to turn over the secondary like this is the luxury they gave themselves by creating a mid-field combination of Thomas Davis and Luke Kuechly. Kuechly, perhaps by virtue of existing at the same time as J.J. Watt, has somehow gone under the radar as a franchise cornerstone. He's not even 25, and he's already on a Hall-of-Fame career path, with three Pro Bowls, a Defensive Player of the Year Award, and first-team All-Pro in back-to-back seasons. Davis is yet another successful data point supporting the trend of converting big safeties to linebackers, though his sudden health was sort of like Gettleman waking up and finding a hundred-dollar bill in his laundry. Gettleman believes so much in reinforcing this strength that he secured the player most likely to grow up and be Davis, Washington hybrid safety-linebacker Shaq Thompson, in the first round.

Then there's the offensive line. Think about everything you learned by reading *The Blind Side*, then punt it out of your brain—because the Panthers disagree with the value of free-agent linemen to the point that they're basically begging someone to step up for them. Gettleman inherited a franchise tackle in Gross and a top-of-the-line center in Ryan Kalil. But after watching helplessly as Gross retired, the Panthers have turned the Carolina offensive line into a place where anybody can come off the street and potentially be the answer. Of the 15 linemen on the roster heading into camp, only two were drafted under Gettleman. Former second-rounder Amini Silatolu, one of Hurney's last busts, is on the final year of his rookie deal. Kalil is still one of the best centers in the league. Everyone else came as a low-grade veteran free agent or undrafted rookie. Gettleman's philosophy seems to be that of a JRPG hero in a new town: you might as well talk to everybody.

It's very easy to point and laugh at Michael Oher and Jonathan Martin being a team's lone offseason acquisitions on the offensive line. Not only have both played poorly over the last few seasons, but they're both high-profile media targets. Oher's failure is particularly emblematic of the hasty criticisms against *The Blind Side* that start by listing out the draft status or pay grade of the left tackles on the last 10 Super Bowl winners. However, perhaps a better way to view Oher and Martin is as the depth signings the Panthers hope they will be.[1]

Carolina's UDFA system at offensive line has, at times, been something of a chicken-and-egg game. Is a player valuable because he starts, or does he start because nobody is ready? Clearly it was very easy to demonize Byron Bell after his abysmal season at left tackle last year, but at the same time, do we acknowledge that few teams have been able to engineer a below-average right tackle out of a UDFA? And, finally, when you weigh that against the actual costs of a franchise tackle—either in free agency or in the draft—are there enough savings to make it worthwhile? For a team that had struggled with financials, you can see the appeal for the Panthers. Peyton Manning has spent his whole career making bad offensive lines look good, and we have mountains of evidence that suggest that a quarterback's sack rate is mostly owned by him. If there's a position to scrimp at, doesn't it make sense that it's this one?

It's a plan borne of both cost-cutting and self-belief. The Panthers haven't necessarily looked foolish while doing this, which is a good sign. Is it a sustainable and reliable process? Perhaps not, especially if the aim is to create a dominant offensive line. Turn to the Dallas chapter, and you'll find a pretty good argument for the opposite strategy. Gettleman has also held back from spending much new money or draft capital on the running back position, perhaps a sign that Gettleman, unlike Hurney, does not believe building a running game is a cost-efficient long-term plan.

So what are the Panthers spending the draft capital on under Gettleman? Wide receivers with size and versatility. Kelvin Benjamin was Gettleman's first-round pick in 2014, and the Panthers traded up in the second round to select Michigan's

---

1 Or, perhaps they won't be. Martin decided to retire right before we went to press.

Devin Funchess in this year's draft. Combine that with Greg Olsen, a tight end as liable to line up out wide as he is in the slot or backfield, and the Panthers truly believe in the philosophy of the "movable chess piece," which means they, too, have watched a lot of *NFL Matchup*.

Table 2. Big Bodies, Flexed Positions

Player	Height	%ile	Weight	%ile	40-Yard Dash	%ile
Kelvin Benjamin	6-foot-5	96	240	99	4.61	17
Devin Funchess	6-foot-4	89	232	98	4.70	4
Greg Olsen	6-foot-6	88	254	46	4.51	97

All numbers from NFL combine, percentiles for their individual positions

Now, these two wideouts have their flaws. Benjamin had a low DVOA his rookie year thanks in part to an ongoing case of the dropsies (not to mention the forcies, as Cam Newton spent the whole season trying to force the ball to his best receiver no matter the coverage). Funchess was dinged for the same basic problem coming out of Michigan, though to his credit he played much of the 2014 season with a severely damaged foot that impacted a lot of his basic functions. As he himself told the *Detroit News*, while referring to himself in the third person, "We never got to see the full Devin Funchess at Michigan because I did play one season at wide receiver, and I was battling through an injury."

It's interesting that at a time when a few NFL teams are scaling back on how much they value wide receivers—espe-

cially in light of how many good ones have flooded into the league over the past two rookie classes—Gettleman has chosen to spend his capital here. It's the kind of philosophy that speaks to how highly he values finding matchup advantages and utilizing them, even if Benjamin and Funchess are flawed players in their own right.

We haven't been able to see the entire story of what Gettleman wants the Panthers to be, but we're almost there. Johnson's contract and Jonathan Stewart's massive overpay are the only two of Hurney's deals that continue to haunt the roster. Newton's extension is now on the payroll to replace some of those savings, and the contract extension for Kuechly will be coming next, but the Panthers so far are scheduled only to have $1.6 million in dead cap space for the 2016 season.

What you have here is a roster that is unlike any other. The Panthers believe in their low-cost systems, especially specific positions like tackle and cornerback, and emphasize mismatches over the middle of the field. They have a quarterback who can effectively run the ball. It's not exactly a grand experiment, but they've created enough unique ways of winning one-on-one battles that this roster stands out in today's NFL.

Carolina, like its fellow NFC South brethren, is expected to get a big boost from finding the AFC South and NFC East on its schedule. While it's an awkward projection on paper, it's not hard to see this franchise improving on last season and making another run to the playoffs. Because, even without all the money at his disposal, Gettleman has at least proven he can scheme his way into a mismatch.

Rivers McCown

2014 Panthers Stats by Week

Wk	vs.	W-L	PF	PA	YDF	YDA	TO	Total	Off	Def	ST
1	at TB	W	20	14	334	264	3	9%	3%	-16%	-10%
2	DET	W	24	7	313	323	3	40%	29%	-9%	2%
3	PIT	L	19	37	349	454	-2	-47%	-3%	36%	-8%
4	at BAL	L	10	38	315	454	-1	-68%	-12%	57%	1%
5	CHI	W	31	24	322	347	1	19%	-4%	-5%	17%
6	at CIN	T	37	37	431	513	1	-10%	34%	25%	-19%
7	at GB	L	17	38	331	363	-1	-30%	-18%	19%	6%
8	SEA	L	9	13	266	310	0	-13%	-24%	-13%	-2%
9	NO	L	10	28	231	375	0	-16%	-36%	-16%	4%
10	at PHI	L	21	45	317	365	-5	-88%	-50%	26%	-12%
11	ATL	L	17	19	391	346	-1	-6%	-10%	-11%	-7%
12	BYE										
13	at MIN	L	13	31	348	210	-1	-48%	-13%	-15%	-49%
14	at NO	W	41	10	497	310	2	33%	22%	-21%	-10%
15	TB	W	19	17	392	287	2	15%	-6%	-15%	7%
16	CLE	W	17	13	404	228	-1	19%	0%	-27%	-8%
17	at ATL	W	34	3	306	288	3	49%	2%	-45%	2%
18	ARI	W	27	16	386	78	0	88%	13%	-77%	-2%
19	at SEA	L	17	31	362	348	-3	3%	9%	10%	4%

Trends and Splits

	Offense	Rank	Defense	Rank
Total DVOA	-4.7%	20	-1.7%	15
Unadjusted VOA	-2.5%	18	1.9%	19
Weighted Trend	-7.3%	20	-8.8%	9
Variance	4.8%	6	7.1%	25
Average Opponent	2.6%	29	2.2%	4
Passing	4.1%	23	0.0%	9
Rushing	-5.5%	16	-4.0%	23
First Down	5.1%	12	-4.9%	11
Second Down	-5.7%	21	-4.6%	12
Third Down	-23.3%	27	9.2%	22
First Half	-6.2%	21	0.5%	16
Second Half	-3.0%	19	-3.6%	11
Red Zone	-13.0%	20	21.0%	31
Late and Close	5.6%	14	-13.7%	6

Five-Year Performance

Year	W-L	Pyth W	Est W	PF	PA	TO	Total	Rk	Off	Rk	Def	Rk	ST	Rk	Off AGL	Rk	Def AGL	Rk	Off Age	Rk	Def Age	Rk	ST Age	Rk
2010	2-14	2.4	2.2	196	408	-8	-36.2%	31	-35.8%	32	-1.1%	16	-1.5%	22	39.8	27	35.1	24	25.7	30	25.4	32	25.0	32
2011	6-10	7.4	6.9	406	429	+1	-4.1%	20	18.2%	4	15.8%	32	-6.5%	32	47.6	29	61.5	32	27.2	15	25.3	32	26.0	25
2012	7-9	7.8	8.8	357	363	+1	5.5%	13	7.2%	10	-3.1%	11	-4.8%	29	23.1	10	53.0	27	27.1	15	25.7	28	26.0	19
2013	12-4	11.7	11.0	366	241	+11	24.6%	3	7.9%	10	-15.7%	3	1.0%	13	42.4	21	28.4	17	28.2	2	26.6	16	26.6	7
2014	7-8-1	7.0	7.4	339	374	+3	-8.5%	24	-4.7%	20	-1.7%	15	-5.5%	30	39.7	25	11.7	1	26.4	26	27.2	8	26.4	6

2014 Performance Based on Most Common Personnel Groups

CAR Offense					CAR Offense vs. Opponents					CAR Defense					CAR Defense vs. Opponents			
Pers	Freq	Yds	DVOA	Run%	Pers	Freq	Yds	DVOA	Run%	Pers	Freq	Yds	DVOA		Pers	Freq	Yds	DVOA
11	49%	5.6	0.4%	29%	Base	48%	5.1	-3.4%	52%	Base	31%	5.2	-17.6%		11	54%	5.9	3.9%
12	36%	5.6	2.7%	47%	Nickel	43%	5.7	4.4%	31%	Nickel	68%	5.8	5.2%		12	20%	5.2	-4.1%
13	6%	3.8	-2.1%	76%	Dime+	8%	5.3	-15.3%	14%	Goal Line	1%	0.8	56.2%		21	11%	4.8	-29.1%
21	4%	4.4	-11.6%	40%	Goal Line	1%	0.0	-21.1%	100%						22	4%	7.4	8.0%
22	3%	4.6	-36.0%	63%	Big	0%	8.8	97.1%	60%						10	3%	6.0	-12.3%

Strategic Tendencies

Run/Pass		Rk	Formation		Rk	Pass Rush		Rk	Secondary		Rk	Strategy		Rk
Runs, first half	41%	8	Form: Single Back	66%	26	Rush 3	3.8%	25	4 DB	21%	25	Play action	28%	5
Runs, first down	47%	19	Form: Empty Back	4%	24	Rush 4	71.1%	8	5 DB	78%	2	Avg Box (Off)	6.40	5
Runs, second-long	38%	5	Pers: 3+ WR	49%	26	Rush 5	19.7%	24	6+ DB	0%	31	Avg Box (Def)	6.16	26
Runs, power sit.	58%	15	Pers: 4+ WR	0%	27	Rush 6+	5.4%	24	CB by Sides	77%	19	Offensive Pace	30.70	20
Runs, behind 2H	32%	7	Pers: 2+ TE/6+ OL	47%	4	Sacks by LB	13.8%	26	DB Blitz	9%	19	Defensive Pace	29.18	7
Pass, ahead 2H	45%	21	Shotgun/Pistol	70%	8	Sacks by DB	5.0%	19	Hole in Zone	5%	17	Go for it on 4th	0.84	21

You would expect a run-heavy offense like Carolina's to be strong in the red zone, but the exact opposite was true in 2014: the Panthers ranked fifth in red zone pass DVOA but 30th when running in the red zone. ☚ This was the second straight season we didn't mark the Panthers with a single play where they used more than five defensive backs. ☚ The Panthers allowed 9.4 yards per pass when blitzing a defensive back; only the Patriots, who didn't use a lot of DB blitzes, were worse. ☚ Carolina's run defense ranked third in the league against the run when three or more wide receivers were on the field, both in terms of DVOA (-19.9%) and yards per carry (3.74). ☚ The Panthers had just 99 penalties last year, including declined and offsetting. Every other NFL team was in triple digits, and it was the second straight year the Panthers were below 100 total penalties. The Panthers have been particularly good avoiding penalties on kickoffs and punts, with just nine last year and just 17 over the last two years. ☚ The Panthers spent an average of 15:38 of each game tied, over a minute more than any other team. (Seattle was second at 14:31, and the playoff game between the two teams was tied for a total of 16:54.)

Passing

Player	DYAR	DVOA	Plays	NtYds	Avg	YAC	C%	TD	Int
C.Newton	-105	-14.5%	485	2841	5.9	4.8	58.7%	18	11
D.Anderson	254	27.8%	102	664	6.5	2.8	68.4%	5	0

Rushing

Player	DYAR	DVOA	Plays	Yds	Avg	TD	Fum	Suc
J.Stewart	72	1.3%	175	810	4.6	3	2	51%
C.Newton	146	16.3%	95	544	5.7	5	2	-
D.Williams*	-17	-15.2%	62	221	3.6	0	1	45%
M.Tolbert	-72	-53.2%	37	78	2.1	0	0	27%
F.Whittaker	33	22.7%	32	145	4.5	1	0	41%
D.Reaves	-27	-29.8%	31	78	2.5	0	0	32%
C.Ogbonnaya*	17	17.8%	14	50	3.6	1	0	57%
C.Brown	63	169.6%	8	95	11.9	0	0	-
D.Anderson	14	34.3%	5	25	5.0	0	0	-
J.Todman	*15*	*3.8%*	*32*	*186*	*5.8*	*1*	*0*	*25%*

Receiving

Player	DYAR	DVOA	Plays	Ctch	Yds	Y/C	YAC	TD	C%
K.Benjamin	9	-11.8%	145	73	1010	13.8	2.3	9	50%
J.Cotchery	55	-3.7%	78	48	571	11.9	4.0	1	62%
J.Avant*	-40	-26.2%	40	21	201	9.6	3.9	1	53%
C.Brown	59	7.7%	36	21	296	14.1	2.5	2	58%
B.Bersin	42	13.0%	20	13	151	11.6	2.6	1	65%
T.Ginn	*-6*	*-15.5%*	*26*	*14*	*190*	*13.6*	*3.3*	*0*	*54%*
J.Boykin	-38	-49.9%	12	3	23	7.7	9.0	0	25%
M.Brown	-43	-50.4%	15	7	88	12.6	2.4	0	47%
G.Olsen	178	14.7%	123	84	1009	12.0	4.0	6	68%
E.Dickson	3	-5.0%	17	10	115	11.5	6.3	1	59%
B.Williams	-10	-22.8%	8	4	44	11.0	2.0	0	50%
J.Stewart	35	7.8%	31	25	181	7.2	8.6	1	81%
M.Tolbert	-21	-39.4%	17	12	93	7.8	8.3	0	71%
D.Reaves	-10	-35.4%	8	5	31	6.2	8.4	0	63%
F.Whittaker	24	53.6%	6	5	60	12.0	15.6	1	83%
D.Williams*	4	-3.3%	6	5	44	8.8	11.4	0	83%
J.Todman	*-35*	*-34.9%*	*37*	*25*	*198*	*7.9*	*7.9*	*1*	*68%*

Offensive Line

Player	Pos	Age	GS	Snaps	Pen	Sk	Pass	Run	Player	Pos	Age	GS	Snaps	Pen	Sk	Pass	Run
Ryan Kalil	C	30	16/16	1075	1	2.0	8.5	3.0	Amini Silatolu	LG	27	7/7	404	4	3.0	6.0	5.0
Byron Bell*	LT	26	15/15	1009	8	9.0	22.5	9.0	Fernando Velasco	RG	30	13/7	397	0	0.0	5.5	2.0
Nate Chandler	RT	26	11/11	690	1	4.5	13.5	0.0	Mike Remmers	RT	26	5/5	357	2	0.5	1.5	0.0
Andrew Norwell	LG	24	10/9	679	1	1.0	6.0	4.0	*Michael Oher*	OT	29	11/11	651	6	5.5	16.5	3.0
Trai Turner	RG	22	13/9	660	3	0.0	3.0	4.0	*Jonathan Martin*	OT	26	15/9	645	2	5.5	17.0	0.5

Year	Yards	ALY	Rk	Power	Rk	Stuff	Rk	2nd Lev	Rk	Open Field	Rk	Sacks	ASR	Rk	Short	Long	F-Start	Cont.
2012	3.88	3.49	30	75%	1	23%	26	1.08	22	0.72	19	36	7.6%	21	2	21	17	25
2013	3.87	3.91	14	72%	8	19%	14	1.04	22	0.54	25	43	8.2%	25	10	21	9	25
2014	3.93	3.60	27	68%	10	20%	17	1.14	18	0.59	25	42	7.9%	22	15	12	17	26

2014 ALY by direction:	Left End 3.77 (19)	Left Tackle 3.26 (28)	Mid/Guard 3.49 (30)	Right Tackle 4.04 (13)	Right End 3.96 (15)

There's a scene in a *King of the Hill* episode where the owner of a pork processing company convinces the young, naive niece of the family, LuAnn, to dress and act as the girl on his product packaging. Upon the audience learning of a deeper plot to have her marry a nondescript extra posing as the male on the packaging, the extra simply explains his decision by delivering the meek line "life is a series of compromises." That's what comes to mind for us when we look at the above stat tables for Jonathan Martin and Michael Oher.

On the other hand, Byron Bell was likely one of the worst five linemen in the NFL last season, so it's not as if the Panthers can't possibly improve at tackle. Per our charting, Bell finished in the top 10 in blown blocks, and he was also abysmal in the run game. The Panthers are clearly hoping that their UDFA program can provide cheap results at the position. Mike Remmers was a nice find towards the end of the season before the Seahawks turned him into a turnstile in the divisional round, and there are some young options with (grisly) NFL experience on hand in David Foucalt and Nate Chandler. Fourth-rounder Daryl Williams (Oklahoma) is an option to get pushed to right tackle, though scouts were split on how his athleticism would hold up at the NFL level and he could eventually wind up at guard. He didn't allow any sacks in his senior season for the Sooners, and the position is so unsettled that the Panthers may as well let him play his way off tackle.

Panthers center Ryan Kalil was named first-team All-Pro in 2013 and is still one of the league's best at his position. 2014 third-rounder Trai Turner looked like a smooth pickup at right guard, despite missing time in the middle of his rookie season to a knee injury. That injury gave some playing time to 2012 second-rounder Amini Silatolu, but another 2014 UDFA find, David Norwell, will probably start ahead of him at the other guard spot this season. The interior of this line wasn't much of an issue last season when those three played together, though Kalil did have some pass-blocking gaffes as evidenced by the high (for him) number of blown blocks.

Defensive Front Seven

Defensive Line	Age	Pos	Overall								vs. Run					Pass Rush			
			G	Snaps	Plays	TmPct	Rk	Stop	Dfts	BTkl	Runs	St%	Rk	RuYd	Rk	Sack	Hit	Hur	Dsrpt
Kawann Short	26	DT	16	587	41	5.1%	39	33	10	3	32	78%	46	2.5	60	3.5	7	17.0	2
Dwan Edwards	34	DT	16	578	39	4.8%	42	30	14	2	29	76%	61	2.5	58	4.0	10	6.5	1
Star Lotulelei	26	DT	14	477	26	3.7%	72	23	9	0	21	86%	17	1.7	25	2.0	2	3.5	1
Colin Cole	35	DT	16	369	28	3.5%	--	21	5	0	24	79%	--	2.3	--	0.0	0	3.0	0

Edge Rushers	Age	Pos	Overall								vs. Run					Pass Rush			
			G	Snaps	Plays	TmPct	Rk	Stop	Dfts	BTkl	Runs	St%	Rk	RuYd	Rk	Sack	Hit	Hur	Dsrpt
Charles Johnson	29	DE	16	784	42	5.2%	38	26	12	2	28	46%	85	3.7	73	8.5	13	29.5	2
Wes Horton	25	DE	16	462	26	3.2%	77	21	6	2	19	84%	15	1.3	8	3.0	0	3.5	1
Mario Addison	28	DE	16	433	22	2.7%	84	16	8	3	13	54%	82	4.5	83	6.5	6	13.5	0
Kony Ealy	24	DE	15	361	12	1.6%	--	11	4	2	8	88%	--	3.1	--	4.0	3	7.5	0

Linebackers	Age	Pos	Overall								Pass Rush			vs. Run					vs. Pass						
			G	Snaps	Plays	TmPct	Rk	Stop	Dfts	BTkl	Sack	Hit	Hur	Runs	St%	Rk	RuYd	Rk	Tgts	Suc%	Rk	AdjYd	Rk	PD	Int
Luke Kuechly	24	MLB	16	989	165	20.5%	2	110	29	6	3.0	1	8.5	86	70%	18	3.3	38	63	59%	12	5.5	16	12	1
Thomas Davis	32	OLB	15	922	103	13.6%	34	59	24	9	2.5	1	7	44	61%	52	3.4	47	42	73%	2	5.4	14	4	0
A.J. Klein	24	OLB	14	283	35	5.0%	--	21	4	1	0.0	0	0	26	65%	--	3.1	--	12	93%	--	1.1	--	0	0
Jason Trusnik	31	MLB	16	393	40	4.9%	--	26	5	2	0.0	0	2	29	76%	--	2.4	--	11	34%	--	9.0	--	1	1

Year	Yards	ALY	Rk	Power	Rk	Stuff	Rk	2nd Level	Rk	Open Field	Rk	Sacks	ASR	Rk	Short	Long
2012	4.45	4.30	23	66%	23	16%	29	1.23	24	0.88	22	39	7.8%	5	9	20
2013	4.07	3.65	9	74%	27	22%	8	1.19	27	0.83	23	60	9.2%	2	20	11
2014	4.51	3.65	10	79%	29	21%	8	1.07	10	1.27	32	40	7.5%	7	14	11
2014 ALY by direction:		Left End 3.26 (8)			Left Tackle 3.29 (10)			Mid/Guard 3.95 (15)			Right Tackle 3.79 (14)			Right End 2.1 (2)		

Dave Gettleman must have been a baseball fan growing up, because he took the theory of "building a team up the middle" to its logical NFL conclusion. He inherited one of the best off-the-ball linebacker combos in the league in young star Luke Kuechly and the injury-prone but talented Thomas Davis. Davis, who signed a two-year extension in the offseason, is one of the best cover linebackers in the NFL. It was clear that Kuechly made a big effort in copying Davis and learning from him in that area, because he began to take smarter drops and react more fluidly in 2014 after some hiccups in previous seasons. Not content to stop there, Gettleman added safety-linebacker hybrid Shaq Thompson (Washington) in the first round, in what was considered a bit of a reach. However, when you consider how important Davis is to the Panthers, and the fact that he's 32, a fully developed Thompson should enable the Panthers to continue to count on no dropoff from their linebackers. In the meantime, Carolina will play Thompson at the Sam, and he'll have to beat out 2013 fifth-rounder A.J. Klein, a jack of all trades type, for the honor. (We're all just glad Thompson doesn't actually play baseball anymore; he went 0-39 with 37 strikeouts for a Red Sox rookie league affiliate in 2012.)

With Kuechly patrolling center field, Gettleman needed his middle infielders to control the ground game. Star Lotulelei and Kawaan Short, his first two draft picks, were defensive tackles aimed at doing just that. Lotulelei was considered one of the top players in the 2013 draft before a heart condition found at the combine made teams uneasy, but it's really surprising just how much of an impact Short has produced. Short had tape full of red flags for effort at Purdue, but since the middle of Short's rookie season, everything you wanted to see on the field at Purdue started occurring in the NFL on a regular basis. Now he's the rare impact player against both the run and the pass, and arguably more important to the Panthers than Loutlelei. Dwan Edwards and Colin Cole, a pair of vets off the scrapheap who make serviceable backups, rotate with the two high picks.

On the outside, Carolina's biggest problem is trying to replace domestic abuser Greg Hardy, an excellent football player who took his wares to Dallas after being suspended most of last season. The vacuum of Hardy's absence left a rotating mélange of players who couldn't get any real pass rush opposite Charles Johnson. Wes Horton played the most snaps of the trio last season, and his run defense looked divine compared to unrefined 2014 second-rounder Kony Ealy. Ealy is probably the favorite to get pass-rushing snaps, as he finished the year with sacks in three straight regular season games. Mario Addison is stretched as a starter, but has shown enough to play a role as a situational pass-rusher. And don't count out former SackSEER sleeper Frank Alexander, who missed 12 games last season due to a substance abuse suspension but excited coaches and the media at OTAs. The Panthers should get more pressure from their edge rushers this year. How much better could determine a lot about how their season unfolds.

Defensive Secondary

Secondary	Age	Pos	G	Snaps	Plays	TmPct	Rk	Stop	Dfts	BTkl	Runs	St%	Rk	RuYd	Rk	Tgts	Tgt%	Rk	Dist	Suc%	Rk	AdjYd	Rk	PD	Int
Roman Harper	33	SS	16	924	72	8.9%	50	38	12	5	34	65%	5	5.2	16	28	7.6%	28	13.1	66%	9	8.3	50	7	4
Antoine Cason*	29	CB	14	673	64	9.1%	31	19	10	2	13	46%	28	8.8	59	65	24.4%	44	10.4	31%	77	9.5	66	7	2
Thomas DeCoud*	30	FS	15	665	48	6.4%	65	15	6	10	19	47%	25	9.9	60	13	4.8%	5	16.1	31%	71	9.1	59	3	1
Josh Norman	28	CB	14	632	57	8.1%	43	26	6	4	17	59%	14	7.6	50	62	24.8%	47	12.3	59%	7	5.1	2	14	2
Melvin White	25	CB	15	505	42	5.6%	--	13	4	5	10	50%	--	3.9	--	39	19.7%	--	12.4	41%	--	8.6	--	7	1
Bené Benwikere	24	CB	10	449	40	8.0%	--	19	4	5	7	43%	--	5.0	--	37	20.7%	--	10.5	64%	--	5.7	--	7	1
Tre Boston	23	FS	11	359	26	4.7%	--	7	4	2	11	36%	--	14.5	--	11	7.8%	--	19.7	54%	--	8.0	--	3	1
Colin Jones	28	SS	16	284	26	3.2%	--	11	4	4	9	67%	--	3.8	--	19	16.6%	--	12.7	32%	--	11.9	--	3	0
Kurt Coleman	27	SS	15	391	35	4.6%	--	9	2	3	12	17%	--	8.1	--	15	9.5%	--	13.4	72%	--	2.4	--	6	3

Year	Pass D Rank	vs. #1 WR	Rk	vs. #2 WR	Rk	vs. Other WR	Rk	vs. TE	Rk	vs. RB	Rk
2012	12	-4.9%	15	10.1%	26	-1.9%	15	-0.1%	19	-6.9%	13
2013	3	-2.3%	15	-20.0%	4	-28.1%	2	-4.0%	12	4.8%	18
2014	9	15.1%	27	-0.6%	16	7.9%	23	-11.6%	7	-29.5%	2

As explained earlier in the chapter, every year this Panthers secondary is dinged for the lack of talent. As far as pedigree goes, there's no question: this is a group of cast-offs and late-round picks. But if they perform well enough with the help of Kuechly and Davis, does that lack of perceived pedigree actually matter? Josh Norman and Bené Benwikere, a pair of late-round picks, both played phenomenally down the stretch. Benwikere in particular stood out as he made a late charge towards the All-Rookie teams. The third corner, though not necessarily the slot corner, will ideally be one of a pair of older corners coming off major injuries. Peanut Tillman is trying to prolong his career outside of Chicago after tearing his triceps early last season, forcing the Bears to finally give up on him. And Chris Houston, who sat out last season recovering from a lingering toe injury after his release in Detroit, was brought on towards the end of OTAs. Melvin White is on-hand should the Panthers find both these players wanting, but whatever they put in the water here for unheralded guys hasn't hit him yet.

2014 fourth-rounder Tre Boston replaced Thomas "Meow Game" DeCoud towards the middle of the season and was such a vast upgrade at free safety that DeCoud was not invited back. Longtime Saints safety Roman Harper, a box run-stuffer who covers as well as CNN covers breaking news, is the other starter. The main depth piece is Colin Jones, who came over in a trade with the 49ers before last season, though Robert Lester has also had some positive bits of play in the past. Knowing Carolina's propensity for finding decent play from the depth at safety, you could throw a dart at a sheet of paper with the names like "Dean Marlowe" and "Brian Blechen" on it and hit someone who plays 400 snaps this year. They might even find a way to make Kurt Coleman useful.

Special Teams

Year	DVOA	Rank	FG/XP	Rank	Net Kick	Rank	Kick Ret	Rank	Net Punt	Rank	Punt Ret	Rank	Hidden	Rank
2012	-4.8%	29	-6.3	30	4.6	8	-6.9	29	-13.4	28	-1.9	17	-15.5	31
2013	1.0%	13	2.4	14	5.0	8	-3.1	20	1.6	16	-1.0	17	-3.8	21
2014	-5.5%	30	-0.2	18	-2.2	20	2.3	9	-23.1	32	-4.1	22	0.0	17

Carolina had the worst weighted DVOA of any special-teams unit in 2014, primarily because they were downright abysmal on punts. Punter Brad Nortman was bad, and the Panthers' punt coverage was worse. Not even counting the two punts they had blocked, the Panthers had a league-low net average of 37.4 yards per punt (average: 39.9), and allowed a league-high 6.2 yards per return (average: 3.9). Norton's gross punt value was even worse in 2012, and with his rookie contract up after the season, he's punting for his job. The coverage teams were also enough of a problem to give the Panthers negative net kickoff value even though Graham Gano led the league with a 77 percent touchback rate.

The Panthers pretty much cornered the market on available return men this offseason, with Philly Brown, Brenton Bersin, and Fozzy Whittaker from last year's team joining Ted Ginn, Jordan Todman, and Mike Brown coming in as free agents. Carolina is just a Roscoe Parrish and Glyn Milburn away from filming the least-interesting *Ocean's Eleven* spinoff movie in history. Ginn is definitely the favorite for the punt return job coming into camp, but the winner of the fourth-string running back competition between Todman and Whittaker might handle kickoffs.

Chicago Bears

2014 Record: 5-11	Total DVOA: -13.8% (26th)	2015 Mean Projection: 6.5 wins	On the Clock (0-4): 23%
Pythagorean Wins: 4.9 (26th)	Offense: -0.1% (14th)	Postseason Odds: 16.1%	Mediocrity (5-7): 43%
Snap-Weighted Age: 27.2 (2nd)	Defense: 10.6% (28th)	Super Bowl Odds: 1.3%	Playoff Contender (8-10): 28%
Average Opponent: 2.2% (6th)	Special Teams: -3.1% (25th)	Proj. Avg. Opponent: 3.3% (4th)	Super Bowl Contender (11+): 6%

2014: Disaster as the locker room goes Full Kotite.

2015: John Fox gets exiled to Guyville.

It seemed reasonable to expect the 2014 Chicago Bears to be a playoff team, with maybe even an outside shot to challenge Green Bay as the best team in the NFC North. General manager Phil Emery looked like a 21st century executive who said intelligent things in public and on the record about his thought process and use of analytics. Head coach Marc Trestman had looked like a quarterback whisperer the year before, coaxing the best performance out of Jay Cutler since he came to Chicago, and fielding one of the best offenses in the league. The defense was dismal in 2013, but improvement, from better health and an influx of talent, seemed almost inevitable. We were bullish on the Bears in *Football Outsiders Almanac 2014*, giving them a mean projection of 9.0 wins and better than even odds of making the postseason.

That narrative actually lasted a few weeks into the season. The opening home loss to Buffalo in overtime was disappointing, but prime-time road wins against the 49ers and Jets the next two weeks more than offset that. A crucial game at Soldier Field with the 1-2 Packers started off with two proficient offenses trading hammer blows. Then Martellus Bennett was stopped at the 1-yard line at the gun to give Green Bay a 21-17 halftime lead and everything went to pot.

When the second half kicked off, Green Bay's offense kept scoring. Chicago's offense did not. A pair of Cutler interceptions led to short Packers touchdown drives, Green Bay never punted, and the Bears were sunk, 38-17. Turnovers would also be their undoing the next week against Carolina. And two weeks after that against Miami. New England showed just how far the defense had to go, taking a 45-7 lead just over two minutes into the second half. When Green Bay bettered that the next game by going up 42-0 at halftime, the season was mostly sunk.

Naturally, false dawn followed in the form of narrow wins over Minnesota and Tampa Bay and an early 14-3 lead over Detroit on Thanksgiving. It didn't last. The offense sputtered, the defense gave up three consecutive long touchdown drives, and Chicago's season was finally over. All that was left were the recriminations and the fallout.

Defensive coordinator Mel Tucker could never right the ship and obviously had to go. Offensive coordinator Aaron Kromer complained to the media about Cutler's miscues and bad decisions, then compounded things by admitting he was the one talking "anonymously" to the media. The professorial Trestman looked like a CFL coach unable to handle the rigors of managing an NFL locker room. Emery's acquisitions failed to perform, which made thoughtfulness in NFL press conferences look even worse. After five losses in a row made it a 3-10 finish, all of them were sent packing.

Enter some adult supervision, in the form of new head coach John Fox. It was certainly an unusual hire for the franchise. The previous nine Bears head coaches were all first-time NFL head coaches. Not since owner George Halas assumed the reins of the team for the fourth time in 1958 had a new Bears head coach had previous NFL head coaching experience. Jettisoned after Denver's postseason exit, Fox's long experience seems the perfect fit for a fractured and fractious locker room. His defensive background made him an even better choice for a team with an illustrious history of defensive play which abruptly ended when the defensive line imploded halfway through 2013.

Fox inherited significant problems on both sides of the ball, an underachieving offense and a dismal defense. Of the two problems, the offense is the trickier.

L'affaire Kromer and Trestman's apparent mismanagement and unceremonious departure camouflaged one very important fact: the Chicago Bears did not have a bad offense in 2014. By DVOA, the Bears came out almost precisely average, at -0.1%. That was good enough to rank 14th overall.

While a comedown from 2013's fine performance, this was superb by franchise standards. By both overall and passing DVOA, this was Chicago's second-best offense since the Dave Krieg-led 1996 unit. Cutler, despite all the criticism for frequently bone-headed play, was still a league-average quarterback (-0.7% DVOA). He put up these numbers despite an underwhelming offensive line, with star wideouts Alshon Jeffery and Brandon Marshall banged up much of the season, and no real third receiver. The job for Fox and new general manager Ryan Pace seemed easy. Keep the scheme intact, add in parental supervision, find a third receiver and some line help, and you should have another top-ten unit.

Naturally, that was not what happened. Kromer was fired, as he had to be. Fox brought Adam Gase with him from Denver as the new offensive coordinator. Marshall, identified as one of the problems in the locker room, was traded to the Jets for a fifth-round pick. Cutler was the subject of incessant trade rumors in the offseason, but Pace found nary a taker thanks to the significant guaranteed money in the contract extension Emery gave the quarterback after the 2013 season.

38

2015 Bears Schedule

Week	Opp.	Week	Opp.	Week	Opp.
1	GB	7	BYE	13	SF
2	ARI	8	MIN	14	WAS
3	at SEA	9	at SD (Mon.)	15	at MIN
4	OAK	10	at STL	16	at TB
5	at KC	11	DEN	17	DET
6	at DET	12	at GB (Thu.)		

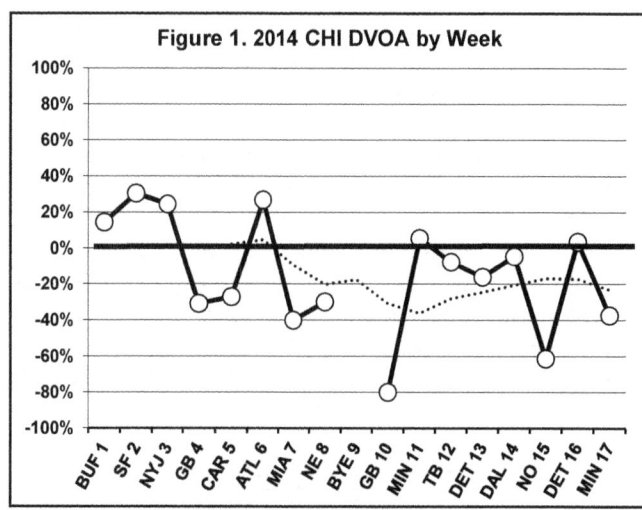

Figure 1. 2014 CHI DVOA by Week

Fox's Carolina days, plus his comment this offseason that what he looks for in a quarterback is "one that wins," make it clear he prefers a reliable veteran quarterback who does not make many mistakes. The forced Cutler marriage is sure to be a rocky one, and there is no guarantee it will last the season. If it does, it will probably be because the Bears have no other real option. Trestman tried benching Cutler for Jimmy Clausen, in the hopes that a more pliant quarterback would have greater success, to no avail. Though less dismal than he was as a rookie for Fox with the 2010 Panthers, Clausen was less productive than Cutler. Surprisingly, the offseason did not see the arrival of another veteran quarterback, so Cutler it will be unless former sixth-rounder David Fales is, like every sixth-round quarterback, the next Tom Brady.

Given the foregoing, the Bears' other moves on offense were surprisingly sensible. They signed free-agent Eddie Royal to be the necessary third wideout, while the seventh overall pick brought Marshall's replacement, Kevin White. Royal is archetypally a slot receiver, but that was what the Bears needed. He was very productive in San Diego the past two seasons, ranking in the top 20 by receiving DVOA, and had a prolific rookie season with Cutler in Denver back in 2008. White is tremendously physically gifted and has drawn comparisons to Larry Fitzgerald. Our Playmaker Score projection, however, is not as high on him as most scouts. He came out as a senior, not the norm among star receivers, and was not especially productive given how much West Virginia threw the ball. Technically, he ran only a limited number of routes in a spread offense, and there were strong reasons to doubt his productivity as a rookie even before a foot injury cost him most of the offseason. He and Jeffery may be a good combination for Chicago's next quarterback, but Cutler will likely have to rely more on Jeffery and Royal.

Dealing with the offense may be trickier because the problems revolve around personality and chemistry, but the challenge of fixing the defense is significantly more difficult. The main problem for Fox and new defensive coordinator Vic Fangio is an almost total absence of significant building blocks. The only player who really qualifies is cornerback Kyle Fuller, who had the rough rookie year we often see from cornerbacks minus the in-season improvement you want to see from a first-round pick.

The arrival of Fangio brought with it its own problems, namely an attempt to take a bunch of 4-3 players and plug them into a 3-4 alignment like the one Fangio ran in San Francisco. The returning defensive linemen are mostly one-gap

penetrators, the defensive ends turned outside linebackers are all players who have rarely if ever rushed from a two-point stance, and the inside linebacker situation made defensive line and outside linebackers look like strengths. Reinforcements were mandatory.

The most interesting arrival is Pernell McPhee, a versatile 6-foot-3, 280-pounder who broke out with 7.5 sacks last year as a part-time player in Baltimore. The Bears also signed Sam Acho away from Arizona, giving them another edge rusher with 3-4 experience. They join Jared Allen, Willie Young, and Lamarr Houston to give Chicago a deep collection of pass-rushers. Then the Bears bolstered their defensive line by using a second-round selection on Eddie Goldman of Florida State. If you liked him going into the draft, you thought he was a natural nose tackle with the versatility to play other than straight up. If you did not, you saw a player whose performance did not consistently match up to his strength and who did all his work at, rather than on the other side of, the line of scrimmage. Goldman has a good chance to start, as does Jarvis Jenkins, who brings 3-4 experience from Washington.

The most marked sign of the Bears' desperate need for talent on the defensive line was their attempt to bring in one of Fangio's San Francisco players, Ray McDonald. McDonald was released by the 49ers in December after a sexual assault accusation followed a domestic violence arrest. Chicago took a chance on a talented player after chairman George McCaskey spoke to his parents, who assured him their son was a solid citizen. And he was, for some two months, until he was arrested again, this time for domestic violence and child endangerment. The Bears rightly released him, leaving McCaskey, Pace, and Fangio, who suggested McDonald had been treated unfairly, with egg on their faces and an empty spot at five-technique.

McDonald's departure (or, more accurately, non-arrival) likely means an even bigger role for Jeremiah Ratliff. Back when he was Jay, he was a highly effective penetrator in Wade Phillips' attacking one-gap 3-4 in Dallas. That was so long ago that Dave Krieg had only been retired for a decade and Jay Cutler was still a promising young quarterback.

The question marks abounding in the front seven put even more pressure on a secondary that went from average to a liability in 2014. Charles Tillman tore his triceps in Week 2, ending his season, and then left for Carolina in free agency. Tim Jennings had a down season. Fuller, as noted earlier, had the usual rookie struggles. The Bears did add safety help this offseason, in the form of Antrel Rolle. He reunites with Ryan Mundy, his partner on the 2013 Giants team that finished eighth in pass defense DVOA. Back then, only one of them was over 30.

Frankly, it is difficult to be too optimistic about the Bears' 2015 prospects. Average play can sneak you into the playoffs in some divisions, but not in the NFC North, where Green Bay sets the tone, Detroit is coming off a playoff appearance, and Minnesota is a young team on the rise. Losing teams generally improve under new head coaches, simply because most teams that fire their head coach are unlucky and/or have straightforward problems that a change at head coach can fix. The Trestman-to-Fox swap is one that seems like it could pay major dividends there. Looking over the roster, though, there are too many holes on the roster and too many apparent mismatches between players and scheme. This year's Bears will likely end up looking a lot like a better-managed version of last season's Bears. The better management will probably translate to an extra win or two, but not much more than that.

Tom Gower

2014 Bears Stats by Week

Wk	vs.	W-L	PF	PA	YDF	YDA	TO	Total	Off	Def	ST
1	BUF	L	20	23	427	360	-2	14%	40%	26%	1%
2	at SF	W	28	20	216	359	4	30%	21%	-22%	-12%
3	at NYJ	W	27	19	257	414	2	24%	-8%	-28%	5%
4	GB	L	17	38	496	358	-2	-31%	7%	36%	-3%
5	at CAR	L	24	31	347	322	-1	-27%	-2%	-1%	-27%
6	at ATL	W	27	13	478	287	1	27%	13%	-22%	-9%
7	MIA	L	14	27	224	393	-3	-40%	-21%	22%	3%
8	at NE	L	23	51	384	487	-2	-30%	23%	41%	-12%
9	BYE										
10	at GB	L	14	55	311	451	-2	-80%	-54%	30%	4%
11	MIN	W	21	13	468	243	-1	5%	13%	-8%	-16%
12	TB	W	21	13	204	367	3	-8%	-27%	-19%	1%
13	at DET	L	17	34	269	474	-1	-16%	15%	44%	13%
14	DAL	L	28	41	376	397	-2	-5%	30%	25%	-9%
15	NO	L	15	31	278	443	-2	-61%	-41%	32%	11%
16	DET	L	14	20	234	367	2	4%	5%	5%	4%
17	at MIN	L	9	13	264	311	1	-37%	-36%	-1%	-3%

Trends and Splits

	Offense	Rank	Defense	Rank
Total DVOA	-0.1%	14	10.6%	28
Unadjusted VOA	-3.1%	19	12.0%	30
Weighted Trend	-6.9%	19	15.6%	32
Variance	7.4%	14	6.1%	16
Average Opponent	-0.8%	12	1.9%	7
Passing	11.6%	16	22.6%	29
Rushing	-1.2%	11	-5.0%	21
First Down	7.4%	11	2.7%	21
Second Down	-6.9%	23	13.2%	30
Third Down	-4.0%	19	21.5%	28
First Half	-5.2%	19	19.2%	32
Second Half	4.9%	13	1.6%	17
Red Zone	21.8%	5	-8.1%	14
Late and Close	3.1%	16	-5.5%	11

Five-Year Performance

Year	W-L	Pyth W	Est W	PF	PA	TO	Total	Rk	Off	Rk	Def	Rk	ST	Rk	Off AGL	Rk	Def AGL	Rk	Off Age	Rk	Def Age	Rk	ST Age	Rk
2010	11-5	9.5	8.3	334	286	+4	2.4%	14	-15.8%	28	-10.9%	4	7.4%	1	6.8	3	5.4	2	27.1	21	28.3	5	27.6	1
2011	8-8	8.3	7.3	353	341	+2	1.3%	15	-21.4%	30	-14.2%	4	8.5%	1	42.2	24	12.4	6	26.9	18	28.0	4	26.5	9
2012	10-6	10.8	11.0	375	277	+20	20.5%	6	-10.9%	26	-26.7%	1	4.7%	6	17.6	8	13.6	4	27.2	12	27.9	4	26.9	6
2013	8-8	7.3	9.2	445	478	+5	6.6%	11	13.3%	6	8.7%	25	2.0%	11	6.9	1	55.6	30	27.5	8	27.3	10	27.5	1
2014	5-11	4.9	6.4	319	442	-5	-13.8%	26	-0.1%	14	10.6%	28	-3.1%	25	41.0	27	60.6	26	27.9	3	27.0	12	26.3	9

2014 Performance Based on Most Common Personnel Groups

CHI Offense					CHI Offense vs. Opponents					CHI Defense					CHI Defense vs. Opponents			
Pers	Freq	Yds	DVOA	Run%	Pers	Freq	Yds	DVOA	Run%	Pers	Freq	Yds	DVOA	Pers	Freq	Yds	DVOA
11	67%	5.4	2.5%	30%	Base	24%	5.6	15.0%	35%	Base	48%	5.7	3.8%	11	47%	6.7	14.8%
12	22%	5.6	24.8%	31%	Nickel	69%	5.1	0.4%	33%	Nickel	50%	6.9	19.1%	12	26%	6.2	10.4%
611	6%	6.5	11.0%	26%	Dime+	7%	7.8	52.3%	7%	Dime+	0%	2.7	-45.5%	21	14%	5.2	-11.2%
21	2%	4.8	-28.6%	53%	Goal Line	0%	-7.0	-215.1%	100%	Goal Line	1%	0.3	-16.7%	22	6%	5.4	24.0%
610	1%	5.0	17.7%	62%										13	2%	6.9	42.1%
612	1%	2.1	-70.3%	75%													

Strategic Tendencies

Run/Pass		Rk	Formation		Rk	Pass Rush		Rk	Secondary		Rk	Strategy		Rk
Runs, first half	30%	32	Form: Single Back	81%	7	Rush 3	1.3%	31	4 DB	37%	6	Play action	21%	18
Runs, first down	39%	32	Form: Empty Back	4%	25	Rush 4	65.9%	13	5 DB	61%	16	Avg Box (Off)	6.04	31
Runs, second-long	20%	32	Pers: 3+ WR	68%	6	Rush 5	29.5%	6	6+ DB	0%	30	Avg Box (Def)	6.34	12
Runs, power sit.	58%	16	Pers: 4+ WR	0%	30	Rush 6+	3.3%	30	CB by Sides	82%	14	Offensive Pace	32.29	27
Runs, behind 2H	27%	14	Pers: 2+ TE/6+ OL	31%	16	Sacks by LB	7.7%	31	DB Blitz	4%	32	Defensive Pace	29.59	9
Pass, ahead 2H	53%	3	Shotgun/Pistol	73%	6	Sacks by DB	2.6%	27	Hole in Zone	7%	10	Go for it on 4th	1.80	2

The Bears used six linemen on 8.7 percent of plays, tied with New England for third in the league behind Denver and Atlanta. Of all the teams to use six linemen on more than a handful of downs, the Bears were the only one to pass more often than they ran (61 percent of plays). The Bears gained 5.5 yards per play with the extra lineman, but that high average comes in part thanks to a couple of particularly long plays, such as a 74-yard pass to Alshon Jeffery against Atlanta in Week 6. Chicago's -3.0% DVOA with the extra lineman roughly matched the NFL average. ☜ The Bears led the league with 50 running back screen passes, and were very good on these plays, with 6.3 average yards and 43.9% DVOA (compared to league averages of 6.1 yards and 14.4% DVOA). ☜ Chicago was both the worst offense and the worst defense in the league on second-and-short (1-2 yards to go). ☜ The Chicago offense inexplicably ranked second in offensive DVOA in the third quarter, even though the Bears ranked 19th or worse in the other three quarters. ☜ The Bears' defense was the worst in the league before halftime, though it was average after halftime. ☜ Chicago's defense had a 7.7 percent adjusted sack rate on first and second down (fifth in NFL) but fell to 3.2 percent on third and fourth down (32nd). ☜ The Bears had the second-fewest total of broken tackles of any defense, though this might have been because they weren't getting close enough to ballcarriers to miss tackles. ☜ Chicago had a league-leading 29 penalties on kickoffs and punts, after just 13 such penalties the year before.

Passing

Player	DYAR	DVOA	Plays	NtYds	Avg	YAC	C%	TD	Int
J.Cutler	398	-0.7%	602	3554	5.9	5.5	66.0%	29	15
J.Clausen	-5	-12.7%	51	203	4.0	4.7	54.2%	2	1

Rushing

Player	DYAR	DVOA	Plays	Yds	Avg	TD	Fum	Suc
M.Forte	113	0.9%	265	1039	3.9	6	1	50%
K.Carey	47	21.2%	36	158	4.4	0	0	53%
J.Cutler	65	38.3%	24	204	8.5	2	1	-
A.Jeffery	-4	-49.8%	6	33	5.5	0	1	-

Receiving

Player	DYAR	DVOA	Plays	Ctch	Yds	Y/C	YAC	TD	C%
A.Jeffery	278	11.1%	145	85	1133	13.3	5.5	11	59%
B.Marshall*	78	-3.3%	106	61	721	11.8	3.8	8	58%
M.Wilson	-31	-25.0%	32	17	140	8.2	3.0	1	53%
J.Morgan*	-27	-30.4%	19	10	70	7.0	5.0	1	53%
S.Holmes*	-4	-16.6%	14	8	67	8.4	3.1	0	57%
M.Bennett	88	3.0%	128	90	916	10.2	5.0	6	70%
D.Rosario	-32	-31.9%	22	16	116	7.3	3.4	0	73%
M.Forte	127	5.0%	131	103	809	7.9	7.7	4	79%
K.Carey	17	43.5%	6	5	57	11.4	8.6	0	83%

Offensive Line

Player	Pos	Age	GS	Snaps	Pen	Sk	Pass	Run	Player	Pos	Age	GS	Snaps	Pen	Sk	Pass	Run
Kyle Long	RG	27	15/15	994	7	0.5	5.5	5.0	Brian De La Puente*	C	30	8/6	488	2	4.0	6.5	1.5
Jermon Bushrod	LT	31	14/14	921	5	3.5	16.0	1.5	Matt Slauson	LG	29	5/5	264	1	1.0	3.5	1.0
Michael Ola	G/T	27	13/12	822	3	6.0	15.0	8.0	Ryan Groy	LG	25	4/3	226	1	1.0	4.0	1.5
Jordan Mills	RT	25	13/13	813	9	5.0	21.5	0.5	Will Montgomery	C	32	16/8	581	4	0.5	0.5	2.5
Roberto Garza*	C	36	12/12	746	4	1.0	4.5	2.0	Vladimir Ducasse	G	28	13/6	406	5	2.0	5.0	2.0

Year	Yards	ALY	Rk	Power	Rk	Stuff	Rk	2nd Lev	Rk	Open Field	Rk	Sacks	ASR	Rk	Short	Long	F-Start	Cont.
2012	4.08	4.05	16	57%	25	21%	25	1.12	19	0.73	18	44	8.0%	24	9	22	24	30
2013	4.37	3.80	20	50%	30	21%	26	1.23	11	1.03	3	30	5.5%	5	8	15	8	48
2014	3.97	3.94	15	68%	10	18%	10	1.21	12	0.38	32	41	6.3%	18	16	9	24	23
2014 ALY by direction:			Left End 3.55 (20)			Left Tackle 3.27 (27)			Mid/Guard 4.14 (8)			Right Tackle 3.86 (17)			Right End 4.28 (9)			

New Bears offensive line coach Dave Magazu followed John Fox and Adam Gase from Colorado to Illinois, and the most vexing question he faces is where it makes the most sense to deploy Kyle Long. The team's most talented offensive lineman, Long has spent his first two years at right guard amidst constant chatter about whether his long-term future will be as a tackle or an interior lineman. That talk intensified this offseason, when Long played both tackle spots in OTAs and minicamp.

Unless injury forces the Bears to reshuffle their line, Long will not be the left tackle in 2015. That job belongs to Jermon Bushrod, pretty much the definition of serviceable. Though Bushrod was absent from OTAs for unspecified reasons, he is expected to be ready for training camp and should not face any competition. Right tackle Jordan Mills is the player who might lose his job to Long. Mills' main asset has been that he was better than what the Bears had trotted out before, but a foot injury from last offseason lingered well into the season and hampered his play. Long would very likely be an upgrade, but the question Fox, Gase, and Magazu have to answer is if a position switch would make the entire line better. Depth comes from last year's seventh-rounder Charles Leno, who worked the tackle spot Long did not in Bushrod's and Mills' offseason absences, and sixth-rounder Tayo Fabujule, a gargantuan (over 350 pounds) road-grader from Texas Christian who needs to improve his motor and footwork.

If Long does move outside to tackle, the Bears will be looking at three new primary starters on the interior line. The situation is better than that sentence makes it seem. Veteran Matt Slauson is healthy after a torn pectoral ended his 2014 season after just five games, and drew plaudits from Fox for taking a step forward in his leadership during OTAs. Roberto Garza was released in April after ten years with the team, and the Bears have two candidates to fill the void at center. The first is veteran Will Montgomery, another who made the thousand-mile trek across I-76/I-80 this offseason. The other is third-round pick Hroniss Grasu, a teammate of Long's at Oregon. Like many collegians, he needs further technique and weight room work to adapt to the NFL game. The best potential right guard candidates beyond Long are Vlad Ducasse, not the answer with the Jets in the past or the Vikings last season, or Michael Ola, who started at every line position except center for last year's Bears and did not excel at any of them. Maybe Mills is not so bad after all.

Defensive Front Seven

Defensive Line	Age	Pos	G	Snaps	Plays	TmPct	Rk	Stop	Dfts	BTkl	Runs	St%	Rk	RuYd	Rk	Sack	Hit	Hur	Dsrpt
						Overall						**vs. Run**					**Pass Rush**		
Stephen Paea*	27	DT	16	700	33	4.2%	57	27	12	2	25	76%	59	2.0	33	6.0	6	18.5	2
Jay Ratliff	34	DT	11	460	37	6.8%	15	27	10	2	28	64%	86	2.7	69	6.5	5	13.5	0
Will Sutton	24	DT	15	458	24	3.2%	77	14	5	2	20	55%	93	3.6	91	0.0	0	2.0	2
Ego Ferguson	24	DT	16	313	25	3.1%	--	18	2	1	20	65%	--	2.7	--	2.0	0	4.0	3
Jarvis Jenkins	27	DE	16	540	29	3.8%	67	23	3	0	29	79%	37	2.6	66	0.0	3	6.5	0

Edge Rushers	Age	Pos	G	Snaps	Plays	TmPct	Rk	Stop	Dfts	BTkl	Runs	St%	Rk	RuYd	Rk	Sack	Hit	Hur	Dsrpt
						Overall						**vs. Run**					**Pass Rush**		
Jared Allen	33	DE	15	886	61	8.2%	8	52	17	3	45	84%	13	2.0	30	5.5	15	27.5	3
Willie Young	30	DE	15	664	41	5.5%	32	34	14	2	28	79%	30	2.8	55	10.0	3	16.5	2
Lamarr Houston	28	DE	8	396	12	3.0%	81	9	5	1	9	67%	69	2.2	34	1.0	6	14.5	1
Pernell McPhee	26	OLB	16	515	31	3.7%	67	28	18	5	15	87%	9	1.5	12	7.5	19	22.5	3
Sam Acho	27	OLB	16	469	31	3.9%	65	26	10	3	20	85%	11	1.5	10	1.0	2	11.0	1

Linebackers	Age	Pos	G	Snaps	Plays	TmPct	Rk	Stop	Dfts	BTkl	Sack	Hit	Hur	Runs	St%	Rk	RuYd	Rk	Tgts	Suc%	Rk	AdjYd	Rk	PD	Int
						Overall						**Pass Rush**				**vs. Run**					**vs. Pass**				
Jon Bostic	24	MLB	13	679	86	13.3%	37	39	13	0	0.0	0	1	47	55%	73	4.7	78	19	43%	49	6.7	41	2	0
Lance Briggs*	35	OLB	8	453	37	9.3%	67	25	8	2	0.0	1	3	23	70%	19	2.4	11	17	51%	35	5.8	21	3	1
Christian Jones	24	MLB	16	433	65	8.2%	74	30	9	3	2.0	1	0	29	52%	80	5.6	86	20	60%	10	5.7	19	2	0
Shea McClellin	26	OLB	4	424	36	6.0%	80	20	8	2	1.0	0	3	25	64%	40	3.6	53	14	44%	--	5.8	--	1	0
D.J. Williams*	33	MLB	12	412	46	7.7%	75	23	3	3	0.0	0	1.5	29	62%	48	3.6	52	10	56%	--	5.1	--	0	0
Mason Foster	26	MLB	10	556	63	11.4%	52	33	11	0	0.0	1	2	37	59%	61	3.9	67	11	32%	--	7.6	--	2	0

Year	Yards	ALY	Rk	Power	Rk	Stuff	Rk	2nd Level	Rk	Open Field	Rk	Sacks	ASR	Rk	Short	Long
2012	4.11	3.52	3	60%	14	24%	5	1.20	19	0.92	24	41	6.4%	15	6	13
2013	5.34	4.45	32	77%	31	20%	14	1.57	32	1.40	32	31	6.3%	23	10	13
2014	4.45	4.38	30	53%	2	15%	31	1.12	13	0.84	24	39	6.4%	22	11	14
2014 ALY by direction:		Left End 2.74 (5)			Left Tackle 4.9 (29)			Mid/Guard 4.38 (29)			Right Tackle 5.55 (32)			Right End 3.73 (14)		

What do you do with a bunch of underachieving 4-3 penetrators when transitioning to a 3-4? Vic Fangio has a difficult question to answer. Stephen Paea was the most proficient of the Chicago tackles last year, and he departed for greener climes (or, more accurately, a greener wallet, now that he signed with Washington). Will Sutton, who didn't play as well when he got much bigger in college, seems like the most obvious misfit between skill set and scheme after an underwhelming rookie season. Ego Ferguson, the other 2014 draft pick at tackle, is also more of a penetrator but has the size and ability to hold up against blockers that Fangio prefers.

Inside linebacker seems about as bleak. Like the fired Mel Tucker, Fangio is high on second-year man Christian Jones, calling him a potential building block. The Florida State alum had a very solid performance for an undrafted rookie, filling in for Lance Briggs on the weak side. He added 10 pounds in the offseason to help with the scheme change. His partner is more of a question mark. The favorite might be Shea McClellin, whose future may be as a read-and-react linebacker rather than the edge rusher the Bears hoped for when they drafted him three years ago. Jon Bostic, who has started roughly half of Chicago's games the past two years, and Mason Foster, signed away from Tampa Bay this offseason, seem to be McClellin's main competition. Of the quartet, only McClellin, at Boise State, has started in a 3-4 before, and that was not on the inside. Patrick Willis and Navorro Bowman, or even Chris Borland, this is not.

Defensive Secondary

Secondary	Age	Pos	G	Snaps	Plays	Overall TmPct	Rk	Stop	Dfts	BTkl	vs. Run Runs	St%	Rk	RuYd	Rk	vs. Pass Tgts	Tgt%	Rk	Dist	Suc%	Rk	AdjYd	Rk	PD	Int
Tim Jennings	32	CB	16	1006	58	7.3%	62	21	8	6	10	30%	50	9.1	62	76	21.7%	24	12.0	49%	43	8.6	52	8	0
Ryan Mundy	30	SS	16	945	107	13.5%	10	44	12	8	52	48%	23	4.8	10	39	11.8%	60	9.4	52%	43	6.6	26	7	4
Kyle Fuller	23	CB	16	858	72	9.1%	32	27	15	7	14	57%	16	5.0	17	98	32.9%	77	12.3	42%	69	9.6	68	10	4
Brock Vereen	23	FS	16	502	35	4.4%	--	3	2	9	11	9%	--	15.6	--	6	3.2%	--	11.7	80%	--	5.2	--	1	1
Chris Conte*	26	FS	12	463	43	7.2%	61	3	3	5	14	0%	71	10.4	64	18	11.3%	56	12.1	36%	66	11.7	68	3	3
Demontre Hurst	24	CB	15	365	33	4.4%	--	12	10	1	7	71%	--	4.0	--	22	17.4%	--	10.5	26%	--	13.5	--	1	1
Antrel Rolle	33	FS	16	1049	93	11.5%	26	37	10	11	42	48%	24	7.1	43	32	9.0%	39	12.0	66%	8	8.9	57	9	3
Alan Ball	30	CB	7	495	25	6.6%	--	9	3	2	4	75%	--	2.5	--	40	26.5%	--	12.8	53%	--	6.2	--	3	1

Year	Pass D Rank	vs. #1 WR	Rk	vs. #2 WR	Rk	vs. Other WR	Rk	vs. TE	Rk	vs. RB	Rk
2012	1	-31.0%	2	-5.2%	11	-30.2%	3	-24.7%	1	-27.2%	3
2013	17	-10.0%	10	6.6%	18	4.0%	19	18.8%	27	-14.3%	6
2014	29	11.2%	25	10.1%	25	-0.3%	17	30.6%	32	3.0%	21

Our mantra at Football Outsiders is that highly drafted corners, even ones who end up very good, usually struggle early in their careers before improving. But the trend of Kyle Fuller's rookie season ended up very unusual. He started out as a fairly average corner, posting an adjusted success rate of 48 percent and allowing 8.9 adjusted yards per pass in the Bears' first eight games. After the bye, he struggled badly. His success rate fell to 40 percent, and he allowed 9.7 adjusted yards per pass. Sometimes, splits just happen; by our metrics, Tim Jennings' performance in the second half of the season improved more than Fuller's declined. We often see the better cornerbacks start to become very good from their first to second season, though sometimes it takes a year or two after that. Jennings' career arc reinforces the point that it would be premature to declare 2015 of supreme importance for the future direction of Fuller's career, but it is a very important season for him and the team.

With Fuller and Jennings starting, depth is the biggest question. First Isaiah Frey, then Demontre Hurst filled the role when Fuller stepped into the starting lineup after Charles Tillman was lost of the year in Week 2. Neither did an adequate job. Hurst will compete for the nickel job with veteran Alan Ball and longtime special-teams standout Sherrick McManis. That Chicago felt the need to sign Tracy Porter to a one-year deal in June is probably a sign of their (lack of) confidence in the depth chart.

Antrel Rolle's addition was a necessary one, with Chris Conte gone to join old coach Lovie Smith in Tampa Bay and Brock Vereen looking overmatched as a rookie. The previous pairing of Rolle and Ryan Mundy on the 2013 New York Giants was very successful, but that Giants team had a better cornerback group and a better pass rush. Fangio showed in San Francisco that his defense does not need a rangy free safety to succeed—but if he's looking for a rangy safety, that might be fifth-round pick Adrian Amos (Penn State), a converted cornerback who ran a 4.56-second 40.

Special Teams

Year	DVOA	Rank	FG/XP	Rank	Net Kick	Rank	Kick Ret	Rank	Net Punt	Rank	Punt Ret	Rank	Hidden	Rank
2012	4.7%	6	-4.4	24	13.0	2	0.5	14	18.8	2	-4.4	23	2.0	13
2013	2.0%	11	4.0	9	-4.1	26	-1.6	18	5.3	11	6.5	7	-5.6	23
2014	-3.1%	25	-5.9	29	0.2	16	1.6	10	-6.9	25	-4.3	23	-1.4	21

Robbie Gould got the glory of the TD Ameritrade commercial, and responded with the worst season of his career. He missed four games with a quad injury. He had his second consecutive mediocre season kicking off, ranking 28th with minus-3.4 points of gross kickoff value. (Injury fill-in Jay Feely nearly matched that in one-fifth as many kicks, but good Chicago coverage teams helped the Bears end up as average in net kickoff value.) Gould also had a lousy season in field goals, missing as many as he did in 2013 despite attempting 17 fewer kicks (dropping from 26-of-29 to 9-of-12). He even flubbed the third extra point of his career.

Punting was just as problematic as kicking. Replacing Adam Podlesh, rookie Pat O'Donnell ranked 29th out of 32 punters with minus-8.3 points of gross punt value. Nevertheless, like Gould, he faces no competition for his job.

Both return jobs seem open to competition, however. November signee Marc Mariani returns. He was good on kickoff returns and underwhelming on punts, just as he was when he made the Pro Bowl for Tennessee back in 2010. Eddie Royal could be the punt returner, a job he split in San Diego the past three seasons, while fellow new arrival Jacquizz Rodgers spent two seasons returning kicks in Atlanta. Running back Senorise Perry, a special-teams mainstay, provides another option.

Cincinnati Bengals

2014 Record: 10-5-1	Total DVOA: 5.0% (12th)	2015 Mean Projection: 8.6 wins	On the Clock (0-4): 7%
Pythagorean Wins: 8.6 (14th)	Offense: -1.4% (18th)	Postseason Odds: 45.3%	Mediocrity (5-7): 28%
Snap-Weighted Age: 26.9 (16th)	Defense: -2.3% (14th)	Super Bowl Odds: 7.5%	Playoff Contender (8-10): 41%
Average Opponent: 0.3% (15th)	Special Teams: 4.2% (6th)	Proj. Avg. Opponent: 1.4% (12th)	Super Bowl Contender (11+): 24%

2014: Over and over and over and over, like a monkey with a miniature cymbal.

2015: For this version of the Bengals, perhaps the last chance to win a tight division race and lose in the first round yet again.

Another trip to the playoffs, another Sisyphean one and done for the Cincinnati Bengals and their fans. If, as noted football expert Karl Marx once said, history repeats the first time as tragedy and the second time as farce, the Bengals broke new ground. History repeated the third time as ennui. The season ended with a punch to a face that was already numb from repeated blows.

But that was a negative way to view the season. In truth, merely making the playoffs was something of an overachievement. The team barely scraped into the top 12 in DVOA thanks mainly to a solid special-teams effort. Cincinnati lost both coordinators to other jobs before 2014. The defense, mostly the front seven, fell off considerably from the heights it had reached under departed defensive guru Mike Zimmer, finishing with but 20 sacks, dead last in the league. On offense, quarterback Andy Dalton had a mediocre season even by his own so-so standards, hindered in part by a raft of injuries to his pass-catchers. The Bengals managed to win ten games (and would have won 11 but for a shanked chip shot at the end of overtime against Carolina) despite much lower expectations from estimated wins (9.0) and Pythagorean wins (8.6—only Arizona had a larger gap between Pythagorean wins and actual wins). If it weren't for a late A.J. Green fumble deep in Pittsburgh territory in the season finale, these flawed Bengals might well have repeated as division champs.

The Striped Cats straggled across the postseason/fishing season divide, only to piss off America once again by flatlining on wild-card weekend. The lineup was so ravaged by injury that fourth-string running back Rex Burkhead saw time at slot receiver. The Bengals still managed to hang around for thirty minutes before the Colts dominated the second half. The NFL-record fourth straight one-and-done was also head coach Marvin Lewis' sixth playoff loss without a win. In the second halves of those games, Cincy has been outscored 84-13. Blecch.

So does eking a postseason berth out of a rather ragtag season, then absorbing yet another playoff loss, constitute a good season or a failure?

How you answer that one suggests your feelings about the follow-up question: should Bengals fans welcome the looming breakup of the core that made it to four straight playoffs, only to be blasted each time? Or, realizing the difficulty of making it to the tournament four straight times regardless of result, should they fear the potential deconstruction?

Just how 2015 plays out should provide a bit of clarity to a conundrum with no easy answers.

No fewer than 13 key Bengals are in the final years of their contracts. That includes three offensive line starters, both starting safeties, the top three wideouts, and three of the cornerbacks who did such a good job in 2014, when the Bengals ranked seventh in pass defense DVOA despite the paucity of pass rush. The structuring of Dalton's contract extension, signed last offseason, allows the team to escape after 2015 without significant cap penalty. Lewis was given a token one-year extension through 2016, but there are signs even from this most loyal (and frugal) of organizations that "Hardly Starvin'" Marvin is coaching for his job this season.

Now, just because this seems like a make-or-break year doesn't necessarily make it so. Lewis has been on and off the hot seat so often his ass is part thermometer by now. Sure, the Bengals *can* get out of Dalton's contract, but the same logic that led to his extension—*who else are they gonna get?*—makes it likely he continues in stripes next year. Similarly, not all of those free agents are going elsewhere in 2016. Green, in particular, will almost definitely be franchised if a long-term deal isn't yet in the offing.

But there is a definite "last hurrah" sensation drifting out of Cincinnati this offseason. "It's now or never," running back Jeremy Hill said in the spring. (And he's only been around for a single season! Backs apparently have become so fungible they view the league through an accelerated lens.) 2015 sets up not only as a "prove it" campaign for the Bengals to show the NFL world they can finally win in January, but also as a showdown for roster spots going forward. The Bengals are unlikely to keep both Reggie Nelson and George Iloka at safety, for example. They certainly won't be retaining both starting tackles, Andrew Whitworth and Andre Smith. Will either stay in stripes? Which promising but flawed receiver drafted in 2012 stays, Marvin Jones or Mohamed Sanu? If both Leon Hall and Adam Jones get offers to take their veteran corner smarts elsewhere, do the Bengals keep either?

Even recently re-signed star players have had their futures questioned. Linebacker Vontaze Burfict's progress after microfracture surgery on his knee has been slow, and full recovery from that particular operation is always chancy. The team drafted what they hope is his clone, and if necessary his replacement, in Paul Dawson out of TCU. Meanwhile, defen-

2015 Bengals Schedule

Week	Opp.	Week	Opp.	Week	Opp.
1	at OAK	7	BYE	13	at CLE
2	SD	8	at PIT	14	PIT
3	at BAL	9	CLE (Thu.)	15	at SF
4	KC	10	HOU (Mon.)	16	at DEN (Mon.)
5	SEA	11	at ARI	17	BAL
6	at BUF	12	STL		

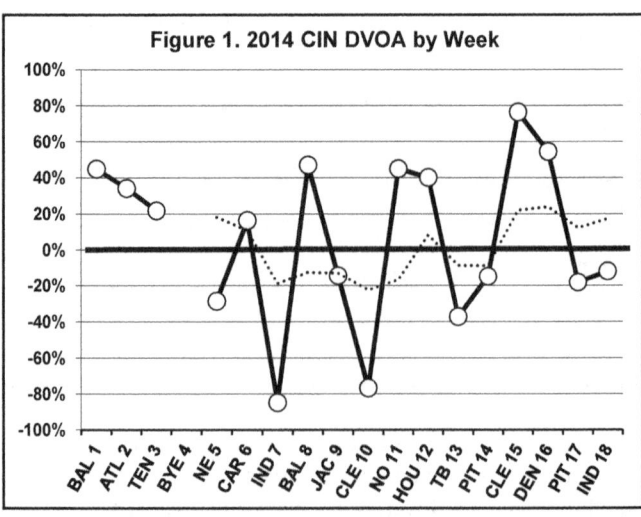

Figure 1. 2014 CIN DVOA by Week

sive tackle Geno Atkins has become so ordinary in the wake of a torn ACL (three sacks and a dozen defeats) that defensive coordinator Paul Guenther very publicly put him on notice, saying that if Atkins could not regain his old dominant form, "we need to go find another inside rusher."

The NFL, she is a fickle lover.

Our projection is somewhat bullish on Cincinnati's Drive for Five, forecasting another tight three-way tussle with Baltimore and Pittsburgh where the losers will still have a good shot at wild cards. Sure, Pythagoras would say the Bengals are headed back to the mean, and yes, the schedule looks harder. The tissue-soft NFC and AFC South divisions are replaced with the respective Western collectives, ensuring much longer road trips (two separate journeys to the Bay Area, among other jaunts). On the other hand, the division rivals have to face the same eight West teams, and finishing second in 2014 takes New England and Indianapolis off the schedule; the Bengals get Buffalo and Houston instead while the Steelers have to tangle with Andrew Luck and (maybe) Tom Brady. There are also a number of key players expected to return to the lineup after injuries cost them some or all of 2014, including Green, Jones, tight end Tyler Eifert, and hopefully Burfict. Yes, the team regressed on both sides of the ball last year, but teams often regress with new coordinators. Guenther and Hue Jackson are bound to improve with seasoning, now that their styles are more ingrained in the personnel. Yes, Dalton is still the quarterback—but then, it could be much worse. Take a drive up I-71 sometime.

As befitting such a schizophrenic bunch, the 2014 Bengals were all over the place, finishing next-to-last in variance. Seven times they were over 30% in single-game DVOA, but there were seven other games with negative DVOA, and the Bengals were the only playoff team with two stinkeroos below -75%. The pessimist would point out that Cincy will always wind up in the negative against the power teams led by great quarterbacks; the half-full type would say many of those lame performances were greatly affected by injuries or circumstances, including a Thursday night debacle versus Cleveland hard on the heels of an intensely physical thriller victory over the Ravens, and a stink job in Tampa when Dalton played through a debilitating case of the upchucks (a game the Bengals won despite playing poorly).

Perhaps the best reason to believe in another year of playoff contention is the strength of the overall operation, still a difficult paradigm for long-time fans of the Bungles to comprehend. The roster, when healthy, is strong and balanced. The team's approach to scouting, drafting, and player development has been mostly exemplary over the last few years, a big reason why the Bengals actually have a number of players approaching free agency that other teams will want. No team has less dead money weighing down its salary cap (a paltry $782,913 as of July 1, per Spotrac). And in an example of its free-agent acumen, Cincy let defensive end Michael Johnson walk a year ago; when he bombed in Tampa and was released, the Bengals reclaimed him at a fraction of the cost, and collected a compensatory draft choice in the bargain.

The franchise even has been getting the little things right of late, as witnessed by its spot-on handling of the Devon Still nightmare. You know the story—the defensive tackle was about to be cut, but was kept on the practice squad for the express purpose of allowing him to keep his medical benefits, ensuring top treatment for Still's cancer-stricken daughter Leah. For an organization that used to sue its players so as not to pay their medical costs, this represents a gigantic leap forward.

Speaking of medical issues, if there is an exception to the Bengals' organizational excellence it may be in the training staff. In this case it wasn't so much the aggregate injuries (the Bengals were 16th in adjusted games lost) but the way ouchies tended to worsen over time compared to the initial diagnoses. Marvin Jones' foot injury was suffered in preseason, and the world was told he would be back in time for the Week 5 encounter with New England. Instead, Jones missed the whole year. The status of Eifert's elbow became a running joke among the team's beat writers, who were asked about it so often by readers because what was supposed to be half-season damage turned out to be full-season trauma. Then there was Burfict, whose health status from a series of concussions changed seemingly quarter-to-quarter until all of sudden he needed major surgery on his knee and was gone for good. And of course, Atkins was no Gronk or Peterson when it came to returning to form after a torn knee ligament. Some of this may be chalked up to standard NFL misinformation rather than malpractice, but it was a worrying trend.

Fortunately, while depth was an issue last year, a hallmark of the Bengals the last several seasons has been being consistently ready with in-house replacements for departing players and coaches. That was true with the duo of coordinators a year ago, and was the impetus behind the double-dipping at offensive tackle during the draft. After grabbing Cedric Ogbuehi of Texas A&M in the first round, an elite talent who fell due to a knee injury in college, the team shocked most observers by using its second-round pick on another highly graded slipper, Oregon's Jake Fisher, who can also play guard. That decision was clearly influenced by the uncertainty of the future at the position, with Whitworth, Smith, and guard Kevin Zeitler all impending free agents. No matter what combination of the three are retained, their replacements will have a season in the system and, theoretically, be ready to step in and start by 2016.

Similarly, the secondary could have a new look in the near future, with former first-round corners Dre Kirkpatrick and Darqueze Dennard champing at the bit to take over from the still-strong starters. One of them will do so this year, since free-agent veteran Terence Newman left to reunite with Mike Zimmer in Minnesota. At safety, Shawn Williams, a promising third-year player, stands ready to replace either Reggie Nelson or George Iloka should one depart, which seems likely. The lone position group without stand-ins is wide receiver. Obviously, losing Green would be catastrophic, but even if only Jones and/or Sanu depart, the lack of quality backups would be felt.

Perhaps the biggest decision ahead may be choosing between Green and Dalton. To keep both long-term would almost certainly lead to major attrition elsewhere. Green has been the exception to the rule that the quarterback makes the wide receiver, not vice-versa. Many fans wonder wistfully about how great A.J. could be with a top-flight passer hurling darts his way. On the other hand, every offseason contract handed to the likes of Josh McCown or Ryan Fitzpatrick is a stark reminder that no matter how good Green may be, he still is probably easier to replace than even a middle-pack signal-caller like the Red Rifle.

This is why the most scrutinized player on the team may well be one who hardly plays. A.J. McCarron has the name recognition, the major college pedigree, and the stunning arm candy of a top quarterback. It has yet to be determined, however, whether he can actually play pro ball, much less do so better than Dalton. The track record of fifth-round talent at the position is poor, and McCarron missed virtually all of 2014 with a bum shoulder. After a supposedly sterling minicamp— has anyone ever publicly been said to have had a bad one?— he has the backup job to himself, and all of Southern Ohio and Northern Kentucky is praying for McCarron to develop into a true competitor for the top gig. Of course, barring an injury to Dalton, virtually all of McCarron's progress or lack of it will take place behind the scenes. So everyone will be forced to read the tea leaves of occasional public utterances from the coaching staff. If there is no "A.J. to A.J." combo in Cincy's future, a very difficult decision will be nigh.

All this focus on 2016 befogs the fact that there is a season to play first. Just how well 2015 goes will determine much about the makeup of future editions of the Bengals. Should they step up, plant their feet, and (*dare to dream!*) actually win a postseason game, the offseason decision-making will take place in the context of being close to the promised land. Finish 7-9, and the spring cleaning will be more thorough, likely starting with the head coach and, quite possibly, the quarterback.

The oddity is that Cincinnati fans would be happy either way. What would be infuriating is yet another one-and-done in January. When the worst-case scenario is reaching the playoffs but not advancing in them, you've reached a rarefied status in football history.

Robert Weintraub

2014 Bengals Stats by Week

Wk	vs.	W-L	PF	PA	YDF	YDA	TO	Total	Off	Def	ST
1	at BAL	W	23	16	380	423	2	45%	20%	-15%	9%
2	ATL	W	24	10	472	309	3	34%	25%	-27%	-18%
3	TEN	W	33	7	300	326	1	22%	10%	-3%	9%
4	BYE										
5	at NE	L	17	43	320	505	-3	-29%	3%	17%	-15%
6	CAR	T	37	37	513	431	-1	16%	31%	29%	14%
7	at IND	L	0	27	135	506	2	-85%	-70%	25%	11%
8	BAL	W	27	24	350	294	0	47%	2%	-36%	9%
9	JAC	W	33	23	423	365	-1	-14%	17%	35%	4%
10	CLE	L	3	24	165	368	-3	-77%	-66%	21%	11%
11	at NO	W	27	10	405	330	1	45%	27%	-8%	10%
12	at HOU	W	22	13	372	248	0	40%	7%	-24%	9%
13	at TB	W	14	13	288	263	-2	-37%	-25%	11%	-1%
14	PIT	L	21	42	408	543	-2	-15%	-4%	20%	9%
15	at CLE	W	30	0	347	107	1	76%	-14%	-80%	10%
16	DEN	W	37	28	353	385	2	54%	-3%	-41%	17%
17	at PIT	L	17	27	337	346	0	-18%	-15%	-18%	-21%
18	at IND	L	10	26	254	482	0	-12%	-11%	8%	8%

Trends and Splits

	Offense	Rank	Defense	Rank
Total DVOA	-1.4%	18	-2.3%	14
Unadjusted VOA	0.0%	14	-0.8%	16
Weighted Trend	-7.4%	21	-2.6%	17
Variance	8.9%	23	9.8%	31
Average Opponent	1.5%	23	0.9%	10
Passing	6.8%	20	-5.0%	7
Rushing	-1.0%	10	1.1%	28
First Down	1.3%	15	-2.8%	14
Second Down	-0.7%	16	4.1%	22
Third Down	-7.9%	22	-11.4%	11
First Half	-0.7%	15	-13.3%	4
Second Half	-2.2%	17	9.2%	27
Red Zone	12.8%	8	-11.1%	10
Late and Close	6.2%	12	-6.7%	9

Five-Year Performance

Year	W-L	Pyth W	Est W	PF	PA	TO	Total	Rk	Off	Rk	Def	Rk	ST	Rk	Off AGL	Rk	Def AGL	Rk	Off Age	Rk	Def Age	Rk	ST Age	Rk
2010	4-12	6.0	6.6	322	395	-8	-3.4%	19	1.7%	17	1.5%	17	-3.5%	28	14.9	7	46.6	30	28.9	1	26.4	22	26.0	21
2011	9-7	8.6	8.5	344	323	0	0.1%	17	-1.4%	17	0.80%	17	2.3%	7	25.2	14	26.5	17	26.5	24	27.4	13	26.4	13
2012	10-6	9.9	8.7	391	320	+4	6.1%	12	-1.8%	17	-3.8%	10	4.1%	7	37.0	21	22.2	13	25.1	32	27.3	11	26.0	17
2013	11-5	11.1	10.1	430	305	+1	14.2%	9	0.4%	17	-12.6%	5	1.2%	12	11.2	2	30.5	19	26.0	29	27.4	8	26.3	9
2014	10-5-1	8.6	9.0	365	344	0	5.0%	12	-1.4%	18	-2.3%	14	4.2%	6	48.5	28	23.2	5	25.9	29	28.1	2	26.1	14

2014 Performance Based on Most Common Personnel Groups

CIN Offense					CIN Offense vs. Opponents					CIN Defense					CIN Defense vs. Opponents			
Pers	Freq	Yds	DVOA	Run%	Pers	Freq	Yds	DVOA	Run%	Pers	Freq	Yds	DVOA		Pers	Freq	Yds	DVOA
11	56%	5.7	0.1%	32%	Base	42%	5.6	3.3%	63%	Base	42%	4.9	-3.4%		11	47%	6.1	6.1%
12	33%	5.7	7.5%	61%	Nickel	46%	5.7	-3.0%	31%	Nickel	52%	5.9	0.9%		12	19%	5.2	-5.6%
13	4%	4.9	6.0%	81%	Dime+	10%	6.0	20.7%	32%	Dime+	5%	7.3	-19.8%		21	11%	4.3	-25.2%
611	2%	3.4	-95.3%	78%	Goal Line	2%	1.6	39.6%	81%	Goal Line	1%	0.4	-0.6%		22	6%	5.2	-0.5%
21	1%	5.9	-16.1%	23%											13	4%	6.6	47.0%
21*	17%	5.2	-4.1%	75%											10	4%	4.4	-68.5%

* 21 personnel with Ryan Hewitt considered FB rather than TE; overlaps with numbers for 12 personnel.

Strategic Tendencies

Run/Pass		Rk	Formation		Rk	Pass Rush		Rk	Secondary		Rk	Strategy		Rk
Runs, first half	46%	2	Form: Single Back	67%	24	Rush 3	2.1%	29	4 DB	28%	15	Play action	23%	12
Runs, first down	58%	4	Form: Empty Back	4%	23	Rush 4	75.2%	2	5 DB	65%	11	Avg Box (Off)	6.38	6
Runs, second-long	29%	18	Pers: 3+ WR	57%	19	Rush 5	14.8%	31	6+ DB	7%	19	Avg Box (Def)	6.24	19
Runs, power sit.	72%	1	Pers: 4+ WR	0%	26	Rush 6+	7.9%	10	CB by Sides	72%	23	Offensive Pace	29.42	11
Runs, behind 2H	24%	21	Pers: 2+ TE/6+ OL	41%	7	Sacks by LB	0.0%	32	DB Blitz	14%	6	Defensive Pace	30.00	12
Pass, ahead 2H	42%	27	Shotgun/Pistol	58%	19	Sacks by DB	17.5%	2	Hole in Zone	7%	8	Go for it on 4th	1.09	12

The addition of Jeremy Hill led to a more run-oriented Bengals offense overall, and their rank went up from 2013 in each of the run/pass ratio categories in the Strategic Tendencies table. ☙ Here's a fun, probably arbitrary split from 2014: the Bengals offense went from 21st in the league at home to ninth on the road, but the defense went from 12th at home to 21st on the road. ☙ Another split that smells like a fluke: Andy Dalton led the league with 11.4 average yards against DB blitzes after being near the bottom of the league with 4.1 yards in 2013 and near league average with 6.8 yards in 2012. ☙ The Bengals used a lot more of just four defensive backs compared to 2013, when they led the league in frequency of nickel (69 percent) and were dead last in using four defensive backs (25 percent). ☙ Cincinnati's "CB by Sides" number requires a bit of clarification. The Bengals were low in this metric because starting cornerback Leon Hall moved into the slot in three-wide sets and thus played all over the field. However, with three cornerbacks on the field, the Bengals tended to strictly use Terence Newman on the defensive left and Adam Jones on the defensive right. ☙ In the red zone, Cincinnati's defense was the best in the league against the pass but ranked 28th against the run.

Passing

Player	DYAR	DVOA	Plays	NtYds	Avg	YAC	C%	TD	Int
A.Dalton	237	-3.7%	502	3284	6.5	5.6	64.2%	19	17
J.Campbell*	-74	-64.4%	20	69	3.5	5.2	57.9%	0	0

Rushing

Player	DYAR	DVOA	Plays	Yds	Avg	TD	Fum	Suc
J.Hill	204	12.6%	222	1127	5.1	9	4	54%
G.Bernard	3	-8.1%	168	680	4.0	5	0	39%
A.Dalton	26	-2.9%	46	181	3.9	4	2	-
C.Peerman	-32	-52.9%	15	43	2.9	0	1	33%
R.Burkhead	-7	-34.9%	9	27	3.0	1	0	22%
M.Sanu	24	28.3%	7	51	7.3	0	0	-

Receiving

Player	DYAR	DVOA	Plays	Ctch	Yds	Y/C	YAC	TD	C%
A.J.Green	158	4.1%	116	69	1041	15.1	4.5	6	59%
M.Sanu	99	0.1%	98	56	790	14.1	5.8	5	57%
B.Tate	42	8.5%	26	17	193	11.4	4.2	1	65%
J.Wright	-27	-34.6%	16	5	91	18.2	7.2	0	31%
D.Sanzenbacher	-23	-31.7%	15	9	105	11.7	4.8	0	60%
G.Little*	-11	-24.9%	12	6	69	11.5	5.5	0	50%
D.Moore	-57	-39.4%	27	12	115	9.6	3.3	0	57%
J.Gresham*	-73	-21.9%	79	62	460	7.4	4.2	5	78%
R.Hewitt	-18	-27.2%	15	10	86	8.6	5.7	0	67%
K.Brock	-10	-33.1%	6	5	21	4.2	2.0	0	83%
G.Bernard	48	0.8%	59	43	349	8.1	8.4	2	73%
J.Hill	17	-3.7%	32	27	217	8.0	8.3	0	84%
R.Burkhead	3	-7.7%	10	7	49	7.0	5.6	0	70%

Offensive Line

Player	Pos	Age	GS	Snaps	Pen	Sk	Pass	Run	Player	Pos	Age	GS	Snaps	Pen	Sk	Pass	Run
Clint Boling	LG	26	16/16	1062	4	2.5	17.5	2.0	Andre Smith	RT	28	9/9	482	7	4.0	7.0	1.0
Russell Bodine	C	23	16/16	1061	5	3.0	8.8	8.5	Mike Pollak*	RG	30	14/6	442	0	0.0	0.3	1.0
Andrew Whitworth	LT	34	16/16	1029	5	0.5	7.5	4.0	Marshall Newhouse*	OT	30	14/6	442	4	2.0	13.0	2.0
Kevin Zeitler	RG	25	12/12	736	2	0.0	3.5	3.5	Eric Winston	OT	32	4/2	176	2	0.0	4.0	1.0

Year	Yards	ALY	Rk	Power	Rk	Stuff	Rk	2nd Lev	Rk	Open Field	Rk	Sacks	ASR	Rk	Short	Long	F-Start	Cont.
2012	4.17	4.15	11	69%	5	17%	9	0.91	31	0.90	10	46	8.3%	28	9	26	16	35
2013	3.70	4.03	11	63%	19	18%	9	0.96	26	0.37	30	29	5.2%	3	11	8	17	32
2014	4.53	4.03	11	68%	9	15%	3	1.16	16	1.04	3	23	4.6%	5	9	7	18	24
2014 ALY by direction:		Left End 3.88 (16)			Left Tackle 3.46 (23)			Mid/Guard 3.99 (17)				Right Tackle 4.96 (2)				Right End 3.73 (16)		

Andrew Whitworth had an exceptional season at left tackle, allowing a mere half-sack all year. One of the team's unquestioned leaders, Big Whit was instrumental in keeping together a unit plagued by injury and breaking in a new center. That was rookie Russell Bodine, who played virtually every snap, giving the line a stable workhorse in the middle. The quality of those snaps were *comme ci, comme ca*. Bodine's scouting report emphasized his physical strength while knocking his football smarts. The reality of his rookie season showed his ability to make calls and adjust to enemy blitzing as a pleasant surprise, while he was often overpowered at the point of attack. Improvement in the run game is mandatory.

The guard play was quality, with Clint Boling re-signing after a sturdy season and Kevin Zeitler excelling after recovery from leg injuries. At right tackle, Andre Smith was effective, particularly in run blocking; his midseason triceps injury left the Bengals in dire straits. Replacement Marshall Newhouse was godawful, to the point Eric Winston was called out of his office at the NFL Players Association to don stripes as an emergency starter through the playoff loss. That lack of depth, plus the fact both Whitworth and Smith are in the final years of their contracts, led the Bengals to double-dip at tackle in the draft. Cedric Ogbuehi would have been a top-ten pick had he not torn a knee ligament in Texas A&M's bowl game. Cincy pounced at 21, willing to slow walk the huge but nimble athlete's recovery. Oregon's Jake Fisher was added in the second round, and can serve as a highly skilled backup at tackle or guard. Both rookies will be molded by Paul Alexander, one of the most respected offensive line coaches in the league. Neither Ogbuehi nor Fisher are AFC North-style mashers, but Alexander's motto is give him the feet and he'll deal with the rest. Meanwhile, look for plenty of six-lineman sets in southern Ohio this season, a tactic the Bengals only used on 3.2 percent of plays (roughly the NFL average) last year.

Defensive Front Seven

Defensive Line	Age	Pos	G	Snaps	Plays	TmPct	Rk	Stop	Dfts	BTkl	Runs	St%	Rk	RuYd	Rk	Sack	Hit	Hur	Dsrpt
						Overall						**vs. Run**					**Pass Rush**		
Geno Atkins	27	DT	16	740	34	3.9%	65	29	12	2	26	88%	12	0.9	7	3.0	6	15.5	1
Domata Peko	31	DT	16	685	46	5.3%	35	33	8	0	43	72%	71	2.6	62	1.0	0	0.5	0
Devon Still	26	DT	12	231	19	2.9%	--	10	0	1	18	50%	--	4.0	--	0.0	0	0.0	0
Brandon Thompson	26	DT	11	227	21	3.5%	--	17	1	1	19	79%	--	2.7	--	1.0	0	2.0	0
Pat Sims	30	DT	16	420	26	3.1%	--	18	2	1	24	67%	--	2.7	--	0.0	1	3.0	1

Edge Rushers	Age	Pos	G	Snaps	Plays	TmPct	Rk	Stop	Dfts	BTkl	Runs	St%	Rk	RuYd	Rk	Sack	Hit	Hur	Dsrpt
						Overall						**vs. Run**					**Pass Rush**		
Carlos Dunlap	26	DE	16	943	70	8.1%	9	53	27	3	46	70%	61	2.9	56	8.0	19	26.0	3
Wallace Gilberry	31	DE	16	826	50	5.8%	30	36	10	5	42	69%	65	2.7	50	1.5	13	17.5	2
Robert Geathers	32	DE	16	592	24	2.8%	83	14	4	1	16	63%	76	3.0	62	1.0	4	9.0	2
Michael Johnson	28	DE	14	629	27	3.5%	70	24	9	3	18	100%	1	0.6	2	4.0	8	9.5	0

Linebackers	Age	Pos	G	Snaps	Plays	TmPct	Rk	Stop	Dfts	BTkl	Sack	Hit	Hur	Runs	St%	Rk	RuYd	Rk	Tgts	Suc%	Rk	AdjYd	Rk	PD	Int
						Overall						**Pass Rush**			**vs. Run**					**vs. Pass**					
Vincent Rey	28	OLB	16	933	126	14.5%	28	53	16	10	0.0	1	2	73	45%	86	4.6	77	40	48%	43	6.9	43	3	0
Emmanuel Lamur	26	OLB	14	888	96	12.7%	44	52	15	4	0.0	2	1.5	46	52%	77	5.5	85	30	66%	5	6.0	27	6	2
Rey Maualuga	28	MLB	12	443	63	9.7%	65	41	9	11	0.0	0	0	39	69%	21	2.7	16	17	63%	8	3.6	2	4	1
Vontaze Burfict	25	OLB	5	217	31	11.4%	51	16	8	5	0.0	3	2	15	60%	57	3.0	24	8	39%	--	6.7	--	2	0
A.J. Hawk	31	ILB	16	837	91	10.8%	56	37	3	3	0.5	0	3.5	51	49%	83	4.3	74	30	50%	41	7.1	45	3	0

Year	Yards	ALY	Rk	Power	Rk	Stuff	Rk	2nd Level	Rk	Open Field	Rk	Sacks	ASR	Rk	Short	Long
2012	4.05	4.04	16	82%	32	18%	21	1.19	17	0.48	6	51	8.7%	2	13	22
2013	3.78	3.82	15	60%	10	15%	29	0.99	5	0.43	3	43	7.0%	14	18	16
2014	4.31	4.24	27	69%	23	17%	24	1.27	27	0.60	12	20	4.5%	31	7	8

2014 ALY by direction:	Left End 4.5 (29)	Left Tackle 4.81 (28)	Mid/Guard 4.19 (26)	Right Tackle 3.55 (9)	Right End 4.1 (19)

The success of the front seven, and to some extent the entire defense, rests on the health of two brittle knees. One belongs to linebacker/wildman Vontaze Burfict, who capped an injury-marred campaign by undergoing microfracture surgery in the offseason. He is a likely candidate to begin the season on the PUP list. Cincinnati desperately missed his physical play and emotional leadership in 2014. The other crucial joint underpins Geno Atkins, as the ACL he tore in 2013 continued to hamper him last year. While he played all 16 games, he was "just a guy," in the dismissive phraseology of defensive coordinator Paul Guenther. Pre-injury, Atkins was the best defensive tackle in football, but his dominance was keyed by puma-like quickness and incredible lower-body leverage. If that is permanently diminished, Cincy's defense is, too.

Only Oakland had a worse adjusted sack rate than the Bengals. Can the return of an end with but 7.5 sacks in the last two years change that? Michael Johnson, with his huge wingspan and excellent run defense, returns from a one-year exile in the wilderness (a.k.a. Tampa Bay). Johnson's departure left rotation players such as Wallace Gilberry in roles too large for their talents, and the Bengals hope now tumblers can click in proper sequence. Johnson reunites with Carlos Dunlap, who had an excellent season without his fellow rush end. Gilberry and promising second-year end Will Clarke will see plenty of action, while injury-prone third-year end Margus Hunt is at a career crossroads. At tackle, Domata Peko is on his last legs alongside Atkins. Run-stuffers Brandon Thompson and another former Bengal returning home, Pat Sims, figure to take plenty of Peko's playing time. Fourth-rounder Marcus Hardison (Arizona State) can back up at end or tackle.

Cincinnati native A.J. Hawk comes over from Green Bay to augment the linebackers, and depending on Burfict's prognosis, he may see more of the field than the Bengals would prefer. This position group was riddled by injury in 2014, and in response Guenther has declared that every linebacker will practice at all three spots. The middle still is held down by Rey Maualuga, who was strong against the run and whose absence was keenly felt when hurt. After a rocky start to his career in stripes, Maualuga has emerged as a key veteran, and played some of his best football last year after returning from injury. Youngsters Vinny Rey and Emmanuel Lamur struggled early but improved as the year progressed. Both will be pressed by rookie Paul Dawson, a tackling machine out of TCU who drew comparisons to Burfict for his on-field omnipresence and off-field character issues. If he comes anywhere close to the Tazmanian Devil, the Bengals will be happy.

Defensive Secondary

Secondary	Age	Pos	G	Snaps	Plays	Overall TmPct	Rk	Stop	Dfts	BTkl	vs. Run Runs	St%	Rk	RuYd	Rk	vs. Pass Tgts	Tgt%	Rk	Dist	Suc%	Rk	AdjYd	Rk	PD	Int
George Iloka	25	SS	16	1115	83	9.6%	45	24	11	7	35	31%	52	7.0	40	26	5.8%	14	18.0	84%	1	3.3	2	9	3
Reggie Nelson	32	FS	16	1097	105	12.1%	21	42	20	7	40	43%	34	6.1	28	45	10.4%	51	14.5	62%	13	5.4	12	15	4
Leon Hall	31	CB	15	910	75	9.2%	28	28	11	4	22	41%	37	4.8	13	68	19.0%	10	12.0	49%	44	9.5	67	8	1
Terence Newman*	37	CB	13	865	85	12.1%	2	40	16	6	19	58%	15	5.3	22	89	26.2%	59	11.7	52%	32	7.0	19	13	1
Adam Jones	32	CB	16	776	74	8.5%	38	28	14	7	15	40%	38	6.0	34	76	24.9%	49	10.6	55%	22	6.1	9	10	3
Dre Kirkpatrick	26	CB	16	244	21	2.4%	--	11	4	2	2	0%	--	22.5	--	29	30.3%	--	15.4	66%	--	8.0	--	7	3

Year	Pass D Rank	vs. #1 WR	Rk	vs. #2 WR	Rk	vs. Other WR	Rk	vs. TE	Rk	vs. RB	Rk
2012	9	-12.3%	9	7.3%	22	9.5%	24	-3.9%	12	-8.4%	10
2013	4	-21.9%	3	-27.6%	3	-19.6%	6	-11.7%	9	8.2%	23
2014	7	-28.9%	1	-32.8%	3	-24.4%	2	-20.4%	4	26.6%	29

The fact the Bengals finished seventh in pass defense DVOA despite their inability to mount a pass rush gives some idea of how superbly the defensive backs played. The unit finished in the top three against all three groups of wide receivers that we track. Teams avoided the boundary against a deep set of cornerbacks. 33 percent of passes were charted as targeting the middle of the field, a figure that no other defense had above 27 percent. The Bengals ranked fifth in DVOA on those middle passes, and all that funneling between the hashmarks helped Cincy rank first in DVOA against short passes (less than 16 yards through the air).

Despite the success, the secondary is in transition. Last year's top draft choice, Darqueze Dennard, scarcely played, even after Marvin Lewis called him the best rookie corner he had ever seen in training camp. With Terence Newman gone and both Leon Hall and Adam Jones over 30, the future belongs to Double-D and Dre Kirkpatrick, who began to live up to his first-round pedigree late last season. Kirkpatrick has shown a nose for the football—he has six interceptions (including a pick-six against Denver that put the Bengals in the playoffs) over the last two seasons in just 546 snaps.

Cincy was equally good at safety, where George Iloka had the league's best adjusted success rate against the pass. Reggie Nelson remains solid, and special-teams ace Shawn Williams is pushing for playing time. Fourth-round rookie Josh Shaw from USC can swing between corner and safety and should crack the roster through versatility. Both Iloka and Nelson are free agents-to-be, so the 2016 Bengals secondary could look far different than the one that begins this season.

Special Teams

Year	DVOA	Rank	FG/XP	Rank	Net Kick	Rank	Kick Ret	Rank	Net Punt	Rank	Punt Ret	Rank	Hidden	Rank
2012	6.1%	2	8.2	4	9.2	4	0.1	16	1.6	13	11.7	3	-4.8	24
2013	0.9%	14	-0.5	19	3.5	10	0.0	13	-2.4	23	4.1	10	-9.4	28
2014	0.4%	14	-6.2	30	10.4	1	-5.5	28	9.9	7	-6.6	30	-10.9	29

Other than an early-season stretch when kicker Mike Nugent went sideways (missing three field goals in one game against Atlanta and the infamous shank at the end of overtime against Carolina), this was a potent unit overall. Punter Kevin Huber had an excellent comeback season after having his jaw broken late in 2013. The coverage teams were very good, led by Cedric Peerman with 14 tackles. And Adam Jones topped the NFL with an estimated 9.3 points worth of field position on kickoff returns while also having an excellent year returning punts. Unfortunately, Brandon Tate was worth minus-5.1 points of value on his kickoff returns, cancelling out a lot of Jones' positive value. Mario Alford, a pocket-sized speedster drafted in the seventh round out of West Virginia, will be given every opportunity to seize the secondary returner role from Tate.

Cleveland Browns

2014 Record: 7-9	**Total DVOA:** -6.7% (23rd)	**2015 Mean Projection:** 6.4 wins	**On the Clock (0-4):** 25%
Pythagorean Wins: 6.9 (25th)	**Offense:** -10.2% (24th)	**Postseason Odds:** 17.1%	**Mediocrity (5-7):** 42%
Snap-Weighted Age: 26.4 (25th)	**Defense:** -3.0% (11th)	**Super Bowl Odds:** 1.5%	**Playoff Contender (8-10):** 27%
Average Opponent: -2.6% (25th)	**Special Teams:** 0.4% (14th)	**Proj. Avg. Opponent:** 2.9% (7th)	**Super Bowl Contender (11+):** 6%

2014: Mike Pettine and Kyle Shanahan somehow will the Browns to 7-9.

2015: There's a tougher schedule and no hope at quarterback, setting up another year of disappointment at the Factory of Sadness.

Winning seven games is an unremarkable season for most franchises. A 7-9 season is just another forgettable year. It doesn't (normally) result in a spot in the playoffs and it still wasn't bad enough to result in a high draft pick.

The Browns are not most franchises.

The Browns have won seven or more games just four times since 2000. Not once during the other 10 seasons did they even manage to win six games. Winning seven games in 2014 was definitely a remarkable season for the franchise.

Those seven victories came with a first-time head coach. Mike Pettine's first year in charge should be considered a positive and a building block for a team that has been perennially rebuilding since 2007. Yet, it doesn't feel like it. That is because the team once again is lacking in continuity. A defense that ranked 11th in DVOA last year made intelligent additions without revamping its identity, but the offense is again entering a major overhaul.

Kyle Shanahan was hired to take over the offense in February of 2014, fewer than 12 months after Rob Chudzinski was brought in to correct the career of Brandon Weeden. Shanahan inherited Brian Hoyer as his starter, but that wasn't what ultimately led to his departure after the 2014 season. Instead, Shanahan left because the Browns' front office was putting pressure on him to start Johnny Manziel. Shanahan didn't want Manziel initially and didn't believe he could win with him moving forward, so he resigned. Ironically, even though Shanahan departed for Atlanta, Manziel still isn't expected to start.

Shanahan may have only been in Cleveland for one season, but he was a huge reason for the team's success. That may seem extreme to say about an offensive coordinator, but offensive coordinators are very important when you don't have high quality quarterback play. The Browns haven't had high quality quarterback play in a very long time, and last season was another disappointing one at the position. Hoyer, Manziel, and Connor Shaw all started games. The veteran Hoyer started every single game that the Browns won before getting benched in Week 14, but those victories were the only reason he kept his job as long as he did.

Even though the Browns were winning games, they were doing so in spite of their quarterback. Hoyer finished the season 24th in DYAR and 25th in DVOA amongst quarterbacks. He completed just 55.7 percent of his passes. Frankly, even those inferior numbers flatter him. Shanahan set his offense up in such a way that Hoyer's assignments were much easier than they typically are for starting quarterbacks in the NFL. Using the same approach that he used with Robert Griffin III during his successful rookie season, Shanahan set up conditions that allowed Hoyer to avoid making difficult reads or mitigating pressure in the pocket. Despite this, Hoyer's decision-making proved to be terrible both inside and outside of the pocket.

Decision-making is hugely important in any NFL offense, but Shanahan was able to minimize the impact of Hoyer's by creatively and aggressively going in search of big plays. Hoyer threw 22 percent of his passes further than 15 yards downfield, which ranked fifth out of 37 qualifying quarterbacks. Shanahan understood the strengths of his offense, though. He wasn't asking Hoyer to push the ball downfield into tight windows. Instead, he committed to running the ball and then built the passing game by moving the pocket and using hard play fakes. The Browns went from running on 41 percent of first downs in 2013 to 58 percent last year. They also ran the ball more than twice as often while losing in the second half of games. Shanahan's scheme worked. It consistently allowed receivers to find wide-open space down the field. Yet, Hoyer's accuracy couldn't even make those plays. He repeatedly underthrew, overthrew, and just plain missed receivers on throws that every NFL passer should expect to make.

Shanahan didn't draft or develop Hoyer, so it's unfair to blame him for the quarterback's inability to execute. Instead, Shanahan needs to be commended for getting the most out of a very limited set of personnel.

A lack of execution from the quarterback position will typically torpedo the overall effectiveness of an offense on its own. Despite Hoyer's incompetence, Shanahan's unit ranked 24th in DVOA last year. A below-average ranking is impressive considering how bad the quarterback play was, but it becomes even more impressive when you consider the rest of the offense. Two of the Browns' three best offensive players combined to play in just 10 games last year, and they never stepped on the field together. Josh Gordon was suspended to start the season, and Alex Mack broke his leg in Week 6.

Mack is perhaps the best center in the NFL, and his loss proved to be massive. He was an integral part of the Browns' zone-blocking scheme early on. Despite his obvious talent and value, his loss impacted the Browns offense as a whole in an unforeseen way. At the time he was injured, the Browns

2015 Browns Schedule

Week	Opp.	Week	Opp.	Week	Opp.
1	at NYJ	7	at STL	13	CIN
2	TEN	8	ARI	14	SF
3	OAK	9	at CIN (Thu.)	15	at SEA
4	at SD	10	at PIT	16	at KC
5	at BAL	11	BYE	17	PIT
6	DEN	12	BAL (Mon.)		

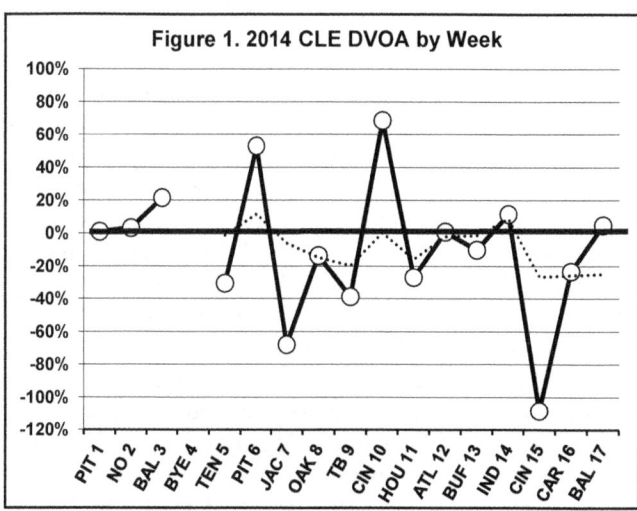

Figure 1. 2014 CLE DVOA by Week

ranked a surprising fourth in the league in offensive DVOA (19.9%), broken down into fifth in passing (44.3%) and eighth in rushing (3.3%). After his injury, those ranks fell to 30th overall (-24.9%), 26th in passing (-12.1%) and 31st in rushing (-25.7%). Particularly specific to Mack's performance, Cleveland's adjusted line yards on runs up the middle or behind the guards fell from 3.82 in Weeks 1-6 to 3.35 in Weeks 7-17. Mack helped the Browns pile up 732 rushing yards in five games—42 percent of their rushing yards in 31 percent of their games.

Mack will be back, but Gordon and Shanahan will not, and the Browns are entering the season with John DeFilippo as their offensive coordinator. DeFilippo was the Oakland Raiders' quarterback coach last season. He has never been an offensive coordinator before, but presented himself as adaptable, fitting himself to the team instead of the other way around. "We're not going to just scrap something just because I'm here," he told Andrew Gribble in an interview with the team's website. "I don't have that type of ego. If something's good that our players do well and they know, we're going to keep doing it. One of the things Mike and I talked about in our interview was if there's something these guys are familiar with in terms of a name, I don't need to change the name just because I see it as, for example, the play's called 'smash' and they call it 'hammer.' I can learn. Let one guy learn the new tag for it."

Even though DeFilippo's words should be seen as a positive for Manziel, they have been drowned out by negatives for the young passer in recent months. After Shanahan departed and was replaced, Manziel entered rehab. Once that happened, reports surfaced that suggested Pettine was in agreement with his departed offensive coordinator that it was time to move on from Manziel. While Pettine refuted those reports, his team's actions this offseason suggest that there may be some truth to them. Not only did the Browns sign Josh McCown as a free agent, but Pettine also wasted no time at OTAs before pegging McCown as the favorite to start in 2015. "If you're taking the starters' reps, I guess that would be fair to say... we're not going to start talking competition," he said to Mary Kay Cabot of the *Cleveland Plain Dealer*. "Josh, like I said, will more than likely be the starter going into camp and in the foreseeable future I don't see that changing."

Adding a veteran option makes sense because Manziel has a potent combination of youth, inexperience and unrefined technique. However, immediately making that player the favorite to start is more damning. Pettine is giving McCown the first crack at the starting job because of what he did with the Chicago Bears two seasons ago. "We just look back to when he was in Chicago, when he had a pretty good supporting cast around him, and he was able to be more than functional," Pettine said in a radio interview on *The Bull and the Fox* show on 92.3 The Fan. "He had a very successful year. When you build the team right, it minimizes the importance of the quarterback." That stretch of positive production for McCown has been a blip in his career rather than the norm. His statistical production also didn't reflect his actual performances during that stretch, as McCown benefited from the perfect storm of poor defensive play from opponents and outstanding play from his supporting cast.

Tampa Bay signed McCown ahead of last season to be their starter using a similar line of thinking. He wilted in that role, and the Buccaneers finished dead last in offensive DVOA. McCown was 36th in DYAR and 37th in DVOA amongst quarterbacks, while playing behind an offensive line that put him under constant pressure. If the 35-year-old quarterback had a track record on which we could rely, his poor play last season would be easier to overlook, but that's not the case. As recently as 2010, he was unable to find a job in the league. Over his 13-year career, he has started just 49 games out of a possible 208. He is a career backup and not a significant upgrade over Hoyer. Pettine and general manager Ray Farmer are reluctantly relying on McCown—reports circled this offseason that they were seeking to acquire Sam Bradford, then Marcus Mariota. That aggressiveness and reluctance to rely on Manziel is likely born out of the need to win in 2015.

If the Browns had limped to three or four wins during Pettine and Farmer's first season, expectations for this year would likely be lower than they are. After winning seven games last season, winning fewer this season will be more easily framed as a step backwards. Jimmy Haslam's willingness to move on from Rob Chudzinski after one season looms as a warning to his current head coach. To keep the status quo, the Browns will likely need to replicate much of what they did last season. In 2014, the Browns relied on their defense to carry the offense. That unit was good overall, but had both major strengths and major weaknesses. The Browns ranked 11th by DVOA, but second against the pass and 31st against the run.

Pettine and Farmar have been aggressive in trying to rectify their leaky run defense this offseason. Selecting Danny Shelton in the first round of the draft is expected to have a huge impact. The nose tackle was a polarizing prospect out of Washington. He was viewed as an inconsistent performer whose reputation was built on his size and athleticism rather than his performances or ability. Pettine vehemently refuted that idea in an interview with the team website, stating "[Combine performance is] not something we were concerned with, especially after you watch the film. He doesn't play to that speed and the college coaches who have gone against him have made the comment they're glad he's gone. He's gone against elite competition and played well. I think he's an example of you believe the tape more than you believe the stopwatch or tape measure." Browns defensive line coach Anthony Weaver echoed Pettine's excitement, stating "He's had success throughout college, and I could see that easily translating to our level."

The Browns are talking about Shelton as a three-down defensive tackle, but just helping them to become competent against the run in 2015 would go a huge way to improving the unit as a whole. He won't be alone in his efforts, as the Browns also added veteran free agent Randy Starks to play defensive end and drafted the versatile Xavier Cooper in the third round. Starks should have more value than Cooper, as the rookie projects to be more of a disruptive pass-rusher than a stout run defender. The Browns also have a deep, versatile secondary that should sustain its effectiveness despite swapping out Buster Skrine for Tramon Williams. Yet, if they can't improve against the run and the offensive performance matches what looks set on paper, then it won't matter how talented the defensive backs are. Cleveland also goes from one of the league's ten easiest schedules to a schedule projected to be one of the ten most difficult. Even going 7-9 again will be a massive task.

So here are the 2015 Cleveland Browns. A team that has made plenty of alterations without making significant change. Maybe 2015 will be different, but as is often said, insanity is doing the same thing over and over again while expecting different results. At this point, it's hard to feel sane predicting anything positive for this franchise.

Cian Fahey

2014 Browns Stats by Week

Wk	vs.	W-L	PF	PA	YDF	YDA	TO	Total	Off	Def	ST
1	at PIT	L	27	30	389	503	1	1%	21%	16%	-4%
2	NO	W	26	24	324	397	2	3%	11%	14%	6%
3	BAL	L	21	23	375	377	1	21%	45%	7%	-17%
4	BYE										
5	at TEN	W	29	28	460	410	-1	-31%	13%	46%	2%
6	PIT	W	31	10	368	359	0	53%	17%	-26%	10%
7	at JAC	L	6	24	266	336	0	-68%	-66%	-6%	-8%
8	OAK	W	23	13	306	387	3	-14%	-9%	9%	5%
9	TB	W	22	17	330	365	0	-39%	-33%	18%	13%
10	at CIN	W	24	3	368	165	3	69%	14%	-68%	-12%
11	HOU	L	7	23	375	424	-1	-27%	-3%	19%	-5%
12	at ATL	W	26	24	475	315	-1	1%	-15%	-12%	3%
13	at BUF	L	10	26	315	287	-1	-10%	-21%	-19%	-9%
14	IND	L	24	25	248	362	2	12%	-30%	-27%	15%
15	CIN	L	0	30	107	347	-1	-109%	-110%	-4%	-3%
16	at CAR	L	13	17	228	404	1	-23%	-29%	-3%	3%
17	at BAL	L	10	20	259	419	-2	5%	-12%	-8%	9%

Trends and Splits

	Offense	Rank	Defense	Rank
Total DVOA	-10.2%	24	-3.0%	11
Unadjusted VOA	-8.6%	23	-3.8%	9
Weighted Trend	-20.7%	28	-9.8%	8
Variance	13.7%	32	6.6%	18
Average Opponent	2.0%	28	-2.0%	25
Passing	5.3%	22	-10.7%	2
Rushing	-15.4%	26	5.2%	31
First Down	-15.0%	28	6.2%	24
Second Down	6.6%	12	-4.7%	11
Third Down	-28.5%	29	-17.0%	7
First Half	-18.2%	29	-1.5%	12
Second Half	-2.2%	18	-4.7%	10
Red Zone	-16.1%	24	-13.4%	8
Late and Close	-2.8%	21	-4.0%	13

Five-Year Performance

Year	W-L	Pyth W	Est W	PF	PA	TO	Total	Rk	Off	Rk	Def	Rk	ST	Rk	Off AGL	Rk	Def AGL	Rk	Off Age	Rk	Def Age	Rk	ST Age	Rk
2010	5-11	6.1	6.7	271	332	-1	-4.0%	20	-5.0%	22	1.7%	18	2.7%	10	42.6	31	51.8	32	27.7	13	27.7	9	27.4	3
2011	4-12	5.0	5.5	218	307	+1	-14.2%	25	-11.2%	25	4.2%	22	1.3%	10	45.5	27	26.3	15	26.1	29	26.6	24	26.1	23
2012	5-11	6.1	6.2	302	368	+3	-13.5%	24	-15.2%	27	4.5%	22	6.1%	2	26.4	13	57.0	29	25.7	30	26.1	26	25.2	30
2013	4-12	5.5	4.4	308	406	-8	-21.8%	28	-14.4%	26	8.2%	24	0.9%	14	24.8	9	16.3	8	26.6	21	25.4	30	24.9	31
2014	7-9	6.9	7.2	299	337	+6	-6.7%	23	-10.2%	24	-3.0%	11	0.4%	14	30.5	16	36.6	14	26.6	18	26.4	22	25.8	23

2014 Performance Based on Most Common Personnel Groups

	CLE Offense					CLE Offense vs. Opponents						CLE Defense					CLE Defense vs. Opponents		
Pers	Freq	Yds	DVOA	Run%		Pers	Freq	Yds	DVOA	Run%		Pers	Freq	Yds	DVOA		Pers	Freq	Yds	DVOA
11	38%	5.1	-8.6%	21%		Base	61%	5.2	-4.8%	60%		Base	35%	5.3	1.4%		11	51%	5.3	-8.7%
12	28%	5.4	5.1%	57%		Nickel	29%	4.9	-19.8%	22%		Nickel	46%	5.4	-5.4%		12	24%	5.6	2.9%
21	27%	5.2	-4.9%	59%		Dime+	10%	6.6	27.8%	13%		Dime+	16%	6.0	-7.8%		21	10%	6.2	6.4%
13	3%	8.2	29.1%	76%		Goal Line	1%	0.7	22.3%	86%		Goal Line	1%	1.0	-0.6%		22	4%	3.7	-19.0%
22	2%	0.7	-98.9%	53%								Big	2%	5.7	-6.3%		10	3%	7.7	38.7%

Strategic Tendencies

Run/Pass		Rk	Formation		Rk	Pass Rush		Rk	Secondary		Rk	Strategy		Rk
Runs, first half	45%	4	Form: Single Back	64%	29	Rush 3	9.0%	8	4 DB	24%	20	Play action	31%	2
Runs, first down	58%	3	Form: Empty Back	4%	17	Rush 4	63.0%	19	5 DB	49%	23	Avg Box (Off)	6.58	2
Runs, second-long	37%	6	Pers: 3+ WR	39%	30	Rush 5	21.8%	19	6+ DB	26%	10	Avg Box (Def)	6.24	18
Runs, power sit.	66%	5	Pers: 4+ WR	0%	23	Rush 6+	6.1%	19	CB by Sides	53%	32	Offensive Pace	27.85	3
Runs, behind 2H	35%	4	Pers: 2+ TE/6+ OL	35%	10	Sacks by LB	67.2%	3	DB Blitz	13%	10	Defensive Pace	28.31	3
Pass, ahead 2H	41%	29	Shotgun/Pistol	41%	31	Sacks by DB	8.6%	11	Hole in Zone	4%	25	Go for it on 4th	1.23	8

Cleveland's low shotgun rate in 2014 is even lower if you only look at Brian Hoyer's plays. Hoyer only used shotgun or pistol on 37 percent of plays; Johnny Manziel was at 76 percent and Connor Shaw 53 percent. And Cleveland (5.1 yards in shotgun/pistol, 5.2 without) was the only offense in the league to average more yards with the quarterback under center. ☻ The Browns threw a league-low 10 percent of passes to running backs. Part of the reason: the Browns went "max protect" on 18 percent of pass plays, the highest rate in the league. ☻ The Browns were excellent at stopping short passes (up to 15 yards in the air). They had the best DVOA in the league against passes in the short middle area of the field and were in the top ten against both short left and short right passes. ☻ Cleveland's defense ranked fifth against the pass in the red zone, but 23rd against the run. Demonstrating the year-to-year variability of stats like this: the Browns had the league's worst DVOA against red zone passes in 2013.

Passing

Player	DYAR	DVOA	Plays	NtYds	Avg	YAC	C%	TD	Int
B.Hoyer*	166	-5.3%	465	3170	6.8	5.6	55.7%	12	12
J.Manziel	-144	-73.2%	38	149	3.9	4.7	51.4%	0	2
C.Shaw	-68	-44.2%	33	148	4.5	8.4	50.0%	0	1
J.McCown	-665	-41.9%	360	1971	5.5	4.0	57.0%	11	14

Rushing

Player	DYAR	DVOA	Plays	Yds	Avg	TD	Fum	Suc
T.West	21	-5.7%	171	673	3.9	4	1	47%
I.Crowell	30	-3.6%	148	609	4.1	8	3	44%
B.Tate*	-39	-18.0%	106	333	3.1	4	0	36%
B.Hoyer*	-59	-64.8%	19	37	1.9	0	1	-
J.Manziel	-9	-36.7%	9	29	3.2	1	0	-
J.McCown	47	35.9%	22	127	5.8	3	0	-

Receiving

Player	DYAR	DVOA	Plays	Ctch	Yds	Y/C	YAC	TD	C%
A.Hawkins	11	-11.4%	113	64	829	13.0	6.4	2	57%
T.Gabriel	21	-9.0%	74	38	633	16.7	7.3	1	51%
M.Austin*	120	10.1%	72	47	568	12.1	4.3	2	65%
J.Gordon	-35	-22.7%	47	24	303	12.6	6.7	0	51%
T.Benjamin	9	-10.2%	46	18	314	17.4	2.4	3	39%
D.Bowe	62	-4.4%	95	60	754	12.6	3.8	0	63%
B.Hartline	77	2.6%	63	39	485	12.4	3.5	2	62%
J.Cameron*	-34	-17.5%	48	24	424	17.7	7.0	2	50%
J.Dray	26	6.6%	28	17	242	14.2	6.0	1	61%
G.Barnidge	10	-0.3%	25	13	156	12.0	3.2	0	52%
R.Housler	8	0.2%	17	9	129	14.3	9.3	0	53%
C.Clay	2	-6.9%	84	58	605	10.4	4.4	3	69%
I.Crowell	8	-3.6%	14	9	87	9.7	7.6	0	64%
T.West	20	17.5%	13	11	64	5.8	4.8	1	85%
B.Tate*	-11	-32.4%	12	9	60	6.7	5.0	0	75%
R.Agnew*	-31	-76.7%	9	3	15	5.0	3.3	0	33%

Offensive Line

Player	Pos	Age	GS	Snaps	Pen	Sk	Pass	Run	Player	Pos	Age	GS	Snaps	Pen	Sk	Pass	Run
Joel Bitonio	LG	24	16/16	1050	5	0.0	8.5	4.0	Nick McDonald	C	31	8/7	469	1	3.0	6.0	6.0
John Greco	RG	30	16/16	1050	5	3.0	11.0	5.5	Alex Mack	C	30	5/5	297	0	0.0	0.0	2.0
Mitchell Schwartz	RT	26	16/16	1050	6	6.5	23.5	7.0	Ryan Seymour	C	25	11/3	169	2	1.0	1.5	4.0
Joe Thomas	LT	31	16/16	1050	10	4.5	15.0	2.5									

Year	Yards	ALY	Rk	Power	Rk	Stuff	Rk	2nd Lev	Rk	Open Field	Rk	Sacks	ASR	Rk	Short	Long	F-Start	Cont.
2012	3.79	4.03	20	53%	29	19%	16	1.08	23	0.40	31	36	6.0%	12	15	15	25	40
2013	3.53	3.83	18	70%	9	20%	18	0.95	28	0.36	31	49	7.5%	17	12	23	23	35
2014	3.79	3.63	25	61%	19	22%	31	1.13	19	0.60	22	31	6.0%	15	10	11	19	31
2014 ALY by direction:		Left End 4.3 (8)			Left Tackle 4.37 (5)			Mid/Guard 3.51 (29)				Right Tackle 3.77 (18)				Right End 2.55 (29)		

There is no doubt that the center of attention in Cleveland is the center position. As pointed out earlier in the chapter, Alex Mack's absence last year did more to highlight his importance to the team than a healthy season possibly could. Just 29 years old, Mack isn't close to the end of his prime. Yet, despite his obvious value and relative youth, the Browns spent a first-round pick on his possible replacement this year. Cameron Erving is versatile enough to play guard or even tackle in a desperate situation, but his true potential at this level will only be reached as a center. Mack can void his contract after this season, and considering his potential value on the open market, it would make little sense for him not to.

Erving's presence will allow the Browns to move on from Mack instead of investing big money into his future, but there are still 16 regular-season games and potential (albeit unlikely) playoff appearances to be made before that point. So for 2015, the Browns need to find a way to accommodate Erving in their starting lineup. The only logical starting spot for him is at right guard, where John Greco is a proven veteran who enjoyed a good season last year. Greco won't simply be replaced by Erving based on potential; Erving will need to force his way onto the top of the depth chart. The Browns aren't in any rush to start Erving because they have so many talented pieces up front. Greco is their worst starting lineman, but he's far from a bad football player.

Apart from the two centers, the Browns are set to carry continuity forward on their offensive line, where none of the other starters missed a snap last season. Joe Thomas continues to play to his reputation as the best offensive tackle in the NFL, while right tackle Mitchell Schwartz enjoyed an improved season in 2014 after a disappointing 2013. Left guard Joel Bitonio was overshadowed by Zack Martin during his rookie season last year, but he elevated the unit as a whole with his outstanding play. Bitonio was a college tackle who moved inside and showed athleticism harnessed by impressive technique and strength. He should be a staple of the offensive line alongside Thomas for many years to come.

Defensive Front Seven

Defensive Line	Age	Pos	G	Snaps	Plays	TmPct	Rk	Stop	Dfts	BTkl	Runs	St%	Rk	RuYd	Rk	Sack	Hit	Hur	Dsrpt
						Overall							vs. Run				Pass Rush		
Desmond Bryant	30	DE	15	733	50	6.0%	24	35	13	2	41	63%	89	2.1	44	5.0	6	9.5	1
Billy Winn	26	DE	13	501	32	4.4%	50	23	10	5	23	74%	67	1.8	28	0.0	2	3.5	1
Ahtyba Rubin*	29	DT	13	450	29	4.0%	62	18	2	1	27	59%	90	3.3	89	1.0	3	5.5	1
Ishmaa'ily Kitchen	27	DT	12	301	43	6.4%	--	28	3	2	42	67%	--	3.6	--	0.0	1	0.0	0
Sione Fua	27	DT	11	251	12	2.0%	--	10	0	0	12	83%	--	3.0	--	0.0	0	0.0	0
Randy Starks	32	DT	15	540	29	3.8%	70	24	12	2	19	89%	9	0.8	4	4.5	1	7.0	1

Edge Rushers	Age	Pos	G	Snaps	Plays	TmPct	Rk	Stop	Dfts	BTkl	Runs	St%	Rk	RuYd	Rk	Sack	Hit	Hur	Dsrpt
						Overall							vs. Run				Pass Rush		
Paul Kruger	29	OLB	16	899	54	6.1%	26	42	18	9	37	70%	58	2.7	51	10.5	9	20.5	2
Jabaal Sheard	26	OLB	16	676	47	5.3%	36	30	17	4	40	63%	76	3.4	69	2.0	4	13.5	2
Barkevious Mingo	25	OLB	15	667	42	5.0%	44	27	11	6	30	57%	80	4.1	77	2.0	7	14.5	2

Linebackers	Age	Pos	G	Snaps	Plays	TmPct	Rk	Stop	Dfts	BTkl	Sack	Hit	Hur	Runs	St%	Rk	RuYd	Rk	Tgts	Suc%	Rk	AdjYd	Rk	PD	Int
						Overall					Pass Rush				vs. Run					vs. Pass					
Karlos Dansby	34	ILB	12	814	95	14.2%	31	59	22	7	3.0	0	3	62	56%	68	5.0	82	22	70%	3	7.0	44	3	1
Christian Kirksey	23	ILB	16	684	77	8.7%	71	41	11	6	2.0	2	3	50	58%	65	4.1	70	20	46%	45	5.3	13	1	0
Craig Robertson	27	ILB	16	661	94	10.6%	58	55	17	5	0.0	3	4.5	70	63%	47	2.7	15	17	53%	26	7.5	51	2	2

Year	Yards	ALY	Rk	Power	Rk	Stuff	Rk	2nd Level	Rk	Open Field	Rk	Sacks	ASR	Rk	Short	Long
2012	4.36	4.31	25	77%	30	15%	31	1.20	20	0.68	14	38	6.3%	18	7	21
2013	3.94	3.83	16	79%	32	18%	15	0.97	2	0.65	18	40	6.5%	21	15	14
2014	4.45	4.36	29	58%	8	15%	29	1.32	28	0.67	14	31	6.1%	25	10	7

2014 ALY by direction:	Left End 4.14 (25)	Left Tackle 2.94 (6)	Mid/Guard 4.63 (32)	Right Tackle 4.86 (28)	Right End 3.77 (15)

An inability to stop the run was a major issue for the Browns last year, and extensive measures have been taken to correct it. Most significantly, the franchise invested a high first-round pick in nose tackle Danny Shelton out of the University of Washington. Shelton has drawn comparisons to Haloti Ngata and Dontari Poe because of his size and ability to play a huge number of snaps. However, he was a more polarizing prospect than Ngata and doesn't appear to have the same incredible physical talent as Poe.

The Browns also added free-agent Randy Starks, who should start at defensive end across from Desmond Bryant. He is a proven player with the bulk to hold up against offensive guards and the athleticism to penetrate past them when given the opportunity. With Starks, Bryant, and Shelton in the starting lineup, the Browns should expect to be much more resilient against the run than they were last season. Furthermore, the depth should be better in 2015 than it was in 2014. John Hughes and Phil Taylor were both quality run-stoppers two years ago before losing much of last season to knee injuries. Third-round pick Xavier Cooper (Washington State) will be competing with the duo for playing time. Cooper has a limited overall skill set, but his burst off the line makes him an intriguing pass-rushing option from the interior.

It's unfair to be too harsh on Barkevious Mingo for his struggles to this point of his career, but this season should be one of expectation rather than hope for the outside linebacker. Mingo's second season was disappointing, but he was dealing with a shoulder issue that eventually required surgery after the season finished. Mingo is the most important piece of the Browns' linebacker group. He is an outstanding athlete with the instincts to become a great pass rusher and run defender. If he can establish himself as a real threat off the edge, he will draw attention away from the defensive linemen in front of him, and from Paul Kruger across the field. That is presuming Kruger can withstand any potential challenge for his spot from second-round pick Nate Orchard. Orchard will need to prove he's not a one-year wonder after 18.5 sacks in his senior year at Utah; he had only six sacks in his other three seasons. SackSEER is also unimpressed with Orchard's combine numbers, and gave him a rating of 41.6 percent, suggesting that his transition to the NFL may take some time.

Karlos Dansby is the Browns' best linebacker. He missed four games last year, giving third-round rookie Christian Kirksey more opportunities to get on the field. Kirksey struggled to play to his potential, but that playing time should prove to be valuable as he attempts to take over more of Craig Robertson's snaps in 2015.

Defensive Secondary

						Overall					vs. Run					vs. Pass						
Secondary	Age	Pos	G	Snaps	Plays	TmPct	Rk	Stop	Dfts	BTkl	Runs	St%	Rk	RuYd	Rk	Tgts	Tgt%	Rk	Dist	Suc%	Rk	AdjYd	Rk	PD	Int
Donte Whitner	30	SS	16	1153	110	12.4%	17	40	18	12	60	42%	35	6.0	25	30	6.6%	22	9.4	52%	44	5.6	15	3	1
Buster Skrine*	26	CB	16	1129	84	9.4%	23	36	14	8	11	36%	41	8.6	58	116	26.5%	62	13.9	50%	41	7.6	32	15	4
Joe Haden	26	CB	15	1022	93	11.1%	5	34	13	7	19	32%	49	7.0	44	112	28.3%	65	15.6	51%	37	7.4	27	18	3
Tashaun Gipson	25	FS	11	771	60	9.8%	42	24	14	7	35	34%	47	7.2	46	16	5.4%	13	11.4	51%	47	7.4	37	7	6
Jim Leonhard*	33	SS	16	503	37	4.2%	--	11	5	4	15	27%	--	10.3	--	16	8.2%	--	9.5	49%	--	8.9	--	4	2
Justin Gilbert	24	CB	14	363	37	4.8%	--	17	8	4	3	67%	--	6.0	--	46	32.4%	--	13.6	54%	--	8.0	--	7	1
K'Waun Williams	24	CB	13	347	39	5.4%	--	22	11	2	9	67%	--	4.3	--	41	30.1%	--	11.4	64%	--	4.8	--	10	0
Tramon Williams	32	CB	16	1012	83	9.9%	18	27	12	7	17	35%	42	5.8	33	80	22.2%	27	10.9	48%	50	7.3	24	12	3

Year	Pass D Rank	vs. #1 WR	Rk	vs. #2 WR	Rk	vs. Other WR	Rk	vs. TE	Rk	vs. RB	Rk
2012	20	-2.9%	17	9.3%	24	10.3%	25	0.7%	20	-2.2%	15
2013	23	-17.8%	5	8.7%	20	2.9%	17	25.3%	31	20.7%	31
2014	2	-17.6%	6	-5.9%	13	-17.6%	5	-5.7%	15	-41.1%	1

Justin Gilbert didn't receive a vote of confidence from the coaching staff after his tough rookie season, as the Browns brought veteran Tramon Williams in to be the team's starter across from Joe Haden. Williams may be on the wrong side of 30 now, but he's still a quality cornerback. His aggressiveness and physicality will give the Browns a second cornerback capable of pressing receivers at the line of scrimmage effectively. Gilbert needs to develop a huge amount to earn his spot on the field. He isn't built to play in the slot, so if the Browns want to use him in the nickel, they'll need to decide about moving Williams or Haden inside.

Gilbert isn't assured of that third cornerback spot, though. Last year, he barely saw the field more often than undrafted free agent K'Waun Williams. Williams isn't as physically talented as Gilbert, but he showed off better ball skills and overall awareness to be a more reliable cover corner. Williams is also more comfortable in the slot, so he would be less limiting to the defense as the nickelback. Pierre Desir, a fourth-round pick last year, is also in position to challenge for that spot. He is arguably just as talented as Gilbert, but he also comes with the same concerns in terms of moving inside, and played even less as a rookie. Desir is comparable to Antonio Cromartie in how he plays as a boundary cornerback.

At the safety spots, the focus will be on how Tashaun Gipson returns from his torn ACL. Gipson was playing phenomenal football during what was turning into a breakout season in 2014. This wasn't a case of a defender masking inconsistent play with a bundle of interceptions: Gipson was disciplined and effective in coverage while also being a strong run defender. He may be unhappy with his contract situation entering the 2015 season—Gipson is playing the year on a restricted free-agent tender, and will hit the open market in 2016 if he doesn't get a rich extension—but he and Donte Whitner's combination on the back end will be crucial for the overall success of the team.

Special Teams

Year	DVOA	Rank	FG/XP	Rank	Net Kick	Rank	Kick Ret	Rank	Net Punt	Rank	Punt Ret	Rank	Hidden	Rank
2012	6.1%	2	8.2	4	9.2	4	0.1	16	1.6	13	11.7	3	-4.8	24
2013	0.9%	14	-0.5	19	3.5	10	0.0	13	-2.4	23	4.1	10	-9.4	28
2014	0.4%	14	-6.2	30	10.4	1	-5.5	28	9.9	7	-6.6	30	-10.9	29

Acquiring punter Andy Lee from the San Francisco 49ers is as risky a move as acquiring any punter can be. Lee was once an outstanding weapon for the 49ers, but his play significantly declined last season. That and a hefty contract ($2 million this season, rising steadily to over $4 million by 2018) motivated the 49ers to move on from the 32-year old. If the Browns don't mind his cap hit, Lee should still prove to be a valuable addition moving forward. Punters aren't particularly old at 32, and some rebound from last year's collapse is likely. The Browns waived Spencer Lanning after acquiring Lee, so he is assured of his spot on the roster.

With a new punter already in place, the Browns are trying out two new kickers in training camp to match with him. Neither Billy Cundiff nor Garrett Hartley (who replaced Cundiff after a knee injury) was retained after last season, leaving the spot up for grabs between second-year players Carey Spear and Travis Coons. Neither Spear nor Coons was drafted, and neither has appeared in a regular-season NFL game yet. Spear was cut by the Philadelphia Eagles after training camp last year, Coons by the Tennessee Titans. Coons punted and kicked at the University of Washington, but his longest field goal was just 48 yards. He will need to prove his accuracy against Spear, who has the more powerful leg. Actually, the Vanderbilt alum is just more powerful in every way; in Madden 15, he somehow ended up as the hardest-tackling kicker in video-game history with a "hit power" of 73, higher than Richard Sherman or Darnell Dockett.

Travis Benjamin should be a very dangerous punt returner, but he hasn't realized his ability in the NFL just yet. Over the past two years, he has fumbled the ball four times on just 37 returns. It doesn't matter how explosive and elusive you are if you have that kind of fumble ratio. Benjamin can also return kicks, but Marlon Moore and Justin Gilbert will be in contention for that role as well.

Dallas Cowboys

2014 Record: 12-4	Total DVOA: 13.7% (6th)	2015 Mean Projection: 8.4 wins	On the Clock (0-4): 7%
Pythagorean Wins: 10.8 (6th)	Offense: 16.8% (4th)	Postseason Odds: 43.8%	Mediocrity (5-7): 30%
Snap-Weighted Age: 26.1 (29th)	Defense: 4.0% (22nd)	Super Bowl Odds: 6.5%	Playoff Contender (8-10): 41%
Average Opponent: -5.3% (31st)	Special Teams: 0.9% (13th)	Proj. Avg. Opponent: -1.1% (19th)	Super Bowl Contender (11+): 22%

2014: How 'bout them Cowboys? Specifically, the ones doing the blocking.

2015: Expect the Cowboys to start slow, finish strong, and end up in a third straight division-title fight with Philadelphia.

Say your team already possesses a veteran franchise quarterback, a pair of very good receiving targets, and enough warm bodies at most other positions to stay relatively competitive. There are a lot of ways to go about making that team better, but doesn't building a great offensive line make the most sense? You could strive for broad-based improvement by drafting and signing players at a variety of positions, you could focus on defense … heck, you could do just about anything. But by saturation-drafting on the offensive line and making hefty investments over multiple seasons, you can:

• Extend the manufacturer's warranty on that pricey veteran quarterback.
• Render your running game bulletproof against injuries, free-agent defections, or overuse-related issues.
• Create a balanced, ball-control offense that can make your defense look better by keeping it off the field, maintaining leads, and so forth.
• Save cap space by getting the greatest possible value out of both rookie contracts and low-cost positions like center and guard.
• Earn the accolades of peers, sportswriters and fans for "building from the inside out."

The Cowboys built a great offensive line by drafting Tyron Smith, Travis Frederick, and Zack Martin in the first rounds of the 2011, 2013 and 2014 drafts. As a result, they currently enjoy all of the benefits listed above.

Extend the manufacturer's warranty on that pricey veteran quarterback.

The entire Tony Romo narrative has changed since the rebuild. A 35-year-old quarterback with back injuries and Romo's reputation should be Purina Troll Chow on the Internet right now. Instead, he's coming off the best season of his career and getting "grizzled warrior" kudos from all but the angriest commenters on the Eagles-Giants-Redskins discussion boards. Tony Romo walked away from a playoff loss where the referees, not the chokity-chokity-choke artist, took the blame.

Render your running game bulletproof against injuries, free-agent defections, or overuse-related issues.

The Cowboys let Offensive Player of the Year DeMarco Murray leave via free agency with minimal hand-wringing, then resisted the urge to rain draft picks on the Vikings for Adrian Peterson, trade up for Todd Gurley, or do anything more drastic than sign Darren McFadden to a bare-bones contract. The Cowboys know Joseph Randle, McFadden and Lance Dunbar can provide more-than-adequate rushing production as long as the Legion of Room is blocking for them.

Create a balanced, ball-control offense that can make your defense look better by keeping it off the field, maintaining leads, and so forth.

DVOA shows that the Cowboys had a below-average defense, on a per-play basis. But the Cowboys defense was not on the field much. The Cowboys finished second in the NFL to the Steelers in time of possession, retaining the ball for an average of 32.2 minutes per game. They averaged 3:02 per drive, also second behind Pittsburgh at 3:03.

The Cowboys not only moved the ball well, but they moved it methodically. They had the league's slowest overall offense at 30.12 seconds per play, and they were second-slowest (to the Rams) in situation-neutral pace at 32.83 seconds per play. The Legion of Room allowed the Cowboys offense to slowly mulch opponents, keeping that not-so-great defense rested and playing with a lead.

Save cap space by getting the greatest possible value out of both rookie contracts and low-cost positions like center and guard.

The Cowboys are always one free agent away from a credit rating of absolute zero, but they now have two Pro Bowlers playing for rookie contracts through 2016, while Tyron Smith obligingly signed a team-friendly contract that should keep him in the fold for years.

Earn the accolades of peers, sportswriters and fans for "building from the inside out."

All of us smart-alecks who used to make fun of Jerry Jones for shooting dollars and draft picks out of a tee-shirt cannon are now genuflecting before his wisdom.

Of course, Jerry Jones did not precisely set out to create the Legion of Room. The Cowboys famously contradicted their own draft board to select Frederick. The Martin selection came down to something out of an old soap-opera-on-the-ponderosa movie like *Giant*, with Stephen Jones staring down Paw and ordering him to drop both the derringer and the card with "Johnny Football" scrawled on it. The Legion of Room was not built by accident, but it was not precisely designed, either. At any rate, powerful men like the Joneses aren't above taking credit for

2015 Cowboys Schedule

Week	Opp.	Week	Opp.	Week	Opp.
1	NYG	7	at NYG	13	at WAS (Mon.)
2	at PHI	8	SEA	14	at GB
3	ATL	9	PHI	15	NYJ (Sat.)
4	at NO	10	at TB	16	at BUF
5	NE	11	at MIA	17	WAS
6	BYE	12	CAR (Thu.)		

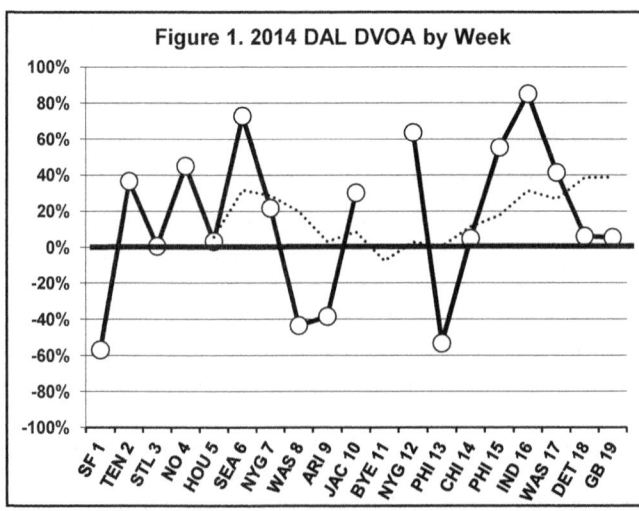

Figure 1. 2014 DAL DVOA by Week

successes they achieved at least partially despite themselves.

Whether by design or otherwise, teams rarely do what the Cowboys did over the last four seasons. You would think that "win in the trenches" is such established conventional wisdom that teams invest first-round picks in offensive linemen across multiple seasons all the time. But even expanding the parameters to three first-round offensive linemen in *five* years, and including supplemental picks in the equation, only 11 teams since the merger have tried to build an offensive line the way the Cowboys built their line.

Here's a rundown of all 11 teams, in order of the effectiveness of their experiment.

Los Angeles Rams 1975-1979

Selections: Dennis Harrah (1975), Doug France (1975), Kent Hill (1979).

This trio started together in Super Bowl XIV. Harrah and Hill went on to block for Eric Dickerson in his finest seasons. Hall of Famer Jackie Slater was also on those lines, though he wasn't considered a star then, and six-time Pro Bowler Rich Saul rounded out the cast. The Rams of the late 1970s were one of the great "trench" teams of history on both sides of the ball, which is how they consistently won 10-12 games with Pat Haden and Vince Ferragamo at quarterback.

San Francisco 49ers 2007-2010

Selections: Joe Staley (2007), Mike Iupati (2010), Anthony Davis (2010).

The 2011-13 49ers success cycle begins with the team's heavy offensive line investments before Jim Harbaugh arrived. Like the Cowboys last year, the 49ers discovered in 2011 that when the blocking is good, suddenly the quarterback storyline and other narratives change.

Houston Oilers 1982-1984

Selections: Mike Munchak (1982), Bruce Matthews (1983), Dean Steinkuhler (1984).

Without a trio of drafts that produced two Hall of Famers and a damn fine starter for many years, there would have been no run 'n' shoot, no Warren Moon, no Jerry Glanville.

New York Giants 1984-1989

Selections: Gary Zimmerman (1984 Supplemental), William Roberts (1984), Eric Moore (1988), Brian Williams (1989).

Roberts and Moore started for the 1990 Super Bowl team. Williams later became a starting center for several seasons.

Zimmerman was a USFL supplemental draft selection who never played a down for the Giants; unable to agree on contract terms, he was traded to Minnesota for two second-round picks. The late-era Parcells Giants weren't known for outstanding offensive lines (though Roberts and Bart Oates made the Pro Bowl in 1990), but one look at their skill position talent proves that the blockers had to be doing something right.

Green Bay Packers 1994-1997

Selections: Aaron Taylor (1994), John Michels (1996), Ross Verba (1997).

Taylor and Verba started for Super Bowl teams. Knee injuries ruined Michels' career after two seasons. The Packers weren't precisely trying to build a powerhouse offensive line with these picks; they were a perennial contender with few other needs grabbing extra guys to protect Brett Favre.

Cincinnati Bengals 1980-1984

Selections: Anthony Muñoz (1980), Dave Rimington (1983), Brian Blados (1984).

Muñoz was a Hall of Famer who played for two AFC Champions. This trio started together for a few of the early Boomer Esiason-Sam Wyche Bengals teams, but Rimington and Blados were gone by the time the Bengals had their Super Bowl run in the late 1980s.

Kansas City Chiefs 1995-1998

Selections: Trezelle Jenkins (1995), Victor Riley (1998), John Tait (1999).

Jenkins was a massive bust. Riley and Tait started as bookend tackles for a few years on a great line that also featured Will Shields and Tim Grunhard. Riley was gone by the time the Chiefs offense got rolling with Trent Green and Priest Holmes. Despite all the high draft picks on the offensive line, two of the key linemen of the Green years were undrafted: Casey Wiegmann and Brian Waters.

Detroit Lions 1999-2001

Selections: Aaron Gibson (1999), Stockar McDougle (2000), Jeff Backus (2001).

The Lions made plenty of bad first-round decisions on the offensive line before they started making bad first-round decisions at wide receiver. Gibson couldn't keep his weight below 400 pounds and ate his way out of Michigan in less than two seasons. McDougle had a few semi-competent seasons as a massive right tackle. Backus played forever; if one of the other two had panned out, Lions history in the 2000s would have been very different.

Denver Broncos 1976-1979

Selections: Tom Glassic (1976), Steve Schindler (1977), Kelvin Clark (1979).

Glassic started at guard from the Craig Morton Super Bowl era to the dawn of the John Elway era, but the others never amounted to much in Denver.

Kansas City Chiefs 1984-1986

Selections: John Alt (1984), Mark Adickes (1984 Supplemental), Brian Jozwiak (1986).

By the time Alt grew into one of the best guards in the NFL, Adickes (chosen in the special 1984 supplemental draft for USFL players[1]) and Jozwiak were already gone.

Philadelphia Eagles 1993-1996

Selections: Lester Holmes (1993), Leonard Williams (1994), Jermaine Mayberry (1996).

The Eagles also drafted Antone Davis in 1991 as part of a string of terrible first-round decisions on the offensive line that dated back to the 1980s and didn't end until the team drafted Tra Thomas in 1998. Mayberry was a decent guard for a few years. The rest were terrible.

Four of the teams listed above reached the Super Bowl with a significant assist from their first-round linemen; a fifth team drafted two Hall of Famers to block for a third and ushered in a new era of strategic experimentation. That's a pretty impressive set of accomplishments for an 11-team list. Drafting offensive linemen in the first round several years in a row appears to be a pretty sound strategy, particularly if the first selection is a hit (as Tyron Smith, Munchack, Harrah, Muñoz, and others were). It's a wonder that so few teams do it.

Circumstances led the Cowboys to make their offensive line even better when La'El Collins, a first-round caliber lineman, fell through the draft due to fears that Collins may have been involved in the shooting death of ex-girlfriend Britney Mills. Mills was shot just days before the draft; Collins was never officially ruled out as a possible culprit, but investigators never named him as a suspect and were clearly satisfied after Collins

produced an alibi and other information. Collins was suddenly a free agent, and Jerry Jones swooped in with both a three-year contract and one of Jones' patented secret-weapon sales pitches. "For the first time, I really felt like somebody had seen me for who I am," Collins said upon signing with the Cowboys. "Somebody understood me."

Collins essentially gives the Cowboys a fourth first-round lineman in five years, this one at the cost of just $1.6 million over three years and one late-night phone courtship. Collins fits the Cowboys offensive line so well that it's scary. The Cowboys need competition at left guard, where Ronald Leary is the line's weak link, and the team also needs an eventual upgrade over re-signed right tackle Doug Free. Collins, whose scouting report downside was an inability to play left tackle, can start his career at guard, then slide out to replace Free.

So the already-great Cowboys offensive line is likely to get even better, both through Collins' arrival and the continued development of Frederick and Martin. Four-fifths of the Cowboys line is still under 25 years old. The team can expect the benefits of the Legion of Room power train—a healthy, well-protected Romo; good running backs looking great; ball control to help the defense; cap consciousness; admiration from the intelligentsia—for years to come. Two years ago, it was impossible to peer past the event horizon of the Romo Salary-Cap Black Hole and see anything but a 4-12 crater. Now, it's easy to imagine the next Cowboys quarterback developing within a Smith-Frederick-Martin-Collins cocoon, and the Cowboys staying competitive even during a dead-money nuclear winter.

It's even easy to imagine the Cowboys reaching the Super Bowl in 2015. They reached the divisional round of the playoffs last year, after all, and beat the Seahawks in the regular season. Murray's departure is a minor setback: after 436 carries last year, including the postseason, he was poised for expensive disappointment, and he's now a division rival's problem. Sean Lee, lost for the year during 2014 minicamp when his on-field introduction to Zack Martin went awry, gives the Cowboys back a needed playmaker in pass coverage. And the Legion of Room provided the team one unforeseen benefit this offseason: it allowed the Cowboys to acquire risky players on defense without accruing that much risk.

The Cowboys signed Greg Hardy to improve their pass rush, although Hardy will start the season with a four-game suspension for the 2014 domestic violence incident that made him available in the first place. Linebacker Rolando McClain, another trouble magnet, will return to the Cowboys at an affordable price this year after a 2014 season of surprising productivity on the field and just-passable reliability off it. McClain is also suspended for the first four weeks, for violating league drug policy.[2]

---

1 This has nothing to do with the 2015 Dallas Cowboys, but an interesting digression: three of the first five picks in that special 1984 supplemental draft came from the Los Angeles Express offense. Steve Young went first to Tampa Bay, Zimmerman third to the Giants, and Adickes fifth to Kansas City. Eleven of the 28 first-round picks in that draft came from the Express. Sounds like the dominant USFL team, right? They went 10-8.

2 These suspensions further contribute to the likely pattern of the Cowboys season: slow start, strong finish. The Dallas schedule is extremely front-loaded. The first eight opponents include the Eagles and Giants twice plus both of last year's Super Bowl teams, and the Cowboys have either the fourth- or sixth-hardest schedule of Weeks 1-9 depending on the status of Tom Brady. Except for a Week 14 trip to Green Bay, things are much easier from Week 10 on, and the Cowboys' schedule ranks 29th in Weeks 10-17.

The Cowboys also drafted undersized edge rusher Randy Gregory, who slipped into the second round due to what were initially described as "character-related issues." Further reporting slowly revealed that Gregory's "character issues" are for the most part mental health issues: anxiety and depression, which Gregory self-medicated with marijuana. That's a very different kind of risk than the risk from employing bad actors such as Hardy and McClain, but it's a risk nonetheless.

Each of these players has the potential to provide high-level talent at a low cost. They are not core players, either: the Cowboys can reach the playoffs without contributions from any of them. But Hardy could bring an extreme pass-rush boost just in time for the playoffs, Gregory has dozen-sack talent if he can overcome his anxiety, and McClain can hammer the middle of the field so Lee can roam in coverage without taking a pounding. Add top pick and combine hero Byron Jones, who is whistle-clean off the field but inexperienced on it, and the Cowboys added tons of raw talent to a defense which, thanks to the Legion of Room, only has to be pretty good.

The Cowboys have signed or drafted their share of Bad Boys in the past, but the new crop fits both within a budget and a recognizable plan for reaching the Super Bowl. That may be the biggest adjustment we have to make when thinking about the Cowboys, bigger than burying the Choko Romo narrative or wishing someone would come up with a better nickname for their line than "Legion of Room." As Stephen Jones has taken an ever-expanding role in team management from his father, the Cowboys have become more analytics-friendly, cap-conscious, sports-science-accepting, judicious, and—for want of a less-loaded term—*progressive* than they were during Paw's free-spending, pick-squandering, coach-contradicting heyday.

If the Cowboys had taken this approach six years ago, just after Bill Parcells filled the cupboards and left —if they spent wisely, drafted prudently, focused their resources and enjoyed slightly better luck—they probably would have a Super Bowl to show for the heights of the careers of Romo, Jason Witten and DeMarcus Ware. As it stands, Romo and Witten still have a chance to saddle up and claim that ring, with the help of some shady rustlers on defense and tons of prize beef on offense.

It's not a great chance; the NFC East is tough, and the Packers and Seahawks still look like better teams than the Cowboys. But thanks to that offensive line, it's a chance that, just two years ago, looked like it would never come.

Mike Tanier

2014 Cowboys Stats by Week

Wk	vs.	W-L	PF	PA	YDF	YDA	TO	Total	Off	Def	ST
1	SF	L	17	28	382	319	-4	-57%	-7%	40%	-10%
2	at TEN	W	26	10	368	314	1	36%	11%	-6%	19%
3	at STL	W	34	31	340	448	1	1%	22%	20%	-2%
4	NO	W	38	17	445	438	3	45%	43%	0%	2%
5	HOU	W	20	17	456	330	-2	3%	17%	9%	-5%
6	at SEA	W	30	23	401	206	-1	73%	39%	-54%	-20%
7	NYG	W	31	21	423	352	1	22%	38%	16%	-1%
8	WAS	L	17	20	395	409	-1	-44%	-19%	24%	0%
9	ARI	L	17	28	266	339	-1	-39%	-27%	8%	-3%
10	vs.JAC	W	31	17	399	333	2	30%	26%	-5%	0%
11	BYE										
12	at NYG	W	31	28	385	417	0	64%	57%	10%	16%
13	PHI	L	10	33	267	464	-2	-53%	-37%	16%	-1%
14	at CHI	W	41	28	397	376	2	5%	34%	36%	7%
15	at PHI	W	38	27	364	294	2	55%	27%	-20%	9%
16	IND	W	42	7	377	229	2	85%	39%	-52%	-6%
17	at WAS	W	44	17	473	413	3	41%	25%	-9%	7%
18	DET	W	24	20	315	397	2	6%	-3%	-2%	7%
19	at GB	L	21	26	315	416	0	5%	31%	22%	-4%

Trends and Splits

	Offense	Rank	Defense	Rank
Total DVOA	16.8%	4	4.0%	22
Unadjusted VOA	15.6%	5	0.2%	18
Weighted Trend	19.1%	4	-0.1%	19
Variance	7.4%	13	7.1%	24
Average Opponent	0.9%	21	-4.0%	30
Passing	35.9%	4	10.1%	22
Rushing	6.6%	3	-4.0%	22
First Down	16.2%	5	2.0%	19
Second Down	19.3%	3	-6.9%	10
Third Down	14.0%	9	23.0%	29
First Half	20.7%	3	8.4%	27
Second Half	11.9%	6	0.7%	15
Red Zone	17.1%	7	3.4%	24
Late and Close	21.5%	6	-5.6%	10

Five-Year Performance

Year	W-L	Pyth W	Est W	PF	PA	TO	Total	Rk	Off	Rk	Def	Rk	ST	Rk	Off AGL	Rk	Def AGL	Rk	Off Age	Rk	Def Age	Rk	ST Age	Rk
2010	6-10	7.0	6.8	394	436	0	-10.5%	23	-4.7%	21	6.3%	27	0.6%	15	20.6	12	11.0	7	28.7	2	27.4	15	25.6	27
2011	8-8	8.6	8.4	369	347	+4	3.5%	14	5.9%	12	0.4%	16	-2.1%	25	43.5	25	19.0	11	26.6	22	28.2	2	26.0	27
2012	8-8	7.4	7.9	376	400	-13	-0.4%	17	6.1%	11	6.7%	23	0.2%	15	29.0	17	57.5	30	27.2	11	26.7	19	25.6	26
2013	8-8	8.2	8.2	439	432	+8	-2.8%	17	7.5%	11	13.8%	30	3.4%	8	16.4	5	50.2	29	26.5	22	26.1	24	25.3	28
2014	12-4	10.8	10.3	467	352	+6	13.7%	6	16.8%	4	4.0%	22	0.9%	13	9.3	2	66.8	28	26.4	25	26.1	25	25.6	29

2014 Performance Based on Most Common Personnel Groups

DAL Offense					DAL Offense vs. Opponents					DAL Defense				DAL Defense vs. Opponents			
Pers	Freq	Yds	DVOA	Run%	Pers	Freq	Yds	DVOA	Run%	Pers	Freq	Yds	DVOA	Pers	Freq	Yds	DVOA
11	42%	6.8	26.2%	29%	Base	51%	5.6	12.2%	70%	Base	27%	5.1	-0.9%	11	65%	6.2	4.7%
12	32%	5.8	14.9%	60%	Nickel	32%	6.7	31.3%	29%	Nickel	68%	6.3	6.6%	12	16%	6.4	1.5%
21	9%	6.5	15.1%	70%	Dime+	15%	7.6	33.7%	10%	Dime+	5%	7.2	3.8%	21	7%	4.7	3.2%
13	6%	4.4	-10.3%	71%	Goal Line	1%	4.2	35.8%	83%	Goal Line	1%	0.7	8.9%	22	4%	3.2	-13.2%
22	4%	4.8	-8.2%	98%	Big	1%	4.0	-11.9%	90%					01	2%	6.0	1.5%
02	3%	9.7	128.8%	3%													

Strategic Tendencies

Run/Pass		Rk	Formation		Rk	Pass Rush		Rk	Secondary		Rk	Strategy		Rk
Runs, first half	46%	3	Form: Single Back	77%	11	Rush 3	5.2%	19	4 DB	17%	30	Play action	17%	28
Runs, first down	68%	1	Form: Empty Back	8%	11	Rush 4	71.8%	7	5 DB	75%	3	Avg Box (Off)	6.33	10
Runs, second-long	26%	25	Pers: 3+ WR	47%	28	Rush 5	18.8%	25	6+ DB	7%	18	Avg Box (Def)	6.15	28
Runs, power sit.	59%	12	Pers: 4+ WR	2%	16	Rush 6+	4.1%	28	CB by Sides	72%	25	Offensive Pace	32.83	31
Runs, behind 2H	38%	3	Pers: 2+ TE/6+ OL	48%	3	Sacks by LB	16.7%	22	DB Blitz	8%	21	Defensive Pace	30.57	24
Pass, ahead 2H	39%	31	Shotgun/Pistol	48%	28	Sacks by DB	7.4%	14	Hole in Zone	6%	16	Go for it on 4th	0.68	25

DeMarco Murray's breakout year meant some big changes in the Cowboys' pass/run ratios. Two years ago, the Cowboys ran just 43 percent of the time on first down, 25th in the league. Last year, they were No. 1. Another huge change: the Cowboys went 24 percent runs when behind in the second half (26th) to 38 percent (third) in 2014, and from 60 percent passes when ahead in the second half (third) to 39 percent passes (31st) in 2014. ☞ If a great running back is supposed to stop defenses from blitzing, nobody gave Dallas opponents the memo. Tony Romo led the league in frequency of DB blitzes (14.1 percent of passes) and big blitzes of six or more (12.6 percent). His average yardage did go down against the blitz, though he was still above average no matter the number of pass rushers. Romo had 8.0 yards per pass against three or four pass rushers, 7.5 yards against five, and 6.9 against six or more. ☞ Dallas had just 12 dropped passes, fewer than any offense in the NFL. ☞ The Cowboys' "CB by Sides" number is a bit confusing because starter Orlando Scandrick moved to the slot with nickel personnel. If we looked at Brandon Carr and Sterling Moore instead of Carr and Scandrick, Dallas would move to around the league average. ☞ The Cowboys went from having the worst defensive DVOA in the league against passes in the middle of the field in 2013 to the best DVOA against such passes in 2014. That's particularly surprising given the injury to Sean Lee. They were strong against both short middle passes (third) and deep middle passes (first). However, their DVOA against passes on the offensive left fell from 12th in 2013 to 31st in 2014. Their DVOA against passes on the offensive right stayed roughly the same. ☞ Dallas opponents threw a league-low 17 percent of passes to the players we identified as No. 1 receivers. On the other hand, they threw a league-high 27.6 percent of passes to tight ends; no other defense was above 23 percent. ☞ The Cowboys' preference to rush only four may have led to some sample-size quirks. The Cowboys allowed a league-high 8.1 yards per play when sending five pass rushers, but a league-low 2.9 yards per play when sending six or more. ☞ Fumble recovery luck suggests the Dallas offense may look even better this year (recovered 5 of 17 fumbles) but the defense may not look quite as good (recovered 10 of 16 fumbles).

Passing

Player	DYAR	DVOA	Plays	NtYds	Avg	YAC	C%	TD	Int
T.Romo	1187	27.6%	465	3441	7.4	5.4	70.3%	34	9
B.Weeden	21	-3.5%	42	294	7.0	6.7	58.5%	3	2

Rushing

Player	DYAR	DVOA	Plays	Yds	Avg	TD	Fum	Suc
D.Murray*	382	14.8%	392	1849	4.7	13	3	54%
J.Randle	68	26.3%	51	344	6.7	3	2	51%
L.Dunbar	-10	-16.9%	29	99	3.4	0	0	45%
T.Romo	23	50.9%	9	76	8.4	0	0	-
D.McFadden	-33	-13.9%	156	534	3.4	2	1	40%
J.Collins	10	10.4%	8	19	2.4	0	0	63%

Receiving

Player	DYAR	DVOA	Plays	Ctch	Yds	Y/C	YAC	TD	C%
D.Bryant	430	27.0%	137	88	1320	15.0	4.6	16	64%
T.Williams	220	30.6%	65	37	621	16.8	3.0	8	57%
C.Beasley	117	16.7%	49	37	420	11.4	6.6	4	76%
D.Harris*	8	-2.3%	11	6	108	18.0	6.0	0	55%
D.Street	-28	-63.3%	7	2	18	9.0	2.5	0	29%
J.Witten	146	17.9%	90	64	703	11.0	3.6	5	71%
G.Escobar	45	37.1%	13	9	105	11.7	2.4	4	69%
J.Hanna	-4	-17.2%	6	4	48	12.0	3.5	0	67%
D.Murray*	58	3.0%	64	57	418	7.3	8.8	0	89%
L.Dunbar	88	60.7%	22	18	217	12.1	10.8	0	82%
D.McFadden	-75	-37.5%	56	36	212	5.9	7.3	0	74%
R.Agnew	-31	-76.7%	9	3	15	5.0	3.3	0	33%
J.Collins	28	72.3%	6	5	39	7.8	7.6	1	83%

Offensive Line

Player	Pos	Age	GS	Snaps	Pen	Sk	Pass	Run	Player	Pos	Age	GS	Snaps	Pen	Sk	Pass	Run
Travis Frederick	C	24	16/16	1059	6	1.0	6.0	6.5	Ronald Leary	LG	26	15/15	991	5	3.0	6.0	6.0
Tyron Smith	LT	25	16/16	1059	9	3.0	12.0	4.5	Doug Free	RT	31	11/11	699	4	2.0	10.0	3.0
Zack Martin	RG	23	16/16	1053	2	1.0	6.0	4.5	Jermey Parnell*	OT	29	16/5	379	1	0.0	3.0	3.0

Year	Yards	ALY	Rk	Power	Rk	Stuff	Rk	2nd Lev	Rk	Open Field	Rk	Sacks	ASR	Rk	Short	Long	F-Start	Cont.
2012	3.78	3.92	22	63%	15	19%	12	1.04	25	0.52	26	36	5.8%	11	11	14	26	28
2013	4.66	4.23	4	68%	11	15%	2	1.29	6	1.02	4	35	6.2%	10	14	12	16	37
2014	4.86	4.40	1	76%	4	18%	11	1.38	2	1.10	2	30	6.1%	16	12	10	13	32
2014 ALY by direction:		Left End 4.36 (7)			Left Tackle 4.56 (3)			Mid/Guard 4.14 (7)			Right Tackle 4.9 (3)			Right End 4.16 (12)				

The Cowboys line got plenty of love earlier in the chapter. Now let's give them each a brief solo album, like the ones KISS put out in 1978. Most of the details come from a series of "10 Things You Didn't Know" articles from the *Dallas Morning News*:

Tyron Smith can bench press between 600 and 700 pounds, at least according to Travis Frederick. "He does crazy things in the weight room that I wish that I could do and I never will be able to do unfortunately," Frederick said in a radio interview. "It wouldn't be unusual to see a small car." In Texas, it's always unusual to see a small car. For the record, a smart car weighs 1,800 pounds. Maybe if Smith, Frederick and Zach Martin work together…

Travis Frederick has shaved his beard twice in his life: once after his eighth-grade graduation (!) and once before his brother's wedding. So … do people who have never seen a clean-shaven, post-middle school Frederick look at his brother's wedding pictures and wonder who the guy with the cut-up chin is? Frederick is also a spokesman for One Wipe Charlies, a moist toilet paper for men. Because all the metrosexuals want to buy hygiene products from a dude who shaves twice per millennium.

Zack Martin is clearly a bad, bad man. The *Morning News* didn't even give him a cute "10 Things You Didn't Know" segment, lest he get riled up and cripple Sean Lee.

Doug Free's nickname in college was Doug Freak; he earned the nickname "for his athleticism and his work ethic," according to the *Morning News*. Umm, no one gets the nickname "freak" because of work ethic. Maybe if he knew about Frederick's wet wipes, his nickname would have been Dougie Fresh. Free signed a two-year contract in the offseason, preventing his nickname from becoming Pete Best, at least for now.

Ronald Leary is the best dressed of the Cowboys linemen, according to Frederick. "He's the only one that comes in matching … or looking any good." That fashion sense will come in handy on job interviews after Leary is replaced by La'El Collins. Leary is the weak link of the line as a pass protector, but there are far worse guards starting in the NFL.

La'El Collins practiced at right tackle and left guard during OTAs, which makes sense when you look at who plays center, right guard and left tackle. After he signed with the Cowboys, he stated that he wants to be part of the greatest offensive line in history. It's an ambitious goal, but not a completely unrealistic one.

Defensive Front Seven

Defensive Line	Age	Pos	G	Snaps	Plays	Overall TmPct	Rk	Stop	Dfts	BTkl	vs. Run Runs	St%	Rk	RuYd	Rk	Pass Rush Sack	Hit	Hur	Dsrpt
Nick Hayden	29	DT	16	571	39	4.9%	41	25	8	1	32	69%	83	3.0	82	0.0	4	4.5	1
Henry Melton*	29	DT	16	424	19	2.4%	88	18	15	0	5	80%	32	1.0	8	5.0	4	8.0	4
Terrell McClain	27	DT	13	322	18	2.8%	--	12	4	0	15	73%	--	3.0	--	1.0	2	5.5	0

Edge Rushers	Age	Pos	G	Snaps	Plays	Overall TmPct	Rk	Stop	Dfts	BTkl	vs. Run Runs	St%	Rk	RuYd	Rk	Pass Rush Sack	Hit	Hur	Dsrpt
Jeremy Mincey	32	DE	16	706	36	4.5%	54	28	12	2	27	74%	46	1.9	24	6.0	9	22.5	0
Tyrone Crawford	26	DE/DT	15	627	34	4.6%	53	29	13	2	25	92%	3	1.0	4	3.0	13	16.0	1
George Selvie*	28	DE	16	500	31	3.9%	64	24	7	2	22	82%	22	2.1	31	3.0	5	13.0	0
Anthony Spencer*	31	DE	13	372	22	3.4%	72	19	6	0	17	82%	21	2.9	58	0.5	6	7.5	1

Linebackers	Age	Pos	G	Snaps	Plays	Overall TmPct	Rk	Stop	Dfts	BTkl	Pass Rush Sack	Hit	Hur	vs. Run Runs	St%	Rk	RuYd	Rk	vs. Pass Tgts	Suc%	Rk	AdjYd	Rk	PD	Int
Rolando McClain	26	MLB	13	633	83	12.9%	40	52	16	5	1.0	2	5.5	48	81%	3	2.3	8	27	37%	59	5.6	17	2	1
Anthony Hitchens	23	OLB	16	531	77	9.7%	64	42	10	6	0.0	2	0.5	50	64%	40	3.0	22	21	43%	52	6.6	36	2	1
Bruce Carter*	27	OLB	13	521	75	11.7%	47	40	17	8	1.0	2	2	36	64%	42	3.6	50	38	45%	47	5.7	20	7	5
Justin Durant*	30	OLB	6	324	53	17.8%	8	36	11	4	0.0	0	2.5	28	82%	1	2.2	7	18	44%	48	7.2	46	3	1
Kyle Wilber	26	OLB	16	212	23	2.9%	--	14	4	2	1.5	1	2.5	11	73%	--	3.1	--	8	38%	--	5.5	--	2	0
Jasper Brinkley	30	MLB	16	460	72	8.6%	73	35	4	3	1.0	0	0.5	54	56%	70	4.8	80	11	28%	--	10.0	--	0	0
Andrew Gachkar	27	ILB	15	382	36	5.0%	--	25	11	3	1.0	0	2	20	70%	--	2.2	--	13	68%	--	3.6	--	0	0

Year	Yards	ALY	Rk	Power	Rk	Stuff	Rk	2nd Level	Rk	Open Field	Rk	Sacks	ASR	Rk	Short	Long
2012	4.37	4.14	19	65%	20	16%	28	1.13	8	0.83	18	34	6.9%	9	10	16
2013	4.84	4.34	29	76%	29	18%	17	1.48	31	0.98	26	34	6.1%	26	12	10
2014	4.46	3.85	17	67%	20	18%	20	1.16	19	1.02	30	28	4.6%	29	7	9
2014 ALY by direction:	Left End 3.5 (11)		Left Tackle 3.82 (18)		Mid/Guard 3.77 (10)			Right Tackle 3.92 (15)			Right End 4.46 (29)					

The Cowboys front seven is undersized along the line and thin at several positions, a byproduct of the team's top-heavy cap structure. Coordinator Rod Marinelli is hoping for a talent injection from some price-cut troublemakers, and one oft-injured returnee, as he tries to create his version of a vintage Tampa-2 defense.

Sean Lee will move from middle linebacker to the weak side this season. The goal is to both give Lee a key defensive role—the "Will" linebacker plays the Derrick Brooks role in Marinelli's faithful interpretation of the Tampa-2—and keep Lee healthy after missing all of 2014 with a Zack Martin-induced ACL injury. Lee will spend more time playing in space or flowing behind the line as a Will than he did as a Mike, who spends more time plugging run gaps. Lee is expected to take some practice sessions off and dial down the training camp intensity in an effort to stay healthy. Coaches should also remind La'el Collins that he has nothing to prove by walloping the weakside linebacker.

While Lee channels Brooks, Tyrone Crawford plays the Warren Sapp role. Crawford was a revelation last year after missing all of 2013 with an Achilles injury: consistent, disruptive, and versatile enough to slide to end when needed. Crawford is one of those pleasant surprises the Cowboys never used to get in the middle rounds of the draft; "third-round pick develops three years later" was not a common storyline back when Jerry Jones flew every offseason by the seat of his pants. Crawford is in the final year of his rookie contract, so he will be playing for a major payday while the Cowboys figure out who they can afford to keep.

Keeping the Tampa-2 metaphor going, the Cowboys incurred a lot of risk in their quest for a Simeon Rice. Greg Hardy is currently scheduled to return to the field before Tom Brady, however we may feel about that. Randy Gregory didn't just slip to the second round because of off-field questions; there are also questions about his on-field effort and his size. But SackSEER loves his combine numbers, and his 235-pound weigh-in is the same as what Trent Cole and Robert Mathis weighed at their combines. They both added bulk as pros, and Gregory needs to do so too, so it's hard to project him as anything more than a situational player as a rookie. Demarcus Lawrence, last year's undersized second-round pass rusher, came on late and had two postseason sacks after missing the first two months with a broken foot. The Cowboys want to keep Lawrence at left end, where he feels most comfortable. At 260 pounds, he is small for that side of the formation. Hustling veteran Jeremy Mincey will man right end while Hardy serves his suspension. Nick Hayden is an undersized nose tackle playing for a one-year tender offer; he's quick, determined, and easy to push around on rushing downs. Terrell McClain is a sturdy rotation tackle. Anthony Hitchens was active and effective as a run defender as a rookie but was often exposed in coverage. Lee's presence will allow

Hitchens to play a more traditional Sam role, with more run fits and easier coverage assignments. Fourth-round pick Damien Wilson (Minnesota) is similar to Hitchens: a stout, smart Big Ten linebacker who hustles but shouldn't be asked to chase many tight ends up the seam.

Rolando McClain was a great story on the field but his off-the-field issues took some of the luster away from his redemption story. McClain was much less consistent than his press clippings suggest: he was a nasty gap penetrator, but the Eagles left him breathless, and he had a midseason stretched when he whiffed on nearly as many tackles as he made. Off the field, ESPN Dallas' Jean-Jacque Taylor reports, "he was a mess." The Cowboys signed McClain to another one-year deal and will be content to pay as they go for a defender with concussions, arrests, substance-abuse violations and sudden retirements on his resume. McClain starts the year with a four-game suspension, and king-sized run-thumper Jasper Brinkley was signed as low-cost McClain flighty insurance.

Defensive Secondary

Secondary	Age	Pos	G	Snaps	Plays	Overall TmPct	Rk	Stop	Dfts	BTkl	vs. Run Runs	St%	Rk	RuYd	Rk	Tgts	Tgt%	Rk	vs. Pass Dist	Suc%	Rk	AdjYd	Rk	PD	Int
Brandon Carr	29	CB	16	1000	61	7.7%	55	25	8	8	18	44%	29	7.6	49	69	18.5%	8	14.8	47%	54	10.7	74	8	0
J.J. Wilcox	24	FS	16	970	75	9.5%	46	25	10	10	36	22%	64	10.4	65	28	7.6%	29	9.7	51%	49	7.3	34	5	3
Barry Church	27	SS	16	890	99	12.5%	14	40	17	11	46	39%	39	6.4	36	31	9.3%	42	11.1	66%	7	6.0	21	7	2
Orlando Scandrick	28	CB	14	861	64	9.2%	27	28	15	3	7	29%	53	5.7	31	52	16.2%	2	8.5	57%	13	7.2	23	8	2
Sterling Moore*	25	CB	16	726	58	7.3%	61	20	8	4	6	33%	44	10.8	71	70	25.9%	56	12.2	41%	73	8.6	51	12	0
Corey White	25	CB	15	758	57	7.5%	58	18	11	7	7	14%	71	16.1	75	69	22.6%	30	11.9	41%	72	9.0	57	7	2

Year	Pass D Rank	vs. #1 WR	Rk	vs. #2 WR	Rk	vs. Other WR	Rk	vs. TE	Rk	vs. RB	Rk
2012	25	-7.0%	12	11.5%	29	19.5%	28	28.9%	32	3.5%	18
2013	27	12.4%	25	17.6%	28	-11.4%	8	26.8%	32	9.6%	24
2014	22	-2.2%	14	29.5%	29	-24.3%	3	-9.0%	11	-6.3%	12

Brandon Carr was one of the worst values in the NFL last year on a dollar-for-dollar basis. He did it all as a cornerback: blow coverages, miss tackles, and incur penalties (five pass interference fouls, three holds), all for the unreasonable price of $12 million in cap space. Carr becomes affordably cuttable next year. Until then, he resides in the DeAngelo Hall zone: just experienced and talented enough to make eating his cap number more palatable than replacing him with a rookie.

Byron Jones is the rookie who will replace Carr in 2016. Jones achieved instantaneous fame when he set a world record in the standing broad jump at the scouting combine. In the old days, we would snicker at Jerry Jones drafting the guy he saw trending on Twitter (not to mention another Jones), but Byron Jones has solid tape from UConn to go with his eye-opening athleticism. He will start the season as the nickel and may keep steady, capable No. 2 corner Orlando Scandrick on the outside. Morris Claiborne has become vaporware, and the perpetually-injured 2012 first-round pick could get released, traded, or (most likely) buried as a bit player until his contract expires. Robert Steeples, a knockaround player who has had stints on the Rams and Vikings practice squads, generated some buzz in minicamp and will push Saints castoff Corey White for the final cornerback job.

Barry Church, J.J. Wilcox, and top reserve Jeff Heath all return to a safety corps that doesn't generate much excitement. All three safeties are adequate at preventing big plays, the primary duty of a safety in the Tampa-2. Danny McCray returned to the Cowboys after a year as part of the Bears comedy troupe at safety. McCray is mostly a special-teamer but gives Marinelli an in-the-box option at safety against run-oriented opponents like the Eagles.

Special Teams

Year	DVOA	Rank	FG/XP	Rank	Net Kick	Rank	Kick Ret	Rank	Net Punt	Rank	Punt Ret	Rank	Hidden	Rank
2012	0.2%	15	7.8	5	-3.1	24	-10.9	32	-1.4	17	8.4	4	2.5	10
2013	3.4%	8	7.0	5	1.2	14	3.2	7	-1.5	21	7.3	5	0.9	14
2014	0.9%	13	5.3	6	5.0	8	-3.0	23	-0.6	19	-2.5	16	3.1	11

Dan Bailey's whopping 2014 contract has been retconned from a reckless splurge by a cap-strapped organization with more pressing needs to the judicious retention of a dependable kicker by a championship contender. (For more Cowboys retcons, see "we always planned to build our offensive line around Travis Frederick, no matter what our draft board said.") Bailey missed a 41-yarder in the Lions playoff game and had a 50-yarder partially blocked (the trajectory of the kick was too low) in the Packers loss, a reminder that "reliable crunch-time veteran kicker" is more a perception than a reality, no matter how much you pay. That said, Bailey is consistent on field goals and adequate on kickoffs.

With Dwayne Harris gone to the Giants, Lance Dunbar and Cole Beasley are the favorites to handle the return chores. Dunbar has returned 15 NFL kickoffs in three years without doing anything noteworthy. Beasley fielded a handful of returns in 2013. Free-agent rookie Lucky Whitehead fielded some punts during OTAs and could win a return job. Whitehead, who lists at 5-foot-10 but just 163 pounds, returned a punt for a touchdown and also returned kickoffs for Florida Atlantic last year. Nick Harwell, another tiny undrafted rookie, returned a punt for a touchdown for Kansas and got some OTA opportunities. Harris was also among the team's best gunners, but core special-teamers like James Hanna and Jeff Heath will keep the coverage units sound. Chris Jones gets the job done at punter.

Denver Broncos

2014 Record: 12-4	**Total DVOA:** 29.5% (2nd)	**2015 Mean Projection:** 9.5 wins	**On the Clock (0-4):** 4%
Pythagorean Wins: 11.0 (4th)	**Offense:** 20.0% (3rd)	**Postseason Odds:** 59.1%	**Mediocrity (5-7):** 20%
Snap-Weighted Age: 26.9 (15th)	**Defense:** -13.2% (4th)	**Super Bowl Odds:** 15.3%	**Playoff Contender (8-10):** 40%
Average Opponent: 1.5% (12th)	**Special Teams:** -3.7% (27th)	**Proj. Avg. Opponent:** 2.8% (8th)	**Super Bowl Contender (11+):** 37%

2014: The best team in the league through October.

2015: Can two old dogs teach each other new tricks?

When are a 46-18 record and four division titles not enough to keep your job? End each season with an inexplicable playoff defeat after some of the highest expectations in the league. That's why John Fox and most of his coaching staff are gone. Denver is only the third team since 1989 to finish in the top two in DVOA in at least three consecutive seasons. The 1992-95 Cowboys won three Super Bowls and the 2012-14 Seahawks were a yard away from a repeat. It's a little bad luck that Denver's historic run is concurrent with Seattle's superiority, but when you are that good in the regular season, you better come away with something better than a 35-point Super Bowl blowout loss as your playoff peak.

Gary Kubiak was hired as the new head coach before the team even knew if Peyton Manning was going to return for an 18th season. Manning's back with the fifth head coach of his career, but which version of Peyton Manning are we getting? If he's healthy, then Denver is a top-three AFC team and expectations are high as usual. Everything this book says about Manning in 2015 should be prefaced with the caveat of "if he stays healthy." It's easier to keep the 39-year-old healthy if he's throwing less and getting more out of the running game, which is Kubiak's area of expertise. That sounds like the perfect marriage, but a patchwork offensive line is threatening to give it a rocky start. However, if Manning and Kubiak each bring their usual modus operandi, there's really no better duo to compensate for a flawed offensive line.

But can the two find the right mesh point in their proven ways of doing things? For the first time, Manning will have a offense-oriented head coach who brings his own schematic history, and some see this as a problem when it comes to who will be calling the shots each week. Kubiak's offense specializes in keeping the quarterback under center, using a fullback, and utilizing bootlegs and play-action passing with a zone-blocking scheme. Manning is a master of the no-huddle offense, has been in shotgun over 73 percent of the time the last two years, and loves having three wide receivers on the field. There is clearly a schematic difference between the two (Table 1) and they will have to combine the two styles to create something that works best for Denver's personnel. It's not like Kubiak wanted to use three wide receivers much in Houston when the front office failed to put anything better than Kevin Walter behind Andre Johnson. Any coach is more likely to give the quarterback some freedom at the line if that quarterback is Manning instead of Matt Schaub.

Manning's on his fourth head coach and fifth offensive co-ordinator since 2008. So far he's always been allowed to run things his way, but this may be the one situation where he has to give in more to what Kubiak and offensive coordinator Rick Dennison like to do. Kubiak has proven he's willing to change an offense dramatically, even with an established head coach and quarterback. The 2013 Ravens used shotgun on 73.1 percent of their plays, but Kubiak reduced that to a league-low 24.1 percent in 2014. Joe Flacco handed off to a running back in the shotgun just nine times all season. *N-I-N-E times*. Denver had 212 such shotgun runs and fared quite well with them (second in DVOA). There has to be some mixing this year or else Denver will have the most predictable offense in the league. If Manning's under center, defend the run. If Manning's in shotgun, he's going to pass. Okay, this is starting to sound worrisome. Is Kubiak going to butcher the Manning-style offense that has produced 14 playoff seasons (each with 10-plus wins) and 14 top-eight finishes in offensive DVOA?

Let's relax for a second. It's still football and things should look familiar to Denver fans this year.

Once upon a time in his physical prime, Manning was big on using play-action and stretch runs. He's used play-action

Table 1. Bad Idea to Cross the Schemes?

Year	Team	Shotgun Pct.	Rk	3+ WR Pct.	Rk	2+ RBs Pct.	Rk	PA Pct.	Rk
2008	HOU	11%	31	36%	30	70%	7	22.0%	7
2009	HOU	19%	30	42%	26	62%	11	21.0%	7
2010	HOU	31%	27	43%	23	65%	7	24.6%	2
2011	HOU	19%	31	24%	32	53%	12	32.5%	1
2012	HOU	22%	32	24%	31	52%	12	25.4%	8
2013	HOU	53%	22	43%	29	47%	14	18.9%	20
2014	BAL	24%	32	38%	31	49%	4	18.4%	23
AVG	*Kubiak*	*25.6%*	*29.3*	*35.8%*	*28.9*	*56.9%*	*9.6*	*23.3%*	*9.7*
2008	IND	47%	5	83%	1	11%	32	18.0%	14
2009	IND	51%	2	70%	1	6%	32	22.1%	6
2010	IND	58%	2	79%	1	5%	32	17.3%	18
2012	DEN	57%	6	67%	4	7%	31	28.6%	5
2013	DEN	78%	2	72%	5	4%	31	24.9%	9
2014	DEN	73%	5	72%	4	7%	30	22.6%	13
AVG	*Manning*	*60.7%*	*3.7*	*73.7%*	*2.7*	*6.7%*	*31.3*	*22.3%*	*10.8*

2015 Broncos Schedule

Week	Opp.	Week	Opp.	Week	Opp.
1	BAL	7	BYE	13	at SD
2	at KC (Thu.)	8	GB	14	OAK
3	at DET	9	at IND	15	at PIT
4	MIN	10	KC	16	CIN (Mon.)
5	at OAK	11	at CHI	17	SD
6	at CLE	12	NE		

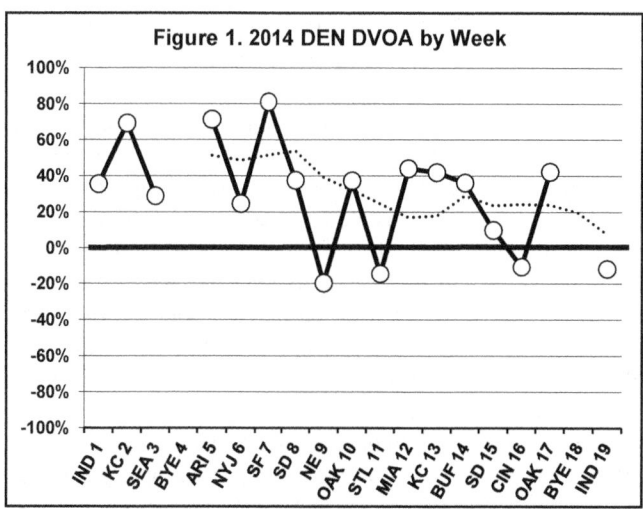

Figure 1. 2014 DEN DVOA by Week

more in Denver than Kubiak's last two offenses have, so no worries there. Manning practiced primarily from under center during OTAs because Kubiak knows the shotgun snaps will be on point. Kubiak has coached John Elway, Brian Griese, Jake Plummer, Schaub, and Flacco to the highest passing DVOA season of each of their careers. Surely he can get Manning functioning at a high level, right? Then again, Denver fans remember the feud between Elway and head coach Dan Reeves. Elway always felt Reeves' style of offense held him back as a player, yet quarterbacks like Roger Staubach, Craig Morton, Phil Simms, Chris Chandler, and Michael Vick all played some of their best ball under Reeves. You just have to hope two professionals will sort out their differences and do what's best for the team to succeed.

Manning is at the stage of his career where he should be doing less, but his control-freak nature and the modern game's rules make it very hard to hold him back from throwing 600 passes in a season. He'll still probably be close to that figure, because Kubiak's offense is not from the prehistoric ages despite its reputation. Even Elway had 586 pass plays under Kubiak, in the long-ago days of 1997. While he's not going to challenge any of his 2013 records this season, Manning will still throw often in this offense.

Of course, Denver's offense already went through some dramatic changes last season with mixed results. Through Week 9, Denver's passing offense ranked first in DVOA (63.9%). In Weeks 10-17, that fell to 16.9% (ninth), which was the biggest midseason decline in the league.[1] Figuring out how much of the second-half decline was on Manning aging versus injury is a huge part of projecting where things are headed in 2015. Some analysts, such as SI's Greg Bedard, suspect Manning was injured as early as the Week 8 game against San Diego. There was no confirmation of that, but FOX's Jay Glazer did report in January that Manning had injuries to both quads, which also was never substantiated.

Here's what we know: through that October game, Manning was leading the league in DVOA, ESPN's QBR, passer rating, touchdown percentage, and various other statistics. He was having another All-Pro season and Denver looked like the class of the AFC. Then he threw 155 passes in a three-game road trip that produced two losses and led to numerous

changes along the bullied offensive line. After C.J. Anderson took over at running back, Denver leaned more on the run, and in Week 12 the offense had arguably its most balanced effort of the last three years against Miami. It's impossible to look at that game and suspect that Manning was injured. Anderson rushed for 167 yards and Manning threw four touchdowns in a 39-36 win. This is really the blueprint for a balanced Kubiak offense, but rarely does an offense perform that well at both styles of attack.

A week later in Kansas City, Manning was nearly flawless in the first half, but played terrible with the lead after halftime, forcing too many deep passes. Manning completed 14-of-20 passes in against both Buffalo and San Diego, relying on the run and deep passes. He entered Week 15's San Diego game with flu-like symptoms and left before halftime to get an IV. This was when the torn quad injury occurred, though Manning returned and finished with one of the highest yards per attempt (11.65) averages he's ever had in a game. Eight days later in Cincinnati, Manning's passes looked noticeably weaker and he struggled with four interceptions in a loss. In the regular-season finale against outmatched Oakland, he mostly did what he wanted, but finished without a touchdown pass for the second time in December. Keep in mind, Anderson led the league with seven rushing touchdowns in December, so the offense was still scoring efficiently.

Then came the brutal playoff loss against the Colts. For the first time in 28 home games with Denver, Manning failed to lead the Broncos to at least 20 points. He didn't even get into the red zone after the opening drive. The game plan was completely nonsensical, with Manning's average pass traveling 16.6 yards in the first half. He didn't have healthy legs to drive the ball with any accuracy. When Manning went to a dink-and-dunk attack in the second half, the Colts were immediately on every receiver. Manning had 15 failed completions, the most for any offense in any game since at least 1989—a

---

1 For those wondering, this is a very large decline, but not historically unprecedented. It doesn't even make the top dozen second-half declines in passing DVOA since 1989. But Denver's decline of 47.0% *was* larger than the biggest decline of the previous year: the 43.8% that Green Bay lost off its passing DVOA after Aaron Rodgers broke his collarbone at midseason. The largest decline ever belongs to the 1999 Patriots, who had 41.7% passing DVOA in Weeks 1-9 (fifth) and then -27.2% in Weeks 10-17 (31st) even though Drew Bledsoe started all 16 games.

span including 13,320 offensive performances.[2] This game screams outlier, but it serves as a very bleak ending to the Fox era in Denver.

Given the type of perfectionist Manning is, he likely would not have returned for the grind of another season if he did not think the struggles were injury-related. Things started so well that it's just not feasible to think he woke up after Halloween and aged dramatically. Think back to Brett Favre in 2008, when the Jets went from looking like the best team in the AFC to 9-7 after Favre tried playing with a torn biceps tendon. He recharged in the offseason, joined the Vikings and played some of his best football at age 40 with Minnesota. That's what Manning should be thinking of with this return.

Everyone's allowed to have a few off games, but Denver's offense had an incredibly weird season. Their top eight games in offensive DVOA were all eight home games. Denver had the fifth-highest home offensive DVOA (45.9%) since 1989, but only ranked 18th on the road (-3.6%) last season. That 49.5% difference in DVOA between home and road is the largest of any of the 797 teams since 1989 (Table 2). All 15 of Manning's previous offenses had ranked in the top 10 in road DVOA, including a dozen top-five finishes. Despite some games of musical chairs along the offensive line, it's not likely that Manning was suddenly unable to audible or communicate with his teammates on the road. It's more likely that the unique schedule wore this team down.[3]

Table 2. Largest Home-Road DVOA Disparity on Offense, 1989-2014

Team	Year	OFF DVOA	Rk	Home DVOA	Rk	Road DVOA	Rk	DIFF
DEN	2014	20.0%	3	45.9%	1	-3.6%	18	-49.5%
PHX	1990	3.5%	14	26.3%	2	-20.5%	23	-46.8%
TB	1998	-7.5%	22	14.6%	8	-28.8%	28	-43.4%
SF	1991	24.0%	2	44.0%	1	1.9%	10	-42.1%
DAL	1990	-23.6%	28	-2.7%	21	-44.1%	28	-41.4%
NYJ	2004	20.8%	4	40.2%	1	0.3%	12	-39.9%
DAL	2008	1.8%	17	22.2%	6	-17.7%	26	-39.9%
GB	2008	7.3%	11	27.7%	1	-11.1%	23	-38.8%
NO	2013	16.0%	5	35.1%	1	-3.7%	16	-38.8%
ARI	1994	-16.3%	27	3.8%	13	-34.3%	28	-38.1%

Denver played five of its first seven games at home, only the ninth team since 1978 to do so (strike seasons excluded). That stretch included an early bye in Week 4. The Broncos paid for the advantageous start by playing six road games in an eight-week stretch. Only one other team since 1978 had to play six of eight on the road after Week 8: the 2007 Broncos, who went 1-5 in those games and finished 7-9. Furthermore, these 2014 Broncos were playing road games against teams that knew them very well, including all three AFC West rivals. The struggles in New England and St. Louis can also be partially attributed to Bill Belichick and Jeff Fisher having 42 games of combined experience against Manning-led offenses. Denver also lost Julius Thomas and Emmanuel Sanders to injuries in the St. Louis game, in addition to starting three offensive linemen in different positions. That's too many changes on the fly against a dominant front seven that was starting to peak. This was a midseason hiccup any team could experience under such circumstances.

Based on the schedule, the Broncos were never as great as they looked early, or as ordinary as they looked later. After the injury, Manning was clearly not the same player, but he's had an offseason to heal. With a more balanced schedule in 2015, Denver should fare better on the road, and the Broncos only have to travel once in the final four games.

Regardless of what you believe happened to Manning and Denver last year, this is still one of the most talented rosters in the NFL. Acquiring all of this talent costs money, so this offseason was more about losses than significant gains, but all of the losses are replaceable.

Wes Welker's concussions became a problem and he was limited to a small number of routes last year. Andre Caldwell can fill that role, and the Broncos will look to get Cody Latimer on the field more this year. Latimer can play outside with Sanders, who was a real home run in free agency, moving to the slot. The big departure is tight end Julius Thomas, the red zone weapon with 24 touchdowns in the last two years. However, Thomas was a total unknown before the 2013 season. In 2012, Manning operated just fine with Jacob Tamme and Joel Dreessen as his tight ends. He still has Virgil Green, and Owen Daniels is a fine pickup who is reuniting with Kubiak on a third team. James Casey, another of Kubiak's former Texans, can line up at fullback or H-back in this offense and catch a few passes as well. Left guard Orlando Franklin, demoted from right tackle after a miserable Super Bowl performance against Seattle, was not a great fit in a zone-blocking scheme since he's not very fleet of foot. But while Franklin is replaceable, the Broncos did not count on losing the entire left side of the offensive line.

Denver had the fewest adjusted games lost to injury in 2014, but things are already regressing quickly in 2015. Ryan Clady was May's big casualty when he tore his ACL in a non-contact drill, leaving right guard Louis Vasquez as the only returning starter on the offensive line. The rest of the line figures to be filled out by largely inexperienced players the Broncos have added since March, but at least they will learn the zone-blocking scheme together. Most are also a good fit for it too, with Shelley Smith, Gino Gradkowski, and Ryan Harris all playing under Kubiak in previous stops. Denver could be starting second-round pick Ty Sambrailo at left tackle, but is starting a rookie that much of a worry given that Manning has won MVP awards

---

2 "Failed completions" are complete passes that do not gain 45 percent of needed yards on first down, 60 percent on second down, or 100 percent on third or fourth down. We wrote more on this incredible game here: http://bit.ly/1InujDv

3 Oddly, the Denver defense had the reverse split, ranking No. 1 in DVOA on the road but only No. 11 at home.

with the likes of Tony Ugoh (bust), Charlie Johnson (moved to guard in Minnesota), and Chris Clark (undrafted journeyman) as his left tackles. Clark, of course, is still in Denver; he replaced Clady in Week 2 of 2013's record-setting offense season but will likely start as right tackle in 2015.

The most stable element to Denver's offensive line is Manning's ability to adjust plays and get rid of the ball quickly. Manning was pressured on 13.1 percent of his passes last year, the lowest rate of any quarterback since 2010. No one who watched the 2014 Broncos would have thought the offensive line was that good, but for an explanation, look no further than who ranks second and third on the pressure list since 2010: Manning in 2012 (13.3 percent) and Manning in his last year with the Colts in 2010 (13.8 percent). He accomplished this with two teams, three offensive coordinators and 18 different starting offensive linemen. That's pure skill and it makes all of his linemen's stats look better.

Manning's ability to negate pressure by getting the offense into the right plays and protection schemes is a huge help to any offensive line. He still gets rid of the ball faster than anyone in the NFL. Denver allowed zero long sacks (more than 3.1 seconds from snap to contact) last year while every other team had at least five. Consider this alongside Kubiak's ability to teach the zone-blocking scheme he learned so well from Alex Gibbs and Mike Shanahan, and it takes away a lot of the concern over this unit's ability to function. The proof is in the numbers: Manning's lines have done an incredible job in adjusted sack rate and Kubiak's lines have dominated on the ground in adjusted line yards (Table 3).

Table 3. Kubiak & Manning: Blocking with Their Minds?

Year	Kubiak			Manning		
	Team	ALY	Rk	Team	ASR	Rk
1995	DEN	4.54	2	-	-	-
1996	DEN	4.43	5	-	-	-
1997	DEN	4.85	1	-	-	-
1998	DEN	4.45	1	IND	4.1%	1
1999	DEN	3.88	18	IND	3.2%	1
2000	DEN	4.38	5	IND	4.2%	2
2001	DEN	4.10	8	IND	5.5%	7
2002	DEN	5.13	1	IND	3.6%	2
2003	DEN	4.43	5	IND	3.6%	2
2004	DEN	4.47	6	IND	3.6%	2
2005	DEN	4.55	2	IND	3.7%	1
2006	HOU	4.21	15	IND	3.4%	1
2007	HOU	4.30	8	IND	4.2%	5
2008	HOU	4.19	10	IND	2.8%	1
2009	HOU	4.13	16	IND	3.1%	1
2010	HOU	4.52	4	IND	2.8%	1
2011	HOU	4.37	4	IND	-	-
2012	HOU	4.17	9	DEN	4.2%	2
2013	HOU	4.10	6	DEN	3.6%	1
2014	BAL	4.25	3	DEN	3.7%	1
AVG	-	4.37	6.5	-	3.7%	1.9

Anderson should be next in the long line of backs that Kubiak's offense has turned into statistical studs: Terrell Davis, Olandis Gary, Mike Anderson, Clinton Portis, Reuben Droughns, Tatum Bell, Steve Slaton, Arian Foster, and Justin Forsett. Maybe backup Montee Ball will even start to shine. And just like Manning, Kubiak has not needed much first-round talent on his offensive line to make his offense work. In Denver, center Tom Nalen was a seventh-round pick and tackle Matt Lepsis (133 starts) was undrafted. Sixth-round pick Chris Myers followed Kubiak from Denver to Houston and became a two-time Pro Bowl center. The line's in great hands with Kubiak and Manning running the offense.

The other pivotal returnee for the 2015 Broncos is defensive coordinator Wade Phillips, who has a long history of turning bad defenses around immediately. His most recent triumph was improving Houston's 31st-ranked defense from 2010 to the sixth-ranked unit in 2011. He's unlikely to improve on Denver's No. 4 DVOA ranking from a year ago, but he should help limit regression towards the mean, and he can do better than ranking 12th in points per drive allowed.

There is plenty of talent here to work with. Not only did Phillips inherit one of the NFL's best pass-rushing duos in Von Miller and DeMarcus Ware, but the Broncos drafted Shane Ray in the first round. Sure, Denver is a tricky landing spot for a player cited for marijuana the week of the draft, but if Ray keeps his head on straight, the Broncos could have some exciting third-down blitz packages with all three players on the field together. Ware, Denver's only starting defender in his thirties, had just one sack in his last seven games. That's why it's important for him to be spelled by Ray, who should get an invaluable learning experience from the player he will eventually replace.

Phillips also can rely on one of the league's strongest secondaries, which featured three Pro Bowl selections in 2014. Thanks to their coverage, Denver had the best pass defense DVOA in the league last year on plays where the quarterback wasn't pressured. However, the Broncos need to be more productive when they do get in the quarterback's face. While Jack Del Rio's unit produced the fifth-highest pressure rate in 2014, the Broncos ranked 29th in DVOA when getting pressure. Del Rio rushed at least five defenders 29.3 percent of the time in his Denver career, dropping down to 22 percent in 2014. Phillips rushed at least five roughly 49 percent of the time in all three of his seasons in Houston. Del Rio's Denver defenses always finished with 24-26 takeaways, a league-average number. Expect Denver to blitz more this season in an effort to generate more big plays.

Phillips' defense should have a fine regular season, but like the offense, it will ultimately be judged by what happens in the postseason. Every Super Bowl winner this century has had its playoff run highlighted by at least one game-changing takeaway. Denver had just three inconsequential takeaways in five playoff games under Del Rio: a fumbled snap by Joe Flacco and two deep Andrew Luck interceptions on third down that effectively served as punts. Champions don't need stars to make those plays—see Tracy Porter (twice) and Malcolm Butler for examples—but they need to get them somehow.

Unless Brock Osweiler is a hidden gem, Kubiak and Phillips have a very small window to deliver a championship in Denver. Six head coaches have reached the Super Bowl in their first season with a team, three of them winning a title. Four of the six were on-staff promotions, including the time Jim Caldwell did his *Weekend at Bernie's* impersonation behind Manning in 2009. The two coaches hired from outside were Red Miller (1977 Broncos) and Jon Gruden (2002 Buccaneers). The latter took over a strong defense and improved the offense enough to get the Buccaneers to the next level. If Kubiak and Phillips can get the running game and defense peaking in the playoffs, then Manning will have all the team support needed for a title run. Maybe he can announce his impending retirement in December to get that extra-effort push from his teammates. Hey, it worked for Ray Lewis, and at the expense of these Broncos.

There is no guarantee this is Manning's final season and he is under contract through 2016, but this could very well be the farewell tour. Elway has done an admirable job of trying to recreate the same perfect ending for Manning that he enjoyed in his own career. Elway set several career-best numbers in passing efficiency in 1998 and won a Super Bowl MVP in his final game. That's as good as it gets, but that only happened because Denver functioned as a complete team. Fox was unable to turn this impressive talent collection into a team that played complementary football against the best competition. Kubiak has no such track record either, but he's also never had this type of talent with which to work. It's a bold experiment, but the Broncos do not want to be remembered as the best team of their era to not win a Super Bowl. Fortune still favors the bold, and the Broncos are still one of the favorites in the AFC.

Scott Kacsmar

2014 Broncos Stats by Week

Wk	vs.	W-L	PF	PA	YDF	YDA	TO	Total	Off	Def	ST
1	IND	W	31	24	361	408	2	35%	40%	-8%	-12%
2	KC	W	24	17	325	380	0	69%	59%	-7%	2%
3	at SEA	L	20	26	332	384	-1	29%	8%	-17%	4%
4	BYE										
5	ARI	W	41	20	568	215	-2	71%	45%	-28%	-1%
6	at NYJ	W	31	17	359	204	2	24%	4%	-17%	4%
7	SF	W	42	17	419	310	1	81%	80%	-8%	-6%
8	SD	W	35	21	425	306	2	37%	36%	-7%	-6%
9	at NE	L	21	43	472	398	-1	-20%	-1%	-13%	-32%
10	at OAK	W	41	17	471	222	1	37%	-6%	-34%	9%
11	at STL	L	7	22	397	337	-2	-14%	-14%	-7%	-8%
12	MIA	W	39	36	450	313	0	44%	66%	11%	-11%
13	at KC	W	29	16	388	151	2	42%	-1%	-43%	-1%
14	BUF	W	24	17	306	415	0	36%	30%	1%	7%
15	at SD	W	22	10	337	288	2	10%	-7%	-19%	-2%
16	at CIN	L	28	37	385	353	-2	-11%	-13%	-15%	-13%
17	OAK	W	47	14	451	199	1	42%	18%	-15%	9%
18	BYE										
19	IND	L	13	24	288	364	1	-12%	-1%	15%	4%

Trends and Splits

	Offense	Rank	Defense	Rank
Total DVOA	20.0%	3	-13.2%	4
Unadjusted VOA	20.6%	2	-10.9%	4
Weighted Trend	14.3%	6	-13.3%	3
Variance	8.9%	22	1.7%	1
Average Opponent	-1.9%	7	-1.3%	22
Passing	40.5%	3	-7.2%	5
Rushing	3.8%	7	-23.6%	3
First Down	8.9%	9	-11.9%	4
Second Down	20.4%	2	-13.6%	3
Third Down	43.0%	1	-15.0%	9
First Half	18.9%	5	-7.2%	11
Second Half	21.3%	3	-18.7%	2
Red Zone	30.4%	2	4.8%	25
Late and Close	25.0%	2	-38.0%	1

Five-Year Performance

Year	W-L	Pyth W	Est W	PF	PA	TO	Total	Rk	Off	Rk	Def	Rk	ST	Rk	Off AGL	Rk	Def AGL	Rk	Off Age	Rk	Def Age	Rk	ST Age	Rk
2010	4-12	4.9	5.3	344	471	-9	-17.1%	26	2.1%	15	16.6%	30	-2.6%	27	10.9	6	40.7	28	26.6	24	28.9	2	25.6	28
2011	8-8	5.8	7.0	309	390	+1	-11.8%	24	-9.9%	23	1.6%	18	-0.2%	18	15.0	4	40.4	24	25.6	32	27.5	10	25.9	28
2012	13-3	12.5	14.7	481	289	-1	36.5%	2	22.1%	2	-13.8%	5	0.6%	13	27.8	15	21.4	11	28.3	5	27.0	15	25.9	21
2013	13-3	11.7	14.1	606	399	0	32.7%	2	33.5%	1	-0.2%	15	-1.0%	21	37.8	19	45.8	26	27.9	3	26.3	18	26.8	5
2014	12-4	11.0	13.3	482	354	+5	29.5%	2	20.0%	3	-13.2%	4	-3.7%	27	11.7	4	25.2	6	28.6	2	25.7	31	25.6	27

2014 Performance Based on Most Common Personnel Groups

DEN Offense					DEN Offense vs. Opponents					DEN Defense					DEN Defense vs. Opponents			
Pers	Freq	Yds	DVOA	Run%	Pers	Freq	Yds	DVOA	Run%	Pers	Freq	Yds	DVOA		Pers	Freq	Yds	DVOA
11	71%	6.8	32.7%	33%	Base	26%	5.5	14.7%	57%	Base	29%	4.4	-21.1%		11	60%	5.1	-13.1%
12	16%	5.7	20.6%	42%	Nickel	57%	6.5	29.6%	35%	Nickel	34%	4.6	-12.7%		12	18%	4.6	-13.2%
611	11%	5.2	1.6%	71%	Dime+	17%	7.1	26.7%	25%	Dime+	36%	5.4	-9.1%		21	8%	4.2	-19.4%
01	1%	6.3	17.8%	0%	Goal Line	1%	0.8	34.6%	100%	Goal Line	1%	4.1	51.7%		13	3%	5.2	-8.4%
02	0%	-1.2	-125.9%	40%						Big	0%	3.6	18.0%		01	2%	6.2	3.5%

Strategic Tendencies

Run/Pass		Rk	Formation		Rk	Pass Rush		Rk	Secondary		Rk	Strategy		Rk
Runs, first half	38%	15	Form: Single Back	89%	2	Rush 3	5.6%	18	4 DB	22%	24	Play action	23%	13
Runs, first down	50%	13	Form: Empty Back	7%	12	Rush 4	72.5%	4	5 DB	34%	27	Avg Box (Off)	6.12	27
Runs, second-long	30%	17	Pers: 3+ WR	72%	4	Rush 5	18.2%	26	6+ DB	43%	5	Avg Box (Def)	6.09	29
Runs, power sit.	53%	22	Pers: 4+ WR	1%	22	Rush 6+	3.7%	29	CB by Sides	82%	15	Offensive Pace	29.28	9
Runs, behind 2H	21%	30	Pers: 2+ TE/6+ OL	29%	18	Sacks by LB	43.9%	13	DB Blitz	6%	27	Defensive Pace	31.13	28
Pass, ahead 2H	49%	12	Shotgun/Pistol	73%	5	Sacks by DB	14.6%	5	Hole in Zone	5%	20	Go for it on 4th	1.07	14

We can get rid of that old book that says not to blitz Peyton Manning. For the third straight year, Manning had more yards per pass against three or four pass rushers (8.1) than against five or more pass rushers (7.6). And once again, Manning struggled against defensive back blitzes even though Denver opponents almost never used this strategy. Manning faced DB blitzes on just 6.8 percent of passes—only Matthew Stafford faced them less often—but had just 5.7 yards per pass on these plays. ☞ Of course, most defensive coordinators are still playing by the old book. Manning faced only three pass rushers on 14 percent of pass plays, when no other quarterback was above 10 percent. He crushed these defenses with 8.9 yards per pass. ☞ For the second straight year, Denver was among the top three teams in using wide receiver screens, but these plays were much less successful. The Broncos averaged 5.5 yards with 0.0% DVOA after averaging 8.3 yards and 99.6% DVOA on wide receiver screens in 2013. ☞ Denver used six linemen more often than any other team: 122 plays by our count, or 11.6 percent of plays. It may not have been the best strategy, as the Broncos had just 4.8 yards per play and -8.0% DVOA on these plays. It was a dramatic change from 2013, when the Broncos were the only team we never recorded using a six-lineman set. ☞ Now that they had DeMarcus Ware and a full year of a healthy Von Miller, the Broncos didn't depend as much on the blitz as they had in years past. In 2013, they had sent five or more pass rushers on 34 percent of pass plays, and blitzed a defensive back 15 percent of the time. Last year, those numbers dropped to 22 percent and 6.4 percent. Oddly, even though DB blitzes dropped by more than half, the Broncos went from having zero sacks from defensive backs in 2013 to six in 2014.

Passing

Player	DYAR	DVOA	Plays	NtYds	Avg	YAC	C%	TD	Int
P.Manning	1412	23.9%	615	4589	7.5	4.8	66.5%	39	15
B.Osweiler	-5	-19.7%	10	42	4.2	7.5	44.4%	1	0

Rushing

Player	DYAR	DVOA	Plays	Yds	Avg	TD	Fum	Suc
C.J.Anderson	196	17.5%	179	849	4.7	8	0	51%
R.Hillman	31	-1.4%	106	434	4.1	3	1	43%
M.Ball	-26	-20.2%	55	172	3.1	1	1	44%
J.Thompson	67	18.0%	54	272	5.0	3	1	61%
E.Sanders	31	43.2%	8	44	5.5	0	0	–
J.Stewart	-7	-32.9%	6	22	3.7	0	0	33%

Receiving

Player	DYAR	DVOA	Plays	Ctch	Yds	Y/C	YAC	TD	C%
D.Thomas	317	9.2%	184	111	1619	14.6	5.8	11	60%
E.Sanders	481	29.6%	141	101	1404	13.9	3.5	9	72%
W.Welker*	86	4.4%	64	49	464	9.5	3.9	2	77%
A.Caldwell	-37	-44.8%	15	5	47	9.4	3.6	0	33%
J.Thomas*	140	24.7%	62	43	489	11.4	3.8	12	69%
J.Tamme	-67	-42.8%	28	14	111	7.9	1.6	2	50%
V.Green	35	71.5%	6	6	74	12.3	7.7	1	100%
O.Daniels	49	2.2%	79	48	527	11.0	3.7	4	61%
C.J.Anderson	65	13.0%	44	34	324	9.5	8.3	2	77%
R.Hillman	-8	-18.3%	34	21	139	6.6	5.1	1	62%
M.Ball	-4	-19.7%	13	9	62	6.9	5.8	0	69%
J.Thompson	-15	-51.4%	7	4	25	6.3	5.3	0	57%

Offensive Line

Player	Pos	Age	GS	Snaps	Pen	Sk	Pass	Run	Player	Pos	Age	GS	Snaps	Pen	Sk	Pass	Run
Manny Ramirez*	C/G	32	16/16	1123	5	1.0	9.0	12.0	Will Montgomery*	C	32	16/8	581	4	0.5	0.5	2.5
Louis Vasquez	G/T	28	16/16	1120	6	3.0	12.0	5.0	Chris Clark	RT	30	13/7	472	7	2.0	5.5	4.5
Orlando Franklin*	LG	28	16/16	1090	10	0.5	7.0	9.5	Paul Cornick	OT	26	12/6	300	4	1.0	4.0	1.0
Ryan Clady	LT	29	16/16	1052	7	2.0	13.5	5.0	Shelley Smith	G	28	11/3	359	3	2.0	7.0	4.0

Year	Yards	ALY	Rk	Power	Rk	Stuff	Rk	2nd Lev	Rk	Open Field	Rk	Sacks	ASR	Rk	Short	Long	F-Start	Cont.
2012	4.07	4.13	12	67%	9	20%	20	1.19	16	0.53	25	21	4.2%	2	10	5	12	29
2013	4.38	4.07	8	64%	17	16%	3	1.30	4	0.63	20	20	3.6%	1	9	6	14	36
2014	4.39	3.98	12	75%	5	18%	9	1.24	10	0.83	7	17	3.7%	1	10	0	18	36
2014 ALY by direction:		Left End 3.38 (24)			Left Tackle 2.98 (31)			Mid/Guard 4.27 (4)			Right Tackle 4.12 (12)				Right End 3.54 (18)			

The offensive line is clearly Denver's biggest weakness heading into training camp, and that was true even before Ryan Clady tore his ACL in May. Right guard Louis Vasquez, 2014's only returning starter, is arguably the only player locked into a starting job. However, as long as Peyton Manning is the maestro, Denver can continue its game of musical chairs along the offensive line, with a constantly changing roster and, this year, a new zone-blocking scheme. Fortunately, there's time for everyone to learn the offense together. Manning's not going to sacrifice what could be his final season behind an offensive line that's not ready to operate at a high level.

Orlando Franklin told *The Denver Post* in May 2014 that "it was a lot easier to play with Kyle Orton and Tim Tebow when I came in." He was not talking about ease of blocking, but there was more information to process after Manning arrived. Franklin moved from right tackle to left guard before last season; we charted him with half as many blown blocks on passes compared to the year before, but he also finished with the second-most blown blocks at his position in the run game. He's made the move to San Diego, so Manning may have to data dump on former Air Force officer Ben Garland instead. Garland spent three years on Denver's military reserve list and then a year on the practice squad before getting his first NFL playing time in 2014, but he still has never started an NFL game. His competition at left guard is veteran Shelley Smith, who was benched in Miami after just two starts last season.

Manny Ramirez started last season at center, but struggles up front led to big changes in Week 10. Will Montgomery took over at center, where he averaged the most snaps per blown block in 2014, but he has moved on to the Bears. Ramirez was moved to right guard, which slid 2013 All-Pro guard Louis Vasquez over to right tackle where he had most of his blown blocks and all of his sacks allowed. He was still better than Chris Clark (fewest snaps per blown block on the roster) and Paul Cornick, but those experiments are over in 2015. Vasquez is returning to guard, which is a more natural position for his mauling style. He is familiar with zone concepts, having playing in Mike Leach's offense at Texas Tech and in San Diego early in his NFL career. Ramirez was traded to Detroit as part of the move to draft Shane Ray, so expect Gino Gradkowski (who learned under Kubiak in Baltimore) or fourth-round rookie Max Garcia (Florida) to take over at center.

The Clady injury opens up some interesting tackle scenarios. Clark is not a lock for right tackle, because Denver still has to take a look at Michael Schofield. No, not the guy from *Prison Break*, but a 2014 third-round pick from Michigan with the footwork and run-blocking ability Kubiak covets in his scheme. Ty Sambrailo (Colorado State) was a second-round pick with the potential to start at left tackle in Week 1, though some scouts saw him as a finesse player. He's already received good practice reps with the first team against Denver's talented front seven. DeMarcus Ware noted he saw Sambrailo's aggressiveness start to come out in OTAs. Ryan Harris was signed after the Clady injury, and he has the experience to start at either tackle position should Clark or the rookie falter.

Defensive Front Seven

Defensive Line	Age	Pos	G	Snaps	Plays	TmPct	Rk	Stop	Dfts	BTkl	Runs	St%	Rk	RuYd	Rk	Sack	Hit	Hur	Dsrpt
Terrance Knighton*	29	DT	16	520	33	4.0%	61	32	11	1	25	100%	1	1.2	15	2.0	4	4.5	3
Sylvester Williams	27	DT	16	426	22	2.7%	--	16	4	0	21	71%	--	2.1	--	0.0	2	7.5	0
Marvin Austin	26	DT	15	274	12	1.6%	--	10	0	0	11	91%	--	2.6	--	0.0	1	2.0	0
Antonio Smith	34	DT	16	757	19	2.3%	91	18	7	1	15	93%	3	1.1	14	3.0	3	19.5	0

Edge Rushers	Age	Pos	G	Snaps	Plays	Overall TmPct	Rk	Stop	Dfts	BTkl	Runs	St%	vs. Run Rk	RuYd	Rk	Sack	Hit	Pass Rush Hur	Dsrpt
DeMarcus Ware	33	DE	16	739	40	4.9%	48	34	19	2	27	78%	34	2.0	26	10.0	11	26.0	0
Derek Wolfe	25	DE	16	718	36	4.4%	56	27	4	2	31	74%	43	2.4	41	2.0	3	13.0	1
Malik Jackson	25	DE	16	565	45	5.5%	33	38	14	2	32	84%	14	1.3	9	3.0	9	22.0	3
Quanterus Smith	26	DE	15	305	13	1.7%	--	10	2	0	8	75%	--	2.6	--	0.0	1	3.5	3

Linebackers	Age	Pos	G	Snaps	Plays	Overall TmPct	Rk	Stop	Dfts	BTkl	Sack	Pass Rush Hit	Hur	Runs	St%	vs. Run Rk	RuYd	Rk	Tgts	Suc%	vs. Pass Rk	AdjYd	Rk	PD	Int
Von Miller	26	OLB	16	910	61	7.5%	76	46	24	4	13.5	12	43	31	77%	7	2.0	6	8	35%	--	6.2	--	0	0
Brandon Marshall	26	OLB	14	870	119	16.6%	15	67	21	6	2.0	1	3.5	62	60%	59	3.8	61	52	50%	37	4.5	5	8	1
Nate Irving*	27	MLB	8	349	45	11.0%	55	22	10	5	1.0	1	3	34	59%	64	3.6	51	16	38%	57	11.6	63	0	0
Steven Johnson	27	MLB	14	210	22	3.1%	--	11	2	2	0.5	1	3	12	67%	--	4.4	--	6	17%	--	13.6	--	0	0

Year	Yards	ALY	Rk	Power	Rk	Stuff	Rk	2nd Level	Rk	Open Field	Rk	Sacks	ASR	Rk	Short	Long
2012	3.69	3.91	14	52%	6	18%	18	1.02	3	0.35	1	52	8.7%	1	19	18
2013	3.61	3.23	3	64%	13	22%	9	1.03	9	0.63	16	41	6.5%	22	11	16
2014	3.55	3.20	2	55%	7	22%	7	0.97	5	0.60	11	41	6.3%	23	15	15
2014 ALY by direction:		Left End 2.65 (4)			Left Tackle 2.89 (4)			Mid/Guard 3.57 (8)			Right Tackle 2.56 (1)			Right End 2.59 (5)		

As a head coach or defensive coordinator, Wade Phillips has coached the likes of Reggie White, Bruce Smith, Elvin Bethea, DeMarcus Ware (twice now), and J.J. Watt. In Buffalo, he made Bryce Paup into the 1995 Defensive Player of the Year. Phillips seems to know something about molding talented pass-rushers into greatness, and how that can help the other pieces in a defense. The Broncos are transitioning from a 4-3 to a 3-4 under Phillips, but either way Von Miller is the best player in this front seven. After dealing with a suspension and serious injury in 2013, Miller returned to form with 43 quarterback hurries, second only to Watt (54). As if Phillips did not have enough pass-rushing talent to work with here, the Broncos also moved up in the draft to select Missouri's Shane Ray, who slid due to a marijuana citation the week of the draft. But is Ray truly the top-10 talent he was thought to be before the slide? His SackSEER rating of 18.5 percent portrays him as another Vernon Gholston. Ray blew up his junior year with 14.5 sacks, but only had 4.5 sacks in his first two seasons with just one pass defensed in his entire college career. He also had a poor pro day, though Ray supporters claim he was hampered by a foot injury suffered during the Citrus Bowl. He's more likely to replace Ware down the road than have a big impact this season, but if anyone can figure out a way to get everything he can out of Ray's talent, it's Phillips.

The outside linebackers get all the pub in the 3-4, but Denver's defensive line deserves attention for its strength against the run. Only Detroit allowed fewer adjusted line yards. Terrance Knighton impressively had a 100 percent stop rate against the run, but he only averaged 32.5 snaps per game. Although the free-agent market never quite materialized for him, he left for Washington on a one-year contract. The Broncos are content to move forward with 2013 first-round pick Sylvester Williams at nose tackle, though he made his average run tackle roughly a yard further downfield than Knighton in both 2013 and 2014. Williams will have strong insulation with Malik Jackson and Derek Wolfe at defensive end. Jackson had a career season with production against the run and pass and should be a nice fit as a five-technique end in the 3-4. Wolfe recovered from the seizure symptoms he suffered in 2013, though his performance still hasn't quite returned to the level he showed in his rookie year. His four-game suspension for performance-enhancing drugs puts the spotlight on Vance Walker and opens an opportunity for Kenny Anunike, a 2014 UDFA from Duke. Antonio Smith provides veteran depth, though his availability is in question due to a criminal investigation in Texas.

It's easy to forget those inside linebackers, but someone has to clean up the line's mistakes and defend the short passes. Danny Trevathan and Brandon Marshall are a strong duo for the job. The greatest trick Trevathan ever pulled was to convince Phil Simms that he sometimes was the best linebacker in football in 2013. He can be very good, but last year was basically a lost season as injuries limited Trevathan to three games. Marshall had a bit of a breakout year even though angry fantasy players still confuse him for the ex-Broncos wide receiver on Twitter. He's had foot surgery this offseason, making health a concern for both linebackers. Compounding that worry is the lack of depth behind Trevathan and Marshall. Nate Irving left for the Colts and Denver did not draft any inside linebackers.

Defensive Secondary

Secondary	Age	Pos	G	Snaps	Plays	TmPct	Rk	Stop	Dfts	BTkl	Runs	St%	Rk	RuYd	Rk	Tgts	Tgt%	Rk	Dist	Suc%	Rk	AdjYd	Rk	PD	Int
Rahim Moore*	25	FS	16	1054	55	6.7%	62	16	8	6	19	26%	58	11.5	69	24	5.1%	7	14.7	47%	55	7.4	40	6	4
T.J. Ward	29	SS	15	1003	79	10.3%	36	41	15	8	29	76%	1	3.3	2	60	13.6%	66	8.6	53%	38	7.1	30	6	2
Chris Harris	26	CB	16	987	71	8.7%	35	35	20	5	10	40%	38	3.7	6	75	17.2%	5	12.3	59%	6	5.1	3	13	3
Aqib Talib	29	CB	15	917	80	10.4%	12	35	15	6	9	44%	29	4.1	8	91	22.4%	28	12.8	55%	20	5.9	6	15	4
Bradley Roby	23	CB	16	805	76	9.3%	25	35	20	7	7	29%	53	5.1	19	81	22.8%	32	12.0	47%	55	8.5	49	13	2
Quinton Carter*	27	FS	11	218	16	2.8%	--	5	4	3	3	0%	--	7.7	--	8	8.3%	--	11.6	16%	--	11.7	--	1	0
David Bruton	28	SS	14	188	23	3.2%	--	13	6	1	6	67%	--	7.2	--	6	7.2%	--	9.2	65%	--	2.6	--	2	0
Kayvon Webster	24	CB	12	130	21	3.4%	--	9	5	0	5	40%	--	6.2	--	14	24.4%	--	12.1	48%	--	7.9	--	1	0
Darian Stewart	27	SS	16	755	56	6.7%	63	21	4	9	27	52%	19	6.3	33	16	5.3%	11	17.5	61%	14	8.4	51	3	1

Year	Pass D Rank	vs. #1 WR	Rk	vs. #2 WR	Rk	vs. Other WR	Rk	vs. TE	Rk	vs. RB	Rk
2012	5	-12.5%	8	-20.3%	3	-18.1%	4	6.9%	24	-7.7%	11
2013	21	-1.1%	17	-4.5%	11	13.7%	27	3.8%	17	-8.7%	13
2014	5	-18.6%	5	-36.0%	2	5.3%	22	-7.0%	13	-1.4%	17

Phillips has the flexibility to bring pressure thanks to one of the best secondary units in the league. Aqib Talib was the big-money signing last offseason, but Chris Harris fared better in charting. He can both cover No. 1 receivers on the outside and defend the slot. What made his season even more remarkable was that he tore his ACL in January against the Chargers in the playoffs and still made it back to start all 16 games and not allow a single touchdown pass.[4] The Broncos and Cardinals were the only two teams to field three cornerbacks with at least 75 charted targets, and Harris was actually targeted the least among Denver's trio. Rookie Bradley Roby had a game-clinching pass breakup against Reggie Wayne on fourth down in Week 1, but he had his share of struggles last year, with some offenses targeting him in coverage instead of Harris and Talib. We see young cornerbacks improve in their second seasons all the time, and there is no reason not to be optimistic about Roby after last year. There's also good depth here with Tony Carter and Kayvon Webster returning, and the addition of fifth-round rookie Lorenzo Doss who displayed good ball skills at Tulane with 33 passes defensed and 15 interceptions in three seasons.

T.J. Ward came as advertised from Cleveland with his ability to stop the run. He led all safeties with a 76 percent stop rate, and while he did have 20 fewer stops than in his 2013 breakout year, the drop is a bit deceiving since the Broncos faced the most passes and fewest runs of any defense in 2014. Ward was also charted with 60 targets, or as many as he had in 2012-13 combined. He cleaned up underneath while Rahim Moore defended the deep passes with a competence fans only wish he had shown that time Jacoby Jones asked him to dance with the devil in the pale moonlight. Moore did not help in the run game and always had average charting metrics at best, so it's not surprising the Broncos did not re-sign him. David Bruton has been with the team since 2009, but veteran Darian Stewart will likely replace Moore as the starting free safety. Stewart brings a more physical edge, though durability is a concern. Last year with Baltimore was the first time he completed a full 16-game season in five tries.

Special Teams

Year	DVOA	Rank	FG/XP	Rank	Net Kick	Rank	Kick Ret	Rank	Net Punt	Rank	Punt Ret	Rank	Hidden	Rank
2012	0.6%	13	-4.7	26	-1.6	20	0.9	12	13.2	5	-4.6	24	-0.1	18
2013	-1.0%	21	10.7	3	-11.7	29	5.4	5	-1.9	22	-7.6	28	20.8	1
2014	-3.7%	27	-4.4	27	-6.3	27	6.3	4	-7.7	26	-6.3	29	7.8	4

The coverage and return units performed relatively similar to 2013, but the significant decline was in kicking field goals. Matt Prater went from etching his name into the record book to seeking a new job after serving a four-game suspension for violating the NFL's substance abuse policy. Brandon McManus, fresh off a preseason trial with the Giants, tried to fill the void but Denver altitude be damned, he never made a field goal longer than 44 yards. His lack of range should have encouraged John Fox let Peyton Manning go for it on fourth down more often, but that never materialized. Veteran kicker Connor Barth was signed in late November and only missed one of his 18 field goals with the team (including playoffs). However, none of Barth's eight kickoffs in Kansas City (Week 13) produced a touchback, so McManus was brought back as the kickoff specialist and finished

---

4 Harris was covering Keenen Allen when Allen scored on a 2-yard touchdown on a screen pass in Week 8, but we don't count screens in our charting stats for cornerbacks. Getting blocked out of a play at the line of scrimmage is certainly not the same as getting beat in coverage downfield.

fourth in touchback rate (70.3 percent). Without a big improvement in range from McManus, the Broncos may need to spend a roster spot on a kickoff specialist again in 2015.

One way to maximize McManus' value may be to try him at punter, given that he averaged 45.1 yards per punt at Temple. Britton Colquitt is one of the highest-paid punters in the NFL, but he declined for the second year in a row, falling to 23rd in gross punt value and 26th in net punt value.

Return specialist Trindon Holliday was another notable departure for last year's team, but the Broncos did not miss his fumbling habits. Omar Bolden and Andre Caldwell split the kick return duties, and Bolden surged late in the season. Even though Bolden had just 12 kick returns, he finished third in the NFL in value behind the Jones not-brothers, Adam and Jacoby. He also led the Broncos with 12 special-teams tackles. Denver might as well give Bolden a shot at punt returns, where Isaiah Burse showed so little last year. Only Ace Sanders of Jacksonville had more negative value than Burse on punt returns.

Detroit Lions

2014 Record: 11-5	**Total DVOA:** 4.4% (14th)	**2015 Mean Projection:** 8.2 wins	**On the Clock (0-4):** 8%
Pythagorean Wins: 9.2 (13th)	**Offense:** -3.8% (19th)	**Postseason Odds:** 37.5%	**Mediocrity (5-7):** 32%
Snap-Weighted Age: 27.0 (7th)	**Defense:** -13.9% (3rd)	**Super Bowl Odds:** 5.6%	**Playoff Contender (8-10):** 40%
Average Opponent: -2.1% (23rd)	**Special Teams:** -5.7% (31st)	**Proj. Avg. Opponent:** 3.8% (3rd)	**Super Bowl Contender (11+):** 20%

2014: The Lions finally roll the boulder up the mountain with their highest win total since 1991.

2015: Actually, the Lions are just at a lean-to halfway up the mountain.

No NFL franchise has starved the way the Detroit Lions have. The current owners of the league's longest championship drought, Detroit's 1957 title came roughly two months before a band called The Quarrymen started fiddling with its name and eventually settled on The Beatles. By those standards, an 11-5 playoff campaign in the first year of a new coaching regime should sound rather promising. So why does it feel like we're watching the same old Lions?

Well, for one thing, the shiny record was partially the by-product of some fool's gold. In 2012 and 2013, the Lions went 7-15 in one-score games, leading the league in such losses and bettering only the Tampa Bay Buccaneers in winning percentage. The pendulum finally swung back last year, and Detroit went 6-3 in one-score contests (including its wild-card loss to Dallas). The Lions were actually playing better in tight contests, as they were one of five teams to rank in the top ten of both offensive and defensive DVOA in late-and-close situations, along with Dallas, New England, Denver and Seattle. Unlike those squads, however, Detroit was escaping against inferior competition. Five of the Lions' six one-score wins came against teams who finished the year with losing records; the other four teams listed had just seven combined one-score wins against sub-.500 level teams. Overall, Detroit's Pythagorean win total jumped minimally from 8.5 to 9.2 despite its actual four-win improvement from 2013, which would suggest oncoming stagnation if the Lions returned the exact same core from last season.

Of course, the most important defender in that core migrated south this offseason. It's quintessentially Lions that, after years of whiffing on Carlos Rogers and Joey Harrington types, Detroit would select a pair of true blue-chippers in Calvin Johnson and Ndamukong Suh, only for both to become *too good* to afford. The Suh-Megatron-Matthew Stafford triumvirate gobbled up a whopping 39 percent of the team's salary cap last year, and that figure would have risen even higher in 2015 had the Lions been able to keep their All-Pro defensive tackle. As it is, the Ghost of Suh (i.e., his dead money) will hold the third-highest cap number on the Lions' 2015 books while the living version stomps away in South Beach. That's an extremely problematic development for Detroit, which built its success on a front seven that anchored last year's top rushing defense by both DVOA and adjusted line yards. Miami and Dallas, the second- and third-best rushing teams

according to DVOA, combined for 123 yards on 40 carries against the Lions, good for a rushing average that would have been the worst among all qualifying running backs last season. Teams quite literally stopped trying to run on the Lions. In one three-week stretch, the Patriots, Bears and Buccaneers combined for 42 carries, eight of which came from LeGarrette Blount on the final drive of a blowout. It's hard to overstate the value of Suh, who is not only a transcendent player in a vacuum, but the fulcrum around which Detroit built its weekly game plans. Despite receiving double-teams most of the time, Suh was still involved in 7.1 percent of Detroit's defensive plays, highest on the team and 11th among interior defenders. Many will remember Suh's time in the Motor City as filled with fines and a general disrespect for others, but they should also remember a two-play sequence from last year's wild-card game. With Dallas in the red zone trailing by six, Tony Romo held the ball for roughly eight seconds on consecutive plays, only for the indefatigable Suh to wrestle past a double-team to drag down Romo for a sack each time. And with the free-agent departures of both Nick Fairley and C.J. Mosley, who each started eight games alongside Suh, even the skeleton of his supporting cast is gone.

So how does defensive coordinator Teryl Austin retool? Haloti Ngata's acquisition should help keep the middle of the line respectable, and the 31-year-old still has game, having accrued the fourth-most disruptions (batted passes plus incompletions caused by QB hits) last season. But Ngata isn't the All-Pro cornerstone he once was; it's telling that Baltimore posted four of its best defensive DVOA figures during Ngata's four-game suspension to end the regular season. Fortunately, Detroit still possesses an exemplary linebacking corps, strengthened this offseason by Stephen Tulloch's return. The Lions' defensive captain tore his ACL while celebrating a sack of Aaron Rodgers in Week 3, a particularly cruel price to pay for Detroit's biggest win in years. Tulloch may have led the Lions with 30 defeats in 2013, but he'll return to find the bar raised by his partner-in-crime DeAndre Levy. Without Tulloch, Levy blossomed into one of the league's most active linebackers. The sixth-year linebacker was involved in 19.5 percent of Detroit's defensive plays, the third-highest rate of any defender last season. Suh may have been Detroit's most famous defender, but Levy was its most omnipresent, whether carrying a receiver down the seam or knifing through the A-

2015 Lions Schedule

Week	Opp.	Week	Opp.	Week	Opp.
1	at SD	7	MIN	13	GB (Thu.)
2	at MIN	8	at KC (U.K.)	14	at STL
3	DEN	9	BYE	15	at NO (Mon.)
4	at SEA (Mon.)	10	at GB	16	SF
5	ARI	11	OAK	17	at CHI
6	CHI	12	PHI (Thu.)		

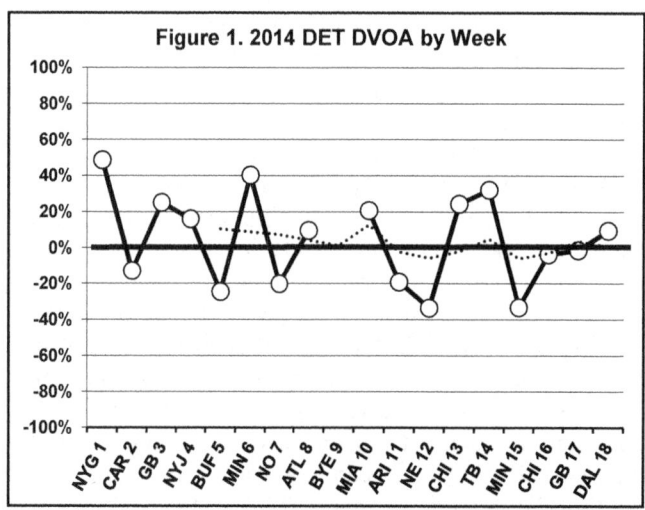

gap. Assuming Tulloch is reasonably effective 11 months removed from knee surgery, few teams can boast a more versatile linebacker duo than Detroit. If we use defeats as a reliable measure of big plays, only three teams have had two different linebackers accrue 30 or more defeats in either of the past two seasons: Baltimore, Carolina, and Detroit (Table 1).

Table 1. Linebackers with 30+ Defeats, 2013-2014

Player	Team	Year	Defeats
Karlos Dansby	ARI	2013	31
Daryl Smith	BAL	2013	32
C.J. Mosley	BAL	2014	30
Thomas Davis	CAR	2013	37
Luke Kuechly	CAR	2013	34
DeAndre Levy	**DET**	**2014**	**35**
Stephen Tulloch	**DET**	**2013**	**30**
Robert Mathis	IND	2013	33
Justin Houston	KC	2014	33
Kevin Burnett	OAK	2013	30
NaVorro Bowman	SF	2013	35
Alec Ogletree	STL	2013	34
Lavonte David	TB	2013	50
Lavonte David	TB	2014	42

No defense is better without Suh, but at least Austin has a clear foundation around which to reprogram the unit as a whole. The linebacking unit is not just the Levy-Tulloch show, as Tahir Whitehead was a pleasant revelation replacing Tulloch, posting a team-high 73 percent run stop rate. With 2014 second-rounder Kyle Van Noy also in the fold, the Lions have more capable linebackers than they can currently provide snaps for. Given that defensive tackle acquisitions Ngata and Tyrunn Walker both played in 3-4 systems last year, there has been speculation that the Lions could be more multiple in their fronts.

And considering Austin's background in Baltimore's versatile scheme, we might reasonably expect further changes to a defense that certainly benefited from fresh leadership last year. For instance, Austin's defense put together more creative pressure schemes than the straight four-man rushes that characterized the Jim Schwartz era. While he wasn't exactly Todd Bowles or Rob Ryan, Austin was more willing to send extra rushers, forcing the ball out of opposing quarterbacks' hands and alleviating pressure off his mediocre secondary personnel. Austin sent five or more rushers on 25.1 percent of opponent dropbacks, a big uptick from Schwartz's 19.7 percent rate in 2013. Though that was still below the NFL average (30.9 percent), Austin could conceivably further escalate the pass-rushing opportunities for the likes of Levy, Tulloch, and James Ihedigbo, all of whom were sent on the occasional blitz last year.

Of course, the Lions defense could afford a little more margin for error if the offense's production matched its talent on a more consistent basis. We've heard this story before, and 2014 was yet another gunslingin', Wrangler-jean-wearin' campaign for Matthew Stafford. No wait, that's not right. While the side-arming, mechanically inconsistent side of Stafford was still recognizable, the Lions quietly underwent significant changes in the passing game under first-year coordinator Joe Lombardi. Coming over from New Orleans, Lombardi installed an offense designed so Stafford could plant and deliver quickly, with route combinations disguised out of a variety of formations. Announcers happily noted these facts within the first 10 minutes of virtually every Lions contest, always insinuating that a grand change was in the offing for Stafford's game.

Stafford did deliver the lowest interception rate of his career (excluding 2010, when he played just three games), while seeing his touchdown rate and per-attempt yardage numbers dip significantly as well. And yet, it would also be wrong to suggest that Stafford has evolved into a more conservative version of his former self. For one, accuracy issues still plagued the former No. 1 pick, as Stafford's 20 percent bad-throw figure (the rate of passes marked as overthrown or underthrown by game charters) ranked 28th out of 36 quarterbacks with at least 200 pass attempts. That included an abysmal 7.7 percent of passes being underthrown, which ranked 32nd. The anecdotal evidence confirms this, for hardly a quarter passed last year without Stafford firing a screen or slant pass behind or at the feet of a poor receiver. Stafford has always had erratic aim, but considering that Detroit's short-pass percentage rose from 78 percent in 2013 to 82 percent under Lombardi, the numbers become a little more concerning.

Still, it's not entirely fair to pile on Stafford for not carrying the same burden as Andrew Luck or Peyton Manning simply because they all share the same draft slot. The Lions receiving corps was extremely thin last season, perilously so while Calvin Johnson battled ankle woes. Megatron posted his lowest DVOA since 2009, and he was essentially out of commission from Weeks 4-9 after getting banged up against Green Bay. (Between Johnson and Tulloch, was there a more underrated Pyrrhic victory last season?) Human pinball Golden Tate, signed away from Seattle before the season, was prolific as the primary beneficiary of Lombardi's system and Megatron's injury, quietly finishing eighth in targets (144) and seventh in receiving yards (1,331). But Tate can only outrun so many defenders on screen passes behind the line, and his production certainly can't fully make up for the Lions' disintegrating supporting cast. Joseph Fauria and Reggie Bush, both new additions to the 2013 squad, produced a combined total of 1,719 yards from scrimmage and 18 touchdowns that season. In 2014, those figures collapsed to 624 yards from scrimmage and five touchdowns. Rookies Eric Ebron and Corey Fuller were occasionally promising but mostly overmatched, though both figure to rank among Stafford's top targets in 2015.

Perhaps seeking relief for Stafford and his motley crew of receivers, general manager Marty Mayhew targeted improvements in the running game this offseason. After a couple promising seasons in 2012 and 2013, Joique Bell essentially became BenJarvus Green-Ellis with poor ball security, which is the same version of the Law Firm that shortly went out of business. Last season, Bell was one of 17 running backs with over 200 carries. Only Andre Williams wasted a greater fraction of his carries on puffs of dust that gained two yards or less (Table 2).

Table 2. Two Yards and a Cloud of Dust, 2014

Player	Team	Runs	Pct 2 Yards or Less
A.Williams	NYG	217	50.7%
J.Bell	**DET**	**223**	**49.3%**
A.Ellington	ARI	200	49.0%
J.Forsett	BAL	234	46.6%
A.Morris	WAS	265	46.4%
L.McCoy	PHI	310	45.2%
E.Lacy	GB	246	44.7%
A.Foster	HOU	260	43.8%
M.Forte	CHI	265	43.0%
M.Ingram	NO	226	42.9%
J.Hill	CIN	222	42.8%
F.Gore	SF	255	41.2%
M.Lynch	SEA	280	41.1%
L.Bell	PIT	290	41.0%
D.Murray	DAL	392	40.8%
J.Charles	KC	205	37.1%
L.Miller	MIA	216	37.0%

Minimum 200 carries

Bell is still around, but it appears Detroit is ready to scale back some of his workload. His best season was 2012, when he finished with a 12.6 % DVOA that would have ranked seventh among running backs had he accrued over 100 carries. Perhaps the point is that he didn't reach that threshold. The first two days of the Lions draft clearly targeted ground-game upgrades. Detroit traded in its old Bush model for the shiny Ameer Abdullah update, while also concocting a trade with Denver that netted them interior linemen Laken Tomlinson and Manny Ramirez. The Lions ditched durable but mediocre starters Dominic Raiola and Rob Sims this offseason, the two players who led the team in blown blocks last year. Between Tomlinson, Ramirez, Larry Warford, and Travis Swanson, the Lions now have a deep interior rotation, especially if Tomlinson and/or Swanson prove capable of handling a full-time starting job on their first try. The Lions ranked just 26th in both second-level yards and open-field yards after placing ninth and 17th, respectively, in each category in 2013. Part of that probably stemmed from both Bell and Bush playing through various injuries last season, but the line also didn't generate a whole lot of interior push. With more talent inside, Detroit should get a better read on what kind of backs Bell and Abdullah really are.

An improved running game wouldn't be a luxury, but rather an important upgrade for a team that will need something different to rely on in 2015. Part of Detroit's success stemmed from players who had career years unlikely to repeat themselves. Take Glover Quin, whose season embodies the fickleness of interception totals: after picking off eight passes through his first five seasons, Quin led the league with seven interceptions in 2014. The aforementioned Ihedigbo, who totaled three interceptions through his first six seasons, chipped in four more. With 11 combined picks, Ihedigbo and Quin broke the franchise record for most interceptions by a safety tandem. Assuming Ed Reed has not split his soul and chosen to use Quin and Ihedigbo as Horcruxes, it's safe to expect a fairly severe decline in that department, especially if the Suhless pass rush doesn't produce as many pressures.

It's also fair to raise your eyebrows at the starting tackle tandem of Riley Reiff and LaAdrian Waddle. If Reiff and Waddle had a meal equivalent, it would be plain yogurt with a side of whole wheat bread. You can stomach it and get what you need, but having that breakfast year after year can turn into a drag. Well, that meal received an unexpected flavor boost last year: Reiff blew just 12 blocks all season, second-best among all left tackles behind only Andrew Whitworth, while Waddle, led all right tackles with a rate of 91.7 snaps per blown block. However, Waddle is returning from a partially torn ACL suffered in Week 15, while Reiff was one of the poorer pass protectors on the blindside each of the previous two seasons. And although Lombardi's system should get the ball out of Stafford's hands and improve those blown block numbers, it's not as though Reiff and Waddle were pancaking defenders left and right like the second and third comings of Anthony Muñoz.

In fairness, it's not as though the Lions are the only team which will need to answer for likely areas of regression, as every team has its share of surprising overachievers. Detroit got no bang for its buck with top draftees Ebron and Van Noy last year. Maybe those two take big sophomore-year leaps and become integral matchup nightmares. Maybe this year's draft class sees Tomlinson and Abdullah re-energize the running game while Day 3 corners Alex Carter and Quandre Diggs offset Quin's return to reality and age-related declines from Ihedigbo and Rashean Mathis. Maybe the borderline comatose Jim Caldwell is the perfect head coach for a franchise that has felt a little frenzied with its week-to-week and year-to-year inconsistency.

But that's a lot of maybes for a team trying to dethrone Aaron Rodgers in its division. Any way you slice it, the Lions are facing fundamental infrastructural changes to how they'll attempt to win games in 2015. Detroit was bound to undergo this kind of offseason at some point given the salary cap situation Mayhew had constructed, and now the Lions are taking their medicine. The organization's controlled approach should ultimately prove beneficial in the long run. Detroit has just $112.3 million currently committed to the 2016 cap, 12th-lowest in the league, and is in line to draw multiple compensatory picks (including a third-rounder for Suh) after skimping in that department for much of the past decade. It's a more prudent approach than the last time the Lions made the postseason in 2011, when they subsequently doubled-down on their stars and left the cupboard of cost-controlled talent bare. Nonetheless, our projections have the Lions falling back into the same DVOA and win-loss record territory they inhabited in 2012 and 2013. Whatever intangible lessons or value Detroit may have derived from last year's playoff run is likely diminished simply because of how different this year's team will be. If the Lions really want to graduate from the kiddie pool and swim with the real contenders, they must become as adaptive as the teams that don't wait a half-century for a championship.

Sterling Xie

2014 Lions Stats by Week

Wk	vs.	W-L	PF	PA	YDF	YDA	TO	Total	Off	Def	ST
1	NYG	W	35	14	417	197	2	49%	21%	-43%	-15%
2	at CAR	L	7	24	323	313	-3	-13%	2%	3%	-12%
3	GB	W	19	7	353	223	-2	25%	-4%	-37%	-9%
4	at NYJ	W	24	17	360	336	2	16%	22%	3%	-3%
5	BUF	L	14	17	273	343	-1	-25%	-30%	-21%	-16%
6	at MIN	W	17	3	255	212	3	40%	-11%	-64%	-13%
7	NO	W	24	23	344	408	0	-20%	-31%	-7%	3%
8	vs. ATL	W	22	21	385	291	0	10%	-7%	-9%	7%
9	BYE										
10	MIA	W	20	16	351	228	1	21%	-3%	-38%	-15%
11	at ARI	L	6	14	262	352	1	-19%	-24%	3%	8%
12	at NE	L	9	34	335	439	0	-34%	-22%	7%	-4%
13	CHI	W	34	17	474	269	1	24%	28%	1%	-3%
14	TB	W	34	17	407	233	2	32%	12%	-11%	9%
15	MIN	W	16	14	233	360	2	-33%	-21%	6%	-6%
16	at CHI	W	20	14	367	234	-2	-4%	-13%	-18%	-9%
17	at GB	L	20	30	313	377	1	-1%	12%	-1%	-14%
18	at DAL	L	20	24	397	315	-2	9%	-17%	-35%	-8%

Trends and Splits

	Offense	Rank	Defense	Rank
Total DVOA	-3.8%	19	-13.9%	3
Unadjusted VOA	1.3%	13	-12.8%	2
Weighted Trend	-5.4%	17	-10.0%	7
Variance	3.6%	4	4.5%	9
Average Opponent	2.6%	30	0.8%	11
Passing	9.9%	17	-3.0%	8
Rushing	-16.9%	29	-31.4%	1
First Down	-8.9%	24	-14.3%	3
Second Down	-15.0%	28	-10.0%	7
Third Down	22.5%	5	-19.2%	5
First Half	-12.6%	26	-12.9%	5
Second Half	4.9%	14	-14.9%	3
Red Zone	-16.0%	23	-30.2%	2
Late and Close	7.0%	10	-14.5%	5

Five-Year Performance

Year	W-L	Pyth W	Est W	PF	PA	TO	Total	Rk	Off	Rk	Def	Rk	ST	Rk	Off AGL	Rk	Def AGL	Rk	Off Age	Rk	Def Age	Rk	ST Age	Rk
2010	6-10	7.8	7.5	362	369	+4	-1.1%	18	-0.8%	19	2.9%	22	2.6%	11	26.5	16	24.3	17	27.7	12	26.1	26	27.2	5
2011	10-6	10.1	9.4	474	387	+11	10.1%	11	7.1%	10	-8.1%	9	-5.1%	29	29.2	15	14.8	8	27.9	7	26.0	28	27.5	1
2012	4-12	6.4	7.6	372	437	-16	0.1%	16	12.3%	8	7.1%	24	-5.1%	30	23.2	11	58.3	31	28.3	4	26.7	17	27.8	1
2013	7-9	8.5	7.7	395	376	-12	-1.5%	16	-1.9%	19	-0.8%	14	-0.4%	20	31.9	14	30.7	20	27.0	14	27.0	13	26.8	6
2014	11-5	9.2	8.7	321	282	+7	4.4%	14	-3.8%	19	-13.9%	3	-5.7%	31	26.4	13	41.1	21	27.0	15	27.5	6	25.9	20

2014 Performance Based on Most Common Personnel Groups

DET Offense					DET Offense vs. Opponents					DET Defense					DET Defense vs. Opponents			
Pers	Freq	Yds	DVOA	Run%	Pers	Freq	Yds	DVOA	Run%	Pers	Freq	Yds	DVOA		Pers	Freq	Yds	DVOA
11	60%	5.5	-0.7%	24%	Base	31%	5.5	4.9%	56%	Base	20%	3.9	-34.3%		11	64%	5.4	-9.5%
21	14%	7.8	24.5%	43%	Nickel	52%	5.3	-4.6%	28%	Nickel	76%	5.4	-8.5%		12	17%	4.7	-21.8%
12	11%	3.9	-21.3%	51%	Dime+	16%	5.8	-6.5%	11%	Dime+	1%	8.9	95.4%		21	7%	4.1	-39.0%
22	6%	4.7	8.7%	86%	Goal Line	1%	1.1	13.6%	69%	Goal Line	1%	0.4	-22.3%		20	3%	4.2	-5.2%
20	3%	4.3	-55.7%	19%	Big	1%	4.3	17.1%	100%	Big	2%	3.7	-16.4%		10	2%	6.8	11.2%

Strategic Tendencies

Run/Pass		Rk	Formation		Rk	Pass Rush		Rk	Secondary		Rk	Strategy		Rk
Runs, first half	33%	30	Form: Single Back	66%	28	Rush 3	2.5%	28	4 DB	18%	29	Play action	19%	21
Runs, first down	49%	15	Form: Empty Back	11%	4	Rush 4	72.4%	5	5 DB	80%	1	Avg Box (Off)	6.11	29
Runs, second-long	23%	29	Pers: 3+ WR	65%	11	Rush 5	20.9%	22	6+ DB	1%	27	Avg Box (Def)	6.01	32
Runs, power sit.	53%	22	Pers: 4+ WR	2%	13	Rush 6+	4.2%	27	CB by Sides	97%	1	Offensive Pace	31.28	22
Runs, behind 2H	27%	16	Pers: 2+ TE/6+ OL	22%	27	Sacks by LB	14.3%	25	DB Blitz	8%	24	Defensive Pace	30.14	15
Pass, ahead 2H	51%	7	Shotgun/Pistol	56%	22	Sacks by DB	4.8%	20	Hole in Zone	4%	26	Go for it on 4th	1.60	3

Matthew Stafford continues to face the blitz less often than any other quarterback. He had the lowest rate in 2014, 24 percent of pass plays, after ranking second-to-last in both 2012 and 2013. After significant struggles with the blitz in 2013, Stafford was actually slightly better when blitzed in 2014: 6.1 yards per pass with three or four pass rushers, 6.7 yards per play with five or more. ☞ In 2013, only 4.3 percent of runs by Lions running backs came out of two-back formations. Last year, that grew all the way to 38 percent. And the fullback was a great help. While NFL teams on average gain 0.5 yards more per carry from one-back sets, the Lions were actually much better from two-back sets (4.5 yards per carry, -0.8% DVOA) than from one-back sets (3.3, -29.7%). ☞ The Lions dropped only 20 passes (3.6 percent, sixth in the NFL) after dropping a league-high 46 passes (7.8 percent) in 2013. ☞ The Lions allowed a league-high 9.4 yards per pass on play-action in 2013, but that dropped all the way down to 5.7 yards per pass in 2014. Only Kansas City allowed fewer yards per pass on play-action. ☞ The Lions faced more running back screens than any other defense last season, and were roughly average against them, allowing 5.7 average yards and 5.1% DVOA. ☞ Problems with dumpoffs, however, meant the Lions were the worst defense in the league against passes thrown behind the line of scrimmage, with 32.4% DVOA. On the other hand, the Lions were fifth in the league against passes thrown beyond the line of scrimmage, allowing 24.3% DVOA. (Both numbers are above 0% because so many negative pass plays don't qualify for either category, including sacks, passes thrown away, and passes batted at the line.)

Passing

Player	DYAR	DVOA	Plays	NtYds	Avg	YAC	C%	TD	Int
M.Stafford	423	-0.7%	645	3998	6.2	6.1	60.9%	22	12

Rushing

Player	DYAR	DVOA	Plays	Yds	Avg	TD	Fum	Suc
J.Bell	-59	-14.9%	223	861	3.9	7	5	45%
R.Bush*	17	-2.4%	75	289	3.9	2	0	43%
M.Stafford	-4	-15.4%	23	107	4.7	2	2	-
T.Riddick	-22	-34.4%	20	51	2.6	0	0	40%
G.Winn	0	-8.6%	19	73	3.8	0	0	53%
J.Collins*	10	10.4%	8	19	2.4	0	0	63%
G.Tate	16	21.1%	5	30	6.0	0	0	-

Receiving

Player	DYAR	DVOA	Plays	Ctch	Yds	Y/C	YAC	TD	C%
G.Tate	214	6.7%	144	99	1333	13.5	7.0	4	69%
C.Johnson	231	10.2%	128	71	1077	15.2	3.3	8	55%
J.Ross	34	0.2%	35	24	314	13.1	5.8	1	69%
C.Fuller	8	-9.5%	31	14	221	15.8	3.6	1	45%
E.Ebron	-65	-28.6%	47	25	248	9.9	5.0	1	53%
B.Pettigrew	-21	-31.3%	15	10	70	7.0	3.1	0	67%
J.Fauria	-25	-34.1%	12	6	74	12.3	5.7	1	50%
R.Bush*	-18	-19.6%	57	41	261	6.4	6.5	0	72%
J.Bell	54	6.2%	52	34	322	9.5	9.9	1	65%
T.Riddick	76	14.7%	50	34	316	9.3	9.0	4	68%
J.Collins*	28	72.3%	6	5	39	7.8	7.6	1	83%

Offensive Line

Player	Pos	Age	GS	Snaps	Pen	Sk	Pass	Run	Player	Pos	Age	GS	Snaps	Pen	Sk	Pass	Run
Rob Sims*	LG	32	16/16	1093	3	6.0	16.0	3.0	Cornelius Lucas	OT	24	15/3	448	3	4.5	7.5	1.0
Dominic Raiola*	C	37	15/15	1024	5	1.5	8.0	4.0	Travis Swanson	C	24	16/5	360	1	1.5	7.5	1.0
Riley Reiff	LT	27	15/15	941	1	2.5	9.0	3.0	Garrett Reynolds*	RT	28	10/4	224	4	3.0	8.0	0.0
Larry Warford	RG	24	13/13	783	1	2.0	6.0	3.0	Manny Ramirez	C/G	32	16/16	1123	5	1.0	9.0	12.0
LaAdrian Waddle	RT	24	10/10	550	6	2.0	5.0	1.0									

Year	Yards	ALY	Rk	Power	Rk	Stuff	Rk	2nd Lev	Rk	Open Field	Rk	Sacks	ASR	Rk	Short	Long	F-Start	Cont.
2012	4.01	4.05	15	56%	27	17%	5	1.10	20	0.49	27	29	3.7%	1	5	18	19	39
2013	4.23	3.94	13	76%	3	19%	12	1.26	9	0.68	17	23	4.5%	2	10	7	11	33
2014	3.75	3.79	21	65%	15	22%	30	0.99	26	0.59	26	45	6.9%	21	18	15	12	23
2014 ALY by direction:			Left End 3.79 (18)			Left Tackle 3.57 (19)			Mid/Guard 4.06 (13)			Right Tackle 3.18 (26)			Right End 4.21 (10)			

Something's not quite right here. The eye test wouldn't make the Lions offensive line class valedictorian, and neither would Detroit's own front office, which released longtime starters Dominic Raiola and Rob Sims this offseason. The numbers also suggest mediocrity, as Detroit has suffered a three-year decline in adjusted line yards and a precipitous 2014 dip in adjusted sack rate.

Yet somehow, our charters found an abnormally low number of blown blocks, suggesting that most of Detroit's stuffed runs did not stem from an individual lineman's mistake. And it's not as if there were tons of assignment busts on passes, as only 18 percent of opposing sacks came from unblocked rushers, a middling rate. In theory, the Lions' mediocre rushing yardage totals should receive a boost after Marty Mayhew attacked the ground game during the early rounds of the draft, selecting Laken Tomlinson and Ameer Abdullah while also trading for the versatile Manny Ramirez. The 6-foot-3, 323-pound Tomlinson is a mauler in short-space areas and should fit nicely into the Lions' power run scheme. While the Duke product's pass blocking remains a work in progress, he could still represent an immediate upgrade over Sims, whose 16 blown blocks in pass protection and six sacks allowed last year were both easily team highs. Ramirez is probably destined for a reserve role after a rough 2014 campaign that saw him rank 33rd among centers in snaps per blown block. Still, the 32-year-old provides playable interior depth in the event that Tomlinson or second-year center Travis Swanson proves too callow for full-time duty, a luxury the Lions didn't enjoy last year. Swanson also filled in at right guard last year during Larry Warford's three-game absence, providing the Lions flexibility in how they arrange their guard-center-guard combinations.

In contrast, the bookends figure to remain static for a third consecutive season. Lions fans are rather lukewarm on left tackle Riley Reiff, who was the guilty party on Demarcus Lawrence's strip-sack that ended Detroit's season. But it's curious that the Lions coaching staff talked openly about moving the former first-rounder to guard this year before reversing course, as Reiff has measurably improved each of his three seasons in the league. The former Iowa Hawkeye doesn't possess the prototypical flexibility you'd like to see from blindside bodyguards, which can create its share of issues in pass protection (hello, Jerry Hughes). Nevertheless, Reiff astoundingly finished third among all offensive linemen with 78.4 snaps per blown block, including just three blown blocks in the running game. Perhaps that level of success is a huge aberration—his 2014 figure looks like a massive outlier compared to the 46.7 and 32.5 snaps per blown block marks from 2013 and 2012, respectively—but more likely, Reiff is maturing into a competent-at-worst left tackle, having committed just a single penalty last year. Coupled with right tackle LaAdrian Waddle, who battled injuries and but nevertheless improved measurably in pass protection last year, the Lions have the makings of a line capable of supporting all that flashy skill-position talent.

Defensive Front Seven

Defensive Line	Age	Pos	G	Snaps	Plays	TmPct	Rk	Stop	Dfts	BTkl	Runs	St%	Rk	RuYd	Rk	Sack	Hit	Hur	Dsrpt
Ndamukong Suh*	28	DT	16	851	56	7.1%	11	49	26	3	40	85%	22	1.0	8	8.5	11	16.0	3
C.J. Mosley	32	DT	15	490	26	3.5%	74	20	6	1	21	76%	57	3.0	84	2.5	5	8.0	0
Nick Fairley*	27	DT	8	288	14	3.5%	73	11	4	0	12	83%	24	1.6	24	1.0	4	4.0	0
Andre Fluellen	30	DT	8	158	10	2.5%	--	6	5	0	7	43%	--	1.3	--	2.0	2	3.0	0
Haloti Ngata	31	DE	12	529	39	6.2%	19	30	12	1	26	77%	53	3.1	86	2.0	2	7.5	5
Tyrunn Walker	25	DE	16	304	18	2.2%	--	15	11	1	11	82%	--	2.2	--	2.5	2	4.5	0

Edge Rushers	Age	Pos	G	Snaps	Plays	Overall TmPct	Rk	Stop	Dfts	BTkl	Runs	vs. Run St%	Rk	RuYd	Rk	Pass Rush Sack	Hit	Hur	Dsrpt
Ezekiel Ansah	26	DE	16	664	47	5.9%	27	38	24	3	30	77%	36	2.0	27	7.5	19	29.5	0
Jason Jones	29	DE	16	645	23	2.9%	82	18	11	2	11	82%	22	4.3	81	5.0	12	14.5	2
George Johnson*	28	DE	16	491	25	3.2%	79	19	13	0	14	71%	57	1.6	17	6.0	6	11.5	1
Darryl Tapp	31	DE	16	283	19	2.4%	--	11	2	0	9	56%	--	2.9	--	0.5	11	9.5	2

Linebackers	Age	Pos	G	Snaps	Plays	Overall TmPct	Rk	Stop	Dfts	BTkl	Pass Rush Sack	Hit	Hur	Runs	vs. Run St%	Rk	RuYd	Rk	Tgts	vs. Pass Suc%	Rk	AdjYd	Rk	PD	Int
DeAndre Levy	28	OLB	16	1045	155	19.5%	3	87	35	13	2.5	1	6	76	68%	26	3.1	29	58	56%	17	6.2	29	5	1
Tahir Whitehead	25	OLB	16	722	82	10.3%	59	40	10	4	0.0	2	3.5	33	73%	16	3.4	46	35	54%	23	6.4	32	4	2
Josh Bynes	26	OLB	13	209	20	3.1%	--	11	3	1	0.0	1	1	10	70%	--	2.1	--	9	41%	--	6.3	--	1	1
Stephen Tulloch	30	MLB	3	138	20	13.5%	--	14	7	3	2.0	0	0	13	69%	--	2.5	--	4	54%	--	12.6	--	0	0

Year	Yards	ALY	Rk	Power	Rk	Stuff	Rk	2nd Level	Rk	Open Field	Rk	Sacks	ASR	Rk	Short	Long
2012	4.30	3.69	5	72%	28	26%	2	1.33	29	1.03	27	34	5.2%	29	5	20
2013	4.08	3.13	2	50%	3	26%	4	1.13	19	1.07	29	33	5.8%	31	7	14
2014	3.17	2.82	1	63%	15	25%	3	0.86	1	0.50	5	42	6.6%	18	17	10

| 2014 ALY by direction: | Left End 2.54 (1) | Left Tackle 3.3 (11) | Mid/Guard 2.68 (1) | Right Tackle 2.87 (3) | Right End 2.51 (4) |

As we've discussed, "replacing" isn't really the right verb for what the Lions will need to do in 2015 without Ndamukong Suh anchoring what was the league's stingiest defense on carries up the middle. Haloti Ngata is certainly no slouch, but his run stop rate fell from 85 percent two years ago to 77 percent last season, 53rd among interior linemen. With Ngata as the anchor, the A- and B-gaps will no longer be impermeable sphinx-guarded passageways. Detroit added an interesting penetrating speed element in 25-year-old former Saints tackle Tyrunn Walker, who compiled nearly as many defeats as Ngata last year in 225 fewer snaps. Hopefully Walker is ready to graduate from sub-package specialist to three-down starter, as the defections of serviceable backups C.J. Mosley and Andre Fluellen have left untested backups like Caraun Reid and Darius Philon as the top interior reserves.

Suh's departure will also shine the spotlight on Ziggy Ansah, a bright young edge defender who has benefited from a distinct lack of double-teams his entire career. Ansah's gaudy sack totals are the sexy numbers most will point out to justify his status as a former No. 5 overall pick, but it's his run defense that really amplifies his value. Ansah's 12 run defeats ranked fifth among all defensive ends and second among 4-3 defensive ends, behind only Michael Bennett. The Lions kept Ansah fresh by using him on just 63.5 percent of snaps, but with reserve right end George Johnson now in Tampa Bay, that figure will rise in 2015. Besides Ansah, Detroit is light on bendy edge-rushers, as Jason Jones, Devin Taylor, and Darryl Tapp all profile as strongside edge-setters.

Ultimately, the strength of this unit will come from the second level, especially if Stephen Tulloch is healthy after last year's Gramátican celebration fail. DeAndre Levy compiled the third-most defeats in the entire league last year, behind only the otherworldly totals of J.J. Watt and Lavonte David. The year before, Tulloch's 79 stops ranked tied for 13th among all defenders. In Tahir Whitehead, the Lions also unearthed a former core special-teamer who proved surprisingly disruptive over 722 snaps of three-down duty. We've yet to even mention 2014 second-rounder Kyle Van Noy, whose rookie campaign was essentially a wash after missing eight games on short-term IR to start the year. Van Noy would benefit significantly if the whispers about Detroit moving to more 3-4 fronts come to fruition, though it's worth noting that Teryl Austin has downplayed those rumors. Regardless, Van Noy projected as a weakside 3-4 OLB coming out of BYU, and utilizing more hybrid fronts with Van Noy rushing off the edge is one way to get the 40th overall pick on the field. Our SackSEER projections portrayed Van Noy as one of the better Day 2 pass-rushing prospects, so surely Austin has a plan to carve out snaps for him. If the Lions stick to 40 fronts, Whitehead and Van Noy should at least compete for the SAM linebacker role that Ashlee Palmer held last season. The cap-strapped Lions are suffering the unfortunate consequences of having been bad at the wrong time, but as Detroit digs itself out of cap hell, it remains fortunate to boast a linebacking corps upon which it can reasonably build a new defensive foundation.

Defensive Secondary

Secondary	Age	Pos	G	Snaps	Plays	Overall TmPct	Rk	Stop	Dfts	BTkl	vs. Run Runs	St%	Rk	RuYd	Rk	vs. Pass Tgts	Tgt%	Rk	Dist	Suc%	Rk	AdjYd	Rk	PD	Int
Glover Quin	29	SS	16	1038	84	10.6%	30	25	14	4	19	26%	58	8.7	56	29	7.3%	25	14.2	61%	18	6.2	23	9	7
Rashean Mathis	35	CB	16	1023	60	7.6%	57	26	12	6	8	25%	59	6.9	41	74	18.8%	9	12.0	58%	10	5.7	4	7	1
Darius Slay	24	CB	16	1011	76	9.6%	20	32	9	6	10	30%	50	6.9	42	104	26.7%	63	12.2	53%	25	7.9	40	16	2
James Ihedigbo	32	FS	13	824	78	12.1%	22	38	22	11	28	64%	6	4.8	10	29	9.0%	40	10.9	63%	11	4.8	4	9	4
Cassius Vaughn*	28	CB	13	382	22	3.4%	--	12	6	6	3	67%	--	1.3	--	23	15.4%	--	11.8	42%	--	11.7	--	5	2
Isa Abdul-Quddus	26	FS	16	294	31	3.9%	--	9	1	5	13	38%	--	7.2	--	14	12.4%	--	13.3	53%	--	5.1	--	2	0
Josh Wilson	30	CB	16	445	35	4.3%	--	19	6	5	8	100%	--	2.5	--	30	18.5%	--	9.0	46%	--	8.9	--	7	1

Year	Pass D Rank	vs. #1 WR	Rk	vs. #2 WR	Rk	vs. Other WR	Rk	vs. TE	Rk	vs. RB	Rk
2012	21	-5.1%	13	24.6%	31	2.0%	20	14.3%	26	-37.1%	2
2013	20	11.2%	24	-8.7%	10	12.5%	23	-20.6%	5	2.9%	16
2014	8	-26.4%	2	-11.9%	9	2.4%	20	-10.0%	8	14.8%	23

Even ignoring their inflated interception totals, the safety tandem of Glover Quin and James Ihedigbo was the defense's most pleasant surprise in 2014. If we lower the minimum qualification to 20 passes charted, both ranked among the top 20 defensive backs in adjusted success rate. The 29-year-old Quin was particularly impressive in his second Lions season, emerging as one of the league's better centerfielders in Detroit's single-high safety coverages. Quin demonstrated outstanding instincts and closing speed—a good example was his fourth-quarter pick off Drew Brees, which led to the game-winning touchdown against the Saints in Week 7—and was easily the best tackler in the Lions secondary, charting with the fewest missed tackles despite playing the most snaps. His partner in crime Ihedigbo might be the slowest safety in the league, as the 31-year-old has surely lost a step since running a torpid 4.77 40 time at his pro day back in 2007. That hasn't diminished his effectiveness, however, as Ihedigbo ranked sixth among all safeties with a 64 percent success rate against the run, playing almost exclusively near the line of scrimmage. Ihedigbo threatened to hold out for a new contract, but ended up reporting to play out the last year of his deal. If Ihedigbo regresses from his surprising 2014 form, the Lions can go to Isa Abdul-Quddus, who proved effective filling his box safety role when the veteran missed the first three games of last season with a neck injury.

Surprisingly strong safety play made life easier for the cornerbacks, who were the most consistent unit on the roster in terms of deployment. Detroit went nickel on 80 percent of its plays, tops in the league, and rarely asked its perimeter corners to cover anything beyond their outside third of the field. Former second-rounder Darius Slay made an important leap, seeing an uptick in adjusted success rate despite playing nearly three times as many snaps and being Detroit's most-targeted cornerback. Slay still has issues tracking the deep ball, as he did concede 7.9 adjusted yards per pass, but it's hard to complain about the results given his previous lack of pedigree covering No. 1 wide receivers on a weekly basis. Opposite Slay will be Rashean Mathis, who continued a remarkable resurgence during his age-34 season. Mathis was a top-ten cornerback last year by our success rate metric, and was also one of the ten least-targeted corners when adjusting for percentage of total snaps played. These numbers are particularly striking since two years ago, Mathis was so clearly toast that hipster restaurants were featuring him on the menu. Though he was roughly average in 2013, Mathis hemorrhaged yardage in 2012, ranking dead last out of 87 qualified corners with 11.2 adjusted yards per pass.

Detroit needs Mathis to hold off the AARP for another year, as the rest of the unit is a huge question mark. Third-round rookie Alex Carter could become Mathis' successor on the perimeter, though the Stanford product might also transition to safety at some point. And while most of our readers know that the Chargers suffered terrible injury luck at center last year, did you also know the Lions used six slot corners in the first month of the season? Nevin Lawson is the only member of that sordid sextet competing with newcomer Josh Wilson (Ex-Washington) and sixth-round pick Quandre Diggs (Texas) for that accursed role in 2015. (Don Carey is more of a safety, and the other four players are no longer on the team.) The slot isn't a particularly glaring issue given the coverage capabilities of Detroit's linebackers, and if all else fails, Levy and Tulloch might actually be better options anyway.

Special Teams

Year	DVOA	Rank	FG/XP	Rank	Net Kick	Rank	Kick Ret	Rank	Net Punt	Rank	Punt Ret	Rank	Hidden	Rank
2012	-5.1%	30	4.5	9	-9.4	30	-4.8	24	-9.1	25	-6.9	29	0.2	16
2013	-0.4%	20	-11.1	30	-1.6	24	5.7	4	-0.7	20	5.8	8	-11.2	31
2014	-5.7%	31	-19.6	32	-4.0	24	-1.7	21	-0.6	17	-2.5	17	-6.6	26

It's hard to do justice to last year's Detroit kicking game without a complicated metaphor involving the words "Cop Rock" and "Diet Crystal Pepsi." The Lions didn't just hit rock bottom; they started out there, as three different kickers combined to miss 10 of Detroit's first 15 field goal attempts. The third of those kickers, Matt Prater, would recover to make 20 of his last 23 field goals, and over the course of the year Prater was only worth minus-1.8 points below average in our placekicking metric. But Nate Freese and Alex Henery were so bad in those first few weeks that the Lions as a whole had the lowest value we've measured on field goals since Seth Marler and the 2003 Jaguars.

Trouble in the third phase went past just the placekicking, as returner Jeremy Ross saw a big dropoff after a 2013 campaign where he ranked sixth in points added from punt returns. Punter Sam Martin was fourth in the league in gross punt value by our metrics, but the Lions gave that value all back with poor punt coverage. Martin had a couple of particularly awesome moments, including a 24-yard fake against Miami and a successful onside free kick against Green Bay following a safety. Nevertheless, his 10-yard shank that catalyzed Dallas' game-winning drive in the playoffs will be the memory that stings longest.

Green Bay Packers

2014 Record: 12-4	Total DVOA: 23.3% (3rd)	2015 Mean Projection: 9.7 wins	On the Clock (0-4): 3%
Pythagorean Wins: 11.2 (3rd)	Offense: 24.7% (1st)	Postseason Odds: 60.2%	Mediocrity (5-7): 18%
Snap-Weighted Age: 26.2 (28th)	Defense: -1.0% (16th)	Super Bowl Odds: 14.6%	Playoff Contender (8-10): 40%
Average Opponent: -0.9% (16th)	Special Teams: -2.3% (22nd)	Proj. Avg. Opponent: 2.5% (10th)	Super Bowl Contender (11+): 39%

2014: For want of an onside kick recovery, the NFC Championship was lost.

2015: It's a quarterback league, and the Packers have the best. The rest is commentary.

Defense wins championships.

You hear it every year, in pretty much every sport. There is even an element of truth to it. Championship teams, most years and in most sports, are excellent defensive teams. That is because championship teams are typically excellent teams, strong both offensively and defensively.

For the Green Bay Packers, defense wins championships. For the past four seasons, their journey has reached the postseason but ended short of another Lombardi Trophy. Not coincidentally, their defense ranked second in DVOA in 2010 but has not fared as well in more recent seasons. Last season's overall average performance (-1.0%, 16th) was a marked improvement on 2013's 31st-place ranking, but short of the heights of NFC champion Seattle (first) and Super Bowl champion New England (fourth).

The reason defense wins championships for the Green Bay Packers is that the presence of Aaron Rodgers virtually guarantees they will have an excellent offense, one of the best in the league. Rodgers led all quarterbacks in DVOA again in 2014 and has ranked among the top six quarterbacks for five straight seasons. He is still only 31 years old. A healthy Rodgers will be an elite-level player in 2015, and in 2016 and 2017 and 2018 and 2019 and... well, given how Tom Brady and Peyton Manning have transformed the NFL track record of older quarterbacks, probably for 2020 and beyond.

Importantly, Rodgers is not alone. His phenomenal connection with Jordy Nelson is a constant threat to opposing defenses. The re-signed Randall Cobb may be "just" a slot receiver, but he is the NFL's best and a deep threat in his own right. Heading into just his second season, Davante Adams has already shown signs he could supplant Nelson the same way Nelson once supplanted Greg Jennings. And there are a number of other promising athletes waiting to graduate from the Green Bay School of Receiver Development, led by explosive third-round pick Ty Montgomery.

Particularly key for Rodgers given his injuries the past two seasons, the re-signing of Bryan Bulaga means his entire offensive line returns intact. The rare black mark on Rodgers' play on the field has been a tendency, common to many scrambling quarterbacks, to get sacked at an above-average rate. Green Bay had an adjusted sack rate of 7.2 percent or worse and ranked in the bottom dozen for five straight years. Last year, with an improved offensive line, they finished 13th

at 5.5 percent. From 2012 to 2014, the percentage of Rodgers dropbacks that ended in a sack we attributed to a blown block fell from 6.3 percent to 2.9 percent.

The offensive line improvement meant not only help for Rodgers but also bigger holes for Eddie Lacy. Ted Thompson's past misadventures, as chronicled in *Football Outsiders Almanac 2014*, included the inability to find a quality chain-moving running back to provide a bit of balance to the Rodgers-led attack. That's no longer a problem. Lacy definitely fills that bill as a violent sustaining runner who learned at Alabama how to stay on the field through thick and thin, while reliable veteran James Starks is still around to help in key situations.

The Packers' offense is not perfect. They could use another Jermichael Finely-like dynamic receiving tight end, instead of the more humdrum Andrew Quarless and Richard Rodgers. More depth at running back in case of a Lacy injury would be useful. Ditto a more certain fourth receiver for a team that ranked in the top five in use of four wide receivers in 2014. Who knows if Scott Tolzien will be good enough to keep things afloat in the event of another Aaron Rodgers injury. In the current NFL, though, Green Bay's offense with Rodgers is as good as it gets and will again be one of the league's best.

The only real uncertainty about Green Bay's 2015 offense is Mike McCarthy's decision to give up play-calling, made after widespread criticism of Green Bay's conservative offensive approach late in the NFC Championship Game. Offensive coordinator Tom Clements takes over the job. The continuity in personnel, plus McCarthy's continued presence—and availability to take the job over again if early returns are too negative—suggests this change should have minimal effect. If it helps McCarthy make better strategic decisions on game day (an occasional weakness of his) and frees him up to help other areas like special teams, it should be an improvement.

The problem is that pesky defense. Ted Thompson's 2014 misadventure, sadly not predicted in last year's book, proved to be the inside linebackers. Seattle's rushing success in the season opener resulted in the excommunication of Brad Jones, who went from playing all 70 snaps in Week 1 to 146 in the last 14 games combined. A.J. Hawk went from every-down player to fewer than 20 snaps a game in the final seven games. Both players were released this offseason.

Jones' and Hawk's struggles posed an interesting question to coordinator Dom Capers: does the Packers' best defense

2015 Packers Schedule

Week	Opp.	Week	Opp.	Week	Opp.
1	at CHI	7	BYE	13	at DET (Thu.)
2	SEA	8	at DEN	14	DAL
3	KC (Mon.)	9	at CAR	15	at OAK
4	at SF	10	DET	16	at ARI
5	STL	11	at MIN	17	MIN
6	SD	12	CHI (Thu.)		

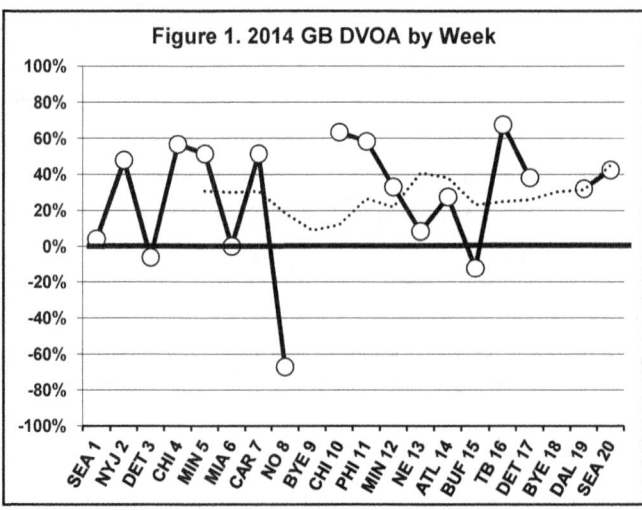

Figure 1. 2014 GB DVOA by Week

feature their best 11 defensive players? The focal point for the answer to that question is Clay Matthews. The third-generation NFL star led the Packers in sacks again in 2014, for the sixth time in his six-year career. It was his move to inside linebacker, though, that directly led to Hawk's late-season reduction in playing time. Heading into 2015, Capers again must answer: does it make sense to have your best pass rusher playing at a position where pass rushing is not the emphasis?

On the whole, the move seemed to pay benefits. Matthews was still a successful rusher after the bye week change. He had 8.5 of his 11 regular season sacks in the final eight games, after the switch (on the other hand, he had 15.5 of his 22.5 hurries in the first eight games, so his overall pressure totals were unchanged). The defense improved overall, against both the run and the pass, and even the pass rush improved (Table 1).

Table 1. Green Bay Defense, Before and After Matthews Move

	Weeks 1-9	Rank	Weeks 10-17	Rank
DVOA vs. Run	0.2%	24	-9.1%	19
DVOA vs. Pass	7.5%	11	-5.2%	13
Adjusted Sack Rate	5.5%	22	8.1%	10

After that success, Matthews seems poised to continue playing inside linebacker in base personnel while playing on the edge in sub. One of the Packers' goals in offseason workouts was to get him more comfortable there, while still letting him play on the edge part of the time. Matthews described his role in the offseason thusly: "They're going to rush me from all over the field, they're going to drop me from all over the field and I expect to do a multitude of things this year."

The inside linebacker issues had a couple effects beyond Matthews that will pose further questions for 2015. Capers has long been an advocate of sub personnel packages, and last year's Packers lined up in base personnel with just four defensive backs on the field a league-low 17 percent of the time. The Packers instead ran more and more dime personnel. At first, this looks like an extreme move, since their use of dime more than doubled from 2013. But it was really just going back to the way Capers had schemed the year before; Green Bay's relative ranks for use of four, five, and six defensive back sets look a lot like the ranks for 2012's successful (until it met Colin Kaepernick and the read-option in the postseason) unit.

If the extensive use of dime continues in 2015, it could feed right into a roster issue that may qualify as Ted Thompson's next misadventure. The Packers were able to play so much dime in recent years because they had outstanding depth at defensive back. That depth took a significant hit this offseason. Veteran mainstay Tramon Williams took his 32-year-old body and a new $7 million per year cap hit to Cleveland. Davon House, who might have been the favorite to replace Admiral Armbar, took the money and ran to Jacksonville.

Thompson clearly did not want this to be his next misadventure, so made sure he had replacements on hand. The first two picks in the draft brought Damarious Randall and Quentin Rollins. Each was worthy of his draft slot. Each carries his own complication that seems likely to limit his ability to be an immediate impact player. Randall was a safety at Arizona State and is being converted to cornerback. Rollins played just one year of college football after four of basketball at Miami of Ohio. He did well enough that season to be named MAC Defensive Player of the Year, but he is understandably raw even by the standards of rookie corners.

Either Randall or Rollins (or both) will need to be reliable contributors for the Packers to reach their ultimate goal. At the season's outset, former nickelback Casey Hayward will likely be Williams' replacement as a starter. But it's likely that the increasing prevalence of three- and four-receiver sets in the NFL will force the Packers to play a lot of sub packages. What will those packages look like? Will the inexperience of Randall and Rollins force Hayward to stay outside with backup safety Micah Hyde as the slot corner in a nickel package? Who are the nickel linebackers? Can Sam Barrington or fourth-round rookie Jake Ryan (Michigan) be reliable enough in sub packages to let Matthews continue to play primarily as an edge rusher, or will the Packers need him more elsewhere? Just who are the Packers' 11 best defensive players, anyway? More importantly, who will they be when Green Bay's real season begins, in early January?

If you think our mean projection of 9.7 wins for the Packers seems a bit pessimistic for a team whose starting quarterback is 64-23 the last six seasons, you are not alone. The compressed nature of our projection system leads to conservative results. Historically, there is a lot more randomness in the NFL schedule than most fans tend to understand. An actual NFL season is played but a single time. Our simulations are run many times, and recognize that every team could fulfill its best- or worst-case scenario, which results in projections closer to 8-8 at both extremes. That being said, there is reason to believe that in the case of the Packers, the conservative nature of our projections might be a bit *too* conservative. Since 2002, 85 different teams have finished 11-5 or better. The next year, on average, these teams dropped from 12.1 wins to 9.4 wins. However, we see a much smaller drop if we only look at teams that employed the five best quarterbacks of the past dozen years, who according to DVOA are Tom Brady, Drew Brees, Peyton Manning, Philip Rivers, and Rodgers. Thirty times, these quarterbacks have led their teams to a record of 11-5 or better, with an average of 12.7 wins. The next year, these teams only dropped to 11.3 wins.[1] Nothing consistently wins games like having a very good quarterback, and the Packers have the best.

What matters more than the projected mean win total is that our forecast clearly identifies the Packers as the second-best team in the NFC, behind only Seattle. An increasingly competitive NFC North and matchups with the two strong West divisions will make it difficult for the Packers to have a historically great win-loss record, but unless Rodgers suffers a major injury, they are going to be playing in the postseason. At that point, bringing the Lombardi Trophy home comes down to postseason performance levels, specific matchups, and not doing dumb things. Don't play too conservatively with the lead. Don't kick field goals instead of scoring touchdowns. Don't go to the ground after an interception when there's plenty of green grass ahead of you. And for the love of all that is holy in the state of Wisconsin, stick to your assignment on the onside kick.

Tom Gower

2014 Packers Stats by Week

Wk	vs.	W-L	PF	PA	YDF	YDA	TO	Total	Off	Def	ST
1	at SEA	L	16	36	255	398	0	4%	19%	15%	0%
2	NYJ	W	31	24	390	313	0	48%	29%	-4%	15%
3	at DET	L	7	19	223	353	2	-6%	-6%	2%	2%
4	at CHI	W	38	17	358	496	2	57%	60%	2%	-1%
5	MIN	W	42	10	320	299	2	51%	22%	-27%	3%
6	at MIA	W	27	24	369	349	3	0%	13%	3%	-11%
7	CAR	W	38	17	363	331	1	51%	42%	-9%	1%
8	at NO	L	23	44	491	495	-2	-67%	-20%	49%	2%
9	BYE										
10	CHI	W	55	14	451	311	2	63%	40%	-38%	-15%
11	PHI	W	53	20	475	429	4	58%	51%	-9%	-2%
12	at MIN	W	24	21	362	308	1	33%	42%	9%	0%
13	NE	W	26	21	478	320	0	8%	33%	19%	-6%
14	ATL	W	43	37	502	465	1	27%	46%	23%	4%
15	at BUF	L	13	21	333	253	-1	-12%	-10%	-20%	-23%
16	at TB	W	20	3	431	109	0	68%	11%	-69%	-13%
17	DET	W	30	20	377	313	-1	38%	39%	9%	7%
18	BYE										
19	DAL	W	26	21	416	315	0	32%	39%	3%	-4%
20	at SEA	L	22	28	306	397	3	42%	-4%	-24%	23%

Trends and Splits

	Offense	Rank	Defense	Rank
Total DVOA	24.7%	1	-1.0%	16
Unadjusted VOA	24.9%	1	-1.5%	14
Weighted Trend	26.8%	1	-2.4%	18
Variance	5.3%	7	7.4%	26
Average Opponent	-0.3%	16	-1.1%	20
Passing	46.5%	2	1.2%	11
Rushing	5.3%	6	-3.7%	24
First Down	26.9%	1	-5.1%	10
Second Down	17.4%	5	5.9%	24
Third Down	31.7%	2	-4.1%	13
First Half	38.4%	1	-8.6%	9
Second Half	6.9%	10	6.5%	25
Red Zone	7.6%	10	-4.8%	15
Late and Close	12.0%	8	5.3%	24

Five-Year Performance

Year	W-L	Pyth W	Est W	PF	PA	TO	Total	Rk	Off	Rk	Def	Rk	ST	Rk	Off AGL	Rk	Def AGL	Rk	Off Age	Rk	Def Age	Rk	ST Age	Rk
2010	10-6	12.1	10.9	388	240	+10	23.0%	4	11.5%	7	-13.9%	2	-2.4%	26	40.3	28	45.8	29	27.2	19	26.5	21	25.8	26
2011	15-1	12.2	13.3	560	359	+24	27.0%	1	33.8%	1	8.6%	25	1.8%	8	21.3	9	37.5	22	26.3	26	26.7	23	25.1	32
2012	11-5	10.5	11.8	433	336	+7	26.3%	5	19.5%	3	-7.0%	8	-0.2%	18	38.7	23	62.8	32	26.9	16	25.8	27	24.9	32
2013	8-7-1	7.8	7.3	417	428	-3	-6.0%	20	8.6%	9	14.4%	31	-0.3%	19	59.1	29	43.9	24	26.0	30	26.3	19	25.2	29
2014	12-4	11.2	10.8	486	348	+14	23.3%	3	24.7%	1	-1.0%	16	-2.3%	22	11.0	3	31.0	9	25.7	30	26.7	18	25.9	19

1 Both figures include the 2008 Patriots, where Brady started Week 1, but not the 2011 Colts where Manning missed the entire season.

2014 Performance Based on Most Common Personnel Groups

GB Offense					GB Offense vs. Opponents					GB Defense					GB Defense vs. Opponents			
Pers	Freq	Yds	DVOA	Run%	Pers	Freq	Yds	DVOA	Run%	Pers	Freq	Yds	DVOA		Pers	Freq	Yds	DVOA
11	63%	6.6	34.5%	28%	Base	26%	6.3	11.3%	56%	Base	24%	5.3	-4.6%		11	60%	5.5	-0.4%
12	13%	7.2	19.2%	56%	Nickel	68%	6.5	32.6%	34%	Nickel	53%	5.1	-4.2%		12	20%	4.9	-8.7%
20	9%	6.4	39.6%	57%	Dime+	4%	9.5	116.8%	0%	Dime+	22%	6.0	11.1%		21	6%	4.5	-3.0%
22	5%	5.5	9.9%	96%	Goal Line	1%	0.6	9.7%	75%	Goal Line	1%	2.8	22.1%		13	4%	4.1	-13.8%
01	4%	6.0	5.0%	15%	Big	1%	1.8	-48.9%	80%	Big	1%	3.3	-11.1%		611	2%	4.7	-35.2%

Strategic Tendencies

Run/Pass		Rk	Formation		Rk	Pass Rush		Rk	Secondary		Rk	Strategy		Rk
Runs, first half	35%	26	Form: Single Back	73%	16	Rush 3	4.8%	22	4 DB	17%	32	Play action	24%	8
Runs, first down	49%	14	Form: Empty Back	4%	21	Rush 4	54.3%	24	5 DB	51%	22	Avg Box (Off)	6.20	25
Runs, second-long	35%	7	Pers: 3+ WR	78%	1	Rush 5	31.9%	3	6+ DB	32%	8	Avg Box (Def)	6.02	31
Runs, power sit.	52%	24	Pers: 4+ WR	6%	5	Rush 6+	9.0%	8	CB by Sides	85%	10	Offensive Pace	29.15	7
Runs, behind 2H	28%	13	Pers: 2+ TE/6+ OL	22%	28	Sacks by LB	65.9%	5	DB Blitz	13%	11	Defensive Pace	29.11	5
Pass, ahead 2H	49%	14	Shotgun/Pistol	64%	15	Sacks by DB	8.5%	12	Hole in Zone	7%	9	Go for it on 4th	1.11	10

Packers fans were used to Mike McCarthy slowing things down with a lead long before the NFC Championship Game. The Packers ranked sixth in pace when trailing (one play every 24.4 seconds) but 29th with a lead (one play every 30.4 seconds). ⬯ The Packers have ranked among the top five teams in offense on second-and-long (7+ yards to go) for five straight seasons. ⬯ Green Bay sent twice as many big blitzes (six or more rushers) than the year before, going from 28th to eighth in frequency. ⬯ How much benefit are the Packers really getting from blitzing their defensive backs? We only recorded a quarterback under pressure on 29 percent of these DB blitz plays, the second straight year the Packers ranked 31st. And yet, the Packers also allowed only 5.0 yards per pass on DB blitzes, better than the NFL average of 6.3. ⬯ Green Bay continued to have a big problem stopping passes up the middle, ranking 28th in DVOA against these passes after ranking 30th in 2013. The Packers have struggled with both short and deep passes in the middle of the field. ⬯ Packers opponents only dropped 16 passes last year after dropping a league-high 42 the year before.

Passing

Player	DYAR	DVOA	Plays	NtYds	Avg	YAC	C%	TD	Int
A.Rodgers	1564	32.2%	550	4168	7.6	6.0	65.8%	38	5
M.Flynn*	-104	-98.1%	18	54	3.0	4.1	50.0%	0	1

Rushing

Player	DYAR	DVOA	Plays	Yds	Avg	TD	Fum	Suc
E.Lacy	189	9.8%	246	1139	4.6	10	3	48%
J.Starks	0	-8.6%	85	340	4.0	2	1	40%
A.Rodgers	104	54.4%	31	283	9.1	2	1	-
J.Kuhn	13	3.1%	24	85	3.5	1	0	58%
D.Harris*	14	11.0%	16	64	4.0	0	0	56%
R.Cobb	9	-22.6%	11	37	3.4	0	0	-

Receiving

Player	DYAR	DVOA	Plays	Ctch	Yds	Y/C	YAC	TD	C%
J.Nelson	482	26.8%	151	98	1519	15.5	5.1	13	65%
R.Cobb	479	35.7%	127	91	1287	14.1	6.4	12	72%
D.Adams	19	-9.0%	66	38	446	11.7	4.6	3	58%
J.Boykin*	-38	-49.9%	12	3	23	7.7	9.0	0	25%
A.Quarless	24	-0.1%	46	29	323	11.1	5.5	3	63%
R.Rodgers	-8	-10.9%	30	20	225	11.3	2.4	2	67%
E.Lacy	112	23.0%	55	42	427	10.2	10.3	4	76%
J.Starks	-20	-27.1%	29	18	140	7.8	6.7	0	62%

Offensive Line

Player	Pos	Age	GS	Snaps	Pen	Sk	Pass	Run	Player	Pos	Age	GS	Snaps	Pen	Sk	Pass	Run
Corey Linsley	C	24	16/16	1050	5	1.0	4.0	5.5	T.J. Lang	RG	28	16/16	947	2	2.0	10.0	1.0
David Bakhtiari	LT	24	16/16	1007	9	4.5	16.0	5.8	Bryan Bulaga	RT	26	15/15	926	5	3.5	10.0	2.0
Josh Sitton	LG	29	16/16	995	3	0.0	0.0	3.3									

Year	Yards	ALY	Rk	Power	Rk	Stuff	Rk	2nd Lev	Rk	Open Field	Rk	Sacks	ASR	Rk	Short	Long	F-Start	Cont.
2012	3.58	3.86	25	68%	7	19%	13	0.97	29	0.28	32	51	8.6%	31	9	29	13	35
2013	4.52	4.11	5	83%	1	16%	5	1.24	10	0.95	8	45	8.3%	26	14	14	13	38
2014	4.39	4.08	8	59%	25	21%	24	1.29	5	0.83	8	30	5.5%	13	9	13	11	43
2014 ALY by direction:				Left End 3.88 (15)			Left Tackle 3.84 (14)			Mid/Guard 4.08 (12)				Right Tackle 4.49 (5)			Right End 4.15 (13)	

Did January's divisional round game feature the two best offensive lines in the NFL? The Cowboys' impressive 2014 performance earned them plenty of plaudits, but the Packers were just as impressive—and their vocal harmonies are far superior.

The season certainly did not begin auspiciously, with Derek Sherrod's turnstile performance against the Seahawks after Bryan Bulaga got hurt early. Once Bulaga returned in Week 3, the line got better and better, and it returns this season completely intact. With Jahri Evans in decline and Ben Grubbs traded out of New Orleans, the Packers now feature the NFL's best pair of guards. Josh Sitton's work in pass protection was nearly as impeccable as that startling figure of 0.0 blown blocks indicates. T.J. Lang drew tougher foes and sometimes tougher assignments. He is plenty good in his own right.

Offensive line coach James Campen gave the succinct statement of David Bakhtiari's 2014 play, saying he "had a good year for a second-year player, and [he] will take another step." Bakhtiari will never be Tyron Smith, but continued technique work should move him into the top ten, possibly the top five, of our left tackle rankings by snaps per blown block instead of in the middle of the pack (14th). Bulaga was a rock, ranking second in fewest snaps per blown block. Don Barclay provides depth and, if forced to play, cannot be any worse than Sherrod was.

For a rookie center, Corey Linsley played fairly well. He got the ball to Rodgers. He flashed quickness in getting up to the second level in the run game. His recognition in picking up the right pass-rusher in protection improved as the season went along. Campen declared him, like Bakhtiari, a "very headstrong accountable player" and is expecting a similar level of improvement in his second season. J.C. Tretter, the favorite to win the job last year until his preseason knee injury, is still around should Linsley falter.

Defensive Front Seven

Defensive Line	Age	Pos	G	Snaps	Plays	Overall TmPct	Rk	Stop	Dfts	BTkl	Runs	vs. Run St%	Rk	RuYd	Rk	Pass Rush Sack	Hit	Hur	Dsrpt
Mike Daniels	26	DE	16	683	40	4.8%	43	33	12	6	32	81%	28	2.6	63	5.5	8	14.5	0
Letroy Guion	28	DT	16	548	32	3.8%	69	25	10	2	24	79%	38	2.8	71	3.5	3	3.5	1
Josh Boyd	26	DE	15	386	22	2.8%	--	18	5	3	21	81%	--	2.2	--	0.0	1	2.5	0
Datone Jones	25	DE	13	314	21	3.1%	--	13	5	1	14	57%	--	4.1	--	1.5	2	13.5	0

Edge Rushers	Age	Pos	G	Snaps	Plays	Overall TmPct	Rk	Stop	Dfts	BTkl	Runs	vs. Run St%	Rk	RuYd	Rk	Pass Rush Sack	Hit	Hur	Dsrpt
Clay Matthews	29	OLB	16	898	69	8.2%	7	50	23	4	32	69%	66	2.3	37	11.0	10	22.5	5
Julius Peppers	35	OLB	16	808	54	6.4%	21	45	23	9	31	74%	43	2.4	39	7.0	10	24.5	6
Mike Neal	28	OLB	16	642	33	3.9%	63	25	11	2	25	72%	54	2.5	43	4.5	6	10.0	0
Nick Perry	25	OLB	15	360	24	3.0%	--	20	6	1	18	89%	--	3.0	--	3.0	0	3.5	2

Linebackers	Age	Pos	G	Snaps	Plays	Overall TmPct	Rk	Stop	Dfts	BTkl	Pass Rush Sack	Hit	Hur	Runs	vs. Run St%	Rk	RuYd	Rk	vs. Pass Tgts	Suc%	Rk	AdjYd	Rk	PD	Int
A.J. Hawk*	31	ILB	16	837	91	10.8%	56	37	3	3	0.5	0	3.5	51	49%	83	4.3	74	30	50%	41	7.1	45	3	0
Sam Barrington	25	ILB	14	355	54	7.3%	--	23	5	2	1.0	3	3	39	44%	--	4.1	--	14	55%	--	5.9	--	0	0
Jamari Lattimore*	27	ILB	11	281	36	6.2%	--	16	2	3	0.0	0	1.5	24	58%	--	3.6	--	7	16%	--	7.8	--	1	1

Year	Yards	ALY	Rk	Power	Rk	Stuff	Rk	2nd Level	Rk	Open Field	Rk	Sacks	ASR	Rk	Short	Long
2012	4.40	4.25	22	51%	4	17%	24	1.17	12	0.80	16	47	8.0%	4	12	23
2013	4.67	4.26	26	77%	30	17%	22	1.38	29	0.88	24	44	8.1%	5	15	20
2014	4.09	4.21	26	63%	14	17%	25	1.19	21	0.42	1	41	6.9%	14	19	10

2014 ALY by direction:	Left End 4.42 (28)	Left Tackle 5.09 (30)	Mid/Guard 4.05 (18)	Right Tackle 4.12 (19)	Right End 3.8 (16)

B.J. Raji's preseason triceps injury helped accelerate Mike Daniels' transition from solid rotational player to regular contributor, and the 2012 fourth-rounder made the move successfully. He is a bit lighter than the traditional 3-4 defensive lineman. The lack of bulk showed at times in run defense, but the Packers were quite willing to make the tradeoff for his pass-rush ability. He had strong pressure numbers for an interior lineman for the second straight season (6.5 sacks and 15 hurries in 2013).

However, an even bigger beneficiary of Raji's injury was Letroy Guion, thrust into the starting lineup at nose tackle. The Packers were satisfied enough with his play to bring him back, even after an offseason arrest for marijuana and firearm possession. Raji was re-signed at the same time, so another training camp competition seems to be the order of the day. A healthy Raji is the better player, but the presence of both of them on the roster will give the Packers a tactical option they did not have last season and probably could have used in some games (against Seattle and New Orleans, perchance). Injury-plagued first-rounder Datone Jones provides pass-rush depth, while Josh Boyd and Mike Pennel provide added bulk.

If Clay Matthews does play on the inside, the Packers could need one of their questionable contributors on the outside to emerge. Julius Peppers was still an effective player last year, at least when the Packers were not throwing him passes on offense, but at 35 he would probably function best playing 50 percent of the snaps instead of 2014's 74 percent. Whether the Packers can afford to take him off the field will depend on the health of Nick Perry. The 2012 first-rounder had his fifth-year option declined and missed OTAs after yet another injury. After hand and wrist injuries as a rookie and foot injuries in his second season, it was a shoulder injury in year three. He only missed one game, but he has yet to become the player the Packers envisioned. If Perry is in the tub again, Mike Neal will again be around to fill in the other snaps, but he's not a difference-maker. It would be very helpful if either 2014 UDFA Jayrone Elliott (66 snaps in 2014) or 2013 UDFA Andy Mulumba (0 snaps in two active weeks before going to injured reserve) develops into at least a rotational player.

Defensive Secondary

Secondary	Age	Pos	G	Snaps	Plays	Overall TmPct	Rk	Stop	Dfts	BTkl	Runs	vs. Run St%	Rk	RuYd	Rk	Tgts	vs. Pass Tgt%	Rk	Dist	Suc%	Rk	AdjYd	Rk	PD	Int
Tramon Williams*	32	CB	16	1012	83	9.9%	18	27	12	7	17	35%	42	5.8	33	80	22.2%	27	10.9	48%	50	7.3	24	12	3
Morgan Burnett	26	SS	15	943	127	16.1%	1	51	18	14	76	50%	20	4.8	12	33	9.8%	46	10.6	41%	61	8.6	55	5	1
Ha Ha Clinton-Dix	23	FS	16	941	95	11.3%	27	27	5	12	50	36%	44	5.7	20	21	6.2%	17	17.4	61%	16	5.7	18	5	1
Sam Shields	28	CB	14	820	49	6.7%	68	20	9	9	6	50%	21	5.3	24	68	23.5%	38	15.3	58%	11	7.8	36	10	2
Micah Hyde	25	FS/CB	16	704	64	7.6%	58	24	11	6	25	32%	51	7.7	50	37	14.7%	68	10.4	56%	32	7.8	45	8	2
Casey Hayward	26	CB	16	426	43	5.1%	--	22	11	9	15	60%	--	5.9	--	25	16.3%	--	7.7	54%	--	6.4	--	7	3
Davon House*	26	CB	13	405	34	5.0%	--	13	5	4	9	11%	--	11.1	--	42	29.0%	--	16.5	68%	--	5.4	--	10	1

Year	Pass D Rank	vs. #1 WR	Rk	vs. #2 WR	Rk	vs. Other WR	Rk	vs. TE	Rk	vs. RB	Rk
2012	7	16.3%	24	-25.1%	2	-31.6%	2	-11.6%	6	22.8%	27
2013	28	20.0%	28	16.7%	27	-8.1%	11	15.4%	25	13.3%	27
2014	11	-1.5%	15	-14.2%	7	-11.4%	9	-5.8%	14	1.0%	19

Ted Thompson liked what Sam Shields did in his first four seasons enough to hand him $9.5 million per season, and got another year of pretty much the same. Whether that was to be expected or a disappointment depends on your view. Shields is certainly a solid starting corner. The salary, however, suggests he should be more of a playmaker than he was in 2014, and it makes the long plays allowed all the more galling. Shields has consistently ranked better by success rate than by adjusted yards per pass in his three seasons as a starter. With the uncertainty at slots two through four on the depth chart (addressed earlier in the chapter), the Packers are counting on at least another Sam Shields-like season in 2015.

The post-Nick Collins wait for quality safety play in Green Bay came to an end in 2014. Morgan Burnett had a standout second half of the season as a force against the run and was a better cover player than our charting metrics indicate. The key was the quick growth of first-round rookie Ha Ha Clinton-Dix. Eased into the lineup, he was a rotational player until Week 7, then barely left the field after that (11 missed snaps over the final 13 games, including postseason). He still had some rookie raggedness that included the normal susceptibility to double moves and route combinations designed to take advantage of the aggressiveness of an inexperienced safety. Even at his worst, though, he was still a big upgrade from M.D. Jennings. Like

Burnett, he missed a few more tackles than you would want but made enough plays against the run that the Packers were willing to live with it. Once again a backup, Micah Hyde also gives Capers a solid slot cover option.

Special Teams

Year	DVOA	Rank	FG/XP	Rank	Net Kick	Rank	Kick Ret	Rank	Net Punt	Rank	Punt Ret	Rank	Hidden	Rank
2012	-0.2%	18	-11.8	31	-1.5	18	0.0	17	9.7	7	2.5	10	3.4	8
2013	-0.3%	19	4.0	10	-12.3	30	-4.2	23	5.4	9	5.6	9	7.5	6
2014	-2.3%	22	-2.9	24	-7.0	28	-2.9	22	-9.4	29	10.5	4	0.1	16

It would be an exaggeration to say that Micah Hyde's two punt return scores were all that separated Green Bay's special-teams unit from being a complete disaster. But not much of one. The defensive back had 12.6 points of value (second in the NFL behind Darren Sproles) while splitting that job with Randall Cobb. The rest of the third unit was as much of a problem as the 2014 figures in the table above indicate. The Packers especially struggled blocking for their kickers, allowing three blocked field goals, two blocked extra points, and two blocked punts. Those struggles led to the firing of special-teams coordinator Shawn Slocum, the first coordinator fired by the Packers since defensive coordinator Bob Sanders got the axe after 2008. His replacement is a familiar face. Ron Zook was brought in as an assistant to Slocum before 2014, and the former college head coach now gets a promotion and more oversight from Mike McCarthy. McCarthy indicated in the offseason that special teams would be more of a priority, and would feature more veterans. The Packers showed their commitment to the unit by retaining Sean Richardson in the face of a restricted free-agent offer sheet from the Raiders, even though the reserve safety has no obvious path to playing time on defense barring injury.

Beyond Richardson, what personnel will Zook have to work with? Third-round rookie Ty Montgomery (Stanford) seems like the strong favorite to return kickoffs after DuJuan Harris was not retained. Cobb's role on offense should make Hyde the full-time punt returner. He was good there in 2013 as well (6.0 points of return value). Mason Crosby should be good enough at kicker. The team's negative placekicking value was solely a result of the blocks, something that should be eliminated by better play in front of the kicker. Crosby's kickoffs were better in 2014 than they were in 2013, though he was still below average. Paired with the league's sixth-worst kick coverage unit, opponents enjoyed good field position too often. Punter Tim Masthay has camp competition in the inexperienced Cody Mandell and needs it; both with and without the blocked punts, he was the worst punter in the league by our numbers over the second half of last season. Punt coverage was no better than kick coverage. Zook seems to have his work cut out for him.

Houston Texans

Texans head coach Bill O'Brien spent the 2014 season doing what the most successful rookie coaches do: steal, borrow, and otherwise twist through history to find the best schemes for his offense. Like *MacGyver*, O'Brien was somehow able to make the 2014 Texans offense more than the sum of its parts. He was able to use the paperclip that was Andre Johnson like so, attach it to the rubber band, and … no, what he really did was send Arian Foster and Alfred Blue into the line. A lot. The Texans finished 24th in offensive rushing DVOA, but first in rushing attempts. They had 26 more than second-place Seattle, and 43 more than third-place Dallas, despite the notable handicap of not having an acceptable Foster backup. (Blue finished dead last in DVOA and DYAR among all qualifying running backs.)

Were this one of those internet columns with 800 .gifs, we could show you how each concept helped the passing offense. But all you really need to know is that, on the macro level, this strategy turned a passing game with one good receiver and zero good quarterbacks into the No. 18 DVOA pass offense. And there are two full games of Case Keenum in that sample! It also includes one game where Ryan Mallett tried to play through a torn pectoral muscle and wound up like the quarterback equivalent of a *Goldeneye* Klobb gun, spraying passes with apparently random trajectories.

Let us show you the two years of Ryan Fitzpatrick's career prior to him joining the Texans, and then show you his 2014 advanced statistics. (Table 1) What O'Brien was able to ring out of a sack- and interception-prone borderline NFL starter was phenomenal.

Table 1. Ryan Fitzpatrick, Before and After Bill O'Brien

Year	DVOA	Rk	DYAR	Rk	Net Y/P	Rk
2012	-7.6%	23	120	23	6.1	20
2013	-3.6%	20	179	21	6.4	14
2014	6.7%	12	383	17	7.2	6

O'Brien was able to churn a lot of offense from a few areas last season. That is a skill. It is not an optimal solution. MacGyver faced problems with clear disadvantages, but they often weren't problems of his own creation. You never saw MacGyver look at a missile launcher, shrug, and start creating a slingshot to clog an intake valve.

O'Brien the head coach is creating a lot of value for his team. Trying to figure out what percentage of the groceries he gets to shop for as compared to what general manager Rick Smith does is like trying to decipher the rules for when the NRG Stadium roof is open. But while we cannot be sure of precisely where the bad seed lies, the harsh truth is that the Texans are failing because their recent drafts have been abysmal, free agency has often yielded small-stakes duds, and O'Brien hasn't had a real quarterback to work with yet.

On the first front, the Texans have selected 27 players between the 2012-2014 drafts. After releasing D.J. Swearinger for unrevealed (read: chemistry) reasons, just two players from their entire 2013 draft are still on the roster. 2012 and 2014 have provided more players still wearing jerseys, but most of those players could best be described as "adequate." DeAndre Hopkins and Brandon Brooks are damn good players. Jadeveon Clowney may be a good player if he comes back from microfracture surgery with his original skill set intact. The rest of this lot hasn't made a noticeable impact yet (Table 2, next page).

Note that the rest of the 2014 class is also not off to a promising start. Left guard Xavier Su'a-Filo barely played at all last year. Nose tackle Louis Nix III went straight to IR. Quarterback Tom Savage, the modern-day king of anonymous scout ass-kissing, made such strides that the Texans signed two quarterbacks ahead of him this offseason. C.J. Fiedorowicz was a first-year tight end who neither blocked nor caught like one.

The Texans have not spent heavily in free agency since reeling in Johnathan Joseph and Danieal Manning in 2011. That's not necessarily a bad thing in a general sense, but on a roster that's quickly becoming bereft of talent, it would be one avenue to jump-start things. Instead, the Texans have spent most of the last few seasons digging in the free-agency bargain bin or, when they do decide to ante up, bringing in old players.

Perhaps the worst decision the team has made under Smith's guidance was letting safety Glover Quin walk to sign future Hall of Famer Ed Reed. Reed was banged up before he even signed, and played in just seven games before being released. Quin was a hallmark member of Detroit's defense, which ranked No. 3 in DVOA last season despite a lack of cornerback talent.

2015 Texans Schedule

Week	Opp.	Week	Opp.	Week	Opp.
1	KC	7	at MIA	13	at BUF
2	at CAR	8	TEN	14	NE
3	TB	9	BYE	15	at IND
4	at ATL	10	at CIN (Mon.)	16	at TEN
5	IND (Thu.)	11	NYJ	17	JAC
6	at JAC	12	NO		

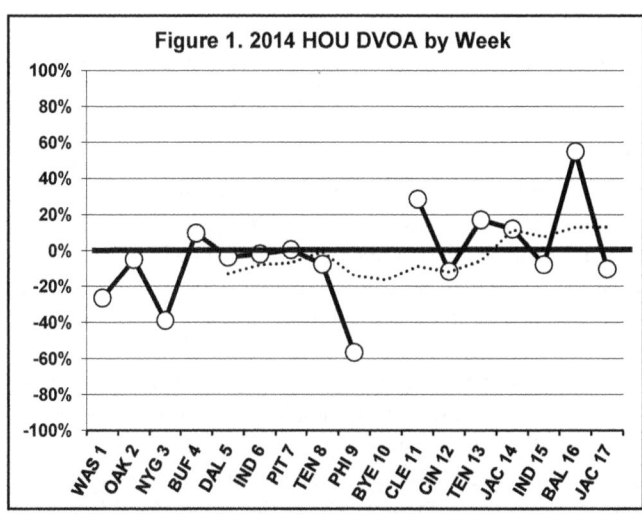

Figure 1. 2014 HOU DVOA by Week

The other major consequence of the Reed move was an everlasting hole at safety. Denver's Rahim Moore is the latest stab at fixing the position, but it should be noted that the reason they need to bring in Moore is that last season's potential fix, Chris Clemons, didn't even make it out of training camp with the Texans.

Signing nose tackle Vince Wilfork away from the Patriots is a move that has the same potential downside, though it is at least at a position where the Texans didn't already have an

Table 2. Recent Texans Draft History

2012 Players	Rd	Pos	Career AV	Comments
Whitney Mercilus	1	OLB	16	Ideally, a sub pass-rusher
DeVier Posey	3	WR	2	Injured, traded to NYJ
Brandon Brooks	3	G	12	Stellar interior lineman
Ben Jones	4	C	13	Adequate interior lineman
Keshawn Martin	4	WR	4	Adequate punt returner
Jared Crick	4	DE	12	Solid 3-4 end
Randy Bullock	5	K	4	Adequate kicker
Nick Mondek	6	OT	0	No NFL playing time

2013 Players	Rd	Pos	Career AV	Comments
DeAndre Hopkins	1	WR	15	Very good receiver
D.J. Swearinger	2	SS	10	Chemistry problem, cut
Brennan Williams	3	OT	0	Microfracture surgery, cut
Sam Montgomery	3	DE	0	Off-field drama, cut
Trevardo Williams	4	DE	0	Injured, cut
David Quessenberry	6	OT	0	Recovering from lymphoma
Alan Bonner	6	WR	0	Total non-entity so far
Chris Jones	6	DT	12	Cut; solid backup for NE
Ryan Griffin	6	TE	2	Decent backup

2014 Players	Rd	Pos	Career AV	Comments
Jadeveon Clowney	1	OLB	1	Microfracture surgery
Xavier Su'a-Filo	2	G	1	Unplayable in his rookie season
C.J. Fiedorowicz	3	TE	0	Block-first TE who couldn't block
Louis Nix	3	DT	0	Straight to IR
Tom Savage	4	QB	0	Incredibly raw in small sample
Jeoffrey Pagan	6	DE	0	Depth 3-4 end
Alfred Blue	6	RB	4	Below replacement level
Jay Prosch	6	FB	0	Fullback
Andre Hal	7	CB	1	Big plays and big mistakes
Lonnie Ballentine	7	FS	0	Straight to IR

established good player. Wilfork missed most of the 2013 season after tearing his Achilles tendon in Week 4. Wilfork bounced back in 2014 with a less impressive performance stuffing the run; the Patriots ranked dead last against short-yardage runs and 28th in stuff rate. He'll turn 34 in November, and is clearly a year-to-year proposition at this point.

Now, a team can contend with poor draft performance and minimal free-agent contributions if it gets good quarterback play. The Texans are not currently poised to receive such a performance without sending their running backs into the line 580 times.

The moves that led to Houston's dismal quarterback situation can be rationalized if you frame them in an ideal light. It made some sense for the Texans to use every draft pick possible to build around Matt Schaub and make a run in 2011-2012, rather than setting aside a pick to find a real Schaub successor. Through that prism, it makes sense that the team collapsed when Schaub imploded in 2013. If the Texans didn't believe that Teddy Bridgewater, Blake Bortles, Derek Carr, or Johnny Manziel were capable of becoming franchise quarterbacks, it makes sense that they didn't use the No. 1 overall pick on one of them that season. If the Texans believed that quarterback Ryan Mallett was a potential starter, and were that down on the other roster options last season, it was fine to part with a seventh-round pick for him. If the Texans believe that they can sneak into a playoff game with steady quarterbacking, and think that O'Brien can do to ex-Browns quarterback Brian Hoyer's career what he did to Fitzpatrick's, there is a logic behind that move as well.

But that is the very problem that faces the Texans right now: they are a team always designed to be viewed in ideal light. Owner Bob McNair has battled cancer and been a tougher quote of late, but when he does speak, you can see that mindset coming out often. McNair often bemoans injuries as if other teams have never suffered them. McNair gives his head coaches and general managers enough rope to climb a mountain, even when they've all firmly decided to camp halfway up rather than head to the summit.

And while each individual move in the process has some sense behind it, there's not really a cohesive long-term plan in place here. No NFL team should be relying on Savage to be its future at quarterback, and yet instead of doubling-down on another interesting arm that fell in the draft like UCLA's Brett Hundley, Houston has Hoyer as a presumptive starter. Ryan Mallett is 27 and has one good NFL start to his name, to go with a backlog of preseason work that says accuracy is still a problem. That uncertainty is a good thing for the Texans right now, because he might still develop into something better than what we've seen so far. But pretending like he may be a star because he was stuck behind Tom Brady for three years is simply unrealistic.

That quarterback carousel was enough to alienate future Hall of Fame receiver Andre Johnson, who missed most of OTAs and training camp and was behind the program to the point that he finished second-to-last in receiving DVOA among qualified wideouts. (Yes, the quarterbacks were a problem, but not enough of a problem to keep DeAndre Hopkins from finishing in the top 25.) Clearly, the Texans believed that Johnson's underwhelming 2014 season was an indicator of declining talent rather than a matter of motivation. That makes sense on its face, and the Texans were going to have to move on from Johnson sooner or later, but Houston didn't spend most of the vacated cap space from Johnson's release. Johnson had limited speed and wasn't a deep threat without a double move, but he's still a talented receiver with the potential to bounce back at a position where we've seen several recent players play well into their 30s. With no backup plan,

the Texans had to spend a third-round pick (and trade up for) Jaelen Strong out of Arizona State just to avoid starting wideouts fresh off the scrapheap.

Despite all this, the Texans have a lot going for them. O'Brien has demonstrated the ability early in his career to really get the most out of limited talent. J.J. Watt, the world's most valuable non-quarterback, is under contract for seven more seasons. Those are two building blocks that any franchise would kill to have. Foster should be considered a star back until proven otherwise, Hopkins is the pre-eminent bad-ball catching wide receiver in the NFL, and Duane Brown is a terrific all-around left tackle with excellent mobility. If Clowney becomes what many thought he would be coming out of South Carolina, the Texans will have the best 1-2 pass-rush combo in the NFL.

But the Texans haven't added many new stars since Watt, are a team with about a 10 percent chance to solve their quarterback problem from the current crop, and are facing roster-wide talent shortages (especially when it comes to depth at non-cornerback positions).

It's not hard to see O'Brien getting the most out of this team, Watt having another historic season, and the Texans remaining on the fringes of the AFC playoff race. It's just that it involves more wishcasting than a team with these main ingredients should have to use.

Rivers McCown

2014 Texans Stats by Week

Wk	vs.	W-L	PF	PA	YDF	YDA	TO	Total	Off	Def	ST
1	WAS	W	17	6	321	372	1	-27%	-12%	12%	-3%
2	at OAK	W	30	14	327	364	4	-5%	14%	12%	-7%
3	at NYG	L	17	30	411	419	-2	-39%	-8%	24%	-7%
4	BUF	W	23	17	301	316	-1	10%	-24%	-30%	3%
5	at DAL	L	17	20	330	456	2	-4%	-2%	-5%	-7%
6	IND	L	28	33	332	456	0	-2%	24%	16%	-10%
7	at PIT	L	23	30	393	328	-2	0%	-4%	-12%	-8%
8	at TEN	W	30	16	405	326	2	-8%	4%	7%	-5%
9	PHI	L	21	31	300	483	3	-57%	-34%	9%	-13%
10	BYE										
11	at CLE	W	23	7	424	375	1	28%	17%	-7%	5%
12	CIN	L	13	22	248	372	0	-12%	-15%	-4%	-1%
13	TEN	W	45	21	457	320	3	17%	12%	-14%	-10%
14	at JAC	W	27	13	304	262	1	12%	-1%	-6%	7%
15	at IND	L	10	17	289	278	0	-8%	-29%	-21%	0%
16	BAL	W	25	13	313	211	2	55%	-30%	-91%	-6%
17	JAC	W	23	17	358	233	-2	-10%	-13%	-4%	-1%

Trends and Splits

	Offense	Rank	Defense	Rank
Total DVOA	-6.8%	21	-6.2%	6
Unadjusted VOA	-4.5%	21	-10.9%	5
Weighted Trend	-8.0%	23	-12.7%	4
Variance	3.1%	3	7.1%	22
Average Opponent	1.8%	27	-5.5%	32
Passing	7.9%	18	-5.3%	6
Rushing	-11.7%	24	-7.4%	16
First Down	-12.4%	26	12.0%	28
Second Down	-1.3%	17	-8.1%	8
Third Down	-5.0%	20	-42.2%	1
First Half	-13.0%	27	-8.8%	8
Second Half	-0.8%	16	-3.3%	12
Red Zone	-16.6%	25	-25.7%	3
Late and Close	-13.1%	25	-3.9%	14

Five-Year Performance

Year	W-L	Pyth W	Est W	PF	PA	TO	Total	Rk	Off	Rk	Def	Rk	ST	Rk	Off AGL	Rk	Def AGL	Rk	Off Age	Rk	Def Age	Rk	ST Age	Rk
2010	6-10	7.1	7.9	390	427	0	2.5%	13	21.7%	2	17.5%	31	-1.7%	23	30.9	20	24.1	16	27.4	15	25.5	30	26.2	15
2011	10-6	10.9	10.0	381	278	+7	18.6%	5	8.4%	9	-9.5%	6	0.7%	13	31.3	17	18.9	10	28.1	2	25.7	29	26.1	24
2012	12-4	10.2	8.3	416	331	+12	6.7%	11	0.1%	16	-14.2%	4	-7.7%	32	6.7	1	30.6	19	28.1	6	26.5	22	26.4	11
2013	2-14	4.2	3.9	276	428	-20	-26.5%	30	-18.9%	29	2.5%	18	-5.1%	29	35.1	18	28.6	18	27.5	9	26.2	22	25.7	26
2014	9-7	9.8	6.7	372	307	+12	-4.5%	19	-6.8%	21	-6.2%	6	-3.9%	28	18.8	6	41.1	20	27.2	12	26.0	28	26.1	17

2014 Performance Based on Most Common Personnel Groups

HOU Offense					HOU Offense vs. Opponents					HOU Defense				HOU Defense vs. Opponents			
Pers	Freq	Yds	DVOA	Run%	Pers	Freq	Yds	DVOA	Run%	Pers	Freq	Yds	DVOA	Pers	Freq	Yds	DVOA
11	57%	6.1	14.5%	40%	Base	40%	4.4	-23.0%	54%	Base	34%	4.9	-9.3%	11	61%	5.6	-3.2%
12	22%	5.0	-17.8%	47%	Nickel	49%	5.8	9.6%	43%	Nickel	22%	5.2	3.1%	12	20%	4.6	-7.7%
21	8%	3.6	-35.2%	65%	Dime+	9%	7.9	39.8%	34%	Dime+	43%	5.7	-9.6%	21	9%	4.7	-16.0%
10	4%	5.4	-17.2%	44%	Goal Line	1%	0.4	1.2%	64%	Goal Line	1%	0.8	4.1%	13	3%	5.0	-20.5%
22	4%	3.1	-26.6%	89%	Big	1%	1.9	-52.5%	86%	Big	1%	3.1	-20.0%	22	2%	3.1	-17.0%

Strategic Tendencies

Run/Pass		Rk	Formation		Rk	Pass Rush		Rk	Secondary		Rk	Strategy		Rk
Runs, first half	45%	6	Form: Single Back	77%	10	Rush 3	7.3%	11	4 DB	25%	17	Play action	19%	20
Runs, first down	60%	2	Form: Empty Back	9%	8	Rush 4	52.8%	27	5 DB	21%	30	Avg Box (Off)	6.28	16
Runs, second-long	40%	3	Pers: 3+ WR	64%	12	Rush 5	23.5%	15	6+ DB	54%	2	Avg Box (Def)	6.28	15
Runs, power sit.	61%	11	Pers: 4+ WR	4%	7	Rush 6+	16.5%	1	CB by Sides	71%	26	Offensive Pace	29.24	8
Runs, behind 2H	38%	2	Pers: 2+ TE/6+ OL	28%	19	Sacks by LB	30.3%	19	DB Blitz	15%	3	Defensive Pace	27.99	1
Pass, ahead 2H	41%	28	Shotgun/Pistol	50%	26	Sacks by DB	2.6%	26	Hole in Zone	6%	14	Go for it on 4th	1.26	7

The Texans used three or more wide receivers 50 percent more often than they did the year before. ☞ There's a reason so many Texans fans get allergic hives whenever they see Arian Foster motion out wide: the Texans once again were terrible when using an empty backfield, averaging 5.5 yards per play with -26.3% DVOA (similar to 5.2 yards, -26.7% DVOA in 2013, and much worse than the NFL average of 6.7 yards, 22.1% DVOA). ☞ The Texans also had by far the NFL's largest gap between performance on runs out of two-back sets (2.4 yards per carry, -49.3% DVOA) and runs out of one-back sets (4.5 yards per carry, -5.6% DVOA). They showed no similar split in other recent seasons. ☞ The Texans led the league in big blitzes (six or more pass rushers) for the third straight season. ☞ Houston opponents threw a league-high 22 percent of passes to the players we identified as No. 3 or "other" receivers.

Passing

Player	DYAR	DVOA	Plays	NtYds	Avg	YAC	C%	TD	Int
R.Fitzpatrick*	383	6.7%	334	2393	7.2	5.5	63.3%	17	8
C.Keenum*	-50	-20.8%	80	422	5.3	5.8	58.4%	2	2
R.Mallett	120	14.5%	74	395	5.3	3.9	56.2%	2	2
T.Savage	-20	-24.2%	21	117	5.6	3.3	52.6%	0	1
B.Hoyer	166	-5.3%	465	3170	6.8	5.6	55.7%	12	12

Rushing

Player	DYAR	DVOA	Plays	Yds	Avg	TD	Fum	Suc
A.Foster	167	7.5%	260	1246	4.8	8	2	46%
A.Blue	-88	-21.3%	169	528	3.1	3	0	39%
J.Grimes	-22	-24.0%	39	153	3.9	0	0	49%
R.Fitzpatrick*	32	2.8%	37	195	5.3	2	0	-
C.Keenum*	9	4.3%	8	37	4.6	0	0	-
R.Brown*	-16	-88.7%	6	4	0.7	0	0	0%
D.Johnson	0	-37.0%	5	19	3.8	0	0	-
B.Hoyer	-59	-64.8%	19	37	1.9	0	1	-

Receiving

Player	DYAR	DVOA	Plays	Ctch	Yds	Y/C	YAC	TD	C%
A.Johnson*	-86	-19.8%	147	85	939	11.0	4.6	3	58%
D.Hopkins	237	10.3%	127	76	1210	15.9	4.9	6	60%
D.Johnson	-39	-23.5%	49	31	331	10.7	5.9	1	63%
K.Martin	-16	-30.4%	12	6	78	13.0	9.5	0	50%
C.Shorts	-183	-33.7%	110	53	557	10.5	4.9	1	48%
N.Washington	97	5.3%	72	40	647	16.2	3.5	2	56%
G.Graham	17	2.3%	28	18	197	10.9	3.5	1	64%
R.Griffin	5	-2.7%	16	10	91	9.1	3.6	1	63%
C.Fiedorowicz	-5	-19.1%	7	4	28	7.0	2.5	1	57%
A.Foster	46	0.7%	59	38	327	8.6	6.8	5	64%
A.Blue	41	25.4%	18	15	113	7.5	5.0	1	83%
J.Grimes	33	72.4%	8	6	86	14.3	12.5	0	75%

Offensive Line

Player	Pos	Age	GS	Snaps	Pen	Sk	Pass	Run	Player	Pos	Age	GS	Snaps	Pen	Sk	Pass	Run
Derek Newton	RT	28	16/16	1107	6	3.0	22.0	5.0	Ben Jones	LG	26	16/16	1047	5	1.5	17.0	10.0
Chris Myers*	C	34	16/16	1100	2	0.0	8.0	9.0	Brandon Brooks	RG	26	15/15	984	5	0.5	7.0	8.0
Duane Brown	LT	30	16/16	1099	6	1.5	14.5	6.5									

Year	Yards	ALY	Rk	Power	Rk	Stuff	Rk	2nd Lev	Rk	Open Field	Rk	Sacks	ASR	Rk	Short	Long	F-Start	Cont.
2012	4.34	4.17	9	61%	18	20%	23	1.26	10	0.85	12	28	5.3%	9	14	7	18	33
2013	4.20	4.10	6	56%	26	20%	17	1.31	3	0.53	26	42	6.6%	11	13	14	19	38
2014	4.07	3.72	23	67%	13	21%	25	1.07	22	0.80	12	26	4.9%	8	8	13	15	39
2014 ALY by direction:		Left End 2.72 (30)			Left Tackle 3.42 (24)			Mid/Guard 4.1 (11)			Right Tackle 3.51 (24)				Right End 3.46 (19)		

Houston had a few decisions to make on one of the better run-blocking offensive lines of 2014. (Yes, the Texans finished only 23rd in adjusted line yards, but that was mostly because opponents were stacking the box against the offense that ran more than any other. ESPN marked 23.5 percent of Houston runs against "loaded" boxes, fifth in the NFL.) Staying is Derek Newton, who parlayed a career year into a five-year, $26.5 million contract with $10 million in guarantees. Note that even in Newton's best season, there were still plenty of blown blocks on passes. This is a deal similar to what Minnesota gave Phil Loadholt, plus interest from the recent salary-cap increases, and the Texans are hoping that Newton can sustain a similar level of performance. If he goes back to what he was before 2014, it'll be a waste of cap space.

The Texans also decided to cut ties with long-time center Chris Myers, who will turn 34 in September and looked a little slower than he had in past seasons. This decision basically hands a starting job to 2014 second-round pick Xavier Su'a-Filo. Su'a-Filo's first season was so raw it made onlookers sick, as his functional strength was poor enough in a small sample size that he received only 45 snaps over the last nine weeks of the season. Remember, this is the player the Texans took with the pick they could've used as bait to trade up for any non-Blake Bortles quarterback in the 2014 draft. Now the starting left guard, Sua-Filo is under a lot of pressure this season to make good on Houston's faith in him.

To make room for Su'a-Filo, Ben Jones switches to his college position of center in the final year of his rookie contract. In extended trials at guard during the 2012 and 2014 seasons, Jones has been acceptable, if not inspiring. Brandon Brooks has been a true War Daddy since being picked in the third round of the 2012 draft, and he faces his own contract season at right guard. All-Pro tackle Duane Brown rounds out the line on the blind side. Brown had a down season in 2013, worn down by injuries. He bounced back in 2014, but at 29, he's getting to the age where any struggles will be watched with scrutiny. The only backup on this line with a drafted pedigree, 2013 sixth-rounder David Quessenberry, is trying to come back from lymphoma that is (thankfully) in remission. Any missed games by the starters could have a huge impact.

Defensive Front Seven

Defensive Line	Age	Pos	Overall								vs. Run					Pass Rush			
			G	Snaps	Plays	TmPct	Rk	Stop	Dfts	BTkl	Runs	St%	Rk	RuYd	Rk	Sack	Hit	Hur	Dsrpt
J.J. Watt	26	DE	16	1050	87	10.2%	1	75	43	4	53	81%	29	0.8	3	20.5	35	54.0	9
Jared Crick	26	DE	16	714	61	7.2%	10	47	12	0	42	79%	43	2.7	69	3.5	9	9.0	5
Tim Jamison	29	DE	13	410	19	2.8%	83	12	3	0	14	64%	86	3.1	87	1.5	1	6.0	0
Ryan Pickett*	36	DT	13	287	23	3.3%	--	21	2	0	19	95%	--	1.5	--	0.0	0	1.0	2
Vince Wilfork	*34*	*DT*	*16*	*802*	*48*	*6.0%*	*21*	*42*	*4*	*4*	*45*	*89%*	*10*	*2.1*	*40*	*0.0*	*1*	*8.0*	*1*

Edge Rushers	Age	Pos	Overall								vs. Run					Pass Rush			
			G	Snaps	Plays	TmPct	Rk	Stop	Dfts	BTkl	Runs	St%	Rk	RuYd	Rk	Sack	Hit	Hur	Dsrpt
Whitney Mercilus	25	OLB	15	804	50	6.3%	24	38	18	2	38	76%	37	2.3	38	5.0	8	16.5	0
Brooks Reed*	28	OLB	16	786	44	5.2%	40	32	15	3	31	74%	43	2.6	49	3.0	9	16.0	1
John Simon	25	OLB	11	235	10	1.7%	--	10	4	1	7	100%	--	0.0	--	1.5	4	2.5	0

Linebackers	Age	Pos	Overall								Pass Rush			vs. Run					vs. Pass						
			G	Snaps	Plays	TmPct	Rk	Stop	Dfts	BTkl	Sack	Hit	Hur	Runs	St%	Rk	RuYd	Rk	Tgts	Suc%	Rk	AdjYd	Rk	PD	Int
Brian Cushing	28	ILB	14	724	74	10.0%	61	41	3	9	1.0	9	11.5	57	54%	75	4.3	73	19	54%	21	6.5	34	2	0
Mike Mohamed	27	MLB	14	511	65	8.7%	69	39	11	4	0.0	1	5.5	38	66%	34	3.4	42	15	59%	--	5.3	--	4	1
Justin Tuggle	25	ILB	16	270	38	4.5%	--	19	3	7	0.0	1	1	26	62%	--	3.9	--	11	43%	--	5.1	--	2	1
Akeem Dent	28	MLB	15	224	27	3.4%	--	17	3	1	1.0	5	5.5	20	75%	--	3.1	--	4	16%	--	8.9	--	0	0

Year	Yards	ALY	Rk	Power	Rk	Stuff	Rk	2nd Level	Rk	Open Field	Rk	Sacks	ASR	Rk	Short	Long
2012	3.93	3.62	4	59%	11	25%	4	1.22	23	0.67	12	44	7.3%	6	11	15
2013	4.27	3.68	12	53%	6	22%	10	1.10	16	1.04	27	32	6.7%	18	12	8
2014	4.13	3.83	14	64%	17	19%	18	1.25	24	0.59	10	38	6.2%	24	10	14
2014 ALY by direction:		Left End 3.61 (15)			Left Tackle 4.42 (26)			Mid/Guard 3.84 (11)			Right Tackle 3.7 (12)			Right End 3.07 (7)		

It says a lot about the value of the quarterback position that, even in a year where no quarterback really separated himself from the crowd, a season like J.J. Watt's still couldn't win the Most Valuable Player award. Watt recorded 20.5 sacks, dominated his blockers one-on-one in run defense, and scored touchdowns on fumble recoveries, interceptions, and even as a goal-line receiver. Houston inked Watt to a six-year, $100 million extension before the season. It may turn out to be the biggest bargain second contract in today's NFL if the salary cap keeps rising.

Watt's historic season helped mask a lot of mediocrity in the rest of this front seven. Going forward, it seems that Houston's guiding strategy in building a unit around Watt is "dream of sunshine and lollipops," because the Texans are banking on a number of gambles working out. For example, Houston spent a second-round pick on Mississippi State middle linebacker Benardrick McKinney to give Brian Cushing an acceptable running mate. This would be great, except that despite McKinney's ideal size (6-foot-4, 246 pounds) and athleticism (4.66 40-yard dash), he struggled as a coverage player in college. If 2010 Brian Cushing was taking the field, that wouldn't matter, but the stalwart linebacker clearly lost a step laterally coming off two consecutive season-ending injuries. Houston had Cushing on a snap count for most of last season, and Bill O'Brien's pre-camp comments suggested he wants McKinney as a pass rusher on third down. It's hard to project either of them as coverage linebackers in 2014, which might lead to more Jeff Tarpinian or Mike Mohamed than anyone would desire.

General manager Rick Smith's pressers and actions seem to suggest last year's No. 1 overall pick Jadeveon Clowney will be ready for the start of the season, despite microfracture surgery after messing up his knee on a divot in the Reliant Stadium turf. That's a very aggressive timetable, especially if the Texans are expecting Clowney to be an impact pass-rusher. Smith also handed out a four-year, $26 million extension to former first-rounder Whitney Mercilus after the draft. Mercilus has had as little impact as a pass-rusher as someone with 18 sacks in three seasons can possibly have, so this looks like a deal where the Texans are projecting improvement that hasn't happened yet. With Brooks Reed gone to Atlanta, there is no drafted depth at outside linebacker unless sixth-rounder Reshard Cliett (South Florida) is to be tried there.

Free-agent signee Vince Wilfork should provide Houston with the nose tackle they've needed since Seth Payne hung up the pads in 2004. This move suggests that 2013 third-rounder Louis Nix III may already be on the outs with the organization, but he otherwise projects as the backup. Five-tech Jared Crick enters the final year of his rookie deal looking to complete a mini-breakout—he really took a step forward over the last half of the season, with 7.5 of his nine hurries and six of his nine hits coming after Week 8.

Defensive Secondary

Secondary	Age	Pos	G	Snaps	Plays	TmPct	Rk	Stop	Dfts	BTkl	Runs	St%	Rk	RuYd	Rk	Tgts	Tgt%	Rk	Dist	Suc%	Rk	AdjYd	Rk	PD	Int
Kendrick Lewis*	27	FS	16	1077	90	10.6%	29	31	14	13	50	28%	57	7.4	48	24	5.3%	10	12.6	67%	5	5.6	16	5	2
D.J. Swearinger*	24	SS	16	1018	79	9.3%	47	29	14	12	45	36%	45	6.1	27	40	9.3%	43	12.0	59%	23	7.3	36	5	2
Johnathan Joseph	31	CB	16	859	86	10.1%	15	27	12	7	13	23%	64	6.9	43	103	28.7%	67	11.6	52%	30	6.0	7	12	2
Kareem Jackson	27	CB	13	773	64	9.3%	26	35	12	12	14	64%	8	3.4	5	66	20.6%	19	10.1	61%	3	5.7	5	10	3
A.J. Bouye	24	CB	14	633	65	8.7%	33	19	12	4	4	0%	77	20.5	77	79	30.0%	71	12.6	45%	63	7.5	31	10	3
Danieal Manning*	33	FS	16	580	39	4.6%	--	8	4	2	16	13%	--	12.3	--	19	7.9%	--	12.1	68%	--	4.0	--	2	0
Darryl Morris	25	CB	11	258	36	6.2%	--	16	6	2	5	80%	--	1.8	--	38	35.0%	--	11.1	52%	--	6.7	--	6	1
Andre Hal	23	CB	14	224	22	3.0%	--	8	5	3	4	0%	--	9.8	--	19	19.9%	--	13.2	45%	--	10.3	--	2	0
Jumal Rolle	25	CB	10	202	19	3.6%	--	8	4	1	3	33%	--	11.7	--	18	21.5%	--	9.8	35%	--	10.6	--	4	3
Rahim Moore	25	FS	16	1054	55	6.7%	62	16	8	6	19	26%	58	11.5	69	24	5.1%	7	14.7	47%	55	7.4	40	6	4
Stevie Brown	28	SS	16	576	37	4.6%	70	11	5	4	21	33%	48	9.4	59	9	4.3%	3	13.9	32%	70	13.6	71	0	0

Year	Pass D Rank	vs. #1 WR	Rk	vs. #2 WR	Rk	vs. Other WR	Rk	vs. TE	Rk	vs. RB	Rk
2012	4	-26.7%	4	11.3%	28	1.8%	19	-12.2%	4	-23.1%	5
2013	24	-1.0%	18	5.4%	17	-10.5%	9	24.9%	30	17.6%	30
2014	6	1.0%	16	-39.4%	1	4.5%	21	-24.1%	3	-8.6%	11

It was a mild surprise that the Texans took a defensive back with their first-round pick, as cornerback would have seemed to be their most set position before the draft. Wake Forest's Kevin Johnson was regarded by some as the most NFL-ready corner in the draft: a finished product who was only held back in the process by a less-than-ideal 188-pound frame. His selection answers a lot of questions about the present and future of Houston's roster construction.

Johnathan Joseph, a very good corner who can no longer escape a game without getting dinged up, is going to see out the last year of his deal before ceding his starting spot to Johnson. Johnson also allows the Texans to continue playing Kareem Jackson in the slot on passing downs. The Texans managed to re-sign Jackson on the precipice of free agency by giving him a slightly Maxwellian four-year, $34 million deal with $20 million in guarantees. Jackson has certainly had an eventful career—he was horrible in his first two seasons, but has been terrific in two of the last three years. There's a surprising amount of depth at corner between A.J. Bouye, Andre Hal, Daryl Morris, and Jumal Rolle, all of whom were at least slightly effective in small sample sizes filling in for Jackson and Joseph last season. Houston's goal this season: find out which of them is should be playing nickel and dime once Johnson replaces Joseph long-term.

At safety, Houston exchanged Kendrick Lewis for the rangy Rahim Moore. Moore found a cold free-agent market, likely because teams are worried about the compartment syndrome that forced him to miss part of the 2013 season. With the surprise May release of third-year player D.J. Swearinger, the Texans have some potential issues at the other safety spot. Stevie Brown, signed away from the Giants in free agency, is a borderline starter with a lengthy injury history. The only other safety on the roster to even have NFL snaps at this point is Eddie Pleasant. Pleasant, a 2012 UDFA out of Oregon, has accumulated a grand total of 219 snaps over the last two years. Romeo Crennel likes to play three-safety sets. This is a potentially flammable situation.

Special Teams

Year	DVOA	Rank	FG/XP	Rank	Net Kick	Rank	Kick Ret	Rank	Net Punt	Rank	Punt Ret	Rank	Hidden	Rank
2012	-7.7%	32	-5.8	29	-25.9	32	-6.9	28	-1.2	16	1.4	13	5.7	4
2013	-5.1%	29	-12.2	31	-1.4	20	-5.0	27	-7.8	27	0.6	13	1.3	13
2014	-3.9%	28	0.5	15	-2.0	19	-5.2	27	-6.5	24	-6.1	27	2.3	13

The Texans have been searching for answers on special teams for the better part of the decade. They have invested multiple late-round picks on players like Trindon Holliday and Randy Bullock, and have emphasized special teams for their other late-round picks. They fired special-teams coordinator Joe Marciano late in 2013 and replaced him with Bob Ligashesky, to no real avail. Bullock had a better season, but he's not exactly battle-tested and had an abnormally low number of 40-yard attempts in 2014. He's also not creating a lot of touchbacks given how many games he plays indoors. Punter Shane Lechler seems basically ageless, and is the only real weapon Houston has on this unit, but weakness on punt coverage is still a problem. Keshawn Martin is the incumbent punt returner, but he is more shifty than fast. He's coming off a down year, likely small sample-size variation rather than decline. Damaris Johnson returned some kickoffs last year—he was better at it than Danieal Manning was, but has no real track record of success. This is a unit that could really use an injection of speed. Or a *Bar Rescue*-themed episode of *Hard Knocks*.

Indianapolis Colts

2014 Record: 11-5	**Total DVOA:** 4.5% (13th)	**2015 Mean Projection:** 9.3 wins	**On the Clock (0-4):** 4%
Pythagorean Wins: 10.2 (7th)	**Offense:** -1.1% (17th)	**Postseason Odds:** 61.1%	**Mediocrity (5-7):** 21%
Snap-Weighted Age: 27.0 (8th)	**Defense:** -2.3% (13th)	**Super Bowl Odds:** 9.9%	**Playoff Contender (8-10):** 42%
Average Opponent: -3.1% (26th)	**Special Teams:** 3.3% (8th)	**Proj. Avg. Opponent:** -4.4% (30th)	**Super Bowl Contender (11+):** 33%

2014: Deflating finish for the AFC's runner-up.

2015: Third prize is you're fired.

Let's take a trip back to the summer of 2013 to see what owner Jim Irsay had to say about the makeup of the Andrew Luck-era Colts. "There was a conscious effort to make sure we had more balance and tighten the special teams up," Irsay said. "It was really a strong theme that I thought was important as Andrew came in and as we started this new era. When we can add that component [a tough ground game and a tough defense] to the Andrew Lucks of the world, I think you really have a chance to win more than one."

More than one Super Bowl win is the goal Irsay has pushed for after expressing his disappointment with the one ring from the Peyton Manning era. But have the Colts come anywhere close to building the balanced team Irsay wants? The Colts have yet to find a consistent ground game and last year they fielded the oldest defense in the league with very few building blocks on the roster. Rather than splurge on a true difference-maker in free agency, general manager Ryan Grigson's solution this year was to sign a bunch of past-their-prime stop-gap veterans in their thirties. Adding new players will become much more difficult given the looming fact that Luck is set to become the highest-paid player in league history at potentially $25 million per season. This is also a contract year for several of the offense's best players, as well as head coach Chuck Pagano.

Essentially, Irsay has a team that is even more dependent on its quarterback to succeed than the Manning-era Colts. If he didn't like the "Star Wars numbers" from Peyton and company, then it must be killing him that Andrew the Giant has to dismantle the damn Death Star on his own.

The Colts are attempting to become the first team in NFL history to advance one step further in the playoffs four years in a row. That would put them in this year's Super Bowl. Not many teams can boast of stacking together three 11-5 seasons and three playoff wins, especially with the kind of roster deficiencies the Colts have overcome. In a sense, this team has overachieved, but we've seen this story before with the Manning-led Colts consistently beating their expected win total. As long as the Colts have a healthy Luck, they are a Super Bowl contender, and some of this year's changes should lead to the best roster put around Luck so far.

So why do we have such a pessimistic view of this team's direction?

It's because when we look at Indianapolis, we don't see a team as much as we see a quarterback asked to keep the ship from sinking. The Colts thought they pressed the "easy button" the day they turned in the card to choose Luck first overall in 2012. The Colts found another franchise quarterback, and the rest of the AFC South was left wanting. Playing in that poor division means Indianapolis pretty much starts each season with five or six wins in the bank, and the Colts have taken full advantage with a 16-2 division record (and 13 straight wins) over the last three years.

Despite the perception of the Colts as a paper tiger in a bad division, the AFC South is not the only source of this team's success. The Colts are one of four teams since 2012 (along with the Seahawks, Patriots and Steelers) to have a winning record against playoff teams at 12-11. Yet the Colts have a reputation of not getting it done against good teams, because in those 11 losses, the Colts have been outscored by 20.5 points per game. The other half of the story is that some of the wins have required monumental comebacks, like an 18-point rally against Green Bay in 2012 and an epic 28-point comeback to beat the Chiefs 45-44 in the 2013 AFC wild-card round. If the Colts aren't getting destroyed, they're squeezing out wins by the tiniest of margins against the best competition. All six of the Colts' losses last year were against teams with double-digit wins, and the Colts allowed at least 30 points in every game. If you want to get really pessimistic, you can question how far the team would have gone last postseason without the luck of the draw. First, they got a Cincinnati team that had no receivers to work with and already had been shut out in Indianapolis during the regular season. When they faced Denver the next week, Peyton Manning was suffering from a torn quad, and Demaryius Thomas admitted in January that some of Denver's players were caught looking ahead to New England.

Where would the Colts be last postseason if their playoff opponents had been Pittsburgh and New England instead? In the regular season, the Colts became the first defense in NFL history to allow a 500-yard passer (Ben Roethlisberger) and 200-yard rusher (Jonas Gray) in the same season. The Andrew Luck Colts are 0-4 against the Patriots, losing by an average of 29 points per game. The figurative Death Star in the AFC may be New England, but firing little rookie receiver Phillip Dorsett into the heart of the beast isn't going to change a thing this season. The obvious criticism of the Colts' first-round

2015 Colts Schedule

Week	Opp.	Week	Opp.	Week	Opp.
1	at BUF	7	NO	13	at PIT
2	NYJ (Mon.)	8	at CAR (Mon.)	14	at JAC
3	at TEN	9	DEN	15	HOU
4	JAC	10	BYE	16	at MIA
5	at HOU (Thu.)	11	at ATL	17	TEN
6	NE	12	TB		

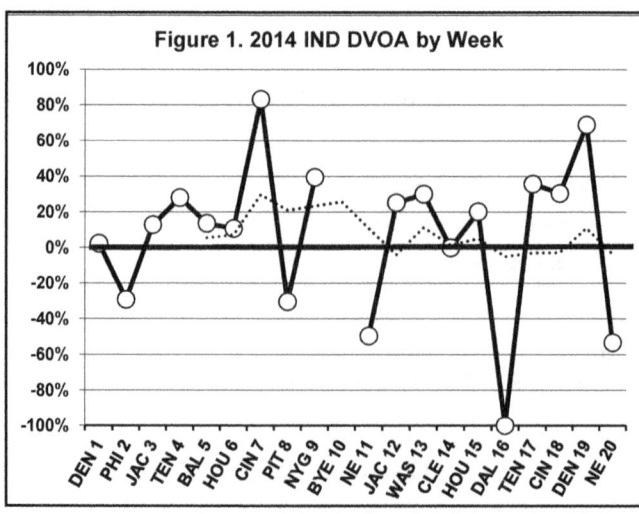

Figure 1. 2014 IND DVOA by Week

pick was that it does nothing to stop the Patriots from rushing for over 150 yards with their back of choice against Indianapolis. However, the Dorsett pick has value for a team that needs upgrades at most positions. This is not a finely-tuned offense in need of a consistent defense like the Manning-era teams. Believe it or not, the 2014 Colts ranked higher in defensive DVOA (13th) than they did on offense (17th).

The single biggest problem Indianapolis has is that four or five times each season the team is completely outdone in every phase of the game. That is only supposed to happen to bad teams. Since 2012 (including playoffs), the Colts have 10 losses by at least 17 points, tied for the sixth-most in that span. Those other six teams have a combined zero playoff appearances in 18 opportunities. In the last three years, the Colts have allowed at least 40 points in 10 games—three more than any other team. Such things rarely happened in the Manning era.

• Indianapolis allowed 40-plus points in nine of Peyton Manning's 227 games (4.0 percent).
• Indianapolis has allowed 40-plus points in 10 of Andrew Luck's 54 games (18.5 percent).
• Indianapolis scored fewer than 10 points in eight of Peyton Manning's 227 games (3.5 percent), including a Week 17 rest game in 2009.
• Indianapolis has scored fewer than 10 points in six of Andrew Luck's 54 games (11.1 percent)

Despite the annual 11-5 pedigree, the Colts have all the hallmarks of a bad team in a bad division. They just also happen to have a young quarterback capable of miraculous things. Since 2012, the Colts are a league-best 20-4 (.833) in games decided by a touchdown or less. That covers up for the abnormal amount of times the Colts are blown out. But all the blowouts speak very poorly for Pagano and Grigson, because consistent playoff teams should not have so many of these lapses. Contenders like the Seahawks, Patriots, and Packers have all recently had streaks of 60-plus games where they were at least within one score in the fourth quarter. That's what you call being competitive, even when the game doesn't start well. The Colts flop hard early and it just snowballs from there. Some holes are even too big for Luck to climb out of.

While the Colts stand out among their current peers for some of the wrong reasons, things really come into perspective when we compare them to other consistent playoff teams from the past. Since 1970, there have been 158 cases of a team

making three consecutive playoff appearances. This includes longer runs with overlap. For example, if the Colts make the playoffs in 2015, we would look at their three-year runs from 2012-14 and 2013-15 as two cases. When we look at historical record of these teams allowing an inordinate amount of points, winning close games, and losing by a big margin, the 2012-14 Colts stick out like a sore thumb (Table 1).

Table 1. The Colts vs. Other 3-Year Playoff Teams Since 1970

Statistic	2012-14 Colts	Rk	NFL Average
Games allowing 40-plus points	10	1st	1.3
Percentage of games allowing 40-plus points	18.5%	1st	2.5%
Games allowing 30-plus points	16	T-1st	6.7
Percentage of games allowing 30-plus points	29.6%	3rd	12.8%
Win percentage in one-score games*	.833 (20-4)	T-2nd	0.614
Losses by 17-plus points	10	1st	3.2
Percentage of games lost by 17-plus points	18.5%	1st	6.2%
*Games decided by 1-7 points in 1970-1993, 1-8 points in 1994-2014			

The Colts have allowed at least 30 points in each of their last 10 losses, dating back to 2013. While it's easy to blame the defense, the offense only averaged 18.8 points per game on those days. The ugly 45-7 loss in January's AFC Championship Game is the marquee example of the Colts simply not showing up on either side of the ball, but it's far from a unique event with this team.

Where do the Colts seek help this year to add variety to their one-man show? We would cite better injury luck, but the Colts have ranked 24th or worse in adjusted games lost for nine straight seasons. We could implore the offensive line to protect better, but by now Luck's playing style seems to be established. He has led all quarterbacks in knockdowns (sacks plus hits) three years in a row, with 59 more than the next-closest passer. He's lowered his sack rate each season, but it's come at the expense of rising hit counts: 83, 87, and then 91 in 2014. As a lover of the deep pass, Luck has no problem holding onto the ball and delivering at the last second before a defender takes him down. A lot of these hits still turn into completions and touchdowns, but the cumulative effect is troublesome when you think about long-term health. So far Luck has shown LeBron-like durability, but he'll need to start taking fewer hits as he gets older (and richer).

How about a running game for a change? In terms of rushing support per game (quarterback runs excluded), the Colts have averaged a pedestrian 22 carries for 85.4 yards in Luck's 54 starts, including just one 100-yard rushing performance (Vick Ballard in 2012). It's not like this offense needs Walter Payton production behind Luck, but a little more of a ground game to take some of the pressure off would be big. One thing that needs to stop is having games with less than five rushing yards, which the Colts have somehow done three times since 2013. Luck handed off 14 times for four yards against the Patriots at home last year. Sure, Ahmad Bradshaw was injured in that game, but *four yards?* Luck led the team with 15 rushing yards that night. A month later in Dallas the Colts had 10 runs for one yard. Again, these things just don't happen to other NFL teams, especially not multiple times.

The Colts are average in run blocking, but what really sunk the ground game the last two years was Trent Richardson. The only thing lower than his yards-per-carry average was the way his Indianapolis tenure ended: serving a team-imposed suspension during the playoffs. Richardson averaged just 3.1 yards per carry with the Colts. Since 2013, the Colts' other six running backs combined for 350 carries for 1,657 yards, which is 4.7 yards per carry. That's great production. The Colts felt forced to play an inferior player because they traded a first-round pick for him and didn't accept it as a sunk cost. Those days are finally over. Richardson was released and the Colts added a back who knows nothing but averaging 4.0 yards per carry. Frank Gore did that in all 10 seasons with San Francisco.

The Colts are not getting the 32-year-old Gore at an ideal time in his career, but this could be an ideal situation for him. In each of the last three years in San Francisco, Gore had the highest percentage of runs against eight or more defenders in the box (Table 2). That's not going to happen in Indianapolis when the safety has to worry about defending the deep pass. Running backs for the Colts have seen loaded boxes roughly half as often as Gore, who still had success anyway. With a better distribution of carries against unloaded boxes, Gore should locate some of the favorable lanes that Richardson struggled to find.

We'll look for that improved running game, but this is still a pass-happy offense with loads of weapons. The 2014 Colts were the seventh offense ever to have at least nine players catch at least 20 passes. Offensive coordinator Pep Hamilton let Luck run the show more last year, and it was fun to watch until a late-season slump saw the Colts fall to 26th in offensive DVOA in Weeks 10-17. Ball security was not sharp last year. The Colts had 31 fumbles and led the league with 34 dropped passes. Reggie Wayne was on his last legs, yet he played more snaps than any receiver on the team. Hakeem Nicks didn't get on the same page with Luck until December, if at all.

This year's supporting cast should be stronger. In fact, the Colts may actually have too many weapons to use after already throwing 42 touchdowns last year. T.Y. Hilton is still the go-to guy for Luck, but you know Andre Johnson is going to command his share of targets. Donte Moncrief had some great flashes as a third-round rookie, including two 100-yard receiving games, and he was on the receiving end of that incredible 36-yard touchdown throw from Luck in the playoffs against the Bengals. The additions of Johnson and Phillip Dorsett could really halt Moncrief's development this year. The Colts only used four wide receivers on 25 plays last year, though the fourth wide receiver did play 411 snaps. One possibility with Dorsett is that he was drafted to eventually replace Hilton, who will be an unrestricted free agent in 2016. But Hilton has been too good to not lock up. He's improved every year and has that rare ability to win contested balls downfield despite 5-foot-10 size. Another big season and he's likely looking to bypass the $10-plus million per year Randall Cobb and Jeremy Maclin received and aim for the $14 million Dez Bryant and Demaryius Thomas earned.

When this season is over, the Colts will have some major decisions to make in regards to which offensive starters return in 2016. Sure, that 2012 draft was really good, but that creates a problem when a star receiver such as Hilton and the two tight ends with eight touchdowns each last year will all be free agents at the same time. We know Luck is going to get paid, but who else? Anthony Castonzo is another impending free

Table 2. Rushing vs. Loaded Box (8-10 Defenders) vs. Standard Front (<8 Defenders)

Running Back	Year	Team	8-10 Runs	Pct.	Rk	YPC	Rk	DVOA	Rk	<8 Runs	YPC	Rk	DVOA	Rk	Rk Out of*
Frank Gore	2012	SF	95	37%	1	3.17	16	-6.2%	16	163	5.60	3	36.3%	1	42
Frank Gore	2013	SF	107	39%	1	3.89	6	4.2%	14	169	4.25	25	-4.8%	32	47
Frank Gore	2014	SF	76	30%	1	3.59	13	-3.6%	12	179	4.65	12	12.7%	13	43
Vick Ballard	2012	IND	32	15%	19	1.59	35	-35.4%	34	179	4.26	23	-1.1%	23	42
Donald Brown	2012	IND	18	17%	15	1.22	40	-77.1%	41	90	4.39	19	2.9%	19	42
Trent Richardson	2013	IND	29	16%	25	1.83	40	-32.9%	37	158	3.20	46	-19.3%	43	47
Donald Brown	2013	IND	19	19%	15	4.84	5	34.2%	1	82	5.38	3	18.3%	4	47
Trent Richardson	2014	IND	25	16%	12	3.00	19	-23.2%	26	134	3.32	41	-15.4%	42	43

*The number of running backs qualifying to be ranked in each season.

agent. He's the team's best offensive lineman, and while he's not in Tyron Smith territory, a serviceable left tackle is going to make money on the open market. Castonzo will likely command a deal worth around $8 million per year. The Colts should keep at least one of Coby Fleener and Dwayne Allen at tight end. Fleener's inconsistency and Allen's injury history should keep the price down for both. Given the Colts' plethora of wide receivers, going with the superior blocker (Allen) might be the smart move.

For now, the Colts are spending roughly the same on offense ($65 million) as they are on defense ($66 million), according to Over the Cap. As you can see, this should change soon. The problem with the defense is that Grigson's method of paying for other people's players has not paid off, whether because of injury (Arthur Jones) or just pure disappointment (LaRon Landry). Only 15.3 percent of the 2014 Colts' defensive snaps were by players the team has drafted. That is alarmingly low, and it's easy to see why this defense was the oldest in snap-weighted age. That was accomplished even without 33-year-old Robert Mathis playing a snap. The fact that the Colts had some success rushing the passer without Mathis was remarkable, but that's a credit to the job defensive coordinator Greg Manusky did in dialing up blitzes to get pressure. The Colts rushed at least five defenders on 46 percent of plays, the third-highest rate in the league. But when the pressure failed to get there, the defense was picked apart despite generally good cornerback play, led by Vontae Davis' excellent season.

Davis is the defense's new best player, because Mathis will be fortunate to see action by September after tearing his Achilles tendon last year. This is where you'd like to see Grigson's lone premium drafted defender, Bjoern Werner, step up, but that hasn't worked out so far. If Mathis is still out, the Colts have another old-man edge rusher in Trent Cole (33) to trot out there. Adding a couple of 29-year-old veterans like Kendall Langford and Dwight Lowery isn't likely to make the team balanced, but it is up to Pagano to get everyone playing together in his system. There has to be some frustration in constantly working with new veterans instead of getting young players to groom from day one of their pro careers. It

will take a few drafts to reload the Colts with young defensive talent for the future. Will Grigson still be making those picks? Will Pagano still be in charge of coaching them up?

This is a pivotal season for the Colts given that Luck's cap number is set to rise to over $16 million in 2016, barring his new deal. It takes more than a quarterback to win it all, which the Colts should know better than any franchise. The window to win championships while Luck was under a rookie contract was always going to be small. This season's schedule gives the Colts an inside track to the AFC's top seed thanks to home games against the Patriots (Week 6) and Broncos (Week 9). Those could be games where Tom Brady makes his season debut after his four-game suspension and Peyton Manning breaks the all-time passing yardage record. It's those national games where the Colts can really build up their reputation with much-needed home wins against contenders.

Of course, the Colts could luck out the way Pittsburgh did last decade; the Steelers never played New England in the playoffs in any of their three Super Bowl seasons (2005, 2008, and 2010). But we know it's about more than just New England for the Colts. It's about limiting those awful performances. If Pagano can get this group into the Super Bowl, then he's locked himself up a new deal. However, 2015 feels eerily like 2001, when the Colts drafted a Miami receiver in the first round and the defensive-minded coach (in his fourth year) failed to turn his side of the ball around. Pagano may just be a midseason losing streak away from having his own "playoffs!?" moment with the media. Then the Colts will be searching for a Tony Dungy type again, bringing a sense of calm and efficiency to this growing monster with just enough discipline on defense.

Irsay has been given a second chance to do things right by his quarterback, but the Colts seem content to repeat the same mistakes of the previous era. When Irsay signs off on making Luck the highest-paid player in history, deep down inside he should know that winning even one ring with this type of team is a hell of an achievement. Asking for two is just arrogance.

Scott Kacsmar

2014 Colts Stats by Week

Wk	vs.	W-L	PF	PA	YDF	YDA	TO	Total	Off	Def	ST
1	at DEN	L	24	31	408	361	-2	2%	12%	9%	-1%
2	PHI	L	27	30	341	458	-1	-29%	-10%	22%	2%
3	at JAC	W	44	17	529	344	3	13%	29%	24%	8%
4	TEN	W	41	17	498	261	2	28%	20%	-6%	1%
5	BAL	W	20	13	432	287	-1	14%	-17%	-28%	3%
6	at HOU	W	33	28	456	332	0	11%	24%	21%	8%
7	CIN	W	27	0	506	135	-2	83%	19%	-55%	10%
8	at PIT	L	34	51	448	639	0	-30%	7%	41%	4%
9	at NYG	W	40	24	443	438	1	39%	16%	-12%	11%
10	BYE										
11	NE	L	20	42	322	503	1	-50%	-26%	30%	7%
12	JAC	W	23	3	389	194	-1	25%	-30%	-49%	6%
13	WAS	W	49	27	487	425	-2	30%	28%	-3%	-1%
14	at CLE	W	25	24	362	248	-2	0%	-16%	-24%	-8%
15	HOU	W	17	10	278	289	0	20%	-10%	-24%	6%
16	at DAL	L	7	42	229	377	-2	-100%	-70%	24%	-7%
17	at TEN	W	27	10	378	192	1	36%	-8%	-40%	4%
18	CIN	W	26	10	482	254	0	30%	12%	-18%	1%
19	at DEN	W	24	13	364	288	-1	69%	33%	-37%	-1%
20	at NE	L	7	45	209	397	-2	-53%	-32%	8%	-14%

Trends and Splits

	Offense	Rank	Defense	Rank
Total DVOA	-1.1%	17	-2.3%	13
Unadjusted VOA	-0.3%	15	-3.5%	10
Weighted Trend	-8.0%	22	-6.7%	11
Variance	7.1%	12	9.1%	29
Average Opponent	0.9%	20	-2.2%	26
Passing	15.3%	13	1.1%	10
Rushing	-16.0%	27	-6.5%	19
First Down	-0.7%	17	9.0%	25
Second Down	-15.0%	27	-2.8%	14
Third Down	20.5%	6	-23.5%	4
First Half	-7.3%	22	-7.2%	10
Second Half	6.0%	12	2.7%	21
Red Zone	-12.1%	19	1.8%	20
Late and Close	6.8%	11	-9.1%	8

Five-Year Performance

Year	W-L	Pyth W	Est W	PF	PA	TO	Total	Rk	Off	Rk	Def	Rk	ST	Rk	Off AGL	Rk	Def AGL	Rk	Off Age	Rk	Def Age	Rk	ST Age	Rk
2010	10-6	9.2	8.2	435	388	-4	1.3%	16	13.1%	6	5.5%	24	-6.3%	31	42.2	30	47.8	31	28.0	8	26.4	23	25.4	31
2011	2-14	3.2	3.0	243	430	-12	-32.8%	31	-17.2%	27	9.3%	26	-6.2%	31	37.5	22	47.2	28	27.9	8	26.0	27	25.4	30
2012	11-5	7.2	6.2	357	387	-12	-16.0%	25	-2.9%	18	14.0%	31	0.9%	12	44.4	24	43.1	24	25.9	28	26.6	20	25.2	31
2013	11-5	9.4	9.5	391	336	+13	3.2%	13	4.3%	13	0.9%	16	-0.1%	18	75.5	30	25.2	11	25.8	31	27.7	4	26.0	20
2014	11-5	10.2	8.8	458	369	-5	4.5%	13	-1.1%	17	-2.3%	13	3.3%	8	56.6	29	48.2	23	26.2	28	28.3	1	26.1	12

2014 Performance Based on Most Common Personnel Groups

IND Offense					IND Offense vs. Opponents					IND Defense					IND Defense vs. Opponents			
Pers	Freq	Yds	DVOA	Run%	Pers	Freq	Yds	DVOA	Run%	Pers	Freq	Yds	DVOA		Pers	Freq	Yds	DVOA
11	52%	6.6	10.2%	22%	Base	38%	5.6	-1.1%	47%	Base	45%	5.3	-6.6%		11	54%	6.0	3.2%
12	26%	5.8	-5.3%	34%	Nickel	42%	6.9	11.2%	24%	Nickel	49%	6.1	3.4%		12	23%	5.7	-3.4%
13	12%	5.2	-2.2%	57%	Dime+	18%	6.1	0.0%	17%	Dime+	2%	6.6	-9.0%		21	10%	4.9	-19.3%
612	3%	3.4	-53.7%	61%	Goal Line	1%	0.9	19.7%	53%	Goal Line	1%	-0.4	-14.6%		22	3%	2.2	-51.5%
10	2%	4.8	-18.0%	37%	Big	1%	0.9	-84.8%	78%	Big	2%	5.0	-2.1%		611	2%	5.9	-8.6%
															621	2%	7.1	11.8%

Strategic Tendencies

Run/Pass		Rk	Formation		Rk	Pass Rush		Rk	Secondary		Rk	Strategy		Rk
Runs, first half	30%	31	Form: Single Back	72%	19	Rush 3	5.9%	16	4 DB	35%	8	Play action	19%	22
Runs, first down	44%	27	Form: Empty Back	6%	13	Rush 4	48.4%	30	5 DB	61%	18	Avg Box (Off)	6.33	9
Runs, second-long	24%	27	Pers: 3+ WR	55%	21	Rush 5	33.6%	1	6+ DB	3%	21	Avg Box (Def)	6.35	10
Runs, power sit.	47%	27	Pers: 4+ WR	2%	10	Rush 6+	12.0%	6	CB by Sides	91%	6	Offensive Pace	27.94	4
Runs, behind 2H	15%	32	Pers: 2+ TE/6+ OL	45%	5	Sacks by LB	58.8%	9	DB Blitz	14%	5	Defensive Pace	28.14	2
Pass, ahead 2H	54%	2	Shotgun/Pistol	59%	18	Sacks by DB	11.3%	8	Hole in Zone	3%	31	Go for it on 4th	0.74	24

The Colts didn't just lead the league with 34 dropped passes; they also benefitted from 29 dropped passes by opponents, second only to New England. ☜ Another stat that was high for the Colts on both sides of the ball: broken tackles. Indianapolis was second behind Seattle with broken tackles registered on 9.5 percent of offensive plays. However, the Colts also ranked third on defense, with broken tackles on 8.7 percent of plays. ☜ The Colts had the No. 1 defense in the league in the first quarter, but ranked 23rd from the second quarter on. This is the kind of split that seems like it is telling us something, but probably isn't. After all, the same Colts team in 2013 had the worst defense in the league in the first quarter, and then ranked 11th from the second quarter on. Despite these radically different splits, the Colts defense ended both seasons with roughly similar DVOA. ☜ This one might be somewhat related: When the Colts were behind or tied, their offense ranked 28th in DVOA and the defense was 23rd. When the Colts had a lead, their offense ranked 11th in DVOA and the defense was 10th.

Passing

Player	DYAR	DVOA	Plays	NtYds	Avg	YAC	C%	TD	Int
A.Luck	879	9.2%	645	4573	7.1	5.8	62.1%	40	16
M.Hasselbeck	71	10.8%	46	286	6.2	6.1	68.2%	2	0

Rushing

Player	DYAR	DVOA	Plays	Yds	Avg	TD	Fum	Suc
T.Richardson*	-59	-17.7%	159	520	3.3	3	2	43%
A.Bradshaw	26	-1.8%	90	428	4.8	2	3	54%
D.Herron	17	-2.9%	78	351	4.5	1	1	53%
A.Luck	40	4.4%	47	275	5.9	3	3	-
Z.Tipton	-29	-71.3%	10	18	1.8	0	0	30%
F.Gore	154	6.3%	255	1106	4.3	4	2	50%

Receiving

Player	DYAR	DVOA	Plays	Ctch	Yds	Y/C	YAC	TD	C%
T.Y.Hilton	303	16.5%	131	82	1348	16.4	4.5	7	63%
R.Wayne*	-3	-13.0%	116	65	797	12.3	4.2	2	56%
H.Nicks*	0	-12.7%	68	38	405	10.7	3.4	4	56%
D.Moncrief	47	-0.2%	49	32	444	13.9	6.5	3	65%
A.Johnson	-86	-19.8%	147	85	939	11.0	4.6	3	58%
V.Brown	-15	-22.5%	21	12	118	9.8	3.9	0	69%
C.Fleener	112	10.1%	92	51	774	15.2	5.8	8	55%
D.Allen	104	22.7%	50	29	395	13.6	5.6	8	58%
J.Doyle	4	-4.6%	22	18	118	6.6	6.0	2	82%
A.Bradshaw	152	38.2%	47	38	300	7.9	8.8	6	81%
T.Richardson*	49	11.9%	34	27	229	8.5	8.9	0	79%
D.Herron	10	-7.1%	26	21	173	8.2	9.2	0	81%
Z.Tipton	44	76.8%	6	6	68	11.3	12.0	1	100%
F.Gore	-1	-14.4%	19	11	111	10.1	9.3	1	58%

Offensive Line

Player	Pos	Age	GS	Snaps	Pen	Sk	Pass	Run	Player	Pos	Age	GS	Snaps	Pen	Sk	Pass	Run
Anthony Castonzo	LT	27	16/16	1155	7	4.0	18.0	7.5	Lance Louis	LG	30	9/7	527	4	1.0	10.0	7.0
Jack Mewhort	LG	24	14/14	986	5	1.5	17.3	5.0	A.Q. Shipley*	C	29	15/5	423	1	0.0	3.8	2.0
Gosder Cherilus*	RT	31	13/13	950	5	5.5	29.3	6.0	Joe Reitz	G	30	10/4	270	1	1.0	4.0	0.0
Jonotthan Harrison	C	24	15/10	693	3	2.0	14.5	7.0	Khaled Holmes	C	25	5/2	171	1	0.5	2.0	1.0
Hugh Thornton	RG	24	10/8	565	4	2.0	12.5	5.0	Todd Herremans	G	33	8/8	577	4	0.5	12.0	1.5

Year	Yards	ALY	Rk	Power	Rk	Stuff	Rk	2nd Lev	Rk	Open Field	Rk	Sacks	ASR	Rk	Short	Long	F-Start	Cont.
2012	3.78	3.76	26	72%	2	25%	30	1.23	13	0.48	28	41	6.8%	17	8	17	10	22
2013	3.96	3.89	15	65%	15	18%	10	1.09	19	0.63	21	32	5.6%	6	12	9	8	29
2014	3.91	3.94	16	52%	31	19%	15	1.20	13	0.46	29	29	4.8%	7	5	9	20	19
2014 ALY by direction:		Left End 4.22 (11)			Left Tackle 3.55 (20)			Mid/Guard 4.15 (6)			Right Tackle 4.18 (9)				Right End 3.02 (25)			

Much of the blame for Andrew Luck's league-leading 352 knockdowns since 2012 will go to a flawed offensive line, but that's also part of his playing style. Though they have ignored the defense, the Colts have invested into the offensive line with premium draft picks that need to stay healthy. Left tackle Anthony Castonzo was the only lineman to start all 16 games last year, and the Colts started at least three different players at each of the other four line positions. Castonzo was just average again when it comes to blown blocks, but 2015 is a huge year for him. He'll make over $7 million after the team picked up his fifth-year option, but a strong performance could lead to a huge deal with the Colts or anyone hungry in 2016 for a 28-year-old left tackle with a first-round pedigree. Just look at how the Colts two years ago made a 29-year-old Gosder Cherilus the highest-paid right tackle in the NFL. Cherlius never played up to that contract, and he had the second-worst rate of blown blocks among right tackles in 2014. Indianapolis released him in late July with three years left on his contract.

In fact, Cherilus was one of three Colts linemen who ranked next to last in snaps per blown block last year. Right guard Hugh Thornton and undrafted rookie center Jonotthan Harrison only edged out Philadelphia backups to avoid the bottom at their positions. Thornton has been replaced by Philadelphia veteran Todd Herremans, signed in March to bolster the run blocking, though the former Eagle is going on 33 and had his share of pass-protection issues. Donald Thomas could return to start at left guard after a season-ending injury last year. Joe Reitz has played well in limited snaps the last two years and would make for a solid Cherilus replacement, but the Colts look content on using Jack Mewhort, last year's second-round pick, in that spot. Mewhort had a respectable rookie season at left guard. The Colts have no shortage of versatility and experience on this line, but few dependable starters. Khaled Holmes, a fourth-round pick in 2013, should have the edge for the starting center job after a solid performance through last year's playoff run.

Defensive Front Seven

Defensive Line	Age	Pos	Overall								vs. Run					Pass Rush			
			G	Snaps	Plays	TmPct	Rk	Stop	Dfts	BTkl	Runs	St%	Rk	RuYd	Rk	Sack	Hit	Hur	Dsrpt
Cory Redding*	35	DE	16	740	36	4.6%	45	31	7	6	28	86%	17	2.0	39	3.5	12	13.5	1
Ricky Jean-Francois*	29	DE	16	636	31	3.9%	64	27	13	2	21	86%	17	1.3	19	3.0	3	7.5	4
Josh Chapman	26	DT	16	378	21	2.7%	--	17	5	3	21	81%	--	1.2	--	0.0	0	0.0	0
Arthur Jones	29	DE	9	362	22	5.0%	40	16	5	3	18	72%	70	2.3	50	1.5	2	1.5	0
Zach Kerr	25	DT	12	286	17	2.9%	--	12	5	1	13	62%	--	3.2	--	3.0	0	0.0	1
Montori Hughes	25	DT	12	196	12	2.0%	--	9	3	0	11	73%	--	1.8	--	0.0	0	1.5	0
Kendall Langford	29	DT	16	482	25	3.0%	81	20	4	1	22	86%	16	1.1	11	1.0	2	2.0	0

Edge Rushers	Age	Pos	Overall								vs. Run					Pass Rush			
			G	Snaps	Plays	TmPct	Rk	Stop	Dfts	BTkl	Runs	St%	Rk	RuYd	Rk	Sack	Hit	Hur	Dsrpt
Bjoern Werner	25	OLB	15	747	50	6.8%	20	38	14	4	35	74%	42	2.6	47	4.0	4	11.8	2
Erik Walden	30	OLB	15	657	36	4.9%	49	27	10	2	23	74%	48	3.2	67	6.0	13	17.5	0
Jonathan Newsome	24	OLB	16	390	28	3.5%	--	24	12	4	20	80%	--	1.8	--	6.5	6	13.8	0
Trent Cole	33	OLB	15	800	52	6.4%	22	31	13	4	38	61%	78	3.1	66	6.5	5	22.0	0

Linebackers	Age	Pos	Overall								Pass Rush			vs. Run					vs. Pass						
			G	Snaps	Plays	TmPct	Rk	Stop	Dfts	BTkl	Sack	Hit	Hur	Runs	St%	Rk	RuYd	Rk	Tgts	Suc%	Rk	AdjYd	Rk	PD	Int
D'Qwell Jackson	32	ILB	16	988	138	17.5%	12	71	19	13	4.0	1	9.8	97	58%	66	3.5	49	36	36%	61	7.9	54	1	0
Jerrell Freeman	29	ILB	12	764	100	16.9%	13	56	16	8	1.5	3	5.5	54	65%	37	3.8	60	33	51%	32	5.8	23	6	0
Josh McNary	27	ILB	15	260	22	3.0%	--	8	1	4	0.5	2	2.5	10	40%	--	5.9	--	8	28%	--	20.1	--	0	0
Nate Irving	27	MLB	8	349	45	11.0%	55	22	10	5	1.0	1	3	34	59%	64	3.6	51	16	38%	57	11.6	63	0	0

Year	Yards	ALY	Rk	Power	Rk	Stuff	Rk	2nd Level	Rk	Open Field	Rk	Sacks	ASR	Rk	Short	Long
2012	5.10	4.32	27	64%	19	16%	30	1.15	10	1.49	32	32	5.8%	27	14	9
2013	4.25	4.30	28	53%	5	16%	26	1.18	24	0.58	14	42	7.6%	8	16	12
2014	4.20	4.05	22	67%	20	20%	15	1.23	23	0.68	15	41	7.3%	9	21	11
2014 ALY by direction:		Left End 4.05 (22)			Left Tackle 3.54 (14)			Mid/Guard 4.08 (20)			Right Tackle 4.47 (24)			Right End 4.16 (21)		

The new March tradition: Ryan Grigson travels to the Island of Misfit Toys to pick out which defenders will help allow 140 rushing yards to a random New England running back. Cory Redding and Ricky Jean-Francois have been returned to the Orphanarium, but Kendall Langford may be putting his durable history at risk—he has never missed any of the 112 games in his career—by taking over at defensive end in the Colts' 3-4 defense. Arthur Jones was supposed to do big things last year coming over from Baltimore, but the injury bug bit his season. Josh Chapman and Montori Hughes are two fifth-round picks who should battle for the nose job, but neither has shown much to this point. Third-round pick Henry Anderson from Stanford had some big fans in the draftnik community, and he could be a future starting five-technique end.

D'Qwell Jackson may or may not have kicked off Deflategate with his interception of Tom Brady in the AFC Championship Game. Jackson notched what was surprisingly the first Pro Bowl selection of his career, getting picked as an alternate in his thirties. (The same could be said for his teammate, safety Mike Adams). He faced more runs than any defender in the league, but did not fare well in stopping them. Jerrell Freeman is the team's best linebacker in coverage and the Colts brought Nate Irving over from Denver for depth.

The Colts rushed five defenders more often than any defense last year, but this roster might have too many edge rushers. Two years ago, the front seven was Robert Mathis or bust. At age 34 and coming off an entire missed season with a torn Achilles, expectations have to be very low for the franchise's all-time sack leader. If the Colts were moving in a youthful direction, Bjoern Werner and Jonathan Newsome would take over at outside linebacker, but they may not even beat out Trent Cole and Erik Walden in snaps played. Cole had a terrible year defending the run in Philadelphia, but he is a veteran pass-rusher. Werner has been a big disappointment as Grigson's lone premium draft pick on defense. His biggest play was a coverage sack of Ryan Fitzpatrick to force a game-clinching fumble in Houston. Two of his other sacks came against Baltimore's rookie backup tackle James Hurst in his first-ever road start. Newsome stunned everyone by leading the team in sacks as a fifth-round rookie with limited playing time. Sure, he picked up two sacks on Charlie Whitehurst when no one blocked him, but he also forced a strip-sack in the playoffs against the hardest quarterback to sack: Peyton Manning. Newsome deserves more playing time if only because he's an actual "horseshoe guy" around whome the team could build, but the competition is deep here.

Defensive Secondary

Secondary	Age	Pos	G	Snaps	Plays	Overall TmPct	Rk	Stop	Dfts	BTkl	vs. Run Runs	St%	Rk	RuYd	Rk	vs. Pass Tgts	Tgt%	Rk	Dist	Suc%	Rk	AdjYd	Rk	PD	Int
Mike Adams	34	SS	16	1014	98	12.4%	16	28	16	14	50	22%	66	9.0	58	30	8.0%	33	11.1	69%	4	5.2	8	9	5
Greg Toler	30	CB	15	965	68	9.2%	29	28	16	15	17	35%	42	11.1	72	94	26.4%	60	14.9	51%	34	8.4	47	11	2
Vontae Davis	27	CB	15	824	60	8.1%	42	32	13	4	10	70%	6	5.5	28	70	22.9%	33	15.5	61%	4	6.8	16	18	4
Darius Butler	29	CB	14	614	52	7.5%	--	20	11	11	9	44%	--	8.6	--	41	18.1%	--	10.8	56%	--	9.0	--	7	0
Sergio Brown*	27	FS	15	530	38	5.1%	69	16	9	6	14	43%	33	7.4	47	21	10.5%	52	12.1	66%	6	2.7	1	5	0
LaRon Landry*	31	SS	11	407	45	8.3%	--	13	6	3	21	38%	--	6.4	--	13	8.3%	--	13.3	41%	--	9.6	--	0	0
Josh Gordy*	28	CB	16	277	28	3.5%	--	8	2	2	9	33%	--	6.0	--	32	31.3%	--	12.8	50%	--	8.6	--	5	1
Dwight Lowery	29	FS	16	1029	83	10.1%	38	23	6	6	26	31%	53	10.0	62	48	12.8%	64	11.1	59%	24	7.1	31	4	2

Year	Pass D Rank	vs. #1 WR	Rk	vs. #2 WR	Rk	vs. Other WR	Rk	vs. TE	Rk	vs. RB	Rk
2012	27	11.0%	22	3.0%	17	28.5%	31	22.2%	30	-22.3%	6
2013	13	-6.5%	14	7.6%	19	13.4%	26	17.7%	26	-0.9%	15
2014	10	-11.8%	9	-7.4%	11	-2.6%	14	16.1%	26	29.0%	31

Ryan Grigson's best move on defense remains trading a second-round pick for Vontae Davis in 2012, a move many observers (including some on the Football Outsiders staff) criticized at the time. Davis and Denver's Chris Harris are the only cornerbacks to rank in the top 10 in adjusted success rate in each of the last two seasons. Consistency is hard to find at this position, but Davis was at his best last season, including a very strong playoff run. Cornerback is the strength of this defense and the Colts return the same top three players from last year. Greg Toler is a quality cover corner, but his tackling left a lot to be desired in 2014. Darius Butler did not coax any of the bad AFC South quarterbacks into a pick-six last year, but he's a solid nickel corner and has fully removed the bust label once given to him as a failed second-round pick in New England. There's a real dearth of experience after the top three, but the Colts did finally draft a cornerback of their own in the third round. D'Joun Smith (Florida Atlantic) wasted no time in telling the Colts website, "I'm probably going to be the best cornerback to play the game." Pagano liked the confidence, saying "you don't want a meek kind of milquetoast type of guy sitting there." The Colts would settle for a guy who doesn't get toasted on double moves and speed routes, which was a concern that many scouts had about Smith.

Safety Mike Adams joined the team in June and surprised everyone with a Pro Bowl (alternate) season at age 33. He struggled with the run, but defended the pass well, which means he's a perfect fit on this defense. LaRon Landry is free to team up with the Steiner Brothers on wrestling circuits after the Colts released him in February. If he does sign anywhere, he will be suspended for the first 10 games of the 2015 season, for reasons evident once you see a picture of him. The Colts are trying to fill that hole with another veteran in Dwight Lowery, who spent last year in Atlanta. Lowery rarely makes it through a 16-game season healthy, so he too is a perfect fit for the Colts. Safety options are limited, as Colt Anderson is primarily a special-teams player and free-agent signing Winston Guy has just five not particularly promising career starts with Jacksonville. Fourth-round pick Clayton Geathers (Central Florida) is a box safety who can learn to eventually replace Adams, but not this season.

Special Teams

Year	DVOA	Rank	FG/XP	Rank	Net Kick	Rank	Kick Ret	Rank	Net Punt	Rank	Punt Ret	Rank	Hidden	Rank
2012	0.9%	12	-3.1	22	4.4	9	0.1	15	-2.4	19	5.3	6	1.4	14
2013	-0.1%	18	2.9	12	4.4	9	-3.3	21	-3.9	26	-0.6	16	6.2	7
2014	3.3%	8	8.4	4	4.9	9	0.4	14	11.2	6	-8.5	31	2.4	12

Here's one thing about the current Colts that's very different from the Peyton Manning era, as 2014 proved it's legal in the state of Indiana to have good special teams. The Colts ranked in the top 10 in special-teams DVOA for the first time since 1996, Adam Vinatieri's rookie year. At age 42, Vinatieri became the first player in NFL history to be named first-team All-Pro in his forties. He converted his first 29 field goals before missing one kick in Week 17. Vinatieri only received four more All-Pro votes than New England's Stephen Gostkowski, perhaps because punter Pat McAfee is the excellent kickoff specialist (seventh in gross value and second in touchback rate) for the Colts. McAfee was also first-team All-Pro for his punting and is the only player who can say 100 percent of his passes were dropped last year, thanks to an ill-advised fake punt in Dallas. However, some Indianapolis gambles paid off, as the Colts recovered all three of McAfee's onside kick attempts. The rest of the NFL was just six-of-56 (10.7 percent) in 2014. Before you get too excited, remember that the first seven onside kick attempts of McAfee's career all failed. Pagano's willingness to try a surprise onside is the bigger takeaway here.

Yes, the Colts have ranked exactly ninth in net kickoff value for three straight seasons, but it was the punt coverage that really improved last season, led by Colt Anderson's nine tackles on punts. The return jobs are completely open to competition in training camp. Josh Cribbs provided some vintage flashes on kick returns, but he was released in May. Griff Whalen struggled on punts and kickoffs. The returner job may be crucial in Whalen keeping a roster spot over Vincent Brown and Duron Carter, son of Cris. First-round rookie Phillip Dorsett also could win the job as another way to get him playing time, but he underwhelmed as a returner at Miami, averaging just 19.5 yards per kick return and 4.9 yards per punt return.

Jacksonville Jaguars

The Jaguars are the NFL franchise that we associate most often with the word "analytics." Senior vice president Tony Khan is among the most vocal proponents of analytics and scientific process, and has put his money where his mouth is while buying up valuable properties in the space such as TruMedia. Analytics have become a bit of a marketing ploy over the past few years, as teams like the Philadelphia 76ers have begun to use the word to explain poor results with a smile. The Jaguars would like you to believe that they have the same sort of dichotomy: that, like every general manager who steps to the podium at the combine will tell you, The Process is working.

And the analytics department does create some great work. Jacksonville has unearthed some gems in the later rounds of the draft over the past few years, finding cheap players with above-average ceilings such as linebacker Telvin Smith and cornerbacks Aaron Colvin and Demetrius McCray. They've also struck gold in the lower rungs of free agency, most notably with defensive tackle Sen'Derrick Marks, who has blossomed into one of the best interior rushers in the league since arriving in Duval County.

But the analytics department, at this point, is supplemental to the big boys: general manager David Caldwell and head coach Gus Bradley. And to state things in a fairly reductionist fashion, the Jaguars have become the very embodiment of the scouts versus stats dynamic that ruled the sports landscape a decade ago. Every big decision that this team has made has been made by Caldwell and Bradley. The Jaguars have had three top-three picks over the past three years. All three players, to this point, have been disappointments. Not one of the

players was highly regarded by analytics, at least outside the Jacksonville organization.

Let's start with quarterback Blake Bortles, because he is the focal point of Jacksonville's plan for building a playoff team. Bortles had an impressive preseason as a rookie, and created a lot of big plays early in the season with his pocket movement. Then he got beat down behind a bad offensive line, and the Jaguars suffered by sticking with him through his struggles. Bortles finished with one of the worst DYAR scores in the DVOA era, narrowly avoiding joining the hallowed -1,000-DYAR club (Table 1).

The Jaguars have all but admitted that this selection was the work of Caldwell and Bradley, who hunkered down together in unison. Depending on how much you want to sell it, the Jaguars either ignored their scouts or didn't unify them with the vision. Pre-draft analytics would have told you—as would any pre-draft scouting report that didn't rely on pro days or pure physical traits—that Lousiville's Teddy Bridgewater was the best quarterback in the draft. Our quarterback projections (both the LCF system used last year and the new QBASE introduced in 2015) had much the same output, though these systems didn't necessarily classify Bortles as a likely bust.

Bortles has spent his offseason being basically rebuilt from the ground up. Bortles worked with mechanics expert Tom House, most famous for being a pitching coach, and we've seen a number of admissions from both Bortles and the Jaguars that he was not prepared for the NFL. From reads and outputs, to Bortles' weight, pretty much anything that could be under scrutiny was.

For Bortles to bounce back and become a good quarterback would not be unprecedented, though most of the examples of such second-year rebounds come from the halcyon days where quarterbacks were not tested so quickly as rookies, and instead spent their time handing off to running backs in two-back sets. The recent examples of breakouts after bad rookie seasons pretty much amount to Matthew Stafford and Eli Manning. Stafford missed most of his second season before performing like a borderline top-10 quarterback in 2011. Manning rose into the top 20 in passing DVOA in his second season, then took another step into the top 10 in 2008. Since 2000, only four rookie quarterbacks have started seven or more games with a negative DYAR and eventually improved enough to have a season worth 500 DYAR: Manning, Staf-

Table 1. Worst Passing DYAR, 1989-2014

Player	Team	Year	DYAR	DVOA	Plays	NY/P	TD	INT
David Carr	HOU	2002	-1130	-47.4%	529	3.98	9	15
Blaine Gabbert	JAC	2011	-1010	-46.5%	457	4.13	12	11
Bobby Hoying	PHI	1998	-962	-68.2%	265	2.88	0	9
Blake Bortles	**JAC**	**2014**	**-955**	**-40.7%**	**530**	**4.82**	**11**	**16**
Alex Smith	SF	2005	-866	-88.6%	194	3.59	1	11
Kelly Stouffer	SEA	1992	-837	-72.7%	218	3.11	3	9
JaMarcus Russell	OAK	2009	-834	-62.0%	278	3.89	3	10
Jimmy Clausen	CAR	2010	-760	-48.0%	336	3.85	3	9
Akili Smith	CIN	2000	-700	-51.4%	303	3.29	3	6
Trent Dilfer	SF	2007	-681	-55.4%	244	4.03	7	11

2015 Jaguars Schedule

Week	Opp.	Week	Opp.	Week	Opp.
1	CAR	7	BUF (U.K.)	13	at TEN
2	MIA	8	BYE	14	IND
3	at NE	9	at NYJ	15	ATL
4	at IND	10	at BAL	16	at NO
5	at TB	11	TEN (Thu.)	17	at HOU
6	HOU	12	SD		

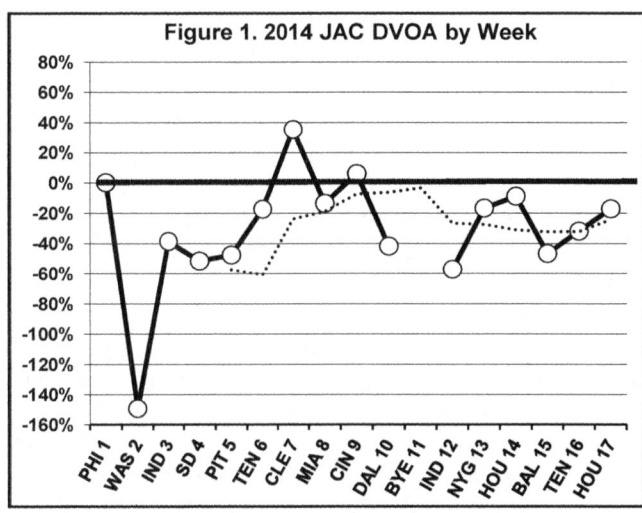

Figure 1. 2014 JAC DVOA by Week

ford, Kyle Orton, and Josh Freeman. Orton and Freeman, combined, only hit the plateau three times.

No matter what you think about the rest of Jacksonville's squad, it's almost impossible to figure out where the franchise goes from here without a real verdict on Bortles that we won't have until we're at least halfway through the 2015 season. Unless you want to go back 25 years, there is very little track record of quarterbacks who start their careers with two straight below-replacement seasons but then turn things around and become legit NFL starters (Table 2). This is a huge year for the bet that the Jaguars made on Bortles. Early indications that he still wasn't comfortable with his throwing motion in training camp are, to put it mildly, concerning.

Table 2. Quarterbacks Below Replacement in First Two Seasons, 1989-2014

Player	Team	Rookie Year	DYAR Year 1	DYAR Year 2	Career High Year	Career High DYAR
T.Aikman	DAL	1989	-299	-251	1995	1358
J.George	IND	1990	-211	-590	1995	1127
D.Klingler	CIN	1992	-174	-118	1995	4
R.Mirer	SEA	1993	-160	-34	2000	20
H.Shuler	WAS	1994	-134	-146	1994	-134
D.Wuerffel	NO	1997	-239	-260	2002	-40
R.Leaf	SD	1998	-661	-539	2001	-188
T.Couch	CLE	1999	-478	-54	2002	98
A.Smith	CIN	1999	-385	-700	2001	13
Q.Carter	DAL	2001	-10	-17	2003	146
M.McMahon	DET	2001	-74	-204	2004	0
J.Harrington	DET	2002	-279	-250	2007	41
K.Boller	BAL	2003	-220	-108	2006	118
L.McCown	CLE	2004	-254	-58	2010	44
C.Frye	CLE	2005	-119	-230	2008	-65
A.Smith	SF	2005	-866	-147	2014	493
J.Beck	MIA	2007	-327	-143	2011	-143
S.Bradford	STL	2010	-186	-325	2012	388
J.Skelton	ARI	2010	-349	-325	2012	-324
B.Gabbert	JAC	2011	-1010	-268	2014	22
B.Weeden	CLE	2012	-291	-443	2014	21
E.Manuel	BUF	2013	-190	-53	2014	-53
G.Smith	NYJ	2013	-371	-33	2014	-33

Minimum 100 passes each season.

The Jaguars also went against analytics when they tabbed Florida's Dante Fowler with the No. 3 overall pick in this year's draft. Our SackSEER projections see Fowler as a far less impressive prospect than Vic Beasley or Bud Dupree (Table 3). Nathan Forster wrote in explaining the projection that "Fowler recorded only 14.5 sacks during his entire three-year career; that's only 2.5 more than Vic Beasley recorded in his senior year alone. Fowler had a nice 4.60-second 40-yard dash, but he performed poorly on the vertical jump, the broad jump, and the three-cone, which are equally important, but often overlooked."

Table 3. First-Round Edge Rushers by SackSEER, 2015

Player	Team	Pick	Projected Sacks Years 1-5	SackSEER Rating
Vic Beasley	ATL	8	34.0	95.7%
Bud Dupree	PIT	22	29.2	94.6%
Dante Fowler	JAC	3	21.7	43.3%
Shane Ray	DEN	23	20.4	18.5%

That's not to say that all of the analytics agree on Fowler. Companies that have done charting of college games, such as Pro Football Focus and STATS Inc., provided data showing that Fowler had plenty of hurries in college, and was great at creating them on third down. There's still plenty of debate about the actual value of those hurries versus actual sacks though, and Fowler's main selling points are his versatility, his ability to stop the run, and his base size-speed measurables. While reasonable minds can disagree on the value of pass pressure versus run defense and overall versatility, the NFL is a passing league and pure analytics simply do not point to Fowler as the best pass-rusher in this draft.

Unfortunately for the Jaguars, Fowler tore his ACL on his first day of rookie minicamp and will miss his entire rookie season. That's going to cloud any actual debate over his talents as we move forward, as draft position is a snapshot in time rather than something that evolves over time.

Finally, there's the case of Luke Joeckel. Joeckel was regarded as probably the best player in the 2013 draft by scouts, and thus it is hard to get much lather up about his selection. We noted earlier that none of these three first-round picks have been highly regarded by analytics, but analytics didn't necessarily disagree with the Joeckel pick either. He was the safe choice when compared to Eric Fisher's Senior Bowl-aided stock boost. The problem for the Jaguars is that they picked a bad time to get the No. 2 overall pick, as the entire top of the 2013 draft class has busted out. Two years later, the only members of the top 10 who have clearly developed into quality starters are Detroit defensive end Ezekiel Ansah and Philadelphia offensive tackle Lane Johnson.

Joeckel, too, suffered from an injury that left the Jaguars without a foundation piece for most of the 2013 season. But when he has played, he's been ineffective as both a pass blocker and a run blocker. Entering his third season, we've yet to see any indication that he's going to be the type of core player the Jaguars thought they were getting when they selected him.

And that is the big problem facing this team at the moment, because they are starting to come out of the doldrums of the Gene Smith era. The overall talent level on the team, thanks to the aforementioned drafts and free-agency splashes, is higher than it's been in any time in recent memory. But winning football games is about having top-tier talent and then supplementing it with other good players. Jacksonville has found the other good players, but thus far has struck out on just about every attempt to find the top-tier talent.

To be fair, the Jaguars did finally find a top-of-the-line player to take their money when they reeled in tight end Julius Thomas to a five-year, $46 million deal with $24 million in guarantees. Thomas has flaws: he's a below-average run blocker who isn't a total burner, but he's shown the ability to make contested catches and should be a nice safety valve for a quarterback who really needed one last season. Before anyone frets about the cost of reeling in Thomas, they should remember that the Jaguars have perpetually hung out near the cap floor over the past few seasons, and there are so many players on releasable contracts that Jacksonville has plenty of flexibility when they need it.

But Caldwell and Bradley didn't find any other home runs in this free-agent class. They tried to reel in running back DeMarco Murray but lost out despite, according to Caldwell, having a competitive offer on the table. If you read that sentence with us, and you thought to yourself "a team with a deep foundation in analytics was trying to reel in a running back that is the latest poster boy for The Curse of 370?"—well, that pretty much sums up the current dichotomy in Jacksonville.

The Jaguars have tried their best to make hay out of what they can, reeling in enough players to create a sustainable power run game around second-round rookie running back T.J. Yeldon. There are plenty of second-year targets on hand who could take a leap up if the Bortleback becomes a quarterback. But to the extent that a playoff run is possible, the contention hopes of this year's Jacksonville squad are relying heavily on big boosts from highly-drafted players who simply haven't performed that well yet.

Downtown Jacksonville is still in the middle of being built. Drive around the area where EverBank Field sits, and you'll find your share of developed commercial space as well as empty grass lots. It's an easy metaphor for the Jaguars themselves, but it's a metaphor that feels just a bit off. If the city of Jacksonville were to be built like the Jaguars, we would instead need a half-built city hall surrounded by beautiful parks, well-designed infrastructure, and quirky stores.

Bradley and Caldwell are not to be cursed for going against what pure numbers would tell them to do. NFL teams need to try underdog tactics when they are in situations as stark as what those two inherited, and that may involve going against ideal team-building best practices. It's better to have a good running game than to have nothing to prop up Bortles at all. It's also not entirely their fault that two of their top three picks immediately suffered season-ending injuries in their rookie seasons, and that they thus have been unable to provide a core for the analytics to supplement.

But, supplementation or not, the Jaguars had better take a step forward this season. It doesn't take analytics to tell you that another 4-12 finish, one that would take Bradley's career record to 11-37, would start to create serious doubt both inside and outside the organization that the Jaguars are actually on the right path.

Rivers McCown

2014 Jaguars Stats by Week

Wk	vs.	W-L	PF	PA	YDF	YDA	TO	Total	Off	Def	ST
1	at PHI	L	17	34	306	420	2	0%	-8%	-26%	-18%
2	at WAS	L	10	41	148	449	-1	-149%	-104%	40%	-5%
3	IND	L	17	44	344	529	-3	-39%	-8%	34%	4%
4	at SD	L	14	33	320	407	-3	-52%	-25%	31%	4%
5	PIT	L	9	17	243	372	-1	-48%	-54%	-8%	-2%
6	at TEN	L	14	16	379	290	-2	-17%	-6%	-1%	-13%
7	CLE	W	24	6	336	266	0	35%	-19%	-50%	4%
8	MIA	L	13	27	377	326	-2	-14%	-17%	-8%	-5%
9	at CIN	L	23	33	365	423	1	6%	28%	11%	-11%
10	vs. DAL	L	17	31	333	399	-2	-42%	-33%	7%	-2%
11	BYE										
12	at IND	L	3	23	194	389	1	-57%	-69%	-18%	-7%
13	NYG	W	25	24	258	329	3	-17%	-27%	-8%	2%
14	HOU	L	13	27	262	304	-1	-9%	-14%	-2%	3%
15	at BAL	L	12	20	248	314	0	-47%	-26%	6%	-15%
16	TEN	W	21	13	288	357	0	-32%	-13%	21%	2%
17	at HOU	L	17	23	233	358	2	-17%	-23%	-7%	-1%

Trends and Splits

	Offense	Rank	Defense	Rank
Total DVOA	-24.3%	31	1.5%	20
Unadjusted VOA	-22.4%	31	0.1%	17
Weighted Trend	-22.4%	29	-3.6%	16
Variance	8.7%	20	5.4%	13
Average Opponent	1.7%	26	-0.3%	17
Passing	-32.1%	32	8.0%	17
Rushing	-8.2%	20	-5.5%	20
First Down	-22.9%	29	2.4%	20
Second Down	-18.0%	29	3.8%	20
Third Down	-36.8%	31	-3.3%	14
First Half	-21.6%	31	1.3%	20
Second Half	-27.1%	32	1.8%	18
Red Zone	-45.2%	32	-19.2%	5
Late and Close	-48.0%	32	-1.8%	18

Five-Year Performance

Year	W-L	Pyth W	Est W	PF	PA	TO	Total	Rk	Off	Rk	Def	Rk	ST	Rk	Off AGL	Rk	Def AGL	Rk	Off Age	Rk	Def Age	Rk	ST Age	Rk
2010	8-8	6.3	6.5	353	419	-15	-9.0%	22	3.9%	14	17.7%	32	4.8%	7	19.7	10	17.8	11	27.2	20	25.8	29	26.0	22
2011	5-11	5.3	5.5	243	329	+5	-17.4%	27	-26.5%	31	-11.3%	5	-2.2%	26	23.5	12	52.8	29	26.2	28	26.9	18	26.5	8
2012	2-14	3.3	2.7	255	444	-3	-33.0%	31	-18.4%	28	11.7%	28	-3.0%	25	63.7	30	36.2	22	26.5	20	27.0	14	25.8	23
2013	4-12	3.1	3.2	247	449	-6	-38.2%	32	-29.8%	32	10.9%	28	2.5%	9	47.3	24	26.8	14	26.6	20	26.2	23	24.7	32
2014	3-13	3.6	3.3	249	412	-6	-29.5%	32	-24.3%	31	1.5%	20	-3.6%	26	33.5	19	44.3	22	24.7	32	26.1	27	25.5	30

2014 Performance Based on Most Common Personnel Groups

JAC Offense					JAC Offense vs. Opponents					JAC Defense					JAC Defense vs. Opponents			
Pers	Freq	Yds	DVOA	Run%	Pers	Freq	Yds	DVOA	Run%	Pers	Freq	Yds	DVOA		Pers	Freq	Yds	DVOA
11	60%	5.1	-21.7%	24%	Base	36%	4.4	-23.2%	51%	Base	38%	5.3	0.6%		11	59%	6.2	2.1%
21	14%	3.8	-35.1%	55%	Nickel	50%	5.0	-27.7%	27%	Nickel	59%	5.9	-0.7%		12	19%	5.2	-2.9%
12	13%	4.9	-11.5%	41%	Dime+	13%	4.9	-7.5%	11%	Dime+	1%	7.3	115.2%		21	8%	4.8	-8.1%
22	4%	3.8	-10.0%	78%	Goal Line	1%	1.5	80.2%	67%	Goal Line	2%	1.3	37.8%		13	4%	5.8	8.1%
20	4%	4.1	-46.9%	26%											22	3%	3.7	-24.1%

Strategic Tendencies

Run/Pass		Rk	Formation		Rk	Pass Rush		Rk	Secondary		Rk	Strategy		Rk
Runs, first half	38%	14	Form: Single Back	72%	21	Rush 3	4.2%	24	4 DB	28%	13	Play action	23%	9
Runs, first down	39%	31	Form: Empty Back	3%	27	Rush 4	80.2%	1	5 DB	70%	7	Avg Box (Off)	6.35	7
Runs, second-long	31%	15	Pers: 3+ WR	66%	9	Rush 5	13.0%	32	6+ DB	1%	26	Avg Box (Def)	6.24	20
Runs, power sit.	69%	3	Pers: 4+ WR	2%	15	Rush 6+	2.6%	32	CB by Sides	91%	5	Offensive Pace	29.41	10
Runs, behind 2H	25%	18	Pers: 2+ TE/6+ OL	19%	31	Sacks by LB	13.3%	27	DB Blitz	5%	31	Defensive Pace	30.34	18
Pass, ahead 2H	53%	4	Shotgun/Pistol	70%	7	Sacks by DB	4.4%	21	Hole in Zone	5%	21	Go for it on 4th	0.92	17

Signing Julius Thomas has even more benefit for the Jaguars if it means they stop running plays with no tight end on the field. It's an area where they have been just abysmal the last couple years: 3.9 yards per play and -49.7% DVOA last year, 4.5 yards per play and -40.1% DVOA the year before. ☺ A league-low 15 percent of Jaguars passes were listed as being in the middle of the field.

This was not an issue with the official scorer in Jacksonville, as an above-average number of passes by Jacksonville opponents (25 percent) were listed as being in the middle. ☞ With Jedd Fisch gone, the Jaguars also should stop running so many go-nowhere screen passes. The Jaguars ranked third in WR/TE screens, but gained just 4.1 yards per play with -19.3% DVOA on these plays. ☞ Maybe it comes from practicing against them so much, but the Jacksonville defense was phenomenal against screens. The Jaguars allowed just 3.2 yards per pass and -34.4% DVOA on wide receiver screens, and 5.3 yards per pass and -39.7% DVOA on running back screens. ☞ Jacksonville opponents threw a league-low 14 percent of passes to the players we identified as No. 2 receivers, but 22.8 percent of passes to running backs (second in the NFL). ☞ The Jaguars ranked eighth in DVOA against passes on the offensive left side, were average against passes listed in the middle of the field, and had the worst defense in the league against passes on the offensive right side. ☞ Jacksonville led the league with 121 broken tackles on defense, although one bright spot was that only three were quarterbacks escaping sacks. ☞ Jacksonville was 27th in the NFL with 109 penalties, but dead last with just 573 penalty yards because 36 of those penalties were declined or offset.

Passing

Player	DYAR	DVOA	Plays	NtYds	Avg	YAC	C%	TD	Int
B.Bortles	-955	-40.7%	530	2554	4.8	5.8	59.1%	11	16
C.Henne	-249	-54.3%	94	393	4.2	5.1	53.8%	3	1

Rushing

Player	DYAR	DVOA	Plays	Yds	Avg	TD	Fum	Suc
D.Robinson	3	-8.1%	135	583	4.3	4	2	38%
T.Gerhart	-35	-16.1%	101	326	3.2	2	1	43%
B.Bortles	100	24.7%	52	422	8.1	0	2	-
J.Todman*	15	3.8%	32	186	5.8	1	0	25%
S.Johnson	-18	-22.1%	29	86	3.0	2	0	34%
B.Pierce	-24	-14.8%	93	366	3.9	2	1	42%

Receiving

Player	DYAR	DVOA	Plays	Ctch	Yds	Y/C	YAC	TD	C%
C.Shorts*	-183	-33.7%	110	53	557	10.5	4.9	1	48%
A.Hurns	-13	-14.4%	97	51	677	13.3	4.2	6	53%
A.Robinson	10	-11.1%	81	48	548	11.4	3.3	2	59%
M.Lee	-41	-20.3%	68	37	422	11.4	4.8	1	54%
M.Brown*	-43	-50.4%	15	7	88	12.6	2.4	0	47%
A.Sanders*	-2	-16.8%	7	6	55	9.2	4.0	0	86%
B.Walters	-12	-27.2%	11	6	57	9.5	6.5	0	55%
C.Harbor	5	-4.8%	35	26	289	11.1	6.9	1	74%
M.Lewis	-5	-9.8%	31	18	206	11.4	7.8	2	58%
J.Thomas	140	24.7%	62	43	489	11.4	3.8	12	69%
J.Todman*	-35	-34.9%	37	25	198	7.9	7.9	1	68%
D.Robinson	-43	-39.2%	31	23	124	5.4	8.7	0	74%
T.Gerhart	53	27.5%	24	20	186	9.3	11.5	0	83%
W.Ta'ufo'ou*	38	70.2%	8	7	81	11.6	9.9	0	88%
B.Pierce	-20	-80.0%	6	2	13	6.5	5.0	0	33%

Offensive Line

Player	Pos	Age	GS	Snaps	Pen	Sk	Pass	Run	Player	Pos	Age	GS	Snaps	Pen	Sk	Pass	Run
Zane Beadles	LG	29	16/16	1037	3	2.5	7.0	5.0	Sam Young	RT	28	9/6	396	3	2.5	6.8	7.0
Luke Joeckel	LT	24	16/16	982	5	8.5	21.3	4.0	Jacques McClendon*	G	28	13/3	207	2	0.5	3.0	4.0
Luke Bowanko	C	24	16/14	922	5	3.0	10.3	2.5	Stefen Wisniewski	C	26	16/16	1010	7	1.0	7.0	5.5
Brandon Linder	RG	23	15/15	901	2	4.5	6.5	1.0	Jermey Parnell	OT	29	16/5	379	1	0.0	3.0	3.0
Austin Pasztor	RT	25	8/8	492	2	4.5	10.0	3.5									

Year	Yards	ALY	Rk	Power	Rk	Stuff	Rk	2nd Lev	Rk	Open Field	Rk	Sacks	ASR	Rk	Short	Long	F-Start	Cont.
2012	3.89	4.05	17	61%	20	19%	15	1.01	28	0.58	23	50	7.8%	22	17	13	16	25
2013	3.43	3.13	31	58%	24	25%	30	0.93	30	0.59	24	50	7.9%	24	23	9	16	30
2014	3.98	3.52	30	58%	26	21%	22	0.96	27	0.81	10	71	11.3%	32	32	19	8	29
2014 ALY by direction:		Left End 3.81 (17)			Left Tackle 3.4 (25)			Mid/Guard 3.52 (28)			Right Tackle 3.67 (22)			Right End 3.17 (24)				

Nature abhors a vacuum. So the giant sucking wound that was last season's Jaguars offensive line has vacuumed up a lot of potential replacements for the problems that occurred in 2014. The big money went to former Cowboys right tackle Jermey Parnell, who signed a five-year, $32 million contract with $13 million in guarantees. That he was able to parlay roughly 400 snaps of good football on a good line into this money speaks volumes about a) how desperate the Jaguars were and b) how light on tackles this year's free-agent market was. At least this pushes overmatched tackles Austin Pastzor and Sam Young into the backup roles they deserved.

After picking up guard A.J. Cann (South Carolina) in the third round of the draft and center Stefen Wisniewski (ex-Oakland) on the damaged goods flea market, the Jaguars should be able to cobble together a better interior combination than they had last season. Cann is regarded as able to step in immediately according to no less of a line expert than NFL.com's Lance Zierlein, though his pass protection needs work. 2013 sixth-rounder Luke Bowanko was thrust into a starting gig quickly after The Jacques McClendon Experiment ended, and was only slightly less worthless in pass protection than McClendon. Miami (Florida) third-rounder Brandon Linder quietly had a solid rookie season in the midst of all the upheaval around him, and as a returning right guard should offer stability while the Jags sort out who should start. 2014 free-agent pickup Zane Beadles did not distinguish himself well, and if the unit looks better in the preseason, he might not make the final roster.

At left tackle, the Jaguars are still trying to be patient rather than proactive, and former No. 2 overall pick Luke Joeckel will again be given plenty of opportunity to fix what ails him. Jaguars supporters are right that it's too soon to call Joeckel a bust. Jaguars critics are also right that he has played like a bust so far. Injuries have been a factor—Joeckel was effectively re-playing his rookie year after fracturing his ankle in Week 4 of the 2013 season—but the Jaguars are still waiting to see a return worth the initial investment. Joeckel returning to the sure-fire All-Pro left tackle he seemed to be in college would be a huge win for a team that could desperately use one.

Defensive Front Seven

Defensive Line	Age	Pos	G	Snaps	Plays	TmPct	Rk	Stop	Dfts	BTkl	Runs	St%	Rk	RuYd	Rk	Sack	Hit	Hur	Dsrpt
						Overall						vs. Run				Pass Rush			
Sen'Derrick Marks	28	DT	16	719	46	5.3%	35	36	23	1	25	80%	32	0.9	6	8.5	9	10.5	3
Roy Miller	28	DT	14	482	32	4.2%	52	30	7	1	30	93%	3	1.6	23	1.0	1	3.5	1
Ziggy Hood	28	DT	16	416	24	2.8%	--	14	2	2	21	57%	--	3.6	--	1.0	2	4.0	0
Abry Jones	24	DT	16	374	39	4.5%	--	26	5	3	33	67%	--	2.6	--	3.0	1	5.0	1
Jared Odrick	28	DT	16	807	34	4.2%	55	26	8	3	25	76%	59	2.1	42	1.0	8	6.5	5

Edge Rushers	Age	Pos	G	Snaps	Plays	TmPct	Rk	Stop	Dfts	BTkl	Runs	St%	Rk	RuYd	Rk	Sack	Hit	Hur	Dsrpt
						Overall						vs. Run				Pass Rush			
Chris Clemons	34	DE	16	789	39	4.5%	55	31	14	4	24	67%	69	4.5	84	8.0	5	17.0	2
Red Bryant*	31	DE	16	519	23	2.7%	85	18	6	3	21	76%	38	1.9	23	1.0	0	2.0	0
Tyson Alualu	28	DE	16	463	30	3.5%	71	24	7	2	28	79%	30	2.6	48	2.0	3	7.0	0
Andre Branch	26	DE	9	329	21	4.3%	58	14	6	2	14	50%	84	4.2	80	3.0	3	6.5	3
Ryan Davis	26	DE	16	305	16	1.8%	--	16	9	1	7	100%	--	2.9	--	6.5	6	11.5	2
Dan Skuta	29	OLB	14	386	28	4.1%	61	18	10	4	15	67%	69	2.9	59	5.0	2	4.0	1

Linebackers	Age	Pos	G	Snaps	Plays	TmPct	Rk	Stop	Dfts	BTkl	Sack	Hit	Hur	Runs	St%	Rk	RuYd	Rk	Tgts	Suc%	Rk	AdjYd	Rk	PD	Int
						Overall					Pass Rush			vs. Run					vs. Pass						
J.T. Thomas*	27	OLB	16	714	85	9.8%	63	51	16	10	0.0	0	0	44	75%	12	3.2	33	36	57%	16	5.8	24	6	2
Telvin Smith	24	OLB	16	705	102	11.8%	45	61	23	11	2.0	0	3	55	62%	49	3.3	39	28	54%	24	5.9	25	4	1
Geno Hayes*	28	OLB	16	572	51	5.9%	82	34	15	2	2.0	0	3	33	82%	2	1.4	1	20	53%	27	8.2	58	0	0
Paul Posluszny	31	MLB	7	485	70	18.5%	5	36	10	3	2.0	1	3.5	41	61%	55	3.1	31	15	35%	--	6.9	--	1	0

Year	Yards	ALY	Rk	Power	Rk	Stuff	Rk	2nd Level	Rk	Open Field	Rk	Sacks	ASR	Rk	Short	Long
2012	4.16	4.31	26	69%	26	18%	20	1.14	9	0.67	10	20	4.0%	32	6	10
2013	4.12	4.01	21	74%	28	18%	19	1.09	15	0.75	19	31	6.0%	30	9	11
2014	4.06	3.61	9	70%	24	21%	9	1.05	9	0.88	27	45	8.5%	2	18	17
2014 ALY by direction:		Left End 3.11 (7)			Left Tackle 2.79 (1)			Mid/Guard 3.95 (16)			Right Tackle 3.24 (6)			Right End 3.58 (13)		

With Dante Fowler on the shelf for the entire season after tearing his ACL in minicamp, the plan to have him replace Chris Clemons also hits the wayside. Clemons, 34, had a rough introduction in Jacksonville, and it shouldn't surprise anyone if the Jaguars turn the Fowler replacement plan into a Ryan Davis replacement plan. Davis was a demon in limited snaps as a pass rusher. Former second-round pick Andre Branch—who missed a big chunk of 2014 with a torn groin muscle—could also see situational pass-rush snaps as a Leo.

The loss of Fowler is an even bigger problem given that Jacksonville's high adjusted sack rate from 2014 has a fool's gold feel to it. The Jaguars had all those sacks despite getting pressure on the quarterback on just 20.1 percent of pass plays, which put them ahead of only Cincinnati. With an inexperienced secondary, Gus Bradley wanted to rush four as often as possible—the Jaguars only blitzed 16 percent of the time, the only defense below 20 percent—but they can't rely on four guys if those four guys can't get to the quarterback. The Jaguars ranked 29th with a 17.4 percent pressure rate rushing four. A league-high 12 coverage sacks helped hide the lack of production from the defensive ends.

So did the fact that Jacksonville's best pass-rusher was a tackle, Sen'Derrick Marks. He's now trying to recover from his own torn ACL from Week 17, which is a shame—Marks has been a terrific story ever since coming over from the Titans, and he was a force to be reckoned with last season. Jared Odrick comes over from Miami on a five-year, $42 million ($17 million guaranteed) deal, and should minimize the loss of Marks on base downs. Sixth-round pick Michael Bennett (Ohio State) could eventually be a solid player in the same role, and many draft experts expected the versatile big man to be gone in the first three rounds. Nose tackle Roy Miller remains a formidable run-stopping force in the middle. Ziggy Hood was a stab at finding the next Marks who could break out in Jacksonville, but it hasn't quite worked out. Hood did show a bit as a pass-rusher a year ago, but he's not in Marks' league. Tyson Alualu also continues to be employed here. Alualu moved to five-tech, and that's nice and all, but his next good year in the NFL will be his first and he's a legacy member of the Gene Smith years that nobody wants to remember.

Middle linebacker Paul Posluszny received a contract extension after he tore a pectoral muscle that ended his season, but at 30 and with nothing but his wits to depend on as a pass defender, he's really just a short-term stopgap at this point. However, Telvin Smith, the sleek ex-Florida State linebacker with safety speed, looks like a piece to build on after his rookie season. The main issue with drafting Smith was if he would be able to handle NFL run defense, and he held his own there in his rookie season. Dan Skuta takes over the "Otto" role for failed experiment Dekoda Watson. At five years and $20.5 million ($8 million guaranteed), it's a lot of Khan Bucks for a player with just 22 career starts. Skuta has played admirably in babysitting Aldon Smith's job over the last two years, but it's hard to see much upside in the 29-year-old.

Defensive Secondary

Secondary	Age	Pos	G	Snaps	Plays	TmPct	Rk	Stop	Dfts	BTkl	Runs	St%	Rk	RuYd	Rk	Tgts	Tgt%	Rk	Dist	Suc%	Rk	AdjYd	Rk	PD	Int
								Overall					vs. Run						vs. Pass						
Johnathan Cyprien	25	SS	15	982	112	13.8%	5	39	8	17	70	47%	28	5.8	22	29	9.5%	45	10.8	51%	51	9.5	61	2	0
Josh Evans	24	FS	16	968	91	10.5%	32	21	5	22	44	30%	56	8.9	57	16	5.2%	9	12.8	52%	45	10.3	64	2	0
Dwayne Gratz	25	CB	15	854	63	7.8%	52	26	8	6	18	72%	5	5.2	20	67	25.5%	53	15.6	43%	68	10.2	71	8	1
Demetrius McCray	24	CB	16	811	49	5.7%	74	14	7	6	8	25%	59	4.9	15	54	21.6%	23	12.2	51%	33	7.0	18	3	0
Alan Ball*	30	CB	7	495	25	6.6%	--	9	3	2	4	75%	--	2.5	--	40	26.5%	--	12.8	53%	--	6.2	--	3	1
Will Blackmon*	31	CB	8	351	28	6.5%	--	11	5	7	9	56%	--	5.1	--	21	19.6%	--	11.5	38%	--	8.8	--	0	0
Aaron Colvin	24	CB	6	277	27	8.3%	--	15	6	1	9	78%	--	9.7	--	18	21.3%	--	10.1	42%	--	7.7	--	1	0
Sergio Brown	27	FS	15	530	38	5.1%	69	16	9	6	14	43%	33	7.4	47	21	10.5%	52	12.1	66%	6	2.7	1	5	0
Davon House	26	CB	13	405	34	5.0%	--	13	5	4	9	11%	--	11.1	--	42	29.0%	--	16.5	68%	--	5.4	--	10	1

Year	Pass D Rank	vs. #1 WR	Rk	vs. #2 WR	Rk	vs. Other WR	Rk	vs. TE	Rk	vs. RB	Rk
2012	29	16.8%	25	4.9%	18	36.6%	32	-1.5%	18	1.7%	17
2013	26	13.3%	26	8.9%	21	16.1%	28	19.9%	28	-9.0%	11
2014	17	37.0%	32	-9.8%	10	22.3%	28	5.9%	22	-5.8%	13

The Jaguars have done a very good job of finding solid, credible players at cornerback. They've yet to find a Richard Sherman. Dwayne Gratz had a nice success rate in his rookie season, but thus far his best attribute is run defense. (It should be noted that he's missed a lot of time with injuries.) Demetrius McCray, a 2013 seventh-rounder, stepped in and played well enough to make veteran Alan Ball expendable. Aaron Colvin came off PUP in Week 12 and immediately showed why he was regarded as a Day 2 pick prior to tearing his ACL at the Senior Bowl. Davon House, another of approximately 800 free-agent additions the Jaguars made this offseason, jumped ship from Green Bay for an opportunity for more playing time. ($10 million guaranteed didn't hurt, though.) House, continuing the chapter theme, has showed well in limited playing time for the Packers. He's the most likely member of this group to start, but there should be plenty of competition for snaps.

Safety is less settled. 2013 second-rounder Johnathan Cyprien improved greatly from where he was in the first six weeks of his rookie season, but is more of a solid-average player than a star at this point. He's got the coverage ability to be better than your usual box safety, but doesn't play that way consistently. Winston Guy (an utter disaster) and Josh Evans (merely bad) were poor as deep safeties, and the Jaguars were outbid for the rights to rumored target Devin McCourty this offseason. So the Jags—you're not gonna believe this—signed a free agent who played well in limited snaps in 2014 to man the spot: Sergio Brown, signed away from the division rival Colts with a three-year, $7 million deal. They also drafted Louisville safety James Sample in the fourth round, though he may be more of a box safety than a threat to Brown. Think Bernard Pollard.

Special Teams

Year	DVOA	Rank	FG/XP	Rank	Net Kick	Rank	Kick Ret	Rank	Net Punt	Rank	Punt Ret	Rank	Hidden	Rank
2012	-3.0%	25	1.9	13	-3.6	25	-3.8	23	-3.2	21	-5.9	28	1.0	15
2013	2.5%	9	1.9	15	7.2	5	2.9	8	7.3	8	-6.6	26	9.2	5
2014	-3.6%	26	-1.8	21	2.6	12	0.5	12	-13.2	31	-6.2	28	-3.0	23

Josh Scobee is a perfectly acceptable big-leg kicker: good for a few silly shanks a year, but with a cannon leg that works from range and produces a credible amount of touchbacks. If we ignore the fact that Bryan Anger came at a marked-up price, he's indistinguishable from most other NFL punters. The Jaguars struggled on punts last year, but that's more about the coverage team than Anger.

With Jordan Todman and Mike Brown both joining the Panthers in the offseason, Ace Sanders was the last man standing with NFL experience at returner. Then the Jaguars cut him too. So if you've been looking for the camp battle of least interest to NFL fans, you've found it. Who will return kicks and punts for the Jaguars? Early training camp hype had rookie wide receiver Rashad Greene lobbying for the job, with Tandon Doss and Bryan Walters hanging out on the fringes of the roster with a chance to win it as well.

Kansas City Chiefs

2014 Record: 9-7	**Total DVOA:** 10.4% (10th)	**2015 Mean Projection:** 7.9 wins	**On the Clock (0-4):** 11%
Pythagorean Wins: 10.1 (8th)	**Offense:** 5.0% (12th)	**Postseason Odds:** 34.3%	**Mediocrity (5-7):** 34%
Snap-Weighted Age: 26.4 (24th)	**Defense:** 1.3% (19th)	**Super Bowl Odds:** 4.9%	**Playoff Contender (8-10):** 38%
Average Opponent: 2.2% (7th)	**Special Teams:** 6.7% (3rd)	**Proj. Avg. Opponent:** 2.0% (11th)	**Super Bowl Contender (11+):** 17%

2014: The best AFC team to miss the playoffs.

2015: One of the better AFC teams to miss the playoffs?

In many ways, Kansas City's step back to 9-7 was the most predictable outcome in the 2014 NFL season. The team's unusual path from 2-14 and a No. 1 pick in 2012 to 11-5 and the playoffs in 2013 was helped by factors that tend to regress to the mean.

Injuries were an area where the Chiefs were hit hardest, both literally and figuratively. After finishing with the second-fewest adjusted games lost in 2013, the 2014 Chiefs limped to 26th. They didn't make it past Week 1 before losing three starters to season-ending injuries: linebacker Derrick Johnson (Achilles), defensive end Mike DeVito (Achilles) and right tackle Jeff Allen (bicep). The most devastating loss came later with safety Eric Berry, who was diagnosed with Hodgkin's lymphoma after getting tested for chest discomfort. Fortunately, his treatment went well and he has returned to practice with his teammates, and will likely play this season.

Turnovers were critical to the Chiefs' turnaround, and the team posted a plus-18 turnover differential in 2013. While the offense held up its end of the bargain last year, the defense slipped from 36 takeaways to just 14, including a franchise-low six interceptions. We are starting to see this more often as modern offenses protect the ball better. Prior to 2012, only two defenses ever had forced fewer than 15 takeaways in a non-strike season. Since 2012, it's happened six times, including both the 2012 Chiefs and the 2012 Eagles (Andy Reid's last team in Philadelphia).

Then there's the uncontrollable factor of the schedule. The Chiefs played the NFL's easiest slate of opponents in 2013, but had the seventh-toughest schedule in 2014 thanks to playing both West divisions. That's why you have to take full advantage of the winnable home games. Sure, the Chiefs knocked off both eventual Super Bowl participants in impressive fashion, but that 26-10 loss at home in Week 1 to a Tennessee team that finished 2-14 was one of the season's biggest upsets. So was the 24-20 loss against an Oakland team that had lost 16 consecutive games. It's maddening how a team can boast the caliber of wins and losses the 2014 Chiefs had. One more win against a scrub and the Chiefs would have been in the exact same position as the previous year: a No. 5 seed playing in Indianapolis on wild-card weekend.

Instead, the Chiefs simply go down as another surprise playoff team that failed to produce an encore the following season. In the Philadelphia chapter of *Football Outsiders Almanac 2014*, we looked at the 21 teams since 2001 which increased their win total by at least six games to make the playoffs. Only six of those 21 teams made the playoffs the following year as well. Obviously the Chiefs missed out, but so did the 2014 Eagles despite going 10-6. It's hard to improve two years in a row, especially when the first year's improvement is so vast.

The good news for the Chiefs in 2015 is that they should expect some positive regression in these areas. You can expect a healthier team, as last year's ranking of 26th in adjusted games lost was easily the worst for the Chiefs since 2002. You can also count on some more takeaways from Bob Sutton's defense. The schedule is still above-average, but the order of games appears more favorable. The Chiefs get Pittsburgh and Buffalo at home this year, they have a bye before the Week 10 game in Denver, and the season ends with home games against Cleveland and Oakland where the Chiefs should be favored.

This is a solid team, but there's an elephant in the room we have ignored to this point.

No, it's not in the front office. Unlike last year when the Chiefs lost Branden Albert and Brandon Flowers while adding almost nothing of value, this offseason the team filled two of its biggest holes with wide receiver Jeremy Maclin and left guard Ben Grubbs. Center Rodney Hudson went to Oakland, but drafting Mitch Morse (Missouri) should allow for a smooth transition. The Chiefs also improved their cornerback depth with first-round pick Marcus Peters (Washington).

We've brought up regression a lot in regards to the Chiefs, so there is an obvious number from last season that has nowhere to go but up: the zero touchdown passes caught by a wide receiver. No offense in the modern NFL (since 1960) had ever done this. It's a comical stat, but has it ever really mattered *how* a team scored its points? The 2014 Chiefs did have six touchdown passes to receivers lined up out wide or in the slot, but those players were all listed as tight ends or running backs on the roster. Dwayne Bowe had a ball in his hands in the end zone in Pittsburgh, but failed to finish the play. That 2010 season when he finished with 15 touchdowns sure looks like an outlier now, and the Chiefs parted ways with the receiver after eight seasons.

Of course any production in the passing game is directly related to the quarterback, and that's the position that is keeping Kansas City in the second tier of AFC teams, just below the top Super Bowl contenders. The elephant man is Alex Smith, and going into his 11th season, it's hard to imagine he will ever lead a team to a championship.

2015 Chiefs Schedule

Week	Opp.	Week	Opp.	Week	Opp.
1	at HOU	7	PIT	13	at OAK
2	DEN (Thu.)	8	DET (U.K.)	14	SD
3	at GB (Mon.)	9	BYE	15	at BAL
4	at CIN	10	at DEN	16	CLE
5	CHI	11	at SD	17	OAK
6	at MIN	12	BUF		

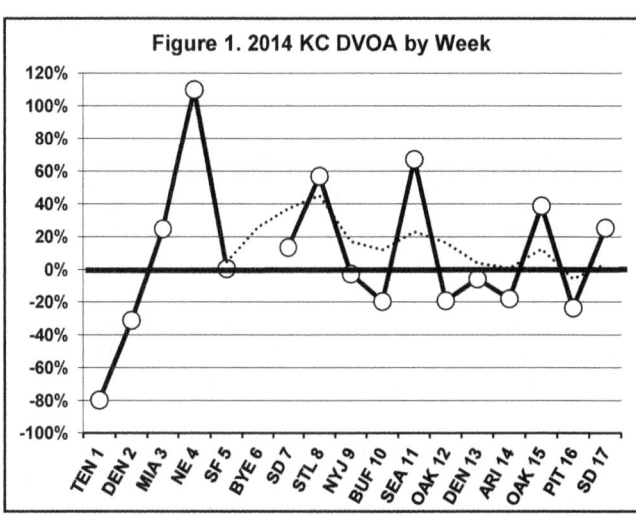

Figure 1. 2014 KC DVOA by Week

During a preseason game last August, FOX analyst John Lynch said Smith is "up there with the Peyton Mannings and Drew Breeses." His justification was *winning*. That's fine if you want to ignore that Smith was 19-31 as a starter before Jim Harbaugh came to San Francisco but is 39-18-1 since 2011 (including playoffs). That's fine if you ignore the huge difference in the contributions those quarterbacks have made to team success compared to what Smith has done. Smith is part of the nouveau riche at quarterback, the $1 million per game club, but he has one of the flimsiest claims for deserving that type of money.

According to Advanced Football Analytics, Smith has accumulated 4.04 win probability added (WPA) since 2011, which ranks 20th in the NFL in that span. Smith trails the likes of Ryan Fitzpatrick (4.79 WPA) and Matt Schaub (4.70 WPA), while barely ranking ahead of Nick Foles (3.60 WPA) despite appearing in 30 more games. Smith's teams may be winning, but he is clearly not the driving force behind those wins, and any comparison to Manning (14.19 WPA in Denver) or Brees (17.46 WPA) is downright foolish.

Plenty of other advanced stats have derided Smith over the years. He never finished higher than 21st in DVOA or 24th in DYAR until 2011. Even in his last four years of relevancy, he's still routinely finished in the 13-20 range among his peers. His Total QBR was always under 40.0 until 2011. Since then he's only had one above-average (greater than 50.0) season: a 69.4 QBR in 2012 when he still lost his job to Colin Kaepernick, who led the 49ers to the Super Bowl.

The career path for Smith has been unusual. Most quarterbacks break out in their first couple of seasons if they're going to be good. Most would never get as many chances as Smith has had to prove his worth. That's the value of being a No. 1 over-all pick. Quarterbacks like Terry Bradshaw, Jim Plunkett, Steve Bartkowski, Vinny Testaverde, and Jeff George kept getting chances to start despite years of below-average results. Eventually the scouts were proven right when the pieces were in place around those quarterbacks, but in Smith's case, it's not like the 49ers weren't a talented team. A lot of quarterbacks would love to throw to Frank Gore, Vernon Davis, and Michael Crabtree, with Joe Staley protecting their blind side. It's not like Smith never had decent coaching either, given Mike McCarthy (2005) and Norv Turner (2006) were his first two offensive coordinators. In 2007-2008, Smith was clearly being outplayed by the undrafted Shaun Hill. It took a great coach like Harbaugh to make San Francisco's talent work while getting better play out of Smith, even if the offense was still trying to hide his flaws.

In Kansas City, Andy Reid has also been known as a coach who maximizes the play of his quarterbacks.

Smith's improvement since 2011 is built on coaching, but let's not pretend Harbaugh had to "teach him how to win." Smith has taken advantage of the great defenses around him. Even the 2014 Chiefs, while not a statistical powerhouse, allowed the second-fewest points in the league. In his career, Smith has been a major liability when forced to score an above-average amount of points to win games. Including playoffs, Smith is 3-33-1 (.095) when his team allows at least 24 points (1-8 in Kansas City). An average team should win at least 20 percent of such games. How do the Chiefs expect to navigate the AFC playoffs when it's likely they will have to outscore at least one team with a quarterback very capable of scoring 24-plus points? Tom Brady (41-42), Joe Flacco (15-22), Andrew Luck (11-16), Peyton Manning (44-71), Philip Rivers (20-37) and Ben Roethlisberger (14-34) all have far better records in that situation than Smith, as do most quarterbacks in this era. Even Andy Dalton is 8-19-1 (.304) with the Bengals, another potential January opponent for the Chiefs.

January play is what some may point to if holding out hope for Smith. In three career playoff games he has thrown nine touchdowns and zero interceptions. Minus a Super Bowl appearance, that kind of makes him the Tony Eason or Jeff Hostetler of this era—surprisingly great playoff stats, albeit on a sample size tinier than Smith's hands if you recall an old narrative. We could point out the three defenses Smith played in the playoffs all ranked 16th or worse in DVOA, but there's a more important point to be made. Even in those big performances against the 2011 Saints and 2013 Colts, Smith's flaws still shined through. In the 36-32 win over the Saints in the 2011 NFC divisional round, Smith really just had two great drives at the end of the game rather than a complete game. New Orleans coughed up five early turnovers on the road, but Smith was only able to build a 23-17 lead before the teams combined for four touchdowns in the final five minutes. Smith contributed just 56 passing yards to the 49ers' first 23 points, and a total of 163 yards to the final two drives.

Smith threw for a career-high 378 yards in the 2013 AFC wild-card round in Indianapolis. He was spectacular in building a 38-10 lead, but a strip-sack by Robert Mathis after Smith held the ball too long really turned that game around. From that point on, Smith's success rate (on both runs and passes) was just 7-for-22 (31.8 percent). Trailing 45-44 with the ball at the Indianapolis 39, Smith looked off a screen to his back side and hesitated with the ball, leading to a huge penalty for intentional grounding that pushed the Chiefs out of field goal range. On fourth-and-11 with the game on the line, Smith's vertical pass down the right sideline didn't give Bowe enough room to get both feet in bounds. While Smith was far from the main reason the Chiefs blew that huge lead, his flaws were still on display, even in one of his best games ever.

We can do better than a sample size of three games against playoff competition by including regular-season games against playoff teams. In his career, Smith is 14-32 (.304) as a starter against playoff teams. An examination of the 14 wins paints a perfect picture of the "game manager" role. Smith's defenses were usually excellent in those games, allowing an average of 14.5 points per game and forcing 43 takeaways (3.1 per game). That aforementioned playoff win over New Orleans is the only time Smith has beaten a playoff team when his team allowed more than 20 defensive points. *Outlier much?* Smith's rushing support has also been outstanding; his teams have averaged 27.1 carries for 149 yards per game (5.49 yards per carry) in those wins. The average Smith stat line was a modest 18-of-29 passing for 197 yards, 1.4 touchdowns and 0.4 interceptions. He exceeded 250 passing yards just three times. In last year's 24-20 win over Seattle, Smith threw just 16 passes for 108 yards, the fewest in the 14-game sample.

Some might suggest this is no different from the successful Seattle model. Play great defense and run the ball with Marshawn Lynch—Russell Wilson has never needed to throw 38 passes in any of his 56 NFL games. Why force the issue with Smith when he's had Gore and Jamaal Charles in the backfield? But there are some major differences between the two quaterbacks and how they have been used. Wilson has had more added to his plate each season, while Reid actually had Smith drop back less in his second season with the Chiefs. Wilson is one of the league's most dynamic rushing threats. Smith has decent mobility, but his rushing yards dropped from 431 in 2013 to 254 last year. But the biggest differences are really Wilson's superior management of pressure and his greater ability to throw down the field. In three seasons Wilson has shown he can sometimes take games over in a way Smith never really has.

In 110 regular-season games, Smith has just four 300-yard passing games (3.6 percent)—the lowest rate for any quarterback with at least 100 starts since Dan Pastorini (2.1 percent). Incredibly, Smith only threw for 303, 309, 310 and 311 yards in those games, barely making the cut. This makes the 378 yards in that Indianapolis playoff loss really stand out. Again, *outlier much?*

Whether it's the last two years in San Francisco or the two in Kansas City, the book is out on this improved version of Smith. He has thrown just 23 interceptions since 2011, but he is so focused on protecting the ball that he will sacrifice chances for big plays. Since 2011, Smith has had a league-low 5.7 percent of his passes defensed, just beating out Aaron

Rodgers (5.7 percent) and Tom Brady (5.8 percent). That sounds great until you remember it's because he's too conservative and his production is nowhere near as prolific as those other quarterbacks.

Cue the "Smith doesn't have any receivers" complaint. Last year, it was somewhat true if you are talking about "wide" receivers, although Charles is a great receiving back and Travis Kelce looked like the real deal after missing nearly his entire first season with an injury. But the Chiefs' seven wide receivers combined for exactly 1 DYAR, compared to 222 DYAR for the incoming Maclin. Maclin was always a good No. 2 when he played for Reid in Philadelphia, but exploded last year in Chip Kelly's system as the unquestioned No. 1. That earned him a five-year deal worth $55 million from the Chiefs. Five different quarterbacks in Philadelphia all had success targeting Maclin, so we'll see how Smith fares. Maclin was the right move for the Chiefs to make once Randall Cobb was off the market, but it's hard to expect him to repeat his 2014 success. On passes thrown more than 20 yards beyond the line of scrimmage in 2014, Smith was 4-of-21 with three interceptions. In Philadelphia last year, Maclin caught 8-of-29 passes thrown more than 20 yards, including five touchdowns. Maclin has been at his best when his quarterbacks have been willing to make throws and give him a chance for a big play. That's never been Smith's game.

What about the offensive line? It certainly has not been a strength in Kansas City's offense, but quarterbacks still play a huge role in managing pressure. Smith's pressure numbers have been fairly consistent over the last five years despite playing in three offensive systems with two teams. He's not as decisive with the ball as he should be, resulting in some really bad sacks. Last year, 75 percent of the Chiefs' sacks came after 2.6 seconds, the third-highest rate in the league. There was a great sign of Smith's absurd conservatism at the end of the Week 13 game against Denver. Down 29-16 and facing fourth-and-19 in the game's final minute with nothing to lose, Smith scrambled to his left and ran out of bounds to give DeMarcus Ware one of the easiest sacks of his career. A lot of quarterbacks would have forced a throw there, but not Smith.

Third down is where Smith's conservatism may hurt his teams the most. Since 2011, Smith has taken the most third-down sacks (69) and has the worst sack rate (13.4 percent) among quarterbacks with at least 200 third-down passes. And when he's not pulling the trigger, he's firing too short. In 2014, Smith's average third-down pass was thrown 2.3 yards short of the first-down marker, the shortest average in the league when compared to the needed yards for a first down. Aaron Rodgers had the longest average pass at 4.0 yards beyond the first-down marker. More than any quarterback in the league, Smith relies on his receivers to break tackles and gain yards after the catch to convert on third down. This metric is called Air Minus Need Differential (AMND). The average starting quarterback has an AMND of plus-1.4 since 2011. Smith's minus-1.7 AMND is the lowest since 2011 among players with at least 300 attempts (Figure 2, next page). It's as if Smith is playing a different sport than his peers.

In one of NFL history's wildest coincidences, Kansas City

Figure 2. Air Minus Need Differential, Third Downs (2011-2014)

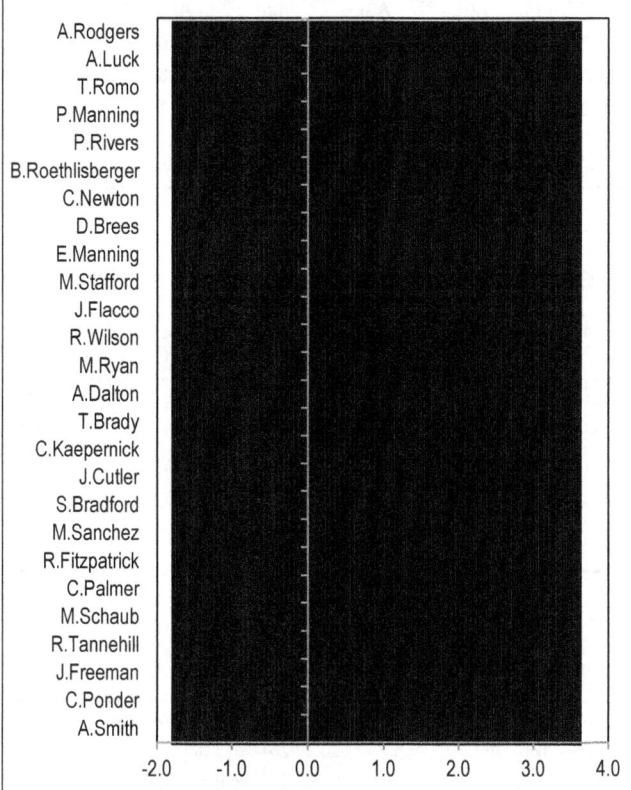

has bought a former San Francisco treat five times in an effort to find a franchise quarterback. Smith is somewhere between Steve Bono and old Joe Montana, but he might need a Trent Dilfer (2000 Ravens) or Brad Johnson (2002 Buccaneers) experience to win a Super Bowl. Kansas City's defense is good, but it's not up to that level yet. With Smith's contract struc-

ture, he has at least the next two seasons to prove to the Chiefs he's the right guy, but the last decade is pretty suggestive that he isn't.

Really, the Chiefs are starving for any playoff win. Remember that old school Royal Rumble finish when Bret Hart and Lex Luger went over the top rope simultaneously? Kansas City's last playoff win happened six days before that on January 16, 1994. For perspective, just think where you were in your life at that time. Feels like eons ago. The depression goes back even further, to be honest. Sure, there's no denying the Chiefs were the best team in the AFL. They had the best record, the most Hall of Famers, and won the last Super Bowl before the merger. Since the 1970 merger, though, Kansas City is 3-13 in the playoffs. Fans have had to savor those two weeks of Joe Montana's January magic from 21 years ago. It's not like the Chiefs have lacked talent over the years or never had impressive regular seasons, but everything comes back to the quarterback. It's no coincidence the two most successful periods in team history featured Len Dawson and Montana. Those guys are hard to find. Dawson bombed in the NFL before finding his way in the AFL. San Francisco traded Montana after injury-plagued years at the end of his career.

In 2015, the Chiefs and Smith should be good enough to keep themselves out of a draft position likely to net a top quarterback prospect. There's certainly nothing to guarantee the right player will be there, but we know the odds decrease the deeper you go into the draft. While most of the league has been loading up on first-round quarterbacks, the Chiefs have not taken one since Todd Blackledge in 1983. With the Chiefs starting to build up an impressive young core, they just may have to join in the first-round fun to shake up the status quo. If your quarterback won't take any risks, then maybe the front office has to do it instead.

Scott Kacsmar

2014 KC Stats by Week

Wk	vs.	W-L	PF	PA	YDF	YDA	TO	Total	Off	Def	ST
1	TEN	L	10	26	245	405	-3	-80%	-56%	32%	8%
2	at DEN	L	17	24	380	325	0	-31%	16%	34%	-14%
3	at MIA	W	34	15	342	332	-2	25%	7%	-16%	2%
4	NE	W	41	14	443	290	3	110%	69%	-40%	1%
5	at SF	L	17	22	265	357	-1	0%	-1%	3%	4%
6	BYE										
7	at SD	W	23	20	365	251	1	13%	16%	8%	5%
8	STL	W	34	7	355	200	0	57%	18%	-18%	22%
9	NYJ	W	24	10	309	364	0	-3%	18%	22%	1%
10	at BUF	W	17	13	278	364	2	-20%	-4%	13%	-2%
11	SEA	W	24	20	298	372	-2	67%	43%	-7%	17%
12	at OAK	L	20	24	313	351	1	-19%	-15%	20%	16%
13	DEN	L	16	29	151	388	-2	-6%	-27%	-19%	2%
14	at ARI	L	14	17	390	366	-2	-18%	-4%	10%	-4%
15	OAK	W	31	13	388	280	0	39%	3%	-8%	27%
16	at PIT	L	12	20	327	282	-1	-24%	-18%	12%	6%
17	SD	W	19	7	251	361	3	25%	-11%	-20%	17%

Trends and Splits

	Offense	Rank	Defense	Rank
Total DVOA	5.0%	12	1.3%	19
Unadjusted VOA	5.6%	12	2.3%	20
Weighted Trend	2.7%	11	0.1%	20
Variance	8.1%	18	4.3%	8
Average Opponent	-2.0%	6	1.2%	9
Passing	12.0%	14	2.6%	13
Rushing	6.0%	5	-0.2%	26
First Down	14.0%	6	22.3%	32
Second Down	-0.3%	15	-14.9%	2
Third Down	-5.0%	21	-12.2%	10
First Half	9.8%	9	8.1%	26
Second Half	-0.1%	15	-5.1%	9
Red Zone	27.8%	3	-23.1%	4
Late and Close	1.7%	18	4.4%	22

Five-Year Performance

Year	W-L	Pyth W	Est W	PF	PA	TO	Total	Rk	Off	Rk	Def	Rk	ST	Rk	Off AGL	Rk	Def AGL	Rk	Off Age	Rk	Def Age	Rk	ST Age	Rk
2010	10-6	9.1	8.3	366	326	+9	0.3%	17	4.4%	13	2.1%	20	-2.1%	24	5.8	2	4.2	1	27.9	10	25.9	28	25.8	24
2011	7-9	4.2	6.3	212	338	-2	-16.9%	26	-19.3%	29	-3.2%	13	-0.9%	19	43.8	26	21.7	13	28.0	5	26.3	25	26.1	22
2012	2-14	2.5	2.4	211	425	-24	-40.1%	32	-25.1%	31	13.0%	30	-2.0%	22	50.0	27	29.3	17	26.3	24	26.1	25	26.0	14
2013	11-5	11.1	10.0	430	305	+18	17.5%	6	3.0%	15	-6.7%	9	7.8%	1	29.4	13	10.6	3	26.1	27	26.4	17	25.8	23
2014	9-7	10.1	9.4	353	281	-3	10.4%	10	5.0%	12	1.3%	19	6.7%	3	36.0	20	62.8	27	26.6	19	26.6	20	25.7	26

2014 Performance Based on Most Common Personnel Groups

KC Offense					KC Offense vs. Opponents					KC Defense				KC Defense vs. Opponents			
Pers	Freq	Yds	DVOA	Run%	Pers	Freq	Yds	DVOA	Run%	Pers	Freq	Yds	DVOA	Pers	Freq	Yds	DVOA
11	41%	5.7	11.6%	29%	Base	45%	5.1	9.7%	54%	Base	30%	4.3	-7.7%	11	55%	5.8	4.9%
12	23%	6.0	14.0%	24%	Nickel	39%	5.6	13.9%	30%	Nickel	31%	5.8	8.2%	12	19%	5.0	-5.5%
21	11%	3.8	-7.5%	66%	Dime+	14%	5.4	-13.1%	12%	Dime+	35%	5.6	-1.6%	21	8%	4.0	-3.4%
22	8%	4.7	1.8%	68%	Goal Line	1%	5.2	45.4%	58%	Goal Line	0%	0.8	28.8%	22	5%	3.5	-17.7%
13	7%	5.6	25.5%	58%	Big	1%	9.3	-5.6%	50%	Big	3%	6.9	33.9%	611	3%	3.7	-27.1%
20	4%	6.1	51.6%	42%													

Strategic Tendencies

Run/Pass		Rk	Formation		Rk	Pass Rush		Rk	Secondary		Rk	Strategy		Rk
Runs, first half	41%	9	Form: Single Back	75%	14	Rush 3	6.8%	12	4 DB	20%	26	Play action	30%	4
Runs, first down	52%	11	Form: Empty Back	5%	16	Rush 4	65.0%	15	5 DB	29%	28	Avg Box (Off)	6.26	19
Runs, second-long	33%	11	Pers: 3+ WR	47%	27	Rush 5	22.3%	17	6+ DB	49%	4	Avg Box (Def)	6.39	7
Runs, power sit.	59%	13	Pers: 4+ WR	2%	12	Rush 6+	5.9%	21	CB by Sides	72%	24	Offensive Pace	32.56	30
Runs, behind 2H	23%	28	Pers: 2+ TE/6+ OL	42%	6	Sacks by LB	66.3%	4	DB Blitz	10%	15	Defensive Pace	30.52	23
Pass, ahead 2H	48%	15	Shotgun/Pistol	57%	20	Sacks by DB	3.3%	22	Hole in Zone	5%	19	Go for it on 4th	0.76	22

The Chiefs have been extremely strong in the red zone since Andy Reid's arrival, on both sides of the ball:

	Offense 2013	Rk	Offense 2014	Rk	Defense 2013	Rk	Defense 2014	Rk
Overall DVOA	3.0%	15	5.0%	12	-6.7%	9	1.3%	19
Red Zone DVOA	18.7%	6	27.8%	3	-15.1%	7	-23.1%	4

Has Reid possibly solved the puzzle of red zone performance and its regression towards the mean from season to season? Probably not. In each of his final three years in Philadelphia, the Eagles were worse in the red zone than overall, on both offense and defense. ⬢ Kansas City dropped 31 passes, more than any offense other than Indianapolis. It worked out to 6.8 percent of passes; no other offense last year was above 6.0 percent. This was the sixth straight season the Chiefs ranked in the top eight in dropped pass rate. ⬢ The Kansas City offense dropped to 3.6 average yards and 0.5% DVOA on running back screens after 7.6 yards and 92.9% DVOA in 2013. ⬢ Kansas City was dead last in the NFL with just 30 defensive penalties and 188 defensive penalty yards. ⬢ In part because of a rotating cast across from Sean Smith, Kansas City opponents threw a league-high 25 percent of passes to the players we identified as No. 2 receivers. No other team was above 22 percent. However, Kansas City opponents threw a league-low 15.2 percent of passes to their running backs. ⬢ The Chiefs allowed a league-low 5.2 yards per pass on play-action passes.

Passing

Player	DYAR	DVOA	Plays	NtYds	Avg	YAC	C%	TD	Int
A.Smith	493	4.1%	511	3039	5.9	6.1	65.5%	19	6
C.Daniel	-28	-24.4%	32	140	4.4	4.1	57.1%	0	0

Rushing

Player	DYAR	DVOA	Plays	Yds	Avg	TD	Fum	Suc
J.Charles	249	19.9%	205	1045	5.1	9	4	54%
K.Davis	-50	-17.7%	134	478	3.6	6	3	37%
A.Smith	38	8.5%	41	260	6.3	1	1	-
D.Thomas	66	62.3%	13	96	7.4	0	0	-
C.Gray	10	20.8%	8	31	3.9	1	0	50%

Receiving

Player	DYAR	DVOA	Plays	Ctch	Yds	Y/C	YAC	TD	C%
D.Bowe*	62	-4.4%	95	60	754	12.6	3.8	0	63%
D.Thomas	-55	-34.9%	32	24	173	7.2	8.0	1	75%
A.Wilson	57	14.8%	28	16	260	16.3	7.4	0	57%
D.Avery*	-13	-19.4%	26	15	176	11.7	2.5	0	58%
J.Avant	22	-0.2%	22	13	152	11.7	4.9	0	59%
J.Hemingway	-14	-21.2%	21	12	108	9.0	5.7	0	57%
A.J.Jenkins	-7	-19.0%	15	9	93	10.3	4.8	0	60%
F.Hammond	-29	-46.7%	11	4	45	11.3	3.8	0	36%
J.Maclin	222	7.4%	143	85	1318	15.5	5.8	10	59%
T.Kelce	174	23.0%	87	67	862	12.9	7.2	5	77%
A.Fasano*	23	2.0%	36	25	226	9.0	3.2	4	69%
J.Charles	1	-13.5%	60	41	282	6.9	7.7	5	68%
K.Davis	-4	-17.2%	25	16	147	9.2	9.8	1	64%
A.Sherman	12	2.0%	14	10	71	7.1	6.5	1	71%
J.McKnight	55	118.7%	7	6	64	10.7	8.7	2	86%

Offensive Line

Player	Pos	Age	GS	Snaps	Pen	Sk	Pass	Run	Player	Pos	Age	GS	Snaps	Pen	Sk	Pass	Run
Rodney Hudson*	C	26	16/16	1007	2	2.0	3.0	3.3	Mike McGlynn*	LG	30	14/13	807	5	5.0	17.0	3.8
Eric Fisher	LT	24	16/16	1006	9	5.0	20.3	2.3	Jeff Linkenbach*	G/T	28	16/3	219	2	2.5	6.8	0.0
Zach Fulton	RG	24	16/16	997	5	2.5	16.5	4.0	*Ben Grubbs*	G	31	16/16	1134	3	2.5	13.5	3.0
Ryan Harris*	RT	30	16/15	958	3	5.5	18.5	2.5	*Paul Fanaika*	G	29	14/14	891	7	0.5	12.0	3.0

Year	Yards	ALY	Rk	Power	Rk	Stuff	Rk	2nd Lev	Rk	Open Field	Rk	Sacks	ASR	Rk	Short	Long	F-Start	Cont.
2012	4.84	4.04	19	59%	23	20%	19	1.33	8	1.25	2	40	8.2%	27	10	20	20	30
2013	4.58	4.33	2	65%	16	16%	7	1.27	8	0.91	9	41	7.7%	20	14	15	19	28
2014	4.47	4.08	7	60%	21	17%	5	1.15	17	0.97	4	49	9.4%	28	12	14	16	40
2014 ALY by direction:		Left End 4.26 (10)			Left Tackle 3.38 (26)			Mid/Guard 4.06 (15)			Right Tackle 3.75 (19)			Right End 5.17 (4)				

Last year, the Chiefs returned just one offensive line starter in the same position as 2013, center Rodney Hudson. Now Hudson is gone too after a strong year led to a lucrative contract with rival Oakland. That means for the second year in a row the Chiefs are bringing back just one starter: Eric Fisher, the only man who can challenge Sam Bradford for the title of Most Irrelevant No. 1 Overall Pick.[1] The decision to pick up Fisher's fifth-year option comes after this season. He made the move to left tackle in 2014 and improved his rate of snaps per blown block to 44.2 (ranked 18th) after a brutal 23.9 snaps per blown block in 2013. That's still not living up to his draft status, nor does it justify letting Branden Albert go, but at least Fisher wasn't a complete disaster last year.

Ben Grubbs takes over at left guard after the Chiefs snagged him for a fifth-round pick to ease some of New Orleans' cap struggles. It's not exactly like picking up Willie Roaf in 2002, but Grubbs is a significant upgrade over Mike McGlynn, who has charted poorly three years in a row with the Chiefs and Colts. Replacing Hudson is hardly a monumental task, but the Chiefs are likely to have inexperience at center no matter who wins the job. Eric Kush has one career start in two years and second-round rookie Mitch Morse played tackle at Missouri. Everyone raves about Morse's intelligence, so he should be able to make the conversion inside and handle protection calls. Right guard is also up in the air. Zach Fulton started every game last year as a sixth-round rookie, but struggled as you might expect a sixth-round rookie to do. He's likely to take a backseat to the winner of the battle between Jeff Allen and Paul Fanaika. Allen has played several positions for the Chiefs and actually started at right tackle in Week 1 last year before a biceps injury ended his season. Fanaika had a myriad of issues in Bruce Arians' offense in Arizona the last two years.

With Ryan Harris off to Denver, Donald Stephenson should have a lock on the right tackle job this year. To this point, he has just been "that guy taken one pick before Russell Wilson." Maybe that's all he'll ever be, but we don't know for sure yet since he has yet to hold down a starting job. He didn't chart well in 2012 or 2013 in limited playing time. He started 2014 with a four-game suspension for performance-enhancing drugs, and when he returned, the Chiefs stuck with Harris.

Few jobs are set in stone, and the opportunities are there for several linemen to earn long-term jobs and finally build up some continuity in this offense. If no one steps up, then the Chiefs have shown they have no problem with starting fresh again next year.

---

1 OK, most irrelevant *active* No. 1 overall pick. We can already hear the Terry Baker admiration society complaining.

Defensive Front Seven

Defensive Line	Age	Pos	G	Snaps	Plays	Overall TmPct	Rk	Stop	Dfts	BTkl	Runs	St%	vs. Run Rk	RuYd	Rk	Sack	Pass Rush Hit	Hur	Dsrpt
Dontari Poe	25	DT	16	944	46	5.7%	29	34	10	3	38	68%	84	2.8	72	6.0	1	8.8	1
Allen Bailey	26	DE	14	748	43	6.0%	22	34	16	6	32	78%	46	1.9	32	5.0	2	3.5	2
Jaye Howard	27	DT	16	436	37	4.5%	47	27	9	1	32	72%	74	2.4	55	1.0	4	3.5	0

Edge Rushers	Age	Pos	G	Snaps	Plays	Overall TmPct	Rk	Stop	Dfts	BTkl	Runs	St%	vs. Run Rk	RuYd	Rk	Sack	Pass Rush Hit	Hur	Dsrpt
Justin Houston	26	OLB	16	1032	73	9.0%	3	59	33	5	40	73%	52	2.4	40	22.0	7	32.8	5
Tamba Hali	32	OLB	16	973	56	6.9%	19	34	12	8	46	57%	81	3.9	75	6.0	9	18.5	0

Linebackers	Age	Pos	G	Snaps	Plays	Overall TmPct	Rk	Stop	Dfts	BTkl	Sack	Hit	Hur	Runs	St%	vs. Run Rk	RuYd	Rk	Tgts	vs. Pass Suc%	Rk	AdjYd	Rk	PD	Int
Josh Mauga	28	ILB	16	1005	105	12.9%	39	56	12	11	0.5	5	7.5	71	55%	74	3.6	57	15	57%	--	5.8	--	2	0
James-Michael Johnson	26	ILB	16	438	48	5.9%	81	26	7	6	0.0	0	0	31	65%	38	2.0	5	16	33%	62	6.6	37	1	0

Year	Yards	ALY	Rk	Power	Rk	Stuff	Rk	2nd Level	Rk	Open Field	Rk	Sacks	ASR	Rk	Short	Long
2012	4.48	4.18	20	52%	5	18%	23	1.17	13	0.99	25	27	6.5%	14	4	17
2013	4.27	3.67	11	56%	7	18%	18	1.03	10	0.94	25	47	7.9%	6	14	20
2014	4.96	4.57	32	55%	4	18%	23	1.57	32	0.84	25	46	8.3%	3	17	13

2014 ALY by direction:	Left End 7.36 (32)	Left Tackle 4.34 (24)	Mid/Guard 4.39 (30)	Right Tackle 4.82 (26)	Right End 4.13 (20)

Studies show marijuana has medicinal purposes, but another of its overlooked benefits is that it allowed the Chiefs to steal Justin Houston in the 2011 draft. That class will go down as one of the best ever for pass-rushers. J.J. Watt, Von Miller, Robert Quinn, Aldon Smith, Ryan Kerrigan, and Cameron Jordan all went in the first 24 picks. Houston fell all the way to 70th thanks to a positive marijuana test at the combine. Kansas City took a chance on him and that gamble has been paying off. Houston was at his best in 2014 with 22 sacks, just one shy of a new NFL record. The Chiefs struck a long-term deal with Houston rather than have him play 2015 on the franchise tag. He gets $52.5 million in guaranteed money and the (temporary) label of richest linebacker contract in NFL history.

Houston's impact was crucial in a difficult season for this front seven. Tamba Hali, at age 31, had his least productive season as a pass-rusher since moving to outside linebacker in 2009. First-round rookie Dee Ford was mostly a spectator with 122 defensive snaps, but he's the plan for the future. With Houston likely to regress a little from his career year, Hali will have to pick up the slack and return to previous form. If he can't, then expect Ford to earn more playing time in his second season.

The star up front remains defensive tackle Dontari Poe, though he had a down year in both run defense and applying interior pressure on quarterbacks. We'll cut the big man some slack since he plays such an unusually high amount of snaps (1,007 in 2014 and 1,030 in 2013) for a defensive lineman. Unfortunately, a minicamp injury led to back surgery in July and Poe could miss much of the regular season. Jaye Howard expects to move into Poe's spot, and he came on late in 2014. He's like a heavier version of Allen Bailey, who could see significant time at defensive end this year. Mike DeVito and Derrick Johnson were supposed to be a big part of 2014's defense, but neither made it past Week 1 before rupturing their Achilles. Both should be back in their roles this year, but there's always some concern about players in their thirties returning from serious injuries. DeVito's not a high-snap player by any means, and the Chiefs can get along fine with Bailey in the rotation.

The linebacker joining Johnson in the middle will be decided by an open competition. Josh Mauga was serviceable in replacing Johnson last season, but he had few impact plays. His 12 defeats were the fewest among the 18 front-seven players with at least 1,000 snaps. James-Michael Johnson is another veteran, but he struggled in coverage, which was thought to be his strength heading into the season. It's possible a rookie starts at inside linebacker. Fourth-round pick Ramik Wilson was productive at Georgia, but scouts are concerned with his coverage against tight ends. Fifth-round pick D.J. Alexander (Oregon State) played on the outside, and his speed makes him a good candidate for special-teams work this season. Wilson certainly has the edge in experience and learning curve for playing inside.

Defensive Secondary

Secondary	Age	Pos	G	Snaps	Plays	Overall TmPct	Rk	Stop	Dfts	BTkl	Runs	vs. Run St%	Rk	RuYd	Rk	Tgts	vs. Pass Tgt%	Rk	Dist	Suc%	Rk	AdjYd	Rk	PD	Int
Sean Smith	28	CB	16	1036	65	8.0%	45	21	10	6	18	6%	76	9.9	66	81	19.9%	12	12.6	55%	21	6.0	8	15	1
Husain Abdullah	30	FS	16	1024	79	9.7%	44	32	13	9	41	39%	40	6.3	32	31	7.8%	30	8.7	59%	22	6.3	24	7	1
Ron Parker	28	SS/CB	16	1011	106	13.0%	13	29	14	20	34	15%	70	10.1	63	78	19.8%	70	10.8	47%	54	7.2	33	10	1
Chris Owens*	29	CB	11	491	34	6.1%	--	15	9	6	8	25%	--	10.8	--	44	22.7%	--	10.5	57%	--	8.3	--	4	0
Kurt Coleman*	27	SS	15	391	35	4.6%	--	9	2	3	12	17%	--	8.1	--	15	9.5%	--	13.4	72%	--	2.4	--	6	3
Phillip Gaines	24	CB	13	371	21	3.2%	--	9	6	6	2	50%	--	10.0	--	29	20.0%	--	15.4	58%	--	5.7	--	5	0
Eric Berry	27	SS	6	361	39	12.8%	--	12	4	5	18	33%	--	8.1	--	13	8.9%	--	7.4	57%	--	5.7	--	2	0
Marcus Cooper	25	CB	13	287	21	3.2%	--	4	1	3	1	0%	--	11.0	--	41	36.6%	--	14.2	40%	--	10.8	--	3	0
Jamell Fleming	26	CB	7	253	29	8.1%	--	9	7	2	4	25%	--	8.0	--	38	38.5%	--	14.1	49%	--	7.2	--	3	0
Tyvon Branch	29	SS	3	190	30	19.2%	--	12	3	1	20	40%	--	4.7	--	3	4.8%	--	6.0	63%	--	9.3	--	1	0

Year	Pass D Rank	vs. #1 WR	Rk	vs. #2 WR	Rk	vs. Other WR	Rk	vs. TE	Rk	vs. RB	Rk
2012	31	22.1%	28	7.0%	21	2.8%	22	-4.0%	11	33.4%	32
2013	7	-11.7%	8	-4.4%	12	2.8%	16	-36.9%	2	-7.1%	14
2014	13	5.9%	22	-3.9%	14	1.6%	19	7.3%	23	-2.4%	15

With Brandon Flowers gone, this secondary had to look towards versatile safety Eric Berry as its veteran leader. Sadly, Berry's season was cut short after a diagnosis of Hodgkin lymphoma. He has concluded treatment and resumed practicing in training camp. If he's healthy to start, he'll be a big upgrade for the defense, which will still have some solid safety depth in Hussain Abdullah and Tyvon Branch. Abdullah charted well in his first year as Kansas City's starting free safety. His season was highlighted by a pick-six against Tom Brady in prime time. That was one of only six interceptions by the defense in 2014, the lowest season total in team history. That's why they need a playmaker like Berry. Branch is a solid veteran, but he has been limited to just five games in the last two seasons due to injuries.

The depth is not so good at cornerback, especially with Sean Smith serving a three-game suspension for a DUI. When active, he's a big (6-foot-3) No. 1 corner coming off a career year. Smith's on a short list of cornerbacks that have charted well in our main metrics for each of the last two years. In his absence, the Chiefs will have to face Peyton Manning (Week 2) and Aaron Rodgers (Week 3) with a very green set of cornerbacks. Phillip Gaines, a 2014 third-round pick, is a player who will have to ascend in role after a rookie campaign where he had solid coverage metrics in limited playing time. His arrow was pointing in the right direction before a concussion ended his season in Week 14. The Chiefs continued to play dime defense at a much higher rate (35 percent) than the average team, but it's hard to field that many defensive backs when Chris Owens departed and Marcus Cooper continues to struggle. Kansas City needed more playmakers in the secondary, so enter first-round cover corner Marcus Peters. He intercepted eight passes in his last two seasons at Washington, but there are concerns about his rawness and maturity that could delay him from being a Week 1 starter. He's likely a nickelback when Smith returns, but the Chiefs don't have many other options to put opposite of Gaines in September. Sanders Commings is always hurt and third-round rookie Steven Nelson (Oregon State) would leave two rookies against two of the best passing offenses in the league in Denver and Green Bay.

Of course the Chiefs could put Abdullah back at safety and rely on the versatile Ron Parker to handle corner duties without Smith. Parker took on the difficult task of replacing Berry last year, and his journeyman story is also one of inspiration. Parker was undrafted in 2011 and has been cut eight times in the NFL, but he made last year's opportunity count, splitting time at cornerback and safety. Parker, who ran a 4.35 40-yard dash years ago, showed up often when you watched film of this defense. Sometimes he made a good stop, but there were also the 20 times he missed a tackle, the third-highest total in the league. In March, the Chiefs signed him to a five-year contract worth $30 million, believed to be the largest deal ever for an undrafted safety. It's realistic to think Parker's best days are ahead of him as last year was his first significant playing time in the NFL. His game was expectedly rough around the edges given he made the conversion from corner to safety, but he's a big part of this secondary now.

Special Teams

Year	DVOA	Rank	FG/XP	Rank	Net Kick	Rank	Kick Ret	Rank	Net Punt	Rank	Punt Ret	Rank	Hidden	Rank
2012	-2.0%	22	-2.2	19	-1.5	19	-9.8	31	8.8	8	-5.4	26	2.4	12
2013	7.8%	1	-5.6	26	3.0	12	19.8	2	4.6	13	17.2	1	5.2	9
2014	6.7%	3	-1.5	20	-2.7	23	12.4	1	11.6	4	13.7	2	0.1	15

The Chiefs were able to sustain their excellent play on special teams from 2013. The most notable feat was ranking in the top two in both kick returns and punt returns for the second year in a row despite losing both primary return specialists (Dexter McCluster and Quintin Demps) from the year before. Knile Davis continued to shine on kick returns (7.5 points of estimated field position value, fourth in the NFL) but rookie De'Anthony Thomas was really the difference-maker. He averaged 30.6 yards per kick return and 11.9 yards per punt return, including an 81-yard punt return touchdown against Oakland. We measured him with 9.5 points worth of value on 34 punt returns, and another 3.9 points on just 13 kick returns.

Punting also improved with Dustin Colquitt having the third-highest rate (43.7 percent) of punts downed inside the opponent's 20. The kicking game is where things took a few steps back. Undrafted free agent rookie Cairo Santos beat out Ryan Succop for the job, and he did okay on field goals after a few early misses. The problem was on kickoffs, where he ranked 30th out of 32 kickers in touchback rate (32.5 percent). He ranked 18th in average kickoff distance, so maybe some better coverage can lead to more touchbacks in 2015, but right now this is a weakness in a league where half the kickers produce touchbacks more than half the time. Colquitt only has five career kickoffs, so the burden is really on Santos to strengthen that kicking leg.

Miami Dolphins

2014 Record: 8-8	Total DVOA: 3.5% (15th)	2015 Mean Projection: 7.5 wins	On the Clock (0-4): 14%
Pythagorean Wins: 8.4 wins (15th)	Offense: 10.1% (8th)	Postseason Odds: 27.7%	Mediocrity (5-7): 37%
Snap-Weighted Age: 26.6 (21st)	Defense: 0.5% (17th)	Super Bowl Odds: 3.1%	Playoff Contender (8-10): 36%
Average Opponent: 2.7% (5th)	Special Teams: -6.1% (32nd)	Proj. Avg. Opponent: -0.5% (18th)	Super Bowl Contender (11+): 13%

2014: Just like the uniforms, things are slightly different but mostly the same as Miami goes 8-8 again.

2015: A franchise that tastes like water gets a flavor burst, but is the Kool-Aid really worth drinking?

First, the urgency: Joe Philbin, who will be going into his fourth season at the helm in Miami, has to be fully aware of the fact that Dave Wannstedt is the only head coach in the post-Shula era to last more than four seasons. And while Wannstedt will never be remembered as the second coming of Vince Lombardi, he at least had three playoff games and a postseason victory on his resume. Philbin has none of those credentials; to this point, he's perhaps best known for presiding over a team wracked by the bullying scandal that ultimately sank the 2013 roster. Now, Philbin's legacy in Miami will be inexorably tied to quarterback Ryan Tannehill, who signed a sizable deal in the offseason that will either see the two of them lead Miami into the playoffs for the first time since 2008 or emerge as the latest AFC East coach-quarterback tandem unable to unseat Bill Belichick and Tom Brady from the top of the division.

When it comes to optimism, the offseason signings of Suh and Jordan Cameron and the trade for Kenny Stills definitely stoked the excitement level in South Florida. The reckless spending of Jeff Ireland has been replaced by a more strategic approach from Dennis Hickey. Replacing tight end Charles Clay with a cost-efficient Jordan Cameron is a smart move, especially when the Bills made Clay one of the highest-paid tight ends in the history of the game (let that statement roll around your brain for a few seconds) and the Dolphins needed to commit most of their offseason financial resources to signing Suh and Tannehill. On the other hand, it's hard to think of Hickey as stingy when the Dolphins came within four million of being the first team in NFL history to hand out two $100 million contracts in the same offseason.

The Suh contract is fascinating because the Dolphins essentially booby-trapped their own 2016 salary cap to get Suh in the door. Suh technically will have a salary below $1 million in 2015, and will count only $6.1 million against the salary cap. He's actually taking up more room on the Detroit cap ($9.7 million) than he is on the Miami cap. But in 2016, Suh's salary is already fully guaranteed at $23.5 million, giving him the highest cap hit in the league at $28.6 million. There's no way the Dolphins can let that stand; they will have to restructure the deal after just one year, which will dump tons of money onto their cap down the line. The Tannehill contract, on the other hand, could help make carrying that Suh money palatable. It's well-structured to give Miami a starting quarterback at a below-market rate for the next few years. The trade-off is that much of the money for the next two seasons is guaranteed. If Tannehill crashes and burns this year, the Dolphins are stuck paying a lot of money to a player they will want to get rid of.

Good thing, then, that there's a lot to like about Tannehill's chances for further improvement in 2015. As he enters his second year with offensive coordinator Bill Lazor, there should be enough shorthand between the offensive coordinator and quarterback to get Tannehill past some dicey situations. And for the first time in his professional career, he's likely going to be playing behind a line that gives him a chance to succeed. Between injuries and personnel shuffling the last two years, Tannehill has had very little stability up front. While that doesn't absolve Tannehill of his own flaws, the lack of continuity along the offensive line has played a central role in his inconsistencies. With Mike Pouncey unavailable at the start of last season, the Dolphins started off 2014 with five brand-new starters across the offensive line. But gradually over the course of the season, the line coalesced and improved, despite losing left tackle Branden Albert to a knee injury at midseason. The Dolphins were ninth in the NFL in adjusted line yards, Miami's first top-10 finish in that category since 2009. The coaches also showed more faith in the line's pass-blocking, going "max protect" on just 9 percent of plays after the Dolphins had led the league at 15.2 percent in 2013. Miami hopes the line can continue its improvement where last year left off, with the added bonus of getting Albert back in the lineup.

There was also massive turnover at receiver this offseason, where three of the top four pass catchers were shipped out and replaced with new targets: third-year receiver Kenny Stills, veteran Greg Jennings, and first-round pick DeVante Parker. Jarvis Landry, the slot receiver who led the team in catches as a rookie last year, is also back for his second season. It's not known if the speedy Stills can make the transition to becoming arguably the lead option in the passing game, but there's no questioning his dependability last season: his astounding 75 percent catch rate was tops among all receivers who were targeted at least 75 times. That's mind-boggling when we consider that Stills is primarily a deep threat. His catch rate was 19.6 percent higher than expected based on average depth of target, the best mark among all wide receivers last year. Stills will almost certainly see his catch percentage dip without the

2015 Dolphins Schedule

Week	Opp.	Week	Opp.	Week	Opp.
1	at WAS	7	HOU	13	BAL
2	at JAC	8	at NE (Thu.)	14	NYG (Mon.)
3	BUF	9	at BUF	15	at SD
4	NYJ (U.K.)	10	at PHI	16	IND
5	BYE	11	DAL	17	NE
6	at TEN	12	at NYJ		

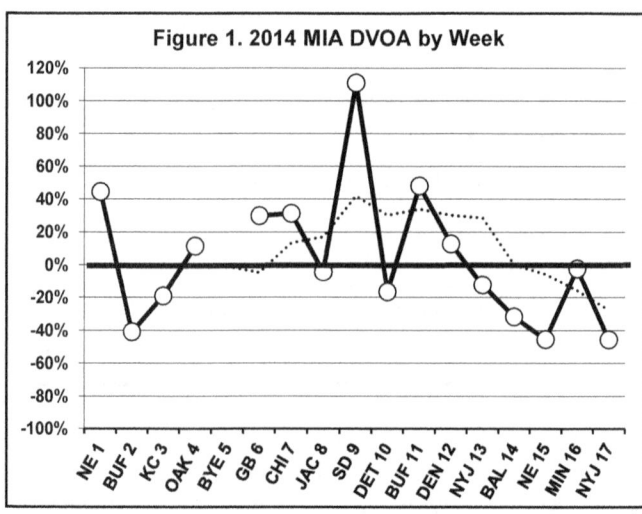

Figure 1. 2014 MIA DVOA by Week

impeccably accurate Drew Brees, but perhaps this deep threat will mesh better with Tannehill than Mike Wallace did. And if Landry can find that extra gear he was looking for all offseason (he spent a sizable amount of time training to increase his surprisingly underwhelming straight-line speed) and Parker is healthy after attempting to square away a foot issue that dogged him last season with Louisville, the Dolphins could have a nice array of young talent at the receiver spot.

Meanwhile, the replacement of Clay with Cameron could pay dividends in several areas, including the red zone. Miami scored touchdowns on just 51.5 percent of its red zone trips in 2014, and the athletic Cameron has always displayed a nice flair when it comes to short and intermediate routes, particularly inside the opposing 20-yard line. The 6-foot-5, 249-pound Cameron isn't Gronktastic, but he does feature a wide catch radius and an ability to get open in short spaces. Seven of his nine touchdown catches the last two years have come in the red zone, thanks in large part to jump balls when matched up against linebackers.

The new faces represent a collective upgrade, but Tannehill needs to develop a cohesive relationship with his new receivers as fast as possible, as a quick start would certainly take some pressure off the quarterback in the early going. The schedule does set up relatively nicely for the Miami passing game out of the gate; while personnel has changed since the end of the 2014 season, four of the Dolphins' first five opponents were in the bottom half of the league last year in pass defense DVOA, including the Titans (26th) and Redskins (32nd).

On defense, the Dolphins need to take a page from the New England squad they're trying to dethrone. The Patriots haven't had a strong all-around defense for most of the Tom Brady era, but they do a better job than most teams when it comes to maximizing their strengths. Miami must do the same, and for the Dolphins, maximizing their strengths means leaning heavily on the defensive line.

Suh, Cameron Wake and Olivier Vernon will draw most of the headlines, and rightfully so. Suh was signed to be a defensive difference-maker, and his 36 sacks are the most in the NFL for a defensive tackle since he entered the league in 2010. If he is able to collapse the pocket with the Dolphins like he did in Detroit, the domino effect will open up one-on-ones for the fearsome edge rushers Wake and Vernon. As for the Ringo figure of this foursome, the departures of Randy Starks and Jared Odrick mean Earl Mitchell will occasionally see time next to Suh at the defensive tackle spot, while Suh's old Detroit teammate C.J. Mosley (who signed a one-year

deal with the Dolphins in the offseason) will provide depth.

The problem with projecting a big defensive improvement lies in the technicality that Miami must line up seven more defenders in addition to the front four. The failure of expensive mistakes Dannell Ellerbe and Phillip Wheeler forced career part-timer Koa Misi into an every-down role at middle linebacker, with 2013 fourth-round pick Jelani Jenkins starting 14 games on the outside after he had barely played as a rookie. Callow youngsters Jamar Taylor and Will Davis are competing for starting roles at cornerback, and they'll be banking on help from a safety with a paper mâché knee (Louis Delmas) and a journeyman nickelback who benefited from an unusually low target percentage in 2014 (Brice McCain). Overall, an average defense—the Dolphins were 17th in the league last year in defensive DVOA the same spot as 2013—isn't guaranteed to improve simply due to Suh's signing. Part of the reason the Miami defense fell short of its potential last season was injuries, including season-enders to the likes of Ellerbe, Davis, and safety Michael Thomas. But this year, when starting linebacker goes down, Miami won't have a Jenkins-quality backup lurking as depth. Instead, it'll be career special-teamers like Chris McCain or Walt Aikens. God forbid something happens to Wake or Vernon, the alternatives are either 2014 seventh-round pick Terrence Fede or Derrick Shelby and his 5.5 career sacks. While the star power can hide some deficiencies, Miami almost certainly needs above-average injury luck to make a big leap forward this season.

One more issue that could hinder Miami's chances of challenging the Patriots: despite having one of the easiest opponent slates on tap for 2015, the Dolphins will log the second-most travel miles in the league. Miami will travel 26,542 miles in 2015, including two road games of at least 2,000 miles each. (Compounding things is the fact that the Dolphins have to forfeit a home game this year for a date in London against the Jets.) Miami travel slate is second only to the 49ers, who will travel 27,998 miles during the regular season. While it's easy to dismiss the impact of travel in the NFL—especially when judged against the other major professional sports—it can still come into play, especially when it's a distance of 1,000 miles or more in one direction. A 2012 study by Bill Barnwell showed that in the 15-season period from 1997-2011, teams that traveled 2,000 miles or more for a road trip won only 39.8 percent of their games. That's slightly worse than the 43 percent of games won by teams that went on road trips that were 1,000 miles or less.

The bottom line is that, at the very least, the 2015 Dolphins project to be a lot more interesting than they've been in recent seasons. For a vanilla-flavored organization that has notched between six and eight wins for six straight years, adding the year's most impactful free-agent defender was guaranteed to shine some limelight onto South Beach. At the same time, the margin for error here is perilously thin, one of the reasons our new and improved projection system is far less enthusiastic about the Dolphins than the "quick and rough" projections we ran on ESPN Insider in May. Though Ryan Tannehill still could fulfill his potential, the Dolphins right now have to be considered average at the most important position in the game. On defense, though the Dolphins match up very nicely across the board with just about any team in the AFC (save maybe at linebacker), they do not have much depth, particularly in the secondary, and will be banking on a few relatively unproven players to emerge as quality contributors. And while Miami has improved on paper, you can certainly say the same thing about fellow Patriots chasers Buffalo and New York.

Ultimately, the narrative on Miami is easy to see coming. The Dolphins are sure to get off to a hot start, as the cumulative winning percentage of their first five foes was .275 in 2014. The real tests will come over the final 11 games, when a squad that has likely suffered a few injuries will face a slate of opponents which posted a .590 winning percentage last season.[1] The Dolphins will get a de facto victory lap for their offseason moves as they wade through shallow waters in September and October, but check back in when the sharks start to circle in the season's latter half.

Christopher Price

2014 Dolphins Stats by Week

Wk	vs.	W-L	PF	PA	YDF	YDA	TO	Total	Off	Def	ST
1	NE	W	33	20	360	315	-1	44%	15%	-30%	-1%
2	at BUF	L	10	29	290	315	-2	-41%	10%	12%	-39%
3	KC	L	15	34	332	342	2	-19%	-3%	1%	-15%
4	vs. OAK	W	38	14	435	317	1	11%	-1%	-9%	3%
5	BYE										
6	GB	L	24	27	349	369	-3	30%	13%	-17%	0%
7	at CHI	W	27	14	393	224	3	31%	29%	-15%	-13%
8	at JAC	W	27	13	326	377	2	-4%	-2%	4%	1%
9	SD	W	37	0	441	178	4	111%	23%	-86%	2%
10	at DET	L	16	20	228	351	-1	-17%	-18%	7%	8%
11	BUF	W	22	9	330	237	-2	48%	41%	-7%	0%
12	at DEN	L	36	39	313	450	0	13%	46%	34%	0%
13	at NYJ	W	16	13	291	326	0	-12%	-11%	-2%	-3%
14	BAL	L	13	28	249	447	1	-32%	-11%	26%	5%
15	at NE	L	13	41	384	395	-1	-45%	-34%	11%	1%
16	MIN	W	37	35	493	357	-1	-2%	45%	19%	-28%
17	NYJ	L	24	37	387	494	0	-46%	4%	30%	-20%

Trends and Splits

	Offense	Rank	Defense	Rank
Total DVOA	10.1%	8	0.5%	17
Unadjusted VOA	10.9%	8	-1.4%	15
Weighted Trend	10.7%	7	5.9%	25
Variance	5.4%	8	8.2%	28
Average Opponent	-2.1%	5	-0.4%	19
Passing	19.4%	11	7.3%	16
Rushing	9.6%	2	-6.8%	18
First Down	8.8%	10	-4.6%	13
Second Down	18.4%	4	3.7%	19
Third Down	-1.5%	18	4.8%	17
First Half	10.7%	8	1.9%	21
Second Half	9.5%	7	-1.0%	13
Red Zone	-0.2%	15	11.4%	29
Late and Close	24.9%	3	4.9%	23

Five-Year Performance

Year	W-L	Pyth W	Est W	PF	PA	TO	Total	Rk	Off	Rk	Def	Rk	ST	Rk	Off AGL	Rk	Def AGL	Rk	Off Age	Rk	Def Age	Rk	ST Age	Rk
2010	7-9	6.2	8.5	273	333	-12	1.8%	15	0.7%	18	-4.8%	9	-3.7%	29	27.0	19	23.9	15	26.5	26	26.3	24	25.8	25
2011	6-10	8.5	7.7	329	313	-6	-1.3%	18	-7.5%	20	-3.7%	12	2.5%	6	22.1	10	9.6	3	26.6	21	27.7	6	26.3	16
2012	7-9	7.1	7.6	288	317	-10	-7.2%	21	-8.4%	22	-0.8%	14	0.4%	14	19.7	9	18.0	7	25.7	29	26.8	16	25.7	25
2013	8-8	7.5	6.8	317	335	-2	-6.5%	22	-1.8%	18	2.4%	17	-2.4%	23	41.3	20	18.6	9	26.5	23	27.3	11	26.0	18
2014	8-8	8.4	8.8	388	373	+2	3.5%	15	10.1%	8	0.5%	17	-6.1%	32	40.3	26	39.1	18	26.2	27	27.3	7	25.7	25

1 Do you prefer our projections to last year's winning percentage? Miami's first eight opponents average -5.6% DVOA, 29th in the NFL. Their final eight opponents average 4.5% DVOA, the fourth hardest schedule of Weeks 10-17.

2014 Performance Based on Most Common Personnel Groups

MIA Offense					MIA Offense vs. Opponents					MIA Defense					MIA Defense vs. Opponents			
Pers	Freq	Yds	DVOA	Run%	Pers	Freq	Yds	DVOA	Run%	Pers	Freq	Yds	DVOA		Pers	Freq	Yds	DVOA
11	75%	5.7	11.6%	33%	Base	25%	5.8	30.8%	46%	Base	40%	5.2	-5.6%		11	53%	5.5	2.7%
12	22%	5.3	24.6%	50%	Nickel	62%	5.5	4.3%	36%	Nickel	58%	5.5	6.8%		12	17%	5.0	-9.8%
10	2%	4.2	24.0%	26%	Dime+	12%	5.7	45.6%	16%	Dime+	2%	4.0	-71.8%		21	13%	5.9	6.9%
					Goal Line	0%	1.0	-119.6%	100%	Goal Line	1%	0.9	-3.9%		22	4%	2.6	-21.6%
					Big	1%	1.4	1.3%	57%						20	3%	6.1	1.2%
															611	3%	4.8	1.7%

Strategic Tendencies

Run/Pass		Rk	Formation		Rk	Pass Rush		Rk	Secondary		Rk	Strategy		Rk
Runs, first half	36%	24	Form: Single Back	87%	3	Rush 3	14.7%	3	4 DB	28%	10	Play action	26%	6
Runs, first down	43%	29	Form: Empty Back	8%	9	Rush 4	49.9%	28	5 DB	69%	8	Avg Box (Off)	5.99	32
Runs, second-long	30%	16	Pers: 3+ WR	77%	2	Rush 5	26.1%	9	6+ DB	3%	22	Avg Box (Def)	6.42	3
Runs, power sit.	54%	19	Pers: 4+ WR	2%	14	Rush 6+	9.3%	7	CB by Sides	84%	12	Offensive Pace	30.06	17
Runs, behind 2H	25%	17	Pers: 2+ TE/6+ OL	22%	26	Sacks by LB	16.7%	22	DB Blitz	13%	9	Defensive Pace	30.44	20
Pass, ahead 2H	49%	13	Shotgun/Pistol	86%	2	Sacks by DB	5.1%	18	Hole in Zone	8%	7	Go for it on 4th	1.07	15

One of our most surprising findings in recent years is that there seems to be no year-to-year consistency in which teams are better or worse when using play-action, and the Dolphins may be the best example from 2013. We thought Miami might be an exception because the Dolphins were far better in both 2012 and 2013 when using play-action. But in 2014, the Dolphins had roughly the same yards per pass with and without play-action, and a much better DVOA without (27.9%, eighth) than with (-4.0%, 28th). ☜ In 2013, 40 percent of running back carries for Miami came out of two-back sets. Last year, that dropped to just 3.6 percent. Only Philadelphia used two-back sets less often, which makes sense since Miami offensive coordinator Bill Lazor had come over from the Eagles. ☜ Although the Dolphins' run defense overall was average, they had a league-worst 11.8% DVOA against the run when opponents spread things out with three or more wide receivers, and ranked 30th with 5.44 yards allowed per carry.

Passing

Player	DYAR	DVOA	Plays	NtYds	Avg	YAC	C%	TD	Int
R.Tannehill	630	4.1%	637	3713	5.8	4.8	66.7%	27	12

Rushing

Player	DYAR	DVOA	Plays	Yds	Avg	TD	Fum	Suc
L.Miller	246	17.8%	216	1099	5.1	8	2	57%
D.Thomas*	34	11.3%	44	168	3.8	2	1	57%
R.Tannehill	51	11.4%	41	323	7.9	1	3	-
D.Williams	-2	-9.7%	36	122	3.4	0	0	47%
K.Moreno*	50	26.9%	31	148	4.8	1	0	65%

Receiving

Player	DYAR	DVOA	Plays	Ctch	Yds	Y/C	YAC	TD	C%
M.Wallace*	221	11.8%	115	67	864	12.9	3.5	10	58%
J.Landry	102	-0.8%	112	84	760	9.0	5.1	5	75%
B.Hartline*	77	2.6%	63	39	485	12.4	3.5	2	62%
B.Gibson*	-56	-27.3%	51	29	295	10.2	3.8	1	57%
R.Matthews	-3	-14.5%	23	13	138	10.6	3.5	2	57%
K.Stills	285	30.3%	84	63	931	14.8	3.0	3	77%
C.Clay*	2	-6.9%	84	58	605	10.4	4.4	3	69%
D.Sims	42	11.1%	36	24	284	11.8	4.6	2	67%
J.Cameron	-34	-17.5%	48	24	424	17.7	7.0	2	50%
L.Miller	9	-10.7%	52	38	262	6.9	6.1	1	73%
D.Williams	90	40.1%	27	21	187	8.9	7.2	1	78%
D.Thomas*	37	19.7%	19	13	121	9.3	9.4	0	68%

Offensive Line

Player	Pos	Age	GS	Snaps	Pen	Sk	Pass	Run	Player	Pos	Age	GS	Snaps	Pen	Sk	Pass	Run
Samson Satele*	C	31	16/16	1075	5	3.5	14.5	8.5	Shelley Smith*	G	28	11/3	359	3	2.0	7.0	4.0
Ja'Wuan James	RT	23	16/16	1038	10	6.0	25.5	10.5	Jason Fox	OT	27	9/2	214	2	0.0	5.5	1.0
Mike Pouncey	RG	26	12/12	771	4	4.0	8.0	3.5	J.D. Walton	C	28	16/16	1118	5	1.0	7.5	12.0
Daryn Colledge*	LG	34	13/13	740	4	5.0	10.5	5.0	Jeff Linkenbach	G/T	28	16/3	219	2	2.5	6.8	0.0
Dallas Thomas	G/T	26	14/9	673	3	7.0	18.5	3.0	Jacques McClendon	G	28	13/3	207	2	0.5	3.0	4.0
Branden Albert	LT	31	9/9	543	4	2.0	5.5	4.0									

Year	Yards	ALY	Rk	Power	Rk	Stuff	Rk	2nd Lev	Rk	Open Field	Rk	Sacks	ASR	Rk	Short	Long	F-Start	Cont.
2012	4.15	3.93	21	63%	17	18%	11	1.14	17	0.76	17	37	6.8%	18	14	14	14	42
2013	3.83	3.62	28	56%	27	21%	27	1.00	23	0.64	19	58	8.6%	30	24	8	9	29
2014	4.63	4.06	9	63%	17	18%	12	1.42	1	0.82	9	46	6.9%	19	23	11	20	26
2014 ALY by direction:			Left End 2.29 (31)			Left Tackle 4.01 (10)			Mid/Guard 4.41 (2)			Right Tackle 3.92 (16)			Right End 4.75 (8)			

Following up on a year where quarterback Ryan Tannehill was sacked a league-high 58 times amid the fallout from the Richie Incognito-Jonathan Martin bullying scandal, the Dolphins' offensive line underwent a massive overhaul last offseason, with Miami acquiring premier left tackle Branden Albert in free agency and using a first-round pick on Ja'Wuan James. As a result, the Dolphins had five new starters to open the year (Mike Pouncey returned to the starting lineup following hip surgery in October), and not surprisingly, things went from awful to not-so-bad. Even with some positional shuffling because of injury, the offensive line cut down on the sacks, and was able to provide some stability for Bill Lazor's offense. The pass protection remained middling overall, though that still represented a big uptick from 2013. On the other hand, Lazor's system drastically increased Miami's rushing efficiency, as evidenced by the team's massive leap in adjusted line yards.

Provided Pouncey and Albert can stay healthy—the latter went down last November with a season-ending ACL tear—this can be a good group in 2015. In part because of the injuries, James became the eighth offensive lineman in Dolphins history to start all 16 games as a rookie, and while he had a shockingly high blown block rate (one for every 28.8 snaps, 66th among 71 ranked tackles), more experience should lead to improvement this season. There's still some question as to whether or not Albert will be healthy enough to start the season-opener, which would allow the Dolphins to move James back to his natural right tackle position. Pouncey remains an imposing presence in the middle. Of the six—of all the Miami offensive linemen who finished the year with 500 or more snaps, he had the best blown-block rate, one every 67 snaps, despite playing out of position at right guard. He'll move back to his natural center spot, where he posted the position's third-best snaps per blown block rate (224.8) back in 2013. The questions for this group are at guard: Daryn Colledge (retired) and Shelley Smith (free agency) have left South Florida, and as a result, youngsters Dallas Thomas, Jamil Douglas and Billy Turner are all in the mix in 2015. In the wake of spring practices, it appears Douglas (a fourth-round rookie out of Arizona State) and Thomas are battling for the left guard job, while second-year lineman Turner has the edge at right guard. The Dolphins also brought in a lot of veteran depth this offseason, but they certainly hope they don't have to give actual starts to guys like Jeff Linkenbach and Jacques McClendon.

Defensive Front Seven

Defensive Line	Age	Pos	G	Snaps	Plays	TmPct	Rk	Stop	Dfts	BTkl	Runs	St%	Rk	RuYd	Rk	Sack	Hit	Hur	Dsrpt
						Overall						**vs. Run**				**Pass Rush**			
Jared Odrick*	28	DT	16	807	34	4.2%	55	26	8	3	25	76%	59	2.1	42	1.0	8	6.5	5
Earl Mitchell	28	DT	16	536	34	4.2%	55	31	11	2	29	93%	5	1.0	10	2.0	0	6.5	1
Ndamukong Suh	28	DT	16	851	56	7.1%	11	49	26	3	40	85%	22	1.0	8	8.5	11	16.0	3

Edge Rushers	Age	Pos	G	Snaps	Plays	TmPct	Rk	Stop	Dfts	BTkl	Runs	St%	Rk	RuYd	Rk	Sack	Hit	Hur	Dsrpt
						Overall						**vs. Run**				**Pass Rush**			
Olivier Vernon	25	DE	16	838	46	5.6%	31	33	13	5	36	69%	63	2.9	60	6.5	7	18.5	0
Cameron Wake	33	DE	16	756	41	5.0%	45	32	16	4	23	70%	61	3.0	65	11.5	12	25.5	1
Randy Starks*	32	DT	15	540	29	3.8%	70	24	12	2	19	89%	9	0.8	4	4.5	1	7.0	1
Derrick Shelby	26	DE	15	418	27	3.5%	69	22	7	3	22	82%	22	2.0	25	3.0	0	11.0	0
Dion Jordan	25	DE	10	221	14	2.7%	--	9	3	0	8	50%	--	5.0	--	1.0	1	2.5	0

Linebackers	Age	Pos	G	Snaps	Plays	TmPct	Rk	Stop	Dfts	BTkl	Sack	Hit	Hur	Runs	St%	Rk	RuYd	Rk	Tgts	Suc%	Rk	AdjYd	Rk	PD	Int
Jelani Jenkins	23	OLB	15	899	108	14.1%	33	59	15	6	3.5	2	3	68	62%	51	5.3	83	26	55%	19	6.3	31	1	0
Koa Misi	28	MLB	11	572	65	11.6%	49	33	11	7	1.0	3	2.5	41	68%	27	3.1	31	11	56%	--	4.8	--	0	0
Jason Trusnik*	31	ILB	16	393	40	4.9%	--	26	5	2	0.0	0	2	29	76%	--	2.4	--	11	34%	--	9.0	--	1	1
Philip Wheeler*	31	OLB	15	379	45	5.9%	--	30	5	1	0.0	0	1.5	33	73%	--	2.8	--	15	47%	--	10.7	--	0	0

Year	Yards	ALY	Rk	Power	Rk	Stuff	Rk	2nd Level	Rk	Open Field	Rk	Sacks	ASR	Rk	Short	Long
2012	3.88	3.85	11	64%	18	21%	10	1.04	5	0.63	9	42	6.3%	19	15	14
2013	4.25	4.24	25	64%	14	15%	28	1.20	28	0.58	13	42	6.8%	16	14	13
2014	4.12	3.85	15	65%	19	21%	10	1.08	11	0.80	20	39	7.5%	8	19	5
2014 ALY by direction:		Left End 3.32 (9)			Left Tackle 3.24 (9)			Mid/Guard 3.84 (12)			Right Tackle 4.28 (20)				Right End 4.32 (24)	

It will be interesting to see what sort of impact Ndamukong Suh will have on Miami's defensive front seven in 2015. There's no question he can be a truly disruptive presence, and his 26 defeats last year were the second-most of any interior defender last year (tops among non-Wattian mortals). However, he needs to continue trying to dial down his occasionally reckless play and penchant for taking bad if he wants to be the once-in-a-generation defensive tackle the Dolphins are paying him to be.

Regardless, Suh's presence—combined with the likes of edge rushers Cameron Wake and Olivier Vernon—means the Dolphins will be one of seven teams to trot out three "front seven" defenders who finished the 2014 season with 16 or more hurries. On the edges. Wake can still be a terrifying presence, and he notched his fifth straight year of at least 20 hurries in 2014. At 33, he might need to transition more into a situational role in the not-too-distant future, though those plans are likely on hiatus for at least one more year following Dion Jordan's year-long PED suspension. On the other side, Vernon is a good complementary player who doesn't offer the same flashy stats as Wake, but is a durable presence who still gets after the quarterback.

It's a good thing that the front looks so talented, because Miami's linebackers are a relatively average, anonymous group. In many spots, the current regime is paying the price for the sins of Jeff Ireland, but maybe no more so than at linebacker. In March 2013, the ex-GM signed Dannell Ellerbe and Philip Wheeler to sizable deals (Ellerbe got a five-year, $34.75 million deal, while Wheeler was gifted with a five-year, $26 million contract), but both turned out to be horrible gaffes. This offseason, the Dolphins dealt Ellerbe to the Saints and cut Wheeler, and started the process of rebuilding the position. Jelani Jenkins took advantage of an opportunity on the weak side after Ellerbe went down early in the year with a hip injury, and ended up leading the Miami linebackers in almost every major category in 2014. He showed a nice ability to work in coverage and get after the passer as needed. On the strong side, it certainly appeared that Chris McCain was going to be a nice complement at the start of 2014, as he blocked a punt and produced an important sack in the opener against the Patriots. However, he was dogged by injury the rest of the way, and produced little down the stretch. He'll get another chance in 2015; behind him is Spencer Paysinger, who signed a one-year deal to move from one unimpressive linebacker group (the Giants) to another. Former part-timer Koa Misi moved into the middle last year, where Kelvin Sheppard also will figure into the mix as well. While rebuilding the Miami linebacking corps will take a few years, the short-term plan is to hope Jenkins can build on his good sophomore season and that the Dolphins can get at least one other player currently on the roster to step forward and make the most of his opportunity.

Defensive Secondary

Secondary	Age	Pos	G	Snaps	Plays	TmPct	Rk	Stop	Dfts	BTkl	Runs	St%	Rk	RuYd	Rk	Tgts	Tgt%	Rk	Dist	Suc%	Rk	AdjYd	Rk	PD	Int
Brent Grimes	32	CB	16	1013	68	8.3%	41	30	12	9	14	64%	8	5.6	29	83	23.5%	37	13.9	49%	48	8.1	43	12	5
Louis Delmas	28	FS	13	834	66	9.9%	40	29	7	5	42	52%	17	6.3	33	12	4.1%	1	10.5	39%	63	6.7	27	2	1
Jimmy Wilson*	29	FS	14	781	59	8.3%	54	19	9	12	19	47%	25	7.7	51	35	12.9%	65	9.7	43%	60	8.5	54	3	1
Reshad Jones	27	SS	12	756	86	14.0%	4	35	13	4	50	50%	20	6.7	38	22	8.4%	37	11.7	58%	25	4.9	6	6	3
Cortland Finnegan*	31	CB	12	704	52	8.5%	39	22	8	7	7	57%	16	5.4	27	50	20.3%	18	12.6	46%	56	9.9	70	7	0
Jamar Taylor	25	CB	12	293	29	4.7%	--	12	7	4	5	80%	--	1.6	--	38	37.4%	--	13.0	52%	--	5.7	--	1	0
Brice McCain	29	CB	14	600	31	4.8%	77	15	9	3	8	75%	3	2.3	1	38	15.7%	1	11.1	50%	42	7.6	33	6	3
Zack Bowman	31	CB	16	450	25	3.1%	--	12	4	2	13	38%	--	7.2	--	33	21.6%	--	20.1	72%	--	5.1	--	6	2

Year	Pass D Rank	vs. #1 WR	Rk	vs. #2 WR	Rk	vs. Other WR	Rk	vs. TE	Rk	vs. RB	Rk
2012	17	5.2%	19	10.0%	25	-2.4%	14	-3.4%	13	22.9%	28
2013	12	-12.6%	7	11.9%	25	-39.3%	1	24.5%	29	4.6%	17
2014	16	5.9%	21	-13.4%	8	29.1%	30	-16.5%	5	15.5%	25

This might be the year Brent Grimes hits his expiration date. He turns 32 in July, and while Grimes is competitive and durable, our charting stats raise questions about his ability at this stage of his career. Grimes bounced back slightly from a subpar 2013, but it was still a far cry from 2012, when he ranked third in adjusted success rate and second in adjusted yards per pass. Analysis we ran on our website this spring found that Grimes was among the 10 worst No. 1 corners in 2014 based on both metrics. Additionally, quarterbacks went after him more, as Grimes saw his estimated target percentage rise from 20.4 percent two years ago to 23.5 percent last season. Our three-year defensive similarity scores compare Grimes to a number of cornerbacks who were nearing the end in their early thirties, including Fernando Bryant (2005-2007), Fakhir Brown (2005-2007) and former Dolphin Andre' Goodman (2007-2009).

There are other questions in the secondary, including who is going to line up opposite Grimes. After a good spring, the leader heading into camp is Jamar Taylor, a 2013 second-round pick out of Boise State who contributed little during his first two injury-plagued seasons. Health has also been an issue for Will Davis, selected out of Utah State one round after Taylor in 2013; Davis played only five games as a rookie and then tore his ACL in the middle of his second season. Another possible starter is veteran Brice McCain, signed away from Pittsburgh in free agency. McCain started a career-high nine games last year, but he's definitely better covering slot receivers; even if he technically ends up as the starter, he'll be moving inside in the nickel. McCain is the poster boy for the year-to-year inconsistency of our cornerback charting numbers. He had some of the best metrics in the league in 2011, then some of the worst in 2012. Then 2013 was a mix (strong in yards per pass, poor in success rate). Last year, he was very middle of the road except for the very strange fact that we somehow measured him as the least-targeted cornerback in the league once we adjusted for snaps played. For example, McCain played 37 snaps against the Bengals in Week 14 and was targeted once, partly because Andy Dalton spent the whole game going after Ike Taylor. But even when Taylor stopped playing, opponents didn't throw at McCain. He played 65 snaps against the Chiefs in Week 16 and was only targeted three times. It was bizarre.

At safety, the big question is whether Louis Delmas can ever stay healthy, and whether it just makes sense to plan ahead for Delmas to miss time. Delmas is coming off a December torn ACL. Considering that he came out of college with concerns about a degenerative knee condition and also experienced recurrent knee issues in Detroit, it's fair to have concern about his availability. If Delmas is out again, his only backups are fifth-round rookie Cedric Thompson (Minnesota) and assorted practice-squadders, unless the Dolphins want to consider a position change for one of their young cornerbacks. The strong safety spot belongs to Reshad Jones, an underrated talent who was frequently around the ball (he was fourth among all safeties by being part of 14 percent of his team's defensive plays) and had one of the best broken-tackle rates of any defensive back in the league at just 4.9 percent.

Special Teams

Year	DVOA	Rank	FG/XP	Rank	Net Kick	Rank	Kick Ret	Rank	Net Punt	Rank	Punt Ret	Rank	Hidden	Rank
2012	0.4%	14	-4.9	27	0.5	16	7.4	6	-2.8	20	2.0	12	3.7	7
2013	-2.4%	23	-10.9	28	0.5	15	-6.1	28	9.4	5	-4.6	24	11.9	3
2014	-6.1%	32	-8.8	31	-12.6	32	0.1	15	-4.3	22	-4.8	26	15.3	2

The Dolphins had some really good individual performances on special teams last season: Jarvis Landry averaged 28.1 yards per kick return, fourth-best in the NFL, and Miami ended up with six blocked kicks—four punts and two field goals. So why did they finish dead last in special-teams DVOA?

First of all, the Dolphins were awful in a number of areas. The Dolphins had two of their own field goals blocked, and Caleb Sturgis only connected on 78 percent of his attempts overall (29-of-37). He was closer to average on kickoffs, but the coverage team was horrible, allowing 28.3 yards per kick return (28th in the NFL, excluding squibs and onside kicks). Punter Brandon Fields was mediocre, a big fall from when he led the league in gross punt value in 2013. Meanwhile, Landry couldn't hold onto the ball. He fumbled away two kick returns and had a fumble and three muffs on punt returns.

As for the Dolphins' own blocked kicks, those get to the issue of what we consider "non-predictive" plays. Blocking a punt or a field goal is not necessary a product of luck. It usually requires good scheming and someone making an impressive play. However, blocking a kick is essentially statistical noise; it doesn't predict that the team will block more kicks in the future, because the sample size is so small. (This works both ways; our numbers consider Sturgis' blocked field goals no different from the ones he just plain missed.) But wait, there are more statistical anomalies involving the Miami special teams last season. Did you notice the Dolphins ranking second in "hidden" value last year? Opposing kickers missed eight field goals against the Dolphins in 2014—not just the two blocks but also six flat-out misses, including a 33-yard miss from Brandon McManus *in Denver*.

The bottom line on all this is that Miami is going to be seeing a ton of regression towards the mean on special teams in 2015. The Dolphins aren't going to block six kicks again, and opponents aren't going to miss as many field goals, but the flip side is that Landry isn't going to fumble six returns and Sturgis should be better—or lose his job. The Dolphins are going to have a higher special-teams DVOA in 2015, but without those big plays that DVOA doesn't measure, it may not actually lead to more wins.

Minnesota Vikings

2014 Record: 7-9	**Total DVOA:** -8.7% (25th)	**2015 Mean Projection:** 8.5 wins	**On the Clock (0-4):** 7%
Pythagorean Wins: 7.5 (19th)	**Offense:** -7.4% (22nd)	**Postseason Odds:** 41.8%	**Mediocrity (5-7):** 29%
Snap-Weighted Age: 26.2 (27th)	**Defense:** 4.3% (23rd)	**Super Bowl Odds:** 6.8%	**Playoff Contender (8-10):** 41%
Average Opponent: -1.6% (18th)	**Special Teams:** 3.0% (10th)	**Proj. Avg. Opponent:** 3.2% (5th)	**Super Bowl Contender (11+):** 23%

2014: September storm clouds give way to sunny post-Thanksgiving days.

2015: They're real, but are they spectacular?

If you're just now looking for a seat on the Minnesota Vikings bandwagon, tickets have been sold out for months. Behind a wave of young talent and a promising head coach-quarterback combination entering its second season, the Vikings are the 2015 version of that annual NFL tradition: the team everyone projects to reach the postseason just to be "trendy."

We shouldn't leap too far on the jump-to-conclusions mat, of course. It's hard to label a team the hot up-and-comer when it still posted a negative DVOA last season and ranked 25th overall, just one spot above where Minnesota sat after posting a 5-10-1 record in 2013. And while the core is young and highly talented, the overall roster was not especially young last year. Minnesota ranked 17th in snap weighted age and has actually gotten older the past two seasons after ranking 31st in 2012 with a snap weighted age of 25.5.

On the other hand, while those already reserving playoff tickets might want to slow down, we shouldn't dampen the enthusiasm too much. The Vikings ended last season 18th in weighted DVOA, illustrating clear progress, and were a blocked 26-yard field goal and blocked punt away from finishing the season on a five-game winning streak. Minnesota spent the year integrating a rookie quarterback while staving off a huge off-field distraction that also blew a giant hole in the middle of the roster. So it's plausible that the strong finish was more indicative of the team's talent and future than the overall 16-game picture. Our projections certainly think so, forecasting this to be the best Minnesota team since Brett Favre's last stand in 2009. Every year, Football Outsiders runs a draft report card report online where we aggregate draft grades from the interwebs and average out the GPAs to see the overall perception surrounding each team's draft class. General manager Rick Spielman has garnered a top-five GPA each of the past three seasons. Seven of his first- or second-rounders are in the projected starting lineup for 2015, as the Vikings have been unafraid to throw their premium prospects into the fire.

The leader of that septet is Teddy Bridgewater, whose development is clearly the highest priority of the Vikings' short-term future. Bridgewater was the most composed and pro-ready prospect in last year's erratic quarterback class, which was the prevailing opinion until pro day hullabaloo caused him to slip to the 32nd pick. FO's Matt Waldman had Bridgewater as his top-ranked quarterback in his *2014 Rookie Scouting Portfolio*, while the QBASE projection system also pegged Bridgewater at the top of his class. We say this less to plug our stats and writers and more to illustrate how both the numbers and tape agreed on Bridgewater more than any of his rookie quarterback peers. The Louisville product experienced plenty of struggles typical of rookie signal-callers, most notably his issues with pressure. Bridgewater's -102.8% DVOA under pressure ranked 32nd out of 37 qualifying quarterbacks, and his 1.8 net yards per pass under pressure ranked 34th. Norv Turner dialed back his vertically oriented passing game, both to simplify Bridgewater's reads and to protect the rookie from an offensive line that conceded eight sacks in his second start and five in his third. Of Bridgewater's 402 pass attempts, 53 were designed screens, often as part of run-pass option packaged plays. That doesn't include the myriad checkdowns Bridgewater threw to running backs Matt Asiata or Jerick McKinnon, who combined for 104 pass targets. Taken as a whole, Bridgewater's rookie year might not appear particularly promising.

And yet, despite injuries and underachievement thinning out the skill positions and offensive line, the Vikings offense still experienced a noticeable second-half leap. After posting a -14.1% DVOA through Week 9, 30th in the league, Minnesota's 1.9% offensive DVOA in Weeks 10-17 ranked 12th. The running game was surprisingly a top-10 unit all season (more on that later), but the passing game jumped from a -20.3% DVOA in the first half of the year (31st overall) to 4.1% DVOA in the second half (17th). That's not necessarily a huge deal on its own, considering that Matt Cassel and Christian Ponder started half of Minnesota's first eight games. However, while Bridgewater's total DYAR would portray him as one of the 10 worst quarterbacks from last season, he accrued 126 DYAR during that aforementioned five-game closing stretch, which ranked him 11th over that span.

Slapping the franchise quarterback label on Bridgewater based on a strong finish feels a little presumptuous, however. Rookie seasons are all about development, but the desire to see progress can also foster overreactions to any quarterback who can walk, talk and take a snap from under center without collapsing like a baby deer. Going back to 2000, 25 quarterbacks have started at least 12 games their rookie seasons, like Bridgewater did in 2014. Eleven of those players, including Bridgewater, improved their DVOA in the second half of the

2015 Vikings Schedule

Week	Opp.	Week	Opp.	Week	Opp.
1	at SF (Mon.)	7	at DET	13	SEA
2	DET	8	at CHI	14	at ARI (Thu.)
3	SD	9	STL	15	CHI
4	at DEN	10	at OAK	16	NYG
5	BYE	11	GB	17	at GB
6	KC	12	at ATL		

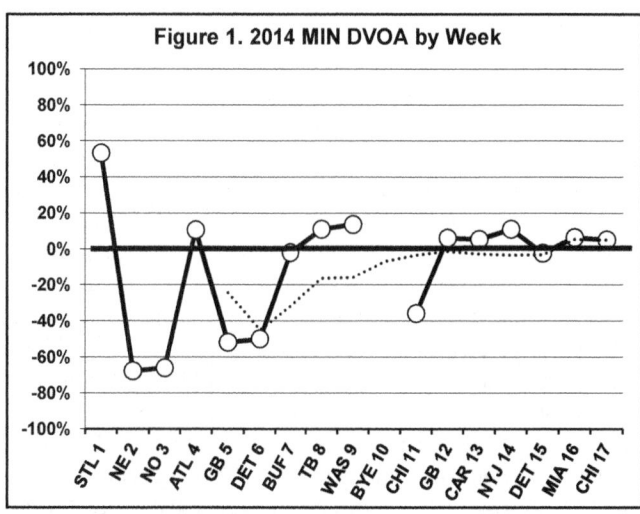

Figure 1. 2014 MIN DVOA by Week

season, if we split the season into Weeks 1-9 and Weeks 10-17 (Table 1). However, the "improvers" didn't actually fare much better than the "regressors" in their sophomore seasons. The overall average gets anchored down by Chris Weinke's atrocious 2002 season, but even excluding Weinke, the "improvers" average -1.3% DVOA in their second seasons, which isn't significantly more promising than the -3.9% DVOA averaged by the "regressors." Moreover, there are massive busts (Blaine Gabbert, Joey Harrington) and big hits (Andrew Luck, Russell Wilson) on both lists, so it doesn't appear as if second-half improvement is really the golden ticket into the franchise quarterback factory.

However, we also cannot dismiss Bridgewater's improvement with his greatest weakness, his deep-ball accuracy. Over his first seven starts, Bridgewater compiled 77 DYAR on passes we charted as deep, with three touchdowns to two interceptions. Conversely, during the last five starts, Bridgewater garnered 235 DYAR on deep passes and tossed three touchdowns with no picks. There's danger of reading too much into this, as we're focusing on a small sample within a small sample. The good stretch came over a grand total of 18 passes. And though two of his five opponents were top-10 pass defenses by DVOA (Detroit and Carolina), his touchdowns convenient-

ly came against the other teams, one each against the Jets, Dolphins, and Bears. However, apart from his apparently Lilliputian hand size, Bridgewater's deep ball was the most popular criticism during his pre-draft browbeating. It's only fair to point out that progress, while also recognizing that he did not suddenly morph into John Elway. Moreover, Bridgewater's deep-ball success coincided with Charles Johnson stealing a starting spot from Cordarrelle Patterson, who caught just three of his 10 deep targets. With speed merchant Mike Wallace arriving via offseason trade, one could reasonably argue that the combination of Bridgewater's development and receiver upgrades should help him sustain something close to the strong deep-ball form he exhibited at the end of 2014.

Of course, the player most meaningful to Bridgewater's development might be the guy he's replacing as the face of the Vikings franchise. Adrian Peterson was the purple elephant in the room that loomed over Minnesota's 2014 season, but the

Table 1. 1st Half/2nd Half Splits of Rookie Quarterbacks, 2000-2014

			Improved in 2nd Half							Regressed in 2nd Half		
Player	Team	Year	DVOA Rise Weeks 10-17	DVOA Full Season	DVOA Next Year	Player	Team	Year	DVOA Fall Weeks 10-17	DVOA Full Season	DVOA Next Year
T. Bridgewater	MIN	2014	21.3%	-16.9%	?	D. Carr	OAK	2014	-18.5%	-5.3%	?
R. Wilson	SEA	2012	41.5%	19.7%	15.6%	B. Bortles	JAC	2014	-15.4%	-33.1%	?
R. Griffin	WAS	2012	25.3%	16.6%	-13.1%	M. Glennon	TB	2013	-8.6%	-7.7%	-3.1%
B. Weeden	CLE	2012	2.5%	2.5%	-36.1%	G. Smith	NYJ	2013	-2.6%	-23.6%	-12.5%
B. Gabbert	JAC	2011	2.3%	-46.5%	-25.3%	A. Luck	IND	2012	-14.6%	-5.1%	4.6%
M. Ryan	ATL	2008	15.5%	25.3%	12.4%	R. Tannehill	MIA	2012	-7.9%	-19.4%	-9.8%
J. Flacco	BAL	2008	3.0%	-3.0%	8.4%	A. Dalton	CIN	2011	-3.3%	5.6%	-5.9%
V. Young	TEN	2006	32.0%	-6.3%	-12.3%	C. Newton	CAR	2011	-14.7%	0.8%	2.0%
C. Palmer	CIN	2004	40.8%	2.6%	33.4%	S. Bradford	STL	2010	-5.5%	-15.6%	-24.2%
B. Leftwich	JAC	2003	2.5%	5.5%	5.1%	M. Sanchez	NYJ	2009	-10.7%	-26.5%	-4.3%
C. Weinke	CAR	2001	3.6%	-25.5%	-70.5%	K. Orton	CHI	2005	-1.7%	-33.5%	DNP
						B. Roethlisberger	PIT	2004	-21.3%	31.7%	35.8%
						J. Harrington	DET	2002	-14.5%	-20.9%	-18.2%
						D. Carr	HOU	2002	-3.0%	-47.4%	-7.0%
Average			**16.9%**	**-0.9%**	**-8.2%**	**Average**			**-9.7%**	**-11.7%**	**-3.9%**

Minimum: 12 starts

jilted running back has since quit his passive-aggressive tango with the organization. Peterson's skeptics would point out that Minnesota's rushing DVOA actually improved from 5.8% in 2013 to 6.5% last season, good for fourth in the NFL. Some of that difference stems from shedding Ponder's -32.3% rushing DVOA from 2013, but Bridgewater's -8.5% DVOA on the ground was also nothing to write home about. Given that two of Minnesota's starting offensive linemen, Brandon Fusco and Phil Loadholt, suffered season-ending injuries, it's tempting to suggest that the McKinnon-Asiata timeshare could make Peterson redundant to the team's long-term plans.

But that view severely discounts the effect Peterson has on how opposing defensive coordinators game plan for Minnesota. We certainly can't reach that conclusion without first seeing what Peterson can do in Turner's power-run scheme. The longtime offensive coordinator has coached a trio of rushing champs in Emmitt Smith, Ricky Williams, and LaDainian Tomlinson; if he could prod a top-10 DVOA rookie season from the converted college quarterback McKinnon, what could Turner do with Peterson? Though his 2013 season (25th in DYAR, 26th in DVOA) was nothing like his historic 2012, there are indications that the 30-year-old veteran should thrive in the new offense. Most notably, the Vikings became much more of a shotgun-oriented offense last year, lining up in the gun on 64 percent of snaps, close to the NFL average. That's a big leap from 2013, when Minnesota was in shotgun just 44 percent of the time, fourth-lowest in the league. When you picture Peterson in your mind, he's running out of the I-formation behind (the now-departed) Jerome Felton, but he also helped Minnesota post a league-high 28.3% DVOA on shotgun runs in 2013. Only the Colts came within a yard of the Vikings' 6.7 yards per shotgun carry that season. The Vikes were similarly successful in 2012 with an 11.0% DVOA on shotgun runs, ninth in the league.

Ideally, a pacified Peterson wreaks havoc in his return, while the 10-carry-per-game range maximizes McKinnon's effectiveness and keeps him healthy after he suffered a season-ending back injury last November. Asiata was 2014's Fantasy Vulture of the Year with his terrific success on the goal line, but outside the red zone he earned minus-2 DYAR. Minnesota has hinted at a more balanced Peterson-McKinnon split in 2015, which seems appropriate. It might come as a disappointment to Vikings fans that the KUBIAK projection for Peterson lines up largely with his 2013 season, rather than approximating his historic 2012 campaign. In truth, though, Peterson would be joining historic company if he does replicate that 2013 campaign. Since the merger, only 11 running backs over the age of 30 have accumulated as many carries (279) and rushing yards (1,266) in a single season as a 29-year-old Peterson did two years ago. Six of them—Barry Sanders, Walter Payton, Emmitt Smith, Curtis Martin, Tony Dorsett, and John Riggins—are in the Hall of Fame. Peterson will surely join them one day, but the Vikings aren't tethered to him despite the misguided notion that his July contract extension brought him long-term security. All of Peterson's fully guaranteed $13.4 million comes this year, and the Vikings can cut bait on him before free agency in either 2016 or 2017 and

walk away with no dead money on the cap. There's a popular narrative that Peterson's return will goose Bridgewater's development, and that might be true for this season. Beyond that, Minnesota will need to invest more dollars and picks into a still-mediocre receiving corps and relatively thin offensive line as they move beyond the Peterson era.

Fortunately, the Vikings should be able to help Bridgewater with a strong defensive foundation. As alluded to earlier, Minnesota was not a particularly young team by snap-weighted age last season, but that was mostly because of the offense. On defense, the Vikings' snap-weighted age of 25.9 was fourth-youngest in the league and a big dip for a franchise that had fielded one of the 12 oldest defenses in five of the six preceding seasons. That number could hold steady if rookie headliners Trae Waynes and Eric Kendricks earn larger roles than over-30 vets Terence Newman and Chad Greenway. Waynes and Kendricks would also give Minnesota seven defensive starters aged 28 or younger who were former first- or second-round picks, an absurd collection of premium young talent that would make everyone besides Nick Saban jealous. Green defenses don't need to be bad—both Super Bowl XLIX participants were among the league's younger defenses last season—but the youth didn't lead to great results in Mike Zimmer's first season at the helm. Unlike Bridgewater, the Vikings defense regressed after a strong start, falling from 10th in DVOA from Weeks 1-9 to 25th in the latter half of the season. The run defense was the primary culprit, as the Vikings finished with their worst DVOA ranking against the run since pre-Williams Wall days. Announcers seemed to constantly praise free-agent signee Linval Joseph, who manned the 1-technique as Minnesota's primary run-stuffer. Truthfully, though, Joseph has been a below-average run defender each of the past three seasons, and has only gotten worse. Take his progression in run stop rate: 72 percent in 2012 (44th among interior defenders), 64 percent in 2013 (79th), and 59 percent in 2014 (91st). His 2.5 average yards per tackle last season was the best of his career, and that was still a below-average mark. Joseph should not be the lone scapegoat here, but it's puzzling that he holds the perception of being Minnesota's best run defender.

Fortunately for the Vikings, defending the run just isn't as important as defending the pass, especially when you play both Aaron Rodgers and Matthew Stafford twice a year. Minnesota's pass defense tailed off, finishing 25th in DVOA from Weeks 10-17, but there's a strong base of rangy athleticism and speed on the back seven. Spielman has particularly emphasized the broad jump, with several of his highly drafted back seven players (Anthony Barr, Eric Kendricks, Xavier Rhodes, and Harrison Smith) all testing well in that particular measure of explosiveness. This defense is built to eat away the spacing that passing schemes crave and nullify the mismatches most offenses exploit. All that is dependent on players like Waynes, Kendricks, and Barr translating their tools into functional skills, of course, but the draft-and-develop culture that Zimmer came from in Cincinnati is clearly at work.

As the talent matures, Zimmer's system has done well to limit big plays. The Vikings ranked 12th in DVOA against deep passes, following the footsteps of a Bengals defense that ranked third in DVOA against deep passes in 2013 and 10th in 2012. Zimmer never employed a shutdown corner or star centerfield safety during that time (though Xavier Rhodes and George Iloka are/were close), and the coverage numbers only further support the notion that his system will concede yards, but not the important ones. Of the 16 qualifying defensive backs to play at least 500 snaps under Zimmer the past three seasons, 10 ranked higher at their position in success rate than they did in adjusted yards per target. This would suggest that the pass defenders are well-coached and will make risk-averse plays that keep the scoreboard operator idle, even if they don't always translate into sexy YouTube highlight reels.

The Vikings defense also performed unusually poorly in some situations that don't appear to hold much annual carryover. Minnesota ranked 29th in goal-to-go defense (27.1% DVOA), but considering that Jacksonville and San Diego were top-five defenses in that category, this doesn't seem particularly indicative of overall skill. Moreover, the Vikings struggled in late-and-close game situations, ranking 28th in defensive DVOA. That performance doesn't necessarily carry over into 2015, even though it obviously holds important implications for the outcomes of games. And to put the cherry on top, the Vikings only generated turnovers on 10.6 percent of drives last year, 24th in the league. Turnovers are notoriously fluky, and the law of averages would suggest more takeaways for the Vikings in 2015. So does all that speed and explosiveness Spielman has drafted.

The optimist will stump for the young defensive talent and buy into the hype portraying Minnesota as the next big thing. The cynic will point out that most of Minnesota's core players are simply recent high draft picks, which are speculative stocks that often get overhyped, while also pleading with Bob from HR to please shut up about how he was the first to say the Vikings are going to the playoffs this year. Team and player development patterns are rarely linear, both in the good and bad sense. At this time two years ago, another team was a trendy up-and-comer following up an impressive season from a new head coach-rookie quarterback duo. That duo was even more promising than the current Zimmer-Bridgewater partnership, because that team actually went to the postseason. Since then, it's been all downhill for the Washington Redskins, who already disposed of Mike Shanahan and are nearing the same breaking point with Robert Griffin III. Then again, maybe the 2014 Vikings go down as this generation's version of the 1992 Packers, who saw Brett Favre take over the reins three games into the season (just like Bridgewater) and lead Green Bay to a promising finish under first-year coach Mike Holmgren. All these teams—the 2014 Vikings, 2012 Redskins and 1992 Packers—finished with roughly similar overall DVOA figures, illustrating how drastically fortunes can change for a franchise still in the embryonic stages of championship contention.

Playing in the same division as Green Bay means playing on an uneven field, at least as long as Aaron Rodgers is in his prime. The Packers can overcome their recent track record of mediocre defensive drafting because they have the best quarterback in the game. The Vikings will need to be better at everything else. In spending top picks on premium positions, Spielman has significantly multiplied Minnesota's future upside since he took the job in 2012, while also creating a base of cost-controlled talent that allows Minnesota to avoid the salary cap conundrums of division rivals Detroit and Chicago. Bridgewater should soon be in position to post a season equal or superior to that of Matthew Stafford and Jay Cutler at roughly 10 percent of the cost. After finishing third in the NFC North last season, moving up one more spot in the pecking order isn't a difficult ask.

That last ascent is a doozy, though, and as long as the Vikes are playing for second in their own division, they will be fighting their way through the wild-card mosh pit simply to earn the right to play three road games en route to the Super Bowl. Our projections have Minnesota playing the league's fifth-toughest schedule, and it's important to remember that last year's baby steps came against an average schedule. The Vikings could be a better team in 2015 and finish with the same 7-9 record. In that case, we will likely still be talking about the Vikings at this time next year with the same kind of anticipation. The Vikings have had recent one-year playoff flashes in 2009 and 2012, but this feels like the organization's first sustainable long-term construction plan in eons. Don't jump off the bandwagon just because it might be a year late to its destination.

Sterling Xie

2014 Vikings Stats by Week

Wk	vs.	W-L	PF	PA	YDF	YDA	TO	Total	Off	Def	ST
1	at STL	W	34	6	355	318	2	53%	21%	-25%	7%
2	NE	L	7	30	217	292	-4	-68%	-53%	1%	-15%
3	at NO	L	9	20	247	396	0	-66%	-36%	30%	0%
4	ATL	W	41	28	558	411	2	11%	32%	28%	7%
5	at GB	L	10	42	299	320	-2	-52%	-46%	4%	-1%
6	DET	L	3	17	212	255	-3	-50%	-60%	-4%	7%
7	at BUF	L	16	17	276	373	2	-2%	-31%	-15%	14%
8	at TB	W	19	13	332	225	2	11%	11%	-5%	-5%
9	WAS	W	29	26	352	347	1	14%	16%	1%	-1%
10	BYE										
11	at CHI	L	13	21	243	468	1	-36%	-23%	10%	-2%
12	GB	L	21	24	308	362	-1	6%	11%	19%	14%
13	CAR	W	31	13	210	348	1	5%	-15%	-6%	14%
14	NYJ	W	30	24	411	410	0	11%	18%	0%	-7%
15	at DET	L	14	16	360	233	-2	-2%	5%	-2%	-9%
16	at MIA	L	35	37	357	493	1	6%	21%	31%	16%
17	CHI	W	13	9	311	264	-1	5%	-18%	-13%	10%

Trends and Splits

	Offense	Rank	Defense	Rank
Total DVOA	-7.4%	22	4.3%	23
Unadjusted VOA	-4.7%	22	4.4%	23
Weighted Trend	-2.6%	16	3.9%	23
Variance	8.9%	21	2.7%	2
Average Opponent	0.7%	19	0.4%	12
Passing	-10.5%	29	8.8%	19
Rushing	6.5%	4	-0.8%	25
First Down	-1.8%	18	-0.6%	18
Second Down	-21.5%	30	8.7%	27
Third Down	4.6%	16	6.5%	18
First Half	-9.3%	24	-1.0%	13
Second Half	-5.5%	21	10.1%	28
Red Zone	20.5%	6	2.3%	23
Late and Close	4.1%	15	10.9%	28

Five-Year Performance

Year	W-L	Pyth W	Est W	PF	PA	TO	Total	Rk	Off	Rk	Def	Rk	ST	Rk	Off AGL	Rk	Def AGL	Rk	Off Age	Rk	Def Age	Rk	ST Age	Rk
2010	6-10	6.0	6.5	281	348	-11	-13.9%	25	-15.1%	27	-2.5%	12	-1.4%	19	35.6	25	19.6	14	28.5	5	28.3	4	27.4	2
2011	3-13	5.3	4.6	340	449	-3	-22.2%	29	-10.2%	24	8.0%	23	-4.1%	27	20.5	8	28.3	19	27.7	10	27.3	14	26.4	15
2012	10-6	8.8	8.8	379	348	-1	2.0%	14	0.3%	15	3.1%	21	4.7%	5	10.4	3	18.5	8	25.5	31	27.2	12	25.5	28
2013	5-10-1	6.1	6.5	391	480	-12	-11.4%	26	-4.7%	21	10.5%	27	3.8%	6	21.4	8	32.5	21	26.6	19	27.1	12	25.8	24
2014	7-9	7.5	7.2	325	343	-1	-8.7%	25	-7.4%	22	4.3%	23	3.0%	10	39.0	23	17.1	3	26.7	17	25.9	29	25.6	28

2014 Performance Based on Most Common Personnel Groups

MIN Offense					MIN Offense vs. Opponents					MIN Defense					MIN Defense vs. Opponents			
Pers	Freq	Yds	DVOA	Run%	Pers	Freq	Yds	DVOA	Run%	Pers	Freq	Yds	DVOA	Pers	Freq	Yds	DVOA	
11	58%	5.7	8.0%	24%	Base	37%	4.5	-20.0%	57%	Base	38%	5.4	7.4%	11	53%	5.5	-2.9%	
12	24%	4.6	-14.2%	42%	Nickel	52%	5.6	6.4%	25%	Nickel	61%	5.7	2.2%	12	25%	6.2	13.4%	
21	8%	4.8	-28.6%	70%	Dime+	9%	6.2	10.8%	13%	Dime+	1%	3.5	-97.0%	21	9%	4.2	-3.8%	
22	6%	4.3	-16.7%	90%	Goal Line	2%	2.6	0.2%	80%	Goal Line	1%	0.8	32.7%	22	4%	3.3	-17.4%	
					Big	1%	10.6	104.1%	86%					20	2%	9.1	71.2%	

Strategic Tendencies

Run/Pass		Rk	Formation		Rk	Pass Rush		Rk	Secondary		Rk	Strategy		Rk
Runs, first half	38%	17	Form: Single Back	77%	12	Rush 3	1.3%	30	4 DB	26%	16	Play action	23%	11
Runs, first down	48%	16	Form: Empty Back	3%	29	Rush 4	69.0%	9	5 DB	73%	5	Avg Box (Off)	6.23	23
Runs, second-long	24%	28	Pers: 3+ WR	59%	18	Rush 5	22.2%	18	6+ DB	1%	25	Avg Box (Def)	6.27	16
Runs, power sit.	63%	8	Pers: 4+ WR	1%	21	Rush 6+	7.4%	16	CB by Sides	76%	21	Offensive Pace	30.70	19
Runs, behind 2H	24%	22	Pers: 2+ TE/6+ OL	33%	12	Sacks by LB	15.9%	24	DB Blitz	9%	20	Defensive Pace	30.64	25
Pass, ahead 2H	47%	18	Shotgun/Pistol	66%	12	Sacks by DB	7.3%	15	Hole in Zone	4%	24	Go for it on 4th	0.85	20

For the most part, Minnesota's pass/run ratios did not change without Adrian Peterson in the lineup, with one exception: second-and-long. The Vikings ran 44 percent of the time in second-and-long in 2013 (second in the NFL) but dropped to 24 percent (28th) in 2014. ☞ In 2013, roughly two-thirds (65 percent) of carries by Minnesota running backs came out of two-back sets. In 2014, that dropped to roughly one-third of carries (36 percent). Vikings backs gained 0.7 yards per carry more out of two-back sets, but with almost exactly the same DVOA as they had on runs from one-back sets. ☜ As a team, the Vikings were average throwing passes listed as either left or right, but the worst team in the league on passes listed in the middle of the field. However, three interceptions by Matt Cassel and Christian Ponder make up a big part of this number; Teddy Bridgewater was merely below average on passes up the middle, not horrendous. ☜ The Vikings fumbled 10 times on offense last year, but only lost the ball once. ☜ On first down, Minnesota ranked third in defensive DVOA on passes (-7.3%) but 31st on runs (5.2%), the only team in the NFL with a better DVOA rating against passes than runs. ☜ The Vikings' defense got killed on running back screens. They faced more than any team except Detroit and allowed 7.8 yards per pass with 42.3% DVOA (compared to NFL averages of 6.1 yards and 10.4% DVOA).

Passing

Player	DYAR	DVOA	Plays	NtYds	Avg	YAC	C%	TD	Int
T.Bridgewater	-159	-16.9%	436	2656	6.1	5.6	65.4%	14	11
M.Cassel*	-147	-40.4%	79	351	4.4	7.2	57.7%	4	4
C.Ponder*	-146	-57.5%	50	188	3.8	4.5	50.0%	0	2
S.Hill	*-31*	*-13.1%*	*248*	*1538*	*6.2*	*5.6*	*63.3%*	*8*	*6*

Rushing

Player	DYAR	DVOA	Plays	Yds	Avg	TD	Fum	Suc
M.Asiata	69	1.0%	164	570	3.5	9	1	52%
J.McKinnon	82	11.5%	113	538	4.8	0	0	42%
T.Bridgewater	8	-8.5%	40	220	5.5	1	0	-
J.Banyard	15	8.6%	21	88	4.2	0	0	52%
A.Peterson	5	-1.8%	21	75	3.6	0	0	43%
B.Tate*	1	-6.7%	13	38	2.9	0	0	38%
C.Patterson	53	47.6%	10	117	11.7	1	0	-
J.Wright	41	126.5%	5	71	14.2	0	0	-
D.Harris	*14*	*11.0%*	*16*	*64*	*4.0*	*0*	*0*	*56%*

Receiving

Player	DYAR	DVOA	Plays	Ctch	Yds	Y/C	YAC	TD	C%
G.Jennings*	125	5.0%	92	59	744	12.6	3.4	7	64%
C.Patterson	-64	-25.0%	67	33	384	11.6	4.8	1	49%
J.Wright	64	0.7%	62	42	588	14.0	7.8	2	68%
C.Johnson	-16	-16.2%	59	31	475	15.3	5.6	2	53%
A.Thielen	43	31.3%	13	8	137	17.1	4.3	1	62%
M.Wallace	*221*	*11.8%*	*115*	*67*	*864*	*12.9*	*3.5*	*10*	*58%*
C.Ford	32	6.8%	35	23	258	11.2	2.7	1	66%
K.Rudolph	17	0.0%	34	24	231	9.6	4.8	2	71%
R.Ellison	31	10.0%	26	19	208	10.9	8.3	1	73%
M.Asiata	-33	-23.9%	63	44	312	7.1	7.7	1	70%
J.McKinnon	-83	-53.1%	41	27	135	5.0	6.4	0	66%
J.Banyard	12	7.1%	11	9	62	6.9	7.9	0	82%

Offensive Line

Player	Pos	Age	GS	Snaps	Pen	Sk	Pass	Run	Player	Pos	Age	GS	Snaps	Pen	Sk	Pass	Run
Matt Kalil	LT	26	16/16	1023	11	12.5	27.8	5.5	Joe Berger	RG	33	16/9	612	1	3.0	8.0	0.5
John Sullivan	C	30	16/16	972	4	0.0	7.0	1.0	Vladimir Ducasse*	G	28	13/6	406	5	2.0	5.0	2.0
Charlie Johnson*	LG	31	14/14	863	1	3.5	11.8	2.0	Michael Harris	RT	27	12/5	362	1	7.0	7.3	1.0
Phil Loadholt	RT	29	11/11	715	3	4.0	19.5	3.5	Brandon Fusco	RG	26	3/3	170	1	0.0	0.0	0.5

Year	Yards	ALY	Rk	Power	Rk	Stuff	Rk	2nd Lev	Rk	Open Field	Rk	Sacks	ASR	Rk	Short	Long	F-Start	Cont.
2012	5.67	4.17	10	53%	30	24%	29	1.41	4	2.08	1	32	6.5%	16	7	15	14	48
2013	4.78	4.04	10	79%	2	20%	20	1.29	7	1.26	1	44	7.8%	23	14	16	11	34
2014	4.11	3.97	13	68%	10	15%	2	1.07	21	0.61	21	51	9.1%	27	16	12	16	28
2014 ALY by direction:		Left End 4.2 (12)			Left Tackle 3.75 (17)			Mid/Guard 4.1 (10)			Right Tackle 3.1 (28)				Right End 4.07 (14)			

It's tough to judge this unit by adjusted line yards or any other rushing metric, since any offensive line is going to look worse blocking for Matt Asiata instead of Adrian Peterson. Even if the Peterson saga had never occurred, though, this unit's performance likely would have regressed simply due to worse injury luck. The Vikings never started the same five-man group more than four consecutive weeks at any point, a far cry from the perfect continuity score they put up two seasons ago.

Pass protection was the line's real undoing. Vikings quarterbacks were under pressure on 29.8 percent of dropbacks, the sixth-highest rate in the league. (It dropped slightly, to 28.3 percent, if we only look at Teddy Bridgewater as quarterback.) The edge was particularly insecure, with Matt Kalil and Phil Loadholt forming a highly underachieving bookend pairing. Both experienced hellacious footwork struggles, exposing them to Catch-22 situations where they would either lose to simple speed rushes around the corner or overset and allow inside counter moves. Kalil was the dictionary definition of embattled last season, ranking 30th out of 32 qualified left tackles in snaps per blown block (30.7). We charted Kalil with 12.5 sacks allowed last season, when no other offensive lineman in the league allowed more than nine. It's been a puzzling fall for the former No. 4 overall pick, who was roughly average during his rookie campaign in 2012 (50.5 snaps per blown block). But there is cautious optimism after Kalil underwent arthroscopic surgery and received platelet-rich plasma injections in both knees this offseason, as the knee surgery he had during the 2014 offseason didn't prevent him from experiencing swelling during the season. Minnesota did pick up his fifth-year option, suggesting an organizational belief that injuries were culpable for his miserable two-year run. Hopefully Kalil rewards the Vikings' faith more so than Loadholt, whose pass protection has regressed since signing a four-year, $25 million deal during the 2013 offseason. A year after posting a slightly below-average rate of 44.4 snaps per blown block, Loadholt's rate of 31.1 snaps per blown block ranked 32nd among 39 qualified right tackles. Loadholt is still a competent run-blocker, and hopes to rebound a bit in 2014 after offseason surgery for a torn pectoral. But in drafting T.J. Clemmings (fourth round, Pitt) and Tyrus Thompson (sixth round, Oklahoma), the Vikings have put both their incumbent starters on notice.

At least the interior should anchor a strong running game, even with an unsettled right guard situation. Brandon Fusco is set to return from a torn pectoral that limited him to three games last season; it was apparently the injury of choice on the Minnesota line last year. Fusco forms one of the league's more underrated guard-center combinations alongside John Sullivan, but he'll be kicking over to the left side this year. Journeyman veterans Mike Harris and Joe Berger will compete for the starting right guard job if the rookie Clemmings isn't ready to play. In front of Peterson, Minnesota was a top-three ALY team in runs up the middle during both the 2012 and 2013 campaigns. Norv Turner's power-run schemes have always complemented his vertically based passing attacks, and with better health on the offensive line, an improved between-the-tackles rushing attack should theoretically have a positive domino effect for Bridgewater's development.

Defensive Front Seven

Defensive Line	Age	Pos	G	Snaps	Plays	TmPct	Rk	Stop	Dfts	BTkl	Runs	St%	Rk	RuYd	Rk	Sack	Hit	Hur	Dsrpt
						Overall						**vs. Run**				**Pass Rush**			
Linval Joseph	27	DT	16	728	48	5.7%	28	30	10	1	41	59%	91	2.5	57	3.0	6	4.5	1
Sharrif Floyd	24	DT	14	568	43	5.9%	25	32	15	2	32	72%	74	2.0	37	4.0	5	10.5	1
Tom Johnson	31	DT	16	440	22	2.6%	85	17	10	2	13	77%	53	2.6	65	6.5	6	7.5	0
Shamar Stephen	24	DT	16	402	23	2.7%	--	16	3	1	21	71%	--	2.7	--	0.0	1	1.5	0

Edge Rushers	Age	Pos	G	Snaps	Plays	TmPct	Rk	Stop	Dfts	BTkl	Runs	St%	Rk	RuYd	Rk	Sack	Hit	Hur	Dsrpt
						Overall						**vs. Run**				**Pass Rush**			
Everson Griffen	28	DE	16	967	61	7.3%	15	54	24	2	35	89%	7	2.1	33	12.5	15	20.5	2
Brian Robison	32	DE	16	906	26	3.1%	80	21	9	3	16	81%	26	2.6	45	4.5	8	26.0	3
Corey Wootton	28	DE	15	271	16	2.0%	--	9	1	0	14	50%	--	3.8	--	1.0	0	3.5	0

Linebackers	Age	Pos	G	Snaps	Plays	TmPct	Rk	Stop	Dfts	BTkl	Sack	Hit	Hur	Runs	St%	Rk	RuYd	Rk	Tgts	Suc%	Rk	AdjYd	Rk	PD	Int
						Overall					**Pass Rush**			**vs. Run**					**vs. Pass**						
Anthony Barr	23	OLB	12	776	73	11.6%	48	41	11	8	4.0	4	8.5	30	53%	76	3.6	55	35	51%	33	5.5	15	2	0
Chad Greenway	32	OLB	12	760	95	15.1%	24	47	13	6	1.0	5	5	59	49%	82	4.8	81	19	43%	50	7.3	48	1	0
Gerald Hodges	23	OLB	14	503	70	9.5%	66	49	13	8	0.5	1	4.5	38	63%	45	3.2	35	23	59%	13	5.0	9	5	1
Jasper Brinkley*	30	MLB	16	460	72	8.6%	73	35	4	3	1.0	0	0.5	54	56%	70	4.8	80	11	28%	--	10.0	--	0	0
Casey Matthews	*26*	*ILB*	*16*	*434*	*52*	*6.0%*	*--*	*26*	*6*	*6*	*1.5*	*1*	*4*	*38*	*61%*	*--*	*3.4*	*--*	*12*	*34%*	*--*	*9.8*	*--*	*0*	*0*

Year	Yards	ALY	Rk	Power	Rk	Stuff	Rk	2nd Level	Rk	Open Field	Rk	Sacks	ASR	Rk	Short	Long
2012	3.75	3.87	12	59%	12	24%	6	1.11	7	0.46	4	44	6.4%	16	9	21
2013	3.89	3.67	10	60%	9	23%	7	1.19	26	0.64	17	41	6.8%	17	12	17
2014	4.49	4.56	31	73%	26	14%	32	1.25	25	0.64	13	41	7.0%	12	18	13
2014 ALY by direction:		Left End 4.05 (23)			Left Tackle 5.12 (31)			Mid/Guard 4.49 (31)			Right Tackle 5.02 (30)			Right End 4.5 (30)		

A year ago, Mike Zimmer made this unit the focal point of his first offseason in Minnesota. With the under-28 quartet of Everson Griffen, Sharrif Floyd, Anthony Barr, and now Butkus Award-winning second-round pick Eric Kendricks, this unit may be fueling the Vikings bandwagon even more than Bridgewater. Griffen actually lived up to the five-year, $42.5 million deal that seemed above market value last offseason. The defensive end ranked fourth with 27 total knockdowns (sacks + hits), blowing away the 11 he accumulated his contract year. Playing more weakside wide-9 technique certainly helped Griffen's pass-rushing, but his 89 percent run stop rate, seventh among edge defenders, made him invaluable on a poor rush defense. Across from him, the eminently reliable Brian Robison shocked everyone… by cutting his signature ponytail in December. On the field, he continued to plug away at strongside end, posting an 81 percent run stop rate for the second consecutive season. The 32-year-old figures to make way for recent third-rounders Scott Crichton and Danielle Hunter at some point, though both are raw prospects who are unlikely to cut into Robison's heavy snap total this year. At defensive tackle, Linval Joseph and Floyd didn't create many disruptive plays with just 25 combined defeats, though Floyd did draw eight holding calls, tied for second-most in the league behind only Jason Pierre-Paul. Neither Joseph nor Floyd ranked in the top 70 in run stop percentage, regularly allowing offensive linemen to block down to the second level.

Linebackers were also a big reason why Minnesota's run defense had its worst DVOA since 2004. Battling through a fractured hand and ribs, Chad Greenway's 49 percent run stop rate was fifth-worst among qualified linebackers. The longtime starter sliced his base salary in half from $7 million to $3.4 million to stay on the roster, but even that amount is likely overpaying him at this point. Gerald Hodges and his 63 percent run stop rate should see more time in base packages next year, especially with two-down linebacker Jasper Brinkley off to Dallas. The Barr-Greenway nickel pairing had trouble shedding blocks all year, playing a big role in the run defense's decline. In fairness, Barr came labeled as a fairly raw prospect with just two collegiate seasons of defensive experience. Minnesota asked a lot by bestowing a three-down role on him right away, and the rookie did hold up well in pass coverage, allowing just 5.5 adjusted yards per attempt. The Vikings figure to similarly challenge the rangy Kendricks in his rookie year, with the hope that the former UCLA roommates harness their functional athleticism and three-down potential to develop into the fulcrum of this defense.

Defensive Secondary

Secondary	Age	Pos	G	Snaps	Plays	Overall TmPct	Rk	Stop	Dfts	BTkl	vs. Run Runs	St%	Rk	RuYd	Rk	vs. Pass Tgts	Tgt%	Rk	Dist	Suc%	Rk	AdjYd	Rk	PD	Int
Harrison Smith	26	FS	16	1070	100	11.9%	24	41	23	6	47	45%	30	5.3	18	30	8.1%	34	12.0	53%	42	8.2	47	9	5
Captain Munnerlyn	27	CB	16	1062	66	7.9%	49	26	11	4	16	44%	32	5.0	17	63	17.2%	4	10.9	47%	52	9.3	61	5	2
Xavier Rhodes	25	CB	16	1027	65	7.7%	53	28	13	4	15	33%	44	5.7	32	78	22.1%	25	15.2	57%	14	6.3	13	18	1
Robert Blanton	26	SS	15	948	108	13.7%	7	29	5	8	58	34%	46	7.2	45	21	6.3%	20	10.1	61%	17	7.3	35	3	1
Josh Robinson	24	CB	16	671	47	5.6%	75	15	6	3	5	60%	11	4.8	14	74	32.3%	76	16.4	49%	45	8.2	45	8	3
Terence Newman	37	CB	13	865	85	12.1%	2	40	16	6	19	58%	15	5.3	22	89	26.2%	59	11.7	52%	32	7.0	19	13	1

Year	Pass D Rank	vs. #1 WR	Rk	vs. #2 WR	Rk	vs. Other WR	Rk	vs. TE	Rk	vs. RB	Rk
2012	24	3.9%	18	38.6%	32	-8.7%	9	4.6%	22	18.4%	25
2013	30	5.1%	22	8.9%	22	44.8%	32	0.1%	15	15.2%	29
2014	19	11.7%	26	-22.3%	5	-15.2%	6	-2.0%	17	15.8%	26

With three first-round investments the past four years, expectations are high for the Vikings secondary. Two of these players, versatile safety Harrison Smith and physical cover cornerback Xavier Rhodes, are on the verge of maturing into blue-chippers. Though technically designated as a free safety, few safeties were as disruptive as Smith behind the line of scrimmage. The third-year pro accumulated 23 defeats, most among all defensive backs and a huge leap from the nine defeats he garnered in 2013. Minnesota might be better off letting Smith wreak havoc in the box full-time while playing single-high coverage. Of course, good centerfielders are in short supply, and though the Vikes waded into the Devin McCourty sweepstakes during free agency, there are worse fates than having a heat-seeking missile move around the field. It's unclear who Smith's partner will be, as Robert Blanton was unspectacular and tied for the team lead with eight missed tackles despite playing the fifth-highest snap total. Last year's third safety Andrew Sendejo is probably a better fit as a special-teamer, which could leave the job to 2014 sixth-rounder Antone Exum (Virginia Tech) or intriguing undrafted rookie Anthony Harris (Virginia), who received mid-round projections before durability concerns sent his stock plummeting.

Rhodes, meanwhile, is rapidly developing a stay-away reputation. Rhodes finished in the top 15 in adjusted yards per pass for the second straight year. He still needs to learn how to toe the line with his physicality; Rhodes picked up 12 penalties, nine of which were for defensive holding or pass interference, after just five total penalties in 2013. Still, the Vikings were pleased enough with Rhodes' development that he started shadowing top receivers like Alshon Jeffery by the end of the year. Curiously, Minnesota's pass defense DVOA was essentially the same on both the right side (with Rhodes) and the left side, where undersized corners Captain Munnerlyn and Josh Robinson typically played. Munnerlyn, who often moved to the slot in nickel, doesn't have a shutdown reputation, but he posted a top-10 adjusted target percentage (which adjusts targets for percentage of snaps played) for the second straight year in 2014. With the offseason cornerback additions, Munnerlyn should thrive in an exclusive slot role. The 5-foot-10 Robinson, on the other hand, might have his roster spot on life support after he was consistently victimized manning left corner in nickel packages. It was hard not to feel second-hand embarrassment during the Week 11 Chicago game, when the Bears targeted Robinson 16 times (!) and came away with 12 receptions and three touchdowns.

In his place will go first-rounder Trae Waynes, selected 11th overall out of Michigan State, or veteran addition Terence Newman. Waynes was the consensus top cornerback in this draft and resembles Rhodes as a long press cover corner who will need to become less handsy to succeed in the NFL. If he needs a season to refine his technique, the ancient Newman should still be adequate. His career appeared to be over following his demise in Dallas, but he revived his game under Zimmer in Cincinnati.

Special Teams

Year	DVOA	Rank	FG/XP	Rank	Net Kick	Rank	Kick Ret	Rank	Net Punt	Rank	Punt Ret	Rank	Hidden	Rank
2012	4.7%	5	9.5	2	2.5	11	7.9	5	4.0	12	-0.1	16	-3.4	23
2013	3.8%	6	-0.6	20	-15.4	32	22.4	1	0.6	17	11.8	3	-4.6	22
2014	3.0%	10	-3.6	25	6.0	7	5.5	5	3.4	9	3.7	10	7.2	5

There aren't many kicking environments worse than a Minnesota winter, so it's not shocking that Blair Walsh saw his field goal accuracy drop from 86.7 percent to 74.3 percent after moving outdoors. After missing just four field goals from under 50 yards during his first two seasons combined, Walsh missed five such kicks in 2014. That included a blocked 26-yarder in the Vikings' 16-14 loss at Detroit, his first career miss from under 30 yards. Though Walsh is in no danger of losing his job, five of his nine misses did come on the road, suggesting that the move outdoors wasn't entirely to blame. Our advanced metrics adjust for weather and altitude, and they suggest that Walsh's dropoff actually came before his second season, not his third.

However, Minnesota ranked in the top 10 in the other four elements of special teams other than placekicking. Punter Jeff Locke didn't have a particularly strong year, with below-average gross punt value, and his most memorable moment was a negative one: a blocked punt against Miami with 45 seconds left which led to the game-winning safety for the Dolphins. However, excellent coverage teams gave the Vikings positive net punting value and added value to Walsh's above-average kickoffs.

Cordarrelle Patterson seemingly regressed in every other way last season, so why not in kickoff returns too? After leading the league in points off kickoff returns in 2013, the disappointing sophomore only took 34 of Minnesota's 54 kickoffs in 2014, and he didn't get past the 50 on a single one of those returns. However, the Vikings benefited from an unusual number of squib kicks stemming from the combination of cold weather and residual fear of Patterson, giving them a sneaky leg up in field position. Even if we don't consider kicks in the final minute of a half, there were 11 instances when an opposing kicker bounced the kickoff so that someone other than Patterson fielded it before it even got to the Minnesota 10. The value of those squibs are reflected in the rating for kick returns listed above. Marcus Sherels had another strong year on punt returns, though not as strong as the year prior.

New England Patriots

2014 Record: 12-4	Total DVOA: 22.1% (4th)	2015 Mean Projection: 10.5 wins[1]	On the Clock (0-4): 1%
Pythagorean Wins: 11.8 (2nd)	Offense: 13.5% (6th)	Postseason Odds: 71.7%	Mediocrity (5-7): 11%
Snap-Weighted Age: 27.0 (10th)	Defense: -3.0% (12th)	Super Bowl Odds: 22.3%	Playoff Contender (8-10): 35%
Average Opponent: 1.5% (11th)	Special Teams: 5.7% (5th)	Proj. Avg. Opponent: -2.8% (25th)	Super Bowl Contender (11+): 52%

2014: Just when it seemed the boulder would again stop inches short of the hilltop, the most influential play in NFL history nudged it over.

2015: The secondary is going to be a lot worse, but everything else on this team may be a little better.

When Seattle snapped the ball with 26 seconds left in Super Bowl XLIX, the Patriots had by our estimates about a 12.6 percent chance of winning their fourth NFL championship. Five seconds later, their chances had risen to about 100 percent. That 87 percent swing makes Malcolm Butler's interception by far the most influential play in NFL history. Forget about finding a competitor in another sport, either. Even Jimmy Chitwood's shot against South Bend Central did not mean as much to Hickory High's championship hopes as Malcolm Butler's pick did to the Patriots' title chances.

Butler's Immaculate Interception epitomizes the knife's edge on which Super Bowls increasingly turn. His play came less than a minute after Jermaine Kearse's catch, which itself would have ranked as one of the five most influential plays ever if Seattle had won. By Brian Burke's Win Probability Calculator at AdvancedFootballAnalytics.com, New England's chances of winning fell from 75 percent to 38 percent after Kearse corralled the pass. That 37 percent change in the Patriots' probability of winning the Super Bowl eerily resembles the 39 percent drop that came with the Helmet Catch seven years earlier. The parallels between those two plays are almost enough to make a stats guy believe in fate. At the snap, the Seahawks had 1:14 left to erase their four-point deficit, the Giants 1:15. The Kearse catch went for 33 yards; the Helmet Catch went for 32.

So the recent Patriots have been a part of two of the top five most influential plays in NFL history, and a third misses out only by virtue of an even bigger play taking its place. That is the first rule of the Most Influential Plays list: to make the cut, a play has to be the most pivotal play in its own game (Table 1). Plays before the Super Bowl can count, but they have a tough time making the list because we are trying to find the plays that had the biggest impact on the eventual champion. Burke's calculator provides the game win probabilities except in a few situations right at the end of games where it does not work well. A play's SBD, or Super Bowl Delta, value is the change in Super Bowl win probability that the play caused. Bart Starr's sneak in the Ice Bowl, for example, has an SBD of 0.25 because it: A) increased Green Bay's chances of winning the NFL championship by about 0.35 from where they were at the snap, and B) the point spread gave the Packers about a 71 percent chance of beating the Chiefs if they advanced to

---

1 Numerous reports suggest that Tom Brady and the NFLPA will seek an injunction in federal court to postpone Brady's four-game suspension until legal proceedings are concluded. In 75 percent of our season simulations, we considered Jimmy Garoppolo the Patriots' quarterback for the first four games. In 25 percent of simulations, Brady plays the entire season barring injury.

Table 1: The Most Influential Plays of the Super Bowl Era

Rank	NFL Year	Game	Play	Time at Snap	Super Bowl Winner	Game WP Change	SBD Value
1	2014	Super Bowl	Immaculate Interception	0:26	Patriots	0.870	87
2	1990	Super Bowl	Wide Right	0:08	Giants	0.450	45
3	2008	Super Bowl	Holmes 40 yards to Arizona 6	1:02	Steelers	0.420	42
4	2007	Super Bowl	Helmet Catch	1:15	Giants	0.390	39
5	1982	Super Bowl	Here Comes the Diesel	10:28	Redskins	0.360	36
6	2012	Super Bowl	Fourth-down incomplete to Crabtree	1:50	Ravens	0.350	35
7	1988	Super Bowl	Montana to Rice, 27 yards on second-and-20	1:15	49ers	0.340	34
8	1979	Super Bowl	Pass to Stallworth over Rod Perry	12:15	Steelers	0.310	31
9	2013	NFC Champ.	Sherman tip-to-INT vs. Crabtree	0:30	Seahawks	0.500	28
10	1970	Super Bowl	Mike Curtis INT of Morton	1:09	Colts	0.270	27
11	1967	NFL Champ.	Starr QB sneak	0:16	Packers	0.350	25
12	1993	Super Bowl	Thomas fumble, James Washington TD return	14:21 (Q3)	Cowboys	0.240	24
13	1972	Div. Round	Immaculate Reception	0:22	Steelers	0.950	24

For more of these plays: http://bit.ly/1U2QreB

2015 Patriots Schedule

Week	Opp.	Week	Opp.	Week	Opp.
1	PIT (Thu.)	7	NYJ	13	PHI
2	at BUF	8	MIA (Thu.)	14	at HOU
3	JAC	9	WAS	15	TEN
4	BYE	10	at NYG	16	at NYJ
5	at DAL	11	BUF (Mon.)	17	at MIA
6	at IND	12	at DEN		

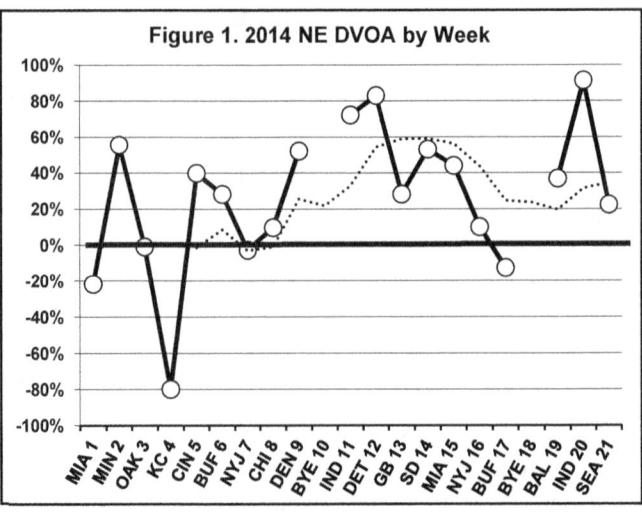

Figure 1. 2014 NE DVOA by Week

Super Bowl II.

The most influential plays include two passes intended for Michael Crabtree (No. 6 and No. 9) and three plays (No. 3, No. 7, and No. 10) that were not even the most memorable plays in those games. For example, Santonio Holmes had a much more famous catch for the go-ahead touchdown in Super Bowl XLIII, but the Steelers were then already in position to at least tie the Cardinals due to his 40-yard catch a few plays earlier. Scott Norwood's miss against the Giants ranked first as the most influential play in the Super Bowl era for over two decades. But even that play swung the Super Bowl needle by less than 50 percent because Norwood was a below-average kicker in an era when 47-yarders were not routine.

So the Immaculate Interception stands alone, looking like Tiger Woods' score atop the 2000 US Open scoreboard. The Patriots' Super Bowl win turned on one great play that will be difficult to top and impossible to forget. In fact, Butler's interception stands out so vividly that it may have impacted how the Patriots constructed their roster for this coming season.

* * * * *

Our brains often fool us with memory. In particular, our brains are hard-wired to evaluate an entire experience based on two attributes: what happened at the most intense point, and what happened at the end. (Google "Daniel Kahneman peak-end" for much more on this theory.) In Super Bowl XLIX, the peak moment *was* the final moment, so it stands out particularly strongly in our memories. Whether you define that moment to be just the final play or the entire final drive including Kearse's catch, Malcolm Butler featured prominently. Butler made three great plays on the ball in the last two minutes. Barring a deflected-and-caught pass like the Kearse catch that went unmarked by our game charters, no other defensive player got his hands on three passes on a single drive all year.

It is hard to think back to that last Seattle drive and not imagine Butler as a potential starting cornerback. But consider other defensive backs, such as Larry Brown and Dexter Jackson, who became overvalued after surprising Super Bowl star-turns. Butler, the fifth cornerback on the depth chart entering the game, made his big plays at exactly the right time for those plays to become how we think of him. And Patriots fans want to think of Butler as a future star, not just a Super Bowl star, because one of the strongest positions on the 2014 Patriots turned into a colossal, steaming crater in the weeks after Super Bowl XLIX.

New England, of course, is in the strange position of being the first team in Super Bowl history to possibly start its title defense without its best player on *either* side of the ball. Tom Brady's Deflategate fate, however, will impact four games at most. The Patriots must figure out how to win without Darrelle Revis for the entire season. And the overhaul of the cornerback position isn't just about Revis. The Patriots said goodbye to the cornerbacks who ended last season second and third on the depth chart, Brandon Browner and Kyle Arrington, as well as 2013 starter Alfonzo Dennard.

Butler's ability to step into a much larger role will play a key part in determining whether the Patriots secondary returns to the dark days of 2011, when the lack of a true top corner contributed to a defense that ranked 30th in DVOA. Butler did flash elite balls skills as a rookie; he did much more on his Super Bowl plays than simply be in the right place at the right time. Still, he faced just 29 targets in 2014 and was only moderately successful in that limited playing time. Despite playing in a defense with a Pro Bowl-caliber safety, Butler showed a vulnerability to the big play, allowing 10.5 adjusted yards per pass. That number is worse than all but four of the 77 cornerbacks who had enough targets to qualify for our rankings. Still, we shouldn't pretend to learn definitive lessons from a small sample of the notoriously inconsistent cornerback charting stats. New acquisition Robert McClain, for example, ranked first in adjusted yards per pass as a nickelback in 2012.

Given his inexperience and uneven record, Butler's potential starting spot comes primarily by process of elimination. The Patriots waited until the seventh round to select a cornerback. The other four corners on the roster who have NFL experience all have significant concerns. Logan Ryan, who is the current best bet to start on the outside with Butler, performed essentially at a replacement level in 2014, as did McClain. Bradley Fletcher should have been wearing a Washington Generals jersey when he went up against the Dez Bryants and Jordy Nelsons of the NFL (although his overall performance, 36th out of 77 qualifying corners in adjusted success rate, was better than his laughingstock reputation would suggest). With Fletcher having struggled at OTAs and recently signed Tarell Brown the only other corner with NFL experience, seventh-round pick Darryl Roberts—who impressed at workouts in some action running with the starters—may not only make the team but see significant playing time. That Butler, with his one NFL start, is perhaps the surest thing says everything about the Patriots' uncertainty at corner.

Even if Butler does not pan out as a starter, the secondary is unlikely to fully revert to 2011 form. That was the season when Devin McCourty had an RG3-like dropoff in his second year at corner before reinventing himself as a safety the following year. McCourty's presence as an elite-level safety now matters even more with the question marks at cornerback. The Patriots will likely avoid that situation, in part by relying on McCourty to provide the kind of support in man-based coverage that he gave to the limited Arrington in the AFC Championship Game, when the pair held T.Y. Hilton to a single catch. Moreover, the Patriots will likely play a higher share of zone-based coverage schemes that will put a higher premium on McCourty's skills and offer him more interception opportunities.

In fact, the better historical parallel for this Patriots defense is probably not 2011 but rather the mid-2000s teams that relied more on zone coverage and a dominant front seven. This front seven should be New England's best since 2007, and their standout attribute plays directly into the Patriots' slogan of "Do Your Job." Over the last three seasons, the Patriots improved from sixth to third to first in the share of plays where opponents break tackles. In 2014, the Patriots allowed a broken tackle on just 4.8 percent of opponents' offensive plays. This year's unit may supplement sure tackling with a potent pass rush. Since the 2007 Patriots ranked second in adjusted sack rate, New England has cracked the top ten only once, when they finished ninth in 2013. Last year, they finished 20th in part due to losing defensive end Chandler Jones for about half the season. This year, in addition to Jones, the Patriots have both the underrated stalwart Rob Ninkovich and newly-acquired Jabaal Sheard to provide pressure off the edge.

Linebackers Jamie Collins and Donta Hightower supplement that edge pressure with selected A-gap blitzes. That pressure up the middle more often came from Hightower (six sacks, 17 hurries), but Collins was the more devastating blitzer, particularly late in the season. Blitzing infrequently in most games, Collins still accumulated four sacks (all from Week 13 on) and 10.5 pressures (7.5 from Week 9 on). Collins excelled in coverage, too, except for a vulnerability to the double moves that Seattle and Baltimore used against him in the playoffs. Despite his strength in coverage, Belichick could look to utilize Collins more frequently as the explosive pass-rusher that flashed in 2014—the same explosive pass-rusher SackSEER saw in Collins' pre-draft numbers.

The Patriots' run defense may also be better in 2015, even with the loss of aging defensive line anchor Vince Wilfork. The return of Wilfork from a 2013 injury helped the Patriots improve last year from 30th to 18th in adjusted line yards. But even with Wilfork, the Patriots' defense ranked dead last in "power" situations, stopping opponents on just 19 percent of important short-yardage runs (which was the underappreciated reason why Pete Carroll should have managed the clock

to run three times). Overall, the Patriots ranked 19th on runs listed as left tackle, 22nd on runs up the middle, and 21st on runs right tackle, the second year in a row that New England was below average in all three categories.

Help for the future arrived in the form of some draft luck. Overconfident Malcom Brown—his boast of "Y'all about to get the best player y'all have ever drafted" sounds like rookie Brady with a twang—fell to pick 32, enabling Belichick to replace his 6-foot-2, 325-pound, 33-year-old run stopper with a 6-foot-2, 320-pound, 21-year-old run stopper. It is certainly not the first time that Belichick has jettisoned an older player for a strikingly similar younger model. Brown's capacity to step into Wilfork's shoes, like Butler's ability to replicate his Super Bowl magic, represents a key unknown for the 2015 Patriots defense.

Just a mediocre defense will suffice if recent history is any guide. The Patriots have not had a top-ten defense since 2006, yet they have ranked in the top five in overall DVOA in each of those seasons except the one that Brady missed. The narrative for the Patriots—great defense in Brady's early years and great offense later on—misses how long the offense has driven the team. In Brady's 13 seasons, the Patriots have ranked higher in offensive DVOA than defensive DVOA every season except one (2003).

The Patriots' offense under Brady has been by far the best single unit of the DVOA era. Not even Peyton Manning's Colts offense comes particularly close. Best five-year run since 1989? The 2007-2011 Patriots, despite a year with Matt Cassel at quarterback, averaged an offensive DVOA of 31.0% and ranked first three times (runner-up among other teams: 25.5% for the 1989-93 49ers). Best ten-year run? The 2004-2013 Patriots averaged a DVOA of 25.9% and never ranked worse than seventh (runner-up: 20.9% for the 1989-98 49ers). Take out the 2007 team, and a recent Patriots' run still wins either race by an American Pharaoh-like margin.

At first glance, however, there appear to be recent signs of slippage. In 2014, the Patriots posted the lowest offensive DVOA (13.5%) for a Tom Brady-quarterbacked team since 2003. That came on the heels of a 2013 campaign where the offense also took a step back in offensive DVOA, posting the merely very good 16.4% for the entire season. While a similar drop-off for the 1995-96 49ers preceded an even bigger decline the following year, the Gronkowski Principle predicts that the Patriots offense will actually improve back towards its 2010-12 form.

Gronkowski Principle: The Patriots always have a top-three offense with a healthy No. 87.

When Gronkowski has been healthy and at full strength, the Patriots' offense has been remarkably consistent since he entered the league. In fact, the 2010-14 Gronkowski-in-the-lineup-and-at-full-strength Patriots would be the best offense of the DVOA era.

From Weeks 5-16 last year (New England rested their starters in Week 17), the Patriots edged out Pittsburgh as the top offense in football (offensive DVOA of 23.9%). In 2013, New England also struggled early without Gronkowski before posting an offensive DVOA of 27.5% in the eight games he played.

Precedents exist to be broken, but the Patriots have yet to field a less-than-elite offense with a full-strength Rob Gronkowski.

The Gronkowski Principle explains the Patriots' offensive variation, but perhaps just as important is the Post-September Rule.

Post-September Rule: Even if the Patriots' offense looks bad in September, it will be elite when the baseball playoffs start.

Only playoff failures in 2012 and 2013 obscured the Patriots' dominance on offense even without Rob Gronkowski late in those seasons. Including the playoffs, in 2012 the Patriots posted an offensive DVOA of 27.3% without Gronkowski after he went down against the Colts in Week 11. In 2013, the Patriots had a 30.9% DVOA after losing Gronkowski in Week 14 against the Browns.

Last year, the even more dramatic offensive turnaround (28th in offensive DVOA in Weeks 1-4, then third in Weeks 5-17) was as much about the offensive line coalescing as it was evidence of the Gronkowski Principle. After throwing together unsuccessful combinations like a blind chef, the Patriots settled on an offensive line in Week 5 that paved the way for the offensive success that followed. Except for injury and six offensive linemen formations, the Patriots went with the quintet of left tackle Nate Solder, left guard Dan Connolly, center Bryan Stork, right guard Ryan Wendell, and right tackle Sebastian Vollmer. In contrast to the earlier lines that included fairly disastrous stints from players such as Jordan Devey, this line delivered competent play that enabled Brady to do what he normally does.

Research by ESPN Stats & Information last October argued that Brady is more dependent than other elite quarterbacks on getting good pass protection. While pressure faced explained 35 percent of Brady's fluctuations in Total QBR from game to game since 2006, it explained less than half that for Drew Brees, Peyton Manning, and Aaron Rodgers. Part of that correlation likely comes from Brady historically getting rid of the ball more quickly than any other quarterback (although Manning has often been about as quick). When Brady was pressured early in 2014, it often came so quickly that receivers had not even gotten downfield into their routes.

Despite all the early-season turmoil, the Patriots still finished second in adjusted sack rate, posting their lowest number (4.4 percent) since 2009. The improved line should get some props for that success at avoiding sacks, but Brady's decisiveness deserves primary credit. His quick release has kept the Patriots in the top ten of adjusted sack rate every year since 2004 except the Matt Cassel season (when they finished 26th). Brady brought a little extra sack avoidance to the table in 2014, proving that you can teach old quarterbacks new skills. In the offseason, Brady aimed to improve his foot speed through drills that asked him to shuffle his feet and make throws on the move. The success of those drills led to the odd sight of a 37-year-old quarterback looking quicker than he had since his first few seasons.

Brady may need all of that new quickness for the Patriots' divisional games in 2015. All three division rivals can generate pass pressure without resorting to the blitzes that Brady eats up. The Bills ranked first in adjusted sack rate in 2014 and figure to dominate again with the same front four. The Jets ranked fourth and then added defensive tackle Leonard Williams. The Dolphins were eighth last season and they just added Ndamukong Suh.

All of the interior pressure coming from players such as Suh, Marcell Dareus, and Sheldon Richardson puts an unusual premium on the Patriots finding competent guard play. On the right side, Ryan Wendell returns. On the left, fourth-round draft pick Tre' Jackson is the most likely candidate to replace Dan Connolly, who retired in July after the Patriots showed little interest in re-signing him. Logan Mankins knows how Bill Belichick seems to feel about 32-year-old guards, but the Patriots are certainly taking a chance if they entrust a starting spot to an unknown commodity in a division that may dominate the All-Pro defensive line spots.

Less risky than letting Connolly leave was the decision to part ways with running backs Stevan Ridley and Shane Vereen. No team better illustrates the replaceable running back than the Patriots. Since 2007, they have employed hesitant backfield dancers (Laurence Maroney), speed-challenged non-fumblers (BenJarvus Green-Ellis), diminutive white guys (Danny Woodhead), and guys who were headaches anywhere but New England (LeGarrette Blount). Not a great player in the bunch, but the Patriots have nonetheless ranked in the top half of the league in rushing DVOA every year since 2006 and in the top ten every season except 2014. The easiest place to pin the blame for last season's drop-off to 14th in rushing DVOA is the offensive line and the absence of longtime line coach Dante Scarnecchia. But last year the Patriots finished in the top five in adjusted line yards for the eighth straight year.

The Patriots' success at running the ball is as much a product of their strategic intelligence as strong line play. When the Patriots have matchups that favor them in the running game, as they did in the AFC Championship Game against the Colts, they run the ball relentlessly. Against opponents who stop the run, the Patriots sometimes abandon it altogether. Despite being completely stonewalled by Baltimore's run defense (9 carries, 20 yards) and having limited success against Seattle (19 carries, 60 yards), the Patriots achieved a respectable 3.8 yards per carry in the postseason because 59 percent of their carries happened in the one game where they could run the ball effectively.

In 2015, the Patriots again will likely rank high in both rushing DVOA and adjusted line yards. Even if their backs and offensive line are no more talented than league-average, the Patriots running game starts on third base with coaches smart enough to run only in favorable situations and a passing game that ensures opponents rarely stack the box.

The driving force behind that passing game is still fighting his battle to ensure that the Case of the Missing 0.4 PSI does not keep him out of regular-season action[2]. If Jimmy Garoppolo has to play, early games would be up in the air, as we would project the Garoppolo-led Patriots as an average team. As the

---

2 We're not going to get into the Wells Report, which can be best described as "jiggery-pokery" and "pure applesauce."

playoff chase heats up, however, the Brady-led offense will likely again be short-passing opponents into submission. The defense may fluctuate all over the rankings. Super Bowls may come down to never-to-be-repeated plays. But little in NFL his-

tory has been more reliably consistent than the Patriots in contention behind a dominant offense. And the run is not done yet.

Andrew Healy

2014 Patriots Stats by Week

Wk	vs.	W-L	PF	PA	YDF	YDA	TO	Total	Off	Def	ST
1	at MIA	L	20	33	315	360	1	-22%	-9%	2%	-11%
2	at MIN	W	30	7	292	217	4	56%	-2%	-41%	16%
3	OAK	W	16	9	297	241	1	-1%	-13%	-12%	0%
4	at KC	L	14	41	290	443	-3	-80%	-34%	49%	4%
5	CIN	W	43	17	505	320	3	40%	31%	4%	13%
6	at BUF	W	37	22	396	336	3	28%	38%	3%	-6%
7	NYJ	W	27	25	323	423	0	-3%	20%	29%	6%
8	CHI	W	51	23	487	384	2	10%	27%	31%	13%
9	DEN	W	43	21	398	472	1	52%	15%	-12%	25%
10	BYE										
11	at IND	W	42	20	503	322	-1	72%	49%	-30%	-7%
12	DET	W	34	9	439	335	0	83%	46%	-18%	19%
13	at GB	L	21	26	320	478	0	28%	39%	2%	-9%
14	at SD	W	23	14	397	216	-1	53%	-12%	-58%	7%
15	MIA	W	41	13	395	384	1	44%	14%	-25%	5%
16	at NYJ	W	17	16	231	307	0	10%	-8%	-6%	12%
17	BUF	L	9	17	260	268	1	-13%	-3%	13%	4%
18	BYE										
19	BAL	W	35	31	422	428	1	37%	47%	8%	-3%
20	IND	W	45	7	397	209	2	91%	32%	-45%	14%
21	vs. SEA	W	28	24	377	396	-1	22%	25%	5%	2%

Trends and Splits

	Offense	Rank	Defense	Rank
Total DVOA	13.5%	6	-3.0%	12
Unadjusted VOA	12.7%	6	-2.7%	13
Weighted Trend	19.3%	3	-6.1%	13
Variance	6.1%	10	7.6%	27
Average Opponent	-1.8%	8	-0.1%	15
Passing	35.0%	5	2.5%	12
Rushing	-3.7%	14	-10.3%	13
First Down	19.0%	4	-2.6%	16
Second Down	5.5%	13	-11.3%	5
Third Down	14.7%	8	9.0%	21
First Half	19.7%	4	-0.1%	15
Second Half	6.5%	11	-6.2%	7
Red Zone	4.9%	11	-8.9%	13
Late and Close	8.1%	9	-3.6%	16

Five-Year Performance

Year	W-L	Pyth W	Est W	PF	PA	TO	Total	Rk	Off	Rk	Def	Rk	ST	Rk	Off AGL	Rk	Def AGL	Rk	Off Age	Rk	Def Age	Rk	ST Age	Rk
2010	14-2	12.6	14.6	518	313	+28	44.6%	1	42.2%	1	2.3%	21	4.7%	8	32.7	23	39.4	27	28.3	6	25.5	31	26.2	18
2011	13-3	11.9	12.2	513	342	+17	22.8%	3	31.9%	3	13.2%	30	4.1%	5	40.0	23	57.5	31	28.5	1	26.7	22	26.1	21
2012	12-4	12.7	13.4	557	331	+25	34.9%	3	30.8%	1	1.4%	15	5.5%	4	46.7	25	28.0	15	27.9	7	25.6	29	26.2	12
2013	12-4	10.5	11.0	444	338	+9	18.9%	5	16.4%	4	4.2%	20	6.7%	2	47.8	25	49.8	28	27.6	6	25.8	29	25.6	27
2014	12-4	11.8	10.8	468	313	+12	22.1%	4	13.5%	6	-3.0%	12	5.7%	5	24.4	9	37.6	16	27.7	5	26.6	19	26.1	16

2014 Performance Based on Most Common Personnel Groups

NE Offense				NE Offense vs. Opponents					NE Defense				NE Defense vs. Opponents			
Pers	Freq	Yds	DVOA	Run%	Pers	Freq	Yds	DVOA	Run%	Pers	Freq	Yds	DVOA	Pers	Freq	Yds	DVOA
12	41%	5.9	23.2%	31%	Base	44%	5.6	13.0%	49%	Base	26%	5.3	5.4%	11	61%	5.8	-9.5%
11	28%	6.0	18.5%	24%	Nickel	42%	6.1	25.9%	29%	Nickel	60%	5.6	-8.0%	12	20%	6.1	14.6%
21	11%	6.2	23.6%	47%	Dime+	10%	5.3	-2.7%	13%	Dime+	13%	6.0	-3.3%	21	6%	3.3	-20.5%
22	4%	3.5	-35.1%	89%	Goal Line	2%	2.6	45.8%	68%	Goal Line	1%	0.9	34.4%	13	4%	4.3	-4.2%
611	4%	4.6	5.9%	67%	Big	2%	5.3	5.1%	94%					22	2%	4.9	1.0%
20	3%	4.8	-18.7%	44%										20	2%	5.4	17.2%

Strategic Tendencies

Run/Pass		Rk	Formation		Rk	Pass Rush		Rk	Secondary		Rk	Strategy		Rk
Runs, first half	36%	20	Form: Single Back	71%	22	Rush 3	14.8%	2	4 DB	17%	31	Play action	25%	7
Runs, first down	46%	24	Form: Empty Back	9%	6	Rush 4	64.4%	17	5 DB	64%	12	Avg Box (Off)	6.29	15
Runs, second-long	26%	24	Pers: 3+ WR	32%	32	Rush 5	17.8%	27	6+ DB	19%	11	Avg Box (Def)	6.08	30
Runs, power sit.	65%	7	Pers: 4+ WR	0%	30	Rush 6+	3.0%	31	CB by Sides	59%	31	Offensive Pace	26.61	2
Runs, behind 2H	30%	9	Pers: 2+ TE/6+ OL	58%	1	Sacks by LB	40.0%	16	DB Blitz	6%	29	Defensive Pace	30.97	27
Pass, ahead 2H	55%	1	Shotgun/Pistol	47%	30	Sacks by DB	2.5%	28	Hole in Zone	7%	13	Go for it on 4th	1.13	9

We have situation-neutral pace tracked for 569 different teams going back to 1997. Four of the eight fastest figures belong to the last four Patriots teams. ☞ Tom Brady has always favored the left side and middle of the field, but never quite as much as he did in 2014. Brady threw a league-high 45 percent of passes to the left and a league-low 31 percent of passes to the right. Twenty-four percent of passes were listed as being in the middle, slightly above the NFL average. ☞ Defensive back blitzes seem to be a strong strategy against Brady and the Patriots' offensive line. In the past two seasons, Brady has averaged just 4.9 (2013) and 4.7 (2014) yards per pass against DB blitzes. In 2012, the first season for which we have these numbers, Brady averaged 6.6 yards per pass, better than the NFL average against DB blitzes but certainly lower than his usual performance. ☞ The Patriots qualified as "max protect" on 15.7 percent of pass plays, second in the league behind Cleveland. ☞ Year after year, the Patriots drop a ton of passes. They were tied for fourth with 28 drops, after 38 drops in 2013 (second) and 39 drops in 2014 (fourth). But they also benefited from 33 dropped passes by opponents last season, more than any other team. ☞ The Patriots' defense faced shotgun (or pistol) on a league-leading 78 percent of plays, even though they were actually better when opponents were in shotgun. No defense last year allowed fewer yards per play against shotgun compared to not shotgun, but the Patriots were closest at 5.5 yards (-3.5% DVOA, 10th) vs. shotgun and 5.4 yards (9.1% DVOA, 31st) otherwise. ☞ The Patriots sent a big blitz of six or more less often than any other team—just 18 plays not counting screen passes. They rarely big blitz because they are terrible at it. Last year, they allowed 8.9 yards per play. There were three sacks but 10 first downs and two touchdowns on the other 15 plays (including a DPI with a minute left in Week 3 that put Oakland near the goal line and almost cost the Patriots a win). ☞ In 2013, the Patriots had 89 penalties, 29th in the NFL. They ranked dead last in penalties on both defense and special teams. In 2014, the Patriots got flag-happy, tied for seventh with 142 penalties including declined and offsetting. But Brandon Browner and close play on defense was not the only issue:

Year	Offense		Defense		Sp. Tms/TO Returns	
	Penalties	Yards	Penalties	Yards	Penalties	Yards
2013	43	262	27	265	13	98
2014	61	413	52	442	29	225

Passing

Player	DYAR	DVOA	Plays	NtYds	Avg	YAC	C%	TD	Int
T.Brady	1176	18.1%	602	3950	6.6	5.0	64.4%	33	9
J.Garoppolo	-5	-13.8%	32	146	4.6	6.3	70.4%	1	0

Rushing

Player	DYAR	DVOA	Plays	Yds	Avg	TD	Fum	Suc
S.Vereen*	4	-7.4%	96	391	4.1	2	0	41%
S.Ridley*	-6	-9.9%	94	340	3.6	2	0	53%
J.Gray	152	29.1%	89	412	4.6	5	0	65%
L.Blount	60	15.2%	60	281	4.7	3	0	45%
B.Bolden	-3	-11.2%	28	89	3.2	1	0	43%
T.Brady	-19	-25.1%	21	73	3.5	0	1	-
J.Edelman	80	95.5%	10	94	9.4	0	0	-
J.White	0	-7.1%	9	38	4.2	0	0	56%
T.Cadet	-18	-55.8%	10	32	3.2	0	1	50%

Receiving

Player	DYAR	DVOA	Plays	Ctch	Yds	Y/C	YAC	TD	C%
J.Edelman	137	0.2%	133	92	974	10.6	4.6	4	69%
B.LaFell	174	5.7%	119	74	953	12.9	5.0	7	62%
D.Amendola	-16	-17.7%	42	27	200	7.4	2.7	1	64%
B.Tyms	6	-5.6%	11	5	82	16.4	0.6	1	45%
K.Thompkins*	-23	-38.9%	11	6	53	8.8	4.8	0	55%
B.Gibson	-56	-27.3%	51	29	295	10.2	3.8	1	57%
R.Gronkowski	237	19.7%	131	82	1124	13.7	5.6	12	63%
T.Wright	89	30.9%	33	26	259	10.0	3.6	6	79%
M.Hoomanawanui	-4	-16.3%	6	3	44	14.7	1.7	0	50%
S.Chandler	17	-3.6%	70	47	497	10.6	4.1	3	67%
S.Vereen*	49	-3.1%	77	52	447	8.6	7.3	3	68%
J.Develin	-17	-45.7%	8	6	43	7.2	5.3	0	75%
B.Bolden	-26	-81.7%	6	2	8	4.0	5.5	0	33%
T.Cadet	57	5.4%	51	38	296	7.8	6.4	1	81%

Offensive Line

Player	Pos	Age	GS	Snaps	Pen	Sk	Pass	Run	Player	Pos	Age	GS	Snaps	Pen	Sk	Pass	Run
Nate Solder	LT	27	16/16	1038	9	5.5	28.5	8.0	Marcus Cannon	G/T	27	16/4	434	6	2.0	12.5	3.0
Sebastian Vollmer	RT	31	15/15	1005	3	2.0	19.0	5.0	Jordan Devey	G	27	7/4	296	5	1.0	5.0	3.0
Ryan Wendell	RG	29	14/12	880	4	1.0	15.0	2.5	Josh Kline	G	26	12/4	289	0	1.5	5.5	0.0
Dan Connolly*	LG	33	13/13	832	3	1.0	12.0	3.0	Cameron Fleming	OT	23	7/2	207	1	1.5	5.0	0.0
Bryan Stork	C	25	13/11	796	5	0.5	7.0	4.5									

Year	Yards	ALY	Rk	Power	Rk	Stuff	Rk	2nd Lev	Rk	Open Field	Rk	Sacks	ASR	Rk	Short	Long	F-Start	Cont.
2012	4.32	4.45	3	66%	13	18%	10	1.33	9	0.63	22	27	4.5%	5	9	8	13	23
2013	4.69	4.63	1	59%	23	16%	4	1.39	2	0.80	12	40	6.1%	9	23	9	11	32
2014	4.11	4.22	5	59%	23	21%	27	1.22	11	0.59	23	26	4.4%	2	15	6	19	28
2014 ALY by direction:			Left End 4.5 (2)			Left Tackle 4.93 (2)			Mid/Guard 3.71 (25)				Right Tackle 4.63 (4)				Right End 5.19 (3)	

The first four weeks of the 2014 season seemed to make a strong case for retired offensive line coach Dante Scarnecchia as a uniquely indispensable position coach. Since 2004, a Tom Brady-led offense had ranked no lower than ninth in adjusted sack rate. Through four weeks last year, the Patriots' adjusted sack rate of 6.7 percent ranked 23rd, a number that would have been even worse with almost any other quarterback. Even Brady's quickest-in-the-NFL release could not cover for how bad the line was last September. But much of that early-season failure seems to have been both an adjustment period and, more importantly, a reflection of the carousel of players who rotated through the lineup. After starting both Marcus Cannon and Jordan Devey in the first three games, then Cameron Fleming in the fourth, the Patriots settled on the lineup that would stay intact for the rest of the season: left tackle Nate Solder, left guard Dan Connolly, center Bryan Stork, right guard Ryan Wendell, and right tackle Sebastian Vollmer. That line registered an adjusted sack rate of 3.5 percent in Weeks 5-16, good enough for second in the league, just behind Denver. Their 4.4 percent adjusted sack rate for the season ended up also ranking second and was their best mark since 2009.

For evaluating the Patriots' offensive line play, those numbers are mainly useful in telling us that the sky did not fall as seemed possible in September. No player deserves more credit for the low sack rate than Brady, and the solid adjusted line yards stat comes in large part from the strategic flexibility mentioned earlier in the chapter. While Vollmer played a solid right tackle and Stork held up well at center for a rookie, some other returning linemen missed blocks at a rate far beyond their peers. According to our charting stats, Wendell ranked 24th out of 34 right guards in the number of snaps per blown block. Solder blew blocks at a higher rate than any other left tackle in the NFL. And Cannon was terrible, ranking 106th out of 108 interior linemen (although he did get snaps at tackle, too). That all sounds pretty bad even without considering Devey, who avoids the bottom ten percent of interior linemen only by virtue of not having enough snaps to qualify.

For 2015, the outlook is again for mediocre play that is mostly good enough. The question mark is at left guard, where fourth-round draft pick Tre' Jackson (Florida State) looks like the most likely replacement for the retired Connolly. The other option is Josh Kline, who played heavily in two playoff games after an injury to Stork and was at least closer to competent than Cannon and Devey.

Defensive Front Seven

Defensive Line	Age	Pos	G	Snaps	Plays	TmPct	Rk	Stop	Dfts	BTkl	Runs	St%	Rk	RuYd	Rk	Sack	Hit	Hur	Dsrpt
						Overall						vs. Run					Pass Rush		
Vince Wilfork*	34	DT	16	802	48	6.0%	21	42	4	4	45	89%	10	2.1	40	0.0	1	8.0	1
Chris Jones	25	DT	15	503	24	3.2%	77	17	6	0	17	71%	79	3.7	92	3.0	3	1.0	0
Dominique Easley	23	DT	11	261	10	1.8%	--	5	3	2	8	38%	--	2.8	--	1.0	2	4.0	0
Sealver Siliga	25	DT	7	235	31	8.9%	3	24	5	1	25	72%	72	2.1	42	2.5	1	1.0	0
Alan Branch	31	DT	8	161	14	3.5%	--	9	2	0	13	62%	--	1.8	--	0.0	2	1.0	1

Edge Rushers	Age	Pos	G	Snaps	Plays	TmPct	Rk	Stop	Dfts	BTkl	Runs	St%	Rk	RuYd	Rk	Sack	Hit	Hur	Dsrpt
						Overall						vs. Run					Pass Rush		
Rob Ninkovich	31	DE	16	1021	63	7.9%	11	46	20	7	38	74%	49	3.0	62	8.0	9	24.0	0
Chandler Jones	25	DE	10	568	44	8.9%	4	31	10	2	33	67%	69	2.7	53	6.0	8	14.5	2

Linebackers	Age	Pos	G	Snaps	Plays	Overall TmPct	Rk	Stop	Dfts	BTkl	Pass Rush Sack	Hit	Hur	vs. Run Runs	St%	Rk	RuYd	Rk	vs. Pass Tgts	Suc%	Rk	AdjYd	Rk	PD	Int
Jamie Collins	25	OLB	15	925	117	15.7%	20	60	22	7	4.0	6	10.5	72	46%	84	4.7	79	36	68%	4	5.1	11	2	2
Dont'a Hightower	25	MLB	12	834	90	15.1%	23	59	17	2	6.0	7	14	55	67%	28	3.4	45	24	64%	6	6.0	28	1	0
Akeem Ayers*	26	OLB	11	392	18	3.3%	86	12	7	0	4.0	2	9.5	9	67%	29	2.3	8	4	30%	--	6.0	--	1	1
Jerod Mayo	29	OLB	6	332	53	17.8%	9	29	7	1	1.0	1	3.5	39	64%	39	4.0	68	9	41%	--	10.3	--	0	0
Jonathan Casillas*	28	OLB	11	261	30	5.0%	--	16	3	1	0.0	2	3.5	17	65%	--	3.1	--	7	59%	--	5.7	--	0	0

Year	Yards	ALY	Rk	Power	Rk	Stuff	Rk	2nd Level	Rk	Open Field	Rk	Sacks	ASR	Rk	Short	Long
2012	3.97	3.83	10	50%	2	19%	13	1.29	27	0.49	7	37	6.0%	24	4	20
2013	4.24	4.37	30	60%	11	13%	32	1.12	17	0.43	4	48	7.5%	9	8	20
2014	4.08	3.95	18	81%	32	16%	28	1.16	20	0.47	3	40	6.5%	20	14	14

2014 ALY by direction:	Left End 2.97 (6)	Left Tackle 3.84 (19)	Mid/Guard 4.1 (22)	Right Tackle 4.33 (21)	Right End 4.29 (23)

Last season, the front seven was a mixed bag. The relative weakness came at defensive tackle, an area of former strength. While Vince Wilfork returned from an Achilles tear to help the run defense improve from 27th to 13th in DVOA, he was still not quite his former self. The limited Chris Jones saw the second-most snaps at tackle, a year after leading the Patriots as a rookie with Wilfork injured. In 2015, the Patriots will no longer have Wilfork, but they may still be able to move Jones into a smaller role. In the short-term, the starting spots will go to Sealver Siliga, who started next to Wilfork in December through the Super Bowl, and veteran Alan Branch. In the long-term, the Patriots will try to build a new line around the two first-round defensive tackles they've chosen in the past two drafts: first two-time ACL-buster Dominique Easley out of Florida in 2014, and then Texas tackle Malcom Brown this year. If Easley can stay healthy, the Easley-Brown pairing puts together two talented tackles whose skills complement each other well. Easley showed some burst as an interior pass rusher last year, before ending the season on injured reserve with knee soreness. Brown should step into the gap-eating run-stopper role that Wilfork filled—if not right away, than at least by the start of 2016.

On the outside, the Patriots have a clearer idea of what to expect, and now more depth with which to work. Chandler Jones only started eight games in 2014. When healthy, he accumulated sacks at about the same rate as 2013, when he notched 11.5. Rob Ninkovich played a very unusual role for the Patriots, as we charted him with 18 pass targets in 2014. No other edge rusher on a nominally 4-3 team faced more than four. Even with his frequent drops into coverage, Ninkovich got 8.0 sacks. The indefatigable Ninkovich—no defensive lineman has played more snaps over the last three years, not even J.J. Watt—remains one of the NFL's biggest veteran bargains at his new cap number of $4.75 million. More rest for Ninkovich and Jones could be coming this year with the arrival of Jabaal Sheard, who led the Browns with 5.5 sacks last year despite having over 200 fewer snaps than Paul Kruger. The 25-year-old edge rusher also had a strong stop rate against the run in a small sample of 23 attempts, so Sheard perhaps has some potential to contribute beyond the situational pass-rusher role ordinarily ascribed to him.

At linebacker, Donta Hightower and Jamie Collins took big steps in 2014 towards joining the Belichick's previous standouts at the position. Donta Hightower looked appropriately Tedy Bruschi-esque in No. 54, leading all inside linebackers with six sacks. Jamie Collins looked a bit like a middle-class man's Lawrence Taylor with his explosiveness on blitzes, although he was primarily used in pass coverage. Both Hightower and Collins did extremely well in their coverage assignments. Facing 24 targets, Hightower ranked sixth (out of 63 qualifying linebackers) with a 64 percent success rate. Collins ranked even higher, finishing fourth with a 68 percent success rate (36 targets).

That full front seven, which will also include the returned-from-injury Jerod Mayo, may not see the field together very often. In 2014, the Patriots played at least seven defensive linemen and linebackers only 27.3 percent of the time. Only two teams (Detroit and Green Bay) did so less frequently. This year, New England might want to shift more towards their relative strength in the front seven, but opponents are likely to spend even more time with three or more wide receivers to force the Patriots out of their base defense.

Defensive Secondary

Secondary	Age	Pos	G	Snaps	Plays	TmPct	Rk	Stop	Dfts	BTkl	Runs	St%	Rk	RuYd	Rk	Tgts	Tgt%	Rk	Dist	Suc%	Rk	AdjYd	Rk	PD	Int
Darrelle Revis*	30	CB	16	1011	61	7.7%	56	28	15	1	10	40%	38	6.7	40	69	17.0%	3	13.2	62%	2	7.3	25	13	2
Devin McCourty	28	FS	16	998	73	9.2%	48	15	9	3	30	20%	68	11.7	70	19	4.6%	4	15.1	54%	34	7.7	44	5	2
Patrick Chung	28	SS	16	839	92	11.6%	25	47	9	5	52	54%	14	4.5	9	39	11.4%	58	10.8	54%	35	7.4	38	8	1
Brandon Browner*	31	CB	9	580	31	6.9%	67	15	6	4	5	100%	1	2.4	2	53	22.5%	29	14.5	56%	16	7.4	28	9	1
Logan Ryan	24	CB	16	509	41	5.2%	76	15	8	1	8	50%	21	6.3	35	52	25.2%	50	12.7	46%	60	9.4	65	7	2
Kyle Arrington	29	CB	14	439	38	5.5%	--	15	6	2	8	75%	--	4.3	--	39	21.8%	--	11.9	55%	--	6.3	--	4	0
Duron Harmon	24	FS	16	279	12	1.5%	--	1	1	0	4	0%	--	10.0	--	3	2.2%	--	24.8	99%	--	0.8	--	1	1
Tavon Wilson	25	SS	16	183	20	2.5%	--	11	4	1	11	36%	--	6.6	--	9	11.5%	--	10.2	78%	--	7.5	--	2	0
Bradley Fletcher	29	CB	15	1047	80	9.8%	19	34	13	8	19	47%	25	4.5	12	115	29.4%	69	16.6	51%	36	8.9	55	22	1
Tarell Brown*	30	CB	14	961	58	8.0%	47	22	7	2	14	50%	21	5.4	26	58	18.3%	7	12.8	52%	31	8.0	42	5	0
Robert McClain	27	CB	16	628	61	7.4%	60	21	5	9	18	44%	29	5.3	21	56	24.4%	45	12.9	45%	62	7.8	39	5	2

Year	Pass D Rank	vs. #1 WR	Rk	vs. #2 WR	Rk	vs. Other WR	Rk	vs. TE	Rk	vs. RB	Rk
2012	23	-5.0%	14	-16.4%	6	27.3%	30	21.3%	29	14.8%	23
2013	14	-1.9%	16	17.9%	29	5.5%	21	-1.1%	13	5.1%	19
2014	12	-14.4%	7	1.8%	17	-13.8%	7	22.0%	30	-4.6%	14

Patriots' fans likely fear the Cornerback Domino Theory, the vicious sequence of events that follows the loss of a No. 1 cornerback. Those dominoes helped derail New England's 2012 and 2013 playoff runs. In those AFC Championship Games, injuries to Aqib Talib forced other corners into roles they could not fill. In 2012, an overmatched Marquice Cole (two career starts) replaced Talib on Anquan Boldin and surrendered five catches on six targets for 60 yards and two touchdowns. In 2013, the Patriots moved No. 2 corner Alfonzo Dennard onto Demaryius Thomas and slid everyone else up accordingly, with similarly disastrous results. Altogether in those games, the Patriots gave up three points on four drives with Talib healthy and 51 points on 12 meaningful drives with him on the sidelines.

So what will the Patriots do now that they have to replace Darrelle Revis? New England fans hope that 2004 is the better parallel than 2012 or 2013. That year, the Patriots lost Ty Law halfway through the season and still posted a top-ten defensive DVOA. Back then, the Patriots had a series of attributes they lacked in those more recent playoff defeats: time to adjust to losing Law, strong safety play, a dominant front seven, and a young corner named Asante Samuel who turned out to be as good as Law once he broke into the starting lineup. The Patriots could have the first three of those, but at least right now they lack anyone on Samuel's level at corner. Samuel, who for a time was arguably the best zone corner in the NFL, became a starter in his second year in 2004 and was the Patriots' top corner during their playoff run that year. Hoping for a similar breakout from second-year corner Malcolm Butler is asking for the improbable but not the impossible.

Along with Butler, Logan Ryan appears likely to start on the outside. After a strong rookie season of making plays on the ball, Ryan regressed in his second year. His Super Bowl struggles, most memorably on Chris Matthews' criminally easy touchdown, helped pave the way for Butler's star turn. Tarell Brown was signed in July to challenge Butler and Ryan. Bradley Fletcher led the league in yardage given up in coverage last year, but our charting also suggests that Fletcher was partly a victim of a vicious series of assignments. (His 9.8 adjusted yards per pass drops to a more respectable 8.9 after accounting for the quality of the receivers he had to cover.) Robert McClain was signed way from Atlanta to replace Kyle Arrington in the slot, but Ryan would be a logical choice there if he doesn't start on the outside.

Seventh-round draft pick Darryl Roberts (Marshall) generated chatter out of OTAs that sounded like the comments Malcolm Butler earned last year. Butler earned the nickname "Scrap" for his energetic play in offseason workouts. In college, Roberts was dubbed "Swagg" for his aggressive play, and his 17 pass breakups in 2014 ranked second in FBS. Roberts could also fill the Brandon Browner penalty accumulation role, as he racked up six penalties for 71 yards last season.

With the uncertainty at corner, one natural thought is that the Patriots could turn to the former Pro Bowl corner already on the roster. As a rookie in 2010, McCourty shined at corner before struggling in 2011 as the Patriots moved to more man-based coverage. McCourty, however, offers more at the safety spot he has manned since 2012, usually offering support to the Patriots' limited cornerback contingent rather than manning up on a tight end or receiver. At safety, McCourty is joined by a host of average players. Patrick Chung started 15 games and received a contract extension late last season. He had a good season in run support (54 percent stop rate, ranked 14th among secondary players). Second-round pick Jordan Richards joins an ever-growing cast of early-round safeties that Belichick selects seemingly just to show he doesn't care about conventional wisdom. Previous Day 2 picks Tavon Wilson and Duron Harmon, who like Richards would probably have been available in the sixth or seventh round, have been adequate but have never lived up to their draft position. Richards may check off the usual Patriots boxes—high intelligence, great three-cone drill time—but there's little reason to expect he will either.

Special Teams

Year	DVOA	Rank	FG/XP	Rank	Net Kick	Rank	Kick Ret	Rank	Net Punt	Rank	Punt Ret	Rank	Hidden	Rank
2012	5.5%	4	-1.8	18	15.0	1	2.2	11	6.2	11	5.9	5	0.0	17
2013	6.7%	2	11.4	1	10.5	2	2.0	9	9.0	6	0.5	14	-9.9	30
2014	5.7%	5	10.8	1	8.4	3	0.5	13	0.2	16	8.4	5	8.9	3

For most of the NFL, special-teams rankings vary even more than offense and defense from year to year. Last year, five of the top ten units by DVOA were in the bottom half of the league the year before. The No. 1 special-teams unit, Philadelphia, ranked 25th in 2013. Buffalo improved last year from 30th to fourth. But these normal rules seemingly do not apply to the Patriots. New England has ranked in the top half of the league in special teams every year in the Belichick era. Last year marked the fourth year in a row that the Patriots ranked in the top five.

Stephen Gostkowski is particularly responsible, leading the NFL in our placekicking measure for a second straight season. After adjusting for weather, Gostkowski's kicks were worth 10.8 points more than what the Patriots would have gotten from an average kicker given the same opportunities. It is important with Gostkowski to separate these last two years from most his previous ones. In 2013 and 2014, he made 73 of 78 kicks (93.6 percent), including a remarkable-even-for-this-era 29 of 33 kicks (87.9 percent) from 40 yards or longer. Last year, he made 13 of 14 from that range (92.9 percent). This sample is big enough to suggest that Gostkowski has improved from his first seven seasons, when he made a much lower percentage (70.8 percent) of his kicks from 40 yards and out.

Gostkowski's kickoffs were another strength, as he helped the Patriots rank in the top five in net kickoff value for the fourth year in a row. Ryan Allen was an average punter, and 2014 was a mediocre year for the punt coverage unit. Gunner Matthew Slater still tied for the league lead with 10 tackles in punt coverage and made the Pro Bowl for the fourth year in a row.

Other than Gostkowski, the Patriots' most important special-teams contributor in 2014 was Julian Edelman. Edelman is the only punt returner in the league to rank in the top five of our rankings in two of the last three years (he was fourth in 2012, though the Patriots ranked fifth as a team). In the 2014 regular season, Edelman averaged 12.0 yards per return. He was even better in the playoffs, averaging 15.9 yards on nine returns. Even in an era that is more favorable to punt returns with longer punts, Edelman deserves consideration for any list of the top-ten returners in NFL history. In the regular season, Edelman ranks second all-time in punt return average during the Super Bowl era, just behind Devin Hester. Including the playoffs, Edelman ranks first all-time with 12.4 yards per return. Not bad for a seventh-round college quarterback whom the whole league passed on in free agency just two years ago.

New Orleans Saints

2014 Record: 7-9	Total DVOA: -0.9% (17th)	2015 Mean Projection: 8.7 wins	On the Clock (0-4): 7%
Pythagorean Wins: 7.4 (20th)	Offense: 10.6% (7th)	Postseason Odds: 45.3%	Mediocrity (5-7): 27%
Snap-Weighted Age: 27.3 (1st)	Defense: 13.1% (31st)	Super Bowl Odds: 6.2%	Playoff Contender (8-10): 40%
Average Opponent: -1.7% (20th)	Special Teams: 1.6% (11th)	Proj. Avg. Opponent: -5.3% (31st)	Super Bowl Contender (11+): 27%

2014: One more data point showing that defense is less consistent than offense.

2015: Saints change things up, hoping to get their veteran leader to one last Super Bowl—just like Denver, but with less national attention.

Drew Brees is 36. He has played 14 seasons in the NFL and thrown more than 7,500 passes. He has been sacked 300 times and hit on countless more occasions. The 6-foot, 209-pound quarterback is physically declining at this point, and it's a decline that is evident on the field. It is not, however, a decline that prevents him from playing quality football. Maybe more importantly, it is not a decline that has made the Saints consider moving on. Despite drafting Garrett Grayson in the third round of this year's draft, both Mickey Loomis and Sean Payton have repeatedly stated that Brees is an integral part of their plans. "I don't see the end for Drew Brees on the short-term horizon, at least I certainly hope not," Loomis said after the team selected Grayson. Payton had previously responded to trade rumors by stating, "Yeah, it's not that time [to trade him]... We're not interested in moving on from Drew Brees. He's going to be a part of our next championship."

Our next championship. That is the focus of Payton. It's ultimately the focus of every head coach in the NFL, but Payton isn't looking to spend years rebuilding his roster in pursuit of his next Super Bowl. He and Loomis have backed that up with their aggressiveness over the past two offseasons. Even though the 2014 offseason didn't pay off with a place in the playoffs, Payton and Loomis reacted to that disappointment with vigor rather than dejection. The first big move was to move on from All-Pro tight end Jimmy Graham. Graham was a pivotal piece of the passing game, but the Saints traded him to the Seattle Seahawks for a first-round pick and center Max Unger. Unger won't be playing alongside left guard Ben Grubbs though, as Grubbs was shipped to the Kansas City Chiefs for a fifth-round pick. Grubbs reportedly got on the wrong side of Brees, as did wide receiver Kenny Stills, who was sent to the Miami Dolphins for a third-round pick and linebacker Dannell Ellerbe. Veteran wide receiver Marques Colston and right guard Jahri Evans were forced to take pay cuts to stay with the team.

Payton offered a succinct summary of the franchise's motivation this offseason: "I think if you're looking closely to when we've been really good, there's been that element defensively, there's been that element in the running game," he said in an interview with Chris Wesseling of NFL.com. When the Saints were really good, they won a Super Bowl, the only Super Bowl in the history of the franchise. That was back in 2009.

In 2009, the Saints offense ranked second in DVOA and first in rushing DVOA. In 2014, the offense ranked seventh overall, but ninth in both rushing and passing DVOA. The running game wasn't dramatically less efficient, but it was dramatically less productive. The Saints running game finished the 2009 regular season averaging 29.2 attempts (seventh in the NFL) for 131.6 yards (sixth). In 2014, those numbers were to 25.4 (19th) and 113.6 (13th). The Saints simply couldn't run the ball as often because their defense was so poor. In 2009, the defense ranked 17th in DVOA, but ninth in pass DVOA while creating 39 turnovers (second in the NFL). In 2014, Rob Ryan's unit dropped to 31st in DVOA, 27th against the pass and 32nd against the run, while creating just 17 turnovers.

Payton accurately assessed the weaknesses of his team, and understands how to make the team more competitive by fixing those weaknesses. However, the team's cap situation put him in a difficult position. The Saints couldn't simply build around their strengths to become a better team. Their lack of cap space meant they had to cut players and redo contracts just to become cap compliant. Adding pieces to the defense and rejuvenating the running game required trading away key components of the passing game. Trading away receiving options and offensive linemen obviously means giving away pieces that have a direct link to the quarterback position. That direct link is easier to see, but it doesn't necessarily make those pieces more significant than the parts of the team that have an indirect link to Brees.

Two years ago, before any of these moves were made, Payton spoke about the importance of the defense and running game for the success of the quarterback. Brees had thrown 19 interceptions in 2012, clouding the perception of what had otherwise been a productive season. "When you tell me a team is last in the league in defense and last in the running game, I'm telling you the quarterback's job description is entirely different," Payton told Larry Holder of the *New Orleans Times-Picayune*. "I'm telling you he's having to play and press and try to do certain things that his counterpart may not have to do based on the way that team is running the ball or playing defense. That's the first thing that I saw. You get one-dimensional, you find yourself in these games where you're not controlling the game."

This is relevant again because Brees threw 17 interceptions last year, but with 10 fewer touchdowns than he threw in 2012. The goal is for the restructuring of the Saints roster to push Brees away from that kind of production.

2015 Saints Schedule

Week	Opp.	Week	Opp.	Week	Opp.
1	at ARI	7	at IND	13	CAR
2	TB	8	NYG	14	at TB
3	at CAR	9	TEN	15	DET (Mon.)
4	DAL	10	at WAS	16	JAC
5	at PHI	11	BYE	17	at ATL
6	ATL (Thu.)	12	at HOU		

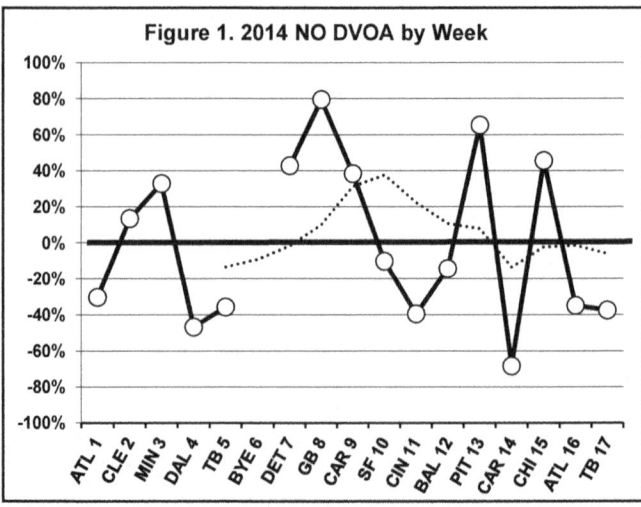

Figure 1. 2014 NO DVOA by Week

Brees won't be relegated to a game-managing role, but like Peyton Manning in Denver, he's likely to have less offensive responsibility than in years past. A lesser workload in more favorable situations is theoretically an easier job for the veteran, but that's not the case. Because the franchise had to send away Stills and Graham to improve their defense and running game, Brees is going to be relied on to elevate a depleted receiving corps this season. Graham didn't lead the Saints in yardage last year, but he was still the team's most important receiving option. Graham drew more attention in coverage than any other player and acted as a matchup nightmare against man coverage. Stills was the team's best deep threat, a player whose ability to consistently adjust to the ball in the air made Brees' deep-passing numbers much more impressive than they should have been. Graham and Stills both boast skill sets that allow them to be very effective against man coverage. As such, opposing defenses played a huge amount of zone against the Saints offense and were reluctant to blitz. The Saints were blitzed 27 percent of the time last season, 24th in the NFL. Forcing defenses into these types of game plans allowed the offense's other receivers to thrive in more favorable situations.

Neither Brandin Cooks nor Marques Colston has a skill set that lends itself favorably to beating man coverage, especially not press-man coverage. Film study of the Saints 2014 season shows that neither player was asked to consistently beat press or man coverage on a regular basis (Table 1).

Table 1. Saints WR vs. Types of Coverage in 2014

Brandin Cooks		Marques Colston	
Receptions	53	Receptions	59
v Press	6	v Press	3
v Off	47	v Off	56
v Man	23	v Man	18
v Zone	30	v Zone	41
v Press Man	3	v Press Man	2
v Off Man	20	v Off Man	16
v Zone from Press	3	v Zone from Press	1
v Zone from Off	27	v Zone from Off	40

Cooks' 47 receptions that didn't come against press coverage last year accounted for 485 of his 550 yards and all three of his touchdowns. Payton was able to consistently hide him from the defense by lining him up 3 yards off the line of scrimmage or tight to teammates. Even though Cooks is an outside receiver (with Colston being the primary slot receiver), he doesn't have the size or strength to fend off the more aggressive cornerbacks in the NFL. Colston is a lanky slot receiver, but he lacks the strength or speed to consistently separate against man coverage. His limitations beating coverage have always been a part of his game, but those limitations have been exacerbated by his declining athleticism over recent years. To worsen matters, he became very unreliable at the catch point in 2015, as he couldn't consistently work through tight coverage to win contested catches. If the Saints can't put Cooks and Colston in situations where they are primarily facing zone coverage and avoiding press situations, Brees will be required to elevate their production by consistently throwing them open with precision and awareness.

The best way for the Saints to take the pressure off of Cooks and Colston is by replacing what Stills and Graham offered to the offense. A cast of receivers will be vying for Stills' spot during training camp and the preseason, but Graham has an obvious heir. Josh Hill is a third-year player who measures 6-foot-5 and 250 pounds, just slightly smaller than Graham's size of 6-foot-7 and 265 pounds. Despite his impressive size, Hill is comfortable in space. He can stretch the field down the seam or catch the ball in space before turning to run with it downfield. His athleticism proved to be very valuable in a limited sample last season. Eight of Hill's 14 receptions last year came after play-action, and those eight receptions accounted for four of his five touchdowns. The Saints asked him to leak out the backside of hard play fakes so he was uncovered and immediately in space. They also had him running deep crosses or seam routes that made the best use of his linear athleticism. To fully replace Graham, Hill will need to prove that he can consistently make receptions on these types of plays, and also prove himself at the catch point. Graham was able to use his size against smaller players by fending off defenders with his strength before attacking the ball in the air. Hill has the size, but not every big player understands how to use his size like Graham.

At this point of his career, Brees has thrown more than 10,000 passes dating back to his college days. It's no surprise that his arm strength is showing signs of decline, but that doesn't mean he can't still be very effective within the structure of Payton's offense. Payton doesn't ask Brees to push the ball downfield a huge amount. He ranked as average last season in both percentage of throws going 16-25 yards and percentage of throws going 26+ yards. Ball placement on deeper throws has become a greater issue for Brees over recent years. The design of Payton's offense and Brees' ability to look off coverage both create more space for his targets, helping him continue to throw catchable passes downfield. This has helped Brees rank first in bad-throw percentage in three of the past four years, and he was second in the year he wasn't first (2012). Only 10.6 percent of his throws were overthrown or underthrown last year, the lowest rate in the league by a significant margin; only one other quarterback was within 3.8 percent of him. When Brees is asked to fit the ball into tighter windows, his ball placement becomes a greater issue. Over the past four seasons, he has ranked 21st, 27th, 31st and 27th in defended pass percentage.

To further close the gap between Brees' bad-throw percentage rating and his defended pass percentage rating, the Saints should incorporate more screens next year. That is the added dimension that Cooks and new running back C.J. Spiller bring to the offense. The Saints threw just 14 screens to wide receivers and tight ends last season. If Cooks plays 16 games next season, they should easily double that number. Spiller is the most dangerous screen receiver on the team, though. He has a similar skill set to the one Reggie Bush boasted when he was in New Orleans. The Saints have ranked first or second in use of running back screen passes for six straight years, but last season those passes were split between Travaris Cadet and Pierre Thomas. Neither running back has the ability to advance screen passes that Spiller does.

The Saints are expecting to complement their altered offense with an improved defense. We constantly bring attention to the fact that defense is less predictable than offense from year to year. Normally, we would be highlighting the strong likelihood that a defense near the bottom of the league is going to improve the next season, especially when that same defense with the same coordinator was 10th in DVOA just two years ago. On the other hand, a defense this poor will usually spend the offseason addressing its biggest weakness, not exacerbating it. Junior Galette's release doesn't cost the franchise an All-Pro player, but the loss of his pass-rushing ability is tough for the Saints to replace. The roster isn't stocked with proven pass-rushers at any spot, but it's especially lacking at outside linebacker. Galette's departure puts the spotlight on Hau'oli Kikaha, an unproven rookie with health and athleticism question marks, and Anthony Spencer, a veteran whose career has been derailed by health issues. At least Spencer and Kikaha will benefit from playing with Cameron Jordan, one of the most talented defensive linemen in the NFL. The new contributors on the outside may also be joined by a new starting duo at inside linebacker. Dannell Ellerbe and rookie Stephone Anthony are more talented than David Hawthorne, but Hawthorne may stay in the starting lineup, either due to Ellerbe's lack of consistency and durability or Anthony's lack of experience. No matter who starts, each of the trio must prove they can be relied on.

The secondary has more proven players, but just as many question marks. Keenan Lewis should be a high-quality starting cornerback this year after struggling while playing hurt last season. Safety Jairus Byrd needs to find the skills he apparently left behind in Buffalo; he looked like the worst free-agent signing in the league last year before landing on IR with a torn meniscus. The Saints will be hoping to pair Byrd and Kenny Vaccaro in the starting lineup, using Vaccaro in a box-safety role that better suits his skill set. Vaccaro played deeper last year than he did during his rookie season and struggled so much that he was benched. Using players in roles that fit their skills will also be very important when it comes to the free-agent additions who will play alongside Lewis. Brandon Browner (ex-Patriots) is a proven player but needs very specific press-man assignments to be effective. Kyle Wilson (ex-Jets) needs to be kept in the slot.

Trading away your best offensive weapons is certainly an unusual approach to helping your quarterback, but Sean Payton and Mickey Loomis appear to have built a better team in New Orleans for the 2015 season. The man at the center of all these moves is on board also, as Brees told ESPN reporter Ed Werder during the offseason that he is "very convinced" that he will win another championship before retiring. Then again, he also believes he's going to be a quarterback in the NFL for another nine years.

Cian Fahey

2014 Saints Stats by Week

Wk	vs.	W-L	PF	PA	YDF	YDA	TO	Total	Off	Def	ST
1	at ATL	L	34	37	472	568	-1	-30%	12%	49%	7%
2	at CLE	L	24	26	397	324	-2	13%	34%	21%	1%
3	MIN	W	20	9	396	247	0	33%	29%	-10%	-6%
4	at DAL	L	17	38	438	445	-3	-47%	5%	44%	-7%
5	TB	W	37	31	511	314	-2	-36%	10%	46%	1%
6	BYE										
7	at DET	L	23	24	408	344	0	43%	20%	-14%	9%
8	GB	W	44	23	495	491	2	79%	55%	-23%	1%
9	at CAR	W	28	10	375	231	0	38%	5%	-27%	6%
10	SF	L	24	27	423	330	-2	-10%	-4%	4%	-2%
11	CIN	L	10	27	330	405	-1	-40%	6%	36%	-9%
12	BAL	L	27	34	525	449	0	-14%	17%	37%	6%
13	at PIT	W	35	32	393	538	2	65%	57%	-3%	6%
14	CAR	L	10	41	310	497	-2	-68%	-36%	34%	2%
15	at CHI	W	31	15	443	278	2	45%	35%	-17%	-6%
16	ATL	L	14	30	328	403	-4	-35%	-33%	26%	24%
17	at TB	W	23	20	338	280	-2	-38%	-26%	6%	-5%

Trends and Splits

	Offense	Rank	Defense	Rank
Total DVOA	10.6%	7	13.1%	31
Unadjusted VOA	10.3%	9	14.6%	31
Weighted Trend	5.2%	9	9.0%	28
Variance	7.6%	15	7.1%	23
Average Opponent	1.6%	24	0.1%	13
Passing	21.6%	9	19.2%	27
Rushing	0.8%	9	6.3%	32
First Down	9.9%	8	12.9%	30
Second Down	23.3%	1	2.9%	18
Third Down	-8.8%	23	30.8%	31
First Half	4.1%	14	13.3%	29
Second Half	16.5%	5	13.0%	29
Red Zone	2.5%	13	23.8%	32
Late and Close	6.1%	13	7.1%	25

Five-Year Performance

Year	W-L	Pyth W	Est W	PF	PA	TO	Total	Rk	Off	Rk	Def	Rk	ST	Rk	Off AGL	Rk	Def AGL	Rk	Off Age	Rk	Def Age	Rk	ST Age	Rk
2010	11-5	9.3	9.2	384	307	-6	9.2%	10	6.4%	11	-4.3%	10	-1.5%	21	19.6	9	25.1	18	28.2	7	27.6	12	27.0	10
2011	13-3	12.4	12.0	547	339	-3	23.8%	2	33.0%	2	10.2%	28	1.0%	12	17.4	6	7.2	1	27.7	11	26.9	19	26.2	18
2012	7-9	8.2	6.4	461	454	+2	-5.2%	19	11.9%	9	14.8%	32	-2.3%	24	11.5	4	23.6	14	28.3	3	26.6	21	25.9	22
2013	11-5	10.8	10.0	414	304	0	19.3%	4	16.0%	5	-5.8%	10	-2.5%	24	12.3	3	59.0	31	28.4	1	26.0	25	26.2	10
2014	7-9	7.4	7.6	401	424	-13	-0.9%	17	10.6%	7	13.1%	31	1.6%	11	26.4	12	31.6	10	29.0	1	26.2	24	25.9	22

2014 Performance Based on Most Common Personnel Groups

NO Offense				NO Offense vs. Opponents					NO Defense				NO Defense vs. Opponents			
Pers	Freq	Yds	DVOA	Run%	Pers	Freq	Yds	DVOA	Run%	Pers	Freq	Yds	DVOA	Pers	Freq	Yds	DVOA
11	48%	6.6	16.4%	20%	Base	38%	5.2	7.3%	56%	Base	39%	5.3	11.0%	11	53%	6.4	13.3%
12	18%	7.3	32.2%	40%	Nickel	52%	6.8	22.6%	24%	Nickel	53%	6.5	10.3%	12	22%	5.7	13.8%
21	14%	4.8	0.4%	56%	Dime+	9%	7.4	0.3%	6%	Dime+	7%	9.0	65.1%	21	10%	5.9	7.3%
22	8%	3.7	-22.8%	68%	Goal Line	1%	0.2	-26.9%	55%	Goal Line	1%	0.8	26.2%	22	5%	4.3	-14.9%
13	7%	6.2	27.1%	48%						Big	1%	4.0	2.3%	10	3%	11.2	110.4%
														13	3%	4.0	1.3%

Strategic Tendencies

Run/Pass		Rk	Formation		Rk	Pass Rush		Rk	Secondary		Rk	Strategy		Rk
Runs, first half	33%	28	Form: Single Back	67%	25	Rush 3	6.1%	15	4 DB	28%	11	Play action	18%	25
Runs, first down	45%	25	Form: Empty Back	8%	10	Rush 4	57.7%	21	5 DB	61%	17	Avg Box (Off)	6.24	22
Runs, second-long	29%	20	Pers: 3+ WR	51%	24	Rush 5	20.0%	23	6+ DB	10%	17	Avg Box (Def)	6.39	6
Runs, power sit.	51%	26	Pers: 4+ WR	1%	19	Rush 6+	16.2%	2	CB by Sides	64%	30	Offensive Pace	29.54	12
Runs, behind 2H	30%	10	Pers: 2+ TE/6+ OL	35%	9	Sacks by LB	55.9%	11	DB Blitz	13%	7	Defensive Pace	29.13	6
Pass, ahead 2H	49%	10	Shotgun/Pistol	52%	24	Sacks by DB	5.9%	17	Hole in Zone	4%	22	Go for it on 4th	2.01	1

One of the subjects we've written on in the past is that contrary to popular belief, the New Orleans Saints don't generally have a larger home-field advantage than the rest of the league. Two years ago was an exception, as the Saints were much better at home than on the road in 2013. Not last year. The Saints' offense went from 5.6% DVOA (10th) at home to 16.6% DVOA (third) on the road. The defense went from 18.4% (32nd) at home to 8.4% (26th) on the road. ☞ The Saints had a league-low 39 penalties on offense. ☞ The Saints' offense started games slow, just 25th in first-quarter DVOA, then ranked fifth in offensive DVOA from the second quarter on. ☞ Drew Brees struggled against defensive back blitzes (6.0 yards per pass) after crushing them the previous two seasons (8.4 yards per pass combined in 2012 and 2013). ☞ Only nine times since 1989 has a head coach who lasted the entire year put up an Aggressiveness Index above 2.0, and Sean Payton was the first coach to do it twice. (He also scored at 2.22 in 2007.)

Passing

Player	DYAR	DVOA	Plays	NtYds	Avg	YAC	C%	TD	Int
D.Brees	1225	15.7%	684	4750	6.9	4.8	69.8%	33	17

Rushing

Player	DYAR	DVOA	Plays	Yds	Avg	TD	Fum	Suc
M.Ingram	108	2.7%	226	964	4.3	9	1	50%
K.Robinson	57	8.9%	76	362	4.8	3	1	58%
P.Thomas*	74	30.9%	45	223	5.0	2	0	58%
D.Brees	27	17.7%	16	77	4.8	1	0	-
T.Cadet*	-18	-55.8%	10	32	3.2	0	1	50%
A.Johnson	10	12.9%	8	22	2.8	0	0	63%
B.Cooks	53	55.3%	7	73	10.4	1	0	-
C.J.Spiller	-76	-33.2%	78	303	3.9	0	3	40%

Receiving

Player	DYAR	DVOA	Plays	Ctch	Yds	Y/C	YAC	TD	C%
M.Colston	201	13.0%	99	59	902	15.3	5.0	5	60%
K.Stills*	285	30.3%	84	63	931	14.8	3.0	3	75%
B.Cooks	124	9.7%	69	53	550	10.4	3.2	3	77%
N.Toon	52	15.7%	23	17	215	12.6	2.5	1	74%
R.Meachem*	-12	-20.2%	20	7	114	16.3	3.0	0	35%
J.Morgan	1	-11.5%	10	4	92	23.0	5.8	0	40%
J.Graham*	124	6.8%	124	85	889	10.5	3.5	10	69%
B.Watson	-29	-21.3%	31	20	136	6.8	3.9	2	65%
J.Hill	57	32.0%	20	14	176	12.6	7.1	5	70%
P.Thomas*	111	22.2%	55	45	378	8.4	9.4	1	82%
T.Cadet*	57	5.4%	51	38	296	7.8	6.4	1	75%
M.Ingram	-54	-40.9%	36	29	145	5.0	5.0	0	81%
K.Robinson	3	-8.8%	11	8	63	7.9	10.8	0	73%
E.Lorig	-23	-45.3%	10	9	27	3.0	3.8	1	90%
C.J.Spiller	28	7.8%	22	19	125	6.6	9.7	1	86%

Offensive Line

Player	Pos	Age	GS	Snaps	Pen	Sk	Pass	Run	Player	Pos	Age	GS	Snaps	Pen	Sk	Pass	Run
Jahri Evans	RG	32	16/16	1140	2	4.5	17.0	2.0	Terron Armstead	LT	24	14/14	837	8	2.0	18.0	1.0
Ben Grubbs*	LG	31	16/16	1134	3	2.5	13.5	3.0	Bryce Harris	OT	26	16/2	387	4	1.0	12.0	1.5
Zach Strief	RT	32	16/16	1059	3	3.0	10.0	4.0	Tim Lelito	C	26	16/2	287	1	0.5	2.0	0.0
Jonathan Goodwin*	C	37	14/14	854	3	2.0	5.5	6.0	Max Unger	C	29	6/6	375	2	1.5	1.5	2.0

Year	Yards	ALY	Rk	Power	Rk	Stuff	Rk	2nd Lev	Rk	Open Field	Rk	Sacks	ASR	Rk	Short	Long	F-Start	Cont.
2012	4.40	4.04	18	71%	3	19%	14	1.25	12	0.90	9	26	4.9%	7	12	7	22	32
2013	4.11	4.08	7	67%	13	21%	23	1.22	12	0.65	18	37	5.3%	4	17	7	13	26
2014	4.36	4.38	2	59%	22	18%	13	1.25	8	0.73	15	30	5.3%	12	10	11	10	33
2014 ALY by direction:		Left End 4.49 (4)			Left Tackle 4.29 (8)			Mid/Guard 4.61 (1)			Right Tackle 4.34 (7)				Right End 3.44 (20)			

Andrus Peat was a surprising first-round pick for the Saints. The Stanford tackle was a highly regarded prospect by most media analysts, but he didn't offer an obvious fit in New Orleans. Offensive line help was obviously a need after a disappointing season in 2014, but the trade of Ben Grubbs suggested that help would come in the form of a left guard rather than a left tackle. Peat could be set to follow in the footsteps of Zack Martin and Joel Bitonio, tackle prospects who were moved to guard as rookies last year. However, Peat has never played guard and is 6-foot-7. That doesn't make it impossible to play on the inside, but it's a huge disadvantage. So the 13th overall pick may be forced to sit as a rookie. Left tackle Terron Armstead doesn't have the skill set to move inside, and right tackle Zach Strief is in the exact same situation as Peat, just with a decade more NFL experience.

Whether Peat beats out Strief or not for the right tackle position will likely be less significant than how the left guard and center positions play out. Tim Lelito and Senio Kelemete will compete for the left guard spot, with Lelito the favorite. An undrafted free agent from 2013, Lelito has played sparingly to this point in his career, mainly as a backup both at guard and at center. Max Unger will be starting at center after coming over from Seattle in the (infamous) Jimmy Graham trade. Knee and ankle injuries limited Unger to just six regular-season starts last year, and he has dealt with injury issues throughout his career. Nonetheless, while Unger struggles with his health and consistency, he offers much more versatility and athleticism than the physically limited veteran he replaces, Jonathan Goodwin. Payton has always highly valued interior linemen and discussed the center position after acquiring Unger. "We talk in certain games about this spot 2 yards behind the center is like the most important piece of property in football," he told reporters at the NFL's annual meeting. "If we can occupy that spot then we're gonna win the game and that sounds kind of simple, but...if that [spot] gets muddied, it's tough to play the [quarterback] position."

Defensive Front Seven

Defensive Line	Age	Pos	G	Snaps	Plays	TmPct	Rk	Stop	Dfts	BTkl	Runs	St%	Rk	RuYd	Rk	Sack	Hit	Hur	Dsrpt
						Overall							vs. Run				Pass Rush		
Cameron Jordan	26	DE	16	999	56	6.9%	13	47	14	2	43	79%	39	2.3	48	7.5	2	16.5	5
Akiem Hicks	26	DE	15	716	41	5.4%	33	32	8	2	38	79%	40	2.1	41	2.0	5	6.5	0
John Jenkins	26	DT	12	390	31	5.1%	38	24	4	0	27	74%	64	2.1	45	1.0	0	2.0	1
Brandon Deaderick	28	DE	13	339	8	1.2%	--	4	0	0	8	50%	--	2.4	--	0.0	0	6.0	0
Tyrunn Walker*	25	DE	16	304	18	2.2%	--	15	11	1	11	82%	--	2.2	--	2.5	2	4.5	0
Brodrick Bunkley*	32	DT	11	274	18	3.2%	--	13	1	1	18	72%	--	2.9	--	0.0	0	0.5	0

Edge Rushers	Age	Pos	G	Snaps	Plays	TmPct	Rk	Stop	Dfts	BTkl	Runs	St%	Rk	RuYd	Rk	Sack	Hit	Hur	Dsrpt
						Overall							vs. Run				Pass Rush		
Junior Galette*	27	OLB	16	795	47	5.8%	29	34	16	4	27	74%	46	3.0	61	10.0	11	32.5	0
Parys Haralson	31	OLB	16	489	33	4.1%	62	25	7	4	26	77%	35	1.6	15	3.0	6	9.5	0
Anthony Spencer	*31*	*DE*	*13*	*372*	*22*	*3.4%*	*72*	*19*	*6*	*0*	*17*	*82%*	*21*	*2.9*	*58*	*0.5*	*6*	*7.5*	*1*

Linebackers	Age	Pos	G	Snaps	Plays	TmPct	Rk	Stop	Dfts	BTkl	Sack	Hit	Hur	Runs	St%	Rk	RuYd	Rk	Tgts	Suc%	Rk	AdjYd	Rk	PD	Int
						Overall					Pass Rush			vs. Run					vs. Pass						
Curtis Lofton*	29	ILB	16	1044	145	18.0%	6	71	16	7	0.0	4	6.5	92	60%	58	3.3	40	43	50%	40	7.3	49	0	0
David Hawthorne	30	ILB	12	743	86	14.2%	32	52	18	13	3.0	2	6	57	65%	36	2.8	18	47	52%	30	6.6	38	3	1
Ramon Humber	28	ILB	15	448	44	5.8%	83	21	4	5	1.0	2	1.5	27	52%	79	3.9	65	18	36%	60	7.6	52	0	0

Year	Yards	ALY	Rk	Power	Rk	Stuff	Rk	2nd Level	Rk	Open Field	Rk	Sacks	ASR	Rk	Short	Long
2012	5.29	4.47	31	60%	15	18%	19	1.38	31	1.48	31	30	5.5%	28	6	18
2013	4.40	3.75	14	69%	23	21%	12	1.06	12	1.13	30	49	8.6%	4	13	16
2014	4.78	3.99	19	74%	28	18%	22	1.32	29	1.17	31	34	6.0%	26	16	8

2014 ALY by direction: Left End 3.93 (21)   Left Tackle 4.4 (25)   Mid/Guard 3.41 (6)   Right Tackle 5.26 (31)   Right End 4.38 (26)

Akiem Hicks and Cameron Jordan were the Saints' two constants on the defensive line last season, but neither played to his potential in 2014. Jordan in particular was the focal point of team's pass rush. He has versatility to play inside and outside, but no matter where Rob Ryan moves him, he still draws added attention from blockers. He still finished the regular season with 7.5 sacks, but his pressure was less constant and those sacks were less impactful than in previous years. One was a blown assignment, one was a coverage sack, and one came when the quarterback ran into him even though he hadn't beaten his blocker. Another 1.5 sacks came in Week 17 when the season had already been lost.

The Saints needed Jordan to be more of an instigator last season… and they'll certainly need him to be more of an instigator *this* season after cutting outside linebacker Junior Galette. Injury, character issue, and off-field controversy eventually pushed the Saints to absorb a huge cap hit just to rid themselves of their top edge rusher. Galette's departure may prove to be addition by subtraction off the field, but the Saints really shouldn't be comfortable with how much they now need to depend on Hau'oli Kikaha and Anthony Spencer. Kikaha is a rookie who had 13 sacks for Washington last year. He fell to the second round of the draft because he has suffered multiple ACL injuries already and there are question marks over his athleticism translating to the NFL. Athleticism is less of an issue against college offensive linemen for obvious reasons. Anthony Spencer also has health issues and durability question marks, but he is on the other end of his career. The 31-year-old former Dallas Cowboys defensive end had microfracture surgery in 2013 and was limited throughout 2014. He showed flashes of his old pass-rushing self toward the end of last season, but expectations should be muted at this point in his career.

The Saints couldn't stop the run in 2014 and the coaching staff identified the inside linebacker spots as places that needed new faces. The departed Curtis Lofton ranked third in the league in run tackles, but didn't make enough of those tackles before the back had already managed a successful gain. The Saints brought in two players to replace Lofton: Stephone Anthony (Clemson) came with the 31st overall pick acquired in the Jimmy Graham trade, while Dannell Ellerbe was acquired in a trade with the Miami Dolphins. Keeping with the theme established at outside linebacker, Ellerbe and Anthony offer the Saints a veteran needing to prove himself and a rookie with significant question marks. Both players are very impressive athletes, but Anthony needs to be refined technically while Ellerbe needs to prove his durability and consistency. Both players have huge upside because of their potential to play both the run and the pass, but both also need a significant amount of work from a coaching staff that hasn't been earning glowing reviews over recent months. David Hawthorne may stay in the starting lineup if Ellerbe isn't healthy or Anthony isn't ready, and everybody will be happier if special-teams captain Ramon Humber can concentrate on special teams instead of getting pushed around on runs as a depth linebacker.

Defensive Secondary

Secondary	Age	Pos	G	Snaps	Plays	Overall TmPct	Rk	Stop	Dfts	BTkl	vs. Run Runs	St%	Rk	RuYd	Rk	vs. Pass Tgts	Tgt%	Rk	Dist	Suc%	Rk	AdjYd	Rk	PD	Int
Kenny Vaccaro	24	SS	15	981	77	10.2%	37	28	13	10	32	44%	31	6.8	39	28	7.1%	24	8.8	57%	30	6.4	25	5	2
Keenan Lewis	29	CB	16	900	53	6.6%	70	22	8	10	6	17%	69	9.0	61	86	23.7%	39	15.2	53%	24	7.8	38	14	2
Corey White*	25	CB	15	758	57	7.5%	58	18	11	7	7	14%	71	16.1	75	69	22.6%	30	11.9	41%	72	9.0	57	7	2
Patrick Robinson*	28	CB	14	612	47	6.7%	69	17	7	4	5	20%	65	6.6	38	51	20.7%	21	11.7	53%	27	7.0	21	10	2
Rafael Bush	28	FS	10	467	57	11.3%	--	12	5	5	24	25%	--	8.5	--	18	9.6%	--	13.7	50%	--	10.2	--	2	0
Pierre Warren	23	FS	6	406	34	11.2%	--	6	3	6	15	0%	--	14.9	--	9	5.5%	--	19.0	59%	--	8.6	--	2	2
Jairus Byrd	29	FS	4	267	24	11.9%	--	10	6	4	9	33%	--	4.9	--	4	3.7%	--	12.0	51%	--	9.7	--	1	0
Brandon Browner	31	CB	9	580	31	6.9%	67	15	6	4	5	100%	1	2.4	2	53	22.5%	29	14.5	56%	16	7.4	28	9	1
Kyle Wilson	28	CB	16	308	21	2.7%	--	9	4	1	5	40%	--	7.4	--	22	19.4%	--	10.0	52%	--	7.8	--	1	0

Year	Pass D Rank	vs. #1 WR	Rk	vs. #2 WR	Rk	vs. Other WR	Rk	vs. TE	Rk	vs. RB	Rk
2012	28	38.3%	32	8.5%	23	-4.1%	12	-7.4%	8	17.5%	24
2013	6	-9.2%	12	10.7%	24	-5.0%	12	-15.6%	7	-10.4%	10
2014	27	25.1%	30	8.6%	24	-5.2%	13	-26.7%	1	40.7%	32

The Saints secondary is going to look very different in 2015. The most significant changes aren't the additions, but rather two veterans returning from injury-plagued seasons. Jairus Byrd was the team's highest-profile free-agent addition before the beginning of last season. In Buffalo, Byrd was widely considered one of the best safeties in the NFL, but he struggled during the initial stages of his first season with New Orleans. He missed tackles and made bad reads in coverage on a regular basis. Then Byrd landed on IR with a torn meniscus before he could correct his play on the field. Cornerback Keenan Lewis played all 16 games last year, but he never looked to be 100 percent healthy. A balky knee stood out more than any other ailment he endured. Lewis and Byrd have the potential to be two of the best players at their respective positions in the NFL, but they need to be fully healthy.

Brandon Browner will join Lewis and Byrd in the starting lineup. The former Seahawks and Patriots cornerback is a talented player, but because of his size and lumbering lateral movement, Browner needs to be used in press coverage and regularly given safety help. The Patriots could afford to use Browner in that way because they had Devin McCourty and Darrelle Revis. The Saints will need Byrd and fellow safety Kenny Vaccaro to be fully effective to get the most out of Browner. Vaccaro was benched last year as he endured an awful season, but he is still young enough to turn his career around as a nickelback/safety. If Byrd can cover enough ground and Vaccaro can handle the types of receivers who cause Browner problems, Browner can be used to nullify bigger receivers. If Browner is overstretched or struggles too much with his consistency, P.J. Williams (2015 third-rounder, Florida State) or Stanley Jean-Baptiste (2014 second-rounder, Nebraska) could be given a crack to force their way into the starting lineup. Williams is more versatile than Browner, but is also primarily built to play as a boundary cornerback. Jean-Baptiste, a former receiver who started just 17 games as a cornerback in college, was the very definition of a "project" cornerback, and played in just four games with just eight defensive snaps.

Former Jets first-round pick Kyle Wilson is the favorite to rotate in the slot with Vaccaro, but Devin Breaux has been impressive in offseason workouts. Breaux is a great story, a local kid who broke his back playing for McDonogh 35 High School and never played at LSU because he was having problems recovering from that injury. He ended up in something called the Gridiron Developmental Football League, then played Arena ball before ending up a 2014 CFL All-Star for the Hamilton Tiger-Cats and then signing with the Saints.

Special Teams

Year	DVOA	Rank	FG/XP	Rank	Net Kick	Rank	Kick Ret	Rank	Net Punt	Rank	Punt Ret	Rank	Hidden	Rank
2012	-2.3%	24	-4.1	23	-7.3	28	-6.2	25	8.6	9	-2.5	18	14.2	3
2013	-2.5%	24	-13.8	32	-2.1	25	-0.5	14	11.1	2	-7.3	27	-8.0	27
2014	1.6%	11	-4.1	26	-2.5	21	4.0	8	13.4	2	-2.6	18	-23.1	32

Thomas Morstead has been the Saints' punter for the past six seasons, and has performed so well in recent years that the Saints didn't even bring in another punter to compete with him in training camp. Morstead also had his most valuable season on kickoffs last year. Unfortunately, the Saints can't seem to find someone they can trust to kick field goals. Garrett Hartley's demise in 2013 left the team with no long-term option. Veteran Shayne Graham was just a stop-gap option for the 2014 season. Dustin Hopkins and Zach Hocker will compete for the job in 2015. Hopkins was a Buffalo seventh-round pick out of Florida State in 2013 but suffered a groin injury and ended up on injured reserve; last year, he couldn't win a camp competition against the guy who replaced him, Dan Carpenter. Hocker was a Washington seventh-round pick out of Arkansas last year, but couldn't beat out Kai Forbath. This would be our annual reminder not to draft kickers, except we're talking about two seventh-round picks here. You might as well throw them at the wall and see what sticks. New Orleans hopes ones of them does.

One of the more intriguing returners in the NFL is Jalen Saunders. He was a 2014 fourth-round pick of the Jets, but New York released him early in the regular season. Saunders bounced around multiple practice squads before the Saints added him to their 53-man roster. In Week 16 against the Atlanta Falcons, Saunders had a 99-yard kick return that highlighted his impressive speed and elusiveness. While his size (5-foot-9, 165 pounds) will likely prevent him from ever being a factor on offense, his return ability will create a lot of excitement in New Orleans.

New York Giants

2014 Record: 6-10	**Total DVOA:** -5.8% (21st)	**2015 Mean Projection:** 7.7 wins	**On the Clock (0-4):** 11%
Pythagorean Wins: 7.5 (18th)	**Offense:** -0.3% (15th)	**Postseason Odds:** 32.9%	**Mediocrity (5-7):** 35%
Snap-Weighted Age: 27.0 (11th)	**Defense:** 4.9% (24th)	**Super Bowl Odds:** 3.2%	**Playoff Contender (8-10):** 38%
Average Opponent: -2.0% (22nd)	**Special Teams:** -0.6% (15th)	**Proj. Avg. Opponent:** -1.3% (20th)	**Super Bowl Contender (11+):** 15%

2014: Ouch.

2015: Ouch?

The story of the 2013 and 2014 Giants was not an Eli Manning story or a Tom Coughlin story. It was an injury story. The 2015 season is shaping up the same way.

For two years in a row, the Giants led the NFL in adjusted games lost. The Giants lost the equivalent of 137.5 starter-games to injuries in 2014 after losing 141.3 starter-games the previous season. The Giants finished 31st in the NFL with 65.9 AGL on offense – the Chargers and their Spinal Tap drummer-centers and running backs topped them – and 30th in the NFL with 71.3 AGL on defense, where the 49ers and Raiders suffered a few more injuries.

The Giants had the third-worst AGL in the league for running backs (the Chargers and Colts nicked them), the worst wide receiver AGL, the sixth-worst linebacker AGL, and the second-worst secondary AGL, behind the Raiders.

Keep in mind that 16 AGL is essentially one lost season by a starter. That means 137.5 AGL is equivalent to eight starters lost for a full season, with another starter out for half the season. The Giants have coped with that for two straight years. That rate goes a little beyond "well, injuries are part of the game." The Giants have suffered so many injuries for so many seasons (they ranked 25th in AGL in 2012) that they are difficult to both evaluate and predict. The team on the field in October usually bears little resemblance to the team on the post-minicamp depth chart, except that Eli Manning is the quarterback.

This year is already shaping up to be another one of those years. Left tackle William Beatty tore a pectoral muscle while lifting weights during OTAs. He is out until late in the season. Victor Cruz is still recovering from the knee injury that erased the second half of last season. By early June, he was running routes during OTAs, but his precise status and timetable remained a source of anxiety. Larry Donnell walked the sidelines during early June's open practices with a protective boot on his left foot. Robert Ayers had to be carted off the field during one series of drills. And Odell Beckham's hamstring flared up ominously; hamstring issues turned the most exciting rookie in the NFL into vaporware for most of 2014 training camp and limited his role early in the season.

Finally, in a late development that necessitated some mid-summer team-chapter edits, Jason Pierre-Paul lost his right index finger after a run-in with a Fourth of July firework. Given the rate at which Giants players comic-tragically injure themselves, Andre Williams will suffer a bad case of late-July acne, attempt to pop a zit in the bathroom mirror, and blind himself with the ricochet by the time you read this. On a positive note, no one accidently shot himself in a nightclub this offseason, so perhaps there's progress.

Ayers' injury turned out to be a sprain, Donnell's Achilles was just a collegiate injury that flairs up now and then, Cruz has suffered no setbacks, and neither Beckham nor the Giants pushed any hamstring panic buttons. Even JPP is expected to play, though nobody's sure if that will be in September or November. The Beatty injury was the most significant one, and it was plenty significant: instead of a veteran coming off a great year at left tackle and first-round rookie Ereck Flowers on the right, the Giants will probably start the year with Flowers on the left and a bunch of questions on the right. But most teams can get through OTAs and a backyard barbecue without constant injury updates about all of their most important non-quarterbacks. Giants injury reports start before the hitting starts, before the pads go on, before the NBA Finals start.

It's important to note that there is nothing intrinsically wrong with the Giants as an organization that causes them to be the league's most injured team year after year. Coughlin is forward-thinking when it comes to conditioning and training; the Giants aren't getting gassed on 100 degree days or pulling muscles because an old-school coach is making them slam into each other on the first day of camp. Players such as Beckham arrive in East Rutherford with clean college injury records and reputations for durability, so it's not like Jerry Reese keeps pulling from the "slightly used" bin. Conditioning coach Jerry Palmieri has been with the club for nine years, so he has two Super Bowl rings to verify that he does something right. He is supported by Markus Paul (a conditioning assistant for the 2001-04 Patriots) and recent arrival Joe Danos. These are well-respected physical trainers, not medieval barbers. The Giants consult with sports-science companies like Catapult, use their practice bubble when Meadowlands conditions reach "sweltering," and at least dabble in other next-generation training techniques. The Giants just seem to have rotten injury luck, the kind that stretches the limits of probability.

With no relief from the hamstring-and-pectoral zombie plague in sight, projecting the Giants is like projecting the real estate market for a village at the base of a volcano. When we started running post-draft calculations, Beatty was healthy,

2015 Giants Schedule

Week	Opp.	Week	Opp.	Week	Opp.
1	at DAL	7	DAL	13	NYJ
2	ATL	8	at NO	14	at MIA (Mon.)
3	WAS (Thu.)	9	at TB	15	CAR
4	at BUF	10	NE	16	at MIN
5	SF	11	BYE	17	PHI
6	at PHI (Mon.)	12	at WAS		

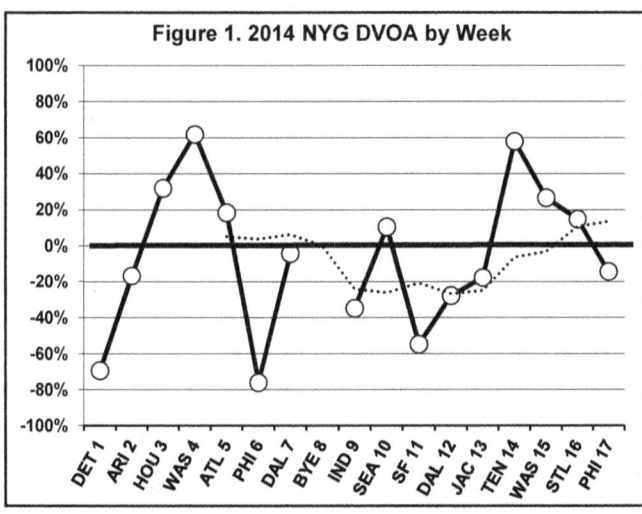

Figure 1. 2014 NYG DVOA by Week

there were no red flags for Beckham or Donnell, and Cruz was a standard veteran receiver on the mend. The Giants had just added Flowers in the draft and Shane Vereen in free agency. The Giants looked stable on the offensive line and deep at the skill positions. With Ben McAdoo's offense more firmly established, they were poised to have one of the best passing attacks in the NFL.

As of June, the Giants were facing discontinuity and inexperience on the offensive line. Even with Cruz still on track, the specter of a limited Beckham loomed, and while Donnell is not the superstar he appeared to be for a few Monday night hours last October, you don't want to watch his backups run routes. Even with the backfield upgraded, the Giants offense looked like it could be another version of the one we saw too often in 2013 and 2014: Eli under pressure, forcing passes to whoever was healthy and competent, launching interceptions when the ball leaves his hand too hot or Rueben Randle decides to run a totally different route than the one in the playbook.

We never got a true look at the McAdoo offense last season. Beckham and Cruz were simultaneously healthy for about 90 minutes of game time. Running back Rashad Jennings, expected to be the chairman of the backfield committee, got hurt in October and was either out or severely limited for the rest of the season. Jerrel Jernigan broke camp as the third receiver and was lost by the middle of Week 3. Beckham became a breakout star, Andre Williams was more Brandon Jacobs than Ron Dayne by the end of the season, and Donnell had his moments, but the Giants were again forced to give meaningful touches to the likes of Peyton Hillis and Kevin Ogletree just to get through games.

Still, there were signs that the new offense was more dynamic and better suited to the Giants' hypothetical personnel than Kevin Gilbride's old scheme. Manning passed for 4,400 yards and 30 touchdowns with half his weapons tied behind his back, after all. McAdoo used the no-huddle in a variety of non-traditional situations, with varying degrees of success. There were times during the Giants' three-game winning streak early in the season when they looked like the NFL's next great up-tempo offense. Then a bunch of guys got hurt, the Giants started facing opponents better than the Redskins and Falcons, and both the pace and effectiveness of McAdoo's attack began to waiver. It's one thing to pressure the defense with tempo when the versatile Jennings and crafty Cruz are on the field, quite another when counting on a pair of rookie playmakers and the easily-befuddled Randle.

While the Giants embrace McAdoo's newfangled offensive concepts, they have brought back a familiar face to helm the defense. Steve Spagnuolo's days as a coaching A-lister are fading into memory; 2007 was a long time ago in football years. Spags spent 2014 keeping the Ravens secondary from falling apart during a Giants-caliber injury rash. It was the perfect warmup for a return to New Jersey.

Spags inherits a front four with talent, though not the kind of Strahan-Tuck-Kiwanuka-Umenyiora talent that made him a coaching superstar eight years ago. Jason Pierre-Paul now fills the Umenyiora role of inconsistent mega-talent with a perpetual contract beef. Jonathan Hankins is a better pure defensive tackle than those Super Bowl lines ever had; pencil him in as the steady Tuck of the group. Cullen Jenkins is no Strahan, but he is a useful veteran pass-rusher. Robert Ayers and Marcus Kuhn are hard-nosed types, Jay Bromley and Owamagbe Odighizua situational pass-rush prospects. Spags can mix and match to get a lot of production out of this unit.

It's the rest of the defense he must worry about, particularly the secondary. (The Giants have cobbled together linebacker corps from oft-injured journeymen and late-round picks for so long that they have forgotten there is another way.) Cornerbacks Prince Amukamara and Trumaine McBride are returning from injuries that ended their 2014 seasons after eight and five games. It's never a good thing when Dominique Rodgers-Cromartie is your steady, dependable cornerback. The cornerback corps is like the receiving corps: if everyone returns healthy, it's dangerous and deep. Another injury outbreak, and Chykie Brown (the Peyton Hillis of defensive backs) ends up covering Dez Bryant.

Meanwhile, the Giants jettisoned all of their safeties from 2013 and 2014. All of them. Only Stevie Brown was a real loss. Antrel Rolle had reached the point where he talked a much better game than he played, while Quintin Demps had never been more than a kick returner and dime safety until the Giants needed him in relief of the injured Brown.

With a nearly-empty safety depth chart on draft weekend, Jerry Reese traded into the top of the second round to grab Landon Collins, the Alabama safety who slipped because he is more of a traditional in-the-box strong defender than most teams prefer these days. Collins was one of Nick Saban's magna cum laude students, so he can be penciled in as an immediate starter. But the candidates to start at free safety are Cooper Taylor, a 2013 draft pick who has had two fine camps but (wait for it) missed all of last season with a foot injury; and Nat Behre, a second-year special-teams standout who may be better suited to back up Collins. Fifth-round pick Mykkele Thompson is also in the mix, and the unsinkable Chykie Brown could conceivably slide over.

If DRC, Amukamara, and McBride stay healthy, the Giants can get by with inexperienced safeties. If Jon Beason has one of his healthy leap years at middle linebacker, the Giants will be in good shape there, too. Of course, it's assumed that projections for all teams come with the *"if everyone stays mostly healthy"* qualifier" For the Giants, we're forced to go hoarse repeating it, all the while wondering if there's even a remote chance that it will happen.

Injuries are never an excuse. That's both the conventional wisdom and the WFAN logic. Angry-fan types beat the drum for Coughlin's departure last season, lost patience with Eli hours after his second Super Bowl win, and have no particular love for Reese and his slow-and-steady roster management. Coughlin, Manning and Reese are hardly blameless—the

sock-flag incident against the Colts and late-game collapse against the Jaguars reflect poorly on Coughlin, Manning has plateaued, and Reese could peek outside the financial box a little more. But it is hard to figure out what the coach, quarterback and general manager are supposed to do when the injury list runs onto the third page except rummage deep into the practice squad, insert whoever is available into the lineup, and cross their fingers.

Injuries are never an excuse for Football Outsiders, either. But sometimes they are a legitimate reason. Our projections are based on a snapshot of the Giants depth chart in late June, plus the usually-reasonable assumption that injury rates will be in the same area code as league norms. We see explosive receivers, a versatile running back, an up-tempo offense, an established quarterback and coaching staff, talent on the front four, and big question marks on the offensive line and in the secondary. If you are reading in August and all of that has already changed because Beckham crashed into Amukamara and they toppled onto Cruz, adjust your expectations accordingly, and wonder when this Giants injury nightmare will end.

Mike Tanier

2014 Giants Stats by Week

Wk	vs.	W-L	PF	PA	YDF	YDA	TO	Total	Off	Def	ST
1	at DET	L	14	35	197	417	-2	-69%	-33%	38%	1%
2	ARI	L	14	25	341	266	-4	-17%	0%	-10%	-27%
3	HOU	W	30	17	419	411	2	32%	33%	-4%	-5%
4	at WAS	W	45	14	449	329	5	62%	20%	-29%	12%
5	ATL	W	30	20	317	397	-1	18%	9%	-9%	1%
6	at PHI	L	0	27	254	448	1	-76%	-65%	8%	-3%
7	at DAL	L	21	31	352	423	-1	-4%	10%	19%	4%
8	BYE										
9	IND	L	24	40	438	443	-1	-35%	-18%	20%	3%
10	at SEA	L	17	38	324	510	1	10%	24%	13%	-1%
11	SF	L	10	16	330	333	-4	-55%	-57%	5%	7%
12	DAL	L	28	31	417	385	0	-28%	7%	29%	-6%
13	at JAC	L	24	25	329	258	-3	-18%	-12%	7%	1%
14	at TEN	W	36	7	402	207	2	58%	-15%	-60%	12%
15	WAS	W	24	13	287	372	0	26%	7%	-13%	7%
16	at STL	W	37	27	514	387	3	15%	57%	36%	-6%
17	PHI	L	26	34	505	426	0	-14%	14%	17%	-11%

Trends and Splits

	Offense	Rank	Defense	Rank
Total DVOA	-0.3%	15	4.9%	24
Unadjusted VOA	-2.3%	17	6.1%	24
Weighted Trend	-1.3%	14	6.1%	26
Variance	10.0%	26	6.3%	17
Average Opponent	-0.5%	14	-2.3%	27
Passing	16.6%	12	8.9%	21
Rushing	-11.5%	23	0.0%	27
First Down	-4.2%	19	4.8%	23
Second Down	-3.5%	19	12.4%	29
Third Down	12.3%	10	-7.2%	12
First Half	14.5%	7	1.1%	18
Second Half	-15.7%	25	8.8%	26
Red Zone	-10.0%	18	-9.2%	12
Late and Close	-18.2%	28	-2.0%	17

Five-Year Performance

Year	W-L	Pyth W	Est W	PF	PA	TO	Total	Rk	Off	Rk	Def	Rk	ST	Rk	Off AGL	Rk	Def AGL	Rk	Off Age	Rk	Def Age	Rk	ST Age	Rk
2010	10-6	10.1	10.4	394	347	-3	13.0%	9	7.5%	10	-11.2%	3	-5.8%	30	39.6	26	18.3	13	27.3	18	27.2	16	26.0	20
2011	9-7	7.8	9.1	394	400	+7	8.5%	12	10.5%	7	2.4%	19	0.3%	15	25.2	13	53.1	30	27.4	13	27.6	8	26.1	20
2012	9-7	10.2	9.5	429	344	+14	13.4%	7	12.8%	7	1.5%	16	2.0%	10	26.1	12	56.6	28	27.8	8	27.2	13	26.2	13
2013	7-9	5.6	5.5	294	383	-15	-15.7%	27	-22.0%	31	-11.4%	6	-5.1%	28	80.9	32	60.3	32	27.4	12	27.4	7	26.1	15
2014	6-10	7.5	7.0	380	400	-2	-5.8%	21	-0.3%	15	4.9%	24	-0.6%	15	65.9	31	71.3	30	26.6	20	27.6	5	26.7	3

2014 Performance Based on Most Common Personnel Groups

NYG Offense					NYG Offense vs. Opponents					NYG Defense					NYG Defense vs. Opponents			
Pers	Freq	Yds	DVOA	Run%	Pers	Freq	Yds	DVOA	Run%	Pers	Freq	Yds	DVOA		Pers	Freq	Yds	DVOA
11	68%	5.8	4.6%	28%	Base	29%	5.0	0.5%	64%	Base	36%	5.8	4.7%		11	52%	6.3	4.0%
12	11%	5.7	8.4%	54%	Nickel	53%	5.6	1.8%	30%	Nickel	55%	6.3	5.3%		12	22%	6.2	6.4%
21	10%	4.3	-3.1%	87%	Dime+	16%	7.2	27.3%	23%	Dime+	9%	6.7	-0.3%		21	9%	7.1	12.0%
22	6%	4.3	-11.0%	85%	Goal Line	2%	0.9	-24.9%	70%	Goal Line	1%	4.1	5.5%		13	5%	5.8	23.6%
02	2%	10.3	47.5%	0%											22	3%	4.0	-11.3%

Strategic Tendencies

Run/Pass		Rk	Formation		Rk	Pass Rush		Rk	Secondary		Rk	Strategy		Rk
Runs, first half	40%	12	Form: Single Back	73%	17	Rush 3	4.9%	21	4 DB	23%	21	Play action	23%	10
Runs, first down	53%	7	Form: Empty Back	3%	30	Rush 4	63.4%	18	5 DB	63%	13	Avg Box (Off)	6.33	11
Runs, second-long	34%	8	Pers: 3+ WR	71%	5	Rush 5	23.9%	12	6+ DB	13%	14	Avg Box (Def)	6.36	9
Runs, power sit.	54%	20	Pers: 4+ WR	1%	20	Rush 6+	7.9%	11	CB by Sides	74%	22	Offensive Pace	29.65	13
Runs, behind 2H	31%	8	Pers: 2+ TE/6+ OL	20%	29	Sacks by LB	17.0%	21	DB Blitz	8%	22	Defensive Pace	29.60	10
Pass, ahead 2H	45%	23	Shotgun/Pistol	60%	17	Sacks by DB	6.4%	16	Hole in Zone	6%	15	Go for it on 4th	0.67	26

They didn't go empty backfield much, but the Giants were phenomenal when they did, leading the NFL with 10.9 yards per play and 91.4% DVOA.   The Giants ranked among the top three teams in number of running back draws for the fourth straight year. They had 4.1 yards per carry on these plays with -14.7% DVOA.   There was a hiccup in 2013 where Eli Manning struggled against big blitzes, but he returned to his usual performance with 8.7 yards per pass last season. In three of the past four years, Manning has ranked as one of the top three quarterbacks against blitzes of six or more pass rushers.   Unfortunately, the Giants defense was bad exactly where their quarterback was good. The Giants didn't big blitz much, but when they did, they allowed a mind-numbing 12.7 yards per play. No other team in the NFL allowed more than 9.0 yards per play on big blitzes.   The Giants ranked 31st in the NFL in both DVOA (10.1%) and yards per carry (5.75) allowed against runs with three or four wide receivers on the field. The year before, the Giants had actually led the league with -28.3% DVOA on these runs.   Big Blue was a big mess against passes in the "short middle" section of the field, allowing a league-worst 120.0% DVOA when no other team was above 100% and the NFL average was 48.6% DVOA.   The Giants had 20 broken tackles that were quarterbacks escaping from sacks; no other team was charted with more than 11 of these.

Passing

Player	DYAR	DVOA	Plays	NtYds	Avg	YAC	C%	TD	Int
E.Manning	642	4.6%	628	4231	6.7	5.1	63.3%	30	14
R.Nassib	-18	-48.8%	7	48	6.9	10.8	80.0%	0	0

Rushing

Player	DYAR	DVOA	Plays	Yds	Avg	TD	Fum	Suc
A.Williams	-24	-11.4%	217	721	3.3	7	1	38%
R.Jennings	112	7.0%	167	639	3.8	4	0	47%
P.Hillis*	6	-1.9%	26	115	4.4	0	0	38%
H.Hynoski	-7	-21.4%	7	13	1.9	0	0	71%
O.Beckham	19	17.7%	7	35	5.0	0	0	-
E.Manning	18	41.3%	6	38	6.3	1	0	-
O.Darkwa	10	35.1%	5	21	4.2	1	0	60%
S.Vereen	4	-7.4%	96	391	4.1	2	0	41%
C.Ogbonnaya	17	17.8%	14	50	3.6	1	0	57%

Receiving

Player	DYAR	DVOA	Plays	Ctch	Yds	Y/C	YAC	TD	C%
O.Beckham	396	25.8%	130	91	1305	14.3	5.3	12	70%
R.Randle	34	-9.3%	127	71	938	13.2	3.3	3	56%
P.Parker	70	3.2%	56	36	418	11.6	3.3	2	64%
V.Cruz	13	-9.0%	41	23	337	14.7	7.7	1	56%
J.Jernigan*	-2	-15.4%	9	6	40	6.7	1.7	0	67%
K.Ogletree*	-8	-24.0%	9	5	50	10.0	2.8	0	56%
C.Washington	13	6.6%	8	5	52	10.4	2.8	1	63%
D.Harris	8	-2.3%	11	6	108	18.0	6.0	0	55%
L.Donnell	-18	-10.2%	92	63	628	10.0	3.5	6	68%
D.Fells	75	42.9%	20	16	188	11.8	5.3	4	80%
A.Robinson	10	10.1%	7	5	50	10.0	10.0	1	71%
R.Jennings	-35	-29.3%	41	30	226	7.5	10.4	0	73%
A.Williams	-48	-37.6%	37	18	130	7.2	8.2	0	49%
P.Hillis*	-16	-34.4%	16	10	87	8.7	9.3	0	63%
S.Vereen	49	-3.1%	77	52	447	8.6	7.3	3	68%

Offensive Line

Player	Pos	Age	GS	Snaps	Pen	Sk	Pass	Run	Player	Pos	Age	GS	Snaps	Pen	Sk	Pass	Run
John Jerry	RG	29	16/16	1126	5	2.0	16.3	6.5	Weston Richburg	LG	24	16/15	1035	7	2.0	17.5	5.0
J.D. Walton*	C	28	16/16	1118	5	1.0	7.5	12.0	Justin Pugh	RT	25	14/14	910	9	5.5	17.5	4.5
William Beatty	LT	30	16/16	1114	9	4.0	19.8	7.0	Marshall Newhouse	OT	30	14/6	442	4	2.0	13.0	2.0

Year	Yards	ALY	Rk	Power	Rk	Stuff	Rk	2nd Lev	Rk	Open Field	Rk	Sacks	ASR	Rk	Short	Long	F-Start	Cont.
2012	4.75	4.47	2	67%	8	19%	18	1.38	7	0.96	7	20	4.4%	3	1	11	13	33
2013	3.48	3.27	30	70%	10	25%	31	1.10	18	0.45	28	40	7.6%	18	10	11	6	23
2014	3.62	3.76	22	61%	20	20%	18	0.94	29	0.47	28	30	5.0%	10	12	10	18	37
2014 ALY by direction:			Left End 3.45 (23)			Left Tackle 3.93 (12)			Mid/Guard 3.86 (21)				Right Tackle 3.67 (20)			Right End 3.34 (22)		

The original post-draft wisdom listed the Giants starting offensive line, right-to-left, as follows: Will Beatty, Jordan Pugh, Weston Richburg, Geoff Schwartz, and Ereck Flowers. This would have given the Giants two quick, experienced pass protectors on the left side and two traditional steamrollers on the right: a classic line configuration.

When Beatty injured himself while lifting weights in OTAs, however, it set off a chain reaction. As of late May, Flowers was taking starter's reps at left tackle, with newcomer Marshall Newhouse at right tackle and Schwartz, still recovering from a late-2014 ankle injury, rotating with John Jerry at right guard. "Our plans are to continue to try to figure out how this line is going to fall out, who is going to be where, and we're going to try some different combinations to get there," Tom Coughlin said in late May. In other words, what we saw in the wake of Beatty's injury is probably not what we will see at the start of training camp or in the season opener against Dallas.

Flowers, the ninth overall selection in this year's draft, is a 6-foot-6, 330-pound mountain of muscle with a hard-nosed disposition and just enough athleticism to play left tackle. That said, a rookie is a rookie, and he had trouble with inside moves and elite speed rushers in his final season at Miami. Pugh played well through nagging injuries last season but did not really build on his 2013 success, which may be why the Giants appear more committed to sliding him from right tackle to guard than giving him a tryout on the left side. Pugh has not played guard since high school but has the tools for the transition.

The Giants drafted Richburg as a center last season but needed him as an emergency starter at left guard. His pass blocking improved as the season wore on, but he will look much better at his natural position: Richburg is a heady "calls and adjustments" center, not a top athlete. Newhouse had a pair of ugly seasons as the Packers' starting left tackle in 2011 and 2012, and is now a multi-position lineman for hire who was last seen starting a handful of midseason games at right tackle for the 2014 Bengals. He's an absolute stopgap.

Schwartz had a typical Giants season last year. A toe injury forced him onto the injured list at the end of camp, he got healthy enough to play a pair of November games, then suffered an ankle injury that ended his season. Schwartz stated in camp that he can play right tackle if needed, though no one in the organization approached him about it. "I won't be playing left tackle," he joked. Jerry and Dallas Reynolds are the only experienced backups; as Jerry showed last season, neither is the kind of lineman you want to count on for multiple starts.

Beatty, who responded well to the new offense last year and bounced back from a dreadful 2013 full of multi-sack meltdowns, could theoretically return by mid-November. The Giants will probably need him.

Defensive Front Seven

Defensive Line	Age	Pos	G	Snaps	Plays	TmPct	Rk	Stop	Dfts	BTkl	Runs	St%	Rk	RuYd	Rk	Sack	Hit	Hur	Dsrpt
Johnathan Hankins	23	DT	16	681	54	6.7%	16	47	13	2	42	86%	17	2.0	34	7.0	6	6.5	3
Mike Patterson*	32	DT	16	422	27	3.3%	76	21	3	2	26	77%	53	3.2	88	0.0	0	1.0	0
Cullen Jenkins	34	DT	12	360	15	2.5%	86	11	4	4	13	69%	81	2.8	75	1.0	6	13.5	1
Markus Kuhn	29	DT	14	248	19	2.7%	--	15	2	2	15	87%	--	2.3	--	1.0	0	3.5	0

Edge Rushers	Age	Pos	G	Snaps	Plays	TmPct	Rk	Stop	Dfts	BTkl	Runs	St%	Rk	RuYd	Rk	Sack	Hit	Hur	Dsrpt
Jason Pierre-Paul	26	DE	16	960	80	9.9%	1	65	27	5	48	75%	39	3.8	74	12.5	10	24.0	4
Mathias Kiwanuka*	32	DE	11	551	28	5.1%	43	21	6	3	20	80%	28	3.5	70	2.5	4	9.0	0
Robert Ayers	30	DE	12	377	23	3.8%	66	17	6	8	15	67%	69	3.9	76	5.0	11	22.5	0
Damontre Moore	23	DE	16	319	25	3.1%	--	18	14	3	12	50%	--	5.2	--	5.5	7	6.5	3
George Selvie	28	DE	16	500	31	3.9%	64	24	7	2	22	82%	22	2.1	31	3.0	5	13.0	0

Linebackers	Age	Pos	G	Snaps	Plays	TmPct	Rk	Stop	Dfts	BTkl	Sack	Hit	Hur	Runs	St%	Rk	RuYd	Rk	Tgts	Suc%	Rk	AdjYd	Rk	PD	Int
				Overall							Pass Rush			vs. Run					vs. Pass						
Jameel McClain	30	ILB	16	972	117	14.5%	29	59	19	8	2.5	4	7.5	71	63%	44	4.2	72	34	43%	51	8.1	57	3	0
Jacquian Williams*	27	OLB	9	563	76	16.8%	14	38	10	8	0.0	1	5.5	36	56%	70	5.4	84	32	52%	31	9.9	62	2	0
Devon Kennard	24	OLB	12	333	44	7.3%	77	27	12	4	4.5	1	4.5	31	61%	53	2.8	17	5	71%	--	2.1	--	0	0
Mark Herzlich	28	MLB	15	313	49	6.5%	--	29	6	3	1.0	1	0	34	68%	--	3.6	--	9	43%	--	8.8	--	1	0
J.T. Thomas	27	OLB	16	714	85	9.8%	63	51	16	10	0.0	0	0	44	75%	12	3.2	33	36	57%	16	5.8	24	6	2
Jonathan Casillas	28	OLB	11	261	30	5.0%	--	16	3	1	0.0	2	3.5	17	65%	--	3.1	--	7	59%	--	5.7	--	0	0

Year	Yards	ALY	Rk	Power	Rk	Stuff	Rk	2nd Level	Rk	Open Field	Rk	Sacks	ASR	Rk	Short	Long
2012	4.65	4.42	30	48%	1	19%	15	1.26	25	0.87	21	33	6.0%	22	9	15
2013	3.56	3.62	8	66%	19	21%	13	1.00	7	0.44	5	34	6.1%	28	6	19
2014	4.81	4.31	28	62%	13	16%	27	1.37	31	1.00	29	47	7.8%	6	21	12
2014 ALY by direction:		Left End 4.56 (31)			Left Tackle 3.77 (16)			Mid/Guard 4.18 (25)			Right Tackle 4.02 (17)				Right End 5.51 (31)	

Jason Pierre-Paul, as you probably know, no longer has an index finger on his right hand thanks to a combination of poor fireworks safety and being a member of the New York Giants. JPP must learn to rush quarterbacks with four fingers on his right hand; the New York Post actually investigated and determined that, no, JPP cannot be fitted with a prosthetic finger that shoots laser beams or gives him the strength to crush a left tackle's facemask. Our extensive database of nine-fingered pass rushers was little help in determining JPP's short-term potential. The firecracker fail eroded Tom Coughlin's seemingly endless patience with his brilliant-but-inconsistent pass rusher, and the Giants reportedly pulled away a lucrative contract extension before JPP could clutch a pen between his thumb and pinkie and sign it. JPP will remain on the Giants roster this season and will probably play; given the Giants injury rate, amputation is not an enough to get you on the IR.

The Giants released veteran Mathias Kiwanuka in February, so Robert Ayers and Demonte Moore will share left end duties. Ayers is considered an early-down run defender but was an effective pass-rusher on first and second downs last year. Moore is a flash player who, like JPP, concentrated many of his sacks into a late-season run against opponents like the Titans and Redskins.

Defensive tackle Jonathan Hankins had three of his eight sacks in the Week 15 dismantling of the Redskins, but he applied consistent pressure throughout the season and played excellent run defense. Expect the Giants to rotate tackles next to Hankins. Sophomore Jay Bromley has become a Pierre-Paul protégé (the Giants are lucky he didn't barbecue his own face during a summer cookout) and could stick as the designated inside pass-rusher, with German-born Markus Kuhn, a coaching-staff favorite, playing on first and second downs. Steve Spagnuolo will have plenty of options when he wants to get creative on third-and-15. Cullen Jenkins is still in the mix as a situational pass rusher inside, and third-round pick Owamagbe Odighizuwa, a raw athlete out of UCLA with sprinter's speed and (OH GOD OH GOD) a history of hip injuries, could grow into a budget-friendly JPP surrogate. George Selvie, two seasons removed from a surprise star turn for the Cowboys, will also battle for a role.

The Giants have assembled their usual motley assortment of linebackers. Jon Beason took a pay cut to remain with the team. He has played one, four, 14, and four games in the last four seasons, so expect Jameel McClain to come off the bench again to try hard, miss tackles, and struggle to cover anyone but the fullback. Sophomore Devon Kennard got hurt (of course) in the season opener last season, but came on strong with five late-season sacks. Again, the Giants faced the Jaguars, Titans, and Surrenderskins at the end of the season, so enthusiasm should be tempered, but Kennard has pass-rush chops. Steady J.T. Thomas arrives from Jacksonville to start on the weak side. The Giants also signed Jonathan Casillias, probably as a human sacrifice to the IR gods. Mark Herzlich remains the first linebacker off the Giants bench, which is like being the fire extinguisher in the kitchen of a halfway house for pyromaniacs.

Defensive Secondary

Secondary	Age	Pos	G	Snaps	Plays	TmPct	Rk	Stop	Dfts	BTkl	Runs	St%	Rk	RuYd	Rk	Tgts	Tgt%	Rk	Dist	Suc%	Rk	AdjYd	Rk	PD	Int
				Overall							vs. Run					vs. Pass									
Antrel Rolle*	33	FS	16	1049	93	11.5%	26	37	10	11	42	48%	24	7.1	43	32	9.0%	39	12.0	66%	8	8.9	57	9	3
D.Rodgers-Cromartie	29	CB	16	751	50	6.2%	72	21	11	4	6	33%	44	10.7	69	66	25.7%	55	13.9	52%	28	7.4	26	11	2
Quintin Demps*	30	FS	16	627	59	7.3%	60	21	10	10	24	38%	43	10.0	61	25	11.7%	59	13.1	44%	57	7.5	41	7	4
Stevie Brown*	28	SS	16	576	37	4.6%	70	11	5	4	21	33%	48	9.4	59	9	4.3%	3	13.9	32%	70	13.6	71	0	0
Chykie Brown	29	CB	15	504	44	5.8%	--	9	2	6	8	25%	--	7.1	--	47	25.5%	--	14.0	42%	--	10.8	--	3	0
Prince Amukamara	26	CB	8	458	57	14.1%	1	30	10	1	19	68%	7	7.7	51	39	24.7%	46	15.2	43%	67	9.2	59	11	3
Zack Bowman*	31	CB	16	450	25	3.1%	--	12	4	2	13	38%	--	7.2	--	33	21.6%	--	20.1	72%	--	5.1	--	6	2
Mike Harris	26	CB	5	216	23	9.1%	--	11	5	0	5	100%	--	3.0	--	18	23.9%	--	8.5	37%	--	6.1	--	2	1
Trumaine McBride	30	CB	6	212	22	7.3%	--	13	6	2	8	75%	--	5.5	--	15	20.1%	--	8.4	55%	--	7.5	--	1	1
Josh Gordy	28	CB	16	277	28	3.5%	--	8	2	2	9	33%	--	6.0	--	32	31.3%	--	12.8	50%	--	8.6	--	5	1

Year	Pass D Rank	vs. #1 WR	Rk	vs. #2 WR	Rk	vs. Other WR	Rk	vs. TE	Rk	vs. RB	Rk
2012	16	11.9%	23	-4.0%	13	18.2%	26	-20.2%	3	-7.6%	12
2013	8	-11.6%	9	-33.7%	2	-22.0%	5	-18.7%	6	14.9%	28
2014	21	7.8%	23	-3.1%	15	1.1%	18	13.9%	25	2.1%	20

Prince Amukamara gives up a lot of productive passes in front of him but is not without his merits. Amukamara plays the run well, makes few deep mistakes, and has the size to match up with bigger receivers. He's a useful defender, but because he plays for the New York Giants, he is always injured. He spent this spring on the mend from a bicep injury that ended his 2014 season in Week 9. The Giants exercised a fifth-year option to keep Amukamara around through 2016 but are not planning a long-term extension.

Dominique Rodgers-Cromartie handled many of the No. 1 coverage assignments last year and generally got the job done, but he was an injury report mainstay with back, ankle and hamstring issues. Trumaine McBride, the team's waiver-wire discovery of 2013, was picking up where he left off before he got shelved with a hand injury after Week 6. If all three Giants cornerbacks are healthy at the same time, they make a formidable, versatile unit. And if you ever hit on a scratch-off, you will tell the boss what you really think. Until then, Jayron Hosley and the ubiquitous jack-of-all-trades Chykie Brown must be ready to contribute. Holsey missed the first four games of last season with a substance-abuse violation, then came back to miss some tackles as the Last Healthy Dime Defender in New York. Unlike Brown, Holsey occasionally flashes brilliance.

The safety situation was covered earlier in the chapter. Landon Collins spoke at length in rookie camp about shedding the "in the box" label after falling to the top of the second round because most NFL coaches prefer safeties who cover like cornerbacks to safeties who can play the run like linebackers. You know how the snowball of draft discussion rolls: a safety goes from "too slow to cover Pierre Garcon one-on-one" to "a nose tackle with a uniform number in the 20s." Collins is a fine multi-purpose safety who will do well in a division with the run-heavy Cowboys and Eagles and offensively confused Redskins.

Special Teams

Year	DVOA	Rank	FG/XP	Rank	Net Kick	Rank	Kick Ret	Rank	Net Punt	Rank	Punt Ret	Rank	Hidden	Rank
2012	2.0%	10	-3.0	21	1.5	13	14.6	1	0.9	15	-4.0	22	-3.1	22
2013	-5.1%	28	0.7	17	3.3	11	-4.2	24	-20.5	31	-4.6	23	-12.8	32
2014	-0.6%	15	3.7	8	7.0	6	-5.9	29	-5.2	23	-2.8	19	-13.3	30

The Giants called for fair catches on their final 11 punt returns of the 2014 season: all the fair catches took place in their final two games except for the Redskins' flag-of-surrender punt late in the fourth quarter in Week 15. Odell Beckham and Rueben Randle shared the chores, and the thought of losing the league's most electrifying rookie or an important often-starter for 2015 on a meaningless December punt return must have given Tom Coughlin the chills. It's precisely the sort of thing that happens to the Giants. Hence, endless fair catches.

Dwayne Harris should handle the return chores for the Giants this season. The Giants signed Harris away from Dallas to contribute on offense, but he is most valuable as an all-purpose special-teamer with dangerous return chops and the coverage skills to make up for the loss of top gunner Spencer Paysinger. Beckham can still replace Harris in win-or-else situations, with Preston Parker as a last resort.

Josh Brown produced touchbacks on a solid 56 percent of his kickoffs, with plenty of high, hard-to-return kicks among the non-touchbacks. Brown was also 8-of-9 beyond 40 yards and went 2-of-3 on onside kicks. Brown's long field goal numbers are as random as most kickers' long field goal numbers (he was amazing in 2008-09, then bad for a while, and then was great again last year) but he remains a top athlete with the seasoning an old coach like Tom Coughlin craves. Steve Weatherford is a reliable punter and another top athlete.

New York Jets

2014 Record: 4-12	**Total DVOA:** -15.5% (27th)	**2015 Mean Projection:** 8.2 wins	**On the Clock (0-4):** 8%
Pythagorean Wins: 4.8 (27th)	**Offense:** -11.2% (27th)	**Postseason Odds:** 37.2%	**Mediocrity (5-7):** 31%
Snap-Weighted Age: 27.0 (9th)	**Defense:** 3.5% (21st)	**Super Bowl Odds:** 4.5%	**Playoff Contender (8-10):** 41%
Average Opponent: 4.5% (3rd)	**Special Teams:** -0.8% (16th)	**Proj. Avg. Opponent:** -2.7% (24th)	**Super Bowl Contender (11+):** 20%

2014: The Rex Ryan era ends with a whimper and a bunch of fifth-string cornerbacks.

2015: The Jets are back! (in ways both good and bad)

Some NFL teams have no clear personality. Can you quickly explain what kind of football the Tennessee Titans play? What kind of teams have the Falcons put on the field throughout their history? Is there anything tying the last couple decades of Detroit Lions football together?

The New York Jets do not have this problem. When the New York Jets are winning, they play great defense. For the last two decades, that's been what the New York Jets are about. The Jets played great defense when Bill Parcells was head coach in the late '90s, and they played great defense when Rex Ryan came to town in 2009.

Unfortunately, that great defense hasn't always led to winning, because the Jets can rarely pair great defense with even average offense. And in this quarterback-driven era, it's easy to see why the Jets have failed to get over the hump. They can't find a quarterback.

Since 2000, the Jets have drafted 10 quarterbacks, more than any other team in the league. That doesn't even begin to take into account the trades they've made for the likes of Tim Tebow and Brett Favre and the signings of free agents both veteran (Michael Vick) and undrafted (Greg McElroy). To be fair, they haven't always gotten it wrong. You could argue that the Jets found a franchise quarterback when they selected Chad Pennington in the first round of the 2000 draft, even if that quarterback couldn't stay healthy. Pennington never made the Pro Bowl, but he led the Jets to the postseason in three of his five seasons as a starter. He led the league in DVOA in 2002, and was the last Jets quarterback to finish with an above-average DVOA in 2006.

Since then, the Jets have two kinds of quarterbacks: struggling youngsters with hints of potential, and just plain bad. Eight straight seasons of below-average performance at the quarterback position is enough to frustrate any fan base. (Although, if you're comparing misery, that's nothing compared to the Bears, who had a whopping 16 straight seasons of below-average passing DVOA from 1997 to 2012.) While there were back-to-back trips to the AFC title game in the first two years with Mark Sanchez, the steady decline of the USC product eventually led to his release prior to the start of the 2014 season. He's been replaced by Geno Smith, who first took control when Sanchez went down with a season-ending injury prior to the start of the 2013 campaign and was under center as the Jets' passing game struggled throughout 2014. Can Smith possibly raise his game enough to follow in the footsteps of the Sanchize and get the Jets back into the postseason?

Well, we have good news and bad news for Jets fans. Our projections for 2015 say that the Jets this year will look a lot more like the Jets as we think of them. Statistical trends and significant roster overhaul both point to the Jets reversing recent decline and once again fielding one of the best defenses in the NFL. That's the good news. But when we say the Jets are going to field a more familiar team this season, we're talking about both sides of the ball. The Jets' offense is going to suck.

Last year, Smith was at or near the bottom of the league in most major passing statistics, and the Jets were at or near the bottom of all the team passing metrics. Smith completed just 60 percent of his passes with 13 touchdowns and 13 interceptions. His DVOA of -12.5% and DYAR of -33 both finished 30th among the 37 quarterbacks with at least 200 pass attempts. The West Virginia product did get some occasional relief from veteran Michael Vick, who played in 10 games (three starts) and was even worse. Vick finished with a 53 percent completion rate, three touchdowns, and two interceptions, good enough for a -36.8% DVOA and -228 DYAR.

So which kind of Jets quarterback is Smith: bad with potential, or just plain bad? Unfortunately, two years of poor play on Smith's resume is probably enough for us to know the answer is the latter. In his first two years in the league, Smith has ranked 37th and 30th in DVOA, and history tells us that very few quarterbacks who begin their career in such a fashion are capable of rounding into something resembling a competitive NFL starter. It's been almost 25 years since any quarterback other than Alex Smith has developed into a quality starter after starting his career with two years below replacement level, and even that assumes you consider Smith to be a quality starter. (You'll find the depressing details in a table in the Jacksonville chapter.) Smith improved down the stretch, but even that improvement is essentially just one game: an improbable Week 17 performance that came out with 14.3 yards per attempt and a perfect 158.3 passer rating. Without that game, even Smith's improved December still resulted in passing DVOA of -3.4%.

And so, entering the 2015 season, the Jets have Smith, veteran backup Ryan Fitzpatrick and fourth-round draft pick Bryce Petty. Petty was the best available Petty left on the board when the Jets drafted him—certainly a better option than Richard,

2015 Jets Schedule

Week	Opp.	Week	Opp.	Week	Opp.
1	CLE	7	at NE	13	at NYG
2	at IND (Mon.)	8	at OAK	14	TEN
3	PHI	9	JAC	15	at DAL
4	at MIA (U.K.)	10	BUF (Thu.)	16	NE
5	BYE	11	at HOU	17	at BUF
6	WAS	12	MIA		

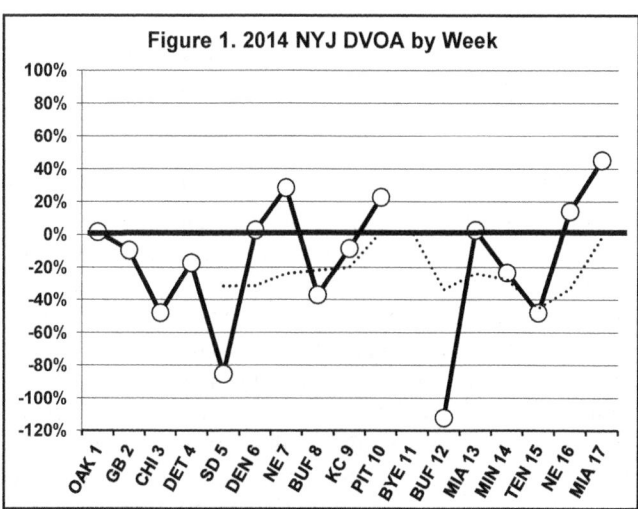

Figure 1. 2014 NYJ DVOA by Week

Tom or Lori—but while he does have an intriguing skill set, our new QBASE projection system considers him a very likely bust, in large part because of the opposition that he faced in 2014. Petty accumulated his college stats against a schedule of opposing defenses which ranked 70th in FBS last year, which certainly doesn't bode well for a quick transition to facing NFL competition. Fitzpatrick, who will now suit up for his sixth team in 11 years, has certainly proven himself to be capable, but he's hardly the type of quarterback to lead a team on a long postseason run. Nonetheless, given Smith's track record to this point—and despite the fact that new head coach Todd Bowles insisted there's no quarterback controversy in the spring—there's the very real likelihood that Smith will be feeling the heat from Fitzpatrick before we get to Halloween.

Whoever is playing quarterback for the Jets at least will have a few new weapons on offense, with the biggest addition being wide receiver Brandon Marshall. Marshall, who has seen his numbers drop the last three seasons as part of the Bears' dysfunctional passing game, should become the No. 1 option in New York. At the same time, it's important to remember that history is littered with veteran free-agent wide receivers that were acquired with an eye toward jumpstarting an offense, but ended up underwhelming in their first year at their new address. Marshall has a history of moving around, and posted very good numbers in his first year after moving from Denver to Miami as well as his initial season after going from Miami to Chicago. This move will be a bit harder, because Marshall is now 31 and he has Geno Smith at quarterback. There are very few cases of a veteran receiver in his thirties making an impact in his first season with a new team. Unless we're talking about Randy Moss in 2007 or Terrell Owens in 2004—guys with Hall-of-Fame resumes joining teams with at least some small measure of talent at the quarterback spot— free-agent receivers generally don't have the seismic impact that some believe.

The best Marshall could hope for is probably to emulate his new teammate Eric Decker. Decker went from a passing attack that ranked first in passing yards to one that ranked 31st, and while his DVOA took a massive hit (he went from 21.3% in his last year with Peyton Manning and the Broncos to 9.4% with the 2014 Jets), his 962 receiving yards was more than double anyone else on the roster and he had a 64 percent catch rate for the second straight season. Marshall and Decker will be augmented at the receiver position by second-round pick Devin Smith, a deep threat out of Ohio State, and Jeremy Kerley, who was fundamentally the only receiver other than

Decker who accomplished anything last season in New York. Still, Kerley's efficiency dropped off significantly last year, in large part because the Jets had him running more midrange routes. Kerley's percentage of passes thrown within five yards of the line of scrimmage have dropped from 42 percent to 29 percent over the last three years, and his share of midrange passes (6-15 yards past the line) have climbed from 36 percent to 52 percent.

The Jets also hope to get more out of their tight-end combination of veteran Jeff Cumberland and last year's second-round pick, Jace Amaro. Amaro struggled early and had six drops (one *New York Post* story quoted an anonymous teammate as saying Amaro "couldn't catch a cold" in July), but gradually emerged as one of the better young tight ends in a class that had a few of them. Cumberland's efficiency numbers have been on a roller-coaster the last three years, down then up and then down again. The additions of Amaro and Decker meant he was thrown shorter passes last year, and thrown them less often, despite going from 675 snaps in 2013 to 910 snaps in 2014.

Of course, the other way to help the quarterback is to get the running game going. The Jets' offensive line is not the strength it was a few years ago, but New York was successful at the most important parts of ground-and-pound. The Jets were only 20th in adjusted line yards but ranked fifth converting 75 percent of their "power" runs. Good blocking helped the offense play well overall in short-yardage situations, ranking ninth in DVOA on second-and-short and 11th on third-and-short. The backfield will look a bit different this year: Chris Johnson is gone, but in his place, the Jets added Stevan Ridley and Zac Stacy this offseason. Ridley, who signed a one-year, "show-me" deal after a season-ending knee injury in October, is one of the more intriguing prospects in the AFC East. He was the most consistent of the Patriots' running backs over the last four years, despite occasional fumble-related benchings, and if his ACL recovery doesn't take too long, he could represent one of the great value signings of the offseason for any team. He'll battle for playing time with Chris Ivory and Stacy; the former of whom was the best and most consistent part of the New York ground game last year.

Of course, the other part of Gang Green's classic "running-and-defense" personality is defense. Their once league-leading defense declined slowly over the last few years, dropping to 12th in DVOA in 2013 and then an unforgivable 21st last season. Former Arizona defensive coordinator Bowles was hired as head coach to reverse that trend, and he's going to get a lot of help from some old familiar faces and some new ones.

The most exciting of the new faces is first-round pick Leonard Williams. One of the reasons the Jets have struggled so much on offense is that they rarely seem to use their top draft picks there. But it was impossible to pass up on the USC star when he was still sitting available at the sixth overall pick, as Williams was considered by many to be the best pure talent available in this year's draft regardless of position. With that selection, the Jets became just the second team since the 1970 merger to use seven straight first-round picks on defensive players. (The Cowboys used eight straight first-round picks on defensive players between 1998 and 2007.)

Williams joins a truly elite group of defensive linemen in New York, one so good that he'll have trouble seeing the field on a regular basis as a rookie. On one end, there's Sheldon Richardson, who followed up a rookie year where he took home AP Defensive Rookie of the Year honors with an eight-sack season that also included 16.5 hurries. On the other side, there's Muhammad Wilkerson, who fell back from a double-digit sack season in 2014, but still had a team-high 13 quarterback hits

and 15.5 quarterback hurries, second to Richardson. Richardson, Wilkerson, and defensive tackle Damon "Big Snacks" Harrison were also a big part of one of the league's top run defenses, which still ranked 11th in DVOA. The Jets yielded more than 100 rushing yards on just six occasions, a remarkable feat considering that many teams were looking to grind down New York in the second half while holding onto a lead.

Of course, the defensive line wasn't the weakness that caused the Jets defense to fall apart last year, and the linebackers weren't a particular weakness either. The problem with last year's Jets was in the secondary. 2013 first-round pick Dee Milliner couldn't get healthy and played only three games all year. Slot cornerback Kyle Wilson finally wore out his welcome. The Jets were stuck moving Antonio Allen over from safety and giving eight starts to undrafted rookie Marcus Williams.

Things will be different this year, and that's where the old familiar faces come in. Darrelle Revis is back after two years in exile, Antonio Cromartie after one year away. The Jets also added free agents who haven't played for them before. Buster Skrine comes over from Cleveland to play the nickel, and Marcus Gilchrist will play free safety. Of the Jets' top five defensive backs, only Calvin Pryor returns from 2014, and he's likely to improve now that he has a year of NFL experience.

The arrival of Revis will certainly improve the man coverage. The Jets corners were competitive enough against No. 1 receivers in 2014—top pass-catchers had a DVOA of 2.7%

Table 1. Biggest Net AV Over Replacement Change on Defense, 2003-2015

Team	Year	Net AV Change	DVOA Y-1	Rk	DVOA	Rk	Change	Players Added	Players Lost
DET	2009	21	24.3%	32	17.9%	32	-6.4%	L.Foote (6), J.Peterson (5), P.Buchanon (5), A.Henry (4), G.Jackson (3), K.Simpson (2), J.David (1), M.Manuel (1)	L.Bodden (2), P.Lenon (2), D.Bullocks (1), C.Redding (1)
NYJ	2015	21	3.5%	21	--	--	--	D.Revis (11), A.Cromartie (6), B.Skrine (4), M.Gilchrist (3)	D.Landry (3)
KC	2005	20	16.0%	30	-2.9%	14	-18.8%	P.Surtain (9), S.Knight (5), D.Washington (5), C.Hall (3)	S.Fujita (2)
DEN	2009	17	20.7%	31	-9.8%	7	-30.5%	B.Dawkins (8), V.Holliday (5), A.Davis (4), A.Goodman (4), R.Hill (3)	D.Bly (2), E.Ekuban (1), M.Manuel (1), D.Robertson (1), N.Webster (1), J.Winborn (1)
ATL	2006	16	11.9%	28	2.8%	18	-9.0%	J.Abraham (4), C.Crocker (4), G.Jackson (4), D.Johnson (4), L.Schulters (4), L.Milloy (2)	K.Carpenter (2), C.Lavalais (2), B.Scott (2)
DET	2003	16	17.5%	31	5.9%	21	-11.5%	D.Bly (6), E.Holmes (5), A.Molden (4), W.Rainer (4), O.Smith (2), D.Wilkinson (2)	C.Claiborne (4), T.Lyght (3)
TB	2014	16	-6.8%	8	1.1%	18	+7.9%	A.Verner (9), M.Johnson (6), M.Jenkins (2), C.McDonald (2), M.Wright (2)	D.Revis (4), D.Te'o-Nesheim (1)
MIN	2005	14	21.6%	32	3.8%	23	-17.8%	F.Smoot (7), P.Williams (6), D.Sharper (4), N.Harris (1)	B.Russell (2), C.Claiborne (1), K.Mixon (1)
BUF	2003	13	10.0%	24	-11.0%	7	-21.0%	L.Milloy (4), T.Spikes (4), S.Adams (3), J.Posey (3), I.Reese (3)	C.Ahanotu (3), E.Robinson (3), K.Newman (1)
MIN	2008	12	-0.1%	17	-19.3%	4	-19.1%	J.Allen (13), M.Williams (2)	D.Smith (3)
PHI	2011	12	-3.6%	11	-3.7%	11	-0.1%	N.Asomugha (9), J.Babin (7), D.Landri (4), D.Rodgers-Cromartie (3), C.Jenkins (2)	Q.Mikell (7), E.Sims (3), S.Bradley (2), D.Patterson (1)
WAS	2015	12	9.9%	27	--	--	--	C.Culliver (4), T.Knighton (4), R.Jean-Francois (3), S.Paea (3), D.Goldson (2)	J.Jenkins (3), B.Meriweather (1)
MIA	2003	11	-15.0%	2	-14.7%	4	+0.3%	J.Seau (5), J.Zgonina (5), S.Knight (4)	D.Rodgers (3)
NYG	2010	11	2.4%	19	-11.2%	3	-13.7%	A.Rolle (5), K.Bulluck (4), D.Grant (4)	D.Clark (1), F.Robbins (1)
AVERAGE			8.2%	22.1	-3.4%	13.5	-11.7%		

against the Jets, 17th in the league. The struggles came against everyone else: the second receivers, slot receivers and the tight ends. Both the arrival of Revis and the hire of Bowles should have a real impact on how the Jets deploy their cornerbacks. The sides vs. man coverage debate rages across the NFL, and Cromartie this offseason was the latest to take shots at Richard Sherman about whether or not he's a true elite corner because he plays sides instead of following the opponent's top receiver. The Jets used a mishmash of both strategies in 2014, moving their cornerbacks around a ton in the first eight weeks of the season ("CB by Sides" rating: 54 percent) and then playing them strictly left and right after Week 9 ("CB by Sides" rating: 98 percent). Regardless of where the Jets corners are slotted in 2015—Skrine figures to line up inside and Cromartie will be opposite Revis—the additions should allow everyone to be properly slotted when it comes to the defensive game plan.

The overhaul of the secondary is a major reason why our new, upgraded projection system is surprisingly high on the Jets this season. One of the problems we had with our team projections in the past was difficulty properly measuring the impact of specific personnel moves. That's been improved significantly this year, by giving defenses credit for the talent they've added (or lost) based on value above replacement level using Pro Football Reference's Approximate Value metric. Each player who moves teams is counted using his AV above a replacement level of 3. Using this measure, the four defensive backs added by the Jets are worth 24 AV above replacement. The loss of Dawan Landry subtracts 3, but that still leaves the Jets with a net add of 21 defensive AV above replacement. This is tied with the 2009 Detroit Lions for the highest figure among teams since 2003 (Table 1, previous page). There were a dozen teams in our dataset that had improved their defensive talent by more than 10 AV over replacement, and these teams

saw their defenses improve by an average of -11.7% DVOA.

Some of this is regression towards the mean by bad defenses, but that doesn't explain why a number of these bad defenses shot past average and became very good. Free agents aren't always the answer to a team's defensive problems, but when you add a lot of talent, you are usually going to get improvement. The Jets have added a lot of talent.

These new defensive backs will also help the Jets get more interceptions than the measly six they picked off opposing quarterbacks last year, and regression towards the mean should help here as well. Last year, the Jets only ended 5.6 percent of opponent drives with a turnover, the lowest figure of any defense in our entire drive stats database (going back to 1997). The only other defenses below 6.0 percent were Washington in 2006 and Houston in 2013. Twelve other defenses since 1997 had turnovers on 8.2 percent of drives or fewer (Table 2). The following year, these teams averaged almost twice as many turnovers. Those additional turnovers meant an average improvement of more than 10 percentage points of defensive DVOA. Only one of these defenses had fewer turnovers the next year. Of course, that defense was the 2013 Jets, so there may be a bit more to this than random chance. But it's very rare for a team to recover fumbles as infrequently as the Jets defense has for two straight years: only 3 of 12 fumbles last season, and only 1 of 13 fumbles two years ago.

There are other metrics that also show the Jets were not as bad as last year's 4-12 record. The Jets lost seven games by a touchdown or less last year, including two defeats at the hands of the Patriots by a total of three points. (Both of those games turned late on blocked or tipped field goals.) The Jets had the third-hardest schedule in the league by average DVOA of opponent. That gets a lot easier in 2015—they have one of the ten easiest schedules based on our projections, and they get to play Miami in London rather than Sun Life Stadium.

All this adds up to a team that is going to be better than it was last year, and will look even better than that. Remember, when the Jets were playing their best in recent years, they didn't need an elite passer to succeed. In his first two seasons, despite the fact that New York reached back-to-back AFC title games, Mark Sanchez was not a good quarterback: in 2009, he ranked 38th with minus-382 DYAR. In 2010, his best season, he was 22nd with 212 DYAR. That example might be enough to give hope to New York fans entering the 2015 campaign. They remember great years when a mediocre offense was carried by a strong front seven and a secondary led by Darrelle Revis. But they don't remember going to the Super Bowl with those teams, because eventually Sanchez could only get them so far.

So while the Jets will be an improved team in 2015—with a defense that's good enough to turn some of last year's narrow losses into victories—this is still an era where the success and failure of most every franchise rides on the shoulders of the quarterback. The Jets are going to surprise a lot of people by competing for a wild card this year, but they simply won't be a serious playoff contender until they manage to get the quarterback situation right. Until then, they're just the same old Jets.

Christopher Price

Table 2. Fewest Defensive Drives Ended by Turnover, 1997-2014

Team	Year	TO/ Drive	Rk	TO/Drive Y+1	Rk	DVOA	Rk	DVOA Y+1	Rk	Change
NYJ	2014	5.6%	32	--	--	3.5%	21	--	--	--
WAS	2006	5.8%	32	12.8%	23	15.0%	32	-7.9%	7	-22.9%
HOU	2013	5.9%	32	16.6%	3	2.5%	18	-6.2%	6	-8.7%
KC	2012	6.4%	32	15.9%	3	13.0%	30	-6.7%	9	-19.7%
PHI	2012	6.8%	31	15.8%	4	9.4%	26	4.9%	23	-4.5%
OAK	2014	7.0%	31	--	--	6.3%	26	--	--	--
KC	2014	7.1%	30	--	--	1.3%	19	--	--	--
HOU	2005	7.8%	32	13.3%	23	20.1%	32	13.7%	31	-6.3%
STL	2004	7.9%	32	13.3%	20	14.2%	28	12.7%	29	-1.5%
GB	2004	8.0%	31	11.1%	26	15.2%	29	2.9%	21	-12.3%
NYJ	2013	8.0%	31	5.6%	32	-5.6%	12	3.5%	21	+9.0%
DEN	2008	8.0%	32	16.2%	7	20.7%	31	-9.8%	7	-30.5%
DEN	2011	8.1%	32	12.4%	16	1.6%	18	-13.8%	5	-15.4%
OAK	2009	8.1%	32	9.4%	31	7.9%	24	-2.3%	13	-10.2%
PHI	1998	8.2%	30	20.8%	1	8.5%	25	-11.1%	4	-19.6%
AVERAGE		**7.2%**	**31.5**	**13.6%**	**15.8**	**8.9%**	**24.7**	**-1.7%**	**14.7**	**-10.6%**

2014 NYJ Stats by Week

Wk	vs.	W-L	PF	PA	YDF	YDA	TO	Total	Off	Def	ST
1	OAK	W	19	14	402	158	-2	2%	-13%	-8%	7%
2	at GB	L	24	31	313	390	0	-10%	2%	4%	-8%
3	CHI	L	19	27	414	257	-2	-48%	-51%	-9%	-5%
4	DET	L	17	24	336	360	-2	-17%	-3%	24%	10%
5	at SD	L	0	31	151	439	-1	-85%	-74%	15%	3%
6	DEN	L	17	31	204	359	-2	3%	-11%	-5%	9%
7	at NE	L	25	27	423	323	0	28%	33%	10%	5%
8	BUF	L	23	43	312	280	-6	-37%	-27%	10%	0%
9	at KC	L	10	24	364	309	0	-9%	7%	14%	-2%
10	PIT	W	20	13	275	362	4	23%	-8%	-33%	-1%
11	BYE										
12	at BUF	L	3	38	218	336	-1	-112%	-58%	32%	-22%
13	MIA	L	13	16	326	291	0	3%	-3%	-17%	-11%
14	at MIN	L	24	30	410	411	0	-23%	-6%	22%	5%
15	at TEN	W	16	11	277	342	1	-48%	-26%	15%	-6%
16	NE	L	16	17	307	231	0	14%	-1%	-22%	-6%
17	at MIA	W	37	24	494	387	0	45%	32%	-2%	12%

Trends and Splits

	Offense	Rank	Defense	Rank
Total DVOA	-11.2%	27	3.5%	21
Unadjusted VOA	-10.3%	24	6.6%	25
Weighted Trend	-6.6%	18	2.6%	22
Variance	8.5%	19	3.2%	3
Average Opponent	-0.9%	11	3.5%	1
Passing	-8.6%	27	15.8%	24
Rushing	-5.6%	17	-12.7%	11
First Down	-24.5%	30	-7.8%	5
Second Down	-4.9%	20	-3.0%	13
Third Down	1.7%	17	33.9%	32
First Half	-2.7%	18	6.9%	25
Second Half	-20.1%	28	0.0%	14
Red Zone	-42.0%	31	7.3%	26
Late and Close	-15.8%	27	1.8%	20

Five-Year Performance

Year	W-L	Pyth W	Est W	PF	PA	TO	Total	Rk	Off	Rk	Def	Rk	ST	Rk	Off AGL	Rk	Def AGL	Rk	Off Age	Rk	Def Age	Rk	ST Age	Rk
2010	11-5	9.8	10.1	367	304	+9	18.7%	6	2.1%	16	-10.9%	5	5.8%	5	8.8	4	32.9	23	27.6	14	28.1	7	26.5	13
2011	8-8	8.4	8.4	377	363	-3	13.5%	10	-8.3%	21	-16.1%	2	5.6%	4	9.2	2	21.2	12	27.6	12	27.5	9	26.2	17
2012	6-10	5.3	5.6	281	375	-14	-18.0%	27	-20.7%	30	-4.2%	9	-1.5%	21	37.7	22	41.0	23	26.6	19	28.1	2	26.0	16
2013	8-8	5.4	7.5	290	387	-14	-7.7%	24	-15.3%	27	-5.6%	12	2.1%	10	33.9	15	9.1	1	26.2	26	26.7	14	26.1	13
2014	4-12	4.8	5.9	283	401	-11	-15.5%	27	-11.2%	27	3.5%	21	-0.8%	16	18.7	5	22.8	4	27.3	9	27.0	11	26.1	13

2014 Performance Based on Most Common Personnel Groups

NYJ Offense					NYJ Offense vs. Opponents					NYJ Defense					NYJ Defense vs. Opponents			
Pers	Freq	Yds	DVOA	Run%	Pers	Freq	Yds	DVOA	Run%	Pers	Freq	Yds	DVOA	Pers	Freq	Yds	DVOA
11	44%	5.1	-0.4%	46%	Base	40%	4.9	-19.6%	55%	Base	59%	5.3	-5.7%	11	47%	6.6	21.0%
12	21%	4.7	-21.4%	26%	Nickel	50%	5.1	-0.8%	40%	Nickel	34%	5.9	16.4%	12	29%	4.8	-7.6%
21	11%	5.1	-2.4%	53%	Dime+	10%	4.9	3.7%	13%	Dime+	4%	9.6	78.9%	21	8%	5.8	3.2%
13	6%	5.2	-29.7%	54%	Goal Line	0%	1.0	117.4%	67%	Goal Line	2%	1.1	-13.8%	13	4%	3.3	-12.4%
20	5%	5.8	8.9%	27%						Big	1%	1.2	-52.6%	22	4%	5.3	-9.8%
10	3%	4.0	2.0%	39%										611	4%	4.1	-27.8%

Strategic Tendencies

Run/Pass		Rk	Formation		Rk	Pass Rush		Rk	Secondary		Rk	Strategy		Rk
Runs, first half	49%	1	Form: Single Back	73%	18	Rush 3	14.9%	1	4 DB	48%	1	Play action	21%	17
Runs, first down	55%	5	Form: Empty Back	5%	15	Rush 4	53.9%	25	5 DB	45%	25	Avg Box (Off)	6.30	13
Runs, second-long	38%	4	Pers: 3+ WR	57%	20	Rush 5	23.6%	13	6+ DB	6%	20	Avg Box (Def)	6.22	23
Runs, power sit.	71%	2	Pers: 4+ WR	5%	6	Rush 6+	7.6%	14	CB by Sides	76%	20	Offensive Pace	30.92	21
Runs, behind 2H	33%	5	Pers: 2+ TE/6+ OL	31%	14	Sacks by LB	50.0%	12	DB Blitz	11%	14	Defensive Pace	30.11	14
Pass, ahead 2H	39%	30	Shotgun/Pistol	73%	4	Sacks by DB	11.1%	9	Hole in Zone	7%	11	Go for it on 4th	0.98	16

Geno Smith averaged a league-low 1.4 yards per pass against defensive back blitzes. ☞ The Jets ran a league-high 43 percent of the time when they had at least three wide receivers on the field. ☞ On the other hand, Jets opponents didn't run from spread formations often, as the Jets were one of only three defenses that faced fewer than 100 running plays with three or more wideouts on the field. However, when spread out like this, the Jets' otherwise stalwart run defense allowed a league-high 6.01 yards per carry and ranked 27th with 5.9% DVOA. ☒ The Jets had the second-best DVOA in the NFL against passes thrown behind the line of scrimmage (-25.1%, behind only Seattle) and the second-worst DVOA in the NFL against passes thrown beyond the line of scrimmage (67.0%, ahead of only Washington).

Passing

Player	DYAR	DVOA	Plays	NtYds	Avg	YAC	C%	TD	Int
G.Smith	-33	-12.5%	395	2328	5.9	5.5	60.2%	13	13
M.Vick*	-228	-36.8%	138	494	3.6	3.9	54.2%	3	2
M.Simms*	0	-11.1%	8	39	4.9	7.7	37.5%	0	0
R.Fitzpatrick	383	6.7%	334	2393	7.2	5.5	63.3%	17	8

Rushing

Player	DYAR	DVOA	Plays	Yds	Avg	TD	Fum	Suc
C.Ivory	69	-0.6%	198	823	4.2	6	2	44%
C.Johnson*	16	-6.0%	155	663	4.3	1	1	45%
G.Smith	-65	-34.3%	54	235	4.4	1	4	-
B.Powell	22	7.6%	33	141	4.3	1	0	45%
M.Vick*	3	-8.9%	23	151	6.6	0	2	-
P.Harvin*	85	24.7%	22	110	5.0	0	0	-
J.Conner*	-6	-29.8%	6	20	3.3	0	0	33%
J.Kerley	62	174.8%	5	88	17.6	0	0	-
R.Fitzpatrick	32	2.8%	37	195	5.3	2	0	-
S.Ridley	-6	-9.9%	94	340	3.6	2	0	53%

Receiving

Player	DYAR	DVOA	Plays	Ctch	Yds	Y/C	YAC	TD	C%
E.Decker	199	9.4%	115	74	962	13.0	4.4	5	64%
J.Kerley	-51	-21.2%	75	38	409	10.8	3.9	1	51%
P.Harvin*	-15	-16.2%	52	29	350	12.1	5.2	1	56%
G.Salas	-13	-20.1%	23	8	167	20.9	14.3	0	35%
D.Nelson*	-76	-74.4%	16	8	70	8.8	1.0	0	50%
T.J.Graham	24	22.7%	8	3	87	29.0	7.0	1	38%
B.Marshall	78	-3.3%	106	61	721	11.8	3.8	8	58%
J.Amaro	1	-7.0%	53	38	345	9.1	4.4	2	72%
J.Cumberland	-66	-29.3%	47	23	247	10.7	4.2	3	49%
Z.Sudfeld	25	48.5%	7	5	85	17.0	11.6	0	71%
C.Johnson*	0	-13.8%	34	24	151	6.3	6.1	1	71%
C.Ivory	-2	-15.4%	27	18	123	6.8	6.7	1	67%
B.Powell	14	2.2%	15	11	92	8.4	8.7	0	73%

Offensive Line

Player	Pos	Age	GS	Snaps	Pen	Sk	Pass	Run	Player	Pos	Age	GS	Snaps	Pen	Sk	Pass	Run
D'Brickashaw Ferguson	LT	32	16/16	1088	2	4.0	20.0	5.5	Oday Aboushi	LG	24	15/10	722	1	3.0	12.0	6.5
Breno Giacomini	RT	30	16/16	1088	8	3.5	26.5	5.0	Brian Winters	LG	24	6/6	371	2	1.0	7.0	2.0
Willie Colon	RG	32	16/16	1080	14	1.0	8.0	7.0	James Carpenter	G	26	13/13	816	9	0.5	8.5	6.0
Nick Mangold	C	31	15/15	979	1	1.0	7.5	0.5									

Year	Yards	ALY	Rk	Power	Rk	Stuff	Rk	2nd Lev	Rk	Open Field	Rk	Sacks	ASR	Rk	Short	Long	F-Start	Cont.
2012	4.00	4.38	5	67%	10	16%	2	1.06	24	0.45	29	47	8.6%	30	16	19	16	48
2013	4.27	3.79	21	68%	12	17%	8	0.95	27	0.80	11	47	8.4%	27	13	21	14	42
2014	4.20	3.84	20	75%	5	18%	8	1.12	20	0.65	19	47	8.8%	25	9	23	17	37
2014 ALY by direction:		Left End 2.87 (28)			Left Tackle 3.2 (29)			Mid/Guard 3.94 (20)			Right Tackle 3.6 (23)				Right End 4.97 (6)			

The center and tackle spots are the areas of strength for the Jets. Center Nick Mangold remains one of the best in the game at his position. The 31-year-old finished the season with just eight blown blocks, and an impressive ratio of 122.4 snaps per blown block, easily the best ratio on the roster among the regulars. Meanwhile, left tackle D'Brickashaw Ferguson had some slippage in his game; he dropped from 60.1 snaps per blown block in 2013 to 42.7 last year, and the Jets struggled to run to the left side. On the other side, Giacomini had an up-and-down year in his first season with the Jets after coming over from Seattle. He was among the top offensive linemen in the league when it came to yielding hits or hurries, but still managed to give up just 3.5 sacks. Free-agent James Carpenter comes over from Seattle and appears to be the favorite to start at left guard, while right guard is the most unsettled position on the line. That's where veteran Willie Colon will be challenged by Oday Aboushi (who played left guard most of last season), Dakota Dozier (a 2014 fourth-rounder out of Furman) and Jarvis Harrison (a rookie fifth-rounder out of Texas A&M). In addition, Brian Winters might figure into the mix as a backup guard at both spots. Colon has a few things working against him here, including his age (he turned 32 in April) and the fact that he was whistled for a whopping 14 penalties last season, tops on the Jets and second-most among all NFL offensive linemen. (That includes 7 false starts, tops in the NFL.)

Defensive Front Seven

Defensive Line	Age	Pos	G	Snaps	Plays	Overall TmPct	Rk	Stop	Dfts	BTkl	vs. Run Runs	St%	Rk	RuYd	Rk	Pass Rush Sack	Hit	Hur	Dsrpt
Sheldon Richardson	25	DE	16	808	68	8.9%	4	47	22	3	52	63%	88	3.3	90	8.0	12	16.5	1
Muhammad Wilkerson	26	DE	13	716	61	9.8%	2	56	23	1	43	91%	6	0.9	5	6.0	13	15.5	5
Damon Harrison	27	DT	16	484	55	7.2%	9	42	3	3	54	78%	48	2.9	81	0.0	2	2.5	0
Leger Douzable	29	DE	16	319	25	3.3%	--	17	6	1	18	72%	--	2.4	--	2.5	2	5.0	0
Stephen Bowen	*31*	*DE*	*8*	*243*	*12*	*3.2%*	*79*	*10*	*2*	*0*	*10*	*90%*	*8*	*2.0*	*35*	*0.0*	*0*	*3.0*	*1*

Edge Rushers	Age	Pos	G	Snaps	Plays	Overall TmPct	Rk	Stop	Dfts	BTkl	vs. Run Runs	St%	Rk	RuYd	Rk	Pass Rush Sack	Hit	Hur	Dsrpt
Calvin Pace	35	OLB	16	821	42	5.5%	34	33	16	4	20	90%	5	1.8	21	5.0	1	12.3	2
Quinton Coples	25	OLB	16	689	35	4.6%	52	26	14	2	25	72%	54	1.6	13	6.5	11	14.0	0
Jason Babin	35	OLB	16	459	25	3.3%	74	19	6	1	20	75%	39	1.7	19	2.0	9	11.8	0

Linebackers	Age	Pos	G	Snaps	Plays	Overall TmPct	Rk	Stop	Dfts	BTkl	Pass Rush Sack	Hit	Hur	vs. Run Runs	St%	Rk	RuYd	Rk	vs. Pass Tgts	Suc%	Rk	AdjYd	Rk	PD	Int
David Harris	31	ILB	16	1010	125	16.4%	16	62	21	6	5.5	0	6	61	59%	62	3.1	27	32	50%	39	6.7	40	1	0
Demario Davis	26	ILB	16	1006	119	15.6%	21	56	15	9	3.5	1	8.8	61	59%	62	3.6	56	33	54%	20	5.2	12	5	0
Jamari Lattimore	*27*	*ILB*	*11*	*281*	*36*	*6.2%*	*--*	*16*	*2*	*3*	*0.0*	*0*	*1.5*	*24*	*58%*	*--*	*3.6*	*--*	*7*	*16%*	*--*	*7.8*	*--*	*1*	*1*

Year	Yards	ALY	Rk	Power	Rk	Stuff	Rk	2nd Level	Rk	Open Field	Rk	Sacks	ASR	Rk	Short	Long
2012	4.33	4.09	18	56%	8	16%	27	1.10	6	0.89	23	30	6.2%	20	9	19
2013	3.21	3.23	4	39%	1	26%	3	0.80	1	0.48	8	41	6.2%	24	14	21
2014	3.81	3.80	13	64%	18	19%	16	0.89	3	0.69	17	45	8.2%	4	24	12

2014 ALY by direction:	Left End 2.64 (3)	Left Tackle 4.33 (23)	Mid/Guard 4.06 (19)	Right Tackle 3.94 (16)	Right End 3.28 (9)

As was the case in 2014, this is the unquestioned strength of the team. Muhammad Wilkerson is a dominant defensive end, and while he didn't hit double digits in sacks in 2014 like he did in 2013, he still led the New York defensive front in stops (56) and defeats (23) and had just one broken tackle. At the other defensive end spot, Sheldon Richardson led the group in total snaps and provided the bulk of the pass rush, leading the team in sacks (8) and quarterback hurries (16.5). In the middle, the massive Damon Harrison continued to serve as the anchor of the Jets' run defense. While he doesn't have the pass-rushing skills of other defensive tackles who might be considered elite, he serves as an excellent complementary player to both Wilkerson and Richardson while frequently occupying two blockers along the interior. Meanwhile, rookie Leonard Williams has the pedigree and skill set needed to become an elite five-technique defensive end, and work in support of Wilkerson and Richardson. The selection of Williams is not just a case of the rich getting richer; it's more like Bill Gates discovering buried treasure in his backyard.

The absolute strength of the front three allows to the Jets to get away with some weakness on the outside. Yes, Calvin Pace and Quinton Coples both had double-digit hurries and at least five sacks last season, but Pace will turn 35 in October and Coples is more of a defensive end than outside linebacker. One place where Pace tends to be underrated is pass coverage: he was third among edge rushers with 16 charted targets last season and allowed only 4.3 yards per pass after just 2.9 yards per pass in 2013.

There's a conspiracy theory that the only reason linebacker David Harris was re-signed was due to how much Darrelle Revis likes him. His 2014 numbers (59 percent run stop rate) didn't live up to his reputation (or his past performance) as a supposed run-stopper, especially considering that opposing backs were slowed down by the great linemen playing in front of him. But considering the fact that the Jets were able to retain Revis, the investment was probably worth it. Demario Davis has developed into a solid, unspectacular starter next to Harris, and Jamari Lattimore comes over from Green Bay to provide depth.

Defensive Secondary

Secondary	Age	Pos	G	Snaps	Plays	TmPct	Rk	Stop	Dfts	BTkl	Runs	St%	Rk	RuYd	Rk	Tgts	Tgt%	Rk	Dist	Suc%	Rk	AdjYd	Rk	PD	Int
Dawan Landry*	33	SS	16	942	105	13.7%	6	37	8	6	49	39%	41	6.5	37	21	5.9%	15	10.1	53%	39	5.8	20	1	0
Darrin Walls	27	CB	14	750	52	7.8%	51	23	5	8	5	60%	11	4.4	11	78	28.0%	64	15.4	48%	51	11.0	76	12	2
Calvin Pryor	23	FS	16	679	57	7.5%	59	27	10	8	30	53%	15	5.3	19	13	5.0%	6	7.4	43%	58	6.1	22	1	0
Antonio Allen	27	CB	15	512	47	6.6%	71	20	8	10	12	25%	59	7.3	47	54	28.6%	66	11.3	46%	58	9.7	69	7	0
Marcus Williams	24	CB	8	446	43	11.3%	4	13	7	3	7	57%	16	3.7	7	33	20.0%	16	9.8	35%	76	8.2	44	6	1
Jaiquawn Jarrett	26	FS	14	383	37	5.5%	--	10	7	4	21	19%	--	5.2	--	12	8.5%	--	14.4	85%	--	1.6	--	3	2
Kyle Wilson*	28	CB	16	308	21	2.7%	--	9	4	1	5	40%	--	7.4	--	22	19.4%	--	10.0	52%	--	7.8	--	1	0
Phillip Adams*	27	CB	12	306	26	4.5%	--	6	3	4	6	33%	--	15.7	--	38	33.2%	--	16.5	43%	--	11.8	--	4	1
Buster Skrine	26	CB	16	1129	84	9.4%	23	36	14	8	11	36%	41	8.6	58	116	26.5%	62	13.9	50%	41	7.6	32	15	4
Darrelle Revis	30	CB	16	1011	61	7.7%	56	28	15	1	10	40%	38	6.7	40	69	17.0%	3	13.2	62%	2	7.3	25	13	2
Marcus Gilchrist	27	SS	16	988	81	10.5%	34	34	17	6	39	38%	42	7.1	44	42	12.0%	62	9.1	54%	36	7.6	42	3	1
Antonio Cromartie	31	CB	16	987	59	7.4%	59	24	13	10	14	43%	33	10.5	67	78	20.0%	15	13.7	49%	46	9.2	60	11	3

Year	Pass D Rank	vs. #1 WR	Rk	vs. #2 WR	Rk	vs. Other WR	Rk	vs. TE	Rk	vs. RB	Rk
2012	10	-19.4%	5	-4.9%	12	-0.9%	16	-3.1%	14	4.1%	19
2013	18	-0.6%	19	13.5%	26	-1.3%	13	5.5%	19	-22.3%	3
2014	24	2.7%	17	19.0%	27	34.0%	31	30.5%	31	-23.0%	4

The Jets have gotten the band back together! There was some talk at the start of 2014 that Darrelle Revis had lost a step, but as the season went on, those doubts were quelled. Revis was targeted less than almost any other cornerback in the league, and while he allowed more adjusted yards per pass than he did in Tampa Bay (7.3 vs. 6.4), he also had a higher success rate (62 percent vs. 57 percent). While Rex Ryan and his blitz-heavy packages are gone from MetLife, new coach Todd Bowles loves to blitz too, which means we should see Revis on a lot of islands this season. (Bowles won't hesitate to put Revis on the other team's No. 1 receiver, and the Cardinals ranked 28th in "CB by Sides" last year.) The other corners who figure to get the lion's share of work alongside Revis in 2015 are both used to being paired with elite corners of their own. After spending a year alongside Patrick Peterson in Arizona—and playing relatively well as a No. 2 corner—returns to town with Bowles and will play second fiddle to Revis again. Buster Skrine will work inside as the nickelback after serving as a No. 2 alongside Joe Haden in Cleveland last year. As is the case with any corner who is opposite someone like Haden, Skrine faced a ton of targets and struggled at times, but going from covering first and second options in the passing games to third and fourth options for a better defense will likely improve his metrics—which have already been above-average the last two seasons. As for Dee Milliner, he's likely to start the year on PUP as he continues to rehab a torn Achilles and the Jets try to figure out if he can finally play up to his potential.

Expect some combination of newcomer Marcus Gilchrist and Calvin Pryor at safety. Gilchrist has some intriguing versatility, having played some corner in his first two years with the Chargers before moving to safety. Gilchrist had 17 defeats last year with the Chargers, a number that would have led the New York secondary if he was in Green and White. Meanwhile, Pryor was asked to play a lot of coverage as a rookie because of the Jets' deficiencies at cornerback. That shouldn't be necessary this year, and instead he gets to spend the 2015 season at his natural spot as an in-the-box safety looking to provide support against the run.

Special Teams

Year	DVOA	Rank	FG/XP	Rank	Net Kick	Rank	Kick Ret	Rank	Net Punt	Rank	Punt Ret	Rank	Hidden	Rank
2012	-1.5%	21	-5.0	28	-0.2	17	4.4	8	-7.9	24	1.3	14	-6.7	26
2013	2.1%	10	8.4	4	1.6	13	0.8	12	-0.4	19	-0.1	15	-3.7	20
2014	-0.8%	16	0.5	14	4.8	10	-0.8	18	0.8	15	-9.0	32	-2.6	22

Included in the Jets' offseason makeover was the addition of special-teams coach Bobby April. April was frequently the best part of the Bills' coaching staff through some recent lean years in Buffalo, and he inherits a middle-of-the-road special-teams unit in New York. In a case of "What might have been?" the Jets lost two games to the Patriots last season in large part because of blocked kicks late in the contest. A year after starting the season by making his first 23 field goal attempts, Nick Folk hit 15 of his first 16 field goal attempts to open 2015. However, he slumped a bit down the stretch, missing five attempts in the last five games of the regular season, due in large part to a hip injury. Nobody in New York is thinking of dumping Folk, but it is also worth noting that he's had below-average gross kickoff value for three straight years. Punter Ryan Quigley was an average punter at best in 2014, and will face a training camp battle with Jake Schum for the second straight summer. Nick Bellore (14 tackles on special teams) leads the kickoff and punt coverage.

There are also questions for the Jets at both return positions. Saalim Hakim handled kick returns prior to Percy Harvin's arrival, and while he didn't reinvent the position, his electric speed should give him the inside track on the job in 2015. (Hakim was worth an estimated minus-3.2 points of field position on 13 returns, but the negative value essentially all comes from one play, where he muffed a Mason Crosby kickoff in Week 2 and it bounced out of bounds at the 5.) Jeremy Kerley and Walter Powell shared punt returns after Jalen Saunders was cut last year, and probably will share them again this season. One thing about Kerley that bears watching: for someone who didn't really have the full-time gig, he took a few too many fair catches (13) than some in the organization would prefer. Despite April's initial trepidation about using a rookie as a returner—and a limited resume as a return man at Ohio State—there's also the possibility that speedy rookie Devin Smith could see some reps at either spot.

Oakland Raiders

Twenty years ago, the late Al Davis moved the Raiders back to Oakland. Today, his son Mark faces questions about whether the team is returning to Los Angeles in a new stadium. Maybe that's the shot in the arm the Raiders need next, because these last 20 years have only produced three winning seasons (2000-02). Oakland's active streak of 12 seasons without a winning record or playoff appearance is the sixth-longest streak since 1960 (Table 1). No matter where Davis decides to physically move the franchise, fans just want the product on the field to move away from the black hole that has sucked up all the excellence to which the Raiders were once so committed.

Table 1. Most Consecutive Seasons without Winning Record or Playoff Berth, 1960-2014

Team	Seasons	Years	10+ Losses	.500 Seasons
New Orleans Saints	1967-1986	20	9	2
Tampa Bay Buccaneers	1983-1996	14	13	0
Cincinnati Bengals	1991-2004	14	9	3
Denver Broncos	1960-1973	13	6	1
St. Louis/Arizona Cardinals	1985-1997	13	8	1
Oakland Raiders	**2003-2014**	**12**	**10**	**2**
Philadelphia Eagles	1967-1977	11	5	1
New York Jets	1970-1980	11	6	4
Detroit Lions	2001-2010	10	9	0
St. Louis Rams	**2005-2014**	**10**	**6**	**1**

The bad news: expect that streak to extend to 13 seasons with Oakland once again among the lowest teams in our 2015 projections. The good news: this is finally a time to feel optimistic about Oakland's *future*—not overflowing confidence at Raiderjoe levels, but definitely more hopeful. General manager Reggie McKenzie is into the actual talent acquisition phase of his massive rebuilding project that started with a total turnover of the roster. In past years, Oakland proceeded with a lot of instability, which is why past wholesale roster changes never stopped the excessive losing. The development process was broken. This year ventures to be different. Some of the fruits of McKenzie's labor were on display last year as

the Raiders had a productive rookie draft class with multiple starters, which is a huge change from past disappointments. It's not the only change either.

Oakland hired another Denver defensive coordinator at head coach, but unlike the bland Dennis Allen, Jack Del Rio brings some identity to the job. He also has past success that's more recent than 12 years ago, so this won't be 2006 Art Shell Part Deux. For the first time since Rich Gannon was MVP in 2002, the Raiders have a quarterback who started every game the year before and will know it's still his job this year. The fact that Derek Carr was not a JaMarcus Russell-sized joke in his rookie season is a good sign, though few things are ever JaMarcus-sized in the NFL. Carr's potential is debatable, but it is huge for this team to have direction at coach and quarterback.

Efforts to build around Carr are underway, with the Raiders actually drafting the player most analysts spent months saying they should take, Alabama wide receiver Amari Cooper. Oakland even picked Michael Crabtree over Darrius Heyward-Bey in free agency, perhaps offering some absolution for past sins when they took the latter ahead of the former in the draft. The Raiders *did* sign another Super Bowl MVP, but Malcolm Smith was a logical addition and not a reactionary move like Larry Brown or Desmond Howard. Smith won't be asked to lead the defense, because last year's top-five pick Khalil Mack delivered as advertised with a fantastic season. Oakland also signed the only running back drafted in the top eight since Darren McFadden, but fortunately Trent Richardson cost them very little and should play second fiddle to speedy Latavius Murray. Raider Nation may want to root extra hard for no injuries this year, because Oakland's backup quarterback (Christian Ponder) is afraid to throw the ball down the field and Richardson might start running backwards if he's told to find the Black Hole. Not every move is a crowd-pleaser, but these are more positives than usual for Oakland.

Oakland's dark ages have seen a steady plague of bad hires, poor drafting, brutal signings, and a hint of bad luck. That collective failure is the only formula to produce so much losing for so long, because some of the individual pieces of those teams have gone on to success after escaping the Black Hole. Norv Turner forged a successful stint as head coach of the Chargers. Oakland offloaded Randy Moss to the Patriots for a 2007 fourth-round pick and watched him go on to have one

2015 Raiders Schedule

Week	Opp.	Week	Opp.	Week	Opp.
1	CIN	7	at SD	13	KC
2	BAL	8	NYJ	14	at DEN
3	at CLE	9	at PIT	15	GB
4	at CHI	10	MIN	16	SD (Thu.)
5	DEN	11	at DET	17	at KC
6	BYE	12	at TEN		

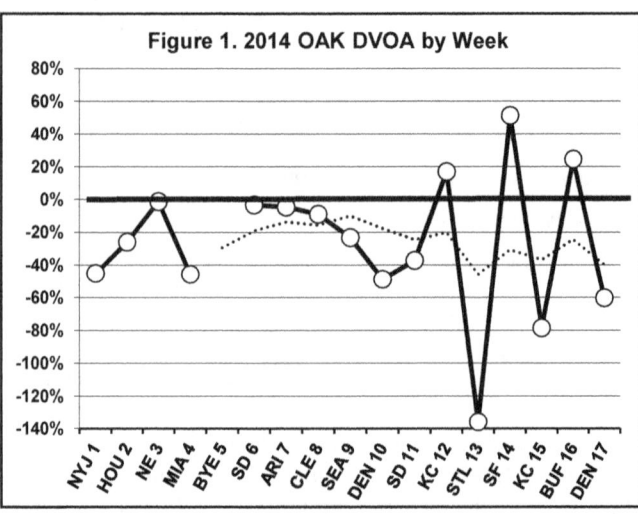

Figure 1. 2014 OAK DVOA by Week

of the greatest receiving seasons ever. Safety Mike Mitchell's notorious seventh-round grade from NFL Network's Mike Mayock added to Oakland's draft day embarrassment in 2009, but he had a career year in 2013 with Carolina. Linebacker Rolando McClain smiled for a photo while being arrested and then retired at age 23, but he returned as a quasi-savior for Dallas in 2014. Carson Palmer, far from the "greatest trade in football" as Hue Jackson once said, has rebounded nicely with Bruce Arians in Arizona.

The Raiders have targeted some of the right pieces, but Oakland never had the system in place to bring out the best in them, or at least to keep certain players motivated through the hard times. This is where a hard-nosed, defensive-minded coach can succeed with discipline. Jim Mora, Tony Dungy, and Marvin Lewi shared some of those traits when they ended the losing streaks of the Saints, Buccaneers, and Bengals, the three longest streaks without a winning season since the merger. Del Rio played linebacker under Mora in New Orleans, made the Pro Bowl in Dungy's defense in Minnesota, and worked with Lewis in Baltimore as part of the Ravens' defensive staff. While those streak-stoppers were in their first head coaching jobs, though, Del Rio is trying to get things right the second time around after he went 68-71 in Jacksonville from 2003-2011.

Davis was hesitant to hire a defensive coach, but Del Rio convinced him he knew offense too. "When we met and he dissected the Raiders roster and was able to tell me about each offensive player and tell me how they ranked and how they did was pretty amazing to me, that he had just spent a whole season up in Denver but knew our offensive roster as well as anybody," Davis told the press. Okay, that strengthens the comparison of Davis to Chris Farley's character in *Tommy Boy*, a 1995 comedy about a dimwitted heir who has to save his company after his father's death. Del Rio *should* know Oakland's offensive personnel given that he spent the last three seasons game-planning against it with the Broncos. Still, Del Rio has not been stubbornly one-dimensional as a head coach and should have an input on the offense.

One appreciable quality Del Rio always had was the boldness to go for it on fourth down. His 2007 Jaguars had 33 fourth-down attempts, still the most of any team since 1997. That's also the only year this century the Jaguars have won a playoff game. Overall, Del Rio's Aggressiveness Index (AI), which measures coaches on fourth-down decisions, is the 11th-highest since 1989 among coaches with three-plus years of experience. Underdog teams need to take chances,

which is something Dennis Allen (ranked 120th out of 140 total coaches in AI since 1989) rarely dared to do. Del Rio also excelled in Jacksonville with the underdog strategy of limiting possessions by running and throwing high-percentage passes to minimize the scoring total of high-powered offenses like Peyton Manning's Colts. From 2003 to 2010, the Colts only lost 12 games against teams without a winning record, and Del Rio pulled off four of those upsets. Thanks to Father Time, Del Rio won't have to spend eight more years competing in the same division with Manning, but he has proven he understands the necessity to help an overmatched defense.

To help turn around this Oakland defense, Del Rio reached out to an old friend in Ken Norton Jr. The two started together at linebacker for the Cowboys in 1989-1991. Norton has since learned under Pete Carroll at USC and Seattle before joining Oakland in February for his first defensive coordinator job. This is a considerable change for both men, because the Raiders lack the star-studded lineups the Broncos and Seahawks have enjoyed. Oakland's defense has one star, and his name is Khalil Mack. Fortunately, linebacker is Norton's specialty; he helped to develop players like Lofa Tatupu, Keith Rivers, Brian Cushing, Clay Matthews, Rey Maualuga, Bruce Irvin, Bobby Wagner, and K.J. Wright. This is also good news for Sio Moore, who was much more active around the ball in his second season and should make for a nice pairing with Mack for years to come.

Mack is already the best pass-rusher on a defense that only had 22 sacks last year. Oakland finished 19th in pressure rate, but ranked an ineffective 30th in DVOA when generating pressure. One reason is the lack of finishing plays. The Raiders tied for a league-low with five long sacks (plays that took more than 3.1 seconds). Too often Oakland was just a hair too late getting to the quarterback to really cause a bad play. Mack's season was a great example of this. He had 30.5 quarterback hurries, but only 4.0 sacks. We have charted 23 players since 2012 with at least 30 quarterback hurries in a season. Nineteen of those players had double-digit sacks; Mack is the only one with fewer than seven. Del Rio likely sees Mack as the Von Miller of his 4-3 defense at strongside linebacker, though Mack also has the strength to line up at defensive end when Oakland brings in extra defensive backs. Mack has already mastered stuffing the run—his 17 run defeats ranked third in the league—but to take his game to the next level, he'll have to finish more sacks.

Del Rio had more to work with to generate pressure in Denver, but the Broncos only ranked 29th in DVOA with pressure, one measly spot above Oakland. That's a bit shocking, but the defenses had radically different results when they failed to generate pressure. The Broncos (8.3%) and Seahawks (8.7%) had the best DVOA without pressure thanks in large part to defensive backfields loaded with stars. The Raiders had a 38-year-old Charles Woodson and some young guys who were trying to prove themselves, and they ranked 21st without pressure (42.7%). Those guys are still trying to prove themselves this season, with D.J. Hayden and T.J. Carrie the young cornerbacks in need of development. Del Rio's defenses have always featured a "shutdown corner," whether it was Rashean Mathis in Jacksonville or Champ Bailey in Denver. Maybe new defensive backs coach Rod Woodson can instill some Hall of Fame knowledge, but time is starting to tick on Hayden after two injury-riddled years. Safety Nate Allen comes over from Philadelphia as the big free-agent signing, but he has not charted well in past years.

Secondary is the biggest weakness in Oakland that must be addressed next offseason. However, this is probably the right weakness to have in a rebuilding project. In 2009 Oakland made cornerback Nnadmi Asomugha the highest-paid defensive back as of that point in NFL history. That's not great value when your defense is usually stuck playing from behind. In Asomugha's last three years with the team (2008-2010), Oakland faced the most runs and fewest passes in the league. So it's really a good thing the Raiders are not tied into any large defensive back contract right now, because the team is not currently configured to make that valuable. The resources are in the front seven, and that's where Del Rio and Norton have to improve the defense the most in 2015.

Some coaches simply do not get things right on the first job, so time to refocus and a change of scenery are needed. We have seen this work before with Marv Levy (whose first job was a failed stint with the Chiefs), Bill Belichick (Browns)

and Mike Shanahan (Raiders) drastically turning their fortunes around at their second stops. Of course, it's not like Del Rio is inheriting a team with Jim Kelly, Tom Brady, or John Elway at quarterback. Or is he?

The jury is very much out on Derek Carr after one season. Some think he is a franchise quarterback while others see a replacement-level player. Supporters will cite the bleak situation around Carr: Oakland's offense faced the toughest schedule of defenses with the worst average starting field position and the 32nd-ranked rushing attack. Suddenly it makes sense how Oakland could go three-and-out on 36.8 percent of its drives, the third highest rate since 1997. The defense ranked 32nd in first-quarter DVOA, putting the offense down early and often. Every time Carr took the field with the offense, the Raiders were losing by an average of 9.45 points, the second-worst average margin since 1997. Of course Carr could have combated this with more third-down conversions and earlier scoring drives, but he was not in a great position to play savior last year.

One thing Carr does not appear to be is a human piñata like his brother David was in Houston. Maybe it was the elder Carr's brutal experience that led to this, but Derek looked poised to not take sacks in 2014. He accomplished this with a lot of quick passes, but he is also mobile enough to escape the pocket and get out of bounds. Oakland's improved offensive line was solid in protection and will be coached this year by another Del Rio comrade in Mike Tice, who did yeoman's work in Atlanta with a line ravaged by injuries. Carr's 3.85 percent sack rate was the sixth lowest for a rookie since 1970 (minimum 200 passes), only trailing Doug Williams, Dan Marino, Drew Bledsoe, Peyton Manning, and Matt Ryan. That's great news, because Manning (first), Marino (second), Williams (third) and Ryan (seventh) rank among the all-time leaders in lowest career sack rate. This is very much a repeatable skill.

There are other statistics that tend to draw a fine line on where people stand with Carr. Those who like him cite his ratio of 21 touchdowns to 12 interceptions, which is strong for a rookie, but still misleading in this case. While Carr threw many quick passes, he also had a lot of dangerous throws, including seven

Table 2. Lowest Passing Yards per Attempt in a Season

Rk	Quarterback	Low YPA Season					Rest of Career After Low YPA Season							
		Year	Team	Age	Season	YPA	Starts	Att.	Comp.	Pct.	Yards	YPA	TD	INT
1	Joey Harrington	2003	DET	25	2nd	5.20	48	1555	900	57.9%	9519	6.12	50	47
2	Jack Trudeau	1986	IND	24	1st	5.34	38	1227	669	54.5%	8018	6.53	34	51
3	Joey Harrington	2002	DET	24	1st	5.35	64	2109	1209	57.3%	12399	5.88	67	69
4	Blaine Gabbert	2011	JAC	22	1st	5.36	13	371	207	55.8%	2181	5.88	11	13
5	Vince Evans	1981	CHI	26	5th	5.40	10	610	328	53.8%	4546	7.45	26	32
6	Chris Weinke	2001	CAR	29	1st	5.43	5	169	93	55.0%	973	5.76	4	7
7	**Derek Carr**	**2014**	**OAK**	**23**	**1st**	**5.46**	-	-	-	-	-	-	-	-
8	Drew Bledsoe	1995	NE	23	3rd	5.51	150	4961	2902	58.5%	34055	6.86	198	148
9	Kyle Boller	2004	BAL	23	2nd	5.52	22	831	487	58.6%	5112	6.15	28	34
10	Jon Kitna	2001	CIN	29	5th	5.54	76	2731	1706	62.5%	18977	6.95	108	98

Minimum 400 passes.

dropped interceptions. Carr often threw into good coverage and 9.1 percent of his passes were defensed, the fourth-highest rate in the league. He's not afraid to try a back-shoulder throw in Seattle against Richard Sherman, though that one was intercepted. Carr threw 18 touchdowns in the red zone and Oakland had the highest red zone passing DVOA in the last nine seasons. Oakland's red zone touchdown percentage (72.4%) was the fourth highest since 1999 and it was very dependent on Carr's passing. Oakland's red zone rushing DVOA was just -25.6%. That difference of 110.0% between the pass and run is the third largest since 1989. That's great, but Carr led the Raiders to the fewest red zone trips in the league (29). Only nine offenses since 1999 have had fewer than 30 red zone trips. Part of the reason Oakland rarely got inside the 20 was that the offense ranked last in DVOA with the ball between the opponent's 21 and 39. These field-zone stats do not have strong yearly correlation. We expect Oakland to get into the red zone more often in 2015, which is the goal anyway, but Carr won't be as efficient.

Those not impressed by Carr only need to mention that he averaged 5.46 yards per pass attempt, the seventh-lowest season average in NFL history (Table 2, previous page). Something the Carr brothers have in common is that their completions just do not gain many yards. Derek's 9.4 yards per completion is the third-lowest season average in history (minimum 400 attempts), sandwiched between two seasons from David that rank first and fourth. Quarterbacks who populate such lists rarely pan out. Drew Bledsoe is one who did, and he led New England to the Super Bowl in 1996 with a better cast of receivers around him. That's the idea in Oakland, but rarely has a top-five pick at wide receiver improved a team's fortunes. David Carr still had miserable seasons with Andre Johnson. The best combinations we've seen of a quarterback and top-five pick wide receiver since the merger are Kurt Warner-to-Larry Fitzgerald in Arizona and Matthew Stafford-to-Calvin Johnson in Detroit.

Perhaps a curious choice to turn this offense around is new offensive coordinator Bill Musgrave, whom Del Rio let go in Jacksonville after two mediocre seasons of building around a young Byron Leftwich. Musgrave fared even worse trying to develop Ponder for three years in Minnesota. He learned some new tricks from Chip Kelly in Philadelphia last year, but Mus-

grave's history suggests that Murray may be the player most likely to have a breakout year in Oakland's offense.

There is no denying Oakland needed better wide receivers for Carr, guys with better hands and more separation so there won't be as many drops and contested passes. James Jones caught some 50/50 balls, but he was never meant to be a No. 1 receiver. Andre Holmes (good size) and Rod Streater (injured in 2014) can make plays, but they only have to be third and fourth receivers with the additions of Cooper and Crabtree. That's a quick improvement to the receiving corps, but the biggest improvement still has to come from the second-year quarterback.

The eternal optimist might look at the Raiders as a team that finished 3-3 down the stretch, with each win spoiling a playoff contender's season. The Thursday night upset over Kansas City to end a 16-game losing streak was a turning point led by the new core. Murray had his breakout performance with a 90-yard touchdown run. Carr led the first game-winning drive of his career. In the season's most hilarious moment, Mack and Moore celebrated a sack about 20 yards away from the action with the Chiefs threatening to run their next play. That youthful enthusiasm and talent is something the Raiders can perhaps bottle and mature for 2015. Then again, this team was blown out 52-0 by the Rams ten days after that breakthrough win.

The growing pains are still coming as the Raiders should struggle just to pull out six wins this year. The schedule will not be kind, as the AFC West is still one of the toughest divisions in the league, while both North divisions are fairly competitive in their own right. Oakland's talent pales in comparison to most of the league, but the key this year is to look for improvement in the players around whom the Raiders are building for the future. Frankly, it is refreshing to talk about this team in a positive light instead of focusing on the latest draft bust or asinine free-agent contract that's continuing to hold them back. Clearly, the Raiders have not been good for the better part of two decades now, but a return to relevancy would be a welcome sight. Even if those moments like the Tuck Rule and the night Jon Gruden was three steps ahead of Rich Gannon's every move still sting to this day, it's better to have losses that make you care instead of being desensitized to losing.

Scott Kacsmar

2014 Raiders Stats by Week

Wk	vs.	W-L	PF	PA	YDF	YDA	TO	Total	Off	Def	ST
1	at NYJ	L	14	19	158	402	2	-45%	-34%	7%	-3%
2	HOU	L	14	30	364	327	-4	-26%	-2%	21%	-3%
3	at NE	L	9	16	241	297	-1	-1%	-21%	-15%	5%
4	vs. MIA	L	14	38	317	435	-1	-46%	-50%	10%	14%
5	BYE										
6	SD	L	28	31	396	423	-1	-3%	40%	34%	-9%
7	ARI	L	13	24	220	365	1	-5%	2%	10%	4%
8	at CLE	L	13	23	387	306	-3	-9%	-1%	17%	10%
9	at SEA	L	24	30	226	326	-3	-23%	-33%	-6%	4%
10	DEN	L	17	41	222	471	-1	-49%	-49%	-5%	-5%
11	at SD	L	6	13	233	300	-1	-37%	-41%	-5%	-1%
12	KC	W	24	20	351	313	-1	17%	14%	-12%	-8%
13	at STL	L	0	52	244	348	-5	-136%	-75%	58%	-4%
14	SF	W	24	13	330	248	2	51%	31%	-15%	5%
15	at KC	L	13	31	280	388	0	-79%	-44%	10%	-25%
16	BUF	W	26	24	347	321	2	24%	13%	-9%	3%
17	at DEN	L	14	47	199	451	-1	-60%	-38%	11%	-12%

Trends and Splits

	Offense	Rank	Defense	Rank
Total DVOA	-19.4%	30	6.3%	26
Unadjusted VOA	-23.7%	32	10.1%	29
Weighted Trend	-19.3%	27	5.7%	24
Variance	10.6%	27	3.8%	5
Average Opponent	-4.6%	1	2.8%	2
Passing	-10.1%	28	21.0%	28
Rushing	-21.6%	32	-9.7%	14
First Down	-29.6%	31	4.6%	22
Second Down	-6.2%	22	7.6%	26
Third Down	-21.1%	25	7.6%	20
First Half	-20.1%	30	8.9%	28
Second Half	-18.7%	26	2.9%	22
Red Zone	34.2%	1	-3.6%	18
Late and Close	-1.2%	20	9.1%	26

Five-Year Performance

Year	W-L	Pyth W	Est W	PF	PA	TO	Total	Rk	Off	Rk	Def	Rk	ST	Rk	Off AGL	Rk	Def AGL	Rk	Off Age	Rk	Def Age	Rk	ST Age	Rk
2010	8-8	9.0	7.1	410	371	-2	-4.1%	21	-8.3%	23	-2.3%	13	1.8%	13	15.0	8	15.3	10	26.6	25	26.2	25	27.1	7
2011	8-8	6.1	7.3	359	433	-4	-8.0%	22	2.6%	14	9.6%	27	-1.0%	20	36.7	21	41.4	26	26.8	19	27.1	16	26.8	4
2012	4-12	4.1	3.7	290	443	-7	-27.8%	29	-9.5%	23	12.5%	29	-5.8%	31	31.8	19	35.0	20	27.1	13	27.5	9	26.6	8
2013	4-12	4.9	2.1	322	453	-9	-34.1%	31	-16.7%	28	10.3%	26	-7.1%	31	49.7	26	27.2	15	26.7	17	27.6	5	26.1	16
2014	3-13	3.1	4.8	253	452	-15	-27.4%	29	-19.4%	30	6.3%	26	-1.7%	18	26.1	11	77.5	32	26.5	22	27.7	4	26.2	11

2014 Performance Based on Most Common Personnel Groups

OAK Offense					OAK Offense vs. Opponents					OAK Defense				OAK Defense vs. Opponents			
Pers	Freq	Yds	DVOA	Run%	Pers	Freq	Yds	DVOA	Run%	Pers	Freq	Yds	DVOA	Pers	Freq	Yds	DVOA
11	49%	5.3	-16.2%	19%	Base	38%	4.1	-12.9%	49%	Base	26%	4.8	-0.9%	11	60%	6.2	10.2%
21	27%	4.0	-16.3%	29%	Nickel	37%	4.5	-31.5%	22%	Nickel	65%	6.1	9.6%	12	21%	5.9	10.6%
22	6%	2.6	-38.6%	63%	Dime+	22%	5.7	7.8%	12%	Dime+	8%	6.8	4.7%	21	7%	4.5	-6.8%
20	5%	4.7	-0.6%	47%	Goal Line	1%	0.9	23.0%	50%	Goal Line	1%	2.6	5.5%	20	3%	4.9	7.8%
621	4%	3.7	-8.7%	74%	Big	3%	5.8	4.0%	82%					611	3%	4.3	-3.1%

Strategic Tendencies

Run/Pass		Rk	Formation		Rk	Pass Rush		Rk	Secondary		Rk	Strategy		Rk
Runs, first half	36%	22	Form: Single Back	66%	27	Rush 3	3.4%	26	4 DB	19%	28	Play action	21%	16
Runs, first down	41%	30	Form: Empty Back	5%	14	Rush 4	65.0%	16	5 DB	67%	9	Avg Box (Off)	6.40	4
Runs, second-long	32%	12	Pers: 3+ WR	54%	22	Rush 5	23.5%	14	6+ DB	13%	15	Avg Box (Def)	6.23	21
Runs, power sit.	39%	31	Pers: 4+ WR	0%	24	Rush 6+	8.0%	9	CB by Sides	84%	13	Offensive Pace	29.80	15
Runs, behind 2H	23%	25	Pers: 2+ TE/6+ OL	18%	32	Sacks by LB	31.8%	18	DB Blitz	6%	26	Defensive Pace	30.40	19
Pass, ahead 2H	51%	9	Shotgun/Pistol	65%	14	Sacks by DB	13.6%	6	Hole in Zone	12%	2	Go for it on 4th	0.88	19

For only the second time since 2007, the Raiders did not finish first or second in total penalties. They were tied for 11th with 138 penalties, including declined and offsetting. ⬬ Oakland's offense averaged just 4.3 yards after the catch, 31st in the NFL. That included 6.3 average YAC on passes thrown behind the line of scrimmage; no other team was below 7.0, and the

NFL average was 8.9. ☜ We also charted the Raiders with a league-low 43 broken tackles (no other team was below 50). ☜ The Raiders sent the standard four pass rushers roughly 50 percent more often than they did in 2013, when they ranked 32nd at 44 percent of plays. ☜ In a connected note, the Raiders dramatically changed their strategy on defensive back blitzes, which plummeted from a league-leading 22 percent of plays in 2013. The Raiders were average when they ran so many DB blitzes two years ago, but last year may have been smart to cut down, as they allowed 9.2 yards per play. ☜ Oakland's "CB by Sides" number is a bit artificially low because starter Carlos Rogers was used as a slot corner so much in the first half of the season. After midseason, Oakland tended to play starters on strict sides, with Tarell Brown on the defensive left and D.J. Hayden on the defensive right. ☜ The Raiders allowed a league-worst average of 6.3 yards after the catch.

Passing

Player	DYAR	DVOA	Plays	NtYds	Avg	YAC	C%	TD	Int
D.Carr	-150	-14.9%	622	3071	4.9	4.2	58.9%	21	12
M.McGloin	-58	-54.4%	20	121	6.1	4.8	63.2%	1	2
M.Schaub*	-158	-220.7%	13	28	2.2	4.8	50.0%	0	2
C.Ponder	-146	-57.5%	50	188	3.8	4.5	50.0%	0	2

Rushing

Player	DYAR	DVOA	Plays	Yds	Avg	TD	Fum	Suc
D.McFadden*	-33	-13.9%	156	534	3.4	2	1	40%
L.Murray	35	1.7%	82	424	5.2	2	1	44%
M.Jones-Drew*	-69	-50.1%	42	107	2.5	0	1	24%
M.Reece	2	-6.1%	21	85	4.0	0	1	48%
D.Carr	40	28.4%	18	106	5.9	0	0	-
T.Richardson	-59	-17.7%	159	520	3.3	3	2	43%
R.Helu	42	15.7%	40	216	5.4	1	0	55%

Receiving

Player	DYAR	DVOA	Plays	Ctch	Yds	Y/C	YAC	TD	C%
J.Jones	-18	-14.7%	112	73	666	9.1	3.0	6	65%
A.Holmes	42	-7.2%	98	47	693	14.7	4.1	4	48%
B.Butler	42	1.9%	36	21	280	13.3	4.0	2	58%
K.Thompkins	-33	-24.9%	36	15	209	13.9	4.3	0	42%
D.Moore*	-57	-39.4%	27	12	115	9.6	3.3	0	44%
V.Brown*	-15	-22.5%	21	12	118	9.8	3.9	0	57%
R.Streater	15	2.0%	13	9	84	9.3	3.3	1	69%
M.Crabtree	24	-9.9%	108	69	702	10.2	3.9	4	64%
M.Rivera	-97	-22.6%	99	58	534	9.2	3.0	4	59%
B.Leonhardt	1	-5.6%	8	6	35	5.8	1.5	1	75%
L.Smith	-2	-11.3%	8	7	42	6.0	3.4	1	88%
M.Reece	10	-10.9%	59	37	265	7.2	5.5	1	63%
D.McFadden*	-75	-37.5%	56	36	212	5.9	7.3	0	64%
L.Murray	8	-6.6%	23	17	143	8.4	9.0	0	74%
M.Jones-Drew*	4	-9.2%	16	11	71	6.5	5.9	0	69%
J.Olawale	28	58.5%	6	5	18	3.6	1.4	2	83%
R.Helu	108	31.2%	47	42	480	11.4	11.6	2	89%
T.Richardson	49	11.9%	34	27	229	8.5	8.9	0	79%

Offensive Line

Player	Pos	Age	GS	Snaps	Pen	Sk	Pass	Run	Player	Pos	Age	GS	Snaps	Pen	Sk	Pass	Run
Austin Howard	RG	28	16/16	1029	2	5.5	18.8	3.8	Khalif Barnes	G/T	33	14/13	762	4	3.0	15.5	0.0
Donald Penn	LT	32	16/16	1017	2	5.5	20.3	1.0	Menelik Watson	RT	27	12/9	485	7	3.0	20.3	1.0
Stefen Wisniewski*	C	26	16/16	1010	7	1.0	7.0	5.5	Rodney Hudson	C	26	16/16	1007	2	2.0	3.0	3.3
Gabe Jackson	LG	24	13/12	809	4	1.0	2.0	3.3									

Year	Yards	ALY	Rk	Power	Rk	Stuff	Rk	2nd Lev	Rk	Open Field	Rk	Sacks	ASR	Rk	Short	Long	F-Start	Cont.
2012	3.90	3.52	29	55%	28	21%	24	1.10	21	0.78	15	27	4.4%	4	10	7	16	32
2013	4.09	3.71	26	61%	20	16%	6	0.88	31	0.83	10	44	8.5%	28	7	24	23	22
2014	3.80	3.56	28	55%	29	21%	21	0.94	31	0.65	18	28	4.4%	3	11	10	17	32
2014 ALY by direction:		Left End 4.37 (6)			Left Tackle 3.9 (13)			Mid/Guard 3.52 (27)			Right Tackle 3.09 (29)				Right End 1.97 (31)			

We need more than one season of data to see if Derek Carr is Peyton Manning-like in his ability to get rid of the ball to avoid contact and make his linemen look a lot better than they really are. Carr had the NFL's third-lowest knockdown rate (8.0 percent) in 2014, but he'll need to hold onto the ball a bit longer if this offense is going to create more big plays with its new receivers.

Oakland has made some curious decisions with its offensive line. Not bringing back left tackle Jared Veldheer a year ago worked out only because veteran Donald Penn surprisingly played at a very similar level for slightly less cash. The only problem there is Veldheer was four years younger and had a chance to stay long-term with Carr. This year, the Raiders had a choice between two 26-year-old centers taken in the second round of the 2011 draft. Rather than re-sign Stefen Wisniewski to a new deal, Oakland opted to snag Rodney Hudson from the Chiefs and make him the second-highest paid center in the league ($8.9 million per year), right between the two Pouncey brothers. Wisniewski is only going to make $2.5 million for one year in Jacksonville. This reeks of a move where the Raiders thought they could hurt the Chiefs and improve the line at the same time, but it's hard to say Hudson is a center with a track record of that kind of impact. Sure, he's coming off a great year where he ranked second in snaps per blown block and Wisniewski was only 18th, but we just have to go back to 2013 to find Wisniewski (seventh) ranked one spot above Hudson (eighth) in the same metric. Center is a position where teams can go cheap, but Oakland made it the centerpiece of this year's free-agent spending.

Oakland repeated a gamble to pay for another team's player over its own; will it also repeat the gamble of starting a rookie guard for the second straight year? Gabe Jackson had an excellent rookie year, and our charters ranked him second in snaps per blown block. He should help solidify the left side of the line for years, but the right side is a problem. Jon Feliciano (Miami) is a fourth-round pick with plenty of experience as a solid run blocker, but scouting reports consistently cite his lack of athleticism and project limited pro success. Nonetheless, the Raiders will consider putting Feliciano right into the starting lineup, because Austin Howard really struggled in his first year with Oakland after starting at right tackle for the Jets. Maybe Howard should move back to right tackle after Menelik Watson had the worst rate of blown blocks in the league last year. You hate to pull the plug so quickly on a second-round pick, but Watson was always known to be a very raw project; he entered the league at age 25 with just one year of major college football experience. If Oakland starts veteran Khalif Barnes, who can play guard or tackle, then it's not unrealistic to think the soundest offensive line in the AFC West belongs to the Raiders.

Defensive Front Seven

Defensive Line	Age	Pos	G	Snaps	Plays	Overall TmPct	Rk	Stop	Dfts	BTkl	Runs	vs. Run St%	Rk	RuYd	Rk	Pass Rush Sack	Hit	Hur	Dsrpt
Antonio Smith*	34	DT	16	757	19	2.3%	91	18	7	1	15	93%	3	1.1	14	3.0	3	19.5	0
Justin Ellis	25	DT	16	623	22	2.6%	84	17	2	0	20	80%	32	2.0	35	0.0	1	4.5	1
Pat Sims*	30	DT	16	420	26	3.1%	--	18	2	1	24	67%	--	2.7	--	0.0	1	3.0	1
Dan Williams	28	DT	16	412	33	4.2%	--	28	4	3	30	87%	--	1.7	--	1.0	3	2.5	1

Edge Rushers	Age	Pos	G	Snaps	Plays	Overall TmPct	Rk	Stop	Dfts	BTkl	Runs	vs. Run St%	Rk	RuYd	Rk	Pass Rush Sack	Hit	Hur	Dsrpt
Justin Tuck	32	DE	15	640	46	5.9%	28	34	21	2	34	65%	74	2.6	46	5.0	10	18.0	4
C.J. Wilson	28	DE	16	364	23	2.8%	--	17	5	0	20	70%	--	3.0	--	2.0	0	1.5	0
Benson Mayowa	24	DE	16	352	12	1.4%	--	9	3	1	8	88%	--	1.1	--	1.0	2	3.5	1

Linebackers	Age	Pos	G	Snaps	Plays	Overall TmPct	Rk	Stop	Dfts	BTkl	Pass Rush Sack	Hit	Hur	Runs	vs. Run St%	Rk	RuYd	Rk	Tgts	vs. Pass Suc%	Rk	AdjYd	Rk	PD	Int
Miles Burris*	27	MLB	16	1063	109	13.1%	38	61	19	10	0.0	1	6.5	64	69%	25	3.7	59	29	42%	54	9.4	61	1	0
Khalil Mack	24	OLB	16	994	77	9.3%	68	58	25	5	4.0	9	30.5	60	80%	4	1.9	4	3	66%	--	3.5	--	1	0
Sio Moore	25	OLB	11	698	91	15.9%	19	59	14	9	3.0	3	9	64	70%	17	3.0	26	20	54%	22	6.9	42	1	0
Curtis Lofton	29	ILB	16	1044	145	18.0%	6	71	16	7	0.0	4	6.5	92	60%	58	3.3	40	43	50%	40	7.3	49	0	0
Malcolm Smith	26	OLB	14	271	33	5.1%	--	14	3	3	0.0	0	1.5	25	48%	--	4.0	--	14	74%	--	3.7	--	1	0

Year	Yards	ALY	Rk	Power	Rk	Stuff	Rk	2nd Level	Rk	Open Field	Rk	Sacks	ASR	Rk	Short	Long
2012	4.27	3.80	6	58%	9	22%	9	1.01	2	1.18	30	25	4.9%	30	8	11
2013	3.96	3.95	18	73%	25	17%	21	1.16	21	0.45	6	38	7.3%	11	15	11
2014	4.08	3.85	16	62%	12	20%	12	1.13	15	0.72	18	22	4.1%	32	9	5
2014 ALY by direction:		Left End 2.56 (2)			Left Tackle 3.79 (17)			Mid/Guard 4.01 (17)				Right Tackle 4.85 (27)			Right End 3.42 (12)	

Oakland's front seven has gone through many changes in recent years, but this season should retain at least four starters from 2014. Justin Ellis was just a fourth-round rookie, but acclimated quickly to a starting role inside. Dan Williams comes over from Arizona and should be an improvement on Pat Sims as a run-stuffing defensive tackle. Mario Edwards was a controversial pick in the second round due to his fluctuating weight and lack of pass-rush ability. He is versatile should the team want to switch it up between a 3-4 and 4-3 defense, but most of Edwards' scouting report reads as a major red flag for the 35th overall pick. Justin Tuck, perhaps slowed by a knee injury, was limited to no more than five sacks for the third time in four years while also struggling against the run. He did have 10 quarterback hits, so his problem was often getting to the quarterback just a hair too late, a common theme for this defense last season.

Take Khalil Mack's season as an example. He only notched four sacks, so some might compare him to overrated linebackers drafted high like Aaron Curry and Brian Bosworth. While he had four sacks, Mack finished sixth in the league with 30.5 hurries. He also drew eight offensive holding penalties, so he was definitely a handful for blockers last year. It's good we have numbers like this, because a lot of standout seasons from a 4-3 outside linebacker—particularly one who plays a Von Miller-like hybrid role, often rushing the passer—can easily be overlooked without sack production. Mack just missed some sacks, but he was dominant at stuffing the run and still generated a lot of pressure.

Sio Moore is Oakland's other young starting linebacker. He defended the run well too, and also helped against short passes. Malcolm Smith comes over from Seattle where he worked with new defensive coordinator Ken Norton Jr., and will provide depth. Nick Roach missed last season and Miles Burris was released after the draft, so veteran Curtis Lofton is leaving the Falcons-Saints rivalry and taking over the middle linebacker job in Oakland. He rarely makes any splash plays, but Lofton has quietly started 111 of a possible 112 games in his career.

Defensive Secondary

Secondary	Age	Pos	G	Snaps	Plays	TmPct	Rk	Stop	Dfts	BTkl	Runs	St%	Rk	RuYd	Rk	Tgts	Tgt%	Rk	Dist	Suc%	Rk	AdjYd	Rk	PD	Int
						Overall					vs. Run								vs. Pass						
Charles Woodson	39	FS	16	1102	121	14.5%	2	48	16	21	55	40%	37	6.4	35	37	10.1%	49	7.7	50%	53	8.4	52	7	4
Tarell Brown*	30	CB	14	961	58	8.0%	47	22	7	2	14	50%	21	5.4	26	58	18.3%	7	12.8	52%	31	8.0	42	5	0
Brandian Ross	26	SS	14	706	60	8.2%	56	22	10	8	20	40%	37	5.7	21	25	10.6%	53	12.3	64%	10	5.7	19	6	2
D.J. Hayden	25	CB	10	581	57	11.0%	8	21	9	5	10	30%	50	5.7	30	60	31.3%	73	11.4	53%	26	8.4	46	9	1
T.J. Carrie	25	CB	13	543	53	7.8%	--	26	12	8	12	25%	--	6.8	--	38	21.1%	--	10.9	53%	--	7.1	--	7	1
Carlos Rogers*	34	CB	7	461	36	9.9%	--	23	9	3	15	67%	--	3.4	--	20	12.9%	--	8.8	47%	--	9.7	--	1	0
Usama Young*	30	FS	6	218	24	7.7%	--	5	2	3	13	15%	--	9.8	--	8	10.5%	--	10.1	56%	--	8.0	--	3	0
Tyvon Branch*	29	SS	3	190	30	19.2%	--	12	3	1	20	40%	--	4.7	--	3	4.8%	--	6.0	63%	--	9.3	--	1	0
Larry Asante	27	SS	6	161	20	6.4%	--	4	1	3	15	20%	--	7.1	--	3	4.8%	--	14.0	70%	--	11.0	--	0	0
Nate Allen	28	FS	15	1076	67	8.2%	55	15	11	4	18	22%	64	8.4	54	33	8.1%	35	13.7	36%	64	9.4	60	5	4

Year	Pass D Rank	vs. #1 WR	Rk	vs. #2 WR	Rk	vs. Other WR	Rk	vs. TE	Rk	vs. RB	Rk
2012	30	25.9%	30	5.0%	19	-13.4%	7	15.3%	28	11.0%	21
2013	29	10.8%	23	20.2%	31	28.4%	31	3.9%	18	10.8%	25
2014	28	16.7%	28	2.5%	18	12.1%	25	-9.1%	10	15.4%	24

When a team has to rebuild on such a mass scale like Oakland, some units are going to improve more slowly than others. The secondary has not been a big part of Oakland's recent drafts and free-agent spending periods, so it is the weakest part of the team. Veteran stop-gaps from last year like Carlos Rogers and Tarell Brown are gone, and the Raiders will be depending on youth, most notably with D.J. Hayden and T.J. Carrie. Hayden has yet to live up to his first-round status, but he showed some improvement last year. He has been heavily targeted in the 18 games he's been healthy for the last two years, but Hayden only has two interceptions and hasn't shown much ability for getting in position to make plays on the ball. He lost first-team reps to Keith McGill in OTAs, so Hayden's not even guaranteed to start this season. Carrie came on late in the season and may already be the best corner on the roster. That's not saying much since the depth consists of inexperienced players such as McGill, Neiko Thorpe, and Chimdi Chekwa. The trio combined for 287 defensive snaps last year. Oakland's only 2015 draft pick used on the secondary was seventh-round selection Dexter McDonald (Kansas).

Charles Woodson played 1,207 snaps at age 38 last year, which is very impressive in a league that keeps getting younger each year. Woodson had four of Oakland's nine interceptions, which made him the 11th player in NFL history to reach 60 interceptions. It could be a long time before we see the 12th, but there's a good reason many players retire well before 38. Woodson's athleticism is just not what it used to be, and we charted him with 21 broken tackles, the second most in the league. But even an older, slower Woodson is still much better than the alternatives for Oakland. Usama Young and Tyvon Branch are gone after injury-shortened seasons. Larry Asante and Brandian Ross are back, but Nate Allen is going to start alongside Woodson after the Raiders paid him $11.8 million guaranteed. Allen had a career-high four interceptions with the Eagles last year, but his coverage has ranked 65th and 64th in adjusted success rate the last two years.

Special Teams

Year	DVOA	Rank	FG/XP	Rank	Net Kick	Rank	Kick Ret	Rank	Net Punt	Rank	Punt Ret	Rank	Hidden	Rank
2012	-5.8%	31	11.8	1	-12.1	31	-2.8	21	-15.3	31	-10.4	32	-7.4	27
2013	-7.1%	31	-11.1	29	6.0	6	-10.4	32	-16.1	30	-4.1	22	13.5	2
2014	-1.7%	18	8.2	5	-5.4	25	-9.3	32	2.7	12	-4.7	24	6.3	6

Oakland crawled back to special-teams mediocrity last year after consecutive next-to-last finishes in DVOA. Any further improvement will be overseen by Brad Seely, the new special teams coordinator. Seely spent the previous four years with San Francisco, which ranked second, 20th, seventh, and 24th in DVOA in that time. Have we mentioned that special teams can be pretty erratic? That is often driven by the lack of consistency in the kicking game, and Sebastian Janikowski is no stranger to that. He rebounded from a 21-of-30 2013 campaign to make 19-of-22 in 2014, including a 12-of-15 record from 40-plus yards, though his 22 total attempts were the fewest in any season of his career. Janikowski also ranked sixth in gross kickoff value, but his coverage unit failed him when he delivered a returnable kickoff. Oakland's opponents averaged a league-high 32.5 yards per kick return.

Oakland's own return game remained stagnant, and ranked dead last in kickoff returns for the second year in a row. The Raiders have not returned a punt or kickoff for a touchdown since 2011, and just finding reliable returners has been a problem. Even Darren McFadden and a 38-year-old Charles Woodson were given a shot last year. T.J. Carrie returned most of the punts and the second-most kickoffs, but the cornerback was not effective at either role. Latavius Murray has great speed, but was worth an estimated minus-3.4 points on kick returns and should focus on his running back duties. The Raiders could give the jobs to veteran Trindon Holliday, signed after seventh-round return specialist Andre Debose tore his Achilles in OTAs.

Marquette King improved to 10th in gross punt value in his second year of replacing Shane Lechler. King had plenty of practice with 109 punts, tied for the fifth most in a season in NFL history. He only had three touchbacks, but could do a better job of placing punts inside the 20 and making more kicks nonreturnable against Oakland's suspect coverage unit. Chimdi Chekwa (nine) was the only Oakland player to rank in the top 85 in special-teams tackles.

Philadelphia Eagles

2014 Record: 10-6	**Total DVOA:** 12.8% (7th)	**2015 Mean Projection:** 8.8 wins	**On the Clock (0-4):** 6%
Pythagorean Wins: 9.7 (10th)	**Offense:** 1.1% (13th)	**Postseason Odds:** 48.5%	**Mediocrity (5-7):** 26%
Snap-Weighted Age: 27.0 (6th)	**Defense:** -3.3% (10th)	**Super Bowl Odds:** 7.1%	**Playoff Contender (8-10):** 42%
Average Opponent: -3.4% (28th)	**Special Teams:** 8.3% (1st)	**Proj. Avg. Opponent:** -2.4% (22nd)	**Super Bowl Contender (11+):** 27%

2014: Running on empty, running blind, running into the sun but running behind.

2015: His name is Kellymandius, King of Kings.

The New Year dawned, and Chip Kelly ceased to be a mere mortal. He became instead a Mesopotamian creator-destroyer god: he who brings life-giving rains and crop-obliterating floods, the granter, taker, and re-granter of life.

Kelly climbed the ziggurat at the NovaCare Center in South Philadelphia and feasted upon Howie Roseman's still-beating heart, obtaining mighty personnel and salary cap omnipotence. Kelly would later claim to be heeding a higher directive: Jeffrey Lurie thrust the crown onto his head, like Jupiter himself descending from heaven to crown Caesar Augustus. But those who attain godhood via bloody coup always claim divine provenance.

Whatever the catalyst, Kelly loosed a cleansing upon the Eagles the likes of which the NFL has never seen. Woe to ye who fitteth not the culture (LeSean McCoy), costeth money that might be spent elsewhere (Jeremy Maclin), skippeth OTAs (Evan Mathis), complaineth about the pace of practice (Cary Williams), or simply be near at hand when the urge to trade doth strike the god-king (Nick Foles, and others)! But blessed be those coming off ACL injuries (Sam Bradford, Kiko Alonso), running backs who be not shady (DeMarco Murray, Ryan Mathews), men who walked the hallowed halls of the University of Oregon (Walter Thurmond, Alonso), and all those who otherwise curried the favor of the football All-Father!

The Eagles offseason raises a lot of questions. Football questions. Fantasy football questions. Philosophical questions. Existential questions. The Eagles offseason was the kind of thing that slips the moorings of what you thought of as football reality. The 2015 Eagles are impenetrable by typical analysis, whether it's statistical analysis, scouting analysis, or fly-by-the-seat-of-the-pants midday talk show analysis. Conventional wisdom does you no good, because it keeps screaming the same thoughts into your ear. *This is too much change. These are too many risks. Nothing even close to this has ever, ever worked.*

Our established Football Outsiders techniques hit a brick wall when faced with an all-new starting quarterback who hasn't played a down since October of 2013 and might not even be ready to start training camp. Once we guesstimate some variables for Sam Bradford, we must let DeMarco Murray's 392-carry workload and Kelly's run-friendly offense wrestle on the spreadsheets, then project a receiving corps expected to feature two starters under 23 years old,

then worry about two new starters at guard. By the time we get to a 75-percent rebuilt secondary, well, maybe we aren't throwing darts, but this isn't the usual offseason of projecting last year's variables onto a slightly different roster. It's more like superimposing an offense so unique that its data hasn't settled yet onto an all-new expansion team of complete strangers.

The best we can do here is take a selection of Eagles talking points, examine them, trim a little of the rhetorical fat, and plate them as a tasting menu with the hope that it all coalesces into a satisfying meal. The only way to think about the Eagles offseason at all is to think differently. After weeks of studying the Eagles offseason from the inside out, it's the only way some of us *can* think about it.

Kelly inherited a cap surplus when he gained absolute power. He has his own theories on how to spend such a surplus, just as he has his own theories about huddling. Kelly adopted a short-term cap model after the Eagles spent a decade operating under the long-term model preferred by Andy Reid and Joe Banner and continued by Howie Roseman. Kelly seeks to spend immediate money to produce immediate results. That sounds potentially disastrous in a last-decade Redskins sort of way, but the Eagles are not doling out many of the huge long-term deals that doomed the Redskins. They are not paying Tuesday for a hamburger today; they are paying today and tomorrow.

At quarterback, Kelly had the choice of spending one last thrifty season deciding if Nick Foles was a "franchise" player or spending some of that cap surplus judging a quarterback with higher upside. He decided to spend $13 million the Eagles had in available budget to swap out Foles for Sam Bradford. The Eagles will still spend 2015 evaluating their quarterback, but they will now be evaluating someone who was considered a top-tier talent not long ago, instead of a mid-round pick who had a 2013 hot streak.

If Bradford pans out, the Eagles must award the same kind of 2016 contract they would have to give Foles or any other young veteran who crosses the Andy Dalton quality threshold. The risk with Foles was that he might max out as a Dalton. Bradford could potentially be much better. He could also be too injured to take the field in 2015. It's an obvious risk, one that Kelly felt was worth taking but most other coaches would run screaming from.

2015 Eagles Schedule

Week	Opp.	Week	Opp.	Week	Opp.
1	at ATL (Mon.)	7	at CAR	13	at NE
2	DAL	8	BYE	14	BUF
3	at NYJ	9	at DAL	15	ARI
4	at WAS	10	MIA	16	WAS (Sat.)
5	NO	11	TB	17	at NYG
6	NYG (Mon.)	12	at DET (Thu.)		

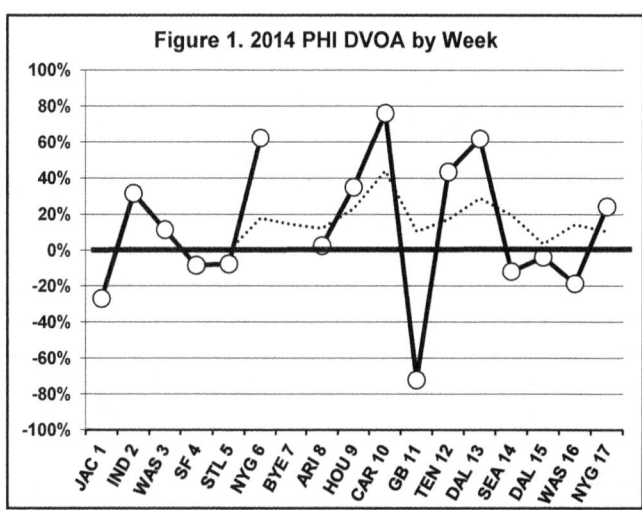

Figure 1. 2014 PHI DVOA by Week

Most of the rest of the offseason represents a clear shifting of cap resources from offense to defense. That includes the LeSean McCoy-Kiko Alonso trade, Jeremy Maclin's departure, the Byron Maxwell signing, and a few minor moves such as Brandon Graham's contract extension. Kelly needed to upgrade a defense, particularly a secondary that ranked 18th against the pass in DVOA including 24th and 20th, respectively, at stopping No. 1 and No. 2 receivers. Kelly reasoned that he could build a new Jeremy Maclin out of Jordan Matthews and perhaps a draft pick (which turned out to be Maclin clone Nelson Agholor). Maxwell-level talents are harder to develop, so the Eagles paid a premium for one, then drafted a second Seahawks-sized cornerback prospect in Eric Rowe. Alonso was one of the top defensive rookies of 2013 before tearing an ACL last year, and he is still under his rookie contract through the end of 2016. Kelly plans to win with scheme on offense and talent on defense: it's a familiar refrain for him, and the Eagles clearly upgraded their defensive talent.

It all made perfect sense, sort of—until Kelly doubled down on DeMarco Murray and Ryan Mathews. Suddenly, the coach whose scheme should produce big numbers for any competent running back was a) overspending for one running back coming off one of the most obvious overuse situations of the last 20 years and b) simultaneously grabbing another who seemed a little too content to settle for contractual sloppy seconds.

Murray and Mathews were obviously not Kelly's first choices; the Eagles thought they had Frank Gore signed, but Gore changed his mind and went to the Colts instead. Gore would have been a short-term offensive solution; it's easy to imagine Kelly drafting a mid-round running back to platoon with Gore in 2015 and completely replace him by 2017. Kelly was forced to adjust on the fly, and he may have overcompensated just a smidge.

It's best to look at this Eagles offseason as neither an act of pure genius or sheer madness, but as a combination of the two. Kelly was an inexperienced trader and general manager with a skeletal staff whose duties were still being redefined when free agency began. The McCoy trade caught even Rex Ryan by surprise, the Gore signing was bungled, and flying both Murray and Mathews into Philly at the same time was a lapse of professionalism that might have ended badly. Some of the organizational and procedural niceties slipped past the Eagles as Kelly tried to do more in one offseason than any general manager has ever done, despite a complete lack of experience: remember that Kelly was never even an NFL assistant before 2013, so some of the basics of scheduling meetings and fram-

ing transaction announcements were new to him. Kelly had a plan at every position, but the running back plan clearly got a little bungled.

As bungles go, obtaining the reigning Offensive Player of the Year at more-or-less market value is fairly mild. Murray's contract is front-loaded, making him potentially cuttable after the 2016 season and easily cuttable after 2017, if-and-when the Eagles get Curse of 370 Buyer's Remorse. Mathews represents a moderate-cost Curse of 370 power-train warranty. That's part of the wisdom underlying the madness of the Kelly system: this year's all-in gamble could fail, and the Eagles would still have a manageable cap situation in 2016 and could easily clean the slates in 2017 without facing a dead-money catastrophe.

A clean salary-cap slate, as the 2014 Raiders will tell you, is not always a good thing. If Bradford proves unworthy to retain—or, possibly, becomes valuable enough to spark a bidding war and leave town—the Eagles enter 2016 with Mark Sanchez and Matt Barkley as the only quarterbacks under contract. Murray is now 27; the down indicators are flashing all over his screen like pop-up ads and will probably crash the hard drive next year. Fletcher Cox, the team's best defensive player, is only signed through 2016. Rookie contracts will start to come due on many important players in the next two seasons: Cedric Thornton and Mychal Kendricks this year, then Cox, Lane Johnson, Zach Ertz and Kiko Alonso the next. Kelly has a young core to start paying, and he may have to simultaneously find a new backfield if Bradford-Murray falters.

The fear—and this is what the little cartoon with the Bill Hader voice is really screaming—is that Kelly will address 2016 and beyond the same way he addressed 2015: more sudden trades, more core players leaving town, another no-tomorrow gamble for the Super Bowl. The Eagles burned a lot of resources to get slightly better in 2015. They spent a lot of money, sweetened the Bradford trade with a second-round pick, let one of the most recognizable and liked veterans on the team walk after a career year, and engendered a little bad blood (the kind that seeps into future free-agent contract discussions if your program is not successful) from the likes of McCoy, Cary Williams and Mathis. A team that tries to keep doing that year after year will end up slaughtering its breeding stock. There were rumors that Kelly considered trading Cox in a draft-day Marcus Mariota frenzy. Maybe that was a smokescreen, but what happens if Bradford fails and Kelly gets a hankering for Colin Kaepernick, Jay Cutler, Robert Griffin or some other affordable top talent? If you don't think Kelly would trade Cox for Cutler, remember that even Rex Ryan was shocked to learn he would trade Shady McCoy for Alonso.

Looking past 2015 is difficult when our brains can process what the Eagles are doing right now. Kelly is counting on his vaunted "culture" to let him outsmart conventional wisdom this season. He believes his sports science staff can rehabilitate Bradford (and Alonso, and some other injured acquisitions) and keep them healthy. The Eagles use state-of-the-art pedagogical techniques to teach the Kelly system, with assistant coaches making offhand remarks about differentiated instruction and reading articles on brain-based learning, so theoretically, all of the newcomers will learn their roles efficiently. Team "chemistry" does not seem to be that big of a problem, because Kelly really does sign the "smart, high-character players" that every team claims to prioritize. Kelly acquisitions of the last two years such as Jordan Matthews, Nelson Agholor, Malcolm Jenkins, Walter Thurmond, Zach Ertz and even Murray all sound a little like Kelly when they talk. None of these guys are going to start complaining about the workout regimen.

If you are fully indoctrinated into the Kellypolitik, you can envision an Eagles Super Bowl. But any skepticism whatsoever starts to unravel the threads. The worst-case scenario is a 4-12 debacle with Tim Tebow running options while Bradford watches from the sideline in a boot, Murray grinds along at a worn-down 3.8 yards per rush, Maxwell proves he's no Richard Sherman, and (here's the scary part) all the Kelly Believers in the clubhouse start to think of themselves as trade fodder.

Just about any outcome in between is also conceivable, even the mundane ones. The no-huddle offense is still novel enough to beat a few weak opponents on sheer lack-of-preparation value. The running game is too deep to not work, and the front seven is strong. The Eagles could go 10-6 again with Bradford and Sanchez taking uninspiring turns, Murray and Mathews splitting 1,400 yards, and the secondary doing just enough to stop the Redskins receivers but not enough to stop the Cowboys receivers. The 2015 Eagles, having changed everything but the team colors, could end up with similar results to the 2014 and 2013 Eagles.

Wouldn't that be anticlimactic? We all want Kelly's grand experiment to either win big or lose big, for Kelly to be some football Orson Wells. He could just as easily turn out to be football's Michael Bay: too creative and clever to fail miserably, but too stubborn to produce much more than noisy pyrotechnics and slick-but-disappointing results. The destroyer god is but a man, and the 2015 Eagles are just another pretty good team with strengths, weaknesses and quarterback questions. If they turn out to be more, 2015 will be remembered as a turning point in NFL history, the year when Kelly taught franchises to rethink everything. If they turn out to be less, well … history is teeming with all-powerful rulers. How many of them can you actually name?

Mike Tanier

2014 Eagles Stats by Week

Wk	vs.	W-L	PF	PA	YDF	YDA	TO	Total	Off	Def	ST
1	JAC	W	34	17	420	306	-2	-27%	-25%	10%	8%
2	at IND	W	30	27	458	341	1	31%	29%	-19%	-17%
3	WAS	W	37	34	379	511	0	11%	5%	26%	33%
4	at SF	L	21	26	213	407	-3	-8%	-31%	-8%	15%
5	STL	W	34	28	352	466	0	-8%	17%	28%	4%
6	NYG	W	27	0	448	254	-1	62%	-3%	-48%	17%
7	BYE										
8	at ARI	L	20	24	521	400	-2	3%	4%	7%	5%
9	at HOU	W	31	21	483	300	-3	35%	10%	-20%	5%
10	CAR	W	45	21	365	317	5	76%	19%	-39%	18%
11	at GB	L	20	53	429	475	-4	-72%	-22%	28%	-21%
12	TEN	W	43	24	462	351	1	43%	0%	-13%	30%
13	at DAL	W	33	10	464	267	2	62%	7%	-51%	3%
14	SEA	L	14	24	139	440	0	-12%	-21%	3%	12%
15	DAL	L	27	38	294	364	-2	-4%	-12%	3%	11%
16	at WAS	L	24	27	495	305	0	-19%	15%	25%	-10%
17	at NYG	W	34	26	426	505	0	24%	8%	5%	21%

Trends and Splits

	Offense	Rank	Defense	Rank
Total DVOA	1.1%	13	-3.3%	10
Unadjusted VOA	-0.5%	16	-3.3%	11
Weighted Trend	1.1%	13	-7.4%	10
Variance	3.1%	2	6.9%	20
Average Opponent	0.2%	17	-1.4%	24
Passing	11.6%	15	8.5%	18
Rushing	-3.0%	13	-17.2%	7
First Down	0.0%	16	-6.3%	6
Second Down	-8.0%	24	0.1%	16
Third Down	18.6%	7	-2.8%	15
First Half	7.6%	10	-0.8%	14
Second Half	-5.6%	22	-6.3%	6
Red Zone	-5.7%	17	-0.5%	19
Late and Close	-3.9%	22	0.8%	19

Five-Year Performance

Year	W-L	Pyth W	Est W	PF	PA	TO	Total	Rk	Off	Rk	Def	Rk	ST	Rk	Off AGL	Rk	Def AGL	Rk	Off Age	Rk	Def Age	Rk	ST Age	Rk
2010	10-6	9.5	11.9	439	377	+9	23.2%	5	17.3%	3	-3.6%	11	2.3%	12	41.3	29	28.5	21	25.6	32	26.6	18	26.2	16
2011	8-8	9.8	9.0	396	328	-14	13.5%	9	9.8%	8	-3.7%	11	0.0%	17	10.5	3	11.4	5	26.7	20	26.9	17	25.7	29
2012	4-12	3.9	4.5	280	444	-24	-22.4%	28	-10.8%	25	9.4%	26	-2.2%	23	65.2	32	8.1	2	26.8	17	26.5	23	25.6	27
2013	10-6	9.4	10.2	442	382	+12	15.2%	8	22.9%	3	4.9%	23	-2.8%	25	21.2	7	11.0	4	27.5	11	26.2	21	26.0	19
2014	10-6	9.7	9.7	474	400	-8	12.8%	7	1.1%	13	-3.3%	10	8.3%	1	32.2	18	16.4	2	27.2	11	26.9	13	26.9	1

2014 Performance Based on Most Common Personnel Groups

PHI Offense					PHI Offense vs. Opponents					PHI Defense				PHI Defense vs. Opponents			
Pers	Freq	Yds	DVOA	Run%	Pers	Freq	Yds	DVOA	Run%	Pers	Freq	Yds	DVOA	Pers	Freq	Yds	DVOA
11	66%	6.1	5.0%	32%	Base	31%	5.2	-4.4%	54%	Base	56%	4.9	-9.9%	11	46%	6.6	9.1%
12	29%	5.3	5.5%	52%	Nickel	55%	6.2	11.8%	34%	Nickel	21%	6.5	17.3%	12	23%	5.1	-22.1%
21	3%	6.9	47.7%	27%	Dime+	14%	5.5	0.6%	25%	Dime+	23%	6.5	-2.4%	21	8%	4.8	-13.9%
13	1%	5.1	16.6%	89%										13	8%	3.7	-15.1%
														22	5%	3.2	-23.2%

Strategic Tendencies

Run/Pass		Rk	Formation		Rk	Pass Rush		Rk	Secondary		Rk	Strategy		Rk
Runs, first half	34%	27	Form: Single Back	98%	1	Rush 3	9.4%	7	4 DB	38%	4	Play action	33%	1
Runs, first down	43%	28	Form: Empty Back	1%	32	Rush 4	57.1%	23	5 DB	28%	29	Avg Box (Off)	6.20	24
Runs, second-long	41%	1	Pers: 3+ WR	66%	8	Rush 5	25.7%	10	6+ DB	34%	7	Avg Box (Def)	6.35	11
Runs, power sit.	65%	6	Pers: 4+ WR	0%	28	Rush 6+	7.8%	12	CB by Sides	94%	3	Offensive Pace	22.22	1
Runs, behind 2H	32%	6	Pers: 2+ TE/6+ OL	31%	15	Sacks by LB	65.3%	6	DB Blitz	7%	25	Defensive Pace	29.97	11
Pass, ahead 2H	45%	24	Shotgun/Pistol	86%	1	Sacks by DB	2.0%	29	Hole in Zone	0%	32	Go for it on 4th	0.65	27

The Eagles were the fastest team in our database (back to 1997) in both total pace (one play every 21.95 seconds) and situation-neutral pace (22.22 seconds). Both numbers broke the record set by the Eagles themselves the year before. ☞ The Eagles had just 5.5 average yards after the catch, close to the league average; the year before they had put up 6.6 average yards after catch, the highest figure going back to 2005 (since surpassed by Washington in 2014). ☞ The Eagles led the league with 60 wide receiver or tight end screens, almost double the number they ran in Chip Kelly's first season. They averaged 6.3 yards and 27.2% DVOA on these plays (vs. NFL averages of 5.7 yards and 14.2% DVOA). ☞ Philadelphia qualified as using "max protect" blocking on just 3.2 percent of pass plays; Philadelphia and San Diego were the only teams below 5.5 percent. ☞ The Eagles ran more often than any other team on second-and-long (scrambles not included), but had just 3.7 yards per carry (-38.4% DVOA) after gaining 5.9 yards per carry (29.9% DVOA) the year before. ☞ Philadelphia was the only offense in the league that we never marked using an extra offensive lineman all season. ☞ On defense, the biggest personnel change for the 2014 Eagles was a shift from nickel to dime when opponents spread out. The Eagles had used six defensive backs on just 0.9 percent of plays in 2013. ☞ The Eagles ranked sixth in the league in DVOA against passes behind the line of scrimmage, and only Denver (7.3) allowed fewer average yards after catch than Philadelphia (7.6) on these passes. However, the Eagles also ranked 29th in DVOA against passes beyond the line of scrimmage, allowing a league-high 5.3 average yards after catch.

Passing

Player	DYAR	DVOA	Plays	NtYds	Avg	YAC	C%	TD	Int
M.Sanchez	210	-1.4%	334	2226	6.7	5.7	64.3%	14	11
N.Foles*	264	1.8%	322	2108	6.5	5.3	60.4%	13	10

Rushing

Player	DYAR	DVOA	Plays	Yds	Avg	TD	Fum	Suc
L.McCoy*	87	-1.6%	310	1317	4.2	5	3	45%
D.Sproles	86	30.4%	56	318	5.7	6	2	41%
C.Polk	43	12.9%	46	172	3.7	4	0	54%
M.Sanchez	-15	-25.9%	21	88	4.2	1	2	-
N.Foles*	15	9.5%	13	71	5.5	0	1	-
T.Burton	-13	-78.5%	5	10	2.0	0	0	40%
D.Murray	382	14.8%	392	1849	4.7	13	3	54%
R.Mathews	62	11.3%	74	333	4.5	3	1	47%

Receiving

Player	DYAR	DVOA	Plays	Ctch	Yds	Y/C	YAC	TD	C%
J.Maclin*	222	7.4%	143	85	1318	15.5	5.8	10	59%
J.Matthews	194	11.6%	103	67	872	13.0	5.8	8	65%
R.Cooper	-38	-17.8%	95	55	577	10.5	2.8	3	58%
J.Huff	-49	-48.9%	18	8	98	12.3	9.6	0	44%
M.Austin	120	10.1%	72	47	568	12.1	4.3	2	65%
S.Ajirotutu	-17	-32.2%	12	4	45	11.3	2.5	0	33%
Z.Ertz	127	13.3%	89	58	702	12.1	3.9	3	65%
B.Celek	-49	-20.8%	51	32	340	10.6	4.1	1	63%
D.Sproles	37	-3.1%	63	41	392	9.6	10.1	0	65%
L.McCoy*	-9	-18.2%	39	30	160	5.3	6.6	0	77%
D.Murray	58	3.0%	64	57	418	7.3	8.8	0	89%
R.Mathews	32	37.6%	10	9	69	7.7	7.0	0	90%

Offensive Line

Player	Pos	Age	GS	Snaps	Pen	Sk	Pass	Run	Player	Pos	Age	GS	Snaps	Pen	Sk	Pass	Run
Jason Peters	LT	33	16/16	1145	12	6.5	24.0	4.5	Todd Herremans*	RG	33	8/8	577	4	0.5	12.0	1.5
Lane Johnson	RT	25	12/12	888	8	2.5	15.0	3.0	Matt Tobin	G	25	13/7	523	0	1.0	14.0	3.5
Jason Kelce	C	28	12/12	827	6	2.0	4.5	7.5	David Molk	C	27	7/4	404	1	0.0	11.0	3.5
Andrew Gardner	G/T	29	16/8	669	5	5.0	18.0	6.0	Dennis Kelly	G	25	3/3	201	1	0.0	1.0	1.0
Evan Mathis*	LG	34	9/9	596	3	3.0	8.0	5.0									

Year	Yards	ALY	Rk	Power	Rk	Stuff	Rk	2nd Lev	Rk	Open Field	Rk	Sacks	ASR	Rk	Short	Long	F-Start	Cont.
2012	4.47	3.56	28	69%	6	26%	31	1.39	6	1.06	6	48	8.1%	25	17	19	15	31
2013	5.02	3.71	25	72%	7	20%	21	1.57	1	1.24	2	46	9.4%	31	10	24	14	48
2014	4.36	3.52	29	81%	1	21%	26	1.24	9	0.93	6	32	4.9%	9	13	11	17	27
2014 ALY by direction:		Left End 3.54 (21)			Left Tackle 3.57 (18)			Mid/Guard 3.81 (23)			Right Tackle 2.68 (32)			Right End 3.33 (23)				

Jason Peters said during OTAs that the Eagles offensive line was better than the Cowboys line. It would be nice to think so. Peters spoke after the Cowboys added La'El Collins but before the Eagles released Evan Mathis in a salary dispute; Peters probably did not take into account the Cowboys adding talent while the Eagles put extra energy into subtracting some. While Peters represents an extreme and biased opinion, the Eagles' 2014 line was excellent when healthy last year and would have looked even better if LeSean McCoy didn't grow so snobbish about the size and quality of his inside-zone holes.

Peters and center Jason Kelce are the anchors and veteran leaders of the line. The Eagles ran around left end on 22 percent of their rushes, the highest figure in the league and more than twice the league average, which illustrates: a) their faith in Peters and b) the insistence with which Shady bounced everything outside. Peters is Exhibit A for anyone seeking proof that 300-pound-plus linemen can maintain their conditioning in an up-tempo offense. Peters was a lumpy, gooey guy with persistent injuries (though a very effective lineman when healthy) when Chip Kelly arrived. He has now played at a high level for two years without missing a game.

Kelce earned Pro Bowl notice last year and deserved it in 2013. He's a good zone-stretch blocker who gets downfield well on the Eagles' many screens, and he's a reliable adjustment-maker in pass protection. The entire Eagles offense suffered when David Molk filled in for four games, though it didn't help that the novice Polk was often on the field with a pair of novice guards. Lane Johnson stabilized into a steady right tackle last season, though his low total of sacks allowed is partially the product of a scheme with lots of rolling-pocket play-action passes. Eagles quarterbacks roll left a lot, giving Johnson some easy protection assignments.

The changing of the guard will take place with the guards. The 33-year-old Mathis may have been reading some dubious scouting reports and developed an inflated sense of his market value. Nevertheless, he was a great system fit who used craftiness to steer defenders into bad positions, then let the tempo do the rest. Todd Herremans is also gone, now in Indianapolis after missing the second half of last season with an ankle injury. Veteran journeyman Allen Barbre is slated to play left guard, with Matt Tobin and Dennis Kelly battling for a job on the right side. All three saw action during the injury rash last season. None were impressive, but the Eagles haven't drafted an offensive lineman for two years, so someone will have to step forward to back up Peters' boast.

Defensive Front Seven

Defensive Line	Age	Pos	G	Snaps	Plays	TmPct	Overall Rk	Stop	Dfts	BTkl	Runs	St%	vs. Run Rk	RuYd	Rk	Sack	Pass Rush Hit	Hur	Tips
Fletcher Cox	25	DE	16	921	61	7.0%	12	47	13	0	56	75%	62	2.4	53	4.0	3	14.5	1
Cedric Thornton	27	DE	16	640	52	6.0%	23	37	7	1	46	72%	76	2.6	67	1.0	0	8.5	2
Bennie Logan	26	DT	16	639	59	6.8%	14	47	14	1	55	78%	45	1.3	18	0.0	1	6.0	1
Vinny Curry	27	DE	16	371	18	2.1%	--	13	10	3	8	50%	--	4.3	--	9.0	5	15.0	0

Edge Rushers	Age	Pos	G	Snaps	Plays	TmPct	Overall Rk	Stop	Dfts	BTkl	Runs	St%	vs. Run Rk	RuYd	Rk	Sack	Pass Rush Hit	Hur	Tips
Connor Barwin	29	OLB	16	1007	68	7.8%	12	48	28	4	34	59%	79	4.1	78	14.5	9	24.5	6
Trent Cole*	33	OLB	15	800	52	6.4%	22	31	13	4	38	61%	78	3.1	66	6.5	5	22.0	0
Brandon Graham	27	OLB	16	499	40	4.6%	51	28	17	6	30	70%	59	2.3	35	5.5	6	23.5	0

Linebackers	Age	Pos	G	Snaps	Plays	TmPct	Overall Rk	Stop	Dfts	BTkl	Sack	Pass Rush Hit	Hur	Runs	St%	vs. Run Rk	RuYd	Rk	Tgts	vs. Pass Suc%	Rk	AdjYd	Rk	PD	Int
Mychal Kendricks	25	ILB	12	761	83	12.8%	42	46	17	12	4.0	5	18.5	48	52%	78	4.1	71	20	63%	9	4.7	7	2	0
DeMeco Ryans	31	MLB	8	513	49	11.3%	53	25	9	4	0.0	1	0.5	36	56%	70	3.9	62	15	52%	--	6.7	--	4	1
Casey Matthews*	26	ILB	16	434	52	6.0%	--	26	6	6	1.5	1	4	38	61%	--	3.4	--	12	34%	--	9.8	--	0	0
Emmanuel Acho	25	ILB	14	261	26	3.4%	--	11	2	3	0.0	0	1.5	20	50%	--	4.1	--	5	54%	--	17.1	--	0	0

Year	Yards	ALY	Rk	Power	Rk	Stuff	Rk	2nd Level	Rk	Open Field	Rk	Sacks	ASR	Rk	Short	Long
2012	4.06	3.82	9	60%	16	22%	8	1.26	26	0.67	13	30	6.5%	12	7	11
2013	3.61	3.89	17	68%	21	18%	20	0.98	3	0.33	1	37	6.7%	19	16	10
2014	3.64	3.72	11	80%	30	21%	11	1.02	7	0.48	4	49	7.1%	10	18	20

| 2014 ALY by direction: | Left End 3.52 (12) | Left Tackle 2.9 (5) | Mid/Guard 4.09 (21) | Right Tackle 4.46 (23) | Right End 3.35 (11) |

The front seven is the last stronghold for players of the Andy Reid-Howie Roseman era. Kelly ejects veterans at other positions like Willie Wonka kicking misbehaving children off the candy factory tour, but in the front seven, last-regime players still hold leadership positions and earn contract extensions.

Fletcher Cox is the Eagles' best defender and one of the two best returning veterans (with Jason Peters) after The Purge. Cox is an exceptional two-gap run defender with bull-rush capability. Kelly exercised a fifth-year rookie-contract option on Cox, which was a no-brainer. Some insiders see Cox's contract situation as a final litmus test of Kelly's long-range plan. If Kelly extends Cox, it's a sign that there is still room for conventional wisdom in the Eagles culture. If Cox has another strong season and Kelly lets him walk, well, it's dogs and cats living together.

Seven of Connor Barwin's 14 sacks came in two games: three against the Giants in Week 6 (Justin Pugh had a long afternoon) and four in a Week 10 humiliation of the Panthers. Barwin has a great talent-and-technique combination as a pass rusher, drops into coverage well (no edge rusher has more charted targets over the last two seasons), and is one of the team's leading citizens in the Philadelphia community. Barwin is at his best when pass rushing in tandem with Vinny Curry, a situational rusher the Eagles want to give an increased role in 2015. Chip Kelly has suggested that Curry might play some outside linebacker, though it sounded suspiciously like he was blowing off a press conference question. It's more likely that run-stopping end Cedric Thornton will rotate inside to nose tackle more often in place of Bennie Logan, who is merely adequate.

Brandon Graham has slowly developed from an oft-injured role player under Reid to an excellent all-purpose outside linebacker. The Eagles rewarded Graham with the only long-term contract the team shelled out to an incumbent this offseason. Graham's role will increase with Trent Cole in Indy. Marcus Smith, a disappointment as a rookie, is competing with Travis Long, Emmanuel Acho and others for Graham's role as the first outside linebacker to rotate off the bench.

Inside linebackers Mychal Kendricks and DeMeco Ryans are two more Reid-era holdovers hanging on to their starting jobs, though newcomer Kiko Alonso is going to play somewhere. Kendricks was the subject of trade rumors—heck, Cox was the subject of trade rumors before the Mariota Fever broke—but he is a speedy, reliable defender coming off a fine year. Ryans plugs run gaps hard, behaves like a hard-working professional, and does little else. Lanky, laconic Alonso looks and acts like the Mayor of Surf City but is incredibly rangy and has the best coverage chops of any linebacker on the team. A Ryans-Alonso platoon of some kind is possible; a run-stuffing inside linebacker is worth having around when you face the Cowboys twice per year.

Defensive Secondary

Secondary	Age	Pos	G	Snaps	Plays	TmPct	Rk	Stop	Dfts	BTkl	Runs	St%	Rk	RuYd	Rk	Tgts	Tgt%	Rk	Dist	Suc%	Rk	AdjYd	Rk	PD	Int
Malcolm Jenkins	28	FS	16	1153	91	10.5%	32	33	17	9	34	32%	50	8.0	53	60	13.8%	67	10.6	56%	31	7.6	43	14	3
Cary Williams*	31	CB	16	1149	67	7.7%	54	21	6	6	16	19%	67	10.8	70	92	21.4%	22	14.0	52%	29	9.1	58	11	2
Nate Allen*	28	SS	15	1076	67	8.2%	55	15	11	4	18	22%	64	8.4	54	33	8.1%	35	13.7	36%	64	9.4	60	5	4
Bradley Fletcher*	29	CB	15	1047	80	9.8%	19	34	13	8	19	47%	25	4.5	12	115	29.4%	69	16.6	51%	36	8.9	55	22	1
Brandon Boykin	25	CB	16	494	50	5.8%	73	30	16	4	4	50%	21	3.3	3	56	30.3%	72	10.0	59%	5	6.2	10	9	1
Nolan Carroll	28	CB	16	369	27	3.1%	--	16	5	3	3	67%	--	6.3	--	29	20.7%	--	11.0	69%	--	6.0	--	4	0
Byron Maxwell	27	CB	13	700	51	8.5%	40	18	11	2	3	33%	44	3.3	4	66	25.4%	52	12.9	51%	39	6.9	17	11	2
E.J. Biggers	28	CB	15	450	31	4.4%	--	11	5	5	4	50%	--	6.3	--	34	20.0%	--	14.5	43%	--	10.3	--	5	0

Year	Pass D Rank	vs. #1 WR	Rk	vs. #2 WR	Rk	vs. Other WR	Rk	vs. TE	Rk	vs. RB	Rk
2012	32	35.5%	31	11.1%	27	19.2%	27	-2.5%	16	11.0%	22
2013	25	2.6%	21	2.3%	16	12.8%	24	10.0%	24	5.8%	21
2014	18	10.2%	24	4.4%	20	-6.1%	11	0.2%	19	19.7%	28

The secondary is the one unit where the Eagles made clear, unequivocal improvements, with no "if he stays healthy," "if the young players develop," or "if DeMarco Murray's legs don't fall off from overuse" qualifiers.

Byron Maxwell was the Seahawks' fourth-best defensive back in 2014 and fifth-best in 2013. But he is also a big, strong, capable defender used to being in the crosshairs as opponents avoided Richard Sherman and company. The Eagles paid a Legion of Boom premium to land Maxwell, but he will provide an immediate upgrade over the many moods, most of them bad, of Cary Williams. Rookie Eric Rowe is slated to start at the other cornerback position, with Brandon Boykin established in the slot. Boykin is reliable, opportunistic, and a sure tackler, but he is tiny. Rowe, chosen 47th overall out of Utah, is tall and well-built in the Seahawks mold. Sixth-round pick JaCorey Shepherd had an excellent minicamp and will push Nolan Carroll and E.J. Biggers for the dime role. Shepherd is a converted receiver out of Kansas who fits best in the slot; he slipped in the draft because of offseason injuries (which resulted in a 4.65-second 40), but he has a great mix of quickness and instincts.

Walter Thurmond, another former Seahawks supporting player, was signed as a cornerback but moved to safety at the start of camp. He and steady veteran Malcolm Jenkins will be the starters. Depth is an issue at safety; Earl Wolff spent most of OTA's stretching and performing rehab drills on a separate field, and coaches were obviously frustrated with his slow return from November knee surgery. The Eagles are emphasizing "cross training" among defensive backs, with cornerbacks learning safety roles and vice-versa, so veteran cornerbacks like Carroll and Biggers could slide over to safety in a system that rarely calls for defensive backs to play in the box and plug the run.

Special Teams

Year	DVOA	Rank	FG/XP	Rank	Net Kick	Rank	Kick Ret	Rank	Net Punt	Rank	Punt Ret	Rank	Hidden	Rank
2012	-2.2%	23	0.9	17	3.3	10	-0.5	18	-18.2	32	3.3	8	-9.1	29
2013	-2.8%	25	-2.8	24	-12.5	31	-0.9	15	5.4	10	-3.4	18	3.3	11
2014	8.3%	1	3.5	9	9.8	2	12.3	2	1.7	14	14.2	1	23.5	1

Ryan Mathews returned kickoffs for the Eagles during OTAs. Yes, a former 1,000-yard rusher, fielding kickoffs. Mathews is just part of an embarrassment of riches for a team that returned two kicks and two punts for touchdowns last year. Darren Sproles is still on board as the primary punt returner, and Mathews' presence should make it easier for Sproles to focus on his returns and third-down responsibilities, rather than serving as the No. 2 committee back. Josh Huff had a kick return touchdown last year and rotated with the returners during OTAs.

The Eagles also blocked five total kicks last year, which is not exactly a repeatable feat. Beau Allen and Bryan Brennan, two of last-year's kick blockers, are both back this year, and both are still over 6-foot-5. Brian Mihalik, a 6-foot-9 defensive end, is also fighting for a job and will be looking to bat down some kicks. Reserve tight end Trey Burton and top gunner Chris Maragos play key roles in blocking kicks, blocking for returns, and tackling opponent's returners. Both are likely to stick around as core special teamers.

Kicker Cody Parkey had two ugly misses in the Week 16 loss to the Redskins but was consistent on field goals for most of the season. Parkey mixes touchbacks with high hangers on kickoffs; his gross value was average, but the coverage team was excellent. Donnie Jones is a standard-issue veteran punter, and former Oklahoma State punter Kip Smith is the designated camp leg in case Jones slips.

Pittsburgh Steelers

2014 Record: 11-5	Total DVOA: 12.1% (8th)	2015 Mean Projection: 8.1 wins	On the Clock (0-4): 9%
Pythagorean Wins: 9.7 (11th)	Offense: 22.5% (2nd)	Postseason Odds: 39.5%	Mediocrity (5-7): 32%
Snap-Weighted Age: 26.9 (13th)	Defense: 11.3% (30th)	Super Bowl Odds: 6.5%	Playoff Contender (8-10): 40%
Average Opponent: -4.2% (29th)	Special Teams: 0.9% (12th)	Proj. Avg. Opponent: 2.6% (9th)	Super Bowl Contender (11+): 19%

2014: With powerful offense and terrible defense, Bizzaro Steelers am finishing last in NFC South, returning to playoffs.

2015: Can a 33-year-old Ben Roethlisberger continue to carry a defense in transition?

Keith Butler has big shoes to fill. The former linebackers coach in Pittsburgh has waited a long time for Dick LeBeau to vacate the defensive coordinator role. Butler attracted a lot of interest from other teams who wanted him to become a defensive coordinator elsewhere, including Indianapolis in 2012 and Tennessee in 2014. Butler held out in Pittsburgh, hoping to one day become another staple in the history of a franchise that is famed for its ability to produce on the defensive side of the ball. Now LeBeau is in Tennessee, and Butler has finally ascended to the position he patiently waited a dozen years to take.

However, the 59-year-old Butler isn't getting an easy transition despite his long history with the Steelers franchise. He's not inheriting the defense that ranked in the top 10 of DVOA from 2004 to 2011. He's not inheriting Casey Hampton, Aaron Smith, James Farrior, LaMarr Woodley, Troy Polamalu or Ryan Clark. He is inheriting James Harrison, but not the one who could compete for the Defensive Player of the Year trophy each season.

No, Butler is inheriting a defense that finished 30th in DVOA last season: a defense that was anchored to the bottom tier of the league by a 24.9% pass defense DVOA, over 35 points of DVOA below the top-ranked Buffalo Bills. LeBeau's final defense was the end result of four years of consistent decline. After leading the league by a huge margin as the top-ranked defense by DVOA in 2010, the Steelers fell to seventh in 2011, 13th in 2012 and 19th in 2013 before dropping down to 30th in 2014. It was a steady descent, with aging superstars either retiring to off-field roles or deteriorating on the field in front of our eyes.

The Steelers have sustained success as well as anyone over the past 25 years because of their ability to continually re-tool their defense without ever entering a full-blown rebuild. In the entire history of DVOA, going back to 1989, the Steelers had never finished below 15th in defense until 2013 and 2014. A two-year absence from the playoffs isn't considered a bad stretch for most teams, but for the Steelers it was a significant aberration from what they've come to expect. The Steelers have not had a losing season since 2003, and they've endured just four losing seasons since 1989. Not a single one of those seasons featured fewer than six victories, and the franchise has not gone more than three consecutive seasons without making the playoffs since 1988.

And yet, that stretch of futility would have been matched in 2014 if not for their outstanding offensive output. The Steelers have transitioned from a team that sustained success on the back of their dominant defense to a team that hopes to sustain success by relying on Ben Roethlisberger and their explosive offense.

Thanks to that inversion, Keith Butler doesn't need to replicate what Dick LeBeau did in Pittsburgh. Obviously every team wishes it could build a dominant defense, but that's not always a realistic goal. The 2015 Steelers have more realistic goals: they need to search for consistent discipline or become a more opportunistic unit. Much like last year's Dallas Cowboys or the Super Bowl champion Saints of 2009, the Steelers will go in search of turnovers as a way of covering for their lack of overall talent.

That's not a suggestion that Butler is going to radically alter Pittsburgh's defensive scheme; instead it is a reflection of the types of moves the Steelers made in the 2015 draft. After selecting exceptionally athletic outside linebacker Alvin "Bud" Dupree in the first round, the Steelers invested two picks in undersized cornerbacks who are celebrated for their ball skills: 5-foot-9 Senquez Golson (Ole Miss) and 5-foot-10 Doran Grant (Ohio State).

It's possible for a shorter player to be a high-quality boundary cornerback in the NFL, but it requires exceptional coverage ability. Finding two cornerbacks of that type is very difficult. The San Diego Chargers may be the only team in the league with two on their roster, Brandon Flowers and Jason Verrett. A cornerback depth chart led by Golson, Grant, and veteran William Gay lacks the athleticism to fend off the talented big receivers that have become more popular across the league lately. The only cornerback over six-feet tall on the current roster is Cortez Allen, who was benched last year for being one of the worst cornerbacks in the NFL. He had a 42 percent adjusted success rate in coverage, good enough for 70th out of 77 qualifying cornerbacks.

It appears that Butler is hoping to trade off mismatches in his secondary for an increase in turnovers. The Steelers have the fewest takeaways (76) since 2011, and interceptions have been especially hard to come by since Mike Tomlin became the head coach eight years ago (Table 1, next page). Pittsburgh is the first team since 1940 to intercept fewer than 12 passes in four consecutive seasons. Only five other teams have had a streak of at least three seasons, including the 2012-14 Raiders.

2015 Steelers Schedule

Week	Opp.	Week	Opp.	Week	Opp.
1	at NE (Thu.)	7	at KC	13	IND
2	SF	8	CIN	14	at CIN
3	at STL	9	OAK	15	DEN
4	BAL (Thu.)	10	CLE	16	at BAL
5	at SD (Mon.)	11	BYE	17	at CLE
6	ARI	12	at SEA		

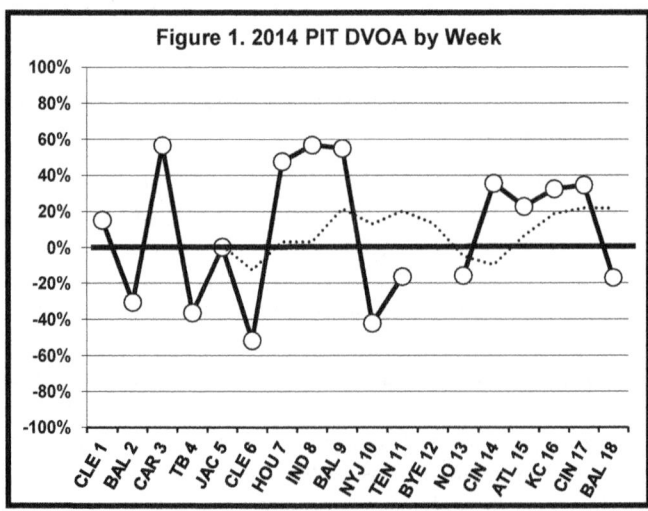

Figure 1. 2014 PIT DVOA by Week

Troy Polamalu's unpredictability and athleticism from the safety position—combined with the heightened pressure from LeBeau's blitzes and quality pass rushers such as Harrison and LaMarr Woodley—used to force mistakes from quarterbacks on a regular basis. But it has been a long time since the Steelers threatened offenses in so many ways. Polamalu had been on the field, but his diminished athleticism made his freelancing more of a hindrance for the defense than a source of intimidation against the offense. Diminishing athleticism for different reasons also neutralized Woodley and Harrison's pass-rushing ability.

Replacing Polamalu is almost impossible. He is a generational talent who will waltz his way into the Hall of Fame in five or six years. Replacing Harrison and Woodley should theoretically have been easier. Neither player was a first-round pick or immediate starter as a rookie. Instead, they were products of the Steelers' developmental philosophy that saw them play special teams and fully learn the scheme before assuming roles they had been prepared for. The quality of Joey Porter and Clark Haggans allowed LeBeau to be patient with Woodley and Harrison. Butler doesn't have that luxury with his young pass-rushers.

To reignite the Steelers' pass rush, Butler needs to find a way to kick-start the career of Jarvis Jones while also fast-tracking the development of Dupree. Jones' career has been a disaster so far. He came out of Georgia as a polarizing prospect because he was a limited athlete who had produced big numbers in a conference the NFL favors. Athleticism is typically very important for edge rushers in the NFL, while college production can be very misleading. Poor pro-day performance, especially in the 40, gave Jones a SackSEER rating of just 58.7 percent, with numbers comparable to players such

Table 1. Pittsburgh Interceptions, 2007-2014

Year	Int	Rank
2007	11	30
2008	20	6
2009	12	25
2010	21	5
2011	11	24
2012	10	27
2013	10	29
2014	11	25

as Casey Dailey, Cheta Ozougwu, and Kroy Biermann. Jones has done nothing in his NFL career to suggest that he can turn his fortunes around and become a valuable player.

The Steelers appear to have recognized their mistake with Jones, and they went completely in the opposite direction by trying to rectify it with Dupree. Dupree never had more than 7.5 sacks in a season at Kentucky, but he electrified this year's combine with outstanding results in the jumps and sprints. Dupree's poor three-cone time suggests that he may be more of a straight-ahead speed-rusher than an all-around player with multiple moves, but SackSEER gave Dupree a rating of 94.6 percent, and similar players such as Will Smith and Michael Johnson have been quite successful in the NFL. As such, Butler's focus should be on getting the most out of Dupree, and that may require Butler to adjust his approach and incorporate more 4-3 looks.

Dupree would be best suited to act as the open-side defensive end in a 4-3 under front. This position would allow Dupree to be aggressive with his burst off the line of scrimmage while using his combination of size and power to work his way to the quarterback. It would also limit the variety of assignments that the Steelers would ask of him, thus allowing him an easier transition to the NFL than if he were trying to play as a 3-4 outside linebacker. The Steelers have been a 3-4 team for a long time, but since Casey Hampton's departure, they haven't been built to do it effectively. Steve McLendon has been the Steelers' nose tackle since Hampton left, but despite his size he is best suited to be a penetrating defensive tackle rather than a space-eating nose tackle. He would fit perfectly at 3-technique alongside Dupree. Second-year player Stephon Tuitt would likely need to play nose guard with Cameron Heyward as the closed defensive end, but these would be similar roles to what Tuitt and Heyward would expect to play in a 3-4 look. With Ryan Shazier, Arthur Moats, James Harrison, Sean Spence, and Lawrence Timmons as options at linebacker, Butler would have plenty of combinations to try out to figure out how to get his best players on the field in this front.

If Butler can create more pressure this way, it should be an alignment that becomes prominent in their defense even if they stick to their 3-4 as the base. Pressure against the pass needs to be Butler's focus because opponents will likely be trying to keep pace in a shootout with the Steelers' prodigious offense.

A year ago, we certainly would not have expected Roethlisberger to lead the NFL in passing DYAR in 2014. Though he still was above average each year, his performance had steadily declined since 2010. However, the quality of the offense around Roethlisberger has lifted his game, because he doesn't have to play hero ball like he once did. Last year, Roethlisberger actually had the second-lowest pressure rate among starting quarterbacks, with pressure marked on just 17.4 percent of pass plays. Roethlisberger's deep ball doesn't look as pretty as it once did, but it's actually more effective because he's more comfortable in Todd Haley's offense and has more time to throw. In 2012, Roethlisberger completed 28 percent of passes thrown 20 or more yards downfield, ranked 26th out of 31 quarterbacks with at least 30 such passes. In 2013, that number was 34 percent, ranked 17th. Last year, Roethlisberger completed 41 percent of these passes, ranking seventh.

Even better, this offense as a whole is set up to sustain its success even as Roethlisberger enters his mid-thirties. Save for tight end Heath Miller, every offensive piece around Roethlisberger is still at least relatively young. Seven of the 11 projected starters for next season are no older than 26 years of age. Antonio Brown, right in his prime at 26, was the top-ranked wide receiver by DYAR last year, with a significant margin over the second-ranked Jordy Nelson. It wasn't a one-off either, as he had ranked fifth overall during the previous season. The two most important pieces past Brown are Martavis Bryant (24 years old) and Le'Veon Bell (23). As a rookie, Bryant had the highest DYAR of any receiver who caught between 10 and 49 passes last season, while Bell was one of the top runners by any measure and a major star as a receiver. Bell ranked first in DYAR for receiving amongst running backs while more than doubling the success of second-place Ahmad Bradshaw.

The Steelers offense ranked second in DVOA last season, second in weighted DVOA, and 12th in rushing DVOA. They can still get better running the football, while sustaining their incredible efficiency as a passing team. Ranking first in passing DVOA is always an impressive achievement, but more so than usual last year. A number of veteran quarterbacks (Tony Romo, Joe Flacco) had career-best seasons while Aaron Rodgers continued to be Aaron Rodgers, superlative in stats and even more impressive in film study. They may not rank No. 1 again, but there's no reason to believe the Steelers can't be near the top unless major injuries hit. The offense should alleviate the pressure on Butler to create a dominant defense. Instead, that pressure will be replaced by expectations that this team can once again compete for a Super Bowl if Butler can create a competent unit that is capable of creating timely turnovers.

2015 may be a year too soon for the Steelers to truly compete for a championship. Pittsburgh is used to tough competition from its division rivals, which doesn't look set to change, but the competition on the rest of the schedule will change. Pittsburgh's schedule ranked 29th by our ratings last year; this year's schedule ranks fourth in our projections, with the Steelers facing both West divisions plus the Colts and Patriots. (If Tom Brady's suspension is delayed by a federal court injunction, Pittsburgh's strength of schedule drops to ninth.) A lot hinges on Butler moving forward as the Steelers have a window with Roethlisberger that should last at least two or three years. It may take until 2016 or 2017 for the Steelers to be one of the most balanced teams in the league again, but their offensive setup suggests they can do it sooner rather than later if Butler can be half the defensive coordinator LeBeau was.

Cian Fahey

2014 Steelers Stats by Week

Wk	vs.	W-L	PF	PA	YDF	YDA	TO	Total	Off	Def	ST
1	CLE	W	30	27	503	389	-1	15%	35%	28%	8%
2	at BAL	L	6	26	301	323	-3	-31%	-20%	6%	-4%
3	at CAR	W	37	19	454	349	2	56%	69%	24%	12%
4	TB	L	24	27	390	350	0	-36%	9%	38%	-8%
5	at JAC	W	17	9	372	243	1	0%	7%	4%	-3%
6	at CLE	L	10	31	359	368	0	-52%	-15%	34%	-3%
7	HOU	W	30	23	328	393	2	47%	26%	0%	21%
8	IND	W	51	34	639	448	0	57%	76%	12%	-7%
9	BAL	W	43	23	376	332	1	55%	53%	-25%	-23%
10	at NYJ	L	13	20	362	275	-4	-42%	-27%	7%	-8%
11	at TEN	W	27	24	386	312	0	-16%	11%	25%	-2%
12	BYE										
13	NO	L	32	35	538	393	-2	-16%	14%	39%	10%
14	at CIN	W	42	21	543	408	2	35%	56%	20%	0%
15	at ATL	W	27	20	398	407	1	23%	31%	12%	3%
16	KC	W	20	12	282	327	1	32%	28%	-6%	-2%
17	CIN	W	27	17	346	337	0	34%	1%	-12%	21%
18	BAL	L	17	30	387	299	-2	-17%	-21%	6%	10%

Trends and Splits

	Offense	Rank	Defense	Rank
Total DVOA	22.5%	2	11.3%	30
Unadjusted VOA	20.1%	3	6.9%	26
Weighted Trend	22.0%	2	8.1%	27
Variance	9.4%	24	3.4%	4
Average Opponent	1.1%	22	-4.5%	31
Passing	47.0%	1	24.9%	30
Rushing	-1.7%	12	-7.3%	17
First Down	26.1%	2	11.2%	27
Second Down	13.3%	6	6.3%	25
Third Down	30.2%	3	19.4%	27
First Half	21.4%	2	4.2%	23
Second Half	23.8%	2	18.0%	31
Red Zone	-3.6%	16	8.8%	27
Late and Close	27.1%	1	16.3%	29

Five-Year Performance

Year	W-L	Pyth W	Est W	PF	PA	TO	Total	Rk	Off	Rk	Def	Rk	ST	Rk	Off AGL	Rk	Def AGL	Rk	Off Age	Rk	Def Age	Rk	ST Age	Rk
2010	12-4	12.1	12.1	375	232	+17	35.4%	2	14.3%	5	-20.7%	1	0.4%	16	32.0	22	17.9	12	27.0	22	29.2	1	26.7	12
2011	12-4	11.1	11.3	325	227	-13	22.6%	4	11.4%	6	-9.4%	7	1.7%	9	33.2	19	27.3	18	26.4	25	29.1	1	26.2	19
2012	8-8	8.7	7.4	336	314	-10	-1.2%	18	-4.0%	19	-2.9%	13	-0.1%	17	64.3	31	19.1	9	26.5	21	29.2	1	25.9	20
2013	8-8	8.2	8.3	379	370	-4	0.9%	15	4.4%	12	4.0%	19	0.5%	16	55.3	28	27.5	16	26.4	25	28.4	1	25.7	25
2014	11-5	9.7	9.4	436	368	0	12.1%	8	22.5%	2	11.3%	30	0.9%	12	4.1	1	38.7	17	26.5	24	27.8	3	26.2	10

2014 Performance Based on Most Common Personnel Groups

PIT Offense					PIT Offense vs. Opponents						PIT Defense					PIT Defense vs. Opponents			
Pers	Freq	Yds	DVOA	Run%	Pers	Freq	Yds	DVOA	Run%		Pers	Freq	Yds	DVOA		Pers	Freq	Yds	DVOA
11	63%	6.5	29.6%	28%	Base	33%	6.4	18.0%	54%		Base	50%	6.1	13.6%		11	44%	6.2	15.9%
22	15%	6.1	30.4%	64%	Nickel	56%	6.3	28.5%	29%		Nickel	48%	6.1	9.1%		12	29%	6.8	21.5%
12	14%	6.4	18.1%	50%	Dime+	7%	8.7	67.7%	14%		Dime+	1%	6.7	75.5%		21	12%	5.6	4.5%
01	3%	6.9	10.1%	34%	Goal Line	1%	-0.8	-19.5%	50%		Goal Line	1%	0.4	-10.2%		13	6%	7.1	27.1%
21	1%	5.7	38.2%	57%	Big	3%	5.9	43.2%	64%							22	3%	2.6	-24.7%

Strategic Tendencies

Run/Pass		Rk	Formation		Rk	Pass Rush		Rk	Secondary		Rk	Strategy		Rk
Runs, first half	36%	21	Form: Single Back	81%	8	Rush 3	11.0%	5	4 DB	35%	7	Play action	22%	15
Runs, first down	46%	21	Form: Empty Back	12%	2	Rush 4	53.1%	26	5 DB	62%	15	Avg Box (Off)	6.24	20
Runs, second-long	32%	13	Pers: 3+ WR	68%	7	Rush 5	29.9%	5	6+ DB	2%	24	Avg Box (Def)	6.40	5
Runs, power sit.	55%	17	Pers: 4+ WR	4%	9	Rush 6+	6.0%	20	CB by Sides	84%	11	Offensive Pace	31.59	24
Runs, behind 2H	25%	19	Pers: 2+ TE/6+ OL	32%	13	Sacks by LB	68.2%	2	DB Blitz	12%	13	Defensive Pace	28.97	4
Pass, ahead 2H	52%	5	Shotgun/Pistol	62%	16	Sacks by DB	0.0%	31	Hole in Zone	5%	18	Go for it on 4th	1.10	11

Pittsburgh opponents traditionally play at a much faster pace than the Steelers do. Last year was the 11th straight season the Steelers ranked in the bottom ten for situation-neutral pace on offense, and the seventh season out of eight where they ranked in the top ten for situation-neutral pace on defense. ⬤ The Pittsburgh offense was the best in the league on third down when passing, but ranked 27th when running. However, the issue was failed scrambles by Ben Roethlisberger and failed conversions by LeGarrette Blount; Le'Veon Bell converted 72 percent of runs on third or fourth down. ⬤ Bell is a phenomenal receiver, but there's some evidence that he's better coming out of the backfield rather than lining up wide. Although only Arizona went empty backfield more often than the Steelers, Pittsburgh's averages of 5.7 yards and 14.0% DVOA on these plays were below the NFL averages of 6.7 yards and 22.1% DVOA. ⬤ Pittsburgh had led the league by using dime personnel 45 percent of the time in 2013; last year, with a much healthier front seven, Dick LeBeau returned to his traditional use of nickel instead of dime in pass situations. ⬤ The Pittsburgh defense allowed a league-high 9.4 yards per play on play-action passes. ⬤ Pittsburgh ranked 29th by allowing 33.4 yards per drive, but ninth in forcing three-and-outs on 23.7 percent of drives.

Passing

Player	DYAR	DVOA	Plays	NtYds	Avg	YAC	C%	TD	Int
B.Roethlisberger	1572	26.8%	636	4761	7.5	5.6	68.2%	32	9

Rushing

Player	DYAR	DVOA	Plays	Yds	Avg	TD	Fum	Suc
L.Bell	205	8.6%	290	1361	4.7	8	0	51%
L.Blount*	-5	-10.1%	65	266	4.1	2	1	48%
B.Roethlisberger	-34	-50.8%	14	36	2.6	0	2	-
D.Archer	9	-23.0%	10	40	4.0	0	0	-
J.Harris	-21	-62.9%	9	16	1.8	0	0	33%
D.Williams	-17	-15.2%	62	221	3.6	0	1	45%

Receiving

Player	DYAR	DVOA	Plays	Ctch	Yds	Y/C	YAC	TD	C%
A.Brown	554	25.7%	181	129	1697	13.2	4.6	13	71%
M.Wheaton	84	-0.2%	86	53	654	12.3	3.2	2	62%
M.Bryant	137	22.9%	49	26	549	21.1	7.3	8	53%
A.Brown	554	25.7%	181	129	1697	13.2	4.6	13	71%
M.Wheaton	84	-0.2%	86	53	654	12.3	3.2	2	62%
M.Bryant	137	22.9%	49	26	549	21.1	7.3	8	53%
L.Moore*	20	-2.8%	26	14	198	14.1	2.9	2	54%
J.Brown*	-54	-45.0%	21	12	94	7.8	1.8	0	57%
D.Archer	-45	-74.0%	10	7	23	3.3	4.0	0	70%
H.Miller	127	13.5%	91	66	761	11.5	4.9	3	73%
L.Bell	316	38.4%	105	83	854	10.3	9.8	3	79%
W.Johnson	-16	-36.6%	11	7	41	5.9	5.3	0	64%
L.Blount*	-2	-17.5%	8	6	36	6.0	8.0	0	75%
D.Williams	4	-3.3%	6	5	44	8.8	11.4	0	83%

Offensive Line

Player	Pos	Age	GS	Snaps	Pen	Sk	Pass	Run	Player	Pos	Age	GS	Snaps	Pen	Sk	Pass	Run
Kelvin Beachum	LT	26	16/16	1111	7	8.0	17.0	7.5	Ramon Foster	LG	29	14/14	963	3	1.0	6.5	2.0
David DeCastro	RG	25	16/16	1111	4	0.0	5.5	2.0	Marcus Gilbert	RT	27	12/12	760	5	6.0	15.0	1.0
Maurkice Pouncey	C	26	16/16	1104	5	1.0	6.0	1.5	Mike Adams	OT	25	16/4	366	2	1.0	11.0	5.0

Year	Yards	ALY	Rk	Power	Rk	Stuff	Rk	2nd Lev	Rk	Open Field	Rk	Sacks	ASR	Rk	Short	Long	F-Start	Cont.
2012	3.71	3.72	27	61%	19	19%	17	0.95	30	0.54	24	37	6.3%	15	12	18	13	26
2013	3.57	3.79	22	60%	21	21%	24	0.94	29	0.39	29	43	7.3%	15	13	15	11	27
2014	4.50	4.10	6	69%	8	15%	1	1.18	15	0.96	5	33	5.8%	14	12	9	15	27
2014 ALY by direction:			Left End 4.49 (3)			Left Tackle 5.53 (1)			Mid/Guard 3.96 (19)			Right Tackle 2.97 (31)				Right End 5.22 (2)		

Last year, years of offensive line investment finally paid off. The Steelers have had this group together for a while now, but figuring out the right combination and keeping everyone healthy proved to be a prolonged process. But in 2014, the Steelers didn't have to rely too much on inadequate backups; yes, there were injuries, but those were minor in both length and impact.

The two linemen who missed time last season were the least difficult to replace. Starting right tackle Marcus Gilbert, who missed four games because of a concussion and ankle injury, had the second-worst blown block rate on the offensive line. He wasn't a liability, as his 47.5 snaps per blown block actually ranked him as average among offensive tackles, but he also didn't excel at anything in particular.[1]

Starting left guard Ramon Foster was the only other starter to miss time, due to a September ankle injury. Foster's numbers can be somewhat misleading in terms of his value to the Steelers. Our charters only listed him with a blown block every 113.3 snaps, which ranked fourth among left guards and 13th among all interior offensive linemen. However, those impressive numbers need to be seen in context. Foster is a converted offensive tackle who went undrafted back in 2009 because of his limited athleticism. He is a disciplined, technically sound player whose greatest strength is his consistency. However, he's also a complementary piece whose weaknesses can be somewhat covered by dominating linemates Maurkice Pouncey and David De-Castro. Asking Foster to be a focal point of a running game or play in space as a pass protector on a regular basis is a recipe for disaster. Asking him to carry out simpler assignments that don't overextend his abilities allows him to flourish. And so Foster flourished, as the Steelers finally got a full season of their two first-round linemen, Pouncey and DeCastro, working in tandem. Athletically superior and technically sound, Pouncey and DeCastro are foundational pieces that allowed offensive line coach Mike Munchak to diversify the Steelers' blocking schemes on both runs and passes. DeCastro blew a block once every 148.1 snaps, the best rate among right guards with at least 500 snaps. Pouncey was just behind, showing no lingering effects from the knee injury that cost him the 2013 season; his rate of one blown block every 147.2 snaps ranked third among centers. The Steelers hope they can write two of the best interior offensive linemen in the NFL onto their depth chart in permanent marker

---

1 When looking for data on Gilbert, don't get too caught up in the strange dichotomy between the Steelers ranking 31st in ALY right tackle but second right end. There's a small sample size because Pittsburgh was listed as running up the middle or behind guard on two-thirds of runs, and a lot of the busted runs listed as right tackle came in the four games started by Mike Adams.

for the next few seasons, and they'll surely hand DeCastro a big extension sometime in the next few months to keep this pair together past 2016.

The left tackle position comes with less certainty moving forward. The failure of Mike Adams to live up to his potential as a second-round pick forced the Steelers to turn to former seventh-rounder Kelvin Beachum as a starter. Beachum solidified the left tackle position within Todd Haley's offense, achieving blown block numbers that rank him exactly average amongst left tackles and amongst all tackles. The problem with Beachum as a long-term starter at left tackle is that he is better built to be a guard. Although he played left tackle in college, the 6-foot-3, 303-pound product out of SMU simply lacks the size and power to be asked to contain pass rushers alone on the outside. Beachum was Pittsburgh's most penalized lineman last year (seven for 54 yards), while also giving up the most sacks (eight) and blowing the most blocks on passing plays (17). It would seem like a natural progression for Beachum to eventually replace the 29-year-old Foster at left guard, although that won't happen in 2015 unless something unforeseen occurs. The Steelers have gotten away with Beachum at left tackle by being smart with their offensive play-calling and design, so let's give credit to Haley and Munchak, but they won't want to live with that for the length of his career. This will create a tough situation for both the team and the player when his contract is up at the end of the 2015 season. Beachum will want to be paid like a tackle if he is playing tackle, but it might not make sense from the franchise's perspective.

Defensive Front Seven

Defensive Line	Age	Pos	G	Snaps	Plays	TmPct	Rk	Stop	Dfts	BTkl	Runs	St%	Rk	RuYd	Rk	Sack	Hit	Hur	Dsrpt
						Overall							vs. Run				Pass Rush		
Cameron Heyward	26	DE	16	858	57	7.7%	6	44	18	0	36	75%	62	1.8	29	7.0	8	16.5	3
Cam Thomas	29	DE	16	439	18	2.4%	87	11	3	0	14	57%	92	3.1	85	0.5	2	2.0	0
Brett Keisel*	37	DE	12	437	22	4.0%	63	16	4	2	14	71%	77	2.9	79	1.0	5	7.5	3
Stephon Tuitt	22	DE	16	398	17	2.3%	90	11	5	1	12	67%	85	2.4	56	1.0	2	5.5	0
Steve McLendon	29	DT	12	304	21	3.8%	--	15	4	1	19	74%	--	2.5	--	1.0	2	2.0	0

Edge Rushers	Age	Pos	G	Snaps	Plays	TmPct	Rk	Stop	Dfts	BTkl	Runs	St%	Rk	RuYd	Rk	Sack	Hit	Hur	Dsrpt
						Overall							vs. Run				Pass Rush		
Jason Worilds*	27	OLB	16	978	61	8.3%	6	47	16	6	41	78%	33	2.9	57	7.5	16	23.5	1
James Harrison	37	OLB	11	432	44	8.7%	5	36	13	1	29	90%	6	2.1	32	5.5	8	13.5	0
Arthur Moats	27	OLB	16	337	23	3.1%	--	15	6	1	14	71%	--	3.3	--	4.0	3	8.5	0

Linebackers	Age	Pos	G	Snaps	Plays	TmPct	Rk	Stop	Dfts	BTkl	Sack	Hit	Hur	Runs	St%	Rk	RuYd	Rk	Tgts	Suc%	Rk	AdjYd	Rk	PD	Int
						Overall					Pass Rush			vs. Run					vs. Pass						
Lawrence Timmons	29	ILB	16	977	132	17.9%	7	75	27	11	2.0	4	3.5	83	66%	32	3.3	37	41	42%	56	8.1	56	1	0
Sean Spence	25	ILB	16	498	49	6.6%	79	29	4	3	1.0	1	4	34	74%	14	3.1	30	15	23%	--	10.2	--	0	0
Ryan Shazier	23	ILB	9	258	36	8.7%	70	14	5	3	0.0	1	2.5	15	67%	29	2.3	8	12	43%	--	6.8	--	1	0
Vince Williams	26	ILB	16	248	28	3.8%	--	9	4	3	0.0	2	3.5	12	42%	--	3.8	--	10	63%	--	5.6	--	0	0

Year	Yards	ALY	Rk	Power	Rk	Stuff	Rk	2nd Level	Rk	Open Field	Rk	Sacks	ASR	Rk	Short	Long
2012	3.78	3.89	13	66%	22	19%	14	1.03	4	0.47	5	37	6.7%	11	11	15
2013	4.07	4.16	24	65%	16	15%	30	0.98	4	0.60	15	34	6.1%	27	6	16
2014	4.36	4.04	21	53%	3	18%	21	1.32	30	0.75	19	33	6.4%	21	6	14

2014 ALY by direction: Left End 3.6 (14)   Left Tackle 4.15 (22)   Mid/Guard 3.64 (9)   Right Tackle 4.9 (29)   Right End 4.43 (28)

Steve McLendon was supposed to be Casey Hampton's replacement, a new-age nose tackle who relied on penetration rather than space-eating to stop the run and harass the quarterback. But while McLendon has been one of the Steelers' best linemen while healthy, the team just doesn't use him much. He's played just 654 snaps in 26 games over the last two years. McLendon playing so few snaps could be explained away by the Steelers' adjusting their approach to feature more nickel packages and two-man defensive lines. However, the Steelers haven't got high quality play from their other options—with the very obvious exception of Cameron Heyward, maybe the most talented player in their front seven—while McLendon's size and athleticism should make him a good fit in those fronts. Expecting McLendon to play more alongside Heyward next season seems like wishful thinking, so instead the most realistic hope for Steelers fans should be a greater role for Stephon Tuitt. The second-rounder out of Notre Dame struggled a lot during his rookie season. He has impressive size and athleticism, but needs to develop better technique to follow in Heyward's footsteps instead of becoming the next Evander Hood. The Steelers lack depth on the defensive line, so they are largely reliant on getting better play from their young starters.

Behind the defensive line, LeBeau focused on incorporating more speed into his defense over recent seasons. That was something he spoke about before the 2014 season, telling reporters, "We're fast. We have good athleticism. Sometimes we don't go in the right direction with it because we're young... Those two safeties we have and those four linebackers we have, at those positions we can run a race with anybody in the NFL. The problem is it ain't a race, it's a football game." Unfortunately, LeBeau's reservations about how his team's speed would translate to being an effective defense were justified. First-round rookie Ryan Shazier was limited to just nine games and five starts because of two injuries: first a knee sprain, then a high ankle sprain. When he was on the field, he proved to be a boom-or-bust player who relied on his speed to get to the football. Shazier was too aggressive and often seemed to be guessing what the defense was going to do instead of diagnosing plays as they developed. He gave up gap integrity and team discipline to go in search of greater individual statistics. Sean Spence also had limited impact because he was basically a rookie after the early stages of his career were derailed by an abnormal knee injury. His discipline and consistency proved to be a better complement to Lawrence Timmons, but it would still be tough to call him a quality starter, and Shazier is likely to return to his place next to Timmons at the top of the Week 1 depth chart.

Incredibly, James Harrison may be the Steelers' best outside linebacker again in 2015. The 37-year-old Harrison was coaxed out of retirement after Jarvis Jones broke his wrist against the Panthers in Week 3. Ironically, Jones himself was drafted two years ago to replace Harrison, but his athletic limitations have made him a non-factor in the NFL. In two seasons, Jones has only registered three sacks, three QB hits, and 12 hurries in 21 games (11 starts). Jones and Arthur Moats will likely be competing for the starting spot across from Harrison, while rookie Alvin "Bud" Dupree will be expected to play a rotational role to help reignite the Steelers' pass rush.

Defensive Secondary

Secondary	Age	Pos	G	Snaps	Plays	Overall TmPct	Rk	Stop	Dfts	BTkl	vs. Run Runs	St%	Rk	RuYd	Rk	vs. Pass Tgts	Tgt%	Rk	Dist	Suc%	Rk	AdjYd	Rk	PD	Int
Mike Mitchell	28	FS	16	958	74	10.0%	39	19	9	9	39	26%	61	11.1	67	24	6.3%	19	12.8	40%	62	8.3	49	2	0
William Gay	30	CB	16	858	76	10.3%	13	30	10	8	15	47%	27	5.3	24	89	26.0%	58	11.8	56%	17	8.7	53	11	3
Troy Polamalu*	34	SS	12	699	61	11.0%	28	26	9	7	38	55%	11	5.3	17	15	5.2%	8	8.8	70%	3	4.9	5	2	0
Brice McCain*	29	CB	14	600	31	4.8%	77	15	9	3	8	75%	3	2.3	1	38	15.7%	1	11.1	50%	42	7.6	33	6	3
Cortez Allen	27	CB	11	452	52	10.2%	14	15	3	7	11	27%	56	12.5	73	58	32.0%	74	14.0	42%	70	10.3	73	10	2
Will Allen	33	FS	16	313	30	4.1%	--	12	8	4	14	64%	--	3.6	--	12	9.7%	--	5.3	56%	--	5.0	--	1	0
Antwon Blake	25	CB	16	273	42	5.7%	--	15	4	5	6	17%	--	7.8	--	40	36.9%	--	12.2	43%	--	7.4	--	5	1

Year	Pass D Rank	vs. #1 WR	Rk	vs. #2 WR	Rk	vs. Other WR	Rk	vs. TE	Rk	vs. RB	Rk
2012	15	-30.1%	3	-1.8%	16	0.5%	17	23.4%	31	4.5%	20
2013	19	23.9%	29	0.6%	15	-24.2%	4	-0.5%	14	-15.2%	5
2014	30	4.4%	20	-6.8%	12	39.3%	32	17.4%	28	13.3%	22

The Steelers rarely make big free-agent moves, but they made one before last season, handing Mike Mitchell a hefty contract because they needed to replace Troy Polamalu's long-time partner Ryan Clark. If the Steelers were hoping Mitchell could replicate what Clark brought to the Steelers secondary, they were gravely mistaken. If they were hoping his different skill set could add a new dimension to the back end of their coverage, they were gravely mistaken. Regardless of what the Steelers expected Mitchell to do, those expectations weren't met. He proved to be the complete opposite of Clark, a liability both against the run and in coverage. Clark was never a great athlete, but he excelled in the Steelers defense because he was a strong tackler and a disciplined player who understood how to read the game. Mitchell was repeatedly drawn out of position and was a big reason why the Steelers ranked 29th in DVOA against deep passes (16 or more yards past the line of scrimmage).

With Polamalu retired, the starting role will be filled by either Will Allen or Shamarko Thomas. Thomas has youth on his side, but he has underwhelmed since he was selected in the fourth round of the 2013 draft. The 33-year-old Allen is in his second stint with the Steelers, a reliable run defender from the strong safety spot with major limitations in coverage. The Steelers will hope that Thomas can surpass him, but they shouldn't expect him to based on his NFL career so far.

At the very least, the Steelers will have the flexibility to keep Thomas as a safety instead of asking him to be some form of nickel cornerback, thanks to two draft picks who can fill that role. Both Senquez Golson and Doran Grant could start for the Steelers outside, but they will initially be expected to earn the nickel role inside. Then again, Cortez Allen's awful play in 2014 has created an opening in the starting lineup across from William Gay. During Gay's prime, he was the fourth best defensive back in a talented secondary. Now, he's the best defensive back in Pittsburgh, but there may not be another roster in the league where that would be true.

Special Teams

Year	DVOA	Rank	FG/XP	Rank	Net Kick	Rank	Kick Ret	Rank	Net Punt	Rank	Punt Ret	Rank	Hidden	Rank
2012	-0.1%	17	6.8	6	-1.8	21	5.6	7	-6.3	23	-4.8	25	-9.4	30
2013	0.5%	16	2.4	13	-1.5	22	1.0	11	-11.1	28	11.8	4	-6.0	24
2014	0.9%	12	2.5	10	-2.6	22	-4.6	26	3.2	10	5.8	9	-13.5	31

When he was at LSU, Brad Wing looked like the type of punter who would be worth a mid-round draft pick, but character questions left him undrafted. He won last year's Pittsburgh punting job primarily because he came cheaper than veteran Adam Podlesh, and he never showed the same impressive accuracy that had him consistently pinning college opponents deep in their own territory. The low point of his 2014 season came in Tampa Bay's Week 4 upset, when a 29-yard punt late in the fourth quarter landed at the Pittsburgh 46 and set up the Bucs' game-winning drive. Wing's failure at the NFL level is a bit bizarre given how "can't miss" he looked in college, and even people around the Pittsburgh organization can't quite pinpoint what physical change or technical problem has caused his struggles. To keep his spot with the Steelers, he'll have to fend off younger competition in training camp: rookie Jordan Berry out of Eastern Kentucky and second-year punter Richie Leone out of the University of Houston.

Kicker Shaun Suisham continues to be a model of consistency as long as Wing isn't botching his holds. Suisham converted 29 of 32 field goal attempts in 2014, his third straight season over 90 percent, while also setting a career high with a 53-yard strike against the Jets in Week 10. Of course, a 53-yard field goal isn't very long for a career-long, and Suisham has hit only three kicks from 50 yards or more in the past six seasons. The limited leg strength contributes to the downside of Suisham's consistency: he's consistently one of the worst kickoff men in the NFL. If he stays unusually reliable as a placekicker, the Steelers seem content to live with this weakness. A powerful offense means a lot of kickoff opportunities, so Terence Garvin and Vince Williams were among the league leaders with 15 special-teams tackles each.

Despite his importance to the offense, Antonio Brown continues to serve as a punt returner for the Steelers. It makes little sense for them to take him off of returns: it gets the ball in his hands an extra 30 times per season, plus he's really good at it. Brown had a 71-yard touchdown return against the Cincinnati Bengals and finished the season with three 20-plus-yard returns (and one fumble) on 30 attempts, plus 16 fair catches. As the primary kick returner, Markus Wheaton was reliable but lacked the explosiveness to truly threaten big plays. Dri Archer may take over the kick return duties full-time in 2015, but he did little with his nine opportunities in 2014. Archer and Wheaton may be pushed aside by rookie wide receiver Sammie Coates, an outstanding athlete who is unlikely to be playing a major role in this year's offense.

St. Louis Rams

Three years ago, the St. Louis Rams hired head coach Jeff Fisher and general manager Les Snead to bring their franchise back to respectability, and they have certainly done that. The duo took over a team that was the laughingstock of the league for the better part of a decade and turned it into a dangerous group of spoilers; since 2012, the Rams have posted six wins and a tie against teams that went on to make the playoffs. But their growth has stagnated, and so the team has hit reset. The timing of that decision makes sense, but the process itself has been puzzling. In a pass-happy era the likes of which the NFL has never seen, the Rams have gone all-in as a running-and-defense team, pairing a dominant front seven with an electrifying rookie running back and hoping that will be enough to get back to the postseason. It might have been a good strategy to win Super Bowl I, but does a team built that way have a chance to win Super Bowl L?

Let's begin by taking a closer look at where the Rams have been. After Mike Martz was fired during the 2005 season, the St. Louis hired Scott Linehan to replace him. Three years later, they hired Steve Spagnuolo to replace Linehan. The six-year period under Linehan and Spagnuolo turned into a half-dozen of the darkest years any NFL team has ever seen. Between 2006 and 2011, the Rams went a league-worst 23-73, never finishing better than 25th in DVOA and four times ending up last or next to last. The 2008 and 2009 clubs are among the six worst teams in DVOA history (since 1989), and the 2007 and 2011 squads also made the bottom 30. Each of those clubs also ranked among the 13 worst teams since 1989 in our "estimated wins" metric.

Considering the mess of a team they inherited, the 20-27-1 record put together by Fisher and Snead looks brilliant, especially their 7-10-1 mark in the brutally tough NFC West. Under Fisher, the Rams have finished 15th, 14th, and 18th in DVOA. That's much better than the horrors of the Spagnuolo regime, but it's also a steady mark of mediocrity. If St. Louis wanted to get better, it was time to make some drastic changes. Not on defense, mind you: the Rams got off to a slow start, ranking 25th in defensive DVOA in the first half of last season, but they were fourth over the second half of the year. Considering they were the NFL's youngest defense by snap-weighted age, there was little need to make major roster moves. All of the Rams' defensive starters from 2014 will return in 2015, though some may get demoted to make

room for players returning from injury (Chris Long) or added in free agency (Akeem Ayers). The front seven, in particular, is a terrifying unit, with first-round draft picks at seemingly every position.

Wholesale changes were required, however, on an offense that has not had a positive DVOA since Marc Bulger, Steven Jackson, and Torry Holt were leading the team in 2006. And so a number of starters from 2014 were either allowed to leave or were shipped out, including three starting offensive linemen. Joe Barksdale and Davin Joseph were not re-signed after the season, while Scott Wells was released. A fourth lineman, Jake Long, was also cut; he started seven games last year before his season ended with a torn ACL. Zac Stacy started five games at running back in 2014, and though the Rams might have had plans for him in 2015, they did not waste time in satisfying his trade requests after the draft.

The biggest departure, though, is quarterback Sam Bradford, the one-time savior who never came close to living up to expectations after he was the first overall draft pick in 2010. Bradford missed more games (31) than he won (18) in five years as a starter. The Rams decided they could no longer rely on a quarterback who had missed time due to shoulder problems, ankle injuries, *and* two torn ACLs dating back to his time at Oklahoma, and was not appreciably better than his backups when he was healthy.

And so Bradford was moved to the Eagles for Nick Foles, with a bevy of draft picks also involved. The best of those picks was a 2016 second-rounder that moved from Philadelphia to St. Louis. That makes it unlikely that this will work out to be a bad trade for the Rams, but that doesn't guarantee Foles will be an effective quarterback for his new team. Our quarterback projections were cautiously optimistic about Foles coming into the league in 2012, mainly because he started for three years at Arizona State, but a poor combine performance and questions about arm strength pushed him down to the end of the third round, 13 picks after Russell Wilson. Foles was underwhelming as a part-time player in his rookie season, with a -20.4% DVOA in 285 dropbacks. Then came 2013, when Chip Kelly brought his run-heavy, fast-break, shotgun offense to the Eagles. Foles hit the field when Michael Vick was injured in Week 5 and went on to enjoy a season for the ages, leading the league in touchdown rate, yards per pass, and passer rating, while throwing only two interceptions and

2015 Rams Schedule

Week	Opp.	Week	Opp.	Week	Opp.
1	SEA	7	CLE	13	ARI
2	at WAS	8	SF	14	DET
3	PIT	9	at MIN	15	TB (Thu.)
4	at ARI	10	CHI	16	at SEA
5	at GB	11	at BAL	17	at SF
6	BYE	12	at CIN		

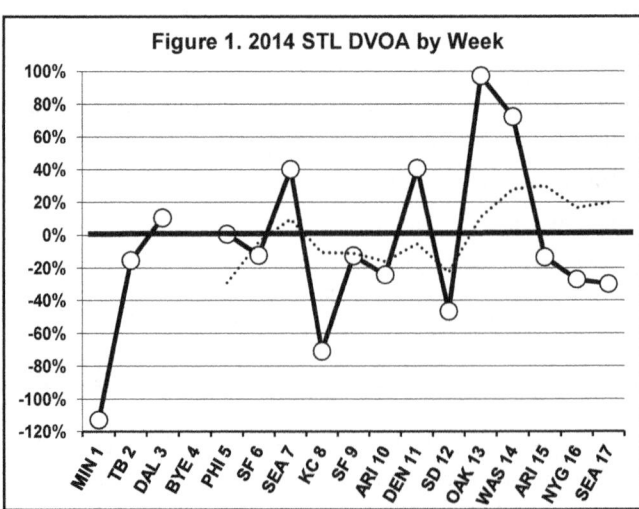

Figure 1. 2014 STL DVOA by Week

finishing second in DVOA behind Peyton Manning. In 2014, though, the league started to figure out Kelly's offense, and Foles fell back to earth. He finished 19th out of 37 quarterbacks in DVOA, and even lower than that in completion rate, interception rate, yards per pass, and passer rating. His year ended abruptly with a broken collarbone suffered in a Week 9 win over Houston. Just eight starts after his miracle season, Kelly and the Eagles had lost faith in him, and were ready to take a chance on Bradford. The Rams were happy to swap two guys who each needed a change in scenery.

Table 1: Least Experienced Offensive Lines, 1989-2014

Team	Year	Avg. Starts	W-L	OFF DVOA	Rank	PASS	Rank	RUSH	Rank
CAR	1995	7.9	7-9	-24.9%	29	-27.1%	29	-14.3%	26
BUF	2009	8.5	6-10	-20.7%	29	-21.1%	27	-3.7%	18
NYG	2003	11.2	4-12	-11.3%	26	-1.2%	21	-9.4%	28
NE	2005	12.5	10-6	17.5%	7	46.6%	2	-2.8%	17
NYJ	1995	12.6	3-13	-30.7%	30	-35.6%	30	-18.3%	29
NYG	2002	12.6	10-6	3.8%	13	23.9%	5	-5.7%	24
NYG	1997	13.2	10-5-1	-4.9%	22	3.1%	19	-2.8%	18
MIA	1990	13.9	12-4	9.3%	8	31.9%	5	-10.9%	23
JAC	1995	14.6	4-12	-9.3%	23	-1.9%	21	-3.2%	18
MIA	2004	15.6	4-12	-29.5%	31	-29.4%	30	-14.5%	30
JAC	2014	15.7	3-13	-24.3%	31	-32.1%	32	-8.2%	20
SEA	1992	16.6	2-14	-41.3%	28	-65.3%	28	-6.6%	23
IND	1999	16.6	13-3	14.2%	5	35.6%	4	0.7%	18
SD	1989	16.7	6-10	-3.7%	18	-5.9%	20	5.9%	7
CLE	2003	16.8	5-11	-8.4%	23	-4.1%	24	-2.8%	20
PIT	2013	16.8	8-8	4.4%	12	23.5%	9	-14.9%	29
BUF	2010	16.8	4-12	-14.5%	26	-9.7%	26	-8.3%	22
SD	1990	17.0	6-10	4.1%	13	-9.4%	19	18.2%	2
STL	1997	17.5	5-11	-14.6%	27	-0.7%	23	-16.5%	29
GB	2001	18.0	12-4	8.5%	6	28.9%	5	-3.8%	22
WAS	1998	18.0	6-10	-0.3%	13	0.1%	18	13.0%	3
SEA	2012	18.4	11-5	18.5%	4	37.3%	4	16.5%	1
BUF	2011	18.5	6-10	0.3%	16	2.3%	19	4.5%	8
CAR	1996	18.8	12-4	0.0%	17	21.7%	7	-7.8%	20
DEN	2010	19.3	4-12	2.1%	15	24.6%	10	-16.2%	30
SD	2014	19.3	9-7	7.0%	11	29.4%	7	-14.2%	25
KC	2013	19.6	11-5	3.0%	15	6.7%	18	11.1%	2
OAK	2006	19.6	2-14	-37.0%	32	-45.4%	32	-12.8%	29
SEA	2011	19.8	7-9	-8.7%	22	0.1%	21	-1.6%	14
AVG			7.0-9.0	-6.6%	19.0	0.9%	17.8	-4.5%	19.1

With their next passer in hand, the Rams went out and got a runner, taking Georgia's Todd Gurley with the tenth overall pick of the draft. Gurley wasn't just the first running back taken in this year's draft; he was the earliest taken since Trent Richardson went third overall in 2012. Gurley is a big back at 6-foot-1, 222 pounds, but he also has speed. He did not run at the combine or the Bulldogs' pro day (for reasons we shall get to shortly), but he has a track background, with a personal best of 10.04 seconds in the 100 meters. In his *Rookie Scouting Portfolio*, Football Outsiders' college scouting guru Matt Waldman called him "the most talented back in this class," citing his agility, acceleration, receiving ability, and blocking prowess.

However, Waldman also asked the most important question of Gurley: "Can he stay on the field?" Gurley's college career ended last November after a torn ACL, an injury that might not be fully healed when the Rams kick off against Seattle in Week 1. He also missed three full games and parts of others in 2013 with a variety of thigh and ankle injuries, and his ankles in particular have given him problems ever since high school.

The Rams still weren't done transmogrifying their offense, as they added four linemen between the second and sixth rounds of the draft. Up to three of those linemen could be starting by opening day. There's a lot here that's going to be unsettled going into training camp, but unless St. Louis adds a veteran player late in the game, the Rams are looking at five starting linemen with an average of no more than 20.6 starts in the NFL. Remember, that is the maximum; the line might be even less experienced depending on who wins what job. That's very low, but not unprecedented. The top five linemen on the expansion Carolina Panthers in 1995 included two rookies and three veterans with a combined total of 55 NFL starts prior to that season. That team went 7-9, but that record came from a strong defense. Carolina's offense ranked 29th that season, broken down into 29th passing and 26th rushing.

All told, we have 29 teams since 1989 whose average lineman (weighted by the number of games they eventually started that season) entered training camp with fewer than 20 starts. (Table 1). Results were mixed. The average rank of these teams in offensive DVOA was 19.0, but keep in mind some of these teams played when the NFL had 28 or 30 teams—with an average ranking of 17.8 in passing offense and 19.1 in rushing offense. About half the teams were positive in passing DVOA and half were negative, with an average rank of 17.8. The good passing teams were generally led by top quarterbacks, including Russell Wilson, Tom Brady, Peyton Manning, Dan Marino, Brett Favre, Philip Rivers and Ben Roethlisberger. So yes, you can put a strong passing game on the field despite a very green line, if your quarterback falls somewhere between a Pro Bowler and a Hall of Famer. Even the Rams themselves don't appear to think Foles is on this level, despite what he did in 2013, which is why they're planning to commit strongly to the ground game. However, these 29 teams with inexperienced lines averaged an even lower 19.1 rank in rushing DVOA. The Rams ranked No. 15 in rushing offense last year, and while it's hard to think they'll be a worse running team with Gurley, the young faces on the line could limit what St. Louis is able to do.

Further making things difficult for the passing game: while they were adding a quarterback and a running back and scads of linemen, St. Louis neglected to overhaul one of the league's worst groups of wide receivers. To be fair, it's not as if the Rams have deliberately ignored the position. The Rams drafted six wideouts in the first four rounds between 2011 and 2013, and they also signed free agent Kenny Britt, a Tennessee first-rounder in 2009. That's a heavy investment of resources in one position, but the Rams still don't have a single receiver who has ever caught 50 passes or gained even 800 yards in a season. The Rams do have talented tight ends, but while Jared Cook and Lance Kendricks are good players, they're not exactly peak Gronkowski and Hernandez (thank goodness, in the latter case). The Rams' game plan looks clear on paper: run Gurley a lot, run Gurley a lot more, use Tre Mason as a change of pace, and hope Foles can find somebody open on the occasional play-action bomb. That won't be a change for Foles, as the Eagles were second in usage of play-action in 2013 and first in 2014. However, he had better get used to spending more time under center. The Eagles led the league in shotgun usage in both of Chip Kelly's seasons, but the Rams were 29th in shotgun usage last year and 31st in 2013.

The Rams are going all-in as a running-and-defense team as the rest of the league is going pass-wacky like never before. Granted, the Seahawks have shown that you can still build a champion around great defense and a brilliant running game. But even they recognized this offseason that a stud receiver like Jimmy Graham would make their offense better. There's no Jimmy Graham in St. Louis; there isn't even a Doug Baldwin. The Rams' fate in 2015 will hinge almost entirely on Gurley's impact as a rookie, and their front seven destroying other team's game plans. Can a roster built this way be successful in this era, or is this a dated strategy?

We can try to use Pro Football Reference's Approximate Value stat to answer that question. You can hit their site for the details, but in a nutshell, AV measures the quality of each team, then uses team and individual statistics to divvy that quality up between each player. It's not a perfect system (and its creators know this—that's why it's called "approximate"

value), but it's by far the best metric available for measuring groups of players, especially in the pre-DVOA days of the 1970s and '80s.

We went back and looked at every team in every season since the 1970 merger, 1,317 team-seasons in all, and measured each team's share of AV that came from their front seven, or from their running back. We then divided that timeframe into three 15-year periods, and looked for teams that were in the top 25 percent of each time period in both front seven AV share and running back AV share. We tallied the number of teams that qualified in each era, and how they fared in the win-loss column (Table 2).

Table 2: Teams In Top 25 Percent of Front Seven Value and Running Back Value, 1970-2014

Timeframe	Qualifying Teams	Winning Teams	Combined Win%	Best	Worst
1970-1984	11	5	0.448	12-4	0-14
1985-1999	17	11	0.551	12-4	5-11
2000-2014	14	8	0.516	11-5	2-14

Based on percentage of Approximate Value coming from running backs, front seven, or both.

The 1970s are often hailed as the era of running and defense, but surprisingly, that's the era where it's most difficult to find teams who got most of their value from these two parts of the roster. They were more frequent in the 1990s, and then slightly less so this century. From a win-loss standpoint, results have been very mixed. Recent qualifying teams include the 2-14 2012 Chiefs and the 5-11 2009 Browns, but also the 2005 Buccaneers and 2008 Ravens, both of whom went 11-5. Both of those teams made the playoffs, with the Bucs losing a wild-card game to Washington, while the Ravens fell to eventual Super Bowl champion Pittsburgh.

So yes, on rare occasions, running-and-defense teams can still make the playoffs and even advance, and our projection system says the Rams have a good chance to be one of those teams. The 2013 version of Foles might have been a product of the Eagles' system, but even the 2014 version of Foles should be an upgrade over what Austin Davis and Shaun Hill did last year, despite the lack of weapons in the passing game. The trio of Gurley, Mason, and Benny Cunningham should be productive on the ground, if not dominant. And the defense, with a spectacular front seven backed up by a promising secondary, could be the best in the league if everything falls into place.

That's a good team in a vacuum, and circumstances outside St. Louis also favor the Rams. The NFC West has been the best division in the league for a few years now, but we foresee declining defenses in Arizona and San Francisco, opening a door for the Rams to (head) butt their way into the playoff race. If the Cardinals and 49ers live up (or rather, down) to our projections, it will also contribute to the Rams' middle-of-the-pack schedule, which sees other softies like Cleveland,

Washington, and Tampa Bay mixed in with tough contests against the two North divisions and, of course, the double-header with Seattle. Weirdly, the Rams will play no average teams this year. Every opponent on the schedule is in either the bottom 10 or the top 10 in mean projected DVOA.

Fisher and Snead have made the Rams respectable again. The next step is to make them admirable. It will take a post-

season berth to make that happen, something the team hasn't earned since 2004. St. Louis' ground-based approach could be enough to get it done even in this age of aerial assault—because while the Rams likely won't be putting up big numbers through the air, neither will their opponents.

Vincent Verhei

2014 Rams Stats by Week

Wk	vs.	W-L	PF	PA	YDF	YDA	TO	Total	Off	Def	ST
1	MIN	W	6	34	318	355	-2	-113%	-65%	47%	-1%
2	at TB	W	19	17	339	332	0	-15%	5%	20%	-1%
3	DAL	L	31	34	448	340	-1	11%	8%	-5%	-3%
4	BYE										
5	at PHI	L	28	34	466	352	0	1%	25%	4%	-21%
6	SF	L	17	31	309	432	0	-12%	-10%	4%	2%
7	SEA	W	28	26	275	463	0	40%	40%	24%	24%
8	at KC	L	7	34	200	355	0	-71%	-45%	5%	-20%
9	at SF	W	13	10	193	263	0	-13%	-33%	-16%	4%
10	at ARI	L	14	31	244	335	-2	-24%	-39%	-11%	3%
11	DEN	W	22	7	337	397	2	41%	0%	-26%	15%
12	at SD	L	24	27	317	410	0	-47%	-40%	17%	10%
13	OAK	W	52	0	348	244	5	97%	27%	-62%	8%
14	at WAS	W	24	0	329	206	2	72%	-6%	-58%	20%
15	ARI	L	6	12	280	274	-2	-13%	-30%	-19%	-3%
16	NYG	L	27	37	387	514	-3	-27%	17%	50%	6%
17	at SEA	L	6	20	245	354	-1	-30%	-63%	-20%	12%

Trends and Splits

	Offense	Rank	Defense	Rank
Total DVOA	-11.1%	25	-3.8%	9
Unadjusted VOA	-13.3%	28	-4.0%	8
Weighted Trend	-14.0%	26	-10.8%	6
Variance	10.7%	28	10.0%	32
Average Opponent	-2.7%	4	-0.1%	14
Passing	-6.8%	26	8.9%	20
Rushing	-4.4%	15	-19.9%	4
First Down	-6.9%	22	-2.8%	15
Second Down	-12.0%	25	2.5%	17
Third Down	-19.0%	24	-15.9%	8
First Half	-1.9%	17	-13.8%	3
Second Half	-20.2%	29	6.5%	24
Red Zone	-22.9%	26	-17.5%	6
Late and Close	-38.5%	31	18.4%	31

Five-Year Performance

Year	W-L	Pyth W	Est W	PF	PA	TO	Total	Rk	Off	Rk	Def	Rk	ST	Rk	Off AGL	Rk	Def AGL	Rk	Off Age	Rk	Def Age	Rk	ST Age	Rk
2010	7-9	6.8	5.4	289	328	+5	-19.4%	28	-18.1%	30	2.1%	19	0.8%	14	26.8	18	12.7	9	25.7	29	26.8	17	26.1	19
2011	2-14	2.3	2.2	193	407	-5	-35.4%	32	-27.2%	32	3.4%	21	-4.8%	28	32.6	18	40.0	23	27.1	16	27.6	7	26.4	11
2012	7-8-1	6.6	8.2	299	348	-1	1.5%	15	-4.2%	21	-9.1%	7	-3.4%	26	30.2	18	19.3	10	26.3	23	26.3	24	25.5	29
2013	7-9	7.6	7.8	348	364	+8	2.4%	14	-9.5%	22	-5.7%	11	6.3%	4	46.3	23	44.8	25	26.1	28	25.0	31	25.0	30
2014	6-10	7.1	6.1	324	354	-2	-3.8%	18	-11.1%	25	-3.8%	9	3.5%	7	82.1	32	37.0	15	26.5	23	25.0	32	25.2	32

2014 Performance Based on Most Common Personnel Groups

STL Offense					STL Offense vs. Opponents					STL Defense				STL Defense vs. Opponents			
Pers	Freq	Yds	DVOA	Run%	Pers	Freq	Yds	DVOA	Run%	Pers	Freq	Yds	DVOA	Pers	Freq	Yds	DVOA
11	47%	5.7	-7.4%	19%	Base	49%	5.1	-3.4%	61%	Base	35%	5.1	-10.4%	11	54%	6.1	0.5%
12	39%	5.2	-12.9%	54%	Nickel	28%	5.8	-8.5%	21%	Nickel	56%	6.1	3.7%	12	17%	6.9	18.5%
13	9%	4.1	-6.8%	75%	Dime+	22%	5.5	-16.7%	15%	Dime+	7%	7.7	-12.2%	21	11%	4.7	0.1%
21*	21%	5.5	-2.2%	66%	Goal Line	1%	0.9	46.9%	43%	Goal Line	1%	3.1	-43.2%	22	5%	4.1	-43.6%
22*	9%	3.8	-9.7%	79%										13	4%	3.4	-53.8%

* 21 and 22 personnel with Cory Harkey considered FB rather than TE; overlaps with numbers for 12 and 13 personnel.

Strategic Tendencies

Run/Pass		Rk	Formation		Rk	Pass Rush		Rk	Secondary		Rk	Strategy		Rk
Runs, first half	45%	5	Form: Single Back	56%	32	Rush 3	4.6%	23	4 DB	22%	23	Play action	18%	24
Runs, first down	52%	10	Form: Empty Back	4%	26	Rush 4	46.7%	32	5 DB	66%	10	Avg Box (Off)	6.35	8
Runs, second-long	28%	21	Pers: 3+ WR	50%	25	Rush 5	33.3%	2	6+ DB	12%	16	Avg Box (Def)	6.38	8
Runs, power sit.	38%	32	Pers: 4+ WR	2%	17	Rush 6+	15.4%	4	CB by Sides	86%	7	Offensive Pace	33.13	32
Runs, behind 2H	22%	29	Pers: 2+ TE/6+ OL	51%	2	Sacks by LB	8.8%	29	DB Blitz	19%	2	Defensive Pace	31.29	29
Pass, ahead 2H	44%	25	Shotgun/Pistol	48%	29	Sacks by DB	15.0%	4	Hole in Zone	8%	5	Go for it on 4th	0.43	31

The Rams were third in the league with 146 penalties, including declined and offsetting, and led the NFL with 1,139 penalty yards. ☞ St. Louis has struggled to convert third downs for years now. Last year was the seventh season in the past eight where the Rams ranked 24th or worse in third-down DVOA. ☞ A league-leading 69 percent of St. Louis runs came with two or more players in the backfield, and they had one of the largest gaps in DVOA between runs with one back (3.9 yards per carry, -23.7% DVOA) and runs with two backs (4.1, -6.8%). ☞ The Rams used a defensive back blitz more than twice as often as they did in 2013, but it wasn't particularly effective: the Rams allowed an average of 7.6 yards on these plays, 27th in the NFL. ☞ St. Louis also blitzed much more in 2014, rising from 19th in frequency of sending five pass rushers (21.9 percent in 2013) to second.

Passing

Player	DYAR	DVOA	Plays	NtYds	Avg	YAC	C%	TD	Int
A.Davis	47	-8.8%	312	1819	5.8	5.0	63.8%	12	9
S.Hill*	-31	-13.1%	248	1538	6.2	5.6	63.3%	8	6
N.Foles	264	1.8%	322	2108	6.5	5.3	60.4%	13	10
C.Keenum	-50	-20.8%	80	422	5.3	5.8	58.4%	2	2

Rushing

Player	DYAR	DVOA	Plays	Yds	Avg	TD	Fum	Suc
T.Mason	55	-0.9%	179	765	4.3	4	2	44%
Z.Stacy*	-1	-8.8%	76	298	3.9	1	2	50%
B.Cunningham	26	1.7%	66	246	3.7	3	0	38%
T.Austin	175	46.7%	36	224	6.2	2	0	-
T.Watts	5	6.3%	7	30	4.3	0	0	57%
A.Davis	5	4.6%	7	43	6.1	0	0	-
N.Foles	15	9.5%	13	71	5.5	0	1	-
C.Keenum	9	4.3%	8	37	4.6	0	0	-

Receiving

Player	DYAR	DVOA	Plays	Ctch	Yds	Y/C	YAC	TD	C%
K.Britt	163	12.4%	84	48	748	15.6	3.5	3	57%
S.Bailey	103	16.8%	46	30	435	14.5	6.1	1	65%
T.Austin	24	-5.8%	44	31	242	7.8	5.5	0	70%
B.Quick	115	24.5%	39	25	375	15.0	2.9	3	64%
C.Givens	0	-12.9%	20	11	159	14.5	4.0	1	55%
A.Pettis*	10	-6.0%	18	12	118	9.8	4.4	1	67%
J.Cook	-39	-13.4%	99	52	634	12.2	5.1	3	53%
L.Kendricks	51	11.8%	38	27	259	9.6	3.9	5	71%
C.Harkey	-6	-14.6%	11	8	55	6.9	4.5	1	73%
B.Cunningham	109	25.7%	53	45	352	7.8	7.0	1	85%
T.Mason	55	28.3%	26	16	148	9.3	10.3	1	62%
Z.Stacy*	48	23.2%	23	18	152	8.4	8.7	0	78%

Offensive Line

Player	Pos	Age	GS	Snaps	Pen	Sk	Pass	Run	Player	Pos	Age	GS	Snaps	Pen	Sk	Pass	Run
Joseph Barksdale*	RT	26	16/16	994	6	7.5	25.5	1.0	Greg Robinson	G/T	23	16/12	725	11	4.0	18.0	6.0
Scott Wells*	C	34	16/16	976	6	3.5	12.5	5.0	Jake Long*	LT	30	7/7	431	1	3.0	10.0	1.5
Rodger Saffold	LG	27	16/16	916	3	0.5	5.5	2.0	Garrett Reynolds	OT	28	10/4	224	4	3.0	8.0	0.0
Davin Joseph*	RG	32	16/13	874	7	4.5	17.5	6.5									

Year	Yards	ALY	Rk	Power	Rk	Stuff	Rk	2nd Lev	Rk	Open Field	Rk	Sacks	ASR	Rk	Short	Long	F-Start	Cont.
2012	4.74	4.50	1	66%	12	17%	7	1.49	1	0.79	14	41	8.5%	29	4	26	13	48
2013	4.05	3.57	29	55%	28	24%	29	1.12	15	0.98	5	39	7.8%	22	9	18	19	39
2014	4.08	3.90	18	53%	30	21%	29	1.18	14	0.71	16	47	8.6%	23	19	16	20	38
2014 ALY by direction:		Left End 4.81 (1)			Left Tackle 4.25 (9)			Mid/Guard 3.58 (26)			Right Tackle 3.67 (21)				Right End 5.12 (5)			

Jeff Fisher and offensive line coach Paul Boudreau have raised the offensive line from the nadir of the Linehan and Spagnuolo regimes, when the Rams were 26th or worse in adjusted line yards a remarkable five years in a row. But that improvement has plateaued, and the line was getting older, not better. So the team hit reset, saying goodbye to three starters. Gone are

Joe Barksdale (23rd among right tackles in blown blocks per snap), Scott Wells (31st among centers), and Davin Joseph (31st among right guards). It's not immediately clear who will be starting in their places, but it's obvious that St. Louis' line is going to be very young and very inexperienced in 2015.

Let's start with the holdovers. Greg Robinson, the second overall pick of the 2014 draft, took over at left tackle for the oft-injured (and also cut) Jake Long halfway through his rookie season. Next to him is left guard Rodger Saffold, the 33rd overall pick in 2010. That's 72 NFL starts on that side of the line, though 60 of them are by Saffold. Only two other linemen on the roster have ever started an NFL game: Tim Barnes has bounced between the practice squad and the bench for four years in St. Louis and started four games in 2013, while Garrett Reynolds has spent five NFL seasons bouncing in and out of the starting lineups in Detroit and Atlanta before joining St. Louis this offseason. And that's it, unless the Rams pick up somebody else's late roster cut. Should all four make the Rams' first string—which is no guarantee for Jones or Reynolds—the Rams' offensive line will have a combined 103 NFL starts. For comparison's sake, Houston left tackle Duane Brown already has 106 career starts, and he didn't turn 30 until August.

The other four veteran linemen on the roster (Barrett Jones, Brandon Washington, Demetrius Rhaney, and Stephen Baker) don't have much of a pedigree. Each has been with the team for one to three years, none drafted any earlier than the fourth round. Jones has the most potential, having won the Outland and Rimington trophies at Alabama, but foot and back injuries have sidelined him for each of his first two NFL seasons. The door is open for any of the four linemen St. Louis drafted this year to make the starting lineup on opening day. The candidates:

- **Rob Havenstein, Wisconsin, second round (57th overall):** Started 42 games in college, all at right tackle. Second-team all-Big Ten as a sophomore in 2012, and first-team in 2014 as a senior. A huge man at 6-foot-7 and 321 pounds (and he actually lost 50 pounds in college), Havenstein is a tenacious mauler; Dane Brugler of CBS Sports noted he likes to "drive defenders into the parking lot." His footwork leaves a lot to be desired, however, as does his upper body strength. Brugler called Havenstein's combine performance of 16 reps on the bench press "inexcusable." Probably a better guard than a tackle.
- **Jamon Brown, Louisville, third round (72nd overall):** Started 40 games at college, seeing roughly equal time at left and right tackle. Similar to Havenstein, Brown struggled with his weight in school (he hit 350 pounds at one point, but weighed 323 at the combine), blocks better in a phone booth than in space, and will likely move from tackle to guard in the NFL.
- **Andrew Donnal, Iowa, fourth round (119th overall):** Only started 16 collegiate games, including 13 at right tackle as a senior, in part because he tore his ACL in October of 2012. As such, he's a developmental pick who probably needs to add muscle mass and improve technique before playing on Sundays. Unlikely to start this year.
- **Cody Wichmann, Fresno State, sixth round (216th overall):** The most experienced of the four, Wichmann started 50 collegiate games, some at right tackle, but mostly at right guard. Stop me if you've heard this before, but his strength is more impressive than his agility, and while he should be fine at the point of attack, he's going to have trouble hitting moving targets or kicking out to take on pass-rushers.

The Rams also selected Clemson's Isaiah Battle in the supplemental draft, but GM Les Snead has said that Battle is a long-term project who will not play in 2015.

Just after OTAs, Brandon Bate at *Turf Show Times* projected a starting lineup of Robinson, Brown, Barnes, Saffold, and Havenstein. That's probably as good a guess as any other.

Defensive Front Seven

Defensive Line	Age	Pos	G	Snaps	Plays	TmPct	Overall Rk	Stop	Dfts	BTkl	Runs	St%	vs. Run Rk	RuYd	Rk	Sack	Pass Rush Hit	Hur	Dsrpt
Aaron Donald	24	DT	16	705	48	5.8%	26	42	25	2	32	88%	13	0.0	1	9.5	5	20.5	1
Michael Brockers	25	DT	16	621	31	3.7%	71	21	7	1	25	72%	72	4.9	93	2.0	2	4.5	2
Kendall Langford*	29	DT	16	482	25	3.0%	81	20	4	1	22	86%	16	1.1	11	1.0	2	2.0	0
Alex Carrington	28	DT	8	146	1	0.2%	--	1	0	0	1	100%	--	1.0	--	0.0	0	1.0	0
Nick Fairley	27	DT	8	288	14	3.5%	73	11	4	0	12	83%	24	1.6	24	1.0	4	4.0	0

Edge Rushers	Age	Pos	G	Snaps	Plays	TmPct	Overall Rk	Stop	Dfts	BTkl	Runs	St%	vs. Run Rk	RuYd	Rk	Sack	Pass Rush Hit	Hur	Dsrpt
Robert Quinn	25	DE	16	786	51	6.2%	25	44	19	2	32	78%	32	2.8	54	10.5	10	18.5	3
William Hayes	30	DE	16	534	41	5.0%	47	32	13	3	33	82%	22	1.5	11	4.0	3	17.5	0
Eugene Sims	29	DE	16	488	27	3.3%	75	21	5	1	17	88%	8	2.0	27	2.5	5	8.5	0

Linebackers	Age	Pos	G	Snaps	Plays	Overall TmPct	Rk	Stop	Dfts	BTkl	Pass Rush Sack	Hit	Hur	vs. Run Runs	St%	Rk	RuYd	Rk	vs. Pass Tgts	Suc%	Rk	AdjYd	Rk	PD	Int
Alec Ogletree	24	OLB	16	1043	122	14.7%	26	72	21	13	0.0	0	8.5	58	78%	6	3.1	28	38	50%	42	8.3	59	6	2
James Laurinaitis	29	MLB	16	1040	111	13.4%	35	55	18	3	3.5	2	6.5	58	64%	43	4.1	69	24	45%	46	7.2	47	2	0
Jo-Lonn Dunbar	30	OLB	16	420	35	4.2%	85	21	6	4	0.0	3	3.5	24	75%	12	1.9	3	12	24%	--	9.8	--	0	0
Akeem Ayers	26	OLB	11	392	18	3.3%	86	12	7	0	4.0	2	9.5	9	67%	29	2.3	8	4	30%	--	6.0	--	1	1

Year	Yards	ALY	Rk	Power	Rk	Stuff	Rk	2nd Level	Rk	Open Field	Rk	Sacks	ASR	Rk	Short	Long
2012	4.09	3.50	2	59%	13	25%	3	1.21	21	1.02	26	52	8.5%	3	18	24
2013	3.80	3.50	5	51%	4	27%	2	1.13	18	0.77	20	53	9.5%	1	20	17
2014	3.88	3.31	3	55%	4	24%	5	1.12	14	0.82	22	40	6.7%	15	17	9
2014 ALY by direction:			Left End 3.74 (19)			Left Tackle 2.84 (3)			Mid/Guard 3.35 (4)			Right Tackle 3.35 (8)			Right End 3.35 (10)	

While the names on the St. Louis offensive line are unfamiliar and unproven, their counterparts on defense are notorious and feared. The Rams have an amazing six former first-round draft picks among their linebackers and linemen, and two more players who were taken in the first seven picks of the second round. Robert Quinn is the two-time Pro Bowler who has drawn a league-high 15 holding penalties in the last two seasons. Aaron Donald is the reigning Defensive Rookie of the Year, who had more defeats last season than any other tackle save Ndamukong Suh and made his average run tackle at the line of scrimmage. Michael Brockers is a man-child who left LSU after his sophomore season and made his 43rd NFL start on his 24th birthday (and one more the next week). Chris Long, son of Hall of Famer Howie Long, missed most of last season with an ankle injury and was ineffective when he did play, but he had 19 defeats, 8.5 sacks, and 20 hurries in 2013. All are former first-round draft picks, and now there's a fifth coming off the bench in Nick Fairley, formerly with the Detroit Lions, who ranked among the top-ten tackles in defeats in 2013. You won't find a more talented defensive line in the league, though there are injury concerns here—Long missed ten games in 2014 after ankle surgery, while Fairley missed the last nine games of the year (including the playoffs) with a knee injury. Fairley has also struggled with weight and off-field issues throughout his career, but he was found not guilty of a DUI in February and weighed 280 pounds in March. Hopefully, for the Rams' sake, he's put those problems behind him. St. Louis also has depth at end, where William Hayes has racked up 24 sacks and 159 tackles in seven years as a part-time player for the Titans and Rams.

Strongside linebacker Alec Ogletree did a little bit of everything last season. He was in the top 20 among all linebackers (including 3-4 outside guys) in successful run tackles and the top ten in successful pass plays (combining tackles and PDs), and he was ninth among all defenders in total successful plays. While he had no sacks and few hurries, he still made an impact as a pass rusher. He tipped seven passes at the line of scrimmage, five more than any other 4-3 linebacker or 3-4 inside linebacker. James Laurinaitis hasn't missed a start in his six-year career and shows no signs of slowing down, making at least three tackles in every game last year and finishing in the top ten at the position for lowest rate of broken tackles. Newly signed Akeem Ayers has already started 47 NFL games and is kind of a poor man's Ogletree, with the ability to do many things competently, but none of them particularly well. He was miscast as the top linebacker in Tennessee, but should have more success in St. Louis in a more limited role.

Defensive Secondary

Secondary	Age	Pos	G	Snaps	Plays	Overall TmPct	Rk	Stop	Dfts	BTkl	vs. Run Runs	St%	Rk	RuYd	Rk	vs. Pass Tgts	Tgt%	Rk	Dist	Suc%	Rk	AdjYd	Rk	PD	Int
T.J. McDonald	24	SS	16	1047	110	13.3%	11	58	20	3	56	63%	7	3.8	3	37	10.8%	54	9.0	61%	15	5.3	11	5	1
Rodney McLeod	25	FS	16	1023	76	9.2%	49	24	12	14	30	23%	63	11.5	68	26	7.9%	32	13.3	54%	33	9.8	62	6	2
E.J. Gaines	23	CB	15	935	84	10.8%	11	39	13	12	21	57%	16	4.2	9	75	24.8%	48	10.0	57%	15	6.2	11	14	2
Janoris Jenkins	27	CB	14	836	63	8.7%	34	26	10	13	17	41%	36	9.8	65	54	19.9%	11	11.8	43%	66	11.1	77	5	2
Mark Barron	26	SS	16	639	71	8.6%	51	28	11	5	24	54%	12	5.8	23	25	12.0%	61	11.8	58%	27	8.7	56	4	0
Trumaine Johnson	25	CB	9	433	42	9.0%	--	14	8	6	5	20%	--	6.0	--	38	27.3%	--	10.6	41%	--	8.5	--	6	3
Lamarcus Joyner	25	CB	10	277	39	7.5%	--	15	7	0	12	42%	--	7.8	--	23	25.8%	--	8.9	51%	--	6.5	--	2	0

Year	Pass D Rank	vs. #1 WR	Rk	vs. #2 WR	Rk	vs. Other WR	Rk	vs. TE	Rk	vs. RB	Rk
2012	8	-17.3%	6	-7.7%	9	5.3%	23	5.4%	23	26.6%	31
2013	15	41.6%	32	-16.1%	5	0.6%	15	-41.6%	1	25.6%	32
2014	20	3.5%	19	33.8%	31	-1.0%	15	-12.2%	6	-9.9%	10

Just in case the Rams' front seven needed help, second-year safety T.J. McDonald was second at his position in successful run tackles, and tied for fourth in total defeats. Rodney McLeod, also in his second year as a starter, was in the top ten for pass defeats. Only Arizona got more defeats from its safeties, and the Cardinals often used four safeties on the field at once.

Cornerback E.J. Gaines was just an anonymous sixth-round draft pick when training camp opened last year, but then he was put into the starting lineup when Trumaine Johnson went down with an MCL sprain. Johnson was ready to go by Week 9, but by then he had been Wally Pipped, and Gaines was clearly the Rams' top corner. In the past three seasons, only 11 rookie corners have started 10 or more games. Gaines had the best adjusted success rate of the bunch, and the third-best adjusted yards per target. Johnson, meanwhile, will be left battling 2014 second-rounder Lamarcus Joyner for the nickel spot.

In last year's St. Louis chapter, we compared Janoris Jenkins to DeAngelo Hall, and his 2014 season can only be described as DeAngelous. Jenkins' horrible charting numbers in 2014 were actually marginal improvements over what he did in 2013. He was embarrassed by 33-year-old Brandon Lloyd for an 80-yard touchdown late in the first half on Monday Night Football, Lloyd's only touchdown in 14 games last year. (Jenkins also gave up a 49-yard catch and a 36-yard DPI to Michael Floyd. Perhaps he just can't cover anyone whose name ends in "oyd.") However, Jenkins is deadly with the ball in his hands. He turned both of his interceptions last season into touchdowns, including a 99-yarder against San Diego, and now has six touchdowns in his three-year career—two more than Rams wide receiver Chris Givens, who was also drafted in 2012.

Special Teams

Year	DVOA	Rank	FG/XP	Rank	Net Kick	Rank	Kick Ret	Rank	Net Punt	Rank	Punt Ret	Rank	Hidden	Rank
2012	-3.4%	26	1.0	16	1.3	14	-8.4	30	-2.3	18	-8.2	30	-1.4	20
2013	6.3%	4	1.4	16	12.6	1	-1.4	17	22.4	1	-3.5	19	11.1	4
2014	3.5%	7	-4.7	28	0.1	17	-1.2	19	11.3	5	12.1	3	4.4	10

The Leg was lousy last year. Greg Zuerlein's kickoff numbers were down from prior seasons, and he missed several short field goals and an extra point. Speaking of kickoffs, Benny Cunningham sure made an adventure out of things. He averaged 27.5 yards per return, one of the ten best numbers in football, but he also ran 28 kicks out of the end zone. Only Devin Hester and Jordan Todman did so more often. The Rams' own kickoff coverage was almost exactly average.

When it came to punts, though, the Rams were excellent on either side of the ball. Tavon Austin upped his punt return average from 8.5 to 11.2 yards, and after negative net value as a rookie he was one of the five most valuable returners last season. On top of that, on his only return of the year, Stedman Bailey scored a 90-yard touchdown against Seattle on a trick play. Actually, that term seems insufficient for what the Rams pulled off; "mass hypnosis" or "Jedi mind trick" would be more appropriate. Meanwhile, Johnny Hekker was second in the league in gross punt value, and his coverage team was also outstanding. Furthermore, Hekker completed passes for critical first downs on fakes against Seattle and San Diego. A high school quarterback, Hekker has now completed five of six passes for 79 yards in his three-year NFL career, with every completion going for a first down or touchdown. Forget trading for Nick Foles, they should have just promoted this guy.

San Diego Chargers

2014 Record: 9-7	Total DVOA: -0.6% (16th)	2015 Mean Projection: 8.5 wins	On the Clock (0-4): 7%
Pythagorean Wins: 8.0 (17th)	Offense: 7.0% (11th)	Postseason Odds: 42.7%	Mediocrity (5-7): 29%
Snap-Weighted Age: 27.2 (3rd)	Defense: 4.9% (25th)	Super Bowl Odds: 6.9%	Playoff Contender (8-10): 41%
Average Opponent: 4.2% (4th)	Special Teams: -2.7% (23rd)	Proj. Avg. Opponent: 1.2% (13th)	Super Bowl Contender (11+): 23%

2014: A short-lived MVP campaign for Philip Rivers.

2015: Too Liuget to quit, but is this the end for several of the team's best players?

Six years ago, the Chargers made Philip Rivers one of the highest-paid quarterbacks in the NFL with an extension worth $15.3 million per season. Rivers turns 34 in December, and as he enters the final year of that extension, he only ranks 17th among quarterbacks in average salary. Whether it happens before the season or shortly after, Rivers is going to get another big contract, likely in the range of what fellow 2004 draftee Ben Roethlisberger got in Pittsburgh: $21.85 million per year and roughly $65 million over the next three years.

But will Rivers be playing for the San Diego Chargers or the Los Angeles Chargers? How about the Buffalo Bills or another team that's just a quarterback away from competing? Pick your poison for rumors, but as the league's L.A. hype has been building, the general thought is that Rivers wants to be sure the Chargers are staying in San Diego before he signs an extension. Rivers has a large family (his wife is pregnant with their eighth child) and it's easy to understand why he would want to stay in San Diego. We also know that the big trade rumor leading into the draft involved Rivers and the Tennessee Titans, likely in a move that would have reunited Rivers with Ken Whisenhunt and made Oregon quarterback Marcus Mariota the new franchise signal-caller in San Diego. Discussions were never denied by Chargers general manager Tom Telesco, but the trade never materialized and the Titans simply drafted Mariota with the No. 2 pick.

If San Diego was very impressed by Mariota, should there have been a stronger effort to move Rivers while his value was still high? If we're being honest, the combination of Rivers and a roster depreciating in talent has not made San Diego much of a serious contender. The Chargers have not won more than nine games since 2009 and have just one playoff win in the last six seasons. That lone triumph came in Cincinnati, where the Bengals hand over wild-card wins easier than the school wimp gives up his lunch money.

We have reached a point where Rivers and his NFC equivalent Tony Romo are the modern day Dan Fouts and Warren Moon, the best quarterbacks to never reach a Super Bowl. That's especially depressing in this era when eight active starting quarterbacks have at least one Super Bowl ring, the most in NFL history. Rivers has a shot to finish with Dan Marino-like numbers (60,000 passing yards and 400 touchdowns), which should get him serious Hall of Fame consideration. But like Marino in 1984, Rivers may have had his best team in his first year as a full-season starter in 2006. Since then he has been asked to do more to carry the team each season, which justifies his salary, but that strategy doesn't help fill San Diego's empty trophy case. Despite some of the gaudier passing numbers of his era, Rivers has yet to be named a first-team All-Pro in any of his nine seasons as a starter. He has received only four MVP votes in his career, or as many as Chad Pennington. For as loud as Rivers can be on the field, he has developed a quiet profile compared to some of his prolific peers.

Table 1. Largest Declines in Passing Yards Per Attempt, Games 1-6 vs. Games 7-16 (1978-2014)

Rk	Quarterback	Year	Team	Age	Games 1-6 YPA	TD	INT	Games 7-17 YPA	TD	INT	YPA Diff.
1	Joe Ferguson	1979	BUF	29	9.91	10	3	6.90	4	12	-3.02
2	David Carr	2004	HOU	25	9.38	8	5	6.49	8	9	-2.88
3	Joe Ferguson	1978	BUF	28	8.12	9	5	5.50	7	10	-2.62
4	Don Majkowski	1989	GB	25	8.89	12	11	6.41	15	9	-2.47
5	Ron Jaworski	1983	PHI	32	8.85	7	3	6.68	13	15	-2.17
6	Eli Manning	2006	NYG	25	7.51	13	8	5.39	11	10	-2.12
7	Philip Rivers	2014	SD	33	8.82	15	2	6.82	16	16	-2.00
8	Drew Bledsoe	2005	DAL	33	8.48	11	4	6.52	12	13	-1.96
9	Boomer Esiason	1993	NYJ	32	8.39	9	6	6.44	7	5	-1.95
10	Randall Cunningham	1988	PHI	25	8.10	11	3	6.16	13	13	-1.94

2015 Chargers Schedule

Week	Opp.	Week	Opp.	Week	Opp.
1	DET	7	OAK	13	DEN
2	at CIN	8	at BAL	14	at KC
3	at MIN	9	CHI (Mon.)	15	MIA
4	CLE	10	BYE	16	at OAK (Thu.)
5	PIT (Mon)	11	KC	17	at DEN
6	at GB	12	at JAC		

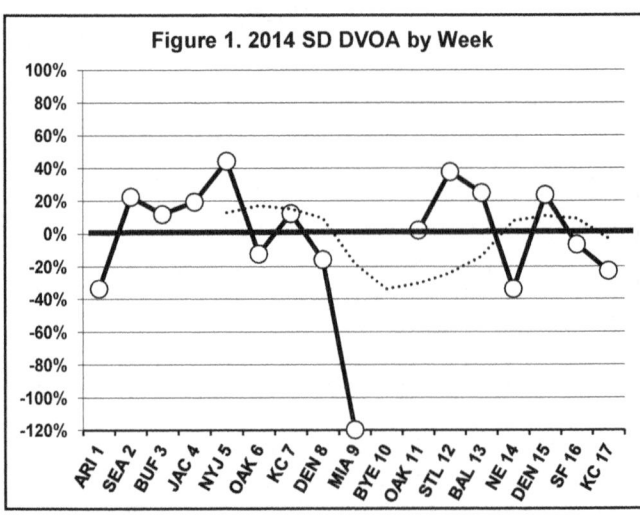

Figure 1. 2014 SD DVOA by Week

Rivers briefly took the NFL's spotlight to start the 2014 season, but had a very uncharacteristic finish. Through six games, he seemed to be in full control of an offense that replaced Whisenhunt with quarterbacks coach Frank Reich at offensive coordinator. Rivers started with an MVP-like ratio of 15 touchdowns to two interceptions while averaging 8.82 yards per pass attempt (YPA). Then came a collapse: first, two divisional losses in five days, followed by one of the worst games of Rivers' career in a 37-0 shutout loss in Miami. In the final 10 games of the season, Rivers threw as many interceptions as touchdowns (16) and only averaged 6.82 YPA. Among the 430 seasons where a quarterback played in 16 games and averaged 15 passes per game, Rivers' decline of 2.0 YPA is the seventh largest since 1978 (Table 1, previous page). Drew Bledsoe is the only other quarterback in the top 10 as old as Rivers, and he was replaced the following season by Romo in Dallas before retiring. From 2006-2013, Rivers' average drop in YPA over the last 10 games was only 0.24, so he had usually been consistent throughout the season.

Known for strong December finishes, Rivers managed to lead the offense to just 24 combined points in losses against AFC contenders like the Patriots, Broncos, and Chiefs. For the second year in a row the Chargers only had to beat the Chiefs in Week 17 to clinch a playoff spot. After barely doing so in 2013, the 2014 Chargers fell 19-7 in Kansas City (who was playing Chase Daniel at quarterback), with Rivers throwing two interceptions to tie him with Jay Cutler for the league lead (18).

Maybe a team *shouldn't* re-sign a quarterback going on 34 when he finishes a season like that. Then again, any quarterback who's still starting at this stage of his career has to be pretty good (or he's like Jon Kitna, a personal piñata for Mike Martz to destroy in Detroit). A total of 25 quarterbacks have attempted at least 1,500 passes after their age-33 season, and 13 of those names should be represented in Canton in the near future. The skilled pocket passer still has a lot of value in his later years. Since taking over the job, Rivers has a streak of 153 consecutive starts (including playoffs) to his name, but clearly something was bothering him last season. We did not see the same quarterback in December that expertly carved up the Bills and Seahawks in September.

The decline was not just randomness or old age setting in. Shortly after Rivers' season went south, reports came out that he was playing for weeks through a "very severe rib injury," which is how tight end Antonio Gates described the injury that only appeared on the official injury report *after* his comments

went public. Rivers once played an AFC Championship Game on a torn ACL, so of course he would gut out a rib injury. But like any player, he still needs his health to be truly effective. If not for some incredible fourth-quarter heroics in Baltimore and San Francisco, the Chargers would have dropped five straight games to close the season. Watching Rivers lead touchdown drive after touchdown drive in those fourth quarters showed he still has plenty left in the tank, but he never had the time to fully heal last season. While Rivers hasn't yet done it in the postseason, he is on the short list of quarterbacks with the talent to go on a hot streak and pace a team through a championship run. It's a lot easier for him to do that when the team around him is built to play at a high level, and the Chargers have made some moves in an effort to do so for Rivers in 2015.

Running back was a troubled position for San Diego last season. Injuries once again limited Ryan Mathews to just six games, and his time in San Diego is over. Donald Brown was a huge disappointment in free agency after a career year in Indianapolis. In 2013, Brown led the league with 2.7 yards per rush *after first contact*. In San Diego, Brown averaged just *2.6 yards per carry* (1.6 after contact). Danny Woodhead was lost after three games to a broken leg and ankle. Branden Oliver was a pleasant surprise, but has limitations as a featured back. About the only thing San Diego did consistently well on the ground was draw plays. The Chargers led the league again with 62 draws (average team: 16.8) and ranked seventh in DVOA on those plays.

On the surface, it's understandable why San Diego was fed up with this committee approach and wanted a workhorse back. One of the draft's boldest moves was trading two mid-round picks to move up two spots to select Wisconsin running back Melvin Gordon at No. 15. (Apparently, the Chargers feared Houston would draft Gordon to replace an aging Arian Foster.) Not a single running back was drafted in the first round in 2013 or 2014, but many people viewed this year's draft as having minimal impact players at other positions. Throw in some recent success for second-round backs like Le'Veon Bell, Eddie Lacy, and Jeremy Hill, all of which would go much higher in a redraft with hindsight, and the atmosphere was more conducive to San Diego going this direction.

We are still going to criticize the pick anyway. This might be a case of a team's past is clouding its future judgment. LaDainian Tomlinson was a fantastic player for San Diego and was at his best in Rivers' early years. Ever since his decline, the running game was never the same around Rivers. Tomlinson was a perfect example of a first-round pick playing at a Hall-of-Fame level for the team that drafted him. There has not been another running back like that since Adrian Peterson in 2007, but even his impact has its limitations. The Vikings are 51-52-1 in the games Peterson has played, but when he was paired with a strong quarterback like Brett Favre in 2009, Minnesota nearly reached the Super Bowl.

That's probably the thought process with pairing Gordon with Rivers, but since 2008 there has been a bit of a drought in first-round running back production, especially if we look at what the 15 players gave the teams that drafted them (Table 2). We looked at their average rank in rushing DVOA (qualified seasons only) and how the team fared in playoff games when each back played. As of July, seven of the 15 backs are either retired or free agents. Injuries have taken their toll on this list, but only three of the backs remain with the team that drafted them. Several of these players were on offenses with future Hall of Fame quarterbacks, but that did not help them achieve their own star status.

Perhaps it's fitting that Chris Johnson tops the list in production, because Gordon plays like a young Johnson with less top-end speed, but more power. Gordon had a very prolific finish to his college career. Last season he rushed for 2,587 yards, second in FBS history to only Barry Sanders (2,628 yards in 1988). Gordon rushed for 408 yards against Nebraska, setting a single-game NCAA record that lasted a week. He should help those yards after contact numbers for the Chargers, but Gordon isn't another Marshawn Lynch. Gordon is very elusive and dynamic in the open field, though there are concerns about his ability to play on every down given his pass protection and limited receiving numbers (just 22 catches) in college. Rivers has always loved to have a receiving back, and he has played with some of the best ever in Tomlinson, Darren Sproles, and Woodhead. That makes Woodhead's return good news for the Chargers. In 2013, Rivers completed 76-of-87 passes to the checkdown demigod and he was surely missed last season. Still, it's not great for creating mismatches if defenses know Gordon has to come off for Woodhead in passing situations. That's why if you draft a running back this high, you hope that he truly is an every-down workhorse, and Gordon will have high expectations right away.

Diversifying the offense is crucial, especially when it appears head coach Mike McCoy has fallen victim to the play-action fallacy. Our research has shown the efficiency of a team's running game does not correlate strongly with the success of its play-action passing game, but we have found some correlation between how often a team runs the ball and how often it *uses* play-action. Coaches think you can't effectively use play-action without a good running game, but McCoy's Chargers are a perfect counterpoint. In 2013 the Chargers used play-action the least of any offense, but ranked second in DVOA when they did use it. With 2014's running game in the dumps, San Diego used play-action on just 8.0 percent of its dropbacks, the second-lowest rate of any team since 2008. Yet Rivers continued to thrive, posting the second-highest DVOA (90.3%) on play-action passes since 2008.

While San Diego's play-action efficiency would likely decrease with a higher usage rate, there's still no excuse to be last in the league at using something you do better than anyone else. If it takes putting a big name like Gordon in the backfield for McCoy to implement more play-action into his offense, then the Chargers should be a better offense in 2015.

Of course you still need an offensive line keeping Rivers upright after those fakes, and opening up holes for Gordon, who was stuffed for a loss or no gain on 19.2 percent of his

Table 2. First-Round Running Backs Since 2008

Year	Pick	Running Back	Draft Team	Seasons	GP	GS	Rush YPG	YPC	Rush TD	Avg Rk Rush DVOA	PO Record	Current Team
2008	24	Chris Johnson	TEN	6	95	93	83.8	4.57	50	25.2	0-1	FA
2012	31	Doug Martin	TB	3	33	33	72.8	4.14	14	30.0	0-0	-
2010	12	Ryan Mathews	SD	5	60	52	67.7	4.40	23	18.8	1-1	PHI
2008	23	Rashard Mendenhall	PIT	5	57	48	62.3	4.11	29	27.0	2-1	Retired
2012	3	Trent Richardson	CLE	2	17	17	62.1	3.54	11	39.0	0-0	OAK
2009	12	Knowshon Moreno	DEN	5	60	45	57.8	4.10	26	23.8	2-2	FA
2008	13	Jonathan Stewart	CAR	7	90	28	53.6	4.63	30	15.2	1-2	-
2008	4	Darren McFadden	OAK	7	83	63	51.2	4.09	25	33.1	0-0	DAL
2011	28	Mark Ingram	NO	4	50	21	48.5	4.17	20	18.3	1-1	-
2009	31	Beanie Wells	ARI	4	51	23	48.5	3.95	24	32.0	1-1	Retired
2010	9	C.J. Spiller	BUF	5	70	36	47.4	4.97	12	19.0	0-0	NO
2010	30	Jahvid Best	DET	3	22	15	43.0	3.71	6	44.0	0-0	Retired
2008	22	Felix Jones	DAL	5	64	23	42.6	4.79	11	20.8	1-1	FA
2009	27	Donald Brown	IND	5	66	20	36.0	4.31	17	18.8	3-2	SD
2012	32	David Wilson	NYG	3	21	6	24.0	4.38	5	N/A	0-0	Retired

carries last season according to NFL.com. San Diego's decision to ignore offensive linemen in the draft was interesting given the struggles up front and the hits that accumulated on Rivers that led to his decline last year. Rivers was actually pressured just as often in the last 10 games (21.5 percent) as the first six (21.7 percent), but the pressure started being more effective. His sack rate went from 4.1 percent to 6.5 percent, and that's mostly on the line allowing quick pressure. The Chargers had the third-highest rate of short sacks (less than 2.6 seconds after the snap) at 56.8 percent.

San Diego's best answer was signing left guard Orlando Franklin from Denver, creating a massive left side of the line with tackle King Dunlap the most reliable player in the starting five. However, Rivers will have to get used to life without center Nick Hardwick and guard Jeromey Clary, a duo that combined to start 229 games for San Diego. Both retired this offseason.

Rivers still has some unrivaled familiarity at receiver. Rivers, Malcom Floyd, and Antonio Gates are teammates for the 12th consecutive season, which ties the NFL record set by the unlikely QB-WR-TE trio of Pat Ryan, Wesley Walker, and Mickey Shuler for the 1978-1989 Jets. San Diego has gotten a lot more production out of its trio, but this is possibly their last waltz together since all three will be unrestricted free agents in 2016. Gates is going on 36 and may just retire after this year. We keep hearing that Ladarius Green will be his successor, but Green had fewer targets (25) last year than he had in 2013 (30).

The 2014 Chargers had a very unique receiving distribution. They are one of four offenses in NFL history with four 750-yard receivers, but they are the only one in that group without any receiver over 860 yards. That's how tight the distribution was. Keenan Allen actually had the least efficient season among the four after a strong rookie performance in 2013, but he's still the No. 1 target. Eddie Royal is gone, but Stevie Johnson seems like a perfect fit for this offense with his ability to get separation in intermediate routes. This is the best quarterback situation Johnson has ever had, so it would not be a surprise to see him return to prominence.

San Diego has to remain an offensive-driven team as coordinator John Pagano continues searching for improvement with a defense that has finished better than average just one time in the past seven years (No. 7 in 2010). Striking a new deal with safety Eric Weddle seems like a good idea heading into 2015, but the Chargers just have not been able to secure the long-term future of their best player on either side of the ball. Instead, in early June San Diego locked up Corey Liuget for five years and over $51 million after four pretty unremarkable seasons. This puts Liuget in an exclusive club of just four 3-4 defensive ends making an average of $10 million per season, but his production in the passing game (top-tier linemen aren't paid just to stop the run) completely pales in comparison to the others according to our charting data (Table 3). No one expects J.J. Watt production, but Liuget has a lot to prove.

In the best-case scenario, Liuget lives up to his new deal immediately with a career season and Weddle honors his contract with another All-Pro performance, while Brandon Flowers and Jason Verrett establish themselves as one of the league's best cornerback duos. Melvin Ingram and Manti Te'o both stay healthy, one providing a steadier pass rush and the other tackling every (living) thing in sight. The new offensive line clicks, sparking Gordon to an Offensive Rookie of the Year award with a great highlight reel full of big plays. Allen returns to his rookie form and Johnson cracks 1,000 yards again. Gates emerges from the Lazarus Pit after his four-game PED suspension. Rivers remains the same immobile, bolo-tie wearin', trash-talkin', shot-put throwin' son of a gun for the whole season, and McCoy never punts on fourth-and-short at midfield in the fourth quarter of a two-score game again.

Even in that best-case scenario, the Chargers still feel like another 9-7 team that will be scrapping for a playoff berth in Week 17. San Diego has finished in third place in the AFC West in both of McCoy's seasons so far. In theory, quarterback is the area where San Diego should gain ground on second-tier AFC contenders like the Chiefs, Dolphins, and Bills. If the Chargers return to their usual trend of finishing strong, then the schedule favors a playoff push. San Diego does not play Denver until December, including a Week 17 meeting at Mile High. The Chargers also have to travel to Kansas City (Week 14) and host playoff hopeful Miami (Week 15). That's a chance to stay relevant, San Diego. There's also that slight chance we are looking at the Carson City Chargers in 2016, complete with none of the team's best players from the last decade.

This is a pivotal year indeed.

Scott Kacsmar

Table 3. The Richest 3-4 Defensive Ends in the NFL, 2011-2014 Production

Player	Team	$/Year	GP	GS	Snaps/Game	Sack	Hit	Hur	FF	Stop	Dfts	BTkl
J.J. Watt	HOU	$16.7 M	64	64	58.2	57	112	143	12	297	153	14
Cameron Jordan	NO	$11 M	64	63	54.8	29	23	80	5	165	55	9
Calais Campbell	ARI	$11 M	59	58	59.2	30.5	35	79	4	223	90	15
Corey Liuget	SD	$10.3 M	63	61	42.2	18	19	46.5	5	134	55	4

2014 Chargers Stats by Week

Wk	vs.	W-L	PF	PA	YDF	YDA	TO	Total	Off	Def	ST
1	at ARI	L	17	18	290	403	1	-34%	-23%	16%	5%
2	SEA	W	30	21	377	288	1	22%	37%	15%	0%
3	at BUF	W	22	10	333	292	0	12%	20%	6%	-2%
4	JAC	W	33	14	407	320	3	19%	19%	-2%	-1%
5	NYJ	W	31	0	439	151	1	44%	21%	-22%	1%
6	at OAK	W	31	28	423	396	1	-12%	38%	52%	1%
7	KC	L	20	23	251	365	-1	12%	18%	13%	7%
8	at DEN	L	21	35	306	425	-2	-16%	19%	31%	-3%
9	at MIA	L	0	37	178	441	-4	-120%	-90%	22%	-8%
10	BYE										
11	OAK	W	13	6	300	233	1	2%	-9%	-5%	7%
12	STL	W	27	24	410	317	0	38%	22%	-24%	-8%
13	at BAL	W	34	33	440	350	-2	25%	45%	15%	-5%
14	NE	L	14	23	216	397	1	-34%	-40%	-20%	-14%
15	DEN	L	10	22	288	337	-2	24%	6%	-22%	-5%
16	at SF	W	38	35	446	447	0	-7%	9%	12%	-4%
17	at KC	L	7	19	361	251	-3	-23%	-21%	-14%	-15%

Trends and Splits

	Offense	Rank	Defense	Rank
Total DVOA	7.0%	11	4.9%	25
Unadjusted VOA	5.7%	11	3.7%	22
Weighted Trend	3.6%	10	2.2%	21
Variance	11.9%	30	4.7%	11
Average Opponent	-4.0%	2	-0.4%	18
Passing	29.4%	7	16.2%	25
Rushing	-14.2%	25	-8.0%	15
First Down	-7.3%	23	9.0%	26
Second Down	11.5%	8	-12.7%	4
Third Down	29.3%	4	24.9%	30
First Half	7.2%	12	5.5%	24
Second Half	6.9%	9	4.1%	23
Red Zone	4.3%	12	-11.6%	9
Late and Close	22.4%	5	9.9%	27

Five-Year Performance

Year	W-L	Pyth W	Est W	PF	PA	TO	Total	Rk	Off	Rk	Def	Rk	ST	Rk	Off AGL	Rk	Def AGL	Rk	Off Age	Rk	Def Age	Rk	ST Age	Rk
2010	9-7	11.0	9.4	441	322	-6	15.4%	8	15.5%	4	-10.0%	7	-10.2%	32	34.2	24	27.1	20	27.4	16	27.5	14	27.1	9
2011	8-8	8.7	7.4	406	377	-7	0.7%	16	13.0%	5	10.8%	29	-1.6%	23	53.4	30	25.2	14	28.0	6	28.0	5	26.4	10
2012	7-9	8.0	6.6	350	350	+2	-9.0%	22	-10.0%	24	2.0%	18	3.0%	8	14.8	6	15.0	6	28.4	2	27.8	6	27.1	2
2013	9-7	9.2	8.8	396	348	-4	6.4%	12	23.1%	2	17.5%	32	0.8%	15	43.8	22	16.2	7	27.5	10	25.8	28	26.0	17
2014	9-7	8.0	8.0	348	348	-5	-0.6%	16	7.0%	11	4.9%	25	-2.7%	23	39.5	24	35.3	13	27.9	4	26.7	17	26.6	4

2014 Performance Based on Most Common Personnel Groups

SD Offense					SD Offense vs. Opponents					SD Defense				SD Defense vs. Opponents			
Pers	Freq	Yds	DVOA	Run%	Pers	Freq	Yds	DVOA	Run%	Pers	Freq	Yds	DVOA	Pers	Freq	Yds	DVOA
11	73%	6.1	19.6%	26%	Base	20%	4.1	-17.5%	71%	Base	36%	5.4	3.7%	11	51%	6.1	11.7%
12	19%	4.4	-14.3%	63%	Nickel	61%	5.9	19.1%	31%	Nickel	45%	5.7	6.7%	12	19%	5.0	-8.4%
13	5%	2.9	-39.3%	82%	Dime+	18%	6.4	20.3%	11%	Dime+	18%	6.3	5.4%	21	13%	6.1	14.3%
02	1%	12.9	199.9%	0%	Goal Line	1%	0.7	-9.2%	57%	Goal Line	1%	0.8	-2.5%	22	5%	3.3	-11.7%
14	1%	0.7	38.1%	33%	Big	1%	4.7	59.5%	71%					13	4%	3.7	-16.1%

Strategic Tendencies

Run/Pass		Rk	Formation		Rk	Pass Rush		Rk	Secondary		Rk	Strategy		Rk
Runs, first half	38%	16	Form: Single Back	84%	4	Rush 3	10.6%	6	4 DB	24%	19	Play action	8%	32
Runs, first down	48%	18	Form: Empty Back	4%	18	Rush 4	58.1%	20	5 DB	49%	24	Avg Box (Off)	6.12	28
Runs, second-long	27%	23	Pers: 3+ WR	74%	3	Rush 5	25.5%	11	6+ DB	26%	9	Avg Box (Def)	6.31	14
Runs, power sit.	42%	29	Pers: 4+ WR	0%	25	Rush 6+	5.8%	22	CB by Sides	70%	27	Offensive Pace	32.18	26
Runs, behind 2H	23%	26	Pers: 2+ TE/6+ OL	27%	23	Sacks by LB	61.5%	7	DB Blitz	12%	12	Defensive Pace	31.50	31
Pass, ahead 2H	52%	6	Shotgun/Pistol	77%	3	Sacks by DB	7.7%	13	Hole in Zone	9%	4	Go for it on 4th	0.53	30

The Chargers had the league's biggest gap between offense from shotgun/pistol and offense from "standard" formations. From shotgun they had 17.8% DVOA (eighth) and 6.2 yards per play (13th). With Rivers under center, they had -22.5% DVOA (29th) and 3.5 yards per play (32nd). ● San Diego was dead last in using max protect schemes, just 3.1 percent of pass plays. San

Diego and Philadelphia were the only teams below 5.5 percent. ☞ Among the many things that killed Ladarius Green's alleged breakout year: San Diego's use of two-tight end sets dropped from 38 percent of plays to 27 percent, while their use of three or more wideouts rose from 56 percent to 74 percent. ☞ Philip Rivers likes to take his time: this was the fifth straight year the Chargers ranked in the bottom ten for situation-neutral pace. ☞ San Diego ranked seventh in defensive DVOA at home, but had the worst defense in the league on the road.

Passing

Player	DYAR	DVOA	Plays	NtYds	Avg	YAC	C%	TD	Int
P.Rivers	918	12.6%	609	4086	6.7	5.1	67.0%	31	16

Rushing

Player	DYAR	DVOA	Plays	Yds	Avg	TD	Fum	Suc
B.Oliver	20	-5.5%	160	582	3.6	3	0	44%
D.Brown	-51	-23.9%	84	221	2.6	0	0	30%
R.Mathews*	62	11.3%	74	333	4.5	3	1	47%
P.Rivers	3	-10.0%	22	112	5.1	0	1	-
D.Woodhead	-14	-30.3%	15	38	2.5	0	0	33%
R.Brown*	25	31.2%	14	59	4.2	0	0	71%
S.Draughn*	-20	-62.7%	10	19	1.9	0	0	40%

Receiving

Player	DYAR	DVOA	Plays	Ctch	Yds	Y/C	YAC	TD	C%
K.Allen	43	-8.0%	122	78	805	10.3	3.9	4	64%
M.Floyd	252	23.1%	91	52	856	16.5	2.4	6	57%
E.Royal*	183	12.8%	91	62	779	12.6	5.8	7	68%
D.Inman	49	24.0%	17	12	158	13.2	1.2	0	71%
S.Ajirotutu*	-17	-32.2%	12	4	45	11.3	2.5	0	33%
S.Johnson	139	23.4%	50	35	435	12.4	5.3	3	70%
J.Jones	11	-4.1%	18	9	131	14.6	9.2	0	50%
A.Pettis	10	-6.0%	18	12	118	9.8	4.4	1	67%
A.Gates	204	24.1%	98	69	821	11.9	3.7	12	70%
L.Green	41	15.9%	25	19	226	11.9	6.0	0	76%
B.Oliver	68	15.3%	45	36	271	7.5	9.4	1	80%
D.Brown	-22	-23.7%	42	30	213	7.1	9.8	0	71%
R.Mathews	32	37.6%	10	9	69	7.7	7.0	0	90%
R.Brown*	-2	-18.2%	7	4	39	9.8	7.3	0	57%
D.Woodhead	24	46.4%	6	5	34	6.8	6.6	0	83%

Offensive Line

Player	Pos	Age	GS	Snaps	Pen	Sk	Pass	Run	Player	Pos	Age	GS	Snaps	Pen	Sk	Pass	Run
Chad Rinehart*	LG	30	16/16	1067	3	3.0	18.0	7.0	Chris Watt	C/G	25	12/5	483	6	1.5	4.5	4.0
King Dunlap	LT	30	16/16	1058	4	2.5	14.3	0.5	Rich Ohrnberger*	C	29	8/7	449	4	0.5	0.5	5.0
D.J. Fluker	RT	24	16/16	1020	9	6.0	29.3	7.5	Trevor Robinson	C	25	3/1	168	1	1.0	5.0	0.0
Johnnie Troutman	RG	28	15/15	774	3	4.5	12.0	4.0	Orlando Franklin	G	28	16/16	1090	10	0.5	7.0	9.5

Year	Yards	ALY	Rk	Power	Rk	Stuff	Rk	2nd Lev	Rk	Open Field	Rk	Sacks	ASR	Rk	Short	Long	F-Start	Cont.
2012	3.71	3.91	23	60%	21	17%	6	1.01	27	0.41	30	49	8.9%	32	14	19	22	22
2013	4.20	4.26	3	74%	5	12%	1	1.10	17	0.50	27	30	5.9%	8	11	12	21	28
2014	3.51	3.29	31	78%	3	21%	28	0.95	28	0.52	27	37	6.1%	17	21	8	14	27
2014 ALY by direction:		Left End 3.91 (14)			Left Tackle 3.08 (30)			Mid/Guard 3.35 (31)				Right Tackle 3.35 (25)				Right End 2.36 (30)		

It would be nearly impossible for San Diego's offensive line to have more injuries than a year ago, when five different centers started at least one game. The 2014 Chargers' 52.6 adjusted games lost to injury is the highest figure in our database for an offensive line. Shocking Eagles fans everywhere, left tackle King Dunlap turned in another consistent year. He averaged 70.7 snaps per blown block in 2013 and remained steady at 71.3 in 2014 (third best among left tackles). His run blocking was really never in question; he has been credited with just half of a blown block in the running game in his 27 starts with San Diego. The Chargers are hoping for similar improvement from left guard Orlando Franklin, a four-year starter in Denver. He's another massive run blocker, but edge rushers gave him problems with speed at right tackle, and he was demoted from that job after an ugly performance in Super Bowl XLVIII. He's an improvement over Chad Rinehart, but keep in mind that Franklin's 9.5 blown blocks in the running game were the second most among left guards in 2014.

Chris Watt appears to be the Last Center Standing in San Diego after Nick Hardwick retired. Those are big shoes to fill and the stage indeed looked too big at times for Watt as a rookie last year. He was a guard at Notre Dame and had to learn center on the fly thanks to the injuries San Diego had. Watt doesn't have top-end athleticism, but he's smart and has experience at multiple positions.

The line's weakness is the right side. Through early reports from minicamps, the Chargers seem content with keeping Johnnie Troutman at right guard and D.J. Fluker at right tackle. Joe Barksdale was signed in May from St. Louis, but he's a backup who barely charted better than Fluker last season. Though he was considerably better in 2013, Barksdale has been working with the second unit this summer. Fluker has been rumored to move to guard for a long time now, but nothing is official yet. The 2013 first-round pick has really struggled in his first two seasons, credited with more blown blocks (71.3) than any right tackle in that span. Troutman was also mediocre in his first year as a full-time starter, ranking 27th among right guards in snaps per blown block in 2014. It is possible Fluker moves to guard and Barksdale to tackle, but as of press time, San Diego looks to be giving last year's duo one more shot.

Defensive Front Seven

Defensive Line	Age	Pos	G	Snaps	Plays	TmPct	Rk	Stop	Dfts	BTkl	Runs	St%	Rk	RuYd	Rk	Sack	Hit	Hur	Dsrpt
						Overall						vs. Run				Pass Rush			
Corey Liuget	25	DE	16	775	58	7.5%	8	46	22	3	46	80%	31	1.3	17	4.5	6	18.5	2
Kendall Reyes	26	DE	16	643	32	4.1%	59	26	6	4	29	83%	27	2.0	38	1.0	5	10.5	0
Sean Lissemore	28	DT	15	331	29	4.0%	--	20	2	1	28	68%	--	3.5	--	1.0	1	2.5	0
Ricardo Mathews	28	DE	12	297	19	3.3%	--	13	4	0	15	73%	--	2.3	--	1.5	3	7.0	0
Tenny Palepoi	25	DE	16	276	16	2.1%	--	12	4	2	16	75%	--	1.4	--	0.0	1	1.0	0

Edge Rushers	Age	Pos	G	Snaps	Plays	TmPct	Rk	Stop	Dfts	BTkl	Runs	St%	Rk	RuYd	Rk	Sack	Hit	Hur	Dsrpt
						Overall						vs. Run				Pass Rush			
Dwight Freeney*	35	OLB	16	573	11	1.4%	87	10	7	4	6	83%	17	1.2	6	3.0	6	25.5	0
Jarret Johnson*	34	OLB	15	548	52	7.2%	17	30	9	0	38	63%	75	3.3	68	1.0	2	6.5	1
Melvin Ingram	26	OLB	9	497	30	6.9%	18	18	10	4	21	52%	83	4.4	82	4.0	4	12.5	1
Jeremiah Attaochu	22	OLB	11	178	9	1.7%	--	7	3	1	6	67%	--	5.5	--	2.0	0	6.5	1

Linebackers	Age	Pos	G	Snaps	Plays	TmPct	Rk	Stop	Dfts	BTkl	Sack	Hit	Hur	Runs	St%	Rk	RuYd	Rk	Tgts	Suc%	Rk	AdjYd	Rk	PD	Int
						Overall					Pass Rush			vs. Run					vs. Pass						
Donald Butler	27	ILB	14	706	73	10.8%	57	31	8	4	1.0	0	1.5	46	46%	85	4.6	76	15	35%	--	9.7	--	2	0
Manti Te'o	24	ILB	10	457	62	12.8%	41	33	9	4	1.5	0	1.5	36	61%	54	3.5	48	14	70%	--	3.4	--	3	1
Andrew Gachkar*	27	ILB	15	382	36	5.0%	--	25	11	3	1.0	0	2	20	70%	--	2.2	--	13	68%	--	3.6	--	0	0
Kavell Conner	28	ILB	16	348	57	7.4%	--	36	4	5	1.0	0	1	43	70%	--	3.2	--	12	34%	--	6.8	--	1	0

Year	Yards	ALY	Rk	Power	Rk	Stuff	Rk	2nd Level	Rk	Open Field	Rk	Sacks	ASR	Rk	Short	Long
2012	3.81	3.80	7	59%	10	23%	7	1.18	15	0.54	8	38	7.0%	8	14	11
2013	4.46	4.45	31	73%	26	16%	27	1.39	30	0.55	11	35	6.9%	15	10	12
2014	4.03	4.02	20	58%	9	20%	14	1.20	22	0.56	7	26	5.5%	27	7	8
2014 ALY by direction:		Left End 3.37 (10)			Left Tackle 4.48 (27)			Mid/Guard 3.94 (14)			Right Tackle 4.79 (25)			Right End 3.95 (17)		

There was a good stretch when writers had it easy with San Diego's front seven. You simply cited them as one of the most talented teams, only needing to point to players like Shawne Merriman, Jamal Williams, Luis Castillo, and Shaun Phillips as the proof. The on-field results spoke loudly as well. But in the last five years, the focus has been stuck on all the players that simply didn't pan out. If we weren't writing about draft busts such as Larry English and Jonas Mouton, we were writing about Melvin Ingram's injuries, or the ghost of Dwight Freeney and the ghosts of Manti Te'o's past. The Chargers have not been able to find a front-seven player worthy of star status for several years now.

However, they think they have one in Corey Liuget after extending him to a five-year deal with over $30 million guaranteed. Liuget simply has not been a player for whom opposing offenses have to game-plan every week, but he's going to get more attention than ever this year from fans expecting more out of him. Kendall Reyes is the other young defensive end and he matched Liuget's 2012-13 production quite well, which is just more reason to be suspicious of Liuget's big contract. Last year was a different story, but Reyes is only going into his third year as a full-time starter. You can stereotype Reyes, Ricardo Matthews, and rarely-used nose tackle Sean Lissemore as 3-4 linemen who are supposed to just occupy blockers and let the linebackers get the glory, though they're not that effective at doing so.

It's not like the stud linebackers were really present to take advantage anyway. For being 34, Freeney actually wasn't that bad last season. His 25.5 quarterback hurries were as many as Jarret Johnson, Melvin Ingram, and rookie Jeremiah Attaochu had combined on 650 more snaps. The problem is that at age 34, that spin move just doesn't spin as fast as it used to, so Freeney only finished three plays for sacks. With Freeney gone, Attaochu (second-round pick in 2014) and Tourek Williams (third-year player with one career sack) have to step up. Both may play often since Ingram has missed 19 games in the last two years. He needs to stay healthy. San Diego traded up to the 50th spot to draft Attaochu, so ideally you'd like to see him get the starting job, but the Chargers will take anyone with a pulse for pass-rushing right now.

At interior linebacker, Donald Butler's poor performance against the run in 2013 only got worse in 2014. Te'o missed six more games due to injury, but was more assertive in his second season and continued to show good awareness when in coverage. The splash plays just haven't come around yet in his game. San Diego drafted Denzel Perryman (Miami) in the second round. Look for him to steal playing time and eventually replace Butler as the heavy-hitter against the run this defense has been lacking.

Defensive Secondary

Secondary	Age	Pos	G	Snaps	Plays	TmPct	Rk	Stop	Dfts	BTkl	Runs	St%	Rk	RuYd	Rk	Tgts	Tgt%	Rk	Dist	Suc%	Rk	AdjYd	Rk	PD	Int
												vs. Run					**vs. Pass**								
Eric Weddle	30	FS	16	1021	112	14.5%	3	45	16	3	58	43%	32	7.1	42	19	5.3%	12	7.7	58%	28	7.2	32	6	1
Marcus Gilchrist*	27	SS	16	988	81	10.5%	34	34	17	6	39	38%	42	7.1	44	42	12.0%	62	9.1	54%	36	7.6	42	3	1
Shareece Wright*	28	CB	14	828	67	9.9%	17	30	8	6	22	59%	13	4.9	16	68	23.3%	36	13.5	46%	57	7.8	37	9	0
Brandon Flowers	29	CB	14	816	62	9.2%	30	28	8	3	12	42%	35	6.5	37	68	23.9%	40	14.7	59%	9	8.9	56	9	3
Jahleel Addae	25	FS	11	431	44	8.3%	--	14	6	7	24	38%	--	6.5	--	8	5.0%	--	8.8	54%	--	8.0	--	1	0
Richard Marshall*	31	CB	8	280	19	4.9%	--	4	1	1	2	100%	--	0.5	--	19	18.9%	--	17.2	32%	--	12.1	--	0	0
Jason Verrett	24	CB	6	219	23	7.9%	--	9	1	0	5	80%	--	4.2	--	25	32.0%	--	14.1	55%	--	5.9	--	3	1
Jimmy Wilson	29	FS	14	781	59	8.3%	54	19	9	12	19	47%	25	7.7	51	35	12.9%	65	9.7	43%	60	8.5	54	3	1
Patrick Robinson	28	CB	14	612	47	6.7%	69	17	7	4	5	20%	65	6.6	38	51	20.7%	21	11.7	53%	27	7.0	21	10	2

Year	Pass D Rank	vs. #1 WR	Rk	vs. #2 WR	Rk	vs. Other WR	Rk	vs. TE	Rk	vs. RB	Rk
2012	18	21.6%	27	-17.3%	5	-11.2%	8	-12.0%	5	23.4%	29
2013	31	24.7%	31	24.5%	32	3.4%	18	-5.1%	11	7.9%	22
2014	25	-3.6%	13	11.2%	26	12.9%	26	-4.0%	16	17.3%	27

The secondary should be the strength of this defense, but every position has some type of question mark hanging over it. Safety Eric Weddle is the Philip Rivers of the defense and he's coming off another All-Pro season. Like Rivers, he will be a free agent in his thirties in 2016, so he's looking for that last monster contract. His attempt at a holdout did not work, and Weddle was likely frustrated to see the team pay Liuget instead. He should return to camp with his teammates and give his best in a contract year, but this could be the end of the road in San Diego for Weddle. The player alongside him at strong safety remains a mystery. Marcus Gilchrist is gone after an unremarkable season. Jahleel Addae has charted well in limited playing time, but keep in mind we're talking about 18 targets in two years. Jimmy Wilson has experience at cornerback and safety, but he missed 12 tackles last season after just one missed tackle in 2013. In a division that added a couple of No. 1 receivers (Jeremy Maclin and Amari Cooper) to go with the entire Denver passing game, the Chargers need to tighten things up on the back end.

Cornerback gets an upgrade as the weak links, Shareece Wright and Richard Marshall, are both gone. Starter Brandon Flowers was an outstanding pickup in June. He proved his value on a one-year deal and signed for four more years and $36 million in March. At 29, Flowers should still have some prime years ahead of him. He also had three of the team's seven interceptions, the lowest total in Chargers history. Flowers is not likely to be a high-pick guy since he is better suited to playing zone coverage instead of pressing receivers physically, but he limits big plays. Flowers has ranked in the top 10 in adjusted success rate in two of his last three seasons with the down year (2013 in Kansas City) related to a poor scheme fit.

While most teams are going for size at cornerback, the Chargers have the 5-foot-10 Flowers and 5-foot-9 Jason Verrett, who saw his stock rising before a shoulder injury ended his season after six games. Some scouts thought the size disadvantage would be too severe, but Verrett showed good ball skills with a game-clinching interception against Oakland. The knock that may have legitimacy is that his small frame could lead to a lack of durability, but if Verrett stays healthy, then the Chargers should have a really solid duo of corners for the next several years. Patrick Robinson comes over from New Orleans with 33 starts and nine interceptions on his resume. He should be a big part of the nickel package this year. San Diego also drafted Texas State cornerback Craig Mager in the third round, but he's more likely to contribute his physicality on special teams in 2015.

Special Teams

Year	DVOA	Rank	FG/XP	Rank	Net Kick	Rank	Kick Ret	Rank	Net Punt	Rank	Punt Ret	Rank	Hidden	Rank
2012	3.0%	8	6.4	7	7.7	6	3.2	9	-4.9	22	2.4	11	2.8	9
2013	0.8%	15	3.4	11	-0.8	17	-2.2	19	7.4	7	-3.8	21	-0.1	15
2014	-2.7%	23	0.6	13	-8.3	29	-1.4	20	-3.0	20	-1.6	13	-0.4	19

Fifteen players had at least 13 tackles on special teams last year, and the Chargers had four of them. Darrell Stuckey (16) ranked second in the league, the departed Seyi Ajirotutu (15) was tied for third, and Kavell Conner (14) and Andrew Gachkar (13) were very active as well. Unfortunately, the Chargers gunners were able to get so many tackles because they had to face so many kickoff and punt returns.

The biggest problem was on kickoffs, where Nick Novak was worth minus-15.8 points of field position less than an average kicker by our gross kickoff value metric. That's the lowest value of any kicker in the past three seasons. Novak only produced a touchback 12.8 percent of the time; the league's other kickers averaged 52.4 percent. This is not a one-year fluke either. Since the NFL moved kickoffs to the 35-yard line in 2011, only four teams have managed a touchback rate under 20 percent, including the 2013 Chargers (19.6 percent). Novak is adequate on field goals and he even played emergency punter when Mike Scifres was injured last year, but he's not getting the job done on kickoffs. Scifres had a mediocre punting season before suffering a fractured clavicle after Donald Brown blew a block against the Patriots. (Goddammit, Donald, again.)

Rookie Chris Davis handled kick return duties, and was slightly below average. Keenan Allen and Eddie Royal split the punt returns again, and each had one return of 29-plus yards after never breaking one for more than 28 yards in 2013. Royal left for Chicago, but the Chargers added Jacoby Jones in free agency. There's a good chance the 31-year-old just takes over both return jobs. He ranked second in kick return value in 2014 with the Ravens.

San Francisco 49ers

2014 Record: 8-8	**Total DVOA:** 6.6% (11th)	**2015 Mean Projection:** 6.8 wins	**On the Clock (0-4):** 20%
Pythagorean Wins: 7.0 (24th)	**Offense:** -0.4% (16th)	**Postseason Odds:** 19.9%	**Mediocrity (5-7):** 41%
Snap-Weighted Age: 27.1 (5th)	**Defense:** -10.1% (5th)	**Super Bowl Odds:** 2.0%	**Playoff Contender (8-10):** 31%
Average Opponent: 2.1% (8th)	**Special Teams:** -3.0% (24th)	**Proj. Avg. Opponent:** 4.4% (2nd)	**Super Bowl Contender (11+):** 9%

2014: It's better to burn out than to fade away.

2015: Maybe nobody wants to play for the 49ers because of the housing prices.

After three straight years of regular season dominance and postseason heartbreak, the San Francisco 49ers crashed back to 8-8 last season. Though it seemed to come out of nowhere, in hindsight the signs of this collapse are plain to see. Years of strange power moves in the front office and poor results in the draft room led to the collapse of 2014, and the strangest move of them all came at the end of the year, with the dismissal of one of the winningest coaches the league has ever seen. The 49ers are confident that they can win without Jim Harbaugh, but we think they're about to learn some much needed lessons in humility.

In some ways, the 49ers resemble Icarus from Greek mythology. For those of you who have forgotten reading Edith Hamilton in high school, Icarus was the son of Daedalus, the master craftsman who built the Labyrinth for King Minos. Father and son attempted to flee the island of Crete with wings of feathers and wax. Daedalus warned his son not to fly too close to the sun, but Icarus paid him no heed, foolishly believing he was too gifted to fail. As he soared higher and higher, the wax in his wings melted, and he fell to the sea to his doom.

No, the analogy isn't perfect. Daedalus specifically warned Icarus to avoid flying too high or too low, which means he wanted his son to go 8-8 every year like the Miami Dolphins. But the point is not that the 49ers' future is bleak specifically because they were oh-so-close to three different Super Bowl wins. The point is, Icarus was too arrogant to see his own limitations, and a similar sort of arrogance might have cost the 49ers their shot at glory.

The problems in San Francisco's front office can be seen in the forced dismissal of a key decision-maker with a strong track record of success, and no, we're not talking about Harbaugh. To truly understand the failures of 2014, we must first go back to 2010. That's when the 49ers parted ways with Scot McCloughan, their top player personnel man since 2005. He drafted most of the players who made San Francisco's three-year championship chase under Harbaugh possible, including Pro Bowlers like Frank Gore, Vernon Davis, Ahmad Brooks, Patrick Willis, Joe Staley, and Dashon Goldson, as well as long-term starters like Alex Smith, Parys Haralson, Delanie Walker, Ray McDonald, and Michael Crabtree. He also signed Justin Smith, perhaps the team's biggest free-agent acquisition since Deion Sanders. McCloughan's last two drafts in San Francisco were less successful, but his tenure in the Bay Area was still one that any general manager would be proud to emulate.

Then, barely a month before the 2010 draft, the 49ers suddenly announced that McCloughan had been given "an extended leave of absence." Public and private messages from both sides made it clear this separation would be permanent. Team owner Jed York, just 28 at the time, issued a statement calling the decision "mutual" and said it was made for "private personnel reasons." He then went deep underground. David White of the *San Francisco Chronicle* wrote that the move had been made "strictly for personal reasons" and "not for football reasons." Michael Silver, then with Yahoo!, reported that McCloughan had been "blindsided" by his dismissal. Silver also suggested it was part of a power move by Paraag Marathe, then San Francisco's Vice President of Football Operations, now the team's president.

With McCloughan unavailable for that year's draft, the 49ers turned to Trent Baalke, who has managed every draft for San Francisco since then. And Baalke had some success early on, as his first two drafts netted Anthony Davis, Mike Iupati, NaVorro Bowman, Aldon Smith, and Colin Kaepernick. (It should be pointed out that McCloughan traded away a 2009 second-round pick for a 2010 first-rounder, and Baalke used that first-rounder on Iupati.) Since 2012, though, things have been dreadful. In the past three drafts, only one player drafted by Baalke has developed into a regular starter, Pro Bowl safety Eric Reid. When you compare McCloughan's track record in San Francisco to Baalke's, it's obvious why the team's fortunes have turned around so quickly (Table 1, next page).

(The table lists McCloughan and Baalke as "GM" because their official job titles changed frequently. McCloughan was Vice President of Player Personnel from 2005-07, and General Manager in 2008-09. Baalke ran his first draft in McCloughan's absence as Director of Player Personnel, then was named Vice President of Player Personnel a month later, but was not officially named as a General Manager until 2011. York even admittedly blanked on Baalke's job title in the press conference following Harbaugh's firing. It's almost as if the front office is shuffling names around and has no idea what it is doing.)

To be sure, this data comes with plenty of caveats. It does not evaluate where a player was drafted, or a team's ability to trade up or down in the draft, or to trade for veteran players.

2015 49ers Schedule

Week	Opp.	Week	Opp.	Week	Opp.
1	MIN (Mon.)	7	SEA (Thu.)	13	at CHI
2	at PIT	8	at STL	14	at CLE
3	at ARI	9	ATL	15	CIN
4	GB	10	BYE	16	at DET
5	at NYG	11	at SEA	17	STL
6	BAL	12	ARI		

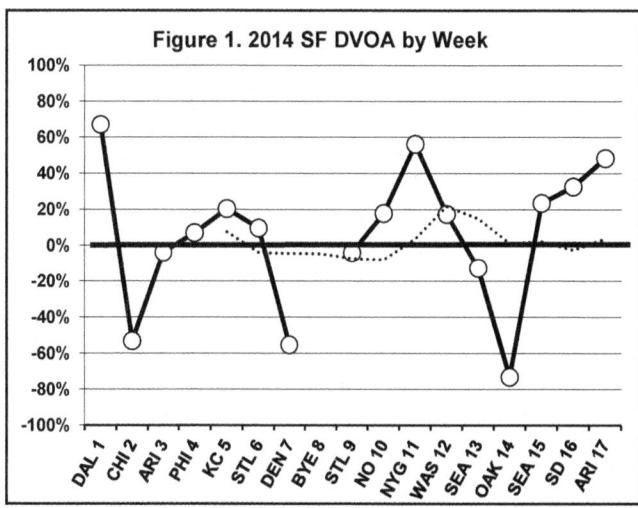

Figure 1. 2014 SF DVOA by Week

It looks only at the players each team has drafted and a rough summary of their careers. Also, the more recent the draft, the more difficult it is going to be to accurately measure its quality. We all have a very good idea of how the 2005 draft worked out, but the fate of the 2014 draft is still to be determined.

With that said, the fact remains that no team has gotten less out of the draft since 2012 than San Francisco. That season was the peak of the Harbaugh era, as the 49ers came within one failed red zone drive of a championship, but in hindsight it was clearly the beginning of the end times. The 49ers' draft that year featured the selections of wide receiver A.J. Jenkins in the first round and running back LaMichael James in the second. Jenkins was traded to Kansas City a year later and has only 17 catches in his career. James, now in Miami, has never started an NFL game and has only 44 career rushes. And then came the third round, which is a fascinating study in "what might have been." Baalke traded his third-round pick to the Colts in exchange for a fourth-rounder in 2012 and a fifth-rounder in 2013, kicking off a bevy of trades that ended up with Baalke trading away three picks to get five, with four other picks passing through his hands in the process. Now, we generally believe in the idea of trading down to get more picks, but only one of the players involved in these transactions turned into a starter for San Francisco, safety Eric Reid. Meanwhile, the two picks that Baalke gave Dallas to move up to get Reid turned into Pro Bowl center Travis Frederick and starting wideout Terrance Williams, while a couple of the

other picks involved in this complex tangle turned into T.Y. Hilton and Lamar Miller. Baalke clearly knows how to work the phones in the draft room, but he hasn't been nearly as successful scouting players in the film room.

McCloughan has since revealed that in his last two years in San Francisco, he was waging a battle with alcoholism that cost him his marriage, so the 49ers could be forgiven for cutting ties with him in 2010. He also said, however, that York had approached him about a separation, and McCloughan had only accepted the deal because he didn't want to work for a team that didn't want him there. Instead, he joined old buddy John Schneider in Seattle (the two were scouts for Green Bay in the 1990s), where he helped the Seahawks have the best draft of 2011 *and* 2012, as measured by approximate value. McCloughan left the team last year and is now GM in Washington, but while he was in Seattle, the team drafted Richard Sherman and Malcolm Smith, the two players involved in the NFC championship game interception that effectively killed the monster McCloughan had created in San Francisco. Eighteen months after that game, only 12 of San Francisco's 22 starters remain. Seven have left in free agency or were released, and three more have retired. And Baalke has failed to find suitable replacements for most of them.

To be brutally honest, it has been all downhill for Baalke since his first week on the job when he made the decision to hire Jim Harbaugh. In a very brief career, Harbaugh accomplished almost everything a coach can in the NFL, with one obvious exception. He finishes with a 44-19-1 regular-season record. Only four coaches (Guy Chamberlin, John Madden, Vince Lombardi, and George Allen) can top a .695 winning percentage, and all four of those guys are in Canton. Harbaugh also went 5-3 in the playoffs, with one loss in overtime and two coming down to failed red zone drives in the final minutes of the game.

And for all that success, there were still signs of trouble brewing. Rumors broke in February of 2014 that the 49ers had considered trading Harbaugh to the Browns. Cleveland owner Jimmy Haslam told *USA Today* that there had been an "opportunity" to get Harbaugh. York first denied the rumors entirely, then admitted that Cleveland had made contact about the deal,

Table 1: San Francisco Drafts Under McCloughan and Baalke

Year	"GM"	Starter Seasons	Rank	Total AV	Rank
2005	McCloughan	27	3	230	3
2006	McCloughan	23	5	158	14
2007	McCloughan	28	1	267	1
2008	McCloughan	4	30	61	27
2009	McCloughan	7	t-22	57	28
2005-09	*McCloughan*	*89*	*1*	*773*	*3*
2010	Baalke	12	7	145	3
2011	Baalke	6	t-18	96	t-7
2012	Baalke	0	32	12	32
2013	Baalke	2	22	31	t-22
2014	Baalke	0	t-24	20	t-11
2010-14	*Baalke*	*20*	*t-25*	*317*	*8*

but he told Matt Barrows of the *Sacramento Bee*, "We want Jim to be our head coach, and we've said that very clearly."

Ten months later, Harbaugh was gone amid reports that he wasn't getting along with Baalke. Harbaugh accepted the head job at Michigan within the week, while York said in a press conference that Harbaugh's dismissal had been a mutual decision. (Sound familiar?)

"This wasn't us saying, 'Jim, you're fired, you're not here anymore," York said. "This wasn't Jim saying, 'I don't want to be there, I'm leaving.' It was a discussion that took place over a decent amount of time to figure out what's best for everybody involved. It was the conclusion that we came to, it wasn't an easy conclusion for anybody, but that's where we ended up."

Taylor Price, covering that press conference for the team's own website, noted that York had "strongly hinted that other NFL teams were interested in trading for [Harbaugh] once the 49ers were eliminated from playoff contention. But rather than entertain such requests, York said he had enough respect for Harbaugh to let him decide where he wanted to coach next."

York did his best to put himself in a good light, as if he had been unfairly forced to manage a disgruntled employee and was doing all he could to make everyone happy. There's only one problem: It's all lies. "I was told I wouldn't be the coach anymore," Harbaugh said two months later in a podcast interview with Tim Kawakami of the *San Jose Mercury News*. "I didn't leave the 49ers. I felt like the 49er hierarchy left me."

Regardless, Harbaugh was out the door, and the team needed a new head coach. That didn't concern York, who said, referring to Harbaugh and Baalke, "I think we've demonstrated that we can make good hires." In York's mind, apparently, it's easy to find a good coach.

Baalke conducted a lengthy search, and flew to Denver to meet with Broncos offensive coordinator Adam Gase. The next day, 49ers assistant Jim Tomsula was promoted to Harbaugh's old position. It was some odd timing, and it at least gave the impression that Baalke had tried and failed to woo Gase, taking Tomsula as Plan B. (Gase ended up as the new offensive coordinator in Chicago.)

Tomsula has coached the San Francisco defensive line since 2007, working not only for Harbaugh but also for Mike Singletary and Mike Nolan. Prior to that he spent nine years as a coach in NFL Europe. His only head coaching experience: guiding the Rhein Fire to a 6-4 record in 2006, and winning one game as interim coach in San Francisco after Singletary was fired in 2010. While he is popular with his players, he is also viewed as a company man who won't meddle in Baalke's moves.

Tomsula isn't the only coach in a new position on the roster.

Offensive coordinator Greg Roman and defensive coordinator Vic Fangio left for those same positions with the Bills and Bears, respectively. Replacing Roman will be Geep Chryst, who has been coaching in the NFL for 23 years, including the last four years working with the quarterbacks in San Francisco. In his only prior experience as coordinator, he guided a Chargers offense which ranked 28th in DVOA in 1999, then 29th in 2000. In his defense, his quarterbacks there were Ryan Leaf and, of all people, Jim Harbaugh, at the very end of his playing career.

Meanwhile, Eric Mangini, who has been coaching San Francisco's tight ends since 2011, takes over as defensive coordinator. He had that same position with New England in 2005, then spent three years as head coach of the Jets and two more in charge of the Browns. That's six years as a head coach or defensive coordinator, but none of his defenses have ever ranked higher than 14th in DVOA, and four of them ranked 25th or worse.

To recap: the 49ers now have an owner who can't be trusted, a GM who can't draft good players, a head coach with almost no experience, and coordinators who have never successfully coordinated anything on either side of the ball. Maybe that's why many of their good players are deciding to retire rather than show up for work. Granted, Justin Smith is 36 this year, and Patrick Willis was forced out by bad feet. But Chris Borland and Anthony Davis are in their mid-20s, and both walked away from the game, citing health concerns over long-term concussion damage. To be fair, Jake Locker and Jason Worilds also shockingly retired this offseason, and neither of them played in San Francisco. Still, you've got to think the toxic environment around the team played a part in some of these decisions. And on top of the retirements, the 49ers lost four other defensive players who started at least 10 games last year. It's the second straight offseason they turned over two of their top three cornerbacks.

If there is hope for 2015, it's that Chryst will be able to reverse Kaepernick's decline, the team's very old receiving corps will fight off Father Time, and Carlos Hyde's tackle-busting ways (he ranked fourth in broken tackle rate among running backs last year) can overcome the shortcomings on the offensive line. And perhaps Mangini's experience will help him manage aging veterans like Darnell Dockett, Glenn Dorsey, Antoine Bethea, and Ahmad Brooks, while Aldon Smith regains his pre-suspension form and NaVorro Bowman recovers from his devastating knee injury.

Or, Icarus fails to repair his wings, and falls into the sea again.

Vincent Verhei

2014 49ers Stats by Week

Wk	vs.	W-L	PF	PA	YDF	YDA	TO	Total	Off	Def	ST
1	at DAL	W	28	17	319	382	4	67%	40%	-26%	1%
2	CHI	L	20	28	359	216	-4	-53%	-39%	15%	0%
3	at ARI	L	14	23	318	338	1	-4%	27%	22%	-10%
4	PHI	W	26	21	407	213	3	7%	-7%	-46%	-33%
5	KC	W	22	17	357	265	1	20%	5%	-12%	3%
6	at STL	W	31	17	432	309	0	10%	4%	-8%	-2%
7	at DEN	L	17	42	310	419	-1	-55%	-8%	48%	2%
8	BYE										
9	STL	L	10	13	263	193	0	-4%	-29%	-38%	-14%
10	at NO	W	27	24	330	423	2	18%	-3%	-18%	3%
11	at NYG	W	16	10	333	330	4	56%	1%	-65%	-10%
12	WAS	W	17	13	312	213	-2	17%	-9%	-26%	1%
13	SEA	L	3	19	164	379	-3	-13%	-26%	-18%	-4%
14	at OAK	L	13	24	248	330	-2	-73%	-35%	42%	3%
15	at SEA	L	7	17	245	290	1	23%	7%	-15%	1%
16	SD	L	35	38	447	446	0	32%	19%	-11%	3%
17	ARI	W	20	17	395	397	3	48%	43%	3%	8%

Trends and Splits

	Offense	Rank	Defense	Rank
Total DVOA	-0.4%	16	-10.1%	5
Unadjusted VOA	-3.3%	20	-6.8%	6
Weighted Trend	-1.8%	15	-11.3%	5
Variance	6.1%	9	9.2%	30
Average Opponent	-0.8%	13	1.4%	8
Passing	5.8%	21	-7.6%	4
Rushing	2.5%	8	-13.5%	10
First Down	-14.7%	27	-18.4%	2
Second Down	9.2%	10	-11.1%	6
Third Down	11.4%	12	7.4%	19
First Half	17.4%	6	-14.7%	2
Second Half	-18.8%	27	-5.4%	8
Red Zone	0.3%	14	-13.6%	7
Late and Close	-10.3%	23	-17.4%	4

Five-Year Performance

Year	W-L	Pyth W	Est W	PF	PA	TO	Total	Rk	Off	Rk	Def	Rk	ST	Rk	Off AGL	Rk	Def AGL	Rk	Off Age	Rk	Def Age	Rk	ST Age	Rk
2010	6-10	6.8	6.9	305	346	-1	-11.2%	24	-11.1%	24	-1.4%	15	-1.5%	20	20.6	11	6.7	3	25.8	28	27.6	11	25.6	29
2011	13-3	12.3	10.8	380	229	+2	18.6%	6	-3.9%	18	-14.6%	3	7.8%	2	29.6	16	8.8	2	26.5	23	26.7	21	26.6	7
2012	11-4-1	11.4	12.5	397	273	+9	29.5%	4	16.5%	5	-14.4%	3	-1.5%	20	11.7	5	4.5	1	27.1	14	27.3	10	26.9	5
2013	12-4	11.5	10.6	406	272	+12	17.4%	7	9.1%	8	-4.6%	13	3.7%	7	34.7	17	46.8	27	27.8	5	27.4	9	26.9	4
2014	8-8	7.0	9.0	306	340	+7	6.6%	11	-0.4%	16	-10.1%	5	-3.0%	24	30.0	15	71.8	31	27.6	6	26.8	16	26.4	8

2014 Performance Based on Most Common Personnel Groups

SF Offense					SF Offense vs. Opponents					SF Defense					SF Defense vs. Opponents			
Pers	Freq	Yds	DVOA	Run%	Pers	Freq	Yds	DVOA	Run%	Pers	Freq	Yds	DVOA	Pers	Freq	Yds	DVOA
11	40%	5.7	14.8%	22%	Base	53%	5.2	0.0%	56%	Base	41%	4.9	-10.2%	11	54%	5.8	-3.8%
21	26%	6.2	11.2%	55%	Nickel	31%	5.5	9.9%	24%	Nickel	46%	5.5	-12.4%	12	20%	4.7	-23.6%
12	12%	4.7	-13.3%	41%	Dime+	13%	6.3	21.7%	13%	Dime+	11%	7.3	10.7%	21	10%	6.0	12.4%
22	11%	4.1	-9.4%	73%	Goal Line	1%	1.8	-48.2%	54%	Goal Line	0%	0.3	4.0%	10	3%	5.5	-20.5%
01	3%	4.8	-41.4%	4%	Big	1%	4.7	-2.5%	86%	Big	2%	1.7	-35.4%	13	3%	3.5	-23.2%

Strategic Tendencies

Run/Pass		Rk	Formation		Rk	Pass Rush		Rk	Secondary		Rk	Strategy		Rk
Runs, first half	39%	13	Form: Single Back	57%	31	Rush 3	11.1%	4	4 DB	28%	14	Play action	20%	19
Runs, first down	52%	9	Form: Empty Back	9%	7	Rush 4	67.3%	11	5 DB	56%	20	Avg Box (Off)	6.50	3
Runs, second-long	31%	14	Pers: 3+ WR	46%	29	Rush 5	16.6%	29	6+ DB	15%	12	Avg Box (Def)	6.20	25
Runs, power sit.	58%	14	Pers: 4+ WR	6%	4	Rush 6+	4.9%	26	CB by Sides	95%	2	Offensive Pace	31.35	23
Runs, behind 2H	29%	11	Pers: 2+ TE/6+ OL	28%	21	Sacks by LB	57.1%	10	DB Blitz	6%	28	Defensive Pace	30.72	26
Pass, ahead 2H	45%	22	Shotgun/Pistol	53%	23	Sacks by DB	2.9%	23	Hole in Zone	4%	23	Go for it on 4th	1.08	13

As expected, the 49ers made significant changes to their personnel tendencies in 2014 after years of Jim Harbaugh holding out against the move to more spread, multiple-wide receiver sets. They went from 22 percent (32nd in 2013) to 46 percent (29th) of plays using three or more wide receivers, and dropped from 52 percent (third in 2013) to 28 percent (21st) of plays using two or more tight ends. However, the 49ers were still the only offense in the NFL using four different packages for at least 10 percent of plays. ☜ The percentage of San Francisco runs coming from two-back sets dropped from 78 percent in 2013 to 58 percent in 2014, but that was still second in the league behind only St. Louis. Running more out of one-back formations worked well for the 49ers, who had one of the largest gaps between performance by running backs out of one-back sets (4.7 yards per carry, 15.3% DVOA) and two-back sets (3.7, -17.1%). ☜ In Jim Harbaugh's first three seasons as head coach, the 49ers had been one of the top play-action teams in the league, with DVOA over 50% on play-action passes each season. In 2014, however, the 49ers were actually better *without* play-action, putting up -1.4% DVOA and 5.3 yards per pass on play-action but 18.7% DVOA and 6.5 on other pass plays. ☜ San Francisco's offensive DVOA disintegrated as the game went on: 23.2% (third) in the first quarter, 12.5% (eighth) in the second quarter, -6.5% (21st) in the third quarter, and -29.3% (29th) in the fourth quarter or overtime. ☜ For the second straight year, opponents blitzed a defensive back on just 8.2 percent of San Francisco pass plays, and for the second straight year, Colin Kaepernick killed these blitzes, with 8.8 yards per pass in 2014. ☜ San Francisco and Tampa Bay tied for the NFL lead with 151 penalties, including declined and offsetting. ☜ The 49ers recovered only 4 of their 15 fumbles on offense last season. ☜ On defense, the 49ers allowed a league-low -23.4% DVOA on play-action passes, along with 6.5 yards per play (seventh). ☜ Random, Inexplicable 49ers Stat of the Year: San Francisco ranked 31st in pace when trailing and 31st in pace when leading but was somehow the fifth fastest offense in the league when the game was tied.

Passing

Player	DYAR	DVOA	Plays	NtYds	Avg	YAC	C%	TD	Int
C.Kaepernick	91	-8.4%	532	3033	5.7	4.8	60.5%	19	10
B.Gabbert	22	37.7%	7	38	5.4	1.7	42.9%	1	0

Rushing

Player	DYAR	DVOA	Plays	Yds	Avg	TD	Fum	Suc
F.Gore*	154	6.3%	255	1106	4.3	4	2	50%
C.Kaepernick	88	7.5%	88	653	7.4	1	4	-
C.Hyde	38	3.0%	83	333	4.0	4	1	46%
A.Smith*	-2	-16.4%	7	19	2.7	0	0	29%
B.Miller	-21	-60.2%	6	12	2.0	0	1	50%
B.Ellington	31	66.4%	6	28	4.7	1	0	-
R.Bush	17	-2.4%	75	289	3.9	2	0	43%

Receiving

Player	DYAR	DVOA	Plays	Ctch	Yds	Y/C	YAC	TD	C%
A.Boldin	222	9.3%	131	83	1062	12.8	4.8	5	63%
M.Crabtree*	24	-9.9%	108	69	702	10.2	3.9	4	64%
S.Johnson*	139	23.4%	50	35	435	12.4	5.3	3	70%
B.Lloyd*	12	-8.1%	35	14	294	21.0	5.3	1	40%
B.Ellington	11	-1.5%	12	6	62	10.3	5.5	2	50%
Q.Patton	-18	-37.2%	8	3	44	14.7	0.0	0	38%
T.Smith*	310	26.8%	92	49	767	15.7	3.4	11	53%
V.Davis	-66	-28.4%	51	26	245	9.4	1.9	2	51%
D.Carrier	-22	-30.6%	14	9	105	11.7	4.1	0	64%
V.McDonald	-46	-99.1%	7	2	30	15.0	13.0	0	29%
B.Miller	95	52.2%	25	18	189	10.5	7.6	2	72%
F.Gore*	-1	-14.4%	19	11	111	10.1	9.3	1	58%
C.Hyde	-21	-38.5%	16	12	68	5.7	5.4	0	75%
R.Bush	-18	-19.6%	57	41	261	6.4	6.5	0	72%

Offensive Line

Player	Pos	Age	GS	Snaps	Pen	Sk	Pass	Run	Player	Pos	Age	GS	Snaps	Pen	Sk	Pass	Run
Joe Staley	LT	31	16/16	1054	12	5.0	23.0	7.0	Daniel Kilgore	C	28	7/7	449	1	0.0	2.0	3.0
Mike Iupati*	LG	28	15/15	944	4	6.0	20.0	5.5	Anthony Davis	RT	26	7/7	428	5	2.5	11.0	0.5
Alex Boone	RG	28	15/14	941	4	5.5	9.5	4.0	Joe Looney	G	25	15/4	328	3	0.0	3.5	1.0
Jonathan Martin*	RT	26	15/9	645	2	5.5	17.0	0.5	Erik Pears	G	33	16/16	1062	5	3.0	13.5	3.0
Marcus Martin	C	22	8/8	512	4	5.5	8.5	0.0									

Year	Yards	ALY	Rk	Power	Rk	Stuff	Rk	2nd Lev	Rk	Open Field	Rk	Sacks	ASR	Rk	Short	Long	F-Start	Cont.
2012	4.30	4.08	14	63%	16	20%	21	1.26	11	0.76	16	35	6.2%	14	8	12	22	26
2013	3.95	3.95	12	58%	25	19%	13	1.05	20	0.68	16	36	6.8%	14	14	7	13	29
2014	4.15	4.05	10	48%	32	21%	19	1.26	6	0.59	24	52	9.8%	30	19	18	14	22

2014 ALY by direction:	Left End 3.53 (22)	Left Tackle 4.53 (4)	Mid/Guard 4.01 (16)	Right Tackle 3.1 (27)	Right End 4.82 (7)

Retirements: 1

The 49ers were prepared for the free agent departures of Mike Iupati and Jonathan Martin, but the retirement of Anthony Davis caught them completely off guard, coming several weeks after the draft and months after free agency began. As a result of all these moves, the 49ers are left with just one sure thing: Joe Staley will still be one of the league's better left tackles, even if he's coming off a down year in 2014, when he blew twice as many blown blocks per snap as he did in either of the prior two seasons.

After Staley, things get murky in a hurry. The favorite to start at left guard is Brandon Thomas, a Clemson product who tore his ACL shortly before the 2014 draft. The 49ers took him 100th overall, knowing he would effectively redshirt his rookie season. He's loaded with talent and size (317 pounds, 34 3/4-inch arms), but he has never taken a snap in an NFL game. Erik Pears comes over from Buffalo, where he alternated between right guard and right tackle, and he will likely play the latter position in San Francisco; he has also played right tackle for the Raiders and Broncos, and even started at left tackle as a rookie in Denver in 2006. Alex Boone has started 46 games at right guard for the 49ers in the last three seasons. He has tackle size at 6-foot-7 and 330 pounds, and there is a chance that he and Pears will swap spots. The center spot looks like a battle between Daniel Kilgore and Marcus Martin. Kilgore, a fifth-round draftee in 2011, never started an NFL game until last year, when he started the first seven games of the year at center before breaking his leg. Martin, a third-round rookie out of USC, took over from there, with Joe Looney also starting one game at the position. Martin is also a candidate to start at either guard spot, though that versatility could actually hurt him if San Francisco opts to keep him on the bench as a multipurpose super sub. Looney is also still around and fighting, though it would be surprising to see him win a first-string role.

The 49ers also spent two late-round picks on linemen, and they have a better than average chance to start this year given the mess in front of them. Sixth-rounder Ian Silberman played tackle at Boston College, but looks more like a guard in the NFL. Seventh-rounder Trent Brown might go the other way; he played guard at Florida, but 6-foot-8 and 355 pounds, he has size to spare if the 49ers want to move him outside.

Defensive Front Seven

Defensive Line	Age	Pos	G	Snaps	Plays	Overall TmPct	Rk	Stop	Dfts	BTkl	Runs	St%	vs. Run Rk	RuYd	Rk	Sack	Pass Rush Hit	Hur	Dsrpt
Justin Smith*	36	DE	16	694	42	5.4%	34	32	10	2	34	76%	56	2.8	73	5.0	9	12.8	0
Ray McDonald*	31	DE	14	693	39	5.7%	27	27	7	1	33	73%	69	2.8	76	3.0	5	10.5	0
Tony Jerod-Eddie	25	DE	16	420	18	2.3%	89	13	2	1	17	71%	79	3.0	83	0.0	3	8.0	0
Quinton Dial	25	DT	14	327	30	4.4%	--	22	4	4	27	70%	--	2.1	--	2.0	2	2.5	1
Ian Williams	26	DT	9	214	23	5.3%	--	19	5	1	19	79%	--	2.2	--	1.0	0	3.5	1

Edge Rushers	Age	Pos	G	Snaps	Plays	Overall TmPct	Rk	Stop	Dfts	BTkl	Runs	St%	vs. Run Rk	RuYd	Rk	Sack	Pass Rush Hit	Hur	Dsrpt
Ahmad Brooks	31	OLB	13	603	33	5.2%	37	27	9	5	20	75%	39	4.2	79	6.0	5	5.5	3
Aaron Lynch	22	OLB	16	514	25	3.2%	78	21	7	1	12	83%	17	3.5	71	6.0	11	20.8	3
Dan Skuta*	29	OLB	14	386	28	4.1%	61	18	10	4	15	67%	69	2.9	59	5.0	2	4.0	1

Linebackers	Age	Pos	G	Snaps	Plays	Overall TmPct	Rk	Stop	Dfts	BTkl	Sack	Pass Rush Hit	Hur	Runs	St%	vs. Run Rk	RuYd	Rk	Tgts	Suc%	vs. Pass Rk	AdjYd	Rk	PD	Int
Michael Wilhoite	29	ILB	16	1014	91	11.7%	46	50	16	8	0.0	3	5.5	51	67%	29	3.4	41	46	55%	18	6.3	30	6	2
Chris Borland*	24	ILB	14	476	104	15.3%	22	68	21	6	1.0	0	4.5	69	75%	11	2.8	20	29	52%	28	5.6	18	5	2
Patrick Willis*	30	ILB	6	343	37	12.7%	43	14	6	1	0.0	2	3.5	18	50%	81	3.6	54	19	63%	7	3.5	1	2	1
Philip Wheeler	31	OLB	15	379	45	5.9%	--	30	5	1	0.0	0	1.5	33	73%	--	2.8	--	15	47%	--	10.7	--	0	0

Year	Yards	ALY	Rk	Power	Rk	Stuff	Rk	2nd Level	Rk	Open Field	Rk	Sacks	ASR	Rk	Short	Long
2012	3.68	3.92	15	60%	17	19%	16	0.97	1	0.42	2	38	6.4%	17	16	10
2013	3.88	4.12	22	66%	18	14%	31	0.99	6	0.42	2	38	6.0%	29	9	14
2014	4.04	4.16	25	71%	25	16%	26	1.00	6	0.59	9	36	6.6%	16	10	17
2014 ALY by direction:		Left End 3.78 (20)			Left Tackle 4.01 (21)			Mid/Guard 4.33 (28)			Right Tackle 3.7 (13)			Right End 4.39 (27)		

Retirements: 3

Justin Smith's retirement was not a surprise. The list of defensive linemen who are still effective past their mid-30s is very short, and the list of men in their mid-30s who want to deal with the pain of recovering from playing professional football each week is even shorter. Pain also pushed Patrick Willis out of the league. His retirement was not expected, but given that he missed ten games last year with foot injuries and turned 30 in the week before the Super Bowl, the 49ers had to suspect that his prime playing years were over. Chris Borland's departure, on the other hand, was completely unpredictable. The Wisconsin product announced his retirement only ten months after San Francisco made him a third-round draft pick. In just 14 games and only eight starts, Borland put together one of the greatest demonstrations of run stuffing since Football Outsiders started tracking defensive stats. The rookie ranked in the NFL's top 20 in run tackles, top 10 in run stops, and top five in run defeats, even though he was not one of the top 350 players in snaps played. Borland started every game from Week 7 on, and in that time-frame, he made 12 more run tackles, 17 more run stops, and two more run defeats than any other player. He also led the NFL in total stops and percentage of team plays in Weeks 7-17, and finished third in defeats, tied with Lavonte David behind top-flight pass rushers J.J. Watt and Justin Houston. Borland was largely a two-down player, but it's not as if his coverage numbers were terrible in a small sample size. He was one of the most brilliant one-year players in league history. And now he's gone.

The good news is that NaVorro Bowman, who missed all of 2014 after shredding his knee in the 2013 NFC Championship Game, will return. Bowman was one of the most active linebackers in the league before his injury, ranking sixth or better in percentage of his team's plays every year from 2011 to 2013. He is expected to be ready to go for the season opener, and though concerns remain about his effectiveness following his knee injury, NaVorro Bowman at 80 percent is still better than many starters in the league. His partner inside will be Michael Wilhoite, who spent several years hanging around the bottom of San Francisco's depth chart and then suddenly started 16 games last year. The club nearly traded him before the draft when it appeared he'd be stuck behind the Willis-Bowman-Borland logjam; thank goodness they couldn't find any takers. There are question marks on the outside. Aldon Smith was a non-factor after his suspension last year, with only two sacks (both against Washington, one of the worst pass-blocking teams in the league) in seven games. Ahmad Brooks has been a rock in San Francisco for four years now, but he missed three games last year and just turned 31. In March, he was accused of sexual assault by the same woman who claimed former 49ers player Ray McDonald raped her, and was named as a co-defendant in her lawsuit against McDonald. In a part-time role, Aaron Lynch tied for the team lead with six sacks, five of them coming in a six-game stretch between October and November. The rookie fell to the fifth round of the draft due to concerns about his work ethic and effort, and after he was drafted, his strength and conditioning coach at South Florida tweeted that integrity and character must not be important in San Francisco. In other words, despite his early success, Lynch still has a lot to prove.

With McDonald and Justin Smith out the door, the 49ers could field a starting defensive line that played a combined zero NFL snaps in 2014. Nose tackle Glenn Dorsey returns after a torn biceps put him on the sidelines. He'll line up next to Darnell Dockett, signed away from Arizona in free agency. Dockett missed only two games in his first ten NFL seasons, but he missed all of 2014 with a torn ACL, and he turned 34 in May. Oregon's Arik Armstead, the 15th pick in this year's draft, has elite athleticism and a 6-foot-7 frame, but he's raw, and it's not clear that he'll be ready to start this year. Tank Carradine, a 2013 second-rounder who had three sacks in just 146 snaps last year, should see plenty of action on passing downs, while Quinton Dial, Ian Williams, and Tony Jerod-Eddie will provide nearly a half-ton of depth.

Defensive Secondary

Secondary	Age	Pos	G	Snaps	Plays	TmPct	Rk	Stop	Dfts	BTkl	Runs	St%	Rk	RuYd	Rk	Tgts	Tgt%	Rk	Dist	Suc%	Rk	AdjYd	Rk	PD	Int
Antoine Bethea	31	SS	16	1039	96	12.4%	18	46	21	11	45	60%	9	5.0	13	33	7.9%	31	14.3	51%	48	6.9	28	9	4
Perrish Cox*	28	CB	15	940	69	9.5%	22	25	9	4	7	14%	71	8.4	55	87	23.1%	35	15.5	51%	38	7.7	35	16	5
Eric Reid	24	FS	15	879	45	6.2%	66	14	10	4	20	15%	69	11.9	71	21	6.0%	16	15.7	59%	21	4.6	3	6	3
Chris Culliver*	27	CB	14	821	59	8.7%	36	22	9	3	9	33%	44	7.1	45	74	22.6%	31	16.0	58%	12	6.2	12	13	4
Dontae Johnson	24	CB	16	490	35	4.5%	--	13	6	4	9	33%	--	8.9	--	46	23.6%	--	14.1	49%	--	6.7	--	6	1
Jimmie Ward	24	CB/FS	8	262	19	4.9%	--	4	0	1	3	0%	--	8.7	--	20	19.2%	--	12.0	34%	--	8.4	--	2	0
Shareece Wright	28	CB	14	828	67	9.9%	17	30	8	6	22	59%	13	4.9	16	68	23.3%	36	13.5	46%	57	7.8	37	9	0

Year	Pass D Rank	vs. #1 WR	Rk	vs. #2 WR	Rk	vs. Other WR	Rk	vs. TE	Rk	vs. RB	Rk
2012	6	-10.3%	10	-16.2%	7	2.1%	21	-9.5%	7	-17.0%	8
2013	10	-9.5%	11	-1.2%	14	-0.6%	14	-15.0%	8	-13.6%	7
2014	4	-6.0%	11	-22.4%	4	-11.8%	8	-9.7%	9	-16.5%	8

Retirements: None, it turns out.

Eric Reid has started every game but one since the 49ers made him the 18th overall pick of the 2013 draft, but that one exception was due to a concussion, one of three Reid has suffered in two seasons. He told the *San Francisco Chronicle* that "If I have another concussion and I don't feel like I can play any more, then I won't." He later claimed the paper had twisted his words and he was not considering retirement, but one can hardly blame anyone in the Bay Area media for jumping to that specific conclusion these days. Reid's game, like his name, is similar to Ed Reed—he plays very deep off the line and specializes in preventing big plays. The 49ers' defense was third in DVOA against deep passes last year, even though a league-leading 26 percent of passes thrown by San Francisco opponents qualified as deep (16-plus yards through the air). Reid's coverage range allows Antoine Bethea to crowd the line of scrimmage. In his first year in San Francisco, Bethea was third among safeties in defeats. Despite his physical style, Bethea has been remarkably durable. Between the 49ers and Colts, Bethea hasn't missed a start since 2007. The 49ers also have good depth here, with former St. Louis starter Craig Dahl; 2014 first-rounder Jimmie Ward, who was limited to eight games last year with assorted foot and leg injuries; and second-round rookie Jaquiski Tartt, a 6-foot-1, 221-pound thumper.

The bad news for the 49ers is that just one year after they lost Carlos Rogers and Tarell Brown, they must once again replace both starting cornerbacks, this time Chris Culliver and Perrish Cox. One replacement will be free-agent signing Shareece Wright, who showed improvement with the Chargers last season. In his first year as a starter in 2013, he ranked in the 80s in both success rate and yards per pass allowed, while finishing third among corners in target rate. In plain English: opponents threw at him early, they threw at him often, and they threw at him with great success. Last year, he was mediocre, which was a huge step in the right direction. Tramaine Brock was supposed to be a starter for the 49ers last season, but he missed 13 games with a myriad of leg woes. He showed promise as a nickelback in 2013, and will get his second chance at starting this year. The 49ers don't have much depth here beyond 2014 fourth-rounder Dontae Johnson. Ward also figures to spend a lot of time in the slot.

Special Teams

Year	DVOA	Rank	FG/XP	Rank	Net Kick	Rank	Kick Ret	Rank	Net Punt	Rank	Punt Ret	Rank	Hidden	Rank
2012	-1.5%	20	-17.8	32	-2.6	23	-0.6	19	13.4	4	0.3	15	-2.0	21
2013	3.7%	7	5.9	6	10.0	3	-4.6	26	10.7	3	-3.6	20	2.0	12
2014	-3.0%	24	-2.0	22	0.7	14	-0.8	17	-8.3	28	-4.8	25	-6.4	25

Retirements: None, but plenty of strange punter-related moves.

Drafting a punter is almost never a good idea, but that has never stopped Trent Baalke before, and so he took Clemson's Bradley Pinion in the fifth round this year. It was especially surprising because the 49ers already had Andy Lee, a three-time All-Pro who currently has the fifth-highest gross average in NFL history. Baalke then traded Lee to Cleveland for a 2017 seventh-round draft pick. That's about as close as you'll ever see to a team giving away a Pro Bowler for nothing, but there are hints of reason behind these moves. Lee was a top-four punter in our coverage-independent gross punt value metric in 2012 and 2013, but fell to 26th last year. Furthermore, Pinion figures to save San Francisco more than $2 million in cap space per season compared to what Lee would have cost, so we might have to give Baalke the benefit of the doubt here. (Of course, if he just wanted to save money, Baalke also could have just signed a college free agent after the draft like most any other team would have done.) Pinion can also kick off, and might get a chance for an extra-long field goal—he has made them from 65 yards.

Phil Dawson's last few years have been similar to Lee's: He was a top-ten kicker in 2012 (with Cleveland) and 2013, but slumped in 2014. Bruce Ellington split return duties with Perrish Cox and Carlos Hyde last season, but with Cox in Tennessee and Hyde starting, Ellington figures to see the bulk of the returns this fall. He was eminently mediocre in both tasks last year. Craig Dahl is the lead tackler on San Francisco's nondescript coverage units.

Seattle Seahawks

2014 Record: 12-4	**Total DVOA:** 31.9% (1st)	**2015 Mean Projection:** 10.7 wins	**On the Clock (0-4):** 1%
Pythagorean Wins: 11.9 (1st)	**Offense:** 16.8% (5th)	**Postseason Odds:** 75.0%	**Mediocrity (5-7):** 10%
Snap-Weighted Age: 25.8 (30th)	**Defense:** -16.8% (1st)	**Super Bowl Odds:** 25.2%	**Playoff Contender (8-10):** 34%
Average Opponent: 0.8% (13th)	**Special Teams:** -1.7% (19th)	**Proj. Avg. Opponent:** 1.2% (14th)	**Super Bowl Contender (11+):** 56%

2014: The most controversial play call in Super Bowl history leads to the greatest change of fortune in Super Bowl history.

2015: It's a long road to redemption, but they clearly enter the season as the best team in football.

They should have run it. Of course they should have run it. It's not the only reason they lost the Super Bowl, and it will have virtually no impact on their upcoming campaign. The fate of the Seattle Seahawks this season will hinge on names like Jimmy Graham and Cary Williams, not Malcolm Butler or Brandon Browner. On paper, the Seahawks are better now than they were when they nearly won a championship in February, and as the rest of the NFC West has fallen off a bit, their path to a third straight appearance in the Super Bowl seems clear. Whether it's fair or not, though, the lasting memory of last year's Seahawks will be the result of their final offensive play. If you're a regular Football Outsiders reader, you probably want to know what the numbers say about it. Well, the numbers are clear: they should have run it. So before we move on to the new developments of 2015, let's end the discussion of the last play of 2014.

Anyone who paid to read this book already knows the basics: trailing 28-24 in the final minute of the game, Seattle had a second-and-goal at the 1. Most expected a Marshawn Lynch run, but Seahawks offensive coordinator Darrell Bevell had other ideas, and Russell Wilson threw a slant pass to Ricardo Lockette. Brandon Browner jammed Jermaine Kearse at the line, and then Malcolm Butler jumped the route, intercepting the ball, and knocking Lockette and the Seahawks flat on their backs.

This would have been a bad call in a vacuum, but given the strengths of this particular offense, and the weaknesses of this specific defense, it is nearly impossible to defend. Seattle's rushing offense DVOA last year was 29.9%, best in the league by an enormous margin and one of the five highest we've recorded in more than a quarter-century of football. New England's defensive DVOA against the run was -10.3%, which ranked 13th last year. Moreover, Seattle's success rate in short-yardage "power" running was 81 percent, tied with Philadelphia for best in the league and one of the 20 best rates we've measured since 1989. And New England? They allowed opponents to convert on power runs 81 percent of the time, the NFL's worst mark in 2014.

Wilson's interception wasn't Seattle's only red zone failure in the Super Bowl. Their first drive in the second half ended in a field goal after Lynch was stuffed on third-and-1. On both that play and the Butler pick, Seattle spread the field with multiple receivers, and New England responded by leaving their corners on islands and packing the box with as many defenders as possible. Seattle's strategy on those plays wasn't unusual—they used three or more wideouts on a league-high 42 percent of short-yardage plays (defined here as any play with 1 or 2 yards to go) in 2014. And it usually worked; their DVOA on those plays was 20.0%, compared to 10.8% with fewer wideouts. Even when opponents responded to these spread formations by stuffing the box, Seattle had great success on rushing plays. Passing plays? Those didn't work out nearly so well (Table 1).

The argument that goal-line interceptions are flukishly rare is accurate, and also completely missing the point. To defend Bevell's play call is to suggest that the pass had a better chance of scoring than a running play, and that is simply false. The Seahawks had a perfect opportunity to win a Super Bowl with their greatest strength matched up against their opponents' most glaring weakness, and they (literally and figuratively) threw it all away.

It might have been those short-yardage incompletions that motivated general manager John Schneider to make the biggest move of Seattle's offseason, trading the team's first-

Table 1: Seattle, Short-Yardage Plays, 2014

	Runs			Passes			All		
	Plays	Suc%	DVOA	Plays	Suc%	DVOA	Plays	Suc%	DVOA
0-1 WR	7	100.0%	39.6%	4	25.0%	-48.5%	11	73.0%	8.4%
2WR	16	68.8%	15.3%	4	50.0%	-4.2%	20	65.0%	12.0%
3+WR	33	72.7%	32.6%	15	46.7%	-10.8%	48	64.6%	20.0%
Loaded Box	24	70.8%	38.9%	7	42.9%	-28.2%	31	64.5%	25.4%
3+WR, loaded	18	72.2%	50.2%	7	42.9%	-28.2%	25	64.0%	29.9%
Overall	56	75.0%	28.2%	23	43.5%	-16.4%	79	65.8%	16.3%

2015 Seahawks Schedule

Week	Opp.	Week	Opp.	Week	Opp.
1	at STL	7	at SF (Thu.)	13	at MIN
2	at GB	8	at DAL	14	at BAL
3	CHI	9	BYE	15	CLE
4	DET (Mon.)	10	ARI	16	STL
5	at CIN	11	SF	17	at ARI
6	CAR	12	PIT		

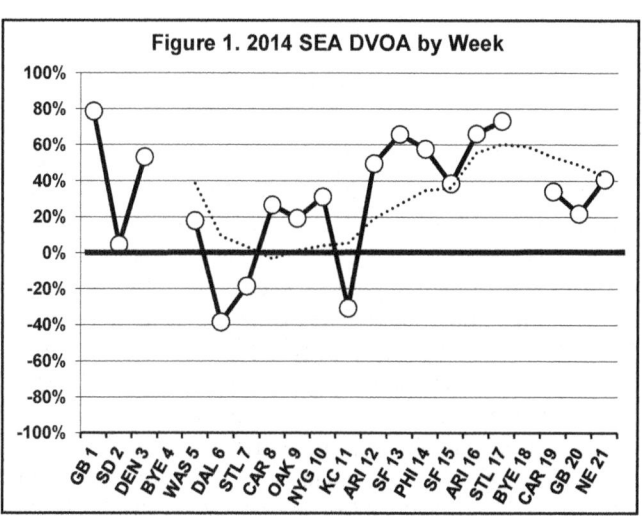

Figure 1. 2014 SEA DVOA by Week

round draft choice and former All-Pro center Max Unger in exchange for New Orleans tight end Jimmy Graham (himself a former All-Pro) and a fourth-rounder. In the last three years, Graham has caught 26 passes in 47 targets with 1 or 2 yards go, leading the league in both categories, and only one of those receptions failed to pick up a first down.

Of course, Graham is a lot more than a short-yardage weapon. He is likely the most talented receiver Seattle has had since Steve Largent retired, and he'll certainly be the most talented receiver with whom Wilson has ever played. He's the most dangerous red zone receiver in the NFL, with a league-high 41 touchdowns inside the 20 since he was drafted in 2010. He also has 111 catches for 1,628 yards and 11 touchdowns over the middle, ranking in the top ten in all three categories over that same timeframe. And though there's some debate over his position—no matter what the NFL's arbitrator ruled, factually Graham is a wide receiver who sometimes plays tight end, not the other way around—the bottom line is that he can put a hand on the ground, flex out to the slot, or split out wide, creating mismatches the likes of which Seattle has never seen before.

It's that versatility that makes Graham so valuable. When he lines up at tight end, he'll draw the defense's attention to the middle of the field, creating opportunities for teammates on the outside. If he splits out wide, that bumps Doug Baldwin down to the second receiver spot and Jermaine Kearse down to third, effectively making the Seahawks better at three positions.

The only question concerning Graham's impact on the Seahawks is how many opportunities he'll get in the passing game. Since Wilson was drafted in 2012, the Seahawks have the most runs and the fewest passes of any team in the league. It's almost certain, though, that they'll be more balanced in 2015. The Graham acquisition cost Seattle not just a top blocker, but also a draft pick which they could have used to replace him. The offensive line hasn't really been a strength in Seattle, and now it's clearly their biggest weakness. Further, there's a question of how many more violent collisions Marshawn Lynch can endure—he'll be 29 this year, and he has a league-high 1,383 carries since he was traded to Seattle in 2010. What happens if he breaks down this year? Christine Michael and Robert Turbin have flashed potential, but they still have fewer than 300 NFL carries between them, and it's impossible to accurately predict how either would fare with a full-time workload. And then there's Graham himself. Seattle didn't pay the cost to get him just so he could set the edge on

zone reads. They won't be passing as frequently as Graham's old team did, but this offense figures to revolve around Russell Wilson more in 2015 than ever before.

Will the fourth-year quarterback be up to the task? Though his standard passing stats have been remarkably consistent in his first three seasons, his advanced stats fell in 2014, and he ranked in the mid-teens in both DYAR and DVOA after finishing in the top ten in both categories two years in a row. That's partly due to the Percy Harvin effect, as Wilson threw more short passes than he ever had before, even after the mercurial (read: dickhead) wideout was traded to New York. All told, 58 percent of Wilson's passes were thrown to receivers within 5 yards of the line of scrimmage in 2014, up from 45 percent the year before. As a result of that, he threw more failed completions (83, up from 60) and averaged fewer yards per pass (7.7, down from 8.2). And it's not just the number of short passes Wilson threw, but when he threw them. On third downs (including fourth-down throws), the average quarterback throws short of the needed yards to go about 40 percent of the time. Wilson threw short a little less than that in 2013, with 38 percent of his third-down passes coming short of the sticks. That number soared to 47 percent of third downs in 2014, as Wilson was suddenly much more willing to dump off. That's bad news—as you'd expect, those short passes are much less likely to pick up a first down (converting 21 percent of the time in 2014) than throws to receivers at or beyond the first-down line (52 percent). That partly explains why Wilson's passing DVOA fell from 12.4% on first downs to 6.0% on second downs, and then to -6.1% on third downs.

Wilson's increased usage of short passes was partly due to a change in offensive philosophy, and partly due to a lack of receivers who were able to get open downfield. Seattle simply didn't have much receiving talent on hand after Golden Tate's departure in free agency and the ensuing Harvin trade. That was abundantly clear in the playoffs. The Seahawks got 78 percent of their postseason receiving yardage from players who entered the league as undrafted free agents, including each of the four wideouts who caught passes in the Super Bowl. This also explains why the front office was so eager to acquire a top-tier target like Graham.

Wilson's passing, of course, is only part of his story. Between option runs and scrambles, Wilson accumulated 849 yards on the ground, good for 269 rushing DYAR. The latter figure is the second-best total for a quarterback in our database, and the highest since Randall Cunningham was terrorizing defensive coordinators in 1990. On the downside, Wilson fumbles a lot—five times on sacks last seasons, four times on snaps or handoffs, and once as a runner. Remarkably, Seattle covered all of those fumbles, and even though Wilson himself recovered half those loose balls (including each blown snap), he obviously won't get that lucky this year. Seattle recovered three of Wilson's six fumbles in 2012, and five of ten in 2013.

While the offense could be evolving before our eyes, the Seahawks have made few changes on defense—and why would they? They weren't as dominant in 2014 as they had been in 2013, but they still led the league in defensive DVOA for the second straight season, the first team to do so since Pittsburgh teams with Rod Woodson and Kevin Greene were running roughshod through the AFC in the early '90s. Nine starters from Super Bowl XLIX will return (and seven of those were starters in Super Bowl XLVIII too). The first of the two changes is at defensive tackle, where Brandon Mebane went on IR in November with a torn hamstring, but is expected back this year. That leaves only one true new starter: Cary Williams, who will take over at cornerback for Byron Maxwell in a free agent "trade" between Seattle and Philadelphia. Williams has started every game the last four seasons between the Eagles and Ravens. His charting numbers have left a lot to be desired, fluctuating wildly and never ranking Williams in the top 25 in either success rate or adjusted yards per pass. In Seattle, he will have the benefit of playing with Earl Thomas, a luxury the likes of which he never enjoyed in Philadelphia. The last time Williams got to play with an All-Pro caliber safety, it was with Ed Reed in Baltimore. That team led the NFL in defensive DVOA in 2011 and then won the Super Bowl in 2012.

Consistency on defense is just one of the many reasons why Seattle starts the 2015 season as clear favorites to win another Super Bowl. The Seahawks have finished first in overall DVOA for three straight years now, the first to do so since the Aikman-Emmitt-Irvin Cowboys dynasty. By snap-weighted age, they were the league's third-youngest team last season, and their key players are all under 30 years old. Their schedule strength is reasonable, and their NFC West rivals look to have taken a collective step backwards, which should clear the way to a division crown and a third consecutive top seed. That would leave them only two wins away from the Super Bowl, at home, where they have gone 26-2 in the last three years, including the playoffs. And even on a neutral field, they would figure to be favored over whichever team emerges from the AFC.

And then, maybe this time, it won't come down to one final yard.

Vincent Verhei

2014 Seahawks Stats by Week

Wk	vs.	W-L	PF	PA	YDF	YDA	TO	Total	Off	Def	ST
1	GB	W	36	16	398	255	0	79%	48%	-31%	-1%
2	at SD	L	21	30	288	377	-1	5%	26%	16%	-5%
3	DEN	W	26	20	384	332	1	53%	21%	-33%	-1%
4	BYE										
5	at WAS	W	27	17	403	307	0	18%	6%	0%	12%
6	DAL	L	23	30	206	401	1	-38%	-53%	1%	15%
7	at STL	L	26	28	463	275	0	-19%	38%	25%	-32%
8	at CAR	W	13	9	310	266	0	27%	-5%	-25%	8%
9	OAK	W	30	24	326	226	3	19%	8%	-36%	-25%
10	NYG	W	38	17	510	324	-1	31%	34%	5%	2%
11	at KC	L	20	24	372	298	2	-31%	5%	24%	-12%
12	ARI		19	3	293	204	1	49%	4%	-31%	14%
13	at SF	W	19	3	379	164	3	66%	14%	-44%	9%
14	at PHI	W	24	14	440	139	0	58%	24%	-46%	-12%
15	SF	W	17	7	290	245	-1	39%	10%	-22%	7%
16	at ARI	W	35	6	596	216	1	66%	53%	-28%	-15%
17	STL	W	20	6	354	245	1	73%	3%	-61%	9%
18	BYE										
19	CAR	W	31	17	348	362	3	34%	28%	-5%	2%
20	GB	W	28	22	397	306	-3	22%	-10%	-38%	-6%
21	vs. NE	L	24	28	396	377	1	41%	31%	-10%	0%

Trends and Splits

	Offense	Rank	Defense	Rank
Total DVOA	16.8%	5	-16.8%	1
Unadjusted VOA	17.7%	4	-12.0%	3
Weighted Trend	15.2%	5	-19.8%	1
Variance	6.1%	11	6.9%	19
Average Opponent	-1.6%	9	-0.2%	16
Passing	21.0%	10	-10.3%	3
Rushing	29.0%	1	-25.1%	2
First Down	22.8%	3	-24.3%	1
Second Down	12.3%	7	0.0%	15
Third Down	11.8%	11	-27.1%	3
First Half	6.1%	13	-11.2%	6
Second Half	27.9%	1	-23.1%	1
Red Zone	23.1%	4	9.8%	28
Late and Close	23.0%	4	-28.4%	2

Five-Year Performance

Year	W-L	Pyth W	Est W	PF	PA	TO	Total	Rk	Off	Rk	Def	Rk	ST	Rk	Off AGL	Rk	Def AGL	Rk	Off Age	Rk	Def Age	Rk	ST Age	Rk
2010	7-9	5.4	6.9	310	407	-9	-22.9%	30	-17.3%	29	12.0%	29	6.4%	2	47.1	32	9.7	4	27.8	11	27.6	10	26.4	14
2011	7-9	8.2	8.1	321	315	+8	-1.5%	19	-8.7%	22	-7.1%	10	0.2%	16	66.5	32	43.5	27	25.8	31	26.2	26	26.0	26
2012	11-5	12.5	13.0	412	245	+13	38.7%	1	18.5%	4	-14.5%	2	5.7%	3	28.0	16	8.3	3	25.9	27	25.6	31	26.0	18
2013	13-3	12.8	13.0	417	231	+20	40.0%	1	9.4%	7	-25.9%	1	4.7%	5	26.1	10	21.4	10	25.7	32	26.0	27	26.1	14
2014	12-4	11.9	12.7	394	254	+10	31.9%	1	16.8%	5	-16.8%	1	-1.7%	19	37.6	21	26.5	7	25.3	31	26.3	23	25.8	24

2014 Performance Based on Most Common Personnel Groups

SEA Offense					SEA Offense vs. Opponents					SEA Defense				SEA Defense vs. Opponents			
Pers	Freq	Yds	DVOA	Run%	Pers	Freq	Yds	DVOA	Run%	Pers	Freq	Yds	DVOA	Pers	Freq	Yds	DVOA
11	50%	6.5	20.4%	33%	Base	39%	6.0	31.3%	60%	Base	41%	4.8	-16.4%	11	58%	5.2	-13.2%
12	16%	6.8	43.8%	47%	Nickel	41%	6.6	29.1%	38%	Nickel	58%	4.9	-18.3%	12	22%	4.5	-20.8%
21	12%	4.6	21.2%	70%	Dime+	17%	5.8	5.5%	22%	Dime+	0%	10.8	66.6%	21	6%	4.3	-24.4%
10	5%	6.8	57.6%	48%	Goal Line	0%	0.3	-58.0%	50%	Goal Line	1%	-0.5	-10.1%	22	5%	3.5	-28.0%
01	3%	5.8	36.8%	24%	Big	2%	2.7	-12.7%	75%					13	3%	6.2	7.0%
20	3%	5.6	3.7%	86%													
22	3%	4.0	24.0%	79%													

Strategic Tendencies

Run/Pass		Rk	Formation		Rk	Pass Rush		Rk	Secondary		Rk	Strategy		Rk
Runs, first half	42%	7	Form: Single Back	68%	23	Rush 3	6.4%	13	4 DB	28%	12	Play action	31%	3
Runs, first down	53%	6	Form: Empty Back	12%	3	Rush 4	66.2%	12	5 DB	71%	6	Avg Box (Off)	6.27	17
Runs, second-long	40%	2	Pers: 3+ WR	64%	13	Rush 5	21.8%	20	6+ DB	1%	29	Avg Box (Def)	6.15	27
Runs, power sit.	67%	4	Pers: 4+ WR	9%	3	Rush 6+	5.6%	23	CB by Sides	85%	9	Offensive Pace	32.38	28
Runs, behind 2H	40%	1	Pers: 2+ TE/6+ OL	26%	24	Sacks by LB	29.2%	20	DB Blitz	6%	30	Defensive Pace	31.80	32
Pass, ahead 2H	47%	19	Shotgun/Pistol	69%	10	Sacks by DB	2.8%	24	Hole in Zone	10%	3	Go for it on 4th	0.92	18

Fumble recovery luck suggests the Seattle offense may look worse this year (recovered 14 of 18 fumbles) but the defense may look even better (recovered seven of 23 fumbles). Another reason to expect the defense to look better: Seattle opponents dropped a league-low 13 passes during the regular season. ⬤ Seattle had 70 offensive penalties, tied for second in the NFL. It was the fourth straight year they ranked first or second in offensive penalties. They had 142 penalties overall, tied with New England for seventh in the league. ⬤ Seattle also had the fewest penalties called against its opponents—by a huge margin. Seattle opponents were flagged only 85 times. Every other team in the league benefited from at least 110 penalties from its opponents. Perhaps the strangest part of this number: opponents were only called for five false starts all year despite all the noise at CenturyLink Field. The good news for Seattle is that this appears to be a one-year fluke, as there is no trend showing similar numbers in other seasons. ⬤ Seattle's offense ranked 20th in DVOA when passing the ball on third or fourth down, but blew away the rest of the league with 77.9% DVOA on third-down runs. (Denver was second at 31.9%.) ⬤ We registered the Seahawks with broken tackles on 12.2 percent of all offensive plays. No other offense was above 10 percent. ⬤ Broken tackles are just one reason Seattle averaged 6.6 yards after the catch. That's the second-highest figure in our data (since 2005), surpassed only by last year's Washington team which had 7.0 average YAC. ⬤ Do Seattle opponents build their game plans around stopping Marshawn Lynch? No problem: Seattle was one of four offenses to go empty backfield at least 10 percent of the time, and the Seahawks gained 7.6 yards per play with 60.4% DVOA on these plays. ⬤ This was the third straight year the Seahawks were 31st or 32nd in situation-neutral pace on defense, as opponents try to keep the ball out of their hands. ⬤ Seattle opponents threw a league-high 23.9 percent of passes to their running backs; the Seahawks have been above-average in this stat for three straight years.

Passing

Player	DYAR	DVOA	Plays	NtYds	Avg	YAC	C%	TD	Int
R.Wilson	503	5.5%	495	3241	6.5	6.6	63.4%	20	7

Rushing

Player	DYAR	DVOA	Plays	Yds	Avg	TD	Fum	Suc
M.Lynch	359	23.1%	280	1310	4.7	14	1	53%
R.Wilson	269	43.7%	97	872	9.0	6	4	-
R.Turbin	57	9.5%	74	310	4.2	0	1	61%
C.Michael	25	10.0%	34	175	5.1	0	1	50%
P.Harvin*	53	60.7%	11	92	8.4	1	0	-

Receiving

Player	DYAR	DVOA	Plays	Ctch	Yds	Y/C	YAC	TD	C%
D.Baldwin	137	5.5%	99	67	833	12.4	5.2	3	68%
J.Kearse	19	-9.1%	69	38	537	14.1	5.9	1	55%
P.Richardson	-8	-15.2%	44	29	271	9.3	2.2	1	66%
P.Harvin*	-40	-31.8%	26	22	133	6.0	4.9	0	85%
R.Lockette	66	50.4%	15	11	195	17.7	6.2	2	73%
B.Walters*	-12	-27.2%	11	6	57	9.5	6.5	0	55%
K.Norwood	25	19.4%	10	9	102	11.3	4.4	0	90%
L.Willson	20	0.6%	40	22	362	16.5	9.7	3	55%
C.Helfet	25	10.2%	24	12	185	15.4	5.8	2	50%
T.Moeaki*	14	9.8%	13	8	134	16.8	9.0	1	62%
Z.Miller*	13	19.2%	7	6	76	12.7	5.7	0	86%
J.Graham	124	6.8%	124	85	889	10.5	3.5	10	
M.Lynch	93	21.8%	48	37	367	9.9	10.9	4	77%
R.Turbin	104	83.3%	20	16	186	11.6	10.5	2	80%

Offensive Line

Player	Pos	Age	GS	Snaps	Pen	Sk	Pass	Run	Player	Pos	Age	GS	Snaps	Pen	Sk	Pass	Run
Justin Britt	RT	24	16/16	1057	8	5.5	30.0	8.5	Max Unger*	C	29	6/6	375	2	1.5	1.5	2.0
J.R. Sweezy	RG	26	16/16	1053	5	4.0	15.5	7.0	Patrick Lewis	C	24	6/4	269	2	1.0	5.0	0.0
Russell Okung	LT	28	14/14	872	10	2.5	18.0	9.0	Lemuel Jeanpierre	C	28	6/3	219	1	0.0	2.0	2.0
James Carpenter*	LG	26	13/13	816	9	0.5	8.5	6.0	Stephen Schilling	G	27	8/3	197	1	0.5	1.5	0.5
Alvin Bailey	G/T	24	14/5	418	5	3.0	7.5	3.0									

Year	Yards	ALY	Rk	Power	Rk	Stuff	Rk	2nd Lev	Rk	Open Field	Rk	Sacks	ASR	Rk	Short	Long	F-Start	Cont.
2012	4.83	4.42	4	70%	4	15%	1	1.42	2	0.94	8	33	7.2%	20	9	19	23	23
2013	4.03	4.05	9	49%	32	19%	15	1.17	13	0.59	23	44	9.6%	32	10	21	21	29
2014	4.62	4.23	4	78%	2	17%	6	1.34	4	0.80	11	42	8.7%	24	15	17	29	25
2014 ALY by direction:		Left End 4.19 (13)			Left Tackle 3.49 (22)			Mid/Guard 4.21 (5)			Right Tackle 4.44 (6)				Right End 5.3 (1)			

For a team that boasted a historically great rushing attack in 2014, the Seahawks had a shockingly bad offensive line. They owe a debt of gratitude to Marshawn Lynch, whose tackle-busting style made their numbers look much better than their actual performance on the field. Out of the 43 backs with at least 100 runs last year, Lynch was second with 2.5 yards after contact per carry, but his 2.2 yards *before* contact was just 22nd. That latter ranking is much more indicative of Seattle's run-blocking prowess, and they were even worse at pass blocking. Russell Wilson was pressured on 39 percent of his dropbacks last season, the highest rate of any starting quarterback. Only one player, left guard James Carpenter, finished in the top 20 at his position in snaps per blown block, and now he's gone, signing with the New York Jets in free agency.

Three starters return from last year's team. Russell Okung has been effective when healthy, but you never know how long that's going to last. He missed most of training camp last season following foot surgery, and was only 80 percent when the season started according to line coach Tom Cable. Then he dealt with shoulder, chest, and calf issues throughout the season, though he only missed two games. Still, he has now missed 21 games in five NFL seasons, and at least one every year. He is entering the final year of his contract, with a very real possibility of moving on in 2016. Rookie right tackle Justin Britt somehow managed to lead the NFL in blown blocks on passing plays even though Seattle had the fewest dropbacks in the NFL. It would have been nice if he had shown some improvement throughout the year, but there wasn't much sign of that—his worst game came in Week 15 against San Francisco, with six blown blocks. Still, he was a rookie, and rookies often struggle. Right guard J.R. Sweezy was a boom-or-bust player in his second year on offense, with several crushing blocks on the second level and many misses at the point of attack, plus a penchant for blowing assignments in pass protection. Still, he remains the most successful of Tom Cable's defense-to-offense conversions—he was one of nine offensive linemen in minicamp who played some defensive line in college, including sixth-round draftee Kristjan Sokoli (SUNY-Buffalo). Alvin Bailey will take over for Carpenter at left guard after three starts at guard and three at tackle (including one in the playoffs) in his first season of significant action. He joined the Seahawks as an undrafted free agent in 2013 after skipping his senior season at Arkansas.

That leaves center, where Patrick Lewis has the edge over Lemuel Jeanpierre (another former defensive lineman) for the spot left vacant by Max Unger's trade to New Orleans and Stephen Schilling's retirement. Lewis spent time on the practice squads in Cleveland and Jacksonville before Seattle signed him a year ago. Jeanpierre is entering his fifth year in Seattle, with 11 starts in his first four seasons. The results of 2014 suggest that either player will be a downgrade from Unger, but a downgrade the Seahawks should be able to afford (Table 3).

Table 3: Seattle's Centers, 2014

Center	Weeks Started	Starts	W-L	Off. DVOA	Rush Off. DVOA	Pass Off. DVOA
Max Unger	1-5, 10-11	6	4-2	23.0%	40.3%	19.7%
Patrick Lewis	9, 12, 16-17	4	4-0	18.4%	31.4%	22.4%
Lemuel Jeanpierre	13-15	3	3-0	16.1%	15.6%	36.6%
Stephen Schilling	6-8	3	1-2	0.2%	17.5%	0.8%

Take a look at Seattle's rushing DVOA, even with their third- and fourth-string centers. Then remember that Miami was the second-best running team in the NFL last year, and their rush offense DVOA was only 9.6%. Now you start to realize how effective the Wilson/Lynch combo was in 2014.

Defensive Front Seven

Defensive Line	Age	Pos	G	Snaps	Plays	TmPct	Rk	Stop	Dfts	BTkl	Runs	St%	Rk	RuYd	Rk	Sack	Hit	Hur	Dsrpt
						Overall							vs. Run				Pass Rush		
Kevin Williams*	35	DT	16	437	33	4.5%	49	25	11	0	27	74%	64	1.9	31	3.0	1	4.0	2
Tony McDaniel	30	DT	16	400	30	4.0%	60	21	2	2	29	69%	82	2.3	49	0.0	0	0.5	1
Jordan Hill	24	DT	13	360	23	3.8%	68	19	10	1	10	80%	32	1.8	27	5.5	4	4.5	4
Brandon Mebane	30	DT	9	278	19	4.6%	46	15	5	0	18	78%	48	1.3	16	1.0	1	2.5	0
Ahtyba Rubin	29	DT	13	450	29	4.0%	62	18	2	1	27	59%	90	3.3	89	1.0	3	5.5	1

Edge Rushers	Age	Pos	G	Snaps	Plays	TmPct	Rk	Stop	Dfts	BTkl	Runs	St%	Rk	RuYd	Rk	Sack	Hit	Hur	Dsrpt
						Overall							vs. Run				Pass Rush		
Michael Bennett	30	DE	16	828	37	5.0%	46	32	20	3	29	83%	20	0.6	1	7.0	13	28.5	0
Cliff Avril	29	DE	16	714	24	3.2%	76	21	13	6	14	86%	10	1.2	7	5.0	14	21.0	1
O'Brien Schofield*	28	DE	16	338	15	2.0%	--	9	4	2	10	70%	--	4.0	--	2.0	5	13.5	0

Linebackers	Age	Pos	G	Snaps	Plays	TmPct	Rk	Stop	Dfts	BTkl	Sack	Hit	Hur	Runs	St%	Rk	RuYd	Rk	Tgts	Suc%	Rk	AdjYd	Rk	PD	Int
						Overall					Pass Rush			vs. Run					vs. Pass						
K.J. Wright	26	OLB	16	919	110	14.8%	25	62	17	12	2.0	0	4	62	60%	59	3.4	44	38	50%	36	5.8	22	1	0
Bruce Irvin	28	OLB	15	692	40	5.8%	84	32	18	6	6.5	6	13	26	77%	8	2.8	21	12	48%	--	8.0	--	2	2
Bobby Wagner	25	MLB	11	658	106	20.8%	1	67	21	7	2.0	4	1.5	62	76%	10	2.7	13	34	42%	55	7.5	50	2	0
Malcolm Smith*	26	OLB	14	271	33	5.1%	--	14	3	3	0.0	0	1.5	25	48%	--	4.0	--	14	74%	--	3.7	--	1	0

Year	Yards	ALY	Rk	Power	Rk	Stuff	Rk	2nd Level	Rk	Open Field	Rk	Sacks	ASR	Rk	Short	Long
2012	4.44	4.22	21	50%	3	18%	22	1.22	22	0.86	20	36	6.1%	21	15	14
2013	3.75	3.73	13	70%	24	21%	11	1.06	11	0.55	12	44	7.6%	7	20	14
2014	3.54	3.41	5	59%	10	23%	6	0.92	4	0.59	8	37	7.0%	13	18	9
2014 ALY by direction:		Left End 3.66 (16)			Left Tackle 3.67 (15)			Mid/Guard 3.51 (7)			Right Tackle 3.31 (7)			Right End 2.08 (1)		

The blueprint for 2015 is the same as it was last year: a quartet of 300-plus-pound tackles getting 20 to 30 snaps each and clogging up the middle; Michael Bennett rushing from the weak side while Cliff Avril attacks from the opposite direction; Bruce Irvin setting the edge on the strong side; Bobby Wagner eliminating anything that gets to the second level; and K.J. Wright taking care of anything that gets past that. The Seahawks place a lot of value on versatility, which is why you'll see Bennett lining up at any spot along the defensive front, Irvin lining up with a hand to the ground, and tackles swapping between nose and three-technique depending on who is available. But no matter who is on the field, the basic plan remains the same.

There are plenty of options at tackle, with Brandon Mebane returning from injury to join Tony McDaniel in the starting lineup. Former Browns starter Ahtyba Rubin replaces Kevin Williams as the veteran backup, with Jordan Hill bringing interior pressure—the 2013 third-rounder finished his second NFL season on a strong note, with 4.5 sacks in December. Depth at end, on the other hand, remains a concern. Seattle's pass rush in the Super Bowl essentially vanished after Avril left the game with a concussion. To that end, the Seahawks used their second-round draft choice on Michigan's Frank Clark, hoping that athletic potential could overcome inexperience and off-field scandals. Clark played defensive back and ran track in high school, and didn't move to end until joining the Wolverines. He collected only 11 sacks in his NCAA career, and was kicked off the team following a domestic violence arrest in November. He then excelled at the scouting combine, ranking seventh or better among defensive line prospects in the broad jump, 40-yard dash, three-cone drill, and vertical jump, and first in both the 20- and 60-yard shuttles. Still, SackSEER was unimpressed with Clark's lack of college production, projecting him with only 5.0 sacks in his first five seasons. Most draft experts expected he would go in the seventh round, not the second. The Seahawks insist they did due diligence investigating Clark's arrest and have claimed it would still be a dealbreaker if they believed he had hit a woman, but Seattle media spoke to several witnesses who claimed the team had never reached out to them. It's a very ugly situation, and at least from a public relations standpoint, Clark is entering the NFL with one strike already against him.

The other concern here might be a handful of players unhappy about their contracts. Bennett has hinted at a holdout just one year after signing a four-year, $32 million contract extension, though he made it clear that he wanted to stay in Seattle. The same can't be said of Bruce Irvin. After the Seahawks declined to pick up the fifth-year option of their 2012 first-round draft pick, Irvin told Samuel Logan of Black Sports Online he wanted to reunite with Falcons coach Dan Quinn, former defensive coordinator in Seattle: "I'm going to be in Atlanta next season... Atlanta is where I want to be. Believe that." While Irvin's agent probably wasn't happy to hear his client harpoon his own market value, Seahawks management probably wasn't happy to hear that their linebacker mentally has one foot out the door. Still, Pete Carroll has put up with worse than this, and it appears Irvin will play out his final year in Seattle.

Finally, there's Wagner, drafted one round after Irvin in 2012 and also entering the final year of his deal. Unlike Irvin, Wagner can legitimately lay claim to being one of the best players at his position. Over his first three seasons, he has ranked third, eighth, and first among all players in percentage of his team's plays, and given his age he's surely the highest defensive priority on Seattle's list of upcoming extensions.

Defensive Secondary

Secondary	Age	Pos	G	Snaps	Plays	TmPct	Rk	Stop	Dfts	BTkl	Runs	St%	Rk	RuYd	Rk	Tgts	Tgt%	Rk	Dist	Suc%	Rk	AdjYd	Rk	PD	Int
						Overall							vs. Run						vs. Pass						
Richard Sherman	27	CB	16	965	64	8.6%	37	26	11	4	19	63%	10	5.3	22	62	17.5%	6	15.1	59%	8	6.5	14	8	4
Earl Thomas	26	FS	16	958	100	13.5%	9	28	15	7	38	26%	58	7.0	41	22	6.2%	18	11.7	62%	12	5.5	14	3	1
Kam Chancellor	27	SS	14	833	81	12.5%	15	40	6	8	47	60%	10	5.8	24	28	9.0%	38	7.9	51%	50	7.4	39	7	1
Byron Maxwell*	27	CB	13	700	51	8.5%	40	18	11	2	3	33%	44	3.3	4	66	25.4%	52	12.9	51%	39	6.9	17	11	2
Marcus Burley	25	CB	13	320	37	6.1%	--	19	9	0	9	33%	--	8.6	--	27	22.9%	--	11.7	58%	--	8.5	--	5	1
Tharold Simon	24	CB	10	298	14	3.0%	--	6	2	0	2	50%	--	4.0	--	21	18.7%	--	14.8	63%	--	4.8	--	2	1
Cary Williams	31	CB	16	1149	67	7.7%	54	21	6	6	16	19%	67	10.8	70	92	21.4%	22	14.0	52%	29	9.1	58	11	2
Will Blackmon	31	CB	8	351	28	6.5%	--	11	5	7	9	56%	--	5.1	--	21	19.6%	--	11.5	38%	--	8.8	--	0	0

Year	Pass D Rank	vs. #1 WR	Rk	vs. #2 WR	Rk	vs. Other WR	Rk	vs. TE	Rk	vs. RB	Rk
2012	3	-37.5%	1	-7.4%	10	-6.0%	10	-1.6%	17	-9.3%	9
2013	1	-18.0%	4	-13.4%	7	-27.1%	3	-34.2%	3	-32.7%	1
2014	3	-22.0%	4	-18.3%	6	-19.2%	4	-0.8%	18	-2.0%	16

If the Legion of Boom is the NFL's answer to the Four Horsemen, it's pretty easy to spot the counterparts. Sherman is Ric Flair (he's got the biggest mouth), Chancellor is Arn Anderson (the Enforcer), and Thomas is Tully Blanchard (uh... he's from Texas). In both factions, the fourth spot was something of a revolving door. Just as the Horsemen went from Ole Anderson to Lex Luger to Barry Windham, it follows that the LOB has gone from Brandon Browner to Byron Maxwell to Cary Williams. Williams figures to see a lot of action playing opposite Sherman, but that's nothing new; we charted him with 93 targets in 2012 (then with Baltimore) and he led the league with 110 targets in 2013, so he's certainly used to a heavy workload. His charting stats, though, have been pretty ugly. He ranked 79th in adjusted success rate and 58th in adjusted yards per target in 2012, and 67th and 28th in those same categories in 2013. Note that until last season, Williams always ranked better in yards per target than success rate. He's used to safety help that keeps him from getting beat deep, and in Seattle, he'll have it.

Earl Thomas' low target rate doesn't do justice to how active he is and how much range he can cover—according to play-by-play data, only two safeties were responsible for a bigger share of their team's pass plays (combining tackles, assists, and passes defensed). Meanwhile, Kam Chancellor was seventh at the position in percentage of his team's run plays. You'll find few safety duos with such a clear deep/box disparity, and even fewer with this kind of talent.

It's not clear in the charting totals, but Richard Sherman probably had his finest season in 2014. Like many other Seahawks, he suffered a midseason slump, surrendering 197 yards (exactly half his season total) in a four-game stretch against the Panthers, Raiders, Giants, and Chiefs. Rookie phenoms Kelvin Benjamin and Odell Beckham both beat him for memorable receptions. And then Sherman caught fire, not allowing a single completion in his next three games, shutting out the Cardinals, 49ers, and Eagles. He gave up only 15 first downs all season, only six third-down conversions, and not a single touchdown. These numbers are even more impressive when we consider that the Seahawks finally took advantage of Sherman's talents and occasionally moved him away from the defensive left to track the opponent's top receiver, such as Dez Bryant in Week 6. (Seattle's "CB by Sides" number in the Strategic Tendencies table was 85 percent after being 99 percent in two of the last three seasons.) And then, somehow, he improved in the playoffs. Cam Newton, Aaron Rodgers, and Tom Brady threw a combined 120 passes against Seattle's defense. Only ten of those passes were thrown in Sherman's direction, resulting in three catches, 26 yards, one first down, and two interceptions. Aaron Rodgers—league MVP, DVOA king, and pretty much everyone's choice for best passer alive—completed one pass against Sherman in two games, and that one catch was a 6-yard gain on third-and-10. It will be very, very hard to top this performance in 2015.

The Seahawks came out of the Super Bowl with some damage. Chancellor played through a deep bone bruise *and* a torn MCL suffered in his final practice, while Thomas battled through a separated shoulder and a torn labrum. Thomas underwent surgery in February, and there's a small but realistic chance he'll miss the start of the regular season. Throw in Sherman's torn elbow ligament suffered in the NFC title game, the broken wrist and torn ACL that knocked nickelback Jeremy Lane out of the Super Bowl (and, likely, part of training camp as well), and backup safety Jeron Johnson's free agent exodus to the Redskins, and depth starts to become an issue. Reserve corners Tharold Simon and Marcus Burley are at least battle-tested, but backup safety DeShawn Shead played only 88 defensive snaps in 16 games last year, 60 of them coming in his only start against Oakland. Seattle's defensive DVOA was -36.2% in that game, for what that's worth.

Special Teams

Year	DVOA	Rank	FG/XP	Rank	Net Kick	Rank	Kick Ret	Rank	Net Punt	Rank	Punt Ret	Rank	Hidden	Rank
2012	5.7%	3	1.9	11	8.5	5	9.1	4	12.0	6	-3.0	19	-6.4	25
2013	4.7%	5	4.3	8	5.6	7	-3.8	22	10.4	4	7.2	6	-2.6	19
2014	-1.7%	19	0.8	12	4.5	11	-7.5	31	-4.0	21	-2.4	15	5.3	8

The natural assumption would be to blame Seattle's horrible kickoff return numbers on the vacuum left by the Percy Harvin trade, but surprisingly, between his stints with the Seahawks and the Jets, Harvin finished last in our kickoff return metric a year ago. He returned a dozen kickoffs in a Seattle uniform last year, and was tackled inside the 20 on half of them. Meanwhile, the Seahawks started the year experimenting with Earl Thomas returning punts, a high-risk strategy with no reward; Thomas was so bad at it he was relieved of the job after just one game. Paul Richardson took over kickoff returns (poorly, but still better than Harvin) while Doug Baldwin and Brian Walters split punt return duties (adequately) the rest of the way. Enter third-round draft pick Tyler Lockett. Lockett returned four kickoffs and two punts for touchdowns in his career at Kansas State, and he figures to take over both jobs in Seattle right away.

Jon Ryan's punts had gross negative value for the second year in a row. The Seahawks ask him to sacrifice distance for hang time in an effort to limit opposing returns, and to a degree it works: Seattle gave up only four punt returns of 10 or more yards, fewest in the league. The Seahawks coverage ranked 23rd in the value of opposing returns, but if we ignore one terrible game against St. Louis, Seattle would jump to seventh in punt coverage, and to 11th in net punt value. Of course, every team would look better if we removed their worst performance, but not every team gives up a 90-yard touchdown on a trick play. Steven Hauschka was third in kickoff value, his third straight season in the top five, but Seattle's kickoff coverage teams were just average. No Seahawks special-teamer made the top 50 in kickoff tackles, or the top 60 in punt tackles.

Hauschka had some struggles with long field goals in 2014, but he has been automatic at shorter ranges. In his last three seasons, he has gone 57-of-58 on kicks shorter than 40 yards.

Tampa Bay Buccaneers

2014 Record: 2-14	**Total DVOA:** -28.3% (30th)	**2015 Mean Projection:** 6.4 wins	**On the Clock (0-4):** 24%
Pythagorean Wins: 4.4 (29th)	**Offense:** -26.3% (32nd)	**Postseason Odds:** 16.1%	**Mediocrity (5-7):** 43%
Snap-Weighted Age: 26.5 (23rd)	**Defense:** 1.1% (18th)	**Super Bowl Odds:** 0.9%	**Playoff Contender (8-10):** 27%
Average Opponent: -1.4% (17th)	**Special Teams:** -0.8% (17th)	**Proj. Avg. Opponent:** -3.4% (26th)	**Super Bowl Contender (11+):** 6%

2014: A franchise that has frequently explored the offensive depths sinks into the abyss.

2015: Another potential savior arrives to try to break the NFL's longest quarterback drought.

Like many of sports' deepest curses, the Curse of Doug Williams starts with parsimony. The strike-shortened 1982 season marked the third time in four years that Williams had quarterbacked the Buccaneers to the playoffs, yet Williams earned the lowest starting quarterback salary in the league and less than 12 NFL backups. In the 1983 offseason, owner Hugh Culverhouse offered Williams—then grieving over recently losing his wife to brain cancer—a new contract that was still far below his market value. After Williams bolted to the USFL, the Bucs fell to 2-14 and then missed the playoffs for 14 consecutive years. Perhaps because Williams was too nice, after that his curse applied only to the offense and, in particular, the quarterback.

First-overall pick Jameis Winston is only the latest talented player who seeks to break the curse. The Buccaneers have spent the equivalent of a first-round pick on a quarterback six times since 1983 (Table 1). Three times the quarterback eventually made a Pro Bowl elsewhere (Steve Young, Vinny Testaverde, and Chris Chandler). Two won a Super Bowl, and another would play in one, but they knew only failure in Tampa.

Table 1: Buccaneers' First-Round Quarterbacks Since Doug Williams

Quarterback	How Acquired	Record as Bucs' Starter
Jack Thompson	Trade for 1984 first-round pick	3-13
Steve Young	First-overall pick in 1984 supplemental draft	3-16
Vinny Testaverde	First pick in 1987 NFL draft	24-48
Chris Chandler	Trade for 1992 first-round pick	0-6
Trent Dilfer	Sixth pick in 1994 NFL draft	38-38
Josh Freeman	17th pick in 2009 NFL draft	24-35

Trent Dilfer made a Pro Bowl in 1997, but he ranked just 16th in DVOA that year. In his other four years as Tampa's main starter, he never ranked higher than 34th. Tampa has never spent a first-round pick on a quarterback who had more than a single successful season there, and only Dilfer and Josh Freeman even had that. If Jameis Winston signs a second contract with the Buccaneers, he will be the first quarterback in the history of the franchise to do so.

Can Winston break the Curse of Doug Williams? There's

plenty of uncertainty involved in predicting early-career performance for young quarterbacks, but we do have some information to go on. This offseason, Football Outsiders introduced an upgraded method for projecting young passers, which we're QBASE. (There's a full introduction to the new system on page 478.) We combine a measure of Winston's experience and his draft position with his college stats, adjusted them for the opposition he faced and the teammates he played. The result predicts the Defense-adjusted Yards Above Replacement (DYAR) he will generate in Years 3-5 of his NFL career.

And the result is not pretty.

Table 2: QBASE Projections for No. 1 Overall Picks Since 1996

Player	Year	Team	Predicted Passing DYAR Yrs 3-5	Actual Passing DYAR Yrs 3-5
Carson Palmer	2005	CIN	2,266	2,268
Peyton Manning	1998	IND	1,463	3,922
Matthew Stafford	2009	DET	1,125	3,021
Andrew Luck	2012	IND	1076	879 (Year 3 only)
Eli Manning	2004	NYG	892	1,179
Cam Newton	2011	CAR	781	316 (Years 3-4 only)
Alex Smith	2005	SF	771	-763
Sam Bradford	2010	STL	617	692
JaMarcus Russell	2007	OAK	535	-834
Tim Couch	1999	CLE	428	-366
Jameis Winston	2015	TB	378	–
David Carr	2002	HOU	365	-215
Michael Vick	2001	ATL	-446	-518

Note: When analyzing players such as Cam Newton and Michael Vick, please note that QBASE does not incorporate rushing value.

Winston has the third-lowest projection of the 13 quarterbacks taken first overall in the last 20 years (Table 2). QBASE is down on Winston because he had a middling 2014 by the numbers—those numbers include completion percentage and adjusted yards per attempt (yards per attempt adjusting for touchdowns and interceptions), but not wins, which turn out not to be particularly useful for predicting how college quarterbacks do as pros—and started only two college seasons.

2015 Buccaneers Schedule

Week	Opp.	Week	Opp.	Week	Opp.
1	TEN	7	at WAS	13	ATL
2	at NO	8	at ATL	14	NO
3	at HOU	9	NYG	15	at STL (Thu.)
4	CAR	10	DAL	16	CHI
5	JAC	11	at PHI	17	at CAR
6	BYE	12	at IND		

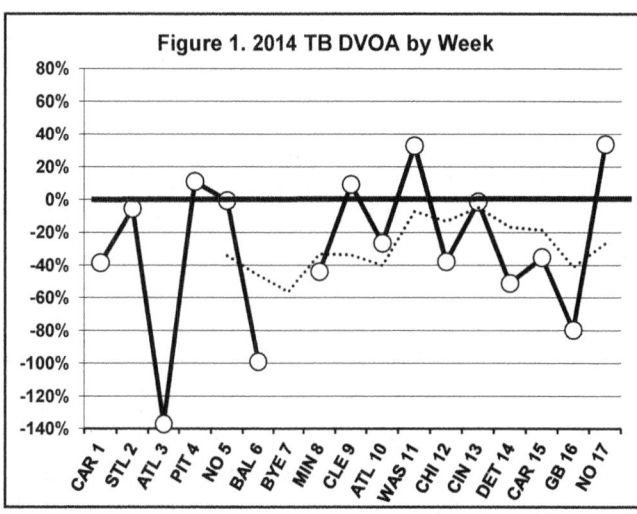

Figure 1. 2014 TB DVOA by Week

He shares these characteristics with many quarterbacks who failed as pros. His college stats look a lot more like David Carr's than Peyton Manning's.

There are so many reasons to be cautious about these kinds of projections that we could write a few thousand words just on the caveats. To reflect that uncertainty, we built into QBASE awareness of its own limitations. For example, Winston's low projection comes with a high variance. QBASE gives a 61 percent chance that Winston is a bust, but still a 13 percent chance that he is upper-tier or elite.

But let's suppose you just naturally distrust statistical models. Instead just take a look at a simple college performance metric: defense-corrected adjusted yards per attempt (DAY/A). Correcting for schedule strength helps Winston because Florida State faced the hardest schedule of opposing defenses in the nation according to FEI ratings. This stat does a very good job of identifying top picks at quarterback. Eight of the 13 No. 1 overall picks finished in the top three in the nation in DAY/A as college seniors. Only three ranked outside the top ten: Eli Manning (18th), Tim Couch (19th), and Jameis Winston (20th).

Winston's sophomore DAY/A might undersell him somewhat because he gets no credit for his freshman year (although QBASE credits him for that) and he may be penalized too harshly for his 18 interceptions. But the DAY/A gap between Winston and his peers who have gone on to have big NFL careers is not a small one. Even taking away a few interceptions would not give Winston a DAY/A close to that of historically strong prospects such as Carson Palmer or Philip Rivers.[1]

Of course, as much as we believe in the value of using stats to make predictions, there's little doubt that intangibles also play a significant role at the quarterback position. And Winston's character is a question mark, Tampa Bay's pre-draft investigation notwithstanding. (One would imagine the girl accusing him of rape—even without charges being filed, the Florida state attorney stated that he thought "things that happened that night were not good"—would at least have been one of the top 75 people worth talking to about Winston's character.) Teams fall in love with players all the time, losing perspective and trading or paying too much to get the apple of their eye. We can't know for sure that Tampa fell prey to that in their vetting of Winston, but there is reason for suspicion.

At the same time, Tampa could reasonably see many assets on Winston's character balance sheet. He seems to have that hard-to-define alpha male thing that people look for in quarterbacks (although there is no clear evidence that this actually matters). Winston was a high school valedictorian, was accepted at Stanford before deciding to attend Florida State, and scored a 27 on the Wonderlic (although there is no correlation between quarterbacks' Wonderlic scores and their NFL performance level). He supposedly eats, drinks, and breathes football (and we have no argument to downplay the importance of that). It would have been pretty shocking for that *not* to be the buzz coming out of Tampa OTAs, given the scrutiny Winston was under—but Johnny Manziel couldn't manage it as a rookie, so Winston has to get some credit for showing up early and staying late. Altogether, Winston's character remains, as Donald Rumsfeld might say, a known unknown. We know it's essential, but whether the pluses outweigh the minuses will only become clear with time.

Betting on No. 1 overall quarterbacks to fail is usually a losing proposition; eight of the 12 chosen in the past two decades made at least one Pro Bowl. Nevertheless, there is enough smoke in Winston's stats to be concerned. An appropriately cautious reading of the stats would put Winston at the low end of the first-overall quarterback range, far below the Peyton tier and even somewhat below the Eli tier. Winston is worthy of optimism, just less than most No. 1 picks.

Winston comes to an offense that was in complete disarray last year. Many times in the past, the Bucs' offensive futility reflected a lack of skill-position talent, but not in 2014. The Bucs came by their impotence more creatively last year. A Week 13 loss against the Bengals symbolized the season. After the generally Gabbert-esque Josh McCown found receiver Louis Murphy with 26 seconds left to set up a potential game-winning field goal attempt, Bengals coach Marvin Lewis illegally threw his challenge flag for no apparent reason. But while the 21-yard catch was clean, referee Bill Leavy found what Lewis wanted

---

1 We should note that before the last 20 years or so, DAY/A was a less consistent indicator of NFL success. Jeff George was the No. 1 pick in 1990 despite ranking 30th in DAY/A. Dan Marino had a Hall-of-Fame career after throwing the most interceptions in Division I in his senior season and ranking 47th in DAY/A.

him to see on review: the Bucs had lined up with 12 men.

The Buccaneers lost more than just the Bengals game due to their propensity to take offensive penalties. Tampa Bay led the league with 82 offensive penalties for 563 yards; no other team had more than 70 offensive penalties or 500 yards. Bucs' drives often ended in a haze of false starts and illegal formation penalties. Demar Dotson was probably the only above-average blocker on the Bucs' offensive line last season, but he took 16 penalties for 127 yards all by himself, tying Cleveland cornerback Buster Skrine for the most penalties by any single player. No other offensive player broke the century mark in penalty yards.

At first glance, this kind of disorganization on offense would seem to be unlikely to repeat, but offensive penalties do correlate a fair bit from year to year. Since 2010, the correlation coefficient between offensive penalties from one year to the next is 0.31. Tampa had about 26 more penalties than the league average in 2014, so that correlation means we would expect them to still have about eight more penalties than the league average this year. That correlation applies even, when like Tampa, a team hires a new offensive coordinator. Across the 28 teams that hired either a new head coach or offensive coordinator from 2010 to 2014, the year-to-year correlation in offensive penalties is actually higher (0.47) than for teams retaining the same head coach and coordinator (0.26). New coaches have tended not to fix offensive penalty problems in their first year.

On the other hand, after last season's disastrous offensive coaching situation, the 2015 Bucs may have unusually strong potential to improve. Last August, first-year offensive coordinator Jeff Tedford had to leave the team in the preseason for health reasons, leaving Marcus Arroyo (the offensive coordinator at 1-11 Southern Miss in 2013) to assume Tedford's position. This year, the much more experienced Dirk Koetter brings almost certain improvement just by virtue of not repeating the 2014 patch-job. Since 2010, Koetter's offenses in Jacksonville and Atlanta committed about seven fewer penalties than the league average each year.

When he's done teaching his linemen to not constantly false start, Koetter will have to figure out how to improve their blocking schemes. Tampa Bay ranked 29th with a 9.4 percent adjusted sack rate in 2014. They were even worse in run blocking, coming in last with 3.21 adjusted line yards. Free-agent signee Anthony Collins was brutal at left tackle, causing Bucs to cut him after a single season. And at right guard, the Bucs got performance that was hide-the-children bad. Patrick Omameh saw most of the snaps and ranked 32nd among 34 right guards with 34.7 snaps per blown block. When Omameh wasn't playing, Garrett Gilkey managed to blow 11.5 blocks in just 206 snaps. At 17.9 snaps per blown block, Gilkey was the only lineman in football to play at least 200 snaps and average under 20 snaps per blown block.

Hope for improvement at these trouble spots comes in the form of second-round picks Ali Marpet and Donovan Smith. Even in the best-case scenario, the new line will take time to coalesce, but there are particular reasons for concern with each of the new additions. There are conflicting press reports over whether the Bucs plan to immediately transition Marpet

from Division III Hobart to Week 1 starter in the NFL. The Bucs seem to prefer that he grow into that role later in the season, though a lack of other good options may accelerate his timetable. Though Smith appears likely to win the left tackle job, many outside scouting experts saw him as a reach with the 34th selection, seeing instead a third-round talent who might need to play either right tackle or guard. Particularly with their new quarterback neither overly mobile nor quick on the release, the Bucs cannot afford to miss on Smith.

Now for the good news: for a team that was bad enough to get the No. 1 pick, the Bucs have an unusual number of near-elite or elite players. From Jameis Winston's perspective, the most important is last year's first-round pick, wide receiver Mike Evans. Despite quarterback play that ranged from terrible (Josh McCown) to mediocre (Mike Glennon), Evans compiled an 11.4% DVOA that ranked him 21st out of 87 wide receivers. Evans and veteran Vincent Jackson provide Winston with a pair of targets that few rookie quarterbacks have had. Winston will be just the fourth first-round quarterback to have two returning 1,000-yard receivers in his first season. Then again, that worked better for Daunte Culpepper (who had Randy Moss and Cris Carter) than it did for Matt Leinart (Larry Fitzgerald, Anquan Boldin) or Patrick Ramsey (Laveranues Coles, Rod Gardner). And as good as Evans could become, nobody should expect Randy Moss-level help for Winston.

On defense, the Bucs have an elite defensive tackle in Gerald McCoy and football's best weakside linebacker in Lavonte David. After a 2013 when McCoy accumulated 9.5 sacks, 13 hits, and an incredible 40 hurries. McCoy came back to Earth a bit in 2014, posting 8.5 sacks, 6 hits, and 15.5 hurries in 13 games last season. As a pass rusher over the last two seasons, McCoy's stat line (18-19-55.5) compares favorably to Ndamukong Suh's (14-26-39). As for David, he led the league in 2013 with 50 defeats (all tackles for a loss, tackles or passes defensed that prevent conversions on third or fourth down, and turnovers caused including batted passes that were intercepted) and posted the second-highest total since 1996. He also pulled the rare Reverse Brandon Meriwether, inexplicably missing out on the Pro Bowl despite making first-team All-Pro (since 2004, only two other non-special teams players, NaVorro Bowman in 2011 and Richard Sherman in 2012, have done that). Last season, David finished second with 42 defeats, one less than J.J. Watt's total of 43.

Almost half of those defeats come on pass plays. Like McCoy's pass rushing skills, David's abilities in coverage give Lovie Smith an ideal piece to make the Tampa-2 work. Smith used two high safeties much less towards the end of his time in Chicago, in large part reflecting a changing league with better precision passing, more three- and four-receiver sets, and rules protecting receivers that made passing over the middle easier than ever. But part of Smith's strategic shift also came because Lance Briggs was aging at weakside linebacker. David's speed enables him to cover the seam routes that are the most notable soft spot of the Tampa-2. With the league having evolved, no coach is likely to use two deep safeties on a majority of opponents' snaps anymore, but David will enable Smith to go to the tactic more often.

That the Buccaneers ranked 23rd in passing defense in 2014 despite having two near-perfect pieces speaks to the ineptitude mostly offered by their highly touted free-agent signings. Tampa generated almost no edge rush, with free-agent signee Michael Johnson notching just four sacks. Fellow 2014 signee Alterraun Verner made the run plays required in the Tampa-2—only Corey Graham had more run tackles among cornerbacks—but charted very poorly against the pass (10.2 adjusted yards per pass, ranked 72nd). And in his second season in Tampa, Dashon Goldson might have been the worst safety in the league by our charting stats. His run stop rate of 21 percent ranked 67th out of 71 safeties, and his 10.5 adjusted yards allowed per pass ranked 65th.

Of those three players, only Verner returns for 2015. While we would expect Verner to regress towards better performance, the outlook for safety and edge rusher has not improved much. The primary addition at edge rusher, George Johnson, had six sacks with Detroit in 2014 but none in four previous years of bouncing around NFL rosters. At best, he's a useful rotation guy, not a starting-quality end. At safety, the Bucs may start Chris Conte, one of Lovie Smith's old Bears who charted even worse against the pass last year (11.7 adjusted yards per pass, ranked 68th) than Goldson did.

Johnson fits an unfortunate pattern of recent free-agent flops in Tampa: one-season or even partial-season wonders. Goldson, signed in 2013, came off of a career year. Verner's 2013 outlier season in Tennessee earned him big Tampa dollars in 2014. They entrusted left tackle last year to Anthony Collins, who shined for half of the 2013 season in Cincinnati. Most notably, they let their season ride on Josh McCown, who proved to be football's worst starting quarterback. His failure in Tampa should be no surprise. Except for his one six-game stretch for the 2013 Bears, McCown has never had even a single season of above-average play (and McCown has thrown passes in eight other NFL seasons). In his five other qualifying seasons, McCown has ranked worse than 40th three times. General manager Jason Licht probably should have avoided the Josh McCown mistake.

Failing so badly last year provides the Bucs with some hidden opportunities this year. Through Week 3, Tampa has first dibs on any player who hits the wire, a right that they have already used this offseason to sign safety D.J. Swearinger and to bring back tight end Tim Wright. Moreover, Licht has set the salary cap up well to enable the Bucs to fit any signees onto this year's team. The Bucs' practice of avoiding signing bonuses in contracts also means they can move on relatively easily from their atrocious recent free-agent signings. By 2016, Collins, Johnson, and Goldson will each be entirely off Tampa's cap, leaving the Bucs in good shape to fill in the roster around their young quarterback.

Licht is already spending almost all his draft resources to support Winston. After spending all six picks on offense in 2014, he used six of his seven picks on offensive players this year. Winston is thus likely to get more help than previous quarterbacks counted on to break the Curse of Doug Williams. At least that should make a repeat of the Steve Young/Vinny Testaverde pattern unlikely. If Winston succeeds in the NFL, it will probably be in Tampa.

Andrew Healy

2014 Buccaneers Stats by Week

Wk	vs.	W-L	PF	PA	YDF	YDA	TO	Total	Off	Def	ST
1	CAR	L	14	20	264	334	-3	-39%	-31%	10%	2%
2	STL	L	17	19	332	339	0	-6%	14%	10%	-10%
3	at ATL	L	14	56	217	488	-1	-137%	-87%	31%	-19%
4	at PIT	W	27	24	350	390	0	11%	-2%	-6%	7%
5	at NO	L	31	37	314	511	2	-1%	-2%	1%	2%
6	BAL	L	17	48	364	475	0	-99%	-17%	66%	-16%
7	BYE										
8	MIN	L	13	19	225	332	-2	-44%	-29%	13%	-2%
9	at CLE	L	17	22	365	330	0	9%	0%	-24%	-15%
10	ATL	L	17	27	373	322	-3	-27%	-13%	14%	1%
11	at WAS	W	27	7	329	322	2	33%	-3%	-27%	8%
12	at CHI	L	13	21	367	204	-3	-38%	-59%	-25%	-4%
13	CIN	L	13	14	263	288	2	-1%	-29%	-24%	3%
14	at DET	L	17	34	233	407	-2	-51%	-32%	22%	2%
15	at CAR	L	17	19	287	392	-2	-35%	-33%	9%	7%
16	GB	L	3	20	109	431	0	-80%	-96%	-8%	8%
17	NO	L	20	23	280	338	2	34%	-18%	-39%	12%

Trends and Splits

	Offense	Rank	Defense	Rank
Total DVOA	-26.3%	32	1.1%	18
Unadjusted VOA	-21.6%	30	2.4%	21
Weighted Trend	-28.8%	32	-4.1%	15
Variance	9.4%	25	7.0%	21
Average Opponent	3.9%	32	2.3%	3
Passing	-22.5%	31	14.9%	23
Rushing	-19.4%	31	-14.5%	8
First Down	-35.7%	32	-5.9%	8
Second Down	-12.4%	26	3.8%	21
Third Down	-31.0%	30	12.0%	24
First Half	-30.7%	32	1.2%	19
Second Half	-22.1%	30	1.1%	16
Red Zone	-30.7%	28	2.2%	22
Late and Close	-31.2%	30	-5.2%	12

Five-Year Performance

Year	W-L	Pyth W	Est W	PF	PA	TO	Total	Rk	Off	Rk	Def	Rk	ST	Rk	Off AGL	Rk	Def AGL	Rk	Off Age	Rk	Def Age	Rk	ST Age	Rk
2010	10-6	8.7	8.4	341	318	+9	3.7%	12	8.0%	8	3.7%	23	-0.5%	18	22.8	14	37.8	25	25.6	31	25.9	27	25.4	30
2011	4-12	3.2	5.5	287	494	-16	-25.1%	30	-11.5%	26	14.2%	31	0.6%	14	17.1	5	34.3	20	26.0	30	25.6	31	25.3	31
2012	7-9	7.9	7.8	389	394	+3	-6.6%	20	0.6%	14	2.9%	20	-4.3%	27	26.7	14	30.1	18	26.4	22	25.6	30	25.7	24
2013	4-12	5.3	6.3	288	389	+10	-5.1%	19	-10.4%	24	-6.8%	8	-1.5%	22	75.6	31	9.6	2	27.0	16	25.0	32	26.2	11
2014	2-14	4.4	4.1	277	410	-8	-28.3%	30	-26.3%	32	1.1%	18	-0.8%	17	31.1	17	56.1	25	27.5	7	25.7	30	26.0	18

2014 Performance Based on Most Common Personnel Groups

TB Offense					TB Offense vs. Opponents					TB Defense				TB Defense vs. Opponents			
Pers	Freq	Yds	DVOA	Run%	Pers	Freq	Yds	DVOA	Run%	Pers	Freq	Yds	DVOA	Pers	Freq	Yds	DVOA
11	50%	5.7	-9.1%	18%	Base	40%	4.7	-18.7%	57%	Base	52%	5.5	0.8%	11	43%	5.6	-0.7%
12	29%	4.7	-22.5%	44%	Nickel	51%	5.3	-24.9%	21%	Nickel	48%	5.8	1.5%	12	24%	6.0	4.3%
21	8%	3.6	-46.7%	57%	Dime+	8%	5.7	-20.6%	1%					21	16%	6.2	13.9%
611	4%	5.6	-1.3%	76%	Goal Line	1%	2.7	17.2%	86%					22	6%	3.5	-20.7%
22	2%	5.3	-90.7%	71%										13	3%	5.1	-21.6%

Strategic Tendencies

Run/Pass		Rk	Formation		Rk	Pass Rush		Rk	Secondary		Rk	Strategy		Rk
Runs, first half	37%	18	Form: Single Back	76%	13	Rush 3	1.1%	32	4 DB	38%	5	Play action	11%	31
Runs, first down	47%	20	Form: Empty Back	3%	31	Rush 4	74.0%	3	5 DB	62%	14	Avg Box (Off)	6.24	21
Runs, second-long	29%	19	Pers: 3+ WR	54%	23	Rush 5	17.3%	28	6+ DB	0%	31	Avg Box (Def)	6.58	1
Runs, power sit.	62%	10	Pers: 4+ WR	2%	11	Rush 6+	7.6%	13	CB by Sides	81%	16	Offensive Pace	30.22	18
Runs, behind 2H	27%	15	Pers: 2+ TE/6+ OL	39%	8	Sacks by LB	8.1%	30	DB Blitz	8%	23	Defensive Pace	30.44	21
Pass, ahead 2H	48%	17	Shotgun/Pistol	56%	21	Sacks by DB	0.0%	31	Hole in Zone	7%	12	Go for it on 4th	0.76	23

As expected, Lovie Smith brought some significant changes to how Tampa Bay lined up on defense. Tampa went from ranking 14th to third in frequency of rushing four, went from 27th to first in the league in average men in the box, and completely stopped using dime personnel after using dime 15 percent of the time (eighth in the NFL) in 2013. ☙ Tampa Bay was the only defense in the league to face more running back carries from two-back sets than one-back sets. This is because teams will spread things out less when they are already beating you by three touchdowns. The Bucs allowed virtually the same yards per carry against one-back and two-back sets, but were much better in DVOA against one-back sets. In fact, only Detroit had a better run defense DVOA (-37.8% DVOA) against runs from one-back sets than Tampa Bay (-32.1% DVOA). ☙ One thing the Bucs defense did really well: they were tied for third in the league with only 64 broken tackles. ☙ The Buccaneers offense has finished dead last in yards after the catch for two straight years, averaging just 3.9 YAC in both 2013 and 2014. ☙ Part of that is that for the past two years, Tampa Bay has run the fewest wide receiver screens in the league. However, the Bucs did start using a lot more running back screens last year, tied for seventh with 32, and they were very successful, averaging 7.3 yards per play with 61.7% DVOA. ☙ Tampa Bay was one of eight teams to use six linemen at least 5.0 percent of the time, but were a lot less successful than they had been the year before, dropping from 4.9 yards per play and 32.6% DVOA to 3.8 yards and -16.5% DVOA.

Passing

Player	DYAR	DVOA	Plays	NtYds	Avg	YAC	C%	TD	Int
J.McCown*	-665	-41.9%	360	1971	5.5	4.0	57.0%	11	14
M.Glennon	107	-3.1%	219	1318	6.0	3.6	57.9%	10	6

Rushing

Player	DYAR	DVOA	Plays	Yds	Avg	TD	Fum	Suc
D.Martin	-21	-12.9%	134	494	3.7	2	0	36%
B.Rainey	14	-4.9%	94	406	4.3	1	1	43%
C.Sims	-84	-42.1%	66	185	2.8	1	2	35%
J.McCown*	47	35.9%	22	127	5.8	3	0	-
M.James	-34	-42.8%	19	37	1.9	0	0	32%
M.Glennon	6	2.2%	7	49	7.0	0	0	-

Receiving

Player	DYAR	DVOA	Plays	Ctch	Yds	Y/C	YAC	TD	C%
V.Jackson	4	-12.3%	142	70	1002	14.3	2.1	2	49%
M.Evans	222	11.4%	123	68	1051	15.5	2.5	12	55%
L.Murphy	-11	-15.3%	56	31	380	12.3	4.1	2	55%
R.Herron	-3	-15.5%	12	6	58	9.7	4.3	1	50%
R.Shepard	1	-11.7%	8	4	63	15.8	5.5	0	50%
A.Seferian-Jenkins	-29	-18.7%	38	21	221	10.5	2.0	2	55%
B.Myers	-23	-18.5%	32	22	190	8.6	2.7	0	69%
L.Stocker	-26	-42.5%	11	7	41	5.9	2.4	0	64%
B.Rainey	31	0.0%	45	33	315	9.5	8.4	1	73%
C.Sims	12	-4.4%	27	19	190	10.0	10.4	0	70%
D.Martin	-35	-47.2%	20	13	64	4.9	4.8	0	65%

Offensive Line

Player	Pos	Age	GS	Snaps	Pen	Sk	Pass	Run	Player	Pos	Age	GS	Snaps	Pen	Sk	Pass	Run
Demar Dotson	RT	30	16/16	979	16	4.5	13.0	4.0	Anthony Collins*	LT	30	10/10	622	10	3.0	14.5	1.0
Evan Dietrich-Smith	C	29	15/15	928	6	2.0	9.0	2.0	Oniel Cousins*	G/T	31	16/7	335	5	3.5	12.5	1.0
Logan Mankins	LG	33	16/16	910	7	1.0	14.0	4.5	Garrett Gilkey	OT	25	16/1	206	9	1.5	8.5	3.0
Patrick Omameh	RG	26	16/16	902	4	7.5	18.0	8.0									

Year	Yards	ALY	Rk	Power	Rk	Stuff	Rk	2nd Lev	Rk	Open Field	Rk	Sacks	ASR	Rk	Short	Long	F-Start	Cont.
2012	4.50	4.09	13	60%	22	20%	22	1.19	15	1.09	5	26	4.8%	6	4	13	17	36
2013	4.00	3.63	27	59%	22	21%	22	1.12	16	0.77	13	47	7.7%	21	16	21	18	33
2014	3.73	3.21	32	69%	7	23%	32	0.99	25	0.79	13	52	9.4%	29	24	13	17	33
2014 ALY by direction:		Left End 3.15 (27)			Left Tackle 3.52 (21)			Mid/Guard 3.24 (32)			Right Tackle 3.01 (30)				Right End 2.86 (28)			

If Josh McCown was the ultimate example of the perils in trusting a veteran backup coming off a hot half-season, left tackle Anthony Collins is a close second. Even including 2013 that included his best stretch as a pro, Collins accumulated just 12 Approximate Value over the first six years of his career, per Pro Football Reference. (By comparison, in his six-year career, Tony Mandarich managed 31 AV.) In Tampa last season, Collins was such a train wreck that the Bucs benched him after ten weeks before finally cutting him in March after failing to trade him (he remains unsigned as of this writing). The silver lining for the Bucs is that Collins will be totally off their salary cap next season, only having received $9 million of the $30 million in the five-year contract he signed last offseason.

This offseason, the Bucs went a different route to fill their left tackle hole, selecting Penn State tackle Donovan Smith in the second round. Smith appears very likely to start in Week 1, with 2013 fifth-rounder Kevin Pamphile his main competition. In a small sample last season, Pamphile showed little reason to think he could be the starting left tackle, blowing five blocks in just 118 snaps. With their other second-round pick, the Bucs drafted Ali Marpet to fill the other yawning void in their 2014 line: right guard. Patrick Omameh started all 16 games for Tampa last season only because he could not be worse than Oniel Cousins or Garrett Gilkey. He may start the 2014 season, but if he does not improve, the Bucs may need to move to Marpet quicker than they would otherwise. But history suggests that Marpet may have a long learning curve. Before Marpet, NFL teams had drafted just 17 Division III players since 1991, and none in the first three rounds. Even the most successful ones, Pierre Garcon and Cecil Shorts of Mount Union, contributed almost nothing as rookies.

Elsewhere on the line, the now more-efficiently named Evan Smith (formerly Dietrich-Smith) will play center, on-the-downside Logan Mankins will man left guard, and underpaid Demar Dotson will start at right tackle. All three project to be competent, although Mankins comes off a down year in which he almost single-handedly lost the Week 5 game against the Saints with a fourth-quarter blown block that led to a safety and a subsequent holding penalty that stopped a potential game-winning drive. Dotson, the line's best player, missed voluntary offseason workouts as he sought a new deal that pays more than the scheduled $2.5 million this season (and just $1.75 million in 2016). Now 29, Dotson understandably wants to get his first big contract. With the Bucs desperate to provide much better protection for Jameis Winston than they did for Glennon last season, Dotson would seem to have the upper hand in the negotiations.

Defensive Front Seven

Defensive Line	Age	Pos	G	Snaps	Plays	TmPct	Rk	Stop	Dfts	BTkl	Runs	St%	Rk	RuYd	Rk	Sack	Hit	Hur	Dsrpt
					Overall							vs. Run					Pass Rush		
Gerald McCoy	27	DT	13	664	37	5.2%	37	29	16	3	22	77%	52	1.5	21	8.5	6	15.5	2
Clinton McDonald	28	DT	13	619	47	6.6%	17	36	12	2	38	74%	68	2.6	64	5.0	3	5.5	1
Akeem Spence	24	DT	16	493	37	4.2%	54	27	12	1	31	71%	78	2.8	74	3.0	4	8.0	0
Henry Melton	*29*	*DT*	*16*	*424*	*19*	*2.4%*	*88*	*18*	*15*	*0*	*5*	*80%*	*32*	*1.0*	*8*	*5.0*	*4*	*8.0*	*4*

Edge Rushers	Age	Pos	G	Snaps	Plays	TmPct	Rk	Stop	Dfts	BTkl	Runs	St%	Rk	RuYd	Rk	Sack	Hit	Hur	Dsrpt
					Overall							vs. Run					Pass Rush		
Michael Johnson*	28	DE	14	629	27	3.5%	70	24	9	3	18	100%	1	0.6	2	4.0	8	9.5	0
William Gholston	24	DE	15	572	45	5.4%	35	38	12	0	38	84%	15	2.0	27	2.0	4	7.5	3
Jacquies Smith	25	DE	15	455	19	2.3%	86	14	12	2	6	33%	87	4.7	86	6.5	5	14.0	2
Da'Quan Bowers	25	DE	11	344	22	3.6%	68	18	6	1	16	94%	2	1.0	4	1.5	1	6.0	2
Larry English	29	DE	12	254	12	1.8%	--	9	2	1	11	73%	--	3.1	--	1.0	3	4.5	0
George Johnson	*28*	*DE*	*16*	*491*	*25*	*3.2%*	*79*	*19*	*13*	*0*	*14*	*71%*	*57*	*1.6*	*17*	*6.0*	*6*	*11.5*	*1*

Linebackers	Age	Pos	G	Snaps	Plays	TmPct	Rk	Stop	Dfts	BTkl	Sack	Hit	Hur	Runs	St%	Rk	RuYd	Rk	Tgts	Suc%	Rk	AdjYd	Rk	PD	Int
					Overall						Pass Rush				vs. Run						vs. Pass				
Lavonte David	25	OLB	14	919	146	18.9%	4	92	42	2	1.0	3	7.5	85	69%	20	2.7	14	40	50%	38	6.4	33	5	0
Danny Lansanah	30	OLB	16	632	87	9.9%	62	50	17	2	1.5	0	2	42	69%	23	2.5	12	27	52%	29	6.6	35	6	3
Mason Foster*	26	MLB	10	556	63	11.4%	52	33	11	0	0.0	1	2	37	59%	61	3.9	67	11	32%	--	7.6	--	2	0
Dane Fletcher*	29	MLB	16	351	30	3.4%	--	12	2	3	0.5	0	1.5	15	47%	--	7.7	--	4	5%	--	21.1	--	0	0
Orie Lemon	28	OLB	10	190	16	2.9%	--	10	4	1	0.0	0	0	13	69%	--	3.2	--	5	46%	--	4.5	--	0	0
Bruce Carter	*27*	*OLB*	*13*	*521*	*75*	*11.7%*	*47*	*40*	*17*	*8*	*1.0*	*2*	*2*	*36*	*64%*	*42*	*3.6*	*50*	*38*	*45%*	*47*	*5.7*	*20*	*7*	*5*

Year	Yards	ALY	Rk	Power	Rk	Stuff	Rk	2nd Level	Rk	Open Field	Rk	Sacks	ASR	Rk	Short	Long
2012	3.58	2.96	1	71%	27	33%	1	1.19	18	0.74	15	27	4.9%	31	10	8
2013	3.95	3.62	7	66%	17	24%	5	1.07	13	0.80	21	35	6.2%	25	14	11
2014	3.94	3.57	8	67%	20	25%	4	1.14	18	0.81	21	36	6.5%	19	19	12
2014 ALY by direction:		*Left End 4.15 (26)*			*Left Tackle 3.1 (8)*			*Mid/Guard 3.91 (13)*			*Right Tackle 3.13 (5)*				*Right End 2.27 (3)*	

How can a team with perhaps the league's best interior pass-rusher be only 19th in adjusted sack rate? Gerald McCoy did not play quite at his All-Pro level of 2013, with double-digit declines in both hits and hurries, but his 8.5 sacks still tied for the third-most at the position (behind Marcell Dareus and Aaron Donald). McCoy was not the problem. Everyone else was. Third-year undrafted defensive end Jacquies Smith was the only other Tampa defender to exceed five sacks or ten hurries. The second-best pass-rusher on the team this year might well be newly-signed Henry Melton, who reunites with the coach who drafted him. In his last healthy season, with Lovie Smith's 2012 Bears, Melton had six sacks and 9.5 hurries.

While the Bucs look to be in good shape for pass pressure from their tackles, pressure off the edge has been key to success for Smith's defenses of the past. Five times in Chicago, Smith had a top-five defense by DVOA (2005, 2006, 2010, 2011, and 2012). In four of those years, the Bears got double-digit sacks from a defensive end. In the other year, 2010, they got eight from a still-in-his-prime Julius Peppers. But Smith's current squad may have the worst set of edge rushers in football. The projected starters are a pair of undrafted players in fourth-year Jacquies Smith and fifth-year George Johnson, each of whom got their first career sack last year. Each posted remarkably similar stat lines in about the same number of snaps as rotational players last year. In 455 snaps, Smith posted 6.5 sacks, five hits, and 14.5 hurries. In 491 snaps, Johnson's stat line was 6.0-6.0-11.5. Both for Smith and Johnson, regression is more likely than continued production at 2014 levels, even though counting stats may increase with more snaps. If Johnson does start in Tampa Week 1, it will be the first start in his NFL career. Behind Smith and Johnson are two players who were drafted but have shown almost nothing as pass-rushers despite having opportunities. Larry English, a former Chargers' first-round pick, has never exceeded three sacks. William Gholston has had two in each of his first two years, giving him at least four more career sacks than his cousin Vernon.

Things look better, if still thin, at linebacker. It is well-established at this point that we love us some Lavonte David. That David has still not made a Pro Bowl is reason enough to dismiss that game as ridiculous. Watching him run down Le'Veon Bell last year brought back memories of Lawrence Taylor chasing down Rueben Mayes. In relentless pursuit, David may be without peer, but teammate Danny Lansanah brought similar energy to the strong side when he got his shot last season. Lansanah, un-drafted in 2008, saw no game action from 2009 through 2013 except with the Hartford Colonials and Las Vegas Locomotives. When he got his NFL shot after almost seven years of waiting, Lansanah played as if he knew it might be his only shot. Bruce

Carter was signed away from Dallas and will move from the outside to the middle to replace Mason Foster and call defensive signals. Fourth-round pick Kwon Alexander (LSU) is also in the mix, and given that Carter has not played 16 games yet in his four NFL seasons, Alexander is likely to see significant playing time. Scouting reports on Alexander praise his strength, quickness, and character, but he has a tendency to overpursue runners and get confused by misdirection.

Defensive Secondary

Secondary	Age	Pos	G	Snaps	Plays	TmPct	Rk	Stop	Dfts	BTkl	Runs	St%	Rk	RuYd	Rk	Tgts	Tgt%	Rk	Dist	Suc%	Rk	AdjYd	Rk	PD	Int
						Overall						vs. Run					vs. Pass								
Johnthan Banks	26	CB	15	908	60	7.3%	63	22	9	5	11	27%	56	7.8	52	79	25.6%	54	11.3	49%	49	7.0	20	11	4
Alterraun Verner	27	CB	14	859	85	11.0%	7	39	22	4	23	78%	2	4.4	10	71	24.1%	41	14.9	41%	74	10.2	72	9	2
Dashon Goldson*	31	FS	14	779	81	10.5%	31	15	3	12	33	21%	67	7.9	52	27	10.0%	48	16.6	44%	56	10.5	65	2	0
Major Wright	27	SS	12	504	52	7.9%	--	16	2	5	28	43%	--	7.5	--	8	4.7%	--	8.3	34%	--	7.0	--	1	0
Bradley McDougald	25	FS	15	445	53	6.4%	64	23	6	7	21	62%	8	4.3	7	24	15.9%	69	11.5	53%	40	5.6	17	6	1
Leonard Johnson	25	CB	16	387	44	5.0%	--	23	8	1	13	85%	--	4.4	--	29	21.6%	--	8.9	43%	--	7.6	--	3	1
Isaiah Frey	25	CB	11	227	22	3.6%	--	5	2	0	4	25%	--	4.8	--	12	15.5%	--	7.7	48%	--	9.1	--	1	0
D.J. Swearinger	24	SS	16	1018	79	9.3%	47	29	14	12	45	36%	45	6.1	27	40	9.3%	43	12.0	59%	23	7.3	36	5	2
Sterling Moore	25	CB	16	726	58	7.3%	61	20	8	4	6	33%	44	10.8	71	70	25.9%	56	12.2	41%	73	8.6	51	12	0
Chris Conte	26	FS	12	463	43	7.2%	61	3	3	5	14	0%	71	10.4	64	18	11.3%	56	12.1	36%	66	11.7	68	3	3

Year	Pass D Rank	vs. #1 WR	Rk	vs. #2 WR	Rk	vs. Other WR	Rk	vs. TE	Rk	vs. RB	Rk
2012	26	6.5%	21	6.7%	20	0.6%	18	12.8%	25	-1.5%	16
2013	11	-6.6%	13	-10.7%	8	20.6%	29	-7.4%	10	-19.5%	4
2014	23	27.1%	31	5.6%	21	-0.9%	16	4.0%	20	-17.9%	7

Alterraun Verner ended up being better than most of Tampa Bay's other 2014 free-agent additions, but he might have been the worst through the first few weeks of the season. Verner was torched by Devin Hester in the Week 3 loss where at one point, Tampa trailed Atlanta 56-0. His terrible charting stats would be even worse if Ben Roethlisberger had not missed a wide-open Antonio Brown on a bomb in the fourth quarter of Week 4. Verner is yet another player who Tampa signed on the basis of a short-term performance spike. Verner's production in 2014 was more in keeping with the player he seemed to be in his first three seasons in Tennessee (when he averaged nine passes defensed and two interceptions) than his outlier 2013 season (when he had 23 PDs and five picks). Tampa Bay's predilection for zone coverage means that Verner is only partially responsible for the Bucs' ranking of 31st against opposing No. 1 receivers. But Lovie Smith does switch up coverage more often than he used to, and he distinctly (and unsuccessfully) moved Verner around to cover certain opposing receivers including Antonio Brown and Steve Smith.

For pass coverage in 2015, we find more reason to be bullish on less-heralded 2013 second-rounder Johnthan Banks. After a poor rookie season both by adjusted yards per pass (79th) and success rate (70th), Banks improved considerably in each category. Run defense is another story: at 6-foot-2 and 185 pounds, Banks is unusually lean and can struggle against bigger runners despite a willingness to attack. New arrival Sterling Moore is yet another defender brought in (like Melton and Carter) from Dallas; he'll compete for the nickelback role with incumbent Leonard Johnson and veteran Mike Jenkins, who missed most of last year with a torn pectoral. Moore looks like another signing of a player coming off an outlier season. In 2012 and 2013, Moore allowed an average of 12.4 adjusted yards per pass on 33 targets. Last year in Dallas, Moore allowed just 8.6 adjusted yards per pass.

The Bucs gave up on free-agent failure Dashon Goldson and will replace him with another free-agent signing: Chris Conte, one of the six safeties who ranked worse than Goldson in adjusted yards per pass. Bradley McDougald, who went undrafted in 2013, appears likely to start ahead of waiver-wire pickup D.J. Swearinger at the other safety spot. McDougald was a pleasant surprise when given his chance in the last six weeks of 2014. In addition to showing consistent aggression and speed against the run, McDougald performed well in pass coverage. Finding both him and Lansanah was the upside of the player experimentation that comes with a 2-14 season.

Special Teams

Year	DVOA	Rank	FG/XP	Rank	Net Kick	Rank	Kick Ret	Rank	Net Punt	Rank	Punt Ret	Rank	Hidden	Rank
2012	-4.3%	27	1.9	12	1.7	12	-6.8	27	-15.1	30	-3.1	20	28.5	1
2013	-1.5%	22	-6.6	27	8.1	4	-7.2	31	-3.5	25	1.8	11	-7.9	26
2014	-0.8%	17	1.7	11	-1.4	18	-3.5	24	-0.6	18	-0.3	12	4.6	9

Tampa Bay's special-teams numbers changed a lot between 2013 and 2014, but the overall result was still mediocrity. One good move was signing kicker Patrick Murray after veteran Rian Lindell struggled in place of the injured Connor Barth in 2013. Murray took longer kicks than Lindell and made more of them, going 5-for-6 from 50 yards or longer. One of those kicks was good from 50 yards despite being deflected at the line by Cameron Heyward, and helped the Bucs upset the Steelers for one of their two wins.

On the other hand, Tampa kickoffs slid back towards average after excelling the year before. Punter Michael Koenen again handled all of the kickoff duties, but the 33-year-old may have lost leg strength. After 41 touchbacks on 69 kicks in 2013, Koenen had only 31 touchbacks on the same number of kicks last year. And while Tampa's net punting value improved overall, Koenen's kicks were often short. He averaged just 40.4 yards per punt, a year after averaging 44.2 yards. Koenen's net punting average fell only 1.2 yards, but the decrease in distance bears watching given his age. He may not make the roster given a price tag ($3.25 million for each of the next two years, no guaranteed money) that does not match his likely production. The Bucs can save $2.67 million in cap money by instead keeping former Browns punter Spencer Lanning (44.3-yard gross average, 39.2-yard net in 2014) for just $585,000. That would seem to be the more likely, and smarter, decision.

To improve on three years of average punt returns and below-average kickoff returns, the Buccaneers may look to Kaelin Clay, a sixth-round draft pick out of Utah. Last season, Clay returned three of 23 punts and one of 22 kickoffs for touchdowns at Utah, although two of those four touchdowns came in the season opener against FCS school Idaho State. Bobby Rainey is also part of the returner mix. He averaged 26.3 yards on six kickoff returns last season. Depth receiver Russell Shepard leads the Tampa coverage units; he had 14 tackles on special teams, 12 of which stopped a return short of what our metrics consider average.

Tennessee Titans

2014 Record: 2-14	**Total DVOA:** -29.3% (31st)	**2015 Mean Projection:** 6.4 wins	**On the Clock (0-4):** 24%
Pythagorean Wins: 3.3 (31st)	**Offense:** -16.4% (29th)	**Postseason Odds:** 18.1%	**Mediocrity (5-7):** 43%
Snap-Weighted Age: 27.0 (12th)	**Defense:** 11.2% (29th)	**Super Bowl Odds:** 0.9%	**Playoff Contender (8-10):** 27%
Average Opponent: -2.4% (24th)	**Special Teams:** -1.8% (20th)	**Proj. Avg. Opponent:** -4.1% (29th)	**Super Bowl Contender (11+):** 6%

2014: Same players, new coaches, what could go wrong? (Hint: Everything.)

2015: Marcus Mariota is now the hottest young thing in Nashville since Juliette Barnes.

When Ken Whisenhunt replaced Mike Munchak as Titans head coach following the 2013 season, it was heralded as new day for an organization whose identity had not really changed since Jeff Fisher's accession to the top job during the 1994 season. Gone was the defensive mindset, the (over-) emphasis on the run game, and the static 4-3 dependent on the defensive line to generate a pass rush. In came Whisenhunt, developer of Ben Roethlisberger, resurrector of Kurt Warner, and the man who took the Arizona Cardinals to the Super Bowl, to bring the Titans into the modern passing era of the NFL. With Whisenhunt came defensive coordinator Ray Horton, who brought the 3-4 back to one of the franchises that helped originate the 3-4 in the NFL, back in the Bum Phillips Luv Ya Blue Houston days of the 1970s.

The Titans neglected only one thing in the 2014 offseason: the acquisition of new players.

When Whisenhunt's offense and Horton's defense took the field Week 1 in Kansas City, you could be forgiven for thinking this was the same old Titans team. Eighteen of the 22 starters that game had previously started for the Titans, and only two starters were making their first appearances in two-tone blue.

With most of the same Titans players that finished 21st in DVOA and went 7-9 in 2013, supposed franchise saviors Whisenhunt and Horton produced a team that regressed across the board. Overall DVOA fell from -7.9% to a -29.3%, barely ahead of Jacksonville to avoid ranking as the worst team in the league. The decline came across the board, on both offense and defense:

- Run offense went from 2.8% DVOA (13th) to -8.9% (21st);
- Pass offense went from 5.6% DVOA (19th) to -12.7% (30th);
- Run defense went from 1.2% DVOA (25th) to 2.6% (29th); and
- Pass defense went from 6.8% DVOA (16th) to 19.1% (26th).

Suddenly, Munchak, the career offensive line coach who did not even know what yard line post-touchdown conversions took place from, did not seem like such a bad head coach.

Whisenhunt's arrival came with a guaranteed five-year contract, so his return was inevitable. General manager Ruston Webster returned, with the opportunity to buy the groceries for another head coach. And buy plenty of groceries the Titans did.

The draft provided the biggest headlines, as the Titans used a top-eight pick on a quarterback for the third time in ten seasons. Marcus Mariota becomes the Titans' latest Quarterback of the Future, following in the footsteps of Vince Young and Jake Locker. There is no question Mariota was a highly accomplished collegiate spread quarterback. Our new QBASE projection system is bullish on his future. He has no statistical red flags, like Locker's dismal completion percentage, and has a 36.7 percent chance of becoming an Upper Tier or Elite starter and only a 22.8 percent chance of being a Bust.

Watching Mariota's transition from Oregon's run-heavy spread to Ken Whisenhunt's traditional pocket-oriented, drop-back passing game will be fascinating. The questions surrounding Mariota are not based on what he has done to date, but what Whisenhunt will ask him to do regularly that he was not asked to do in college. That includes not just the ballyhooed "taking a snap from center" but progression reading, throwing with anticipation, and navigating a muddied pocket rather than escaping it.

Hitching the franchise's wagon to Mariota was a surprising decision for a couple reasons. First, one of his trademarks is his mobility, which was also a distinguishing feature of the failed Young and Locker, and a trait Whisenhunt has indicated he does not value highly. Second, Whisenhunt over the course of his career has shown a definitive preference for strong-armed pocket passers. Matt Leinart, who did not fit the mold, lost favor to Warner, who did. The parade of Derek Anderson, John Skelton, and Ryan Lindley that followed Warner did. Ditto Rivers, and Zach Mettenberger, the sixth-round rookie thrust into the lineup in Week 8 of last season.

Mettenberger drew many plaudits for his strong arm and willingness to throw the pull the trigger on tight window throws. What he did not do was sustain offense or string together a couple good quarters of football in a single game. Mettenberger produced zero first downs on over half of his drives as Tennessee's quarterback (34 of 64). Overall, those 64 drives produced 13 scores and 13 turnovers. The Titans have not won a game where they lost the turnover battle since Week 3 of 2012, so it comes as no surprise the Titans went 0-6 with Mettenberger as the starter and five of those games were decided by at least two scores.

Before and after Mettenberger got his shot, the Titans became the first team to finally give journeyman backup Char-

2015 Titans Schedule

Week	Opp.	Week	Opp.	Week	Opp.
1	at TB	7	ATL	13	JAC
2	at CLE	8	at HOU	14	at NYJ
3	IND	9	at NO	15	at NE
4	BYE	10	CAR	16	HOU
5	BUF	11	at JAC (Thu.)	17	at IND
6	MIA	12	OAK		

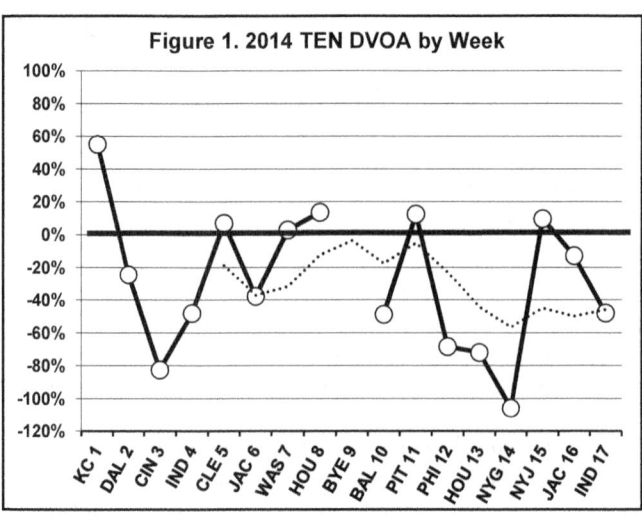

Figure 1. 2014 TEN DVOA by Week

lie Whitehurst an extended chance to start. Clipboard Jesus demonstrated that his main virtue was the willingness to take a sack rather than throw an interception. This is a fine main virtue for a journeyman backup.

Young began his career playing behind Kerry Collins, and Locker started his behind Matt Hasselbeck. But with Mettenberger and Whitehurst as the other options, Mariota starts his NFL career not only as Quarterback of the Future but also as Quarterback of the Present. Whisenhunt the head coach knows Whisenhunt the play-caller will not want to rely on Mariota to win games for him if he does not have to, so the rest of the draft was devoted to making Mariota's life easier.

When Whisenhunt had his success developing Ben Roethsliberger, Roethlisberger threw the ball early as part of a scripted offense, but was not asked to throw the ball frequently. Rather, the Steelers relied on a powerful running game to carry the offensive load. That sort of size and power was what the Titans went looking for with the rest of their draft:

• Second-round wideout Dorial Green-Beckham is 6-foot-5, 237 pounds, an inch taller and more than 30 pounds heavier than each of the Titans' top three receivers before the draft;
• Third-round tackle Jeremiah Poutasi, a mauler who will compete for the right tackle job as a rookie;
• Fourth-round fullback Jalston Fowler, who confessed he was not even sure he would be drafted because of the de-emphasis on fullbacks in today's NFL;
• Fifth-round running back David Cobb, a physical 229-pound between the tackles runner;
• Sixth-round center Andy Gallik, another mauler; and
• Seventh-round receiver Tre McBride, who like Green-Beckham is bigger than the Titans' previous top three receivers.

If you believe in revealed preference, then the Titans' draft picks are screaming they want to run a power run game as much as Whisenhunt and Webster's pre-draft press conference (60 questions about quarterbacks and two about Shane Ray) screamed they would in fact be selecting Marcus Mariota.

The 2004 Pittsburgh Steelers were able to effectively operate their offense under Whisenhunt the play-caller because they had the quality defense needed to sustain a run-heavy attack in the modern NFL. The same man who ran that defense will be tasked with making the 2015 Titans defense a similar sort of unit.

Ray Horton, an assistant on that Steelers team, still holds the title of defensive coordinator. Nevertheless, the Titans made it clear when they hired him that Dick LeBeau, while formally Assistant Head Coach/Defense, will be the one calling the shots.

If the second year is when a team undergoing to a scheme change starts to gel (itself a proposition probably more repeated in the telling than actually true), then LeBeau's arrival and insertion may push that gelling back another year. Horton's 3-4 had significant one-gap elements and was in some ways not much of a change from some of the Gregg Williams-inspired elements of 2013's 4-3 scheme. LeBeau's 3-4 is of a different stripe, placing more emphasis on two-gapping and relying on the outside linebackers for a pass rush the way the Titans of yore relied on 4-3 defensive ends for a pass rush. There's also a lot less emphasis on Horton's preferred press-man technique in the secondary. LeBeau and Horton's long association means the changes might not be quite as dramatic as this makes it seem, but another transition it will be.

The good news for LeBeau and Horton is that while the draft concentrated on the offense, free agency helped bring an overhaul to the defense.

Diving into free agency for big improvements is a chancy proposition. Webster already should know this; after all, he handed out $100 million worth of contracts before 2013 only to see the team's record improve all the way from 6-10 to 7-9 before last season's Whisenhunt swan dive. With smarter contract structuring, trawling the free-agency pond in the modern NFL means a mélange of strategies. You've got retaining your own players (outside linebacker Derrick Morgan, who drew interest from Atlanta and Tampa Bay before returning to the team that drafted him); hoping an aging player from another team can squeeze another year or three of top level production before injuries and Father Time take their toll (outside linebacker Brian Orakpo, late of Washington); gambling on an emerging player without even a season's worth of experience as a full-time starter (safety Da'Norris Searcy, a part-time player in Buffalo's loaded secondary); and signings that combine the last two concepts (cornerback Perrish Cox from San Francisco). The only free-agency boxes the Titans didn't check were paying somebody else's star like a superstar and signing a player who played in last season's Super Bowl and therefore "knows what it takes to win," though they did try for a McCourty Twins reunion before Devin re-signed with the Patriots.

Are these moves a recipe for transition from dreadful back to mediocre, or can a defense with no glaring weaknesses and just enough high-end talent in Orakpo and defensive end Jurrell Casey allow the offense to play the way it needs to?

The Titans are clearly hoping for the latter. Our numbers are more skeptical. The defense has not been above the league average since 2010. The best-case scenario for the offense is a rebound to 2013's league-average performance, not a quick climb to the heights of the 2004 Steelers team that finished in DVOA's

top six both running and passing in Ben Roethlisberger's rookie year. The Titans still play in the AFC South, though, and they face the NFC South in interconference play. That softness in the schedule means a return to the mediocrity of 6-10 or 7-9 is a real possibility. Transcending that barrier will require extremely fast development for Mariota and the renewal of the Dick LeBeau Defensive Academy that seemed to have lost its education license in Pittsburgh in recent years. Both those are unlikely to happen in 2015, which means the Tennessee playoff drought seems likely to reach its seventh season.

Tom Gower

2014 Titans Stats by Week

Wk	vs.	W-L	PF	PA	YDF	YDA	TO	Total	Off	Def	ST
1	at KC	W	26	10	405	245	3	55%	16%	-43%	-4%
2	DAL	L	10	26	314	368	-1	-25%	-25%	-5%	-4%
3	at CIN	L	7	33	326	300	-1	-83%	-33%	26%	-24%
4	at IND	L	17	41	261	498	-2	-48%	-11%	40%	3%
5	CLE	L	28	29	410	460	1	7%	41%	26%	-8%
6	JAC	W	16	14	290	379	2	-38%	-9%	31%	2%
7	at WAS	L	17	19	236	351	0	3%	-9%	-7%	5%
8	HOU	L	16	30	326	405	-2	14%	15%	19%	17%
9	BYE										
10	at BAL	L	7	21	210	312	-2	-49%	-40%	12%	3%
11	PIT	L	24	27	312	386	0	12%	17%	3%	-1%
12	at PHI	L	24	43	351	462	-1	-68%	-35%	7%	-26%
13	at HOU	L	21	45	320	457	-3	-72%	-44%	36%	7%
14	NYG	L	7	36	207	402	-2	-106%	-94%	0%	-13%
15	NYJ	L	11	16	342	277	-1	10%	-6%	-4%	12%
16	at JAC	L	13	21	357	288	0	-13%	8%	20%	-1%
17	IND	L	10	27	192	378	-1	-48%	-51%	-1%	3%

Trends and Splits

	Offense	Rank	Defense	Rank
Total DVOA	-16.4%	29	11.2%	29
Unadjusted VOA	-15.7%	29	8.5%	27
Weighted Trend	-24.0%	31	11.2%	29
Variance	11.0%	29	4.3%	7
Average Opponent	0.5%	18	-2.8%	28
Passing	-12.7%	30	19.1%	26
Rushing	-8.9%	21	2.6%	29
First Down	-6.3%	21	12.2%	29
Second Down	-25.0%	31	10.8%	28
Third Down	-22.9%	26	9.5%	23
First Half	-10.5%	25	0.9%	17
Second Half	-22.1%	31	21.8%	32
Red Zone	-14.8%	21	15.9%	30
Late and Close	1.4%	19	26.8%	32

Five-Year Performance

Year	W-L	Pyth W	Est W	PF	PA	TO	Total	Rk	Off	Rk	Def	Rk	ST	Rk	Off AGL	Rk	Def AGL	Rk	Off Age	Rk	Def Age	Rk	ST Age	Rk
2010	6-10	8.5	8.6	356	339	-4	6.6%	11	-4.5%	20	-5.8%	8	5.3%	6	20.9	13	10.5	5	27.4	17	26.5	20	26.2	17
2011	9-7	8.2	8.3	325	317	+1	6.6%	13	0.6%	15	0.3%	15	6.3%	3	20.0	7	17.7	9	28.1	3	25.7	30	26.4	14
2012	6-10	4.6	3.3	330	471	-4	-29.4%	30	-20.5%	29	7.5%	25	-1.4%	19	49.9	26	14.6	5	27.7	9	25.3	32	26.0	15
2013	7-9	7.5	6.6	362	381	0	-6.1%	21	1.4%	16	4.2%	22	-3.2%	26	28.3	12	15.6	6	27.3	13	26.2	20	26.4	8
2014	2-14	3.3	4.0	254	438	-10	-29.3%	31	-16.4%	29	11.2%	29	-1.8%	20	38.8	22	40.9	19	27.0	14	27.0	10	26.7	2

2014 Performance Based on Most Common Personnel Groups

TEN Offense					TEN Offense vs. Opponents					TEN Defense					TEN Defense vs. Opponents			
Pers	Freq	Yds	DVOA	Run%	Pers	Freq	Yds	DVOA	Run%	Pers	Freq	Yds	DVOA	Pers	Freq	Yds	DVOA
11	63%	5.7	-7.9%	21%	Base	33%	5.0	-9.2%	58%	Base	53%	5.7	9.0%	11	50%	5.7	7.8%
12	19%	4.9	-18.7%	54%	Nickel	50%	5.9	-2.1%	24%	Nickel	7%	4.0	-7.1%	12	22%	6.0	17.0%
21	9%	4.8	-14.8%	41%	Dime+	16%	4.5	-43.7%	14%	Dime+	39%	6.0	17.0%	21	11%	5.2	11.5%
22	3%	3.7	-35.2%	90%	Goal Line	0%	1.5	-22.8%	100%	Goal Line	1%	1.1	32.9%	22	6%	6.5	37.9%
612	2%	6.9	-13.0%	87%	Big	1%	7.4	-41.8%	88%	Big	1%	4.9	-7.5%	13	3%	5.4	16.5%

Strategic Tendencies

Run/Pass		Rk	Formation		Rk	Pass Rush		Rk	Secondary		Rk	Strategy		Rk
Runs, first half	36%	23	Form: Single Back	84%	5	Rush 3	7.7%	10	4 DB	41%	2	Play action	16%	29
Runs, first down	46%	23	Form: Empty Back	4%	22	Rush 4	49.7%	29	5 DB	8%	31	Avg Box (Off)	6.18	26
Runs, second-long	25%	26	Pers: 3+ WR	64%	14	Rush 5	26.5%	8	6+ DB	50%	3	Avg Box (Def)	6.48	2
Runs, power sit.	47%	28	Pers: 4+ WR	0%	30	Rush 6+	16.1%	3	CB by Sides	64%	29	Offensive Pace	32.56	29
Runs, behind 2H	25%	20	Pers: 2+ TE/6+ OL	27%	22	Sacks by LB	43.6%	14	DB Blitz	14%	4	Defensive Pace	30.28	17
Pass, ahead 2H	49%	11	Shotgun/Pistol	69%	9	Sacks by DB	20.5%	1	Hole in Zone	3%	30	Go for it on 4th	1.30	5

Offensively, the Titans were near league average on second-and-long, defined as 7 or more yards to go. But they were oddly abysmal on second-and-medium, defined as 3-6 yards to go. The Titans averaged 2.1 yards in these situations, when the NFL average was 5.1 and the next-worst team (Pittsburgh) averaged 3.7. The Titans' -62.8% DVOA on second-and-medium was the worst for any team in this century; the only teams in our database that were worse in this situation were the 1990 Bucs (-86.5% DVOA) and the 1997 Saints (-79.8% DVOA). Overall, the Titans have ranked 24th or worse on second downs for six straight seasons. 👈 As for third down, last year's Tennessee offense ranked fifth running the ball but 28th passing. 👈 Tennessee used a sixth lineman on 4.2 percent of plays, and actually was very successful. Both 7.7 yards per play and 33.2% DVOA were the highest in the league among the dozen offenses that used an extra lineman on at least 20 plays. 👈 The Titans doubled their frequency of defensive back blitzes, which led the percentage of sacks coming from defensive backs to shoot up from 28th in the league in 2013 to first last year. ESPN Stats & Information only recorded pass pressure on 27 percent of Tennessee's DB blitzes, the lowest figure in the league (NFL average: 42 percent). Yet, despite the lack of quarterbacks under duress, overall the strategy seemed to work, as the Titans allowed just 5.7 yards per pass on these plays compared to 7.4 yards per pass the rest of the time. 👈 Most teams haven't seen much year-to-year consistency when we compare run defense against one-back sets and two-back sets, but Tennessee is a big exception. For four straight seasons, the Titans have allowed significantly more yardage against runs from single-back formations, with a gap roughly twice as large as the NFL average. For 2014, that means 4.7 yards per carry on runs from single-back formations and 3.5 yards per carry with two backs, compared to NFL averages of 4.3 and 3.8.

Passing

Player	DYAR	DVOA	Plays	NtYds	Avg	YAC	C%	TD	Int
C.Whitehurst	49	-7.2%	200	1208	6.0	5.2	58.0%	7	2
Z.Mettenberger	-211	-28.7%	197	1277	6.5	6.2	59.8%	8	7
J.Locker*	-171	-27.8%	162	912	5.6	5.5	59.2%	5	7

Rushing

Player	DYAR	DVOA	Plays	Yds	Avg	TD	Fum	Suc
B.Sankey	24	-4.5%	152	575	3.8	2	2	44%
S.Greene	14	-5.2%	94	392	4.2	2	1	47%
D.McCluster	-19	-20.2%	39	125	3.2	0	0	41%
J.Locker*	53	46.1%	17	146	8.6	1	0	-
C.Whitehurst	5	-5.9%	15	94	6.3	0	1	-
L.Washington*	-18	-49.4%	13	57	4.4	0	0	8%
J.Battle*	11	20.3%	5	9	1.8	1	0	80%

Receiving

Player	DYAR	DVOA	Plays	Ctch	Yds	Y/C	YAC	TD	C%
K.Wright	67	-3.3%	93	57	715	12.5	6.4	6	61%
N.Washington*	97	5.3%	72	40	647	16.2	3.5	2	56%
J.Hunter	-4	-13.4%	67	28	498	17.8	6.4	3	42%
D.Hagan*	0	-12.5%	34	19	254	13.4	1.5	1	56%
K.Durham*	-28	-46.1%	11	6	54	9.0	2.5	0	55%
H.Douglas	108	5.9%	74	51	556	10.9	4.7	2	69%
D.Walker	12	-5.6%	106	63	857	13.6	6.0	4	59%
C.Coffman	-32	-40.5%	14	6	64	10.7	3.2	1	43%
A.Fasano	23	2.0%	36	25	226	9.0	3.2	4	69%
D.McCluster	26	-0.8%	37	27	203	7.5	7.2	1	73%
L.Washington*	14	-4.6%	31	22	159	7.2	6.3	2	71%
B.Sankey	26	7.0%	23	18	133	7.4	8.2	0	78%

Offensive Line

Player	Pos	Age	GS	Snaps	Pen	Sk	Pass	Run	Player	Pos	Age	GS	Snaps	Pen	Sk	Pass	Run
Andy Levitre	LG	29	16/16	965	10	6.5	12.0	1.5	Michael Roos*	LT	33	5/5	290	3	0.0	3.0	0.0
Chance Warmack	RG	24	16/16	964	8	1.5	8.5	5.0	Byron Stingily	RT	27	10/5	242	2	0.0	5.0	1.0
Michael Oher*	RT	29	11/11	651	6	5.5	16.5	3.0	Jamon Meredith	OT	29	7/3	209	3	2.0	5.5	0.0
Brian Schwenke	C	24	11/11	646	2	1.0	10.0	1.0	Will Svitek*	OT	33	5/3	187	0	6.5	11.5	1.0
Taylor Lewan	LT	24	11/6	353	4	4.0	6.0	1.5	Byron Bell	OT	26	15/15	1009	8	9.0	22.5	9.0
Chris Spencer*	G	33	16/5	331	2	0.5	1.5	0.0									

Year	Yards	ALY	Rk	Power	Rk	Stuff	Rk	2nd Lev	Rk	Open Field	Rk	Sacks	ASR	Rk	Short	Long	F-Start	Cont.
2012	4.21	3.35	31	67%	11	24%	28	1.13	18	1.19	3	39	7.1%	19	13	13	17	28
2013	3.83	3.82	19	55%	29	20%	19	1.05	21	0.60	22	37	6.7%	12	14	13	9	29
2014	3.82	3.91	17	63%	17	17%	4	1.06	23	0.39	31	50	8.9%	26	16	15	16	29
2014 ALY by direction:			Left End 3.27 (25)			Left Tackle 4.3 (7)			Mid/Guard 4.06 (14)			Right Tackle 3.99 (15)			Right End 3.01 (27)			

Eventually, the Tennessee Titans believe their investments in the offensive line will pay off. They certainly did not in 2014, which led them to return to the drawing board in 2015. The best position was probably left tackle. Michael Roos was his normal efficient self before blowing out his knee in Week 5 and retiring. First-round pick Taylor Lewan then came in and was solid for a rookie before getting hurt himself. His 47.1 snaps per blown block would have ranked him 14th among left tackles if he had enough snaps (400) to qualify for our rankings.

The big position battle for 2015 is at right tackle, where holdover swing tackle Byron Stingily, free-agent addition Byron Bell, and third-round rookie Jeremiah Poutasi (Utah) are the contenders. Bell showed with Carolina in 2014 he is definitely not a left tackle, but as a right tackle he could be acceptable while Poutasi grows into the position. The huge (6-foot-5, 335-pound) Poutasi also could move inside. Many draft experts doubted whether he has the athleticism to play at tackle, and incumbent left guard Andy Levitre has been a bit of a disappointment after signing a $46 million deal in free agency before 2013. Injuries the past two offseasons have limited his production. His biggest issue has been strength and holding up against power rushers. Levitre ranked among the top-ten left guards in blown block rate a year ago, but his bad plays were very, very bad. Losing one-on-one battles the way he did was particularly concerning to an offense that otherwise is filled with power players whose concern is not core strength.

That group includes two third-year players, right guard Chance Warmack and center Brian Schwenke. Warmack finally started to play up to his top-ten overall draft status late last year, but Schwenke failed to take the expected step forward from his rookie season, ranking in the bottom quarter of centers in snaps per blown block. He also missed significant time with an injury for the second straight year, leading to the selection of Boston College center Andy Gallik, yet another power player, in the sixth round of this year's draft.

Defensive Front Seven

Defensive Line	Age	Pos	G	Snaps	Plays	TmPct	Rk	Stop	Dfts	BTkl	Runs	St%	Rk	RuYd	Rk	Sack	Hit	Hur	Dsrpt
Jurrell Casey	26	DE	16	911	67	7.6%	7	54	21	2	58	78%	50	2.5	59	5.0	13	18.5	0
Sammie Lee Hill	29	DT	15	588	39	4.7%	44	34	10	1	30	83%	24	1.8	26	3.0	1	2.5	4
Ropati Pitoitua	30	DE	12	391	30	4.5%	48	23	6	1	27	74%	64	2.9	78	2.0	0	4.5	1
Mike Martin	25	DE	12	348	13	2.0%	--	6	1	0	13	46%	--	4.0	--	0.0	1	1.5	0
Karl Klug	27	DE	16	329	22	2.5%	--	18	10	2	18	78%	--	2.4	--	2.0	0	3.0	0
Al Woods	28	DT	16	288	26	3.0%	--	22	6	0	25	84%	--	1.4	--	1.0	0	3.5	0

Edge Rushers	Age	Pos	G	Snaps	Plays	TmPct	Rk	Stop	Dfts	BTkl	Runs	St%	Rk	RuYd	Rk	Sack	Hit	Hur	Dsrpt
Derrick Morgan	26	OLB	16	1004	70	8.0%	10	54	20	5	47	72%	53	2.5	44	6.5	3	15.5	3
Kamerion Wimbley*	32	OLB	13	538	30	4.2%	60	12	5	1	22	41%	86	4.6	85	2.0	3	3.0	0
Shaun Phillips*	34	OLB	16	446	26	3.0%	--	17	6	3	16	69%	--	3.1	--	2.0	0	9.5	2
Brian Orakpo	29	OLB	7	385	25	7.5%	14	20	5	2	21	81%	27	2.5	42	0.5	6	8.5	0
Jonathan Massaquoi	27	OLB	15	328	23	3.0%	--	11	4	3	14	36%	--	4.3	--	2.0	5	12.0	1

Linebackers	Age	Pos	G	Snaps	Plays	TmPct	Rk	Stop	Dfts	BTkl	Sack	Hit	Hur	Runs	St%	Rk	RuYd	Rk	Tgts	Suc%	Rk	AdjYd	Rk	PD	Int
Wesley Woodyard	29	MLB	16	879	97	11.0%	54	63	15	8	2.5	4	6.5	68	69%	22	3.2	34	25	53%	25	5.0	8	4	2
Avery Williamson	23	ILB	16	813	76	8.6%	72	46	18	4	3.0	2	6	53	60%	56	2.8	19	12	48%	--	8.8	--	3	0
Zaviar Gooden	25	ILB	15	156	20	2.4%	--	12	2	2	0.0	0	1	14	71%	--	3.5	--	3	61%	--	6.8	--	0	0

Year	Yards	ALY	Rk	Power	Rk	Stuff	Rk	2nd Level	Rk	Open Field	Rk	Sacks	ASR	Rk	Short	Long
2012	4.35	4.39	29	67%	24	20%	12	1.36	30	0.67	11	39	6.5%	13	16	9
2013	4.03	4.15	23	61%	12	17%	23	1.17	22	0.52	10	36	6.6%	20	11	11
2014	4.41	4.08	23	73%	27	19%	17	1.25	26	0.84	26	39	7.0%	11	13	13
2014 ALY by direction:			Left End 3.67 (17)			Left Tackle 5.17 (32)			Mid/Guard 4.12 (23)			Right Tackle 2.9 (4)			Right End 4.22 (22)

This offseason's personnel makeover largely bypassed the defensive line, where every player who took a regular season snap returns and the only addition came on the third day of the draft (fourth-round pick Angelo Blackson, a defensive end out of Auburn). The lack of change was a curious decision, as this position group seemed underwhelming as a whole. The best player in the group, by a significant margin, is Jurrell Casey. An elite penetrator who can split double teams, he adapted just fine to Ray Horton's defensive scheme. His sack total predictably declined from the double digits he hit in 2013, but his other pressure numbers increased from 5 hits and 14 hurries in 2013 to 13 and 18.5 a year ago. LeBeau indicated Casey will again be mostly asked to play one-gap, like he was under both Horton and the Titans' previous regimes.

Horton also wildly praised Sammie Hill's work at nose tackle, declaring him to be a Pro Bowl-caliber player. Hill's lack of pass-rushing success or draft pedigree obviously means he would never make the actual Pro Bowl, but he had some very solid performances against some of the weaker interior lines the Titans faced. The rest of the group has reached a comfortable level of mediocrity. That was a disappointment considering the three-year extension the Titans gave Ropati Pitoitua for his work on run downs. He may lose his starting spot to DaQuan Jones, a Penn State product and 2014 fourth-round pick who played just 137 snaps as a rookie. For passing downs, the Titans surprisingly brought back Karl Klug, an undersized pure penetrator with a tendency to feast on poor foes and be routinely shut down by good ones.

Derrick Morgan's transition from 4-3 end to 3-4 outside linebacker started out with uncertainty and ended up with Morgan having another very Derrick Morgan-like season. As always, Morgan played solid run defense and had a disproportionate number of hurries, only with 150 snaps of pass coverage instead of a handful. The Titans hope that finally adding a quality rusher opposite him turns more of those hurries into sacks. When healthy, Brian Orakpo is that player, a power rusher with better speed and burst than Morgan who also lacks the softness against the run that plagued the retired Kamerion Wimbley. The question is whether the Titans will get a healthy Orakpo. He has missed 22 games the past three seasons and was on the injury report every week he played in 2014. They need him healthy, because their other options are Jonathan Massaquoi, not good enough for Atlanta's anemic pass rush, and sixth-round rookie Deiontrez Mount (Louisville).

By Week 8, rookie inside linebacker Avery Williamson had advanced from special teams only to platoon player to starter to defensive signal-caller. He heads into his second NFL season as a starter on the inside and likely an every-down player once again. As long as the Titans don't ask him to take on many one-on-one assignments in pass coverage, and the defensive line prevents him from having to take on and defeat offensive linemen, he should be successful. Next to him will be either Zach Brown or Wesley Woodyard. Brown is the more physically gifted of the two and can run with any tight end in the league. A pure space player, he played only four snaps in 2014 before a shoulder injury sent him to injured reserve. If he's learned to play football since 2013, Titans fans could stop thinking of him as "the weakside linebacker picked with Lavonte David still on the board." If Brown wins the starting job, the veteran Woodyard will back up both spots.

Defensive Secondary

Secondary	Age	Pos	G	Snaps	Plays	TmPct	Rk	Stop	Dfts	BTkl	Runs	St%	Rk	RuYd	Rk	Tgts	Tgt%	Rk	Dist	Suc%	Rk	AdjYd	Rk	PD	Int
						Overall							vs. Run						vs. Pass						
Michael Griffin	30	FS	16	1131	115	13.1%	12	41	12	17	60	42%	35	6.0	26	41	9.8%	47	10.5	35%	67	10.5	66	5	2
Jason McCourty	28	CB	16	1077	96	10.9%	9	25	10	1	11	18%	68	17.2	76	116	29.2%	68	13.1	43%	65	8.5	50	11	3
George Wilson*	34	SS	16	809	74	8.4%	52	35	10	9	50	52%	18	5.0	14	25	8.2%	36	5.5	57%	29	5.4	13	3	1
Coty Sensabaugh	27	CB	13	721	50	7.0%	66	19	7	10	12	25%	59	7.5	48	53	19.9%	13	10.7	46%	61	8.0	41	6	0
Blidi Wreh-Wilson	26	CB	11	668	67	11.1%	6	24	7	4	19	42%	34	8.4	54	74	29.8%	70	14.0	46%	59	9.3	63	10	1
Bernard Pollard*	31	SS	5	344	28	10.2%	--	10	5	2	14	21%	--	8.4	--	9	6.7%	--	10.3	74%	--	2.6	--	1	0
Daimion Stafford	24	SS	15	274	28	3.4%	--	12	7	5	10	50%	--	8.0	--	11	10.9%	--	6.8	44%	--	6.8	--	2	1
Marqueston Huff	23	FS/SS	14	269	14	1.8%	71	6	5	2	2	50%	20	4.0	5	20	20.2%	71	7.6	51%	46	5.2	9	2	1
Perrish Cox	28	CB	15	940	69	9.5%	22	25	9	4	7	14%	71	8.4	55	87	23.1%	35	15.5	51%	38	7.7	35	16	5
Da'Norris Searcy	27	SS	15	648	62	8.0%	57	23	9	1	39	46%	29	6.2	29	10	4.2%	2	18.6	61%	19	5.1	7	4	3

Year	Pass D Rank	vs. #1 WR	Rk	vs. #2 WR	Rk	vs. Other WR	Rk	vs. TE	Rk	vs. RB	Rk
2012	19	24.3%	29	-13.5%	8	-5.4%	11	-5.5%	10	23.5%	30
2013	16	-13.2%	6	10.0%	23	-14.9%	7	8.6%	22	12.1%	26
2014	26	-6.3%	10	53.9%	32	-8.1%	10	9.0%	24	0.5%	18

The biggest question with the LeBeau-Horton dynamic concerns the corners and how much they will be asked to do. Historically, LeBeau has called more zone coverages while Horton has relied heavily on press corners who can hold up in man coverage. In 2014, the Tennessee corners emphatically did not. Following the league's best young receivers proved too tall a task for Jason McCourty, strictly an outside player with mediocre ball skills and limited agility. Tennessee opponents threw a league-high 30 percent of passes to the players we identified as No. 1 receivers. The Titans had a reasonable DVOA against No.

1 receivers in total because McCourty was much better shutting down older possession receivers we classified as No. 1s, such as Steve Smith and Andre Johnson. But he was burned repeatedly by A.J. Green and Antonio Brown, and will live forever on Odell Beckham's highlight reel.

Across from McCourty, in his first year as a starter, Blidi Wreh-Wilson was better than his lowlights would suggest. However, those lowlights were pretty low; he was annihilated by DeAndre Hopkins on a double move and, in the 2014 Titans' Garo Ypremian moment, gave up a touchdown to Andy Dalton on a throwback pass. Yes, that Andy Dalton. The Titans added Perrish Cox from San Francisco in free agency; he'll replace Wreh-Wilson in the starting lineup and then shift to the slot to replace the disappointing Coty Sensabaugh in sub packages. Cox was a starter last season for the first time since he was a rookie with the 2010 Broncos, and he faded badly over the course of the season, with 60 percent adjusted success rate and 6.7 adjusted yards per pass in the first eight games, then 43 percent and 8.2 thereafter.

What do Dick LeBeau safeties do without Troy Polamalu? Not since Bill Clinton was president has LeBeau coordinated a defense without the recently-retired Dandruff Knight. Michael Griffin is a prototype free safety who is inconsistent in man coverage and has struggled at strong safety in the past. He tends to perform best in ideal situations but persevered in 2014 through a bad team, a separated shoulder, and the loss in Week 5 of Bernard Pollard to a season-ending Achilles injury. Da'Norris Searcy, formerly of the Bills, fits more of the strong safety prototype and the void created by Pollard's offseason release. In OTAs, though, he and a still-rehabbing Griffin were playing left and right safety rather than strong and free. Griffin should be full go by training camp, sending Marqueston Huff back to a backup and sub package role.

Special Teams

Year	DVOA	Rank	FG/XP	Rank	Net Kick	Rank	Kick Ret	Rank	Net Punt	Rank	Punt Ret	Rank	Hidden	Rank
2012	-1.4%	19	-4.6	25	-9.1	29	2.3	10	-13.1	27	17.8	1	2.4	11
2013	-3.2%	26	-1.8	22	-4.5	27	-1.3	16	0.6	18	-9.1	29	5.3	8
2014	-1.8%	20	-0.1	17	-9.4	30	1.1	11	2.7	11	-3.3	20	-9.5	28

Ryan Succop came in to bail the Titans out of last summer's kicking competition and stabilized the position well enough to earn an extension this offseason. He was average on place kicks and average on kickoffs. Tennessee's poor overall ranking on kickoffs was due to the league's second-worst kick coverage unit, which allowed 9.9 points of return value. Like Succop, punter Brett Kern earned an extension. He had perhaps the best season of his career, ranking ninth in gross punting value, and his coverage unit did not suffer from the same breakdowns as the kickoff unit.

Dexter McCluster was the league's most valuable punt returner with Kansas City in 2013, but found space in Tennessee much harder to come by. He spent too much time dancing and trying to avoid gunners, and ended up with below-average value, just like primary kickoff returner Leon Washington. Better blocking should help McCluster, whose skill set is suited well for punt returns, and whoever ends up being the kick returner with Washington unsigned. Candidates for the job include running backs Antonio Andrews and Bishop Sankey, both unimpressive in limited 2014 sample sizes, and everybody else on the roster. [1]

---

1 Except for Jeremiah Poutasi, we assume. Although watching Jeremiah Poutasi return kickoffs would be huge amounts of fun for everybody.

Washington Redskins

2014 Record: 4-12	**Total DVOA:** -27.0% (28th)	**2015 Mean Projection:** 6.0 wins	**On the Clock (0-4):** 30%
Pythagorean Wins: 4.5 (28th)	**Offense:** -11.8% (28th)	**Postseason Odds:** 14.5%	**Mediocrity (5-7):** 42%
Snap-Weighted Age: 26.8 (18th)	**Defense:** 9.9% (27th)	**Super Bowl Odds:** 0.9%	**Playoff Contender (8-10):** 23%
Average Opponent: -1.6% (19th)	**Special Teams:** -5.4% (29th)	**Proj. Avg. Opponent:** -0.2% (17th)	**Super Bowl Contender (11+):** 5%

2014: Between Griffin, Cousins, and McCoy, the Redskins were the NFL's version of a three-ring circus.

2015: Circuses are never quite as fun the second time around.

Checking back in on the Redskins after a few months away is like returning home for your high school reunion and discovering that no one has changed. All of the old grudges, resentments, unfulfilled expectations and dysfunctional relationships have been preserved in amber since the day you left.

There's ol' Bobby the Star Quarterback, still living off already-faded accomplishments. Plucky Kirk is still working in the convenience store and dreaming of buying a bus ticket out of town. Old Man Snyder is still the only employer in town, and while the Redskins football factory brings a living wage, everyone knows that the only thing the old mill really grinds away is hope.

The Redskins you know and love are back. The three-headed quarterback controversy, the closest thing science will ever create to a perpetual motion machine, is back. Supporting characters like Alfred Morris, Pierre Garcon, DeAngelo Hall, Trent Williams, Ryan Kerrigan and Jordan Reed are back. Jay Gruden, who ended every press conference in his rookie season as head coach by stepping on a rake and thwapping himself in the head, is also back. Dan Snyder is back, because owners cannot be fired. There are no big-name newcomers, and only a few medium-name ones. A team that won seven combined games in 2013 and 2014 is back for a second encore.

It almost makes you long for the days when Snyder spent a bazillion dollars and reimagined the roster every year. The Redskins used to make the same mistake every year. Now they spend three years prolonging the same mistake. It's a subtle difference.

Not everything is exactly the same in Washington. No Redskins season would be complete without a new savior: Gruden last year, Robert Griffin in 2012, Mike Shanahan and Donovan McNabb in 2010, and so on, back to Steve Spurrier. The latest messianic figure is Scot McCloughan, tortured NFL genius. McCloughan was the architect of the 2005-09 drafts that turned the 49ers into a powerhouse. He then discovered late-round superstars Russell Wilson and Richard Sherman (among others), helping John Schneider and Pete Carroll create the current Seahawks juggernaut. In between, he drank a lot, sometimes on the job, and a festering alcohol problem led to a quiet dismissal from San Francisco and may have led to a worn-out welcome in Seattle.

A December article on McCloughan by *ESPN The Magazine*'s Seth Wickersham became the defining source text for McCloughan. Unemployed at the time of Wickersham's profile, McCloughan suddenly became a buzzy name in media and fan circles. Snyder may well have had McCloughan on his radar before the article was published, but if there is any owner in the NFL likely to hire a new general manager based on something he read in a magazine, it's Snyder.

Like any new Redskins general manager, McCloughan inherited all of the problems caused by his predecessor—or more precisely, by his predecessor's inability to overcome Snyder's influence. With Griffin in a state of arrested development, the Redskins have virtually nothing to show for three consecutive drafts except Alfred Morris and some oft-injured peripherals like Reed. While division rivals acquired instant difference makers like Odell Beckham and Zack Martin in last year's draft, the Redskins sat out the first round, then grabbed a pair of prospects so unimpressive (Trent Murphy and Morgan Moses) that they doubled down at the same positions this year. The 2014 starting lineup was a hodgepodge of leftovers from 2011, some mid-round picks from 2012-14 who weren't doing anything extraordinary on the field, and the usual collection of veteran free agents who cling to the Redskins depth chart, plus DeSean Jackson, grabbed off the wire last offseason after Chip Kelly cut him in one of the first tremors of what eventually became this offseason's Chipquake.

With minimal star power and an almost complete dearth of mid-tier talent, the 2014 Redskins finished 27th or lower in DVOA on offense, defense, special teams, passing offense, passing defense, adjusted sack rank on offense, and a wide variety of split categories. The Redskins had one of the worst third-down offenses in history (See Table 1, next page), particularly on third-and-long (-144.3% DVOA). The three-quarterback juggling routine generated all of the attention, but the Redskins were rotten in every phase of the game.

McCloughan could not hope to overhaul the Redskins roster in one offseason. He spent judiciously in free agency, adding Terrance Knighton and Stephen Paea to beef up the defensive line and Dashon Goldson and Chris Culliver to professionalize the secondary while fulfilling an "old 49ers" quota. McCloughan extended DeAngelo Hall, the mistake the Redskins plan to keep making until their foolishness starts to look like cockamamie wisdom. Goldson and Culliver aside, McCloughan was in no hurry to stock the roster with "his guys," perhaps in part because many of his guys (Frank Gore, Brandon Browner) were fetching premium open-market prices.

The veteran buttressing will help the Redskins become more competitive, but many of the acquisitions were the kind an expansion team makes just to prevent weekly embarrassment.

2015 Redskins Schedule

Week	Opp.	Week	Opp.	Week	Opp.
1	MIA	7	TB	13	DAL (Mon.)
2	STL	8	BYE	14	at CHI
3	at NYG (Thu.)	9	at NE	15	BUF
4	PHI	10	NO	16	at PHI
5	at ATL	11	at CAR	17	at DAL
6	at NYJ	12	NYG		

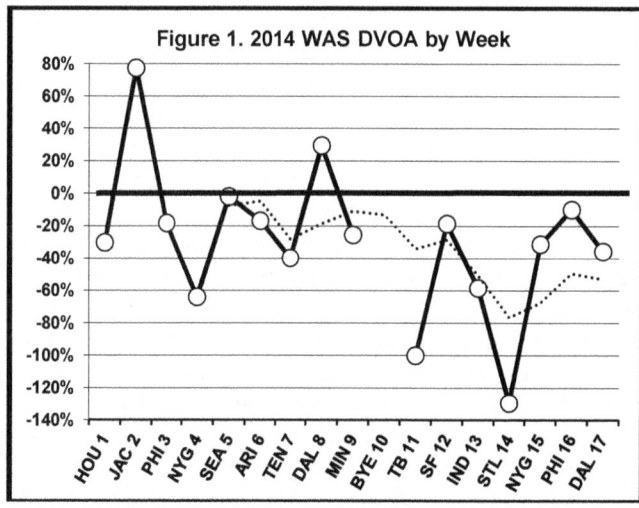

Figure 1. 2014 WAS DVOA by Week

McCloughan's draft was only slightly more illuminating. Right tackle Brandon Scherff, the Redskins' first pick in the first round since Griffin, solves an immediate need and joins Trent Williams to bookend a line that has not seen high-quality reinforcements in years. Pass rusher Preston Smith offsets the free agent loss of Brian Orakpo. Running back Matt Jones decreases the offense's reliance on Morris, who has shouldered a heavy burden for three years. Jamison Crowder and Evan Spencer add competition at wide receiver and could solve a perennial return-game problem. The late rounds brought reinforcements in the secondary and on the offensive lines; because the late rounds are supposed to be McCloughan's "Sherman Zone," the burgundy-and-gold faithful are already penciling in contributions from guys like Tevin Mitchell and Austin Reiter.

Even if you assume that there is a Sherman or Gore lurking among McCloughan's late-round picks, it's hard to muster any immediate excitement about the 2015 Redskins. The draft brought building blocks, just as free agency brought short-term structural support. There's not a playoff-caliber unit on the depth chart, and there's a lingering sense of dysfunctionality between the underwater-mortgage quarterback and the coach who was supposed to breathe fresh air into the organization but spent 2014 recycling the previous year's lingering odor.

Ah, Gruden and Griffin. Every day in the offseason, Gruden woke, brushed his teeth, perhaps savored a soft-boiled egg, then announced to the Washington media that *Robert Griffin is still the Redskins quarterback, as of right now.* It was like entering the codes on *Lost*: if Gruden did not reaffirm Griffin's status daily, complete with a passive-aggressive undermining clause

at the end of the sentence (*if the season started today, if he continues to make progress, If Robert and I were the last two humans on earth*), the global infrastructure would crumble.

It's tempting to take sides in a dysfunctional relationship like Griffin-Gruden (Grudiffin? Griffuden? Have the shippers skipped this one?) Either Gruden has been saddled with a coach killer or Griffin is once again stuck with a coach who has a quick hook and a penchant for public mind games. The truth is probably much simpler and more depressing: the Redskins have a difficult quarterback puzzle to solve and the wrong man trying to solve it.

Gruden managed his three quarterbacks last year as if he was taking requests from message board trolls. Griffin was not the only quarterback who had to deal with Gruden's postgame and midweek forays into giftwrapping sports-talk content. After the October loss to the Cowboys, Gruden publically dressed down Colt McCoy as if the former third-stringer had rear-ended him in the parking lot. Some selected post-game quotes: "Terrible decision by McCoy … McCoy has to take charge of the huddle … He missed the throw … not clean on his audible mechanics …"

McCoy was only in the lineup because Kirk Cousins went from America's favorite backup to interception-prone stumble-bum in six weeks. There weren't enough leash posts in Gruden's quarterback doghouse for all three starters, so McCoy was back

Table 1: Worst Offensive DVOA on Third/Fourth Downs, 1989-2014

Team	Year	3rd/4th Down	Rank	3rd/4th Down Y+1	Rank	Off DVOA	Rank	Off DVOA Y+1	Rank
HOU	2002	-70.5%	32	19.1%	10	-43.3%	32	-14.7%	28
CHI	2004	-65.4%	32	-45.9%	28	-36.5%	32	-17.1%	28
SEA	1992	-63.2%	28	-57.1%	25	-41.3%	28	-7.8%	20
WAS	2014	-62.7%	32	--	--	-11.8%	28	--	--
SF	2005	-58.7%	32	12.3%	15	-40.4%	32	-8.2%	23
CAR	2002	-58.3%	31	-0.9%	15	-25.2%	31	-5.0%	18
OAK	2008	-58.1%	32	-19.8%	20	-26.1%	31	-25.8%	30
SEA	1998	-57.1%	30	-8.8%	18	-10.4%	25	-3.0%	17
ARI	2010	-55.4%	32	-128.1%	32	-35.6%	31	-18.4%	28
BUF	1997	-54.3%	30	106.4%	3	-18.0%	28	19.4%	4
IND	1993	-53.2%	28	-17.8%	19	-20.3%	27	-5.8%	20
ARI	2012	-51.1%	32	-6.2%	18	-31.0%	32	-2.4%	20

in the huddle a few weeks after the Cowboys game. He suffered a neck injury during a six-sack drubbing at the hands of the Rams, but Gruden threw him back on the field after a week of severely limited practice to face the Giants. Griffin replaced McCoy in the first quarter, once it became clear that a clean hit might cripple the starter. Despite McCoy's obvious infirmity, Cousins wasn't even dressed for the Giants game. That made sense.

Gruden's game management was also amateurish. He was generally aggressive on fourth downs, but in a random, indecisive way. The Colts loss hinged on a changed fourth-and-1 call: Gruden scrapped an inside run and ordered McCoy (a month removed from his public castigation) to launch a play-action bomb to single-covered DeSean Jackson. An unblocked Erik Walden strip-sacked McCoy, and the resulting Colts touchdown put the game out of reach.

Gruden called a third-quarter fake punt against the Rams: not a terrible idea in a game when Jackson was hurt and the Redskins needed to manufacture points. But rookie punter Tress Way had never run a fake before, not even in college, and he ignored a Niles Paul block to the outside and barreled straight into a crowd of Rams instead. Way blamed himself. Gruden blamed him too in the postgame presser, as well as special-teams coordinator Ben Kotwica.

And then there was the Giants game in Week 15. The Redskins trailed by 11 points and were out of timeouts with 2:28 to play when they got the ball at their own 18-yard line. After a few short passes and the two-minute warning, Gruden ordered Griffin and the team into slow-down mode. They ran on third-and-8. They took a delay of game penalty. They punted. And when the Giants muffed the punt, Gruden ordered Griffin to throw a short pass to Jackson with nine seconds left instead of a Hail Mary for pride or a kneel for health and safety. Remember that McCoy had already left the game and was headed for injured reserve. Gruden coached the end of the game like he was the Madden AI, not an intelligent adult whose decisions are supposed to achieve some kind of comprehensible goal.

Griffin, for his part, could have done something to inspire Gruden's confidence. On the previous two fourth-quarter drives of the Giants loss, Griffin got dinged after a one-yard scramble on third-and-four and took a strip sack that set up fourth-and-29. The Redskins' historically-awful third-and-long DVOA was the result of synergy between all three quarterbacks' terrible third-down habits (the trio was sacked 19 times on third down with more than six to go) and Gruden's knack for making sure all three quarterbacks faced as many untenable down-and-distance situations as possible. The Redskins were 0-for-20 on conversions of third-and-15 or more, 5-of-68 with four turnovers on third-and-10 or more.

Griffin now has the footwork of a newborn baby deer, with legs sprawling in all directions when he attempts basic maneuvers in or out of the pocket. His stat sheet for 2014 was like a straw-man argument against completion percentage as a measure of quality. Griffin completed 68.7 percent of his passes, which would rank in the all-time top 20 if he had played a little more. But Griffin led the NFL in failed completion rate: exactly one-third (47 of 149) of his completions were essentially useless. Griffin's scrambling brought little value; de-signed runs netted 60 yards on 17 carries, plus a fumble. Griffin's late-season revival was more narrative than reality: he played well against the unravelling Eagles but otherwise just completed short passes and mopped up while Gruden threw in a whole Bed, Bath and Beyond's worth of towels.

There was not much McCloughan could do about the Gruden-quarterback mess. Gruden had already received several votes of confidence before the new general manager came aboard, and firing a coach after one season is generally a bad idea. The free-agent and draft quarterback markets were weak. Cousins' trade value was nonexistent, thanks in part to Gruden burying him in mulch, and of course the Griffin investment requires an extra-slow trigger. Retaining McCoy can be interpreted as a classy move from the you-break-it, you-buy-it standpoint. A token tidying of the quarterback situation—trading Cousins for a conditional seventh-round pick in 2018, or something—would have clarified the organization's quarterback priorities, both in Ashburn and the rest of the country. It did not happen.

Instead, the Redskins refreshed Gruden's coaching staff. Defensive coordinator Jim Haslett was fired after years of fawning by television announcers (Haslett is a generous and open interview subject) but mediocre defensive performances. Joe Barry, defensive coordinator of the 0-16 2008 Lions and son-in-law of Cowboys defensive coordinator Rob Marinelli, replaces Haslett after three seasons as the Chargers linebackers coach.

Bill Callahan also joined Gruden's staff as offensive line coach after three seasons as line coach and running game coordinator for the Cowboys. Like McCloughan, Callahan comes with "savior" bona fides: maybe he can do to the Redskins line what he did to the Cowboys line, turning Scherff into a star like Travis Frederick/Zach Martin, etc. Of course, Callahan also has the resume of an interim head coach if Snyder and McCloughan decide enough is enough after Thanksgiving. Gruden's expendability went up in the offseason. Meanwhile, the Redskins exercised their fifth-year option on Griffin: he won't be going anywhere until after the 2016.

Everyone is now relying on everyone else in the Redskins organization, not to compete for a wild card, but to just claw out of the latest sinkhole. Griffin needs Gruden to help him stabilize his mechanics, draw up some viable game plans, and ditch the public frenemy routine. Gruden needs Griffin to make gains he has spent two seasons failing to make. Gruden and Griffin need Callahan to upgrade the line, and Callahan needs Scherff to mature as quickly as Cowboys rookies did. Gruden needs Barry to coach up the defense; Barry needs McCloughan's low-cost veterans to buy in. Everyone needs McCloughan to be as clever a talent evaluator as advertised and—let's be blunt about a guy who wasn't exactly toeing the 12-stepper line in the Wickersham article—to stay on the wagon. McCloughan needs his coach and quarterback to be better versions of themselves or else no one will care who he discovered in the sixth round. Everyone needs Snyder to stay the heck out of the way.

All teams rely on multiple coaches, players and execs for success, of course. Only Washington is relying on so many people with an obvious capacity for failure.

Mike Tanier

2014 Redskins Stats by Week

Wk	vs.	W-L	PF	PA	YDF	YDA	TO	Total	Off	Def	ST
1	at HOU	L	6	17	372	321	-1	-30%	-3%	7%	-20%
2	JAC	W	41	10	449	148	1	77%	30%	-46%	1%
3	at PHI	L	34	37	511	379	0	-18%	26%	10%	-34%
4	NYG	L	14	45	329	449	-5	-64%	-42%	27%	5%
5	SEA	L	17	27	307	403	0	-2%	12%	7%	-8%
6	at ARI	L	20	30	407	317	-4	-17%	-15%	1%	-1%
7	TEN	W	19	17	351	236	0	-40%	-36%	7%	3%
8	at DAL	W	20	17	409	395	1	29%	-1%	-23%	7%
9	at MIN	L	26	29	347	352	-1	-26%	-6%	25%	5%
10	BYE										
11	TB	L	7	27	322	329	-2	-100%	-42%	41%	-17%
12	at SF	L	13	17	213	312	2	-19%	-31%	-5%	8%
13	at IND	L	27	49	425	487	2	-59%	-15%	39%	-4%
14	STL	L	0	24	206	329	-2	-130%	-77%	16%	-36%
15	at NYG	L	13	24	372	287	0	-31%	-25%	13%	6%
16	PHI	W	27	24	305	495	0	-10%	7%	16%	-1%
17	DAL	L	17	44	413	473	-3	-36%	-20%	17%	1%

Trends and Splits

	Offense	Rank	Defense	Rank
Total DVOA	-11.8%	28	9.9%	27
Unadjusted VOA	-11.7%	27	9.0%	28
Weighted Trend	-22.8%	30	13.5%	30
Variance	7.7%	16	4.7%	12
Average Opponent	-0.9%	10	-3.2%	29
Passing	-5.3%	25	29.5%	32
Rushing	-7.5%	19	-14.2%	9
First Down	3.9%	14	-1.5%	17
Second Down	-2.0%	18	20.9%	32
Third Down	-62.7%	32	14.3%	25
First Half	-8.5%	23	16.9%	31
Second Half	-14.9%	24	2.6%	20
Red Zone	-27.7%	27	2.0%	21
Late and Close	-12.2%	24	3.2%	21

Five-Year Performance

Year	W-L	Pyth W	Est W	PF	PA	TO	Total	Rk	Off	Rk	Def	Rk	ST	Rk	Off AGL	Rk	Def AGL	Rk	Off Age	Rk	Def Age	Rk	ST Age	Rk
2010	6-10	5.9	4.7	302	377	-4	-19.4%	28	-11.3%	25	5.8%	26	-2.3%	25	31.4	21	38.1	26	28.6	3	28.5	3	27.3	4
2011	5-11	5.7	6.3	288	367	-14	-7.0%	21	-7.0%	19	-1.2%	14	-1.2%	21	54.3	31	13.2	7	27.3	14	27.3	15	26.9	3
2012	10-6	9.2	9.8	436	388	+17	9.3%	9	15.3%	6	1.7%	17	-4.3%	28	34.8	20	48.8	26	26.1	26	27.8	5	27.1	3
2013	3-13	4.8	4.2	334	478	-8	-26.2%	29	-10.0%	23	4.2%	21	-12.0%	32	14.6	4	26.8	13	27.0	15	28.0	3	27.1	2
2014	4-12	4.5	4.4	301	438	-12	-27.0%	28	-11.8%	28	9.9%	27	-5.4%	29	21.9	7	67.6	29	27.1	13	26.9	14	25.9	21

2014 Performance Based on Most Common Personnel Groups

WAS Offense					WAS Offense vs. Opponents					WAS Defense					WAS Defense vs. Opponents			
Pers	Freq	Yds	DVOA	Run%	Pers	Freq	Yds	DVOA	Run%	Pers	Freq	Yds	DVOA	Pers	Freq	Yds	DVOA
11	61%	5.7	-13.4%	23%	Base	37%	6.0	3.0%	57%	Base	55%	5.3	-3.7%	11	47%	7.1	25.0%
12	16%	6.5	8.4%	48%	Nickel	43%	5.5	-13.6%	26%	Nickel	43%	7.0	28.2%	12	27%	5.1	3.0%
21	13%	5.8	7.2%	63%	Dime+	18%	6.4	-6.6%	19%	Dime+	1%	7.2	64.8%	21	14%	5.3	-9.4%
22	4%	4.5	-9.5%	70%	Goal Line	1%	1.2	10.1%	73%	Goal Line	1%	1.0	44.1%	22	3%	5.6	-11.0%
13	2%	4.4	-39.0%	63%										10	2%	4.8	-6.6%
														13	2%	3.5	-28.6%

Strategic Tendencies

Run/Pass		Rk	Formation		Rk	Pass Rush		Rk	Secondary		Rk	Strategy		Rk
Runs, first half	40%	11	Form: Single Back	72%	20	Rush 3	5.8%	17	4 DB	40%	3	Play action	22%	14
Runs, first down	51%	12	Form: Empty Back	4%	20	Rush 4	57.4%	22	5 DB	57%	19	Avg Box (Off)	6.30	12
Runs, second-long	22%	31	Pers: 3+ WR	63%	15	Rush 5	30.4%	4	6+ DB	2%	23	Avg Box (Def)	6.42	4
Runs, power sit.	55%	17	Pers: 4+ WR	1%	18	Rush 6+	6.4%	18	CB by Sides	93%	4	Offensive Pace	31.81	25
Runs, behind 2H	29%	12	Pers: 2+ TE/6+ OL	24%	25	Sacks by LB	61.1%	8	DB Blitz	13%	8	Defensive Pace	30.50	22
Pass, ahead 2H	51%	8	Shotgun/Pistol	65%	13	Sacks by DB	9.7%	10	Hole in Zone	4%	27	Go for it on 4th	1.28	6

Washington averaged 7.0 yards after the catch, the highest figure in our data (since 2005). The issue here isn't just that there were so many short passes. Washington led the league with 11.1 average YAC on passes behind the line of scrimmage (average: 8.9) but was also second in the NFL with 5.4 average YAC on passes beyond the line of scrimmage (average: 4.2). Robert Griffin had the highest average YAC of Washington's three quarterbacks, at 7.5, in part because a league-leading 73 percent of his passes were thrown within five yards of the line of scrimmage. Washington averaged 7.1 YAC with Kirk Cousins at quarterback, and 6.0 with Colt McCoy—a number which still would have been tied for fourth in the NFL over the full season. ☞ Thanks to all that YAC, the Redskins actually led the NFL with 7.8 yards per pass on passes thrown behind the line of scrimmage, and their 42.6% DVOA trailed only Dallas. (NFL average for plays behind the line of scrimmage was 5.5 yards and 10.0% DVOA.) Washington's problem with short passes was more about the passes within a few yards of the line of scrimmage, not the passes thrown behind it. ☞ Washington's overall play-action rate dropped from past years, but it was higher with Griffin at quarterback (26 percent) than with Cousins or McCoy (20 percent). Washington gained 10.2 yards per pass with play-action and had the league's biggest gap between DVOA with play-action (55.1%, fourth) and DVOA without (-23.0%, 31st). ☞ Washington's defense was almost as bad on play-action as the offense was good, allowing 8.4 yards per play (28th) and 52.6% DVOA (31st). ☞ Ranking fourth in the "CB by Sides" metric represented a major change for Washington's defense, which had been dead last in 2013. Of course, Washington couldn't use DeAngelo Hall to trail the opposition's No. 1 receiver with Hall injured, but the decision to play cornerbacks on specific sides was actually made before Hall's injury, and Hall played only left cornerback in the first three weeks. ☞ Washington's defense had a 5.4 percent adjusted sack rate on first and second down (28th) but jumped to 9.3 percent on third and fourth down (fourth). ☞ One bright spot for the Washington defense: after having more broken tackles than any other defense in 2013, Washington was one of the top tackling teams in the league in 2014. ☞ Washington benefitted from a league-high 165 penalties by its opponents, and was second with 1,164 opponent penalty yards.

Passing

Player	DYAR	DVOA	Plays	NtYds	Avg	YAC	C%	TD	Int
R.Griffin	-374	-34.2%	250	1452	5.8	7.5	69.2%	4	6
K.Cousins	223	4.6%	212	1625	7.7	7.1	62.1%	10	9
C.McCoy	-43	-15.9%	145	947	6.5	6.0	71.1%	4	3

Rushing

Player	DYAR	DVOA	Plays	Yds	Avg	TD	Fum	Suc
A.Morris	77	-1.4%	265	1079	4.1	8	2	46%
R.Helu*	42	15.7%	40	216	5.4	1	0	55%
R.Griffin	-23	-25.5%	34	174	5.1	1	2	-
S.Redd	24	31.8%	16	75	4.7	1	1	56%
C.McCoy	-13	-33.0%	14	67	4.8	1	2	-
D.Young	21	21.4%	9	22	2.4	3	0	67%
K.Cousins	7	9.0%	5	22	4.4	0	0	-

Receiving

Player	DYAR	DVOA	Plays	Ctch	Yds	Y/C	YAC	TD	C%
P.Garcon	-15	-14.6%	105	68	752	11.1	5.0	3	65%
D.Jackson	306	27.0%	95	57	1171	20.5	8.5	6	60%
A.Roberts	-9	-14.2%	73	36	453	12.6	5.7	2	49%
S.Moss*	15	1.4%	15	10	116	11.6	7.4	0	67%
R.Grant	-27	-37.3%	15	7	68	9.7	3.3	0	47%
J.Reed	-15	-10.8%	65	50	465	9.3	5.7	0	77%
N.Paul	110	24.4%	52	39	507	13.0	6.6	1	75%
L.Paulsen	-32	-36.5%	16	13	78	6.0	3.5	1	81%
R.Helu*	108	31.2%	47	42	480	11.4	11.6	2	89%
A.Morris	7	-8.7%	26	17	155	9.1	9.1	0	65%
D.Young	40	34.2%	14	11	81	7.4	4.6	2	79%
S.Redd	39	59.7%	10	8	107	13.4	12.9	0	80%
C.Thompson	1	-12.4%	7	6	27	4.5	6.0	1	86%

Offensive Line

Player	Pos	Age	GS	Snaps	Pen	Sk	Pass	Run	Player	Pos	Age	GS	Snaps	Pen	Sk	Pass	Run
Chris Chester*	RG	32	16/16	1051	3	4.0	11.0	4.0	Trent Williams	LT	27	15/15	877	12	7.0	12.0	2.0
Kory Lichtensteiger	C	30	16/16	1051	3	1.5	7.0	5.5	Tom Compton	RT	26	16/9	651	5	5.5	12.0	4.0
Shawn Lauvao	LG	28	15/15	950	5	1.5	5.5	5.0	Tyler Polumbus*	RT	30	11/7	471	3	6.5	10.5	1.0

Year	Yards	ALY	Rk	Power	Rk	Stuff	Rk	2nd Lev	Rk	Open Field	Rk	Sacks	ASR	Rk	Short	Long	F-Start	Cont.
2012	4.72	4.24	8	58%	24	16%	3	1.40	5	0.85	13	33	7.8%	23	9	18	26	43
2013	4.51	3.75	23	76%	4	22%	28	1.29	5	0.95	7	43	7.6%	19	11	22	16	48
2014	4.22	3.87	19	58%	27	20%	16	1.26	7	0.75	14	58	9.8%	31	22	12	20	29
2014 ALY by direction:		Left End 3.22 (26)			Left Tackle 3.95 (11)			Mid/Guard 3.96 (18)			Right Tackle 4.12 (11)			Right End 4.18 (11)				

New line coach Bill Callahan and general manager Scot McCloughan both prefer big drive blockers to smaller tacticians. The Redskins, of course, are just two years removed from a Mike Shanahan scheme that required quick zone blockers, and the team has not had any serious resources to commit to an offensive line overhaul. Only left tackle Trent Williams is scheme-transcendent; everyone else faces transition or competition.

Right tackle is where the competition is particularly interesting. Morgan Moses, a third-round pick last year, earned a spot start at left tackle against the 49ers when Williams was hurt and got a school-of-hard-knocks education from Justin Smith and Aldon Smith. He's a likely competitor for 2015 first-round pick Brandon Scherff at right tackle. Moses could also move inside, but he has a tackle's body type. Scherff earned the obligatory minicamp praise and should start sooner than later. Iowa offensive linemen arrive in the NFL relatively polished, and the move from left to right tackle will take some pressure and expectations off him. Still, the Redskins don't need to rush him with Moses available to soak up early starts. The Redskins also re-signed Tom Compton to a one-year deal after Compton took over at right tackle in the second half of last season. He's a stopgap player who could start a few games if Scherff is unready and Moses is otherwise obligated.

The Redskins released Chris Chester after the draft, saving $4.8 million in cap space while clearing away a 32-year-old poor fit (though a still-capable craftsman). Spencer Long, chosen a dozen picks after Moses in last year's third round, is the favorite to replace Chester at right guard. Long's rookie year was a wash; he missed half of his final season at Nebraska with a leg injury and looked tentative in training camp last year. Long is quicker than big, but he was a decorated scholar-athlete who gets high marks on the intangible report card. Kory Lichtensteiger is probably safe at center, where seventh-round pick Austin Reiter (South Florida) is the only competition. Lichtensteiger played at two cupcakes below 300 pounds in the past but bulked up in the offseason. Shawn Lauvao, signed away from the Browns last season, is reasonably priced and adequate at left guard.

Williams and the Redskins were working on a contract extension at press time, which explains where some of those $4.8 smackeroos in cap space the Redskins saved on Chester might wind up.

Defensive Front Seven

Defensive Line	Age	Pos	G	Snaps	Plays	TmPct	Overall Rk	Stop	Dfts	BTkl	Runs	St%	vs. Run Rk	RuYd	Rk	Sack	Hit	Pass Rush Hur	Dsrpt
Jarvis Jenkins*	27	DE	16	540	29	3.8%	67	23	3	0	29	79%	37	2.6	66	0.0	3	6.5	0
Chris Baker	28	DT	15	504	39	5.5%	32	31	7	2	38	79%	40	2.4	54	1.0	3	7.0	0
Jason Hatcher	33	DE	13	500	26	4.2%	53	24	13	2	16	88%	13	2.3	47	5.5	5	14.5	1
Frank Kearse	27	DE	15	259	13	1.8%	--	11	3	0	7	86%	--	1.7	--	3.0	1	2.0	0
Barry Cofield*	31	DT	8	249	7	1.8%	93	6	3	0	6	83%	24	2.7	68	1.0	2	1.0	0
Stephen Bowen*	31	DE	8	243	12	3.2%	79	10	2	0	10	90%	8	2.0	35	0.0	0	3.0	1
Stephen Paea	27	DT	16	700	33	4.2%	57	27	12	2	25	76%	59	2.0	33	6.0	6	18.5	2
Ricky Jean-Francois	29	DE	16	636	31	3.9%	64	27	13	2	21	86%	17	1.3	19	3.0	3	7.5	4
Terrance Knighton	29	DT	16	520	33	4.0%	61	32	11	1	25	100%	1	1.2	15	2.0	4	4.5	3

Edge Rushers	Age	Pos	G	Snaps	Plays	TmPct	Overall Rk	Stop	Dfts	BTkl	Runs	St%	vs. Run Rk	RuYd	Rk	Sack	Hit	Pass Rush Hur	Dsrpt
Ryan Kerrigan	27	OLB	16	975	59	7.8%	13	50	22	2	35	83%	19	2.7	52	13.5	7	30.0	1
Trent Murphy	25	OLB	15	579	33	4.6%	50	23	10	1	25	68%	68	3.0	64	2.5	5	8.5	1
Brian Orakpo*	29	OLB	7	385	25	7.5%	14	20	5	2	21	81%	27	2.5	42	0.5	6	8.5	0

Linebackers	Age	Pos	G	Snaps	Plays	TmPct	Overall Rk	Stop	Dfts	BTkl	Sack	Hit	Pass Rush Hur	Runs	St%	Rk	RuYd	Rk	Tgts	Suc%	Rk	AdjYd	Rk	PD	Int
Perry Riley	27	ILB	14	886	96	14.5%	30	53	16	6	2.0	2	7.5	55	62%	49	3.9	63	44	42%	53	7.9	55	3	0
Keenan Robinson	26	ILB	13	810	108	17.5%	11	58	22	6	1.5	7	10	72	57%	67	3.9	64	38	58%	14	4.5	6	2	1
Will Compton	26	ILB	16	359	52	6.9%	--	25	8	3	0.0	2	2	31	58%	--	3.7	--	15	43%	--	5.6	--	0	0

Year	Yards	ALY	Rk	Power	Rk	Stuff	Rk	2nd Level	Rk	Open Field	Rk	Sacks	ASR	Rk	Short	Long
2012	4.35	4.08	17	79%	31	17%	26	1.19	16	0.86	19	32	5.9%	25	9	11
2013	4.02	3.58	6	68%	22	23%	6	1.18	25	0.82	22	36	7.0%	13	14	11
2014	3.97	3.77	12	60%	11	20%	13	1.04	8	0.69	16	36	6.6%	17	18	8

2014 ALY by direction: Left End 4.1 (24)   Left Tackle 3.09 (7)   Mid/Guard 4.15 (24)   Right Tackle 3.64 (11)   Right End 3.07 (6)

In addition to the usual "faster and more aggressive" boilerplate, Redskins defenders said during OTAs that new coordinator Joe Barry plans to play more one-gap schemes along the front seven, with defensive linemen penetrating while linebackers do a little more gap-shooting and a little less reading and reacting. "We might have more linemen on us, but we also will have gaps to shoot and other things that we can be able to make more plays," inside linebacker Keenan Robinson told the local CBS affiliate in April. "You might see more splash plays out of the linebackers this year."

The Redskins don't necessarily need "splash" plays from Robinson and fellow inside linebacker Perry Riley this season.

Consistent ordinary plays will do. Robinson showed athleticism after missing 2013 with an ACL tear, but his recognition was a beat slow, and he has never seen a blocker that he did not want to try to run around. Riley was a coverage disaster, though Jim Haslett didn't often put him in position to succeed: few inside linebackers are going to chase Marshawn Lynch into the flat and make a successful solo open-field tackle, coach. Robinson and Riley are Barry's only real options on the inside; backup Will Compton was terrible when Robinson was banged up last year. These are the starters a team must rely upon after skipping the first halves of multiple drafts.

The rest of the front seven is much better. Ryan Kerrigan had four sacks in Week 2 against the Jaguars, then took over several other games (both Eagles games, the Rams game) without necessarily racking up high sack totals. Second-round rookie Preston Smith was technically a defensive end at Mississippi State, but he dropped into coverage frequently and handled option-read duties well, so he should adjust smoothly to outside linebacker. At 270 pounds, Smith won't be washed out against the run. Trent Murphy, last year's second-round pick, showed some flashes while starting eight games for the injured (now departed) Brian Orakpo, but he's likely to rotate onto the field as a situational rusher while Smith gets the starting gig. Trevardo Williams, a practice-squad frequent flyer since 2013, was a productive pass-rusher since his UConn days and earned minicamp kudos.

Stephen Paea was one of the few Bears defenders to survive 2014 with his dignity intact. Paea is a quick 300-pounder who should have no trouble sliding from three-tech tackle to 3-4 defensive end. Terrance Knighton is a pot roast. With Paea and Knighton joining Jason Hatcher, Barry will have the one-gap disrupters he needs on the defensive line to free his linebackers to make more plays. Better play from the front three should keep Barry from calling the all-out blitzes Haslett started relying upon, to disastrous effect, late in the season. Creating splash plays will be good for the Redskins defense, but preventing them will be even better.

Defensive Secondary

Secondary	Age	Pos	G	Snaps	Plays	Overall TmPct	Rk	Stop	Dfts	BTkl	vs. Run Runs	St%	Rk	RuYd	Rk	vs. Pass Tgts	Tgt%	Rk	Dist	Suc%	Rk	AdjYd	Rk	PD	Int
Ryan Clark*	36	FS	16	1011	104	13.7%	8	28	10	16	49	31%	54	6.3	31	25	6.5%	21	10.1	53%	37	8.2	48	2	1
David Amerson	24	CB	15	903	68	9.6%	21	19	5	6	5	20%	65	6.6	38	76	22.1%	26	11.6	39%	75	8.4	48	6	0
Bashaud Breeland	23	CB	16	863	76	10.0%	16	34	16	7	17	53%	20	10.5	68	83	25.4%	51	14.3	44%	64	8.8	54	13	2
Brandon Meriweather*	31	SS	10	596	57	12.0%	23	33	11	3	30	70%	2	3.8	4	25	11.1%	55	15.3	60%	20	7.0	29	4	0
E.J. Biggers*	28	CB	15	450	31	4.4%	--	11	5	5	4	50%	--	6.3	--	34	20.0%	--	14.5	43%	--	10.3	--	5	0
Phillip Thomas	26	SS	8	270	26	6.9%	--	15	4	4	15	73%	--	3.5	--	9	8.3%	--	12.1	53%	--	13.3	--	0	0
Chris Culliver	27	CB	14	821	59	8.7%	36	22	9	3	9	33%	44	7.1	45	74	22.6%	31	16.0	58%	12	6.2	12	13	4
Dashon Goldson	31	FS	14	779	81	10.5%	31	15	3	12	33	21%	67	7.9	52	27	10.0%	48	16.6	44%	56	10.5	65	2	0

Year	Pass D Rank	vs. #1 WR	Rk	vs. #2 WR	Rk	vs. Other WR	Rk	vs. TE	Rk	vs. RB	Rk
2012	14	-3.1%	16	-3.3%	14	-17.5%	5	14.5%	27	-24.1%	4
2013	22	13.6%	27	-14.1%	6	12.9%	25	7.5%	21	5.1%	20
2014	32	19.9%	29	32.5%	30	22.8%	29	21.7%	29	-18.0%	6

Scot McCloughan splurged in the secondary, bringing some of his old 49ers discoveries to Washington via trades and free agency. Chris Culliver is coming off an outstanding season in San Francisco and immediately stabilizes one cornerback position. Free safety Dashon Goldson was comically inept for the Buccaneers last season. He seemed to think "Tampa 2" meant "stand exactly 17 yards behind the line of scrimmage and wait for someone to run into you." Goldson was an All-Pro in 2012 and can still be effective in a system that isn't quite so conservative. Oft-injured Seahawks reserve safety Jeron Johnson also climbed into McCloughan's shopping cart. He is expected to compete for a starting job with Duke Ihenacho (former Broncos starter, hurt all of last year) and conceivably DeAngelo Hall.

Thinking about Hall for too long causes migraines. Hall is signed through 2017; he waived a roster bonus in February to make himself a little more cap-friendly, perhaps realizing that he's about as marketable outside the Beltway as a subscription to *Roll Call*. In Washington, however, the delusion persists that he is a quality cover corner, not the football equivalent of a slugging outfielder who bats .235 with 120 strikeouts but 19 tape-measure homers on hanging curveballs. (Hall ranked 50th or lower in both cornerback charting metrics each year from 2010 to 2013.) Hall injured his Achilles tendon against the Eagles on a play where he wasn't even touched, then re-aggravated the injury when he slipped in his home kitchen while getting a late-night pizza snack. Most teams would have moved on long ago from an aging, overrated player with a gift for bonehead mistakes. The Redskins are mulling a move to safety instead. Using Hall as precedent, the Redskins will probably give up on Robert Griffin in the year 2249.

David Amerson and Bashaud Breeland are also hanging around the cornerback depth chart. Breeland committed 14 penalties for a league-high 161 yards last season, including four pass interference fouls, but the rookie at least showed flashes in coverage. Amerson was a scorch mark on the grass. The Redskins released veteran Tracy Porter after drafting cornerback Tevin Mitchel (Arkansas) and nickel safety Kyshoen Jarrett (Virginia Tech) in the sixth round. We are obligated by law to mention here that Scot McCloughan found both Richard Sherman and Kam Chancellor in the fifth round, and therefore all of his late-round defensive backs will be considered future All-Pros until proven otherwise.

Special Teams

Year	DVOA	Rank	FG/XP	Rank	Net Kick	Rank	Kick Ret	Rank	Net Punt	Rank	Punt Ret	Rank	Hidden	Rank
2012	-4.3%	28	1.2	14	0.6	15	-3.6	22	-13.8	29	-5.9	27	-9.0	28
2013	-12.0%	32	-2.5	23	-8.3	28	-6.4	29	-33.3	32	-9.4	30	-0.4	16
2014	-5.4%	29	-0.5	19	-10.1	31	-4.0	25	-8.0	27	-4.1	21	-8.4	27

Kai Forbath is a mediocre but reliable kicker. The Redskins re-signed him in the offseason. This concludes the complementary portion of the Redskins special-teams comment.

Tress Way was an effective punter when not put in untenable situations. Way had a punt blocked, got stopped on a fake against the Rams, and booted a low line drive that was returned for a touchdown on the next series after getting stopped on the fake. Given better support, Way could be part of the Redskins' special-teams solution. Andre Roberts was a fair-catch machine on punt returns and didn't do much on kickoffs. Rookie Jamison Crowder has the punt-returner skill set and could push Roberts out of the role. DeSean Jackson can be a dangerous critical-situation returner, but he fielded just three punts and called for two fair catches.

Last year, Washington ranked 21st in snap-weighted age on special teams. That's a big change: because of all the constant trading of draft picks and cutting of rookies, Washington had ranked among the four oldest special teams every year since 2006. Now that they've solved the problem of always being old, the Washington special teams must solve the problem of always being horrible. An attempt to professionalize kick coverage last season by adding Akeem Jordan and Adam Heyward backfired when both players missed several critical special-teams tackles, then ended up on injured reserve; Hayward will return this season. Late-round picks Tevin Mitchel, Evan Spencer and Kyshoen Jarrett will get opportunities to add to Scot McCloughan's reputation by dousing the Redskins' perennial kick-coverage wildfire. Spencer was a well-regarded special-teams blocker in college, which is the kind of detail you notice when writing about a team that hasn't had a return touchdown since 2010.

Quarterbacks

On the following pages, we provide the last three years' statistics for the top two quarterbacks on each team's depth chart, as well as a number of other quarterbacks who played significant time in 2014.

Each quarterback gets a projection from our KUBIAK fantasy football projection system, based on a complicated regression analysis that takes into account numerous variables, including projected role, performance over the past two years, performance on third down vs. all downs, experience of the projected offensive line, historical comparables, collegiate stats, height, age, and strength of schedule.

It is difficult to accurately project statistics for a 162-game baseball season, but it is exponentially more difficult to accurately project statistics for a 16-game football season because of the small size of the data samples involved. With that in mind, we ask that you consider the listed projections not as a prediction of exact numbers, but the mean of a range of possible performances. What's important is not so much the exact number of yards and touchdowns we project, but whether or not we're projecting a given player to improve or decline. Along those same lines, rookie projections will not be as accurate as veteran projections due to lack of data.

Our quarterback projections look a bit different than our projections for the other skill positions. At running back and wide receiver, second-stringers see plenty of action, but, at quarterback, either a player starts or he does not start. We recognize that, when a starting quarterback gets injured in Week 8, you don't want to grab your *Football Outsiders Almanac* to find out if his backup is any good only to find that we've projected that the guy will throw 12 passes this year. Therefore, each year we project all quarterbacks to start all 16 games. If Ben Roethlisberger goes down in November, you can look up Bruce Gradkowski, divide the stats by 16, and get an idea of what we think he will do in an average week (and then, if you are a Pittsburgh fan, pass out). There are full-season projections for the top two quarterbacks on all 32 depth charts.

The first line of each quarterback table contains biographical data—the player's **name**, **height**, **weight**, **college**, **draft** position, **birth date**, and **age**. Height and weight are the best data we could find; weight, of course, can fluctuate during the offseason. Age is very simple: the number of years between the player's birth year and 2015, but birthdate is provided if you want to figure out exact age.

Draft position gives draft year and round, with the overall pick number with which the player was taken in parentheses. In the sample table, it says that Cam Newton was chosen in the first round of the 2011 NFL Draft, with the first overall pick. Undrafted free agents are listed as "FA" with the year they came into the league, even if they were only in training camp or on a practice squad.

To the far right of the first line is the player's **Risk** variable for fantasy football in 2015, which measures the likelihood of the player hitting his projection. The default rating for each player is Green. As the risk of a player failing to hit his projection rises, he's given a rating of Yellow or, in the worst cases, Red. The Risk variable is not only based on injury probability, but how a player's projection compares to his recent performance as well as our confidence (or lack thereof) in his offensive teammates. A few players with the strongest chances of surpassing their projections are given a Blue rating. Most players marked Blue will be backups with low projections, but a handful are starters or situational players who can be considered slightly better breakout candidates.

Next, we give the last three years of player stats. The majority of these statistics are passing numbers, although the final five columns on the right are the quarterback's rushing statistics.

The first few columns after the **year** and **team** the player played for are standard numbers: games and games started (**G/GS**), offensive **Snaps**, pass attempts (**Att**), pass completions (**Cmp**), completion percentage (**C%**), passing yards (**Yds**), passing touchdowns (**TD**). These numbers are official NFL totals and therefore include plays we leave out of our own metrics, such as clock-stopping spikes, and omit plays we include in our metrics, such as sacks and aborted snaps. (Other differences between official stats and Football Outsiders stats are described in the "Statistical Toolbox" introduction at the front of the book.)

The column for interceptions contains two numbers, representing the official NFL total for interceptions (**Int**) as well as our own metric for adjusted interceptions (**Adj**). For example, if you look at our sample table, Cam Newton had 12 interceptions and 14 adjusted interceptions in 2014. Adjusted interceptions use game charting data to add dropped interceptions, plays where a defender most likely would have had an interception but couldn't hold onto the ball. Then we remove Hail Mary passes and interceptions thrown on fourth down when losing in the final two minutes of the game. We also remove "tipped interceptions," when a perfectly catchable ball deflected off the receiver's hands or chest and into the arms of a defender.

Cam Newton				Height: 6-5		Weight: 248		College: Auburn					Draft: 2011/1 (1)		Born: 11-May-1989		Age: 26	Risk: Yellow					
Year	Team	G/GS	Snaps	Att	Cmp	C%	Yds	TD	INT/Adj	FUM	ASR	NY/P	Rk	DVOA	Rk	DYAR	Rk	YAR	Runs	Yds	TD	DVOA	DYAR	QBR
2012	CAR	16/16	1019	485	280	57.7%	3869	19	12/15	14	7.6%	7.0	6	2.0%	15	422	14	422	127	741	8	11.3%	149	54.1
2013	CAR	16/16	1015	473	292	61.7%	3379	24	13/18	3	8.2%	5.9	23	1.7%	19	421	17	321	111	585	6	5.7%	102	56.2
2014	CAR	14/14	927	448	262	58.5%	3127	18	12/14	9	8.4%	5.9	30	-14.5%	32	-105	32	-46	103	539	5	16.3%	146	56.9
2015	CAR			511	317	62.0%	3617	24	12	7		6.1		-1.7%					106	512	5	14.6%		
	2013:	41% Short		39% Mid		12% Deep		8% Bomb		YAC: 5.5 (18)			2014:		47% Short		35% Mid		10% Deep		7% Bomb	YAC: 4.8 (34)	

Overall, adjusted interception rate is higher than standard interception rate, so most quarterbacks will have more adjusted interceptions than standard interceptions. On average, a quarterback will have one additional adjusted interception for every 120 pass attempts. Once this difference is accounted for, adjusted interceptions are a better predictor of next year's interception total than standard interceptions.

The next column is fumbles (**FUM**), which adds together all fumbles by this player, whether turned over to the defense or recovered by the offense (explained in the essay "Pregame Show"). Even though this fumble total is listed among the passing numbers, it includes all fumbles, including those on sacks, aborted snaps, and rushing attempts. By listing fumbles and interceptions next to one another, we're giving readers a general idea of how many total turnovers the player was responsible for.

Next comes Adjusted Sack Rate (**ASR**). This is the same statistic you'll find in the team chapters, only here it is specific to the individual quarterback. It represents sacks per pass play (total pass plays = pass attempts + sacks) adjusted based on down, distance, and strength of schedule. For reference, the NFL average was 6.5 percent in 2012, 7.0 percent in 2013, and 6.6 percent in 2014.

The next two columns are Net Yards per Pass (**NY/P**), a standard stat but a particularly good one, and the player's rank (**Rk**) in Net Yards per Pass for that season. Net Yards per Pass consists of passing yards minus yards lost on sacks, divided by total pass plays.

The five columns remaining in passing stats give our advanced metrics: **DVOA** (Defense-Adjusted Value Over Average), **DYAR** (Defense-Adjusted Yards Above Replacement), and **YAR** (Yards Above Replacement), along with the player's rank in both DVOA and DYAR. These metrics compare each quarterback's passing performance to league-average or replacement-level baselines based on the game situations that quarterback faced. DVOA and DYAR are also adjusted based on the opposing defense. The methods used to compute these numbers are described in detail in the "Statistical Toolbox" introduction at the front of the book. The important distinctions between them are:

• DVOA is a rate statistic, while DYAR is a cumulative statistic. Thus, a higher DVOA means more value per pass play, while a higher DYAR means more aggregate value over the entire season.
• Because DYAR is defense-adjusted and YAR is not, a player whose DYAR is higher than his YAR faced a harder-than-average schedule. A player whose DYAR is lower than his YAR faced an easier-than-average schedule.

To qualify for a ranking in Net Yards per Pass, passing DVOA, and passing DYAR in a given season, a quarterback must have had 200 pass plays in that season. (We have raised that threshold from the 100 pass plays we have used in the past to focus on key starters and not part-timers.) 38 quarterbacks ranked for 2012, 39 quarterbacks ranked for 2013, and 37 ranked in 2014.

The final five columns contain rushing statistics, starting with **Runs**, rushing yards (**Yds**), and rushing touchdowns (**TD**). Once again, these are official NFL totals and include kneeldowns, which means you get to enjoy statistics such as Peyton Manning rushing 24 times for minus-24 yards. The final two columns give **DYAR** and **DVOA** for quarterback rushing, which are calculated separately from passing. Rankings for these statistics, as well as numbers that are not adjusted for defense (YAR and VOA) can be found on our website, FootballOutsiders.com.

The last number listed is the Total **QBR** metric from ESPN Stats & Information. Total QBR calculates the expected points added by the quarterback on each play, then adjusts the numbers to a scale of 0-100. There are five main differences between Total QBR and DVOA:

• Total QBR incorporates information from game charting, such as passes dropped or thrown away on purpose.
• Total QBR splits responsibility on plays between the quarterback, his receivers, and his blockers. Drops, for example, are more on the receiver, as are yards after the catch, and some sacks are more on the offensive line than others.
• Total QBR has a clutch factor which adds (or subtracts) value for quarterbacks who perform best (or worst) in high-leverage situations.
• Total QBR combines passing and rushing value into one number and differentiates between scrambles and planned runs.
• Total QBR is not adjusted for strength of opponent.

The italicized row of statistics for the 2015 season is our 2015 KUBIAK projection, as detailed above. Again, in the interest of producing meaningful statistics, all quarterbacks are projected to start a full 16-game season, regardless of the likelihood of them actually doing so.

The final line below the KUBIAK projection represents data from the Football Outsiders game charting project. First, we break down charted passes based on distance: **Short** (5 yards or less), **Mid** (6-15 yards), **Deep** (16-25 yards), and **Bomb** (26 or more yards). These numbers are based on distance in the air only and include both complete and incomplete passes. Passes thrown away or tipped at the line are not included, nor are passes on which the quarterback's arm was hit by a defender while in motion. We also give average yards after catch (**YAC**) with the Rank in parentheses for the 45 quarterbacks who qualify.

A number of third- and fourth-string quarterbacks are briefly discussed at the end of the chapter in a section we call "Going Deep."

Top 20 QB by Passing DYAR (Total Value), 2014

Rank	Player	Team	DYAR
1	Ben Roethlisberger	PIT	1572
2	Aaron Rodgers	GB	1564
3	Peyton Manning	DEN	1412
4	Drew Brees	NO	1225
5	Tony Romo	DAL	1187
6	Tom Brady	NE	1176
7	Matt Ryan	ATL	1101
8	Joe Flacco	BAL	987
9	Philip Rivers	SD	918
10	Andrew Luck	IND	879
11	Eli Manning	NYG	642
12	Ryan Tannehill	MIA	630
13	Russell Wilson	SEA	503
14	Alex Smith	KC	493
15	Matthew Stafford	DET	423
16	Jay Cutler	CHI	398
17	Ryan Fitzpatrick	HOU	383
18	Carson Palmer	ARI	285
19	Nick Foles	PHI	264
20	Drew Stanton	ARI	238

Minimum 200 passes.

Top 20 QB by Passing DVOA (Value per Pass), 2014

Rank	Player	Team	DVOA
1	Aaron Rodgers	GB	32.2%
2	Tony Romo	DAL	27.6%
3	Ben Roethlisberger	PIT	26.8%
4	Peyton Manning	DEN	23.9%
5	Tom Brady	NE	18.1%
6	Drew Brees	NO	15.7%
7	Joe Flacco	BAL	15.5%
8	Matt Ryan	ATL	14.9%
9	Philip Rivers	SD	12.6%
10	Andrew Luck	IND	9.2%
11	Carson Palmer	ARI	8.5%
12	Ryan Fitzpatrick	HOU	6.7%
13	Russell Wilson	SEA	5.5%
14	Kirk Cousins	WAS	4.6%
15	Eli Manning	NYG	4.6%
16	Drew Stanton	ARI	4.2%
17	Ryan Tannehill	MIA	4.1%
18	Alex Smith	KC	4.1%
19	Nick Foles	PHI	1.8%
20	Matthew Stafford	DET	-0.7%

Minimum 200 passes.

Derek Anderson
Height: 6-6   Weight: 229   College: Oregon State   Draft: 2005/6 (213)   Born: 15-Jun-1983   Age: 32 Risk: Yellow

Year	Team	G/GS	Snaps	Att	Cmp	C%	Yds	TD	INT/Adj	FUM	ASR	NY/P	Rk	DVOA	Rk	DYAR	Rk	YAR	Runs	Yds	TD	DVOA	DYAR	QBR
2012	CAR	2/0	9	4	4	100.0%	58	0	0/0	0	1.4%	14.5	--	132.9%	--	47	--	48	0	0	0	--	--	91.6
2013	CAR	4/0	15	0	0	0.0%	0	0	0/0	0	0.0%	0.0	--	0.0%	--	0	--	0	5	0	0	27.7%	3	4.3
2014	CAR	6/2	177	97	65	67.0%	701	5	0/2	2	5.2%	6.7	--	27.8%	--	254	--	282	8	24	0	34.3%	14	82.8
2015	CAR			498	290	58.3%	3379	20	17	9		5.9		-7.0%					39	112	1	-1.6%		

	2014:	40% Short	39% Mid	15% Deep	7% Bomb	YAC: 2.8 (--)

Anderson spent the last six seasons making his 2007 Pro Bowl appearance look like a really funny joke. Then, out of no-where, 2014 happened. Anderson had to come in and play for Cam Newton while Newton dealt with a case of everything that could possibly go wrong going wrong, and frankly, he was awesome. It was just as you remembered the 2007 Anderson—130 of his 254 DYAR came on 11 deep balls that averaged about 1 YAC. A fascinating thought experiment, given that this offseason included an actual bidding war for Josh McCown, is how much money Anderson could have bilked out of some team based on this small sample size. Instead, he just gets to throw balls up for Kelvin Benjamin and Devin Funchess. Pretty nice fit for Anderson's skills.

Blake Bortles
Height: 6-4   Weight: 232   College: Central Florida   Draft: 2014/1 (3)   Born: 16-Dec-1991   Age: 24 Risk: Red

Year	Team	G/GS	Snaps	Att	Cmp	C%	Yds	TD	INT/Adj	FUM	ASR	NY/P	Rk	DVOA	Rk	DYAR	Rk	YAR	Runs	Yds	TD	DVOA	DYAR	QBR
2014	JAC	14/13	896	475	280	58.9%	2908	11	17/20	7	10.5%	4.8	37	-40.7%	36	-955	37	-935	56	419	0	24.7%	100	21.9
2015	JAC			547	341	62.3%	3611	22	14	10		5.5		-12.0%					61	333	1	9.7%		

	2014:	57% Short	30% Mid	7% Deep	5% Bomb	YAC: 5.8 (7)

Bortles ultimately spent the 2014 season looking like a handsome young man hidden as the Jaguars quarterback by the Wit-ness Protection Program. The start was more promising than the finish, with Bortles generating a few spectacular plays on pure athleticism before getting beaten down behind a poor offensive line. We're still looking for a Rosetta Stone on quarterback development, which remains one of the great mysteries. One person's "David Carr wasn't very talented" is another's "David Carr was ruined because he started too early and got crushed behind a bad offensive line." That said, it's hard to imagine the Jaguars could have put Bortles into a worse rookie situation than the one he had last year.

We've written in the past about how quarterbacks generally show if they can succeed in the NFL after two seasons. Players who start off with two years below replacement level almost never develop further, though there are a few exceptions (Alex Smith, Troy Aikman). Anybody who pretends they know what to expect from Bortles is kidding themselves—he's essentially a blank slate after last season—but he doesn't have much time left to show us he can be a major cog for the Jaguars.

Sam Bradford   Height: 6-4   Weight: 236   College: Oklahoma   Draft: 2010/1 (1)   Born: 8-Nov-1987   Age: 28   Risk: Red

Year	Team	G/GS	Snaps	Att	Cmp	C%	Yds	TD	INT/Adj	FUM	ASR	NY/P	Rk	DVOA	Rk	DYAR	Rk	YAR	Runs	Yds	TD	DVOA	DYAR	QBR
2012	STL	16/16	1034	551	328	59.5%	3702	21	13/12	7	6.3%	6.0	22	-0.8%	16	388	16	245	37	127	1	29.6%	42	50.3
2013	STL	7/7	450	262	159	60.7%	1687	14	4/5	3	6.0%	5.8	28	5.2%	14	304	19	387	15	31	0	-70.1%	-25	48.0
2015	PHI			594	368	61.9%	4173	26	19	6		6.3		4.0%					52	107	2	-3.8%		

2013:	58% Short	27% Mid	9% Deep	7% Bomb	YAC: 5.7 (12)

It wouldn't be entirely fair to say that Bradford has been outplayed by his own backups since St. Louis made him the first pick in the 2010 draft. The Austin Davises and Kellen Clemenses of the world have generally thrown more interceptions and taken more sacks than their more highly paid colleague, and they have usually had worse DVOAs. Still, they have done a better job moving the ball, with higher completion rates and more yards per pass, which has to be concerning to the fans in Philadelphia.

St. Louis Quarterbacks, 2010-2014

Name	G	GS	Cmp	Att	C%	Yds	Yd/At	TD	INT	INT%	Sk	Sk%	W-L	Pct	DVOA
Sam Bradford	49	49	1032	1760	58.6%	11065	6.3	59	38	2.2%	120	6.4%	18-30-1	0.378	-9.8%
Other Rams QBs	39	31	569	946	60.1%	6464	6.8	31	27	2.9%	87	8.4%	11-20	0.355	-14.1%

This table does undersell Bradford a bit, because it doesn't credit him for the growth he has shown in his career. He showed significant improvement from his first and second seasons (34th and 38th in DVOA) to his third and fourth (16th and 14th), and likely would have a better career statline if he had been healthy in 2014. It will be interesting to see if Bradford is able to hit big plays in Philadelphia's offense, because that was the biggest hole in his game in St. Louis, where he never ranked higher than 24th in yards per completion. Chip Kelly has all but admitted that he would have preferred to get Marcus Mariota but found the asking price too steep, and that Bradford is Plan B, but even he might be pleasantly surprised. Remember that Bradford's glory days at Oklahoma came in a spread offense, so he should be familiar with some of what the Eagles will want him to do. Bradford's health, however, will be a concern throughout the season. That's what happens when you tear your ACL twice in two years. Kelly was asked in July if Bradford would be a full participant in training camp, and the best reply he could offer was "God, we hope so."

Tom Brady   Height: 6-4   Weight: 225   College: Michigan   Draft: 2000/6 (199)   Born: 3-Aug-1977   Age: 38   Risk: Red

Year	Team	G/GS	Snaps	Att	Cmp	C%	Yds	TD	INT/Adj	FUM	ASR	NY/P	Rk	DVOA	Rk	DYAR	Rk	YAR	Runs	Yds	TD	DVOA	DYAR	QBR
2012	NE	16/16	1213	637	401	63.0%	4827	34	8/10	6	4.6%	7.0	5	35.1%	1	2035	1	1910	23	32	4	40.3%	56	77.7
2013	NE	16/16	1197	628	380	60.5%	4343	25	11/8	9	6.1%	6.2	18	10.9%	11	979	6	859	32	18	0	-19.4%	-5	61.1
2014	NE	16/16	1062	582	373	64.1%	4109	33	9/11	6	3.9%	6.6	16	18.1%	5	1176	6	1096	36	57	0	-25.1%	-19	74.3
2015	NE			590	383	65.0%	4198	31	11	8		6.4		17.9%					32	67	1	-8.4%		

2013:	47% Short	33% Mid	13% Deep	7% Bomb	YAC: 5.3 (22)	2014:	51% Short	32% Mid	11% Deep	5% Bomb	YAC: 5.0 (28)

Brady's DVOA has been at least 25.0% and ranked fifth or higher seven times in his last ten full seasons. Two of the exceptions have come in the past three years, and with Brady turning 38 in August, the natural progression would be to expect further decline in Brady's forecast. But while betting on older players to decline is usually a winning proposition—one that seems to drive Patriots' personnel decisions every offseason—Brady doesn't necessarily fit the usual pattern. After four weeks of offensive line musical chairs and a limited Rob Gronkowski, Brady resumed his spot near the top of the league, posting a 30.9% DVOA (ranked third) from Weeks 5 through 17.

Other than Gronkowski's health, the primary concern for Brady in 2015 is the decline in his effectiveness as a deep passer:

Tom Brady on Deep Passes, 2010-2014

Year	C%	Yd/At
2010	49.3%	14.2
2011	49.0%	14.7
2012	32.5%	9.6
2013	38.6%	10.5
2014	37.5%	9.4

The Patriots offense can still succeed without those deep throws, but the margin for error is smaller now with the deep pass only a changeup and not a primary weapon.

Drew Brees   Height: 6-0   Weight: 209   College: Purdue   Draft: 2001/2 (32)   Born: 15-Jan-1979   Age: 36 Risk: Yellow

Year	Team	G/GS	Snaps	Att	Cmp	C%	Yds	TD	INT/Adj	FUM	ASR	NY/P	Rk	DVOA	Rk	DYAR	Rk	YAR	Runs	Yds	TD	DVOA	DYAR	QBR
2012	NO	16/16	1095	670	422	63.0%	5177	43	19/23	6	4.9%	7.1	3	19.8%	5	1441	3	1397	15	5	1	34.2%	11	66.5
2013	NO	16/16	1110	650	446	68.6%	5162	39	12/14	5	5.3%	7.2	6	26.9%	5	1701	3	1550	35	52	3	33.6%	36	70.5
2014	NO	16/16	1140	659	456	69.2%	4952	33	17/19	7	5.2%	7.0	8	15.7%	6	1225	4	1224	27	68	1	17.7%	27	71.6
2015	NO			619	406	65.6%	4612	36	15	5		6.6		19.7%					26	45	0	5.0%		

| 2013: | 52% Short | 30% Mid | 10% Deep | 8% Bomb | YAC: 5.5 (19) | 2014: | 56% Short | 27% Mid | 11% Deep | 7% Bomb | YAC: 4.8 (33) |

As a 35-year-old quarterback, it was no surprise that Drew Brees' arm began to show signs of physical decline last season. That physical decline combined with less effective protection in the pocket had a negative effect on Brees' ability to push the ball down the field. He could still connect with his receivers when they were open or when they could make impressive adjustments at the catch point, but he was an inconsistent deep passer who benefited a lot from Kenny Stills' ability to make plays on the ball in the air. Nonetheless, Brees' continued accuracy on short passes kept the Saints offense ranked in the top ten for passing DVOA. No quarterback had a lower rate of passes marked as "Overthrown" or "Underthrown" in the game charting data.

The question for Brees' 2015 season: how much will the offense ask him to do? He has thrown the ball at least 650 times in each of the past five seasons. Throwing the ball that often obviously stresses the quarterback a lot. That can be offset by focusing more on the running game, but also by heavily relying on C.J. Spiller's ability in the screen game. Brees already throws a large number of short passes, but the Saints can push that number even further next season.

Teddy Bridgewater   Height: 6-2   Weight: 214   College: Louisville   Draft: 2014/1 (32)   Born: 10-Nov-1992   Age: 23 Risk: Yellow

Year	Team	G/GS	Snaps	Att	Cmp	C%	Yds	TD	INT/Adj	FUM	ASR	NY/P	Rk	DVOA	Rk	DYAR	Rk	YAR	Runs	Yds	TD	DVOA	DYAR	QBR
2014	MIN	13/12	794	402	259	64.4%	2919	14	12/11	3	9.1%	6.1	23	-16.9%	34	-159	34	-82	47	209	1	-8.5%	8	50.2
2015	MIN			499	321	64.3%	3670	24	13	7		6.4		2.7%					56	254	2	12.7%		

| | | | | | | 2014: | 61% Short | 23% Mid | 9% Deep | 7% Bomb | YAC: 5.6 (12) |

So this is what happens when teams have too much time to think before the draft. The consternation surrounding Bridgewater's now-infamous pro day, in which the gloveless quarterback sprayed passes like Clark Kent without his cape, was always bizarre. Andrew Healy's QBASE projection system saw Bridgewater as easily the best quarterback prospect of the 2014 class, and the 17th-best of the 65 quarterbacks taken in the top 100 since 1997. Despite lukewarm rookie-year numbers—Derek Carr actually outpaced him slightly in both DVOA and DYAR—Bridgewater exhibited demonstrable progress after posting a 1-to-5 touchdown-to-interception ratio over first three starts. In particular, a hot five-game stretch in Weeks 13-17 saw Bridgewater rank seventh in adjusted yards per attempt (8.32) and second in quarterback rating (103.0) among quarterbacks with at least 100 attempts in that span. Obviously that's a small sample, and though he did carve up two top-10 DVOA pass defenses in Detroit and Carolina, there were a couple freebies mixed in against the woeful Bears and Jets secondaries. Nonetheless, what's most impressive in that stretch is that Bridgewater completed 72 percent of deep pass attempts, compared to just 38 percent in his first eight games. Considering that our own Matt Waldman labeled Bridgewater's deep-ball accuracy "the worst aspect" of his game, it's hard to deny that as progress. Those leaps came amidst a dilapidated offensive line with a Browns practice-squader serving as his top target and Adrian Peterson in exile. So can we all agree now that it's gotta be the gloves?

Derek Carr   Height: 6-3   Weight: 220   College: Fresno St.   Draft: 2014/2 (36)   Born: 3/28/1991   Age: 24   Risk: Green

Year	Team	G/GS	Snaps	Att	Cmp	C%	Yds	TD	INT/Adj	FUM	ASR	NY/P	Rk	DVOA	Rk	DYAR	Rk	YAR	Runs	Yds	TD	DVOA	DYAR	QBR
2014	OAK	16/16	986	599	348	58.1%	3270	21	12/16	10	4.0%	5.0	36	-14.9%	33	-150	33	-355	29	92	0	28.4%	40	38.4
2015	OAK			590	356	60.3%	3869	21	16	10		5.6		-10.5%					36	124	1	2.2%		
		2014:	54% Short		29% Mid			10% Deep			7% Bomb		YAC: 4.2 (35)											

Carr was unusually good in the red zone—not just for a rookie, but for an NFL quarterback, period. His 57.1% DVOA led all quarterbacks in the red zone (minimum 30 passes), and the difference between Carr and second-ranked Alex Smith (31.0%) was striking. Of course, as pointed out in the Oakland chapter, Carr rarely led the Raiders into the red zone (53 passes), but there's another nit to pick about Oakland's red zone success: how much of it really mattered? Carr threw four 1-yard touchdown passes in the second half of games when trailing by at least two touchdowns. The *career* record for similar plays is six touchdowns by Jim "Chris" Everett. Stuff like that is why it's hard to buy into his touchdown-to-interception ratio. Carr has a decent feel for the short-passing game, so he may prove to be a solid red zone quarterback, but we need to see the bigger plays. Carr had seven games last season where he averaged less than 5.0 yards per pass attempt (minimum 10 attempts). Peyton Manning has also done that seven times... in 277 games. Philip Rivers has done that eight times in 153 games. Are those bars too high? OK, the other AFC West quarterback, Alex Smith, has done it only 14 times in 109 opportunities. We know the receivers have been upgraded, but there is a reason they call the NFL a passing league, not a catching league. The ball has to get there first. Carr doesn't seem to have that Smith-type fear of giving his receivers chances, but he has to work on his accuracy.

Matt Cassel   Height: 6-5   Weight: 230   College: USC   Draft: 2005/7 (230)   Born: 17-May-1982   Age: 33   Risk: Red

Year	Team	G/GS	Snaps	Att	Cmp	C%	Yds	TD	INT/Adj	FUM	ASR	NY/P	Rk	DVOA	Rk	DYAR	Rk	YAR	Runs	Yds	TD	DVOA	DYAR	QBR
2012	KC	9/8	578	277	161	58.1%	1796	6	12/10	9	7.3%	5.8	27	-30.4%	36	-353	36	-275	27	145	1	17.8%	35	36.4
2013	MIN	9/6	459	254	153	60.2%	1807	11	9/10	3	6.1%	6.4	16	-5.9%	23	92	23	-7	18	57	1	5.2%	10	48.7
2014	MIN	3/3	140	71	41	57.7%	425	3	4/3	3	7.7%	4.9	--	-40.4%	--	-147	--	-150	9	18	0	-10.5%	0	28.9
2015	BUF			506	290	57.2%	3322	20	16	6		5.7		-10.6%					35	65	0	-14.3%		
		2013:	47% Short		30% Mid		17% Deep			6% Bomb		YAC: 5.2 (25)		2014:	61% Short		25% Mid		9% Deep		5% Bomb		YAC: 7.2 (--)	

When a team starts a retread veteran over a first-round pick, they're typically trying to protect the rookie from failure. You wouldn't know that from the way the Vikings treated Matt Cassel in his three starts, however. Cassel went 0-for-9 on deep pass attempts, as Minnesota's passing scheme was essentially "get the ball to Cordarrelle ASAP!" Last year's Bills squad threw 25 percent of its passes behind the line of scrimmage, the highest rate in the league, so Cassel should be right at home playing hot potato with Sammy Watkins and Percy Harvin if he can win the world's most depressing camp battle over checkdown apprentice EJ Manuel and dark horse Tyrod Taylor.

Jimmy Clausen   Height: 6-3   Weight: 222   College: Notre Dame   Draft: 2010/2 (48)   Born: 21-Sep-1987   Age: 28   Risk: Green

Year	Team	G/GS	Snaps	Att	Cmp	C%	Yds	TD	INT/Adj	FUM	ASR	NY/P	Rk	DVOA	Rk	DYAR	Rk	YAR	Runs	Yds	TD	DVOA	DYAR	QBR
2014	CHI	4/1	89	48	26	54.2%	223	2	1/1	0	5.7%	4.0	--	-12.7%	--	-5	--	-37	3	9	0	15.2%	5	40.6
2015	CHI			567	314	55.3%	3584	17	18	11		5.0		-21.7%					36	103	1	-5.0%		
		2014:	57% Short		27% Mid			6% Deep			10% Bomb		YAC: 4.7 (--)											

As a sign of the Bears' desperation, Clausen was allowed to start for a healthy Jay Cutler in Week 16 against the Lions. This apparently actually created some optimism among Bears players and followers, who believed simply executing the offense would be enough to be productive. Clausen got the ball out quickly, letting his receivers battle in contested catch situations. When the Lions started sitting on quick passes, he did not have an answer for what to do next, and we did not find out what would happen the next week as a concussion ended his season.

Kellen Clemens   Height: 6-2   Weight: 224   College: Oregon   Draft: 2006/2 (49)   Born: 6-Jun-1983   Age: 32   Risk: Yellow

Year	Team	G/GS	Snaps	Att	Cmp	C%	Yds	TD	INT/Adj	FUM	ASR	NY/P	Rk	DVOA	Rk	DYAR	Rk	YAR	Runs	Yds	TD	DVOA	DYAR	QBR
2012	STL	2/0	8	3	1	33.3%	39	0	1/0	1	1.0%	13.0	--	-207.0%	--	-62	--	-62	2	5	0	89.8%	5	1.6
2013	STL	10/9	554	242	142	58.7%	1673	8	7/9	7	7.7%	5.8	24	-7.5%	24	60	25	-133	23	64	0	-52.9%	-35	38.2
2014	SD	2/0	15	3	1	33.3%	10	0	0/0	0	23.6%	0.3	--	-92.7%	--	-20	--	-20	0	0	0	--	--	1.3
2015	SD			538	320	59.5%	3627	18	16	10		5.6		-10.8%					36	77	1	-7.5%		
	2013:	49% Short		30% Mid		15% Deep		5% Bomb		YAC: 5.2 (24)		2014:		50% Short		50% Mid		0% Deep		0% Bomb		YAC: 2.0 (--)		

Mike McCoy has been good at adjusting to his quarterback's strengths, but after nine years we're still trying to figure out what Kellen Clemens' strengths are. He's not particularly accurate, he won't stretch the field, he doesn't take good care of the ball, and he's prone to sacks. But hey, 10 years in the league! It's nice when you can settle behind a quarterback that hasn't missed a start since 2006, and for San Diego's sake that streak will hopefully continue.

Kirk Cousins   Height: 6-3   Weight: 214   College: Michigan State   Draft: 2012/4 (102)   Born: 19-Aug-1988   Age: 27   Risk: Red

Year	Team	G/GS	Snaps	Att	Cmp	C%	Yds	TD	INT/Adj	FUM	ASR	NY/P	Rk	DVOA	Rk	DYAR	Rk	YAR	Runs	Yds	TD	DVOA	DYAR	QBR
2012	WAS	3/1	95	48	33	68.8%	466	4	3/3	1	8.2%	8.4	--	6.4%	--	59	--	55	3	22	0	74.5%	10	75.2
2013	WAS	5/3	238	155	81	52.3%	854	4	7/7	3	4.1%	5.1	--	-42.6%	--	-314	--	-300	4	14	0	-6.6%	1	26.5
2014	WAS	6/5	357	204	126	61.8%	1710	10	9/9	2	3.8%	7.7	14	4.6%	14	223	22	213	7	20	0	9.0%	7	46.9
2015	WAS			570	353	61.8%	4133	27	24	7		6.3		-4.2%					36	69	0	-16.2%		
	2013:	42% Short		44% Mid		11% Deep		3% Bomb		YAC: 4.0 (--)		2014:		51% Short		30% Mid		12% Deep		8% Bomb		YAC: 7.1 (2)		

Better to remain on the bench and be thought of as strictly a sports talk radio phenomenon than to step onto the field and erase all doubt. Cousins has a career interception rate of 4.7 percent in 407 attempts. Rex Grossman's career interception rate was 3.8 percent. Mark Sanchez's is 3.7 percent. If we look only at quarterbacks of note whose careers extended into the 2000s—remember, interception rates have declined steadily through modern NFL history—the only passers close to Cousins are Vinny Testaverde (4.0 percent) and Trent Dilfer (4.1 percent).

Jay Gruden benched Cousins for Robert Griffin after his midseason interception rash; if Griffin was in the doghouse, Cousins was under the rickety porch that's propped up on cinder blocks. There was lots of offseason trade scuttlebutt, but wouldn't ya know it, teams weren't interested in an interception-happy quarterback held in lower esteem by the Redskins coaches than Robert Griffin. Cousins always manages to look good in his first carefully scripted start of the year. If the Redskins ever tire of their juggling act and release Cousins, some contender may dust him off for precisely the purpose of getting them through spot starts.

Jay Cutler   Height: 6-3   Weight: 220   College: Vanderbilt   Draft: 2006/1 (11)   Born: 29-Apr-1983   Age: 32   Risk: Yellow

Year	Team	G/GS	Snaps	Att	Cmp	C%	Yds	TD	INT/Adj	FUM	ASR	NY/P	Rk	DVOA	Rk	DYAR	Rk	YAR	Runs	Yds	TD	DVOA	DYAR	QBR
2012	CHI	15/15	919	434	255	58.8%	3033	19	14/20	8	7.8%	5.9	24	-13.8%	27	-81	28	-42	41	233	0	96.2%	114	50.2
2013	CHI	11/11	636	355	224	63.1%	2621	19	12/13	4	6.0%	6.7	10	5.5%	13	392	18	423	23	118	0	58.4%	48	66.4
2014	CHI	15/15	969	561	370	66.0%	3812	28	18/22	12	6.3%	6.0	26	-0.7%	21	398	16	351	39	191	2	38.3%	65	54.0
2015	CHI			572	363	63.4%	3986	27	15	10		6.1		0.3%					39	157	1	9.1%		
	2013:	48% Short		31% Mid		11% Deep		10% Bomb		YAC: 4.1 (39)		2014:		60% Short		26% Mid		8% Deep		7% Bomb		YAC: 5.5 (16)		

In many ways, the Jay Cutler of 2014 wasn't much different from the Jay Cutler of 2013. He has always been a mistake-prone gunslinger, and his adjusted interception percentage was 3.9 percent, but that was only a touch worse than 2013's 3.7 percent. In 2013, Cutler had 1.9% DVOA under center and 15.9% DVOA in shotgun; in 2014, things didn't change much, with -3.7% DVOA under center and 12.7% DVOA in shotgun. In the red zone, Cutler actually improved his DVOA from 12.0% to 17.9%. He improved on first and second down as well, going from -1.7%/-7.0% to 4.1%/0.6%. Third down? Ah, there's the rub. Cutler was excellent on third and fourth downs in 2013, with a DVOA of 32.4%. In 2014, he struggled, posting a DVOA of -11.4%. The key change came in third-and-not too long (7-10 yards to go). He was outstanding in 2013, converting 44 percent of the time and posting a DVOA of 41.9%. That changed in 2014, with a DVOA of -10.4% and just a 30 percent conversion rate. On such events the fates of coaches change.

Andy Dalton   Height: 6-2   Weight: 215   College: TCU   Draft: 2011/2 (35)   Born: 29-Oct-1987   Age: 28   Risk: Green

Year	Team	G/GS	Snaps	Att	Cmp	C%	Yds	TD	INT/Adj	FUM	ASR	NY/P	Rk	DVOA	Rk	DYAR	Rk	YAR	Runs	Yds	TD	DVOA	DYAR	QBR
2012	CIN	16/16	1025	528	329	62.3%	3669	27	16/19	8	8.5%	6.0	21	-5.9%	20	194	20	339	47	120	4	18.9%	53	48.9
2013	CIN	16/16	1117	586	363	61.9%	4293	33	20/21	4	5.2%	6.7	11	2.3%	18	541	16	612	61	183	2	13.0%	52	55.8
2014	CIN	16/16	1031	481	309	64.2%	3398	19	17/21	3	4.3%	6.5	19	-3.7%	24	237	21	238	60	169	4	-2.9%	26	55.2
2015	CIN			525	332	63.2%	3665	25	17	5		6.1		-1.4%					41	187	2	20.4%		
	2013:	44% Short		35% Mid		12% Deep		8% Bomb		YAC: 5.7 (8)		2014:		54% Short		29% Mid		11% Deep		6% Bomb		YAC: 5.6 (10)	

The replacement of Jay Gruden as Dalton's offensive coordinator with "run-first" Hue Jackson seemed to bode well for Red's efficiency. Instead, Dalton regressed in his first year without Gruden calling the plays, mainly thanks to his continuing penchant for throwing interceptions. His mysterious ineptitude in prime time continues to be an issue, one that that descended into farce at times in 2014, notably during a Thursday night pratfall against Cleveland. To his credit, Dalton continued to display the resiliency that has marked his career. He followed the Browns debacle with an excellent performance at New Orleans. A three-pick first-half nightmare in Tampa (brought on in part by a vicious stomach flu) was followed by a second half rally to victory. An early pick-six in a must-win Monday night encounter with Denver was followed by 20 unanswered points and an eventual victory.

Similarly, Dalton compensated in part for his downturn by being solid on third down (8.0% DVOA), much better than he was on the first two downs. It sometimes seems as though Dalton deliberately tests fans to see how much they can withstand before pulling back from the edge—he's like a football version of Chuck Yeager, always pushing the envelope without actually cratering the airplane.

In fairness, Dalton was hamstrung by injuries to his big-play threats all season. That particularly showed up in his deep passing numbers—his accuracy on such passes fell from 42.4 percent to 30.5 percent, on virtually the same number of throws. In the last four games, including the playoff loss at Indianapolis, he was 0-for-15 on long passes, notably including a flea-flicker underthrow against the Colts that should have been a touchdown. The lack of downfield proficiency was especially disappointing given the excellent protection Dalton received from his line, and his improved play under duress, where he has finally developed subtleties such as sliding up in the pocket to buy time. With a full complement of healthy targets, he should be in line to bounce back in 2015, though fantasy-wise he almost certainly peaked in 2013.

Chase Daniel   Height: 6-0   Weight: 225   College: Missouri   Draft: 2009/FA   Born: 7-Oct-1986   Age: 29   Risk: Red

Year	Team	G/GS	Snaps	Att	Cmp	C%	Yds	TD	INT/Adj	FUM	ASR	NY/P	Rk	DVOA	Rk	DYAR	Rk	YAR	Runs	Yds	TD	DVOA	DYAR	QBR
2012	NO	16/0	13	1	1	100.0%	10	0	0/0	0	-2.1%	10.0	--	579.9%	--	34	--	36	3	17	0	108.0%	7	100.0
2013	KC	5/1	100	38	25	65.8%	248	1	1/1	0	4.7%	5.9	--	-13.6%	--	-6	--	22	14	52	0	47.0%	18	78.7
2014	KC	3/1	67	28	16	57.1%	157	0	0/0	0	13.2%	4.4	--	-24.4%	--	-28	--	-18	4	15	0	84.8%	9	46.4
2015	KC			511	303	59.3%	3277	18	13	10		5.3		-15.1%					49	147	1	-7.2%		
	2013:	75% Short		11% Mid		11% Deep		3% Bomb		YAC: 5.9 (--)		2014:		63% Short		25% Mid		6% Deep		6% Bomb		YAC: 4.1 (--)	

There aren't many better coaches for a quarterback to learn from than Sean Payton and Andy Reid. If Alex Smith suffered an injury, the Chiefs would likely be in better shape than most to handle that transition at starting quarterback. Daniel has thrown 75 regular-season passes in his NFL career. Sixty-three of those passes have come in Week 17 games, including back-to-back starts against the Chargers with Kansas City, where he has done a solid job. Daniel thought he finally had the 2014 Chiefs' first touchdown pass to a wide receiver in that San Diego game, but Dwayne Bowe fumbled the ball at the 1-yard line and the Chiefs ended up recovering for the score. So close.

Austin Davis   Height: 6-2   Weight: 221   College: Southern Mississippi   Draft: 2012/FA   Born: 2-Jun-1989   Age: 26   Risk: Green

Year	Team	G/GS	Snaps	Att	Cmp	C%	Yds	TD	INT/Adj	FUM	ASR	NY/P	Rk	DVOA	Rk	DYAR	Rk	YAR	Runs	Yds	TD	DVOA	DYAR	QBR
2014	STL	10/8	548	284	180	63.4%	2001	12	9/12	5	9.5%	5.9	32	-8.8%	29	47	29	-2	16	36	0	4.6%	5	37.6
2015	STL			494	317	64.2%	3398	22	16	10		5.9		-9.8%					42	80	1	-17.0%		
													2014:		59% Short		22% Mid		9% Deep		10% Bomb		YAC: 5.0 (26)

Davis broke many of Brett Favre's records at Southern Miss. He is unlikely to break any of Favre's records in the NFL. The former collegiate walk-on and undrafted free agent spent two seasons trying to stick as a practice squad player with the Dolphins and Rams. Sam Bradford's torn ACL followed by a Week 1 injury to Shaun Hill opened the door for Davis as an NFL starter, and for a while things went OK. His peak came in a 28-26 win over Seattle, when Davis went 17-of-20 for 155 yards with two touchdowns and no sacks or turnovers against the reigning Super Bowl champs. It didn't last, though. Davis threw five picks in his next three games, and after two interceptions and a lost fumble in the fourth quarter against Arizona, he was benched for Hill and didn't throw another pass all year. With Hill joining Minnesota in free agency, Davis will battle Case Keenum for the primary backup job behind Nick Foles.

Ryan Fitzpatrick Height: 6-2 Weight: 221 College: Harvard Draft: 2005/7 (250) Born: 24-Nov-1982 Age: 33 Risk: Red

Year	Team	G/GS	Snaps	Att	Cmp	C%	Yds	TD	INT/Adj	FUM	ASR	NY/P	Rk	DVOA	Rk	DYAR	Rk	YAR	Runs	Yds	TD	DVOA	DYAR	QBR
2012	BUF	16/16	993	505	306	60.6%	3400	24	16/21	9	5.6%	6.1	20	-7.6%	23	120	23	161	48	197	1	0.5%	22	44.9
2013	TEN	11/9	680	350	217	62.0%	2454	14	12/13	9	5.8%	6.4	14	-3.6%	20	179	21	112	43	225	3	34.8%	85	55.4
2014	HOU	12/12	727	312	197	63.1%	2483	17	8/13	5	5.8%	7.2	6	6.7%	12	383	17	485	50	184	2	2.8%	32	55.3
2015	NYJ			483	303	62.7%	3403	23	17	10		6.2		-8.7%					57	193	2	-5.7%		

2013:	44% Short	37% Mid	11% Deep	8% Bomb	YAC: 5.1 (26)	2014:	51% Short	31% Mid	14% Deep	5% Bomb	YAC: 5.5 (17)

Ryan Fitzpatrick is the Rasputin of the NFL. He looks like a peasant, he lives in uncertain times, and there's something magical about how he managed to play last season despite a total lack of pocket awareness. Every good game he plays makes you think there might be just enough here to settle down, and then come the bad starts. As Fitzpatrick is only attracted to hemophiliac quarterback situations, it was almost a given he would wind up with the Jets. Geno Smith and Bryce Petty make for the kind of depth chart Fitzpatrick can top, and for the low price of a sixth-rounder, the Jets now have a quarterback who can lead them to 9-7 if everything breaks right.

Joe Flacco Height: 6-6 Weight: 236 College: Delaware Draft: 2008/1 (18) Born: 16-Jan-1985 Age: 30 Risk: Yellow

Year	Team	G/GS	Snaps	Att	Cmp	C%	Yds	TD	INT/Adj	FUM	ASR	NY/P	Rk	DVOA	Rk	DYAR	Rk	YAR	Runs	Yds	TD	DVOA	DYAR	QBR
2012	BAL	16/16	1002	531	317	59.7%	3817	22	10/17	9	6.1%	6.3	18	-1.3%	17	358	17	403	32	22	3	-35.1%	-32	46.3
2013	BAL	16/16	1129	614	362	59.0%	3912	19	22/29	8	7.4%	5.4	37	-18.1%	33	-296	36	-242	27	131	1	37.4%	53	46.7
2014	BAL	16/16	1070	554	344	62.1%	3986	27	12/16	5	4.5%	6.7	13	15.5%	7	987	8	962	39	70	2	-12.9%	-1	67.3
2015	BAL			569	355	62.4%	3937	25	14	7		6.0		-0.3%					26	82	1	9.9%		

2013:	48% Short	28% Mid	13% Deep	10% Bomb	YAC: 4.9 (32)	2014:	45% Short	38% Mid	8% Deep	8% Bomb	YAC: 5.1 (24)

How well Flacco plays in 2015 depends in large part on how well he adapts to the loss of two men: offensive coordinator Gary Kubiak and receiver Torrey Smith. Flacco had the best season of his career under Kubiak, whose offense attacked defenses by kneecapping blitzes with quick-hitting passes, often with the quarterback on the move. Sure enough, Flacco improved when five or more rushers came after him, from 4.3 yards per attempt to 7.6. It wasn't a small sample, either—only Tampa Bay's quarterbacks were blitzed more often. We don't know if Marc Trestman can help Flacco continue that performance against the blitz, but he may be able to improve Flacco in the red zone, the one area where the Ravens' quarterback comparatively struggled last year. In two seasons under Trestman, Jay Cutler put up red zone DVOA ratings of 12.9% and 17.0%, despite inferior numbers in the other 80 yards of gridiron.

As for Smith, Rookie Breshad Perriman may be able to replace him as a receiver, but can he replace Smith as a magnet for Defensive Pass Interference flags? Flacco has gained over 280 yards from DPI in three of the past four seasons, leading all quarterbacks with 14 DPI flags in both 2013 and 2014. A big reason for that is Smith, who drew 11 DPI flags last year when no other receiver had more than six.

Nick Foles Height: 6-5 Weight: 243 College: Arizona Draft: 2012/3 (88) Born: 20-Jan-1989 Age: 26 Risk: Green

Year	Team	G/GS	Snaps	Att	Cmp	C%	Yds	TD	INT/Adj	FUM	ASR	NY/P	Rk	DVOA	Rk	DYAR	Rk	YAR	Runs	Yds	TD	DVOA	DYAR	QBR
2012	PHI	7/6	453	265	161	60.8%	1699	6	5/11	8	8.2%	5.5	32	-20.4%	30	-166	30	-158	11	42	1	11.7%	11	43.1
2013	PHI	13/10	703	317	203	64.0%	2891	27	2/4	4	9.2%	7.9	2	35.6%	2	1011	5	1111	57	221	3	23.1%	72	69.0
2014	PHI	8/8	545	311	186	59.8%	2163	13	10/12	4	2.7%	6.5	18	1.8%	19	264	19	280	16	68	0	9.5%	15	62.2
2015	STL			510	321	62.8%	3499	23	15	6		6.0		-2.5%					29	74	1	-0.7%		

2013:	49% Short	24% Mid	15% Deep	13% Bomb	YAC: 6.8 (1)	2014:	50% Short	24% Mid	16% Deep	10% Bomb	YAC: 5.3 (20)

Foles threw seven interceptions and lost five fumbles in the four games from Week 4 through Week 8 (the Eagles' bye was in Week 7). Those were the David Molk/Matt Tobin games for the interior Eagles line, and while Foles had some serious ball-security issues when he took a hit, he also suffered from the massive dropoff in protection when Jason Kelce and Evan Mathis were hurt. Foles' ten picks last year were a cosmic readjustment after his two-pick 2013 season. Foles' career interception rate is now 1.9 percent, precisely the mean of his 2013 and 2014 rates and well below the NFL average of 2.5 percent. He's neither the historical mistake avoider of two years ago nor the interception machine of last year, but a player whose rates have not yet stabilized. Isn't it funny how it always works out that way?

Foles can stand in the pocket and sling it, throws a pretty deep ball, and fits Jeff Fisher's two-handoffs-and-a-play-fake philosophy better than he fit any system built from rolling pockets and read-options. A conservative system and tough divisional opponents will depress his already modest fantasy value, but a healthy Foles could lead the Rams to the playoffs.

Blaine Gabbert Height: 6-4   Weight: 234   College: Missouri   Draft: 2011/1 (10)   Born: 15-Oct-1989   Age: 26 Risk: Green

Year	Team	G/GS	Snaps	Att	Cmp	C%	Yds	TD	INT/Adj	FUM	ASR	NY/P	Rk	DVOA	Rk	DYAR	Rk	YAR	Runs	Yds	TD	DVOA	DYAR	QBR
2012	JAC	10/10	515	278	162	58.3%	1662	9	6/6	5	6.9%	5.0	35	-25.3%	34	-268	32	-309	18	56	0	-6.8%	5	39.7
2013	JAC	3/3	159	86	42	48.8%	481	1	7/5	2	11.0%	4.2	--	-84.1%	--	-429	--	-480	9	32	0	-29.2%	-8	1.8
2014	SF	1/0	9	7	3	42.9%	38	1	0/0	0	0.3%	5.4	--	37.7%	--	22	--	18	1	5	0	-34.2%	-1	91.4
2015	SF			509	295	57.8%	3171	15	15	10		5.1		-24.5%					44	96	0	-19.8%		

| 2013: | 49% Short | 36% Mid | 10% Deep | 4% Bomb | YAC: 6.6 (--) | 2014: | 38% Short | 25% Mid | 25% Deep | 13% Bomb | YAC: 1.7 (--) |

Despite an actual positive DYAR total in seven attempts last season, Gabbert's -1,865 career passing DYAR remains the worst total on record. There are two viable contenders to the throne active this year. Josh McCown had a career-worst -665 DYAR in 2014; think of how much ground that covers! He was 47th-worst in career DYAR entering the season, but is now seventh-worst at -1,172 DYAR. Blake Bortles, Gabbert's replacement in Jacksonville, fared hardly any better than Gabbert did in black-and-teal, with -955 DYAR as a rookie, and he is now 12th from the bottom in the career standings. If either McCown or Bortles plays as badly in 2015 as he did in 2014, he will pass Gabbert for the Worst Quarterback Of The DVOA Era crown—unless, of course, Gabbert sees significant playing time and performs as badly as he always has, which would leave McCown and Bortles chasing a sinking target. The 49ers re-signed Gabbert after the season to a two-year deal worth up to $4 million, so there are certainly worse fates in life than to be the worst starting quarterback of a generation. The 49ers' only offseason addition at the position was undrafted free agent Dylan Thompson, who completed less than 60 percent of his passes at South Carolina, so Gabbert's grip on the No. 2 job seems secure.

Jimmy Garoppolo Height: 6-2   Weight: 226   College: Eastern Illinois   Draft: 2014/2 (62)   Born: 11-Feb-1991   Age: 24 Risk: Yellow

Year	Team	G/GS	Snaps	Att	Cmp	C%	Yds	TD	INT/Adj	FUM	ASR	NY/P	Rk	DVOA	Rk	DYAR	Rk	YAR	Runs	Yds	TD	DVOA	DYAR	QBR
2014	NE	6/0	69	27	19	70.4%	182	1	0/0	0	14.0%	4.6	--	-13.8%	--	-5	--	-28	10	9	0	-14.3%	-1	19.2
2015	NE			544	337	61.9%	3778	25	18	10		5.9		-5.5%					42	85	1	4.1%		

| | | | | | | | | 2014: | 67% Short | 18% Mid | 12% Deep | 3% Bomb | YAC: 6.3 (--) |

If Tom Brady has to miss any time this season, the projected downgrade New England will experience with Garoppolo at the helm depends on how you account for the defenses the young quarterback faced at Eastern Illinois. Garoppolo's raw stats (66 percent completion rate with a 53-9 TD-INT split as a senior) project well, but came against weak competition. We built our new QBASE projection system without considering FCS quarterbacks, so it has no projection for Garoppolo. But if we were to create a projection by treating his schedule as equivalent to one of the worst in FBS, Garoppolo's QBASE projection of 514 DYAR in Years 3-5 of his career would rank him as a marginal NFL starter, higher than Jameis Winston but well below Marcus Mariota. And, of course, even more caveats than usual surround this projection. Right now, all we know about Garoppolo is that he has looked good in preseason action (7.8 yards per pass, 5 TD, 1 INT) and even better in a suit—79 percent of voters in an Outsports.com poll chose Garoppolo as the Patriots' best-looking quarterback.

Mike Glennon

Height: 6-6   Weight: 218   College: North Carolina State   Draft: 2013/3 (73)   Born: 12-Dec-1989   Age: 26 Risk: Red

Year	Team	G/GS	Snaps	Att	Cmp	C%	Yds	TD	INT/Adj	FUM	ASR	NY/P	Rk	DVOA	Rk	DYAR	Rk	YAR	Runs	Yds	TD	DVOA	DYAR	QBR
2013	TB	13/13	842	416	247	59.4%	2608	19	9/11	7	8.3%	5.1	40	-7.7%	25	99	22	-73	27	37	0	-45.6%	-22	45.6
2014	TB	6/5	363	203	117	57.6%	1417	10	6/8	2	7.7%	6.1	24	-3.1%	23	107	26	161	10	49	0	2.2%	6	56.0
2015	TB			510	300	58.8%	3289	22	15	8		5.5		-11.9%					40	116	1	-6.0%		

2013:	43% Short	38% Mid	11% Deep	8% Bomb	YAC: 3.7 (40)	2014:	39% Short	35% Mid	18% Deep	8% Bomb	YAC: 3.6 (37)

Our college quarterback projection system hated Mike Glennon before the 2013 draft, and the new QBASE system feels the same. His projection of -486 DYAR for Years 3-5 is higher than just six other quarterbacks selected in the first three rounds since 1997. Yet Glennon is on a path to outperform that projection. Given the state of last year's Tampa Bay offensive line, playing at replacement level is a sign of potential consistent competence for a second-year quarterback. Glennon improved last year at going through his progressions and showing poise in the pocket. He certainly should have started ahead of Josh McCown. Starting him ahead of Jameis Winston is a potentially good idea that has no chance of happening.

Bruce Gradkowski

Height: 6-1   Weight: 220   College: Toledo   Draft: 2006/6 (194)   Born: 27-Jan-1983   Age: 32 Risk: Red

Year	Team	G/GS	Snaps	Att	Cmp	C%	Yds	TD	INT/Adj	FUM	ASR	NY/P	Rk	DVOA	Rk	DYAR	Rk	YAR	Runs	Yds	TD	DVOA	DYAR	QBR
2012	CIN	3/0	30	11	5	45.5%	65	0	0/0	1	0.0%	5.9	--	-14.9%	--	-3	--	-8	4	-2	0	--	--	54.7
2014	PIT	1/0	7	0	0	0.0%	0	0	0/0	0	--	--	--	--	--	--	--	--	2	-2	0	--	--	--
2015	PIT			564	309	54.7%	3658	21	17	10		5.5		-14.4%					41	89	0	-12.1%		

If it weren't for the cleanly shaven head, it would be tough to tell the difference between Charlie Batch and Bruce Gradkowski. They don't look alike physically, but they are essentially one and the same to Steelers fans: beloved backups who rarely have to play and, in a perfect world, never will. Gradkowski hasn't had more than 20 attempts in a season since 2010.

Robert Griffin

Height: 6-2   Weight: 223   College: Baylor   Draft: 2012/1 (2)   Born: 12-Feb-1990   Age: 25 Risk: Red

Year	Team	G/GS	Snaps	Att	Cmp	C%	Yds	TD	INT/Adj	FUM	ASR	NY/P	Rk	DVOA	Rk	DYAR	Rk	YAR	Runs	Yds	TD	DVOA	DYAR	QBR
2012	WAS	15/15	937	393	258	65.6%	3200	20	5/10	11	7.7%	7.0	7	16.6%	7	727	11	811	120	815	7	7.8%	109	73.2
2013	WAS	13/13	906	456	274	60.1%	3203	16	12/15	10	8.8%	6.0	21	-13.1%	29	-60	30	98	86	489	0	-0.9%	42	40.1
2014	WAS	9/7	457	214	147	68.7%	1694	4	6/6	9	13.7%	5.9	29	-34.2%	35	-374	35	-372	38	176	1	-25.5%	-23	30.8
2015	WAS			547	351	64.2%	4059	24	16	15		6.3		-4.6%					87	406	2	-0.8%		

2013:	47% Short	35% Mid	12% Deep	6% Bomb	YAC: 5.6 (15)	2014:	73% Short	17% Mid	4% Deep	6% Bomb	YAC: 7.5 (1)

Griffin led the NFL in failed completion rate among quarterbacks who completed 100 or more passes: 49 of his 147 completions, or precisely 33.3 percent, were essentially empty calories. (Failed completions gain less than 45 percent of necessary first down yardage on first down, 60 percent of the necessary yardage on second down, or fail to convert altogether on third or fourth down.) Griffin finished second in the NFL (behind Drew Brees) in "bad throw rate," with only 12.1 percent of his attempts charted as either underthrown or overthrown. Griffin's "string of good games" at the end of the season was a mix of statistical padding and optimistic narrative-spinning. His performance against the Eagles was solid, but the Giants and Cowboys games were master classes in how to throw 6-yard passes on third-and-9. And of course, Griffin only started those last few games because Gruden couldn't figure out a *Weekend at Bernie's* scenario for Colt McCoy's lifeless cadaver.

The Redskins picked up Griffin's fifth-year option before the draft, because when you are stuck driving on a rutted mountain path it often seems to make more sense to keep going than to turn around. Yes, the Griffin we swooned over in 2012 could still reemerge. It just becomes harder and harder to imagine that happening in his current environment. The KUBIAK equations are more optimistic, at least when it comes to his fantasy value.

Matt Hasselbeck

Height: 6-4   Weight: 223   College: Boston College   Draft: 1998/6 (187)   Born: 25-Sep-1975   Age: 40   Risk: Green

Year	Team	G/GS	Snaps	Att	Cmp	C%	Yds	TD	INT/Adj	FUM	ASR	NY/P	Rk	DVOA	Rk	DYAR	Rk	YAR	Runs	Yds	TD	DVOA	DYAR	QBR
2012	TEN	8/5	395	221	138	62.4%	1367	7	5/11	3	5.7%	5.4	33	-11.5%	26	-6	26	20	13	38	0	24.9%	9	46.0
2013	IND	3/0	23	12	7	58.3%	130	0	1/1	0	0.6%	10.8	--	-28.6%	--	-15	--	-9	2	-2	0	--	--	38.1
2014	IND	4/0	82	44	30	68.2%	301	2	0/1	1	5.3%	6.2	--	10.8%	--	71	--	96	8	-11	0	-216.5%	-9	71.6
2015	IND			597	384	64.2%	4080	25	17	10		5.7		-5.3%					24	59	0	-3.5%		

| 2013: | 40% Short | 50% Mid | 10% Deep | 0% Bomb | YAC: 12.9 (--) | 2014: | 50% Short | 31% Mid | 15% Deep | 4% Bomb | YAC: 6.1 (--) |

Hasselbeck turns 40 in September, which will make the Colts the rare NFL roster with two 40-year-old players; Adam Vinatieri (43 in December) is the other. That's surely rare, but not unique; just recently, the 2011 Texans had Jeff Garcia (41) and Matt Turk (43) on the roster together for a brief time late in the season. This duo is much better, since Hasselbeck is one of the best backup quarterbacks in the league. It's nice to have a guy with more than 5,000 pass attempts as your backup behind Andrew Luck. (Well, as long as he's not Kerry Collins.)

Chad Henne

Height: 6-2   Weight: 230   College: Michigan   Draft: 2008/2 (57)   Born: 2-Jul-1985   Age: 30   Risk: Red

Year	Team	G/GS	Snaps	Att	Cmp	C%	Yds	TD	INT/Adj	FUM	ASR	NY/P	Rk	DVOA	Rk	DYAR	Rk	YAR	Runs	Yds	TD	DVOA	DYAR	QBR
2012	JAC	10/6	545	308	166	53.9%	2084	11	11/14	3	8.5%	5.7	29	-24.6%	33	-286	33	-171	19	64	1	-33.3%	-17	26.1
2013	JAC	15/13	897	503	305	60.6%	3241	13	14/21	2	7.4%	5.6	34	-13.9%	31	-94	31	-149	27	77	0	-39.9%	-37	31.9
2014	JAC	3/3	141	78	42	53.8%	492	3	1/2	1	16.2%	4.2	--	-54.3%	--	-249	--	-210	4	25	0	38.3%	10	16.1
2015	JAC			536	305	56.8%	3381	17	18	6		4.8		-24.4%					30	109	0	3.6%		

| 2013: | 53% Short | 32% Mid | 9% Deep | 5% Bomb | YAC: 5.9 (4) | 2014: | 55% Short | 28% Mid | 8% Deep | 9% Bomb | YAC: 5.1 (--) |

To come out of the analyst's chair for just a few seconds, it was really disheartening watching the Jaguars offensive line allow Henne to get crushed in his first few games. Washington sacked Henne 10 times in Week 2 alone. Jedd Fisch's offense often did not give easy dumpoffs to his quarterbacks. Mix that scheme with a bad offensive line, and Henne was the one who paid the price. The coaching staff still loves Henne, so he should make it through this year, but at this point he's a below-average backup at best.

Shaun Hill

Height: 6-5   Weight: 210   College: Maryland   Draft: 2002/FA   Born: 9-Jan-1980   Age: 36   Risk: Yellow

Year	Team	G/GS	Snaps	Att	Cmp	C%	Yds	TD	INT/Adj	FUM	ASR	NY/P	Rk	DVOA	Rk	DYAR	Rk	YAR	Runs	Yds	TD	DVOA	DYAR	QBR
2012	DET	1/0	19	13	10	76.9%	172	2	0/0	0	0.7%	14.3	--	136.4%	--	128	--	137	1	-1	0	-97.7%	-7	76.8
2013	DET	1/0	2	0	0	0.0%	0	0	0/0	0	--	--	--	--	--	--	--	--	2	-2	0	--	--	--
2014	STL	9/8	452	229	145	63.3%	1657	8	7/5	7	7.5%	6.2	21	-14.1%	31	-46	31	-35	10	10	1	-41.0%	-8	38.1
2015	MIN			480	302	63.0%	3317	20	13	11		5.8		-5.6%					14	46	0	3.6%		

| | | | | | | | | | | | | | | | | 2014: | 58% Short | 22% Mid | 11% Deep | 9% Bomb | YAC: 5.6 (13) |

It only seems as if Shaun Hill has been around the league forever. He signed his first contract with the Vikings in 2002. First-round quarterbacks that year included David Carr, Joey Harrington, and Patrick Ramsey, none of whom lasted as long as Hill has. The only other member of the quarterback class of 2002 still playing: Josh McCown. It's admirable those two could last so long in such a demanding profession, but that doesn't mean you actually want either guy starting for your team this fall. Hill, at least, won't be taking meaningful snaps unless Teddy Bridgewater gets hurt. As for McCown, read on.

Brian Hoyer

Height: 6-2   Weight: 215   College: Michigan State   Draft: 2009/FA   Born: 13-Oct-1985   Age: 30   Risk: Yellow

Year	Team	G/GS	Snaps	Att	Cmp	C%	Yds	TD	INT/Adj	FUM	ASR	NY/P	Rk	DVOA	Rk	DYAR	Rk	YAR	Runs	Yds	TD	DVOA	DYAR	QBR
2012	2TM	2/1	81	53	30	56.6%	330	1	2/2	1	7.2%	5.3	--	-26.5%	--	-60	--	-119	1	6	0	63.7%	5	37.7
2013	CLE	3/3	151	96	57	59.4%	615	5	3/4	0	7.1%	5.5	--	-10.4%	--	5	--	27	6	16	0	20.4%	4	47.5
2014	CLE	14/13	911	438	242	55.3%	3326	12	13/20	4	5.4%	6.8	10	-5.3%	25	166	24	255	24	39	0	-64.8%	-59	43.1
2015	HOU			505	292	57.8%	3285	18	20	5		5.6		-18.3%					32	49	1	-17.9%		

| 2013: | 49% Short | 30% Mid | 16% Deep | 6% Bomb | YAC: 5.5 (--) | 2014: | 44% Short | 35% Mid | 13% Deep | 9% Bomb | YAC: 5.6 (11) |

Plenty of quarterbacks in the NFL struggle to effectively run their offenses. Being an NFL quarterback isn't easy by any measure. However, what Hoyer did last year was different. Hoyer spectacularly failed in a climate that was set up for him to succeed. Sure, the Browns receivers were limited, but they were consistently open. Hoyer was asked to make throws on the move and push the ball downfield to open receivers—two things that aren't easy, but pale in comparison to what other quarterbacks are forced to do: playing under pressure from the pocket while anticipating tight-window throws. It was a season that suggested Hoyer is an NFL backup at best. He was benched late in the season, but could easily have been benched after the first couple of weeks. Hoyer is the presumed starter in Houston at this point, and Bill O'Brien did manage some minor miracles with Ryan Fitzpatrick's efficiency, but don't mistake good scheming for actual improvement.

Tarvaris Jackson   Height: 6-2   Weight: 226   College: Alabama State   Draft: 2006/2 (64)   Born: 21-Apr-1983   Age: 32   Risk: Red

Year	Team	G/GS	Snaps	Att	Cmp	C%	Yds	TD	INT/Adj	FUM	ASR	NY/P	Rk	DVOA	Rk	DYAR	Rk	YAR	Runs	Yds	TD	DVOA	DYAR	QBR
2013	SEA	3/0	39	13	10	76.9%	151	1	0/0	0	1.3%	11.6	--	81.9%	--	83	--	93	4	1	1	96.1%	9	89.0
2014	SEA	1/0	3	1	1	100.0%	0	0	0/0	0	1.3%	0.0	--	-131.3%	--	-4	--	-4	0	0	0	--	--	43.9
2015	SEA			465	286	61.4%	3183	19	14	9		5.9		-10.9%					51	94	1	-17.3%		
	2013:	46% Short		31% Mid		8% Deep		15% Bomb		YAC: 7.5 (--)			2014:	100% Short		0% Mid		0% Deep		0% Bomb		YAC: 0.0 (--)		

Jackson spent a decent chunk of the offseason unemployed, and when Russell Wilson missed part of OTAs, it left R.J. Archer taking first-string snaps for the two-time defending NFC champs. Jackson then re-signed with the team as soon as OTAs ended, suggesting that he had a handshake deal with the team all along but waited to sign so he could enjoy an extended vacation. We call this kind of thing "veteran savvy." Jackson's average DVOA over his career has been about -8.0%, and he has a 17-17 record as a starter (10-10 in Minnesota, 7-7 in Seattle). You could do a lot worse for a backup. If you're Cleveland, you could do a lot worse for a starter.

Colin Kaepernick   Height: 6-5   Weight: 233   College: Nevada   Draft: 2011/2 (36)   Born: 3-Nov-1987   Age: 28   Risk: Green

Year	Team	G/GS	Snaps	Att	Cmp	C%	Yds	TD	INT/Adj	FUM	ASR	NY/P	Rk	DVOA	Rk	DYAR	Rk	YAR	Runs	Yds	TD	DVOA	DYAR	QBR
2012	SF	13/7	525	218	136	62.4%	1814	10	3/6	7	6.8%	7.2	2	25.8%	3	555	13	462	63	415	5	-1.5%	31	72.2
2013	SF	16/16	968	416	243	58.4%	3197	21	8/10	6	7.8%	6.5	12	16.6%	7	791	8	650	92	524	4	11.8%	91	68.6
2014	SF	16/16	1049	478	289	60.5%	3369	19	10/12	8	9.9%	5.7	34	-8.4%	28	91	27	176	104	639	1	7.5%	88	55.9
2015	SF			493	296	60.0%	3452	22	13	10		6.0		-11.2%					96	544	2	-0.1%		
	2013:	38% Short		39% Mid		16% Deep		6% Bomb		YAC: 5.5 (20)			2014:	53% Short		29% Mid		10% Deep		7% Bomb		YAC: 4.8 (30)		

Kaepernick and Robert Griffin were the 16th and 17th quarterbacks on record to see their passing DVOA decline by at least 9.0% two years in a row with at least 200 passes in all three years. It happened to Troy Aikman twice, while Philip Rivers actually had a decline that sharp for four years in a row from 2009 to 2012. The good news is, many of these quarterbacks (including Aikman and Rivers) rebounded with multiple successful seasons later in their careers. The poster child for that might be John Elway, whose DVOA fell from 11.1% in 1990 to -5.5% in 1991 and then -23.5% in 1992. Elway would go on to be top ten in DVOA five more times, including a third-place finish in his last season in 1998.

The most concerning pattern for Kaepernick might be how his performance declined as games progressed. His DVOA fell from 25.8% in the first quarter to 13.5% in the second, -23.3% in the third, and -50.9% in the fourth quarter or overtime. Kaepernick and the 49ers will need to learn to make better in-game adjustments if they're going to turn things around in 2015.

Case Keenum   Height: 6-2   Weight: 209   College: Houston   Draft: 2012/FA   Born: 17-Feb-1988   Age: 27   Risk: Yellow

Year	Team	G/GS	Snaps	Att	Cmp	C%	Yds	TD	INT/Adj	FUM	ASR	NY/P	Rk	DVOA	Rk	DYAR	Rk	YAR	Runs	Yds	TD	DVOA	DYAR	QBR
2013	HOU	8/8	461	253	137	54.2%	1760	9	6/8	6	7.4%	5.8	25	-22.4%	36	-191	34	-201	14	72	1	23.8%	27	34.5
2014	2TM	2/2	165	77	45	58.4%	435	2	2/2	1	2.8%	5.3	--	-20.8%	--	-50	--	-43	10	35	0	4.3%	9	43.7
2015	STL			488	284	58.3%	3209	15	12	10		5.7		-12.3%					40	139	1	-0.8%		
	2013:	48% Short		33% Mid		8% Deep		10% Bomb		YAC: 5.0 (30)			2014:	60% Short		26% Mid		7% Deep		6% Bomb		YAC: 5.8 (--)		

If you want to think long and hard about how insulated and overworried about age the NFL is, ponder this: the Texans had to release Andre Johnson—one of the best receivers in NFL history—because nobody would trade for him, but they had no problems finding a team to trade a seventh-round pick for Case Keenum.

Ryan Lindley Height: 6-4 Weight: 229 College: San Diego State Draft: 2012/6 (185) Born: 22-Jun-1989 Age: 26 Risk: N/A

Year	Team	G/GS	Snaps	Att	Cmp	C%	Yds	TD	INT/Adj	FUM	ASR	NY/P	Rk	DVOA	Rk	DYAR	Rk	YAR	Runs	Yds	TD	DVOA	DYAR	QBR
2012	ARI	7/4	303	171	89	52.0%	752	0	7/9	3	5.7%	3.6	39	-55.8%	39	-482	38	-601	4	7	0	-21.8%	-1	9.3
2014	ARI	3/2	163	93	45	48.4%	562	2	4/8	1	6.0%	5.2	--	-16.5%	--	-32	--	-116	0	0	0	--	--	37.8
											2014:	35% Short		32% Mid		18% Deep		14% Bomb		YAC: 3.4 (--)				

As a rookie in 2012, Lindley had the worst DVOA of any quarterback with at least 100 passes. He spent the next year and a half on the practice squad in Arizona and San Diego, basically a warm body who could give the defenses some reps against real live throws. Then Carson Palmer's knee imploded in November, and the Cardinals re-signed Lindley to back up Drew Stanton. And then Stanton suffered his own leg injury, and the Cardinals opted to start Lindley ahead of Logan Thomas in the last three games of the season, including the wild-card game. His regular-season games were bad, though that was partly because he played excellent pass defenses in Seattle and San Francisco (note the drastic difference between his DYAR and YAR). Then came the playoff game against Carolina, when Lindley went 16-of-28 for 106 yards (not counting 26 lost yards on laterals on the last play of the game) with one touchdown, two interceptions, two fumbles, and four sacks. It worked out to -166 DYAR, one of the ten worst playoff games we have ever measured, and the worst since Jake Delhomme's infamous six-turnover meltdown with Carolina in 2008. After the game, Lindley noted that the worst part of the loss was that he wouldn't get to play with his new/old teammates anymore. And he was right—Lindley was not re-signed after the season, and remained unemployed in early July.

Jake Locker Height: 6-3 Weight: 231 College: Washington Draft: 2011/1 (8) Born: 15-Jun-1988 Age: 27 Risk: N/A

Year	Team	G/GS	Snaps	Att	Cmp	C%	Yds	TD	INT/Adj	FUM	ASR	NY/P	Rk	DVOA	Rk	DYAR	Rk	YAR	Runs	Yds	TD	DVOA	DYAR	QBR
2012	TEN	11/11	595	314	177	56.4%	2176	10	11/13	4	8.2%	5.9	25	-23.6%	32	-265	31	-198	41	291	1	20.4%	54	44.5
2013	TEN	7/7	395	183	111	60.7%	1256	8	4/6	3	8.3%	5.8	26	-5.7%	22	69	24	130	24	155	2	20.7%	32	58.1
2014	TEN	7/5	299	146	86	58.9%	993	5	7/9	3	9.4%	5.7	--	-27.8%	--	-171	--	-215	22	142	1	46.1%	53	51.1
	2013:	38% Short		39% Mid		13% Deep		10% Bomb		YAC: 5.1 (29)		2014:	51% Short		30% Mid		10% Deep		9% Bomb		YAC: 5.5 (--)		

Locker's NFL career came to a close this offseason, when he retired after his rookie deal expired rather than trying find another team. Find another team he surely would have, given the paucity of veteran signal-callers around the NFL. Instead, his NFL career ends defined by injuries and inconsistency, with some thrilling scrambles and a few good throws, but not too many of them and not enough for someone who doesn't love football to continue his NFL career.

Andrew Luck Height: 6-4 Weight: 234 College: Stanford Draft: 2012/1 (1) Born: 12-Mar-1989 Age: 26 Risk: Green

Year	Team	G/GS	Snaps	Att	Cmp	C%	Yds	TD	INT/Adj	FUM	ASR	NY/P	Rk	DVOA	Rk	DYAR	Rk	YAR	Runs	Yds	TD	DVOA	DYAR	QBR
2012	IND	16/16	1169	627	339	54.1%	4374	23	18/30	15	6.8%	6.2	19	-5.1%	19	257	19	366	62	255	5	41.0%	123	65.2
2013	IND	16/16	1046	570	343	60.2%	3822	23	9/14	6	5.7%	6.0	22	4.6%	16	650	14	623	63	377	4	47.6%	151	62.0
2014	IND	16/16	1072	616	380	61.7%	4761	40	16/21	13	4.8%	7.1	7	9.2%	10	879	10	829	64	273	3	4.4%	40	63.8
2015	IND			619	392	63.4%	4788	35	16	8		7.0		16.0%					62	246	2	16.2%		
	2013:	49% Short		30% Mid		13% Deep		7% Bomb		YAC: 5.6 (14)		2014:	51% Short		30% Mid		12% Deep		7% Bomb		YAC: 5.8 (8)		

Andrew Luck holds the NFL records for the most total passing yards after a quarterback's first, second, and third seasons. He only needs 3,462 yards this year to wipe Peyton Manning out of the fourth-year spot too. He has come as advertised, but he still has room for improvement, especially in eliminating negative plays. That's more than just turnovers, but turnovers seem to be the sticking point for Luck. "That touchdown to interception ratio I think is very important," Luck said in June. "Cutting down on turnovers I think is my No. 1 goal for myself as a quarterback going into next season besides the obvious, winning a Super Bowl."

Luck had 22 turnovers last season, including five that were returned for touchdowns. More troubling than the 16 interceptions were the 13 fumbles (six lost), the second time Luck has fumbled at least 10 times in a season. You live with the picks because of how much Luck throws the ball, the way he attacks downfield, and how often he plays from behind, but he needs to protect the ball better when there's traffic around him. We'll look for any style changes to his game this year, but hopefully he doesn't start getting conservative to avoid interceptions. They're not always a big deal. Since 2012, Luck has 18 giveaways when trailing by 17-plus points. The closest quarterback is Matt Cassel (11). Luck has also already led the Colts to three comeback wins from such deficits, so his style produces results. He just needs to tighten up some things and let that neckbeard be the roughest part of his game.

Ryan Mallett

Height: 6-7 Weight: 253 College: Arkansas Draft: 2011/3 (74) Born: 5-Jun-1988 Age: 27 Risk: Yellow

Year	Team	G/GS	Snaps	Att	Cmp	C%	Yds	TD	INT/Adj	FUM	ASR	NY/P	Rk	DVOA	Rk	DYAR	Rk	YAR	Runs	Yds	TD	DVOA	DYAR	QBR
2012	NE	4/0	24	4	1	25.0%	17	0	1/0	0	-3.2%	4.3	--	-237.3%	--	-44	--	-46	8	-9	0	--	--	0.9
2014	HOU	3/2	157	75	41	54.7%	400	2	2/5	0	3.6%	5.3	--	14.5%	--	120	--	37	6	-2	0	31.6%	6	48.2
2015	HOU			502	274	54.6%	3359	19	20	9		5.6		-20.7%					22	55	0	-7.0%		
	2014:	45% Short		36% Mid			11% Deep			8% Bomb			YAC: 3.9 (--)											

Mallett's free agency was a lot like Matt Flynn's. Each quarterback had a resume with one good start and one poor start, and each had one major quarterback skill where the other was deficient. Mallett has great arm strength but problematic accuracy, which makes him the exact opposite of Flynn. Unfortunately for Mallett, teams appear to have wised up to this act, and he had to settle for just two years and $7 million to return to Houston. Last year's brief trial suggested that Mallett will never develop into an above-average NFL starter. His accuracy is just too scattershot. But the Texans should be praised for taking a chance on Mallett rather than settling for known mediocrities like Josh McCown or Ryan Fitzpatrick. There's at least some question about Mallett's true long-term ability. He could prove us wrong. Brian Hoyer can't.

Eli Manning

Height: 6-4 Weight: 218 College: Mississippi Draft: 2004/1 (1) Born: 3-Jan-1981 Age: 35 Risk: Yellow

Year	Team	G/GS	Snaps	Att	Cmp	C%	Yds	TD	INT/Adj	FUM	ASR	NY/P	Rk	DVOA	Rk	DYAR	Rk	YAR	Runs	Yds	TD	DVOA	DYAR	QBR
2012	NYG	16/16	1003	536	321	59.9%	3948	26	15/24	4	4.3%	6.8	9	9.0%	13	753	10	779	20	30	0	-40.5%	-15	68.9
2013	NYG	16/16	986	551	317	57.5%	3818	18	27/31	7	7.7%	6.0	20	-20.2%	35	-335	37	-202	18	36	0	-76.6%	-27	36.5
2014	NYG	16/16	1109	601	379	63.1%	4410	30	14/20	7	4.7%	6.7	14	4.6%	15	642	11	735	12	31	1	41.3%	18	70.9
2015	NYG			603	380	63.0%	4194	29	14	6		6.3		9.7%					20	41	0	-0.2%		
	2013:	40% Short		39% Mid		14% Deep		8% Bomb		YAC: 4.6 (35)		2014:	47% Short		35% Mid		12% Deep		7% Bomb		YAC: 5.1 (23)			

Manning said in a pre-draft conference call that he hoped to get his interception total below eight. He was not clear what his interception goals are for October, November, or December.

But seriously folks, Manning threw five interceptions in one oil spill of a game against the 49ers but just nine the rest of the year, four of them in his first two games in Ben McAdoo's system. Manning had his best raw statistical season since 2011 and one of the best of his career. DVOA would have liked his performance better if so much of his production (including seven touchdowns, 550 yards, and lots of high-percentage passing) had not come against the lowly Redskins. Interception goals aside, Manning will always sail some throws over a receiver's head and into a free safety's arms. But he has the job security of a tenured professor, and from a fantasy standpoint his production is practically supporting cast-proofed. Also, the 20-plus interception seasons only happen every three years, like clockwork, and Manning is nothing if not predictable.

Peyton Manning

Height: 6-5 Weight: 230 College: Tennessee Draft: 1998/1 (1) Born: 24-Mar-1976 Age: 39 Risk: Yellow

Year	Team	G/GS	Snaps	Att	Cmp	C%	Yds	TD	INT/Adj	FUM	ASR	NY/P	Rk	DVOA	Rk	DYAR	Rk	YAR	Runs	Yds	TD	DVOA	DYAR	QBR
2012	DEN	16/16	1111	583	400	68.6%	4659	37	11/14	2	4.2%	7.5	1	32.8%	2	1805	2	1956	23	6	0	-5.4%	2	82.4
2013	DEN	16/16	1156	659	450	68.3%	5477	55	10/12	10	3.4%	7.9	1	43.2%	1	2475	1	2674	32	-31	1	-110.6%	-30	82.9
2014	DEN	16/16	1092	597	395	66.2%	4727	39	15/19	6	3.5%	7.5	4	23.9%	4	1412	3	1358	24	-24	0	-236.4%	-30	77.3
2015	DEN			571	386	67.5%	4396	34	12	8		7.0		21.0%					23	31	1	-14.0%		
	2013:	55% Short		26% Mid		13% Deep		6% Bomb		YAC: 5.7 (9)		2014:	54% Short		26% Mid		12% Deep		8% Bomb		YAC: 4.8 (31)			

When Peyton Manning makes his likely final trip to Indianapolis in Week 9, he should walk away with the record for most passing yards in NFL history. Hopefully that walk won't include a limp. Only Warren Moon, Doug Flutie, and Brett Favre (twice) have started a full 16-game season at age 39 or older. Yes, Manning is 39, but he is still held to the highest standard. One bad half (Chiefs), two interceptions he'd like to have back (Bills), and two rotten games after tearing his quad (Bengals, Colts) have been enough for many to start shoveling dirt on his grave. As we detailed in the Denver chapter, hold up for a second. The totals here may fall, but the efficiency is likely to still be pretty good.

Manning once started 227 consecutive games in Indianapolis, missing just one play due to injury. He was an ironman like Favre, but then he had four neck surgeries, played on a high ankle sprain midway thru 2013, and tore his quad while he had the flu in Week 15 last year. He has become a big injury risk, which is why expectations are for Denver to lean on the running game more. However, Manning's injury happened in the middle of two games where he attempted just 20 passes, reminding us that injuries can happen on any play. Gary Kubiak doesn't have the secret sauce to prevent injuries. Recall that Bubby Brister went 4-0 as a starter on the 1998 Broncos. John Elway missed time for a sore hamstring and a sore back he hurt while lifting weights, and he even strained a rib muscle in pre-game warmups. There's no way to guarantee Manning's health for the full season, and there's certainly no question that the arm strength now doesn't match the arm strength from his Indianapolis days. But as long as he's healthy, he's going to play at a high level thanks to his brain and anticipation. (Note that Manning's Risk Factor is Yellow, not Red, because the KUBIAK projection already has built in a decline in his stat totals due to a more run-heavy scheme.)

EJ Manuel Height: 6-5   Weight: 240   College: Florida State   Draft: 2013/1 (16)   Born: 19-Mar-1990   Age: 25 Risk: Red

Year	Team	G/GS	Snaps	Att	Cmp	C%	Yds	TD	INT/Adj	FUM	ASR	NY/P	Rk	DVOA	Rk	DYAR	Rk	YAR	Runs	Yds	TD	DVOA	DYAR	QBR
2013	BUF	10/10	694	306	180	58.8%	1972	11	9/10	6	8.9%	5.5	35	-19.9%	34	-190	33	-87	53	186	2	11.0%	49	42.3
2014	BUF	5/4	259	131	76	58.0%	838	5	3/3	1	5.5%	5.8	--	-17.1%	--	-53	--	-36	16	52	1	-26.3%	-10	19.8
2015	BUF			512	306	59.7%	3306	18	14	8		5.6		-15.8%					59	221	3	2.6%		

| | 2013: | 52% Short | 29% Mid | 12% Deep | 7% Bomb | YAC: 5.1 (28) | 2014: | 61% Short | 20% Mid | 14% Deep | 5% Bomb | YAC: 7.0 (--) |

Manuel is right on track for what his college stats would have predicted: roughly replacement-level play as he enters his make-or-break third season. Based on his draft position and college stats, our QBASE projection system forecast Manuel for just 170 DYAR in Years 3-5. Poor defenses helped Manuel post a high completion percentage as a college senior, when Florida State faced a defensive slate ranking 67th according to our Fremeau Efficiency Ratings.

Last year, Manuel threw mostly the short passes on which he relied in college. He threw passes in the intermediate range (6 to 15 yards downfield) just 20 percent of the time, less than every quarterback with 100 attempts except Robert Griffin. His inability to complete those intermediate throws resulted in a -39.8% DVOA on third downs, almost identical to the -39.5% he posted as a rookie in 2013. And no quarterback with 100 attempts threw passes within a yard of the line of scrimmage more frequently than Manuel (32 percent). J.J. Watt was just waiting on that Week 4 swing pass he took 80 yards for a touchdown, which helped to beat the Bills and end Manuel's run as starter.

Johnny Manziel Height: 6-0   Weight: 207   College: Texas A&M   Draft: 2014/1 (22)   Born: 6-Dec-1992   Age: 23 Risk: Yellow

Year	Team	G/GS	Snaps	Att	Cmp	C%	Yds	TD	INT/Adj	FUM	ASR	NY/P	Rk	DVOA	Rk	DYAR	Rk	YAR	Runs	Yds	TD	DVOA	DYAR	QBR
2014	CLE	5/2	75	35	18	51.4%	175	0	2/2	1	9.0%	3.9	--	-73.2%	--	-144	--	-180	9	29	1	-36.7%	-9	5.1
2015	CLE			463	242	52.2%	3001	15	19	9		5.5		-27.8%					88	392	3	8.7%		

| | | | | | | | | | | | | | 2014: | 60% Short | 28% Mid | 13% Deep | 0% Bomb | YAC: 4.7 (--) |

It was brief. It was a disaster. Manziel simply wasn't ready to run an NFL offense as a rookie. That was to be expected because he was a raw prospect coming out, but the degree of his struggles still frustrated the Browns coaching staff. Those struggles reflected Manziel's reluctance to focus on refining his craft during his rookie season. He spent two months in rehab after the regular season concluded, highlighting his need to change his life off the field.

On the field, Manziel needs to become a refined pocket passer. He doesn't have the athleticism to get away with working outside of the design of his system the way he did in college. In college, he made defenders miss by making different moves that take time. When you do that in the NFL, you are just giving the pursuit time to get two or three more players to the tackle point. Only players with great athleticism or players who are already far downfield can afford to use slow-burning moves to beat defenders in the NFL.

Marcus Mariota Height: 6-4   Weight: 222   College: Oregon   Draft: 2015/1 (2)   Born: 30-Oct-1993   Age: 22 Risk: Red

Year	Team	G/GS	Snaps	Att	Cmp	C%	Yds	TD	INT/Adj	FUM	ASR	NY/P	Rk	DVOA	Rk	DYAR	Rk	YAR	Runs	Yds	TD	DVOA	DYAR	QBR
2015	TEN			516	315	61.2%	3476	23	15	10		5.9		-9.8%					108	493	5	15.2%		

There is no question Mariota was a phenomenally effective player at Oregon. He completed 68 percent of his passes in 2014, hardly ever threw an interception, and averaged both 9.0 yards per attempt and over 9.0 yards per carry. The Ducks finished in the top ten in the NCAA in passing S&P+ and passing downs S&P+ all three years he was a starter. Any statistical projection system, like QBASE, should and will love him. Ken Whisenhunt will ask him to be the same sort of executor of an offense, but how well he transitions from a Chip Kelly spread to a dropback passing game will be an open question until he takes the field Week 1.

A.J. McCarron   Height: 6-3   Weight: 220   College: Alabama   Draft: 2014/5 (164)   Born: 13-Sep-1990   Age: 25   Risk: Yellow

Year	Team	G/GS	Snaps	Att	Cmp	C%	Yds	TD	INT/Adj	FUM	ASR	NY/P	Rk	DVOA	Rk	DYAR	Rk	YAR	Runs	Yds	TD	DVOA	DYAR	QBR
2015	CIN			487	287	59.0%	3282	21	17	9		5.7		-12.5%					29	43	1	-9.5%		

McCarron injured his throwing shoulder as a senior at Alabama, which dogged him throughout 2014, to the point where he hardly threw a practice pass. Healthy now, McCarron impressed at OTAs, and seems to have a hammerlock on the Bengals' backup job. Despite fan hopes, he has a ways to go before he can even dream of adequately replacing Andy Dalton, but if McCarron continues to develop, he will be the best second-stringer Cincy has had since Jon Kitna backed up Carson Palmer.

Josh McCown   Height: 6-4   Weight: 215   College: Sam Houston State   Draft: 2002/3 (81)   Born: 4-Jul-1979   Age: 36   Risk: Yellow

Year	Team	G/GS	Snaps	Att	Cmp	C%	Yds	TD	INT/Adj	FUM	ASR	NY/P	Rk	DVOA	Rk	DYAR	Rk	YAR	Runs	Yds	TD	DVOA	DYAR	QBR
2013	CHI	8/5	421	224	149	66.5%	1829	13	1/3	3	4.8%	7.6	5	32.1%	4	659	13	773	13	69	1	10.9%	10	85.1
2014	TB	11/11	630	327	184	56.3%	2206	11	14/13	10	10.4%	5.5	35	-41.9%	37	-665	36	-576	25	127	3	35.9%	47	35.7
2015	CLE			517	313	60.5%	3593	15	14	11		5.8		-10.8%					28	117	0	3.8%		
	2013:	41% Short		42% Mid		12% Deep		5% Bomb		YAC: 5.6 (16)		2014:		47% Short		33% Mid		11% Deep		9% Bomb		YAC: 4.0 (36)	

If McCown's 2014 were a wine, the vintage would be Blaine Gabbert 2011. He threw two of the worst interceptions of the season just in Week 1. In the first quarter, he rolled right and lofted a strange softball while being sacked, but that was nothing compared to what was coming in the third quarter. First, the ball slipped out of McCown's hand as he tried to throw a wide receiver screen. Then, he did a 360 to pick up a ball that bounced right to him. He tried to throw the screen again as he was hit and the ball fluttered. If McCown had not been hit, it might have been a pick-six because the receiver was so covered. Terrible execution and decision-making all in one play: nothing could capture McCown's 2014 better. By our numbers, he was the worst quarterback in football. McCown will have to get unbelievably lucky a second time to succeed in Cleveland.

Luke McCown   Height: 6-3   Weight: 208   College: Louisiana Tech   Draft: 2004/4 (106)   Born: 12-Jul-1981   Age: 34   Risk: Green

Year	Team	G/GS	Snaps	Att	Cmp	C%	Yds	TD	INT/Adj	FUM	ASR	NY/P	Rk	DVOA	Rk	DYAR	Rk	YAR	Runs	Yds	TD	DVOA	DYAR	QBR
2012	ATL	2/0	10	0	0	0.0%	0	0	0/0	0	--	--	--	--	--	--	--	--	2	-3	0	--	--	--
2013	NO	16/0	16	1	0	0.0%	0	0	0/0	0	-5.4%	0.0	--	-89.2%	--	-3	--	-4	3	-4	0	--	--	85.1
2015	NO			574	335	58.4%	3758	24	22	10		5.4		-11.6%					23	48	1	-1.1%		
	2013:	0% Short		0% Mid		100% Deep		0% Bomb		YAC: 0.0 (--)															

Luke McCown has one of the most comfortable jobs in the NFL. He has thrown just one pass over the past three seasons and he's unlikely to throw more this year. McCown has performed well in preseason games over the past two seasons, but this year the 33-year-old quarterback will face stiff competition for his role as top backup to Drew Brees. Not only did Ryan Griffin show flashes of his ability during last year's preseason, but rookie Garrett Grayson will also join the competition. McCown's experience should give him the edge over both players, and they are more likely to compete with each other for the third spot on the depth chart. But a big injury to Brees would likely knock the Saints out of the playoff race, and at that point, what makes more sense: sticking Luke McCown on the field, or giving Grayson (or Griffin) a chance to show he's the heir apparent?

Colt McCoy   Height: 6-1   Weight: 216   College: Texas   Draft: 2010/3 (85)   Born: 5-Sep-1986   Age: 29   Risk: Red

Year	Team	G/GS	Snaps	Att	Cmp	C%	Yds	TD	INT/Adj	FUM	ASR	NY/P	Rk	DVOA	Rk	DYAR	Rk	YAR	Runs	Yds	TD	DVOA	DYAR	QBR
2012	CLE	3/0	39	17	9	52.9%	79	1	0/0	0	16.6%	2.6	--	-2.7%	--	10	--	-23	4	15	0	67.7%	9	13.1
2013	SF	4/0	22	1	1	100.0%	13	0	0/0	0	-1.8%	13.0	--	256.6%	--	14	--	13	6	-6	0	--	--	95.0
2014	WAS	5/4	240	128	91	71.1%	1057	4	3/4	6	11.8%	6.5	--	-15.9%	--	-43	--	-9	16	66	1	-33.0%	-13	46.1
2015	WAS			558	372	66.6%	4046	21	16	14		6.0		-8.3%					51	134	1	-15.0%		
	2013:	100% Short		0% Mid		0% Deep		0% Bomb		YAC: 13 (--)		2014:		61% Short		25% Mid		7% Deep		6% Bomb		YAC: 6.0 (--)	

McCoy's impressive raw stat totals came mostly from relief work in the Titans game (he went 11-of-12) and a three-touchdown performance in a lopsided Colts loss. McCoy got sacked six times and fumbled four times in that Colts game, then suffered a neck injury enduring six more sacks at the hands of the Rams. The Redskins training staff got their medical degrees from

Denial State University (see: Robert Griffin, 2012 playoffs), so an obviously ailing McCoy took the field against the Giants. He only lasted through the opening drive before ending the season on IR.

McCoy's career as a starter essentially ended when the Browns left him in the game against the Steelers despite an obvious concussion in 2011. No one questions McCoy's toughness, but by re-signing for another year of Redskins stuntman duty, he may just be turning into a glutton for punishment.

Matt McGloin

Height: 6-1   Weight: 210   College: Penn State   Draft: 2013/FA   Born: 2-Dec-1989   Age: 26   Risk: Green

Year	Team	G/GS	Snaps	Att	Cmp	C%	Yds	TD	INT/Adj	FUM	ASR	NY/P	Rk	DVOA	Rk	DYAR	Rk	YAR	Runs	Yds	TD	DVOA	DYAR	QBR
2013	OAK	7/6	378	211	118	55.9%	1547	8	8/10	4	3.1%	6.9	8	-11.9%	27	-11	27	62	11	27	0	21.1%	7	49.5
2014	OAK	1/0	24	19	12	63.2%	129	1	2/1	0	4.7%	6.1	--	-54.4%	--	-58	--	-63	2	3	0	8.1%	2	10.3
2015	OAK			575	332	57.7%	3879	16	23	11		5.7		-20.9%					39	90	1	-15.4%		

2013:	45% Short	32% Mid	15% Deep	8% Bomb	YAC: 5.5 (17)	2014:	40% Short	45% Mid	5% Deep	10% Bomb	YAC: 4.8 (--)

McGloin showed pretty solid pocket awareness in 2013, particularly for an undrafted rookie, and he got the ball downfield. Oakland apparently still wanted a veteran backup, so Matt Schaub was brought in via trade for one miserable season. Schaub is gone now but was replaced by Christian Ponder, a first-round flameout who doesn't threaten any defense down the field and takes too many sacks. Looks like McGloin will have tablet duty again, because clipboards are so passé.

Zach Mettenberger

Height: 6-4   Weight: 224   College: Louisiana St.   Draft: 2014/6 (178)   Born: 16-Jul-1991   Age: 24   Risk: Red

Year	Team	G/GS	Snaps	Att	Cmp	C%	Yds	TD	INT/Adj	FUM	ASR	NY/P	Rk	DVOA	Rk	DYAR	Rk	YAR	Runs	Yds	TD	DVOA	DYAR	QBR
2014	TEN	7/6	305	179	107	59.8%	1412	8	7/9	4	8.7%	6.5	--	-28.7%	--	-211	--	-235	5	4	0	64.8%	5	30.1
2015	TEN			498	297	59.6%	3600	23	18	10		6.0		-12.2%					27	50	0	-17.1%		

						2014:	50% Short	29% Mid	16% Deep	5% Bomb	YAC: 6.2 (--)

Do you like strong arms? Is overall mobility a negative? Do you like flashes, but only that, of pocket presence? Do you hate first downs? Are you fine with interceptions? Do you wish it was still the 1970s? If you answered yes to all of those questions, Zach Mettenberger may be the quarterback for you! If not, you should probably look elsewhere. Expecting success from a sixth-round rookie is fairly ridiculous, but Mettenberger was particularly horrid on the money down, converting just 12 of 55 third-down opportunities (22 percent). Mettenberger has said and done all the right things this offseason but seems unlikely to play unless (and maybe even if) Marcus Mariota gets hurt. He really did not show enough as a rookie for any team to consider giving the Titans anything of value to get him in trade.

Matt Moore

Height: 6-3   Weight: 202   College: Oregon State   Draft: 2007/FA   Born: 9-Aug-1984   Age: 31   Risk: Red

Year	Team	G/GS	Snaps	Att	Cmp	C%	Yds	TD	INT/Adj	FUM	ASR	NY/P	Rk	DVOA	Rk	DYAR	Rk	YAR	Runs	Yds	TD	DVOA	DYAR	QBR
2012	MIA	10/0	55	19	11	57.9%	131	1	0/0	0	9.7%	5.8	--	15.5%	--	40	--	31	5	-3	0	-110.2%	-4	59.7
2013	MIA	1/0	6	6	2	33.3%	53	0	2/2	1	-2.7%	8.8	--	-120.6%	--	-36	--	-45	0	0	0	--	--	1.3
2014	MIA	2/0	30	4	2	50.0%	21	0	0/0	0	0.0%	5.3	--	28.4%	--	8	--	13	2	-2	0	--	--	72.4
2015	MIA			564	343	60.8%	3570	23	17	13		5.1		-17.1%					37	62	0	-18.9%		

2013:	17% Short	33% Mid	17% Deep	33% Bomb	YAC: 6.5 (--)	2014:	25% Short	25% Mid	0% Deep	50% Bomb	YAC: 5.0 (--)

Moore actually leads all Dolphins "skill position players" in seniority, having arrived in 2011 after three seasons with the Panthers. He will never be a standout NFL quarterback and has taken just 91 snaps the last three seasons (including 36 the last two years), but if Tannehill has to miss a game here or there, Moore is a good option as a short-term, get-you-over quarterback. If circumstances dictate any more than that, Miami will be in trouble.

Ryan Nassib Height: 6-2 Weight: 229 College: Syracuse Draft: 2013/4 (110) Born: 10-Mar-1990 Age: 25 Risk: Yellow

Year	Team	G/GS	Snaps	Att	Cmp	C%	Yds	TD	INT/Adj	FUM	ASR	NY/P	Rk	DVOA	Rk	DYAR	Rk	YAR	Runs	Yds	TD	DVOA	DYAR	QBR
2014	NYG	4/0	19	5	4	80.0%	60	0	0/0	1	28.0%	6.9	--	-48.7%	--	-18	--	-18	2	-3	0	--	--	29.4
2015	NYG			550	337	61.4%	3554	19	18	11		5.3		-14.4%					41	94	1	0.4%		
	2014:	71% Short		29% Mid			0% Deep			0% Bomb		YAC: 10.8 (--)												

Nassib threw five touchdowns and no interceptions in the 2014 preseason, including four touchdowns in the "dress rehearsal" games against the Colts and Jets. (The Giants played in the Hall of Fame Game, giving them extra rehearsals.) There was some speculation early in 2014 training camp that Nassib was in danger of losing his backup job, but that sounds like a case of the New York beat reporters (all 134 of them) getting carried away after a bad practice or two. Tom Coughlin is comfortable with Nassib, and we have one year left before the *Logan's Run* light flashes and Nassib goes from young prospect to milk that was left in the back of the fridge too long. Expect competent backup play if Nassib is called upon.

Cam Newton Height: 6-5 Weight: 248 College: Auburn Draft: 2011/1 (1) Born: 11-May-1989 Age: 26 Risk: Yellow

Year	Team	G/GS	Snaps	Att	Cmp	C%	Yds	TD	INT/Adj	FUM	ASR	NY/P	Rk	DVOA	Rk	DYAR	Rk	YAR	Runs	Yds	TD	DVOA	DYAR	QBR
2012	CAR	16/16	1019	485	280	57.7%	3869	19	12/15	14	7.6%	7.0	6	2.0%	15	422	14	422	127	741	8	11.3%	149	54.1
2013	CAR	16/16	1015	473	292	61.7%	3379	24	13/18	3	8.2%	5.9	23	1.7%	19	421	17	321	111	585	6	5.7%	102	56.2
2014	CAR	14/14	927	448	262	58.5%	3127	18	12/14	9	8.4%	5.9	30	-14.5%	32	-105	32	-46	103	539	5	16.3%	146	56.9
2015	CAR			511	317	62.0%	3617	24	12	7		6.1		-1.7%					106	512	5	14.6%		
	2013:	41% Short		39% Mid		12% Deep		8% Bomb		YAC: 5.5 (18)			2014:		47% Short		35% Mid		10% Deep		7% Bomb	YAC: 4.8 (34)		

As our own Mike Tanier eloquently put it in a Bleacher Report column, they don't give out awards for the kind of season Cam Newton went through in 2014. Car accident. Wisdom tooth extraction. Broken ribs. An offensive line that tapped out faster than Foot Soldiers against the Ninja Turtles. Newton came through it all with toughness, mental and physical, and with a smile. The Panthers decided to give him a five-year, $103 million deal that guarantees Newton $60 million. Monetary gifts are often the first sign of forgiveness. Carolina hasn't quite souped up the offensive line all the way, but at least Devin Funchess and some shrewd small-stakes free-agent signings should keep Newton from having to force-feed Kelvin Benjamin at every opportunity. It's probably more about the offense around him, but the only quarterback with a worse DVOA on third-down passes last season was Josh McCown.

The talent is there for Newton to become one of the best quarterbacks of his generation. He has been gifted with the body to make it so, and everyone talks about his running talent and how that jump-starts Carolina's offense. But here's the thing: Newton actually had 108 passing DYAR in his first five games, when he wasn't trying to run. Nature versus nurture is one of the big black boxes of quarterback development—this sort of focus didn't exactly pay off for Colin Kaepernick last season—but it would be interesting to see how Newton would fare solely as a pocket passer.

Dan Orlovsky Height: 6-5 Weight: 230 College: Connecticut Draft: 2005/5 (145) Born: 18-Aug-1983 Age: 32 Risk: Yellow

Year	Team	G/GS	Snaps	Att	Cmp	C%	Yds	TD	INT/Adj	FUM	ASR	NY/P	Rk	DVOA	Rk	DYAR	Rk	YAR	Runs	Yds	TD	DVOA	DYAR	QBR
2012	TB	1/0	12	7	4	57.1%	51	0	0/0	0	1.3%	7.3	--	0.4%	--	5	--	10	0	0	0	--	--	34.9
2013	TB	2/0	4	0	0	0.0%	0	0	0/0	0	--	--	--	--	--	--	--	--	0	0	0	--	--	--
2015	DET			562	327	58.2%	3580	20	18	10		5.5		-12.3%					30	59	1	-7.9%		

The tragicomic emblem of Detroit's winless 2008 season, Orlovsky returned to his old stomping grounds last year but didn't take a single snap. The 32-year-old hasn't attempted a pass since his glorious 2012 stint with Tampa Bay, and last started a game during the 2011 Colts campaign. While Orlovsky will always have a place in Indy lore sandwiched between the Peyton Manning and Andrew Luck eras, he's unlikely to see playing time behind Matthew Stafford, who has overcome early-career injury woes to start every game each of the past four seasons.

Kyle Orton Height: 6-4 Weight: 226 College: Purdue Draft: 2005/4 (106) Born: 14-Nov-1982 Age: 33 Risk: N/A

Year	Team	G/GS	Snaps	Att	Cmp	C%	Yds	TD	INT/Adj	FUM	ASR	NY/P	Rk	DVOA	Rk	DYAR	Rk	YAR	Runs	Yds	TD	DVOA	DYAR	QBR
2012	DAL	1/0	11	10	9	90.0%	89	1	0/0	0	1.0%	8.9	--	110.7%	--	95	--	79	0	0	0	--	--	99.4
2013	DAL	3/1	78	51	33	64.7%	398	2	2/3	0	1.1%	7.8	--	4.0%	--	51	--	71	1	8	0	104.4%	7	37.3
2014	BUF	12/12	803	447	287	64.2%	3018	18	10/12	3	7.4%	5.9	31	-6.8%	26	131	25	87	15	14	1	-11.2%	0	42.6
2013:	46% Short		35% Mid		13% Deep		6% Bomb		YAC: 6.7 (--)		2014:	59% Short		23% Mid		11% Deep		6% Bomb	YAC: 5.4 (18)					

And so, the least interesting quarterback in the NFL has called it a career. Relentlessly average, Orton's DVOA has fallen between 10.0% and -10.0% in each of his last five qualifying seasons. In all four seasons where he started at least 12 games, Orton threw 18 to 21 touchdowns and nine to 12 interceptions. His low-ceiling, high-floor play would still be a noticeable improvement at quarterback for some teams—including Buffalo—but he would rather spend time with his family and his new career as Dave Grohl's stunt double.

Brock Osweiler Height: 6-7 Weight: 242 College: Arizona State Draft: 2012/2 (57) Born: 22-Nov-1990 Age: 25 Risk: Yellow

Year	Team	G/GS	Snaps	Att	Cmp	C%	Yds	TD	INT/Adj	FUM	ASR	NY/P	Rk	DVOA	Rk	DYAR	Rk	YAR	Runs	Yds	TD	DVOA	DYAR	QBR
2012	DEN	5/0	33	4	2	50.0%	12	0	0/0	0	-1.5%	3.0	--	-1.4%	--	2	--	7	8	-13	0	--	--	10.4
2013	DEN	4/0	51	16	11	68.8%	95	0	0/0	0	11.3%	4.8	--	-8.5%	--	3	--	18	3	2	0	29.9%	3	43.3
2014	DEN	4/0	37	10	4	40.0%	52	1	0/0	0	11.3%	4.2	--	-19.7%	--	-5	--	1	8	0	0	-85.5%	-6	10.2
2015	DEN			538	330	61.4%	3681	27	18	11		5.6		-8.0%					24	49	1	1.4%		
2013:	75% Short		13% Mid		6% Deep		6% Bomb		YAC: 6.2 (--)		2014:	70% Short		10% Mid		20% Deep		0% Bomb	YAC: 7.5 (--)					

Not many quarterbacks can say their first NFL touchdown pass came after the two-minute warning in the fourth quarter with a 26-point lead in Week 17. As he enters the final year of his rookie contract, we still know very little about Osweiler's readiness to play. His preseasons have gradually improved, if that even means anything. When Denver has to decide on a second contract, it could be signing its next starting quarterback at a bargain rate, because it's not like Osweiler has earned anything up to this point. Or the Broncos could be throwing money away; Osweiler's QBASE projection (-791 DYAR in Years 3-5) is the second-lowest of any quarterback drafted in the first three rounds since 1997. (We hate to keep piling on the poor guy at this point in the chapter, but Josh McCown has the worst projection, an unfathomable -1,304 DYAR.)

Carson Palmer Height: 6-5 Weight: 230 College: USC Draft: 2003/1 (1) Born: 27-Dec-1979 Age: 36 Risk: Green

Year	Team	G/GS	Snaps	Att	Cmp	C%	Yds	TD	INT/Adj	FUM	ASR	NY/P	Rk	DVOA	Rk	DYAR	Rk	YAR	Runs	Yds	TD	DVOA	DYAR	QBR
2012	OAK	15/15	953	565	345	61.1%	4018	22	14/20	8	4.8%	6.5	16	-2.2%	18	340	18	447	18	36	1	17.1%	23	46.8
2013	ARI	16/16	1081	572	362	63.3%	4274	24	22/26	6	6.8%	6.5	13	2.7%	17	547	15	361	27	3	0	-30.4%	-3	51.9
2014	ARI	6/6	410	224	141	62.9%	1626	11	3/5	3	4.1%	6.7	15	8.5%	11	285	18	400	8	25	0	-94.8%	-20	64.8
2015	ARI			571	349	61.2%	4193	23	15	5		6.3		4.3%					22	63	0	1.2%		
2013:	41% Short		36% Mid		15% Deep		8% Bomb		YAC: 4.9 (31)		2014:	54% Short		26% Mid		12% Deep		9% Bomb	YAC: 5.3 (21)					

Palmer took part in 11-on-11 drills in OTAs, so the knee injury that ended his 2014 season should not be a factor this fall. What might be a factor is Palmer's sudden aversion to throwing midrange passes. The average quarterback throws about one-third of his passes to targets 6 to 15 yards past the line of scrimmage, and Palmer has been at or above that level every year of his career. At least, he had been, until last season, when he threw midrange passes 10 percent less frequently than he had in 2013, and six percent less frequently than he ever had before. Drew Stanton and Ryan Lindley were close to average in this metric, so this had nothing to do with Arizona's general play-calling philosophy. Palmer also threw more short passes than he ever had before. His most frequent target on those short throws, not surprisingly, was Andre Ellington, who averaged 6.3 targets per game when Palmer started, but only 4.3 when Drew Stanton or Ryan Lindley did. A healthy Palmer might make Ellington (or another running back who takes his job) worth watching in PPR leagues.

Bryce Petty Height: 6-3 Weight: 230 College: Baylor Draft: 2015/4 (103) Born: 31-May-1991 Age: 24 Risk: Yellow

Year	Team	G/GS	Snaps	Att	Cmp	C%	Yds	TD	INT/Adj	FUM	ASR	NY/P	Rk	DVOA	Rk	DYAR	Rk	YAR	Runs	Yds	TD	DVOA	DYAR	QBR
2015	NYJ			469	268	57.2%	2625	16	16	11		4.7		-33.5%					71	228	2	-5.4%		

Throughout the pre-draft process, Petty became the chic under-the-radar possibility at the quarterback position. The Baylor product put up crazy stats in the high-octane Bears offense, completing 63 percent of his passes and throwing for 8,195 yards and 62 touchdowns in four seasons as a collegian. But a closer look at the numbers suggests that Petty was able to fatten up against some less-than-substantial competition last season: our QBASE formula reveals that he projects to be substantially worse than replacement level in the NFL because Baylor faced the No. 70 slate of opposing defenses in FBS. Despite all of that, he'll still likely be a part of the quarterback conversation this year in New York at some point, given that the new coaching staff will likely have a quick hook with Geno Smith, and veteran backup Ryan Fitzpatrick—though still a palatable short-term possibility if the situation is right—is on his sixth team in 11 years.

Christian Ponder

Height: 6-2　Weight: 229　College: Florida State　Draft: 2011/1 (12)　Born: 25-Feb-1988　Age: 27 Risk: Yellow

Year	Team	G/GS	Snaps	Att	Cmp	C%	Yds	TD	INT/Adj	FUM	ASR	NY/P	Rk	DVOA	Rk	DYAR	Rk	YAR	Runs	Yds	TD	DVOA	DYAR	QBR
2012	MIN	16/16	1032	483	300	62.1%	2935	18	12/19	7	6.5%	5.3	34	-6.1%	21	173	21	66	60	253	2	4.2%	36	51.7
2013	MIN	9/9	511	239	152	63.6%	1648	7	9/11	7	10.6%	5.7	30	-13.5%	30	-42	29	19	34	151	4	-32.3%	-31	51.2
2014	MIN	2/1	89	44	22	50.0%	222	0	2/2	0	11.3%	3.8	--	-57.5%	--	-146	--	-169	4	16	1	35.7%	9	4.7
2015	OAK			578	333	57.6%	3593	14	19	11		4.8		-25.7%					43	110	2	-5.7%		
	2013:	51% Short		26% Mid		14% Deep		9% Bomb		YAC: 4.7 (34)			2014:		57% Short		27% Mid		8% Deep		8% Bomb		YAC: 4.5 (--)

We've mentioned our new QBASE system numerous times in this year's book, so here's our chance to point out that, like all other attempts to project NFL performance from college stats, it is not perfect. Christian Ponder was the top-rated quarterback in the 2011 draft, with a QBASE projection that nearly rivaled those for stars like Andrew Luck and Matthew Stafford. Ponder has not combusted as spectacularly as fellow 2011 first-round quarterbacks Blaine Gabbert and Jake Locker, but he's barely cleared that awfully low bar. The former 12th overall pick posted -156 passing DYAR in his lone start last year, a Thursday night massacre at Lambeau Field. Ponder had largely been below-average rather than atrocious over 35 previous career starts, but No. 36 was an indelible stain on his Vikings tenure. Having accepted a demotion to back up Derek Carr, Ponder will now embark on the clipboard-carrying carousel phase of his career. (Well, tablet-carrying. This is a modern world.)

Philip Rivers

Height: 6-5　Weight: 228　College: North Carolina State　Draft: 2004/1 (4)　Born: 8-Dec-1981　Age: 34 Risk: Yellow

Year	Team	G/GS	Snaps	Att	Cmp	C%	Yds	TD	INT/Adj	FUM	ASR	NY/P	Rk	DVOA	Rk	DYAR	Rk	YAR	Runs	Yds	TD	DVOA	DYAR	QBR
2012	SD	16/16	1023	527	338	64.1%	3606	26	15/18	14	8.9%	5.7	30	-7.3%	22	138	22	124	27	40	0	-46.5%	-19	41.5
2013	SD	16/16	1100	544	378	69.5%	4478	32	11/13	3	5.9%	7.6	4	34.8%	3	1799	2	1884	28	72	0	-17.6%	-5	71.7
2014	SD	16/16	1052	570	379	66.5%	4286	31	18/18	8	6.0%	6.8	12	12.6%	9	918	9	803	37	102	0	-10.0%	3	66.8
2015	SD			569	375	65.9%	4238	27	11	5		6.4		12.2%					36	87	0	-3.4%		
	2013:	52% Short		29% Mid		13% Deep		5% Bomb		YAC: 5.7 (13)			2014:		55% Short		27% Mid		10% Deep		8% Bomb		YAC: 5.1 (25)

Let's hit the "reset" button in San Diego after last year's poor ending. Start by giving Rivers back his health, which has rarely been a problem in his career. Add a potentially explosive running back in Melvin Gordon, which hopefully gives Mike McCoy the common sense to use more play-action, where Rivers was the best quarterback in the league last year, but used it the least. Welcome back the returning Danny Woodhead, the checkdown demigod Rivers always looks to find when in trouble. Keenan Allen and Malcom Floyd give him familiar faces, and Antonio Gates will get on the field eventually. Until then, Ladarius Green, come out and play. Then you add Stevie Johnson, who really could be the perfect midrange receiver in this offense. Rivers has a new left guard in Orlando Franklin, and he shouldn't have to take snaps from five different centers this year. Everything points to Rivers having a more effective and efficient 2015. Maybe he won't reach the level of 2013 and the start of 2014, but the usual Philip Rivers season is good enough to keep San Diego competitive through December. You just wonder how contract talks, if they even happen during the season, will unfold with the team's future so uncertain. This could be the end of an era for the Chargers if Rivers truly does not want to play in Los Angeles, as has been reported. Enjoy him while you can.

Aaron Rodgers

Height: 6-2　Weight: 223　College: California　Draft: 2005/1 (24)　Born: 2-Dec-1983　Age: 32 Risk: Green

Year	Team	G/GS	Snaps	Att	Cmp	C%	Yds	TD	INT/Adj	FUM	ASR	NY/P	Rk	DVOA	Rk	DYAR	Rk	YAR	Runs	Yds	TD	DVOA	DYAR	QBR
2012	GB	16/16	1069	552	371	67.2%	4295	39	8/11	7	8.7%	6.7	13	23.4%	4	1395	4	1276	54	259	2	30.6%	94	74.7
2013	GB	9/9	582	290	193	66.6%	2536	17	6/5	4	7.6%	7.8	3	25.4%	6	740	10	762	30	120	0	6.8%	23	68.7
2014	GB	16/16	983	520	341	65.6%	4381	38	5/7	10	5.3%	7.6	2	32.2%	1	1564	2	1581	43	269	2	54.4%	104	82.6
2015	GB			559	376	67.3%	4625	38	12	9		7.5		29.1%					38	160	2	23.3%		
	2013:	48% Short		30% Mid		14% Deep		8% Bomb		YAC: 6.5 (2)			2014:		54% Short		29% Mid		13% Deep		5% Bomb		YAC: 6.0 (6)

Someday soon, we'll develop *Football Outsiders Almanac* as some sort of iPad program instead of a PDF/print book, and then the Aaron Rodgers comment will just be a series of gifs of Rodgers making inconceivable throws into tiny windows that no other quarterback with single-digit interceptions would ever even attempt. That ability, combined with Rodgers' proficiency from the pocket and his ability to extend plays and then make throws, makes him the best quarterback in the NFL. The only real nit in Rodgers' game is average performance in the red zone the last two years, with a DVOA rating of just 0.2% in 2014 after -7.0% in 2013. This is one area where the change at offensive coordinator might help, with more rushing attempts closer to the goal line, where the Packers threw more than they ran, and fewer in the deeper part of the red zone, where they ran twice as often as they passed on first downs.

Ben Roethlisberger   Height: 6-5   Weight: 240   College: Miami (Ohio)   Draft: 2004/1 (11)   Born: 2-Mar-1982   Age: 33 Risk: Yellow

Year	Team	G/GS	Snaps	Att	Cmp	C%	Yds	TD	INT/Adj	FUM	ASR	NY/P	Rk	DVOA	Rk	DYAR	Rk	YAR	Runs	Yds	TD	DVOA	DYAR	QBR
2012	PIT	13/13	832	449	284	63.3%	3265	26	8/13	5	6.5%	6.5	15	13.2%	11	761	9	764	26	92	0	-6.2%	5	62.8
2013	PIT	16/16	1051	584	375	64.2%	4261	28	14/15	9	7.2%	6.4	15	6.6%	12	724	11	764	27	99	1	-41.5%	-26	54.3
2014	PIT	16/16	1104	608	408	67.1%	4952	32	9/14	8	5.8%	7.6	3	26.8%	3	1572	1	1505	33	27	0	-50.8%	-34	72.5
2015	PIT			588	381	64.8%	4597	29	13	8		7.0		13.7%					41	66	1	-11.6%		
	2013:	48% Short		32% Mid		12% Deep		8% Bomb		YAC: 5.4 (21)		2014:	50% Short		31% Mid		11% Deep		8% Bomb		YAC: 5.6 (14)		

33-year-old quarterbacks aren't supposed to enjoy rebirths, but that is what Ben Roethlisberger did in 2014. The Steelers' quarterback jumped to the top of DVOA and DYAR amongst passers last year, after spending the second half of his career hovering around 10th place. That leap is a direct result of a transformation that the quarterback has undergone under offensive coordinator Todd Haley.

The much-maligned Haley has turned a creative, reckless quarterback who relied on his physical strength and elusiveness into a smart, efficient pocket passer who works in rhythm with the rest of his teammates. This is reflected by the way Roethlisberger spends less and less time outside of the pocket. Just 8.0 percent of his passes in 2014 came on plays outside of the pocket, down from 10.2 percent in 2013 and 11.2 percent in 2012. This development becomes even more significant when you consider that his pass attempts have gone up in each of the last two seasons.

Playing this way has helped a supporting cast that also does a lot to help its quarterback. Maybe the most significant piece for Roethlisberger moving forward is Martavis Bryant. The long, athletic receiver was able to mask some of Roethlisberger's declining deep accuracy with his ability to adjust at the catch point in 2014.

The greatest compliment you can pay to Roethlisberger right now is pointing to the extension he earned—not his own inevitable new deal, but the new contract Haley signed. Fans, analysts, and one notable rapper called for Haley's head on a regular basis up until the beginning of this season. After signing his new deal, one can easily picture Haley sipping tea like Kermit.

Tony Romo   Height: 6-2   Weight: 219   College: Eastern Illinois   Draft: 2003/FA   Born: 21-Apr-1980   Age: 35 Risk: Green

Year	Team	G/GS	Snaps	Att	Cmp	C%	Yds	TD	INT/Adj	FUM	ASR	NY/P	Rk	DVOA	Rk	DYAR	Rk	YAR	Runs	Yds	TD	DVOA	DYAR	QBR
2012	DAL	16/16	1089	648	425	65.6%	4903	28	19/25	5	5.9%	6.8	10	14.8%	10	1156	7	1036	30	49	1	-14.9%	-2	63.4
2013	DAL	15/15	919	535	342	63.9%	3828	31	10/10	4	6.7%	6.3	17	11.5%	10	839	7	898	20	38	0	44.3%	17	59.5
2014	DAL	15/15	971	435	304	69.9%	3705	34	9/12	7	6.3%	7.5	5	27.6%	2	1187	5	1266	26	61	0	50.9%	23	82.8
2015	DAL			526	344	65.4%	4067	33	15	5		6.8		15.9%					30	77	0	10.4%		
	2013:	48% Short		36% Mid		11% Deep		5% Bomb		YAC: 5.2 (23)		2014:	48% Short		33% Mid		11% Deep		8% Bomb		YAC: 5.4 (19)		

Romo has given up golf in the offseason in an effort to keep his back healthy. What a depressing thought: a wealthy, successful, athletic 35-year-old giving up even the occasional round of golf to save himself for his grueling profession. If a corporate manager gave up moderate-intensity outdoor recreation because it was eating into his effectiveness in the boardroom, you would stage an intervention. But we expect our quarterbacks to give up everything in the name of entertaining us. There's a deep, disturbing metaphor for approaching middle age in the first world coded within the saga of offseason Romo:

Age 27: Trip to Cabo at the height of "busy season!" Why not?

Age 28: Watching *American Idol* contestants and thinking: *got her, got her, need her, got her…*

Age 30: Carrie Underwood is writing whole albums about you. Time to settle down.

Age 31: Marry Candace Crawford. We said "settle down," not "settle."

Age 32: High-altitude jogging: a healthier way to get a head rush than jetting off to Cabo.

Age 34: No carousing, less mountain jogging, more getting your butt kicked around a golf course by a kid 12 years younger than you. Granted, he's Jordan Speith, but still…

Age 35: No more golf. Time to start trolling the early-bird dinner specials for mashed potatoes and applesauce.

Romo's back should not cause this level of vicarious midlife crisis. Maybe if the Cowboys get a better backup, he can give up midweek transatlantic flights to face the Jaguars. That should be more effective than cancelling the mid-May golf tournaments.

Matt Ryan   Height: 6-4   Weight: 228   College: Boston College   Draft: 2008/1 (3)   Born: 17-May-1985   Age: 30 Risk: Green

Year	Team	G/GS	Snaps	Att	Cmp	C%	Yds	TD	INT/Adj	FUM	ASR	NY/P	Rk	DVOA	Rk	DYAR	Rk	YAR	Runs	Yds	TD	DVOA	DYAR	QBR
2012	ATL	16/16	1048	615	422	68.6%	4719	32	14/16	4	5.1%	7.0	4	16.5%	8	1196	5	1315	34	141	1	39.7%	54	74.8
2013	ATL	16/16	1065	651	439	67.4%	4515	26	17/16	5	5.9%	6.1	19	13.3%	9	1124	4	825	17	55	0	54.5%	23	61.1
2014	ATL	16/16	1064	628	415	66.1%	4694	28	14/18	5	5.1%	6.9	9	14.9%	8	1101	7	1072	29	145	0	4.8%	23	67.0
2015	ATL			593	389	65.6%	4303	28	14	5		6.3		14.5%					33	111	0	12.3%		

2013:	53% Short	35% Mid	8% Deep	4% Bomb	YAC: 4.8 (33)	2014:	57% Short	25% Mid	14% Deep	4% Bomb	YAC: 5.0 (27)

Ryan has spent the last two years getting thrown down the franchise quarterback depth charts because his team hasn't been winning. Don't let that distract you from the truth: other than Aaron Rodgers, Ryan is the most consistent passer of his generation. A penchant for slightly underthrowing some deep balls aside, Ryan has every skill you want in a prototype franchise quarterback, up to and including his ability to keep the chains moving without Julio Jones in 2013 and his ability to give interview answers that are as interesting as week-old chicken in the fridge. Atlanta's decline in the last two seasons says more about the horrendous defense they've played than it does about Ryan.

Mark Sanchez   Height: 6-2   Weight: 227   College: USC   Draft: 2009/1 (5)   Born: 11-Nov-1986   Age: 29 Risk: Red

Year	Team	G/GS	Snaps	Att	Cmp	C%	Yds	TD	INT/Adj	FUM	ASR	NY/P	Rk	DVOA	Rk	DYAR	Rk	YAR	Runs	Yds	TD	DVOA	DYAR	QBR
2012	NYJ	15/15	938	453	246	54.3%	2883	13	18/21	10	6.9%	5.5	31	-29.4%	35	-593	39	-480	22	28	0	-85.4%	-67	25.8
2014	PHI	9/8	625	309	198	64.1%	2418	14	11/11	7	7.2%	6.8	11	-1.4%	22	210	23	255	34	87	1	-25.9%	-15	58.2
2015	PHI			581	364	62.7%	4206	28	21	8		6.4		1.2%					58	116	2	-8.9%		

						2014:	52% Short	33% Mid	12% Deep	4% Bomb	YAC: 5.7 (9)

Sanchez had four two-interception games last year, and the Sanchez-led Eagles generally beat the teams that can be beat by a quarterback having a two-interception day (Texans, Titans) and lost to the opponents too good to truck such nonsense (Packers, Cowboys). The book on Sanchez hasn't changed much since 2011. He has his hot streaks, and he can throw strikes to his first and maaaaaybe his second read, but the longer he stays in the pocket, the more likely he is to do something ridiculous. Chip Kelly's system can hide a quarterback like Sanchez, to a degree, with lots of screens and quick throws off play-action. Sanchez made more sense as the Eagles' backup than any of the wares at the McCown FitzCasselHoyer thrift shop, so Kelly's two-year investment was prudent.

Sanchez is one Sam Bradford setback from starting on Opening Day, which is scary. But then, maybe the rebuilt Falcons can be beaten by a quarterback who coughs up two interceptions.

Tom Savage   Height: 6-4   Weight: 228   College: Pittsburgh   Draft: 2014/4 (135)   Born: 26-Apr-1990   Age: 25 Risk: Yellow

Year	Team	G/GS	Snaps	Att	Cmp	C%	Yds	TD	INT/Adj	FUM	ASR	NY/P	Rk	DVOA	Rk	DYAR	Rk	YAR	Runs	Yds	TD	DVOA	DYAR	QBR
2014	HOU	2/0	60	19	10	52.6%	127	0	1/0	2	4.2%	6.1	--	-24.2%	--	-20	--	-33	6	-6	0	-183.1%	-31	12.7
2015	HOU			473	251	53.1%	3209	17	20	10		5.4		-24.3%					21	37	0	-8.0%		

						2014:	45% Short	25% Mid	10% Deep	20% Bomb	YAC: 3.3 (--)

Savage got a brief cup of coffee after Ryan Fitzpatrick went down to injury in a Week 15 game in Indianapolis, and showed the reasons he was selected with a fourth-round pick, both good and bad. As advertised, his arm does enable him to push the ball downfield. He made a few really nice passes to Texans receivers straddling the sideline. He also ran into Arian Foster twice while trying to hand the ball off, and had touch problems on balls that weren't easy underneath throws. Savage's biggest adjustment to the NFL will be speeding up his mental clock. He handled everything a step too slowly, and took some 1990s-caliber hits from defenders because of it (including the one that damaged his knee and put him on injured reserve). The small sample gave both his detractors and his supporters something to which they could latch on, but there's a lot to overcome for Savage to be more than a backup.

Matt Schaub

Height: 6-5 Weight: 235 College: Virginia Draft: 2004/3 (90) Born: 25-Jun-1981 Age: 34 Risk: Red

Year	Team	G/GS	Snaps	Att	Cmp	C%	Yds	TD	INT/Adj	FUM	ASR	NY/P	Rk	DVOA	Rk	DYAR	Rk	YAR	Runs	Yds	TD	DVOA	DYAR	QBR
2012	HOU	16/16	1105	544	350	64.3%	4008	22	12/15	4	5.2%	6.7	12	7.5%	14	697	12	882	21	-9	0	-68.2%	-8	64.0
2013	HOU	10/8	610	358	219	61.2%	2310	10	14/19	2	6.1%	5.7	31	-16.2%	32	-123	32	-115	5	24	0	52.6%	9	37.3
2014	OAK	11/0	19	10	5	50.0%	57	0	2/3	2	22.9%	2.2	--	-220.7%	--	-158	--	-158	0	0	0	--	--	0.1
2015	BAL			551	336	61.0%	3494	20	18	5		5.6		-13.0%					35	33	0	-29.3%		
	2013:	47% Short		35% Mid		13% Deep		5% Bomb		YAC: 4.2 (38)		2014:	64% Short		27% Mid		9% Deep		0% Bomb	YAC: 4.8 (--)			

Rarely can you pinpoint the exact moment an NFL player lost his confidence, but we might have it for Schaub. When Richard Sherman intercepted that horrible pass for a game-tying pick-six in 2013, that was the end of Schaub as we knew him. He has been broken ever since. His first meaningful play for Oakland was a fake field goal, as he served as the team's holder last year. He fumbled a low snap before throwing a desperation pass that was intercepted. His only other quarterback snaps came in the 52-0 rout Oakland suffered in St. Louis, where Schaub contributed two more turnovers on just 12 plays. Talk about $8 million well spent. Now Schaub will back up Joe Flacco, who has never missed a game for the Ravens. That's likely $10 million over a two-year period where Schaub will contribute nothing positive. In other words, he has become the Ryan Reynolds of the NFL.

Connor Shaw

Height: 6-1 Weight: 210 College: South Carolina Draft: 2014/FA Born: 19-Sep-1991 Age: 24 Risk: Green

Year	Team	G/GS	Snaps	Att	Cmp	C%	Yds	TD	INT/Adj	FUM	ASR	NY/P	Rk	DVOA	Rk	DYAR	Rk	YAR	Runs	Yds	TD	DVOA	DYAR	QBR
2014	CLE	1/1	65	28	14	50.0%	177	0	1/1	1	11.2%	4.7	--	-44.2%	--	-68	--	-73	7	9	0	-24.2%	-3	14.8
2015	CLE			489	262	53.6%	2952	12	16	9		5.2		-26.8%					67	201	2	-1.8%		
													2014:	58% Short		21% Mid		9% Deep		12% Bomb	YAC: 8.4 (--)			

Connor Shaw's lone start was graded favorably by most onlookers. As an undrafted rookie, he had no actual expectations to meet, so that was always likely to happen. When you dig deeper into his Week 17 performance against the Ravens, you find a quarterback with decent arm talent, a reluctance to stay in the pocket, and some impressive athleticism. He is not a good enough athlete to get away with being such a problematic pocket passer, so he will be fighting for his roster spot rather than a starting spot this season.

Alex Smith

Height: 6-4 Weight: 212 College: Utah Draft: 2005/1 (1) Born: 7-May-1984 Age: 31 Risk: Green

Year	Team	G/GS	Snaps	Att	Cmp	C%	Yds	TD	INT/Adj	FUM	ASR	NY/P	Rk	DVOA	Rk	DYAR	Rk	YAR	Runs	Yds	TD	DVOA	DYAR	QBR
2012	SF	10/9	484	218	153	70.2%	1737	13	5/5	3	9.7%	6.6	14	14.8%	9	418	15	365	31	132	0	26.0%	36	70.1
2013	KC	15/15	978	508	308	60.6%	3313	23	7/11	7	7.9%	5.7	29	-3.7%	21	262	20	416	76	431	1	18.7%	96	49.4
2014	KC	15/15	940	464	303	65.3%	3265	18	6/6	4	9.1%	5.9	28	4.1%	18	493	14	527	49	254	1	8.5%	38	49.4
2015	KC			508	330	65.0%	3375	22	12	7		5.7		-5.7%					59	281	2	15.6%		
	2013:	56% Short		27% Mid		12% Deep		5% Bomb		YAC: 5.7 (10)		2014:	62% Short		27% Mid		8% Deep		3% Bomb	YAC: 6.1 (5)			

Since we have bashed him everywhere else in the book, let's point out some things Alex Smith did well in 2014. He was second in red zone DVOA (31.0%) despite the lack of wide receiver production. Andy Reid had designed some really good plays to get the ball to backs and tight ends on short throws with yards after the catch. After three interceptions in Week 1, Smith threw just three interceptions the rest of the season (429 attempts). Smith instantly clicked with Travis Kelce, completing 59 of 78 passes (75.6 percent) to the tight end. Kelce's average target came 6.0 air yards beyond the line of scrimmage, the fourth-shortest average among tight ends in 2014. Kansas City's receivers had the highest rate of dropped passes (6.8 percent) in the league, so Smith's 65.0 completion percentage could have been noticeably better. Each of these stats, though, is a backhanded compliment and another symptom of the short pass blues. Smith's average dropped pass only traveled 3.2 air yards, the lowest of any quarterback in 2014. There is no denying Smith limits turnovers, but he does it at the expense of scoring more points.

The data compiled over the last four years with Smith on two different teams paints the same picture of a quarterback who plays the game too safely. It's not about the receivers around him. Jeremy Maclin is an expensive bullet for a gun Smith isn't willing to fire. To succeed with Smith is to marginalize him, and no team has been able to do that with a quarterback and win a Super Bowl since the 2000 Ravens.

Geno Smith

Height: 6-3   Weight: 208   College: West Virginia   Draft: 2013/2 (39)   Born: 10-Oct-1990   Age: 25 Risk: Yellow

Year	Team	G/GS	Snaps	Att	Cmp	C%	Yds	TD	INT/Adj	FUM	ASR	NY/P	Rk	DVOA	Rk	DYAR	Rk	YAR	Runs	Yds	TD	DVOA	DYAR	QBR
2013	NYJ	16/16	985	443	247	55.8%	3046	12	21/26	8	8.3%	5.6	32	-23.6%	37	-371	38	-434	72	366	6	9.5%	65	35.9
2014	NYJ	14/13	816	367	219	59.7%	2525	13	13/15	8	7.5%	6.0	27	-12.5%	30	-33	30	-21	59	238	1	-34.3%	-65	35.4
2015	NYJ			482	301	62.5%	3271	22	15	11		5.8		-15.8%					64	280	2	6.5%		

2013:	43% Short	35% Mid	13% Deep	9% Bomb	YAC: 5.1 (27)	2014:	55% Short	29% Mid	11% Deep	6% Bomb	YAC: 5.5 (15)

Rex Ryan had a stake in Smith's success—he invested a second-round pick in the West Virginia product, and if Smith succeeded, by extension, Ryan would look like the sort of guy who might have a clue when it came to evaluating quarterbacking play. Todd Bowles has no such stake in Smith, and history tells us that quarterbacks in Smith's situation get a half-season at most to prove their worth before the new coach moves on to one of his guys. As we noted in the Jets chapter, Smith had some good moments last year, but he's going to have to really put together an impressive streak out of the gate if he wants to win over Bowles and the coaching staff, who refused to acknowledge Smith as the starter throughout the spring workouts.

Matthew Stafford

Height: 6-2   Weight: 225   College: Georgia   Draft: 2009/1 (1)   Born: 7-Feb-1988   Age: 27 Risk: Green

Year	Team	G/GS	Snaps	Att	Cmp	C%	Yds	TD	INT/Adj	FUM	ASR	NY/P	Rk	DVOA	Rk	DYAR	Rk	YAR	Runs	Yds	TD	DVOA	DYAR	QBR
2012	DET	16/16	1181	727	435	59.8%	4967	20	17/23	8	3.7%	6.3	17	12.2%	12	1160	6	891	35	126	4	0.9%	23	57.1
2013	DET	16/16	1125	634	371	58.5%	4650	29	19/27	12	4.5%	6.9	9	4.9%	15	690	12	838	37	69	2	-40.3%	-41	52.5
2014	DET	16/16	1093	602	363	60.3%	4257	22	12/15	8	7.0%	6.2	22	-0.7%	20	423	15	544	43	93	2	-15.4%	-4	55.1
2015	DET			579	357	61.7%	4192	29	16	6		6.3		5.4%					36	96	1	2.6%		

2013:	47% Short	32% Mid	15% Deep	7% Bomb	YAC: 6.1 (3)	2014:	56% Short	28% Mid	10% Deep	6% Bomb	YAC: 6.1 (4)

Matthew Stafford may have become a newlywed this offseason, but it's unclear if he'll ever make a similar commitment to the reigned-in playing style called for by Joe Lombardi's scheme. Part of Stafford's decline in statistical volume surely stemmed from playing with a battered supporting cast all year—most remember Megatron's ankle woes, but the Lions also had two separate games in which they were missing their top three running backs and top three tight ends. And to be sure, the sidearming gunslinger still made his fair share of appearances, both good (the game-winning touchdown vs. Miami) and bad (two red zone picks at Chicago). However, the new three-step-drop version of Stafford finished with his lowest DVOA and DYAR rankings since his rookie year (excluding the 2010 campaign where he played just three games). It's curious that Stafford experienced such a noticeable decline, for while his yardage and touchdown numbers declined, so too did his turnover rate. The culprit might lie in the red zone, where Stafford went from the fourth-best DVOA among starters in 2013 to ranking among the ten worst red zone quarterbacks in 2014. One would think that playing with Calvin Johnson and an assortment of big tight ends would make Stafford deadly inside the 20, but in truth, his excellent 2013 red zone DVOA looks like the outlier over the last three seasons. Obviously that's a tiny sample of throws, but it certainly plays into the narrative that Stafford's high variance is untenable for Super Bowl contention. While the impossibly gorgeous throws will still be there, hitting the easy ones all the time remains Stafford's biggest bugaboo.

Drew Stanton

Height: 6-3   Weight: 230   College: Michigan State   Draft: 2007/2 (43)   Born: 7-May-1984   Age: 31 Risk: Yellow

Year	Team	G/GS	Snaps	Att	Cmp	C%	Yds	TD	INT/Adj	FUM	ASR	NY/P	Rk	DVOA	Rk	DYAR	Rk	YAR	Runs	Yds	TD	DVOA	DYAR	QBR
2014	ARI	9/8	469	240	132	55.0%	1711	7	5/13	1	4.3%	6.5	20	4.2%	16	238	20	185	25	63	0	36.2%	27	58.0
2015	ARI			567	328	57.9%	3937	19	19	7		6.0		-15.4%					46	128	1	-10.5%		

						2014:	42% Short	35% Mid	14% Deep	10% Bomb	YAC: 4.9 (29)

Stanton was the luckiest player in the NFL last year. He threw eight passes that should have been intercepted but were dropped by defenders, tied with Andrew Luck for second-most in the NFL behind Brian Hoyer's nine. He was the only quarterback with at least 200 passes who threw more dropped picks than actual interceptions. Now remember that Hoyer threw 438 passes last year, and Luck threw 616, but Stanton only threw 240. It is completely absurd for someone with so few passes to finish so high in any counting stat. Think of it this way: to finish second in the league in passing yards last year, Stanton would have needed to average better than 20 yards per attempt. Stanton's average pass last year traveled 11.4 yards past the line of scrimmage, highest of any regular quarterback, so it's easy to see how defenders got their hands on so many balls. Assuming they actually hold onto those passes in the future, Stanton will look less like a borderline starter and more like the career backup that he has always been.

Ryan Tannehill

Height: 6-4   Weight: 221   College: Texas A&M   Draft: 2012/1 (8)   Born: 27-Jul-1988   Age: 27 Risk: Yellow

Year	Team	G/GS	Snaps	Att	Cmp	C%	Yds	TD	INT/Adj	FUM	ASR	NY/P	Rk	DVOA	Rk	DYAR	Rk	YAR	Runs	Yds	TD	DVOA	DYAR	QBR
2012	MIA	16/16	980	484	282	58.3%	3294	12	13/16	7	6.7%	5.9	23	-9.9%	25	39	25	86	49	211	2	-11.0%	2	50.4
2013	MIA	16/16	1020	588	355	60.4%	3913	24	17/26	9	8.7%	5.5	36	-9.8%	26	54	26	22	40	238	1	19.0%	46	45.8
2014	MIA	16/16	1065	590	392	66.4%	4045	27	12/15	8	7.0%	5.8	33	4.1%	17	630	12	566	56	311	1	11.4%	51	59.1
2015	MIA			576	373	64.8%	4089	27	15	8		6.0		0.8%					50	220	1	14.0%		
	2013:	41% Short		42% Mid		10% Deep		7% Bomb		YAC: 4.4 (37)		2014:		55% Short		30% Mid		10% Deep		4% Bomb	YAC: 4.8 (32)		

It appears that, fair or not, the Dolphins' 2015 season will be a referendum on Tannehill and whether or not he's capable of being a true franchise quarterback. Miami has fortified its depth on the offensive line and added a number of talented receivers. The signing of Ndamukong Suh means the fans are unlikely to blame another 8-8 season on the defense. All that, set against the backdrop of this new $96 million deal, means Tannehill will be in the spotlight from the beginning of camp. He did take a sizable leap forward in several statistical categories in 2014, including DVOA, but most of those improvements just moved him from the bottom-third of the league to middle-of-the-pack. The next step for Tannehill is to work on his deep throws, so he can properly use the talents of his new teammates Kenny Stills and Jordan Cameron. Speaking of which, according to our similarity scores system, the most similar quarterback to Tannehill over the first three years of his career is Andy Dalton in 2011-2013.

Tyrod Taylor

Height: 6-1   Weight: 216   College: Virginia Tech   Draft: 2011/6 (180)   Born: 3-Aug-1989   Age: 26 Risk: Yellow

Year	Team	G/GS	Snaps	Att	Cmp	C%	Yds	TD	INT/Adj	FUM	ASR	NY/P	Rk	DVOA	Rk	DYAR	Rk	YAR	Runs	Yds	TD	DVOA	DYAR	QBR
2012	BAL	6/0	92	29	17	58.6%	179	0	1/1	1	6.8%	4.7	--	-28.3%	--	-34	--	-56	14	73	1	13.8%	18	45.0
2013	BAL	3/0	21	5	1	20.0%	2	0	1/2	0	0.4%	0.4	--	-236.3%	--	-75	--	-75	8	64	0	26.2%	15	44.8
2014	BAL	1/0	6	0	0	0.0%	0	0	0/0	0	--	--	--	--	--	--	--	--	4	-3	0	--	--	--
2015	BUF			479	281	58.6%	2871	18	18	9		5.2		-22.9%					89	464	2	9.0%		
	2013:	60% Short		40% Mid		0% Deep		0% Bomb		YAC: 1 (--)														

Early in offseason workouts, Taylor got significant snaps with the first-team offense. Is there a real chance that Rex Ryan is telling the truth, and Taylor will get a shot at the starting gig? Taylor's college passing stats were different from EJ Manuel's, but not necessarily worse. (Taylor had a lower completion percentage than Manuel, but higher yards per attempt.) Taylor also faced a difficult set of defenses at Virginia Tech. On the other hand, it is questionable whether Taylor is really as much of a dual threat as some have claimed. Taylor ran a lot in college, but he was not that good at it, averaging 4.4 yards on 501 carries.

Scott Tolzien

Height: 6-3   Weight: 205   College: Wisconsin   Draft: 2011/FA   Born: 9-Jan-1987   Age: 28 Risk: Yellow

Year	Team	G/GS	Snaps	Att	Cmp	C%	Yds	TD	INT/Adj	FUM	ASR	NY/P	Rk	DVOA	Rk	DYAR	Rk	YAR	Runs	Yds	TD	DVOA	DYAR	QBR
2013	GB	3/2	158	90	55	61.1%	717	1	5/8	0	4.2%	7.6	--	-9.1%	--	13	--	19	5	55	1	117.5%	33	24.3
2015	GB			537	339	63.1%	4027	25	18	10		6.7		2.2%					50	113	1	-8.7%		
	2013:	52% Short		27% Mid		13% Deep		8% Bomb		YAC: 6.1 (--)														

The Packers believe the Tolzien who floundered in 2013 is a thing of the past, a product of being thrown into the mix too quickly. Mike McCarthy, quarterbacks coach Alex Van Pelt, and Aaron Rodgers were all suitably effusive in the offseason, praising Tolzien's improved mechanics, greater velocity, and time put in to learn the offense. We will get our chance in preseason to see just how improved Tolzien is, and McCarthy, Van Pelt, Rodgers, the citizenry of Wisconsin, and probably Tolzien himself all hope it stops with that.

Michael Vick

Height: 6-0   Weight: 215   College: Virginia Tech   Draft: 2001/1 (1)   Born: 26-Jun-1980   Age: 35 Risk: N/A

Year	Team	G/GS	Snaps	Att	Cmp	C%	Yds	TD	INT/Adj	FUM	ASR	NY/P	Rk	DVOA	Rk	DYAR	Rk	YAR	Runs	Yds	TD	DVOA	DYAR	QBR
2012	PHI	10/10	667	351	204	58.1%	2362	12	10/14	8	8.0%	5.8	28	-14.4%	28	-78	27	-108	62	332	1	-11.1%	3	45.8
2013	PHI	7/6	325	141	77	54.6%	1215	5	3/3	4	10.5%	7.2	--	-6.9%	--	40	--	49	36	306	2	70.0%	128	58.8
2014	NYJ	10/3	272	121	64	52.9%	604	3	2/5	5	13.5%	3.6	--	-36.8%	--	-228	--	-273	26	153	0	-8.9%	3	22.2
	2013:	35% Short		34% Mid		23% Deep		8% Bomb		YAC: 7.4 (1)		2014:		63% Short		24% Mid		3% Deep		10% Bomb	YAC: 3.9 (--)		

Vick was still capable of waking up the echoes at times last year, and the juke he put on Pittsburgh's Brice McCain on the way to a November win over the Steelers was one of the best moves of the year for any quarterback. Still, at the age of 35 and without a job, it's reasonable to wonder if this is it for him. The Artist Formerly Known As Ron Mexico still has designs on finding a job somewhere, but he will likely have to wait until there's an opening because of an injury, and then hope a myopic general manager can see past his steadily declining skill set and absurd insistence that he can still start in the NFL.

Brandon Weeden — Height: 6-4   Weight: 221   College: Oklahoma State   Draft: 2012/1 (22)   Born: 14-Oct-1983   Age: 32 Risk: Yellow

Year	Team	G/GS	Snaps	Att	Cmp	C%	Yds	TD	INT/Adj	FUM	ASR	NY/P	Rk	DVOA	Rk	DYAR	Rk	YAR	Runs	Yds	TD	DVOA	DYAR	QBR
2012	CLE	15/15	929	517	297	57.4%	3385	14	17/26	5	5.3%	5.8	26	-19.4%	29	-291	34	-210	27	111	0	8.0%	24	27.0
2013	CLE	8/5	452	267	141	52.8%	1731	9	9/11	6	9.7%	5.3	39	-36.1%	40	-443	40	-429	12	44	0	12.4%	11	24.7
2014	DAL	5/1	89	41	24	58.5%	303	3	2/2	1	3.2%	7.0	--	-3.5%	--	21	--	25	6	-1	0	-158.1%	-26	15.4
2015	DAL			539	317	58.8%	3512	21	17	6		5.7		-8.0%					35	77	1	-3.4%		

2013:   47% Short   29% Mid   17% Deep   8% Bomb   YAC: 4.5 (36)   2014:   42% Short   44% Mid   5% Deep   9% Bomb   YAC: 6.7 (--)

Weeden is basically Brian Doyle Murray's character in *Caddyshack* or Benson from *Regular Show*. He's the aging guy stuck in a dead-end job because his only qualification is that he is slightly more mature and responsible than your basic twenty-something slacker. Weeden's lone start was a comical disaster against the Cardinals, and the Cowboys rushed Tony Romo back from a back injury to face the Jaguars in London rather than risk international humiliation. Weeden padded his stats with relief-appearance productivity, including a 43-yard fourth quarter touchdown pass to Terrance Williams to give the Cowboys a 42-7 win over the Colts. Beware of 31-year-olds who need self-esteem boosters in blowouts, and look for Mordecai and Rigby to steal a golf cart and run amok if Weeden is called upon to do anything more than mop up a game.

Charlie Whitehurst — Height: 6-4   Weight: 220   College: Clemson   Draft: 2006/3 (81)   Born: 6-Aug-1982   Age: 33 Risk: Red

Year	Team	G/GS	Snaps	Att	Cmp	C%	Yds	TD	INT/Adj	FUM	ASR	NY/P	Rk	DVOA	Rk	DYAR	Rk	YAR	Runs	Yds	TD	DVOA	DYAR	QBR
2014	TEN	7/5	357	185	105	56.8%	1326	7	2/4	3	8.8%	6.0	25	-7.2%	27	49	28	80	20	90	0	-5.9%	5	39.6
2015	TEN			489	282	57.6%	3470	18	18	10		6.0		-16.9%					47	136	1	-8.6%		

2014:   53% Short   24% Mid   17% Deep   7% Bomb   YAC: 5.2 (22)

Given his most extended chance to play in his ninth NFL season, Charlie Whitehurst showed he was actually an average backup quarterback, not the dismal spot starter he was with the Seahawks. Beyond knowledge of the offense and helping April installs run more smoothly, his main virtue was avoiding interceptions. He did that by waiting for throws to become fully defined and not taking many risks. With a defense and a strong run game, you can make the playoffs even with a -18.6% third-down DVOA and -31.8% red zone DVOA. On a team like the 2014 Titans, those stats will lead to a single win at home against another bad team in a close game (16-14 over Jacksonville). Whitehurst, not Zach Mettenberger, is probably the man to come off the bench if Marcus Mariota suffers an unfortunate injury.

Russell Wilson — Height: 5-11   Weight: 204   College: Wisconsin   Draft: 2012/3 (75)   Born: 29-Nov-1988   Age: 27 Risk: Green

Year	Team	G/GS	Snaps	Att	Cmp	C%	Yds	TD	INT/Adj	FUM	ASR	NY/P	Rk	DVOA	Rk	DYAR	Rk	YAR	Runs	Yds	TD	DVOA	DYAR	QBR
2012	SEA	16/16	979	393	252	64.1%	3118	26	10/12	10	7.4%	6.8	8	19.7%	6	872	8	741	94	489	4	22.3%	147	71.7
2013	SEA	16/16	973	407	257	63.1%	3357	26	9/9	10	9.8%	6.9	7	15.6%	8	770	9	699	96	539	1	23.3%	134	58.9
2014	SEA	16/16	1054	452	285	63.1%	3475	20	7/12	11	8.8%	6.6	17	5.5%	13	503	13	488	118	849	6	43.7%	269	62.5
2015	SEA			448	289	64.4%	3562	25	11	12		7.1		7.0%					98	508	5	21.2%		

2013:   45% Short   31% Mid   14% Deep   10% Bomb   YAC: 5.7 (11)   2014:   58% Short   26% Mid   11% Deep   6% Bomb   YAC: 6.6 (3)

A partial list of the news items Wilson generated following the Super Bowl loss: joining the Texas Rangers for spring training; flying teammates to Hawaii for player-organized offseason practies; escorting his grandmother (*his grandmother!*) and Ciara to separate events at the White House; later making it known that he and Ciara were limiting their relationship to holding hands and mild necking; upgrading random soldiers to first-class seats; making a cameo appearance in *Entourage*; taking an absence from OTAs to accompany new teammate Jimmy Graham to the funeral of Graham's longtime mentor; getting slimed on Nickelodeon; and making weekly visits to Seattle Children's Hospital. Of course this is all deliberate. Wilson takes image-consciousness to heights of which Peyton Manning can only dream, and his sponsorship deal with Alaska Airlines no doubt helps out with those plane tickets and seat upgrades. All this activity also served as a smokescreen so nobody would notice Wilson was entering the last year of his contract, and it worked—for a few months. When his negotiations with the team stretched into July, and he publicly stated he would be willing to play out his last year for $1.5 million and take his chances in 2016, questions about his demands started to rise. Does he want to be the league's highest-paid player? Does he want a fully guaranteed deal? Does he want to hit the open market? Wilson doesn't play football like any other quarterback in the league, spending about a third of his time outside the pocket. It's starting to look like he doesn't manage his business like any other quarterback in the league, either.

Jameis Winston

Height: 6-4 Weight: 230 College: Florida State Draft: 2015/1 (1) Born: 6-Jan-1994 Age: 21 Risk: Red

Year	Team	G/GS	Snaps	Att	Cmp	C%	Yds	TD	INT/Adj	FUM	ASR	NY/P	Rk	DVOA	Rk	DYAR	Rk	YAR	Runs	Yds	TD	DVOA	DYAR	QBR
2015	TB			519	298	57.4%	3763	23	22	11		6.0		-15.8%						49	106	2	-8.7%		

Winston's two seasons at Florida State were remarkably different. As a freshman, Winston finished second in the nation with 9.1 total yards per play, just behind Marcus Mariota. The next year, Winston fell to 7.6 yards per play, ranking tenth. That stat does not even penalize Winston for his 18 interceptions, which ranked second in FBS. Is Winston the quarterback who tore up college football as a freshman (with Kelvin Benjamin, against the No. 64 schedule of defenses according to our Fremeau Efficiency Ratings)? Or is he the quarterback who eked out wins and often struggled as a sophomore (without Benjamin and facing the toughest slate of defenses in FBS)? On the positive side for Winston, he was an elite high school player, so his sophomore season is the outlier. On the negative side, one great season and one not-so-great season is generally a sign of a player who got lucky in the great season.

To figure out how much weight to put on Winston's rave workout reviews so far, consider these quotes:

"His hard word and determination are paying off."

"High character franchise quarterback."

"Vocal leader and hard worker."

Those quotes refer to David Carr, Joey Harrington, and Blaine Gabbert, respectively. Before even preseason snaps have happened, we can safely put exactly zero weight on news reports about Winston. He will remain a high-variance proposition until meaningful footballs are in the air.

T.J. Yates

Height: 6-3 Weight: 195 College: North Carolina Draft: 2011/5 (152) Born: 28-May-1987 Age: 28 Risk: Green

Year	Team	G/GS	Snaps	Att	Cmp	C%	Yds	TD	INT/Adj	FUM	ASR	NY/P	Rk	DVOA	Rk	DYAR	Rk	YAR	Runs	Yds	TD	DVOA	DYAR	QBR
2012	HOU	4/0	23	10	4	40.0%	38	0	1/1	3	8.6%	3.1	--	-128.3%	--	-85	--	-89	2	-1	1	56.0%	8	2.1
2013	HOU	3/0	50	22	15	68.2%	113	0	2/2	1	6.6%	4.4	--	-78.0%	--	-109	--	-112	1	0	0	--	--	12.2
2014	ATL	1/0	17	4	3	75.0%	64	0	1/1	0	0.0%	16.0	--	-44.3%	--	-8	--	-4	0	0	0	--	--	21.1
2015	ATL			584	367	62.9%	3811	23	19	14		5.6		-8.4%					48	144	1	-2.8%		

2013:	60% Short	40% Mid	0% Deep	0% Bomb	YAC: 3.0 (--)	2014:	50% Short	25% Mid	25% Deep	0% Bomb	YAC: 8.7 (--)

The extent of Yates' playing time in 2014 was an appearance in probably the ugliest game of the season, Atlanta's 56-14 Thursday night blowout of Tampa Bay. Yates immediately threw a pick-six, proving that you can take a quarterback off the Texans, but you can't take the Texans out of a quarterback. Headed into his late twenties, Yates is no better than several free-agent quarterbacks that are older than him. His saving grace may be that Kyle Shanahan's offense should be pretty familiar to a Gary Kubiak disciple, since the two worked together in Houston for a few seasons.

Going Deep

R.J. Archer, SEA: Archer had a 6:1 touchdown-to-interception ratio the last two seasons for Jacksonville—the Jacksonville Sharks of the Arena League. He has spent four seasons in arena football, and also spent time on the practice squad (the *practice squad*) of the CFL's Winnipeg Blue Bombers. Before that, his only NFL experience came with the Vikings in 2010 (where he was at times active but never made it into a game), and in training camp with the Lions in 2012 and Seattle in 2014. And yet, with Russell Wilson at a funeral, Tarvaris Jackson unsigned, and B.J. Daniels moving to wide receiver, Archer was taking first-team snaps for Seattle in OTAs. Wilson eventually returned and Jackson eventually re-signed, and Archer continued to walk the fine line between practice squad and third-stringer.

Matt Barkley, PHI: Maybe it was the presence of Tim Tebow making every well-timed spiral look like an accomplishment, but Barkley's velocity and location looked pretty good during minicamp. The quarterback-of-the-future luster is long gone, but Barkley has also moved past his disastrous 2013 performance and looks worthy of a roster spot. That Tebow sure is generous. (2013 stats: 30-for-49, 300 yards, 0 TD, 4 INT, -84 DYAR, -34.9% DVOA)

McLeod Bethel-Thompson, MIA: McLeod Bethel-Thompson must be a nice guy to have around camp, because we can't figure out why else he keeps getting hired as a third-string quarterback. Miami is only going to carry two, and even if one of the others is injured in training camp, we can guarantee you they will sign a veteran or make a trade instead of having Bethel-Thompson on the actual active roster during the regular season.

Matt Blanchard, GB: Blanchard led Wisconsin-Whitewhater to back-to-back Division III Championships with a 25-0 record, a 70.4 percent completion rate, and a 44:5 TD:INT ratio. The NFL, if you hadn't noticed, is not Division III. Blanchard has seen sparse preseason action as end-of-the-roster fodder for Chicago and Carolina. He has taken 11 sacks in 55 dropbacks—in preseason fourth quarters. Green Bay signed him because offseason rosters contain 90 players.

Tajh Boyd, PIT: Maybe the only quarterback associated with the Jets last year that emerged with some semblance of his reputation intact, mostly because he was cut before the regular season. Last year marked quite the odyssey for Boyd, who did everything he could to stay in football shape, including playing semi-pro football in the Boston suburbs. It's unclear how much that'll help when it comes to his spot on the Pittsburgh depth chart—after signing in March, he's currently fourth behind Ben Roethlisberger, Bruce Gradkowski, and Landry Jones—but you have to admire the former All-American for swallowing his pride and taking a gig that was probably beneath him just to stay in the game.

Jason Campbell, FA: Campbell turned down overtures for a camp invite from Cincinnati and Baltimore, and is on the brink of retirement. If he is done, the former first-round draft choice goes out with more regrets (injury, endless coaching changes, no postseason passes) than accomplishments (87 touchdowns, more than 16,000 yards). (2014 stats: 11-for-19, 74 yards, -74 DYAR, -64.4% DVOA)

Zac Dysert, DEN: Dysert's tenure in Denver would have ended years ago under normal circumstances, but the older version of Peyton Manning needs more than one backup ready behind him. Of course we can debate how ready Dysert is to play given that he has yet to appear in a regular-season game. He has thrown 41 passes in the last two preseasons combined. Expect another forgettable August to conclude his on-field presence in 2015.

David Fales, CHI: Fales came out of San Jose State as a West Coast Offense-only fit, with good accuracy and a quick release but not much arm strength. The Bears' gave Jimmy Clausen a chance when they tried to move on from Jay Cutler, and when Clausen got hurt it was back to Cutler rather than giving Fales his shot. Don't expect much.

Matt Flynn, NE: The Packers needed their Aaron Rodgers insurance for precisely one attempt in 2014. Scott Tolzien's development made him expendable in Green Bay, but Roger Goodell vs. The Deflator created a potential need for a quarterback who knows how to take a snap and execute an offense in New England. (2013 stats: 124-for-200, 1,253 yards, 8 TD, 5 INT, -196 DYAR, -24.5% DVOA)

Garrett Gilbert, DET: Gilbert is the poor man's Matt Barkley, the other top high school quarterback from 2009. After floundering at Texas and leading them to their first losing season in a decade, Gilbert transferred to Southern Methodist. He had one good season as a senior, albeit against an unusually forgiving set of opposing defenses (ranked 74th in FBS by FEI ratings). The Lions claimed Gilbert after the Patriots waived him in June.

Garrett Grayson, NO: The third quarterback off the board in a two-quarterback draft, chosen out of Colorado State 75th overall. The Saints are hedging their bets with a potential Drew Brees replacement, investing enough equity to make him a developmental prospect but not someone who will threaten the starter spot anytime soon. Grayson has a big arm to throw deep and makes poor decisions when throwing short.

Ryan Griffin, NO: The Tulane product is entering an important preseason, because places on the quarterback depth chart are limited. Drew Brees and Garrett Grayson are assured of their spots, while Luke McCown is a well-respected backup. Griffin may be auditioning for jobs with other teams in preseason games.

Brett Hundley, GB: Hundley faces a significant learning curve in adjusting to an NFL world where he is not locked into a play called before the snap. Navigating a muddied pocket was sometimes a major challenge for Hundley, and his 8.6 percent sack rate was the worst among all drafted quarterbacks. He is a good bet for Mike McCarthy's Quarterback Development School, but think 2017 for results.

Josh Johnson, CIN: Johnson hasn't thrown a pass in the NFL since 2011, but he's still athletic enough that he has found work in San Francisco (twice), Cincinnati (also twice), and Cleveland as a backup and occasional Wildcat option. He will battle 2014 sixth-rounder Keith Wenning for the third spot in Cincinnati behind Andy Dalton and A.J. McCarron.

Landry Jones, PIT: With Ben Roethlisberger entrenched as a starter and Bruce Gradkowski available to be the backup, it never made sense for the Steelers to spend a fourth-round pick on the scattershot accuracy of Landry Jones. Jones has predictably been buried on the depth chart during the regular season and made no positive impression during the preseason.

Mike Kafka, MIN: In Tampa Bay's 2014 preseason, Kafka went 2-for-7 for 86 yards in the first game, 4-for-11 for 55 yards in the second game, and then 7-for-14 in the 86 yards in the fourth. That performance got him cut. At the veteran combine this offseason, Kafka showed enough of a metamorphosis to earn a contract with Minnesota, but the Vikings do not generally carry three quarterbacks.

Thad Lewis, CLE: Picked up by Houston during the great Quarterback Injury Purge of 2015, Lewis is probably a better quarterback than Case Keenum, but had the notable handicap of not learning Bill O'Brien's offense during training camp. Lewis is an acceptable backup quarterback. In some situations that would mean a season of holding clipboards and teaching professionalism. In Cleveland, it means he'd better be ready. (2013 stats: 93-for-157, 1,092 yards, 4 TD, 3 INT, -84 DYAR, -18.7% DVOA)

Seth Lobato, TB: Like Vincent Jackson, Lobato is tall (6-foot-6) and went to Northern Colorado. A lot of teams like his physical tools, but he went undrafted in 2014 because he's very raw. Spent last year on the Miami practice squad, then signed with Tampa Bay this offseason.

Sean Mannion, STL: Mannion set a Pac-12 record with 13,600 passing yards at Oregon State, but the Beavers ranked a dismal 80th in Passing S&P+ in 2014. Mannion also has problems with mobility (minus-804 rushing yards, and though that includes sacks, his 12 non-sack runs in 2014 still totaled minus-8 yards) or ball security (54 interceptions, 30 fumbles). The Rams drafted him near the end of the third round.

Kellen Moore, DET: Over the last three years, you have been active for as many NFL games as Kellen Moore. Unless you actually played in the NFL during that time, in which case, you have been active for *more* games than Kellen Moore. The Boise State folk hero turned that resume into a two-year, $1.85 million extension this March, perhaps the reward for his shiny 108.4 passer rating last preseason. Moore will again attempt to scale Mount Orlovsky in his fourth season, but even if he fails, he can take solace in the knowledge that he earned one more contract with Detroit than Ndamukong Suh.

Stephen Morris, JAC: Morris is a player built for UDFA puff pieces, the kind of quarterback with every physical tool that a coaching staff can "fix" in a passable player. The problem is that, for most of those players, this is the last time we hear about them. Thankfully, we have Going Deep to tell you that, yes, Morris is still exactly the same guy you heard about in 2014.

Aaron Murray, KC: It's hard to say if we'll ever see Murray get a chance to start in Kansas City, but Andy Reid has a history of maximizing his quarterbacks. A fifth-round pick in 2014, Murray had an 87.1 Total QBR at Georgia in 2013. That's the 13th-highest QBR out of the 1,309 qualified seasons in ESPN's database going back to 2004. Quarterbacks not named Kellen Moore (or gimmicky runners like Pat White) that rank that high in QBR have usually been given a shot to shine in the NFL, but we'll see. Murray's still behind Chase Daniel on the depth chart.

Sean Renfree, ATL: The former Duke signal-caller comes with a Matt Waldman Seal of Interesting, but thus far has gravitated towards the No. 3 quarterback slot after being selected in the seventh round in 2013. Renfree probably is a better long-term bet than T.J. Yates. If that ever actually matters for the Falcons, they're probably in trouble.

Jameill Showers, DAL: Showers got stuck behind Johnny Manziel at Texas A&M, so he used the Russell Wilson Exemption (get an undergraduate degree, and the NCAA won't make you sit a year when you transfer as a grad student) to travel across the state and earn the UTEP starting job. He's a short, well-built, mobile quarterback with mediocre numbers in a run-heavy system (12 passing touchdowns in his final season) but a good rep as a worker/scholar/leader. Showers and Dustin Vaughn will compete for the role of hard-working homegrown Texan third-stringer for the Cowboys.

Trevor Siemian, DEN: Siemian threw seven touchdowns and 11 interceptions in his senior year at Northwestern before tearing his ACL in November. His 43.3 Total QBR also doesn't scream NFL success, but Zac Dysert needed company in the "seventh-round picks who won't replace Peyton Manning" club.

Matt Simms, BUF: Simms asked for and was granted his release by the Jets after New York drafted Bryce Petty. He reunited with Rex Ryan and will head into training camp as the fourth quarterback on the Bills' depth chart, which should guarantee that the 2011 argument between his father and Desmond Howard will remain the most notable event attached to his name in an otherwise unremarkable quarterbacking career. (2013 stats: 16-for-31, 156 yards, 1 TD, 1 INT, -27 DYAR, -24.6% DVOA)

Brad Sorensen, SD: Sorensen became the first player ever drafted out of Southern Utah in 2013. San Diego released him last August, leading to a brief stint with Ken Whisenhunt in Tennessee, then a return to San Diego's practice squad. The only person who thinks Sorensen is a better backup option than Kellen Clemens is Bernie Kosar.

Ricky Stanzi, NYG: Best-known for his "love it or leave it" diatribe about America to FOX's Chris Myers following the 2010 Orange Bowl, Stanzi's NFL career has proven that, without a doubt, he is still best-known for that diatribe.

Tim Tebow, PHI: Tebow looked like a passable third quarterback in OTAs and minicamp. Yes, that is indeed an improvement from what we saw in 2012 and 2013. The mechanics have improved marginally—one out of three passes wobbles and hangs in the air, as opposed to three out of five—but the inability to process coverage and pull the trigger was still obvious, even during 7-on-7s in early June. Quarterbacks who have been in the NFL (on and off) since 2010 don't usually hold the ball for eight seconds like it's 7-on-7 bull riding. The Eagles practice tons of read-options every day, and when Tebow faked to Ryan Matthews or Kenjon Barmer and took off, you couldn't help but wonder for a moment … No! Tebow will not make the Eagles roster. Unless Chip Kelly has some two-point conversion science up his sleeve. Or plans to go options-only if down to his third quarterback. Or just wants to prove how smart he is. Away from me, oh serpent!

Logan Thomas, ARI: Save for one snap in a blowout loss to Seattle in Week 16, Thomas' only rookie action came in Week 5 against Denver after Drew Stanton left the game with a concussion. His numbers on the season: two sacks, eight incompletions, and one pass that never should have been thrown but somehow slipped through a defender's hands into Andre Ellington's, resulting in an 81-yard touchdown. Even with Stanton and Carson Palmer down, Cardinals coach Bruce Arians watched Ryan Lindley throw the season away in the wild-card loss to Carolina, and never gave Thomas a chance to win the game, saying. "I was not going to let him fail because once you fail those scars never go away." That's fine, but to think that a quarterback will somehow develop from sub-Lindley to starting caliber seems wildly optimistic.

Dustin Vaughan, DAL: The Cowboys contacted Vaughan as a rookie free agent literally five minutes after the 2014 draft. "It was very short-lived," Vaughan told the *Dallas News* of his post-draft disappointment. Vaughan is 6-foot-5, excelled in a Division II spread offense at East Texas A&M, and played well enough in 2014 training camp that the Cowboys activated him when Tony Romo was injured instead of dragging Jon Kitna out of a middle school faculty lounge or something. Vaughan isn't expected to challenge Brandon Weeden for the second string this season, but stranger things have happened.

Joe Webb, CAR: *A lot of people say, "What celeb?" It's Webb! / A lot of people ask, "Receiver? Or QB?" / A passer or a receiver, accept him for a thrower or whatever it might be. / It's time for end-of-depth-chart androgyny. / It's Webb!* (2013 receiving stats: 5-for-11, 33 yards, -25 DYAR, -42.6% DVOA)

Keith Wenning, CIN: This former Baltimore practice-squadder is an alum of Ball State, just like David Letterman. Both were unemployed at one point this year, but then the Bengals signed Wenning to compete with Josh Johnson for their third quarterback spot. The odds Dave plays in a regular-season NFL game this season are surprisingly close to the odds Keith will do so, which isn't good considering the former talk show host is 68.

Running Backs

In the following section we provide the last three years' statistics, as well as a 2015 KUBIAK projection, for every running back who either played a significant role in 2014 or is expected to do so in 2015.

The first line contains biographical data—each player's **name**, **height**, **weight**, **college**, **draft** position, **birth date**, and **age**. Height and weight are the best data we could find; weight, of course, can fluctuate during the offseason. **Age** is very simple, the number of years between the player's birth year and 2014, but birthdate is provided if you want to figure out exact age.

Draft position gives draft year and round, with the overall pick number with which the player was taken in parentheses. In the sample table, it says that Alfred Morris was chosen in the 2012 NFL Draft in the sixth round with the 173rd overall pick. Undrafted free agents are listed as "FA" with the year they came into the league, even if they were only in training camp or on a practice squad.

To the far right of the first line is the player's **Risk** for fantasy football in 2015. As explained in the quarterback section, the standard is for players to be marked Green. Players with higher than normal risk are marked Yellow, and players with the highest risk are marked Red. Players who are most likely to match or surpass our forecast—primarily second-stringers with low projections—are marked Blue. Risk is not only based on injury probability, but how a player's projection compares to his recent performance as well as our confidence (or lack thereof) in his offensive teammates.

The first few columns after the **year** and **team** the player played for are standard numbers. First come games played and games started (**G/GS**). Games played is the official NFL total and may include games in which a player appeared on special teams, but did not carry the ball or catch a pass. We also have a total of offensive **Snaps** for each season. The next four columns are familiar: **Runs**, rushing yards (**Yds**), yards per rush (**Yd/R**) and rushing touchdowns (**TD**).

The entry for fumbles (**FUM**) includes all fumbles by this running back, no matter whether they were recovered by the offense or defense. Holding onto the ball is an identifiable skill; fumbling it so that your own offense can recover it is not. (For more on this issue, see the essay "Pregame Show" in the front of the book.) This entry combines fumbles on both carries and receptions.

The next five columns give our advanced metrics for rushing: **DVOA** (Defense-Adjusted Value Over Average), **DYAR** (Defense-Adjusted Yards Above Replacement), and **YAR** (Yards Above Replacement), along with the player's rank (**Rk**) in both **DVOA** and **DYAR**. These metrics compare every carry by the running back to a league-average baseline based on the game situations in which that running back carried the ball. DVOA and DYAR are also adjusted based on the opposing defense. The methods used to compute these numbers are described in detail in the "Statistical Toolbox" introduction in the front of the book. The important distinctions between them are:

- DVOA is a rate statistic, while DYAR is a cumulative statistic. Thus, a higher DVOA means more value per play, while a higher DYAR means more aggregate value over the entire season.
- Because DYAR is defense-adjusted and YAR is not, a player whose DYAR is higher than his YAR faced a harder-than-average schedule. A player whose DYAR is lower than his YAR faced an easier-than-average schedule.

To qualify for ranking in rushing DVOA and DYAR, a running back must have had 100 carries in that season. Last year, 43 running backs qualified to be ranked in these stats, compared to 47 running backs in 2013 and 42 backs in 2012.

Success Rate (**Suc%**), listed along with rank, represents running back consistency as measured by successful running plays divided by total running plays. (The definition for success is explained in the "Statistical Toolbox" introduction in the front of the book.) A player with high DVOA and a low Success Rate mixes long runs with plays on which he was stuffed at or behind the line of scrimmage. A player with low DVOA and a high Success Rate generally gets the yards needed, but rarely gets more. The league-average Success Rate in 2014 was 46 percent. Success Rate is not adjusted for the defenses a player faced.

We also give a total of broken tackles (**BTkl**) according to the Football Outsiders game charting project. This total includes broken tackles on both runs and receptions. Please note that Football Outsiders charters marked roughly 25 percent more broken tackles in 2014 than in previous seasons because of a change in our methodology, described further in the Statistical Toolbox. So most running backs with consistent playing time will be listed with more broken tackles in 2014; it doesn't necessarily mean they suddenly became more powerful or elusive.

Alfred Morris   Height: 5-10   Weight: 219   College: Florida Atlantic   Draft: 2012/6 (173)   Born: 12-Dec-1988   Age: 27   Risk: Yellow

Year	Team	G/GS	Snaps	Runs	Yds	Yd/R	TD	FUM	DVOA	Rk	DYAR	Rk	YAR	Suc%	Rk	BTkl	Rec	Pass	Yds	C%	Yd/C	TD	YAC	DVOA	Rk	DYAR	Rk
2012	WAS	16/16	728	335	1613	4.8	13	4	10.3%	8	254	5	273	52%	7	27	11	16	77	69%	7.0	0	5.9	-14.6%	--	-1	--
2013	WAS	16/16	605	276	1275	4.6	7	6	2.0%	21	121	13	133	48%	20	24	9	12	78	75%	8.7	0	8.8	-12.0%	--	1	--
2014	WAS	16/16	595	265	1074	4.1	8	2	-1.4%	23	77	17	77	46%	18	28	17	26	155	65%	9.1	0	9.1	-8.7%	36	7	38
2015	WAS			274	1129	4.1	7	3	1.3%								22	33	170	67%	7.7	0		-8.3%			

The columns to the right of broken tackles give data for each running back as a pass receiver. Receptions (**Rec**) counts passes caught, while Passes (**Pass**) counts total passes thrown to this player, complete or incomplete. The next four columns list receiving yards (**Yds**), catch rate (**C%**), yards per catch (**Yd/C**), receiving touchdowns (**TD**), and average yards after the catch (**YAC**).

Our research has shown that receivers bear some responsibility for incomplete passes, even though only their catches are tracked in official statistics. Catch rate represents receptions divided by all intended passes for this running back. The average NFL running back caught 73 percent of passes in 2014. Unfortunately, we don't have room for receiving plus-minus in the running back tables, but you'll find the top 10 and bottom 10 running backs in this metric listed in the statistical appendix.

Finally we have receiving DVOA and DYAR, which are entirely separate from rushing DVOA and DYAR. To qualify for ranking in receiving DVOA and DYAR, a running back must have 25 passes thrown to him in that season. There are 57 running backs ranked for 2014, 49 backs for 2013, and 47 backs for 2012. Numbers without opponent adjustment (YAR, and VOA) can be found on our website, FootballOutsiders.com.

The italicized row of statistics for the 2015 season is our 2015 KUBIAK projection based on a complicated regression analysis that takes into account numerous variables including projected role, performance over the past two years, projected team offense and defense, historical comparables, height, age, experience of the offensive line, and strength of schedule.

It is difficult to accurately project statistics for a 162-game baseball season, but it is exponentially more difficult to ac-

Top 20 RB by Rushing DYAR (Total Value), 2014

Rank	Player	Team	DYAR
1	DeMarco Murray	DAL	382
2	Marshawn Lynch	SEA	359
3	Jamaal Charles	KC	249
4	Lamar Miller	MIA	246
5	Le'Veon Bell	PIT	205
6	Jeremy Hill	CIN	204
7	C.J. Anderson	DEN	196
8	Eddie Lacy	GB	189
9	Arian Foster	HOU	167
10	Frank Gore	SF	154
11	Justin Forsett	BAL	149
12	Matt Forte	CHI	113
13	Rashad Jennings	NYG	112
14	Mark Ingram	NO	108
15	LeSean McCoy	PHI	87
16	Jerick McKinnon	MIN	82
17	Alfred Morris	WAS	77
18	Jonathan Stewart	CAR	72
19	Steven Jackson	ATL	70
20	Matt Asiata	MIN	69

Top 20 RB by Rushing DVOA (Value per Rush), 2014

Rank	Player	Team	DVOA
1	Marshawn Lynch	SEA	23.1%
2	Jamaal Charles	KC	19.9%
3	Lamar Miller	MIA	17.8%
4	C.J. Anderson	DEN	17.5%
5	DeMarco Murray	DAL	14.8%
6	Jeremy Hill	CIN	12.6%
7	Jerick McKinnon	MIN	11.5%
8	Eddie Lacy	GB	9.8%
9	Le'Veon Bell	PIT	8.6%
10	Arian Foster	HOU	7.5%
11	Rashad Jennings	NYG	7.0%
12	Justin Forsett	BAL	6.7%
13	Frank Gore	SF	6.3%
14	Mark Ingram	NO	2.7%
15	LeGarrette Blount	2TM	1.6%
16	Jonathan Stewart	CAR	1.3%
17	Matt Asiata	MIN	1.0%
18	Matt Forte	CHI	0.9%
19	Steven Jackson	ATL	-0.3%
20	Chris Ivory	NYJ	-0.6%

Minimum 100 carries.

Top 10 RB by Receiving DYAR (Total Value), 2014

Rank	Player	Team	DYAR
1	Le'Veon Bell	PIT	316
2	Ahmad Bradshaw	IND	152
3	Matt Forte	CHI	127
4	Eddie Lacy	GB	112
5	Pierre Thomas	NO	111
6	Benny Cunningham	STL	109
7	Roy Helu	WAS	108
8	Bruce Miller	SF	95
9	Marshawn Lynch	SEA	93
10	Damien Williams	MIA	90

Top 10 RB by Receiving DVOA (Value per Pass), 2014

Rank	Player	Team	DVOA
1	Bruce Miller	SF	52.2%
2	Damien Williams	MIA	40.1%
3	Le'Veon Bell	PIT	38.4%
4	Ahmad Bradshaw	IND	38.2%
5	Roy Helu	WAS	31.2%
6	Tre Mason	STL	28.3%
7	Bryce Brown	BUF	28.0%
8	Benny Cunningham	STL	25.7%
9	Eddie Lacy	GB	23.0%
10	Pierre Thomas	NO	22.2%

Minimum 25 passes.

curately project statistics for a 16-game football season. Consider the listed projections not as a prediction of exact numbers, but the mean of a range of possible performances. What's important is less the exact number of yards we project, and more which players are projected to improve or decline. Actual performance will vary from our projection less for veteran starters and more for rookies and third-stringers, for whom we must base our projections on much smaller career statistical samples. Touchdown numbers will vary more than yardage numbers.

There are three metrics tracked by ESPN Stats & Information which you will see mentioned in some player comments. ESPN tracks the number of defenders in the box for each snap, and tags each play as either "loaded" or "not loaded." A loaded box is when the defense has more players in the box than the offense has available blockers for running plays. Some player comments may reference how well a back performed in 2014 against loaded vs. not loaded formations, or how many average men in the box he faced.

ESPN also marks **yards after contact** for each play. In the end, we decided not to include this number in the player tables because most running backs are packed surprisingly close in this metric, and we need to do more research on how much these small differences between running backs matter. However, 2014 saw a bit more spread in yards after contact than in previous seasons. 36 of 43 qualifying running backs fell between 1.3 and 2.2 yards after contact on runs; outliers are highlighted in a table below.

For many rookie running backs, we'll also include statistics from our college football arsenal, notably **POE** (Points Over Expected) and **Highlight Yards**. POE analyzes the output of college football running backs by comparing the expected EqPts value of every carry for a given ballcarrier (based on the quality of the rushing defense against which he's running) to the actual output. A positive POE indicates an above-average runner, with an average runner accruing exactly 0 POE. Highlight Yards are those yards not included in Adjusted Line Yards. So, for example, if a runner gains 12 yards in a given carry, and we attribute 7.0 of those yards to the line (the ALY formula gives the offensive line 100 percent credit for all yards gained between zero and four yards and 50 percent credit between five and 10), then the player's highlight yardage on the play is 5.0 yards. Highlight Yards are shown as an average per opportunity, which means Highlight Yards divided by the total number of carries that went over four yards. For more details on these stats, see the college football section of the book (p. TK).

Finally, in a section we call "Going Deep," we briefly discuss lower-round rookies, free-agent veterans, and practice-squad players who may play a role during the 2015 season or beyond.

Ameer Abdullah

Height: 5-10 Weight: 205 College: Nebraska Draft: 2015/2 (54) Born: 13-Jun-1993 Age: 22 Risk: Yellow

Year	Team	G/GS	Snaps	Runs	Yds	Yd/R	TD	FUM	DVOA	Rk	DYAR	Rk	YAR	Suc%	Rk	BTkl	Rec	Pass	Yds	C%	Yd/C	TD	YAC	DVOA	Rk	DYAR	Rk
2015	DET			146	608	4.2	4	2	2.7%								30	40	280	75%	9.3	1		9.8%			

Abdullah was a top combine performer in just about every drill except the 40-yard dash, where his nondescript 4.60 time portrayed the diminutive back as a Day 3 prospect by our Speed Score metric. However, detractors would point to his three-cone drill (6.79) and short shuttle (3.95) times, each of which topped all running back prospects at Indianapolis and better reflect his elusiveness in tight spaces. Concerns about his body type have been the most common fear surrounding the Nebraska product, but it's hard to ignore a resume that includes nearly 4,000 yards from scrimmage the past two seasons. The Lions will likely bestow Reggie Bush's old passing back role onto Abdullah as he transitions to the pros, but a team can only stomach so many 1-yard Joique Bell carries. While Detroit will drive the Honda Civic as long as it can, the Corvette is coming out of the garage at some point.

Jay Ajayi

Height: 5-10 Weight: 221 College: Boise State Draft: 2015/5 (149) Born: 15-Jun-1993 Age: 22 Risk: Yellow

Year	Team	G/GS	Snaps	Runs	Yds	Yd/R	TD	FUM	DVOA	Rk	DYAR	Rk	YAR	Suc%	Rk	BTkl	Rec	Pass	Yds	C%	Yd/C	TD	YAC	DVOA	Rk	DYAR	Rk
2015	MIA			49	220	4.5	1	1	2.7%								10	12	62	83%	6.2	0		-8.1%			

Miami's fifth-round pick may be the new poster boy for medical disinformation campaigns. It's now been four years since he tore his ACL during Boise State's 2011 season, but a number of media reports before the draft declared that teams had taken Ajayi off their boards because his knee never fully healed. Adam Schefter reported that one team doctor told him Ajayi's knee was "bone on bone." Other reports said he would need microfracture surgery. Was this all real, or a smokescreen where certain teams were trying to keep other teams from drafting Ajayi? If it was a disinformation campaign, you wonder why the teams who apparently wanted the guy so badly let the whole third and fourth rounds go by without selecting him.

Anyway, somebody's loss is Miami's gain. Ajayi is a big back who can move (101.3 Speed Score) and has a nice ability to work out of the backfield as a pass-catcher (50 receptions last season at Boise State). With Miami's reticence to lean too heavily on starter Lamar Miller, who has had more than 20 carries in a game just once in his three-year career, Ajayi could see some quality snaps in 2015.

C.J. Anderson — Height: 5-8   Weight: 224   College: California   Draft: 2013/FA   Born: 2-Feb-1991   Age: 24   Risk: Yellow

Year	Team	G/GS	Snaps	Runs	Yds	Yd/R	TD	FUM	DVOA	Rk	DYAR	Rk	YAR	Suc%	Rk	BTkl	Rec	Pass	Yds	C%	Yd/C	TD	YAC	DVOA	Rk	DYAR	Rk
2013	DEN	5/0	21	7	38	5.4	0	0	53.0%	--	19	--	20	86%	--	1	0	1	0	0%	0.0	0	--	-91.1%	--	-5	--
2014	DEN	15/7	495	179	849	4.7	8	1	17.5%	4	196	7	215	51%	10	46	34	44	324	77%	9.5	2	8.3	13.0%	14	65	13
2015	DEN			254	1105	4.4	10	3	9.6%								48	63	433	76%	9.0	2		24.0%			

That Montee Ball breakout year we gushed about last season? We're much more confident C.J. Anderson will deliver this year as Denver's featured back. He already kind of broke out in the second half of 2014. Denver finally gave him a shot in situations that weren't garbage time, and he displayed some impressive vision and tackle-breaking skills on a 51-yard touchdown catch against Oakland. That play was one of the highlights of the year, but Anderson had another miraculous effort on a fourth-and-1 against the Colts in the playoffs. Not getting much blocking from his line that day, Anderson had to break multiple tackles in the backfield for a big conversion. He's a tough runner and decent enough in receiving and pass protection to play every down. Our projection system is trying to stay calm over an undrafted player having a hot half season, but when you consider the success backs have had in Kubiak's system going back to the Terrell Davis days, that forecast might be a bit low. The offensive line be damned, Anderson is the best back on the roster when it comes to creating his own yardage.

Cameron Artis-Payne — Height: 5-10   Weight: 212   College: Auburn   Draft: 2015/5 (174)   Born: 23-Jun-1992   Age: 23   Risk: Red

Year	Team	G/GS	Snaps	Runs	Yds	Yd/R	TD	FUM	DVOA	Rk	DYAR	Rk	YAR	Suc%	Rk	BTkl	Rec	Pass	Yds	C%	Yd/C	TD	YAC	DVOA	Rk	DYAR	Rk
2015	CAR			62	285	4.6	2	2	4.1%								15	18	100	83%	6.6	0		-5.1%			

Panthers general manager Dave Gettleman described Artis-Payne as a "good tackle box runner" on Panthers.com, while also praising his off-field character. It's true that Artis-Payne overcame a lot to get to the NFL, a journey that took him from a minimum-wage job at the age of 20 to a California junior college and then Auburn. It's also true that there's not much physical upside here. The best-case scenario is that Artis-Payne becomes a bowling ball at the goal line, because his Auburn tape showed a player who may need a year or two before he's ready to play on passing downs. Nonetheless, it looks like the Panthers are ready to make him Jonathan Stewart's main backup despite a number of veterans (Jordan Todman, Fozzy Whittaker) taking up space on a messy Carolina depth chart.

Matt Asiata — Height: 5-11   Weight: 220   College: Utah   Draft: 2011/FA   Born: 24-Jul-1987   Age: 28   Risk: Green

Year	Team	G/GS	Snaps	Runs	Yds	Yd/R	TD	FUM	DVOA	Rk	DYAR	Rk	YAR	Suc%	Rk	BTkl	Rec	Pass	Yds	C%	Yd/C	TD	YAC	DVOA	Rk	DYAR	Rk
2013	MIN	11/1	117	44	166	3.8	3	1	12.9%	--	41	--	24	55%	--	3	5	8	13	63%	2.6	0	4.4	-67.7%	--	-26	--
2014	MIN	15/9	524	164	570	3.5	9	1	1.0%	17	69	20	75	52%	6	10	44	63	312	70%	7.1	1	7.7	-23.9%	48	-33	48
2015	MIN			34	122	3.6	0	1	-11.4%								10	13	81	77%	8.1	0		6.9%			

From the 5-yard line and closer, Asiata received 17 carries and scored seven times. Only DeMarco Murray and Mark Ingram received more goal-line carries, and Murray was the only player to eclipse that touchdown total. Asiata demonstrated similar promise in limited 2013 snaps, scoring on three out of five goal-line carries and posting a 62.1% DVOA in the red zone. The 3.5 career yards per attempt mark is probably more indicative of Asiata's true talent level. With Adrian Peterson back and Jerrick McKinnon earning the backup job with last year's promise, we assume that Asiata will turn back into a pumpkin—or a fullback and frustrating goal-line vulture.

Vick Ballard — Height: 5-10   Weight: 219   College: Mississippi State   Draft: 2012/5 (170)   Born: 16-Jul-1990   Age: 25   Risk: Red

Year	Team	G/GS	Snaps	Runs	Yds	Yd/R	TD	FUM	DVOA	Rk	DYAR	Rk	YAR	Suc%	Rk	BTkl	Rec	Pass	Yds	C%	Yd/C	TD	YAC	DVOA	Rk	DYAR	Rk
2012	IND	16/12	579	211	814	3.9	2	3	-7.4%	27	10	27	-10	48%	18	22	17	27	152	63%	8.9	1	6.9	10.7%	15	38	24
2013	IND	1/1	39	13	63	4.8	0	0	34.3%	--	22	--	18	46%	--	0	1	2	-5	50%	-5.0	0	-1.0	-131.0%	--	-18	--
2015	IND			52	214	4.1	1	2	-1.8%								6	8	67	75%	11.2	0		24.5%			

Ballard has the only 100-yard rushing performance for the Colts since 2012. After his promising rookie year, Ballard tore his ACL in the 2013 season opener. Last July he tore his Achilles tendon in training camp, missing yet another full season. What makes those injuries even worse is that they fueled the Trent Richardson trade and then subjected us to watching more T-Rich last year. Ballard won't be the lead back with Frank Gore in town, but hopefully he can stay healthy and resume his playing career with the Colts.

Montee Ball   Height: 5-10   Weight: 214   College: Wisconsin   Draft: 2013/2 (58)   Born: 5-Dec-1990   Age: 25   Risk: Green

Year	Team	G/GS	Snaps	Runs	Yds	Yd/R	TD	FUM	DVOA	Rk	DYAR	Rk	YAR	Suc%	Rk	BTkl	Rec	Pass	Yds	C%	Yd/C	TD	YAC	DVOA	Rk	DYAR	Rk
2013	DEN	16/0	312	120	559	4.7	4	3	7.5%	14	86	21	89	54%	4	12	20	27	145	74%	7.3	0	7.0	-18.3%	41	-7	40
2014	DEN	5/3	191	55	172	3.1	1	1	-20.2%	--	-26	--	-30	44%	--	7	9	13	62	69%	6.9	0	5.8	-19.7%	--	-4	--
2015	DEN			81	337	4.2	2	4	-0.3%							11	14	88	79%	8.0	0		6.9%			

It was the breakout season that only made you want to break things if you were a Denver fan or took Ball in your fantasy draft. Not only did injuries cost him 11 games, but he just never looked the part of a featured back in 2014. The most telling game came against Arizona, when Ball had six carries for seven yards before leaving with an injury. In the second half, Denver's other backs carried 17 times for 80 yards. Ball never touched the ball the rest of the season. He's clearly behind C.J. Anderson on the depth chart now, and he should have to prove his value over Ronnie Hillman for the lead backup role.

Joique Bell   Height: 5-11   Weight: 220   College: Wayne State   Draft: 2010/FA   Born: 4-Aug-1986   Age: 29   Risk: Yellow

Year	Team	G/GS	Snaps	Runs	Yds	Yd/R	TD	FUM	DVOA	Rk	DYAR	Rk	YAR	Suc%	Rk	BTkl	Rec	Pass	Yds	C%	Yd/C	TD	YAC	DVOA	Rk	DYAR	Rk
2012	DET	16/0	381	82	414	5.0	3	1	12.6%	--	71	--	65	54%	--	20	52	69	485	75%	9.3	0	8.3	32.8%	3	193	2
2013	DET	16/4	547	166	650	3.9	8	4	2.0%	20	78	24	75	51%	10	24	53	69	547	77%	10.3	0	10.3	40.3%	3	196	2
2014	DET	15/6	615	223	860	3.9	7	5	-14.9%	38	-59	42	-19	45%	23	24	34	52	322	65%	9.5	1	9.9	6.2%	17	54	18
2015	DET			182	748	4.1	6	3	0.9%							29	42	184	69%	6.3	1		-14.1%			

It only feels like every other Lions offensive play last year was a 1-yard Joique Bell run. No, really. Bell had 35 carries last season that went for exactly 1 yard, fifth-most in the league and 15.1 percent of Bell's total carries for the season. Needless to say, 2014 was a disappointing step backwards for the former Harlon Hill Trophy winner. Ball security is Bell's most pressing issue at the moment, as his nine fumbles over the past two seasons are the most among all running backs in that span. We certainly can't blame degree of difficulty for Bell's struggles, as he faced a loaded box on just 6 percent of carries, tied with Steven Jackson for the lowest percentage among running backs with over 100 carries. And yet, Bell's -15.8% DVOA against non-loaded boxes was the second-worst in the league, bettering only Alfred Blue. Bell did look more spry at the end of the season—he averaged 4.51 yards per carry over Detroit's last four games, including the wild-card loss—so hopefully the concussion and ankle woes he dealt with were the real culprits behind his malaise. Otherwise, he's going to lose his starting job to Ameer Abdullah.

Le'Veon Bell   Height: 6-1   Weight: 230   College: Michigan State   Draft: 2013/2 (48)   Born: 18-Feb-1992   Age: 23   Risk: Yellow

Year	Team	G/GS	Snaps	Runs	Yds	Yd/R	TD	FUM	DVOA	Rk	DYAR	Rk	YAR	Suc%	Rk	BTkl	Rec	Pass	Yds	C%	Yd/C	TD	YAC	DVOA	Rk	DYAR	Rk
2013	PIT	13/13	677	244	860	3.5	8	1	-7.0%	28	17	28	15	47%	23	21	45	65	399	68%	8.9	0	10.0	-5.9%	30	28	28
2014	PIT	16/16	927	290	1361	4.7	8	0	8.6%	9	205	5	283	51%	9	59	83	105	854	79%	10.3	3	9.8	38.4%	3	316	1
2015	PIT			249	1122	4.5	9	2	11.3%							60	86	536	70%	8.9	2		11.9%			

Post-draft development is a concept not typically associated with running backs, but when it is mentioned, it usually concerns weight loss. That was the case for Le'Veon Bell after his rookie season. Bell was a big back in 2013 with impressive quickness and balance to create yardage both between the tackles and outside the edge. In 2014, he was still big, but no longer heavy. He was able to sustain the power he showed off as a rookie while adding more explosiveness in space and elusiveness in tight quarters.

Bell's broken tackles went way up in 2014, even accounting for the overall rise in our broken tackle numbers. (While the league-wide rate in broken tackles per touch went up by about 25 percent, Bell's rate doubled.) Breaking those tackles gave him more opportunities to show off his revitalized athleticism. After averaging 1.6 yards after contact in 2013, he improved by 0.5 yards per carry in 2014. Bell's elusiveness and explosiveness also played a key role in making him the definitive best receiving back in the NFL last year. He also lined up wide or in the slot more often than any back in the game.

The only negative hanging over Bell entering the 2014 season is his impending three-game suspension for a DUI. We're expecting that suspension to be at least somewhat reduced on appeal, and the projection above is for 14 games.

Giovani Bernard

Height: 5-8   Weight: 202   College: North Carolina   Draft: 2013/2 (37)   Born: 22-Nov-1991   Age: 24   Risk: Green

Year	Team	G/GS	Snaps	Runs	Yds	Yd/R	TD	FUM	DVOA	Rk	DYAR	Rk	YAR	Suc%	Rk	BTkl	Rec	Pass	Yds	C%	Yd/C	TD	YAC	DVOA	Rk	DYAR	Rk
2013	CIN	16/0	614	170	695	4.1	5	1	-4.5%	27	28	27	69	48%	21	28	56	71	514	79%	9.2	3	9.4	29.4%	5	167	5
2014	CIN	13/9	509	168	680	4.0	5	0	-8.1%	32	3	32	8	39%	38	19	43	59	349	73%	8.1	2	8.4	0.8%	22	48	21
2015	CIN			108	475	4.4	1	2	-0.7%								60	74	457	81%	7.6	1		9.9%			

Nagging injuries and the emergence of Jeremy Hill caused Bernard's sophomore slump. His decline in receiving stats is particularly worrisome. Opposing defenses keyed on Gio's forays out of the backfield, causing him to absorb some hellacious shots in addition to the regression in his numbers. Injuries elsewhere on the offense played a role in this; in some games Bernard was essentially the Bengals' No. 2 receiver.

2014 determined officially that Bernard, despite his toughness, is not equipped to be an every-down back. He is meant to be Darren Sproles, and the Bengals should deploy him as such. With Hill taking the brunt of the workload, and a full complement of receiving threats returning to the offense, Bernard should have more room to operate in space, where he remains extremely elusive.

LeGarrette Blount

Height: 6-0   Weight: 247   College: Oregon   Draft: 2010/FA   Born: 5-Dec-1986   Age: 29   Risk: Yellow

Year	Team	G/GS	Snaps	Runs	Yds	Yd/R	TD	FUM	DVOA	Rk	DYAR	Rk	YAR	Suc%	Rk	BTkl	Rec	Pass	Yds	C%	Yd/C	TD	YAC	DVOA	Rk	DYAR	Rk
2012	TB	13/0	92	41	151	3.7	2	0	-9.5%	--	-2	--	2	37%	--	2	1	2	2	50%	2.0	0	7.0	-102.8%	--	-11	--
2013	NE	16/7	286	153	772	5.0	7	3	9.4%	10	117	16	131	54%	3	17	2	5	38	40%	19.0	0	20.5	-5.0%	--	3	--
2014	2TM	16/1	231	125	547	4.4	5	1	1.6%	15	56	22	54	46%	19	14	10	12	54	83%	5.4	0	6.1	-15.3%	--	-1	--
2015	NE			157	789	5.0	7	2	20.4%								24	32	168	75%	7.0	1		12.5%			

Last season, Blount did poorly with the Steelers, accumulating a -10.1% DVOA on his 65 carries over the first ten weeks. It got worse towards the end. From Weeks 5-10, Blount averaged just 2.5 yards per carry and had a -36.9% DVOA. Cutting him at the first sign of discontent seemed to have little downside.

As in 2013, however, a move to Foxborough reinvigorated Blount. He ran for 78 yards on 12 carries against the Lions' top-ranked run defense in his first game with the Patriots. Over the last five weeks, he rang up a 15.2% DVOA and 4.7 yards per carry. As the likely Week 2 starter—not Week 1 starter, because he'll be serving a one-game suspension for a marijuana arrest—Blount is a bargain with a $1 million cap hit.

Alfred Blue

Height: 6-2   Weight: 223   College: Louisiana St.   Draft: 2014/6 (181)   Born: 27-Apr-1991   Age: 24   Risk: Green

Year	Team	G/GS	Snaps	Runs	Yds	Yd/R	TD	FUM	DVOA	Rk	DYAR	Rk	YAR	Suc%	Rk	BTkl	Rec	Pass	Yds	C%	Yd/C	TD	YAC	DVOA	Rk	DYAR	Rk
2014	HOU	16/3	336	169	528	3.1	2	0	-21.3%	43	-88	43	-60	39%	36	6	15	18	113	83%	7.5	1	5.0	25.4%	--	41	--
2015	HOU			56	203	3.6	0	1	-9.7%								21	30	137	70%	6.5	0		-5.1%			

Blue finished last among all running backs in DYAR and DVOA, which is about what you'd expect from an unheralded back with a tendency to close his eyes and let his physicality do the talking. Blue is a willing special-teamer, and isn't too poor as a blocker, but it will take some offseason improvement for him to fend off Chris Polk for the No. 2 running back slot in Houston.

Brandon Bolden

Height: 5-11   Weight: 220   College: Mississippi   Draft: 2012/FA   Born: 26-Jan-1990   Age: 25   Risk: Green

Year	Team	G/GS	Snaps	Runs	Yds	Yd/R	TD	FUM	DVOA	Rk	DYAR	Rk	YAR	Suc%	Rk	BTkl	Rec	Pass	Yds	C%	Yd/C	TD	YAC	DVOA	Rk	DYAR	Rk
2012	NE	10/0	99	56	274	4.9	2	0	12.8%	--	53	--	54	54%	--	5	2	2	11	100%	5.5	0	5.0	6.3%	--	2	--
2013	NE	12/2	266	55	271	4.9	3	0	13.1%	--	54	--	54	49%	--	5	21	29	152	72%	7.2	0	7.6	-14.6%	37	-1	37
2014	NE	16/2	72	28	89	3.2	1	0	-11.2%	--	-3	--	-6	43%	--	3	2	6	8	33%	4.0	0	5.5	-81.7%	--	-26	--
2015	NE			30	132	4.4	0	1	3.9%								10	14	89	71%	8.9	0		8.9%			

Bolden provided most of his value on special teams in 2014, posting six tackles, two forced fumbles, and a blocked punt against the Chargers. As a runner, there is little reason to think that Bolden is the back who posted such poor numbers in a small sample in 2014. In his first three years, Bolden averaged 4.6 yards per carry on 134 attempts, running mostly in favorable situations. Since the Patriots only run in favorable situations, Bolden could probably play Jonas Gray for a day if needed. Of course, the Patriots have as many people who could fill that role as the Republican party has presidential candidates.

Ahmad Bradshaw

Height: 5-11 Weight: 195 College: Marshall Draft: 2007/7 (250) Born: 19-Mar-1986 Age: 29 Risk: N/A

Year	Team	G/GS	Snaps	Runs	Yds	Yd/R	TD	FUM	DVOA	Rk	DYAR	Rk	YAR	Suc%	Rk	BTkl	Rec	Pass	Yds	C%	Yd/C	TD	YAC	DVOA	Rk	DYAR	Rk
2012	NYG	14/12	598	221	1015	4.6	6	3	15.8%	5	230	6	194	52%	8	14	23	31	245	74%	10.7	0	11.9	8.5%	18	35	25
2013	IND	3/2	102	41	186	4.5	2	0	9.3%	--	33	--	47	54%	--	3	7	8	42	88%	6.0	0	5.6	8.6%	--	10	--
2014	IND	10/1	382	90	425	4.7	2	3	-1.8%	--	26	--	28	54%	--	33	38	47	300	81%	7.9	6	8.8	38.2%	4	152	2

Before coming to Indianapolis, where even the most durable players go down with injuries, Bradshaw played at least 12 games every year. He was limited to three games in 2013 and 10 games last year before breaking his leg. That one especially hurt because, as usual, a healthy Bradshaw was an effective Bradshaw. He even had six touchdown catches and was eyeing the single-season record for a running back. Now he's 29 and unemployed, and whenever he is eventually signed by someone, he will have to serve a one-game suspension for marijuana possession. The league's just not taking many chances on older backs these days, though we may not have seen the last of Bradshaw in the NFL just yet.

Bryce Brown

Height: 6-0 Weight: 220 College: Kansas State Draft: 2012/7 (229) Born: 14-May-1991 Age: 24 Risk: Green

Year	Team	G/GS	Snaps	Runs	Yds	Yd/R	TD	FUM	DVOA	Rk	DYAR	Rk	YAR	Suc%	Rk	BTkl	Rec	Pass	Yds	C%	Yd/C	TD	YAC	DVOA	Rk	DYAR	Rk
2012	PHI	16/4	334	115	564	4.9	4	4	-2.2%	23	29	24	29	39%	39	17	13	19	56	68%	4.3	0	7.0	-38.9%	--	-26	--
2013	PHI	16/1	194	75	314	4.2	2	0	-1.2%	--	23	--	12	48%	--	10	8	13	84	62%	10.5	0	11.8	8.7%	--	12	--
2014	BUF	7/2	118	36	126	3.5	0	1	-22.9%	--	-21	--	-25	50%	--	7	16	25	176	64%	11.0	0	11.1	28.0%	7	55	16
2015	BUF			13	53	4.1	1	1	5.4%								7	10	53	70%	7.5	0		-3.0%			

In the movie version of the Bills' season, Brown would have to carry around a football while we went to the library for Halle Berry-led tutoring sessions. In an ominous sign for Brown's roster hopes, Rex Ryan has said that "I'm not gonna learn his name until he holds on to the football." Brown's butterfingered reputation is not entirely deserved. After fumbling four times in just 115 carries as a rookie in 2012 (the highest rate for any running back with at least 100 attempts), Brown has fumbled only once in 111 carries over the last two seasons. Alas, that error that stood out, as it helped cost the Bills a Week 9 game against the Chiefs last year. Brown's bigger problem is declining effectiveness as he has increased his ball security. His average has fallen by more than half a yard each of the last two seasons.

Donald Brown

Height: 5-11 Weight: 210 College: Connecticut Draft: 2009/1 (27) Born: 11-Apr-1987 Age: 28 Risk: Green

Year	Team	G/GS	Snaps	Runs	Yds	Yd/R	TD	FUM	DVOA	Rk	DYAR	Rk	YAR	Suc%	Rk	BTkl	Rec	Pass	Yds	C%	Yd/C	TD	YAC	DVOA	Rk	DYAR	Rk
2012	IND	10/4	299	108	417	3.9	1	0	-9.8%	31	-5	31	-5	44%	30	5	9	13	93	69%	10.3	0	11.0	0.9%	--	11	--
2013	IND	16/5	373	102	537	5.3	6	0	19.2%	2	117	14	122	54%	2	17	27	36	214	78%	7.9	2	8.8	6.2%	19	44	22
2014	SD	13/3	358	85	223	2.6	0	1	-23.9%	--	-51	--	-74	30%	--	9	29	42	211	71%	7.3	0	9.8	-23.7%	47	-22	47
2015	SD			40	153	3.8	1	2	-1.1%								17	23	158	74%	9.3	1		10.9%			

San Diego running back coach Ollie Wilson has been working with Brown to get better at making defenders miss after such a disappointing 2014 season. "If you don't rep the situations, then you don't get better at it. So we're going to put him in those situations," Wilson told ESPN. That's great, but in which situations will Brown see the field? He's arguably the fourth-best running back on the team. Melvin Gordon will take the majority of the carries, Danny Woodhead is better as a receiver and pass protector, and Branden Oliver outplayed Brown last season. This might be a situation where money dictates playing time, which is why you have to avoid bad contracts in the first place. Brown's cap hit is more than $4 million this season, yet he's suited for a role you can pay an undrafted rookie the league minimum to perform. Goddammit, Donald.

Reggie Bush

Height: 6-0 Weight: 200 College: USC Draft: 2006/1 (2) Born: 2-Mar-1985 Age: 30 Risk: Green

Year	Team	G/GS	Snaps	Runs	Yds	Yd/R	TD	FUM	DVOA	Rk	DYAR	Rk	YAR	Suc%	Rk	BTkl	Rec	Pass	Yds	C%	Yd/C	TD	YAC	DVOA	Rk	DYAR	Rk
2012	MIA	16/16	572	227	986	4.3	6	4	-8.3%	30	3	30	18	51%	10	24	35	51	292	69%	8.3	2	7.8	7.9%	19	54	17
2013	DET	14/14	610	223	1006	4.5	4	5	-7.8%	32	7	29	38	47%	24	22	54	80	506	68%	9.4	3	8.7	5.8%	20	94	13
2014	DET	11/9	277	76	297	3.9	2	0	-2.4%	--	17	--	24	43%	--	11	40	57	253	72%	6.3	0	6.5	-19.6%	45	-18	45
2015	SF			97	379	3.9	2	1	-4.5%								32	47	258	68%	8.1	1		-5.0%			

After setting a career-high in yards from scrimmage during his first Lions campaign, Bush slumped to his worst season since he last dated a Kardashian. Ankle woes plagued Bush the entire season and robbed him of the agility and speed so crucial to his game. Like his backfield mate Joique Bell, Bush was strangely poor against non-loaded boxes, with a wretched -15.1% DVOA that would hint at his reduced elusiveness. Jim Tomsula has insisted that Bush will receive snaps in San Francisco, as the 30-year-old is quite stylistically distinct from Carlos Hyde, Kendall Hunter, and Mike Davis. Still, Bush is going from one quarterback with notorious touch issues to another, so offseason optimism could go the way of his Heisman Trophy come the regular season.

Travaris Cadet   Height: 6-1   Weight: 210   College: Appalachian State   Draft: 2012/FA   Born: 1-Feb-1989   Age: 26   Risk: Red

Year	Team	G/GS	Snaps	Runs	Yds	Yd/R	TD	FUM	DVOA	Rk	DYAR	Rk	YAR	Suc%	Rk	BTkl	Rec	Pass	Yds	C%	Yd/C	TD	YAC	DVOA	Rk	DYAR	Rk
2012	NO	13/0	28	1	5	5.0	0	0	45.0%	--	2	--	2	100%	--	1	5	8	44	63%	8.8	0	10.8	4.9%	--	8	--
2013	NO	13/0	11	0	0	0.0	0	--	--	--	--	--	--	--	--	--	2	2	5	100%	2.5	1	3.0	76.1%	--	11	--
2014	NO	15/1	205	10	32	3.2	0	2	-55.8%	--	-18	--	-16	50%	--	0	38	51	296	75%	7.8	1	6.4	5.4%	18	57	15
2015	NE			13	58	4.4	0	1	6.7%								30	39	221	77%	7.4	1		1.7%			

Even though he is listed as a running back, Travaris Cadet essentially has the skill set of a wide receiver. That is how the Saints used him in 2014. Only 11 of Cadet's 38 receptions last year came on screen plays. For a running back, he ran an abnormal number of routes downfield and into both flats. The Saints didn't let Cadet run the ball, and they were right not to. If the Patriots are expecting him to replace exactly what Shane Vereen brought to their offense, they are likely to be disappointed. Vereen was a much more physically gifted athlete.

Top 10 Running Backs Lined up as Wide Receivers, 2014

Player	Team	Wide	Slot	Both	Snaps	Pct
Le'Veon Bell	PIT	36	80	116	927	13%
Marcel Reece	OAK	34	71	105	385	27%
Shane Vereen	NE	53	26	79	595	13%
Arian Foster	HOU	34	41	75	621	12%
Kyle Juszczyk	BAL	48	25	73	454	16%
Andre Ellington	ARI	32	25	57	528	11%
Travaris Cadet	NO	37	20	57	205	28%
Dexter McCluster	TEN	23	23	46	233	20%
Reggie Bush	DET	15	29	44	277	16%
Marshawn Lynch	SEA	35	9	44	704	6%

Ka'Deem Carey   Height: 5-9   Weight: 207   College: Arizona   Draft: 2014/4 (117)   Born: 30-Oct-1992   Age: 23   Risk: Green

Year	Team	G/GS	Snaps	Runs	Yds	Yd/R	TD	FUM	DVOA	Rk	DYAR	Rk	YAR	Suc%	Rk	BTkl	Rec	Pass	Yds	C%	Yd/C	TD	YAC	DVOA	Rk	DYAR	Rk
2014	CHI	14/0	98	36	158	4.4	0	0	21.2%	--	47	--	48	53%	--	8	5	6	57	83%	11.4	0	8.6	43.5%	--	17	--
2015	CHI			60	213	3.6	1	2	-15.0%								8	10	50	80%	6.3	0		-2.4%			

Carey seemed like a great fit with Matt Forte, thanks to a similar build and skills. Once the regular season began, though, the significant quality difference between a veteran like Forte and a rookie became apparent. Carey struggled on passing downs, though at least he ran better than was suggested by his horrid 84.8 Speed Score. He will have to show his worth to a new regime, or else will lose playing time to rookie Jeremy Langford or veterans Jacquizz Rodgers and Daniel Thomas.

Jamaal Charles   Height: 5-11   Weight: 200   College: Texas   Draft: 2008/3 (73)   Born: 27-Dec-1986   Age: 29   Risk: Green

Year	Team	G/GS	Snaps	Runs	Yds	Yd/R	TD	FUM	DVOA	Rk	DYAR	Rk	YAR	Suc%	Rk	BTkl	Rec	Pass	Yds	C%	Yd/C	TD	YAC	DVOA	Rk	DYAR	Rk
2012	KC	16/15	577	285	1509	5.3	5	5	1.4%	17	109	12	158	46%	29	16	35	49	236	73%	6.7	1	7.3	-13.8%	32	0	32
2013	KC	15/15	845	259	1287	5.0	12	4	13.7%	7	247	3	258	51%	11	39	70	104	693	67%	9.9	7	9.4	8.5%	17	135	8
2014	KC	15/15	650	206	1033	5.0	9	5	19.9%	2	249	3	212	54%	2	30	40	60	291	68%	7.3	5	7.7	-13.5%	39	1	39
2015	KC			229	1121	4.9	10	4	13.9%								57	75	419	76%	7.4	2		3.4%			

The fact that the Chiefs have replaced four of the five starters on the offensive line for the second year in a row won't bother Charles one bit. Every season of his career he has averaged at least 5.0 yards per carry, and his 5.5 career average is the best in NFL history for a running back (minimum 750 rushes). While he won't win over any purists with his speed-based game, Charles has truly had a historic career in an era where the quarterback is king. He doesn't turn 29 until two days after Christmas and he has yet to log 300 carries in any season, so he's a bit fresher than most backs are at this stage of their careers. Andy Reid and Alex Smith are a perfect fit for Charles' talents as a dual-threat back, and he has scored 12 receiving touchdowns the last two years. He didn't have to do as much as a receiver last year, but it's certainly part of his skill set.

David Cobb   Height: 5-10   Weight: 229   College: Minnesota   Draft: 2015/5 (138)   Born: 3-Jun-1993   Age: 22   Risk: Yellow

Year	Team	G/GS	Snaps	Runs	Yds	Yd/R	TD	FUM	DVOA	Rk	DYAR	Rk	YAR	Suc%	Rk	BTkl	Rec	Pass	Yds	C%	Yd/C	TD	YAC	DVOA	Rk	DYAR	Rk
2015	TEN		119	431	3.6	3	2	-8.0%									22	31	164	71%	7.5	1		-5.9%			

The mainstay of the Minnesota Gophers' offense with over 1600 yards his final season, Cobb will compete for the power-back committee job formerly held by the released Shonn Greene. Despite averaging 4.6 highlight yards per opportunity, he lacks real breakaway speed. That likely limits his overall upside to a committee role. Tennessee's running back situation seems fluid enough that Cobb could win that opportunity right from the start in 2015, but a hamstring injury limited his offseason work.

Tevin Coleman   Height: 5-10   Weight: 206   College: Indiana   Draft: 2015/3 (73)   Born: 16-Apr-1993   Age: 22   Risk: Yellow

Year	Team	G/GS	Snaps	Runs	Yds	Yd/R	TD	FUM	DVOA	Rk	DYAR	Rk	YAR	Suc%	Rk	BTkl	Rec	Pass	Yds	C%	Yd/C	TD	YAC	DVOA	Rk	DYAR	Rk
2015	ATL		160	641	4.0	5	2	-1.8%									33	40	191	83%	5.8	1		-11.6%			

It was an extremely curious fit that saw the Falcons tab Coleman to play in offensive coordinator Kyle Shanahan's zone-based scheme, because his patience on inside zone plays was perhaps his biggest bugaboo coming out of Indiana. If Coleman actually is able to vary his pace and read the blocks well, he's got home-run speed. Coleman ran a 4.39 40-yard dash at his pro day that more than shows up on the field. He's clearly the player the current coaching staff have the most invested in. However, given his inability to absorb contact well at Indiana, our Ouija board narrative believes he'll start slowly and look to gain control of the starting job as the year proceeds.

Isaiah Crowell   Height: 5-11   Weight: 225   College: Alabama State   Draft: 2014/FA   Born: 8-Jan-1993   Age: 22   Risk: Green

Year	Team	G/GS	Snaps	Runs	Yds	Yd/R	TD	FUM	DVOA	Rk	DYAR	Rk	YAR	Suc%	Rk	BTkl	Rec	Pass	Yds	C%	Yd/C	TD	YAC	DVOA	Rk	DYAR	Rk
2014	CLE	16/4	382	148	607	4.1	8	3	-3.6%	25	30	25	43	44%	28	6	9	14	87	64%	9.7	0	7.6	-3.6%	--	8	--
2015	CLE			169	676	4.0	6	3	-4.4%								18	27	133	67%	7.4	0		-11.0%			

Crowell went undrafted in 2014, but that was because of concerns over his character, not the caliber of his talent. He was always considered one of the more talented runners from his class, and he backed that up once he stepped onto an NFL field. He fit perfectly behind the zone-blocking that the Browns offensive line relied on so heavily. His ability to anticipate and set up running lanes allowed him to be dangerous to every area of the field. Crowell isn't a big back, but he is compact and powerful with an aggressive running style that allows him to punish bigger defenders. His vision and overall quickness should keep him ahead of Terrance West on the depth chart, but he could lose a significant number of snaps due to Duke Johnson's value in the passing game.

Benny Cunningham   Height: 5-10   Weight: 217   College: Middle Tennessee State   Draft: 2013/FA   Born: 7-Jul-1990   Age: 25   Risk: Blue

Year	Team	G/GS	Snaps	Runs	Yds	Yd/R	TD	FUM	DVOA	Rk	DYAR	Rk	YAR	Suc%	Rk	BTkl	Rec	Pass	Yds	C%	Yd/C	TD	YAC	DVOA	Rk	DYAR	Rk
2013	STL	14/0	138	47	261	5.6	1	2	-5.7%	--	5	--	20	45%	--	6	6	10	59	60%	9.8	0	10.2	3.6%	--	8	--
2014	STL	16/2	396	66	246	3.7	3	1	1.7%	--	26	--	7	38%	--	12	45	53	352	85%	7.8	1	7.0	25.7%	8	109	6
2015	STL			65	251	3.9	1	3	-8.2%								50	69	347	72%	7.0	1		-2.5%			

Cunningham is just the third runner in our database (and the first this century) to have a positive DVOA on at least 50 carries while averaging less that 4.0 yards per rush with a success rate below 40 percent. (The others were Ki-Jana Carter in 1996 and Rashaan Shehee in 1999.) He pulled that off by playing great inside scoring range, with a 41.0% DVOA and three touchdowns in 15 carries inside the opposing 40. His DVOA in the rest of the field was just -15.0%.

Cunningham was just average at rushing and kick returns last season, but he was an outstanding receiver, putting up at least 20 receiving yards eight times. Those weren't just easy dumpoffs at the end of blowouts, either. He had 46 yards receiving in the win over Seattle, 38 in the win over San Francisco, and 31 in the win over Denver, catching each of the 12 passes thrown his way in those three games. Obviously Cunningham will be the third runner this year behind Todd Gurley and Tre Mason, but that receiving ability means he might be worth a flyer in PPR leagues.

Knile Davis					Height: 5-11			Weight: 227		College: Arkansas				Draft: 2013/3 (95)			Born: 5-Oct-1991		Age: 24		Risk: Green	
Year	Team	G/GS	Snaps	Runs	Yds	Yd/R	TD	FUM	DVOA	Rk	DYAR	Rk	YAR	Suc%	Rk	BTkl	Rec	Pass	Yds	C%	Yd/C	TD	YAC	DVOA	Rk	DYAR	Rk
2013	KC	16/1	170	70	242	3.5	4	2	-19.4%	--	-29	--	-15	34%	--	7	11	15	75	73%	6.8	0	8.3	-27.0%	--	-11	--
2014	KC	16/1	304	134	463	3.5	6	4	-17.7%	42	-50	40	-70	37%	41	13	16	25	147	64%	9.2	1	9.8	-17.2%	42	-4	42
2015	KC			104	448	4.3	6	3	6.2%								24	35	182	69%	7.6	0		-4.6%			

Davis has been an explosive kick returner (29.5 yards per return), but only averages 3.5 yards per carry. There's some disconnect here, as Davis' tape seems to be better than his stats. It's not like he's dragging down his average with lots of short-yardage runs, because his success rate has also been poor the last two years. And it's not like defenses are defending Davis differently than they defend Jamaal Charles. Last year, 13 percent of Davis' runs came against a loaded box (more defenders than blockers) compared to 12 percent for Charles. The difference is that Davis has been very poor the last two years when facing a loaded box, posting a -60.5% DVOA in 2014 and -52.3% DVOA in 2013. Still, if Charles went down with an injury, the Chiefs wouldn't panic too much with Davis filling in like he did in that playoff game in Indianapolis, or when Davis scored two touchdowns in Denver last year and rushed for 132 yards in Miami. He has already had some good moments for a young backup.

Mike Davis					Height: 5-10			Weight: 217		College: South Carolina				Draft: 2015/4 (126)			Born: 19-Feb-1993		Age: 22		Risk: Blue	
Year	Team	G/GS	Snaps	Runs	Yds	Yd/R	TD	FUM	DVOA	Rk	DYAR	Rk	YAR	Suc%	Rk	BTkl	Rec	Pass	Yds	C%	Yd/C	TD	YAC	DVOA	Rk	DYAR	Rk
2015	SF			44	192	4.3	0	2	-3.9%								6	9	40	67%	6.7	0		-17.6%			

The 49ers just can't resist drafting running backs. They took Davis out of South Carolina in the fourth round this year, even with question marks elsewhere and plenty of depth at the position. It's the seventh straight year the 49ers drafted a running back. Davis was a much better player in 2013 (1,183 rushing yards, 40 percent opportunity rate, 6.3 highlight yards per opportunity) than he was in 2014 (982, 39 percent, 4.1), but that may be because the Gamecocks declined overall, dropping from 11-2 to 7-6.

Anthony Dixon					Height: 6-1			Weight: 233		College: Mississippi State				Draft: 2010/6 (173)			Born: 24-Sep-1987		Age: 28		Risk: Red	
Year	Team	G/GS	Snaps	Runs	Yds	Yd/R	TD	FUM	DVOA	Rk	DYAR	Rk	YAR	Suc%	Rk	BTkl	Rec	Pass	Yds	C%	Yd/C	TD	YAC	DVOA	Rk	DYAR	Rk
2012	SF	16/0	32	21	78	3.7	2	0	15.9%	--	23	--	24	67%	--	0	0	--	0	--	0.0	0	--	--	--	--	--
2013	SF	16/1	79	28	56	2.0	2	0	-17.5%	--	-13	--	-31	39%	--	1	3	3	30	100%	10.0	0	9.3	71.1%	--	14	--
2014	BUF	16/0	219	105	432	4.1	2	1	-7.7%	31	4	31	19	49%	14	13	8	9	49	89%	6.1	0	5.5	2.5%	--	8	--
2015	BUF			42	124	2.9	1	2	-21.6%								6	9	31	67%	5.2	0		-18.9%			

Boobie Dixon acquired his nickname for displaying the kind of versatility in college that Boobie Miles showed in the movie *Friday Night Lights.* He never threw the ball in 2014, but he provided value both as a runner and on special teams. Out of the backfield, Dixon cracked four yards per carry for the first time in his career. With the offensive line ranking 26th in adjusted line yards, no other Bills back broke the 4.0-yard barrier. Dixon also blocked two punts on special teams, the first Bills player to do so in one season since Steve Tasker in 1990. Against the Jets, Dixon got a block when the Bills seemingly were playing for a return, plowing his blocker back into the punter on a solo bull rush. The play likely made an impression on his future head coach.

Lance Dunbar

| | Height: 5-8 | Weight: 191 | College: North Texas | Draft: 2012/FA | Born: 25-Jan-1990 | Age: 25 | Risk: Green |

Year	Team	G/GS	Snaps	Runs	Yds	Yd/R	TD	FUM	DVOA	Rk	DYAR	Rk	YAR	Suc%	Rk	BTkl	Rec	Pass	Yds	C%	Yd/C	TD	YAC	DVOA	Rk	DYAR	Rk
2012	DAL	12/0	91	21	75	3.6	0	0	-13.9%	--	-5	--	-2	52%	--	2	6	12	33	50%	5.5	0	4.0	-41.4%	--	-20	--
2013	DAL	9/0	51	30	150	5.0	0	1	16.8%	--	31	--	22	60%	--	3	7	7	59	100%	8.4	0	8.7	-17.3%	--	-1	--
2014	DAL	16/0	138	29	99	3.4	0	0	-16.9%	--	-10	--	-13	45%	--	7	18	22	217	82%	12.1	0	10.8	60.7%	--	88	--
2015	DAL			71	320	4.5	1	2	1.8%								30	40	275	75%	9.2	1		12.9%			

Underused receiving back. Dunbar had four 20-plus-yard gains on 18 receptions last season, but DeMarco Murray was a darn good receiver, and the Cowboys had an insane need to throw to Murray when leading by 17 points in the fourth quarter (see the Jaguars and Bears games) instead of giving Dunbar a little more playing time. With Murray gone, Dunbar should be promoted into a more traditional third-down back role. He's also first in line to replace Dwayne Harris as the kickoff returner.

Andre Ellington

| | Height: 5-9 | Weight: 199 | College: Clemson | Draft: 2013/6 (187) | Born: 3-Feb-1989 | Age: 26 | Risk: Yellow |

Year	Team	G/GS	Snaps	Runs	Yds	Yd/R	TD	FUM	DVOA	Rk	DYAR	Rk	YAR	Suc%	Rk	BTkl	Rec	Pass	Yds	C%	Yd/C	TD	YAC	DVOA	Rk	DYAR	Rk
2013	ARI	15/1	405	118	652	5.5	3	1	17.5%	4	117	15	107	46%	30	28	39	57	371	68%	9.5	1	6.7	22.3%	10	117	10
2014	ARI	12/12	528	201	660	3.3	3	2	-12.3%	35	-29	36	-87	39%	37	13	46	65	395	72%	8.6	2	7.7	-2.6%	27	44	23
2015	ARI			178	709	4.0	4	3	-4.3%								46	72	399	64%	8.7	1		-6.0%			

If anyone was more disappointed in Ellington's drop-off last year than the Cardinals, it was us—he topped our Top 25 Prospects list last year. Then Ellington injured his foot in practice before Week 1. That injury affected Ellington for months until his season ended with a hip injury in November. Further, he underwent sports hernia surgery after the season. Ellington was reportedly at 100 percent in OTAs, but the Cardinals will likely give third-round pick David Johnson plenty of action in an attempt to keep Ellington fresh and healthy this year.

Justin Forsett

| | Height: 5-8 | Weight: 194 | College: California | Draft: 2008/7 (233) | Born: 14-Oct-1985 | Age: 30 | Risk: Yellow |

Year	Team	G/GS	Snaps	Runs	Yds	Yd/R	TD	FUM	DVOA	Rk	DYAR	Rk	YAR	Suc%	Rk	BTkl	Rec	Pass	Yds	C%	Yd/C	TD	YAC	DVOA	Rk	DYAR	Rk
2012	HOU	16/0	121	63	374	5.9	1	0	13.2%	--	53	--	69	48%	--	7	3	5	38	60%	12.7	0	14.3	14.3%	--	9	--
2013	JAC	9/0	99	6	31	5.2	0	1	20.8%	--	7	--	9	33%	--	3	15	16	82	94%	5.5	0	7.2	-28.0%	--	-11	--
2014	BAL	16/14	707	235	1266	5.4	8	1	6.7%	12	149	11	207	44%	29	25	44	60	263	75%	6.0	0	7.4	-33.5%	51	-64	55
2015	BAL			234	1120	4.8	7	4	10.3%								50	66	352	76%	7.0	1		-5.3%			

Forsett became the latest unheralded back to explode in Gary Kubiak's zone-blocking scheme, but last year was also his first crack at a starting role. Prior to joining the Ravens, Forsett averaged 4.9 yards per carry in his career with a low success rate, so he's always been a boom-or-bust type of runner. Kubiak's gone, but Forsett still has a strong offensive line in front of him and little competition behind him. He's going on 30, but still hasn't hit 600 career carries. Under new offensive coordinator Marc Trestman, Forsett will be expected to catch the ball more, but that hasn't been a strength in his game or for the Ravens in recent years. Forsett could lose some snaps to rookie Javorius Allen, a more skilled receiver, but he's still a safe bet to touch the ball 250-plus times this year.

Matt Forte

| | Height: 6-2 | Weight: 218 | College: Tulane | Draft: 2008/2 (44) | Born: 10-Dec-1985 | Age: 30 | Risk: Green |

Year	Team	G/GS	Snaps	Runs	Yds	Yd/R	TD	FUM	DVOA	Rk	DYAR	Rk	YAR	Suc%	Rk	BTkl	Rec	Pass	Yds	C%	Yd/C	TD	YAC	DVOA	Rk	DYAR	Rk
2012	CHI	15/15	692	248	1094	4.4	5	2	3.1%	15	109	11	81	44%	32	15	44	60	340	73%	7.7	1	6.7	-1.1%	25	40	23
2013	CHI	16/16	928	289	1339	4.6	9	3	7.4%	15	193	4	191	47%	26	24	74	96	594	79%	8.0	3	6.8	8.5%	16	113	11
2014	CHI	16/16	975	266	1038	3.9	6	2	0.9%	18	113	12	112	50%	12	30	102	131	808	79%	7.9	4	7.7	5.0%	19	127	3
2015	CHI			246	999	4.1	7	6	-5.1%								70	92	591	76%	8.4	2		9.0%			

Forte skipped Phase I of OTAs, leading to speculation he wanted a contract extension as he heads into the final year of his deal. However, he told the media that he was more interested in speed training of the kind they didn't normally do at Halas Hall, because he felt something missing. Our projections do, too, seeing a veteran back who turns 30 in December. He was a lousy goal-line runner again in 2014, scoring 2.5 touchdowns fewer than an average back would on carries from the 5-yard line or closer. He's scored fewer goal-line touchdowns than expected every year except 2013, and could lose goal-line snaps to rookie Jeremy Langford. The arrival of Jacquizz Rodgers could limit his work on passing downs, especially since our game charting suggests Forte has a real problem with blitz pickup. We marked him with seven sacks allowed last year, twice as many as any other running back; he also led all backs with four sacks allowed in 2013. John Fox has often preferred a committee approach at running back, and it would make sense to more carefully distribute Forte's workload.

Arian Foster

Height: 6-1   Weight: 225   College: Tennessee   Draft: 2009/FA   Born: 24-Aug-1986   Age: 29   Risk: Red

Year	Team	G/GS	Snaps	Runs	Yds	Yd/R	TD	FUM	DVOA	Rk	DYAR	Rk	YAR	Suc%	Rk	BTkl	Rec	Pass	Yds	C%	Yd/C	TD	YAC	DVOA	Rk	DYAR	Rk
2012	HOU	16/16	831	351	1424	4.1	15	3	-1.6%	20	105	13	139	47%	27	28	40	58	217	69%	5.4	2	6.9	-28.0%	41	-43	43
2013	HOU	8/8	327	121	542	4.5	1	0	11.4%	8	99	19	85	50%	16	9	22	35	183	63%	8.3	1	9.5	-9.2%	33	9	33
2014	HOU	13/13	621	260	1246	4.8	8	2	7.5%	10	167	9	159	46%	21	43	38	59	327	64%	8.6	5	6.8	0.7%	23	46	22
2015	HOU			301	1383	4.6	9	2	13.2%								36	52	274	69%	7.6	3		1.9%			

This is a post-peak Arian Foster season. At 29, with six years of tread on the tires, there are two places this can go. The nagging injuries can become long-term injuries that force Foster to the sideline more, effectively ending his career. Or, he can continue to pull the balancing act he's pulled for his whole career, mixing his hang-glider running style with natural smarts to be an effective back who misses three or four games. The fact that he doesn't rely heavily on his physicality should be a positive for his staying power, but with any running back, the first step down can start the tumble that ends a career. Foster is on the precipice, but for now, he's still balancing on the top of that first stair.

Devonta Freeman

Height: 5-8   Weight: 206   College: Florida St.   Draft: 2014/4 (103)   Born: 15-Mar-1992   Age: 23   Risk: Yellow

Year	Team	G/GS	Snaps	Runs	Yds	Yd/R	TD	FUM	DVOA	Rk	DYAR	Rk	YAR	Suc%	Rk	BTkl	Rec	Pass	Yds	C%	Yd/C	TD	YAC	DVOA	Rk	DYAR	Rk
2014	ATL	16/0	234	65	248	3.8	1	1	-22.9%	--	-38	--	-47	31%	--	15	30	37	225	81%	7.5	1	5.7	4.1%	20	33	26
2015	ATL			178	740	4.2	6	2	5.9%								42	55	307	76%	7.3	2		8.2%			

"All hair and ass" is the description of Freeman from our friend Cecil Lammey of FootballGuys.com. The dreads and big hips betray a back that quite a few people thought highly of coming out last season. Having to split the passing-down duties with Jacquizz Rodgers for most of the season didn't help him, and he struggled running the ball behind a suspect offensive line. But with Kyle Shanahan in town, Freeman should do better with more zone runs, and he's got the ability to be a terrific passing-down back. He had an 88 percent catch rate in his senior year at Florida State, catching passes from Jameis Winston. No matter how Tevin Coleman plays, look for Freeman on third downs.

Toby Gerhart

Height: 6-0   Weight: 231   College: Stanford   Draft: 2010/2 (51)   Born: 18-Mar-1987   Age: 28   Risk: Green

Year	Team	G/GS	Snaps	Runs	Yds	Yd/R	TD	FUM	DVOA	Rk	DYAR	Rk	YAR	Suc%	Rk	BTkl	Rec	Pass	Yds	C%	Yd/C	TD	YAC	DVOA	Rk	DYAR	Rk
2012	MIN	16/0	240	50	169	3.4	1	2	-26.0%	--	-34	--	-44	44%	--	4	20	27	155	74%	7.8	0	7.3	25.0%	6	55	16
2013	MIN	14/0	196	36	283	7.9	2	1	73.6%	--	105	--	102	50%	--	8	13	19	88	68%	6.8	0	6.4	10.7%	--	22	--
2014	JAC	14/7	302	101	326	3.2	2	1	-16.1%	39	-35	38	-27	43%	33	15	20	24	186	83%	9.3	0	11.5	27.5%	--	53	--
2015	JAC			45	178	3.9	1	2	-4.9%								14	18	86	78%	6.2	0		-3.9%			

Game of Thrones plotlines can unfold in the time it takes Gerhart to chug to the line of scrimmage. The Jags, to their credit, have guaranteed no more money to Gerhart. The idea of plucking Adrian Peterson's backup out of obscurity and letting his fresh legs help create the bullying run game the Jaguars desired was a credible gamble. It became clear by about Week 7 that watching the gamble play out any further would be torture worthy of Ramsay Bolton.

Melvin Gordon

Height: 5-10   Weight: 215   College: Wisconsin   Draft: 2015/1 (15)   Born: 13-Apr-1993   Age: 22   Risk: Green

Year	Team	G/GS	Snaps	Runs	Yds	Yd/R	TD	FUM	DVOA	Rk	DYAR	Rk	YAR	Suc%	Rk	BTkl	Rec	Pass	Yds	C%	Yd/C	TD	YAC	DVOA	Rk	DYAR	Rk
2015	SD			223	946	4.2	7	3	3.6%								27	37	220	73%	8.2	1		-6.7%			

Expectations for rookie running backs used to be sky high due to the frequency of instant success at that position. As 300-carry seasons have dwindled, it feels as though rookie expectations also are not what they used to be. No one expects Gordon to come in and rush for 1,500 yards in 2015, but a 1,000-yard season is a realistic goal. We have seen 20 rookie running backs rush for 1,000 yards since 2000, including Jeremy Hill (2014) and Eddie Lacy (2013) the last two years. While Gordon may give up some of his third-down snaps to Danny Woodhead, he is still expected to be on the field a lot in an offense that has invested in him in an attempt to help Philip Rivers. Gordon should be a preseason favorite for Offensive Rookie of the Year given that the first-round contenders include two quarterbacks on bad teams, a running back coming off an ACL injury, and a number of wide receivers added to struggling passing games. A first-round pick has won the award in 10 of the last 11 years.

Frank Gore

Height: 5-9 Weight: 215 College: Miami Draft: 2005/3 (65) Born: 14-May-1983 Age: 32 Risk: Red

Year	Team	G/GS	Snaps	Runs	Yds	Yd/R	TD	FUM	DVOA	Rk	DYAR	Rk	YAR	Suc%	Rk	BTkl	Rec	Pass	Yds	C%	Yd/C	TD	YAC	DVOA	Rk	DYAR	Rk
2012	SF	16/16	728	258	1214	4.7	8	3	17.4%	4	268	4	212	48%	17	27	28	36	234	78%	8.4	1	7.9	13.1%	12	50	18
2013	SF	16/16	745	276	1128	4.1	9	3	-0.8%	24	91	20	40	42%	38	15	16	26	141	62%	8.8	0	6.3	-16.3%	39	-3	39
2014	SF	16/16	647	255	1106	4.3	4	2	6.3%	13	154	10	118	50%	11	19	11	19	111	58%	10.1	1	9.3	-14.4%	--	-1	--
2015	IND			220	944	4.3	8	1	9.8%								28	41	201	68%	7.2	1		-2.8%			

The Colts haven't had a running back rush for 1,000 yards and average 4.0 yards per carry since Joseph Addai in 2007. Frank Gore has eight such seasons in his career, only trailing Barry Sanders (10), Walter Payton (nine) and Emmitt Smith (nine) for the most in NFL history. A good finish to help push the Colts over the top could be the final push Gore needs for Canton. Indianapolis signed the 32-year-old Gore to a three-year deal worth up to $12 million, beating Philadelphia in a bidding war for his services. Gore doesn't have to be a 1,000-yard back in an offense led by Andrew Luck, but he should provide the young quarterback with stability in the backfield that hasn't been there the last three years. With Luck's trust, Gore should also see more targets in the passing game after they disappeared significantly in his four years under offensive coordinator Greg Roman in San Francisco. Before 2011, Gore averaged 3.2 catches and 27.2 receiving yards per game. In the last four years he averaged roughly a third of that: 1.1 catches and 9.4 receiving yards per game.

Jonas Gray

Height: 5-10 Weight: 225 College: Notre Dame Draft: 2012/FA Born: 27-Jun-1990 Age: 25 Risk: Green

Year	Team	G/GS	Snaps	Runs	Yds	Yd/R	TD	FUM	DVOA	Rk	DYAR	Rk	YAR	Suc%	Rk	BTkl	Rec	Pass	Yds	C%	Yd/C	TD	YAC	DVOA	Rk	DYAR	Rk
2014	NE	8/3	158	89	412	4.6	5	0	29.1%	--	152	--	152	65%	--	3	1	3	7	33%	7.0	0	3.0	-38.7%	--	-4	--
2015	NE			71	304	4.3	1	3	2.4%								12	16	85	75%	7.1	0		0.4%			

What odds would you want to bet on Jonas Gray as the first player in NFL history with a 200-yard rushing game that was also his only 100-yard rushing game? (Even Timmy Smith had a couple of 100-yard games after his big performance in the Super Bowl.) Four days after Gray's big game against the Colts, the Patriots signed LeGarrette Blount. The day after that, Gray overslept a team meeting and earned a Belichick timeout. He got just 24 carries the rest of the season and was inactive for the Super Bowl. Healthy for the first offseason in his NFL career, Gray is fighting to not be a one-hit wonder. He was effective even beyond the Colts game in 2014, posting a 12.7% DVOA on his other carries.

Shonn Greene

Height: 6-0 Weight: 227 College: Iowa Draft: 2009/3 (65) Born: 21-Aug-1985 Age: 30 Risk: N/A

Year	Team	G/GS	Snaps	Runs	Yds	Yd/R	TD	FUM	DVOA	Rk	DYAR	Rk	YAR	Suc%	Rk	BTkl	Rec	Pass	Yds	C%	Yd/C	TD	YAC	DVOA	Rk	DYAR	Rk
2012	NYJ	16/14	567	276	1063	3.9	8	5	-4.5%	24	49	22	84	52%	9	10	19	31	151	61%	7.9	0	6.9	-41.4%	45	-47	44
2013	TEN	11/0	155	77	295	3.8	4	0	8.9%	--	61	--	58	61%	--	3	6	7	39	86%	6.5	0	10.2	-28.5%	--	-7	--
2014	TEN	13/5	164	94	392	4.2	2	1	-5.2%	--	14	--	16	47%	--	7	1	3	13	33%	13.0	0	10.0	-5.7%	--	1	--

A between the tackles grinder on a team with a struggling offensive line who struggled to grind out yards and bounced a few too many runs early in the season, Greene seemed like a longshot to collect his $3.25 million base salary from Tennessee in 2015 even before the Titans drafted David Cobb in the fifth round and he skipped OTAs to deal with family obligations. If he lands elsewhere after the Titans let him go in June, expecting more than an inconsistently effective "thunder" back in a committee is too much.

Todd Gurley Height: 5-10 Weight: 222 College: Georgia Draft: 2015/1 (10) Born: 3-Aug-1994 Age: 21 Risk: Red

Year	Team	G/GS	Snaps	Runs	Yds	Yd/R	TD	FUM	DVOA	Rk	DYAR	Rk	YAR	Suc%	Rk	BTkl	Rec	Pass	Yds	C%	Yd/C	TD	YAC	DVOA	Rk	DYAR	Rk
2015	STL			191	801	4.2	7	2	3.1%							22	32	158	69%	7.3	1		-16.7%			

The 2015 NFL season kicks off just nine months after Gurley tore his ACL, and there's no guarantee that Gurley will be ready to play when the Rams host the Seahawks in Week 1. The Rams said in May that they hoped Gurley would be ready to participate in the second week of training camp, but then word broke in mid-June that Gurley was planning on visiting Dr. James Andrews in Alabama for a re-evaluation of the knee injury, hoping to get clearance for camp. Our projection above assumes that Gurley has about 12 full-time games worth of action, which probably will be a month of ramp-up and then a couple of months as a workhorse back.

Gurley is a bruising, power runner, and he showed more consistency than explosiveness last year. His 7.9 highlight yards per opportunity were very good, but notably behind Tevin Coleman (9.8) and Melvin Gordon (9.3) in this year's draft class. However, none of the ten highest-drafted running backs had a better opportunity rate than Gurley's 46 percent, meaning that he frequently got at least the first few yards that were blocked for him. Which is not to say that Gurley never showed burst in college—of his 35 rushing touchdowns at Georgia, ten came from outside the red zone, and five came from across midfield. And while he only returned 11 kickoffs for the Bulldogs, he averaged 38.4 yards on those returns and took two of them back for scores.

Roy Helu Height: 5-11 Weight: 216 College: Nebraska Draft: 2011/4 (105) Born: 7-Dec-1988 Age: 27 Risk: Green

Year	Team	G/GS	Snaps	Runs	Yds	Yd/R	TD	FUM	DVOA	Rk	DYAR	Rk	YAR	Suc%	Rk	BTkl	Rec	Pass	Yds	C%	Yd/C	TD	YAC	DVOA	Rk	DYAR	Rk
2012	WAS	3/0	44	2	2	1.0	0	0	-107.9%	--	-10	--	-9	0%	--	1	7	7	45	100%	6.4	0	6.7	14.8%	--	10	--
2013	WAS	16/0	526	62	274	4.4	4	2	8.5%	--	48	--	51	45%	--	9	31	42	251	74%	8.1	0	6.1	-15.0%	38	-3	38
2014	WAS	14/0	364	40	216	5.4	1	2	15.7%	--	42	--	43	55%	--	21	42	47	477	89%	11.4	2	11.6	31.2%	5	108	7
2015	OAK			79	338	4.3	2	3	0.7%							45	57	343	79%	7.6	1		9.4%			

Helu is a solid committee back: productive as a receiver, decent as a pass protector, useful as a change-up. Seventeen of his 42 receptions last year came in the fourth quarter, so his receiving numbers are padded with plenty of checkdown passes in blowouts. But Helu also converted six first downs on third-and-4 or longer; yes, he was targeted a whopping 19 times in those situations by quarterbacks (OK, by Robert Griffin) terrified of throwing downfield, but he at least did something with some of those targets. Helu had 13 carries for 84 yards in one three-game stretch in midseason, then earned just four total carries in the following four games. Redskins game plans in 2014 were not renowned for their clarity.

Dan Herron Height: 5-9 Weight: 213 College: Ohio State Draft: 2012/6 (191) Born: 21-Mar-1989 Age: 26 Risk: Red

Year	Team	G/GS	Snaps	Runs	Yds	Yd/R	TD	FUM	DVOA	Rk	DYAR	Rk	YAR	Suc%	Rk	BTkl	Rec	Pass	Yds	C%	Yd/C	TD	YAC	DVOA	Rk	DYAR	Rk
2012	CIN	3/0	15	4	5	1.3	0	0	-95.4%	--	-12	--	-12	0%	--	2	0	1	0	0%	0.0	0	0.0	-97.2%	--	-4	--
2013	IND	6/0	11	5	33	6.6	0	0	63.6%	--	19	--	14	60%	--	1	1	1	57	100%	57.0	0	60.0	363.2%	--	22	--
2014	IND	16/3	245	78	351	4.5	1	2	-2.9%	--	17	--	34	53%	--	12	21	26	173	81%	8.2	0	9.2	-7.1%	35	10	36
2015	IND			71	297	4.2	1	1	0.4%							32	40	319	80%	10.0	1		18.5%			

"Boom" Herron is just the latest back to outshine Trent Richardson in Indianapolis. He had several productive games in Ahmad Bradshaw's absence late in the season. Herron literally saved the Colts from a Week 14 defeat in Cleveland by powering his way to convert fourth down in the final minute. That's a guaranteed loss if the Colts go all stupid and give Richardson the ball in an attempt to exact revenge on his former team. Herron was stopped dead in the backfield, but found a way to spin and get the first down. Herron also proved to be a good receiver, as Andrew Luck fell in love with dumpoffs to substitute for a weak running game and subpar pass protection. Including the playoffs, Herron caught 41 of 49 passes, and all but two of those plays came in a span of nine games. If Vick Ballard is still slow to recover from his injuries, Herron has a nice path to the No. 2 running back job behind Frank Gore.

Peyton Hillis

Height: 6-0 Weight: 240 College: Arkansas Draft: 2008/7 (227) Born: 21-Jan-1986 Age: 29 Risk: N/A

Year	Team	G/GS	Snaps	Runs	Yds	Yd/R	TD	FUM	DVOA	Rk	DYAR	Rk	YAR	Suc%	Rk	BTkl	Rec	Pass	Yds	C%	Yd/C	TD	YAC	DVOA	Rk	DYAR	Rk
2012	KC	13/2	210	85	309	3.6	1	2	-27.5%	--	-71	--	-42	40%	--	7	10	13	62	77%	6.2	0	7.4	-29.1%	--	-10	--
2013	NYG	7/1	202	73	247	3.4	2	2	-13.3%	--	-14	--	-20	49%	--	4	13	21	96	62%	7.4	0	7.9	-13.5%	--	0	--
2014	NYG	9/0	109	26	115	4.4	0	0	-1.9%	--	6	--	2	38%	--	8	10	16	87	63%	8.7	0	9.3	-34.4%	--	-16	--

It's time for the SAT section of the running back comments!

Lord Carnavon : Curse of the Pharaohs :: Peyton Hillis : Curse of the Madden Cover.

Hillis recovered a few shreds of dignity with a handful of non-terrible performances when Rashad Jennings got hurt early in the season for the Giants. Hillis was unsigned at press time, but Jerry Reese has his phone number saved as "Last Resort" in his contact list.

Jeremy Hill

Height: 6-1 Weight: 233 College: Louisiana St. Draft: 2014/2 (55) Born: 10/20/1992 Age: 23 Risk: Green

Year	Team	G/GS	Snaps	Runs	Yds	Yd/R	TD	FUM	DVOA	Rk	DYAR	Rk	YAR	Suc%	Rk	BTkl	Rec	Pass	Yds	C%	Yd/C	TD	YAC	DVOA	Rk	DYAR	Rk
2014	CIN	16/8	501	222	1124	5.1	9	5	12.6%	6	204	6	231	54%	4	26	27	32	215	84%	8.0	0	8.3	-3.7%	30	17	31
2015	CIN			274	1250	4.6	10	5	5.8%								32	44	208	73%	6.5	1		-11.5%			

Some people wondered why the Bengals would spend a valuable second-round choice on Hill when they had a serviceable back on the roster in BenJarvus Green-Ellis. Hill showed them why as soon as he became the top option in the Cincy backfield midway through the season (and Law Firm disappeared from the league). Despite just eight starts, Hill cracked 140 yards in a game four times and led the NFL over the last half of the season in both rushing yards and yards per carry. He consistently made tacklers miss in the backfield, and was speedy enough to peel off three runs of 60-plus yards, including a memorable 85-yarder against Denver in a crucial late-season Monday night game. Cincinnati improved from 30th in open-field yards to third, in large part because of Hill's innate ability to set up and use downfield blocking.

Hill provided just what the offense needed with its wideouts and tight ends banged up: first-and-10 prowess, to the tune of 5.7 yards per carry and a 16.8% DVOA. Hill did fumble five times (losing two), so ball security is an element of his game that needs improvement, but he is the main man going forward in what figures to be a run-heavy attack. His efficiency should nosedive as a result, but Hill is a top fantasy target, and if he avoids injury he should compete for the rushing title.

Ronnie Hillman

Height: 5-9 Weight: 200 College: San Diego State Draft: 2012/3 (67) Born: 14-Sep-1991 Age: 24 Risk: Green

Year	Team	G/GS	Snaps	Runs	Yds	Yd/R	TD	FUM	DVOA	Rk	DYAR	Rk	YAR	Suc%	Rk	BTkl	Rec	Pass	Yds	C%	Yd/C	TD	YAC	DVOA	Rk	DYAR	Rk
2012	DEN	14/0	206	84	327	3.9	1	2	-15.7%	--	-24	--	-15	51%	--	3	10	12	62	83%	6.2	0	6.9	-17.0%	--	-2	--
2013	DEN	10/0	157	55	218	4.0	1	2	-6.9%	--	4	--	3	55%	--	2	12	14	119	86%	9.9	0	6.3	41.1%	--	45	--
2014	DEN	8/4	311	106	434	4.1	3	1	-1.4%	22	31	24	10	43%	31	6	21	34	139	62%	6.6	1	5.1	-18.3%	44	-8	43
2015	DEN			56	234	4.2	2	2	4.8%								29	37	219	78%	7.5	1		4.2%			

The Denver backfield is another example of how teams can get away with minimal investment in the running back position. Ronnie Hillman was drafted 67th overall in 2012 and Montee Ball was drafted 58th overall in 2013, yet it's undrafted C.J. Anderson who holds the starting job and all the promise in Denver right now. Hillman might be the second-best back though, and he had a very encouraging four-game stretch last season after Ball disappointed and before Anderson broke out. Hillman's not built to be a workhorse, but he is the change-of-pace back in Denver and should benefit from Gary Kubiak's zone-blocking scheme.

Kendall Hunter

Height: 5-7 Weight: 199 College: Oklahoma State Draft: 2011/4 (115) Born: 16-Sep-1988 Age: 27 Risk: Green

Year	Team	G/GS	Snaps	Runs	Yds	Yd/R	TD	FUM	DVOA	Rk	DYAR	Rk	YAR	Suc%	Rk	BTkl	Rec	Pass	Yds	C%	Yd/C	TD	YAC	DVOA	Rk	DYAR	Rk
2012	SF	11/0	170	72	371	5.2	2	0	29.1%	--	109	--	108	60%	--	5	9	12	60	75%	6.7	0	6.3	17.7%	--	21	--
2013	SF	16/0	189	78	358	4.6	3	1	-3.0%	--	16	--	2	36%	--	8	2	4	13	50%	6.5	0	8.0	-40.9%	--	-6	--
2015	SF			43	172	4.0	0	2	-7.7%								20	28	167	71%	8.4	0		3.9%			

Hunter tore his ACL during training camp in 2014, but the 49ers were confident enough in his health to re-sign him to a one-year extension in November. Hunter is best used as a receiver—he was among the top-ten running backs in receiving DVOA in 2011, and would have been in 2012 if he had seen enough targets to qualify. Given all that, it's surprising that San Francsico only threw him four passes in 2013, and the Reggie Bush acquisition might limit Hunter's targets again in 2015.

Carlos Hyde Height: 6-0 Weight: 230 College: Ohio St. Draft: 2014/2 (57) Born: 9/20/1991 Age: 24 Risk: Green

Year	Team	G/GS	Snaps	Runs	Yds	Yd/R	TD	FUM	DVOA	Rk	DYAR	Rk	YAR	Suc%	Rk	BTkl	Rec	Pass	Yds	C%	Yd/C	TD	YAC	DVOA	Rk	DYAR	Rk
2014	SF	14/0	292	83	333	4.0	4	1	3.0%	--	38	--	25	46%	--	21	12	16	68	75%	5.7	0	5.4	-38.5%	--	-21	--
2015	SF			214	834	3.9	6	3	-6.0%								20	30	163	67%	8.1	1		-2.1%			

Hyde had some weird splits last year—the worse he played, the more San Francisco gave him the ball. His DVOA in his four games with nine or more carries was just -38.8%, with 2.7 yards per rush, but he had a 41.3% DVOA and 5.2 yards per run in his other ten appearances. It goes without saying that Hyde will be getting a heavier workload in 2015, so for his sake and San Francisco's, let's hope that's a small sample-size fluke. Hyde lost 10 pounds this offseason, which should help him last longer in games this fall. Hopefully he'll be able to maintain his physical style—among running backs with at least 80 touches, only Marshawn Lynch, Ahmad Bradshaw, and Roy Helu had better broken tackle rates than Hyde last year.

Mark Ingram Height: 5-11 Weight: 215 College: Alabama Draft: 2011/1 (28) Born: 21-Dec-1989 Age: 26 Risk: Green

Year	Team	G/GS	Snaps	Runs	Yds	Yd/R	TD	FUM	DVOA	Rk	DYAR	Rk	YAR	Suc%	Rk	BTkl	Rec	Pass	Yds	C%	Yd/C	TD	YAC	DVOA	Rk	DYAR	Rk
2012	NO	16/5	266	156	602	3.9	5	0	0.8%	19	62	19	56	49%	15	13	6	10	29	60%	4.8	0	5.3	-45.4%	--	-21	--
2013	NO	11/3	168	78	386	4.9	1	0	4.6%	--	45	--	41	49%	--	15	7	11	68	64%	9.7	0	10.9	-5.4%	--	5	--
2014	NO	13/9	470	226	964	4.3	9	3	2.7%	14	108	14	129	50%	13	30	29	36	145	81%	5.0	0	5.0	-40.9%	56	-54	54
2015	NO			214	962	4.5	4	5	1.1%								42	52	313	81%	7.5	1		3.9%			

Mark Ingram has been on the verge of breakout for two years. It almost came last year, but injury prevented him from topping 1,000 yards for the first time. Ingram's decisive and aggressive running style paired with his versatile athleticism makes him one of the most dangerous between-the-tackles runners in the NFL. He will be a focal point of the offense in 2015 and, at 25, he is still a young back with very little wear and tear on his body. The Saints didn't get what they expected from Ingram over the first four years of his career, but it's hard to blame them for investing in the next four.

Chris Ivory Height: 6-0 Weight: 222 College: Tiffin Draft: 2010/FA Born: 22-Mar-1988 Age: 27 Risk: Yellow

Year	Team	G/GS	Snaps	Runs	Yds	Yd/R	TD	FUM	DVOA	Rk	DYAR	Rk	YAR	Suc%	Rk	BTkl	Rec	Pass	Yds	C%	Yd/C	TD	YAC	DVOA	Rk	DYAR	Rk
2012	NO	6/2	67	40	217	5.4	2	0	12.5%	--	33	--	34	48%	--	14	2	3	15	67%	7.5	0	14.0	-7.3%	--	1	--
2013	NYJ	15/6	331	182	833	4.6	3	2	-8.3%	33	2	33	38	44%	33	20	2	7	10	29%	5.0	0	4.0	-58.2%	--	-19	--
2014	NYJ	16/10	446	198	821	4.1	6	2	-0.6%	20	69	21	60	44%	25	33	18	27	123	67%	6.8	1	6.7	-15.4%	41	-2	41
2015	NYJ			187	759	4.1	5	1	1.7%								23	28	158	82%	6.9	0		6.4%			

There figure to be zero guarantees in the New York backfield going into the 2015 season, and despite the fact that Ivory has always run hard—he ranked among the top-ten backs with 33 broken tackles last season—he figures to be the wildest of wild cards. In the spring, Todd Bowles anointed him as the lead back for a few reasons, not the least of which is the fact that he led all Jets running backs in snaps, carries, rushing yards, and yards per carry. But if Stevan Ridley proves himself healthy after a season-ending knee injury in 2014, or if newcomer Zac Stacy is able to pick up the offense quicker than anticipated, would anyone be surprised if Ivory was supplanted by either player? Ivory never offered much in the passing game before last season, which makes his skill set a questionable fit with new offensive coordinator Chan Gailey. Ultimately, like many of the middle-of-the-road offensive holdovers from the Rex Ryan Era, Ivory could find himself out of a gig if he proves to be ineffective in the early going.

Fred Jackson | Height: 6-1 | Weight: 215 | College: Coe College | Draft: 2007/FA | Born: 20-Feb-1981 | Age: 34 | Risk: Green

Year	Team	G/GS	Snaps	Runs	Yds	Yd/R	TD	FUM	DVOA	Rk	DYAR	Rk	YAR	Suc%	Rk	BTkl	Rec	Pass	Yds	C%	Yd/C	TD	YAC	DVOA	Rk	DYAR	Rk
2012	BUF	10/8	329	115	437	3.8	3	5	-14.3%	35	-27	32	-38	47%	26	19	34	42	217	81%	6.4	1	6.5	-8.4%	28	13	27
2013	BUF	16/6	663	206	890	4.3	9	3	9.1%	11	163	8	170	51%	9	27	47	66	387	71%	8.2	1	8.8	0.8%	23	52	20
2014	BUF	14/9	548	141	525	3.7	2	4	-4.7%	27	23	27	26	46%	20	25	66	90	501	73%	7.6	1	8.8	-21.5%	46	-38	51
2015	BUF			45	196	4.3	0	2	0.6%								33	53	263	62%	8.0	1		-8.2%			

Jackson is impossible not to root for. Originally undrafted out of Coe College, Jackson bounced around indoor football leagues and NFL Europe before finding NFL success. He won the 2010 Walter Payton NFL Man of the Year Award. Unfortunately, not even Payton was a productive NFL running back at age 34. Payton (who retired at that age) and Jackson actually posted almost identical numbers in their age-33 seasons. Both averaged 3.7 yards per carry. Payton gained 533 yards, Jackson 525. In the last 50 years, just one running back has posted a season of at least 500 yards and four yards per carry past age 33. The odds are against Jackson becoming the second. While he may win on overall good guy-ness, Fred Jackson is not quite Marcus Allen on the field. Keeping Fred Jackson at the behest of owner Terry Pegula is just the latest example of the Bills' apparent plan to do the opposite of what Bill Belichick would do in all personnel decisions. (Note that Jackson's Risk Factor is Green because with LeSean McCoy's arrival, the decline is already built into this projection.)

Steven Jackson | Height: 6-3 | Weight: 229 | College: Oregon State | Draft: 2004/1 (24) | Born: 22-Jul-1983 | Age: 32 | Risk: N/A

Year	Team	G/GS	Snaps	Runs	Yds	Yd/R	TD	FUM	DVOA	Rk	DYAR	Rk	YAR	Suc%	Rk	BTkl	Rec	Pass	Yds	C%	Yd/C	TD	YAC	DVOA	Rk	DYAR	Rk
2012	STL	16/16	706	257	1042	4.1	4	0	5.3%	11	147	10	59	47%	28	21	38	53	321	72%	8.4	0	7.4	11.7%	14	72	12
2013	ATL	12/12	417	157	543	3.5	6	0	-8.8%	35	-2	35	-9	40%	40	15	33	49	191	67%	5.8	1	6.1	-26.0%	46	-36	47
2014	ATL	15/15	420	190	707	3.7	6	0	-0.3%	19	70	19	66	51%	8	20	20	27	148	74%	7.4	0	6.1	-0.2%	25	20	29

Of all the running backs that debuted in 1991 or later, Jackson finished his career 19th in total DYAR, sandwiched between Ahman Green and Kevin Faulk. That alone doesn't begin to tell the cursed tale of Jackson, who made the playoffs just three times in an 11-year career wasted on teams that couldn't fully utilize him. Jackson's teams went 54-121-1 over the course of his career, including just 32 wins over the last eight seasons. Just when he thought he was finally getting to a contender, the Falcons fell apart. Jackson really only had one transcendent season—2006, when he finished fifth in DYAR and led the NFL in yards from scrimmage—but was a steadily good back who took a pounding behind some really bad Rams offensive lines. You know the ones we're talking about. The ones with Alex Barron and Jason Brown. With just three Pro Bowls and no first-team All-Pro appearances, it's more of a Hall of Very Good career, but there's a lot of "what if" involved.

Rashad Jennings | Height: 6-1 | Weight: 231 | College: Liberty | Draft: 2009/7 (250) | Born: 26-Mar-1985 | Age: 30 | Risk: Yellow

Year	Team	G/GS	Snaps	Runs	Yds	Yd/R	TD	FUM	DVOA	Rk	DYAR	Rk	YAR	Suc%	Rk	BTkl	Rec	Pass	Yds	C%	Yd/C	TD	YAC	DVOA	Rk	DYAR	Rk
2012	JAC	10/6	330	101	283	2.8	2	3	-31.8%	42	-97	41	-81	38%	40	15	19	26	130	73%	6.8	0	8.2	-22.6%	37	-11	37
2013	OAK	15/8	548	163	733	4.5	6	0	15.8%	5	164	7	158	47%	25	9	36	46	292	76%	8.1	0	8.7	3.3%	22	44	21
2014	NYG	11/9	418	167	639	3.8	4	1	7.0%	11	112	13	75	47%	16	26	30	41	226	73%	7.5	0	10.4	-29.3%	50	-35	49
2015	NYG			207	819	3.9	6	3	-1.4%								33	49	248	67%	7.5	1		-3.8%			

Jennings was sporadically effective between knee injuries, which is just about the only kind of "effective" a Giants running back is capable of these days. He was productive as a rusher, and while he caught a lot of passes that went nowhere, he rarely made negative plays and blocked well enough. That's Jennings' game: low downside, with minimal upside. Assuming the Giants avoid their usual zombie apocalypse at running back, Jennings will now be a committee back, with Shane Vereen catching most of the passes and Andre Williams as the designated power back. A pro's pro who is always prepared, Jennings will look much better as a swing man than as a starter.

Chris Johnson | Height: 5-11 | Weight: 197 | College: East Carolina | Draft: 2008/1 (24) | Born: 23-Sep-1985 | Age: 30 | Risk: N/A

Year	Team	G/GS	Snaps	Runs	Yds	Yd/R	TD	FUM	DVOA	Rk	DYAR	Rk	YAR	Suc%	Rk	BTkl	Rec	Pass	Yds	C%	Yd/C	TD	YAC	DVOA	Rk	DYAR	Rk
2012	TEN	16/15	815	276	1243	4.5	6	4	-11.3%	32	-30	33	-6	41%	38	16	36	49	232	76%	6.4	0	6.5	-17.6%	35	-9	36
2013	TEN	16/16	798	279	1077	3.9	6	3	1.5%	22	110	17	75	46%	31	18	42	52	345	81%	8.2	4	9.4	10.8%	14	66	16
2014	NYJ	16/6	398	155	663	4.3	1	1	-6.0%	30	16	30	31	45%	24	10	24	34	151	71%	6.3	1	6.1	-13.8%	40	0	40

The veteran hasn't drawn much interest after being cut loose by the Jets at the end of last season, and it's easy to see why teams have shied away from him. He may have hit the wall that most running backs smack into around age 30, and he's had some troubles off the field, including getting wounded in a drive-by shooting in March. Nevertheless, if he could ever tweak his game to the point where he gave a damn about working as a blocker, Johnson could set himself up for a nice second act as a veteran third-down back. He still has the wheels, and has demonstrated that he has a dependable set of hands with a consistently good catch rate over the years. Johnson will also need to ditch the third-person chatter and any pretense that he has another 2,000-plus-yard season in his future, and take a deal below market value.

David Johnson | Height: 5-10 | Weight: 224 | College: Northern Iowa | Draft: 2015/3 (86) | Born: 16-Dec-1991 | Age: 24 | Risk: Yellow

Year	Team	G/GS	Snaps	Runs	Yds	Yd/R	TD	FUM	DVOA	Rk	DYAR	Rk	YAR	Suc%	Rk	BTkl	Rec	Pass	Yds	C%	Yd/C	TD	YAC	DVOA	Rk	DYAR	Rk
2015	ARI			111	447	4.0	3	2	-4.1%							23	34		179	68%	7.8	1		-13.2%			

Johnson was a big fish in a small pond at Northern Iowa, running for at least 1,291 yards and 5.4 yards per carry in both 2013 and 2014, but the defenses of the NFC West are tougher than those in the Missouri Valley Conference. Johnson has lots of size and plenty of speed, but he has trouble improvising and lacks the instincts to adjust when blocking schemes don't work as intended. Andre Ellington's struggles and injury concerns mean that Johnson will get some opportunities this fall, but he looks like a clear No. 2 back in Arizona.

Duke Johnson | Height: 5-10 | Weight: 207 | College: Miami | Draft: 2015/3 (77) | Born: 23-Sep-1993 | Age: 22 | Risk: Green

Year	Team	G/GS	Snaps	Runs	Yds	Yd/R	TD	FUM	DVOA	Rk	DYAR	Rk	YAR	Suc%	Rk	BTkl	Rec	Pass	Yds	C%	Yd/C	TD	YAC	DVOA	Rk	DYAR	Rk
2015	CLE			120	535	4.4	6	2	5.1%							23	29		161	79%	7.0	1		-3.7%			

What a difference a couple of pounds and inches can make. If Duke Johnson were just slightly heavier and bigger, he would have had a chance of cracking the first round of the 2015 draft. Instead, he fell to the third round. His skill set is such that he could be a very effective three-down back in the NFL, if his durability can hold up. He has the vision, creativity, and footwork to be effective between the tackles or outside. Fortunately, the Browns don't need Johnson to be a full-time player from the start of his rookie season, so they will be able to test him to see what his best role will be. He should definitely be the Browns' primary receiving back. Johnson's explosiveness and elusiveness in space allows him to eat up space quickly. Plenty of backs in the NFL are elusive and explosive in space, but how they find that space is what separates the most dangerous receiving options. Johnson is a natural and consistent catcher of the ball, with the versatility to line up all over the field, including the slot.

Maurice Jones-Drew | Height: 5-8 | Weight: 205 | College: UCLA | Draft: 2006/2 (60) | Born: 23-Mar-1985 | Age: 30 | Risk: N/A

Year	Team	G/GS	Snaps	Runs	Yds	Yd/R	TD	FUM	DVOA	Rk	DYAR	Rk	YAR	Suc%	Rk	BTkl	Rec	Pass	Yds	C%	Yd/C	TD	YAC	DVOA	Rk	DYAR	Rk
2012	JAC	6/5	240	86	414	4.8	1	1	-0.9%	--	27	--	42	48%	--	9	14	18	86	78%	6.1	1	5.1	5.8%	--	18	--
2013	JAC	15/15	647	234	803	3.4	5	1	-13.6%	38	-49	42	-66	37%	43	20	43	60	314	72%	7.3	0	7.7	-3.7%	28	32	27
2014	OAK	12/1	204	43	96	2.2	0	1	-50.1%	--	-69	--	-66	24%	--	3	11	16	71	69%	6.5	0	5.9	-9.2%	--	4	--

Remember when "Pocket Hercules" won the rushing title with Blaine Gabbert as his quarterback in 2011? That's about the last time we saw greatness from Jones-Drew. In March, Jones-Drew announced his retirement from the NFL just a few weeks shy of turning 30. In his prime in Jacksonville he was a fun back to watch, and a complete back with production as a receiver and kick returner.

Matt Jones

| | Height: 5-10 | | Weight: 231 | | College: Florida | | | Draft: 2015/3 (95) | | Born: 7-Mar-1993 | | Age: 22 | | Risk: Blue |

Year	Team	G/GS	Snaps	Runs	Yds	Yd/R	TD	FUM	DVOA	Rk	DYAR	Rk	YAR	Suc%	Rk	BTkl	Rec	Pass	Yds	C%	Yd/C	TD	YAC	DVOA	Rk	DYAR	Rk
2015	WAS		49	222	4.5	0	2	-0.1%								13	15	79	87%	6.1	0		-6.5%			

Jones looks like Roy Helu's replacement as the Steady Eddie off the Redskins bench, though with less use as a receiver. Jones is burly and gets high marks as a pass protector, but he rushed for just 819 yards in his final season at Florida, caught just 19 passes in his college career, and didn't exactly set the combine on fire. Jones would be written off as a reach if Scot McCloughan didn't have a reputation for blowing our minds in the third round.

John Kuhn

| | Height: 6-0 | | Weight: 255 | | College: Shippensburg | | | Draft: 2006/FA | | Born: 9-Sep-1982 | | Age: 33 | | Risk: Yellow |

Year	Team	G/GS	Snaps	Runs	Yds	Yd/R	TD	FUM	DVOA	Rk	DYAR	Rk	YAR	Suc%	Rk	BTkl	Rec	Pass	Yds	C%	Yd/C	TD	YAC	DVOA	Rk	DYAR	Rk
2012	GB	14/3	374	23	63	2.7	1	0	-7.9%	--	1	--	-3	39%	--	1	15	18	148	83%	9.9	0	8.5	47.8%	--	60	--
2013	GB	15/6	320	10	38	3.8	1	0	51.1%	--	32	--	33	70%	--	0	13	19	81	68%	6.2	0	6.4	-19.7%	--	-6	--
2014	GB	16/2	192	24	85	3.5	1	0	3.1%	--	13	--	8	58%	--	1	4	4	23	100%	5.8	0	6.3	22.1%	--	8	--
2015	GB			13	47	3.6	2	1	19.6%								15	18	110	83%	7.3	1		7.8%			

Most of Kuhn's carries are simple fullback dives, and nearly half (11 of 24) came in the red zone, but Kuhn was actually less effective near the goal line than either James Starks or Eddie Lacy. The Packers also selected a fullback, Aaron Ripkowski, in the sixth round, so Kuhn might face some competition for his job. Then again, the Packers do not currently have their normal plethora of H-back types, so there may be room on the roster for both.

Eddie Lacy

| | Height: 5-11 | | Weight: 231 | | College: Alabama | | | Draft: 2013/2 (61) | | Born: 1-Jan-1990 | | Age: 26 | | Risk: Green |

Year	Team	G/GS	Snaps	Runs	Yds	Yd/R	TD	FUM	DVOA	Rk	DYAR	Rk	YAR	Suc%	Rk	BTkl	Rec	Pass	Yds	C%	Yd/C	TD	YAC	DVOA	Rk	DYAR	Rk
2013	GB	15/15	680	284	1178	4.1	11	1	5.3%	18	160	9	171	46%	27	29	35	44	257	80%	7.3	0	8.9	-3.5%	27	26	29
2014	GB	16/16	687	246	1139	4.6	9	3	9.8%	8	189	8	159	48%	15	51	42	55	427	76%	10.2	4	10.3	23.0%	9	112	4
2015	GB			274	1275	4.7	10	3	12.4%								39	54	317	72%	8.1	2		12.6%			

Based on similarity scores, the most similar running backs to Lacy in their first two seasons include Marshawn Lynch, Greg Bell, and Corey Dillon. The biggest growth in Lacy's game between his first and second seasons came in the passing game, where the DVOA change was the result of real improvement in his performance after the catch. As a rusher, the record was more mixed. A full season of Aaron Rodgers resulted in fewer loaded boxes and better rate stats, including DVOA and success rate. Lacy did his best work when he had some room to get started, breaking most of his tackles at the second and third levels after he had a head of steam going. With the Packers bringing back the same offensive line, there's no reason to expect things to be different in 2015.

Marshawn Lynch

| | Heiht: 5-11 | | Weight: 215 | | College: California | | | Draft: 2007/1 (12) | | Born: 22-Apr-1986 | | Age: 29 | | Risk: Green |

Year	Team	G/GS	Snaps	Runs	Yds	Yd/R	TD	FUM	DVOA	Rk	DYAR	Rk	YAR	Suc%	Rk	BTkl	Rec	Pass	Yds	C%	Yd/C	TD	YAC	DVOA	Rk	DYAR	Rk
2012	SEA	16/15	675	315	1590	5.0	11	5	19.2%	3	361	2	267	50%	11	26	23	30	196	77%	8.5	1	8.8	13.2%	11	50	19
2013	SEA	16/16	710	301	1257	4.2	12	4	5.9%	17	185	5	146	48%	19	59	36	44	316	82%	8.8	2	7.9	9.1%	15	55	19
2014	SEA	16/14	704	280	1306	4.7	13	3	23.1%	1	359	2	307	53%	5	88	37	48	367	77%	9.9	4	10.9	21.8%	11	93	9
2015	SEA			275	1270	4.6	12	3	14.9%								33	45	267	73%	8.1	2		8.6%			

Marshawn Lynch has led the NFL in broken tackles two years in a row now, and he was in the top 10 in 2012. He led all running backs in rushing DVOA in 2014 despite facing a loaded box more often than any of his peers. Is it fair to say that no runner in the league deserves a greater share of the credit for his accomplishments?
We're just writing this comment so we don't get fined.
Lynch joined Seattle since 2010, and since then he is first or second in the NFL in carries, rushing yards, rushing touchdowns, and total touchdowns. He has multiple "BeastQuake" highlight runs. He has been the best offensive player on two Super Bowl teams, and of course he won a championship. Is this a Hall of Fame player we're looking at here?
We're just writing this comment so we don't get fined.
While the NFL was docking Lynch's check for his refusal to participate in Super Bowl press conferences, Lynch was busy

producing and selling "I'm just here so I won't get fined" t-shirts, with no trademarks so he wouldn't have to split profits with the NFL. He's actually a savvy businessman, isn't he?

We're just writing this comment so we don't get fined.

Lynch didn't want to do NFL media, but he had no problem making multiple appearances on Conan O'Brien's talk show, playing Mortal Kombat with Rob Gronkowski, laughing at the ridiculously bad commercials he shot for a Seattle plumber, brushing off the last play of the Super Bowl, and diving into a pile of Skittles while grabbing what he called his "ding-ding." Is it possible that Lynch, while definitely a weirdo, doesn't take himself too seriously after all?

We're just writing this comment so we don't get fined.

Lynch's refusal to speak to the press was far and away the most interesting thing to happen during Super Bowl media week in years. Doesn't this prove that Super Bowl media week, and really most press conferences and interviews in sports, are useless, cliché-filled wastes of time that only warrant mention when someone shuts up or brings their daughter or something?

We're just writing this comment so we don't get fined.

Doug Martin   Height: 5-9   Weight: 210   College: Boise State   Draft: 2012/1 (31)   Born: 13-Jan-1989   Age: 26   Risk: Green

Year	Team	G/GS	Snaps	Runs	Yds	Yd/R	TD	FUM	DVOA	Rk	DYAR	Rk	YAR	Suc%	Rk	BTkl	Rec	Pass	Yds	C%	Yd/C	TD	YAC	DVOA	Rk	DYAR	Rk
2012	TB	16/16	821	319	1454	4.6	11	1	3.9%	14	155	9	204	48%	20	41	49	70	472	70%	9.6	1	8.9	3.1%	24	66	13
2013	TB	6/6	303	127	456	3.6	1	1	-14.9%	40	-31	38	-53	39%	41	6	12	24	66	50%	5.5	0	4.8	-54.2%	--	-45	--
2014	TB	11/11	345	134	494	3.7	2	0	-12.9%	36	-21	34	5	36%	43	7	13	20	64	65%	4.9	0	4.8	-47.2%	--	-35	--
2015	TB			181	664	3.7	3	1	-5.5%								12	18	84	67%	7.0	0		-11.0%			

The Muscle Hamster apparently doesn't like to be called Muscle Hamster. Muscle Hamster is such a perfect nickname for a guy who stands 5-foot-9 but is chiseled at 223 pounds, it's hard to figure why Martin chooses not to embrace it. In his rookie season, Martin earned a nickname of Muscle Hamster quality. His 1,454 yards ranked tenth all-time for rookie running backs. However, of the 13 rookie running backs to rush for more than 1,400 yards as a rookie, Martin ran for the fewest total yards and yards per carry in his second and third season. With their 2012 first-rounder unproductive and slowed by injuries, the Buccaneers declined Martin's fifth-year option this offseason, choosing a wait-and-see approach. The Muscle Hamster broke tackles on less than 5 percent of his touches in both 2013 and 2014, ranking in the bottom ten of running backs each year. Time to show more muscle and less hamster.

Tre Mason   Height: 5-8   Weight: 207   College: Auburn   Draft: 2014/3 (75)   Born: 8-Jun-1993   Age: 22   Risk: Blue

Year	Team	G/GS	Snaps	Runs	Yds	Yd/R	TD	FUM	DVOA	Rk	DYAR	Rk	YAR	Suc%	Rk	BTkl	Rec	Pass	Yds	C%	Yd/C	TD	YAC	DVOA	Rk	DYAR	Rk
2014	STL	12/9	368	179	765	4.3	4	2	-0.9%	21	55	23	10	44%	30	14	16	26	148	62%	9.3	1	10.3	28.3%	6	55	17
2015	STL			140	602	4.3	2	3	-0.2%								26	34	189	76%	7.4	0		2.9%			

Mason started every game from Week 9 onward, and he was 13th in the NFL in rushing yards in the second half of the year. His biggest game came against Oakland, when he gained 117 yards (including touchdowns of 89 and 8 yards) on only 14 carries, while adding 47 yards and a touchdown on three catches. The drafting of Todd Gurley means Mason won't have much of a chance to follow up on his rookie year, though Mason might get a heavy workload early in the season as the Rams bring Gurley along slowly after his torn ACL.

Ryan Mathews   Height: 6-0   Weight: 218   College: Fresno State   Draft: 2010/1 (12)   Born: 1-May-1987   Age: 28   Risk: Green

Year	Team	G/GS	Snaps	Runs	Yds	Yd/R	TD	FUM	DVOA	Rk	DYAR	Rk	YAR	Suc%	Rk	BTkl	Rec	Pass	Yds	C%	Yd/C	TD	YAC	DVOA	Rk	DYAR	Rk
2012	SD	12/9	402	184	707	3.8	1	2	-7.7%	28	6	28	25	47%	23	17	39	57	252	68%	6.5	0	8.8	-15.4%	34	-5	34
2013	SD	16/14	472	285	1255	4.4	6	2	3.6%	19	141	10	120	49%	17	13	26	33	189	79%	7.3	1	7.3	19.9%	11	61	17
2014	SD	6/6	165	74	330	4.5	3	1	11.3%	--	62	--	37	47%	--	8	9	10	69	90%	7.7	0	7.0	37.6%	--	32	--
2015	PHI			109	480	4.4	3	3	5.1%								17	25	108	68%	6.4	0		-12.2%			

This offseason Chip Kelly acquired Kiko Alonso, Sam Bradford, and Ryan Mathews after all three had season-ending injuries. Maybe Tim Tebow's role is to be the team's healer. Mathews in particular has carried the "injury-prone" tag for years, but 2014 was the first time he didn't play at least 12 games. He's now in a superior system, he has always been a solid back when healthy, and DeMarco Murray (hey, even more injury concerns) is expected to be the workhorse this year. This is no doubt a demotion for Mathews, since he may be fortunate to see 100 carries based on the way Kelly has distributed carries the last two years, but it's a cozy spot to be in and one that should keep him healthier.

Dexter McCluster | Height: 5-9 | Weight: 172 | College: Mississippi | Draft: 2010/2 (36) | Born: 26-Aug-1988 | Age: 27 | Risk: Green

Year	Team	G/GS	Snaps	Runs	Yds	Yd/R	TD	FUM	DVOA	Rk	DYAR	Rk	YAR	Suc%	Rk	BTkl	Rec	Pass	Yds	C%	Yd/C	TD	YAC	DVOA	Rk	DYAR	Rk
2012	KC	16/6	573	12	70	5.8	0	0	38.7%	6	42	2	42	0%	0	0	52	76	452	68%	8.7	1	3.9	-21.1%	81	-34	79
2013	KC	15/6	581	8	5	0.6	0	0	-89.6%	8	-25	8	-27	0%	0	6	53	83	511	64%	9.6	2	4.9	-16.0%	78	-22	76
2014	TEN	14/2	233	40	131	3.3	0	0	-20.2%	--	-19	--	-7	41%	--	8	26	37	197	73%	7.6	1	7.2	-0.8%	26	26	28
2015	TEN			25	107	4.3	1	1	3.9%								32	47	251	68%	7.8	1		-8.9%			

On a team that kept most of its roster intact, McCluster's arrival and shift from slot receiver to running back was Ken Whisenhunt's dramatic declaration of how different things would be in Tennessee. They weren't, and McCluster was just a satellite back, running best (but not well) on the perimeter and occasionally flashing shiftiness in space, but rarely doing more than that. A crowded slot receiver depth chart will keep him in the backfield in 2015, but finding regular offensive snaps for him there should not be a priority.

LeSean McCoy | Height: 5-11 | Weight: 198 | College: Pittsburgh | Draft: 2009/2 (53) | Born: 12-Jul-1988 | Age: 27 | Risk: Green

Year	Team	G/GS	Snaps	Runs	Yds	Yd/R	TD	FUM	DVOA	Rk	DYAR	Rk	YAR	Suc%	Rk	BTkl	Rec	Pass	Yds	C%	Yd/C	TD	YAC	DVOA	Rk	DYAR	Rk
2012	PHI	12/12	694	200	840	4.2	2	4	-12.6%	33	-34	35	7	48%	19	44	54	68	373	81%	6.9	3	8.9	9.2%	17	90	9
2013	PHI	16/16	873	314	1607	5.1	9	1	18.1%	3	341	1	321	52%	8	51	52	64	539	81%	10.4	2	11.3	23.8%	9	137	7
2014	PHI	16/16	775	312	1319	4.2	5	4	-1.6%	24	87	15	93	45%	22	40	28	39	155	77%	5.5	0	6.6	-18.2%	43	-9	44
2015	BUF			302	1252	4.1	7	4	0.8%								28	43	180	65%	6.4	0		-25.6%			

McCoy rushed for 701 yards on plays marked as "left end" or "right end" but just 610 on plays within the tackle box. That's a very unusual split for a modern workhorse running back. Most teams only run outside about 20 percent of the time, but the Eagles were listed as running outside 42 percent of the time. (Some of that comes because the official scorer in Philadelphia is more likely to mark runs as "end" rather than "tackle," but even on the road, 35 percent of runs by Philadelphia backs were marked "left end" or "right end.") The Eagles ran to the outside frequently because Shady ran to the outside frequently. His tendency to bounce every zone rush to the sideline became a crippling addiction when Jason Kelce and Evan Mathis got hurt in the middle of the Eagles line and Shady carried 29 times for 41 yards against the 49ers and Redskins. Shady got his groove back for a string of very good midseason games, but even in his best moments during 2014, he was a boom-or-bust back with his boom frequency beefed up by his line and his system. McCoy was the best running back in the NFL in 2011 and 2013, so the Bills may enjoy another odd-year resurgence, assuming he sticks his nose in the hole more often and comes to terms with the fact that he was traded to the NFL's equivalent of a Siberian gulag.

Darren McFadden | Height: 6-1 | Weight: 211 | College: Arkansas | Draft: 2008/1 (4) | Born: 27-Aug-1987 | Age: 28 | Risk: Yellow

Year	Team	G/GS	Snaps	Runs	Yds	Yd/R	TD	FUM	DVOA	Rk	DYAR	Rk	YAR	Suc%	Rk	BTkl	Rec	Pass	Yds	C%	Yd/C	TD	YAC	DVOA	Rk	DYAR	Rk
2012	OAK	12/12	591	216	707	3.3	2	2	-26.7%	41	-153	42	-132	36%	41	14	42	64	258	69%	6.1	1	6.2	-36.7%	43	-82	47
2013	OAK	10/7	336	114	379	3.3	5	1	-17.0%	42	-38	40	-31	34%	46	6	17	25	108	68%	6.4	0	7.4	-8.8%	32	7	34
2014	OAK	16/12	513	155	534	3.4	2	1	-13.9%	37	-33	37	-40	40%	35	14	36	56	212	64%	5.9	0	7.3	-37.5%	53	-75	56
2015	DAL			126	564	4.5	4	2	8.2%								23	32	178	72%	7.7	1		-1.5%			

More than ever, we want the "if he stays healthy" disclaimer for Darren McFadden to work out, because McFadden's 2015 performance could be an important data point in the on-going debate about running backs vs. offensive lines. McFadden is the first running back to average less than 3.5 yards per carry in three consecutive seasons (with at least 100 carries in each) since Kevan Barlow in 2004-06. But if the Dallas offensive line is as good as advertised, then he could see a real resurgence this season. There's no guarantee he'll win the starting job with Joseph Randle and Lance Dunbar holding tenure in Dallas, but the opportunity's there. Even the most optimistic Dallas fan has no reason to expect a repeat of Murray's success, because McFadden doesn't run with that type of vision. He's going to rely on this offensive line to get him to the second level where he still has some speed left. So while the big games may be there, the consistency is unlikely to follow.

Jerick McKinnon

| | | | Height: 5-9 | | Weight: 209 | | College: Georgia Southern | | Draft: 2014/3 (96) | | Born: 5-Mar-1992 | | Age: 23 | Risk: Blue |

Year	Team	G/GS	Snaps	Runs	Yds	Yd/R	TD	FUM	DVOA	Rk	DYAR	Rk	YAR	Suc%	Rk	BTkl	Rec	Pass	Yds	C%	Yd/C	TD	YAC	DVOA	Rk	DYAR	Rk
2014	MIN	11/6	331	113	538	4.8	0	0	11.5%	7	82	16	72	42%	34	12	27	41	135	66%	5.0	0	6.4	-53.1%	57	-83	57
2015	MIN			73	336	4.6	1	3	0.6%								15	20	109	75%	7.2	1		3.3%			

Quick, who finished with the highest rushing DVOA last year among Eddie Lacy, Le'Veon Bell, Arian Foster, and Jerick McKinnon? You probably didn't need to think too long considering this is McKinnon's player comment, but that doesn't make the fact any less surprising or impressive. Matt Waldman highlighted the former Georgia Southern quarterback as one of the more intriguing projects in his 2014 *Rookie Scouting Portfolio*, noting that McKinnon "flashed the jukes, cuts and speed of a top running back." Those agility-related points may have been McKinnon's biggest selling points, but the most impressive aspect of his rookie season was actually his power. The 5-foot-9 back surprisingly averaged 2.2 yards after contact per attempt, the eighth-best mark among running backs with at least 100 carries. McKinnon is not a pure scatback, despite what his measurables might suggest, and if his receiving efficiency improves, he could be the cost-controlled (and non-controversial) asset that gives Minnesota leverage next offseason with Adrian Peterson.

Christine Michael

| | | | Height: 5-10 | | Weight: 220 | | College: Texas A&M | | Draft: 2013/2 (62) | | Born: 9-Nov-1990 | | Age: 25 | Risk: Green |

Year	Team	G/GS	Snaps	Runs	Yds	Yd/R	TD	FUM	DVOA	Rk	DYAR	Rk	YAR	Suc%	Rk	BTkl	Rec	Pass	Yds	C%	Yd/C	TD	YAC	DVOA	Rk	DYAR	Rk
2013	SEA	4/0	26	18	79	4.4	0	0	10.6%	--	14	--	17	78%	--	0	0	0	0	0%	--	0	--	0.0%	--	0	--
2014	SEA	10/0	73	34	175	5.1	0	1	10.0%	--	25	--	19	50%	--	8	1	2	12	50%	12.0	0	18.0	23.8%	--	3	--
2015	SEA			34	162	4.7	1	1	10.5%							6	8	48	75%	7.9	0		5.2%			

Michael has been very effective in the rare instances when he has been given the ball, but he remains the clear third running back in Seattle behind Marshawn Lynch and Robert Turbin. Michael had character and injury concerns coming into the NFL, but so far he has been a model citizen for the Seahawks. He's just waiting for a chance at significant playing time.

Lamar Miller

| | | | Height: 5-11 | | Weight: 212 | | College: Miami | | Draft: 2012/4 (97) | | Born: 25-Apr-1991 | | Age: 24 | Risk: Green |

Year	Team	G/GS	Snaps	Runs	Yds	Yd/R	TD	FUM	DVOA	Rk	DYAR	Rk	YAR	Suc%	Rk	BTkl	Rec	Pass	Yds	C%	Yd/C	TD	YAC	DVOA	Rk	DYAR	Rk
2012	MIA	13/1	143	51	250	4.9	1	0	7.5%	--	35	--	48	55%	--	5	6	9	45	67%	7.5	0	6.7	-2.0%	--	6	--
2013	MIA	16/15	622	177	709	4.0	2	1	-7.7%	31	6	31	5	46%	29	16	26	35	170	74%	6.5	0	6.8	-7.9%	31	11	32
2014	MIA	16/16	642	216	1099	5.1	8	2	17.8%	3	246	4	239	57%	1	24	38	52	275	73%	7.2	1	6.1	-10.7%	37	9	37
2015	MIA			218	1024	4.7	7	2	13.9%							39	56	312	70%	8.0	1		2.0%			

Three running backs were chosen in the first round of the 2012 draft, yet a sixth-round pick (Alfred Morris) and a fourth-round pick (Lamar Miller) look like the best of the bunch after three years. Morris has cooled down since that hot rookie start, but Miller just continues to get better. Both players show the importance of scheme. Miami offensive coordinator Bill Lazor came from Philadelphia and utilized Miller much as the Eagles did with LeSean McCoy in Chip Kelly's offense. Miller doesn't have all the moves of McCoy, but he's a good speed back and he upped his broken tackles last year. He's only carried the ball 20-plus times in one of his 45 career games, but he's effective on limited touches.

Spacing is very crucial to this offense, and getting into the open field is where Miller's speed can be most deadly. He had a 97-yard touchdown run against the Jets in Week 17 that was the result of a bad angle in the open field by a defensive back. You might note that play is boosting his season averages, but Miller's not a boom-and-bust runner: he led all backs in rushing success rate in 2014. When the Dolphins used three wide receivers last year, Miller averaged 6.1 yards per carry on 141 carries, still averaging 5.4 yards per carry without the 97-yard sprint. Miami should feature that formation more in 2015, with the intriguing new trio of Jarvis Landry, Kenny Stills and rookie DeVante Parker. 81 percent of Miller's runs were out of the shotgun, up from 41 percent in 2013. Miami used him properly last year and he should be able to repeat his success in an offense with better weapons and a healthier offensive line.

Knowshon Moreno

Height: 5-11   Weight: 200   College: Georgia   Draft: 2009/1 (12)   Born: 16-Jul-1987   Age: 28   Risk: N/A

Year	Team	G/GS	Snaps	Runs	Yds	Yd/R	TD	FUM	DVOA	Rk	DYAR	Rk	YAR	Suc%	Rk	BTkl	Rec	Pass	Yds	C%	Yd/C	TD	YAC	DVOA	Rk	DYAR	Rk
2012	DEN	8/6	337	139	525	3.8	4	1	1.1%	18	56	20	67	56%	2	10	21	26	167	81%	8.0	0	6.0	25.3%	5	58	15
2013	DEN	16/15	703	241	1038	4.3	10	1	8.4%	13	171	6	199	50%	14	18	60	74	548	81%	9.1	3	7.9	31.0%	4	192	3
2014	MIA	3/0	68	31	148	4.8	1	0	26.9%	--	50	--	45	65%	--	3	1	1	8	100%	8.0	0	9.0	78.3%	--	5	--

Moreno came out like gangbusters in 2014, dragging New England defenders all over the field in Miami's Week 1 upset. He made sharp cuts and at one point had at least two yards after contact on seven straight carries. But early the next week, Nigel Bradham of the Bills dislocated Moreno's elbow on a tackle, costing him three weeks. In his first game back, he tore his ACL. So much for that one-year prove-it contract he signed in Miami. Currently a free agent, Moreno could return to the Dolphins as a complementary presence to new starter Lamar Miller, but if Jay Ajayi shows anything at all over the course of the summer, Moreno's future will likely be elsewhere.

Alfred Morris

Height: 5-10   Weight: 219   College: Florida Atlantic   Draft: 2012/6 (173)   Born: 12-Dec-1988   Age: 27   Risk: Yellow

Year	Team	G/GS	Snaps	Runs	Yds	Yd/R	TD	FUM	DVOA	Rk	DYAR	Rk	YAR	Suc%	Rk	BTkl	Rec	Pass	Yds	C%	Yd/C	TD	YAC	DVOA	Rk	DYAR	Rk
2012	WAS	16/16	728	335	1613	4.8	13	4	10.3%	8	254	5	273	52%	7	27	11	16	77	69%	7.0	0	5.9	-14.6%	--	-1	--
2013	WAS	16/16	605	276	1275	4.6	7	6	2.0%	21	121	13	133	48%	20	24	9	12	78	75%	8.7	0	8.8	-12.0%	--	1	--
2014	WAS	16/16	595	265	1074	4.1	8	2	-1.4%	23	77	17	77	46%	18	28	17	26	155	65%	9.1	0	9.1	-8.7%	36	7	38
2015	WAS			274	1129	4.1	7	3	1.3%								22	33	170	67%	7.7	0		-8.3%			

Jay Gruden confirmed after the draft that Alfred Morris was still the featured running back, despite the arrival of Matt Jones; about half of Gruden's offseason energy was spent publically confirming the offseason depth chart. Morris' yards per carry have dropped from 4.8 as a rookie to 4.1 last year, but he remains effective after contact and has cut down on his fumbles.

Morris is at the mercy of the rest of the Redskins offense: if the Redskins are out of the game, he's out of the game, and defenses like the Seahawks (13 carries, 29 yards) will continue to easily bottle him up until there is someone else on the Redskins to genuinely worry about. New offensive line coach Bill Callahan is expected to help boost Morris' production, because Callahan is supposed to have magical powers after one great year with a bunch of first-round picks in Dallas.

DeMarco Murray

Height: 6-0   Weight: 213   College: Oklahoma   Draft: 2011/3 (71)   Born: 12-Feb-1988   Age: 27   Risk: Red

Year	Team	G/GS	Snaps	Runs	Yds	Yd/R	TD	FUM	DVOA	Rk	DYAR	Rk	YAR	Suc%	Rk	BTkl	Rec	Pass	Yds	C%	Yd/C	TD	YAC	DVOA	Rk	DYAR	Rk
2012	DAL	10/0	466	161	663	4.1	4	4	1.7%	16	72	15	65	54%	5	26	34	42	247	83%	7.3	0	6.9	10.4%	16	60	14
2013	DAL	14/14	672	217	1121	5.2	9	3	24.0%	1	295	2	288	53%	6	35	53	66	350	80%	6.6	1	7.2	-3.5%	26	40	24
2014	DAL	16/16	782	392	1845	4.7	13	5	14.8%	5	382	1	369	54%	3	51	57	64	416	89%	7.3	0	8.8	3.0%	21	58	14
2015	PHI			270	1208	4.5	9	1	12.1%								45	59	360	76%	8.0	3		17.4%			

Here's a Curse of 370 pu-pu platter for those who can't decide on which reason why Murray won't repeat his 2014 performance:

• Murray's yards per carry dipped from 5.4 in September to 4.9 in October, 4.5 in November and 4.0 in December. Murray was clearly suffering from overuse late in the season, though he bounced back in the playoff game against the Packers.

• Including the playoffs, Murray carried 436 times last season, passing the 370-carry manufacturer's warranty cap by 18.8 percent.

• Murray leaves behind the best offensive line in the NFL for a line that finished 29th in adjusted line yards last season. Yes, the Eagles had a lot of injuries on the offensive line last season, but with two starters in their thirties (Jason Peters and Allen Barbre), injuries may be a fact of life on the Eagles line.

• Ryan Mathews wasn't signed just because the Murray talks slowed down and Chip Kelly got impatient to sign a running back. At least, that's the operating theory. Mathews and Darren Sproles will siphon carries from Murray, no matter how healthy and productive he may be.

• Murray is 27 years old, carried the ball 759 times in college, and missed significant time in each of his first three NFL seasons.

Heard enough? Murray is immensely talented, of course, and he looked both phenomenal and eager to make a great impression in Eagles minicamp. The Eagles can also use creativity in the running game the way the Cowboys used brute blocking force. Murray could be dinged up for a few games, ordinary in a few others, and still finish with 1,200 yards and ten touchdowns. Fantasy owners and Eagles fans must get used to the idea that those numbers are more of an upside than a downside.

Latavius Murray   Height: 6-2   Weight: 223   College: UCF   Draft: 2013/6 (181)   Born: 21-Feb-1991   Age: 24   Risk: Yellow

Year	Team	G/GS	Snaps	Runs	Yds	Yd/R	TD	FUM	DVOA	Rk	DYAR	Rk	YAR	Suc%	Rk	BTkl	Rec	Pass	Yds	C%	Yd/C	TD	YAC	DVOA	Rk	DYAR	Rk
2014	OAK	15/3	275	82	424	5.2	2	1	1.7%	--	35	--	26	44%	--	3	17	23	143	74%	8.4	0	9.0	-6.6%	--	8	--
2015	OAK			203	896	4.4	5	5	0.3%								30	43	227	70%	7.6	1		-2.4%			

Board the Murray bandwagon at your own risk. Most of the excitement about him stems from a 90-yard touchdown run (which was worth about 28 DYAR) against the Chiefs in a prime-time game. Otherwise, Murray has carried the ball 81 times for 334 yards (4.12 yards per carry) and 7 DYAR in his brief career. He's another long scamper and a second sport away from Bo Jackson territory, but that kind of outlier play combined with a lack of a track record should give you some pause in thinking this guy's the next Jamaal Charles. He has nice speed, and he doesn't have Darren McFadden in his way anymore, but Oakland still has to prove its run blocking has improved and that its defense is capable of making the game more conducive to running instead of forcing Derek Carr to throw to catch up. Roy Helu and Trent Richardson are likely to eat into Murray's touches too, since he's not a guy who will carry the ball 20 times per game. The potential is enticing, but never fall in love with one play.

Branden Oliver   Height: 5-8   Weight: 203   College: Buffalo   Draft: 2014/FA   Born: 7-May-1991   Age: 24   Risk: Blue

Year	Team	G/GS	Snaps	Runs	Yds	Yd/R	TD	FUM	DVOA	Rk	DYAR	Rk	YAR	Suc%	Rk	BTkl	Rec	Pass	Yds	C%	Yd/C	TD	YAC	DVOA	Rk	DYAR	Rk
2014	SD	14/7	373	160	582	3.6	3	0	-5.5%	28	20	29	24	44%	26	29	36	45	271	80%	7.5	1	9.4	15.3%	12	68	12
2015	SD			40	142	3.5	2	2	-4.9%							22	28	168	79%	7.7	1		5.6%			

"He's short and he wears No. 34 for San Diego, so let's compare him to Darren Sproles." That was the basic storyline on Oliver last season when he emerged as the team's leading rusher as an undrafted free-agent rookie. He has a bit more power than Sproles, but not the same dynamic speed. Oliver had the third-most broken tackles (29) among backs with fewer than 200 touches last year. He only needs to be a secondary runner this year with Melvin Gordon taking over the starting job.

Adrian Peterson   Height: 6-2   Weight: 217   College: Oklahoma   Draft: 2007/1 (7)   Born: 21-Mar-1985   Age: 30   Risk: Red

Year	Team	G/GS	Snaps	Runs	Yds	Yd/R	TD	FUM	DVOA	Rk	DYAR	Rk	YAR	Suc%	Rk	BTkl	Rec	Pass	Yds	C%	Yd/C	TD	YAC	DVOA	Rk	DYAR	Rk
2012	MIN	16/16	770	348	2097	6.0	12	4	24.9%	2	458	1	357	49%	14	44	40	51	217	78%	5.4	1	4.7	-14.9%	33	-3	33
2013	MIN	14/14	674	279	1266	4.5	10	5	-3.1%	26	60	25	135	44%	32	42	29	41	171	73%	5.9	1	5.5	-22.8%	45	-20	43
2014	MIN	1/1	43	21	75	3.6	0	0	-1.8%	--	5	--	-4	43%	--	1	2	3	18	67%	9.0	0	10.0	53.4%	--	10	--
2015	MIN			290	1320	4.6	11	6	5.3%							38	48	303	79%	8.0	1		7.5%			

At this time last year, Adrian Peterson was the consensus best running back alive. Now, after his season in exile, the only consensus expectation is that Peterson will don purple after blinking first during his offseason staredown against the Vikings. Given that he essentially rested his body for a year, there's little reason to expect much slippage from Peterson's 2013 form. However, that player was far from the MVP version of 2012, as Peterson posted his first negative rushing DVOA since 2008. Still, in his age-30 season, there's reason to believe that a motivated Peterson could thrive in Norv Turner's back-friendly system. The offense Peterson returns to is far unlike the fullback-heavy sets Minnesota has traditionally utilized, as the Vikes evolved into a shotgun-based 11 personnel offense under Teddy Bridgewater. In theory, that should lead to lighter boxes for Peterson, who saw big DVOA drops facing loaded boxes versus non-loaded boxes in both 2013 (-24.4% lower) and 2012 (-32.5% lower). Re-integrating Peterson into a Bridgewater-centric offense is a precarious challenge for a Vikings franchise that generated positive momentum in his absence last season. With 2,279 career touches, 39th all-time and third-most among active players, Peterson is the outlier on a team full of ascending young cornerstones. Still, Peterson was a hop, skip and a jump away from breaking the single-season rushing record the last time he faced widespread doubt before a season. After what's transpired the past 12 months, hardly anything Peterson does on the field would be surprising.

Bernard Pierce

Height: 6-0		Weight: 218		College: Temple				Draft: 2012/3 (84)			Born: 10-May-1991			Age: 24			Risk: Red								

Year	Team	G/GS	Snaps	Runs	Yds	Yd/R	TD	FUM	DVOA	Rk	DYAR	Rk	YAR	Suc%	Rk	BTkl	Rec	Pass	Yds	C%	Yd/C	TD	YAC	DVOA	Rk	DYAR	Rk
2012	BAL	16/0	218	108	532	4.9	1	0	4.1%	13	54	21	52	47%	24	19	7	11	47	64%	6.7	0	6.1	1.8%	--	10	--
2013	BAL	16/1	398	152	436	2.9	2	0	-29.3%	47	-131	46	-125	38%	42	15	20	25	104	80%	5.2	0	5.7	-33.3%	47	-27	46
2014	BAL	13/2	159	93	366	3.9	2	1	-14.8%	--	-24	--	-13	42%	--	6	2	6	13	33%	6.5	0	5.0	-80.0%	--	-20	--
2015	JAC			23	93	4.0	1	1	3.8%								4	5	19	80%	4.8	0		-11.8%			

A couple of field notes from Pierce's DUI arrest in March, according to TMZ Sports: when asked how much he weighed, Pierce replied "530 pounds" twice before finally getting it right with "230." Then Pierce moaned to the cops, "I'm getting cut tomorrow, not like you care." Nostra-Pierce was indeed let go by the Ravens the following day, a decision made easier by his injury-hit, subpar last two seasons. The Jags picked him up off waivers, leading Pierce to say, "God works in mysterious ways." The only mystery is whether Pierce will make the Jaguars roster in the first place.

Chris Polk

Height: 5-11		Weight: 222		College: Washington				Draft: 2012/FA			Born: 16-Dec-1989			Age: 26			Risk: Red								

Year	Team	G/GS	Snaps	Runs	Yds	Yd/R	TD	FUM	DVOA	Rk	DYAR	Rk	YAR	Suc%	Rk	BTkl	Rec	Pass	Yds	C%	Yd/C	TD	YAC	DVOA	Rk	DYAR	Rk
2012	PHI	7/0	0	0	0	0.0	0	--	--	--	--	--	--	--	--	0	0	--	0	--	0.0	0	--	--	--	--	--
2013	PHI	15/0	46	11	98	8.9	3	0	120.4%	--	64	--	59	64%	--	4	4	5	61	80%	15.3	0	12.3	81.6%	--	22	--
2014	PHI	14/0	97	46	172	3.7	4	0	12.9%	--	43	--	42	54%	--	3	2	3	16	67%	8.0	0	10.5	-19.9%	--	-1	--
2015	HOU			77	309	4.0	1	1	-4.5%								16	24	105	67%	6.6	0		-4.8%			

Polk could easily overtake Alfred Blue as Arian Foster's top backup. Blue was a two-game wonder who wilted down the stretch; Polk has been insanely productive with minimal touches and adds value as a return man. If you want a backup running back to come off the bench for five touches and potentially provide 40 yards, Polk is your man. The Eagles initially tendered Polk for 2015, then rescinded the offer when Kelly invited all the free agent running backs on the market to team headquarters, locked the doors, and released $100 bills into the air vents. In an alternate universe, Frank Gore and Polk are the Eagles running backs, with Darren Sproles for third downs. While that combination lacks sizzle, you don't even want to think about what Kelly spent the extra money on.

Bilal Powell

Height: 5-10		Weight: 205		College: Louisville				Draft: 2011/4 (126)			Born: 27-Oct-1988			Age: 27			Risk: Green								

Year	Team	G/GS	Snaps	Runs	Yds	Yd/R	TD	FUM	DVOA	Rk	DYAR	Rk	YAR	Suc%	Rk	BTkl	Rec	Pass	Yds	C%	Yd/C	TD	YAC	DVOA	Rk	DYAR	Rk
2012	NYJ	14/2	397	110	437	4.0	4	0	5.6%	10	63	17	71	50%	13	9	17	36	140	47%	8.2	0	7.1	-24.7%	39	-22	40
2013	NYJ	16/11	618	176	697	4.0	1	1	-8.7%	34	-1	34	37	43%	35	13	36	57	272	63%	7.6	0	8.7	-20.2%	44	-20	44
2014	NYJ	15/1	237	33	141	4.3	1	0	7.6%	--	22	--	24	45%	--	3	11	15	92	73%	8.4	0	8.7	2.2%	--	14	--
2015	NYJ			97	371	3.8	1	4	-5.9%								35	49	252	71%	7.2	1		-5.5%			

For years, the Jets have tried to shoehorn Powell into a number of roles for which he was ill-suited, including the role of every-down, between-the-tackles back. But now, with the Jets moving to a running-back-by-committee approach, Powell figures to have the inside track on the third-down job for a few reasons, not the least of which is that he's the only one on the roster who has shown an ability to catch the ball on anything resembling a regular basis. He's a below-average pass catcher (his catch rate the last three years is 59 percent, which is abysmal for a running back), but skilled enough as a pass blocker to likely be considered a favorite for the job going into camp.

Bobby Rainey

Height: 5-7		Weight: 206		College: Western Kentucky				Draft: 2012/FA			Born: 16-Oct-1987			Age: 28			Risk: Green								

Year	Team	G/GS	Snaps	Runs	Yds	Yd/R	TD	FUM	DVOA	Rk	DYAR	Rk	YAR	Suc%	Rk	BTkl	Rec	Pass	Yds	C%	Yd/C	TD	YAC	DVOA	Rk	DYAR	Rk
2013	2TM	15/6	326	150	566	3.8	5	1	-14.2%	39	-31	39	-43	31%	47	13	15	19	46	79%	3.1	1	4.5	-34.8%	--	-23	--
2014	TB	15/5	381	94	406	4.3	1	3	-4.9%	--	14	--	23	43%	--	14	33	45	315	73%	9.5	1	8.4	0.0%	24	31	27
2015	TB			51	214	4.2	1	2	-1.3%								17	24	118	71%	7.0	1		-2.6%			

Rainey was Tampa's best running back in 2014, averaging 0.6 yards more per carry than Doug Martin and 1.5 more than Charles Sims. Rainey (who ran a 4.42-second 40-yard dash in college) showed consistent explosion. His average likely would have been higher had Rainey not been saddled with the NFL's worst offensive line by adjusted line yards. His DVOA would have been higher if he had not fumbled once every 42 touches. Tampa has been looking at Rainey on kickoffs (he returned six kickoffs last year) and he might be their best option—Rainey ranked second in FBS in kickoff return average in 2008.

Joseph Randle

Height: 6-0　Weight: 204　College: Oklahoma State　Draft: 2013/5 (151)　Born: 29-Dec-1991　Age: 24　Risk: Red

Year	Team	G/GS	Snaps	Runs	Yds	Yd/R	TD	FUM	DVOA	Rk	DYAR	Rk	YAR	Suc%	Rk	BTkl	Rec	Pass	Yds	C%	Yd/C	TD	YAC	DVOA	Rk	DYAR	Rk
2013	DAL	13/2	119	54	164	3.0	2	0	-8.1%	--	1	--	-9	44%	--	2	8	10	61	80%	7.6	0	7.6	-10.6%	--	2	--
2014	DAL	16/0	93	51	343	6.7	3	2	26.3%	--	68	--	63	51%	--	13	4	5	23	80%	5.8	0	6.8	-19.8%	--	-2	--
2015	DAL			225	1003	4.5	7	4	4.1%								20	28	139	71%	6.9	1		-8.3%			

Randle lined up with the Cowboys starters early in OTAs. The conventional wisdom is that Randle and Darren McFadden will chair a running back committee, with Randle's role dependent on his ability to stay off the police blotter and in the good graces of the coaching staff. Domestic abuse charges against Randle were dropped in May (anyone who dusts their hands and says "that settles that" hasn't been following much NFL lately) and Randle got off with a fine after shoplifting cologne and underwear in October. But… this is a guy who makes $500,000 per year but shoplifts underwear and feels compelled to take parting shots at DeMarco Murray. Cowboys coaches made soothing sounds about how much Randle has matured in minicamp. The team would love to see him grow up enough to handle a 20-touch role after watching him average 6.7 yards per carry between brain cramps last season.

Darrin Reaves

Height: 5-10　Weight: 209　College: Alabama-Birmingham　Draft: 2014/FA　Born: 17-Apr-1993　Age: 22　Risk: Green

Year	Team	G/GS	Snaps	Runs	Yds	Yd/R	TD	FUM	DVOA	Rk	DYAR	Rk	YAR	Suc%	Rk	BTkl	Rec	Pass	Yds	C%	Yd/C	TD	YAC	DVOA	Rk	DYAR	Rk
2014	CAR	6/1	152	31	78	2.5	0	0	-29.8%	--	-27	--	-29	32%	--	3	5	8	31	63%	6.2	0	8.4	-35.4%	--	-10	--
2015	CAR			14	55	4.0	1	1	2.5%								5	7	36	71%	7.1	0		-4.1%			

It was only a matter of time before the Panthers somehow managed to align injuries for Jonathan Stewart and DeAngelo Williams together, so for a weird month-long stretch there, Darrin Reaves was the de facto starting back for the Panthers. An undrafted free agent, Reaves simply didn't offer anything to the Panthers, to the point where Fozzy Whittaker and Chris Ogbonnaya, depth players at best, eventually absorbed his role. Reaves was immediately waived as Stewart and Williams got healthy. He'll be lucky to remain on the practice squad this year.

Silas Redd

Height: 5-10　Weight: 200　College: USC　Draft: 2014/FA　Born: 1-Mar-1992　Age: 23　Risk: Green

Year	Team	G/GS	Snaps	Runs	Yds	Yd/R	TD	FUM	DVOA	Rk	DYAR	Rk	YAR	Suc%	Rk	BTkl	Rec	Pass	Yds	C%	Yd/C	TD	YAC	DVOA	Rk	DYAR	Rk
2014	WAS	15/0	55	16	75	4.7	1	1	31.8%	--	24	--	24	56%	--	4	8	10	107	80%	13.4	0	12.9	59.7%	--	39	--
2015	WAS			34	128	3.8	1	1	-7.4%								19	26	139	73%	7.3	0		-2.7%			

Redd carried eight times for 41 yards in Washington's Week 2 blowout of the Jaguars, then caught six passes for 98 yards in two late-season games when Roy Helu was injured. Redd also happened to be the player who was injured in the Redskins bus crash, but it turned out to be nothing serious, just typical Redskins humiliation. Redd is a quick, compact dart of a runner who could rotate with burly rookie Matt Jones in the role vacated by Roy Helu. Redd's pass protection has been questioned, but he looked OK in a handful of opportunities last year.

Marcel Reece

Height: 6-3　Weight: 240　College: Washington　Draft: 2008/FA　Born: 23-Jun-1985　Age: 30　Risk: Red

Year	Team	G/GS	Snaps	Runs	Yds	Yd/R	TD	FUM	DVOA	Rk	DYAR	Rk	YAR	Suc%	Rk	BTkl	Rec	Pass	Yds	C%	Yd/C	TD	YAC	DVOA	Rk	DYAR	Rk
2012	OAK	16/14	659	59	271	4.6	0	2	-6.9%	--	4	--	21	54%	--	15	52	73	496	71%	9.5	1	6.3	7.6%	21	90	8
2013	OAK	16/15	505	46	218	4.7	2	0	7.0%	--	31	--	21	39%	--	5	32	54	331	59%	10.3	2	7.1	-1.1%	24	38	25
2014	OAK	15/15	385	21	85	4.0	0	1	-6.1%	--	2	--	1	48%	--	3	37	59	265	63%	7.2	1	5.5	-10.9%	38	10	35
2015	OAK			25	104	4.1	1	1	6.1%								20	27	153	74%	7.7	1		7.0%			

A 30-year-old fullback? That's like being a 55-year-old actress in Hollywood. Reece's snaps have shrunk each season, but he still made last year's Pro Bowl, because he's one of the few fullbacks people can actually name in today's game. He certainly didn't make it because of 350 yards from scrimmage (the lowest since his rookie year) or his efforts to block for the league's worst rushing attack. We'll have to see if Reece's touches continue to drop now that Oakland signed a better receiving back in Roy Helu.

Trent Richardson

Height: 5-9 Weight: 228 College: Alabama Draft: 2012/1 (3) Born: 10-Jul-1991 Age: 24 Risk: Green

Year	Team	G/GS	Snaps	Runs	Yds	Yd/R	TD	FUM	DVOA	Rk	DYAR	Rk	YAR	Suc%	Rk	BTkl	Rec	Pass	Yds	C%	Yd/C	TD	YAC	DVOA	Rk	DYAR	Rk
2012	CLE	15/15	702	267	950	3.6	11	3	-13.3%	34	-51	37	-21	43%	36	31	51	70	367	73%	7.2	1	8.6	4.4%	23	73	11
2013	2TM	16/10	592	188	563	3.0	3	2	-22.2%	44	-108	45	-124	43%	36	24	35	52	316	67%	9.0	1	8.8	-2.6%	25	34	26
2014	IND	15/12	483	159	519	3.3	3	2	-17.7%	41	-59	41	-46	43%	32	32	27	34	229	79%	8.5	0	8.9	11.9%	15	49	19
2015	OAK			80	292	3.7	1	2	-10.4%								15	18	119	83%	7.9	0		12.2%			

"It just wasn't a good fit there." That's what Trent Richardson told reporters about his time in Indianapolis after the team cut him following two disastrous seasons. The perfect follow-up question would have been "do you mean here or the NFL in general?" We may not see another running back drafted in the top three for a long time for fear of another T-Rich situation. He was great at Alabama on a loaded team, but wasn't worth activating over Zurlon Tipton by the end of his third season. As detailed in the Indianapolis chapter, the Colts had success with every running back not named Richardson the last two years. The most holes he ever found in Indy were on his sex tape. It's fitting that the 2015 salary the Colts chose to void was $3.184 million, since Richardson averaged 3.1 yards per carry with the Colts. It's hard to see Richardson turning things around in Oakland, where Darren McFadden struggled against non-loaded boxes in a very similar fashion the past few years. Richardson is good as a receiver—he catches the ball well in space, and a lot of his broken tackles come on receptions, not runs—but Roy Helu is a better option for that, and Latavius Murray should be getting the most carries in Oakland. Richardson has made it to Year 4, but it's doubtful he'll ever get that average up to 4.0 in the NFL. He's just not a good fit.

Theo Riddick

Height: 5-10 Weight: 201 College: Notre Dame Draft: 2013/6 (199) Born: 4-May-1991 Age: 24 Risk: Green

Year	Team	G/GS	Snaps	Runs	Yds	Yd/R	TD	FUM	DVOA	Rk	DYAR	Rk	YAR	Suc%	Rk	BTkl	Rec	Pass	Yds	C%	Yd/C	TD	YAC	DVOA	Rk	DYAR	Rk
2013	DET	14/0	43	9	25	2.8	1	0	16.2%	--	9	--	5	44%	--	3	4	8	26	50%	6.5	0	4.3	-22.0%	--	-4	--
2014	DET	14/2	172	20	51	2.6	0	0	-34.4%	--	-22	--	-17	40%	--	4	34	50	316	68%	9.3	4	9.0	14.7%	13	76	11
2015	DET			40	160	4.0	0	2	-5.5%								26	33	221	79%	8.5	1		17.6%			

It was all going so swimmingly for Riddick, who appeared set to inherit the high-upside passing back role in Detroit's offense following Reggie Bush's free-agent departure. But the Lions plucked out the former Golden Domer's lucky shamrock and drafted Ameer Abdullah, thus leaving Riddick in roster purgatory. In fairness, the third-year back has just 67 career touches over two seasons, most of which came in Weeks 8-13 last year. Still, his receiving DVOA belies his promising skill set, which might not get a chance to shine with Abdullah and Joique Bell presumably ahead of him on the depth chart.

Stevan Ridley

Height: 6-0 Weight: 223 College: Louisiana St. Draft: 2011/3 (73) Born: 27-Jan-1989 Age: 26 Risk: Red

Year	Team	G/GS	Snaps	Runs	Yds	Yd/R	TD	FUM	DVOA	Rk	DYAR	Rk	YAR	Suc%	Rk	BTkl	Rec	Pass	Yds	C%	Yd/C	TD	YAC	DVOA	Rk	DYAR	Rk
2012	NE	16/12	549	290	1263	4.4	12	4	6.1%	9	192	8	191	55%	4	12	6	14	51	43%	8.5	0	7.8	-38.4%	--	-19	--
2013	NE	14/6	333	178	773	4.3	7	4	10.2%	9	135	11	133	52%	7	14	10	12	62	83%	6.2	0	5.7	-27.6%	--	-9	--
2014	NE	6/5	187	94	340	3.6	2	0	-9.9%	--	-6	--	17	53%	--	3	4	5	20	80%	5.0	0	7.8	-20.2%	--	-2	--
2015	NYJ			79	305	3.9	1	2	-6.1%								9	13	52	71%	5.8	0		-12.8%			

Ridley could flourish away from Bill Belichick's benching mind games. Through Week 9 in 2013, Ridley had posted a 17.2% DVOA, which led the league for running backs with at least 100 attempts. Then Ridley was benched for fumbling in Week 10 against Carolina. From Week 11 on, Ridley posted a -3.6% DVOA in limited action. Oh, and he fumbled the following week against the Broncos on just his fourth carry. The Jets will have to hope that Ridley has recovered not only from his torn ACL and MCL, but also Belichick's counterproductive yo-yoing. He's likely to start the year on PUP.

Denard Robinson   Height: 5-11   Weight: 190   College: Michigan   Draft: 2013/5 (135)   Born: 22-Sep-1990   Age: 25   Risk: Green

Year	Team	G/GS	Snaps	Runs	Yds	Yd/R	TD	FUM	DVOA	Rk	DYAR	Rk	YAR	Suc%	Rk	BTkl	Rec	Pass	Yds	C%	Yd/C	TD	YAC	DVOA	Rk	DYAR	Rk
2013	JAC	16/0	52	20	66	3.3	0	3	-86.1%	--	-61	--	-60	35%	--	0	0	1	0	0%	0.0	0	--	-102.0%	--	-2	--
2014	JAC	13/9	391	135	582	4.3	4	2	-8.1%	33	3	33	31	38%	40	9	23	31	124	74%	5.4	0	8.7	-39.2%	55	-43	52
2015	JAC			86	328	3.8	3	3	-7.0%								36	45	214	80%	6.0	0		-6.4%			

Robinson, a converted quarterback, showed the between-the-tackles physicality and natural athleticism to get positive results behind a bad Jaguars offensive line. He overcame the 2013 fumble problems that were caused by an injury-hindered weak grip, and has shed the too-cute role of Offensive Weapon to become Actual Football Running Back. It's a great story. The Jaguars decided they couldn't bet on him long-term, and brought in T.J. Yeldon in the second round. Still, Robinson is a nice back with some productive carries in his future—it's a nice return on a player nobody was sure about on draft day.

Khiry Robinson   Height: 6-0   Weight: 220   College: West Texas A&M   Draft: 2013/FA   Born: 28-Dec-1989   Age: 26   Risk: Green

Year	Team	G/GS	Snaps	Runs	Yds	Yd/R	TD	FUM	DVOA	Rk	DYAR	Rk	YAR	Suc%	Rk	BTkl	Rec	Pass	Yds	C%	Yd/C	TD	YAC	DVOA	Rk	DYAR	Rk
2013	NO	10/0	73	54	224	4.1	1	0	-11.9%	--	-7	--	4	41%	--	5	0	--	0	--	0.0	0	--	--	--	--	--
2014	NO	10/3	156	76	362	4.8	3	1	8.9%	--	57	--	67	58%	--	16	8	11	63	73%	7.9	0	10.8	-8.8%	--	3	--
2015	NO			56	243	4.3	1	2	0.2%								9	12	70	75%	7.8	1		4.9%			

Khiry Robinson may have missed his chance. The second-year back played in just 10 games last year, missing time because of an arm injury. Even though he impressed on the field when given opportunities, something he has done throughout his short career to this point, Robinson doesn't have an obvious route to the field this season. Mark Ingram is expected carry most of the load, while C.J. Spiller will be the receiving back and spell Ingram. Robinson isn't a great receiver either way, but he would have expected more touches if Pierre Thomas was the other complement to Ingram. Robinson will likely need an injury to either Spiller or Ingram to get extended playing time.

Jacquizz Rodgers   Height: 5-6   Weight: 196   College: Oregon State   Draft: 2011/5 (145)   Born: 6-Feb-1990   Age: 25   Risk: Green

Year	Team	G/GS	Snaps	Runs	Yds	Yd/R	TD	FUM	DVOA	Rk	DYAR	Rk	YAR	Suc%	Rk	BTkl	Rec	Pass	Yds	C%	Yd/C	TD	YAC	DVOA	Rk	DYAR	Rk
2012	ATL	16/0	464	94	362	3.9	1	0	-10.9%	--	-9	--	-12	38%	--	26	53	59	402	90%	7.6	1	8.2	26.1%	4	135	4
2013	ATL	15/4	435	96	332	3.5	2	1	-8.1%	--	2	--	-7	45%	--	16	52	62	341	84%	6.6	2	7.0	7.8%	18	72	15
2014	ATL	16/1	350	58	217	3.7	1	1	-11.4%	--	-7	--	7	40%	--	12	29	40	173	73%	6.0	1	6.4	-5.8%	33	18	30
2015	CHI			25	108	4.3	1	1	1.3%								26	32	197	81%	7.6	1		9.9%			

'Quizz is what he is at this point: a depth running back who has seen his efficiency on his main skill—catching the ball—decline for two straight seasons. Chicago no longer employs Marc Trestman, which would have made this skill set interesting. Instead, as the only running back on the depth chart after Matt Forte with experience, Rodgers figures to tickle the veteran fetish of new head coach John Fox. That means, in the event of a Forte injury, about three weeks of people calling for Jeremy Langford and Ka'Deem Carey before they actually hit the field.

Bishop Sankey   Height: 5-9   Weight: 209   College: Washington   Draft: 2014/2 (54)   Born: 9/15/1992   Age: 23   Risk: Green

Year	Team	G/GS	Snaps	Runs	Yds	Yd/R	TD	FUM	DVOA	Rk	DYAR	Rk	YAR	Suc%	Rk	BTkl	Rec	Pass	Yds	C%	Yd/C	TD	YAC	DVOA	Rk	DYAR	Rk
2014	TEN	16/9	354	152	569	3.7	2	2	-4.5%	26	24	26	34	44%	27	18	18	23	133	78%	7.4	0	8.2	7.0%	--	26	--
2015	TEN			197	856	4.3	3	4	-0.5%								34	48	256	71%	7.5	1		-7.6%			

The most reliable guide to what players will do well in the NFL is what they did well in college. At Washington, Sankey often ran from the shotgun. In the NFL, he ran well from the shotgun, posting 5.6% DVOA compared to -12.9% DVOA with the quarterback under center. His 2015 offseason included more work on tracking, getting a rhythm for the steps and timing of run plays, reflective of his difficulty operating out of old-school, quarterback-under-center sets. That and improved third-down work could lead to a regular role instead of him potentially getting squeezed out on a team going in a more power-oriented direction that does not fit him.

Charles Sims Height: 6-0 Weight: 214 College: West Virginia Draft: 2014/3 (69) Born: 9/19/1990 Age: 25 Risk: Yellow

Year	Team	G/GS	Snaps	Runs	Yds	Yd/R	TD	FUM	DVOA	Rk	DYAR	Rk	YAR	Suc%	Rk	BTkl	Rec	Pass	Yds	C%	Yd/C	TD	YAC	DVOA	Rk	DYAR	Rk
2014	TB	8/0	231	66	185	2.8	1	2	-42.1%	--	-84	--	-77	35%	--	9	19	27	190	70%	10.0	0	10.4	-4.4%	31	12	33
2015	TB			133	561	4.2	2	4	-2.0%								39	56	313	70%	8.0	0		-3.6%			

While Sims showed very little in a small sample as a runner in his rookie season, Tampa is more interested in him as a pass-catching back. The 2014 third-round pick had more than 2,000 receiving yards in college. Mike Mayock called him "as good a receiver out of the backfield as any in (that) draft." Sims appears likely to start the season as the Buccaneers' third-down back, but if Doug Martin doesn't get back on track, a more regular role could be in his future.

Antone Smith Height: 5-9 Weight: 190 College: Florida State Draft: 2009/FA Born: 17-Sep-1985 Age: 30 Risk: Green

Year	Team	G/GS	Snaps	Runs	Yds	Yd/R	TD	FUM	DVOA	Rk	DYAR	Rk	YAR	Suc%	Rk	BTkl	Rec	Pass	Yds	C%	Yd/C	TD	YAC	DVOA	Rk	DYAR	Rk
2012	ATL	13/0	6	0	0	0.0	0	--	--	--	--	--	--	--	--	0	1	0	0%	0.0	0	0.0	-76.6%	--	-2	--
2013	ATL	15/0	25	5	145	29.0	2	0	392.3%	--	78	--	79	100%	--	2	2	3	10	67%	5.0	0	2.5	-32.0%	--	-2	--
2014	ATL	10/0	93	23	144	6.3	2	1	27.3%	--	35	--	33	57%	--	6	13	15	222	87%	17.1	3	17.9	91.6%	--	96	--
2015	ATL			25	120	4.8	1	0	16.9%								15	21	156	71%	10.4	0		15.7%			

All Antone Smith does is create touchdowns. Literally. On 43 touches over the past two years, he has scored seven times, and all seven scores went for at least 38 yards. It's odd that you suddenly just find a home-run hitting back all of a sudden at 28. Usually players with this kind of speed draw some earlier attention. Coming off a broken leg suffered in November, Smith is definitely the X-factor on the Atlanta running back chart. It'd be hard for any player to recreate the stat lines that Smith has made over the past few seasons, but if he continues to score at will, there's nothing saying he can't seize the job and become the fast man's Fred Jackson.

C.J. Spiller Height: 5-11 Weight: 195 College: Clemson Draft: 2010/1 (9) Born: 15-Aug-1987 Age: 28 Risk: Yellow

Year	Team	G/GS	Snaps	Runs	Yds	Yd/R	TD	FUM	DVOA	Rk	DYAR	Rk	YAR	Suc%	Rk	BTkl	Rec	Pass	Yds	C%	Yd/C	TD	YAC	DVOA	Rk	DYAR	Rk
2012	BUF	16/9	568	207	1244	6.0	6	3	27.6%	1	301	3	291	55%	3	34	43	57	459	75%	10.7	2	11.8	16.3%	9	91	7
2013	BUF	15/10	389	202	933	4.6	2	4	-17.8%	43	-70	43	-49	36%	44	18	33	40	185	83%	5.6	0	6.9	-17.8%	40	-8	41
2014	BUF	9/5	188	78	300	3.8	0	3	-33.2%	--	-76	--	-80	40%	--	10	19	22	125	86%	6.6	1	9.7	7.8%	--	28	--
2015	NO			117	510	4.3	3	4	-0.8%								62	81	492	77%	7.8	3		2.2%			

It is not hard to come up with a case for Spiller matching Darren Sproles' numbers with the Saints, probably with a few more carries. Since 1960, six running backs have averaged 6.0 yards per carry and rushed for more than 1,000 yards in a season: Jim Brown, O.J. Simpson, Barry Sanders, Jamaal Charles, Adrian Peterson, and Spiller. For his career, Spiller has averaged 5.0 yards per carry, despite not exactly playing behind the 2014 Cowboys' offensive line. In fact, Spiller is moving from a Bills offensive line that ranked 26th in adjusted line yards to one that ranked second last year.

With his elite speed (he was the 100- and 200-meter sprint champion as a Florida high schooler), Spiller also brings value as a returner, as he showed repeatedly in college at Clemson. The Bills rarely used Spiller as a punt returner, but his 12.1-yard average on 25 returns showed glimpses of the talent. (For comparison, Devin Hester has averaged 12.3 yards on punt returns in his career.) Spiller also has two touchdowns in 60 career kickoff returns.

Spiller's basic stats (yards per carry) look better than his advanced stats (DVOA) due to his often-low success rate and his high fumble rate (once every 50 touches). He has had 11 runs of 40-plus yards (compared to none for Mark Ingram), which have inflated his yards per carry. His statistical profile and injury history make Spiller the ultimate boom-or-bust back.

Darren Sproles Height: 5-6 Weight: 181 College: Kansas State Draft: 2005/4 (130) Born: 20-Jun-1983 Age: 32 Risk: Green

Year	Team	G/GS	Snaps	Runs	Yds	Yd/R	TD	FUM	DVOA	Rk	DYAR	Rk	YAR	Suc%	Rk	BTkl	Rec	Pass	Yds	C%	Yd/C	TD	YAC	DVOA	Rk	DYAR	Rk
2012	NO	13/6	444	48	244	5.1	1	0	10.9%	--	34	--	25	44%	--	12	75	104	667	72%	8.9	7	8.9	21.5%	7	214	1
2013	NO	15/4	357	53	220	4.2	2	1	1.4%	--	21	--	25	49%	--	14	71	89	604	80%	8.5	2	7.3	23.9%	8	174	4
2014	PHI	15/0	337	57	329	5.8	6	2	30.4%	--	86	--	87	41%	--	18	40	63	387	65%	9.7	0	10.1	-3.1%	28	37	24
2015	PHI			42	212	5.0	2	2	24.0%								51	79	414	65%	8.1	2		-8.4%			

Chip Kelly kept giving Sproles six or seven change-up carries per game in the first half of the year, as if to say, "see, Shady, there really is room to run on those inside zones if you just hit the darn hole!" It was a risky way to use such a valuable-but-aging role player. Only three players in NFL history have gained more than 2,000 rushing yards, receiving yards, punt return yards, and kickoff return yards in their careers: Browns and Raiders great Greg Pruitt; Falcons and Browns all-purpose player Eric Metcalf; and Sproles. It's an exclusive list populated with underrated contributors who didn't fit the mold. Pruitt somehow rushed for more than 1,000 yards three times as a 190-pound scatback in the mid-1970s. Metcalf bounced from I-formation halfback to run-'n'-shoot receiver, never quite finding the sweet spot in between. Sproles never enjoyed a 1,000-yard rushing or receiving season like the others, but he got to play for two of the most innovative offensive coaches in modern NFL history. Who knows what Sean Payton or Chip Kelly might have done with Pruitt or Metcalf?

Players like Sproles often enter a "returner only" stage late in their careers, where the touches from scrimmage dry almost completely up. With Ryan Mathews on board for the Eagles' change-up role, Sproles is almost there.

Zac Stacy Height: 5-8   Weight: 216   College: Vanderbilt   Draft: 2013/5 (160)   Born: 9-Apr-1991   Age: 24   Risk: Blue

Year	Team	G/GS	Snaps	Runs	Yds	Yd/R	TD	FUM	DVOA	Rk	DYAR	Rk	YAR	Suc%	Rk	BTkl	Rec	Pass	Yds	C%	Yd/C	TD	YAC	DVOA	Rk	DYAR	Rk
2013	STL	14/12	566	250	973	3.9	7	1	-0.7%	23	80	23	55	42%	39	15	26	35	141	74%	5.4	1	5.7	-19.7%	43	-11	42
2014	STL	13/5	201	76	293	3.9	1	2	-8.8%	--	-1	--	3	50%	--	7	18	23	152	78%	8.4	0	8.7	23.2%	--	48	--
2015	NYJ			56	216	3.9	1	2	-4.8%								14	19	92	75%	6.4	0		-3.3%			

The Rams were all like "We take Todd Gurley," and then Zac goes on Twitter and he's all like, "Yikes," and then he's all like asking for a trade, and the Rams were like "Whatever, you were our third runner at best anyway, #SeeYa" and now Zac is a Jet. Stacy and the Rams both later laughed off Stacy's joke, and St. Louis exec Kevin Demoff told Don Banks of *Sports Illustrated* that the Rams were getting trade offers before they ever heard from Stacy or his agent. And there's no doubt that the Jets' back-field, while crowded, gives Stacy a better chance at starting than he would have had in St. Louis.

James Starks Height: 6-2   Weight: 218   College: Buffalo   Draft: 2010/6 (193)   Born: 25-Feb-1986   Age: 29   Risk: Green

Year	Team	G/GS	Snaps	Runs	Yds	Yd/R	TD	FUM	DVOA	Rk	DYAR	Rk	YAR	Suc%	Rk	BTkl	Rec	Pass	Yds	C%	Yd/C	TD	YAC	DVOA	Rk	DYAR	Rk
2012	GB	6/2	124	71	255	3.6	1	1	-4.3%	--	13	--	-3	51%	--	5	4	6	31	67%	7.8	0	10.5	-24.9%	--	-4	--
2013	GB	13/1	220	89	493	5.5	3	1	19.2%	--	110	--	130	54%	--	13	10	13	89	77%	8.9	1	10.9	38.0%	--	36	--
2014	GB	16/0	260	85	333	3.9	2	1	-8.6%	--	0	--	-8	40%	--	14	18	29	140	62%	7.8	0	6.7	-27.1%	49	-20	46
2015	GB			82	348	4.3	3	3	4.4%								19	23	170	83%	9.0	1		15.3%			

Befitting a complementary back, most of Starks' work came in games where the Packers took a commanding lead. He had a dozen carries in the 42-10 win over Minnesota, ten in the Monday night affair against Atlanta where Green Bay held a 31-7 halftime lead, and eight more, all in the second half, in the 53-20 destruction of Philadelphia. Eddie Lacy's growth meant he was less needed on passing downs, though the target numbers show that Aaron Rodgers did use Starks when he was on the field.

Jonathan Stewart Height: 5-10   Weight: 235   College: Oregon   Draft: 2008/1 (13)   Born: 21-Mar-1987   Age: 28   Risk: Yellow

Year	Team	G/GS	Snaps	Runs	Yds	Yd/R	TD	FUM	DVOA	Rk	DYAR	Rk	YAR	Suc%	Rk	BTkl	Rec	Pass	Yds	C%	Yd/C	TD	YAC	DVOA	Rk	DYAR	Rk
2012	CAR	9/6	312	93	336	3.6	1	2	-18.4%	--	-36	--	-55	42%	--	5	17	23	157	74%	9.2	1	10.5	15.0%	--	34	--
2013	CAR	6/1	110	48	180	3.8	0	1	-7.4%	--	2	--	1	48%	--	4	7	7	44	100%	6.3	0	6.0	30.1%	--	18	--
2014	CAR	13/8	546	175	809	4.6	3	2	1.3%	16	72	18	71	51%	7	32	25	31	181	81%	7.2	1	8.6	7.8%	16	35	25
2015	CAR			192	876	4.6	5	2	6.0%								37	45	262	82%	7.1	0		10.5%			

Nobody has ever doubted that Stewart could play. The problem has been injuries, as Stewart hasn't played a full 16-game season since 2011. Down the stretch, he carried the Carolina running game in the absence of DeAngelo Williams, showing reverberations of his old, healthy self. At this point, think of Stewart like Ahmad Bradshaw with the physical attributes scouts actually desire. Stewart is signed long-term, because without an injury-prone running back making tons of money it wouldn't be an official Panthers football season. At 28, and with the Panthers finally able to shed his salary next season and gain cap space, this will be a crucial campaign for the talented back. It would help if he were able to stay on the field.

Lorenzo Taliaferro

Height: 6-0 | Weight: 229 | College: Coastal Carolina | Draft: 2014/4 (138) | Born: 19-Jun-1992 | Age: 23 | Risk: Yellow

Year	Team	G/GS	Snaps	Runs	Yds	Yd/R	TD	FUM	DVOA	Rk	DYAR	Rk	YAR	Suc%	Rk	BTkl	Rec	Pass	Yds	C%	Yd/C	TD	YAC	DVOA	Rk	DYAR	Rk
2014	BAL	13/0	136	68	292	4.3	4	1	-7.2%	--	4	--	32	49%	--	11	8	10	114	80%	14.3	0	11.8	61.1%	--	33	--
2015	BAL			95	370	3.9	2	4	-8.9%								21	27	192	78%	9.1	1		12.0%			

A small school project, Taliaferro benefitted from the chaos on the depth chart to work his way into the backup role in Baltimore. The drafting of Javorius Allen, a superior pass-catcher, is problematic for Taliaferro, who might be consigned to short-yardage and goal-line carries.

Ben Tate

Height: 5-11 | Weight: 220 | College: Auburn | Draft: 2010/2 (58) | Born: 21-Aug-1988 | Age: 27 | Risk: N/A

Year	Team	G/GS	Snaps	Runs	Yds	Yd/R	TD	FUM	DVOA	Rk	DYAR	Rk	YAR	Suc%	Rk	BTkl	Rec	Pass	Yds	C%	Yd/C	TD	YAC	DVOA	Rk	DYAR	Rk
2012	HOU	11/0	143	65	279	4.3	2	1	-2.2%	--	18	--	33	49%	--	9	11	11	49	100%	4.5	0	3.6	-27.7%	--	-9	--
2013	HOU	14/7	481	181	771	4.3	4	5	-2.0%	25	50	26	51	51%	12	19	34	50	140	70%	4.1	0	4.7	-62.9%	49	-125	49
2014	3TM	11/6	282	119	371	3.1	4	0	-16.8%	40	-38	39	-29	36%	42	11	9	12	60	75%	6.7	0	5.0	-32.4%	--	-11	--

It will be a surprise if Ben Tate's time in the NFL is already over, but the second chapter of his career definitely had an abrupt ending. Tate was rightfully squeezed out of Cleveland by two younger, arguably more talented backs before landing in Minnesota and then moving on to Pittsburgh for the postseason. He remained unsigned into July, but he will only be 27 entering next season. Tate still has the physical talent to break off big runs. His vision and consistency are the only concerns, but those shouldn't be great enough to keep him off a roster completely.

Stepfan Taylor

Height: 5-9 | Weight: 214 | College: Stanford | Draft: 2013/5 (140) | Born: 9-Jun-1991 | Age: 24 | Risk: Green

Year	Team	G/GS	Snaps	Runs	Yds	Yd/R	TD	FUM	DVOA	Rk	DYAR	Rk	YAR	Suc%	Rk	BTkl	Rec	Pass	Yds	C%	Yd/C	TD	YAC	DVOA	Rk	DYAR	Rk
2013	ARI	16/0	131	36	115	3.2	0	0	-14.7%	--	-9	--	-11	39%	--	5	8	9	71	89%	8.9	0	7.5	-10.7%	--	2	--
2014	ARI	14/4	210	63	208	3.3	1	0	-4.4%	--	11	--	-6	41%	--	7	11	15	79	73%	7.2	3	5.9	41.9%	--	48	--
2015	ARI			34	133	3.9	0	1	-8.8%								8	10	61	80%	7.6	0		7.0%			

Stanford's all-time leading rusher, Taylor has found defenses to be much tougher in the NFL than they were in the Pac-12. He started the final four games of the regular season and the wild-card game against Carolina, in the process doing nothing to indicate he deserved more playing time in the future. The Cardinals spent a third-round pick on David Johnson to back up Andre Ellington, leaving Taylor to battle Kerwynn Williams, Marion Grice, and Robert Hughes for the third spot.

Daniel Thomas

Height: 6-2 | Weight: 228 | College: Kansas State | Draft: 2011/2 (62) | Born: 29-Oct-1987 | Age: 28 | Risk: Yellow

Year	Team	G/GS	Snaps	Runs	Yds	Yd/R	TD	FUM	DVOA	Rk	DYAR	Rk	YAR	Suc%	Rk	BTkl	Rec	Pass	Yds	C%	Yd/C	TD	YAC	DVOA	Rk	DYAR	Rk
2012	MIA	12/0	323	91	325	3.6	4	3	-10.8%	--	-9	--	3	51%	--	13	15	22	156	68%	10.4	0	9.6	0.8%	--	14	--
2013	MIA	15/1	339	109	406	3.7	4	0	-7.7%	30	4	32	34	47%	22	14	15	17	63	88%	4.2	2	5.6	12.3%	--	27	--
2014	MIA	12/0	209	44	168	3.8	2	1	11.3%	--	34	--	30	57%	--	2	13	19	121	68%	9.3	0	9.4	19.7%	--	37	--
2015	CHI			13	46	3.5	1	1	-6.4%								7	9	39	78%	5.5	0		-9.1%			

In four NFL seasons, Thomas has averaged just 3.6 yards on about 100 carries a year, so you'd think that there would be something else there that would keep him gainfully employed—great red zone potential, good hands in the passing game, or outstanding blocking ability. Thomas has none of these skills in abundance, and so after four years of relentless mediocrity, Miami let him walk, and he signed with the Bears. He's part of a packed depth chart below Matt Forte as the clear No. 1 back. If he gets 100 carries this season with the Bears, there will be something really wrong with the Chicago offense, Forte, or new Bears coach John Fox.

Pierre Thomas Height: 5-11 Weight: 210 College: Illinois Draft: 2007/FA Born: 18-Dec-1984 Age: 31 Risk: N/A

Year	Team	G/GS	Snaps	Runs	Yds	Yd/R	TD	FUM	DVOA	Rk	DYAR	Rk	YAR	Suc%	Rk	BTkl	Rec	Pass	Yds	C%	Yd/C	TD	YAC	DVOA	Rk	DYAR	Rk
2012	NO	15/4	385	105	473	4.5	1	0	15.1%	6	97	14	80	53%	6	11	39	53	354	74%	9.1	1	9.3	18.7%	8	99	6
2013	NO	16/9	564	147	549	3.7	2	1	-7.6%	29	6	30	32	53%	5	16	77	84	513	92%	6.7	3	8.3	13.2%	13	128	9
2014	NO	11/3	300	45	222	4.9	2	0	30.9%	--	74	--	73	58%	--	16	45	55	378	82%	8.4	1	9.4	22.2%	10	111	5

Playing running back in the NFL is a young man's game. At 30 years of age, Thomas isn't that old, but his overall lack of athleticism will obviously concern teams. The former Saints back was always more reliant on his vision and technical ability as a receiver than any truly great athletic traits. He still showed flashes of his athletic ability in 2014, but he has little margin for error if he loses a step or two physically. Thomas is the kind of running back who could still be effective in a good situation, but he's more reliant on his teammates than ever now.

Juwan Thompson Height: 5-10 Weight: 225 College: Duke Draft: 2014/FA Born: 13-May-1992 Age: 23 Risk: Green

Year	Team	G/GS	Snaps	Runs	Yds	Yd/R	TD	FUM	DVOA	Rk	DYAR	Rk	YAR	Suc%	Rk	BTkl	Rec	Pass	Yds	C%	Yd/C	TD	YAC	DVOA	Rk	DYAR	Rk
2014	DEN	15/0	123	54	272	5.0	3	1	18.0%	--	67	--	70	61%	--	6	4	7	25	57%	6.3	0	5.3	-51.4%	--	-15	--
2015	DEN			33	136	4.1	1	1	3.5%								8	10	51	80%	6.3	0		-1.1%			

A camp standout last year, Thompson had the fifth-most rushing DYAR for anyone with 20 to 99 carries, after injuries to Montee Ball and Ronnie Hillman earned him more carries than expected as a rookie. He's likely to be no higher than No. 4 on the depth chart this season.

Jordan Todman Height: 5-9 Weight: 203 College: Connecticut Draft: 2011/6 (183) Born: 24-Feb-1990 Age: 25 Risk: Green

Year	Team	G/GS	Snaps	Runs	Yds	Yd/R	TD	FUM	DVOA	Rk	DYAR	Rk	YAR	Suc%	Rk	BTkl	Rec	Pass	Yds	C%	Yd/C	TD	YAC	DVOA	Rk	DYAR	Rk
2012	JAC	1/0	7	3	8	2.7	0	0	-42.4%	--	-4	--	-5	33%	--	0	1	1	0	100%	0.0	0	3.0	-94.3%	--	-6	--
2013	JAC	16/2	263	76	256	3.4	2	0	-4.2%	--	13	--	6	37%	--	5	14	26	116	54%	8.3	1	6.9	-12.6%	36	2	36
2014	JAC	16/1	307	32	186	5.8	1	0	3.8%	--	15	--	20	25%	--	6	25	37	198	68%	7.9	1	7.9	-34.9%	52	-35	50
2015	CAR			28	115	4.1	1	1	2.4%								11	16	76	69%	6.9	0		-7.6%			

Todman, a Dave Caldwell waiver-wire find, was a solid kick returner and fresh legs for a Jaguars team that needed them. But the Jaguars didn't bother tendering him as a restricted free agent, and he fled to Carolina. Ted Ginn is a better returner, Cameron Artis-Payne is the future at running back, and Fozzy Whittaker already has experience as the special teams/adequate backup option. Todman is a niche back on a team that won't need his niche unless injuries strike.

Mike Tolbert Height: 5-9 Weight: 243 College: Coastal Carolina Draft: 2008/FA Born: 23-Nov-1985 Age: 30 Risk: Red

Year	Team	G/GS	Snaps	Runs	Yds	Yd/R	TD	FUM	DVOA	Rk	DYAR	Rk	YAR	Suc%	Rk	BTkl	Rec	Pass	Yds	C%	Yd/C	TD	YAC	DVOA	Rk	DYAR	Rk
2012	CAR	16/5	445	54	183	3.4	7	0	25.8%	--	103	--	106	65%	--	10	27	39	268	69%	9.9	0	10.2	7.7%	20	48	20
2013	CAR	16/13	599	101	361	3.6	5	0	9.0%	12	86	22	69	50%	13	11	27	32	184	84%	6.8	2	7.1	29.0%	6	77	14
2014	CAR	8/6	220	37	78	2.1	0	0	-53.2%	--	-72	--	-68	27%	--	2	12	17	93	71%	7.8	0	8.3	-39.4%	--	-21	--
2015	CAR			89	369	4.1	3	4	1.6%								24	35	202	69%	8.4	1		3.2%			

No touchdowns? Are you sure this comment is for Mike Tolbert? Tolbert suffered a hairline leg fracture against the Steelers in Week 3 and was placed on short-term IR. When he returned, he played very much like a player who wasn't fully healthy yet. The former All-Pro fullback should be back at full strength this season, and in a backfield with more questions than answers, he will continue to draw plenty of goal-line carries.

Robert Turbin   Height: 5-10   Weight: 222   College: Utah State   Draft: 2012/4 (106)   Born: 2-Dec-1989   Age: 26   Risk: Green

Year	Team	G/GS	Snaps	Runs	Yds	Yd/R	TD	FUM	DVOA	Rk	DYAR	Rk	YAR	Suc%	Rk	BTkl	Rec	Pass	Yds	C%	Yd/C	TD	YAC	DVOA	Rk	DYAR	Rk
2012	SEA	16/0	224	80	354	4.4	0	0	-5.2%	--	11	--	8	46%	--	7	19	23	181	83%	9.5	0	6.7	21.2%	--	48	--
2013	SEA	16/0	231	77	264	3.4	0	0	-17.0%	--	-25	--	-28	44%	--	4	8	12	60	67%	7.5	0	8.0	-24.2%	--	-6	--
2014	SEA	16/3	260	74	310	4.2	0	1	9.5%	--	57	--	41	61%	--	5	16	20	186	80%	11.6	2	10.5	83.3%	--	104	--
2015	SEA			86	347	4.1	2	3	-2.5%								13	17	106	76%	8.2	0		6.2%			

While Marshawn Lynch has led the NFL in broken tackles two years in a row, Turbin had one of the ten lowest broken-tackle rates last season. Turbin saw most of his action late in the year (30 carries for 131 yards in December), when Seattle had little to play for and Lynch needed more time to rest before the playoffs. Turbin had hip surgery in May, but was expected to be ready for training camp, when he'll once again try to hold off Christine Michael for the No. 2 running back job.

Shane Vereen   Height: 5-10   Weight: 205   College: California   Draft: 2011/2 (56)   Born: 2-Mar-1989   Age: 26   Risk: Green

Year	Team	G/GS	Snaps	Runs	Yds	Yd/R	TD	FUM	DVOA	Rk	DYAR	Rk	YAR	Suc%	Rk	BTkl	Rec	Pass	Yds	C%	Yd/C	TD	YAC	DVOA	Rk	DYAR	Rk
2012	NE	13/1	161	62	251	4.0	3	1	9.6%	--	47	--	52	52%	--	4	8	13	149	62%	18.6	1	17.5	69.6%	--	64	--
2013	NE	8/1	295	44	208	4.7	1	1	-5.0%	--	6	--	6	39%	--	11	47	69	427	68%	9.1	3	5.9	25.1%	7	151	6
2014	NE	16/6	595	96	391	4.1	2	0	-7.4%	--	4	--	-2	41%	--	15	52	77	447	68%	8.6	3	7.3	-3.1%	29	49	20
2015	NYG			55	227	4.1	2	2	-1.5%								43	55	343	78%	8.0	1		2.8%			

In February, Vereen became just the sixth player in NFL history to catch more than ten passes in a Super Bowl. He is the only one of those six to gain fewer than 100 yards. As valuable as Vereen's 11 catches were, the Patriots could reasonably think that any number of other backs would have done the same. Vereen also provides almost no value as a runner (his 1.23 yards after initial contact ranked 69th among 73 running backs with at least 50 carries). Vereen now makes considerably more money (average of $4.12 million over three years, $4.75 million guaranteed) than the receiving back he originally replaced in New England, Danny Woodhead (average of $2.75 million over two years, $3 million guaranteed), but he's simply not as good. The idea that he's going to become a major weapon for the Giants seems a bit misplaced.

Terrance West   Height: 5-9   Weight: 225   College: Towson   Draft: 2014/3 (94)   Born: 1/28/1991   Age: 24   Risk: Blue

Year	Team	G/GS	Snaps	Runs	Yds	Yd/R	TD	FUM	DVOA	Rk	DYAR	Rk	YAR	Suc%	Rk	BTkl	Rec	Pass	Yds	C%	Yd/C	TD	YAC	DVOA	Rk	DYAR	Rk
2014	CLE	14/6	401	171	673	3.9	4	1	-5.7%	29	21	28	39	47%	17	21	11	13	64	85%	5.8	1	4.8	17.5%	--	20	--
2015	CLE			86	322	3.7	1	1	-11.9%								10	14	56	71%	5.6	0		-10.7%			

West was impressive during his rookie season, showing flashes of very quick, precise footwork with the vision to anticipate holes while consistently making good decisions between the tackles. Still, it's going to be tough for him to carve out a prominent role in the Browns' backfield unless something unforeseen happens to either Isaiah Crowell or Duke Johnson. West simply didn't show off the same level of consistency or explosiveness as Crowell. He is a bigger back who can create forward momentum through the point of contact, but he lacks the ability to break tackles and take advantage of the space in behind the defenders once he passes them. He should be able to carve out a role on the field as a short-yardage back. It may not be what the Browns envisioned when they drafted him, but there is definite value in getting West the ball in the right situations.

James White   Height: 5-9   Weight: 204   College: Wisconsin   Draft: 2014/4 (130)   Born: 3-Feb-1992   Age: 23   Risk: Yellow

Year	Team	G/GS	Snaps	Runs	Yds	Yd/R	TD	FUM	DVOA	Rk	DYAR	Rk	YAR	Suc%	Rk	BTkl	Rec	Pass	Yds	C%	Yd/C	TD	YAC	DVOA	Rk	DYAR	Rk
2014	NE	3/0	31	9	38	4.2	0	0	-7.1%	--	0	--	4	56%	--	0	5	5	23	100%	4.6	0	4.8	4.0%	--	5	--
2015	NE			109	435	4.0	4	1	1.5%								47	62	324	76%	6.9	2		-4.8%			

The Patriots likely expected a bigger contribution from their fourth-round pick in 2014. White played just three games and had just nine rushing attempts in his rookie season. Since 2000, the list of drafted Wisconsin running backs includes: Ron Dayne (2000, first round), Michael Bennett (2001, first round), Anthony Davis (2005, seventh round), Brian Calhoun (2006, third round), Montee Ball (2013, second round), and Melvin Gordon (2015, first round). The jury is still out on Ball and obviously Gordon, but rushing for over 6.0 yards per carry, as White did during his Badgers career, may say much more about

Wisconsin's blocking than White's running ability. Reports say White will take the Shane Vereen role in the Patriots offense, but he'll need to hold off Travaris Cadet.

Fozzy Whittaker   Height: 5-10   Weight: 202   College: Texas   Draft: 2012/FA   Born: 2-Feb-1989   Age: 26   Risk: Green

Year	Team	G/GS	Snaps	Runs	Yds	Yd/R	TD	FUM	DVOA	Rk	DYAR	Rk	YAR	Suc%	Rk	BTkl	Rec	Pass	Yds	C%	Yd/C	TD	YAC	DVOA	Rk	DYAR	Rk
2013	2TM	14/2	167	28	79	2.8	0	0	-25.2%	--	-17	--	-11	43%	--	1	21	35	155	60%	7.4	2	7.4	-5.5%	29	18	30
2014	CAR	10/1	84	32	145	4.5	1	0	22.7%	--	33	--	37	41%	--	2	5	6	60	83%	12.0	1	15.6	53.6%	--	24	--
2015	CAR			35	117	3.4	1	1	-11.3%								9	13	52	69%	5.8	0		-15.0%			

Foswhitt Whittaker has played three NFL seasons on four teams. He's a willing special-teamer, which helps him stay employed in times of crisis, but when he carries the ball it is usually more about injuries than any validation of his talent. If you have need for a versatile fourth back who can return kicks, he will answer the phone. The Panthers acquired Jordan Todman, another back with experience returning kicks, so he and Whittaker may be playing for one roster spot behind Jonathan Stewart, Cameron Artis-Payne, and Mike Tolbert.

Andre Williams   Height: 5-11   Weight: 230   College: Boston College   Draft: 2014/4 (113)   Born: 28-Aug-1992   Age: 23   Risk: Green

Year	Team	G/GS	Snaps	Runs	Yds	Yd/R	TD	FUM	DVOA	Rk	DYAR	Rk	YAR	Suc%	Rk	BTkl	Rec	Pass	Yds	C%	Yd/C	TD	YAC	DVOA	Rk	DYAR	Rk
2014	NYG	16/7	520	217	721	3.3	7	1	-11.4%	34	-24	35	-54	38%	39	23	18	37	130	49%	7.2	0	8.2	-37.6%	54	-48	53
2015	NYG			135	523	3.9	5	1	2.2%								22	32	155	69%	7.0	0		-6.8%			

A pair of 100-yard games against the Titans and Rams pulled Williams out of "lost rookie season" mode and demonstrated his potential as a featured runner. The power-speed combo is as good as advertised, and after dropping some passes early in the season, Williams eventually proved that he was capable of at least gobbling up a screen pass and doing something with it (though that screen had better land right in his belly). Williams also appeared to develop as a short-yardage runner, with (tiny sample size alert!) eight 1-yard conversions for first downs or touchdowns in ten tries from Week 7 onward. Williams will never be mistaken for Brian Westbrook in the passing game, but he blocks well enough to not be a liability, and the Giants now have Shane Vereen to handle third-and-long chores. Williams will start as part of a committee but has a good chance to eat away at Rashad Jennings' role.

Damien Williams   Height: 5-11   Weight: 221   College: Oklahoma   Draft: 2014/FA   Born: 3-Apr-1992   Age: 23   Risk: Green

Year	Team	G/GS	Snaps	Runs	Yds	Yd/R	TD	FUM	DVOA	Rk	DYAR	Rk	YAR	Suc%	Rk	BTkl	Rec	Pass	Yds	C%	Yd/C	TD	YAC	DVOA	Rk	DYAR	Rk
2014	MIA	16/0	158	36	122	3.4	0	0	-9.7%	--	-2	--	-6	47%	--	12	21	27	187	78%	8.9	1	7.2	40.1%	2	90	10
2015	MIA			63	236	3.7	2	3	-7.0%								23	27	149	85%	6.5	0		3.2%			

The 2014 Speed Score champion (113.2) made good after going undrafted, getting playing time after Knowshon Moreno went down for the Dolphins. His rushing average was disappointing, but he showed promise as a pass-catching presence out of the backfield. His playing time this year also depends on the health of another man's knee, but this time it's rookie Jay Ajayi instead of Moreno.

DeAngelo Williams   Height: 5-8   Weight: 210   College: Memphis   Draft: 2006/1 (27)   Born: 25-Apr-1983   Age: 32   Risk: Red

Year	Team	G/GS	Snaps	Runs	Yds	Yd/R	TD	FUM	DVOA	Rk	DYAR	Rk	YAR	Suc%	Rk	BTkl	Rec	Pass	Yds	C%	Yd/C	TD	YAC	DVOA	Rk	DYAR	Rk
2012	CAR	16/10	417	173	737	4.3	5	2	-6.7%	26	14	25	19	48%	22	9	13	20	187	65%	14.4	2	16.4	38.9%	--	60	--
2013	CAR	15/15	470	201	843	4.2	3	3	7.2%	16	126	12	76	43%	34	17	26	36	333	72%	12.8	1	14.3	16.0%	12	57	18
2014	CAR	6/6	135	62	219	3.5	0	1	-15.2%	--	-17	--	-22	45%	--	7	5	6	44	83%	8.8	0	11.4	-3.3%	--	4	--
2015	PIT			110	474	4.3	4	4	5.2%								32	42	283	77%	8.7	2		13.0%			

Marty Hurney's greatest folly was giving a five-year, $43 million contract to Williams during the 2011 offseason. And here's the strange thing: it actually went about as well as it could have. From age 28 to age 31, Williams gave the Panthers 281 DYAR. Williams was often hurt, but that's not bad production from an aging back. Of course, the contract kept Carolina from addressing a lot of issues that probably should have been higher on the priority list than running back, but 591 carries and 2,635 yards is likely above the median forecast that any projection system would have given you on Williams after he missed most of 2010 to injuries. Now in Pittsburgh, Williams will get the first crack at being the guy who immediately is benched after Le'Veon Bell's suspension is over.

Kerwynn Williams Height: 5-8 Weight: 195 College: Utah State Draft: 2013/7 (230) Born: 9-Jun-1991 Age: 24 Risk: Green

Year	Team	G/GS	Snaps	Runs	Yds	Yd/R	TD	FUM	DVOA	Rk	DYAR	Rk	YAR	Suc%	Rk	BTkl	Rec	Pass	Yds	C%	Yd/C	TD	YAC	DVOA	Rk	DYAR	Rk
2013	IND	1/0	0	0	0	0.0	0	--	--	--	--	--	--	--	--	--	0	--	0	--	0.0	0	--	--	--	--	--
2014	ARI	5/0	89	53	246	4.6	0	1	2.6%	--	23	--	31	58%	--	5	2	6	11	33%	5.5	0	6.5	-56.6%	--	-12	--
2015	ARI			13	64	4.9	0	1	11.3%								7	8	64	88%	9.1	0		21.5%			

Williams spent a year and a half on practice squads in Indianapolis, San Diego, and Arizona before the Cardinals brought him to the main roster in November, and in December he got his first NFL carry, a 5-yard gain against Kansas City. Then Arizona gave him the ball again, and again, and when the final gun fired Williams had run 19 times for 100 yards. He followed that up with 75 yards on 15 carries against St. Louis, but then gained just 94 yards on 29 runs in three games against Seattle, San Francisco, and (in the postseason) Carolina. The Cardinals have a lot of candidates fighting for the third spot on the depth chart behind Andre Ellington and David Johnson, but none has had more success in the NFL than Williams.

Danny Woodhead Height: 5-9 Weight: 200 College: Chadron State Draft: 2008/FA Born: 25-Jan-1985 Age: 30 Risk: Red

Year	Team	G/GS	Snaps	Runs	Yds	Yd/R	TD	FUM	DVOA	Rk	DYAR	Rk	YAR	Suc%	Rk	BTkl	Rec	Pass	Yds	C%	Yd/C	TD	YAC	DVOA	Rk	DYAR	Rk
2012	NE	16/2	417	76	301	4.0	4	1	22.4%	--	101	--	75	55%	--	5	40	55	446	73%	11.2	3	9.3	35.9%	2	149	3
2013	SD	16/2	491	106	429	4.0	2	1	13.7%	6	104	18	105	60%	1	12	76	87	605	87%	8.0	6	6.1	41.2%	2	282	1
2014	SD	3/0	68	15	38	2.5	0	0	-30.3%	--	-14	--	-21	33%	--	2	5	6	34	83%	6.8	0	6.6	46.4%	--	24	--
2015	SD			86	350	4.0	2	3	0.4%								54	75	509	72%	9.4	2		10.8%			

Even though he has a "Welcome to Hot Topic" appearance, Woodhead is a valuable receiving back and one that Philip Rivers certainly missed last season. Even though Melvin Gordon will be all the rage in San Diego this year, Woodhead is still the best receiving back on the roster and should take a lot of those third-down snaps from Gordon, when Rivers will be looking for a checkdown option.

T.J. Yeldon Height: 5-10 Weight: 226 College: Alabama Draft: 2015/2 (36) Born: 2-Oct-1993 Age: 22 Risk: Yellow

Year	Team	G/GS	Snaps	Runs	Yds	Yd/R	TD	FUM	DVOA	Rk	DYAR	Rk	YAR	Suc%	Rk	BTkl	Rec	Pass	Yds	C%	Yd/C	TD	YAC	DVOA	Rk	DYAR	Rk
2015	JAC			200	818	4.1	6	3	0.5%								25	35	219	71%	8.7	1		-5.2%			

After spending most of NFL draftnik season behind backs like Tevin Coleman and Duke Johnson on big boards, Yeldon was the third back to be actually selected. NFL Films' Greg Cosell compared him to Frank Gore, and praised his ability between the tackles. Our Matt Waldman compared him to Stephen Davis, and said he has the talent to take a job and not look back once he gets the opportunity. Jacksonville desperately needs that to be true, which should make Yeldon one of the safer rookie picks as long as he stays healthy. Don't get caught scouting college positions and comparing Yeldon to Trent Richardson—the talent is here and has been evident since his freshman season.

Going Deep

Javorius Allen, BAL: Baltimore's fourth-round pick has good hands, and averaged 11.3 yards per reception at USC. New Ravens offensive coordinator Marc Trestman likes to throw to his backs, and Allen could find a role easing Justin Forsett's snap count by being as much receiver as runner.

Antonio Andrews, TEN: The Titans cared enough about Andrews to add him to the active roster from the practice squad when the Bills offered the undrafted rookie from Western Kentucky the same chance. He will compete with David Cobb for the power back role in the committee formerly held by Shonn Greene.

Joe Banyard, MIN: After two years on the practice squad, Banyard showed some life jump-starting Minnesota's depleted backfield. The UTEP product received 30 touches from Week 12 onward, spelling starter Matt Asiata after Jerick McKinnon's season-ending back injury. Banyard is likely competing with ex-Packer DuJuan Harris for the final running back spot, but having averaged 5.0 yards per touch last year in addition to playing special teams, he has shown enough to warrant a spot on someone's roster. (2014 stats: 21 carries for 88 yards, 15 DYAR, 8.6% DVOA; receiving stats: 9-for-11, 62 yards, 12 DYAR, 7.1% DVOA)

Kenjon Barner, PHI: One of Chip Kelly's Bench Ducks. Barner took a lot of second and third running back reps during OTAs and minicamp—Darren Sproles isn't called upon to run drills with the backups much, and both DeMarco Murray and Ryan Mathews got some "get acclimated" breaks. Barner left Oregon as a frail third-down back but now looks thicker. He still moves well. Barner could contribute if called upon, but let's face it: the top three spots on the Eagles depth chart are set in granite.

Jackie Battle, FA: Transitioned to fullback and short-yardage back by team necessity, Battle blocked like a career running back transitioned to fullback out of team necessity. That adds to his versatility, which along with special-teams value are the only things that might earn him another NFL job. (2014 stats: 5 carries, 9 yards, 1 TD, 11 DYAR, 20.3% DVOA; receiving stats: 5-for-5, 28 yards, 10 DYAR, 19.0% DVOA)

Tommy Bohanon, NYJ: The days of ground-and-pound in New York are over, but fullback Bohanon—who was limited last season with a broken clavicle—will still carry the flag for the Jets' running game this year as the lead blocker, and he's also a decent pass-catcher. (2013 stats: 17 carries for 62 yards, 5 DYAR, -2.7% DVOA; receiving stats: 11-for-16, 69 yards, -6 DYAR, -20.3%)

Malcolm Brown, STL: A between-the-tackles grinder, Brown is reliable (just one fumble in more than 600 carries at Texas) but lacks breakaway speed (3.9 highlight yards per opportunity in 2014). He went undrafted and will be one of the dozen or so backs fighting to make the Rams roster.

Ronnie Brown, FA: Can you believe it was just a decade ago that three running backs went in the top five of the 2005 draft? Ronnie Brown went to Miami, Cedric Benson to Chicago, and Cadillac Williams to Tampa Bay. At least Miami picked the best of the three, though Frank Gore (65th overall) had the best career for a running back in that class. Brown peaked years ago in Miami, though he did some recent spot duty for the Texans and Chargers. He's not likely to find a suitor at age 34. (2014 stats: 20 carries for 63 yards, 9 DYAR, 2.3% DVOA; receiving stats: 5-for-8, 44 yards, -3 DYAR, -21.5% DVOA)

Rex Burkhead, CIN: The versatility Burkhead displayed while lining up as a wideout in the wild-card game against the Colts is prized in Cincinnati, and the Bengals plan on expanding the long-striding back's role this season. (2014 stats: 9 carries for 27 yards, 1 TD, -7 DYAR, -34.9% DVOA; receiving stats: 7-for-10, 49 yards, 3 DYAR, -7.7% DVOA)

Tyler Clutts, DAL: DeMarco Murray's lead blocker for about 15 snaps per game last season, Clutts did nothing noteworthy and will compete with the more versatile Ray Agnew for a job this season. Behind the Legion of Room, a fullback is often just a guy looking for anyone left to block.

Michael Cox, FA: Activated in October, broken leg in November, waived in April, unsigned in July. To every Giants running back, there is a season. (2013 stats: 22 carries for 43 yards, -27 DYAR, -41.3% DVOA; receiving stats: 3-for-3 for 12 yards, -5 DYAR, -44.9% DVOA)

Orleans Darkwa, NYG: Gifted with an ironically awesome name for a voodoo priest in a cheesy vampire movie, Darkwa stood out in the 2014 preseason for Miami—25-112-1 as a rusher, with seven catches—and earned some carries when the Dolphins were shorthanded early in the season. The Dolphins waived Darkwa when Knowshon Moreno got (briefly) healthy, but the Giants are always in need of a warm body in October. Darkwa was the No. 2 running back behind Andre Williams by December, rushing four times for 21 yards (plus a 12-yard touchdown) and catching two passes in Week 16. Darkwa has the all-around skill set to stick as a No. 2 running back, which is what the Giants' fifth running back inevitably becomes before Halloween. (2014 stats: 9 carries for 23 yards, 1 TD, 10 DYAR, 35.1% DVOA; receiving stats: 5-for-6, 48 yards, 0 DYAR, -14.0% DVOA)

Shaun Draughn, CLE: Draughn bounced around the league last season and only had four carries for the Ravens in 2013, but he's not a bad depth signing for Cleveland. He has experience, plays on special teams, and is still in his prime at 27 years of age. (2014 stats: 10 carries, 19 yards, -20 DYAR, -62.7% DVOA)

Jerome Felton, BUF: As devalued as the running back position is, fullback is even more so. But not in Buffalo. The Bills gave the 2012 second-team All-Pro $9.2 million ($3.6 million guaranteed) to sign him away from Minnesota in free agency. While the Vikings did rank fourth in rushing DVOA, Felton only saw the field for 10.6 snaps per game, down by more than half from the previous two seasons.

Tyler Gaffney, NE: The Patriots picked up Gaffney when Carolina tried to sneak the injured rookie runner through waivers last July, stashing him away on injured reserve. Gaffney can do a little bit of everything and may particularly figure in the plan to replace Shane Vereen. Gaffney is a much bigger back (6-foot-1, 227 pounds), but showed pass-catching abilities at Stanford. He may shine most on third downs as a blocker, a responsibility he fulfilled ably in college. If his left knee has recovered, Gaffney's versatility could make him a real sleeper in the Patriots backfield.

Cyrus Gray, KC: Gray scored his first career touchdown last season, and is firmly entrenched as the No. 3 back behind Jamaal Charles and Knile Davis. Only a rash of injuries is going to make him fantasy viable. He easily saw more special teams snaps (163) than offensive snaps (29) before ending the season with a torn ACL. (2014 stats: 8 carries for 31 yards, 1 TD, 10 DYAR, 20.8% DVOA)

Marion Grice, ARI: Grice was the target on one of the weirdest play designs of the year, a backwards screen pass against Kansas City that was caught 11 yards behind the line of scrimmage, resulting in a 4-yard loss on second-and-goal from the 4. That wasn't atypical for Grice; half of his eight receptions in his rookie year went for no gain or a loss. He also averaged just 2.7 yards per carry, though his DVOA poked into positive numbers thanks to some short-yardage conversions. If he still has any of the burst he showed at Arizona State (5.7 yards per rush, 24.1 yards per kickoff return), he could push for more playing time behind Andre Ellington. (2014 stats: 14 carries for 45 yards, 1 TD, 7 DYAR, 1.0% DVOA)

Jonathan Grimes, HOU: Some running backs get lobster for dinners, and others live above a bowling alley and below another bowling alley. Grimes is a solid bottom-of-the-depth-chart zone runner who was one of Houston's best on special teams. If the Texans move away from being primarily a zone-blocking team, Grimes will probably move on to a different team. Or perhaps a nuclear power plant. (2014 stats: 39 carries for 153 yards, -24.0% DVOA; receiving stats: 6-for-8, 86 yards, 72.4% DVOA)

DuJuan Harris, MIN: Harris was a surprise contributor in the 2012 postseason, but after a knee injury wiped out 2013 he could not find a role in the Packers backfield in 2014. Half of his 16 carries came in the second half of Week 10's game against Chicago where Green Bay led 42-0 at halftime. He was the Packers' primary kick returner, but was below average at that (minus-2.9 points of return value), and was non-tendered as an exclusive rights free agent. The Vikings signed him, but with Adrian Peterson back and Cordarrelle Patterson to return kicks, there may not be a role for him. (2014 stats: 16 carries, 64 yards, 14 DYAR, 11.0% DVOA)

Josh Harris, PIT: Considering he was an undrafted free agent on a relatively stacked depth chart entering the season, Josh Harris was fortunate to get the few chances he did in 2014. He proved to be a very limited back without the explosiveness or strength to offer much upside. The Steelers signaled their lack of excitement when they added Ben Tate to play ahead of him late in the year, but he'll be DeAngelo Williams' backup while Le'Veon Bell serves an early-season suspension. (2014 stats: 9 carries for 16 yards, -21 DYAR, -62.9% DVOA)

Kenny Hilliard, HOU: Drafting an LSU running back with bad measurables in the late rounds of the draft: a Bill O'Brien tradition! Hilliard follows Alfred Blue, to take a stab at a power back role that Chris Polk should be able to fill on his own. Hilliard's agility and second-level speed are question marks, and per MockDraftable, his 40 time of 4.83 seconds (leading to an 83.1 Speed Score) was in the *second* percentile of all running backs since 1999.

Robert Hughes, ARI: In his first three and a half seasons as a blocking fullback for Chicago, Indianapolis, and Arizona, Hughes caught six passes for 36 yards. Then he had an 18-yard reception against Dallas in Week 9, followed by catches for 49 yards against Detroit and 36 yards against Kansas City. Bruce Arians noted Hughes' success as a receiver and said he'd like to expand Hughes' role in the passing game, but the Notre Dame alumnus still fits best in Arizona as a short-yardage option; six of his seven carries last year came on third-and-1, with three conversions. (2014 stats: 6 carries for 7 yards, -4 DYAR, -17.3% DVOA; receiving stats: 8-for-12, 140 yards, 61 DYAR, 66.9% DVOA)

Henry Hynoski, NYG: The Giants re-signed Hynoski for two years in the offseason. He's an excellent lead blocker who doesn't trip over his own feet when he takes a handoff. He's Ben McAdoo's John Kuhn surrogate, complete with a cute Hynocerous nickname to give him fan-favorite cred—but he has scored just one touchdown in four seasons and was never targeted on a pass in 2014. (2014 stats: 7 carries for 13 yards, -7 DYAR, -21.4% DVOA)

LaMichael James, MIA: James was a depth signing by the Dolphins last year after Knowshon Moreno went down, but with the emergence of Lamar Miller, he spent most of the year on the sidelines. He'll battle to work as the backup again this year, and could also end up as a threat to Jarvis Landry at kick returner—James averaged 28.4 yards per return in his two-plus years with the Niners. (2014 stats: 5 carries, 9 yards, -4 DYAR, -30.1% DVOA)

Mike James, TB: If the Bucs choose to keep either of the two fullbacks on the roster, Jorvorskie Lane or 2015 seventh-rounder Joey Iosefa, James may be the odd man out at running back. The 2013 sixth-rounder had one great game as a rookie, throwing a touchdown pass and rushing for 158 yards on 28 carries in an overtime loss to Seattle. That game is responsible for almost half of his career rushing yardage. (2014 stats: 19 carries for 37 yards, -34 DYAR, -42.8% DVOA)

Storm Johnson, JAC: Let's give Storm Johnson credit: if you were desperate enough to need a Jaguars running back in Week 6 or 7, at least he gave your fantasy team a touchdown. He's now no better than third on a depth chart behind a second-round pick and a more intriguing speed back. Hey, some storms do blow over in a few minutes. (2014 stats: 29 carries for 86 yards, 2 TD, -18 DYAR, -22.1% DVOA)

Will Johnson, PIT: Fullback Johnson played 18.5 percent of the Steelers' offensive snaps in 2014, which is a relatively high number for a player on an offense with so many weapons. Johnson isn't a dominant blocker, but he offers the offense some versatility in space and in the passing game. (2014 receiving stats: 6-for-9, 41 yards, -16 DYAR, -36.6% DVOA)

Jeremy Langford, CHI: Le'Veon Bell's replacement at Michigan State, Langford ran for over 2,900 yards his two seasons as the Spartans' feature back, posting 16 consecutive 100-yard games against Big Ten foes. His great 40 time of 4.42 seconds (109.0 Speed Score) is mostly long speed and he is not an outstandingly quick runner. Despite lacking great size and a tendency to run too upright, he was an effective goal-line back and could see a role there. He was also an effective screen back in East Lansing.

Erik Lorig, NO: Lorig is a versatile fullback who can be used in space as a receiver. Even though the Saints pass the ball a lot, the arrival of C.J. Spiller makes it unlikely that his workload will grow in 2015. (2014 stats: 3 carries for 4 yards, -25 DYAR, -154.4% DVOA; receiving stats: 9-for-10, 27 yards, -23 DYAR, -45.3% DVOA)

Joe McKnight, FA: McKnight was a solid back at USC, but never really found a niche with the Jets. In his second game with the Chiefs last year in Miami, he caught six passes for 64 yards and two touchdowns in Jamaal Charles' absence. It was great production for someone with just 15 offensive snaps in 2014, and a total fluke. McKnight ruptured his Achilles just days later in practice, and remains a free agent this summer.

Bruce Miller, SF: On the field, there are no concerns about the 49ers' bruising fullback. He had the best receiving DVOA of any qualifying running back in 2014, albeit with exactly the minimum of 25 pass targets. Off the field, there are problems, and Miller is facing the possibility of suspension after an arrest on suspicion of domestic violence in February. Miller was convicted of a misdemeanor vandalism charge and will remain on the roster. The NFL's new domestic violence policy states that first-time offenders will be suspended for six games, but it's anyone's guess whether Miller's will count as a domestic violence offense. (2014 stats: 6 carries, 12 yards, -21 DYAR, -60.2% DVOA; receiving stats: 18-for-25, 189 yards, 2 TD, 95 DYAR, 52.2% DVOA).

Marcus Murphy, NO: This seventh-round pick out of Missouri is an undersized running back with impressive feet and a short-area burst to escape defenders in space. Maybe most importantly, he's a natural receiver at the running back spot. Darren Sproles may no longer be in New Orleans, but Sean Payton is making plenty of efforts to find someone like him.

Rajion Neal, GB: The favorite for the No. 3 spot in Green Bay, Neal spent 2014 on the practice squad. Coming out of Tennessee, he showed good speed but needed to be more decisive as a runner and needed more technique work to be a good passing-game player.

Chris Ogbonnaya, FA: Officially retired after brief stints with the injury-desperate Panthers and Giants last year. Ogbonnaya pretty much defines the replacement-level running back, which means he can be easily replaced. It also means he might be lured out of retirement by a coach who would rather use a veteran than a late-round pick to soak up emergency carries. (2014 stats: 14 carries for 50 yards, 1 TD, 17 DYAR, 17.8% DVOA)

Isaiah Pead, STL: A second-round pick in 2012, Pead was a disappointment even before a torn ACL cost him the entire 2014 season. Pead only carried the ball 17 times in 25 games in his first two years, and it's very hard to see him sticking with a team that now has Todd Gurley, Benny Cunningham, and Tre Mason. (2013 stats: 7 carries for 21 yards, -4 DYAR, -21.2% DVOA; receiving stats: 11-for-15, 78 yards, 8 DYAR, -5.2% DVOA)

Cedric Peerman, CIN: An important locker room voice and special-teams captain, Peerman remains on the roster by doing things other than carrying the ball, which he does roughly a dozen times a season. (2014 stats: 15 carries for 43 yards, -32 DYAR, -52.9% DVOA; receiving stats: 3-for-5, 27 yards, 0 DYAR, -15.6% DVOA)

Thomas Rawls, SEA: With Seattle's top three running backs unavailable for various reasons, Rawls took snaps with the first-team offense in OTAs and drew praise from Pete Carroll, starting rumors that this undrafted rookie might take Christine Michael's roster spot. It's a cute story, but unlikely, given Rawls' limited athleticism (92.0 Speed Score) and off-field red flags (he was suspended for two games at Central Michigan over a purse-snatching incident, and missed the Chippewas' bowl game due to academic reasons).

Daryl Richardson, NYJ: After two seasons backing up Stephen Jackson in St. Louis, Richardson spent the bulk of the 2014 season on the New York practice squad. While he does have some value as a third-down option (he had 38 catches between 2012-2013) and a potential special-teamer, he'll be a part of a large crowd of running backs fighting for snaps this year with the Jets. (2013 stats: 69 runs for 215 yards, -34 DYAR, -19.4% DVOA; receiving stats: 14-for-18, 121 yards, 9 DYAR, -3.6% DVOA)

Josh Robinson, IND: The Colts won't ask Robinson to touch the ball much this season unless the usual rash of absurd injuries strikes again. The Mississippi State alum is a quality power back with an ability to break tackles and catch the ball, but he lacks elite vision. So he's basically going to be a better version of Trent Richardson, but at the cost of just a sixth-round pick. Now you understand, Ryan Grigson?

Lache Seastrunk, DAL: The Cowboys settled on Seastrunk as a depth acquisition after trying out Felix Jones, Ben Tate, and possibly Walt Garrison at the start of OTAs. They could have done worse: Seastrunk averaged 7.7 yards per carry over two seasons at Baylor and had a fine preseason for Washington last year before landing on the Titans practice squad. Seastrunk is battling Ryan Williams to be the first running back off the practice squad if Darren McFadden gets hurt.

Anthony Sherman, KC: Sherman played the fourth-most snaps (249) among fullbacks last year. He's basically the AFC's version of San Francisco's Bruce Miller. He'll reliably catch a short pass from time to time—he has caught 41 of 55 career targets—and do a solid job in run blocking. (2014 receiving stats: 10-for-14, 71 yards, 1 TD, 12 DYAR, 2.0% DVOA)

Chris Thompson, WAS: Thompson was a dynamic all-purpose back at Florida State before tearing an ACL in 2012. He then tore a labrum in 2013 and suffered a low ankle sprain late in training camp in 2014. He spent the year on the practice squad before earning a late-season call-up and a few carries when Roy Helu was hurt. Thompson remains in the Redskins' plans until the next injury, which should not be long in coming. (2014 stats: 3 carries for 12 yards, 3 DYAR, 18.5% DVOA; receiving stats: 6-for-7, 27 yards, 1 DYAR, -12.4% DVOA)

Zurlon Tipton, IND: Was this guy on *Star Trek* or is he a new brand of soup? Either way, the Colts felt more comfortable with an undrafted free agent in the postseason than they did Trent Richardson. Tipton really didn't show anything exceptional and might be camp fodder this summer with Frank Gore, Dan Herron, Vick Ballard, and rookie Josh Robinson competing for roster spots. (2014 stats: 10 carries for 18 yards, -29 DYAR, -71.3% DVOA; receiving stats: 6-for-6, 68 yards, 1 TD, 44 DYAR, 76.8% DVOA)

Fitzgerald Toussaint, BAL: The UDFA rookie out of Michigan put up 103 yards in the Ravens' final preseason game of 2014, leading to a practice-squad berth that became a promotion when the almost-as-spectacularly named Lorenzo Taliaferro got hurt. Fans of nomenclature are rooting for Fitz to have a second act. (2014 stats: 6 carries for 12 yards, -10 DYAR, -52.0% DVOA; receiving stats: 3-for-6, 27 yards, -2 DYAR, -19.7% DVOA)

Leon Washington, FA: The veteran kick returner also earned a job as the Titans' third-down back in 2014, where he got the occasional draw or dumpoff and three inexplicable third-and-short carries. Overall, he had 21 targets and nine carries on third or fourth down, and only converted six times. He's a free agent and could conceivably show up wherever a kick returner gets injured at midseason. (2014 stats: 13 carries for 57 yards, -18 DYAR, -49.4% DVOA; receiving stats: 22-for-31, 159 yards, 2 TD, 14 DYAR, -4.6% DVOA)

Trey Watts, STL: Watts was active for 14 games as a rookie, but all of his runs and two of his three receptions came in back-to-back games against Dallas and Philadelphia early in the year. The Rams took nine running backs into OTAs and Watts will face a tough battle to earn a roster spot. A four-game suspension for substance abuse levied in late May won't help his cause. (2014 stats: 7 carries for 30 yards, 5 DYAR, 6.3% DVOA)

Nikita Whitlock, NYG: 1991: The foxy Soviet sleeper agent leapt through the window to what she thought was the ambassador's secret love nest, only to find a tubby, loudmouthed sports-talk personality eating a huge mound of beef brisket alone in bed. The assassin was at once repulsed and strangely attracted; her superspy infiltration programming, designed to penetrate America's political power centers, forced her to find overweight know-it-alls charming. The assassin and the sports-talk personality embraced, and nine months later she bore a child she knew would one day bounce from Bengals to Cowboys to Giants training camps as a practice-squad fullback. "You will be great, my child," she cooed to him at night, "so long as you never come face-to-face with your greatest rival, Natasha Kornheiser."

Karlos Williams, BUF: Despite having this year's top Speed Score at 114.2, this fifth-round pick has red flags both on and off the field. Williams averaged 8.0 yards on 93 attempts with Florida State in 2013, but then gained weight last year and saw his average drop to 4.6 yards on 150 carries. Williams' output last year is concerning because he played behind a quality offensive line and had good support at quarterback, but Florida State did face the nation's toughest slate of opposing defenses according to FEI. Williams was also investigated in a domestic battery case. Williams has a high ceiling, but his downside is just as severe. Anything from significant rookie contributor to training camp cut is in play.

Ryan Williams, DAL: Williams was the Cardinals' second-round pick in 2011; you are excused for thinking that this is some different Ryan Williams from that guy, who rushed for 1,655 yards for the Hokies in 2009. Williams tore his patella tendon in his rookie training camp and hasn't been truly healthy since. He appeared in a handful of games in 2012, spent 2013 on injured reserve, and spent all of last season on the Cowboys' practice squad. The Cowboys thought enough of Williams to give him a two-year contract with more guaranteed money than they gave Darren McFadden. That's a sign that either the Cowboys saw glimpses of 2009 Williams during weekly workouts, or they still have moments when they have no idea at all what to do with their money.

Trey Williams, WAS: Williams is a well-built little scatback with home run potential. He averaged 6.6 yards per carry in three seasons at Texas A&M (with only a season's worth of carries, however) and was an effective kick returner. An undrafted rookie signing, Williams should overtake Chris Thompson and compete with Silas Redd as Washington's third running back. Returning kickoffs could seal the deal for him.

George Winn, DET: Winn somehow found himself as Detroit's only healthy tailback by the end of his career debut, a Week 5 loss against Buffalo. After toting the ball 11 times for 48 yards against the Bills' stingy front, he reverted to a reserve role the rest of the season. Winn was a bit of a surprising roster keep over former second-rounder Mikel Leshoure, though special teams likely played a role in that decision. In 2015, he'll again compete for one of the last roster spots, probably against small-school (South Dakota State) darling Zach Zenner. (2014 stats: 19 carries for 73 yards, 0 DYAR, -8.6% DVOA)

Darrel Young, WAS: Young helped kick-start Kirk Cousins Mania by splitting wide against the Jaguars and sprinting uncovered into the end zone for a 20-yard touchdown reception. Late in the year, he spoiled the Eagles' playoff party with a pair of 1-yard fullback-dive touchdowns against a defense that had given up shedding blocks or tackling for the winter. Easy touchdowns aside, Young was a quality role player on an offense short on quality or easily-defined roles. He's a fast fullback who can catch, so an increased role is possible with Roy Helu gone. (2014 stats: 9 carries for 22 yards, 3 TD, 21 DYAR, 21.4% DVOA; receiving stats: 11-for-14, 81 yards, 2 TD, 40 DYAR, 34.2% DVOA)

Wide Receivers

In the following two sections we provide the last three years' statistics, as well as a 2015 KUBIAK projection, for every wide receiver and tight end who either played a significant role in 2014 or is expected to do so in 2015.

The first line contains biographical data—each player's **name**, **height**, **weight**, **college**, **draft** position, **birth date**, and **age**. Height and weight are the best data we could find; weight, of course, can fluctuate during the off-season. **Age** is very simple, the number of years between the player's birth year and 2015, but birth date is provided if you want to figure out exact age.

Draft position gives draft year and round, with the overall pick number with which the player was taken in parentheses. In the sample table, it says that A.J. Green was chosen in the 2011 NFL Draft with the fourth overall pick in the first round. Undrafted free agents are listed as "FA" with the year they came into the league, even if they were only in training camp or on a practice squad.

To the far right of the first line is the player's **Risk** for fantasy football in 2015. As explained in the quarterback section, the standard is for players to be marked Green. Players with higher than normal risk are marked Yellow, and players with the highest risk are marked Red. Players who are most likely to match or surpass our forecast—primarily second- stringers with low projections—are marked Blue. Risk is not only based on injury probability, but how a player's projection compares to his recent performance, as well as our confidence (or lack thereof) in his offensive teammates.

Next we give the last three years of player stats. Note that rushing stats are not included for receivers, but that any receiver with at least five carries last year will have his 2014 rushing stats appear in his team's chapter.

The first few columns after the **year** and **team** the player played for are standard numbers: First come games played and games started (**G/GS**). Games played represents the official NFL total and may include games in which a player appeared on special teams, but did not play wide receiver or tight end. We also have a total of offensive **Snaps** for each season. Receptions (**Rec**) counts passes caught, while Passes (**Pass**) counts passes thrown to this player, complete or incomplete. Receiving yards (**Yds**) is the official NFL total for each player.

Catch rate (**C%**) includes all passes listed in the official play-by-play with the given player as the intended receiver, even if those passes were listed by our game charters as "Thrown Away," "Tipped at Line," or "Quarterback Hit in Motion." The average NFL wide receiver has caught between 58 and 60 percent of passes over the last three seasons; tight ends caught between 64 and 65 percent of passes over the last three seasons.

Plus/minus (+/-) is a new metric that we introduced in *Football Outsiders Almanac 2010*. It estimates how many passes a receiver caught compared to what an average receiver would have caught, given the location of those passes. Unlike simple catch rate, plus/minus does not consider passes listed as "Thrown Away," "Tipped at Line," or "Quarterback Hit in Motion." Player performance is compared to a historical baseline of how often a pass is caught based on the pass distance, the distance required for a first down, and whether it is on the left, middle, or right side of the field. Note that plus/minus is not scaled to a player's target total.

Yards per catch (**Yd/C**) and receiving touchdowns (**TD**) are standard stats. Drops (**Drop**) list the number of dropped passes according to our game charting project. Our totals may differ from the drop totals kept by other organizations.

Next we list yards after catch (**YAC**), rank (**Rk**) in yards after catch, and **YAC+**. YAC+ is similar to plus-minus; it estimates how much YAC a receiver gained compared to what we would have expected from an average receiver catching passes of similar length in similar down-and-distance situations. This is imperfect—we don't specifically mark what route a player runs, and obviously a go route will have more YAC than a comeback—but it does a fairly good job of telling you if this receiver gets more or less YAC than other receivers with similar usage patterns. We also give a total of broken tackles (**BTkl**) according to the Football Outsiders game charting project.

The next five columns include our main advanced metrics for receiving: **DVOA** (Defense-Adjusted Value Over Average), **DYAR** (Defense-Adjusted Yards Above Replacement), and **YAR** (Yards Above Replacement), along with the player's rank in both DVOA and DYAR. These metrics compare every pass intended for a receiver and the results of that pass to a league-average baseline based on the game situations in which passes were thrown to that receiver. DVOA and DYAR are also adjusted based on the opposing defense and include Defensive Pass Interference yards on passes intended for that receiver. The methods used to compute these numbers are described in detail in the "Statistical Toolbox" introduction in the front of the book. The important distinctions between them are:

A.J. Green			Height: 6-4		Weight: 207		College: Georgia				Draft: 2011/1 (4)		Born: 31-Jul-1988		Age: 27		Risk: Green	
Year	Team	G/GS	Snaps	Rec	Pass	Yds	C%	+/-	Yd/C	TD	Drop	YAC	Rk	YAC+	BTkl	DVOA	Rk	DYAR	Rk	DYAR	Rk	YAR	Short	Mid	Deep	Bomb
2012	CIN	16/16	958	97	164	1350	59%	+4.9	13.9	11	8	3.9	47	-0.5	9	4.1%	33	205	22	233	34%	32%	15%	18%
2013	CIN	16/16	1055	98	178	1426	55%	-1.6	14.6	11	5	4.1	65	-0.6	7	1.9%	41	207	20	185	27%	44%	14%	15%
2014	CIN	13/13	648	69	116	1041	59%	+4.2	15.1	6	2	4.5	46	+0.3	9	4.1%	38	158	29	161	23%	45%	20%	12%
2015	CIN			84	144	1187	58%	--	14.1	9							1.9%							

• DVOA is a rate statistic, while DYAR is a cumulative statistic. Thus, a higher DVOA means more value per pass play, while a higher DYAR means more aggregate value over the entire season.

• Because DYAR is defense-adjusted and YAR is not, a player whose DYAR is higher than his YAR faced a harder-than-average schedule. A player whose DYAR is lower than his YAR faced an easier-than-average schedule.

To qualify for ranking in YAC, receiving DVOA, or receiving DYAR, a wide receiver must have had 50 passes thrown to him in that season. We ranked 87 wideouts in 2014, 90 wideouts in 2013, and 86 wideouts in 2012. Tight ends qualify with 25 targets in a given season; we ranked 50 tight ends in 2014, 51 tight ends in 2013, and 49 tight ends in 2012.

The final four columns break down pass length based on the Football Outsiders charting project. The categories are **Short** (5 yards or less), **Mid** (6-15 yards), **Deep** (16-25 yards), and **Bomb** (26 or more yards). These numbers are based on distance in the air only and include both complete and incomplete passes.

The italicized row of statistics for the 2015 season is our 2015 KUBIAK projection based on a complicated regression analysis that takes into account numerous variables including projected role, performance over the past two years, projected team offense and defense, projected quarterback statistics, historical comparables, height, age, and strength of schedule.

It is difficult to accurately project statistics for a 162-game baseball season, but it is exponentially more difficult to accurately project statistics for a 16-game football season. Consider the listed projections not as a prediction of exact numbers, but as the mean of a range of possible performances. What's important is less the exact number of yards we project, and more which players are projected to improve or decline. Actual performance will vary from our projection less for veteran starters and more for rookies and third-stringers, for whom we must base our projections on much smaller career statistical samples. Touchdown numbers will vary more than yardage numbers. Players facing suspension or recovering from injury have those missed games taken into account.

Note that the receiving totals for each team will add up to higher numbers than the projection for that team's starting quarterback, because we have done KUBIAK projections for more receivers than will actually make the final roster.

A few low-round rookies, guys listed at seventh on the depth chart, and players who are listed as wide receivers but really only play special teams are briefly discussed at the end of the chapter in a section we call "Going Deep."

Two notes regarding our advanced metrics: we cannot yet fully separate the performance of a receiver from the performance of his quarterback. Be aware that one will affect the other. In addition, these statistics measure only passes thrown to a receiver, not performance on plays when he is not thrown the ball, such as blocking and drawing double-teams.

Top 20 WR by Receiving DYAR (Total Value), 2014

Rank	Player	Team	DYAR
1	Antonio Brown	PIT	554
2	Jordy Nelson	GB	482
3	Emmanuel Sanders	DEN	481
4	Randall Cobb	GB	479
5	Dez Bryant	DAL	430
6	Odell Beckham	NYG	396
7	Julio Jones	ATL	356
8	Demaryius Thomas	DEN	317
9	Torrey Smith	BAL	310
10	DeSean Jackson	WAS	306
11	T.Y. Hilton	IND	303
12	Kenny Stills	NO	285
13	Alshon Jeffery	CHI	278
14	Malcom Floyd	SD	252
15	DeAndre Hopkins	HOU	237
16	Calvin Johnson	DET	231
17	Mike Evans	TB	222
18	Jeremy Maclin	PHI	222
19	Anquan Boldin	SF	222
20	Mike Wallace	MIA	221

Top 20 WR by Receiving DVOA (Value per Pass), 2014

Rank	Player	Team	DVOA
1	Randall Cobb	GB	35.7%
2	Terrance Williams	DAL	30.6%
3	Kenny Stills	NO	30.3%
4	Emmanuel Sanders	DEN	29.6%
5	Dez Bryant	DAL	27.0%
6	DeSean Jackson	WAS	27.0%
7	Torrey Smith	BAL	26.8%
8	Jordy Nelson	GB	26.8%
9	Odell Beckham	NYG	25.8%
10	Antonio Brown	PIT	25.7%
11	Stevie Johnson	SF	23.4%
12	Malcom Floyd	SD	23.1%
13	Cole Beasley	DAL	16.7%
14	T.Y. Hilton	IND	16.5%
15	Julio Jones	ATL	16.2%
16	Marques Colston	NO	13.0%
17	Eddie Royal	SD	12.8%
18	Kenny Britt	STL	12.4%
19	Mike Wallace	MIA	11.8%
20	Jordan Matthews	PHI	11.6%

Minimum 50 targets

Davante Adams

			Height: 6-1		Weight: 212		College: Fresno St.			Draft: 2014/2 (53)			Born: 12-Dec-1992		Age: 23		Risk: Red	

Year	Team	G/GS	Snaps	Rec	Pass	Yds	C%	+/-	Yd/C	TD	Drop	YAC	Rk	YAC+	BTkl	DVOA	Rk	DYAR	Rk	YAR	Short	Mid	Deep	Bomb
2014	GB	16/11	738	38	66	446	58%	+1.0	11.7	3	4	4.6	44	+0.2	2	-9.0%	59	19	63	28	32%	50%	11%	6%
2015	GB			58	91	803	64%	--	13.8	7						11.4%								

Adams had a tantalizing rookie season, displaying flashes of ball-winning, route adjustments, and big-play potential. His two best games were two of the highest profile ones, six catches for 121 yards in the home win against the Patriots and 7-117-1 in the playoff win over the Cowboys. The rest of the time, you saw why tantalizing potential is as much curse as promise, with too many missed route adjustments and rookie raggedness adapting to the NFL game. Offseason reviews of his performance were ecstatic, even beyond the normal "everything is awesome" nature of offseason quotes. If he really has improved that much, Green Bay's challenging duo of wide receivers could be a trio.

Nelson Agholor

			Height: 6-0		Weight: 198		College: USC			Draft: 2015/1 (20)			Born: 24-May-1993		Age: 22		Risk: Red	

Year	Team	G/GS	Snaps	Rec	Pass	Yds	C%	+/-	Yd/C	TD	Drop	YAC	Rk	YAC+	BTkl	DVOA	Rk	DYAR	Rk	YAR	Short	Mid	Deep	Bomb
2015	PHI			55	91	789	60%	--	14.3	5						4.0%								

CHIP KELLY: Fetch me Jeremy Maclin!
WAYLON SMITHEROWICZ: He signed with the Chiefs while you were trying to trade a kidney for Marcus Mariota, sir.
CHIP KELLY: Then fetch me his rookie-salaried equivalent!
Agholor is so much like the young Maclin that it can cause flashbacks. At minicamp, he was slippery and precise on short routes and gave smarter interviews than the typical Philadelphia mayoral candidate. Maclin posted 56-773-4 as a rookie, and those sound like reasonable Agholor numbers: he's more a possession receiver than a burner, and there are only so many footballs to go around, even for a team that snaps three of them per minute.

Kamar Aiken

			Height: 6-2		Weight: 219		College: UCF			Draft: 2011/FA			Born: 30-May-1989		Age: 26		Risk: Yellow	

Year	Team	G/GS	Snaps	Rec	Pass	Yds	C%	+/-	Yd/C	TD	Drop	YAC	Rk	YAC+	BTkl	DVOA	Rk	DYAR	Rk	YAR	Short	Mid	Deep	Bomb
2012	NE	1/0	3	0	--	0	--	--	--	0	--	--	--	--	--	--	--	--	--	--	--	--	--	--
2014	BAL	16/0	273	24	32	267	75%	+3.5	11.1	3	1	2.5	--	-1.4	0	29.7%	--	106	--	100	22%	56%	13%	9%
2015	BAL			31	48	364	65%	--	11.7	2						-1.5%								

Aiken's quality numbers in spot duty last season earned him the right to run with the starters during OTAs, but his destiny seems to be competing with another well-regarded but inexperienced wideout, Marlon Brown, for the No. 3 role behind Steve Smith and rookie Breshad Perriman. Aiken and Brown will be key in 2015—with an old man and a newbie starting, the next two on the depth chart need to provide some quality or the passing game could take a hit.

Keenan Allen

			Height: 6-2		Weight: 206		College: California			Draft: 2013/3 (76)			Born: 27-Apr-1992		Age: 23		Risk: Green	

Year	Team	G/GS	Snaps	Rec	Pass	Yds	C%	+/-	Yd/C	TD	Drop	YAC	Rk	YAC+	BTkl	DVOA	Rk	DYAR	Rk	YAR	Short	Mid	Deep	Bomb
2013	SD	15/14	946	71	104	1046	68%	+8.6	14.7	8	2	5.9	13	+1.5	10	28.2%	5	343	8	351	37%	43%	17%	3%
2014	SD	14/14	837	77	122	783	63%	+1.4	10.2	4	1	3.9	57	-0.8	6	-8.0%	57	43	55	29	46%	38%	11%	4%
2015	SD			78	117	911	67%	--	11.7	5						2.5%								

In the B.B. (Before Beckham) era, Allen enjoyed one of the better rookie seasons we have seen from a wide receiver. He then had a strong postseason, but things just never got rolling in 2014. Sure, there was that comical hype when he had three catches for 38 yards against Richard Sherman in Week 2, but Allen didn't find the end zone until Week 8. He had 21 total yards against the Patriots and Broncos late in the season before sitting out the final two games with a broken collarbone. You assume better help will lead to better play in 2015, but it was troubling to see Allen's average gain drop from 14.7 yards to 10.2. That's the third-largest sophomore decline among the 69 qualified wide receivers that had at least 50 catches as a rookie. The biggest drops were Billy Howton (minus-4.7) and Frank Sanders (minus-5.2), but these players usually pick things back up. Then again, there are some troubling names on the list near Allen's, quick career faders like Michael Clayton (minus-3.3) and the Tampa Bay model of Mike Williams (minus-3.0). If Allen continues to struggle with making big plays and staying healthy, then he'll just confirm his scouting report and third-round status.

Danny Amendola   Height: 5-11   Weight: 186   College: Texas Tech   Draft: 2008/FA   Born: 2-Nov-1985   Age: 30   Risk: Green

Year	Team	G/GS	Snaps	Rec	Pass	Yds	C%	+/-	Yd/C	TD	Drop	YAC	Rk	YAC+	BTkl	DVOA	Rk	DYAR	Rk	YAR	Short	Mid	Deep	Bomb
2012	STL	11/8	498	63	101	666	62%	+1.3	10.6	3	2	3.8	48	-0.7	4	-7.6%	67	80	45	10	52%	36%	4%	8%
2013	NE	12/6	571	54	83	633	65%	+0.9	11.7	2	4	4.7	43	-0.2	2	12.3%	21	163	27	116	45%	40%	9%	6%
2014	NE	16/4	456	27	42	200	64%	-1.3	7.4	1	2	2.7	--	-2.6	0	-17.7%	--	-16	--	-14	49%	30%	12%	9%
2015	NE			20	34	214	59%	--	10.7	0							-15.5%								

In 2013, Amendola did not live up to a contract that paid him like Wes Welker's heir apparent. With a groin injury limiting him for most of the season, improvement was a reasonable expectation in 2014. But while Amendola stayed healthy last season, his production nosedived to the lowest levels of his career, dipping below two catches per game.

Then he seemingly saved his season—and likely his roster spot, which still required a contract restructuring—with a star turn in the playoffs (31.5% DVOA over three games). His three playoff touchdowns matched his total from his first two seasons in New England. All of a sudden, Amendola was breaking tackles, leaping for the end zone, and reaching for crucial fourth-quarter first downs. It didn't make a ton of sense, and it's not likely to continue.

Dri Archer   Height: 5-8   Weight: 173   College: Kent St.   Draft: 2014/3 (97)   Born: 8-Sep-1991   Age: 24   Risk: Blue

Year	Team	G/GS	Snaps	Rec	Pass	Yds	C%	+/-	Yd/C	TD	Drop	YAC	Rk	YAC+	BTkl	DVOA	Rk	DYAR	Rk	YAR	Short	Mid	Deep	Bomb
2014	PIT	12/0	50	7	10	23	70%	-1.5	3.3	0	1	4.0	--	-4.4	2	-74.0%	--	-45	--	-47	90%	10%	0%	0%
2015	PIT			12	18	116	67%	--	9.7	0							-10.6%								

It was an underwhelming rookie season for Dri Archer in 2014. Injury early in the year prevented him from making an immediate impact, while the offense never really made a strong effort to feature him in the game plan after that. He was effective on the handful of touches he had, but he will essentially be a rookie entering his second season in the NFL.

Interestingly, the Steelers added a player this offseason who could prove to be similar to Archer. Sammie Coates isn't physically built the same way as Archer, and he's not going to be lining up in the backfield, but both players figure to have skill sets that need to be accommodated by the offense rather than just being plugged into a specific position to play.

Miles Austin   Height: 6-3   Weight: 215   College: Monmouth   Draft: 2006/FA   Born: 30-Jun-1984   Age: 31   Risk: Green

Year	Team	G/GS	Snaps	Rec	Pass	Yds	C%	+/-	Yd/C	TD	Drop	YAC	Rk	YAC+	BTkl	DVOA	Rk	DYAR	Rk	YAR	Short	Mid	Deep	Bomb
2012	DAL	16/15	860	66	119	943	55%	-3.0	14.3	6	4	4.4	37	+0.1	6	3.3%	36	184	25	151	25%	43%	23%	9%
2013	DAL	11/8	524	24	49	244	49%	-6.8	10.2	0	3	4.2	--	-0.2	0	-25.9%	--	-51	--	-61	43%	48%	4%	4%
2014	CLE	12/11	535	47	72	568	65%	+3.9	12.1	2	3	4.3	49	-0.2	0	10.1%	25	120	35	127	37%	51%	10%	1%
2015	PHI			11	17	107	65%	--	9.8	0							-7.7%								

There was once a time when Miles Austin appeared set to enjoy a long, productive career as one of the more intimidating receivers in the NFL. But after a short peak, injuries derailed much of his career and sapped him of his explosiveness. He returned to health, if not full effectiveness, in 2014 and proved to be a productive receiver in Kyle Shanahan's offense. Austin probably shouldn't be a starter at this point of his career, but as veteran depth with the ability to be effective on intermediate routes, he could prove to be good value in Philadelphia.

Tavon Austin   Height: 5-8   Weight: 174   College: West Virgina   Draft: 2013/1 (8)   Born: 15-Mar-1991   Age: 24   Risk: Green

Year	Team	G/GS	Snaps	Rec	Pass	Yds	C%	+/-	Yd/C	TD	Drop	YAC	Rk	YAC+	BTkl	DVOA	Rk	DYAR	Rk	YAR	Short	Mid	Deep	Bomb
2013	STL	13/3	422	40	69	418	58%	-4.3	10.5	4	6	5.8	17	+0.2	7	-19.4%	81	-36	80	-38	54%	30%	7%	9%
2014	STL	15/8	534	31	44	242	70%	-1.8	7.8	0	2	5.5	--	-0.9	8	-5.8%	--	24	--	13	67%	20%	7%	7%
2015	STL			37	57	396	65%	--	10.7	1							-7.2%								

Twenty games played, 6 rushing yards per game, 6 yards per carry, 10 receiving yards per game. Doesn't sound like much, but Austin is one of five players in league history to achieve those minimums. Contemporaries Percy Harvin and Cordarrelle Patterson, runner/receiver types similar to Austin, have also done it. The other two: Jerris McPhail (a Dolphins and Lions running back in the mid-'90s whose rushing average is skewed by one 71-yard gain in 23 career runs) and Frank Jackson (an AFL oddity who played two years at running back for the Dallas Texans, then five years at flanker for the Chiefs and Dolphins).

Austin didn't have much success as an actual running back, though that's partly because the Rams were so predictable when they used him that way. We counted 19 times that Austin lined up in the backfield. They handed him the ball on 14 of those plays for 2.9 yards per carry, a long gain of only 8 yards, and only two first downs. They also threw him one pass out of the backfield, which resulted in a catch for no gain. Meanwhile, his 22 runs on end-arounds or fly sweeps averaged 8.3 yards each, with seven gains of 10-plus yards and nine first downs, including both of his touchdowns. The Rams are loaded at running back with Todd Gurley, Benny Cunningham, and Tre Mason on board. There's really no reason for Austin to line up there anymore. He's not much of a wide receiver either, but he's a very dangerous weapon in the misdirection game. And it wouldn't kill the Rams to line their blazing speedster out wide and lob him the ball on a 9-route once in a while, either. He was targeted on only three "bomb" routes at least 26 yards downfield last season, resulting in one catch and two DPIs for 84 total yards.

You'd like to get more than fly sweeps, bombs, and kick returns out of the eighth overall pick in the draft, but at this point it's pretty clear that's all that Austin has to offer.

(Note: while not listed above, Austin's projection also includes 31 carries for 160 yards.)

Jason Avant

Height: 6-0   Weight: 210   College: Michigan   Draft: 2006/4 (109)   Born: 20-Apr-1983   Age: 32   Risk: Green

Year	Team	G/GS	Snaps	Rec	Pass	Yds	C%	+/-	Yd/C	TD	Drop	YAC	Rk	YAC+	BTkl	DVOA	Rk	DYAR	Rk	YAR	Short	Mid	Deep	Bomb
2012	PHI	14/6	656	53	77	648	70%	+7.3	12.2	0	0	2.7	76	-1.6	2	6.8%	28	137	33	118	33%	48%	16%	3%
2013	PHI	16/13	789	38	76	447	50%	-3.4	11.8	2	0	2.1	88	-2.2	1	-24.5%	85	-68	85	-55	26%	41%	24%	9%
2014	2TM	16/0	554	34	62	353	55%	-4.9	10.4	1	2	4.3	48	-1.2	1	-16.5%	79	-18	78	-29	37%	46%	10%	7%
2015	KC			18	28	214	64%	--	11.9	1							0.6%							

One of the great things about free agency is that it makes it easier for coaches to reconnect with past players who have proven success in their system. Avant did not gel with Chip Kelly and he was released in Carolina so Philly Brown could get more reps. Andy Reid snatched him up last November, and Avant had 152 receiving yards in five games after just 201 yards in 11 games with the Panthers. At this stage of his career he is just a role player and possession receiver with good hands (three drops on his last 296 targets), but Avant may fit in anywhere from a No. 2 to a No. 5 wide receiver given this Kansas City depth chart.

Donnie Avery

Height: 5-11   Weight: 183   College: Houston   Draft: 2008/2 (33)   Born: 12-Jun-1984   Age: 31   Risk: N/A

Year	Team	G/GS	Snaps	Rec	Pass	Yds	C%	+/-	Yd/C	TD	Drop	YAC	Rk	YAC+	BTkl	DVOA	Rk	DYAR	Rk	YAR	Short	Mid	Deep	Bomb
2012	IND	16/15	1025	60	125	781	48%	-8.0	13.0	3	6	3.5	63	-1.4	2	-19.1%	79	-75	83	-41	29%	42%	15%	14%
2013	KC	16/14	706	40	72	596	56%	-2.3	14.9	2	4	4.6	49	-0.0	3	-0.8%	52	68	54	72	44%	27%	11%	18%
2014	KC	6/3	232	15	26	176	58%	+0.8	11.7	0	0	2.5	--	-1.7	2	-19.4%	--	-13	--	-12	38%	29%	17%	17%

Before having sports hernia surgery, Avery struggled to get separation, often wearing defenders like fine fur coats. Who would want him now given his extensive injury history and failure to hang on with four different teams? So far this offseason, the answer is "nobody."

Stedman Bailey

Height: 5-10   Weight: 193   College: West Virginia   Draft: 2013/3 (92)   Born: 11-Nov-1990   Age: 25   Risk: Green

Year	Team	G/GS	Snaps	Rec	Pass	Yds	C%	+/-	Yd/C	TD	Drop	YAC	Rk	YAC+	BTkl	DVOA	Rk	DYAR	Rk	YAR	Short	Mid	Deep	Bomb
2013	STL	16/2	188	17	25	226	68%	+3.3	13.3	0	0	2.7	--	-1.1	1	7.5%	--	36	--	33	33%	43%	24%	0%
2014	STL	14/3	404	30	46	435	65%	+3.7	14.5	1	2	6.1	--	+1.5	8	16.8%	--	103	--	98	29%	44%	12%	15%
2015	STL			29	47	398	62%	--	13.7	2							1.9%							

Bailey has spent his entire adulthood unfairly hidden in Tavon Austin's shadow. He was clearly the superior wide receiver (and we stress the words *wide receiver*, not football player) when the two played at West Virginia, but he went 84 picks later in the draft, only to wind up stuck behind Austin on the Rams' depth chart. Then, while Austin spent two seasons trying to translate his freakish athleticism to the football field with decidedly mixed results, Bailey was relegated to third wideout, even after injury knocked Brian Quick out of the starting lineup. Bailey doesn't have Austin's talent, but he has more *skill*, and he's much better at getting open and catching passes. On the other hand, he's something of a garbage-time champion, with nearly one-third of his total yardage coming with the Rams down by more than eight points in the fourth quarter.

Bailey saw most of his action after Quick's injury in 2014, only catching five passes for 60 yards in the first ten weeks of the year. The Rams' depth chart at wideout remains unchanged from last season, but there's a good shot Bailey will develop and assume a larger role in his third season.

Doug Baldwin

Height: 5-11   Weight: 189   College: Stanford   Draft: 2011/FA   Born: 21-Sep-1988   Age: 27   Risk: Green

Year	Team	G/GS	Snaps	Rec	Pass	Yds	C%	+/-	Yd/C	TD	Drop	YAC	Rk	YAC+	BTkl	DVOA	Rk	DYAR	Rk	YAR	Short	Mid	Deep	Bomb
2012	SEA	14/4	434	29	50	366	58%	+0.1	12.6	3	3	2.7	77	-2.0	0	0.0%	47	45	58	38	33%	48%	9%	11%
2013	SEA	16/9	749	50	73	778	68%	+7.3	15.6	5	3	4.6	47	-0.2	2	33.3%	2	274	13	269	27%	45%	18%	11%
2014	SEA	16/16	879	66	99	825	68%	+6.1	12.5	3	3	5.2	24	-0.2	8	5.5%	34	137	32	140	38%	38%	18%	6%
2015	SEA			62	94	834	66%	--	13.4	4						8.1%								

It may be unwise to criticize a guy whose nickname is "Angry Doug" and is known for shouting at reporters who disrespect his team, but here goes: Doug Baldwin is not a No. 1 NFL wide receiver. As an offense's top weapon, he represents little threat, and defenses aren't forced to adjust to him. That was especially true in the playoffs, when he amassed just 102 yards in regulation in three games (though he did have 45 more on the overtime drive against Green Bay). Nor is he particularly dangerous with the ball in his hands. The Seahawks spent about a month after the Percy Harvin trade trying to use Baldwin as a slants-and-flats guy, and as a result Baldwin averaged 7.1 yards per catch with a -21.2% DVOA in Weeks 9-12. As a second or third option, Baldwin is a very effective possession receiver, specializing in the toe-dragging sideline catch. He's also an eager blocker, and volunteers for dirty work on Seattle's kick return units. It shouldn't be surprising that a guy named "Angry Doug" likes to hit people. The Jimmy Graham trade may cause Baldwin's raw receiving totals to dip, but his rate stats should be closer to 2013 levels.

Cole Beasley

Height: 5-8   Weight: 177   College: Southern Methodist   Draft: 2012/FA   Born: 26-Apr-1989   Age: 26   Risk: Green

Year	Team	G/GS	Snaps	Rec	Pass	Yds	C%	+/-	Yd/C	TD	Drop	YAC	Rk	YAC+	BTkl	DVOA	Rk	DYAR	Rk	YAR	Short	Mid	Deep	Bomb
2012	DAL	10/0	124	15	24	128	63%	-2.0	8.5	0	1	3.9	--	+0.1	1	-17.4%	--	-4	--	-6	67%	33%	0%	0%
2013	DAL	14/3	242	39	54	368	72%	+3.4	9.4	2	1	4.7	40	-0.3	3	1.5%	42	59	58	74	61%	37%	2%	0%
2014	DAL	16/2	434	37	49	420	76%	+4.0	11.4	4	0	6.6	6	+2.1	4	16.7%	13	117	36	134	47%	45%	4%	4%
2015	DAL			49	65	521	75%	--	10.6	2						9.8%								

Beasley on third downs in 2014: 13 catches on 17 targets, 164 yards, two touchdowns, nine first downs, and one 26-yard pass interference penalty. All four of the incomplete passes to Beasley were overthrows, which is one of the pitfalls of targeting a 5-foot-8 receiver frequently on third downs. Beasley's productivity is limited by the fact that the Cowboys are just as likely to use two or three tight ends (478 snaps last year) as three or four wide receivers (473), making him one of the NFL's lesser-used slot receivers. On a per-play basis, he's a heck of a role player.

Odell Beckham

Height: 5-11   Weight: 198   College: Louisiana St.   Draft: 2014/1 (12)   Born: 5-Nov-1992   Age: 23   Risk: Green

Year	Team	G/GS	Snaps	Rec	Pass	Yds	C%	+/-	Yd/C	TD	Drop	YAC	Rk	YAC+	BTkl	DVOA	Rk	DYAR	Rk	YAR	Short	Mid	Deep	Bomb
2014	NYG	12/11	771	91	130	1305	70%	+11.1	14.3	12	2	5.3	20	+0.2	14	25.8%	9	396	6	429	33%	40%	14%	12%
2015	NYG			92	145	1235	63%	--	13.4	11						12.3%								

Beckham's 91 receptions ranked second all-time among rookies, behind Anquan Boldin's 101 receptions in 2003. His 1,305 yards ranked fourth all-time among rookies, behind AFL curiosity Bill Groman in 1960 (1,473), Boldin in 2003 (1,377), and Randy Moss in 1998 (1,313). He is one of nine rookie receivers ever to catch 12 or more touchdown passes. Beckham fits snuggly between Moss and Boldin as a long-range prospect: he combines Moss' big-play capability and flair with Boldin's steadier productivity. If the hype fooled you into thinking Beckham is a one-catch wonder, examine the stats above and recalibrate.

Beckham was given the Madden cover in May and promptly suffered a flare-up in his right hamstring. His left hamstring kept him out of most of training camp and slowed him at the start of last season, but any orthopedist will tell you that an injury to one leg can cause overcompensation injuries to the other. Beckham downplayed the severity of the hammy soreness, but when it comes to injury curses, putting a Giants player on the cover of Madden is like putting instant coffee in a microwave.

Kelvin Benjamin

Height: 6-5 Weight: 240 College: Florida St. Draft: 2014/1 (28) Born: 5-Feb-1991 Age: 24 Risk: Yellow

Year	Team	G/GS	Snaps	Rec	Pass	Yds	C%	+/-	Yd/C	TD	Drop	YAC	Rk	YAC+	BTkl	DVOA	Rk	DYAR	Rk	YAR	Short	Mid	Deep	Bomb
2014	CAR	16/15	925	73	145	1008	50%	-7.8	13.8	9	7	2.3	86	-2.0	3	-11.8%	67	9	67	33	18%	49%	15%	18%
2015	CAR			74	141	1082	52%	--	14.6	9						-1.1%								

Cam Newton spent the whole season forcing the ball to Benjamin, a raw receiver forced into the spotlight a little too early due to a barren depth chart. It's easy to focus on the negatives, but Benjamin's size and speed combination did play immediately. Carolina's offensive game plan focuses a lot on creating mismatches, and what Benjamin offers physically will create issues for just about every defensive back in the league. His task in the second year will be to elevate the efficiency in his game, because as incredible as he looks on the field, nobody wants to pay big bucks for a taller Chris Chambers.

Travis Benjamin

Height: 5-10 Weight: 172 College: Miami Draft: 2012/4 (100) Born: 29-Dec-1989 Age: 26 Risk: Green

Year	Team	G/GS	Snaps	Rec	Pass	Yds	C%	+/-	Yd/C	TD	Drop	YAC	Rk	YAC+	BTkl	DVOA	Rk	DYAR	Rk	YAR	Short	Mid	Deep	Bomb
2012	CLE	14/3	297	18	37	298	49%	-2.2	16.6	2	1	3.6	--	+0.4	1	-1.5%	--	33	--	32	17%	47%	17%	19%
2013	CLE	8/3	143	5	13	105	38%	-1.8	21.0	0	1	12.0	--	+7.7	1	-8.3%	--	4	--	-2	23%	31%	23%	23%
2014	CLE	16/0	383	18	46	314	39%	-6.5	17.4	3	3	2.4	--	-2.6	2	-10.2%	--	9	--	5	20%	35%	15%	30%
2015	CLE			14	25	218	56%	--	15.6	0						-2.2%								

Early on during Travis Benjamin's career, there were signs that suggested he could develop into a viable starter. He flashed a natural ability to adjust to the football and the willingness to work through routes over the middle of the field. Yet, after his third season, it appears that Benjamin's career is going to be limited to that of a deep threat and special-teams option. He may benefit from being in a better situation, much like Ted Ginn in his early days, but the ceiling for Benjamin definitely isn't as high as it once appeared to be.

Anquan Boldin

Height: 6-1 Weight: 218 College: Florida State Draft: 2003/2 (54) Born: 3-Oct-1980 Age: 35 Risk: Yellow

Year	Team	G/GS	Snaps	Rec	Pass	Yds	C%	+/-	Yd/C	TD	Drop	YAC	Rk	YAC+	BTkl	DVOA	Rk	DYAR	Rk	YAR	Short	Mid	Deep	Bomb
2012	BAL	15/15	878	65	112	921	58%	+0.0	14.2	4	2	3.6	54	-0.7	5	3.4%	35	122	39	133	29%	47%	18%	7%
2013	SF	16/16	803	85	129	1179	66%	+9.9	13.9	7	4	5.0	30	+0.6	9	25.8%	9	386	3	409	30%	48%	20%	2%
2014	SF	16/16	952	83	131	1062	63%	+3.6	12.8	5	7	4.8	34	+0.6	12	9.3%	28	222	19	240	33%	48%	14%	5%
2015	SF			82	129	1029	64%	--	12.5	6						0.5%								

Boldin appeared to be nearing the end of his career when he left Baltimore, but he has found a fountain of youth in San Francisco. His 2,241 yards in the past two years are among the ten best figures ever by any player in his age 33 and 34 seasons, while his DYAR and DVOA numbers have been his best since his days in Arizona. Still, Father Time is undefeated, and Boldin is now in some rarefied air. There have been 21 1,000-yard seasons by 34-year-olds in league history, but only 12 such seasons at age 35, and only five by players older than that (three of those by the incomparable Jerry Rice). Boldin was a clear WR1 over Torrey Smith when the two played in Baltimore together, but it wouldn't be a surprise to see Smith take a lead role in San Francisco this year.

Dwayne Bowe

Height: 6-2 Weight: 221 College: Louisiana St. Draft: 2007/1 (23) Born: 21-Sep-1984 Age: 31 Risk: Green

Year	Team	G/GS	Snaps	Rec	Pass	Yds	C%	+/-	Yd/C	TD	Drop	YAC	Rk	YAC+	BTkl	DVOA	Rk	DYAR	Rk	YAR	Short	Mid	Deep	Bomb
2012	KC	13/12	739	59	114	801	52%	-2.5	13.6	3	4	4.0	43	+0.1	6	-4.1%	56	60	56	76	17%	54%	18%	11%
2013	KC	15/15	837	57	103	673	55%	-7.7	11.8	5	5	3.4	77	-0.6	6	-4.4%	61	71	52	76	33%	46%	19%	2%
2014	KC	15/15	791	60	95	754	63%	+1.6	12.6	0	7	3.8	59	+0.2	5	-4.4%	52	62	52	57	23%	62%	13%	1%
2015	CLE			61	102	724	60%	--	11.9	4						-9.9%								

Bowe leaves Kansas City with more receptions (532) than any wide receiver in team history. He had this pretty awesome touchdown against the Colts in 2011. He had… 531 other catches that probably included some other good ones. Meh, it was just an unmemorable career in a not-so-memorable time in Kansas City Chiefs history. Bowe would have been great in the previous era with Trent Green, Tony Gonzalez, Priest Holmes, and an incredible offensive line, but timing is everything. Now Bowe goes to Cleveland where he'll get plenty of targets in an offense that could rival the time he played with Tyler Palko.

Kenny Britt

Height: 6-3 Weight: 218 College: Rutgers Draft: 2009/1 (30) Born: 19-Sep-1988 Age: 27 Risk: Green

Year	Team	G/GS	Snaps	Rec	Pass	Yds	C%	+/-	Yd/C	TD	Drop	YAC	Rk	YAC+	BTkl	DVOA	Rk	DYAR	Rk	YAR	Short	Mid	Deep	Bomb
2012	TEN	14/11	600	45	90	589	50%	-4.8	13.1	4	7	2.8	74	-1.2	6	-23.7%	82	-46	81	-71	24%	48%	10%	17%
2013	TEN	12/3	299	11	35	96	31%	-9.2	8.7	0	5	1.2	--	-2.1	3	-48.5%	--	-101	--	-108	20%	46%	17%	17%
2014	STL	16/13	783	48	84	748	57%	+2.9	15.6	3	2	3.5	67	-1.2	2	12.4%	18	163	28	161	35%	22%	13%	30%
2015	STL			45	83	590	54%	--	13.1	5						-8.1%								

St. Louis signed Britt to a one-year, $1.4 million prove-it deal in March of 2014. Britt showed significant improvement throughout his first season with the Rams. In the team's first eight games, he had 45 DYAR with a 3.9% DVOA and 38.1 yards per game. Those numbers climbed to 119 DYAR, 18.3% DVOA, and 61.9 yards per game in the second half of the year, peaking with a four-catch, 128-yard game in the win over Denver. It was a nice rebound season for Britt, who was coming off three straight seasons ruined by injuries and arrests. Britt was among the top ten at his position in both DVOA and DYAR in 2010, and he's still only 27 years old. He definitely has the highest upside among the Rams' receivers, and St. Louis was wise to re-sign him to a two-year deal worth up to $14 million (but with only $4.3 million guaranteed) after the season.

Antonio Brown

Height: 5-10 Weight: 186 College: Central Mighican Draft: 2010/6 (195) Born: 10-Jul-1988 Age: 27 Risk: Green

Year	Team	G/GS	Snaps	Rec	Pass	Yds	C%	+/-	Yd/C	TD	Drop	YAC	Rk	YAC+	BTkl	DVOA	Rk	DYAR	Rk	YAR	Short	Mid	Deep	Bomb
2012	PIT	13/10	652	66	106	787	63%	+3.9	11.9	5	3	5.3	21	-0.3	4	-1.9%	50	88	43	93	38%	38%	15%	9%
2013	PIT	16/14	954	110	167	1499	66%	+10.1	13.6	8	6	5.2	27	-0.2	15	15.0%	15	361	5	346	40%	35%	12%	13%
2014	PIT	16/16	1061	129	181	1698	71%	+16.5	13.2	13	5	4.6	39	-0.2	18	25.7%	10	554	1	525	36%	39%	15%	10%
2015	PIT			112	165	1481	68%	--	13.2	10						11.3%								

"Controlled aggression" is a term that is most often associated with linebackers. Antonio Brown isn't a linebacker, but at times he plays like one. His listed size is deceiving. Brown shows off incredible strength that is highlighted both at the catch point and when running through his routes, as defensive backs often bounce off of him. Brown's hands and feet are exceptionally precise and quick, allowing him to consistently create separation on any type of route against any caliber of defensive back. He is a key piece of the Steelers' quick passing game, with 75 percent of his passes coming within 15 yards of the line of scrimmage. And yet, while only 25 percent of his passes traveled further than 15 yards downfield, Brown was still able to compile 19 receptions of 20-plus yards last year, with four receptions of 40-plus yards. Defensive backs can't press Brown. They can't sit off him. Double-teaming him is an option, but it's not certain to be effective and it's very difficult to do considering the other weapons in the Pittsburgh offense. At 27 years of age, Brown is an established superstar who is in his prime. He should continue to be one of the best receivers in the NFL over the next couple of seasons.

Corey Brown

Height: 5-11 Weight: 180 College: Ohio State Draft: 2014/FA Born: 16-Dec-1991 Age: 24 Risk: Blue

Year	Team	G/GS	Snaps	Rec	Pass	Yds	C%	+/-	Yd/C	TD	Drop	YAC	Rk	YAC+	BTkl	DVOA	Rk	DYAR	Rk	YAR	Short	Mid	Deep	Bomb
2014	CAR	13/3	307	21	36	296	58%	-0.2	14.1	2	1	2.5	--	-2.4	2	7.7%	--	59	--	67	24%	42%	16%	18%
2015	CAR			10	19	130	53%	--	13.0	1						-10.0%								

What the Panthers have in Brown is a speedy deep receiver with special-teams ability. He took over the third receiver job following the release of Jason Avant, and even showed some toughness come playoff time, gutting it out against the Seahawks with a separated shoulder. The acquisitions of Ted Ginn and Devin Funchess could mean we see less of Brown on offense next season, but kick returns should give him a leg up on the rest of Carolina's end-of-roster depth at the position.

Jaron Brown

Height: 6-2 Weight: 205 College: Clemson Draft: 2013/FA Born: 8-Jan-1990 Age: 25 Risk: Yellow

Year	Team	G/GS	Snaps	Rec	Pass	Yds	C%	+/-	Yd/C	TD	Drop	YAC	Rk	YAC+	BTkl	DVOA	Rk	DYAR	Rk	YAR	Short	Mid	Deep	Bomb
2013	ARI	16/0	155	11	18	140	61%	+0.9	12.7	1	0	2.9	--	-2.3	0	2.5%	--	20	--	22	29%	41%	12%	18%
2014	ARI	16/2	230	22	32	229	69%	+1.7	10.4	2	1	2.9	--	-1.6	4	-2.0%	--	27	--	28	50%	25%	16%	9%
2015	ARI			38	63	459	60%	--	12.1	1						-9.4%								

Twenty-five of Brown's 32 targets last season came in the second half of the year, including 15 in back-to-back losses against Seattle and Atlanta. He suffered a fractured scapula (shoulder blade) in the wild-card loss to Carolina, but was able to avoid surgery and was participating in OTAs without any issue. Most of Brown's value comes in the kicking game—he was fourth on the Cardinals with 261 special-teams snaps last year. Since Arizona's tight end spot is such a black hole, we're expecting to see more four-wide sets in 2015, which explains Brown's projection increase.

John Brown

Height: 5-10 | Weight: 179 | College: Pittsburg St. (KS) | Draft: 2014/3 (91) | Born: 4-Mar-1990 | Age: 25 | Risk: Red

Year	Team	G/GS	Snaps	Rec	Pass	Yds	C%	+/-	Yd/C	TD	Drop	YAC	Rk	YAC+	BTkl	DVOA	Rk	DYAR	Rk	YAR	Short	Mid	Deep	Bomb
2014	ARI	16/5	633	48	103	696	47%	-7.3	14.5	5	2	3.8	62	-1.7	0	-12.5%	69	1	69	-5	21%	43%	22%	15%
2015	ARI			64	111	930	58%	--	14.5	6						1.1%								

Brown only scored five touchdowns in his rookie season, but all five were memorable. They averaged 36.2 yards apiece. All came in the second half. Four were go-ahead scores, and the fifth pulled Arizona within one point of San Francisco. He's lucky to be playing for Bruce Arians, who had success developing smaller wideouts in Pittsburgh (Antonio Brown) and Indianapolis (T.Y. Hilton). There were rumors this offseason that both Larry Fitzgerald and Michael Floyd were on the trading block, and though neither of those players were ever dealt, it's clear the organization has great faith in Brown and believes he can be their most dangerous receiver.

Amazing coincidence department: Brown's targets by quarterback last season were virtually identical to those of teammate Larry Fitzgerald. Brown was targeted 45 times by Drew Stanton, 40 by Carson Palmer, 20 by Ryan Lindley, and once by Logan Thomas. Fitzgerald's targets from those same quarterbacks: 45, 40, 19, 2.

Marlon Brown

Height: 6-4 | Weight: 205 | College: Georgia | Draft: 2013/FA | Born: 22-Apr-1991 | Age: 24 | Risk: Yellow

Year	Team	G/GS	Snaps	Rec	Pass	Yds	C%	+/-	Yd/C	TD	Drop	YAC	Rk	YAC+	BTkl	DVOA	Rk	DYAR	Rk	YAR	Short	Mid	Deep	Bomb
2013	BAL	14/12	791	49	83	524	59%	-2.4	10.7	7	2	4.8	35	+0.4	6	4.9%	31	117	41	106	44%	32%	16%	8%
2014	BAL	14/1	375	24	31	255	77%	+5.0	10.6	0	0	4.1	--	+0.0	1	13.9%	--	61	--	59	38%	52%	0%	10%
2015	BAL			57	91	566	66%	--	9.9	3						-2.6%								

Brown seemed poised for a 2014 breakout after a strong rookie year, which included a memorable game-winning touchdown catch in the snow against Minnesota. But his playing time was cut in half instead, thanks to the signing of Steve Smith. Brown's smaller-sample numbers were excellent (he caught every pass thrown his way in Weeks 8-15), and the team likes his size and attitude, so he should see his action rebound at least to 2013 levels, especially if top draft choice Breshad Perriman falters.

Dez Bryant

Height: 6-2 | Weight: 225 | College: Oklahoma State | Draft: 2010/1 (24) | Born: 4-Nov-1988 | Age: 27 | Risk: Green

Year	Team	G/GS	Snaps	Rec	Pass	Yds	C%	+/-	Yd/C	TD	Drop	YAC	Rk	YAC+	BTkl	DVOA	Rk	DYAR	Rk	YAR	Short	Mid	Deep	Bomb
2012	DAL	16/14	922	92	138	1282	67%	+9.0	13.9	12	9	4.9	30	+0.4	16	18.3%	17	392	3	352	34%	38%	14%	15%
2013	DAL	16/16	933	93	160	1233	58%	-1.7	13.3	13	6	5.7	18	+1.4	7	3.7%	33	215	18	242	32%	42%	17%	9%
2014	DAL	16/16	896	88	137	1320	64%	+6.7	15.0	16	4	4.6	41	+0.1	18	27.0%	5	430	5	456	31%	39%	17%	13%
2015	DAL			95	152	1336	63%	--	14.1	14						16.8%								

Dez Bryant spent the early summer insisting, through anonymous channels and not-so anonymous tweets, that he would sit out most of the regular season rather than play for the franchise tag. Meanwhile, Stephen Jones reportedly chatted with John Elway about keeping the Bryant and Demaryius Thomas contracts in roughly the same non-Megatron range, and Jones reportedly passed the gist of the conversation along to Bryant. ("Colluded w Broncos. U mad bro?") Then, in a pair of shocking developments, the threat to squander roughly $750,000 per week by staying home on Sundays proved to be just a negotiation tactic, the ugly collusion scandal wafted away once Bryant and Thomas signed (near identical) contracts, and while the nation's calls for a weekly Dez Bryant/Stephen Jones podcast went unheeded, the prevailing Cowboys summer story went from "How will Cole Beasley fare as a starter for two months" to "Everything is A-OK."

There was also excessive late-winter rumor-mongering on Twitter about a supposed "Dez Tape" showing Bryant perpetrating some form of violence against a woman in a shopping center parking lot. Investigations about the tape turned into a Marcellus Wallace briefcase situation: there may or may not exist footage of an act of violence perpetrated by someone who may or may not be Dez Bryant in front of a shopping center several years ago, and said tape may or may not be in the possession of shady individuals who are holding the tape to persuade Bryant (blackmail is such an ugly word) into retaining associates of these individuals as agents/promoters. Got that? If the Dez Tape really did impact the Cowboys' contract offers, Demaryius Thomas should be fuming.

In summary, it's unlikely that there is a Ray Rice situation brewing beneath a pile of Big Kahuna Burger wrappers in a flophouse somewhere, Bryant will arrive for camp happy and motivated, and after that offseason, we're about as tired of covering him as Brandon Fletcher must be.

Martavis Bryant Height: 6-4   Weight: 211   College: Clemson   Draft: 2014/4 (118)   Born: 20-Dec-1991   Age: 24   Risk: Red

Year	Team	G/GS	Snaps	Rec	Pass	Yds	C%	+/-	Yd/C	TD	Drop	YAC	Rk	YAC+	BTkl	DVOA	Rk	DYAR	Rk	YAR	Short	Mid	Deep	Bomb
2014	PIT	10/3	295	26	49	549	53%	-0.8	21.1	8	3	7.3	--	+1.7	2	22.9%	--	137	--	129	31%	22%	14%	33%
2015	PIT			55	99	923	56%	--	16.8	7						5.8%								

"Sometimes players lose their confidence if you throw them to the wolves. We didn't want to give him too much at once." Those were the words of Richard Mann, Pittsburgh Steelers wide receivers coach, when asked about Martavis Bryant being inactive during the first six weeks of the 2014 season. Bryant was challenged to dominate against the scout team by head coach Mike Tomlin before he would be given a chance to play in a regular-season game. Mental mistakes during the preseason and an inability to play special teams dropped the rookie behind Justin Brown and Lance Moore on the depth chart before the season began, but neither player inspired confidence in the coaching staff, and Bryant ultimately got his shot in Week 7.

Bryant may or may not have dominated the scout team, but he definitely dominated a few NFL teams. Six touchdowns over his first four games and an ability to repeatedly get behind the secondary suggested that he should have been used earlier than he was. While there were examples of mental errors and sloppy routes, Bryant's rookie season as a whole suggests that he can be a major part of the Steelers' passing attack moving forward and the perfect complement to Antonio Brown.

Brice Butler Height: 6-3   Weight: 205   College: San Diego State   Draft: 2013/7 (209)   Born: 29-Jan-1990   Age: 25   Risk: Blue

Year	Team	G/GS	Snaps	Rec	Pass	Yds	C%	+/-	Yd/C	TD	Drop	YAC	Rk	YAC+	BTkl	DVOA	Rk	DYAR	Rk	YAR	Short	Mid	Deep	Bomb
2013	OAK	10/2	210	9	17	103	53%	-1.5	11.4	0	2	3.4	--	-2.2	0	-28.1%	--	-19	--	-20	35%	24%	41%	0%
2014	OAK	15/0	271	21	36	280	58%	-0.1	13.3	2	1	4.0	--	-0.4	2	1.9%	--	42	--	24	26%	57%	9%	9%
2015	OAK			10	19	108	53%	--	10.8	0						-24.5%								

Butler is a marginal receiving talent who will have to compete with the likes of Kenbrell Thompkins, Kris Durham, and Josh Harper for Oakland's final receiver spot. Unlike that trio, Butler doesn't have a signature catch or the past affection of his quarterback to aid him.

Andre Caldwell Height: 6-0   Weight: 190   College: Florida   Draft: 2008/3 (97)   Born: 15-Apr-1985   Age: 30   Risk: Green

Year	Team	G/GS	Snaps	Rec	Pass	Yds	C%	+/-	Yd/C	TD	Drop	YAC	Rk	YAC+	BTkl	DVOA	Rk	DYAR	Rk	YAR	Short	Mid	Deep	Bomb
2012	DEN	8/0	75	1	4	18	25%	-1.4	18.0	0	1	2.0	--	-2.0	0	-50.2%	--	-14	--	-11	25%	25%	50%	0%
2013	DEN	16/2	260	16	29	200	55%	-0.0	12.5	3	1	2.6	--	-2.4	0	2.0%	--	35	--	44	30%	33%	10%	27%
2014	DEN	16/2	180	5	15	47	33%	-4.7	9.4	0	3	3.6	--	-0.2	0	-44.8%	--	-37	--	-44	40%	33%	20%	7%
2015	DEN			5	9	67	56%	--	13.4	1						-4.2%								

Caldwell is in the final year of his second two-year contract with the Broncos. He has done very little in that time, though Wes Welker has vacated the slot position. Welker's absence in a 2013 game against San Diego saw Caldwell step up with two touchdown catches in his most memorable Denver performance. However, Gary Kubiak has to show he shares Manning's three-wide fetish, and the Broncos may still be better off with Cody Latimer seeing the field more than Caldwell.

Randall Cobb Height: 5-11   Weight: 190   College: Kentucky   Draft: 2011/2 (64)   Born: 22-Aug-1990   Age: 25   Risk: Green

Year	Team	G/GS	Snaps	Rec	Pass	Yds	C%	+/-	Yd/C	TD	Drop	YAC	Rk	YAC+	BTkl	DVOA	Rk	DYAR	Rk	YAR	Short	Mid	Deep	Bomb
2012	GB	15/8	631	80	104	954	77%	+11.3	11.9	8	8	5.7	18	-0.1	13	24.1%	9	357	6	303	55%	23%	20%	3%
2013	GB	6/4	333	31	47	433	66%	+4.8	14.0	4	1	5.6	--	+0.0	5	21.1%	--	121	--	105	43%	35%	15%	8%
2014	GB	16/16	922	91	127	1287	72%	+8.4	14.1	12	2	6.4	7	+1.9	10	35.7%	1	479	4	501	46%	32%	21%	2%
2015	GB			87	129	1227	67%	--	14.1	8						21.6%								

Randall Cobb is the NFL's best slot receiver. His body control and speed let him take advantage of the free release and two-way go to create separation. The big step in his game might have come in the red zone, where he was targeted nearly as often as Jordy Nelson and was the only Packers regular to post a positive DVOA (18.1%). He was phenomenal on third downs as well (55.4% DVOA), where he also ran deeper routes (average target: 13.3 yards downfield, compared to 7.3 yards otherwise). The emergence of additional options could see a decline in his overall fantasy numbers, but the Packers valued him enough to pay him $40 million over four years to continue doing what he's done.

Marques Colston

Height: 6-4   Weight: 225   College: Hofstra   Draft: 2006/7 (252)   Born: 5-Jun-1983   Age: 32   Risk: Green

Year	Team	G/GS	Snaps	Rec	Pass	Yds	C%	+/-	Yd/C	TD	Drop	YAC	Rk	YAC+	BTkl	DVOA	Rk	DYAR	Rk	YAR	Short	Mid	Deep	Bomb
2012	NO	16/13	832	83	130	1154	64%	+7.1	13.9	10	9	3.5	61	-0.1	1	19.7%	15	327	11	339	27%	56%	12%	5%
2013	NO	15/11	750	75	110	943	68%	+9.3	12.6	5	2	3.4	78	-0.6	4	19.5%	14	276	12	283	32%	47%	17%	4%
2014	NO	16/13	876	59	99	902	60%	-1.8	15.3	5	6	5.0	30	+1.0	3	13.0%	16	201	23	211	32%	39%	22%	7%
2015	NO			55	92	755	60%	--	13.7	7						8.3%								

It wasn't a surprise that the Saints asked Marques Colston to take a pay cut this offseason and, rather unusually, it wasn't a surprise that Colston was happy to accept it. "At this point in my career, it's not necessarily about maximizing every penny of every contract," he said to ESPN.com's Mike Triplett. "I know for me it came down to, 'What's my priority?'…You look at the position I play, I'm kind of dependent on everyone else along the offense to have success. I've seen guys at my position chase every penny and not really have the career or the success that they've been accustomed to. So I always say I'm never gonna be in a hurry to leave a Hall of Fame quarterback."

The former seventh-round pick understands that the Saints have maximized his skill set over the years. If Colston had landed elsewhere, his career likely wouldn't have lasted this long, so he has shown some loyalty to the franchise, and quarterback, that made him who he is today.

Who he is today is a much lesser receiver than who he was during his prime. Colston was never great at beating man coverage because he lacked great athleticism, but that athleticism continues to decline now that he is a 32-year-old receiver. Colston will be dependent on finding space after play-action and adjusting to zone coverages to be productive next season.

Chris Conley

Height: 6-2   Weight: 213   College: Georgia   Draft: 2015/3 (76)   Born: 25-Oct-1992   Age: 23   Risk: Red

Year	Team	G/GS	Snaps	Rec	Pass	Yds	C%	+/-	Yd/C	TD	Drop	YAC	Rk	YAC+	BTkl	DVOA	Rk	DYAR	Rk	YAR	Short	Mid	Deep	Bomb
2015	KC			32	56	441	57%	--	13.8	3						2.1%								

When you run the 40-yard dash in 4.35 seconds, you're going to open some eyes. Conley's combine was an athletic tour de force, but he concerned some teams with all the passes he dropped in drills. The third-round pick can fly, but that sounds like a reason for Alex Smith to underthrow him, or ignore him when he is open deep. Conley is not as skilled at getting open quickly underneath or generating yards after the catch, which makes him sound like a poor fit for this offense, or at least for this quarterback. By the way, Conley was the No. 1 receiver at Georgia in 2013 playing with Aaron Murray, who is now the third-string quarterback for the Chiefs.

Brandin Cooks

Height: 5-10   Weight: 189   College: Oregon St.   Draft: 2014/1 (20)   Born: 25-Sep-1993   Age: 22   Risk: Green

Year	Team	G/GS	Snaps	Rec	Pass	Yds	C%	+/-	Yd/C	TD	Drop	YAC	Rk	YAC+	BTkl	DVOA	Rk	DYAR	Rk	YAR	Short	Mid	Deep	Bomb
2014	NO	10/7	534	53	69	550	77%	+9.7	10.4	3	1	3.2	75	-2.3	1	9.7%	26	124	34	125	51%	29%	9%	11%
2015	NO			70	102	926	69%	--	13.2	7						15.5%								

The rookie wide receiver was expected to be a perfect fit in Sean Payton's offense, and Brandin Cooks definitely lived up to expectations. The Saints found ways to put the ball in his hands on a regular basis by featuring him prominently on screen plays and end-arounds, but he also proved to be an effective wide receiver running routes down the field. Cooks' speed meant that he could often get in and out of breaks faster than any defensive back trying to cover him, so he was able to avoid contested catch situations instead of trying to fight through them with his small frame. The only significant issues Cooks had creating separation came when he was pressed outside. His Week 11 injury limited his opportunities to show off any potential development in that area as the season developed. Cooks is now the Saints' No. 1 receiver; he'll mostly be used the way he was used as a rookie, but we are expecting him to see a few more deep routes as well.

Amari Cooper Height: 6-1   Weight: 211   College: Alabama   Draft: 2015/1 (4)   Born: 18-Jun-1994   Age: 21   Risk: Red

Year	Team	G/GS	Snaps	Rec	Pass	Yds	C%	+/-	Yd/C	TD	Drop	YAC	Rk	YAC+	BTkl	DVOA	Rk	DYAR	Rk	YAR	Short	Mid	Deep	Bomb
2015	OAK			74	123	991	60%	--	13.4	7						5.7%								

The Raiders have not drafted a receiver that produced a 1,000-yard season for them since Tim Brown in 1988, easily the longest streak in the NFL (though it should be noted that the Jaguars have never drafted a 1,000-yard receiver since coming into the league in 1995). Twenty-two teams had a receiver they drafted gain 1,000 yards in either 2013 or 2014. Brown's last 1,000-yard season was 2001, so it has been a long time for Oakland. Cooper comes in with very high expectations, and he had the highest Playmaker Score among this year's receiver prospects, but the bar for rookie performance has been fairly low for wide receivers drafted in the top five. Only A.J. Green (2011) surpassed 1,000 yards as a rookie, with 1,057 yards for Cincinnati. Derek Carr's brother David was paired with Andre Johnson in his sophomore season, but Johnson finished with 976 yards in 2003. Even Larry Fitzgerald (780) and Calvin Johnson (756) were held under 800 yards. The Cooper pick was all about the long-term implications, so it's not a problem if Cooper doesn't dazzle the way Odell Beckham did last season. Few ever have.

Riley Cooper Height: 6-4   Weight: 222   College: Florida   Draft: 2010/5 (159)   Born: 9-Sep-1987   Age: 28   Risk: Yellow

Year	Team	G/GS	Snaps	Rec	Pass	Yds	C%	+/-	Yd/C	TD	Drop	YAC	Rk	YAC+	BTkl	DVOA	Rk	DYAR	Rk	YAR	Short	Mid	Deep	Bomb
2012	PHI	11/5	486	23	48	248	48%	-4.6	10.8	3	1	4.0	--	-0.3	2	-22.8%	--	-15	--	-25	27%	51%	16%	7%
2013	PHI	16/15	981	47	84	835	56%	+0.5	17.8	8	4	4.9	32	+0.1	4	20.6%	13	212	19	214	26%	37%	20%	18%
2014	PHI	16/16	956	55	95	577	58%	-1.7	10.5	3	2	2.8	81	-2.2	2	-17.8%	80	-38	80	-20	33%	36%	19%	12%
2015	PHI			35	65	477	54%	--	13.6	3						-9.1%								

Cooper had a miserable 2014 season. He jumped offsides a few times early in the year, lost a fumble against the Niners, and caught too many 2- to 4-yard passes that would have netted longer gains in the hands of a better after-catch runner. He was the targeted receiver for four interceptions between Week 8 and Week 12, then got shut down by the Seahawks (who allowed more opportunities to the No. 3 receiver than the other two) and Cowboys (who allowed solid opportunities to all receivers). Cooper was less popular in Philly than Rubén Amaro, Jr. and Donovan McNabb singing a duet of "Empire State of Mind," so Eagles fans may not want to hear that Cooper had a strong offseason, looked good in OTAs, and is likely to stick as the third or fourth receiver. But then, part of being the local sports whipping boy in Philly is sticking around for two or three extra years like a toothache that won't go away.

Jerricho Cotchery Height: 6-1   Weight: 200   College: North Carolina State   Draft: 2004/4 (108)   Born: 16-Jun-1982   Age: 33   Risk: Yellow

Year	Team	G/GS	Snaps	Rec	Pass	Yds	C%	+/-	Yd/C	TD	Drop	YAC	Rk	YAC+	BTkl	DVOA	Rk	DYAR	Rk	YAR	Short	Mid	Deep	Bomb
2012	PIT	14/2	266	17	27	205	63%	+0.8	12.1	0	0	2.5	--	-1.2	0	2.8%	--	35	--	37	27%	46%	27%	0%
2013	PIT	16/6	635	46	76	602	61%	-0.8	13.1	10	3	4.7	41	+0.4	7	26.2%	8	235	16	214	32%	49%	14%	5%
2014	CAR	15/13	783	48	78	580	62%	+0.7	12.1	1	2	4.0	54	-0.6	4	-3.7%	50	55	53	49	34%	41%	20%	5%
2015	CAR			31	57	386	54%	--	12.5	2						-7.8%								

A really odd career. Cotchery was the go-to receiver for the late 2000s Jets, basically disappeared for three years, then caught 10 touchdowns for the 2013 Steelers. Signed by the Panthers last season, touchdown regression hit hard. At 33, there's probably not much left here. Then again, Cotchery has surprised us before. He'll likely serve as the third or fourth receiver, depending on how much Ted Ginn the Panthers want in their lives.

Michael Crabtree Height: 6-2   Weight: 215   College: Texas Tech   Draft: 2009/1 (10)   Born: 14-Sep-1987   Age: 28   Risk: Green

Year	Team	G/GS	Snaps	Rec	Pass	Yds	C%	+/-	Yd/C	TD	Drop	YAC	Rk	YAC+	BTkl	DVOA	Rk	DYAR	Rk	YAR	Short	Mid	Deep	Bomb
2012	SF	16/16	674	85	127	1105	68%	+6.4	13.0	9	5	6.5	9	+1.9	14	21.9%	13	334	10	336	53%	32%	12%	4%
2013	SF	5/5	237	19	33	284	58%	+1.8	14.9	1	1	7.2	--	+3.0	1	3.7%	--	42	--	42	38%	41%	14%	7%
2014	SF	16/16	722	68	108	698	64%	-0.8	10.3	4	5	3.9	58	-1.2	9	-9.9%	63	24	59	50	47%	30%	17%	6%
2015	OAK			53	91	628	58%	--	11.8	3						-10.1%								

Well, Richard Sherman was right, but even a mediocre receiver could be the best pass-catcher the Raiders have seen in years. Crabtree hasn't been the same since tearing his Achilles in 2013, and by the end of his 49ers run he was almost exclusively running screens and slants. In his last five games in a San Francisco uniform (including two contests against arch-nemesis Sherman), 20 of his 25 targets came within 7 yards of the line of scrimmage. Crabtree was probably expecting a better deal in free agency than the one-year prove-it offer he signed with Oakland. The contract will pay Crabtree $3 million in base salary with another $2.2 million available if he meets some high incentives, such as 70-catch or 900-yard thresholds. Again, though, mediocrity will be a welcome sight for Oakland, which hasn't seen a wide receiver finish in the top 20 in DYAR since Jerry Porter and Jerry Rice did it in 2002. Crabtree will start the season as Oakland's primary receiver, but the sooner Amari Cooper is ready for that role, the better it will be for the silver and black.

Victor Cruz Height: 6-1 Weight: 200 College: Massachusetts Draft: 2010/FA Born: 11-Nov-1986 Age: 29 Risk: Red

Year	Team	G/GS	Snaps	Rec	Pass	Yds	C%	+/-	Yd/C	TD	Drop	YAC	Rk	YAC+	BTkl	DVOA	Rk	DYAR	Rk	YAR	Short	Mid	Deep	Bomb
2012	NYG	16/16	902	86	143	1092	60%	+1.6	12.7	10	9	3.8	50	-0.1	6	1.2%	41	165	28	166	33%	48%	8%	11%
2013	NYG	14/12	785	73	121	998	60%	+2.4	13.7	4	3	3.4	76	-0.8	7	1.0%	44	133	35	172	25%	52%	12%	11%
2014	NYG	6/6	372	23	41	337	56%	-1.4	14.7	1	6	7.7	--	+2.5	7	-9.0%	--	13	--	21	29%	37%	22%	12%
2015	NYG			70	117	872	60%	--	12.5	6						-1.0%								

Offseason Cruz headlines usually contained percentages. After the draft, Jerry Reese estimated that Cruz was "probably 85, close to 90 percent" of full speed after last season's patellar tendon injury. Three weeks later during OTAs, Cruz himself said he was at 80 percent. Using regression analysis on those data points, Cruz will be paralyzed by Labor Day. Actually, Cruz claimed to be 75 percent healthy between the draft and late-May OTAs; Giants injury mathematics requires a postgraduate degree.

Cruz attended Eli Manning's passing-game workouts at Duke University in April, but he was limited to a little jogging and a lot of watching. That's a shame, because nobody should have to watch the Giants passing game without Victor Cruz.

But seriously folks, Cruz is targeting a Week 1 return the lineup; he probably expects to be 110 percent by then. Eli, Cruz, and Odell Beckham could form the most dangerous passing attack in the NFC East, assuming everyone is healthy and five able-bodied offensive linemen can be found. Beckham will be the No. 1 option, but Cruz is at his best when working out of the slot anyway, and Ben McAdoo's system offers plenty of opportunities for the Greg Jennings type and the Jordy Nelson type. With a little luck, the big numbers Cruz generates in autumn will be catch totals, not health percentages.

Eric Decker Height: 6-3 Weight: 217 College: Minnesota Draft: 2010/3 (87) Born: 15-Mar-1987 Age: 28 Risk: Green

Year	Team	G/GS	Snaps	Rec	Pass	Yds	C%	+/-	Yd/C	TD	Drop	YAC	Rk	YAC+	BTkl	DVOA	Rk	DYAR	Rk	YAR	Short	Mid	Deep	Bomb
2012	DEN	16/15	1048	85	123	1064	69%	+13.0	12.5	13	7	3.1	69	-0.7	3	27.2%	8	392	4	401	32%	45%	11%	12%
2013	DEN	16/16	1050	87	136	1288	64%	+4.3	14.8	11	7	4.3	58	-0.4	5	21.3%	12	381	4	382	35%	39%	17%	9%
2014	NYJ	15/15	812	74	115	962	64%	+5.4	13.0	5	5	4.4	47	-0.2	1	9.4%	27	199	24	176	33%	44%	15%	9%
2015	NYJ			66	105	838	63%	--	12.7	6						3.1%								

The challenge of going from Peyton Manning to Geno Smith was noticeable for Decker, and though the overall numbers (DVOA, DYAR) were down, he did show that he was more than just a system receiver with the Broncos. The former Denver pass catcher held steady in a number of areas, including catch rate and yards after catch, all while lowering his drops and becoming a more consistent midrange threat in the passing game. It's unclear whether or not Brandon Marshall has taken his role as the No. 1 target for the Jets, but unlike the other offensive holdovers from the Ryan/Idzik era, Decker shouldn't worry about his job in 2015.

Phillip Dorsett Height: 5-10 Weight: 185 College: Miami Draft: 2015/1 (29) Born: 5-Jan-1993 Age: 23 Risk: Yellow

Year	Team	G/GS	Snaps	Rec	Pass	Yds	C%	+/-	Yd/C	TD	Drop	YAC	Rk	YAC+	BTkl	DVOA	Rk	DYAR	Rk	YAR	Short	Mid	Deep	Bomb
2015	IND			38	63	631	60%	--	16.6	4						18.9%								

Really, Ryan Grigson, another receiver over defense? At least Dorsett averaged 24.2 yards per catch at Miami in 2014, and scored 10 touchdowns on 36 catches. He doesn't have to be anything more than a deep threat and No. 3 (or possibly No. 4) wide receiver in an offense that's going to spread the ball around with Andrew Luck. But just for fun, let's look at the impact rookie receivers have had on Super Bowl-winning teams, since the Colts have very high expectations.

Historically, the top four receivers on Super Bowl winners have averaged four seasons with the team and five or six seasons in the NFL. The only eight rookies to finish in the top four in receiving yards on a Super Bowl champion are John Stallworth (1974 Steelers), Lynn Swann (1974 Steelers), Tony Dorsett (1977 Cowboys), Charlie Brown (1982 Redskins), Torry Holt (1999 Rams), Jamal Lewis (2000 Ravens), Travis Taylor (2000 Ravens), and Heath Miller (2005 Steelers). You'll notice two teams double-dipped, and all eight players were third or fourth options. Only Brown (690), Holt (788), and Miller (459) exceeded 300 receiving yards, so it's pretty rare to win a championship with a rookie making a big contribution in the passing game.

Harry Douglas

Height: 5-11 Weight: 176 College: Louisville Draft: 2008/3 (84) Born: 16-Sep-1984 Age: 31 Risk: Green

Year	Team	G/GS	Snaps	Rec	Pass	Yds	C%	+/-	Yd/C	TD	Drop	YAC	Rk	YAC+	BTkl	DVOA	Rk	DYAR	Rk	YAR	Short	Mid	Deep	Bomb
2012	ATL	15/1	585	38	59	396	64%	+2.6	10.4	1	1	4.0	44	-1.0	3	-16.6%	77	-6	76	-4	52%	22%	20%	6%
2013	ATL	16/11	926	85	132	1067	64%	+1.0	12.6	2	7	6.0	9	+1.2	8	3.6%	34	171	26	147	48%	38%	8%	6%
2014	ATL	12/6	557	51	74	556	69%	+1.7	10.9	2	1	4.7	38	+0.1	3	5.9%	32	108	38	102	49%	31%	15%	5%
2015	TEN			50	74	585	68%	--	11.7	3						3.7%								

A veteran slot receiver who has proven he can soak up a lot of volume, Douglas was a fine replacement for Nate Washington. Given how uncertain the Tennessee depth chart is with Dorial Green-Beckham and Justin Hunter's development still up in the air, they very well may need a target sponge. Douglas is never going to blow anyone away on the field, and his 5.9% DVOA last year was actually a career high, but he should at least be a functional cog for the Titans if they need him to be one.

Julian Edelman

Height: 6-0 Weight: 198 College: Kent State Draft: 2009/7 (232) Born: 22-May-1986 Age: 29 Risk: Green

Year	Team	G/GS	Snaps	Rec	Pass	Yds	C%	+/-	Yd/C	TD	Drop	YAC	Rk	YAC+	BTkl	DVOA	Rk	DYAR	Rk	YAR	Short	Mid	Deep	Bomb
2012	NE	9/3	295	21	32	235	66%	-0.5	11.2	3	1	6.7	--	+0.5	3	10.3%	--	65	--	62	55%	32%	6%	6%
2013	NE	16/11	1021	105	151	1056	70%	+5.7	10.1	6	6	4.7	42	-0.8	11	4.3%	32	204	22	164	52%	29%	13%	6%
2014	NE	14/13	805	92	133	972	69%	+7.1	10.6	4	10	4.6	40	-0.1	8	0.2%	42	137	31	102	53%	34%	9%	4%
2015	NE			99	142	1005	70%	--	10.2	5						1.7%								

On NFL Films' Super Bowl footage, Edelman cornered Bill Belichick and told him, "You gave me the best year of my life. I would do anything for you, coach." Then he repeated, "I would do anything." With that beard and his insistent tone, he could have been Robin Williams telling Matt Damon that it wasn't his fault. That tearjerker moment concluded Edelman's dream season. The touchdown that won the Super Bowl, another 12-yard average as a punt returner, the most catches (26) in the play-offs, even his first NFL touchdown pass in the comeback against the Ravens. Plus the whole thing started off with Edelman finally getting paid after the league largely ignored him in free agency two years ago, as he signed a new four-year, $17 million contract before last season began.

Bruce Ellington

Height: 5-9 Weight: 197 College: South Carolina Draft: 2014/4 (106) Born: 22-Aug-1991 Age: 24 Risk: Yellow

Year	Team	G/GS	Snaps	Rec	Pass	Yds	C%	+/-	Yd/C	TD	Drop	YAC	Rk	YAC+	BTkl	DVOA	Rk	DYAR	Rk	YAR	Short	Mid	Deep	Bomb
2014	SF	13/0	95	6	12	62	50%	-1.1	10.3	2	0	5.5	--	+0.0	1	-1.5%	--	11	--	4	45%	27%	9%	18%
2015	SF			24	42	316	57%	--	13.2	2						-15.7%								

Sometimes bad teams do crazy things late in the year. The 49ers were 7-7 and out of the playoffs when they faced San Diego in Week 16, and with nothing to lose, they decided to build their offense around Bruce Ellington. Ellington entered that game with only eight targets and three rushes on the season. Then the 49ers gave him four targets and three runs in the first half. Results of those plays were mixed, as they resulted in three incompletions and only 20 total yards, but Ellington did score twice: an 8-yard gain on a play-action pass after Ellington faked a fly sweep, and a 1-yard run on a fly sweep that saw Ellington break two tackles in the backfield and knife into the end zone to put San Francisco ahead 28-7. The 49ers were penalized for excessive celebration on that play, and apparently the coaches blamed Ellington, who didn't touch the ball on offense the rest of the night. Perhaps not coincidentally, the 49ers scored just one more touchdown, and the Chargers came roaring back to win 38-35 in overtime. This fall, Ellington is the favorite to win the 49ers' third receiver job, while also serving as the primary kick returner.

Mike Evans

Mike Evans — Height: 6-5 — Weight: 231 — College: Texas A&M — Draft: 2014/1 (7) — Born: 21-Aug-1993 — Age: 22 — Risk: Red

Year	Team	G/GS	Snaps	Rec	Pass	Yds	C%	+/-	Yd/C	TD	Drop	YAC	Rk	YAC+	BTkl	DVOA	Rk	DYAR	Rk	YAR	Short	Mid	Deep	Bomb
2014	TB	15/15	768	68	123	1051	55%	+3.8	15.5	12	4	2.5	82	-2.3	4	11.4%	21	222	17	234	21%	38%	22%	19%
2015	TB			77	149	1230	52%	--	16.0	9						2.5%								

Since 2000, just eight rookie receivers (Evans, Odell Beckham, Kelvin Benjamin, Keenan Allen, A.J. Green, Marques Colston, Michael Clayton, and Anquan Boldin) have posted 1,000-yard seasons. That three of them happened to do it last year, one in spectacular fashion, should not diminish Mike Evans' accomplishment in reaching that mark. Reaching 1,000 yards and posting solid advanced stats while mostly catching passes from Josh McCown is even more impressive. Of the other seven rookie receivers to break 1,000 yards, six had much better quarterback situations. Only Anquan Boldin overcame quarterbacking as poor as Evans did last season. In the end zone, Evans even caught it like Beckham, the only other player among these eight to catch double-digit touchdowns as a rookie.

With his size, physicality, and ability to highpoint throws, Evans should be one of the league's top red zone threats for many years. The only warning sign might be that so much of his production came in a four-week span, Weeks 8-11.

Mike Evans by Week, 2014

Weeks	G	Rec	Yds	TD	Yd/Rec	C%	DVOA
Weeks 1-6	5	21	258	2	12.3	60%	0.2%
Weeks 8-11	4	25	536	5	21.4	69%	69.8%
Weeks 12-17	6	22	257	5	11.7	42%	-19.4%

Larry Fitzgerald

Larry Fitzgerald — Height: 6-3 — Weight: 225 — College: Pittsburgh — Draft: 2004/1 (3) — Born: 31-Aug-1983 — Age: 32 — Risk: Yellow

Year	Team	G/GS	Snaps	Rec	Pass	Yds	C%	+/-	Yd/C	TD	Drop	YAC	Rk	YAC+	BTkl	DVOA	Rk	DYAR	Rk	YAR	Short	Mid	Deep	Bomb
2012	ARI	16/16	1029	71	156	798	46%	-19.6	11.2	4	1	3.8	49	-0.3	8	-23.8%	83	-218	86	-186	38%	38%	18%	5%
2013	ARI	16/16	998	82	136	954	62%	+0.3	11.6	10	1	4.2	61	-0.9	6	-0.6%	49	132	36	152	37%	37%	20%	6%
2014	ARI	14/13	857	63	104	784	61%	-1.2	12.4	2	1	5.3	22	+0.4	8	-5.8%	55	54	54	58	37%	37%	20%	6%
2015	ARI			65	111	812	59%	--	12.5	6							-5.7%								

Through age 31, no player has ever caught more passes than Fitzgerald. Only Randy Moss has more yards, and only four players have more touchdowns. However, Fitzgerald's decline appears to be well underway, as his 2014 numbers were his worst since his rookie season. It would be easy to blame that on Carson Palmer's injury, but remember that Fitzgerald once produced 1,411 yards and eight touchdowns with John Skelton as his primary quarterback. Amid reports that the Browns were trying to trade for Fitzgerald (a move that would be indefensibly bad from Cleveland's point of view, for the record), the Cardinals re-signed their all-time leading receiver to an extension that guarantees him $22 million over the next two seasons. That's an absurd amount of money for an aging wideout coming off his worst season, especially on a team that has other quality options in Michael Floyd and John Brown. If Fitzgerald can't turn things around in a hurry, the Cardinals may soon wish they had taken the Browns' offer.

All hope is not lost, however. Bruce Arians said that Fitzgerald struggled with option routes, and suggested that he would do better with another year in the system. And many players similar to Fitzgerald over the past three years were productive well into their thirties, including Art Monk, Keyshawn Johnson, Irving Fryar, and Hines Ward. It would take an amazing player to improve at Fitzgerald's age, but we have been watching him do amazing things for more than a decade now.

Malcom Floyd

Malcom Floyd — Height: 6-5 — Weight: 201 — College: Wyoming — Draft: 2004/FA — Born: 8-Sep-1981 — Age: 34 — Risk: Yellow

Year	Team	G/GS	Snaps	Rec	Pass	Yds	C%	+/-	Yd/C	TD	Drop	YAC	Rk	YAC+	BTkl	DVOA	Rk	DYAR	Rk	YAR	Short	Mid	Deep	Bomb
2012	SD	14/14	845	56	84	814	67%	+10.2	14.5	5	1	1.8	86	-2.2	0	36.0%	3	281	15	303	16%	46%	26%	12%
2013	SD	2/2	88	6	11	149	55%	-0.5	24.8	0	0	2.0	--	-3.8	0	40.9%	--	47	--	45	25%	17%	50%	8%
2014	SD	16/16	942	52	91	856	57%	+7.2	16.5	6	1	2.4	84	-2.0	2	23.1%	12	252	14	245	13%	46%	16%	25%
2015	SD			41	77	642	53%	--	15.7	5							9.8%								

It's hard to believe Floyd will be 34 years old on opening day against Detroit, putting him in a group with Steve Smith, Anquan Boldin, and Andre Johnson as the oldest active wide receivers on a roster at press time. He has not had nearly the kind of career success that those other three have enjoyed, as 2014 was actually the first time he ever finished a 16-game season as a starter. Still, 4,989 receiving yards (at 17.1 yards per catch) is a very nice career for an undrafted player. When healthy, Floyd has been reliable for about 750 yards and five touchdowns every year, which he could do again as Philip Rivers' top deep threat. Last season, Floyd's average depth of target was 17.0 yards, second only to the 17.7 of Arizona's Michael Floyd (no relation).

Michael Floyd   Height: 6-3   Weight: 220   College: Notre Dame   Draft: 2012/1 (13)   Born: 27-Nov-1989   Age: 26   Risk: Red

Year	Team	G/GS	Snaps	Rec	Pass	Yds	C%	+/-	Yd/C	TD	Drop	YAC	Rk	YAC+	BTkl	DVOA	Rk	DYAR	Rk	YAR	Short	Mid	Deep	Bomb
2012	ARI	16/3	555	45	86	562	52%	-0.5	12.5	2	4	3.5	62	-0.9	4	-10.3%	71	-3	74	-20	24%	51%	11%	14%
2013	ARI	16/16	930	65	112	1041	58%	+3.5	16.0	5	4	4.3	57	-0.2	5	12.9%	20	220	17	229	18%	49%	20%	13%
2014	ARI	16/14	944	47	100	841	48%	-5.2	17.9	6	3	2.5	83	-2.4	2	-1.9%	47	81	44	81	15%	41%	16%	29%
2015	ARI			66	116	974	57%	--	14.8	6						-0.6%								

Floyd had an interesting few months after the season ended. First, the Cardinals hemmed and hawed before picking up the fifth-year option on Floyd's contract. They eventually did, locking Floyd up for 2016. However, word then broke that Arizona was taking trade offers for the receiver. No deal came to pass, and Floyd was there in OTAs, with Bruce Arians going out of his way to praise Floyd's conditioning—which was odd, because nobody noticed that Floyd had ever been out of shape. Floyd was drafted to be the heir apparent to Larry Fitzgerald in Arizona, but that title is now John Brown's to lose.

Fun fact: Six different players threw passes to Michael Floyd last year, including all four of Arizona's quarterbacks, plus Ted Ginn and Marion Grice.

Corey Fuller   Height: 6-2   Weight: 204   College: Virginia Tech   Draft: 2013/6 (171)   Born: 23-Jun-1990   Age: 25   Risk: Yellow

Year	Team	G/GS	Snaps	Rec	Pass	Yds	C%	+/-	Yd/C	TD	Drop	YAC	Rk	YAC+	BTkl	DVOA	Rk	DYAR	Rk	YAR	Short	Mid	Deep	Bomb
2014	DET	16/2	410	14	31	212	45%	-3.0	15.1	1	0	3.6	--	-0.6	0	-9.5%	--	8	--	23	19%	41%	22%	19%
2015	DET			25	46	328	54%	--	13.1	1						-9.9%								

The Lions might not be a primary 11-personnel team if their tight ends stay healthy in 2015, but Corey Fuller has an opportunity to shine whenever Detroit does roll out its three-receiver personnel. After redshirting his rookie season, the former sixth-rounder emerged as an interesting prospect. On a per-target basis, Fuller easily received the highest percentage of deep ball targets among Detroit wide receivers, making him the outlier in a passing game where the throws mostly got shorter. Fuller's brother Kyle has the first-round pedigree, but Corey could give his cornerback brother plenty of issues if he carves out a role as the recipient of a few Matthew Stafford bombs every week.

Devin Funchess   Height: 6-4   Weight: 232   College: Michigan   Draft: 2015/2 (41)   Born: 21-May-1994   Age: 21   Risk: Green

Year	Team	G/GS	Snaps	Rec	Pass	Yds	C%	+/-	Yd/C	TD	Drop	YAC	Rk	YAC+	BTkl	DVOA	Rk	DYAR	Rk	YAR	Short	Mid	Deep	Bomb
2015	CAR			36	56	425	64%	--	11.8	3						4.6%								

Funchess spent a lot of the pre-draft process being pegged as a potential tight end, but in the end wound up with the team that already had the most comparable player from the 2014 draft, Kelvin Benjamin. Funchess is a size-and-speed mismatch with the versatility to line up all over the formation. He is not going to run past defensive backs outside, but utilizes his height well and varies his stride enough to set the big body up to win contested catches. There's a lot to like here as a long-term project, though tape nitpickers will argue that Funchess didn't have the "my ball" mentality that Benjamin did in college. Both of them on the same field could create some nice matchups for Carolina, especially if the Panthers can smooth out some of Funchess' process flaws.

Playmaker Score sees a downside to Funchess, who was much less productive in college than other highly-drafted wideouts. Obviously, the quarterback situation at Michigan played a role, but since 2000, only four junior wide receivers have been drafted in the top 100 picks despite never topping 750 yards or six touchdowns in a college season: Brian Hartline, Greg Little, Yamon Figurs, and Funchess.

Taylor Gabriel | Height: 5-8 | Weight: 167 | College: Abilene Christian | Draft: 2014/FA | Born: 17-Feb-1991 | Age: 24 | Risk: Yellow

Year	Team	G/GS	Snaps	Rec	Pass	Yds	C%	+/-	Yd/C	TD	Drop	YAC	Rk	YAC+	BTkl	DVOA	Rk	DYAR	Rk	YAR	Short	Mid	Deep	Bomb
2014	CLE	16/2	610	36	74	621	51%	-5.4	17.3	1	2	7.3	3	+1.2	4	-9.0%	60	21	61	19	32%	33%	17%	18%
2015	CLE			27	49	420	55%	--	15.6	2						-3.5%								

Gabriel went undrafted because he lacks the physical traits to be a quality NFL starter. When you're 5-foot-8, you need elite quickness and speed to be considered in the draft. Nevertheless, it's hard to think of a better landing spot than Cleveland for an undrafted receiver hoping to prove himself. Josh Gordon's suspension and Cleveland's failure to draft a replacement gave Gabriel an opportunity for playing time, and he took it. He was effective relying on his ball skills and precise route running in 2014. Maybe more significant, he also showed off enough athleticism and aggressiveness to suggest that he could be a quality third option, primarily playing in the slot. His main problem is that Andrew Hawkins already appears to be an ideal fit for that role in Cleveland.

Pierre Garcon | Height: 6-0 | Weight: 210 | College: Mount Union | Draft: 2008/6 (205) | Born: 8-Aug-1986 | Age: 29 | Risk: Yellow

Year	Team	G/GS	Snaps	Rec	Pass	Yds	C%	+/-	Yd/C	TD	Drop	YAC	Rk	YAC+	BTkl	DVOA	Rk	DYAR	Rk	YAR	Short	Mid	Deep	Bomb
2012	WAS	10/10	394	44	68	633	66%	+1.0	14.4	4	4	7.1	5	+1.1	3	8.2%	26	131	35	131	36%	38%	21%	5%
2013	WAS	16/16	978	113	181	1346	62%	+0.2	11.9	5	6	5.8	15	+0.5	7	-5.2%	62	104	45	132	44%	36%	14%	6%
2014	WAS	16/14	872	68	105	752	65%	+0.1	11.1	3	0	5.0	29	-0.1	6	-14.6%	75	-15	76	0	49%	33%	9%	9%
2015	WAS			81	128	1024	63%	--	12.6	6						3.4%								

Forty-one of Garcon's 68 catches occurred within 5 yards of the line of scrimmage. He produced just three gains of 15-plus yards in those 41 receptions (including one 47-yarder), so Garcon wasn't exactly juking the world after the catch. Garcon was just 6-of-19 on passes labeled "deep" in the play-by-play (more than 15 yards downfield). The low target total is a result of the arrival of DeSean Jackson, the futility of the Redskins quarterbacks and their pass protection, Jay Gruden's own reluctance to make Garcon a focal point of his unfocused offense, and Garcon's own lack of downfield sizzle.

Gruden spent almost as many press conferences last year talking about getting Garcon more involved as he did sending garbled passive-aggressive messages about Robert Griffin. Look for another season of "we need to get Garcon the ball more" following close on the heels of "Robert is our starter for as long as I can stomach it" in the city where every presser is a rag soaked in kerosene.

Brandon Gibson | Height: 6-1 | Weight: 210 | College: Washington State | Draft: 2009/6 (194) | Born: 13-Aug-1987 | Age: 28 | Risk: Blue

Year	Team	G/GS	Snaps	Rec	Pass	Yds	C%	+/-	Yd/C	TD	Drop	YAC	Rk	YAC+	BTkl	DVOA	Rk	DYAR	Rk	YAR	Short	Mid	Deep	Bomb
2012	STL	16/13	761	51	82	691	62%	+8.5	13.5	5	4	2.2	84	-1.3	3	23.3%	11	214	21	204	23%	52%	17%	8%
2013	MIA	7/3	252	30	43	326	70%	+1.5	10.9	3	2	3.9	--	-0.4	3	16.3%	--	103	--	99	56%	35%	7%	2%
2014	MIA	14/5	503	29	51	295	57%	-2.1	10.2	1	4	3.8	61	-0.8	3	-27.3%	86	-56	84	-59	38%	45%	11%	6%
2015	NE			10	16	104	63%	--	10.4	0						-9.1%								

The Patriots have had a long history of bringing in veteran receivers at a relatively reasonable rate and seeing if they can stick with Tom Brady. Some of them work (Brandon LaFell turned out to be a terrific addition last year), while some of them don't (Joey Galloway, Michael Jenkins, Lavelle Hawkins). If it doesn't work out, there are no worries, as there's relatively no money at stake. Gibson is this year's model: a vet who suffered a torn patella tendon in 2013, he has been a steady contributor when he has been healthy, particularly in 2012. In New England, his positional versatility will play in his favor. He'll also have a year with Patriots offensive coordinator Josh McDaniels under his belt, as the two were together with the Rams in 2011.

Ted Ginn | Height: 5-11 | Weight: 178 | College: Ohio State | Draft: 2007/1 (9) | Born: 12-Apr-1985 | Age: 30 | Risk: Green

Year	Team	G/GS	Snaps	Rec	Pass	Yds	C%	+/-	Yd/C	TD	Drop	YAC	Rk	YAC+	BTkl	DVOA	Rk	DYAR	Rk	YAR	Short	Mid	Deep	Bomb
2012	SF	13/0	64	2	2	1	100%	+0.3	0.5	0	0	2.5	--	-6.7	0	-89.0%	--	-12	--	-13	100%	0%	0%	0%
2013	CAR	16/2	502	36	68	556	53%	-0.1	15.4	5	3	5.9	14	+0.8	2	0.3%	47	65	56	68	31%	42%	3%	24%
2014	ARI	16/0	151	14	26	190	54%	-0.7	13.6	0	2	3.3	--	-1.9	1	-15.5%	--	-6	--	-4	35%	27%	19%	19%
2015	CAR			22	39	310	56%	--	14.1	2						0.1%								

The Panthers are a much better fit for Ginn than the Cardinals ever were. While he would never have been more than a fifth receiver in Arizona, he could be the third wideout in Carolina, where he posted the only positive receiving DVOA of his career two years ago. And while his kick return numbers have slipped in recent years (only Percy Harvin had less value on kickoff returns in 2014), he's still a dangerous threat with the ball in his hands—witness his 71-yard go-ahead punt return touchdown against the Giants in Week 2.

Chris Givens   Height: 5-11   Weight: 198   College: Wake Forest   Draft: 2012/4 (96)   Born: 6-Dec-1989   Age: 26   Risk: Red

Year	Team	G/GS	Snaps	Rec	Pass	Yds	C%	+/-	Yd/C	TD	Drop	YAC	Rk	YAC+	BTkl	DVOA	Rk	DYAR	Rk	YAR	Short	Mid	Deep	Bomb
2012	STL	15/12	615	42	80	698	53%	-4.5	16.6	3	4	6.6	7	+1.2	2	0.0%	48	80	44	52	37%	28%	9%	27%
2013	STL	16/13	779	34	83	569	41%	-9.2	16.7	0	3	7.6	3	+2.9	1	-22.8%	82	-68	84	-66	31%	33%	24%	12%
2014	STL	14/0	197	11	20	159	55%	+1.1	14.5	1	0	4.0	--	-2.5	0	-12.9%	--	0	--	-4	41%	12%	24%	24%
2015	STL			9	17	134	53%	--	14.9	1						-5.6%								

Givens used to be the Rams' only big-play threat. He had 23 catches of 20-plus yards in his first two seasons, 14 more than anyone else on the team. Then Kenny Britt arrived and produced 13 20-plus-yard catches last year, while Givens had only three. Going deep is the one thing Givens is good at, and with Britt taking sole possession of that role in the Rams' playbook, Givens found himself catching less than a pass per game in 2014. He's a likely camp cut in 2015.

Josh Gordon   Height: 6-4   Weight: 220   College: Baylor   Draft: 2012/2 (SUP)   Born: 12-Apr-1991   Age: 24   Risk: N/A

Year	Team	G/GS	Snaps	Rec	Pass	Yds	C%	+/-	Yd/C	TD	Drop	YAC	Rk	YAC+	BTkl	DVOA	Rk	DYAR	Rk	YAR	Short	Mid	Deep	Bomb
2012	CLE	16/13	815	50	95	805	53%	-2.7	16.1	5	5	5.9	12	+1.5	2	-3.6%	54	64	53	79	34%	34%	15%	17%
2013	CLE	14/14	900	87	159	1646	55%	+1.8	18.9	9	10	7.3	4	+2.8	6	14.4%	17	336	9	321	25%	38%	23%	14%
2014	CLE	5/5	233	24	47	303	51%	-3.9	12.6	0	1	6.7	--	+1.5	1	-22.7%	--	-35	--	-38	33%	40%	16%	11%

Josh Gordon will miss the 2015 season because he is suspended again. He only played five games in 2014 because of a previous suspension, and his play wasn't exactly inspired when he was on the field. Part of his struggles could be linked to his conditioning, which obviously needed time to be rebuilt after missing so much time before his Week 12 debut. Little of predictive value can be gleaned from Gordon's 2014 season. At this point, it's hard to carry any future expectations for his career.

A.J. Green   Height: 6-4   Weight: 207   College: Georgia   Draft: 2011/1 (4)   Born: 31-Jul-1988   Age: 27   Risk: Green

Year	Team	G/GS	Snaps	Rec	Pass	Yds	C%	+/-	Yd/C	TD	Drop	YAC	Rk	YAC+	BTkl	DVOA	Rk	DYAR	Rk	YAR	Short	Mid	Deep	Bomb
2012	CIN	16/16	958	97	164	1350	59%	+4.9	13.9	11	8	3.9	47	-0.5	9	4.1%	33	205	22	233	34%	32%	15%	18%
2013	CIN	16/16	1055	98	178	1426	55%	-1.6	14.6	11	5	4.1	65	-0.6	7	1.9%	41	207	20	185	27%	44%	14%	15%
2014	CIN	13/13	648	69	116	1041	59%	+4.2	15.1	6	2	4.5	46	+0.3	9	4.1%	38	158	29	161	23%	45%	20%	12%
2015	CIN			84	144	1187	58%	--	14.1	9						1.9%								

Green missed three entire regular-season games, and the bulk of a couple of others, plus (disastrously) the playoff game against Indy. When fully healthy, Green was in his usual spot near the top of the wideout heap. Andy Dalton's utter reliance on Adriel Jeremiah will always hold down Green's efficiency and catch rates, but he is the engine that makes the Cincinnati offense go. Off-field questions about his contract extension numbers and the negotiation chicken that may surround the deal are a potential concern, but it's unlikely the Bengals will mess around with their meal ticket.

Dorial Green-Beckham   Height: 6-5   Weight: 237   College: Oklahoma   Draft: 2015/2 (40)   Born: 12-Apr-1993   Age: 22   Risk: Yellow

Year	Team	G/GS	Snaps	Rec	Pass	Yds	C%	+/-	Yd/C	TD	Drop	YAC	Rk	YAC+	BTkl	DVOA	Rk	DYAR	Rk	YAR	Short	Mid	Deep	Bomb
2015	TEN			41	76	582	54%	--	14.2	4						-6.9%								

When we last saw Green-Beckham, he was the top receiver on a Missouri team that made the SEC Championship Game, where he impressed as a physical presence against Auburn. But for a No. 1 receiver, he was only moderately productive, with just 883 receiving yards. Green-Beckham also carries major off the field question marks, with marijuana citations and a nasty domestic violence allegation that resulted in his dismissal from Missouri and transfer to Oklahoma. Although he never played for the Sooners due to NCAA transfer regulations, Oklahoma coaches gave him a positive review, and the Titans know there aren't many players of his size who can break 4.50 in the 40.

Leonard Hankerson   Height: 6-2   Weight: 209   College: Miami   Draft: 2011/3 (79)   Born: 7-May-1988   Age: 27   Risk: Yellow

Year	Team	G/GS	Snaps	Rec	Pass	Yds	C%	+/-	Yd/C	TD	Drop	YAC	Rk	YAC+	BTkl	DVOA	Rk	DYAR	Rk	YAR	Short	Mid	Deep	Bomb
2012	WAS	16/5	573	38	57	543	67%	+3.8	14.3	3	4	3.9	45	-0.8	3	11.6%	21	129	37	128	32%	40%	14%	14%
2013	WAS	10/7	390	30	50	375	60%	+1.8	12.5	3	2	4.4	55	-0.0	1	-0.6%	50	46	61	72	40%	40%	20%	0%
2014	WAS	1/0	21	0	1	0	0%	+0.0	0.0	0	0	0.0	--	+0.0	0	-118.9%	--	-9	--	-7	--	--	--	--
2015	ATL			28	47	350	60%	--	12.5	2						-0.7%								

Hankerson spent the first two months of 2014 recovering from an ACL tear he suffered in 2013. He then became a weekly healthy scratch, getting into only one game and receiving just one pass target. Hankerson was a solid big man in the slot in 2012 and 2013, and it's not like the Redskins were in the thick of the playoff chase or loaded at wide receiver, so it was not clear why Hankerson did not at least get a look at the end of the year. He may have had a case of "Last Regime's Guy." Sure enough, Kyle Shanahan brought Hankerson to Atlanta, where he should compete for a role as a hard-working size-speed troublemaker in the slot.

Justin Hardy   Height: 6-0   Weight: 188   College: East Carolina   Draft: 2015/4 (107)   Born: 21-Oct-1991   Age: 24   Risk: Yellow

Year	Team	G/GS	Snaps	Rec	Pass	Yds	C%	+/-	Yd/C	TD	Drop	YAC	Rk	YAC+	BTkl	DVOA	Rk	DYAR	Rk	YAR	Short	Mid	Deep	Bomb
2015	ATL			26	40	294	65%	--	11.3	2						3.3%								

Tabbed in the fourth round of the draft to replace the departed Harry Douglas, Hardy is an interesting slot prospect in that he's not quite as technically sound as you'd like an interior receiver to be. He flashed the skills, but did not deliver them on a consistent basis at East Carolina. Of course, as Devin Hester showed last season, you don't necessarily need to be a dominant receiver to be productive as a lower-rung Matt Ryan option. Don't expect great things right away, but there's enough smoke here to merit watching Hardy's progress.

Brian Hartline   Height: 6-2   Weight: 195   College: Ohio State   Draft: 2009/4 (108)   Born: 22-Nov-1986   Age: 29   Risk: Yellow

Year	Team	G/GS	Snaps	Rec	Pass	Yds	C%	+/-	Yd/C	TD	Drop	YAC	Rk	YAC+	BTkl	DVOA	Rk	DYAR	Rk	YAR	Short	Mid	Deep	Bomb
2012	MIA	16/15	893	74	131	1083	56%	+4.1	14.6	1	6	3.2	67	-0.7	3	0.6%	43	158	29	146	25%	50%	11%	14%
2013	MIA	16/15	907	76	133	1016	57%	-2.9	13.4	4	7	3.7	71	-0.3	6	-0.7%	51	123	38	135	26%	54%	14%	6%
2014	MIA	16/16	813	39	63	474	62%	-0.1	12.2	2	4	3.5	66	-0.5	1	2.6%	40	77	47	73	37%	43%	14%	6%
2015	CLE			41	73	492	56%	--	12.0	2						-12.3%								

Hartline has forged a career as a dependable and consistent presence in the Miami passing game, but he has continually baffled with his inability to reach the end zone. He has just 12 touchdown catches in six years in the NFL. From 2011-2013, he became the first receiver in two decades to catch over 180 passes over a three-year period with seven or fewer touchdowns—and with just two scores last year, he managed this statistical oddity in 2012-2014 as well. The only other receivers to do this since 1978 all did it around the same time: Curtis Duncan with the 1990-1992 Oilers, Reggie Langhorne in 1991-1993 with the Browns and Colts, and Drew Hill in 1991-1993 with the Oilers and Falcons. By the way, Langhorne and Hill never played again after these three-year spans, and Duncan had just one more season left.

Percy Harvin   Height: 5-11   Weight: 192   College: Florida   Draft: 2009/1 (22)   Born: 28-May-1988   Age: 27   Risk: Green

Year	Team	G/GS	Snaps	Rec	Pass	Yds	C%	+/-	Yd/C	TD	Drop	YAC	Rk	YAC+	BTkl	DVOA	Rk	DYAR	Rk	YAR	Short	Mid	Deep	Bomb
2012	MIN	9/8	420	62	86	677	73%	+2.2	10.9	3	0	8.5	1	+1.8	19	4.6%	31	194	24	148	67%	19%	12%	1%
2013	SEA	1/0	19	1	1	17	100%	+0.4	17.0	0	0	5.0	--	+1.7	0	102.4%	--	8	--	9	0%	100%	0%	0%
2014	2TM	13/12	541	51	78	483	65%	-1.7	9.5	1	2	5.1	28	-1.0	10	-21.4%	84	-55	83	-65	62%	22%	7%	9%
2015	BUF			48	72	473	67%	--	9.9	2						-8.3%								

When Harvin is healthy, he is a dynamic offensive option who can be a difference-maker, an explosive presence capable of truly great things. Between 2009 and 2012, he was ninth in the league with 280 catches, ahead of the likes of Anquan Boldin, Steve Smith, and Dwayne Bowe. When he's not, he's an inconsistent gadget guy, a luxury item who might not be worth it because of a history of injuries and off-field nonsense. There is a reason that the Percy Harvin World Tour has now visited four teams in four seasons. When it comes to a reasonable level of expectations this year with the Bills, it's anyone's guess. While he has made his bones in the slot, he does have some positional versatility, and could ultimately be the No. 2 or No. 3 option in the passing game behind a Sammy Watkins/LeSean McCoy combo. But how realistic is that, considering Buffalo will likely go with a run-heavy scheme? If Harvin is healthy and buys in, he could be that massive game-changer for the Bills, a terrific complementary presence to Watkins and McCoy and an offensive chess piece who could potentially give defensive coordinators headaches. He certainly has every reason to want to buy in, as the Bills have structured his contract in a way where both sides could walk away from the deal after one year.

(Note: while not listed above, Harvin's projection also includes 29 carries for 132 yards.)

Andrew Hawkins — Height: 5-7 — Weight: 175 — College: Toledo — Draft: 2008/FA — Born: 10-Mar-1986 — Age: 29 — Risk: Yellow

Year	Team	G/GS	Snaps	Rec	Pass	Yds	C%	+/-	Yd/C	TD	Drop	YAC	Rk	YAC+	BTkl	DVOA	Rk	DYAR	Rk	YAR	Short	Mid	Deep	Bomb
2012	CIN	14/2	518	51	80	533	64%	-2.2	10.5	4	4	6.7	6	+1.4	5	-9.2%	70	13	71	20	59%	26%	13%	1%
2013	CIN	8/0	118	12	18	199	67%	-0.1	16.6	0	2	11.3	--	+4.1	0	8.7%	--	31	--	30	53%	24%	18%	6%
2014	CLE	15/15	647	63	113	824	57%	-5.2	13.1	2	3	6.4	9	+1.1	9	-11.4%	66	11	65	29	40%	41%	15%	4%
2015	CLE			59	96	724	61%	--	12.3	3						-7.0%								

Andy Dalton to Brian Hoyer to Johnny Manziel to Connor Shaw. None of the quarterbacks with whom Andrew Hawkins has played were capable of getting the most out of his skill set. Hawkins is lightning quick and precise through his routes, but it's hard to see except in offseason highlight reels. This type of receiver needs a quarterback who can anticipate throws and play to the timing of the offense. If Hawkins got that kind of service, he could easily become a very productive and effective receiver. He may never be a consistent deep threat or option outside of the slot, but he can still be a very dangerous player in spite of that.

Junior Hemingway — Height: 6-1 — Weight: 225 — College: Michigan — Draft: 2012/7 (238) — Born: 27-Dec-1988 — Age: 27 — Risk: Green

Year	Team	G/GS	Snaps	Rec	Pass	Yds	C%	+/-	Yd/C	TD	Drop	YAC	Rk	YAC+	BTkl	DVOA	Rk	DYAR	Rk	YAR	Short	Mid	Deep	Bomb
2012	KC	1/0	0	0	--	0	--	--	--	0	--	--	--	--	--	--	--	--	--	--	--	--	--	--
2013	KC	16/2	312	13	19	125	68%	+1.5	9.6	2	0	1.9	--	-2.5	0	-22.9%	--	-15	--	-8	61%	17%	22%	0%
2014	KC	14/1	255	12	21	108	57%	-2.6	9.0	0	3	5.7	--	+0.7	2	-21.2%	--	-14	--	-16	57%	33%	0%	10%
2015	KC			8	14	84	57%	--	10.5	0						-18.6%								

At Michigan, Hemingway averaged 18.6 yards per reception in an unconventional offense with Denard Robinson at quarterback. In the last two years with Smith as his quarterback, Hemingway has averaged 9.3 yards per catch, exactly half his college average. None of his 25 career catches have gone for more than 24 yards. Maybe he's just miscast, but he's also about the sixth-best wide receiver on the roster, so his days are likely numbered in Kansas City.

Devin Hester — Height: 5-10 — Weight: 185 — College: Miami — Draft: 2007/2 (57) — Born: 4-Nov-1982 — Age: 33 — Risk: Yellow

Year	Team	G/GS	Snaps	Rec	Pass	Yds	C%	+/-	Yd/C	TD	Drop	YAC	Rk	YAC+	BTkl	DVOA	Rk	DYAR	Rk	YAR	Short	Mid	Deep	Bomb
2012	CHI	15/5	361	23	40	242	58%	-2.6	10.5	1	4	4.5	--	-1.4	2	-28.8%	--	-37	--	-51	50%	30%	8%	13%
2013	CHI	16/0	0	0	0	0	--	--	--	0	--	--	--	--	--	--	--	--	--	--	--	--	--
2014	ATL	16/1	388	38	59	504	64%	-1.9	13.3	2	2	6.8	5	+1.3	2	-4.3%	51	38	57	48	51%	29%	19%	2%
2015	ATL			27	41	320	66%	--	11.9	1						4.6%								

The best return man in NFL history, Hester broke Deion Sanders' touchdown return record last season with his 20th score. That was something expected last season. What was unexpected was Hester becoming a big part of the Atlanta passing game after being completely phased out of the offense by Marc Trestman in Chicago. If Leonard Hankerson can't bounce back after a lost year, Hester could very well be the third wideout in Atlanta this year. It's not an optimal solution, but Hester did look better with Matt Ryan at quarterback than he did with Jay Cutler.

T.Y. Hilton

Height: 5-10 Weight: 183 College: Florida International Draft: 2012/3 (92) Born: 14-Nov-1989 Age: 26 Risk: Green

Year	Team	G/GS	Snaps	Rec	Pass	Yds	C%	+/-	Yd/C	TD	Drop	YAC	Rk	YAC+	BTkl	DVOA	Rk	DYAR	Rk	YAR	Short	Mid	Deep	Bomb
2012	IND	15/1	673	50	90	861	56%	-4.4	17.2	7	7	7.7	2	+2.0	6	10.7%	23	151	30	169	26%	43%	19%	11%
2013	IND	16/10	759	82	140	1083	60%	+0.1	13.2	5	5	4.8	39	-0.7	7	1.1%	43	155	29	152	36%	34%	17%	13%
2014	IND	15/15	831	82	131	1345	63%	+11.9	16.4	7	5	4.5	45	-0.1	5	16.5%	14	303	11	283	22%	45%	14%	19%
2015	IND			80	134	1178	60%	--	14.7	8						7.4%								

Each season Hilton has increased his production and improved his catch rate as he develops along with Andrew Luck. The only player with more 100-yard receiving games in his first three seasons than Hilton (16) was Randy Moss (19). The most similar receiver to Hilton in his first three seasons is departed teammate Hakeem Nicks in 2009-2011, but of course Hicks and Hilton are very different body types. Looking at receivers of Hilton's size, the most similar at the start of their careers include Lee Evans (2004-2006) and Mark Carrier (1987-1989) and, if we go a little taller, John Jefferson (1978-1980) and Torry Holt (1999-2001).

The Colts certainly have enough receiving options for Hilton to not have to hit 1,500 yards, but he's capable. In a weird way, the Colts may hope he doesn't have another career year so that his free-agent price stays closer to the Randall Cobb/Jeremy Maclin range instead of asking for the kind of money Dez Bryant and Demaryius Thomas have earned. Andre Johnson has been a great player, but it's hard not to see Hilton still leading the Colts in most receiving categories this year. It's also hard to believe they can let him go play somewhere else in 2016.

Chris Hogan

Height: 6-1 Weight: 220 College: Monmouth Draft: 2012/FA Born: 24-Oct-1988 Age: 27 Risk: Blue

Year	Team	G/GS	Snaps	Rec	Pass	Yds	C%	+/-	Yd/C	TD	Drop	YAC	Rk	YAC+	BTkl	DVOA	Rk	DYAR	Rk	YAR	Short	Mid	Deep	Bomb
2013	BUF	16/0	187	10	17	83	59%	-0.5	8.3	0	1	2.7	--	-1.5	2	-25.3%	--	-17	--	-23	44%	44%	13%	0%
2014	BUF	16/2	461	41	61	426	67%	+1.0	10.4	4	2	4.6	43	-0.6	5	-8.1%	58	21	60	10	51%	32%	14%	3%
2015	BUF			8	13	74	62%	--	9.3	0						-19.3%								

Hogan's coach at Penn State said he might be the best player at his position in Division I, and "certainly the most dangerous with the ball." In 2009, he made first-team all-conference. He also led the Nittany Lions with 133 shots taken and collected 17 ground balls. Those are apparently impressive statistics in lacrosse, but Hogan had no other college experience to attract NFL scouts. So he enrolled at Division III Monmouth University to play one year of college football before latching on in the NFL as an undrafted free agent. Hogan ended up playing a shockingly large role in last year's Buffalo offense because guys like Mike Williams and T.J. Graham couldn't get out of their own way, but the Bills didn't give all that money to Charles Clay and Percy Harvin so they could give Chris Hogan 61 targets again. Slushee time is over, and 7-11 is closed.

Andre Holmes

Height: 6-5 Weight: 206 College: Hillsdale Draft: 2011/FA Born: 16-Jun-1988 Age: 27 Risk: Green

Year	Team	G/GS	Snaps	Rec	Pass	Yds	C%	+/-	Yd/C	TD	Drop	YAC	Rk	YAC+	BTkl	DVOA	Rk	DYAR	Rk	YAR	Short	Mid	Deep	Bomb
2012	DAL	7/0	16	2	2	11	100%	+0.6	5.5	0	0	1.5	--	-3.6	0	17.9%	--	7	--	5	50%	50%	0%	0%
2013	OAK	10/4	380	25	52	431	48%	-3.6	17.2	1	4	4.4	51	+0.1	0	-2.1%	54	42	64	46	21%	42%	23%	15%
2014	OAK	16/13	714	47	98	693	48%	-4.6	14.7	4	4	4.1	52	-0.4	1	-7.2%	56	42	56	22	25%	36%	22%	18%
2015	OAK			20	39	285	51%	--	14.3	2						-10.4%								

Believe it or not, Holmes led the Raiders in receiving yards in 2014. Holmes flashed on tape at times last year with his size helping him win battles for contested passes, which is certainly a skill that can keep a fringe guy on the roster. Think of Holmes as a poor man's Plaxico Burress—or, more accurately, a younger, holster-owning man's Plaxico Burress. Holmes will definitely not lead the Raiders in receiving yards again this season; Oakland only offered him the lowest tender as a restricted free agent, and Holmes is battling to be the No. 4 wide receiver after a major overhaul at that position.

DeAndre Hopkins

Height: 6-1 Weight: 214 College: Clemson Draft: 2013/1 (27) Born: 6-Jun-1992 Age: 23 Risk: Green

Year	Team	G/GS	Snaps	Rec	Pass	Yds	C%	+/-	Yd/C	TD	Drop	YAC	Rk	YAC+	BTkl	DVOA	Rk	DYAR	Rk	YAR	Short	Mid	Deep	Bomb
2013	HOU	16/16	995	52	91	802	57%	+2.6	15.4	2	1	3.5	75	-1.1	1	6.9%	28	139	34	132	28%	38%	19%	15%
2014	HOU	16/16	1053	76	127	1210	60%	+4.4	15.9	6	2	4.9	32	+0.3	7	10.3%	23	237	15	223	22%	43%	23%	13%
2015	HOU			83	152	1269	55%	--	15.3	7						-2.3%								

Hopkins' breakout season was driven by a weird combination of supporting factors. The Texans ran the ball into the line enough to free up Hopkins deep, so he made plays on the balls that Ryan Fitzpatrick actually put on point. Andre Johnson received more targets, so Hopkins generally wasn't drawing the top coverage corners. He also happens to be a really good football player. Hopkins is another data point to prove that size isn't the most important trait in making contested catches, because that's the biggest strength of his game. Just don't expect the same level of efficiency this year without Johnson.

Josh Huff

Height: 5-11 Weight: 206 College: Oregon Draft: 2014/3 (86) Born: 10/14/1991 Age: 24 Risk: Green

Year	Team	G/GS	Snaps	Rec	Pass	Yds	C%	+/-	Yd/C	TD	Drop	YAC	Rk	YAC+	BTkl	DVOA	Rk	DYAR	Rk	YAR	Short	Mid	Deep	Bomb
2014	PHI	12/0	210	8	18	98	44%	-3.7	12.3	0	3	9.6	--	+3.8	6	-48.9%	--	-49	--	-51	41%	29%	24%	6%
2015	PHI			13	25	156	52%	--	12.0	1						-15.2%								

Huff is a speedy slot receiver with plenty of Oregon Ducks apparel in his closet, precisely the kind of guy Chip Kelly would like to see catch two or three screens per game, plus the occasional sneaky bomb. A shoulder injury limited Huff in the first half of 2014, and inconsistent hands plagued him through OTAs in 2015. A 107-yard kickoff return and a 44-yard catch-and-run against the Cowboys offer hints of Huff's big-play potential; heaven knows he can do more with a slot screen than Riley Cooper, if only he catches it. There's a role waiting for Huff. All he has to do is claim it.

Justin Hunter

Height: 6-4 Weight: 196 College: Tennessee Draft: 2013/2 (34) Born: 20-Apr-1991 Age: 24 Risk: Red

Year	Team	G/GS	Snaps	Rec	Pass	Yds	C%	+/-	Yd/C	TD	Drop	YAC	Rk	YAC+	BTkl	DVOA	Rk	DYAR	Rk	YAR	Short	Mid	Deep	Bomb
2013	TEN	14/0	334	18	42	354	43%	-3.2	19.7	4	1	5.1	--	-0.1	2	-3.6%	--	30	--	45	12%	44%	17%	27%
2014	TEN	12/8	593	28	67	498	42%	-8.7	17.8	3	2	6.4	10	+1.7	5	-13.4%	72	-4	72	-22	21%	34%	30%	15%
2015	TEN			29	60	466	48%	--	16.1	3						-8.3%								

Fantasy pundits are dreaming about Justin Hunter the 6-foot-4 receiver who ran a 4.44 40-yard dash at the combine and can make spectacular leaping catches. At some point, either they'll stop dreaming about him or Hunter will finally develop from the player he is right now: a player who fails to separate on deep routes, can't win against physical coverage, struggles making contested catches, and doesn't make sharp breaks on routes. Oh, and in July we got to add "stabs, cuts, and wounds with malicious intent" to that list of Hunter attributes after he was arrested for assault in Virginia Beach. We expect him to be cut by the time you read this, but we left his KUBIAK projection here for those who might be curious.

Allen Hurns

Height: 6-3 Weight: 195 College: Miami Draft: 2014/FA Born: 12-Nov-1991 Age: 24 Risk: Yellow

Year	Team	G/GS	Snaps	Rec	Pass	Yds	C%	+/-	Yd/C	TD	Drop	YAC	Rk	YAC+	BTkl	DVOA	Rk	DYAR	Rk	YAR	Short	Mid	Deep	Bomb
2014	JAC	16/8	788	51	97	677	53%	-6.8	13.3	6	5	4.2	51	-0.7	5	-14.4%	74	-13	75	-16	38%	37%	13%	11%
2015	JAC			56	96	653	58%	--	11.7	4						-10.7%								

Hurns was an interesting find as an undrafted free agent. His hands come and go. He doesn't have one real standout skill. Still, had an NFL-ready quarterback been under center last season, Hurns was open enough to put up much better numbers than the ones he ended up with. In his second season, Hurns is on more uncertain ground: he no longer has the advantage of playing in his college offense now that former Hurricanes offensive coordinator Jedd Fisch has been let go by the Jaguars. Physically, Hurns can play. The question is if the quarterback and the depth chart will give him the opportunity.

Dontrelle Inman

Height: 6-3 Weight: 205 College: Virginia Draft: 2011/FA Born: 31-Jan-1989 Age: 26 Risk: Green

Year	Team	G/GS	Snaps	Rec	Pass	Yds	C%	+/-	Yd/C	TD	Drop	YAC	Rk	YAC+	BTkl	DVOA	Rk	DYAR	Rk	YAR	Short	Mid	Deep	Bomb
2014	SD	7/0	120	12	17	158	71%	+2.5	13.2	0	1	1.2	--	-2.7	1	24.0%	--	49	--	42	12%	47%	35%	6%
2015	SD			14	23	179	61%	--	12.8	1						-0.9%								

Inman didn't even get a Going Deep comment in last year's book, because to that point he had never played in a regular-season game in the NFL after going undrafted in 2011 and spending two years with the Toronto Argonauts. He made the Chargers' 53-man roster following a good preseason, but didn't get his first career target until Week 16. Then Keenan Allen got hurt and missed the last two games of the year. Inman took full advantage of the opportunity with back-to-back games of 79 receiving yards. Inman will compete with the more established Austin Pettis for the role of No. 4 wide receiver, but Pettis has never had 79 receiving yards in any of his 51 career games. There's more upside with Inman at this point.

DeSean Jackson					Height: 5-9		Weight: 169		College: California			Draft: 2008/2 (49)			Born: 1-Dec-1986			Age: 29		Risk: Green	
Year	Team	G/GS	Snaps	Rec	Pass	Yds	C%	+/-	Yd/C	TD	Drop	YAC	Rk	YAC+	BTkl	DVOA	Rk	DYAR	Rk	YAR	Short	Mid	Deep	Bomb
2012	PHI	11/11	698	45	88	700	51%	+1.9	15.6	2	1	5.1	25	+0.7	8	-10.6%	72	42	61	14	21%	42%	17%	20%
2013	PHI	16/16	987	82	125	1332	66%	+12.2	16.2	9	4	5.9	12	+0.4	5	23.7%	10	358	6	374	36%	26%	22%	17%
2014	WAS	15/13	755	56	95	1169	60%	+0.8	20.9	6	1	8.5	1	+2.5	3	27.0%	6	306	10	300	36%	33%	6%	24%
2015	WAS			58	110	1019	53%	--	17.6	6						3.2%								

There have only been five seasons since 2001 in which a receiver averaged 20-plus yards per reception while catching 40 or more passes. Jackson has had two of those seasons: in 2010 (47-1,056-22.5) and last year. The other seasons: Ashley Lelie in 2004 (54-1,084-20.1), Bernard Berrian in 2008 (48-964-20.1), and Mike Wallace in 2010 (60-1,257-21.0).

The fact that Jackson has twice eclipsed 20 yards per catch on two different teams in two very different situations, while the other deep threats on that list quickly devolved into disappointments or decoys, shows that Jackson is one of the most unique players in the NFL right now. There are better receivers, but there may not be a more consistent pure deep threat, capable of gliding past defenders and producing three 40-yard pass plays per month no matter who is throwing the football.

Jackson earns a $3.75 million roster bonus this year and will earn another one next year, so he will have a hard time grousing about his pay scale as long as he stays productive. Paying Jackson on the installment plan is a smart move; when it comes to his finances, he has a short-term memory problem.

Vincent Jackson					Height: 6-5		Weight: 241		College: Northern Colorado		Draft: 2005/2 (61)			Born: 14-Jan-1983			Age: 32		Risk: Yellow	
Year	Team	G/GS	Snaps	Rec	Pass	Yds	C%	+/-	Yd/C	TD	Drop	YAC	Rk	YAC+	BTkl	DVOA	Rk	DYAR	Rk	YAR	Short	Mid	Deep	Bomb
2012	TB	16/16	976	72	147	1384	49%	-2.6	19.2	8	3	5.0	27	+0.8	6	10.5%	24	224	20	288	12%	41%	25%	21%
2013	TB	16/16	968	78	161	1224	49%	-13.2	15.7	7	11	4.2	63	-0.2	5	-3.3%	57	122	39	138	21%	52%	13%	13%
2014	TB	16/16	903	70	142	1002	49%	-7.8	14.3	2	1	2.1	87	-1.8	5	-12.3%	68	4	68	30	11%	56%	19%	15%
2015	TB			62	121	935	51%	--	15.1	7						-2.0%								

In 2008 and 2009, Jackson ranked second and first, respectively, in DVOA for wide receivers. Jackson was fortunate enough to play with Philip Rivers at that time, and he also was the right age to peak as a wideout. Now Jackson is on the downside at age 32. His DVOA rating has declined every single year since that 2009 peak, and Mike Evans' much better advanced stats last season indicate that Jackson's decline is not entirely about the quarterbacks he has dealt with in Tampa. Jackson posted almost identical DVOA last year on passes from Josh McCown (-11.3%) or Mike Glennon (-12.0%), while Mike Evans was better on passes from Glennon (18.6%) than McCown (8.1%).

Alshon Jeffery					Height: 6-3		Weight: 216		College: South Carolina		Draft: 2012/2 (45)			Born: 14-Feb-1990			Age: 25		Risk: Green	
Year	Team	G/GS	Snaps	Rec	Pass	Yds	C%	+/-	Yd/C	TD	Drop	YAC	Rk	YAC+	BTkl	DVOA	Rk	DYAR	Rk	YAR	Short	Mid	Deep	Bomb
2012	CHI	10/6	431	24	48	367	50%	-1.7	15.3	3	1	2.7	--	-1.3	0	6.7%	--	97	--	77	15%	40%	21%	25%
2013	CHI	16/14	962	89	150	1421	59%	+7.1	16.0	7	6	4.7	44	-0.3	8	8.3%	26	248	14	255	26%	43%	17%	13%
2014	CHI	16/16	956	85	145	1133	59%	+0.1	13.3	10	5	5.5	19	+0.1	7	11.1%	22	278	13	266	38%	31%	12%	18%
2015	CHI			85	141	1169	60%	--	13.8	9						2.5%								

The Jeffery run mostly disappeared from the playbook (6 carries, down from 16) as Brandon Marshall's injury struggles forced his transition to the role of No. 1 receiver. Hamstring injuries hampered him throughout 2014, but John Fox believes better training could help him stay healthy. Marshall's departure means Jeffery now looks like Cutler's binky, and with Cutler that is a very important job. By the way, Football Outsiders similarity scores say the most similar receiver to Alshon Jeffery in the first three years of his career was... Brandon Marshall in 2006-2008. (Dwight Clark 1979-1981 is second, with Chad Johnson 2001-2003 third.)

Greg Jennings   Height: 5-11   Weight: 195   College: Western Michigan   Draft: 2006/2 (52)   Born: 21-Sep-1983   Age: 32   Risk: Green

Year	Team	G/GS	Snaps	Rec	Pass	Yds	C%	+/-	Yd/C	TD	Drop	YAC	Rk	YAC+	BTkl	DVOA	Rk	DYAR	Rk	YAR	Short	Mid	Deep	Bomb
2012	GB	8/5	416	36	62	366	58%	-1.7	10.2	4	2	4.6	35	+0.1	4	-5.2%	58	37	63	21	37%	44%	12%	7%
2013	MIN	15/15	742	68	105	804	65%	+4.7	11.8	4	3	5.0	29	+0.1	4	2.6%	38	127	37	112	39%	34%	18%	9%
2014	MIN	16/13	870	59	92	742	64%	+3.6	12.6	6	4	3.4	70	-1.1	4	5.0%	36	125	33	148	32%	40%	18%	10%
2015	MIA			41	69	428	59%	--	10.4	3						-13.4%								

In their Oprah-inspired offseason, the Dolphins handed out $3 million in guaranteed money for Greg Jennings to serve as sensei for the young receiving trio of Jarvis Landry, Kenny Stills, and DeVante Parker. However, even approaching his age-32 season, Jennings' DVOA and DYAR rankings in his past two Minnesota campaigns have suggested that he's still capable of No. 2 receiver production. That wouldn't be his optimal usage, of course, but as a slot receiver he became Teddy Bridgewater's favorite target, garnering 25 more passes than any other Vikings player. Jennings also led the Vikes in red zone targets for the second consecutive season, and his 78.0% DVOA inside the 20 was a huge leap from his -5.9% DVOA in 2013. His volume numbers will almost certainly set career lows this season, but who among us wouldn't gladly cash in and get a jump start on retirement in South Beach?

Andre Johnson   Height: 6-3   Weight: 219   College: Miami   Draft: 2003/1 (3)   Born: 11-Jul-1981   Age: 34   Risk: Green

Year	Team	G/GS	Snaps	Rec	Pass	Yds	C%	+/-	Yd/C	TD	Drop	YAC	Rk	YAC+	BTkl	DVOA	Rk	DYAR	Rk	YAR	Short	Mid	Deep	Bomb
2012	HOU	16/16	977	112	163	1598	69%	+13.3	14.3	4	7	4.9	29	+0.6	5	19.5%	16	461	2	464	31%	44%	13%	11%
2013	HOU	16/16	994	109	181	1407	60%	+2.6	12.9	5	5	3.7	70	-0.7	8	-2.3%	55	150	31	178	31%	45%	17%	8%
2014	HOU	15/15	926	85	147	936	58%	-6.9	11.0	3	6	4.6	42	-0.7	6	-19.8%	81	-86	86	-81	34%	43%	16%	6%
2015	IND			76	122	868	62%	--	11.4	6						-0.6%								

So here's the question: how much did Andre Johnson want to play last season? He sulked all offseason about Gary Kubiak's firing. He didn't get any familiarity with Ryan Fitzpatrick after missing a lot of offseason reps, and it showed on the field. Johnson had the second-lowest DVOA and DYAR of any qualifying receiver, and was one of two wideouts with more than 115 targets and a negative DYAR. (Reggie Wayne was the other.) We've seen great wide receivers have down years with bad quarterbacks and bounce back before—think Steve Smith's year with Matt Moore and Jimmy Clausen, or Wayne's year with Kerry Collins and company. Johnson's hands were bad last season, but physically he looked fine once you accept the fact that he's only getting open deep with a double move. Is this move going to re-energize him, or were the Texans smart to bail on him? We're about to find out.

Calvin Johnson   Height: 6-5   Weight: 239   College: Georgia Tech   Draft: 2007/1 (2)   Born: 25-Sep-1985   Age: 30   Risk: Red

Year	Team	G/GS	Snaps	Rec	Pass	Yds	C%	+/-	Yd/C	TD	Drop	YAC	Rk	YAC+	BTkl	DVOA	Rk	DYAR	Rk	YAR	Short	Mid	Deep	Bomb
2012	DET	16/16	1152	122	203	1964	60%	+9.5	16.1	5	8	4.1	40	+0.1	6	16.0%	19	488	1	459	26%	36%	27%	11%
2013	DET	14/14	877	84	156	1492	54%	+0.3	17.8	12	10	5.5	22	+1.2	6	14.9%	16	347	7	343	15%	46%	30%	9%
2014	DET	13/13	695	71	128	1077	55%	-0.1	15.2	8	3	3.3	72	-0.7	1	10.2%	24	231	16	253	16%	53%	19%	12%
2015	DET			98	165	1487	59%	--	15.2	12						11.1%								

Despite what his Megatron moniker would suggest, Calvin Johnson was far from indestructible in 2014, hobbling his way through ankle and elbow woes en route to his lowest DVOA and DYAR rankings since 2009, the year before he made his first Pro Bowl. Megatron also saw a big dip in deep targets in Joe Lombardi's system, though he still received plenty of frantic "throw it up" jump balls from Matthew Stafford. The middle of the season was essentially a wash for Johnson, who first hurt his ankle Week 3 against Green Bay and hobbled around the next two weeks, catching just three passes for 19 yards in that time. After a three-game absence, Johnson was essentially himself from his Week 11 return onwards. Pro-rated to 16 games, that pace would equate to a stat line of 96 catches for 1,408 yards and 11 touchdowns, a slightly less explosive version of his 2013 campaign. Johnson should continue to bring a steady deluge of slants and 15-yard dig routes, but better health could also reestablish Megatron as the league's premier deep threat and help him reclaim the Best Receiver title belt.

Charles Johnson — Height: 6-2 — Weight: 215 — College: Grand Valley State — Draft: 2013/7 (216) — Born: 27-Feb-1989 — Age: 26 — Risk: Yellow

Year	Team	G/GS	Snaps	Rec	Pass	Yds	C%	+/-	Yd/C	TD	Drop	YAC	Rk	YAC+	BTkl	DVOA	Rk	DYAR	Rk	YAR	Short	Mid	Deep	Bomb
2014	MIN	12/6	440	31	59	475	53%	-3.1	15.3	2	2	5.6	18	+1.2	1	-16.2%	78	-16	77	2	26%	41%	16%	17%
2015	MIN			47	82	690	57%	--	14.7	5						2.5%								

This is why the Browns can't have nice things. Johnson went from practice-squad afterthought in Cleveland to the best receiver on the Vikings in just a few weeks; he signed with Minnesota in late September and gradually surpassed Cordarrelle Patterson to become the Vikings' starting split end, steadily siphoning off more snaps starting in the Week 8 contest against Tampa Bay. Johnson was essentially the lone deep threat on Minnesota's roster last season, with a team-high 33 percent of his targets on coming on passes that traveled at least 16 yards beyond the line of scrimmage. His catch rate is low in part because of a single Week 12 game against Green Bay, in which he caught just three of 11 targets. Not coincidentally, Johnson was the main beneficiary of Teddy Bridgewater's five-game hot streak to end the season, when he averaged 17.3 yards per catch. Johnson isn't necessarily a 9-route one-trick pony, as his long strides and 6-foot-2 frame also allow him to establish body position over the middle. With Mike Wallace now around to distract the opponent's top cornerback, Johnson's impressive small-sample 2014 performance makes him one of the more intriguing No. 2 receivers for the coming season.

Damaris Johnson — Height: 5-8 — Weight: 175 — College: Tulsa — Draft: 2012/FA — Born: 22-Nov-1989 — Age: 26 — Risk: Yellow

Year	Team	G/GS	Snaps	Rec	Pass	Yds	C%	+/-	Yd/C	TD	Drop	YAC	Rk	YAC+	BTkl	DVOA	Rk	DYAR	Rk	YAR	Short	Mid	Deep	Bomb
2012	PHI	14/1	231	19	31	256	61%	+1.2	13.5	0	0	5.3	--	+1.4	3	5.8%	--	69	--	45	29%	61%	7%	4%
2013	PHI	13/0	53	2	3	14	67%	+0.3	7.0	0	0	0.5	--	-3.6	0	-35.4%	--	-5	--	-5	33%	33%	0%	33%
2014	HOU	16/8	576	31	49	331	63%	-2.2	10.7	1	6	5.9	--	-0.5	6	-23.5%	--	-39	--	-46	67%	20%	4%	9%
2015	HOU			16	27	160	59%	--	10.0	0						-17.7%								

Johnson was one target from qualifying for our wideout leaderboards last season. Had he done so, his DVOA would have ranked 85th out of 88 receivers. Johnson has a very thin frame without enough speed to horizontally threaten anyone. Despite this, the Texans were so in on Johnson that they re-signed him on the first day of free agency. He's a fine bottom-of-the-roster player, but making Johnson your third receiver on purpose is a cry for help.

Stevie Johnson — Height: 6-2 — Weight: 202 — College: Kentucky — Draft: 2008/7 (224) — Born: 22-Jul-1986 — Age: 29 — Risk: Red

Year	Team	G/GS	Snaps	Rec	Pass	Yds	C%	+/-	Yd/C	TD	Drop	YAC	Rk	YAC+	BTkl	DVOA	Rk	DYAR	Rk	YAR	Short	Mid	Deep	Bomb
2012	BUF	16/16	936	79	148	1046	53%	-6.7	13.2	6	5	4.6	33	+0.7	6	-4.7%	57	67	49	73	27%	53%	14%	6%
2013	BUF	12/12	701	52	102	597	52%	-9.1	11.5	3	8	4.2	60	-0.3	7	-15.6%	77	-25	78	-29	46%	39%	12%	4%
2014	SF	13/1	292	35	50	435	70%	+4.1	12.4	3	1	5.3	22	+1.1	4	23.4%	11	139	30	140	41%	43%	12%	4%
2015	SD			56	91	694	62%	--	12.4	4						0.0%								

You could be forgiven for forgetting that Stevie Johnson existed. The 49ers coaches did. He started off on fire, catching 13 of 15 passes for 162 yards in his first three games, including a 9-9-103 statline in Week 3 against Arizona. Then he had only two targets in each of the next two games, and only 33 after that. San Francisco released Johnson after the season, and he signed a three-year deal with San Diego. He'll compete with Austin Pettis and Dontrelle Inman for the third receiver spot behind Keenan Allen and Malcom Floyd.

James Jones — Height: 6-1 — Weight: 208 — College: San Jose State — Draft: 2007/3 (78) — Born: 31-Mar-1984 — Age: 31 — Risk: N/A

Year	Team	G/GS	Snaps	Rec	Pass	Yds	C%	+/-	Yd/C	TD	Drop	YAC	Rk	YAC+	BTkl	DVOA	Rk	DYAR	Rk	YAR	Short	Mid	Deep	Bomb
2012	GB	16/16	1000	64	98	784	65%	+8.2	12.3	14	3	3.6	56	-0.4	2	22.6%	12	318	12	295	33%	45%	12%	11%
2013	GB	14/14	846	59	93	817	63%	+3.3	13.8	3	3	6.2	6	+1.1	8	2.1%	40	110	42	114	38%	37%	12%	13%
2014	OAK	16/10	717	73	112	666	65%	+4.3	9.1	6	2	3.0	79	-2.2	7	-14.7%	76	-18	79	-45	47%	36%	10%	7%

Derek Carr tried to play "back-shoulder throw" like he was Aaron Rodgers last year, but he was throwing to a used James Jones action figure. Perhaps the craziest stat line of 2014 was Jones catching eight passes for 20 yards against Denver in Week 10. No wide receiver since 1960 has had that many catches go for so few yards in a game. That's what some poor screens and dumpoffs against a good secondary can do to you. Jones led all receivers with 27 failed receptions in 2014. He remains a free agent, but he could still help an offense with a solid quarterback.

Julio Jones Height: 6-3   Weight: 220   College: Alabama   Draft: 2011/1 (6)   Born: 3-Feb-1989   Age: 26   Risk: Green

Year	Team	G/GS	Snaps	Rec	Pass	Yds	C%	+/-	Yd/C	TD	Drop	YAC	Rk	YAC+	BTkl	DVOA	Rk	DYAR	Rk	YAR	Short	Mid	Deep	Bomb
2012	ATL	16/15	835	79	129	1198	61%	+5.2	15.2	10	8	5.9	13	+1.1	10	16.0%	20	340	9	320	38%	32%	17%	14%
2013	ATL	5/5	296	41	60	580	68%	+5.3	14.1	2	2	6.0	10	+0.3	4	0.4%	45	60	57	71	50%	21%	20%	9%
2014	ATL	15/15	868	104	163	1593	64%	+7.2	15.3	6	4	5.2	25	+0.4	14	16.2%	15	356	7	353	34%	26%	30%	10%
2015	ATL			100	156	1403	64%	--	14.0	9						12.5%								

Jones came back from his 2013 torn ACL and ho-hummed his way to 1,600 yards despite being the only effective receiver on his team. We're entering a golden age for physically dominant wideouts, and Jones belongs in the conversation with Dez Bryant and Calvin Johnson as the players most likely to be deemed "beastly." As long as he's healthy, he'll be the focal point of the Atlanta offense. There has been some speculation that Kyle Shanahan's offense will lock in on Jones and create even more targets for him. While it's true that Pierre Garcon saw 30 percent of Washington's targets in 2013, the No. 1 receiver in Shanahan's offenses have averaged 26.6 percent of the targets over the past three years. In his 15 games last year, Jones averaged... 28 percent of the targets. Don't buy Jones in fantasy based on the idea that he might get 190 targets. Buy him because he's consistently excellent.

Marvin Jones Height: 6-2   Weight: 199   College: California   Draft: 2012/5 (166)   Born: 12-Mar-1990   Age: 25   Risk: Green

Year	Team	G/GS	Snaps	Rec	Pass	Yds	C%	+/-	Yd/C	TD	Drop	YAC	Rk	YAC+	BTkl	DVOA	Rk	DYAR	Rk	YAR	Short	Mid	Deep	Bomb
2012	CIN	11/5	354	18	32	201	56%	+0.3	11.2	1	1	1.9	--	-1.9	3	-2.1%	--	36	--	34	29%	42%	19%	10%
2013	CIN	16/3	542	51	80	712	64%	+4.2	14.0	10	2	4.4	53	-0.3	11	32.4%	3	279	11	269	24%	54%	14%	8%
2015	CIN			47	77	558	61%	--	11.9	4						-5.5%								

Jones' spectacular 2013 put him ahead of Mohamed Sanu as Venus Flytrap to A.J. Green's Johnny Fever, but a foot injury in training camp led to a worse ankle injury when Jones tried to come back too soon. Instead of building on his success, Jones was gone for the entire season, and he was badly missed. Now that he's healthy again, the Bengals hope Jones' deep speed, huge catch radius, and toughness in the screen game help to revive their offense. Like Sanu, Jones is in the last year of his rookie deal. It seems probable that the Bengals will choose one or the other to re-sign to an extension. May the best man win.

Jermaine Kearse Height: 6-1   Weight: 209   College: Washington   Draft: 2012/FA   Born: 6-Feb-1990   Age: 25   Risk: Green

Year	Team	G/GS	Snaps	Rec	Pass	Yds	C%	+/-	Yd/C	TD	Drop	YAC	Rk	YAC+	BTkl	DVOA	Rk	DYAR	Rk	YAR	Short	Mid	Deep	Bomb
2012	SEA	7/1	80	3	7	31	43%	-0.4	10.3	0	2	0.3	--	-3.4	0	-22.9%	--	-1	--	-6	0%	50%	33%	17%
2013	SEA	15/5	469	22	38	346	58%	+1.5	15.7	4	3	1.7	--	-3.0	0	26.2%	--	116	--	108	16%	42%	24%	18%
2014	SEA	15/14	792	38	69	537	55%	-1.0	14.1	1	3	5.9	11	+0.4	4	-9.1%	61	19	62	22	31%	33%	23%	13%
2015	SEA			31	57	420	54%	--	13.6	2						-8.3%								

Kearse may be the worst player in the league with the best highlight reel. He has caught nine touchdowns in his career, four of them in the playoffs. Those touchdowns have averaged 33.4 yards apiece, and six of them have been go-ahead scores, including game winners in back-to-back conference championship games. And that's not even counting his greatest catch, the 33-yard juggler on his back that set up the finish of the Super Bowl against New England. In his first season as a full-time starter, however, his advanced stats were horrible, and he nearly single-handedly lost the NFC title game against Green Bay when he was the target on four interceptions, two of which hit him in the hands. Kearse is a third-year pro who has never caught more than five passes or gained even 80 yards in a single game, but Seattle signed him to a second-round tender after the season and he stands to make almost $2.4 million this year. That's a lot of money for a guy who should probably be a fourth wideout, not a starter.

Jeremy Kerley

Height: 5-9   Weight: 188   College: TCU   Draft: 2011/5 (153)   Born: 8-Nov-1988   Age: 27   Risk: Green

Year	Team	G/GS	Snaps	Rec	Pass	Yds	C%	+/-	Yd/C	TD	Drop	YAC	Rk	YAC+	BTkl	DVOA	Rk	DYAR	Rk	YAR	Short	Mid	Deep	Bomb
2012	NYJ	16/7	664	56	97	827	59%	+0.7	14.8	2	3	5.3	22	+0.4	4	-8.1%	69	14	70	42	42%	36%	14%	8%
2013	NYJ	12/8	567	43	72	523	60%	+1.3	12.2	3	0	4.1	64	-1.0	1	6.0%	29	97	46	95	37%	38%	20%	5%
2014	NYJ	16/7	734	38	75	409	51%	-4.3	10.8	1	3	3.9	55	-0.7	2	-21.2%	83	-51	82	-67	29%	52%	15%	3%
2015	NYJ			37	64	448	58%	--	12.1	2						-9.2%								

It's difficult to fathom the fact that, at least among the offensive fantasy position players, Kerley and Jeff Cumberland have the most seniority of anyone in a Jets uniform, having both arrived in 2011. While he was an underrated slot presence a few seasons ago, a combination of a few different things—including injury and changeover at quarterback, specifically the departure of Mark Sanchez, with whom he grew close—have meant his numbers have dipped as of late. While he'll probably lose opportunities in the passing game to rookie Devin Smith and free-agent pickup Brandon Marshall, Kerley's special teams value as a punt returner and his experience in the slot will likely allow him to stick around New York for 2015.

Brandon LaFell

Height: 6-3   Weight: 211   College: Louisiana St.   Draft: 2010/3 (78)   Born: 4-Nov-1986   Age: 29   Risk: Yellow

Year	Team	G/GS	Snaps	Rec	Pass	Yds	C%	+/-	Yd/C	TD	Drop	YAC	Rk	YAC+	BTkl	DVOA	Rk	DYAR	Rk	YAR	Short	Mid	Deep	Bomb
2012	CAR	14/12	756	44	76	677	58%	-1.5	15.4	4	2	7.1	4	+2.2	4	2.8%	37	106	40	105	42%	32%	17%	8%
2013	CAR	16/16	907	49	85	627	58%	-2.2	12.8	5	6	5.2	25	+0.5	2	-6.2%	64	44	63	50	26%	44%	23%	7%
2014	NE	16/13	913	74	119	953	62%	-0.2	12.9	7	3	5.0	31	+0.3	8	5.7%	33	174	27	158	34%	43%	16%	7%
2015	NE			69	113	896	61%	--	13.0	6						2.2%								

With the Panthers in 2011, LaFell showed glimpses of being a viable starting receiver, averaging 11 yards on 56 targets with 17 yards per reception. Since then, LaFell has mostly been used on shorter routes. In 2011, throws to LaFell traveled an average of 12.9 yards through the air. That number dropped to 10.7 over his last two years in Carolina. Last year, Brady's passes to LaFell traveled 10.6 yards.

LaFell lacks the lateral quickness to create separation over the middle. His game-winning touchdown down the sideline in the playoffs against Baltimore showcased the benefits of his size. Even there, despite winning off the line, LaFell created little separation—and that was against replacement-level cornerback Rashaan Melvin.

Jarvis Landry

Height: 5-11   Weight: 205   College: Louisiana St.   Draft: 2014/2 (63)   Born: 11/28/1992   Age: 23   Risk: Green

Year	Team	G/GS	Snaps	Rec	Pass	Yds	C%	+/-	Yd/C	TD	Drop	YAC	Rk	YAC+	BTkl	DVOA	Rk	DYAR	Rk	YAR	Short	Mid	Deep	Bomb
2014	MIA	16/11	683	84	112	758	75%	+8.7	9.0	5	3	5.1	26	-0.3	10	-0.8%	45	102	39	86	58%	36%	4%	2%
2015	MIA			89	123	861	72%	--	9.7	6						0.7%								

He didn't produce the same highlight-film catches that fellow LSU alum Odell Beckham offered in 2014, but Landry's numbers were pretty good for a rookie receiver who wasn't his team's lead option in the passing game. While there has been talk about him playing some on the outside, Landry will stay in the slot for a few reasons, not the least of which is the fact that the Dolphins have Kenny Stills, DeVante Parker, and Greg Jennings slated as the primary options outside the numbers. And while Landry is quick, he simply doesn't have the straight-line speed to work effectively anywhere else. (He was the only wide receiver in the league to finish with 80 or more catches, but average less than 10 yards per reception.) Developing that separation speed was his No. 1 priority in the offseason: if he can somehow get to that next level—and acquire the necessary positional versatility—he could go from being a nice player who piles up numbers with short catches to a feared part of the Dolphins' offense.

Cody Latimer

Height: 6-2   Weight: 215   College: Indiana   Draft: 2014/2 (56)   Born: 10-Oct-1992   Age: 23   Risk: Red

Year	Team	G/GS	Snaps	Rec	Pass	Yds	C%	+/-	Yd/C	TD	Drop	YAC	Rk	YAC+	BTkl	DVOA	Rk	DYAR	Rk	YAR	Short	Mid	Deep	Bomb
2014	DEN	8/0	37	2	4	23	50%	+0.2	11.5	0	0	8.0	--	+0.8	0	-17.5%	--	-1	--	-2	25%	50%	0%	25%
2015	DEN			35	57	526	61%	--	15.0	4						9.8%								

The Latimer bandwagon was filling up rather quickly a year ago, but even non-believers had to be surprised with how little he saw the field in 2014. This year, however, Latimer received all the first-team reps in OTAs thanks to Demaryius Thomas' holdout. Now that Thomas is fully back in the fold, Latimer is Peyton Manning's No. 3 option at best. The team says he'll be on the outside, with Emmanuel Sanders moving into the slot in three-wide formations, but make no mistake—after what he did last year, Emmanuel Sanders is the No. 2 receiver, even if he's in the slot. Since 2006, only two No. 3 wide receivers had more than 500 receiving yards in a Kubiak offense, and one of those cases (André Davis in 2007) was purely due to an Andre Johnson injury. Still, it's a Manning offense too, and it's one that lost Wes Welker, Jacob Tamme, and Julius Thomas this offseason.

Marqise Lee

Height: 6-0　Weight: 192　College: USC　Draft: 2014/2 (39)　Born: 11/25/1991　Age: 24　Risk: Yellow

Year	Team	G/GS	Snaps	Rec	Pass	Yds	C%	+/-	Yd/C	TD	Drop	YAC	Rk	YAC+	BTkl	DVOA	Rk	DYAR	Rk	YAR	Short	Mid	Deep	Bomb
2014	JAC	13/8	492	37	68	422	54%	-5.7	11.4	1	4	4.8	36	-0.4	7	-20.3%	82	-41	81	-37	48%	38%	6%	8%
2015	JAC			49	84	617	58%	--	12.6	3						-7.5%								

Lee's first season in Jacksonville was more "senior season at USC" than "junior season at USC." Twenty-yard games were too common, and the package somehow seemed to be less than the sum of its parts. Lee spent his offseason suing Lloyd's of London after they voided his loss-of-value insurance policy despite the fact that he *did* tumble in the draft after his mediocre senior year. The Jags would probably prefer Lee spend his time on the future rather than the past. He's penciled in for a starting slot, but now it's time to see more than just flashes of that junior season.

Brandon Lloyd

Height: 6-0　Weight: 192　College: Illinois　Draft: 2003/4 (124)　Born: 5-Jul-1981　Age: 34　Risk: N/A

Year	Team	G/GS	Snaps	Rec	Pass	Yds	C%	+/-	Yd/C	TD	Drop	YAC	Rk	YAC+	BTkl	DVOA	Rk	DYAR	Rk	YAR	Short	Mid	Deep	Bomb
2012	NE	16/15	1038	74	130	911	57%	+0.0	12.3	4	8	2.3	82	-1.6	2	1.8%	40	130	36	123	14%	55%	21%	10%
2013		--	--	--	--	--	--	--	--	--	--	--	--	--	--	--	--	--	--	--	--	--	--	--
2014	SF	14/3	335	14	35	294	40%	-1.6	21.0	1	0	5.3	--	+0.4	0	-8.1%	--	12	--	-5	12%	36%	12%	39%

Brandon Lloyd is the Nicolas Cage of the NFL. While Cage has *Leaving Las Vegas*, an all-time classic dramatic performance on an otherwise embarrassing resume, Lloyd had 2010, when he led the NFL with 1,448 receiving yards playing for Denver. He never had another season in the top 20, and he only had four other seasons in the top 100. It's a similar story in advanced stats, where he was top 10 in DVOA and DYAR in 2010 but otherwise usually ranked in the 50s or worse, and half the time he failed to even qualify. Lloyd always had tantalizing talent, which is why six teams kept him in the NFL for 11 seasons, but he was almost never productive on the field. He took a year off from football in 2013, made little impact in 2014, and was unemployed as of early July, meaning one of the weirder NFL careers in recent memory may have finally ended.

Ricardo Lockette

Height: 6-2　Weight: 211　College: Fort Valley State　Draft: 2011/FA　Born: 21-May-1986　Age: 29　Risk: Green

Year	Team	G/GS	Snaps	Rec	Pass	Yds	C%	+/-	Yd/C	TD	Drop	YAC	Rk	YAC+	BTkl	DVOA	Rk	DYAR	Rk	YAR	Short	Mid	Deep	Bomb
2013	SEA	8/1	87	5	7	82	71%	+1.8	16.4	0	0	2.4	--	-2.7	0	41.3%	--	27	--	28	14%	29%	14%	43%
2014	SEA	16/0	168	11	15	195	73%	+1.6	17.7	2	0	6.2	--	+0.7	1	50.4%	--	66	--	65	27%	47%	7%	20%
2015	SEA			9	15	148	60%	--	16.4	1						12.7%								

Life is unfair. 2014 was Ricardo Lockette's best season, but he'll always be remembered as the guy who was knocked on his ass while Malcolm Butler made the game-winning interception in the Super Bowl. Up to that point, Lockette was starting to look like the football player that a man with his size, speed (10.0-second 100-meter dash in college, 4.37-second 40 time at the 2011 NFL combine), and hustle (watch him sprint downfield to throw three different blocks on Marshawn Lynch's 79-yard touchdown run against Arizona) should be. He had a 33-yard touchdown against Green Bay, a 39-yard score against Denver, and a 48-yard gain against Arizona. Seattle didn't offer Lockette a free-agent tender, which would have meant a $1.5 million base salary, but they did re-sign him in free agency for $660,000. At that price, and with Lockette's gritty play on special teams, he's a very safe bet to make the roster this year and get a shot at redemption.

Tyler Lockett Height: 5-10 Weight: 182 College: Kansas State Draft: 2015/3 (69) Born: 28-Sep-1992 Age: 23 Risk: Red

Year	Team	G/GS	Snaps	Rec	Pass	Yds	C%	+/-	Yd/C	TD	Drop	YAC	Rk	YAC+	BTkl	DVOA	Rk	DYAR	Rk	YAR	Short	Mid	Deep	Bomb
2015	SEA			30	46	414	65%	--	13.8	2						9.6%								

The most important numbers for Lockett aren't his 11.14-second 60-yard shuttle, best among receivers at this year's combine, nor his 4.4-second 40-yard dash or 4.07-second 20-yard shuttle, which were both in the top five. They aren't the Big 12-leading 1,515 receiving yards and 11 receiving touchdowns he put up last season, or the 3,710 yards and 29 touchdowns he produced in his career. No, the most important numbers for Lockett are his four touchdowns on kickoff returns and two scores on punt returns in his time at Kansas State. The Seahawks were well below average in kick returns last season, and haven't been anything special there since Leon Washington scored three touchdowns in 2010. Lockett automatically makes the NFL's best team better at one of its few weak spots. Which is not to say that he's all wheels and no hands—his 71 percent catch rate last season attests to his receiving ability, and his 16 career red zone touchdowns (nine of them inside the 10) show that he can get open when space is limited too. Lockett's small size likely limits him to a slot role in the NFL, and his Playmaker score was lukewarm, mainly because he stayed at Kansas State through his junior year. Still, the Seahawks had a clear need for a player who can do the things Lockett can do, and he should be a key contributor from Day One.

Jeremy Maclin Height: 6-0 Weight: 198 College: Missouri Draft: 2009/1 (19) Born: 11-May-1988 Age: 27 Risk: Green

Year	Team	G/GS	Snaps	Rec	Pass	Yds	C%	+/-	Yd/C	TD	Drop	YAC	Rk	YAC+	BTkl	DVOA	Rk	DYAR	Rk	YAR	Short	Mid	Deep	Bomb
2012	PHI	15/15	974	69	121	857	56%	-5.2	12.4	7	5	3.8	51	-0.9	1	-6.5%	62	132	34	73	43%	33%	14%	10%
2013	PHI	0/0	0	0	--	0	--	--	--	0	--	--	--	--	--	--	--	--	--	--	--	--	--	--
2014	PHI	16/16	1022	85	143	1318	59%	-1.5	15.5	10	2	5.8	12	+0.8	4	7.4%	30	222	18	245	31%	39%	16%	14%
2015	KC			70	113	921	62%	--	13.2	6						1.4%								

Prior to the ACL tear that erased 2013, Maclin was a textbook example of a very good No. 2 possession receiver. After the injury, Maclin suddenly became a high-volume, high-risk big play guy: more targets, a competitive catch rate, 21 receptions of 20 or more yards, and seven interceptions on passes headed his way. It was a strange transition: no one expected Maclin's yards per catch to increase nearly 2 yards from his prior career high, despite a career high in targets, after a major injury. Maclin was like himself and DeSean Jackson combined at times last year, so of course Chip Kelly ditched him in favor of a rookie so he could sign (among other luxuries) the best third-string running back in the NFL.

Andy Reid hopes he is getting that Maclin/DeSean mix for Clark Hunt's $55 million. The risk is that he is just getting 2010-12 Maclin, the smooth-cutting, hard-working possession guy, and that the 15.5 yards per catch secret spices are actually stirred into Kelly's no-huddle secret recipe. The jury is still out on whether Maclin can consistently beat top cornerbacks without Kelly's time-warp tactics. Even the worst-case scenario, however, isn't terrible: a younger, quicker, more-versatile Dwayne Bowe for roughly the same high price.

Brandon Marshall Height: 6-4 Weight: 229 College: UCF Draft: 2006/4 (119) Born: 23-Mar-1984 Age: 31 Risk: Red

Year	Team	G/GS	Snaps	Rec	Pass	Yds	C%	+/-	Yd/C	TD	Drop	YAC	Rk	YAC+	BTkl	DVOA	Rk	DYAR	Rk	YAR	Short	Mid	Deep	Bomb
2012	CHI	16/16	968	118	195	1508	61%	+8.8	12.8	11	9	2.9	72	-1.3	13	0.0%	46	267	16	205	27%	40%	22%	11%
2013	CHI	16/16	987	100	163	1295	61%	+4.7	13.0	12	12	2.8	83	-2.0	9	9.5%	22	284	10	291	26%	47%	14%	13%
2014	CHI	13/13	753	61	106	721	58%	-2.1	11.8	8	4	3.8	60	-0.8	7	-3.3%	48	78	46	82	31%	49%	8%	13%
2015	NYJ			74	123	898	60%	--	12.1	7						-1.5%								

A standout veteran who gives an impassioned postgame speech and talks about the need for a team to come together and avoid "let[ting] little small groups begin to form in our locker room," as Marshall did after the Week 8 loss to Miami that dropped the Bears to 3-5, is often hailed as a leader. In Marshall's case, it was seen by many as evidence of his divisiveness, which combined with an interest in off-the-field activities like broadcasting and a gig on "Inside the NFL," made him undesirable to the new Chicago regime. The Jets were happy to get him for just a fifth-round pick, and he projects as their top receiver with Eric Decker in the Alshon Jeffery role, to the extent Marshall has dubbed Decker "Alshon."

Jordan Matthews   Height: 6-3   Weight: 212   College: Vanderbilt   Draft: 2014/2 (42)   Born: 7/16/1992   Age: 23   Risk: Yellow

Year	Team	G/GS	Snaps	Rec	Pass	Yds	C%	+/-	Yd/C	TD	Drop	YAC	Rk	YAC+	BTkl	DVOA	Rk	DYAR	Rk	YAR	Short	Mid	Deep	Bomb
2014	PHI	16/10	764	67	103	872	65%	+0.1	13.0	8	3	5.8	15	+0.8	6	11.6%	20	194	25	214	47%	37%	13%	4%
2015	PHI			75	124	1001	60%	--	13.3	8						4.0%								

Matthews' 67 receptions would have led all rookies in 2012, 2011, 2009, 2005 … You get the idea. His 872 yards were the 26th highest total in NFL history for a rookie. So Matthews wasn't chopped liver last year, but he couldn't even wrest all-rookie notice away from Odell Beckham, Sammy Watkins, Kelvin Benjamin, and Mike Evans. Matthews is not as talented as those four, but he has a size-speed package that would have stood out in a typical rookie class, plus fine route chops, hands that got better after some rookie drops, and work habits inspired by cousin Jerry Rice. Those are the tools of a No. 1 receiver, or at least the chair of a receiving committee. Ready or not, Matthews steps into one of those roles this year. He won't be the best sophomore receiver in the NFL, but he has the tools to stay in the top five.

Rishard Matthews   Height: 6-0   Weight: 217   College: Nevada   Draft: 2012/7 (227)   Born: 12-Oct-1989   Age: 26   Risk: Blue

Year	Team	G/GS	Snaps	Rec	Pass	Yds	C%	+/-	Yd/C	TD	Drop	YAC	Rk	YAC+	BTkl	DVOA	Rk	DYAR	Rk	YAR	Short	Mid	Deep	Bomb
2012	MIA	8/1	232	11	20	151	55%	+0.4	13.7	0	0	2.7	--	-1.4	0	-1.4%	--	20	--	25	28%	33%	33%	6%
2013	MIA	16/5	519	41	67	448	61%	+0.7	10.9	2	2	3.9	68	-0.6	0	-7.7%	68	27	67	43	38%	46%	14%	2%
2014	MIA	14/0	210	12	23	135	57%	-0.3	11.3	2	1	3.5	--	-1.0	2	-14.5%	--	-3	--	-15	35%	35%	26%	4%
2015	MIA			9	15	97	60%	--	10.8	0						-12.9%								

With the free-agent additions of Kenny Stills and Greg Jennings, the drafting of DeVante Parker, and the continued emergence of Jarvis Landry in the slot, Matthews will face an uphill battle for opportunities in the passing game in 2015. As a result, it's no surprise that he has already made his dissatisfaction known, boycotting voluntary workouts and pushing for a trade. He's not without value—a general manager in the market for a big slot presence could be persuaded if they pop in some of his highlights from 2013, particularly his two 24-yard catches in a Week 15 contest against the Patriots. But the days of him catching 40-plus passes in the Miami offense are probably done.

Donte Moncrief   Height: 6-2   Weight: 221   College: Mississippi   Draft: 2014/3 (90)   Born: 8-Jun-1993   Age: 22   Risk: Yellow

Year	Team	G/GS	Snaps	Rec	Pass	Yds	C%	+/-	Yd/C	TD	Drop	YAC	Rk	YAC+	BTkl	DVOA	Rk	DYAR	Rk	YAR	Short	Mid	Deep	Bomb
2014	IND	16/2	411	32	49	444	65%	+3.1	13.9	3	2	6.5	--	+1.2	9	-0.2%	--	47	--	61	48%	20%	11%	22%
2015	IND			50	77	672	65%	--	13.4	5						9.8%								

Offensive coordinator Pep Hamilton joked that he ripped up some of his packages involving three tight ends and only two wide receivers once he learned the Colts had drafted Phillip Dorsett. Does he have any four-wide packages, or is Moncrief going to ride the bench after a promising rookie season? He was a third-round pick in 2014 and showed some big-play potential with a few 100-yard games of his own. Most teams would be perfectly content to roll with a trio of T.Y. Hilton, Andre Johnson, and Moncrief, but that's just another reason why the Dorsett pick was so shocking. Even if Johnson is a two-year rental, it's hard to see the Colts not giving their first-round pick some considerable playing time this year. Even in the most prolific passing offenses, which the Colts have a chance to be, the No. 4 wide receiver is going to be fortunate to play 400 snaps and gain more than 400 yards. If it's Moncrief, then he's likely to repeat his rookie season rather than take any big steps forward. But we think the raw rookie will take a back seat to the second-year receiver and Moncrief should be on the receiving end of more Andrew Luck highlights like that touchdown against the Bengals in the playoffs.

Denarius Moore   Height: 6-0   Weight: 191   College: Tennessee   Draft: 2011/5 (148)   Born: 9-Dec-1988   Age: 27   Risk: Green

Year	Team	G/GS	Snaps	Rec	Pass	Yds	C%	+/-	Yd/C	TD	Drop	YAC	Rk	YAC+	BTkl	DVOA	Rk	DYAR	Rk	YAR	Short	Mid	Deep	Bomb
2012	OAK	15/15	793	51	114	741	45%	-12.6	14.5	7	6	5.0	26	+0.6	5	-12.4%	73	-33	78	-5	26%	38%	26%	10%
2013	OAK	13/10	590	46	86	695	53%	-2.9	15.1	5	4	5.6	19	+0.8	2	3.1%	35	107	43	113	30%	48%	16%	6%
2014	OAK	10/2	229	12	27	115	44%	-3.5	9.6	0	2	3.3	--	-1.8	2	-39.4%	--	-57	--	-54	38%	35%	19%	8%
2015	CIN			11	22	146	50%	--	13.2	1						-17.7%								

Moore's Wikipedia page has an amusing blurb about how he only caught one of seven targets in a 2012 game. That's such an Oakland thing these days. Moore (46.9 percent), Darrius Heyward-Bey (46.6 percent), and Louis Murphy (45.1 percent), all drafted by the Raiders, have the three lowest catch rates among active wide receivers (minimum 100 catches). Neither Heyward-Bey nor Murphy have improved much since leaving the Black Hole. Moore gets his shot after a solid run as a fifth-round pick, but he fell completely out of favor with Derek Carr's style of passing last year. A big-play receiver, Moore went from averaging 15.8 yards per catch in his first three seasons to just 9.6 yards per catch in 2014. He'll see more erratic quarterback play in Cincinnati with Andy Dalton, although he'll mostly see it in practice rather than in games unless there are injuries. Moore is not the high-percentage threat the Bengals offense needs, but they definitely needed the depth.

Lance Moore Height: 5-9 Weight: 177 College: Toledo Draft: 2005/FA Born: 31-Aug-1983 Age: 32 Risk: Red

Year	Team	G/GS	Snaps	Rec	Pass	Yds	C%	+/-	Yd/C	TD	Drop	YAC	Rk	YAC+	BTkl	DVOA	Rk	DYAR	Rk	YAR	Short	Mid	Deep	Bomb
2012	NO	15/7	608	65	104	1041	63%	+6.6	16.0	6	5	2.2	83	-1.9	0	31.2%	5	356	7	344	21%	46%	18%	15%
2013	NO	13/5	441	37	54	457	69%	+6.4	12.4	2	3	1.8	90	-2.2	0	22.1%	11	150	30	153	28%	50%	15%	7%
2014	PIT	14/2	262	14	26	198	54%	-1.2	14.1	2	2	2.9	--	-1.2	1	-2.8%	--	20	--	16	35%	27%	31%	8%
2015	DET			8	13	95	62%	--	11.9	--						-3.2%								

Lance Moore was expecting to play a greater role for the Steelers in 2014. He didn't manage to do that because younger, more athletic players were given chances in the slot ahead of him. Even though Moore is still a technically sound receiver with impressive ball skills, he has lost a step physically—a step that he couldn't afford to lose because he has never been an above average athlete. The Lions shouldn't have high expectations for Moore in 2015, and he may not even make the final roster, although he does have experience working with offensive coordinator Joe Lombardi in New Orleans.

Josh Morgan Height: 6-0 Weight: 219 College: Virginia Tech Draft: 2008/6 (174) Born: 20-Jun-1985 Age: 30 Risk: Red

Year	Team	G/GS	Snaps	Rec	Pass	Yds	C%	+/-	Yd/C	TD	Drop	YAC	Rk	YAC+	BTkl	DVOA	Rk	DYAR	Rk	YAR	Short	Mid	Deep	Bomb
2012	WAS	16/15	708	48	74	510	65%	-0.4	10.6	2	5	4.9	31	-0.1	7	-6.9%	65	17	68	39	41%	45%	8%	6%
2013	WAS	14/7	385	20	35	214	63%	+0.5	10.7	0	2	5.2	--	+0.2	1	-14.1%	--	-4	--	3	45%	39%	15%	0%
2014	CHI	14/7	422	10	19	70	53%	-2.3	7.0	1	1	5.0	--	-0.4	2	-30.4%	--	-27	--	-27	72%	17%	0%	11%
2015	NO			15	24	164	63%	--	10.9	1						-2.9%								

As statements about wide receivers go, 422 snaps and only 19 targets is about as clear as you can get. Morgan was a decoy and mini-tight end rather than one of those wide receivers who catches passes. The Saints signed him in May, reuniting him with John Morton, his receivers coach with San Francisco. Morgan said after signing with the Saints he "just [wanted] to go to a team where I could have an impact." New Orleans' depth chart gives him the opportunity, though his best role might be that already occupied by Marques Colston.

Santana Moss Height: 5-10 Weight: 185 College: Miami Draft: 2001/1 (16) Born: 1-Jun-1979 Age: 36 Risk: N/A

Year	Team	G/GS	Snaps	Rec	Pass	Yds	C%	+/-	Yd/C	TD	Drop	YAC	Rk	YAC+	BTkl	DVOA	Rk	DYAR	Rk	YAR	Short	Mid	Deep	Bomb
2012	WAS	16/1	454	41	63	573	67%	+2.3	14.0	8	3	5.8	16	+0.5	5	11.6%	22	98	41	126	47%	35%	12%	7%
2013	WAS	16/1	550	42	79	452	54%	-7.4	10.8	2	6	4.3	59	-0.5	1	-28.3%	87	-97	87	-74	39%	47%	11%	3%
2014	WAS	10/0	131	10	15	116	67%	+0.4	11.6	0	1	7.4	--	+2.0	1	1.4%	--	15	--	16	50%	36%	7%	7%

You probably assumed that Moss was retired and covering preseason games for the Redskins Television Network when suddenly you saw him, wearing a uniform and pads but the official burgundy wool cap of the Paid-but-Forgotten Redskins Veteran, shouting at referees until he drew two penalties and an ejection for arguing a call before halftime of the Week 15 Giants game. The penalties set up an easy onside kick for the Giants after halftime, which led to a Giants field goal, which led to... look, a lot of engineering goes into these incomprehensible Redskins failures, okay? A quick scan of the bottom of the Redskins depth chart in July shows no Santana Moss, Joey Galloway, Peerless Price, or Plaxico Burress types drawing a paycheck and taking a job away from a potential prospect. It's as encouraging a sign of progress in Washington as you are going to find.

Louis Murphy

		Height: 6-3		Weight: 203		College: Florida			Draft: 2009/4 (124)		Born: 11-May-1987			Age: 28		Risk: Green	
Year	Team	G/GS	Snaps	Rec	Pass	Yds	C%	+/-	Yd/C	TD	Drop	YAC	Rk	YAC+	BTkl	DVOA	Rk	DYAR	Rk	YAR	Short	Mid	Deep	Bomb
2012	CAR	16/5	666	25	62	336	42%	-5.5	13.4	1	2	2.6	79	-2.0	0	-37.2%	85	-118	84	-109	23%	43%	16%	18%
2013	NYG	14/0	99	6	13	37	46%	-1.6	6.2	1	1	1.0	--	-2.9	0	-61.2%	--	-50	--	-48	38%	54%	0%	8%
2014	TB	11/3	456	31	56	380	55%	-3.1	12.3	2	5	4.1	53	-0.2	4	-15.3%	77	-11	74	-3	24%	48%	20%	7%
2015	TB			18	38	209	47%	--	11.6	1						-25.3%								

Louis Murphy's Law would say that Tampa's No. 18 cannot rank in the top 60 of wide receivers in DVOA. In six NFL seasons, Murphy has never posted a DVOA higher than his -8.7% rating that ranked 69th in 2010. Quarterbacks and coaching can't entirely account for numbers that bad. Last season, Murphy caught four of 18 third-down targets for a DVOA of -56.1%. Yikes.

Jordy Nelson

		Height: 6-2		Weight: 217		College: Kansas State			Draft: 2008/2 (36)		Born: 31-May-1985			Age: 30		Risk: Green	
Year	Team	G/GS	Snaps	Rec	Pass	Yds	C%	+/-	Yd/C	TD	Drop	YAC	Rk	YAC+	BTkl	DVOA	Rk	DYAR	Rk	YAR	Short	Mid	Deep	Bomb
2012	GB	12/10	593	49	73	745	67%	+8.1	15.2	7	6	5.1	24	+1.2	3	30.8%	6	292	13	264	24%	54%	10%	13%
2013	GB	16/16	1083	85	127	1314	67%	+14.2	15.5	8	4	4.8	37	-0.1	11	26.7%	6	402	2	408	37%	33%	20%	10%
2014	GB	16/16	959	98	151	1519	65%	+11.6	15.5	13	3	5.1	27	+0.6	11	26.8%	8	482	2	487	27%	45%	16%	12%
2015	GB			88	139	1239	63%	--	14.1	10							17.9%								

Nelson was an ineffective red zone receiver in 2014, which makes his 13 touchdowns an all the more remarkable figure. His 46 percent catch rate and -13.1% DVOA were the result of too many isolation routes where his only option was to win one-on-one. Good thing, then, that he scored five touchdowns from the far side of midfield to make up for just four red zone scores. Offseason hip surgery limited his offseason workload and he is now 30, but he still has that mystical connection with Aaron Rodgers that serves them both so well when improvising so many of those big plays.

Hakeem Nicks

		Height: 6-3		Weight: 212		College: North Carolina			Draft: 2009/1 (29)		Born: 14-Jan-1988			Age: 27		Risk: Green	
Year	Team	G/GS	Snaps	Rec	Pass	Yds	C%	+/-	Yd/C	TD	Drop	YAC	Rk	YAC+	BTkl	DVOA	Rk	DYAR	Rk	YAR	Short	Mid	Deep	Bomb
2012	NYG	13/11	668	53	100	692	53%	-2.6	13.1	3	3	3.7	52	-0.2	2	-5.9%	60	67	50	55	25%	51%	15%	9%
2013	NYG	15/15	833	56	101	896	55%	+1.5	16.0	0	7	4.8	38	+0.3	7	-2.4%	56	83	50	121	24%	47%	18%	12%
2014	IND	16/6	576	38	68	405	56%	-4.4	10.7	4	2	3.4	68	-1.7	4	-12.7%	70	0	70	3	38%	37%	17%	8%
2015	TEN			20	39	218	51%	--	10.9	1							-25.3%								

This guy looked like the real deal after winning a Super Bowl with the Giants in his third season. After two subpar seasons, we thought he just needed his health and better quarterback play to get back on track. Nicks found both of those things in a one-year deal with Indianapolis, but he really struggled to get on the same page with Andrew Luck. Things really didn't click until December, and even then it was in a minor role. Nicks has moved on to Tennessee in the form of another one-year deal, but it's hard to generate any real expectations for him as a secondary receiver with a rookie quarterback (though playing-time expectations went up a bit with Justin Hunter's July arrest).

DeVante Parker

		Height: 6-3		Weight: 209		College: Louisville			Draft: 2015/1 (14)		Born: 20-Jan-1993			Age: 22		Risk: Red	
Year	Team	G/GS	Snaps	Rec	Pass	Yds	C%	+/-	Yd/C	TD	Drop	YAC	Rk	YAC+	BTkl	DVOA	Rk	DYAR	Rk	YAR	Short	Mid	Deep	Bomb
2015	MIA			36	66	556	55%	--	15.5	3							-2.3%								

When it comes to a realistic level of expectations for Parker in 2015, there are some serious issues to consider. In addition to the usual rookie curve, he is coming off offseason foot surgery for an issue that dogged him going back a couple of seasons, and remains a question mark for Week 1. In addition, despite the fact that he was a first-round pick of the Dolphins, his college numbers were surprisingly low for a receiver taken 14th overall: although Parker had some impressive per-game numbers in a shortened senior year, he never topped 1,000 yards once in his collegiate career, despite the fact that he had Teddy Bridgewater throwing him the ball as a junior. That puts his Playmaker Score pretty low at 45.9 percent. While there's always a possibility for a surprise, it appears that his prospects for success in the Miami offense in 2015 are dicey.

Preston Parker

Height: 6-0 — Weight: 200 — College: North Alabama — Draft: 2010/FA — Born: 13-Feb-1987 — Age: 28 — Risk: Green

Year	Team	G/GS	Snaps	Rec	Pass	Yds	C%	+/-	Yd/C	TD	Drop	YAC	Rk	YAC+	BTkl	DVOA	Rk	DYAR	Rk	YAR	Short	Mid	Deep	Bomb
2012	TB	2/0	35	0	2	0	0%	-1.5	0.0	0	0	0.0	--	0.0	0	-104.4%	--	-13	--	-14	100%	0%	0%	0%
2014	NYG	16/7	593	36	56	418	64%	+1.0	11.6	2	1	3.3	74	-0.9	5	3.2%	39	70	49	82	32%	46%	16%	5%
2015	NYG			17	28	197	61%	--	11.6	1						-5.7%								

Parker caught seven passes for 79 yards and a touchdown against the Seahawks in Week 10 last season. Kam Chancellor was out and Byron Maxwell was limited in that game, so slot receiver Parker had surprisingly easy sailing against the Substitute Legion of Boom. After that, he settled into a role as a rarely-targeted third receiver who catches a pass or two per game, reappearing on the news feed late in the year when he went berserk defending Odell Beckham after a late hit out of bounds in the Rams game. Parker brings little to the table as a receiver or returner and will fight for a roster spot now that Dwayne Harris is in town and Victor Cruz is coming back. Of course, the Giants' injury woes make the distinction between depth-chart fodder and starter pretty blurry.

Cordarrelle Patterson

Height: 6-2 — Weight: 216 — College: Tennessee — Draft: 2013/1 (29) — Born: 17-Mar-1991 — Age: 24 — Risk: Blue

Year	Team	G/GS	Snaps	Rec	Pass	Yds	C%	+/-	Yd/C	TD	Drop	YAC	Rk	YAC+	BTkl	DVOA	Rk	DYAR	Rk	YAR	Short	Mid	Deep	Bomb
2013	MIN	16/6	436	45	77	469	58%	-2.5	10.4	4	3	6.1	8	-0.4	18	-12.0%	74	4	73	-3	49%	23%	15%	13%
2014	MIN	16/7	566	33	67	384	49%	-4.8	11.6	1	1	4.8	35	+0.1	7	-25.0%	85	-64	85	-46	39%	37%	12%	12%
2015	MIN			21	40	228	53%	--	10.8	0						-23.6%								

Before illness, injury, and irascibility took hold, Percy Harvin was once the embodiment of how a Swiss Army knife could elevate an offense rather than languish as an ill-fitting tweener. Minnesota enjoyed the best of Harvin and attempted to replicate that experience with Patterson, but the former first-rounder has skipped straight to the Jets phase of Harvin's career. Among receivers to receive at least 50 targets each of the past two seasons, only Patterson, Jason Avant, and Cecil Shorts have finished with bottom-20 DVOA rankings in both seasons. That doesn't even account for Patterson's decline on gadget run plays (from 118 DYAR to 53 DYAR) and kick returns (from 19.9 points above average to -2.6 points below) after leading his position in both categories his rookie year. Few receivers were as consistently blanketed in coverage, as his raw route-running doesn't appear to have matured much from his collegiate days. The Vikings seem unlikely to cut bait on Patterson so soon, but he'll need to prove capable of handling more than the odd jet sweep to avoid the bust label.

Breshad Perriman

Height: 6-2 — Weight: 212 — College: UCF — Draft: 2015/1 (26) — Born: 10-Sep-1993 — Age: 22 — Risk: Red

Year	Team	G/GS	Snaps	Rec	Pass	Yds	C%	+/-	Yd/C	TD	Drop	YAC	Rk	YAC+	BTkl	DVOA	Rk	DYAR	Rk	YAR	Short	Mid	Deep	Bomb
2015	BAL			53	89	882	60%	--	16.6	5						9.4%								

The son of former Lions standout Brett, Perriman enters the league with a top-notch Playmaker Score (87.7 percent) and a gaudy yards per reception average (20.9 as a junior). Drops were a concern, however, and he had just a 53 percent catch rate in college. Perhaps the best indicator of Perriman's readiness for the NFL is that he put up consistent numbers even though his quarterback at Central Florida changed from future top draft pick Blake Bortles to future drywall deliveryman Justin Holman. Perriman will be asked to slot into Torrey Smith's deep threat role immediately, and is probably worth scooping up in the late rounds of your fantasy draft.

Austin Pettis

Height: 6-3 — Weight: 209 — College: Boise State — Draft: 2011/3 (78) — Born: 7-May-1988 — Age: 27 — Risk: Green

Year	Team	G/GS	Snaps	Rec	Pass	Yds	C%	+/-	Yd/C	TD	Drop	YAC	Rk	YAC+	BTkl	DVOA	Rk	DYAR	Rk	YAR	Short	Mid	Deep	Bomb
2012	STL	14/2	374	30	48	261	63%	+1.4	8.7	4	1	2.6	--	-1.5	1	0.6%	--	35	--	44	53%	33%	4%	9%
2013	STL	16/6	579	38	63	399	60%	+0.7	10.5	4	2	3.1	80	-1.1	1	5.1%	30	90	49	85	39%	40%	13%	8%
2014	STL	5/0	135	12	18	118	67%	+0.1	9.8	1	2	4.4	--	-0.2	2	-6.0%	--	10	--	18	56%	22%	22%	0%
2015	SD			16	26	171	62%	--	10.7	0						-10.0%								

Pettis specializes in effective short catches. Eleven of his 12 receptions last year came within 10 yards of the line of scrimmage, but only one of those was a failed reception. Still, no team with Tavon Austin, Benny Cunningham, Jared Cook, and

Lance Kendricks among its leading receivers needs a dink-and-dunk guy out wide, and Pettis was deactivated for the Week 7 win against Seattle and then released the following week. In January he signed with San Diego where he could have value as a complement to Keenan Allen with Malcom Floyd stretching defenses deep.

Brian Quick Height: 6-4   Weight: 220   College: Appalachian State   Draft: 2012/2 (33)   Born: 5-Jun-1989   Age: 26   Risk: Red

Year	Team	G/GS	Snaps	Rec	Pass	Yds	C%	+/-	Yd/C	TD	Drop	YAC	Rk	YAC+	BTkl	DVOA	Rk	DYAR	Rk	YAR	Short	Mid	Deep	Bomb
2012	STL	15/1	182	11	27	156	41%	-4.0	14.2	2	3	2.1	--	-2.0	0	-25.0%	--	-33	--	-35	30%	37%	26%	7%
2013	STL	16/5	353	18	34	302	53%	-1.4	16.8	2	2	5.8	--	+1.3	3	12.6%	--	72	--	67	44%	29%	15%	12%
2014	STL	7/7	339	25	39	375	64%	+4.1	15.0	3	1	2.9	--	-1.0	1	24.5%	--	115	--	119	16%	42%	21%	21%
2015	STL			56	100	787	56%	--	14.1	5						-4.2%								

Quick was actually ranked amoong the top 20 wideouts in both DVOA and DYAR when he dislocated his shoulder and tore his rotator cuff against Kansas City in Week 8. Latest word on his recovery is that he will probably miss part of training camp, but should be healthy enough to play in Week 1. Quick still trailed Jared Cook in both targets and receptions even before his injury, and three years into his career he has never had a 100-yard game (99 yards against Minnesota in the season opener was his best), so he was never a dominant player, but it's not too hard to imagine a healthy Quick teaming with Kenny Britt as an effective starting duo in 2015. Statistically, the most similar player to Brian Quick in 2014 was Michael Irvin in 1989, which is about the best career a big-body type like Quick could hope to emulate. The rest of Quick's one-year matches, though, aren't nearly as impressive, including names like Reche Caldwell and Chaz Schilens and whoever the hell Matt Bouza was. The top three-year comps—Brandon Stokley, Riley Cooper, David Dunn, Trevor Gaylor, and Leonard Hankerson—suggest modest potential for Quick to develop into a decent starter, while still leaving plenty of room for the bottom to totally drop out.

Rueben Randle Height: 6-3   Weight: 210   College: Louisiana St.   Draft: 2012/2 (63)   Born: 7-May-1991   Age: 24   Risk: Green

Year	Team	G/GS	Snaps	Rec	Pass	Yds	C%	+/-	Yd/C	TD	Drop	YAC	Rk	YAC+	BTkl	DVOA	Rk	DYAR	Rk	YAR	Short	Mid	Deep	Bomb
2012	NYG	16/1	245	19	32	298	59%	-0.2	15.7	3	1	3.8	--	-1.0	2	16.3%	--	96	--	87	34%	44%	13%	9%
2013	NYG	16/3	578	41	79	611	52%	-2.1	14.9	6	4	4.8	36	+0.1	6	-1.5%	53	71	53	87	22%	39%	24%	15%
2014	NYG	16/13	961	71	127	938	56%	-4.8	13.2	3	4	3.3	72	-0.9	9	-9.3%	62	34	58	54	26%	51%	13%	10%
2015	NYG			46	81	595	57%	--	12.9	4						-3.3%								

Randle was late for a handful of meetings last season and ended up getting benched in first quarters as punishment several times late in the year. The benchings may have woken Randle up, because he caught 12 passes for 290 yards and a touchdown in his final two games. Randle had a hard time mastering Kevin Gilbride's system and tested Ben McAdoo's patience a few times last season, but Tom Coughlin can be surprisingly tolerant of wifty receivers (see Plaxico Burress, Mario Manningham). Randle fits best as a No. 3 receiver behind Odell Beckham and Victor Cruz (with Cruz in the slot for three-wide situations), but he can be a solid No. 2 if the light bulb has been properly screwed in.

Paul Richardson Height: 6-0   Weight: 175   College: Colorado   Draft: 2014/2 (45)   Born: 4/13/1992   Age: 23   Risk: Red

Year	Team	G/GS	Snaps	Rec	Pass	Yds	C%	+/-	Yd/C	TD	Drop	YAC	Rk	YAC+	BTkl	DVOA	Rk	DYAR	Rk	YAR	Short	Mid	Deep	Bomb
2014	SEA	15/6	497	29	44	271	66%	+4.1	9.3	1	1	2.2	--	-2.6	2	-15.2%	--	-8	--	-1	35%	43%	8%	15%
2015	SEA			21	32	231	66%	--	11.0	0						-2.5%								

Richardson is tiny and fast, running a 4.33-second 40-yard dash at the 2014 combine. That suggests either a Dexter McCluster-esque screen player or DeSean Jackson-type bomb threat. Instead, he specialized as a rookie in midrange passes 6 to 15 yards downfield. His DVOA on 18 targets there was 42.9%; on his other 26 targets, it was -56.9%. Richardson tore his ACL in the divisional playoff game against Carolina, and though the team was holding out hope he would be healthy in time for training camp, it's more likely that he spends most of August (and perhaps even September or October) on the sidelines.

Andre Roberts

Height: 5-11 Weight: 195 College: The Citadel Draft: 2010/3 (88) Born: 9-Jan-1988 Age: 27 Risk: Yellow

Year	Team	G/GS	Snaps	Rec	Pass	Yds	C%	+/-	Yd/C	TD	Drop	YAC	Rk	YAC+	BTkl	DVOA	Rk	DYAR	Rk	YAR	Short	Mid	Deep	Bomb
2012	ARI	15/15	837	64	114	759	56%	-2.3	11.9	5	8	3.5	60	-0.4	3	-6.5%	63	12	72	25	36%	47%	13%	5%
2013	ARI	16/2	605	43	76	471	57%	-3.2	11.0	2	1	2.6	86	-2.3	2	-15.3%	76	-15	75	-5	31%	40%	17%	12%
2014	WAS	16/4	693	36	73	453	49%	-7.0	12.6	2	5	5.7	17	+0.8	3	-14.2%	73	-9	73	-27	36%	41%	17%	6%
2015	WAS			39	67	480	58%	--	12.3	3						-7.1%								

Roberts dropped five passes and was the targeted receiver on six interceptions. After 20 receptions in the first six games, he slowly slid off the back of the game plan, catching just nine passes in the final six Redskins games. Roberts has been going backward steadily since his impressive 2013 season with the Cardinals. He is expected to compete for the No. 3 receiver role with Jamison Crowder and others but looks like a very replaceable part.

Allen Robinson

Height: 6-2 Weight: 220 College: Penn St. Draft: 2014/2 (61) Born: 8/24/1993 Age: 22 Risk: Yellow

Year	Team	G/GS	Snaps	Rec	Pass	Yds	C%	+/-	Yd/C	TD	Drop	YAC	Rk	YAC+	BTkl	DVOA	Rk	DYAR	Rk	YAR	Short	Mid	Deep	Bomb
2014	JAC	10/8	516	48	81	548	59%	-0.2	11.4	2	1	3.3	71	-1.0	3	-11.1%	64	10	66	9	27%	53%	9%	11%
2015	JAC			70	118	870	59%	--	12.4	5						-5.6%								

The second of Jacksonville's two second-round receivers from 2014, Robinson had a better rookie season than his comrade Marquise Lee. Robinson showed off the versatility to run anywhere in the route tree, and also played more technically sound than he looked coming out of Penn State. A broken foot sidelined him through most of November and December, but he was fine—if you consider glowing reviews from the AP as "fine"—for OTAs. Someone in this Jacksonville offense is going to have to soak up Cecil Shorts' targets, and they're not all going to Julius Thomas. Robinson is where the smart money is. The next step in his development is to better use his frame to shield the ball while absorbing contact. If he pulls that off, he could grow up to be the next Anquan Boldin.

Jeremy Ross

Height: 5-11 Weight: 213 College: California Draft: 2011/FA Born: 16-Mar-1988 Age: 27 Risk: Green

Year	Team	G/GS	Snaps	Rec	Pass	Yds	C%	+/-	Yd/C	TD	Drop	YAC	Rk	YAC+	BTkl	DVOA	Rk	DYAR	Rk	YAR	Short	Mid	Deep	Bomb
2012	GB	5/0	2	0	--	0	--	--	--	0	--	--	--	--	--	--	--	--	--	--	--	--	--	--
2013	2TM	13/2	185	6	12	67	50%	-2.1	11.2	1	2	3.2	--	-0.9	4	-6.8%	--	6	--	6	67%	25%	8%	0%
2014	DET	16/13	709	24	35	314	69%	+2.8	13.1	1	2	5.8	--	+0.4	7	0.2%	--	34	--	41	41%	35%	12%	12%
2015	DET			9	14	97	64%	--	10.8	0						-5.1%								

Though he was technically the Lions' No. 3 receiver in name, it never really felt like Ross carved out a meaningful offensive role in 2014. While he easily set career-highs in every major receiving category besides touchdowns, Ross never compiled more than three catches in a single game. And if not for a 59-yard touchdown against the Jets on an apparent coverage bust, he would never have had more than 35 receiving yards in any game. Ross' main value is on special teams, though, so the real issue is the career-low 8.9 yards per punt return average he posted last season, as well as his five fumbles. Detroit doesn't seem inclined to give Golden Tate return opportunities given his importance to the offense, but it would behoove Ross to recapture his 2012-13 return form so that the coaching staff doesn't need to reconsider his roster spot.

Eddie Royal

Height: 5-9 Weight: 184 College: Virginia Tech Draft: 2008/2 (42) Born: 21-May-1986 Age: 29 Risk: Green

Year	Team	G/GS	Snaps	Rec	Pass	Yds	C%	+/-	Yd/C	TD	Drop	YAC	Rk	YAC+	BTkl	DVOA	Rk	DYAR	Rk	YAR	Short	Mid	Deep	Bomb
2012	SD	10/2	272	23	44	234	52%	-4.4	10.2	1	0	3.9	--	-1.2	1	-22.7%	--	-56	--	-46	44%	42%	9%	5%
2013	SD	15/3	705	47	67	631	70%	+4.3	13.4	8	2	7.1	5	+1.6	4	31.6%	4	238	15	255	43%	28%	19%	10%
2014	SD	16/11	760	62	91	778	68%	+7.0	12.5	7	3	5.8	13	-0.1	6	12.8%	17	183	26	159	51%	22%	16%	11%
2015	CHI			41	63	459	65%	--	11.2	2						-3.9%								

If Jay Cutler's reunion with Brandon Marshall had to end, why not start another one with Eddie Royal in Chicago? The last time we saw the two together was in the 2008 Denver season finale against San Diego. Down 52-21 in the final minute of a game that decided the AFC West, Cutler threw four in-cuts to Royal for 34 meaningless yards. Those meaningless catches moved Royal past Terry Glenn for the second-most catches by a rookie (91) in NFL history, so the garbage-time hero prevailed again. Last season in San Diego, Royal finished with 778 yards, tied for the second-most receiving yards ever by a team's fourth-leading receiver. Wes Welker had 778 yards on the 2013 Broncos, and Curtis Duncan had 785 yards on the 1990 Oilers. Royal should fit right in the slot in this Chicago offense with Alshon Jeffery and rookie Kevin White on the outside. He's an improvement over Marquess Wilson and the *My Left Foot* version of Santonio Holmes.

Emmanuel Sanders

Height: 5-11   Weight: 186   College: Southern Methodist   Draft: 2010/3 (82)   Born: 17-Mar-1987   Age: 28   Risk: Green

Year	Team	G/GS	Snaps	Rec	Pass	Yds	C%	+/-	Yd/C	TD	Drop	YAC	Rk	YAC+	BTkl	DVOA	Rk	DYAR	Rk	YAR	Short	Mid	Deep	Bomb
2012	PIT	16/7	721	44	74	626	59%	+1.0	14.2	1	4	4.8	32	+0.1	3	9.5%	25	124	38	121	36%	28%	30%	6%
2013	PIT	16/10	796	67	113	740	60%	-0.5	11.0	6	2	4.4	54	-0.9	7	-10.2%	71	22	69	-1	37%	35%	14%	15%
2014	DEN	16/16	1000	101	141	1404	72%	+16.3	13.9	9	0	3.5	65	-1.4	6	29.6%	4	481	3	457	40%	27%	15%	19%
2015	DEN			85	134	1142	63%	--	13.4	8						8.8%								

Last offseason Sanders was finding it hard to believe he was in wide receiver heaven with Peyton Manning as his quarterback. We got our first glimpse of the duo in a preseason game against Houston when Sanders caught five passes for 128 yards and two touchdowns in a half, two things he never did in any of his 56 regular-season games with the Steelers during the previous four years. "Never did that before" remained a theme throughout the season as Sanders reinvented himself as a deep threat fully capable of playing both outside and from the slot. Sanders' 1,404 receiving yards are the most ever by a free agent in his team debut, beating out the old record of 1,397 yards by Henry Ellard on the 1994 Redskins. Sanders and Demaryius Thomas became the fourth pair of teammates in NFL history to each have at least 1,400 receiving yards in the same season. It's not crazy to say Sanders was more impressive last season than Thomas. Sanders had the most targets (141) in the league without an uncontested dropped pass, though he did have two passes marked in our charting as "dropped/defensed," meaning Sanders had the ball in his hands but lost it when hit by a defender. His plus/minus (plus-16.3) was the second highest in the league behind only Antonio Brown (plus-16.5). Sanders has expressed doubt in his ability to put up big numbers in Kubiak's new offense, and it's only logical that he'll see some regression after such a career year. He should still be a very effective receiver in this offense even if the volume isn't as great.

Mohamed Sanu

Height: 6-2   Weight: 211   College: Rutgers   Draft: 2012/3 (83)   Born: 22-Aug-1989   Age: 26   Risk: Green

Year	Team	G/GS	Snaps	Rec	Pass	Yds	C%	+/-	Yd/C	TD	Drop	YAC	Rk	YAC+	BTkl	DVOA	Rk	DYAR	Rk	YAR	Short	Mid	Deep	Bomb
2012	CIN	9/3	204	16	25	154	64%	+0.6	9.6	4	1	4.4	--	-0.8	0	13.8%	--	42	--	54	42%	50%	8%	0%
2013	CIN	16/14	749	47	78	455	60%	+1.2	9.7	2	6	5.4	23	+0.1	2	-10.0%	69	17	71	2	45%	33%	11%	11%
2014	CIN	16/13	986	56	98	790	57%	-6.7	14.1	5	6	5.8	16	+0.7	6	0.1%	43	99	40	91	35%	40%	12%	12%
2015	CIN			41	67	519	61%	--	12.7	3						-3.0%								

Sanu was arguably Cincinnati's MVP in the first half of the season, picking up the slack in the wake of injuries to A.J. Green, Marvin Jones, and Tyler Eifert. But carrying the passing game seemed to tucker him out. The drops mounted badly (our six charted drops are extremely conservative—other counters, including the Bengals themselves, had him in double-digits), and Andy Dalton clearly lost trust in the receiver he counted on the most before fall turned to winter. Sanu does contribute in other ways, notably throwing passes (he's a career 5-for-5 with two touchdowns as a gimmick play quarterback), and if he plays a more natural role as a third wideout, he is valuable. He needs to be, for this is a contract year; he has to be more reliable to earn a new bounty.

Cecil Shorts

Height: 6-0 Weight: 200 College: Mount Union Draft: 2011/4 (114) Born: 22-Dec-1987 Age: 28 Risk: Red

Year	Team	G/GS	Snaps	Rec	Pass	Yds	C%	+/-	Yd/C	TD	Drop	YAC	Rk	YAC+	BTkl	DVOA	Rk	DYAR	Rk	YAR	Short	Mid	Deep	Bomb
2012	JAC	14/9	654	55	105	979	52%	-3.3	17.8	7	8	6.5	8	+2.7	9	5.2%	30	138	32	164	29%	39%	21%	11%
2013	JAC	13/13	759	66	125	777	53%	-5.5	11.8	3	7	4.2	62	-0.7	3	-16.3%	79	-36	79	-32	36%	36%	18%	10%
2014	JAC	13/12	741	53	110	557	48%	-13.2	10.5	1	4	4.9	33	+0.0	5	-33.7%	87	-183	87	-187	39%	44%	13%	4%
2015	HOU			44	79	564	56%	--	12.8	3						-8.6%								

The Texans replaced Andre Johnson with the one qualifying receiver in the NFL with less DYAR and a lower DVOA. Shorts was not done any favors by Blake Bortles and the Jacksonville scheme last season, but his subpar hands also played a big role in his poor year. Treated like a leper in free agency, Shorts has arrived on a depth chart he should be able to top. Can he do better with the Houston quarterback carousel? That's less likely to be a happy result. Still, Shorts is only a year removed from being regarded as a solid receiver. This is a solid buy-low by the Texans.

Devin Smith

Height: 6-0 Weight: 196 College: Ohio State Draft: 2015/2 (37) Born: 3-Mar-1992 Age: 23 Risk: Yellow

Year	Team	G/GS	Snaps	Rec	Pass	Yds	C%	+/-	Yd/C	TD	Drop	YAC	Rk	YAC+	BTkl	DVOA	Rk	DYAR	Rk	YAR	Short	Mid	Deep	Bomb
2015	NYJ			10	19	181	53%	--	18.1	2						6.3%								

The Jets are lacking a traditional burner, so please welcome second-round pick Devin Smith. Smith's numbers at Ohio State are certifiably insane, particularly as a senior: he only caught 33 passes, but had 931 yards and 12 touchdowns because he was gaining a mind-numbing 28.2 yards per pass. He also ran his combine 40 in 4.42 seconds. Smith certainly has the ability to stretch the field, and does a nice job tracking the ball, but he doesn't offer much in the way of short and intermediate offerings at this stage of his career. He'll have to take a couple years to learn the whole route tree; in the meantime, the deep ball is one of Geno Smith's better skills. Devin Smith also brings extra value on special teams, as NFL.com called him the best gunner in college football last season.

Steve Smith

Height: 5-9 Weight: 185 College: Utah Draft: 2001/3 (74) Born: 12-May-1979 Age: 36 Risk: Yellow

Year	Team	G/GS	Snaps	Rec	Pass	Yds	C%	+/-	Yd/C	TD	Drop	YAC	Rk	YAC+	BTkl	DVOA	Rk	DYAR	Rk	YAR	Short	Mid	Deep	Bomb
2012	CAR	16/16	910	73	138	1174	53%	-2.6	16.1	4	8	3.7	53	-0.5	6	4.0%	34	171	27	161	18%	46%	26%	10%
2013	CAR	15/15	770	64	110	745	58%	-0.3	11.6	4	5	2.8	84	-1.7	12	-3.7%	58	74	51	80	27%	52%	13%	8%
2014	BAL	16/16	822	79	134	1065	59%	-3.7	13.5	6	5	4.7	37	+0.3	13	-5.4%	53	79	45	57	33%	44%	12%	11%
2015	BAL			71	122	867	58%	--	12.2	6						-5.1%								

Smith's 2014 was less a football season than a stand-up comedy tour. When he was cut by the Panthers as part of Carolina's salary-cap butchery, Smith said that should he play against his old team, fans would need to "put their goggles on, because there's going to be blood and guts everywhere." When he indeed tangled with Carolina in his Vengeance Is Mine game, he scored a pair of touchdowns, then told the Panthers to "mow his lawn" when they got back to Charlotte. Asked about his stamina before a game, he replied, "You can ask my wife about my stamina." On playing on *Monday Night Football*—"Ex-girlfriends that wish they didn't dump you are questioning themselves right now. That's why I'm not on Facebook." And on and on. It's as though the Ravens signed a receiver and got Louis C.K. instead.

And like the comic born Louis Szekaly, the wideout adopted a stage name, suddenly becoming "Steve Smith, Sr." He played like a man reborn, at least during the first half of the season. Then in Week 8, he caught an apparent game-winning bomb against the Bengals, only to be flagged for offensive pass interference. After that, the jokes dried up, and his numbers cratered, hardly surprising for a 35-year-old wideout. Smith went from 11.2% DVOA in Weeks 1-8 to -22.3% DVOA in Weeks 9-17. His catch rate and the average distance of his passes stayed the same; the problem is that his YAC dropped from 6.6 per catch to 2.6, a number much more in line with the gradual decline of his career in Carolina.

With Torrey Smith gone, Triple-S will now line up across from a collection of receivers with just 104 NFL receptions combined. If this is Smith's swan song, he should contact Comedy Central about developing a pilot.

Torrey Smith Height: 6-1   Weight: 204   College: Maryland   Draft: 2011/2 (58)   Born: 26-Jan-1989   Age: 26   Risk: Yellow

Year	Team	G/GS	Snaps	Rec	Pass	Yds	C%	+/-	Yd/C	TD	Drop	YAC	Rk	YAC+	BTkl	DVOA	Rk	DYAR	Rk	YAR	Short	Mid	Deep	Bomb
2012	BAL	16/16	919	49	110	855	45%	-5.9	17.4	8	5	4.6	34	+0.1	4	0.7%	42	143	31	132	21%	34%	15%	30%
2013	BAL	16/16	1099	65	137	1128	47%	-4.3	17.4	4	3	5.5	21	+0.7	2	0.0%	48	139	33	98	25%	32%	22%	21%
2014	BAL	16/16	788	49	92	767	53%	-3.0	15.7	11	5	3.4	69	-1.0	6	26.8%	7	310	9	304	16%	46%	17%	22%
2015	SF			49	94	810	52%	--	16.5	6						-4.0%								

No one caused the yellow hankies to fly more often last season than Smith, who drew a remarkable 11 pass interference penalties totaling 229 yards. That's five flags and an even hundred yards more than the next most-fouled receiver, Jordy Nelson. It's not a number that is likely to be repeated for his new employers in San Francisco, but clearly, Smith knows how to sell the drama. In the last two seasons, Smith has 17 DPIs for 324 yards. All of the 49ers wideouts combined only drew six interference calls in 2014. The hidden yardage offset his counting stats, which took an expected hit from the targets soaked up by that other Smith.

Few other quarterbacks can chuck the long ball like Joe Flacco, but Colin Kaepernick is one of them. The Niners quarterback badly needed a deep threat to help open up defenses and aid his ability to throw underneath. Smith is hardly consistent, but his big-play capability and underrated red zone efficiency make him a viable fantasy option—especially if your league counts pass interference yardage. (We know, it doesn't, but it should.)

Kenny Stills Height: 6-0   Weight: 194   College: Oklahoma   Draft: 2013/5 (144)   Born: 22-Apr-1992   Age: 23   Risk: Green

Year	Team	G/GS	Snaps	Rec	Pass	Yds	C%	+/-	Yd/C	TD	Drop	YAC	Rk	YAC+	BTkl	DVOA	Rk	DYAR	Rk	YAR	Short	Mid	Deep	Bomb
2013	NO	16/10	689	32	51	641	65%	+6.4	20.0	5	1	6.2	7	+1.5	1	40.1%	1	206	21	218	31%	24%	22%	22%
2014	NO	15/7	617	63	84	931	75%	+15.5	14.8	3	3	3.0	80	-1.6	2	30.3%	3	285	12	301	32%	35%	19%	15%
2015	MIA			57	97	762	59%	--	13.4	4						-4.0%								

Here's another SAT analogy. Kenny Stills : Tony Romo :: Mike Wallace : Colin Kaepernick. Stills, like Romo, is a plus athlete but also an outstanding technician with the ability to elevate his teammates. Wallace, like Kaepernick, is a great athlete who makes his teammates worse by showcasing consistently awful technique. While Wallace wasn't helped by Ryan Tannehill's iffy deep ball, that should be less of an issue for Stills because of his outstanding ball skills. Stills repeatedly bailed Drew Brees out last year by winning at the catch point. He tracks the ball as well as any receiver in the league and has the ball skills to manipulate defensive backs without illegally interfering with them.

Rod Streater Height: 6-3   Weight: 200   College: Temple   Draft: 2012/FA   Born: 9-Feb-1988   Age: 27   Risk: Green

Year	Team	G/GS	Snaps	Rec	Pass	Yds	C%	+/-	Yd/C	TD	Drop	YAC	Rk	YAC+	BTkl	DVOA	Rk	DYAR	Rk	YAR	Short	Mid	Deep	Bomb
2012	OAK	16/2	580	39	75	584	52%	-3.1	15.0	3	4	3.6	57	-0.7	0	-1.9%	51	43	60	61	19%	53%	16%	11%
2013	OAK	16/14	748	60	100	888	61%	+4.4	14.8	4	4	5.1	28	+0.3	3	13.6%	18	204	23	203	31%	42%	17%	10%
2014	OAK	3/3	86	9	13	84	69%	+0.4	9.3	1	0	3.3	--	-1.2	0	2.0%	--	15	--	18	31%	54%	0%	15%
2015	OAK			42	72	571	58%	--	13.6	3						-3.6%								

Anytime an Oakland wide receiver catches more than 60 percent of his targets, it's worth taking notice. Unfortunately Streater was unable to make further strides in his third season as he was limited to just three games after fracturing his foot. He'll likely start the 2015 season as the No. 3 wide receiver behind Amari Cooper and Michael Crabtree, but don't be surprised if he earns his share of production.

Jaelen Strong Height: 6-2   Weight: 217   College: Arizona State   Draft: 2015/3 (70)   Born: 25-Jan-1994   Age: 21   Risk: Red

Year	Team	G/GS	Snaps	Rec	Pass	Yds	C%	+/-	Yd/C	TD	Drop	YAC	Rk	YAC+	BTkl	DVOA	Rk	DYAR	Rk	YAR	Short	Mid	Deep	Bomb
2015	HOU			30	58	389	52%	--	13.0	2						-14.7%								

Jaelen Strong had a 80.7 percent Playmaker Score, which is just average for a first-round wide receiver prospect. Of course, that made it a pretty good move when Houston traded up for Strong in the third round. Much like DeAndre Hopkins, Strong's No. 1 ability as a receiver is his penchant for making contested catches in traffic, and head coach Bill O'Brien has said he'll be groomed purely as an outside receiver. With only Cecil Shorts and Nate Washington in his way, any signs of life should put

Strong on the fast track to starting. If his short-area burst succeeds, think of him as a successor to Marques Colston. If it doesn't, think of him more like Malcom Floyd. His possession skills should be valuable either way, but how "sudden" he'll be on the field is the question mark for his upside.

Brandon Tate							Height: 5-10		Weight: 183		College: North Carolina			Draft: 2009/3 (83)			Born: 5-Oct-1987			Age: 28		Risk: Blue	
Year	Team	G/GS	Snaps	Rec	Pass	Yds	C%	+/-	Yd/C	TD	Drop	YAC	Rk	YAC+	BTkl	DVOA	Rk	DYAR	Rk	YAR	Short	Mid	Deep	Bomb
2012	CIN	16/3	271	13	25	211	52%	-1.2	16.2	1	0	4.9	--	-0.2	3	-6.2%	--	18	--	10	33%	38%	8%	21%
2013	CIN	16/0	69	1	2	6	50%	-0.4	6.0	0	0	0.0	--	-2.9	0	-29.1%	--	-3	--	-5	0%	100%	0%	0%
2014	CIN	16/4	484	17	26	193	65%	+0.7	11.4	1	1	4.2	--	-1.6	1	8.5%	--	42	--	46	35%	42%	8%	15%
2015	CIN			7	12	82	58%	--	11.7	0						-11.2%								

Almost as unloved by Bengals Nation as Jermaine Gresham, Tate was made to look worse and worse every time Adam Jones returned a kick. As a wideout, Tate has never developed beyond a 9-route specialist. Since Cincy didn't draft a wideout in the early rounds, Tate still has a shot at the final roster simply through institutional memory.

Golden Tate							Height: 5-10		Weight: 199		College: Notre Dame			Draft: 2010/2 (60)			Born: 2-Aug-1988			Age: 27		Risk: Green	
Year	Team	G/GS	Snaps	Rec	Pass	Yds	C%	+/-	Yd/C	TD	Drop	YAC	Rk	YAC+	BTkl	DVOA	Rk	DYAR	Rk	YAR	Short	Mid	Deep	Bomb
2012	SEA	15/15	715	45	70	688	69%	+7.6	15.3	7	2	5.9	11	+0.3	14	31.6%	4	245	19	249	41%	25%	10%	24%
2013	SEA	16/13	762	64	100	898	66%	+5.4	14.0	5	4	7.6	1	+2.0	23	12.9%	19	196	24	206	44%	30%	11%	14%
2014	DET	16/16	924	99	144	1331	69%	+4.9	13.4	4	2	7.0	4	+1.5	18	6.7%	31	214	22	244	49%	33%	13%	4%
2015	DET			80	123	1007	65%	--	12.6	6						4.7%								

Your 2014 YAC leader among wide receivers, Tate was a lone wolf at times last season, serving as Matthew Stafford's only viable target during a midseason stretch in which Detroit's suffered a spate of injuries at the fantasy football positions. Tate's surface numbers suggest a breakout, as he blew away his previous career-highs in receptions and receiving yards, but increased volume hid a decrease in efficiency. Indeed, Tate ranked fourth in the NFL with 24 failed completions (catches that failed to generate a successful play), nearly a quarter of his total receptions. The decline is a bit curious, given that Tate should have been the main beneficiary of Detroit's successful screen game (36.9% DVOA, 10th-best in the league). But the Lions largely limited his route tree to short-to-intermediate in-breaking routes, eliminating the big downfield chunks Tate picked up in Seattle's vertically oriented aerial attack. Despite his relatively diminutive frame, Tate has shown the ability to high-point the ball outside the numbers. Slants, screens, and drags will still be his bread and butter in 2015, but hopefully the Lions sprinkle in a few more change-ups to showcase Tate's full receiving arsenal.

De'Anthony Thomas							Height: 5-9		Weight: 174		College: Oregon			Draft: 2014/4 (124)			Born: 5-Jan-1993			Age: 23		Risk: Yellow	
Year	Team	G/GS	Snaps	Rec	Pass	Yds	C%	+/-	Yd/C	TD	Drop	YAC	Rk	YAC+	BTkl	DVOA	Rk	DYAR	Rk	YAR	Short	Mid	Deep	Bomb
2014	KC	12/3	188	23	32	156	75%	-0.3	6.8	0	2	8.0	--	-0.4	4	-34.9%	--	-55	--	-44	93%	0%	3%	3%
2015	KC			31	47	239	66%	--	7.7	1						-25.8%								

The Chiefs have converted Thomas into a full-time wide receiver, but it's hard to view him as anything more than a gadget player (reverses and Wildcat) who can be great on special teams. While defenses have to account for his athleticism, Thomas has a long way to go in becoming a solid receiver capable of running a variety of routes. Last season, 17 of his 32 targets were screen passes. His average target traveled 0.2 yards beyond the line of scrimmage. He only caught one pass that was thrown more than three yards down the field, and that was a 30-yard pass thrown by Chase Daniel. Oops, guess we slipped in another dig at Alex Smith. (Note: while not listed above, Thomas' projection also includes 20 carries for 85 yards.)

Demaryius Thomas

| | | | Height: 6-3 | | Weight: 224 | | College: Georgia Tech | | | Draft: 2010/1 (22) | | Born: 25-Dec-1987 | | Age: 28 | | Risk: Yellow | |

Year	Team	G/GS	Snaps	Rec	Pass	Yds	C%	+/-	Yd/C	TD	Drop	YAC	Rk	YAC+	BTkl	DVOA	Rk	DYAR	Rk	YAR	Short	Mid	Deep	Bomb
2012	DEN	16/16	1019	94	141	1434	67%	+11.4	15.3	10	6	5.7	17	+0.9	9	21.4%	14	354	8	401	42%	31%	12%	15%
2013	DEN	16/16	1106	92	142	1430	65%	+6.2	15.5	14	4	7.6	2	+2.5	8	26.5%	7	430	1	465	48%	24%	17%	11%
2014	DEN	16/16	1021	111	184	1619	60%	-3.8	14.6	11	8	5.8	14	+1.2	7	9.2%	29	317	8	282	43%	32%	19%	6%
2015	DEN			107	164	1474	65%	--	13.8	11							14.8%								

Imagine this career for a wide receiver: 16 seasons, 250 games, 15 Pro Bowls, four-time first-team All-Pro, 1,579 catches, 21,752 receiving yards and 175 touchdowns. That's on the level of Jerry Rice in the G.O.A.T. department. Well, these numbers *actually have happened*, but it's been done by the composite trio that makes up Peyton Manning's No. 1 wide receiver: Marvin Harrison (1998-2006), Reggie Wayne (2007-2010) and Demaryius Thomas (2012-2014). Each was a great receiver in his own right, but those staggering numbers have a lot to do with where the ball is coming from. That's why the Broncos had to be fair and smart with Thomas' new contract. Sure, he's excellent after the catch and quite good before it, but his value is not the same without Manning as his quarterback. Thomas was the last Denver player on the current roster that John Elway did not personally draft, sign, trade for or re-sign to a contract. The Broncos were close to letting Thomas play the season on the franchise tag, but they made sure the fax machine was plugged in and inked Thomas to a new deal just before the deadline on July 15. Thomas' five-year deal worth up to $70 million is almost identical to the one Dez Bryant received on the same day, and only Calvin Johnson makes more money among wide receivers. Thomas has set his eyes on breaking Johnson's single-season receiving yardage record, as he expects many big plays in Gary Kubiak's offense. We're a bit more skeptical of Manning's 39-year-old arm strength.

Kenbrell Thompkins

| | | | Height: 6-1 | | Weight: 196 | | College: Cincinnati | | | Draft: 2013/FA | | Born: 29-Jul-1988 | | Age: 27 | | Risk: Yellow | |

Year	Team	G/GS	Snaps	Rec	Pass	Yds	C%	+/-	Yd/C	TD	Drop	YAC	Rk	YAC+	BTkl	DVOA	Rk	DYAR	Rk	YAR	Short	Mid	Deep	Bomb
2013	NE	12/8	574	32	70	466	46%	-10.5	14.6	4	5	4.3	56	-0.1	4	-11.9%	73	4	74	8	32%	43%	17%	7%
2014	2TM	12/6	394	21	47	262	45%	-6.8	12.5	0	2	4.5	--	-0.2	3	-28.4%	--	-56	--	-66	30%	46%	9%	15%
2015	OAK			14	25	182	56%	--	13.0	1							-8.9%								

Thompkins has received some minicamp buzz, but doesn't that always happen for some team's No. 5 wide receiver? Then when the real games start, you never hear about him again. Since catching that game-winning touchdown from Tom Brady to beat the Saints in 2013, Thompkins has caught 32 of 68 passes for 410 yards and zero scores. He didn't impress last year after the Raiders claimed him off waivers two days after New England released him. With the receivers Oakland has now, you may never hear from him again.

Nick Toon

| | | | Height: 6-2 | | Weight: 215 | | College: Wisconsin | | | Draft: 2012/4 (122) | | Born: 4-Nov-1988 | | Age: 27 | | Risk: Yellow | |

Year	Team	G/GS	Snaps	Rec	Pass	Yds	C%	+/-	Yd/C	TD	Drop	YAC	Rk	YAC+	BTkl	DVOA	Rk	DYAR	Rk	YAR	Short	Mid	Deep	Bomb
2013	NO	8/3	196	4	12	68	33%	-1.1	17.0	0	2	2.3	--	-3.3	0	-39.9%	--	-23	--	-23	10%	40%	20%	30%
2014	NO	8/2	239	17	23	215	74%	+3.1	12.6	1	0	2.5	--	-1.5	2	15.7%	--	52	--	61	26%	43%	22%	9%
2015	NO			30	50	383	60%	--	12.8	3							2.1%								

Nick Toon will get another chance to establish himself as an NFL receiver this season, after he has repeatedly failed to take advantage of the opportunities that have gone his way to this point in his career. Toon is a big receiver who needs to win at the catch point to be successful in the NFL, but isn't as dominant as he should be because he lacks the fluidity to adjust to the ball through contact. That lack of fluidity also limits the precision and speed of his routes, making it much easier for defensive backs to stick with him in space.

Mike Wallace

| | | | Height: 6-0 | | Weight: 199 | | College: Mississippi | | | Draft: 2009/3 (84) | | Born: 1-Aug-1986 | | Age: 29 | | Risk: Yellow | |

Year	Team	G/GS	Snaps	Rec	Pass	Yds	C%	+/-	Yd/C	TD	Drop	YAC	Rk	YAC+	BTkl	DVOA	Rk	DYAR	Rk	YAR	Short	Mid	Deep	Bomb
2012	PIT	15/14	833	64	119	836	54%	-3.7	13.1	8	6	4.2	39	-0.8	4	-17.4%	78	-19	77	-25	33%	38%	12%	17%
2013	MIA	16/16	951	73	141	930	52%	-4.2	12.7	5	7	3.9	67	-0.9	5	-14.8%	75	-24	77	-37	26%	44%	9%	22%
2014	MIA	16/16	819	67	115	862	58%	+3.2	12.9	10	4	3.5	63	-1.0	10	11.8%	19	221	20	216	27%	39%	19%	15%
2015	MIN			69	116	958	59%	--	13.9	6							3.5%								

After a steady statistical decline the last few years, Wallace rebounded slightly in 2014, posting improved numbers on several levels. But now, he's off to his third team in four seasons, joining the Vikings after he wore out his welcome in South Florida. Early reports have him developing a nice cohesiveness with Teddy Bridgewater, and if Wallace and Adrian Peterson are mentally and physically healthy going into the 2015 season, the Vikings offense could have a pair of really dynamic playmakers to make things easier on their young signal-caller. But given the slide he endured, it'll take more than a few good throws in camp to show that Wallace has again regained the form that made him one of the better deep threats in the league from 2009 through 2011, when he spent three years ranked in the top six of receiving DVOA.

Nate Washington

Height: 6-1 Weight: 185 College: Tiffin Draft: 2005/FA Born: 28-Aug-1983 Age: 32 Risk: Yellow

Year	Team	G/GS	Snaps	Rec	Pass	Yds	C%	+/-	Yd/C	TD	Drop	YAC	Rk	YAC+	BTkl	DVOA	Rk	DYAR	Rk	YAR	Short	Mid	Deep	Bomb
2012	TEN	16/14	790	46	90	746	51%	-1.0	16.2	4	4	5.3	20	+1.1	3	-3.2%	53	66	51	70	26%	36%	26%	12%
2013	TEN	16/15	886	58	104	919	56%	+3.7	15.8	3	3	4.0	66	-0.4	3	7.4%	27	162	28	165	13%	58%	14%	15%
2014	TEN	16/11	765	40	72	647	56%	-0.5	16.2	2	4	3.5	64	-0.7	2	5.3%	35	97	41	94	18%	46%	24%	11%
2015	HOU			12	21	150	57%	--	12.5	0						-7.6%								

Washington transitioned into elder statesman with the Titans, a needed one given the youth and lack of quality around him, and posted a fourth straight season with an admirably consistent DVOA around 0%. He'll be a better fit as a third option in Houston than he was as the first or second one in Tennessee, but he'll have to compete with Damaris Johnson, Cecil Shorts, and rookie Jaelen Strong for playing time.

Sammy Watkins

Height: 6-1 Weight: 211 College: Clemson Draft: 2014/1 (4) Born: 14-Jun-1993 Age: 22 Risk: Yellow

Year	Team	G/GS	Snaps	Rec	Pass	Yds	C%	+/-	Yd/C	TD	Drop	YAC	Rk	YAC+	BTkl	DVOA	Rk	DYAR	Rk	YAR	Short	Mid	Deep	Bomb
2014	BUF	16/16	1027	65	128	982	51%	-8.5	15.1	6	2	5.3	21	+0.9	9	-5.7%	54	71	48	48	30%	33%	23%	14%
2015	BUF			61	120	927	51%	--	15.2	9						-3.6%								

In a normal receiver class, Watkins might be the future star. His first-year advanced stats are similar to Calvin Johnson's (-1.2% DVOA, ranked 52nd) and better than Larry Fitzgerald's (-18.7% DVOA, ranked 72nd). With his hair and skill set, Watkins evokes Fitzgerald with every route. Neither came into a good situation at quarterback, either. Fitzgerald endured a first year with Josh Mc-Cown, Shaun King, and John Navarre; this was somehow *not* the worst quarterback quicksand that would drag Fitzgerald down in his career. Watkins entered a similarly hopeless situation that was spackled over last year with the midseason signing of Kyle Orton. Watkins did considerably better last year with Orton at quarterback (16.4 yards per reception, -2.7% DVOA) than with EJ Manuel (11.6 yards per reception, -14.4% DVOA), though he also improved because he had been playing with slight rib fractures early in the season. Unless another Orton-like band-aid arrives, Watkins will have a worse quarterback situation in 2015, as the Cassel-Manuel-Tyrod Taylor trio projects about as well as McCown-King-Navarre. Last year, Watkins showed uncommon explosion, body control, and run-after-the-catch ability at times, despite the quarterback situation. With the quarterback downgrade this year, glimpses may be more fleeting even if Watkins plays up to his potential, and transcendent numbers will be hard to come by.

Reggie Wayne

Height: 6-0 Weight: 198 College: Miami Draft: 2001/1 (30) Born: 17-Nov-1978 Age: 37 Risk: N/A

Year	Team	G/GS	Snaps	Rec	Pass	Yds	C%	+/-	Yd/C	TD	Drop	YAC	Rk	YAC+	BTkl	DVOA	Rk	DYAR	Rk	YAR	Short	Mid	Deep	Bomb
2012	IND	16/15	1079	106	196	1355	55%	-1.7	12.8	5	7	3.4	65	-1.2	4	-6.8%	64	73	47	118	29%	44%	22%	4%
2013	IND	7/7	427	38	59	503	66%	+2.6	13.2	2	3	4.6	48	+0.1	5	8.6%	25	104	44	115	34%	40%	21%	5%
2014	IND	15/15	859	64	116	779	56%	-6.4	12.2	2	8	4.2	50	-0.6	3	-13.0%	71	-3	71	-9	32%	45%	21%	2%

The writing may have been on the wall in the postseason. In three games, Wayne caught just one pass on five targets. He seemed to be defying Father Time to start the season, but a torn triceps caused him to be rarely productive after Week 5 despite gutting out a lot of snaps. The Colts chose not to re-sign Wayne and he has been a free agent since March. He doesn't want to retire, but going on 37 years old, there just may not be any offers out there. Wayne ranks seventh all time in receptions (1,070) and eighth in receiving yards (14,345). There's always a lot of debate about wide receivers in the Hall of Fame, but Wayne will be a big part of that debate for this recent era. Coming back to pad the numbers on a random team shouldn't do anything to strengthen that case. Hang those cleats up with your pride intact, Reggie.

Wes Welker — Height: 5-9 — Weight: 190 — College: Texas Tech — Draft: 2004/FA — Born: 1-May-1981 — Age: 34 — Risk: N/A

Year	Team	G/GS	Snaps	Rec	Pass	Yds	C%	+/-	Yd/C	TD	Drop	YAC	Rk	YAC+	BTkl	DVOA	Rk	DYAR	Rk	YAR	Short	Mid	Deep	Bomb
2012	NE	16/12	1074	118	175	1354	67%	+5.1	11.5	6	12	5.8	14	+0.9	8	6.1%	29	251	18	231	46%	38%	10%	6%
2013	DEN	13/13	770	73	111	778	66%	+1.7	10.7	10	8	4.4	52	-0.4	7	9.3%	24	194	25	209	54%	28%	14%	5%
2014	DEN	14/8	743	49	64	464	77%	+4.1	9.5	2	2	3.9	56	-0.7	0	4.4%	37	86	42	76	60%	31%	8%	2%

A 33-year-old slot receiver with lingering concussion problems doesn't make for a high-volume player anymore. Welker had his least productive season since 2005 and watched his Denver teammates gobble up all the short touchdowns he scored so easily in 2013. After three concussions in roughly nine months, Welker's playing days may be over. He remains unsigned as of press time and has generated little interest in the free-agency process. His legacy is that many teams have gone out to find their own Welker for the slot, but the original just may be too worn down to purchase.

Markus Wheaton — Height: 5-11 — Weight: 189 — College: Oregon — Draft: 2013/3 (79) — Born: 7-Feb-1991 — Age: 24 — Risk: Green

Year	Team	G/GS	Snaps	Rec	Pass	Yds	C%	+/-	Yd/C	TD	Drop	YAC	Rk	YAC+	BTkl	DVOA	Rk	DYAR	Rk	YAR	Short	Mid	Deep	Bomb
2013	PIT	12/1	159	6	13	64	46%	-1.4	10.7	0	0	6.0	--	+0.6	0	-30.5%	--	-18	--	-14	33%	42%	8%	17%
2014	PIT	16/11	745	53	86	644	62%	+4.7	12.2	2	1	3.2	76	-1.2	8	-0.2%	44	84	43	69	20%	52%	17%	11%
2015	PIT			40	69	518	58%	--	13.0	3						-7.5%								

It appears inevitable that Martavis Bryant will usurp Markus Wheaton as the Steelers' No. 2 receiver, but Wheaton should continue to have a prominent role. His versatility and refined technique will keep him ahead of the raw Sammie Coates in 2015, while his overall talent level suggests that he is worthy of being a long-term starter in an offense that heavily relies on more than just two wide receivers.

Kevin White — Height: 6-3 — Weight: 215 — College: West Virginia — Draft: 2015/1 (7) — Born: 25-Jun-1992 — Age: 23 — Risk: Yellow

Year	Team	G/GS	Snaps	Rec	Pass	Yds	C%	+/-	Yd/C	TD	Drop	YAC	Rk	YAC+	BTkl	DVOA	Rk	DYAR	Rk	YAR	Short	Mid	Deep	Bomb
2015	CHI			53	93	714	57%	--	13.5	5						-5.8%								

White is a fascinating test of Playmaker Score and the different ways a wide receiver can develop. Many of the best NFL prospects are like Amari Cooper, top recruits who excelled from their freshman season. Few go to junior college, play part-time as juniors, and then explode with such a huge senior year (1447 yards, 13.3 yards per reception, and a 69 percent catch rate) that they earn a top-ten overall selection. Will that be enough to overcome the dismal record of wide receivers who don't enter the draft until their college eligibility is exhausted? White's problems are exacerbated because he comes from a Mountaineers program where routes were not complex and it was the quarterback's job to adjust to coverage, not the receiver's. Add in off-season injuries, and a slow start to his NFL career would be no surprise.

Roddy White — Height: 6-1 — Weight: 201 — College: Alabama-Birmingham — Draft: 2005/1 (27) — Born: 2-Nov-1981 — Age: 34 — Risk: Yellow

Year	Team	G/GS	Snaps	Rec	Pass	Yds	C%	+/-	Yd/C	TD	Drop	YAC	Rk	YAC+	BTkl	DVOA	Rk	DYAR	Rk	YAR	Short	Mid	Deep	Bomb
2012	ATL	16/15	987	92	143	1351	64%	+10.5	14.7	7	3	3.5	59	-0.5	4	16.3%	18	360	5	360	28%	46%	17%	9%
2013	ATL	13/13	782	63	97	711	65%	+2.6	11.3	3	4	1.8	89	-2.3	0	2.7%	37	118	40	117	34%	45%	14%	6%
2014	ATL	14/14	870	80	125	921	64%	+3.0	11.5	7	5	2.3	85	-1.7	1	-1.3%	46	113	37	115	34%	46%	16%	4%
2015	ATL			80	125	943	64%	--	11.8	7						4.3%								

It feels odd that we're already here, but after two subpar seasons riddled with injury, is it time to close the book on White's prime? While it's true that players like Steve Smith and Reggie Wayne have perpetually bounced back after down seasons, it's also true that Smith and Wayne had much better careers than White has had. White is no slouch—he's racked up enough DYAR to be in the top 20 of all wide receivers who debuted after 1991—but his career fits more in the mold of Wes Welker or Marques Colston than a true No. 1 receiver. And it certainly doesn't help his reputation that Julio Jones showed up mid-career and was empirically better than White in every way. Atlanta won't be asking as much out of their non-Jones receivers this year if all goes according to plan, but given the lack of third options behind White, it really is necessary for him to continue to push his body as much as he has the last two years if Atlanta has hopes of competing this year.

Terrance Williams

Height: 6-2 Weight: 208 College: Baylor Draft: 2013/3 (74) Born: 18-Sep-1989 Age: 26 Risk: Green

Year	Team	G/GS	Snaps	Rec	Pass	Yds	C%	+/-	Yd/C	TD	Drop	YAC	Rk	YAC+	BTkl	DVOA	Rk	DYAR	Rk	YAR	Short	Mid	Deep	Bomb
2013	DAL	16/8	677	44	75	736	60%	+1.9	16.7	5	2	4.6	46	-0.1	3	3.0%	36	92	48	128	28%	41%	16%	15%
2014	DAL	16/16	811	37	65	621	57%	+3.4	16.8	8	2	3.0	78	-1.4	2	30.6%	2	220	21	239	17%	39%	19%	25%
2015	DAL			48	82	755	59%	--	15.7	6						7.6%								

The Alvin Harper of the modern Cowboys. Harper, readers over 35 may recall, was the second receiver behind Michael Irvin for the early-'90s Wowboys. He usually only caught about two passes per game, but one of them was inevitably a 45-yarder, the result of a fast-but-erratic receiver burning single coverage while two defenders worried about Irvin and the other eight dealt with Emmitt Smith. Williams had nine two-catch games in the regular season, with a 47-yard catch, a pair of 43-yarders, and several 20-yarders scattered among these low-productivity games. He was limited with a finger injury for several midseason games and should see a few more opportunities this season. He'll never be an 80-catch performer for the Cowboys, but he could crack 1,000 yards and ten touchdowns if the Cowboys pass a little more this year.

Albert Wilson

Height: 5-9 Weight: 200 College: Georgia State Draft: 2014/FA Born: 12-Jul-1992 Age: 23 Risk: Yellow

Year	Team	G/GS	Snaps	Rec	Pass	Yds	C%	+/-	Yd/C	TD	Drop	YAC	Rk	YAC+	BTkl	DVOA	Rk	DYAR	Rk	YAR	Short	Mid	Deep	Bomb
2014	KC	12/2	215	16	28	260	57%	-0.9	16.3	0	1	7.4	--	+2.7	6	14.8%	--	57	--	56	38%	38%	12%	12%
2015	KC			26	40	314	65%	--	12.1	3						3.0%								

If your offense is built to feed the ball to Jamaal Charles, Jeremy Maclin, and Travis Kelce, then having Wilson as the next option is not so bad. It's especially preferable at his salary compared to keeping Dwayne Bowe around at his high price. Let's remember Wilson was an undrafted rookie who basically had a hot three-game stretch in December against two awful defenses (Oakland and Pittsburgh). He's not ready to be a star, but he has desirable slot skills and will give the Chiefs yards after the catch on the various screens and drag routes he'll be running. He only needs to go deep occasionally, and we know that will naturally be a rare occurance given who the quarterback is. Wilson can stand to get better at catching contested passes, but he's still a very young prospect with time to improve.

Marquess Wilson

Height: 6-3 Weight: 194 College: Washington State Draft: 2013/7 (236) Born: 14-Sep-1992 Age: 23 Risk: Green

Year	Team	G/GS	Snaps	Rec	Pass	Yds	C%	+/-	Yd/C	TD	Drop	YAC	Rk	YAC+	BTkl	DVOA	Rk	DYAR	Rk	YAR	Short	Mid	Deep	Bomb
2013	CHI	10/1	75	2	3	13	67%	+0.5	6.5	0	0	4.5	--	-2.7	3	-38.5%	--	-7	--	-5	33%	67%	0%	0%
2014	CHI	7/6	373	17	32	140	53%	-2.8	8.2	1	3	3.0	--	-1.0	1	-25.0%	--	-31	--	-34	45%	36%	9%	9%
2015	CHI			17	29	213	59%	--	12.5	1						-6.8%								

2014 seemed like would be Wilson's breakout season, especially given Chicago's thin depth chart at receiver. A fractured clavicle in training camp ended those plans by sending him to short-term injured reserve, and he was unimpressive in his return to the lineup. He is still an intriguing and very young player for his third NFL season, but the offseason additions of Eddie Royal and Kevin White ensure his likely role is as the No. 4 receiver.

Robert Woods

Height: 6-0 Weight: 201 College: USC Draft: 2013/2 (41) Born: 10-Apr-1992 Age: 23 Risk: Green

Year	Team	G/GS	Snaps	Rec	Pass	Yds	C%	+/-	Yd/C	TD	Drop	YAC	Rk	YAC+	BTkl	DVOA	Rk	DYAR	Rk	YAR	Short	Mid	Deep	Bomb
2013	BUF	14/14	910	40	85	587	47%	-6.0	14.7	3	1	2.8	85	-1.4	2	-11.7%	72	6	72	-6	19%	46%	23%	12%
2014	BUF	16/15	899	65	104	699	63%	-0.3	10.8	5	5	3.1	77	-1.9	2	-11.4%	65	11	64	12	43%	32%	19%	7%
2015	BUF			45	82	543	55%	--	12.1	4						-13.4%								

Like EJ Manuel, Woods has posted almost identical crappy advanced stats in his first two seasons. Not only did Woods' overall DVOA barely budge, in 2014 he posted similar poor numbers on first down (-9.5%), second down (-11.0%), and third down (-13.7%). In 2013, however, Woods succeeded more with EJ Manuel (56 percent catch rate, 47 targets) than without him (37 percent catch rate, 38 targets). Last year, that pattern flipped. Woods caught 38 percent of his targets from Manuel but 72 percent from Kyle Orton. The biggest change in his targets came from the depth of his routes. On average, balls thrown to Woods traveled 9.4 yards through the air in 2014, compared to 13.4 yards in 2013. Last year, 43 percent of Woods' targets were thrown within five yards of the line of scrimmage, compared to 21 percent in his rookie year. The deeper throws were less effective in 2014, in addition to being less frequent. On throws beyond five yards from Manuel, Woods had a catch rate of 62 percent (39 targets) in 2013 compared to just 21 percent (19 targets) in 2014.

Jarius Wright   Height: 5-10   Weight: 182   College: Arkansas   Draft: 2012/4 (118)   Born: 25-Nov-1989   Age: 26   Risk: Green

Year	Team	G/GS	Snaps	Rec	Pass	Yds	C%	+/-	Yd/C	TD	Drop	YAC	Rk	YAC+	BTkl	DVOA	Rk	DYAR	Rk	YAR	Short	Mid	Deep	Bomb
2012	MIN	7/1	206	22	36	310	61%	-0.4	14.1	2	1	5.0	--	-0.0	4	4.4%	--	68	--	32	54%	23%	9%	14%
2013	MIN	16/3	417	26	43	434	60%	+3.4	16.7	3	1	4.5	--	-0.4	4	22.7%	--	117	--	109	30%	28%	30%	13%
2014	MIN	16/7	512	42	62	588	68%	+3.3	14.0	2	3	7.8	2	+2.2	3	0.7%	41	64	51	86	44%	31%	12%	14%
2015	MIN			36	55	466	65%	--	12.9	2						2.3%								

With the Vikings swapping out Greg Jennings for Mike Wallace, Wright appears likely to inherit a full-time slot role in 2015. Wright was a favored Teddy Bridgewater target on screens, highlighted by a game-winning 87-yard overtime scamper against the Jets that helped boost Wright to 7.8 average yards after the catch (second among qualifying wideouts). The former Razorback deserves the bulk of the credit for the Vikings' sterling 73.7% DVOA on wide receiver and tight end screens, the second-best mark on such passes behind only Baltimore. Of course, Wright has to go 87 yards if he wants to score a touchdown because he doesn't get the ball near the goal line (only 13 red zone targets over his entire three-year career). With a pair of vertically inclined receivers on the outside, Wright's complementary short-area skill set should prevent too much of a backslide in production.

Kendall Wright   Height: 5-10   Weight: 196   College: Baylor   Draft: 2012/1 (20)   Born: 12-Nov-1989   Age: 26   Risk: Green

Year	Team	G/GS	Snaps	Rec	Pass	Yds	C%	+/-	Yd/C	TD	Drop	YAC	Rk	YAC+	BTkl	DVOA	Rk	DYAR	Rk	YAR	Short	Mid	Deep	Bomb
2012	TEN	15/5	557	64	104	626	62%	-1.4	9.8	4	4	4.9	28	-0.4	8	-14.4%	75	15	69	-2	55%	34%	7%	3%
2013	TEN	16/12	808	94	140	1079	67%	+2.3	11.5	2	8	5.9	11	+0.6	14	-3.7%	59	95	47	96	49%	33%	13%	5%
2014	TEN	14/11	662	57	93	715	61%	-1.2	12.5	6	1	6.4	8	+0.8	14	-3.3%	49	67	50	48	46%	26%	18%	9%
2015	TEN			68	115	835	59%	--	12.3	6						-4.9%								

2013 felt like a breakout season for Wright, but he chafed under a coaching staff that reined in some of his "streetballer" instincts and insisted he greatly increase his route precision rather than getting him the ball however he felt like because have you actually seen the Titans' other receivers? His production declined less precipitously on third down than it did for other Titans receivers, and he did good work in the red zone (86.8% DVOA). If he establishes a rapport with Mariota and plays to the coaches' demands, he could see a bit of a rebound in his catch total even with the team's transition to a more ground-oriented attack.

Going Deep

Jared Abbrederis, GB: A torn ACL wiped out Abbrederis' rookie season after Green Bay used a 2014 fifth-round pick on him. The former Wisconsin star projects best as a slot receiver. Green Bay currently has the league's best in Cobb, but the depth chart after the top three is open enough that Abbrederis could please the hometown fans by carving out a role.

Seyi Ajirotutu, PHI: Ajirotutu was a name that popped up a few times in San Diego just to remind everyone of how stretched the depth was in certain years. He was one of 13 Chargers to catch at least 10 passes in 2010. He caught a beautiful game-winning touchdown in Kansas City in 2013, but otherwise has been pretty silent in his five NFL seasons. Philadelphia's not a bad landing spot for a receiver with some skills down the field. (2014 stats: 4-for-12, 45 yards, -17 DYAR, -32.2% DVOA)

Mario Alford, CIN: A tiny (5-foot-8) sprinter out of West Virginia, Alford has the speed to help in the deep passing game and on kick returns—his 100-yard touchdown against Alabama in the 2014 season opener was an apt demonstration of his jets. The seventh-round rookie needs plenty of work in the finer points of receiving, however.

Dres Anderson, SF: The knee injury that ruined Anderson's senior season at Utah might have scared teams away in the draft, as Anderson went unselected despite a fifth-round grade from some scouts. As a junior, Anderson averaged 18.9 yards on 53 catches. Perhaps big-play ability runs in the family; Anderson's father, former Rams wideout Willie "Flipper" Anderson, led the NFL in yards per catch in 1989 and 1990.

Josh Bellamy, CHI: If I told you you were a marginal receiver who didn't have a shot to rise above fifth on the depth chart, would you hold it against me? NFL teams see something here—Kansas City in 2012, Washington in 2013, Chicago in 2014 and still now—but not enough to stick with it.

Kenny Bell, TB: A fifth-round pick out of Nebraska with a Randy Moss-quality afro, Bell ran a 4.37-second 40 at his pro day. He could potentially replace Vincent Jackson in 2016, when cutting the then-33-year-old would save almost $10 million in cap space. There is not much room for Bell now with Jackson and Mike Evans around; Bell's straight-line skill set projects better outside than in the slot.

Brenton Bersin, CAR: Bersin's introduction to the NFL's big stage in the Arizona-Carolina wild-card game involved him frantically waving for a fair catch at any opportunity, up to and including school bus stop signs pilfered from the Charlotte suburbs. Bersin's flowing blonde locks are an unusual sight at the wide receiver position, though they did help our game charters out. In the end, you have a player that got supplemental playing time because the Carolina wideout depth chart was barren. The Panthers have spent a lot of time improving the wideout depth chart, even going as far as to start the Stephen Hill OTA Hype Machine, so you'll more likely see Bersin (retained on a cheap one-year deal) solely a special-teamer going forward. (2014 stats: 13-for-20, 151 yards, 1 TD, 42 DYAR, 13.0% DVOA)

Justin Blackmon, JAC: There tend to be four types of players who get Going Deep comments: the ones who may be, the ones who never were, the ones who already have been, and the ones who can't get out of their own way. Some of the players who can't get out of their own way have deficient traits that keep them from being good on a football field. Justin Blackmon is not one of those. Blackmon was suspended per his third strike on the substance abuse policy, and his reinstatement is a matter of lots of conjecture and little concrete detail. General manager Dave Caldwell shared in December that the Jaguars were treating Blackmon's return as a "luxury" rather than a certainty. This is your yearly reminder that it takes a lot of talent to be a top-10 pick and that, should this all clear up, perhaps Blackmon will make a fine NFL wideout again.

Josh Boyce, NE: After seeing action in just one game last season, the 2013 fourth-rounder may struggle to make the roster this year. He had the second-highest score (23) on the Wonderlic for receivers in his draft class, potentially a sign that he would find it easier to get on the same page with Tom Brady on all the Patriots' option routes. A decade earlier, Deion Branch led his receiver draft class with a 26. But Boyce's test score and speed (4.38 in the 40) have not translated to on-field production in his first two seasons. (2013 stats: 9-for-19, 121 yards, 9 DYAR, -6.9% DVOA)

Jarrett Boykin, CAR: Boykin began the season as Richard Sherman bait, playing most snaps and getting completely ignored. By Week 4, a groin injury sent him to the shelf and he had been supplanted by Davante Adams. After playing 119 snaps the first three games, he played just 119 the rest of the season. Carolina presents a much friendlier depth chart, but Jerricho Cotchery already fills the "big body, not much speed" role and offseason reviews were not positive. That 680-yard season from 2013 looks like a one-hit wonder. (2014 stats: 3-for-12, 23 yards, -38 DYAR, -49.9% DVOA)

Da'Ron Brown, KC: A seventh-round pick out of Northern Illinois, Brown has good hands, but projects as a marginal possession receiver at the pro level. In other words, he's just another guy who won't be catching touchdowns from Alex Smith this season, if he makes the team.

Justin Brown, BUF: Justin Brown was the Steelers' big receiver entering the regular season last year. He was eventually replaced because of his limited impact. Brown wasn't targeted deep down the field much, as 90 percent of his catches came within 15 yards of the line of scrimmage. He caught just 57 percent of his passes with two drops and offered very little YAC potential, averaging 1.8 yards per catch. (2014 stats: 12-for-21, 94 yards, -54 DYAR, -45.0% DVOA)

Mike Brown, CAR: 15 years from now, Brown will be the kind of guy Jaguars fans remember as part of the bridge years. "Remember those games where we had Chad Henne throwing to Mike Brown? Those were dark days." In Carolina, he's not likely to get much of a sniff on a crowded depth chart. (2014 stats: 7-for-15, 88 yards, -43 DYAR, -50.4% DVOA)

Vincent Brown, IND: Injuries plagued Brown's short-lived tenure as a third-round pick in San Diego. Oakland quickly picked him up last year after the Chargers waived him with an injury settlement. Now he's in Indianapolis, where the Colts really need to petition the league to let them use six receivers instead of the maximum allotment of five. There's just not much room for Brown as he competes with the likes of Duron Carter and Griff Whalen for a roster spot. (2014 stats: 12-for-21, 118 yards, -15 DYAR, -22.5% DVOA)

Ryan Broyles, DET: At least he'll always have Oklahoma. The second all-time leading receiver in FBS history has seen his body badly betray him at the pro level, with two ACL tears and a ruptured Achilles robbing Broyles of the explosiveness that made him such a dangerous Sooner. Broyles showed glimpses of life last preseason with a team-high 11 receptions for 144 yards, but never carved out a real role in the offense when the games counted and ended the year with just two catches. The former second-rounder has the type of measurables and pedigree that will get him a contract as long as he can pass a physical, but that might not be a given for much longer.

Isaiah Burse, DEN: It looked like Omar Bolden had taken away the Denver kick returner job from Burse late last year, though Burse may still hold the team's punt returner job. He really does not play on offense (18 snaps last year), so his roster spot is special teams or bust at this point.

LaRon Byrd, MIA: LaRon Byrd is a big receiver with some athletic ability. He has sparsely seen the field throughout his career, and considering the state of the Browns' receiving corps last year, it's hard to think he'll find a better chance than he did in 2014.

Michael Campanaro, BAL: With four catches in the playoff game against New England, this 2014 seventh-rounder from Wake Forest showed some of the promise that has the Ravens excited. The slot man was hit by hamstring issues in his rookie year, but openings at receiver and kick returner in Baltimore could see a rapid expansion of his role in 2015. (2014 stats: 7-for-9, 102 yards, 1 TD, 50 DYAR, 60.5% DVOA)

Duron Carter, IND: Cris Carter's path to Canton wasn't the easiest one. Now his son Duron is trying to go from the CFL to the NFL. Several teams showed interest in Carter earlier this year, but the Colts struck the deal. It's going to be hard for Carter to make the team, let alone see any playing time with T.Y. Hilton, Andre Johnson, Phillip Dorsett, and Donte Moncrief ahead of him on the depth chart.

Kaelin Clay, TB: Clay's most likely way to make the roster and contribute in 2015 is as a kick returner, where he made four different All-American teams for Utah in 2014. He returned three punts for touchdowns in just 23 chances and also returned one kickoff for six, becoming the most notable Kaelin since Kato. Clay also fits the Bucs' need at receiver as he would operate primarily out of the slot, but he had four drops to go with his 43 receptions last year.

Sammie Coates, PIT: The selection of Sammie Coates in the third round of the 2015 draft was a confusing one from Kevin Colbert. Coates doesn't appear to fit either an immediate or long-term need. He is a very raw receiver who will likely need to be used on screens and gadget plays to be effective early in his career. Although he is very athletic, he has major struggles tracking the ball in the air, something that contributed to his 45 percent catch rate during his final season at Auburn. Coates could ultimately just be a bigger version of Dri Archer and see similarly few snaps on the field.

Jamison Crowder, WAS: Crowder is a Wes Welker type (but he's African-American, so there) who had three-straight 1,000-yard seasons for the Blue Devils and proved he could compete with the big boys during a fine Senior Bowl week. He's tough, dedicated, and knows his craft, and can return punts if called upon. Two inches taller and he would have been a second-round pick, but at 5-foot-8 he lasted until the fourth round. Three years ago, we would have dreamed of Crowder catching slot screens and wreaking havoc as teams crowded the box in fear of Robert Griffin-Alfred Morris options. It's still OK to dream a little.

B.J. Daniels, SEA: The 49ers drafted Daniels out of South Florida in the seventh round in 2013, and he has since been waived by both San Francisco and Seattle. Still, he was the No. 2 quarterback on Seattle's roster going into OTAs, and Pete Carroll said he could also play wide receiver or kick returner this season. After OTAs, they scratched quarterback off that list. Daniels never caught a pass or returned kicks in college, but he was athletic enough to rush for 2,068 yards and 25 touchdowns in his Bulls career.

Geremy Davis, NYG: The Giants' sixth-round pick out of UConn, Davis caught 71 passes in 2013 but tailed off as a senior, catching just 44 passes as the Huskies changed coaches, changed quarterbacks, and basically went belly-up at the bottom of a weak conference. The buzzword for Davis in Giants circles is "David Tyree." Davis is a big, tough possession receiver with special-teams chops who can fill several roles on the bench. Tyree, it must be pointed out, never caught more than 19 passes in a regular season. But if the Giants can find their way to the fourth quarter of the Super Bowl again, they're set.

Titus Davis, SD: Davis followed in Antonio Brown's footsteps at Central Michigan and fared quite well. He caught at least eight touchdowns in all four seasons. Expected by some to be a mid-round pick, he'll instead try to catch on as an undrafted free agent with San Diego thanks to his strong route-running and ball skills.

Stefon Diggs, MIN: Diggs has a little Percy Harvin to his game, a Swiss Army knife-type who is a home-run hitter after the catch and excels when given the ability to work in space. Injuries are a legitimate concern for the diminutive Diggs, who has seen his past two seasons at Maryland end with a lacerated kidney and broken leg. If he can take pro-level punishment over the middle, the fifth-round rookie is a dark horse to win the slot receiver gig after Greg Jennings' migration to South Beach.

Aaron Dobson, NE: After two seasons, Dobson seems set to join Chad Jackson and Bethel Johnson in the Patriots "Hall of Second-Round Flops." As a rookie in 2013, Dobson finished 63rd in DVOA. Nine drops in just 72 targets contributed to a 51 percent catch rate. Last season, Dobson barely saw any playing time, a combination of injuries and coaches' decisions. While Dobson has a combination of size and speed that current Patriots' receivers lack, he has looked lost when on the field. The Patriots cut their last second-round flop (Ras I-Dowling) before his third season, and Dobson is headed to the same exit. By the way, the Patriots' Hall of Second-Round Flops is located in the basement of the Somerville Theatre, next to the Museum of Bad Art (museumofbadart.org) and the bathrooms. (2013 stats: 37-for-72, 519 yards, 4 TD, 46 DYAR, -5.4% DVOA)

Kris Durham, OAK: After he failed to make the Lions out of training camp, the Titans claimed Durham off waivers. He finally cracked the lineup after Justin Hunter went to injured reserve and caught a couple passes from someone other than his old college roommate Matthew Stafford. He'll get another chance to do the same thing on Oakland's more crowded depth chart—in the preseason, at least. (2014 stats: 6-for-11, 54 yards, -28 DYAR, -46.1% DVOA)

Marcus Easley, BUF: A year after leading the NFL with 23 special-teams tackles, Easley missed six games but was still productive when healthy, making 11 tackles in ten games. Like Matthew Slater of the Patriots, Easley brings elite speed to the gunner role (4.39 seconds in the 40 at the combine) and almost never actually lines up at wide receiver.

Shaquelle Evans, NYJ: New York's fourth-round pick out of UCLA spent the year on IR after suffering a shoulder injury in August, and faces an uphill battle to make the roster in 2015. Even before he was hurt, the Jets quickly realized they had badly overdrafted Evans, who had a 10.1 percent Playmaker Rating.

George Farmer, DAL: Burly possession-receiver type from USC; tore his ACL and MCL in 2013, then came back for 25 receptions in 2014. Farmer signed with Dallas as a UDFA, hoping to stick as a fifth receiver and special-teams standout.

Devin Gardner, PIT: Gardner split time between quarterback and receiver at Michigan, finishing his Wolverines career with 6,336 passing yards, 916 rushing yards, and 286 receiving yards. He also led the Big 10 in interceptions thrown in 2014. The Patriots signed Gardner after the draft but waived him in May. The Steelers then picked him up with intentions to play him at quarterback. We doubt it will last.

Brittan Golden, ARI: Golden ran a 4.48-second 40-yard dash at his West Texas A&M pro day in 2012, and almost exclusively due to that 120-foot run he has lasted three years in the NFL, mostly on practice squads in Chicago, Jacksonville, and Arizona. He was never active in 2014, but could return kicks in 2015.

Antwan Goodley, DAL: Goodley, signed by Dallas as a UDFA, is built like a third-down running back at 5-foot-11, 220 pounds. He caught 131 passes in his final two seasons at Baylor, mixing screen-and-go plays with sideline bombs to average an impressive 16.6 yards per catch. He has a strange skill set for his stat profile and vice versa, in other words. The Cowboys need a versatile fourth or fifth receiver stout enough to cover kicks and nifty enough to return some. Goodley is as likely a candidate as any.

Marquise Goodwin, BUF: If Al Davis still ran the show in Oakland, Goodwin would probably be a Raider. Goodwin posted one of the fastest ever times at the combine in 2013 (4.27 in the 40), enough to get Buffalo to take him in the third round. Last year, Goodwin caught one pass in nine targets, posting a -95.0% DVOA. Yes, that is a small sample and his quarterbacks were EJ Manuel and Kyle Orton. Still, the third-year burner is in danger of not making the roster. He might be better off, as he won a silver medal in the long jump at the Pan-Am Games and quitting football would free him up to pursue a trip to Rio for the 2016 Olympics.

T.J. Graham, NYJ: This former college track star has crazy, next-level speed, but outside of a modest 31-catch performance as a rookie with the Bills in 2012, he has never been able to put it together with actual football skills. When he joined the Jets last season, it marked his third team in as many years. While he does have some value as a return man—he had four special-teams touchdowns in four years at N.C. State—he could be facing an uphill battle at both spots this year with the Jets. (2014 stats: 3-for-8, 87 yards, 1 TD, 24 DYAR, 22.7% DVOA)

Ryan Grant, WAS: Grant, a fifth-round pick in 2014, caught five passes after DeSean Jackson got hurt against the Jaguars in Week 2 and then disappeared for the rest of the season, catching two more passes despite semi-regular playing time in the Buccaneers, Rams, and Cowboys games. Grant is a route technician with so-so tools, the kind of player who can excel in a functional system but is doomed to run around and not be open for a team playing quarterback roulette. Jamison Crowder, smaller but niftier and just as determined, could push Grant off the back of the depth chart. (2014 stats: 7-for-15, 68 yards, -27 DYAR, -37.3% DVOA)

Rashad Greene, JAC: Jameis Winston's main target at Florida State, Greene also got to stay in-state for his professional career when Jacksonville took him in the fifth round. Though he's limited physically at 5-foot-11, 189 pounds, he mixes average NFL physical tools with good on-field intelligence and an integrated skill set. Greene could play in the slot for the Jaguars right away, but he'll have to beat out Allen Hurns to make it happen.

Derek Hagan, FA: After sitting out all of 2013, Hagan began training camp as the Titans' "you must be at least this good to make the team" benchmark. Nobody was, so he made the team and provided a reliable veteran presence on special teams. When injuries took out the starting receivers late in the season, Hagan ended up getting 27 targets in Weeks 13-17. This did not encourage the Titans to re-sign him. (2014 stats: 19-for-34, 254 yards, 1 TD, 0 DYAR, -12.5% DVOA)

Saalim Hakim, NYJ: Az-Zahir's brother is probably more of a special-teamer than a wide receiver at this point, he lost the kick returner job when the Jets acquired Percy Harvin last October. His ridiculous speed still makes him a threat to land somewhere on the roster.

Frankie Hammond, KC: Hammond did his best work on punt returns in relief of De'Anthony Thomas. As a receiver he dropped two of his 11 targets, so his work on special teams is really the best way to ensure he'll still have a roster spot in 2015. (2014 stats: 4-for-11, 45 yards, -29 DYAR, -46.7% DVOA)

Dwayne Harris, NYG: Harris is an exceptional all-around special-teamer in the Josh Cribbs mold. He is dangerous and sure-handed as a return man, but he is also a demon on kick coverage with 19 special-teams tackles and three fumble recoveries in the last two seasons. The Giants are looking for more than special-teams productivity from Harris, particularly if Victor Cruz is limited early in the season or five other Giants receivers get hurt while you are reading this comment. Harris has provided sporadic big plays on offense, but the Cowboys simply don't throw to their third or fourth receivers much (or their second receiver, for that matter). Harris' special-teams value is guaranteed; his usefulness as anything other than a fourth receiver who runs fly routes on offense is more of a mystery. (2014 stats: 6-for-11, 108 yards, 8 DYAR, -2.3% DVOA)

Matt Hazel, MIA: Hazel spent his rookie season on the practice squad. With the Dolphins doing a bit of a remake at the wide receiver spot this offseason, the 2014 sixth-rounder out of Coastal Carolina will battle a number of other backups for reps in training camp. One thing in his favor is that he does have some positional versatility—he has spent some time in the slot, which will likely help his chances in a crowded field of receivers.

Robert Herron, TB: The 2014 sixth-rounder did not have a catch after Week 6. Herron was inactive for six of the last seven contests and may not make the final 53 this year. He combines excellent straight-line speed (4.39-second 40-yard dash) with less impressive short-distance quickness. (2014 stats: 6-for-12, 58 yards, 1 TD, -3 DYAR, -15.5% DVOA)

Darrius Heyward-Bey, PIT: In 2014, Darrius Heyward-Bey played more special-teams snaps than offensive snaps. Those special-teams snaps will likely give him an edge competing for a roster spot in 2015. Heyward-Bey is a veteran at this point and it may be better for his career if he doesn't make the Steelers roster so he can instead try to land somewhere where he is more likely to play on offense. (2014 stats: 3-for-5, 37 yards, -7 DYAR, -26.0% DVOA)

Santonio Holmes, FA: The Bears gave up on Holmes when Marques Wilson returned from injury. Unsigned at press time, and with no teams showing apparent interest in taking a chance on his foot or his attitude. (2014 stats: 8-for-14, 67 yards, -4 DYAR, -16.6% DVOA)

Jeff Janis, GB: This seventh-round rookie from Saginaw Valley State was beloved by fans of both athletic testing scores and Division II football even before housing both of his preseason receptions in 2014. Finding the field in the regular season was a more elusive goal (15 snaps, 15 games as a healthy inactive). Jordy Nelson's absence gave him work with the top offense in OTAs, and the depth chart beyond the top three is cloudy enough for him to earn a role.

A.J. Jenkins, DAL: Following Alex Smith from city to city is probably a bad idea for a young wide receiver trying to develop, but by now we all agree the 49ers just goofed when they made Jenkins the 30th overall pick in 2012. He really couldn't hold off Junior Hemingway or Albert Wilson in Kansas City last year. If he struggles to catch on in Dallas, where Tony Romo can make anyone look viable, he might as well hang up the cleats for good. (2014 stats: 9-for-15, 93 yards, -7 DYAR, -19.0% DVOA)

Jerrel Jernigan, FA: Jernigan had a classic Giants career. He got drafted, got hurt, got healthy, got hurt again, got healthy, fumbled a few times, finally started flashing potential, got really really hurt, and got released after four long seasons of waiting. See also Dominick Hixon, David Wilson, Andre Brown, et al. (2014 stats: 6-for-9, 40 yards, -2 DYAR, -15.4% DVOA)

Jacoby Jones, SD: A top kick returner, and somewhat less impressive Dancer With The Stars, Jones left the scene of his best NFL moments for San Diego, which has nicer weather than Baltimore, anyway. He caught just nine of 18 passes for 131 yards and no touchdowns in 2014 (11 DYAR, -4.1% DVOA), and at age 30 his kick-returning shelf life is dwindling rapidly as well.

T.J. Jones, DET: A lingering arm injury from Notre Dame's bowl game never healed and ended up costing this Detroit sixth-round pick his entire rookie season. Jones appears healthy this summer after undergoing shoulder surgery and getting cleared in time for rookie minicamps in May. In the *2014 RSP*, Matt Waldman essentially described Jones as a poor man's Marqise Lee, noting that he needed "a lot of work with routes" and labeled his hands "too iffy for me to endorse." Jones should have a chance to compete with Ryan Broyles and Lance Moore for one or two roster spots. As a native of Winnipeg, Jones has a long CFL career ahead of him if (when) he washes out of the NFL.

Tavarres King, TB: The 2013 fifth-round pick bounced around three teams before finally seeing game action with Tampa in Week 15 last season. King set the Georgia state record for high school receiving with 1,632 yards in 2007. With the Bucs' log-jam at wide receiver, King faces an uphill battle to make the roster and may start another season on the practice squad.

Dezmin Lewis, BUF: The seventh-round receiver out of Central Arkansas—the mention of which will cause anyone of a certain age to hear the Bulls' public address announcer revving up for Scottie Pippen—was projected to go as early as the fourth round of the draft after an impressive combine. At 6-foot-4, Lewis is a big target with unusual upside for his draft position. He shined at times against stronger competition, leading all receivers in yardage at the Senior Bowl. A leg injury could put him on the reserve/PUP list to start the season.

Greg Little, FA: According to TMZ, Little is involved in a legal battle with his Hollywood Hills landlord over rent payments on his $15,000 per month mansion. He may want to relocate, given his football status. Little was a drop machine in Cleveland for years; signed out of midseason injury desperation by the Bengals, he naturally dropped the first pass sent his way. He has been released, and his only worry now is whether his property lawsuit is likewise dropped. (2014 stats: 6-for-12, 69 yards, -11 DYAR, -24.9% DVOA)

Jeff Maehl, PHI: One of Chip Kelly's Bench Ducks, or more precisely a Practice-Squad Duck. Maehl caught five passes in a handful of early-season games when Josh Huff was recovering from a shoulder injury, then faded from the active roster. He's skinny and not that elusive, eliminating most of his special teams value, but he clung to Texans practice squads for two years before landing with Kelly, so he must be a swell guy to keep around during training camp.

Marc Mariani, CHI: We noted in *Football Outsiders Almanac 2011* that return specialist Mariani was chasing Jimmy Farris' record of seven catches by a Montana wide receiver. He is still two short of tying that mark but remains a good kickoff returner and average punt returner.

Keshawn Martin, HOU: Martin, in the final year of his rookie deal, has barely been allowed on the field as a receiver for two separate coaching staffs. This offseason, the Texans signed veteran flotsam like Nate Washington and Cecil Shorts to prevent Martin from getting another shot. As a returner, Martin has mixed good (2013) with bad (2014). It would not at all be surprising if Martin didn't survive training camp. (2014 stats: 6-for-12, 78 yards, -16 DYAR, -30.4% DVOA)

Chris Matthews, SEA: After stints with the L.A. Harbor College Seahawks, Kentucky Wildcats, Cleveland Browns, Iowa Barnstormers, and Winnipeg Blue Bombers (CFL's Most Outstanding Rookie in 2012), Matthews was working at Foot Locker when the Seahawks (NFL version) called and offered him a tryout that night. He spent most of the season on the practice squad, then recovered the onside kick in Seattle's NFC title game comeback. His four catches in the Super Bowl, the first catches of his career, produced 109 yards and a touchdown, and he might have won the MVP award if the fourth quarter had gone differently. Matthews' size stands out among Seattle's undersized wide receiver corps, and he could see significant playing time in 2015.

Vince Mayle, CLE: A junior college basketball player who eventually became a record-breaking receiver for Mike Leach at Washington State, Mayle was taken by Cleveland in the fourth round of the 2015 draft, but he is a raw receiver who likely won't make any real impact until 2016 and beyond.

Tre McBride, TEN: Good news, bad news. The bad news: McBride was a seventh-round pick on a team that has not had a seventh-round pick do anything in the NFL since 2006. The good news: McBride was one of the draft's inexplicable fallers, a FCS wide receiver who excelled at William & Mary and did not look out of place against higher-level competition. If you liked him, he was a less polished version of Amari Cooper. He'll have an opportunity in Tennessee.

Robert Meachem, FA: Robert Meachem has just 37 receptions over the past three seasons for San Diego and New Orleans. He isn't a spectacular receiver, but he has shown the ability to create separation down the field with precise route running. The question is, as a 30-year-old receiver, can he muster up enough athleticism to make those routes effective? (2014 stats: 7-for-20, 114 yards, -12 DYAR, -20.2% DVOA)

Ty Montgomery, GB: Green Bay's third-round pick is a fascinating prospect. A rare gamebreaker in Stanford's offense, he looked like a potential future superstar back when Andrew Luck was throwing him the ball. The next three seasons, he was an outstanding return man but looked too stiff running routes, struggled against zone coverage, and did not catch the ball consistently. Ted Thompson has an excellent history with wide receivers, and Montgomery should not have to be more than a kick returner and fourth receiver in 2015.

Marlon Moore, CLE: Moore is at the point of his career where he must embrace his role on special teams. That appears to be all the Browns are expecting from him, at least. He didn't catch a pass last year but did have eight special-teams tackles, all of them stopping a return short of average value.

Joseph Morgan, NO: The health of Joseph Morgan, a player who has missed multiple seasons because of knee injuries, will go a long way in determining if he can help replace the lost production of Kenny Stills. Morgan had a big season for the Saints in 2012 as a deep threat, but he was suspended and waived by the team late last season. He was re-signed in the offseason for what is likely his last chance at carving out a career in the NFL. (2014 stats: 4-for-10, 92 yards, 1 DYAR, -11.5% DVOA)

Keith Mumphery, HOU: Mumphery said after he was drafted in the fifth round that the Texans were the only team to work him out before the draft, which is a sign of where his stock was around the league. Mumphery caught just 26 balls for Michigan State last season, and projects more as a special-teamer than anyone who should give the Texans receiver depth chart a run for their money.

J.J. Nelson, ARI: At just 156 pounds, Nelson is nine pounds lighter than any player who caught a pass in the NFL in 2014. However, this little fella can *run*. He was the fastest player at the combine with a 4.28-second 40-yard dash, and that's not just track speed: his 116 receptions at Alabama-Birmingham averaged 19.6 yards apiece, and he returned five kickoffs for touchdowns in his career, including four in his senior season. The Cardinals took him in the fifth round, and though he probably won't see much time at receiver this year, he should be a big help to a team that ranked 30th in kickoff returns in 2014.

Kevin Norwood, SEA: Norwood is best known for what he did at Alabama, where he won multiple national championships as a sidekick to Julio Jones and Amari Cooper. It's also where he returned this spring to publicly propose to girlfriend Kayla Williams, herself a national champion on the Crimson Tide's gymnastics team. She accepted, and they should produce amazingly athletic babies in the future. In the meantime, the 2014 fourth-rounder will compete in a battle royal for Seattle's No. 3 and No. 4 receiver spots this summer.

Kassim Osgood, FA: Osgood spent 12 NFL seasons as an elite special-teamer with the Chargers, Jaguars, Lions, and 49ers, making the Pro Bowl three times and being named All-Pro in 2009. He was cut by San Francisco three times last year, but still played 13 games, making five tackles. He was unsigned as of mid-July. If this is the end, it has been a hell of a career for a guy who went undrafted out of San Diego State.

Chris Owusu, NYJ: Picked up by the Jets after the Bucs cut him last season, Owusu played sparingly for New York in 2014, though he did catch all six of his pass targets and scored a rushing touchdown on a jet sweep. He was pushed down the depth chart because of the arrival of Brandon Marshall and drafting of Devin Smith, but if he can show flashes of the special-teams value he occasionally displayed last year, it might be enough to win the No. 5 receiver gig. (2014 stats: 6-for-6, 78 yards, 1 TD, 40 DYAR, 65.0% DVOA)

Quinton Patton, SF: In two seasons since the 49ers drafted Patton in the fourth round in 2013, he has 124 yards from scrimmage (including 46 yards on two runs) in ten NFL games. That's partly because he has missed time with foot injuries, but that's still a terribly thin resume for a guy who could open the season as San Francisco's third wideout.

Solomon Patton, DEN: Patton set the Florida record for single-season kickoff return average with a 29.2-yard mark in 2013. As an undrafted rookie, he returned kickoffs and punts for Tampa Bay; the Bucs cut him in May and the Broncos picked him up to fight for their returner spot.

DeVier Posey, NYJ: Thrown in to the trade-up for Jaelen Strong like the floormats on a new car, Posey hasn't done much since tearing his Achilles against the Patriots in the 2012 playoffs. Jets general manager Mike Maccagnan drafted Posey when he was the scouting director for the Texans, but unless Devin Smith needs more developmental time than expected, it's hard to see Posey handling anything but special teams in New York. (2013 stats: 15-for-25, 155 yards, -38 DYAR, -33.7% DVOA)

Terrelle Pryor, CLE: Three teams have taken a shot at Pryor since he washed out as the starting quarterback in Oakland, but none of them held onto him very long. So this time, when the Bengals cut him in June, Pryor announced that he would be open to a position change. The Browns made a waiver claim and will try to develop Pryor as a wide receiver. At 6-foot-4 with a 4.4-second 40, he's a pretty sweet piece of raw clay. Even if he only makes the active roster for one game this year, we want a wide receiver option pass.

Tevin Reese, CIN: This smallish waterbug was a seventh-round pick out of Baylor by the Chargers last season. They cut him before the season and he hooked up with Cincinnati's practice squad, but the drafting of similarly-built Mario Alford likely leaves Reese's future in pieces.

Da'Rick Rogers, FA: Rogers has had some off-field issues, like the DUI that was the final straw for the Colts, but he has also flashed big-play potential in limited playing time. His 46-yard catch against the Chiefs in the 2013 AFC wild-card game really helped to energize that 28-point comeback by the Colts, but it's the last catch we have seen him make in the NFL. The Chiefs signed him shortly after the season but then cut him in June.

Greg Salas, DET: After spending two seasons with the Jets, the Hawaii product signed with the Lions in the offseason, making it five teams in five years. Known as a 3-cone star coming out of Oregon—his quick feet were one of the reasons he found a home with Josh McDaniels in St. Louis, and then again in New England—he's a relatively dependable target with good hands who is likely a depth signing for Detroit. (2014 stats: 8-for-23, 167 yards, -13 DYAR, -20.1% DVOA)

Ace Sanders, FA: A shifty player in space with a tendency to fake out unsuspecting defensive backs, Sanders doesn't offer much as a receiver beyond guile. The Jaguars stacked the depth chart at the position over the last two drafts, so Sanders was cut in July. (2014 stats: 6-for-7, 55 yards, -2 DYAR, -16.8% DVOA)

Dane Sanzenbacher, FA: Jon Gruden's favorite preseason broadcast filler had the slot receiver position open up for him last year after Andrew Hawkins departed Cincinnati. But Dane was hardly great, or even good. There's a Hamlet joke in here somewhere, but Sanzenbacher really isn't worth hunting for it. (2014 stats: 9-for-15, 105 yards, -23 DYAR, -31.7% DVOA)

Bud Sasser, FA: The Rams took Sasser after with the 201st pick in the draft this year, but released him after he was diagnosed with a heart condition before rookie camp. Sasser sought a second opinion from the Mayo clinic and received a clean bill of health, and is seeking a team to give him a chance.

Jalen Saunders, NO: Drafted by the Jets but employed by three different teams as a rookie, Saunders is a return specialist who is unlikely to feature on offense. The Saints may build some packages for him, but he will need the offense to create space for him rather than create it himself by running routes downfield.

Russell Shepard, TB: Shepard was considered one of the top quarterback prospects in the country coming out of high school before he converted to wide receiver at LSU. Despite having a tough depth chart to crack, Shepard may make the 53-man roster if the Buccaneers keep six receivers. In contrast to competitor Robert Herron, Shepard was seeing more action at the end of 2014 and coaches apparently feel he may have more upside. (2014 stats: 4-for-8, 63 yards, 1 DYAR, -11.7% DVOA)

Jerome Simpson, SF: The former second-rounder ran out of chances in Minnesota last season, as the Vikes cut bait on him in September following a citation for drug possession… during a three-game DUI-related suspension… which came two years after a three-game marijuana-related suspension. Simpson was fortunate to receive a two-year contract from the Niners after sitting out the entire 2014 season, but making San Francisco's roster likely isn't the toughest battle he's currently facing. (2013 stats: 48-for-100, 726 yards, 1 TD, 20 DYAR, -10.1% DVOA)

Matthew Slater, NE: For the fourth straight year, Slater made the Pro Bowl as a special-teamer. By comparison, Steve Tasker made seven Pro Bowls (six in a row from 1990 to 1995). Slater has made 25 special-teams tackles the last two seasons, which is fewer than Arizona's Justin Bethel (38 tackles), but that's partly because the Patriots have such an effective offense that they don't punt very often. The Patriots have apparently given up on the occasional random long pass to [Matthew] Slater, having only tried the play twice in the past four seasons. Oddly enough, both were in the playoffs.

DeAndre Smelter, SF: Smelter is the latest in a long line of oversized freak athlete wideouts from Georgia Tech who are difficult to evaluate because they played in the Yellow Jackets' run-heavy offense, a list that includes Stephen Hill, Demaryius Thomas, and Calvin Johnson. (No, Georgia Tech was not running the triple-option when Johnson played there, but they still ran far more than they passed.) Smelter comes with extra questions because he played only two years of college football after a shoulder injury ended his baseball career, and then he tore his ACL last December. He will miss at least the first six weeks of the 2015 season, and given his lack of experience, it would probably make most sense just to put him on the shelf for the whole year and give him a chance to mature physically and mentally. Still, Smelter was Tech's top receiver last year, and has great potential as a downfield threat—he averaged 18.9 yards on 56 collegiate catches, and added a 75-yard rushing touchdown against North Carolina.

Brad Smith, FA: A free agent at press time. The Eagles didn't even use Smith as a kickoff returner last year, so the end of the line has surely come. Smith's career stat line looks like something transplanted from the 1930s. He has thrown 10 career passes to go with 972 rushing yards, 104 receptions, lots of kickoff returns (including four touchdowns), and 72 tackles stretched across a decade. All that's missing are a few extra points and an interception or two. Pro Football Reference still lists Smith as a quarterback, which is more an homage than a fact, but it makes as much sense as any classification. Some guys are just football players. If the Patriots draft them, they become stars. If the Jets draft them, they become Brad Smith.

Rodney Smith, CLE: There's no doubting Smith's ability to tower over defensive backs at 6-foot-5, but he lacks the bulk and athleticism to be an effective NFL receiver. In his third year as a pro, he's still a project, and will need to earn his roster spot through training camp.

Evan Spencer, WAS: The Redskins' sixth-round pick is a 6-foot-2 possession receiver who caught 52 passes in his final season at Ohio State. Not an elite measurables prospect, and below slot-ready Jamison Crowder in the queue for offensive playing time, but an upgrade over keeping Santana Moss on the sideline in a knit cap to berate officials.

Neal Sterling, JAC: A 6-foot-3, 238-pound target from Monmouth, Sterling wasn't invited to the combine and ran a 4.58 40-yard dash at his pro day. Jacksonville drafted him in the seventh round and his weight has given some scouts the thought that he might be able to play tight end. Trying to find detailed scouting notes on how a Monmouth wide receiver blocks is like trying to chisel granite with your teeth, but there have been worse ideas on how to spend a seventh-round pick.

Devin Street, DAL: A fifth-round rookie out of Pitt, Street caught two passes for 18 yards in the season opener, then disappeared from the Cowboys' game plan for the rest of the season. He took first-team reps in OTAs during Dez Bryant's kinda-sorta holdout and would conceivably leapfrog over slot specialist Cole Beasley on the depth chart if anything happened to Bryant or Terrance Williams. Then again, the Cowboys signed failed 49ers and Chiefs prospect A.J. Jenkins in May, which is not a ringing endorsement for Street. The Cowboys don't have much of a role for a fourth receiver, so an ace special-teamer is more likely to land a job on the bottom of the team's depth chart than a low-yield Dez insurance policy. Street did little on special teams last year and will need to step up.

Julian Talley, NYG: Talley attended Winslow High School in South Jersey, which was called Edgewood High School in the mid-1990s, when Football Outsiders' own Mike Tanier taught there. But for a few years and some job relocations, Talley could have joined Ron Dayne and Joe Flacco on the exclusive "NFL Players Taught by Tanier" list. Also, Talley hasn't gotten into a game yet; the Giants have kept him on their practice squad for two years (the Giants keep guys on their practice squad for a long time), but has only been activated in the most extreme injury emergencies. By the way, did you know Tanier also taught Josh Trovato of the reality show *Hell's Kitchen*? Have you noticed that none of Tanier's math students ever seem to excel at mathematics? It may because he was too busy writing capsules like this one to focus on his many talented students.

Adam Thielen, MIN: Thielen's 2014 season sounds like a made-for-television Disney movie. After starring locally at Division II Minnesota State-Mankato, Thielen broke through onto the Vikings active roster, surpassing hotshot first-rounder Cordarrelle

Patterson on the depth chart and catching the game-winning touchdown in the final game of the season. The sequel probably won't feature many receptions, but perhaps Thielen gets a longer look at punt returner, where he averaged 25.4 yards on five chances last preseason. (2014 stats: 8-for-13, 137 yards, 1 TD, 43 DYAR, 31.3% DVOA)

Deonte Thompson, BUF: The Bills have considerable receiver depth and Thompson, signed from the Ravens' practice squad last December, has only a small chance of making the roster. The third-year undrafted receiver can fly (4.31 in the 40 on his pro day), but appeared in just one game last year. (2013 stats: 10-for-20, 96 yards, 13 DYAR, -4.3% DVOA)

Brian Tyms, NE: In 2014, Tyms filled the replaceable role of the guy who mostly does not play but occassionly comes on the field for a random deep pass. All of his catches came against Buffalo: a 43-yard touchdown in Week 6, then the rest in Week 17 when the Patriots were resting starters. Late in the year, Tyms saw some action on special teams, and any contribution there could be important in the fight to make the 2015 roster. (2014 stats: 5-for-11, 82 yards, 1 TD, 6 DYAR, -5.6% DVOA)

Darren Waller, BAL: Classic Georgia Tech wideout size (6-foot-6), but Waller was nowhere near as productive on the Flats as Megatron or BayBay. He has good hands, though, and could develop into a red zone threat. Baltimore snagged him in the sixth round.

Bryan Walters, JAC: Walters was Seattle's last resort in 2014. He was their primary punt returner after their bizarre experiment with Earl Thomas failed, and they were forcing passes to him at the end of the Dallas loss when Percy Harvin refused to take the field. He followed the ever-common Seattle-to-Jacksonville pipeline and will serve as the Jaguars' Swiss Army Knife—a rusty, dull Swiss Army Knife. (2014 stats: 6-for-11, 57 yards, -12 DYAR, -27.2% DVOA)

Corey Washington, NYG: Washington, a 6-foot-4 leaper from Newberry College, stood out in training camp last year the way 6-foot-4 receivers from tiny colleges so often do. After four preseason touchdowns, Washington settled in to life as a back-of-the-roster receiver who barely knew the route tree and lacked special-teams experience. When asked what Washington must do to get more snaps in December, Coughlin was blunt: "Do a better job on the practice field. Do a better job all around… He does have to, obviously, become better at his job." That sounds pessimistic, but if Coughlin is criticizing you, it means he still cares about you. (2014 stats: 5-for-8, 52 yards, 1 TD, 13 DYAR, 6.6% DVOA)

Eric Weems, ATL: Weems, back in Atlanta after a short journey to try to help fix Chicago's special teams, continues to be one of the better gunners in the league going on age 30. He won't be returning kicks again barring a surprise Devin Hester release, but there are much worse uses of a roster spot. Weems also caught his first two regular-season touchdown passes since 2009, but his 2014 receiving numbers scream "small sample-size fluke." (2014 stats: 10-for-11, 102 yards, 2 TD, 50 DYAR, 41.5% DVOA)

Griff Whalen, IND: True story: if you search for Griff Whalen on Football Outsiders, the search engine asks if you meant "grief whale." How great of a nickname is that for a teetering No. 5 wide receiver? The Colts' upgrades at receiver last year put "Stanford Connection: Part II" on the backburner as Whalen worked mostly on special teams. He wasn't too successful there, but that has to be his leg up on the competition with four roster spots already locked in at wide receiver. Whalen has to beat out the likes of Vincent Brown and Duron Carter just to make the team this year. (2014 stats: 2-for-3, 23 yards, 3 DYAR, -1.9% DVOA)

Damian Williams, STL: Williams registered a small blip on the radar with Tennessee when he scored five touchdowns in eight games in 2011, but he hasn't scored one since. After two more forgettable seasons with the Titans, he had one catch in three games with Miami and St. Louis in 2014. He's a long shot to make the Rams' roster this fall.

Mike Williams, FA: Six weeks before the 2013 season opener, Williams signed a six-year, $40.3 million contract with Tampa Bay. Even for the NFL, the numbers for that contract were about as meaningful as Soviet economic growth statistics. Given his contract structure, Williams would have had to play at or beyond his 2012 level to see past the contract's second season, with a reported $14.6 million in "guarantees" not coming to Williams if he were cut before 2015. In the end, Williams' contract became a predictable two years for just $11.8 million. After 30 catches in two injury-plagued seasons, Williams now is just looking for a job. (2014 stats: 8-for-19, 142 yards, 1 TD, -26 DYAR, -30.7% DVOA)

James Wright, CIN: Drafted for his special-teams acumen, Wright didn't do much receiving as a rookie, though all five of his grabs went for first downs, and he was oddly missed after a late-season knee injury. (2014 stats: 5-for-16, 91 yards, -27 DYAR, -34.6% DVOA)

Tight Ends

Top 20 TE by Receiving DYAR (Total Value), 2014

Rank	Player	Team	DYAR
1	Rob Gronkowski	NE	237
2	Antonio Gates	SD	204
3	Greg Olsen	CAR	178
4	Travis Kelce	KC	174
5	Jason Witten	DAL	146
6	Julius Thomas	DEN	140
7	Heath Miller	PIT	127
8	Zach Ertz	PHI	127
9	Jimmy Graham	NO	124
10	Coby Fleener	IND	112
11	Niles Paul	WAS	110
12	Dwayne Allen	IND	104
13	Tim Wright	NE	89
14	Martellus Bennett	CHI	88
15	Lance Kendricks	STL	51
16	Owen Daniels	BAL	49
17	Dion Sims	MIA	42
18	Ladarius Green	SD	41
19	Chase Ford	MIN	32
20	Rhett Ellison	MIN	31

Top 20 TE by Receiving DVOA (Value per Pass), 2014

Rank	Player	Team	DVOA
1	Tim Wright	NE	30.9%
2	Julius Thomas	DEN	24.7%
3	Niles Paul	WAS	24.4%
4	Antonio Gates	SD	24.1%
5	Travis Kelce	KC	23.0%
6	Dwayne Allen	IND	22.7%
7	Rob Gronkowski	NE	19.7%
8	Jason Witten	DAL	17.9%
9	Ladarius Green	SD	15.9%
10	Greg Olsen	CAR	14.7%
11	Heath Miller	PIT	13.5%
12	Zach Ertz	PHI	13.3%
13	Lance Kendricks	STL	11.8%
14	Dion Sims	MIA	11.1%
15	Coby Fleener	IND	10.1%
16	Rhett Ellison	MIN	10.0%
17	Jimmy Graham	NO	6.8%
18	Chase Ford	MIN	6.8%
19	Jim Dray	CLE	6.6%
20	Martellus Bennett	CHI	3.0%

Minimum 25 targets

Dwayne Allen

Height: 6-3   Weight: 255   College: Clemson   Draft: 2012/3 (64)   Born: 24-Feb-1990   Age: 25   Risk: Green

Year	Team	G/GS	Snaps	Rec	Pass	Yds	C%	+/-	Yd/C	TD	Drop	YAC	Rk	YAC+	BTkl	DVOA	Rk	DYAR	Rk	YAR	Short	Mid	Deep	Bomb
2012	IND	16/16	905	45	66	521	68%	+1.7	11.6	3	2	5.4	9	+0.9	1	14.9%	9	67	15	86	47%	45%	3%	5%
2013	IND	1/1	30	1	2	20	50%	-0.1	20.0	1	0	5.0	--	+1.0	1	84.3%	--	12	--	14	0%	50%	50%	0%
2014	IND	13/13	619	29	50	395	58%	-2.7	13.6	8	4	5.6	13	+1.2	3	22.7%	6	104	12	91	34%	46%	16%	4%
2015	IND			37	57	458	65%	--	12.4	5						18.7%								

Though Coby Fleener played with Andrew Luck at Stanford, the consensus since 2012 has been that Allen is the superior tight end in Indianapolis. He is valuable in the red zone and down the seam, and he is a better blocker. His only problem is staying healthy. Since he was drafted in 2012 like Fleener, he is also set to become an unrestricted free agent after this season. Allen is the smarter investment, especially given the resources the Colts have put into adding wide receivers, but both tight ends will have another year to prove their value. Both actually caught eight touchdowns last season, an NFL first for tight ends on the same team.

Jace Amaro

Height: 6-5   Weight: 265   College: Texas Tech   Draft: 2014/2 (49)   Born: 6/26/1992   Age: 23   Risk: Yellow

Year	Team	G/GS	Snaps	Rec	Pass	Yds	C%	+/-	Yd/C	TD	Drop	YAC	Rk	YAC+	BTkl	DVOA	Rk	DYAR	Rk	YAR	Short	Mid	Deep	Bomb
2014	NYJ	14/4	374	38	53	345	72%	+2.3	9.1	2	6	4.4	23	-0.7	2	-7.0%	32	1	32	-1	58%	33%	8%	2%
2015	NYJ			50	76	571	66%	--	11.4	4						1.6%								

The rookie out of Texas Tech got off to a bad start with some hands issues, and struggled to shake them over the course of his first season in the league. He was third among tight ends with six drops, a number that looks worse when you consider the two tight ends who had more drops in 2014 (Martellus Bennett had eight with Chicago and Mychal Rivera had seven in Oakland) had far more chances in the passing game than Amaro. The good news is that tight ends don't usually burst onto the scene as rookies, but they get better with experience. If we look at the ten most similar rookie seasons by tight ends taken in the first three rounds, we see a number of eventual stars: Ben Troupe is the most similar rookie, but the list includes Jason Witten (35-347-1), Greg Olsen (39-391-2) and even Tony Gonzalez (33-368-2). The ten most similar rookies averaged 58 receptions for 616 yards and 5 touchdowns in their second years.

Gary Barnidge   Height: 6-6   Weight: 243   College: Louisville   Draft: 2008/5 (141)   Born: 22-Sep-1985   Age: 30   Risk: Green

Year	Team	G/GS	Snaps	Rec	Pass	Yds	C%	+/-	Yd/C	TD	Drop	YAC	Rk	YAC+	BTkl	DVOA	Rk	DYAR	Rk	YAR	Short	Mid	Deep	Bomb
2012	CAR	16/5	138	6	6	78	100%	+1.7	13.0	1	0	7.2	--	+1.2	0	96.5%	--	42	--	40	67%	17%	17%	0%
2013	CLE	16/12	529	13	18	127	72%	+0.7	9.8	2	0	7.0	--	+2.1	0	-10.7%	--	-4	--	3	71%	18%	6%	6%
2014	CLE	13/2	358	13	25	156	52%	-2.8	12.0	0	0	3.2	43	-1.4	2	-0.3%	27	10	29	-5	46%	29%	21%	4%
2015	CLE			18	28	198	64%	--	11.0	1						-5.8%								

Tying your career high for receptions is never a bad thing. However, when "career high" means the lofty heights of 13 catches in 13 games, it's not necessarily a good thing either. Barnidge was once considered an excellent prospect as a seam-stretcher, but it turned out to be the other way around in the NFL: he's a blocker who shouldn't be asked to run routes often. He simply lacks the physical traits to create separation downfield, and doesn't naturally adjust to the ball in the air. At one point it looked like Barnidge would finally get a starting job in 2014, but it's gradually become clear the team wants to give more snaps to Rob Housler.

Martellus Bennett   Height: 6-6   Weight: 259   College: Texas A&M   Draft: 2008/2 (61)   Born: 10-Mar-1987   Age: 28   Risk: Green

Year	Team	G/GS	Snaps	Rec	Pass	Yds	C%	+/-	Yd/C	TD	Drop	YAC	Rk	YAC+	BTkl	DVOA	Rk	DYAR	Rk	YAR	Short	Mid	Deep	Bomb
2012	NYG	16/16	928	55	90	626	61%	-1.3	11.4	5	8	3.6	35	-0.9	3	4.6%	20	85	11	64	31%	48%	13%	9%
2013	CHI	16/15	951	65	94	759	69%	+5.9	11.7	5	5	5.7	11	+0.4	14	3.4%	23	65	16	59	51%	38%	7%	5%
2014	CHI	16/15	954	90	128	916	70%	+1.6	10.2	6	8	5.0	17	-0.1	19	3.0%	20	88	14	51	57%	31%	12%	1%
2015	CHI			66	101	750	65%	--	11.4	5						1.9%								

When you only have two receivers and one of them gets hurt, it's good to be the tight end. Bennett in 2014 was mostly the same player he had been in the recent past, a good blocker with some ability to stretch the field who can play in-line or be split out. The arrivals of Eddie Royal and Kevin White will likely see his numbers return to a more normal level. An offseason holdout (at least until the mandatory part of it) indicates his future in Chicago may not last beyond the expiration of his current contract in March 2016, but he is one of the league's better complete tight ends.

Jordan Cameron   Height: 6-5   Weight: 220   College: USC   Draft: 2011/4 (102)   Born: 7-Aug-1988   Age: 27   Risk: Red

Year	Team	G/GS	Snaps	Rec	Pass	Yds	C%	+/-	Yd/C	TD	Drop	YAC	Rk	YAC+	BTkl	DVOA	Rk	DYAR	Rk	YAR	Short	Mid	Deep	Bomb
2012	CLE	14/6	329	20	40	226	50%	+0.4	11.3	1	0	5.4	8	+1.1	1	-13.5%	39	-28	39	-30	48%	35%	10%	6%
2013	CLE	15/14	969	80	118	917	68%	+11.6	11.5	7	1	3.0	45	-1.6	0	5.6%	21	99	9	79	39%	40%	15%	6%
2014	CLE	10/9	475	24	48	424	50%	-5.0	17.7	2	1	7.0	5	+1.9	0	-17.5%	38	-34	40	-30	45%	28%	19%	9%
2015	MIA			57	83	710	69%	--	12.5	7						15.0%								

Jordan Cameron wasn't the biggest name in free agency—he's not even as big as Cameron Jordan, the Saints defensive lineman with whom he is often confused—but he can be a major difference maker for the Dolphins. His talent has never been a concern. Cameron has the size and athleticism to stretch the defense with ease, as well as the ball skills to go up and win it in the air above defensive backs. Cameron became famous with fantasy football addicts with a huge 2013, but otherwise his NFL production hasn't matched his talent because of the problematic Cleveland offense and constant injury issues. Cameron has three confirmed concussions over the past two seasons, including one that cost him six games of the 2014 regular season. Cameron only got $5 million guaranteed from the Dolphins over two years, primarily because of that durability concern. 2015 will likely be a make-or-break year.

John Carlson Height: 6-4   Weight: 255   College: Notre Dame   Draft: 2008/2 (38)   Born: 12-May-1984   Age: 31   Risk: N/A

Year	Team	G/GS	Snaps	Rec	Pass	Yds	C%	+/-	Yd/C	TD	Drop	YAC	Rk	YAC+	BTkl	DVOA	Rk	DYAR	Rk	YAR	Short	Mid	Deep	Bomb
2012	MIN	14/6	249	8	14	43	57%	-1.8	5.4	0	1	2.3	--	-2.9	0	-49.6%	--	-38	--	-44	50%	50%	0%	0%
2013	MIN	13/8	497	32	47	344	68%	+1.5	10.8	1	1	4.8	25	-0.6	1	-14.6%	47	-24	44	-11	47%	44%	9%	0%
2014	ARI	16/12	734	33	55	350	60%	-2.8	10.6	1	5	4.3	24	-0.9	0	-20.0%	41	-43	42	-37	54%	34%	10%	2%

On Monday, May 4, Carlson was working out with the Cardinals during OTAs. The next day he retired. It sounds weird on the surface, but when you put yourself in Carlson's shoes, it starts to make sense. *I turn 31 years old this month, I have earned more than $10 million in my career, why the hell am I running wind sprints in the sun?* Really, the only thing surprising about retirements like this is that they don't happen more often. On a less jovial note, Carlson has suffered multiple brain injuries over the years, and an ESPN.com story noted that he was in "scary concussion territory" in October of 2012. No doubt health concerns also played a role in Carlson's decision. The Cardinals were caught off guard by Carlson's retirement, but his departure is not a great loss—he hasn't finished above replacement level in receiving DYAR since 2009, and his -219 total DYAR over the past five years is the worst of any tight end in the league.

Brent Celek Height: 6-4   Weight: 261   College: Cincinnati   Draft: 2007/5 (162)   Born: 25-Jan-1985   Age: 30   Risk: Green

Year	Team	G/GS	Snaps	Rec	Pass	Yds	C%	+/-	Yd/C	TD	Drop	YAC	Rk	YAC+	BTkl	DVOA	Rk	DYAR	Rk	YAR	Short	Mid	Deep	Bomb
2012	PHI	15/14	861	57	87	684	66%	-0.1	12.0	1	8	5.4	10	+0.0	4	-12.8%	38	23	30	15	46%	36%	17%	1%
2013	PHI	16/15	845	32	51	502	63%	+0.7	15.7	6	3	8.8	5	+3.2	2	18.3%	10	89	12	100	52%	23%	21%	4%
2014	PHI	16/15	815	32	51	340	63%	-0.0	10.6	1	2	4.1	27	-1.1	2	-20.8%	42	-49	43	-58	53%	26%	15%	6%
2015	PHI			22	35	194	63%	--	8.8	1						-18.0%								

Celek had a fine offseason and is still a big part of the Eagles' plans, though Zach Ertz has supplanted him as the top receiving tight end and should win the nominal starting job. The Eagles use lots of two-tight end sets, and Celek is both an excellent positional blocker (great for the system) and a fine receiver in traffic. He even has a little open-field capability left in the tank. Celek looked like toast when he was shut out on seven targets in three September games, but 29 catches in his final 12 games made him one of the league's more productive second options at tight end.

Celek is the last guy left in Philly to have shared a huddle with Donovan McNabb, Brian Westbrook, and Kevin Curtis; he played for Eagles teams that still had Jim Johnson at defensive coordinator and John Harbaugh coaching special teams. He's a living Philadelphia fossil, like a horseshoe crab that catches passes. It's surprising Chip Kelly kept him around, because "still a productive player" hasn't exactly been a compelling argument for retention lately. Maybe Celek is the only person who knows how to fix the photocopier jams.

Scott Chandler Height: 6-7   Weight: 270   College: Iowa   Draft: 2007/4 (129)   Born: 23-Jul-1985   Age: 30   Risk: Yellow

Year	Team	G/GS	Snaps	Rec	Pass	Yds	C%	+/-	Yd/C	TD	Drop	YAC	Rk	YAC+	BTkl	DVOA	Rk	DYAR	Rk	YAR	Short	Mid	Deep	Bomb
2012	BUF	15/13	746	43	74	571	58%	-1.4	13.3	6	3	4.4	18	+0.6	0	1.2%	25	52	20	61	27%	57%	14%	1%
2013	BUF	16/7	918	53	81	655	65%	+3.6	12.4	2	4	5.2	15	+0.7	3	-1.3%	33	32	28	26	39%	44%	16%	1%
2014	BUF	16/5	749	47	70	497	67%	+2.6	10.6	3	5	4.1	28	-0.7	1	-3.6%	28	17	26	36	52%	34%	12%	1%
2015	NE			26	39	310	67%	--	11.9	4						16.4%								

Against the Dolphins in Week 2, Chandler took off on a wheel route down the left sideline. As the pass came over his shoulders to the outside, Chandler went full extension and tapped his toes down, showing Gronkowski-like hands at 6-foot-7. Compared to his new teammate, Chandler is slower (he ran a 4.87-second 40-yard dash), less effective as a blocker (he can struggle against heavier and quicker players), and apparently less worthy of a place in erotic fiction (Google it, but not at work), but he does have a rare combination of size and hands. In fact, Chandler has shown those hands consistently, and particularly against the Patriots. He has averaged 43 yards receiving in nine games against the Pats compared to 26 in his 66 other games. Four of his 17 career touchdowns have come against New England.

Chandler is at his best against zone coverages where he can find holes. He is fairly plodding and struggles to create separation against man coverage. He is the kind of player who particularly needs a precision quarterback who can take advantage of his wide catch radius. That makes him a perfect match for Tom Brady, who tends to put the ball slightly wide of his receivers in order to avoid interceptions.

Charles Clay

Height: 6-3   Weight: 239   College: Tulsa   Draft: 2011/6 (174)   Born: 13-Feb-1989   Age: 26   Risk: Red

Year	Team	G/GS	Snaps	Rec	Pass	Yds	C%	+/-	Yd/C	TD	Drop	YAC	Rk	YAC+	BTkl	DVOA	Rk	DYAR	Rk	YAR	Short	Mid	Deep	Bomb
2012	MIA	14/9	333	18	33	212	55%	-0.4	11.8	2	2	4.5	17	-1.1	1	-16.0%	41	-19	38	-14	50%	21%	25%	4%
2013	MIA	16/15	855	69	102	759	68%	+3.5	11.0	6	5	5.2	16	+0.5	13	6.0%	20	88	13	92	49%	40%	9%	2%
2014	MIA	14/14	745	58	84	605	69%	+3.6	10.4	3	1	4.4	22	-1.0	6	-6.9%	31	2	31	8	52%	34%	14%	0%
2015	BUF			49	88	608	56%	--	12.4	4						-7.8%								

Charles Clay is a really underrated tight end who became a key part of the Miami passing game the last three seasons. He can play multiple spots, is a decent enough locker room guy who works hard, and has a good rep around the league as a blocker and pass catcher. But let's get one thing straight: there's no way he deserves to be the NFL's highest-paid tight end over the next two seasons, especially in what figures to be a run-centric Buffalo offense. It'll be really interesting to see what new Buffalo offensive coordinator Greg Roman has in store for Clay, as Roman was an advocate of using tight ends in new and intriguing ways when he was with the Niners, particularly employing multiple tight ends in the run game. If Roman can do that, maybe Clay will be able to justify the whopping $24.5 million over two seasons Buffalo is giving him.

Jared Cook

Height: 6-6   Weight: 246   College: South Carolina   Draft: 2009/3 (89)   Born: 7-Apr-1987   Age: 28   Risk: Green

Year	Team	G/GS	Snaps	Rec	Pass	Yds	C%	+/-	Yd/C	TD	Drop	YAC	Rk	YAC+	BTkl	DVOA	Rk	DYAR	Rk	YAR	Short	Mid	Deep	Bomb
2012	TEN	13/5	471	44	72	523	61%	+0.4	11.9	4	4	3.8	30	-0.5	3	-3.7%	33	9	34	13	45%	37%	12%	6%
2013	STL	16/13	718	51	86	671	59%	+0.5	13.2	5	6	5.1	19	+0.7	1	2.8%	24	58	21	65	39%	41%	16%	5%
2014	STL	16/6	682	52	99	634	53%	-8.1	12.2	3	3	5.1	16	+0.6	6	-13.4%	37	-39	41	-47	40%	43%	13%	3%
2015	STL			51	77	647	66%	--	12.7	5						17.1%								

Cook has led St. Louis in receptions in each of the past two seasons, and he has 32 more catches for 557 more yards than any other Rams receiver since he joined the team. Now, Cook is a nice player, but that says more about St. Louis than it does about Cook. In four seasons in Tennessee, he never led the Titans in either category, and its not as if those teams were stacked with Pro Bowl wideouts. St. Louis didn't do anything to bolster their wide receiving corps over the offseason, so there's a good shot Cook will be their leading receiver again in 2015. Cook gets good YAC for a tight end, thanks in part to his physical style. Cook only had one "broken" tackle, but he led the league with five plays where he dragged defenders 5 yards or more before going down.

Jeff Cumberland

Height: 6-4   Weight: 249   College: Illinois   Draft: 2010/FA   Born: 2-May-1987   Age: 28   Risk: Green

Year	Team	G/GS	Snaps	Rec	Pass	Yds	C%	+/-	Yd/C	TD	Drop	YAC	Rk	YAC+	BTkl	DVOA	Rk	DYAR	Rk	YAR	Short	Mid	Deep	Bomb
2012	NYJ	15/12	592	29	53	359	55%	-4.1	12.4	3	3	3.9	29	-0.4	2	-8.5%	36	-12	37	-8	36%	36%	25%	4%
2013	NYJ	15/12	675	26	39	398	67%	+2.1	15.3	4	2	5.9	7	+0.9	3	38.0%	2	112	8	118	33%	36%	26%	5%
2014	NYJ	16/14	910	23	47	247	49%	-4.8	10.7	3	4	4.2	26	-0.9	2	-29.3%	48	-66	46	-51	40%	40%	14%	7%
2015	NYJ			17	26	153	65%	--	9.0	0						-18.1%								

Cumberland's numbers the last three years look like the EKG of a heart patient—after a poor 2012, he was off the charts in 2013, then fell back to earth in 2014. His DVOA in particular took a stunning plunge; he went from No. 2 in overall tight end DVOA at 38.0% in 2013 to 48th at -29.3% last year. One aspect of Cumberland's game hasn't fluctuated because it has always been a problem: Cumberland was charted with more blown blocks (16.5) than any other non-offensive lineman in 2014, and he also ranked in the top five with 11.5 the year before. While he would appear to be on the metaphorical hot seat, he has two things in his favor. One, he signed a three-year, $5.7 million deal in the offseason, which should buy him some time with the new regime. And two, other than Jace Amaro (who was underwhelming at times last year), New York doesn't have many other options at tight end. One interesting note out of spring workouts: it was reportedly hard to discern how new offensive coordinator Chan Gailey is going to utilize the tight ends. Compounding things is the fact that Todd Bowles told reporters that Cumberland is the starting tight end and Amaro is more of an H-back, which would mean they may not be competing for the same starting snaps.

Owen Daniels

Height: 6-3   Weight: 245   College: Wisconsin   Draft: 2006/4 (98)   Born: 9-Nov-1982   Age: 33   Risk: Green

Year	Team	G/GS	Snaps	Rec	Pass	Yds	C%	+/-	Yd/C	TD	Drop	YAC	Rk	YAC+	BTkl	DVOA	Rk	DYAR	Rk	YAR	Short	Mid	Deep	Bomb
2012	HOU	15/14	864	62	104	716	60%	-3.4	11.5	6	5	5.0	13	+0.5	4	0.6%	27	33	26	52	43%	42%	11%	3%
2013	HOU	5/5	352	24	41	252	59%	-1.4	10.5	3	0	3.5	40	-1.1	2	-2.4%	34	14	35	4	42%	50%	8%	0%
2014	BAL	15/13	818	48	79	527	61%	-2.4	11.0	4	3	3.7	35	-0.9	0	2.2%	22	49	16	42	32%	59%	7%	3%
2015	DEN			56	75	601	75%	--	10.7	5						17.3%								

A quintessential coach's pet, Daniels would follow Gary Kubiak to Pluto if Kubiak got a job there. After a valuable season in Baltimore, Daniels is off with his sensei to Denver, where he will help replace Julius Thomas, far larger shoes to fill (literally and figuratively) than Dennis Pitta's. But with Kubiak designing the plays and Peyton Manning executing them, Daniels, despite his age, should provide quality snaps in a platoon alongside Virgil Green.

Vernon Davis

Height: 6-3   Weight: 250   College: Maryland   Draft: 2006/1 (6)   Born: 31-Jan-1984   Age: 31   Risk: Red

Year	Team	G/GS	Snaps	Rec	Pass	Yds	C%	+/-	Yd/C	TD	Drop	YAC	Rk	YAC+	BTkl	DVOA	Rk	DYAR	Rk	YAR	Short	Mid	Deep	Bomb
2012	SF	16/16	917	41	61	548	67%	+7.5	13.4	5	4	4.1	24	+0.2	6	17.5%	8	104	8	103	39%	30%	18%	13%
2013	SF	15/15	810	52	84	850	62%	+5.6	16.3	13	3	5.1	20	+0.2	3	29.3%	3	199	3	189	30%	34%	21%	15%
2014	SF	14/14	830	26	51	245	51%	-3.5	9.4	2	4	1.9	49	-2.2	3	-28.4%	46	-66	45	-71	29%	44%	17%	10%
2015	SF			44	70	529	63%	--	12.0	5						5.9%								

Last season was Davis' worst in terms of yardage, yards per catch, touchdowns, DYAR, and DVOA. Is there hope he can rebound at age 31? We found ten previous tight ends in their thirties whose production declined by at least 500 yards from one season to the next. Only Shannon Sharpe rebounded from his down year with several more good seasons, which is part of the reason he's in the Hall of Fame now. Five never played again, while the others bounced around the league another year or two without making much impact.

It was especially rough for Davis because his first game of 2014 was his best. He had four catches for 44 yards and two scores in the season opener against Dallas, but he never matched any of those numbers again. It didn't help that he missed two games with a back injury, but Davis would later blame his down season on the coaching staff, saying they tried to emphasize wide receivers at the expense of himself and the other tight ends. Davis has a point—San Francisco used three or more wide receivers on 46 percent of all plays last year, the first time they have been higher than 30 percent in this category since 2010—but given the decline in his advanced numbers, it's safe to say that the 49ers stopped throwing to Davis because they, too, could see him getting older right in front of their eyes.

Ed Dickson

Height: 6-4   Weight: 249   College: Oregon   Draft: 2010/3 (70)   Born: 25-Jul-1987   Age: 28   Risk: Green

Year	Team	G/GS	Snaps	Rec	Pass	Yds	C%	+/-	Yd/C	TD	Drop	YAC	Rk	YAC+	BTkl	DVOA	Rk	DYAR	Rk	YAR	Short	Mid	Deep	Bomb
2012	BAL	13/11	538	21	33	225	64%	+1.3	10.7	0	1	4.0	28	-0.4	1	-5.8%	34	2	35	-6	52%	26%	16%	6%
2013	BAL	16/14	629	25	43	273	58%	-2.9	10.9	1	5	4.0	35	-0.6	1	-10.8%	41	-10	41	-2	41%	36%	20%	2%
2014	CAR	16/10	522	10	17	115	59%	-0.6	11.5	1	2	6.3	--	+2.1	1	-5.0%	--	3	--	-2	73%	13%	13%	0%
2015	CAR			11	17	103	65%	--	9.3	1						-9.9%								

Dickson was the winner of a "deck chairs on the Titanic" battle between playing a second tight end who can't block, or playing a third wide receiver who can't catch. Carolina spent heavily to try bring in enough receiving options to make sure the battle is not re-enacted this year. And, frankly, Dickson doesn't offer anything that Brandon Williams doesn't, besides higher draft stock. On a good team, Dickson would be the third tight end.

Larry Donnell

Height: 6-6   Weight: 269   College: Grambling State   Draft: 2011/FA   Born: 1-Nov-1988   Age: 27   Risk: Yellow

Year	Team	G/GS	Snaps	Rec	Pass	Yds	C%	+/-	Yd/C	TD	Drop	YAC	Rk	YAC+	BTkl	DVOA	Rk	DYAR	Rk	YAR	Short	Mid	Deep	Bomb
2013	NYG	16/1	105	3	6	31	50%	-0.5	10.3	0	0	3.3	--	-0.0	0	-19.2%	--	-5	--	-6	0%	67%	17%	17%
2014	NYG	16/12	866	63	92	623	68%	+4.2	9.9	6	2	3.5	39	-1.2	0	-10.2%	34	-18	36	-16	44%	40%	13%	3%
2015	NYG			48	67	506	72%	--	10.5	3						5.7%								

Sorry if you blew all your waiver points to sign Donnell after his three-touchdown game in Week 4, then settled for just two touchdowns and less than 400 yards the rest of the way. But really, you should have seen that coming. You know: tight end you never heard of, big game against the Redskins, New York media acts like Mike Ditka 1962 just stepped out of a time machine in Central Park. If you fell for Donnell, frankly, you were looking to get taken. So really, we aren't sorry.

Donnell had a few solid performances as a receiver after his star turn, but he is nothing special as a blocker and lost four fumbles last season. The Giants re-signed him to a one-year, $585,000 contract, so he's not exactly the centerpiece of their organizational plan. Daniel Fells is a better blocker, Jerry Reese loves Adrien Robinson for some reason, and the Giants have enough weapons at receiver and in the backfield to marginalize the tight end in the passing game if they wish.

Donnell was walking around OTAs in a protective boot at the start of June. The Giants did not seem too concerned about the injury, because the Giants find it encouraging when their players can walk at all.

Jim Dray Height: 6-5   Weight: 246   College: Stanford   Draft: 2010/7 (233)   Born: 31-Dec-1986   Age: 29   Risk: Green

Year	Team	G/GS	Snaps	Rec	Pass	Yds	C%	+/-	Yd/C	TD	Drop	YAC	Rk	YAC+	BTkl	DVOA	Rk	DYAR	Rk	YAR	Short	Mid	Deep	Bomb
2012	ARI	13/0	34	2	2	15	100%	+0.6	7.5	0	0	0.5	--	-3.1	0	28.3%	--	3	--	2	50%	50%	0%	0%
2013	ARI	16/15	686	26	32	215	81%	+3.4	8.3	2	1	4.0	36	-0.9	2	2.3%	26	21	33	12	69%	31%	0%	0%
2014	CLE	16/8	598	17	28	242	61%	-0.2	14.2	1	1	6.0	8	+1.5	0	6.6%	19	26	21	25	42%	42%	12%	4%
2015	CLE			12	19	144	63%	--	12.0	0						-3.4%								

Jim Dray is definitely more of a blocking tight end than a dangerous receiver, but an argument can be made that he hasn't been used enough as a receiver over the course of his career. Dray has the athleticism to get out and run in space after play-action. That is how the Browns used him last season, and he was impressive even if not overly productive. Dray's size doesn't allow for fluid movement though, which means he has limited route-running ability.

Eric Ebron Height: 6-4   Weight: 250   College: North Carolina   Draft: 2014/1 (10)   Born: 10-Apr-1993   Age: 22   Risk: Yellow

Year	Team	G/GS	Snaps	Rec	Pass	Yds	C%	+/-	Yd/C	TD	Drop	YAC	Rk	YAC+	BTkl	DVOA	Rk	DYAR	Rk	YAR	Short	Mid	Deep	Bomb
2014	DET	13/7	445	25	47	248	53%	-4.0	9.9	1	4	5.0	18	+0.3	1	-28.6%	47	-65	44	-49	50%	26%	11%	13%
2015	DET			46	72	565	64%	--	12.3	6						14.6%								

Like many first-years, Eric Ebron admitted to hitting the rookie wall… in August. So you can imagine the consternation the Lions must have felt when the 10th overall pick lamented about "turning into a zombie mentally" just one month into the regular season. FO's Matt Waldman liked Ebron's game coming out of North Carolina, ranking him second overall among tight ends in his 2014 *Rookie Scouting Portfolio*, but noted that he was at his worst "when he's in traffic with a lot of bodies flashing across his field of vision." It's thus questionable why Detroit confined him to a phone booth so often, often lining him up as an H-back or tethering him to the line of scrimmage. There were a few interesting wrinkles where he lined up as the backside receiver of a 3x1 "Dakota" alignment, but it still makes little sense that the 6-foot-4 Ebron should have had a -37.7% red zone DVOA. Ebron never had more than four catches or 40 yards in any game last season, so hopefully the Detroit coaching staff takes a little bit of the blocking off his plate and lets him showcase why he was a top-10 pick in the first place.

Tyler Eifert Height: 6-6   Weight: 251   College: Notre Dame   Draft: 2013/1 (21)   Born: 8-Sep-1990   Age: 25   Risk: Yellow

Year	Team	G/GS	Snaps	Rec	Pass	Yds	C%	+/-	Yd/C	TD	Drop	YAC	Rk	YAC+	BTkl	DVOA	Rk	DYAR	Rk	YAR	Short	Mid	Deep	Bomb
2013	CIN	15/15	673	39	59	445	66%	+1.3	11.4	2	2	5.8	9	+1.2	6	-14.0%	45	-27	47	-6	54%	29%	13%	5%
2014	CIN	1/1	8	3	3	37	100%	+1.1	12.3	0	0	2.7	--	-1.6	0	47.1%	--	11	--	13	33%	33%	33%	0%
2015	CIN			48	74	526	65%	--	11.0	5						3.6%								

Eifert's 2014 season didn't even last a full quarter. Counted on to be a big part of Hue Jackson's multiplicity of formations, Eifert dislocated his elbow stretching for extra yardage early in the opener against the Ravens, and wound up lost for the season. Eifert took the opportunity to get surgery on the shoulder that ailed him the season before, too. Thus far, he has been as brittle as he is talented, with more sutures than receptions. That makes 2015 a big year for the former first-rounder. Jermaine Gresham is gone, clearing the way for Eifert to be the main man, if only he can stay on the field. A big and maneuverable security blanket with great hands is not a weapon Andy Dalton has been able to bank on in his career. If Eifert can provide him with even Owen Daniels-like reliability, the Bengals offense will be much better.

Zach Ertz

Height: 6-5				Weight: 249			College: Stanford				Draft: 2013/2 (35)				Born: 10-Nov-1990				Age: 25			Risk: Green	

Year	Team	G/GS	Snaps	Rec	Pass	Yds	C%	+/-	Yd/C	TD	Drop	YAC	Rk	YAC+	BTkl	DVOA	Rk	DYAR	Rk	YAR	Short	Mid	Deep	Bomb
2013	PHI	16/3	450	36	56	469	64%	+3.3	13.0	4	2	4.4	30	-0.5	0	9.8%	17	60	20	71	34%	42%	17%	8%
2014	PHI	16/5	587	58	89	702	65%	+3.5	12.1	3	2	3.9	31	-0.5	3	13.3%	12	127	8	130	34%	37%	23%	6%
2015	PHI			63	94	801	67%	--	12.7	4							11.2%								

A 15-catch performance in Week 16 against the Redskins bulked up Ertz's stats. He was still technically the second tight end behind Brent Celek last year, and the pair split targets roughly equally in most games prior to that Redskins loss. Ertz was far more productive and both Chip Kelly and DVOA liked his 12-for-24 conversion rate on third-and-6 or more.

Ertz worked out with Darren Sproles and Sproles' Amazing Rolodex in San Diego this offseason (Russell Wilson and Drew Brees were among the special guests), and he talked shop with Tony Gonzalez about the finer points of tightendery, a detail the Eagles press corps will not let you forget. All the extra work, plus a de facto promotion to the starting lineup, should turn all of Ertz's four-catch, 40-something-yard games into something more fantasy productive. You shouldn't have to wait until late December for him to generate a quarter of his production.

Anthony Fasano

Height: 6-4				Weight: 255			College: Notre Dame				Draft: 2006/2 (53)				Born: 20-Apr-1984				Age: 31			Risk: Green	

Year	Team	G/GS	Snaps	Rec	Pass	Yds	C%	+/-	Yd/C	TD	Drop	YAC	Rk	YAC+	BTkl	DVOA	Rk	DYAR	Rk	YAR	Short	Mid	Deep	Bomb
2012	MIA	16/16	899	41	69	332	59%	-0.1	8.1	5	1	2.2	49	-1.7	2	-19.4%	44	-44	43	-38	51%	44%	5%	0%
2013	KC	9/9	503	23	33	200	70%	+1.3	8.7	3	2	3.2	44	-1.4	2	-12.7%	43	-12	42	5	45%	48%	0%	6%
2014	KC	15/13	671	25	36	226	69%	+0.6	9.0	4	2	3.2	42	-1.8	0	2.0%	23	23	23	21	50%	31%	17%	3%
2015	TEN			19	27	181	70%	--	9.5	2							-0.4%								

Fasano was drafted by the last team Bill Parcells coached (the 2006 Cowboys), so he's really a dad runner at this point of his career. The Titans already have a very solid receiving tight end in Delanie Walker, and Craig Stevens has tenure as the team's blocking tight end. It's hard to see Fasano having much of an impact here, but this is the NFL and crazy things happen. For example, Fasano played more snaps than Travis Kelce in Kansas City last year.

Coby Fleener

Height: 6-6				Weight: 247			College: Stanford				Draft: 2012/2 (34)				Born: 20-Sep-1988				Age: 27			Risk: Green	

Year	Team	G/GS	Snaps	Rec	Pass	Yds	C%	+/-	Yd/C	TD	Drop	YAC	Rk	YAC+	BTkl	DVOA	Rk	DYAR	Rk	YAR	Short	Mid	Deep	Bomb
2012	IND	12/10	450	26	48	281	54%	-3.5	10.8	2	3	4.0	27	-0.1	0	-3.6%	32	-2	36	-10	56%	20%	20%	4%
2013	IND	16/12	815	52	87	608	60%	-2.3	11.7	4	1	4.9	23	+0.4	0	-11.3%	42	-24	45	-21	44%	40%	15%	1%
2014	IND	16/12	787	51	92	774	55%	-3.6	15.2	8	5	5.8	11	+1.3	3	10.1%	15	112	10	115	35%	38%	19%	8%
2015	IND			49	82	602	60%	--	12.3	5							6.8%								

Indianapolis' experiment of drafting a college quarterback and his college tight end together has somewhat paid off, even if Fleener's inconsistencies can be troubling. Fleener and Andrew Luck are certainly the most successful quarterback-tight end duo to play together in college and the NFL, but that's not saying much given the competition. Fleener may have never been better than he was against the Patriots last year when he had 144 receiving yards, often matched up with cornerback Brandon Browner. It's hard to find good receiving tight ends who can match up with starting cornerbacks, but Fleener has not been crucial to an offense that loves to spread the ball around. When someone like Charles Clay gets nearly $40 million from Buffalo, it's just not feasible for the Colts to keep both Fleener and Dwayne Allen when they hit free agency after the season. Fleener should be the guy allowed to walk. His 57 percent catch rate is the lowest among active tight ends, and while Luck is partially responsible for that, it also shows how the Colts like to use Fleener in ways that may be better suited for players like Donte Moncrief and rookie Phillip Dorsett. Fleener had five drops last season, and the average depth of those drops was 16.8 yards beyond the line of scrimmage. (For a particularly bad example, check out Fleener dropping a wide-open 37-yard pass with 10:00 left in the second quarter against Washington in Week 13.) Those are big plays not being made by a player who was at his best last year, because sometimes your best isn't good enough.

Chase Ford   Height: 6-6   Weight: 255   College: Miami   Draft: 2012/FA   Born: 19-Jul-1990   Age: 25   Risk: Green

Year	Team	G/GS	Snaps	Rec	Pass	Yds	C%	+/-	Yd/C	TD	Drop	YAC	Rk	YAC+	BTkl	DVOA	Rk	DYAR	Rk	YAR	Short	Mid	Deep	Bomb
2013	MIN	9/0	149	11	16	133	69%	+2.1	12.1	0	0	5.5	--	+0.6	1	-1.2%	--	6	--	0	43%	36%	21%	0%
2014	MIN	11/5	339	23	35	258	66%	+1.6	11.2	1	1	2.7	46	-1.5	2	6.8%	18	32	19	26	33%	45%	15%	6%
2015	MIN			18	25	186	72%	--	10.3	2						5.1%								

Though starter Kyle Rudolph has a Pro Bowl appearance under his belt, Chase Ford posted a higher receiving DVOA and DYAR last season than Rudolph has at any point in his four-year career. Ford was Minnesota's best receiving option at the tight end position when the Bridgewater era began, and ended up lining up out wide or in the slot on 44.2 percent of his snaps. Minnesota seemed to isolate Ford on a wheel route at least once every game, allowing the 6-foot-6 tight end to use his frame against an outleveraged defender on the perimeter. The Vikes seem intent on Rudolph developing a rapport with Bridgewater, and they also drafted red zone threat MyCole Pruitt. But if Ford is on the outs, the 25-year-old should get a look elsewhere based on his 2014 resume.

Antonio Gates   Height: 6-4   Weight: 260   College: Kent State   Draft: 2003/FA   Born: 18-Jun-1980   Age: 35   Risk: Red

Year	Team	G/GS	Snaps	Rec	Pass	Yds	C%	+/-	Yd/C	TD	Drop	YAC	Rk	YAC+	BTkl	DVOA	Rk	DYAR	Rk	YAR	Short	Mid	Deep	Bomb
2012	SD	15/15	857	49	80	538	61%	+2.6	11.0	7	4	2.7	45	-1.4	1	4.6%	19	79	12	89	29%	51%	11%	9%
2013	SD	16/15	970	77	113	872	68%	+4.0	11.3	4	5	4.8	24	+0.3	8	0.7%	29	63	18	62	54%	36%	7%	3%
2014	SD	16/14	770	69	98	821	70%	+7.8	11.9	12	1	3.7	34	-0.5	1	24.1%	4	204	2	224	45%	39%	8%	8%
2015	SD			50	74	529	67%	--	10.7	5						12.3%								

Gates is the first tight end to ever produce more than 700 receiving yards and double-digit touchdowns and not make the Pro Bowl. Sure, those numbers aren't as impressive these days as they were in the past, but six tight ends got credit for a strong season last year and Gates somehow did not. It's not like he needs a ninth Pro Bowl for his solid Hall of Fame case. He has surpassed 10,000 receiving yards, and he'll get his 800th catch and 100th touchdown this season—though not until October, due to a four-game suspension for PED use (which is reflected in the projecton above). Once the season is over, Gates will have to make a decision as a 36-year-old free agent heading into 2016. Ideally, the Chargers get to celebrate Gates' milestones and his early-season absence helps Ladarius Green finally break out, but not so much so that he demands an absurd new contract. Gates then retires and the Chargers still have their tight end of the future, who got to learn from one of the best to ever play the game.

Crockett Gillmore   Height: 6-6   Weight: 260   College: Colorado St.   Draft: 2014/3 (99)   Born: 11/16/1991   Age: 24   Risk: Green

Year	Team	G/GS	Snaps	Rec	Pass	Yds	C%	+/-	Yd/C	TD	Drop	YAC	Rk	YAC+	BTkl	DVOA	Rk	DYAR	Rk	YAR	Short	Mid	Deep	Bomb
2014	BAL	15/1	372	10	15	121	67%	+0.5	12.1	1	1	5.9	--	+1.0	0	11.2%	--	20	--	21	54%	46%	0%	0%
2015	BAL			18	27	193	67%	--	10.7	2						-1.7%								

Nothing says, "rent, don't buy" like your team drafting two players at your position, as the Ravens did with Gilmore. Perhaps it's the team's way of pushing him toward his destiny as a Z-level movie star. "Action has a new name... Crockett Gilmore!" He can't be worse than the Boz was.

Garrett Graham   Height: 6-3   Weight: 243   College: Wisconsin   Draft: 2010/4 (118)   Born: 4-Aug-1986   Age: 29   Risk: Yellow

Year	Team	G/GS	Snaps	Rec	Pass	Yds	C%	+/-	Yd/C	TD	Drop	YAC	Rk	YAC+	BTkl	DVOA	Rk	DYAR	Rk	YAR	Short	Mid	Deep	Bomb
2012	HOU	15/9	611	28	40	263	70%	+2.6	9.4	3	3	4.1	23	-0.8	1	6.8%	18	36	24	33	67%	19%	11%	3%
2013	HOU	13/11	772	49	89	545	55%	-6.1	11.1	5	4	4.2	33	-0.4	1	-21.3%	50	-84	50	-95	53%	35%	7%	5%
2014	HOU	11/9	552	18	28	197	64%	-0.1	10.9	1	0	3.5	38	-0.9	1	2.3%	21	17	27	15	35%	58%	8%	0%
2015	HOU			48	78	487	62%	--	10.1	1						-20.1%								

It may surprise you to learn that the Texans had tight ends on the roster last year—it certainly surprised those of us who watched them! Graham was handed a three-year, $11.25 million deal before last season, then was somehow was targeted just 28 times all season. This, after a 2013 season where he was targeted 89 times in just 13 games. There's a healthy middle ground somewhere in here. Graham is not a good enough blocker to be worth this contract unless he's regularly catching passes.

Jimmy Graham   Height: 6-6   Weight: 260   College: Miami   Draft: 2010/3 (95)   Born: 24-Nov-1986   Age: 29   Risk: Yellow

Year	Team	G/GS	Snaps	Rec	Pass	Yds	C%	+/-	Yd/C	TD	Drop	YAC	Rk	YAC+	BTkl	DVOA	Rk	DYAR	Rk	YAR	Short	Mid	Deep	Bomb
2012	NO	15/9	695	85	135	982	63%	-0.4	11.6	9	14	3.6	35	-0.6	4	2.7%	23	105	7	104	33%	52%	14%	1%
2013	NO	16/12	755	86	143	1215	60%	+5.1	14.1	16	4	4.7	26	+0.3	9	15.7%	12	223	1	212	36%	44%	11%	9%
2014	NO	16/13	775	85	124	889	69%	+3.7	10.5	10	5	3.5	40	-0.7	7	6.8%	17	124	9	113	41%	46%	10%	2%
2015	SEA			74	105	889	70%	--	12.0	9						16.6%								

Comparing Jimmy Graham to Rob Gronkowski was always an act of desperation rather than a result of informed minds coming together. Graham's production in the passing game was phenomenal in 2013, but he is a player who relies on a narrow skill set to be effective. He is essentially an oversized deep threat who can be put into space on shorter routes when used correctly by the offense. The Saints were able to get the most out of him by accommodating his strengths and minimizing his weaknesses within the offense. The Seahawks will now need to show the same understanding, instead of blindly fitting him into a standard tight end position where he must block and run precision routes or adjust to passes below his shoulders.

Ladarius Green   Height: 6-6   Weight: 237   College: Louisiana-Lafayette   Draft: 2012/4 (110)   Born: 29-May-1990   Age: 24   Risk: Yellow

Year	Team	G/GS	Snaps	Rec	Pass	Yds	C%	+/-	Yd/C	TD	Drop	YAC	Rk	YAC+	BTkl	DVOA	Rk	DYAR	Rk	YAR	Short	Mid	Deep	Bomb
2012	SD	4/1	37	4	4	56	100%	+1.1	14.0	0	0	10.5	--	+5.6	1	52.5%	--	10	--	11	100%	0%	0%	0%
2013	SD	16/10	365	17	30	376	57%	-0.1	22.1	3	1	9.8	1	+5.0	0	45.3%	1	113	7	109	23%	45%	26%	6%
2014	SD	14/4	289	19	25	226	76%	+2.8	11.9	0	1	6.0	8	+0.5	1	15.9%	9	41	18	32	60%	20%	20%	0%
2015	SD			36	57	439	63%	--	12.2	3						4.1%								

Green led all tight ends in DVOA in 2013, and had more DYAR than Antonio Gates. The breakout year was a given, right? Well that hype died around Week 2 when Gates had a masterpiece performance against the Seahawks and Green didn't even get a target. Green had a couple of 60-yard games shortly after that, but finished the season with just 70 yards in his final eight games, an afterthought in the offense at best. Naturally, the Chargers again think this could be Green's breakout year. Green still has a lot to prove, as he told ESPN this offseason. "I've got a lot to work on, from route-running, to blocking and catching—everything. [2014] could have been a lot better. I was hurt. I've got to try and stay healthy. And I've got to try and do what I can for the team. I've still got a lot to improve on." Green and Gates are both free agents in 2016, but with Gates' four-game suspension, we're going to see Green thrust right into a starting role from the get-go. Maybe he never gives it back.

Virgil Green   Height: 6-5   Weight: 240   College: Nevada   Draft: 2011/7 (204)   Born: 3-Aug-1988   Age: 27   Risk: Green

Year	Team	G/GS	Snaps	Rec	Pass	Yds	C%	+/-	Yd/C	TD	Drop	YAC	Rk	YAC+	BTkl	DVOA	Rk	DYAR	Rk	YAR	Short	Mid	Deep	Bomb
2012	DEN	12/2	176	5	6	63	83%	+0.4	12.6	0	0	12.4	--	+6.3	2	22.7%	--	14	--	16	100%	0%	0%	0%
2013	DEN	16/3	319	9	12	45	75%	+0.0	5.0	0	0	1.9	--	-2.7	0	-61.0%	--	-44	--	-44	92%	8%	0%	0%
2014	DEN	13/9	394	6	6	74	100%	+1.7	12.3	1	0	7.7	--	+2.8	0	71.5%	--	35	--	41	83%	0%	17%	0%
2015	DEN			29	37	225	78%	--	7.7	2						-0.1%								

Green actually showed some big-play potential in his final year at Nevada (2010) and had some good measurables coming into the NFL, but he has only caught 23 passes for 206 yards in his first four seasons with Denver. The Broncos re-signed him in March after losing the other tight ends on the roster. That means higher expectations for Green, not only as a blocker, but also as a receiver, though Owen Daniels will still likely earn the most targets.

Jermaine Gresham   Height: 6-5   Weight: 261   College: Oklahoma   Draft: 2010/1 (21)   Born: 16-Jun-1988   Age: 27   Risk: N/A

Year	Team	G/GS	Snaps	Rec	Pass	Yds	C%	+/-	Yd/C	TD	Drop	YAC	Rk	YAC+	BTkl	DVOA	Rk	DYAR	Rk	YAR	Short	Mid	Deep	Bomb
2012	CIN	16/15	1002	64	94	737	68%	+2.8	11.5	5	6	6.5	2	+1.3	6	3.2%	22	24	29	48	49%	37%	12%	2%
2013	CIN	14/14	891	46	67	458	69%	+1.3	10.0	4	3	5.8	10	-0.1	9	-18.5%	49	-47	49	-23	52%	30%	17%	0%
2014	CIN	15/15	875	62	79	460	78%	+5.2	7.4	5	2	4.2	25	-1.3	12	-21.9%	44	-73	48	-76	71%	25%	3%	1%
2015				--	--	--	--	--	--	--						--								

A mystifying, frustrating player. Gresham has oodles of talent and will occasionally make the spectacular catch or the tough block. But his time in Cincinnati was marked by ill-timed drops, woeful inconsistency, and killer penalties. Worse, he got a reputation for not being willing to play through pain, most notably in the playoff loss against Indianapolis, when the Bengals were crippled by injuries to playmakers. In fairness, Gresham had offseason surgery to repair a herniated disk in his back, but that didn't stop the exasperated Bengals front office from moving on. A free agent at press time, Gresham will most likely catch on with a team needing a body at the position (New Orleans is a rumored—and natural—fit), and a change of scenery could work wonders.

Ryan Griffin			Height: 6-6		Weight: 247		College: Connecticut			Draft: 2013/6 (201)		Born: 11-Jan-1990		Age: 25		Risk: Blue	
Year	Team	G/GS	Snaps	Rec	Pass	Yds	C%	+/-	Yd/C	TD	Drop	YAC	Rk	YAC+	BTkl	DVOA	Rk	DYAR	Rk	YAR	Short	Mid	Deep	Bomb
2013	HOU	15/8	362	19	28	244	68%	+2.1	12.8	1	0	5.2	17	+0.2	0	13.9%	13	38	26	43	50%	23%	15%	12%
2014	HOU	16/2	334	10	16	91	63%	-1.1	9.1	1	2	3.6	--	-1.0	0	-2.7%	--	5	--	7	56%	19%	19%	6%
2015	HOU			9	15	84	60%	--	9.3	0						-22.0%								

339 snaps, 13 targets. Griffin hasn't shown anything in his first two seasons that would lead you believe he's a bad player. He's a little slight of build, but he blocks at least as well as Garrett Graham does and was much better than rookie C.J. Fiedoro-wicz. He's not going to stretch the seam or threaten a defense, but he can be a nice underneath valve as a lower-rung receiver. Given the talent around him, it's a little surprising we haven't seen him get more of an extended trial.

Rob Gronkowski			Height: 6-6		Weight: 264		College: Arizona			Draft: 2010/2 (42)		Born: 14-May-1989		Age: 26		Risk: Yellow	
Year	Team	G/GS	Snaps	Rec	Pass	Yds	C%	+/-	Yd/C	TD	Drop	YAC	Rk	YAC+	BTkl	DVOA	Rk	DYAR	Rk	YAR	Short	Mid	Deep	Bomb
2012	NE	11/11	731	55	80	790	69%	+5.7	14.4	11	5	5.5	7	+1.1	2	41.2%	1	279	2	279	34%	45%	16%	5%
2013	NE	7/6	383	39	66	592	59%	-0.2	15.2	4	1	5.0	21	+1.0	4	12.9%	14	91	11	115	25%	45%	22%	7%
2014	NE	15/10	825	82	131	1124	63%	+2.3	13.7	12	5	5.6	14	+1.3	24	19.7%	7	237	1	253	34%	45%	17%	4%
2015	NE			85	129	1106	66%	--	13.0	11						24.1%								

The Patriots started slow in part because Gronk started slow, and the advanced stats reflect this. He came out as slightly below replacement level through four weeks, then from Week 5 onwards had 241 DYAR. Pro-rated to a full season, that would be 321 DYAR, which would rank as the No. 7 season by a tight end since 1989. The actual total ranks as the No. 25 season; all four seasons where Gronk has played at least half the year rank in the top 25, including his 2011 season, which has the highest DYAR ever by a tight end.

Perhaps the most remarkable feat Gronk pulled off in 2014 was staying healthy. Since 1970, only seven other players had a season with Approximate Value of at least 13 (according to Pro Football Reference) and then missed at least a quarter of both Year 3 and Year 4.

Excellent Young (And Then Injured) Players

Player	Pos	First Year	Team	Career AV	Best Early AV	AV Year 5
Steve Owens	RB	1970	DET	40	17	6
Wesley Walker	WR	1977	NYJ	91	16	7
Charlie Brown	WR	1982	WAS/ATL	40	15	7
Tony Reed	RB	1977	KC/DEN	35	14	4
John Riggins	RB	1971	NYJ	121	13	14
Natrone Means	RB	1993	SD/JAC	42	13	7
Michael Bennett	RB	2001	MIN	38	13	4
Rob Gronkowski	TE	2010	NE	46	14	12

Only one of those other seven players played as well as Gronk after returning from two years of injuries. John Riggins may not have been a Party Rocker, but he was also a famously weird and tough dude.

Clay Harbor

Height: 6-3　Weight: 252　College: Missouri State　Draft: 2010/4 (125)　Born: 2-Jul-1987　Age: 28　Risk: Green

Year	Team	G/GS	Snaps	Rec	Pass	Yds	C%	+/-	Yd/C	TD	Drop	YAC	Rk	YAC+	BTkl	DVOA	Rk	DYAR	Rk	YAR	Short	Mid	Deep	Bomb
2012	PHI	14/9	340	25	39	186	64%	-1.2	7.4	2	2	2.8	44	-2.2	1	-37.2%	49	-66	47	-71	55%	39%	3%	3%
2013	JAC	16/7	358	24	35	292	69%	+3.8	12.2	2	0	5.3	14	+0.6	0	0.4%	30	18	34	15	35%	55%	6%	3%
2014	JAC	13/8	482	26	35	289	74%	+1.2	11.1	1	1	6.9	6	+1.2	1	-4.8%	29	5	30	12	57%	34%	6%	3%
2015	JAC			14	23	150	61%	--	10.7	1						-12.7%								

Clay seems like a really poor choice with which to build a harbor. May we suggest concrete? Oh, this isn't Minecraft? Well, Clay Harbor the football player is a replacement-level tight end who has decent hands and isn't much of blocker. The fact that he was one of Jacksonville's most efficient options says a lot about the kind of offense they built last season. Now if you'll excuse us, we need to write the comment for Jake Stoneburner.

Josh Hill

Height: 6-5　Weight: 229　College: Idaho State　Draft: 2013/FA　Born: 21-May-1990　Age: 25　Risk: Red

Year	Team	G/GS	Snaps	Rec	Pass	Yds	C%	+/-	Yd/C	TD	Drop	YAC	Rk	YAC+	BTkl	DVOA	Rk	DYAR	Rk	YAR	Short	Mid	Deep	Bomb
2013	NO	14/3	176	6	10	44	60%	-0.8	7.3	1	1	5.5	--	+0.5	0	-14.7%	--	-6	--	-6	60%	30%	10%	0%
2014	NO	16/3	288	14	20	176	70%	+0.9	12.6	5	1	7.1	--	+2.2	0	32.0%	--	57	--	58	68%	11%	16%	5%
2015	NO			52	78	639	67%	--	12.3	5						15.7%								

The Saints are turning to a relative unknown to replace Jimmy Graham. Josh Hill is entering the third season of his career and has caught just 20 passes in regular season games. He is a 25-year old, 6-foot-5, 250-pound tight end with the athleticism to stretch the defense down the seam and attack space from an in-line position after play-action. Hill showed off his athleticism repeatedly for his five touchdowns last season. He should be able to adequately fill the role of Graham, but he lacks the same bulk and strength at the catch point that Graham used to dominate safeties and cornerbacks on high passes deep down the field. On the other hand, a slighter frame means more flexibility, so Hill should be a more valuable middle-of-the-field receiver for Drew Brees than Graham was.

Rob Housler

Height: 6-6　Weight: 249　College: Florida Atlantic　Draft: 2011/3 (69)　Born: 17-Mar-1988　Age: 27　Risk: Green

Year	Team	G/GS	Snaps	Rec	Pass	Yds	C%	+/-	Yd/C	TD	Drop	YAC	Rk	YAC+	BTkl	DVOA	Rk	DYAR	Rk	YAR	Short	Mid	Deep	Bomb
2012	ARI	15/9	617	45	68	417	66%	+2.2	9.3	0	4	4.0	25	-0.5	6	-17.1%	43	-60	46	-41	51%	37%	11%	2%
2013	ARI	13/10	520	39	57	454	68%	+2.6	11.6	1	3	5.1	18	-0.4	1	0.8%	28	32	27	19	43%	34%	17%	5%
2014	ARI	15/7	320	9	17	129	53%	-2.2	14.3	0	0	9.3	--	+3.2	0	0.2%	--	8	--	-2	41%	35%	24%	0%
2015	CLE			39	58	454	67%	--	11.6	4						7.2%								

Two years into his career, Housler was already among the bottom 40 tight ends in career DYAR (since 1989), but he showed significant improvement in a smaller role in 2013 and 2014. Mike Pettine has told the media Housler is "ideal" as a tight end who can play in the slot and be an effective receiver, which makes you wonder how low the bar for ideal players has gotten in Cleveland these days. Regardless, even if Housler is Cleveland's top tight end, he still figures to be rotated out of the lineup frequently, and has little fantasy value this year.

Travis Kelce

Height: 6-5　Weight: 255　College: Cincinnati　Draft: 2013/3 (63)　Born: 5-Oct-1989　Age: 26　Risk: Green

Year	Team	G/GS	Snaps	Rec	Pass	Yds	C%	+/-	Yd/C	TD	Drop	YAC	Rk	YAC+	BTkl	DVOA	Rk	DYAR	Rk	YAR	Short	Mid	Deep	Bomb
2013	KC	1/0	0	0	--	0			--	0	--	--	--	--	--	--	--	--	--	--	--	--	--	--
2014	KC	16/11	668	67	87	862	77%	+9.9	12.9	5	4	7.2	4	+2.2	12	23.0%	5	174	4	196	53%	35%	12%	0%
2015	KC			74	103	826	72%	--	11.2	5						9.4%								

On May 14, 1989, Skynet sent back a terminator named Rob Gronkowski. John Connor and the resistance countered by sending their own terminator, but Travis Kelce did not arrive until October 5, 1989. "Baby Gronk" is older than you might expect, but Kelce had a breakout season in his first true attempt at the NFL after missing most of 2013 due to microfracture surgery. Combine Alex Smith's fondness for short passes with the absence of a quality No. 2 tight end, and Kelce's ceiling is very high this year. The only troubling issue last year was Kelce's four fumbles, even if the crucial one in Arizona (Week 14) was highly debatable. He is already one fumble away from tying Jason Witten (five) and two away from tying Tony Gonzalez and Antonio Gates (six) for as many fumbles as they've had in their entire careers. Kelce needs to tighten that grip, but he's a very promising young player.

Lance Kendricks			Height: 6-3		Weight: 243		College: Wisconsin			Draft: 2011/2 (47)			Born: 30-Jan-1988			Age: 27		Risk: Green	
Year	Team	G/GS	Snaps	Rec	Pass	Yds	C%	+/-	Yd/C	TD	Drop	YAC	Rk	YAC+	BTkl	DVOA	Rk	DYAR	Rk	YAR	Short	Mid	Deep	Bomb
2012	STL	16/14	843	42	64	519	66%	+0.7	12.4	4	4	5.4	11	+0.9	3	13.0%	12	67	16	54	50%	35%	13%	2%
2013	STL	15/13	575	32	46	258	70%	+0.7	8.1	4	3	3.4	42	-1.4	1	-6.4%	38	3	38	0	72%	23%	5%	0%
2014	STL	16/14	594	27	38	259	71%	+1.4	9.6	5	2	3.9	32	-1.0	0	11.8%	13	51	15	52	64%	25%	11%	0%
2015	STL			30	47	290	64%	--	9.7	3							-3.2%								

What's more surprising, that the Rams re-signed their No. 2 tight end to a four-year deal worth up to $18.5 million, or that Kendricks actually turned down more cash from Atlanta to stay in St. Louis? That's awfully good money for a guy who plays about 35 or 40 snaps per game. Defenders of the contract cited Kendricks' versatility, and sure, he typically played three or four snaps per game at fullback, and another three or four in the slot or out wide. Still, even though he fared OK when the Rams threw him the ball, he was never more than the fourth or fifth option on the field. Both Kendricks and the Rams have talked about a bigger role in the passing game going forward, but if that happens, it would be almost unprecedented. Of the ten tight ends most statistically similar to Kendricks over the last three years, only one ever gained even 300 yards in a season again: Ken Dilger, who was a nice option for Peyton Manning early in the quarterback's career and then lasted another three seasons in Tampa Bay.

Marcedes Lewis			Height: 6-6		Weight: 255		College: UCLA			Draft: 2006/1 (28)			Born: 19-May-1984			Age: 31		Risk: Yellow	
Year	Team	G/GS	Snaps	Rec	Pass	Yds	C%	+/-	Yd/C	TD	Drop	YAC	Rk	YAC+	BTkl	DVOA	Rk	DYAR	Rk	YAR	Short	Mid	Deep	Bomb
2012	JAC	16/15	830	52	77	540	68%	+1.6	10.4	4	5	4.7	16	-0.3	1	0.0%	28	21	31	31	50%	38%	12%	0%
2013	JAC	11/11	582	25	47	359	53%	-5.8	14.4	4	3	9.0	2	+4.0	8	-8.1%	39	-3	39	6	46%	41%	13%	0%
2014	JAC	8/8	432	18	31	206	58%	-2.5	11.4	2	2	7.8	3	+2.4	2	-9.8%	33	-5	33	-12	62%	24%	14%	0%
2015	JAC			26	44	268	59%	--	10.3	3							-10.6%								

Nothing will get you in a more political mood than the career of Marcedes Lewis. Lewis was given a five-year, $35 million deal off the franchise tag in 2011. In a league where most players are thought of as attrition, and in a good organization every contract dollar is essentially a fighting point between agent and team, Lewis was able to collect paycheck after paycheck because the Jaguars needed to hit the minimum salary floor the new CBA provided. Despite contributing just 11 Approximate Value (per Pro-Football-Reference) over the first four injury-plagued years of the deal, there was never a second thought given to his contract because Jacksonville had to spend that money somewhere. Lewis took a paycut in Year 5, where he'll make merely $3.8 million. Lewis was a fine player in his prime: a great blocker, and a tall red zone threat with the ability to post up defenders. His contract is the sort of thing that makes you question the fairness of the system.

Heath Miller			Height: 6-5		Weight: 256		College: Virginia			Draft: 2005/1 (30)			Born: 22-Oct-1982			Age: 33		Risk: Green	
Year	Team	G/GS	Snaps	Rec	Pass	Yds	C%	+/-	Yd/C	TD	Drop	YAC	Rk	YAC+	BTkl	DVOA	Rk	DYAR	Rk	YAR	Short	Mid	Deep	Bomb
2012	PIT	15/15	994	71	101	816	70%	+5.2	11.5	8	3	4.8	14	+0.5	1	21.0%	6	165	4	172	50%	35%	14%	1%
2013	PIT	14/14	901	58	78	593	74%	+8.1	10.2	1	3	3.9	38	-0.9	3	-2.8%	35	23	29	22	53%	33%	11%	3%
2014	PIT	16/16	1081	66	91	761	73%	+5.9	11.5	3	4	4.9	19	+0.2	2	13.5%	11	127	7	110	43%	45%	11%	0%
2015	PIT			55	79	605	70%	--	11.0	4							3.9%								

The 2014 season was a quiet but effective campaign for Heath Miller. It's likely that his role within the Steelers' passing offense is going to diminish moving forward, but he should still provide his quarterback with what he has always provided: a safety blanket. Miller is comfortable working the middle of the field and has been a staple of Ben Roethlisberger's offense for a decade now. Miller's value as a blocker will prolong his career, but the explosive plays are likely to be limited as the Steelers look to shift a greater workload onto Martavis Bryant and Markus Wheaton, with the potential for Sammie Coates to also be a contributor.

Brandon Myers Height: 6-4 Weight: 250 College: Iowa Draft: 2009/6 (202) Born: 4-Sep-1985 Age: 30 Risk: Green

Year	Team	G/GS	Snaps	Rec	Pass	Yds	C%	+/-	Yd/C	TD	Drop	YAC	Rk	YAC+	BTkl	DVOA	Rk	DYAR	Rk	YAR	Short	Mid	Deep	Bomb
2012	OAK	16/16	1009	79	105	806	75%	+8.1	10.2	4	6	3.6	34	-1.0	2	10.7%	13	112	6	123	42%	50%	8%	0%
2013	NYG	16/14	848	47	75	522	63%	+0.4	11.1	4	2	3.6	39	-0.7	1	-5.9%	37	7	36	16	39%	44%	17%	0%
2014	TB	14/6	465	22	32	190	69%	+1.3	8.6	0	1	2.7	45	-2.0	0	-18.5%	39	-23	37	-30	64%	29%	7%	0%
2015	TB			21	34	213	62%	--	10.1	1						-13.4%								

Myers posted eerily similar advanced stats to Austin Seferian-Jenkins in both DVOA (ASJ: -18.7%) and DYAR (ASJ: -29). But a better overall comparison for Myers is former 49ers tight end Eric Johnson, In 2004, his third NFL season, the former seventh-round pick caught 82 passes on a bad 49ers offense. He never again caught 50 passes in a season. In Myers' fourth year, the former sixth-round pick caught 79 passes on a bad Raiders offense. Like Johnson, Myers seems unlikely to approach that mark again. He will almost certainly will not approach it in 2015 with Seferian-Jenkins, Vincent Jackson, and Mike Evans fighting for targets.

Troy Niklas Height: 6-6 Weight: 270 College: Notre Dame Draft: 2014/2 (52) Born: 9/18/1992 Age: 23 Risk: Green

Year	Team	G/GS	Snaps	Rec	Pass	Yds	C%	+/-	Yd/C	TD	Drop	YAC	Rk	YAC+	BTkl	DVOA	Rk	DYAR	Rk	YAR	Short	Mid	Deep	Bomb
2014	ARI	7/2	89	3	3	38	100%	+0.8	12.7	0	0	6.0	--	+1.7	0	80.8%	--	17	--	14	67%	33%	0%	0%
2015	ARI			22	31	249	71%	--	11.3	2						5.3%								

Sixteen months after being drafted, Niklas has undergone surgery three times: two to repair his sprained ankle, the third to mend a hernia. He has also struggled with a bad hamstring and suffered a broken finger that got caught in a jersey. Niklas only played tight end for two seasons at Notre Dame and is still learning the position. He has great athletic gifts, though it's unclear whether he'll ever be healthy enough to develop them. He enters training camp as the top tight end on the roster because somebody has to be.

Greg Olsen Height: 6-6 Weight: 254 College: Miami Draft: 2007/1 (31) Born: 11-Mar-1985 Age: 30 Risk: Green

Year	Team	G/GS	Snaps	Rec	Pass	Yds	C%	+/-	Yd/C	TD	Drop	YAC	Rk	YAC+	BTkl	DVOA	Rk	DYAR	Rk	YAR	Short	Mid	Deep	Bomb
2012	CAR	16/16	1005	69	104	843	66%	+6.7	12.2	5	2	3.5	38	-0.7	2	13.6%	10	157	5	147	30%	53%	12%	5%
2013	CAR	16/16	1001	73	111	816	66%	+7.7	11.2	6	5	4.5	29	-0.1	4	3.8%	22	83	14	65	39%	44%	13%	5%
2014	CAR	16/16	1067	84	123	1008	68%	+5.1	12.0	6	1	4.0	29	-0.3	1	14.7%	10	178	3	183	37%	49%	12%	3%
2015	CAR			77	110	926	70%	--	12.0	6						18.8%								

You likely don't think of Olsen as the focal point of an offense, mostly because he's not an offensive dynamo of the likes of Jimmy Graham or Rob Gronkowski. But Olsen was the fulcrum point for everything Carolina did last season. He's a tough receiver with enough speed to run the seam, he's a solid blocker on both run and pass plays, and he's got the versatility to line up as a wide receiver, in the backfield, or as a traditional tight end. (Olsen was the only player to appear among the top-ten tight ends lining up in both fullback or wide receiver positions.) The Panthers probably won't have to lean on him quite as much this season, but it's a luxury to have a player who can contribute in so many different ways.

Top 12 Tight Ends Lined Up as Fullbacks, 2014

Player	Team	FB	Snaps	Pct
Cory Harkey	STL	301	333	90%
Ryan Hewitt	CIN	225	466	48%
Jack Doyle	IND	162	399	41%
Ed Dickson	CAR	116	522	22%
Dante Rosario	CHI	116	314	37%
Greg Olsen	CAR	95	1067	9%
David Johnson	SD	92	177	52%
Luke Stocker	TB	70	325	22%
Andrew Quarless	GB	58	630	9%
Dwayne Allen	IND	48	619	8%
Lance Kendricks	STL	46	594	8%
Richard Rodgers	GB	43	478	9%

Top 12 Tight Ends Lined Up as Wide Receivers, 2014

Player	Team	Wide	Slot	Both	Snaps	Pct
Jimmy Graham	NO	124	210	334	775	43%
Greg Olsen	CAR	38	269	307	1067	29%
Antonio Gates	SD	30	270	300	770	39%
Martellus Bennett	CHI	47	239	286	954	30%
Travis Kelce	KC	95	186	281	668	42%
Levine Toiololo	ATL	42	223	265	940	28%
Zach Ertz	PHI	48	214	262	587	45%
Jared Cook	STL	54	203	257	682	38%
Delanie Walker	TEN	26	210	236	769	31%
Vernon Davis	SF	34	198	232	830	28%
Jason Witten	DAL	7	216	223	1047	21%
Mychal Rivera	OAK	14	199	213	818	26%

Yes, it makes no sense that the Rams list Harkey as a tight end.

Niles Paul

| | Height: 6-1 | | Weight: 225 | | College: Nebraska | | | Draft: 2011/5 (155) | | Born: 9-Aug-1989 | | Age: 26 | | Risk: Green |

Year	Team	G/GS	Snaps	Rec	Pass	Yds	C%	+/-	Yd/C	TD	Drop	YAC	Rk	YAC+	BTkl	DVOA	Rk	DYAR	Rk	YAR	Short	Mid	Deep	Bomb
2012	WAS	16/4	224	8	15	152	53%	-1.2	19.0	1	2	7.0	--	+2.1	0	-3.9%	--	4	--	5	47%	20%	33%	0%
2013	WAS	15/4	150	4	8	51	50%	-0.7	12.8	0	0	5.5	--	+0.6	0	-26.8%	--	-11	--	-14	57%	29%	14%	0%
2014	WAS	16/7	562	39	52	507	75%	+3.5	13.0	1	3	6.6	7	+1.6	4	24.4%	3	110	11	87	62%	20%	14%	4%
2015	*WAS*			*44*	*62*	*434*	*71%*	*--*	*9.9*	*2*						*-0.4%*								

Paul started the 2014 season with 18 catches for 253 yards in relief of injured Jordan Reed, then settled into one of those non-role roles that defined the undefinable Redskins offense. Paul really is a 6-foot-1, 225-pound tight end, as opposed to a slot receiver listed as a tight end for depth-chart convenience purposes. He often lines up next to the right tackle and lead blocks, especially when Reed is unavailable. Paul isn't a bad run blocker, but sometimes Jay Gruden felt the need to ask him to do the ridiculous: control Bruce Irvin on the back side of an end-around against the Seahawks, for example. (Result: 5-yard loss). Most coaches would do more to keep a woefully undersized tight end from getting eaten alive by defensive ends and linebackers, but Gruden is not most coaches.

The Redskins re-signed Paul in the offseason. His reception totals are at the mercy of Reed's health, the quarterbacks' viability, and Gruden's whims. He might be the best replacement for Roy Helu catching passes out of the backfield.

Logan Paulsen

| | Height: 6-5 | | Weight: 264 | | College: UCLA | | | Draft: 2010/FA | | Born: 26-Feb-1987 | | Age: 28 | | Risk: Yellow |

Year	Team	G/GS	Snaps	Rec	Pass	Yds	C%	+/-	Yd/C	TD	Drop	YAC	Rk	YAC+	BTkl	DVOA	Rk	DYAR	Rk	YAR	Short	Mid	Deep	Bomb
2012	WAS	16/10	675	25	36	308	69%	+1.8	12.3	1	2	4.4	20	+0.3	2	23.7%	4	69	14	76	37%	49%	11%	3%
2013	WAS	16/14	809	28	50	267	56%	-2.3	9.5	3	3	3.4	41	-1.2	1	-36.4%	51	-96	51	-100	56%	31%	11%	2%
2014	WAS	16/12	390	13	16	78	81%	+0.4	6.0	1	0	3.5	--	-1.9	2	-36.5%	--	-32	--	-38	81%	19%	0%	0%
2015	*WAS*			*20*	*30*	*159*	*67%*	*--*	*7.9*	*1*						*-19.1%*								

The Redskins' designated blocking tight end, Paulsen racked up four false starts, three holding penalties, a block below the waist, and an unsportsmanlike conduct penalty in part-time duties last year. That's 62 penalty yards, counting some "half the distance" stuff. Paulsen only had 78 receiving yards, so he almost ended up moving the Redskins backwards overall.

Brandon Pettigrew

| | Height: 6-6 | | Weight: 263 | | College: Oklahoma State | | | Draft: 2009/1 (20) | | Born: 23-Feb-1985 | | Age: 30 | | Risk: Green |

Year	Team	G/GS	Snaps	Rec	Pass	Yds	C%	+/-	Yd/C	TD	Drop	YAC	Rk	YAC+	BTkl	DVOA	Rk	DYAR	Rk	YAR	Short	Mid	Deep	Bomb
2012	DET	14/11	770	59	102	567	58%	-7.1	9.6	3	8	4.0	26	+0.1	1	-25.3%	45	-123	49	-126	55%	35%	9%	0%
2013	DET	14/14	888	41	63	416	65%	-0.2	10.1	2	3	4.6	27	-0.5	2	-16.6%	48	-37	48	-18	59%	25%	13%	3%
2014	DET	14/9	587	10	15	70	67%	-0.6	7.0	0	1	3.1	--	-2.3	0	-31.3%	--	-21	--	-28	71%	29%	0%	0%
2015	*DET*			*17*	*27*	*165*	*63%*	*--*	*9.7*	*2*						*-10.6%*								

After suffering through four years of heinous inefficiency, the Lions finally wised up and siphoned off Pettigrew's opportunities in the passing game. Pettigrew has 11 career games in which he compiled more receiving yards than he did all of 2014, as Detroit cut deep into his snap count despite injuries to Eric Ebron and Joseph Fauria. General manager Marty Mayhew suggested that Pettigrew would have a bigger role in 2015, but given that the former first-rounder was also the subject of trade rumors around draft time, it seems just as likely that he'll take a backseat, so long as one or both of the young tight ends doesn't totally crater.

Dennis Pitta

| | Height: 6-5 | | Weight: 245 | | College: BYU | | | Draft: 2010/4 (114) | | Born: 29-Jun-1985 | | Age: 30 | | Risk: Red |

Year	Team	G/GS	Snaps	Rec	Pass	Yds	C%	+/-	Yd/C	TD	Drop	YAC	Rk	YAC+	BTkl	DVOA	Rk	DYAR	Rk	YAR	Short	Mid	Deep	Bomb
2012	BAL	16/5	639	61	94	669	65%	+1.2	11.0	7	3	4.1	22	-0.4	7	4.3%	21	51	21	68	43%	39%	10%	8%
2013	BAL	4/1	158	20	33	169	61%	-0.4	8.5	1	3	2.6	50	-1.8	0	-4.6%	36	6	37	-18	44%	44%	9%	3%
2014	BAL	3/3	166	16	21	125	76%	+1.1	7.8	0	1	3.4	--	-1.8	2	-3.5%	--	5	--	0	55%	40%	5%	0%
2015	*BAL*			*21*	*33*	*208*	*64%*	*--*	*9.9*	*2*						*-8.4%*								

Serious hip injuries have derailed a promising career, but after two years spent mostly on the shelf, Pitta is optimistic about playing in 2015. He looked fluid in limited work during OTAs, for what that is worth. He is still a likely candidate for the PUP list to begin the season. Maxx Williams' advancement may determine how quickly Pitta decides to test his fragile hips.

Andrew Quarless   Height: 6-5   Weight: 254   College: Penn State   Draft: 2010/5 (154)   Born: 6-Oct-1988   Age: 27   Risk: Yellow

Year	Team	G/GS	Snaps	Rec	Pass	Yds	C%	+/-	Yd/C	TD	Drop	YAC	Rk	YAC+	BTkl	DVOA	Rk	DYAR	Rk	YAR	Short	Mid	Deep	Bomb
2013	GB	16/10	693	32	53	312	60%	+0.6	9.8	2	2	4.3	32	+0.0	1	-14.4%	46	-25	46	-19	53%	38%	6%	2%
2014	GB	16/11	630	29	46	323	63%	-1.2	11.1	3	1	5.5	15	+1.1	2	-0.1%	26	24	22	26	65%	23%	12%	0%
2015	GB			23	35	240	66%	--	10.4	2						-1.0%								

A July firearms arrest could complicate Quarless's 2015 season, with possible league discipline or even his release by the Packers. Green Bay's early reaction was to stand by Quarless, who is by far the best blocking tight end with experience on the roster. Rodgers praised the development in his game as a receiver, but Quarless will never be confused with Jermichael Finley as a receiving threat and should remain in a committee role with limited receiving totals.

Jordan Reed   Height: 6-2   Weight: 236   College: Florida   Draft: 2013/3 (85)   Born: 3-Jul-1990   Age: 25   Risk: Yellow

Year	Team	G/GS	Snaps	Rec	Pass	Yds	C%	+/-	Yd/C	TD	Drop	YAC	Rk	YAC+	BTkl	DVOA	Rk	DYAR	Rk	YAR	Short	Mid	Deep	Bomb
2013	WAS	9/4	379	45	60	499	75%	+3.5	11.1	3	3	5.5	12	+0.5	2	19.5%	9	98	10	124	48%	45%	5%	2%
2014	WAS	11/2	364	50	65	465	77%	+1.9	9.3	0	0	5.7	12	+0.5	10	-10.8%	35	-15	35	-8	66%	28%	6%	0%
2015	WAS			62	84	631	74%	--	10.2	4						8.9%								

Reed had three big games last year, all of them after he missed time for injuries: an 8-92-0 performance against the Cardinals in October, a 9-123-0 effort against the Colts at the end of November, and a 9-70-0 game in the season finale against the Cowboys. In between, Reed alternated between hamstring injuries and Jay Gruden's *Game Plan Twilight Zone*, where no one who can do anything with the football gets the football. Reed has vowed to stop trying to hurdle defenders as a way to cut down on the hamstring injuries, but he has been injury-prone since college, so eradicating one of the moves that makes him special might not be worth it. Like Pierre Garcon and a number of other players in Washington, Reed needs a settled quarterback situation and a coherent offense, in addition to some better health, before he takes the next step toward stardom.

Mychal Rivera   Height: 6-3   Weight: 242   College: Tennessee   Draft: 2013/6 (184)   Born: 8-Sep-1990   Age: 25   Risk: Yellow

Year	Team	G/GS	Snaps	Rec	Pass	Yds	C%	+/-	Yd/C	TD	Drop	YAC	Rk	YAC+	BTkl	DVOA	Rk	DYAR	Rk	YAR	Short	Mid	Deep	Bomb
2013	OAK	16/3	592	38	60	407	63%	+2.5	10.7	4	4	2.4	51	-2.1	3	8.1%	19	60	19	57	42%	44%	11%	4%
2014	OAK	16/10	818	58	99	534	59%	-2.7	9.2	4	7	3.0	44	-1.8	1	-22.6%	45	-97	49	-112	51%	31%	14%	4%
2015	OAK			53	86	586	62%	--	11.1	3						-3.9%								

Rivera has followed in the footsteps of Brandon Myers: an Oakland tight end that only catches your attention in the second halves of bad losses. Too many drops hurt his catch rate last year, but he's still likely to see a lot of the tight end targets this season. Just don't count on many more of those 1-yard touchdown passes in fantasy football.

Richard Rodgers   Height: 6-4   Weight: 257   College: California   Draft: 2014/3 (98)   Born: 1/22/1992   Age: 23   Risk: Yellow

Year	Team	G/GS	Snaps	Rec	Pass	Yds	C%	+/-	Yd/C	TD	Drop	YAC	Rk	YAC+	BTkl	DVOA	Rk	DYAR	Rk	YAR	Short	Mid	Deep	Bomb
2014	GB	16/5	478	20	30	225	67%	-0.1	11.3	2	1	2.4	47	-2.5	1	-10.9%	36	-8	34	-7	59%	24%	10%	7%
2015	GB			28	40	336	70%	--	12.0	4						18.6%								

Rodgers may be one of the league's more polarizing players. The believers see a third-round pick by Ted Thompson playing on one of the best offenses in the league and a field-stretching tight end who could make a big step forward in his second season. The doubters see a player who plays to his 4.8 40-yard dash, is a far cry from a matchup threat at tight end, and is a woeful blocker unable to set the edge in the run game. Andrew Quarless' offseason troubles could give him more opportunity to prove the doubters wrong, because the Packers wouldn't have drafted him in the third round if they weren't believers.

Dante Rosario

| Height: 6-3 | | | | Weight: 244 | | College: Oregon | | | Draft: 2007/5 (155) | | Born: 25-Oct-1984 | | Age: 31 | | Risk: Red |

Year	Team	G/GS	Snaps	Rec	Pass	Yds	C%	+/-	Yd/C	TD	Drop	YAC	Rk	YAC+	BTkl	DVOA	Rk	DYAR	Rk	YAR	Short	Mid	Deep	Bomb
2012	SD	13/2	190	10	18	95	56%	-1.6	9.5	3	0	4.3	--	+0.1	0	-18.3%	--	-6	--	-10	39%	50%	0%	11%
2013	CHI	15/3	183	1	4	13	25%	-2.0	13.0	0	0	15.0	--	+6.1	0	-56.8%	--	-13	--	-14	75%	25%	0%	0%
2014	CHI	16/3	314	16	22	116	73%	+1.4	7.3	0	0	3.4	--	-1.9	1	-31.9%	--	-32	--	-38	65%	25%	10%	0%
2015	CHI			18	31	165	58%	--	9.2	2						-21.6%								

There comes a time in a man's life where … oh, heck, we hired John Fox? Time to give him a familiar face and re-sign Dante Rosario for his third tour of vulpine duty. When not backing up Martellus Bennett and serving as an H-back, he can reminisce about the Queen and Mile High Cities. (Note to the pedantic: Charlotte and Cincinnati city officials agreed to a challenge where last October's Panthers-Bengals game would determine the real "Queen City." Yes, the 34-34 tie.)

Kyle Rudolph

| Height: 6-6 | | | | Weight: 265 | | College: Notre Dame | | | Draft: 2011/2 (43) | | Born: 9-Nov-1989 | | Age: 26 | | Risk: Red |

Year	Team	G/GS	Snaps	Rec	Pass	Yds	C%	+/-	Yd/C	TD	Drop	YAC	Rk	YAC+	BTkl	DVOA	Rk	DYAR	Rk	YAR	Short	Mid	Deep	Bomb
2012	MIN	16/16	951	53	94	493	56%	-6.1	9.3	9	3	5.2	12	+0.2	4	-3.4%	31	64	17	8	53%	39%	7%	1%
2013	MIN	8/8	424	30	46	313	65%	+0.3	10.4	3	1	4.0	37	-0.7	6	-13.9%	44	-21	43	-13	44%	36%	20%	0%
2014	MIN	9/8	434	24	34	231	71%	+1.8	9.6	2	3	4.8	20	+0.3	1	0.0%	25	17	25	11	65%	26%	6%	3%
2015	MIN			58	85	579	68%	--	10.0	5						5.5%								

Fool me once, shame on you; fool me twice, shame on me. Fool me thrice and your name might be Kyle Rudolph. The former second-rounder has missed 15 games the past two seasons with a litany of injuries—a broken foot, knee sprain, ankle sprain and hamstring and abdominal strains. Still, the words "tight end" and "Norv Turner offense" are enough to keep Rudolph firmly on everyone's radar, especially given how Turner utilized him in limited snaps last season. Rudolph lined up in the slot 147 times last year, more than a third of his total snaps, insinuating Minnesota's plans to provide him with more receiving opportunities. The Vikings have plenty of perimeter speed but not much in the way of possession receivers who will control the middle of the field. Thus, if Rudolph's body cooperates, we could see a campaign similar to 2012, when he scored nine times and posted a 68.7% red zone receiving DVOA.

Austin Seferian-Jenkins

| Height: 6-5 | | | | Weight: 262 | | College: Washington | | | Draft: 2014/2 (38) | | Born: 9/29/1992 | | Age: 23 | | Risk: Yellow |

Year	Team	G/GS	Snaps	Rec	Pass	Yds	C%	+/-	Yd/C	TD	Drop	YAC	Rk	YAC+	BTkl	DVOA	Rk	DYAR	Rk	YAR	Short	Mid	Deep	Bomb
2014	TB	9/9	447	21	38	221	55%	-0.0	10.5	2	2	2.0	48	-1.8	1	-18.7%	40	-29	38	-30	30%	55%	15%	0%
2015	TB			48	80	591	60%	--	12.3	5						6.2%								

Seferian-Jenkins did catch five more passes than there are letters on the back of his jersey—yes, we count the hyphen here—but he did not burst on the scene as the Buccaneers might have hoped. Battling through injuries in his rookie season, Seferian-Jenkins actually fared better as a receiver with the awful Josh McCown at quarterback (-10.9% DVOA) than with the serviceable Mike Glennon (-24.5% DVOA). He showed little improvement statistically over the season, with injuries playing a part in that.

Seferian-Jenkins was charted with just two blown blocks in 447 snaps, ranking tenth among tight ends in snaps per blown block. But the Buccaneers aren't looking for him to block like Vernon Davis; they're looking for Seferian-Jenkins to become the receiving tight end that gives Jameis Winston a complete set of weapons.

Dion Sims

| Height: 6-5 | | | | Weight: 262 | | College: Michigan State | | | Draft: 2013/4 (106) | | Born: 18-Feb-1991 | | Age: 24 | | Risk: Green |

Year	Team	G/GS	Snaps	Rec	Pass	Yds	C%	+/-	Yd/C	TD	Drop	YAC	Rk	YAC+	BTkl	DVOA	Rk	DYAR	Rk	YAR	Short	Mid	Deep	Bomb
2013	MIA	15/5	278	6	10	32	60%	-0.1	5.3	1	1	0.7	--	-3.4	0	-22.0%	--	-12	--	-13	50%	50%	0%	0%
2014	MIA	14/2	507	24	36	284	67%	+2.1	11.8	2	1	4.6	21	-0.3	1	11.1%	14	42	17	56	55%	24%	18%	3%
2015	MIA			19	27	224	70%	--	11.8	2						9.4%								

With the Dolphins fundamentally replacing Charles Clay with Cameron Jordan, Sims should fall back into his role as backup tight end. A good blocker who has shown to be a dependable pass catcher if need be, he's a nice complimentary piece in the Miami offense.

Jacob Tamme

Height: 6-3   Weight: 236   College: Kentucky   Draft: 2008/4 (127)   Born: 15-Mar-1985   Age: 30   Risk: Red

Year	Team	G/GS	Snaps	Rec	Pass	Yds	C%	+/-	Yd/C	TD	Drop	YAC	Rk	YAC+	BTkl	DVOA	Rk	DYAR	Rk	YAR	Short	Mid	Deep	Bomb
2012	DEN	16/8	530	52	84	555	62%	+0.7	10.7	2	2	3.8	31	-0.3	1	-5.8%	35	18	32	34	43%	42%	15%	0%
2013	DEN	16/1	264	20	25	184	80%	+3.9	9.2	1	0	3.3	43	-0.7	1	23.7%	7	56	22	53	44%	48%	4%	4%
2014	DEN	15/0	275	14	28	109	50%	-3.9	7.8	2	1	1.6	50	-3.2	1	-42.8%	50	-67	47	-70	34%	41%	17%	7%
2015	ATL			31	42	294	74%	--	9.5	4						11.8%								

He runs like his cleats are made out of cement and 86.5 percent of his career catches came from Peyton Manning, but Jacob Tamme is actually a minor upgrade at tight end for the Falcons. He has reliable hands and can play in the slot to complement Levine Toilolo's inline-blocker role.

Julius Thomas

Height: 6-5   Weight: 251   College: Portland State   Draft: 2011/4 (129)   Born: 27-Jun-1988   Age: 27   Risk: Red

Year	Team	G/GS	Snaps	Rec	Pass	Yds	C%	+/-	Yd/C	TD	Drop	YAC	Rk	YAC+	BTkl	DVOA	Rk	DYAR	Rk	YAR	Short	Mid	Deep	Bomb
2012	DEN	4/0	2	0	--	0	--	--	--	0	--	--	--	--	--	--	--	--	--	--	--	--	--	--
2013	DEN	14/14	901	65	90	788	72%	+6.0	12.1	12	3	6.2	6	+1.5	6	27.0%	4	214	2	214	58%	24%	18%	0%
2014	DEN	13/10	691	43	62	489	69%	+4.3	11.4	12	1	3.8	33	-0.5	3	24.7%	2	140	6	142	58%	31%	8%	3%
2015	JAC			61	97	715	63%	--	11.7	7						4.6%								

Some day you are going to see an NFL Films clip of Julius Thomas screaming "It's so easy!" after scoring a touchdown against the Jets last season. That will quickly be followed by a shot of him in his Jacksonville uniform, either shaking his head in disbelief or completely numb to what's going on around him. Thomas is now the second-highest paid tight end in the NFL, but he has gone from the penthouse to the swamp in Jacksonville. Gone are Peyton Manning's superior pre-snap reads and ability to throw into tight windows in the red zone. Thomas was part of a record-setting offense, but he rarely had to be a focal point. He's not much of a blocker and he also had some injury issues the last two years. Thomas only surpassed 60 receiving yards once in his last 10 games. The Jaguars have an interesting mix of young wide receivers, so Thomas likely won't have to be a dominant force like, say, Tony Gonzalez in his Kansas City days, but he comes with a big contract and high expectations to be a difference-maker in the red zone after back-to-back seasons with 12 touchdowns. If he's only able to give them some prime Marcedes Lewis-type production, then we're going to look back at this as another awful free-agent contract. The difficulty just shot way up for Thomas.

Levine Toilolo

Height: 6-8   Weight: 260   College: Stanford   Draft: 2013/4 (133)   Born: 30-Jul-1991   Age: 24   Risk: Green

Year	Team	G/GS	Snaps	Rec	Pass	Yds	C%	+/-	Yd/C	TD	Drop	YAC	Rk	YAC+	BTkl	DVOA	Rk	DYAR	Rk	YAR	Short	Mid	Deep	Bomb
2013	ATL	16/3	192	11	14	55	79%	+0.9	5.0	2	1	2.5	--	-2.5	0	-22.4%	--	-19	--	-19	73%	27%	0%	0%
2014	ATL	16/16	940	31	53	238	58%	-4.9	7.7	2	4	3.2	41	-1.7	1	-37.5%	49	-115	50	-106	66%	26%	8%	0%
2015	ATL			21	31	185	68%	--	8.8	2						-1.7%								

It wasn't a mere "dropoff" from Tony Gonzalez to Levine Toilolo. It was like diving into the Grand Canyon. Toilolo is one of only two tight ends to crack -100 DYAR in the last three seasons—Brandon Pettigrew pulled off the trick in 2012. If he had been freakishly tall or short, we could have easily confused Toilolo for a *Breaking Madden* character. And, oh by the way, Toilolo was a brutal run blocker last season, which became even more amusing when he had to play out of position at right tackle in a September game because the Falcons ran out of offensive tackles. The upside is that Toilolo probably won't have another year quite as bad as this. The downside is that it will be because it takes Trent Richardson-level delusion for a front office to let someone play this poorly without a challenge.

Clive Walford

Height: 6-4   Weight: 251   College: Miami   Draft: 2015/3 (68)   Born: 21-Oct-1991   Age: 24   Risk: Green

Year	Team	G/GS	Snaps	Rec	Pass	Yds	C%	+/-	Yd/C	TD	Drop	YAC	Rk	YAC+	BTkl	DVOA	Rk	DYAR	Rk	YAR	Short	Mid	Deep	Bomb
2015	OAK			18	29	184	62%	--	10.2	1						-1.7%								

Oakland brass has raved about Walford as a "complete tight end," in that he can catch and block. NFL.com compared Walford to Dwayne Allen of the Colts. Right now the Raiders have a receiving tight end in Mychal Rivera and a blocker in Lee Smith, but if Walford can acclimate quickly as a dual-threat in the offense, then the Raiders can get their best players on the field more often in 11 personnel. Walford's one of those players who has better game speed than combine speed, and he just may be the answer to a position that has not been strong for Oakland for a long time.

Delanie Walker — Height: 6-0 — Weight: 248 — College: Central Missouri — Draft: 2006/6 (175) — Born: 12-Aug-1984 — Age: 31 — Risk: Yellow

Year	Team	G/GS	Snaps	Rec	Pass	Yds	C%	+/-	Yd/C	TD	Drop	YAC	Rk	YAC+	BTkl	DVOA	Rk	DYAR	Rk	YAR	Short	Mid	Deep	Bomb
2012	SF	16/4	570	21	39	344	54%	-0.8	16.4	3	7	2.7	47	-1.4	0	-2.8%	30	32	27	26	30%	35%	27%	8%
2013	TEN	15/11	762	60	86	571	70%	+6.8	9.5	6	4	2.9	47	-1.5	4	-0.7%	31	38	25	37	45%	36%	14%	5%
2014	TEN	15/14	769	63	106	890	59%	-1.2	14.1	4	3	6.0	10	+1.4	14	-5.6%	30	12	28	9	40%	40%	14%	6%
2015	TEN			60	93	717	65%	--	11.9	5						10.5%								

Walker put up the best numbers of his career despite the mostly dysfunctional nature of Tennessee's offense. The YAC total was partly the product of the two longest receptions of his career, and DVOA was less impressed by his performance than most observers. He was mostly the same player he'd been in years past, minus the surprising speed on the big plays. He was ineffective in the red zone, catching just four of the dozen passes thrown his direction, and posted a negative DVOA on every down. One cautionary note: the closest comp for his most recent season is Todd Christensen's 1987. Another receiving tight end who broke out late in his career, Christensen had just 15 catches the next season and retired after that.

Benjamin Watson — Height: 6-3 — Weight: 255 — College: Duke — Draft: 2004/1 (32) — Born: 18-Dec-1980 — Age: 35 — Risk: Yellow

Year	Team	G/GS	Snaps	Rec	Pass	Yds	C%	+/-	Yd/C	TD	Drop	YAC	Rk	YAC+	BTkl	DVOA	Rk	DYAR	Rk	YAR	Short	Mid	Deep	Bomb
2012	CLE	16/14	853	49	81	501	60%	-2.9	10.2	3	0	4.4	19	+0.2	5	-12.8%	37	-37	42	-30	46%	45%	8%	1%
2013	NO	15/7	494	19	30	226	63%	+2.2	11.9	2	0	4.9	22	-0.0	0	2.5%	25	22	31	21	46%	25%	14%	14%
2014	NO	16/8	571	20	31	136	65%	+0.5	6.8	2	2	3.9	30	-1.5	1	-21.3%	43	-29	39	-29	68%	21%	11%	0%
2015	NO			31	47	334	66%	--	10.8	4						9.7%								

As a 34-year-old tight end, expectations for Benjamin Watson shouldn't be high next season. Even with the departure of Jimmy Graham, Watson's days as a high-volume pass catcher won't be reborn. Watson can still play a large number of snaps, but he will need to prove his value and consistency as a run blocker to stay on the field.

Maxx Williams — Height: 6-4 — Weight: 249 — College: Minnesota — Draft: 2015/2 (55) — Born: 12-Apr-1994 — Age: 21 — Risk: Red

Year	Team	G/GS	Snaps	Rec	Pass	Yds	C%	+/-	Yd/C	TD	Drop	YAC	Rk	YAC+	BTkl	DVOA	Rk	DYAR	Rk	YAR	Short	Mid	Deep	Bomb
2015	BAL			46	68	521	68%	--	11.3	4						2.6%								

A tremendous athlete, Williams would have been a monster had Gary Kubiak remained in charge of Baltimore's offense. As it is, he fills a dire need with the departure of Owen Daniels and the injuries to Dennis Pitta. For a player with a reputation for great hands, Williams had a slightly worrying 56 percent catch rate at Minnesota. Still, he was the consensus top tight end in the draft, and the Ravens have a history of strong play at the position. The GM himself can come down to the practice field to give pointers. Maxx is already the best pro to have two X's in his name—unless you count Jamie Foxx, a.k.a. "Steamin'" Willie Beamon from *Any Given Sunday*, which we at Football Outsiders most certainly do.

Luke Willson — Height: 6-5 — Weight: 250 — College: Rice — Draft: 2013/5 (158) — Born: 15-Jan-1990 — Age: 25 — Risk: Green

Year	Team	G/GS	Snaps	Rec	Pass	Yds	C%	+/-	Yd/C	TD	Drop	YAC	Rk	YAC+	BTkl	DVOA	Rk	DYAR	Rk	YAR	Short	Mid	Deep	Bomb
2013	SEA	16/7	404	20	28	272	71%	+2.5	13.6	1	1	8.9	4	+4.2	3	18.2%	11	48	24	43	64%	24%	8%	4%
2014	SEA	15/10	556	22	40	362	55%	-2.2	16.5	3	4	9.7	1	+4.0	5	0.6%	24	20	24	21	42%	26%	18%	13%
2015	SEA			28	42	343	67%	--	12.3	3						10.7%								

An unusual deep-ball specialist, Willson was tied for 40th among tight ends in short targets, but only 14 tight ends had more deep targets 16 or more yards past the line of scrimmage. The Cardinals know all about what Willson can do—he burned them for 20- and 80-yard touchdowns in Week 16. Jimmy Graham's arrival in Seattle bumps Willson down the depth chart (duh), but

Seattle uses a fair amount of two-tight end sets, and of course Graham will also see time in the slot or out wide. So the dent in Willson's opportunities shouldn't be too great.

Jason Witten   Height: 6-6   Weight: 265   College: Tennessee   Draft: 2003/3 (69)   Born: 6-May-1982   Age: 33   Risk: Yellow

Year	Team	G/GS	Snaps	Rec	Pass	Yds	C%	+/-	Yd/C	TD	Drop	YAC	Rk	YAC+	BTkl	DVOA	Rk	DYAR	Rk	YAR	Short	Mid	Deep	Bomb
2012	DAL	16/16	1078	110	149	1039	74%	+14.2	9.4	3	7	2.8	42	-1.1	3	10.0%	14	192	3	147	43%	46%	10%	1%
2013	DAL	16/16	984	73	111	851	66%	-0.2	11.7	8	4	4.3	31	-0.2	7	11.2%	15	134	5	120	39%	44%	15%	2%
2014	DAL	16/16	1047	64	90	703	71%	+6.0	11.0	5	2	3.6	37	-0.7	3	17.9%	8	146	5	171	31%	53%	12%	3%
2015	DAL			71	103	804	69%	--	11.3	5						9.6%								

Witten ranks 13th on the all-time reception list; he's second all-time to Tony Gonzalez (naturally) in receptions by a tight end. Fifty-seven more receptions this season will push Witten into the top 10 with 1,000 catches, tying Hines Ward and passing Randy Moss and Andre Reed. (Anquan Boldin, Steve Smith and a few others could also crash the 1,000-catch party this year.)

Witten's production dip last season was less a result of declining skills than of declining opportunities. He caught 26 passes with the Cowboys leading last year, and 24 with the team trailing. In the previous five seasons, he averaged 23.8 catches per year with the Cowboys leading and 49.8 when trailing. That's a long way of saying that the Cowboys got to sit on more leads last season, a trend which should continue this season. It used to be ridiculous to even expect 50 catches and a half-dozen touchdowns from a tight end at age 33, but Witten's generation of tight ends has changed all of that.

Tim Wright   Height: 6-3   Weight: 220   College: Rutgers   Draft: 2013/FA   Born: 7-Apr-1990   Age: 25   Risk: Green

Year	Team	G/GS	Snaps	Rec	Pass	Yds	C%	+/-	Yd/C	TD	Drop	YAC	Rk	YAC+	BTkl	DVOA	Rk	DYAR	Rk	YAR	Short	Mid	Deep	Bomb
2013	TB	16/8	608	54	75	571	72%	+7.1	10.6	5	3	2.6	49	-1.9	0	21.8%	8	133	6	86	35%	53%	13%	0%
2014	NE	16/2	351	26	33	259	79%	+4.6	10.0	6	1	3.6	36	-1.0	0	30.9%	1	89	13	97	47%	38%	16%	0%
2015	TB			22	34	217	65%	--	9.9	2						2.7%								

Wright shows the difficulty of separating receivers' statistics from the effects of their environment. His top spot in DVOA for tight ends comes courtesy of Tom Brady, Rob Gronkowski, and Josh McDaniels. Most of his success came when he was wide open due to defensive inattention on passes that came his way. Wright is also only loosely a tight end, since at his size he basically can't block in the box. He's plenty big enough to force mismatches in the passing game, though, and his combination of size, speed, and route-running make him a potentially valuable receiving threat for a Tampa Bay offense looking to help Jameis Winston. Wright is not the best receiving tight end in football, but he did succeed as a rookie in Tampa Bay with teammates and coaches who were not quite on the Brady-Gronkowski-McDaniels level.

Going Deep

Rory Anderson, SF: It's not clear why a team with seven tight ends on board would draft an eighth, but that's what the 49ers did when they took Anderson in the seventh round. At 6-foot-5 and 227 pounds, he would fit best flexed off the line of scrimmage. He showed nice red zone ability in his first two years at South Carolina (eight touchdowns in 22 receptions), but was a non-factor as a junior and senior (one touchdown in 39 catches).

David Ausberry, DET: The emergence of Mychal Rivera pushed Ausberry further down the Oakland depth chart. He played just six offensive snaps per game in 2014 after missing the entire 2013 season with a shoulder injury. He signed with Detroit in June, but is a long shot to make the roster. (2014 stats: 2-for-4, 14 yards, -10 DYAR, -46.5% DVOA)

Kennard Backman, GB: A sixth-round pick out of Alabama-Birmingham, Backman is the latest in the Packers' long line of H-backs. He can stretch the seam and play special teams, but doesn't block well.

Blake Bell, SF: Bell's transition at Oklahoma from short-yardage runner to full-time quarterback to tight end was an odd one, to say the least. San Francisco couldn't resist Bell's size (6-foot-6, 252 pounds) and athleticism (second among tight ends at the combine in both the 20-yard and 60-yard shuttles) in the fourth round, even though they were already stacked at the position. Obviously, he is something of a project. This year, he's most likely to see playing time if the 49ers decide to break out the Belldozer for some short-yardage runs.

Rob Blanchflower, PIT: A seventh-round pick and practice-squadder in 2014, Rob Blanchflower will be hoping to crack the Steelers' final 53 in 2015. He's not much of a receiving threat, and his best hope of making a roster is finding a team that will value his size (6-foot-4 and 256 pounds) and blocking skills.

Ted Bolser, ARI: The Redskins drafted Bolser out of Indiana in the seventh round last year, but cut him before the season. He later spent some time on Tampa Bay's practice squad. On most rosters Bolser would be lucky to make the practice squad. In Arizona he could be the third tight end. He does have some goal-line ability, with 15 collegiate touchdowns in only 117 catches.

Brandon Bostick, MIN: Bostick flashed in the preseason, but failed to crack the lineup in Green Bay in the regular season. Following his moment of infamy after fielding, and coughing up, the onside kick in the NFC Championship game, the Packers released him. Minnesota scooped up him despite bringing back their top three tight ends, then subsequently drafted another. Well, at least his eventual release will twist the knife into Packer fans' hearts again. (2013 stats: 7-for-14, 120 yards, -3 DYAR, -11.0% DVOA)

Nick Boyle, BAL: The Ravens love to develop small-school talent, and Boyle, drafted in the fifth round out of Delaware, fits the mold. At an athletic 6-foot-4, 268 pounds, he has the frame to compete, though his blocking struggles in the Colonial Athletic Conference don't bode well for the NFL. He'll hope to progress in the shadows cast by Maxx Williams' spotlight.

Trey Burton, PHI: The Eagles' third tight end, sometime H-back, and core special-teamer. Burton carried the ball five times in the first Giants game, when Chris Polk was injured and the Eagles needed someone to soak up blowout carries in a 27-0 win. Burton was a high school quarterback and Urban Meyer all-purpose weapon in college, so he can handle the occasional touch. But if third-string tight ends start taking handoffs for the Eagles this year, something really horrible has happened.

Derek Carrier, SF: After time on practice squads in Oakland, Philadelphia, and San Francisco, Carrier made the 49ers' active roster for 16 games in the last two seasons. San Francisco signed him to a two-year extension in March, so they clearly see potential in this product of Division III Beloit College in Wisconsin. He missed the final five games of 2014 with foot injuries, and was still wearing a protective boot in OTAs. (2014 stats: 9-for-14, 105 yards, -22 DYAR, -30.6% DVOA)

James Casey, DEN: Casey caught a 4-yard touchdown, a 19-yard pass on second-and-11, and a 26-yard touchdown in three targets. He is now reunited with Gary Kubiak in Denver, where he will introduce Peyton Manning to the "fullback" concept and probably be targeted more than thrice.

Garrett Celek, SF: Celek missed most of 2014 with back and ankle injuries. His roster spot in 2014 will likely come down to which asset the 49ers prefer: his blocking, or Derek Carrier's receiving.

Orson Charles, NO: Orson Charles is a talented, versatile player, who never could quite fit right in Cincinnati and ended up on the New Orleans practice squad last year. He can play tight end, but his best chance of making the roster will likely be at fullback. If Benjamin Watson's play drops off, Charles could take over the blocking tight end role in the offense.

Gerald Christian, ARI: This year's Mr. Irrelevant goes from the Cardinals (Louisville) to the Cardinals (Arizona). At just 244 pounds, Christian's blocking ability is limited. He's got more talent as a receiver, especially at catching passes in traffic, but his routes need work and he doesn't adjust well to poorly thrown balls.

Kellen Davis, NYJ: The Lions snuck Davis through customs in time for their Wembley Stadium matchup against the Falcons, as the seventh-year vet inked a deal with Detroit's top three tight ends all injured. His value is entirely tied to his blocking ability at this point, and if uber-athletic undrafted rookie Wes Saxton flashes, Davis might not be long for Broadway either.

A.J. Derby, NE: The sixth-round tight end out of Arkansas brings some surprisingly physical attributes for a Day 3 pick. Derby ran a 4.69 40 at his pro day, impressive for a player who goes 6-foot-4 and 255 pounds. In addition, Derby has the kind of versatility that Bill Belichick often likes, having played both quarterback and linebacker.

Jack Doyle, IND: Oh, Doyle rules? Doyle was the Stanley Havili of the 2014 Colts, except he actually made some positive contributions with his blocking and 18 catches. If Doyle caught two more passes he would have helped the Colts tie the NFL record of 10 receivers at 20 catches. Better luck next year for the Indianapolis native. (2014 stats: 18-for-22, 118 yards, 2 TD, 4 DYAR, -4.6% DVOA)

Rhett Ellison, MIN: Ellison actually played the most snaps among Vikings tight ends last season, receiving a big uptick in playing time after Kyle Rudolph's injury, and was often a leakout option in the flat for Teddy Bridgewater. Ellison wore a variety of hats last season and will mostly occupy a role as an H-back lead blocker in 2015. (2014 stats: 19-for-26, 208 yards, 31 DYAR, 10.0% DVOA)

Gavin Escobar, DAL: Six touchdowns in 18 receptions over two years make Escobar a classic fantasy touchdown leech, but he was supposed to be much more. The Cowboys tinker with Escobar as a slot threat every offseason and talk about getting him more involved in the passing game. But once the games start mattering, Escobar splits the second tight end role with James Hanna and rarely sees a target outside the red zone. Escobar's role may expand this season with Jason Witten getting older and no DeMarco Murray around to soak up all of the offensive touches, but there is a lot of middle ground between "leeching No. 2 tight end" and "productive fantasy No. 2 tight end." (2014 stats: 9-for-13, 105 yards, 4 TD, 45 DYAR, 37.1% DVOA)

Joseph Fauria, DET: In an attempt to stop his dog from urinating in his home, Fauria tripped over his pet and badly injured his ankle, hampering his sophomore season. No, that was not a Mad Libs. During his rookie year, Fauria ranked third on the Lions in red zone targets and posted a 17.0% DVOA in such situations. But Fauria is stuck in an awkward middle ground of offering neither Brandon Pettigrew's blocking value nor Eric Ebron's receiving upside, so it's hard to imagine him recapturing his 2013 level production on this roster. (2014 stats: 6-for-12, 74 yards, 1 TD, -25 DYAR, -34.1% DVOA)

Daniel Fells, NYG: Standard-issue second tight end: good run blocker and pass protector, decent short-catching skills. Fells was out of the NFL for a year after the Patriots cut him at the end of 2013 training camp, but he leapt over Adrien Robinson on the Giants' depth chart and into a steady role. Fells scored four touchdowns last season but projects strictly as a 1-yard play-action guy in the red zone. (2014 stats: 16-for-20, 188 yards, 4 TD, 75 DYAR, 42.9% DVOA)

Darren Fells, ARI: Fells played basketball, not football, at UC Irvine, and spent five years after college playing hoops overseas. He then gave football a try, making Arizona's practice squad as a 27-year-old rookie in 2013 and catching 5-of-11 passes for 71 yards last year (-2 DYAR, -10.7% DVOA). John Carlson's retirement leaves Fells the top backup behind 2014 second-rounder Troy Niklas. Zot!

C.J. Fiedorowicz, HOU: In his rookie season, Fiedorowicz was a blocking tight end who couldn't block. While that's not the return on investment you'd like to see on a third-round pick, he's still got three years to prove the Texans right. A full offseason in an NFL strength and conditioning program couldn't hurt. (2014 stats: 4-for-7, 28 yards, -5 DYAR, -19.1% DVOA)

Richard Gordon, KC: Gordon is an infrequently used blocking tight end and an even more infrequent pass catcher. He has caught four passes for 14 yards in 34 career games. Blink and you might miss his contributions this year. He spent some time with the Titans in 2014.

Chris Gragg, BUF: Gragg's roster spot could be in trouble, with the Bills now having four tight ends on the roster that project to an H-back role. Scouting reports have Gragg as a better receiver than blocker. (2014 stats: 7-for-10, 48 yards, 1 TD, -1 DYAR, -8.4% DVOA)

MarQueis Gray, BUF: Gray, a college quarterback at times for Minnesota, finds himself in a similar situation as teammate Chris Gragg. His strength is also as a receiver rather than a blocker. (2014 stats: 9-for-11, 134 yards, 52 DYAR, 55.0% DVOA)

James Hanna, DAL: The Cowboys' official blocking tight end, Hanna saw more action than Gavin Escobar in most games but received just six scattered targets. Hanna's longest play last year was a 27-yard catch on third-and-1 from a three-tight end mega-jumbo package play-action pass. He's probably good for another one of those this year.

Cory Harkey, STL: In the past two seasons, Harkey has lined up in the backfield for 575 of his 690 offensive snaps. He wears No. 46. And yet the Rams still insist on arbitrarily listing him as a tight end, even though they have two perfectly fine tight ends on the roster in Jared Cook and Lance Kendricks. Regardless, the Rams already led the NFL in two-back sets in 2014, and that usage (and Harkey's playing time) only figures to increase in 2015 with Todd Gurley's arrival.

Demetrius Harris, KC: Harris was the rarely used (60 snaps) No. 3 tight end last year. He should return to that role assuming everything goes right this summer with his recovery from a broken foot. He could even assume No. 2 duties behind Travis Kelce with a strong preseason. (2014 stats: 3-for-5, 20 yards, -14 DYAR, -50.8% DVOA)

Cooper Helfet, SEA: The Seahawks like versatile athletes, and Helfet started his college career as a lacrosse player before transitioning to football. He's also a promising model, which is interesting if not especially useful in his current profession. He spent two years bouncing on and off Seattle's practice squad before debuting in 2014, peaking in Week 7 when he gained 61 yards and a touchdown against St. Louis. He had only 81 yards the rest of the year, and none in the postseason. Outsports still ran his picture in their Super Bowl preview, because his hair is just too nice to ignore. (2014 stats: 12-for-24, 185 yards, 2 TD, 25 DYAR, 10.2% DVOA)

Jeff Heuerman, DEN: The third-round pick from Ohio State had a good shot to play this year with the departures of Julius Thomas and Jacob Tamme at tight end, but Heuerman tore his ACL at a rookie minicamp in May. The Broncos still signed him to a four-year deal, but Heuerman will miss the entire 2015 season.

Ryan Hewitt, CIN: Hewitt was tremendously effective working as an H-back, throwing thunderous lead blocks and showing just enough as a receiver to keep defenses honest. (He was wide open for a long touchdown against Cleveland, but Andy Dalton painfully underthrew him.) His particular niche may not be prized in many NFL outposts, but under Hue Jackson in Cincy he is an important cog. (2014 stats: 10-for-15, 86 yards, -18 DYAR, -27.2% DVOA)

Michael Hoomanawanui, NE: In 2014, the fourth-year tight end saw the most action of his career, playing in every game for the first time. Primarily used as a blocker, Hoomanawanui had about 105 snaps per blown block, ranking 31st among 49 qualifying tight ends. He had an unusual season as a pass-catcher. After catching just three passes in the regular season, Hoomanawanui caught six passes in the playoffs, two of them on the drive when running back Shane Vereen declared himself ineligible.

Jesse James, PIT: Adding Penn State's Jesse James in the fifth round of the 2015 draft gave the Steelers another blocking tight end with limited ability as a receiver. Because they apparently didn't already have enough of them.

David Johnson, SD: Johnson was healthier in 2014, but still only played 177 snaps with one catch for four yards. His role is to block, and he's essentially San Diego's fullback should they choose to use one in this modern era of offense.

Malcolm Johnson, CLE: It appears that John DeFilippo appreciated the work of Marcel Reese during his time in Oakland. Sixth-round draftee Malcolm Johnson (Mississippi State) appears similar to Reese in that he is a tight end/fullback who has a strong, compact frame and a surprising burst of speed. The Browns should move him around the field if he makes the roster.

Ben Koyack, JAC: After making a bit of noise as a potential NFL pick early in the season, Koyack was a forgotten man come draft time. Jacksonville eventually took the Notre Dame product in the seventh round. There's a nice body to work with here, as well as some of the biggest (10 3/4 inches) hands in recent memory for a tight end. But the blocking was inconsistent, the ability to read defenses as a receiver was lacking, and Koyack probably needs a redshirt year before he's ready to take on the league.

Tyler Kroft, CIN: Kroft had a strong 2013 at Rutgers, but his targets tailed off last season under new offensive coordinator Ralph Friedgen. He worked on his blocking to compensate, and a burly in-line tight end is what the Bengals could really use. The talent is there; the worry is that Kroft's receiving/blocking blend isn't quite good enough to justify a third-round selection. Cincy's recent woes at developing tight ends can't help, either.

Brian Leonhardt, OAK: The good news: Leonhardt was the second-most productive tight end in Oakland's passing game last year. The bad news: he only had eight targets, compared to 99 for Mychal Rivera. (2014 stats: 6-for-8, 35 yards, 1 TD, 1 DYAR, -5.6% DVOA)

Arthur Lynch, MIA: Lynch, a fifth-round pick out of Georgia last year, was on injured reserve all season with a back injury. An in-line tight end who lacks speed to get separation at the NFL level, he will compete for a spot at the back end of the depth chart behind Jordan Cameron and Dion Sims.

Vance McDonald, SF: McDonald had more starts (four) than catches (two) last year, after eight catches in four starts in his rookie year. That doesn't mean he can't catch; he had 36 receptions as a senior at Rice in 2012, playing primarily in the slot. The 49ers are cartoonishly deep at tight end, but they liked McDonald enough to draft him in the second round in 2013, and he might wind up on top of the heap if Vernon Davis struggles again this fall.

Trey Millard, SF: Millard was an all-Big 12 fullback before tearing his ACL in October of 2013. The 49ers took a flyer on him in the seventh round, but Millard never made it onto the field. He was healthy for OTAs this year and saw time at fullback and tight end, and will likely be used as a multipurpose H-back this year.

Zach Miller, FA: Only the Percy Harvin fiasco prevents Zach Miller from being the biggest misstep of the Schneider-Carroll regime in Seattle. The Seahawks signed Miller to a five-year, $34 million contract in 2011 with $17 million guaranteed. He was actually the highest-paid player on the roster when they won the Super Bowl in 2013, but he never gained even 400 yards in a season in Seattle. Ankle surgeries limited him to three games in 2014, and he was released after failing a physical in March. By the way, the "other" Zach Miller (the ex-Jaguars guy) hasn't played in a regular-season game since 2011 but will be in training camp with Chicago, where he spent last year on injured reserve.

Tony Moeaki, ATL: After a promising rookie season in 2010 in Kansas City, Moeaki missed all of 2011 with a torn ACL and has never really been the same since. He missed most of 2013 with a fractured shoulder, then joined Seattle mid-2014 after Zach Miller injured his ankle. Moeaki's 63-yard catch against San Francisco was the first 40-plus-yard play of his career. He's now in Atlanta, where he should get a chance to compete for a role given that Levine Toilolo was last among tight ends in DYAR last year. (2014 stats: 8-for-13, 134 yards, 1 TD, 14 DYAR, 9.8% DVOA)

Nick O'Leary, BUF: An All-American at Florida State and the Mackey Award winner as college football's top tight end, O'Leary was projected to be drafted in the fourth round. His measurables at the combine—O'Leary ran markedly slower and jumped shorter than fellow tight end Maxx Williams—forced a slide that finally ended in the sixth round. With Jack Nicklaus as his grandfather, O'Leary needs to make the Bills roster just so he can take on Rick Rhoden in a celebrity golf match to the death.

James O'Shaughnessy, KC: Last season the Chiefs played Travis Kelce and Anthony Fasano over 650 snaps each. With Fasano gone, this fifth-round pick from FCS Illinois State has a decent shot at seeing the field this year as a "move" tight end in Andy Reid's offense. He has some of those "basketball tight end" skills teams highly covet.

Michael Palmer, PIT: Michael Palmer was active for 15 games last year and is just in Pittsburgh to block. His only catch last year was a 1-yard touchdown. He won't move up the depth chart unless Matt Spaeth or Heath Miller are injured and may not even make this year's roster.

Bear Pascoe, CHI: Some people say you don't need blocking tight ends in today's NFL. But we say, if you do need one, he might as well be named Bear Pascoe, right? He had only two targets for the 2014 Falcons, one of which was a 1-yard touchdown. (2013 stats: 12-for-20, 81 yards, -54 DYAR, -52.0% DVOA)

John Phillips, SD: A blocking tight end, Phillips played 197 snaps on offense last year, but that's only 92 less than "receiving tight end" Ladarius Green played. Phillips caught a 1-yard touchdown against the Chiefs on his only target of the season. News broke in May that Phillips had torn his ACL in December, making him likely to start the 2015 season on the reserve/PUP list.

MyCole Pruitt, MIN: Pruitt became the first Missouri Valley Conference tight end drafted since Pat Dunsmore in 1983 after garnering first-team All-FCS selections each of the past two seasons. As Southern Illinois' top target, Pruitt snagged an eye-opening 13 touchdowns his senior season, relying on his ability to outmuscle defenders for position in traffic rather than sheer superior athleticism. Pruitt's receiving skill set and red zone efficiency might allow him to compete with Chase Ford for a handful of tight end snaps deep on the Minnesota depth chart.

Adrien Robinson, NYG: A Jerry Reese fixation. Reese has called Robinson "the JPP of tight ends" and kept him on the roster for three seasons. Robinson responded by starting training camp as the fifth tight end on the depth chart last year and defaulting his way up to third, where he watched Larry Donnell have a breakout season while Daniel Fells did No. 2 tight end stuff. Robinson only caught 29 passes in four college seasons, making Reese's fetish even creepier. Robinson ended the season with five scattered catches, most of them in lopsided games, and the 1-yard touchdown all No. 3 tight ends receive as a kind of participation trophy. Old college coaches often talk about "Booster's Kid" plays: plays designed to make sure a wealthy, influential parent gets to see his kid do something that looks semi-special once in a while. The NFL equivalent would be "GM's Pet Project Plays," and Robinson got his share of them. (2014 stats: 5-for-7, 50 yards, 1 TD, 10 DYAR, 10.1% DVOA)

Gerell Robinson, MIA: The 6-foot-3, 220-pound Robinson is a WR/TE tweener out of Arizona State who has struggled to find a fit at the NFL level. If everything breaks right for him, the former college receiver has the potential to be a Tim Wright-type, a noble set of aspirations for a guy who is now on his fourth team since 2012.

Wes Saxton, NYJ: One of Jameis Winston's high school teammates, Saxton struggled with injury at South Alabama and caught just 20 passes for 155 yards and no touchdowns as a senior. He impressed at the combine with a 4.65 40 and excellent broad and vertical jumps, but went undrafted and signed with the Jets as an H-back. When you have to tell not only teams but the draft media, "I am willing to block," you probably are not going to be depended on for much blocking.

Alex Smith, CIN: A reliable pro but injury-prone. After a broken wrist in 2013 and a torn biceps that cost him all of 2014, the Bahamanian Bomber will struggle to fend off the healthier camp bodies in Cincinnati.

Lee Smith, OAK: Smith is essentially a sixth offensive lineman, with almost no use as a receiver. In the blocking tight end role, Smith is effective. If he played enough snaps to qualify, his 335 snaps per blown block in 2014 would have ranked fifth among tight ends. Still, Oakland's contract for Smith (three years, $9.1 million, $3.1 million guaranteed) is a substantial overpay for a player with 20 receptions in four NFL seasons. (2014 stats: 7-for-8, 42 yards, 1 TD, -2 DYAR, -11.3% DVOA)

Matt Spaeth, PIT: Matt Spaeth does the grunt work for the Steelers offense, and his value comes in the running game as he offers consistency and versatility working outside. He played 30.7 percent of the team's snaps last year, but only saw four pass targets. Somehow, one of them was a 33-yard touchdown where Spaeth beat Daryl Smith, one of the best coverage linebackers in the league. It was like one of those old Statis Pro "Z" plays.

Craig Stevens, TEN: The veteran blocker went out for the year in Week 5. He has only four catches in the last two years, and the addition of Anthony Fasano puts him on the roster bubble.

Luke Stocker, TB: Given that Stocker is almost exclusively utilized as a blocker, only four blown blocks charted in 325 snaps is an impressive number that reflects his strength in that area. Stocker is currently the only member of Tampa Bay's 2011 draft class still on the team. (2014 stats: 7-for-11, 41 yards, -26 DYAR, -42.5% DVOA)

Zach Sudfeld, NYJ: A wildly raw, towering (6-foot-7) tight end, Sudfeld impressed in camp with the Patriots in 2013 before being cut loose midway through the year after botching a play on special teams. He hasn't played much for the Jets since he signed there, and he tore his ACL in OTAs and will miss the 2015 season. (2014 stats: 5-for-7, 85 yards, 25 DYAR, 48.5% DVOA)

Phillip Supernaw, TEN: The son of a country music singer, Supernaw should feel right at home in Nashville; he signed with the Titans after the Ravens cut him in March. He's just the seventh NFL player to come out of Division II Ouachita Baptist, best known for All-Pro safety Cliff Harris from the '70s Cowboys. (2014 stats: 3-for-3, 30 yards, 0 DYAR, -6.3% DVOA)

Geoff Swaim, DAL: This late seventh-round pick is a size-speed-athleticism prospect from University of Texas who caught just 13 passes in his college career. Another James Hanna for the Cowboys, who can never have too much James Hanna.

Randall Telfer, CLE: Telfer is a younger version of Jim Dray, and the sixth-round rookie from USC will compete for playing time with Dray and Gary Barnidge.

C.J. Uzomah, CIN: An intriguing prospect, Uzomah was as misplaced in Auburn's fast-paced spread rushing attack as grits in an Acela dining car. He didn't even have a position coach in college, and wasn't invited to the NFL combine. The massive (6-foot-5, 265 pounds) former high school wideout then ran a 4.63 40 at his pro day, second-best of any tight end in the draft. Cincinnati used a fifth-round pick on him, but he'll need to show promise quickly in a crowded Bengals camp.

Brandon Williams, CAR: Welcome to the 998th installment of "Football Team Tries to Make Basketball Player a Tight End," starring Brandon Williams. Actually, this is a little different from the tale you're used to. Oregon football wouldn't let Williams play after diagnosing him with a rare spinal condition, so he switched to basketball. Williams went as far as becoming a Portland bike cop before getting discovered at one of the NFL's regional combines. It's anyone's guess as to why the Panthers decided they'd rather roll with Ed Dickson as the No. 2 tight end over Williams, who has all the physical tools to be a player (a chiseled 6-foot-4, 260-pound body, a sub-4.6 40-yard dash), but every hit he takes should be watched cautiously. (2014 stats: 4-for-8, 44 yards, -10 DYAR, -22.8% DVOA)

2015 Kicker Projections

listed below are the 2015 KUBIAK projections for kickers. Due to the inconsistency of field-goal percentage from year to year, kickers are projected almost entirely based on team forecasts, although a handful of individual factors do come into play:

• More experience leads to a slightly higher field-goal percentage in general, with the biggest jump between a kicker's rookie and sophomore seasons.

• Kickers with a better career field-goal percentage tend to get more attempts, although they are not necessarily more accurate.

• Field-goal percentage on kicks over 40 yards tends to regress to the mean.

Kickers are listed with their total fantasy points based on two different scoring systems. For Pts1, all field goals are worth three points. For Pts2, all field goals up to 39 yards are worth three points, field goals of 40-49 yards are worth four points, and field goals over 50 yards are worth five points. Kickers are also listed with a Risk of Green, Yellow, or Red, as explained in the introduction to the section on quarterbacks.

Note that field-goal totals below are rounded, but "fantasy points" are based on the actual projections, so the total may not exactly equal (FG * 3 + XP).

Fantasy Kicker Projections, 2015

Kicker	Team	FG	Pct	XP	Pts1	Pts2	Risk
Stephen Gostkowski	NE	31-36	87%	44	135	150	Green
Mason Crosby	GB	28-30	93%	51	132	146	Yellow
Mike Nugent	CIN	31-35	90%	38	131	145	Yellow
Connor Barth	DEN	29-34	84%	46	131	146	Red
Randy Bullock	HOU	33-40	84%	32	131	146	Red
Cody Parkey	PHI	29-34	86%	43	129	142	Red
Adam Vinatieri	IND	29-35	84%	41	128	141	Green
Blair Walsh	MIN	30-36	83%	38	126	142	Green
Matt Bryant	ATL	29-33	89%	39	126	139	Green
Greg Zuerlein	STL	31-36	85%	34	125	143	Yellow
Dan Bailey	DAL	27-33	82%	44	123	135	Yellow
Steven Hauschka	SEA	27-33	83%	43	122	134	Green
Sebastian Janikowski	OAK	30-34	89%	33	122	140	Yellow
Caleb Sturgis	MIA	29-35	81%	38	122	136	Red
Justin Tucker	BAL	28-35	82%	35	119	135	Green
Josh Brown	NYG	27-31	88%	39	119	131	Green
Matt Prater	DET	27-34	81%	37	117	129	Green
Shaun Suisham	PIT	25-29	87%	42	117	129	Green
Graham Gano	CAR	26-32	83%	39	115	127	Yellow
Phil Dawson	SF	27-33	83%	35	114	126	Yellow
Dustin Hopkins	NO	24-29	82%	44	113	124	Red
Nick Folk	NYJ	27-31	88%	34	112	124	Green
Chandler Catanzaro	ARI	28-33	83%	32	112	126	Yellow
Nick Novak	SD	24-28	88%	40	111	123	Yellow
Cairo Santos	KC	25-28	89%	37	111	123	Yellow
Dan Carpenter	BUF	28-34	80%	30	110	124	Yellow
Kai Forbath	WAS	27-30	87%	32	109	121	Red
Robbie Gould	CHI	24-29	83%	34	103	116	Yellow
Travis Coons	CLE	26-34	76%	26	103	115	Red
Ryan Succop	TEN	23-27	86%	34	101	112	Green
Josh Scobee	JAC	25-28	88%	30	101	114	Red
Patrick Murray	TB	24-28	85%	27	97	108	Yellow

Other kickers who may win jobs:							
Kicker	Team	FG	Pct	XP	Pts1	Pts2	Risk
Zach Hocker	NO	24-29	82%	44	113	124	Red
Carey Spear	CLE	25-33	76%	26	104	118	Red

406

2015 Fantasy Defense Projections

isted below are the 2015 KUBIAK projections for fantasy team defense. The projection method is discussed in an essay in Pro Football Prospectus 2006, the key conclusions of which were:

• Schedule strength is very important for projecting fantasy defense.
• Categories used for scoring in fantasy defense have no consistency from year-to-year whatsoever, with the exception of sacks and interceptions.

Fumble recoveries and defensive touchdowns are forecast solely based on the projected sacks and interceptions, rather than the team's totals in these categories from a year ago. This is why the 2015 projections may look very different from the fantasy defense values from the 2014 season. Safeties and shutouts are not common enough to have a significant effect on the projections. Team defenses are also projected with Risk factor of Green, Yellow, or Red; this is based on the team's projection compared to performance in recent seasons.

In addition to projection of separate categories, we also give an overall total based on our generic fantasy scoring formula: one point for a sack, two points for a fumble recovery or interception, and six points for a touchdown. Remember that certain teams (in particular, the Jets) will score better if your league also gives points for limiting opponents' scoring or yardage. Special-teams touchdowns are listed separately and are not included in the fantasy scoring total listed.

Fantasy Team Defense Projections, 2015

Team	Fant Pts	Sack	Int	Fum Rec	Def TD	Risk	ST TD	Team	Fant Pts	Sack	Int	Fum Rec	Def TD	Risk	ST TD
SEA	123	45.4	17.9	11.6	3.0	Yellow	0.6	SF	104	37.6	15.4	9.9	2.7	Yellow	0.8
BUF	118	49.8	16.0	11.5	2.3	Yellow	0.8	CIN	103	36.1	16.6	11.0	1.9	Yellow	0.8
DEN	117	45.3	16.3	10.4	3.0	Yellow	0.7	NO	103	35.3	14.8	11.3	2.6	Red	1.0
NE	116	42.9	17.0	11.3	2.8	Yellow	0.8	DAL	102	33.3	14.2	11.4	2.9	Green	1.0
BAL	115	42.3	15.9	11.7	3.0	Red	0.9	CAR	101	36.6	14.6	9.8	2.5	Green	0.9
KC	115	44.4	13.8	11.2	3.4	Yellow	1.2	ATL	100	32.9	14.8	11.5	2.3	Yellow	1.3
STL	114	44.8	14.8	11.5	2.7	Yellow	0.8	TEN	100	34.8	13.2	9.9	3.1	Yellow	1.0
NYJ	113	46.5	14.6	11.5	2.3	Red	0.9	PIT	99	38.7	12.9	8.8	2.8	Yellow	0.7
DET	112	41.2	15.2	12.8	2.4	Red	0.7	TB	98	34.6	13.4	11.4	2.3	Green	0.9
GB	110	40.1	16.7	10.3	2.7	Yellow	0.9	JAC	98	35.7	13.6	10.7	2.2	Yellow	1.0
MIA	109	36.6	15.1	10.9	3.4	Yellow	0.9	IND	97	39.1	13.4	10.6	1.7	Yellow	0.8
MIN	109	38.8	15.1	12.2	2.5	Red	1.1	WAS	96	35.9	13.4	9.3	2.5	Yellow	0.9
PHI	108	40.4	15.5	8.9	3.2	Green	1.1	CLE	95	34.3	14.3	8.8	2.4	Green	0.6
NYG	107	38.3	14.6	12.1	2.6	Red	0.8	OAK	90	32.8	12.8	10.0	1.9	Yellow	0.7
HOU	107	39.1	16.1	10.5	2.5	Green	0.5	SD	90	34.9	11.6	8.4	2.5	Yellow	1.0
ARI	105	39.4	15.5	10.5	2.3	Green	0.7	CHI	87	33.3	13.5	8.8	1.5	Green	0.9

Projected Defensive Leaders, 2015

Solo Tackles			Total Tackles			Sacks			Interceptions		
Player	Team	Tkl	Player	Team	Tkl	Player	Team	Sacks	Player	Team	INT
P.Posluszny	JAC	108	L.Kuechly	CAR	151	J.Houston	KC	13.8	R.Sherman	SEA	3.8
L.David	TB	100	P.Posluszny	JAC	145	J.J.Watt	HOU	13.5	H.Smith	MIN	3.6
L.Kuechly	CAR	99	L.David	TB	131	V.Miller	DEN	12.7	T.Gipson	CLE	3.5
N.Bowman	SF	96	D.Jackson	IND	130	M.Williams	BUF	11.8	D.Revis	NYJ	3.5
D.Levy	DET	95	P.Worrilow	ATL	129	C.Jones	NE	11.1	T.Newman	MIN	3.3
K.Alonso	PHI	90	K.Alonso	PHI	128	R.Quinn	STL	10.9	A.Talib	DEN	3.1
A.Ogletree	STL	89	D.Levy	DET	127	R.Kerrigan	WAS	10.9	P.Amukamara	NYG	3.0
C.J.Mosley	BAL	88	N.Bowman	SF	126	C.Wake	MIA	10.6	G.Quin	DET	3.0
D.Trevathan	DEN	88	C.J.Mosley	BAL	125	T.Suggs	BAL	10.6	C.Conte	TB	3.0
S.Tulloch	DET	84	D.Smith	BAL	124	E.Dumervil	BAL	10.5	A.Cromartie	NYJ	3.0
E.Weddle	SD	83	D.Trevathan	DEN	124	V.Beasley	ATL	10.4	A.Bethea	SF	3.0
C.Lofton	OAK	83	L.Timmons	PIT	121	E.Griffen	MIN	10.2	M.Jenkins	PHI	2.9

College Football Introduction
and Statistical Toolbox

ollege football preseason polls are often mocked for their predictability. Some voters appear to approach their ranking process for the upcoming season is as follows: 1.) Copy and paste the final rankings from the previous season; 2.) Shuffle a few teams around to hide the evidence; 3.) Add in a blue-blood program or two that struggled the previous year (Notre Dame, Michigan, and Texas are all eligible candidates for 2015); 4.) Pat yourself on the back, your work is done.

Of course, the predictability approach paid off last season. The four teams that were selected to play in the inaugural College Football Playoff—Alabama, Oregon, Florida State, and Ohio State—each started the year ranked in the top five of the Associated Press poll. A few surprises like Mississippi State's run to the top of the midseason polls and Oklahoma's unexpected nosedive certainly kept thinks interesting in 2014, but the four programs with the strongest recent pedigrees ruled in the end. The Crimson Tide, Ducks, Seminoles, and Buckeyes have topped all Power 5 conference teams in winning percentage since 2010, and each program is well positioned to be a winner over the next five seasons as well.

Year-over-year success begets next-year success. Our projection formula starts with five years of play-by-play and drive efficiency data, and we gave each of the eventual 2014 playoff teams at least a 20 percent chance of making the playoff in last year's *Football Outsiders Almanac*. Those four programs each rank among the seven teams most likely to make the playoff this year as well, but the loss of key personnel to the NFL among many of the top programs suggests this year's playoff race may be cracked wide open. Or maybe only three of the spots are up for grabs.

The defending champion Ohio State Buckeyes appear to be as primed for an undefeated regular season, conference championship, and playoff berth as any program could reasonably expect to be. In addition to steamrolling top opponents down the stretch last fall, head coach Urban Meyer has only lost three games total since his arrival in Columbus in 2012, and Ohio State brings back a loaded roster to face an exceptionally manageable schedule. According to our F/+ ratings, No.1 Ohio State is ten times more likely to go undefeated against its conference slate than No. 2 Alabama is against its own. You may not want to write the Buckeyes into the playoff with a Sharpie just yet, but you should probably prepare to have a scarlet one in hand when the time comes.

Our projections are higher on the UCLA Bruins (F/+ No. 5, 10-2 regular season record) than the consensus this year, making them a solid dark-horse pick to crash the playoff party. UCLA will face the weakest schedule in the Pac-12 and our metrics project at least a 90 percent win likelihood for the Bruins against seven FBS opponents. Our pick to fall short of consensus expectations is the Auburn Tigers (F/+ No. 11, 8-4 regular season record). In addition to a showdown with Alabama on Thanksgiving weekend, a particularly brutal stretch from October 24 to November 14 (at Arkansas, vs. Ole Miss, at Texas A&M, vs. Georgia) is when their championship aspirations are most vulnerable. Our metrics give them a 67 percent chance of going 2-2 or worse in those four games.

The safest wager for the year ahead is that the College Football Playoff race will once again dominate media coverage and tailgate conversations throughout the year. The inaugural committee process was tirelessly debated in 2014, and each week a different set of peculiarities in the rankings challenged our expectations of which teams were actually best positioned to reach the playoff. The rankings were a blessing and a curse—informing our approach as analysts to better predict future committee decisions, and frustrating us as fans hoping fall Saturdays and the games themselves would outshine the postseason politics. College football's new era is underway and the championship crown won by Ohio State was well-earned. Here's hoping this year's title chase is as predictably thrilling as ever.

* * * * *

Welcome to the Football Outsiders Almanac college football section, and our deep dive into the numbers that will shape the 2015 season. Since 2003, Brian Fremeau has been developing and enhancing the drive-based Fremeau Efficiency Index (FEI) and its companion statistics; for the last eight years, Bill Connelly's research has explored play-by-play and drive data, developing measures of efficiency and explosiveness and creating his system, the S&P+ ratings. Both systems are opponent-adjusted and effective in both evaluating teams and uncovering strengths and weaknesses. The combination of the two ratings, F/+, provides the best of both worlds.

The College Statistical Toolbox section that follows this introduction explains the methodology of FEI, S&P+, F/+, and other stats you will encounter in the college chapters of this book. There are similarities to Football Outsiders' NFL-based DVOA ratings in the combined approach, but college football presents a unique set of challenges different from the NFL. All football stats must be adjusted according to context, but how? If Team A and Team B do not play one another and don't share any common opponents, how can their stats be effectively compared? Should a team from the SEC or Big 12 be measured against that of an average team in its own conference, or an average FBS team? With ten years of full data, we are still only scratching the surface with these measures, but the recent progress has been both swift and exciting.

This book is particularly focused on the Playoff and conference contenders for the year ahead. This year, we've put aside previews of the also-rans in the Power 5 conferences in order to concentrate on the top 50 teams in our preseason rankings. Each team capsule provides a snapshot of the team's statistical profile in 2014 and projections for 2015. Supplementing the stat work, college football staff writer Chad Peltier explores player and coaching personnel changes, offensive and defensive advantages and deficiencies, and schedule highlights and pitfalls in a thorough summary of each team's keys to the upcoming season.

Each of our team capsules also includes a statistical graphic illustrating the five-year trajectory for the program's offense, defense, special teams, and overall ratings. We've also included a game-by-game graphic highlighting our projected win likelihoods for the year ahead.

For each of the 128 FBS teams, we project the likelihood of every possible regular-season record, conference and non-conference alike. We've included division, overall conference, and College Football Playoff projections for every team as well. The Playoff projections are based not only on the win probabilities, but also schedule-strength factors we expect will weigh significantly in the selection committee's process.

By taking two different statistical approaches to reach one exciting series of answers to college football's most important questions, we feel we are at the forefront of the ongoing debates. Enjoy the college football section of *Football Outsiders Almanac 2015*, and join us at www.FootballOutsiders.com/college throughout the season.

College Statistics Toolbox

Regular readers of FootballOutsiders.com may be familiar with the FEI and Varsity Numbers columns and their respective stats published throughout the year. Others may be learning about our advanced approach to college football stats analysis for the first time by reading this book. In either case, this College Statistics Toolbox section is highly recommended reading before getting into our 50 team profiles. The stats that form the building blocks for F/+, FEI, and S&P+ are constantly being updated and refined.

Each team profile begins with a statistical snapshot (defending Pac-12 champion Oregon is presented here as a sample). The projected overall and conference records—rounded from the team's projected Mean Wins—are listed alongside the team name in the header. Estimates of offensive and defensive starters returning in 2015 were collected from team websites, spring media guides, and other reliable sources. All other stats and rankings provided in the team snapshot are explained below.

No. 3 Oregon Ducks (10-2, 8-1)

Five-Year F/+ Rating Trend

2010 2011 2012 2013 2014

Five-Year F/+ Offense Rank

15 · 3 · 3 · 10 · 2

Five-Year F/+ Defense Rank

17 · 21 · 17 · 35 · 20

Five-Year ST Efficiency Rank

34 · 39 · 18 · 26 · 17

2015 Projected Win Likelihood by Game

Date	Opponent (Proj Rank)	PWL	Projected Loss	Projected Win
Sep 5	vs E. Washington (FCS)	100%		
Sep 12	at Michigan St. (9)	59%		
Sep 19	vs Georgia St. (118)	99%		
Sep 26	vs Utah (31)	91%		
Oct 3	at Colorado (85)	99%		
Oct 10	vs Washington St. (75)	99%		
Oct 17	at Washington (52)	95%		
Oct 29	at Arizona St. (19)	70%		
Nov 7	vs California (62)	98%		
Nov 14	at Stanford (10)	61%		
Nov 21	vs USC (12)	77%		
Nov 27	vs Oregon St. (70)	99%		

2014: 13-2 (8-1) / F/+ #3 / FEI #1 / S&P+ #3 / Program F/+: #2

2014 Offense			2014 Defense		
Offensive FEI	0.747	3	Defensive FEI	-0.441	14
Off. S&P+ (Adj. PPG)	46.1	2	Def. S&P+ (Adj. PPG)	22.4	28
Rushing S&P+	133.5	5	Rushing S&P+	105.6	52
Passing S&P+	142.6	4	Passing S&P+	109.9	36
Standard Downs S&P+	129.5	5	Standard Downs S&P+	111.8	27
Passing Downs S&P+	154.2	3	Passing Downs S&P+	101.4	62

2015 Projections		
Returning Starters: 7 OFF, 5 DEF		
Proj. F/+	52.5%	3

SOS Rk	35
Mean Wins / Conf Wins	10.5 / 7.9
Conf. / Div. Title Odds	37.4% / 74.8%

2014 Five Factors

Efficiency	Off Success Rate+	124.8	8
	Def Success Rate+	104.9	46
Explosiveness	Off IsoPPP+	152.8	2
	Def IsoPPP+	116.7	27
Field Position	Field Pos. Adv. (FPA)	0.550	7
Finishing Drives	Off Red Zone S&P+	119.6	17
	Def Red Zone S&P+	108.1	39
Turnovers	Turnover Margin	+23.0	1
	Exp. TO Margin	+15.4	1
	Difference	+7.6	12

Drive-by-Drive Data

Fremeau Efficiency Index: Fremeau Efficiency Index (FEI) analysis begins with drive data instead of play-by-play data and is processed according to key principles. A team is rewarded for playing well against a strong opponent, win or lose, and is punished more severely for playing poorly against bad teams than it is rewarded for playing well against bad teams.

To calculate FEI, the nearly 20,000 possessions in every season of major college football are filtered to eliminate first-half clock-kills and end-of-game garbage drives and scores. A scoring rate analysis of the remaining possessions then determines the baseline possession efficiency expectations against which each team is measured. Game Efficiency is the composite possession-by-possession efficiency of a team over the course of a game, a measurement of the success of its offensive, defensive, and special-teams units' essential goals: to maximize the team's own scoring opportunities and to minimize those of its opponent. Finally, each team's FEI rating synthesizes its season-long Game Efficiency data, adjusted for the strength of its opposition; special emphasis is placed on quality performance against good teams, win or lose.

Offensive and Defensive FEI: Game Efficiency is a composite assessment of the possession-by-possession performance of team over the course of a game. In order to isolate the relative performance of the offense and defense, more factors are evaluated.

First, we ran a regression on the national scoring rates of tens of thousands of college football drives according to starting field position. The result represents the value of field position in terms of points expected to be scored by an average offense against an average defense—1.4 points per possession from its own 15-yard line, 2.1 points per possession from its own 40-yard line, and so on. These expected points are called Field Position Value (FPV).

Next, we ran a regression on the value of drive-ending field position according to national special teams scoring expectations. To determine the true national baseline for field-goal range, we took into account not only the 2,200 field goals attempted annually, but also the 1,400 punts kicked from opponent territory each year. In other words, if a team has an average field goal unit and a coach with an average penchant for risk-taking, the offensive value of reaching the opponent's 35-yard line is equal to the number of made field goals from that distance divided by the number of attempts plus the number of punts from that distance.

Touchdowns credit the offense with 6.96 points of drive-ending value, the value of a touchdown adjusted according to national point-after rates. Safeties have a drive-ending value of negative two points. All other offensive results are credited with a drive-ending value of zero.

Offensive efficiency is then calculated as the total drive-ending value earned by the offense divided by the sum of its offensive FPV over the course of the game. Defensive efficiency is calculated the same way using the opponent's offensive drive-ending value and FPV. Offensive and defensive efficiency are calibrated as a rating above or below zero—a good offense has a positive rating and a good defense has a negative one. These numbers are represented in the college chapters as Unadjusted Offense and Unadjusted Defense.

Offensive FEI and Defensive FEI are the opponent-adjusted values of offensive and defensive efficiency. As with FEI, the adjustments are weighted according to both the strength of the opponent and the relative significance of the result. Efficiency against a team's best competition is given more relevance weight in the formula.

Other offensive and defensive possession efficiency measures are defined as follows:

- Available yards are a function of the total yards earned divided by the total yards available based on starting field position.
- Explosive drives are possessions that average at least 10 yards per play.
- Methodical drives are possessions that last at least 10 plays.
- Value drives are possessions that begin on the offense's own side of midfield and reach the opponent's 30-yard line.

Field Position Advantage (FPA): FPA was developed in order to more accurately describe the management of field position over the course of a game. For each team, we calculate the sum of the FPV for each of its offensive series. Then, we add in a full touchdown value (6.96 points) for each non-offensive score earned by the team. (This accounts for the field-position value of special teams and defensive returns reaching the end zone versus tripping up at the one-yard line.) Special-teams turnovers and onside kicks surrendered have an FPV of zero. The sum of the FPV of every possession in the game for both teams represents the total field position at stake in the contest. FPA represents each given team's share of that total field position.

FPA is a description of which team controlled field position in the game and by how much. Two teams that face equal field position over the course of a game will each have an FPA of .500. Winning the field position battle is quite valuable. College football teams that play with an FPA over .500 win two-thirds of the time. Teams that play with an FPA over .600 win 90 percent of the time.

Play-by-Play Data

Success Rates: Our play-by-play analysis was introduced throughout the 2008 season in Bill Connelly's Varsity Numbers columns. Nearly one million plays over eight seasons in college football have been collected and evaluated to determine baselines for success for every situational down in a game. Similarly to DVOA, basic success rates are determined by national standards. The distinction for college football is in defining the standards of success. We use the following determination of a "successful" play:

- First down success = 50 percent of necessary yardage
- Second down success = 70 percent of necessary yardage

- Third/Fourth down success = 100 percent of necessary yardage

On a per play basis, these form the standards of efficiency for every offense in college football. Defensive success rates are based on preventing the same standards of achievement.

Equivalent Points and Points per Play: All yards are not created equal. A 10-yard gain from a team's own 15-yard line does not have the same value as a 10-yard gain that goes from the opponent's 10-yard line into the end zone. Based on expected scoring rates similar to FPV described above, we can calculate a point value for each play in a drive. Equivalent Points (EqPts) are calculated by subtracting the value of the resulting yard line from the initial yard line of a given play. This assigns credit to the yards that are most associated with scoring points, the end goal in any possession.

With EqPts, the game can be broken down and built back up again in a number of ways. With the addition of penalties, turnovers and special teams play, EqPts provides an accurate assessment of how a game was played on a play-by-play basis. We also use it to create a measure called Isolated Points per Play (IsoPPP), which represents the explosiveness of a team's or an individual player's successful plays.

S&P: Like OPS (on-base percentage plus slugging average) in baseball, we created a measure that combines consistency with power. S&P represents a combination of efficiency (Success Rates) and explosiveness (IsoPPP) to most accurately represent the effectiveness of a team or individual player. Success Rates carry about 80 percent of the weight in the formula, however, as efficiency is a more consistent, projectable measure.

A boom-or-bust running back may have a strong yards per carry average and IsoPPP, but his low Success Rate will lower his S&P. A consistent running back that gains between four and six yards every play, on the other hand, will have a strong Success Rate but possibly low IsoPPP. The best offenses in the country can maximize both efficiency and explosiveness on a down-by-down basis. Reciprocally, the best defenses can limit both.

S&P+: As with the FEI stats discussed above, context matters in college football. Adjustments are made to the S&P unadjusted data with a formula that takes into account a team's production, the quality of the opponent, and the quality of the opponent's opponent. To eliminate the noise of less-informative blowout stats, we filtered the play-by-play data to include only those that took place when the game was "close." This excludes plays where the score margin is larger than 28 points in the first quarter, 24 points in the second quarter, 21 points in the third quarter, or 16 points in the fourth quarter.

Beginning in 2015, we also began factoring in other components of what we deem the Five Factors of college football. In January 2014, Bill Connelly introduced this new set of concepts for analysis and debate within the realm of college football stats. At Football Study Hall, a college football stats site within the SB Nation network, he wrote the following:

"Over time, I've come to realize that the sport comes down to five basic things, four of which you can mostly control. You make more big plays than your opponent, you stay on schedule, you tilt the field, you finish drives, and you fall on the ball. Explosiveness, efficiency, field position, finishing drives, and turnovers are the five factors to winning football games."

Unlike the Four Factors used by ESPN's Dean Oliver for discussion of basketball, these factors are heavily related to each other. But they work together to create high-level analysis. Creating quality field position, executing in scoring opportunities, and consistently forcing passing downs (which lead to more sacks, forced fumbles, and passes defensed) are among the factors that have been eased into the overall S&P+ formulas.

This overall combination of play-by-play and drive data gives us S&P+, a comprehensive measure that represents a team's efficiency and explosiveness as compared to all other teams in college football. S&P+ values are calibrated to reflect percentiles and yearly scoring averages. A below-average team will have a percentile rating under 50 percent and a negative adjusted scoring margin. An above-average team will be above 50 percent with a positive adjusted scoring margin.

In the team capsules in each conference chapter, the S&P+ ratings are broken down further as follows:

- Rushing S&P+ includes only running plays, and unlike standard college statistics, does not include sacks.
- Passing S&P+ includes sacks and passing plays.
- Passing Downs S&P+ includes second-and-8 or more, third-and-5 or more, and fourth-and-5 or more. These divisions were determined based on raw S&P data showing a clear distinction in Success Rates as compared with Standard Downs.
- Standard Downs S&P+ includes all close-game plays not defined as Passing Downs.

These measures are all derived only from play-by-play data; drive efficiency data is only factored into the final, overall S&P+ figure.

Second-Order Wins: Second-order wins compare the Five Factors components of a given game, and the single-game win expectancy they create ("Given these stats, you would have won this game X percent of the time"), to the actual results of the game. This projected win total is a cousin of the Pythagorean record, a concept common in many sports.

Highlight Yards: Highlight yards represent the yards gained by a runner outside of those credited to the offensive line through adjusted line yards. The ALY formula, much like the same stat in the NFL, gives 100 percent credit to all yards gained between zero and four yards and 50 percent strength to yards between five and 10. If a runner gains 12 yards in a given carry, and we attribute 7.0 of those yards to the line, and the player's highlight yardage on the play is 5.0 yards. Beginning in 2013, we began calculating highlight yardage averages in a slightly different manner: instead of dividing total highlight yardage by a player's overall number of carries, we divide it only by the number of carries that gain more than four yards; if a line is given all credit for gains smaller than that, then it makes sense to look at highlight averages only for the carries on which a runner got a chance to create a highlight.

Opportunity Rate: Opportunity Rate represents the percentage of a runner's carries that gained at least five yards. This gives us a look at a runner's (and his line's) consistency and efficiency to go along with the explosiveness measured by Highlight Yards.

Combination Data

F/+: Introduced in *Football Outsiders Almanac 2009*, the F/+ measure combines FEI and S&P+. There is a clear distinction between the two individual approaches, and merging the two diminishes certain outliers caused by the quirks of each method. The resulting metric is both powerfully predictive and sensibly evaluative.

Program and Projected F/+: Relative to the pros, college football teams are much more consistent in year-to-year performance. Breakout seasons and catastrophic collapses certainly occur, but generally speaking, teams can be expected to play within a reasonable range of their baseline program expectations. The idea of a Football Outsiders program rating began with the introduction of Program FEI in *Pro Football Prospectus 2008* as a way to represent those individual baseline expectations.

As the strength of the F/+ system has been fortified with more seasons of full drive-by-drive and play-by-play data, the Program F/+ measure has emerged. Program F/+ is calculated from five years of FEI and S&P+ data. The result not only represents the status of each team's program power, but provides the first step in projecting future success.

Projected F/+ for 2015 begins by combining Program F/+ (weighted more toward recent seasons) with measures of two-year recruiting success (using Rivals.com ratings for signees who actually ended up enrolling at each school) and offensive and defensive performance. We adjust that baseline with transition factors like returning offensive and defensive starters, talent lost to the NFL draft, and disproportional success on passing downs. The result, Projected F/+, is a more accurate predictor of next-year success than any other data we have tested or used to date.

Strength of Schedule: Unlike other rating systems, our Strength of Schedule (SOS) calculation is not a simple average of the Projected F/+ data of each team's opponents. Instead, it represents the likelihood that an elite team (typical top-five team) would win every game on the given schedule. The distinction is valid. For any elite team, playing No. 1 Ohio State and No. 128 Eastern Michigan in a two-game stretch is certainly more difficult than playing No. 64 Georgia Southern and No. 65 Western Michigan. An average rating might judge these schedules to be equal.

The likelihood of an undefeated season is calculated as the product of Projected Win Expectations (PWE) for each game on the schedule. PWEs are based on an assessment of five years of FEI data and the records of teams of varying strengths against one another. Roughly speaking, an elite team may have a 65 percent chance of defeating a team ranked No. 10, a 75 percent chance of defeating a team ranked No. 20, and a 90 percent chance of defeating a team ranked No. 40. Combined, the elite team has a 44 percent likelihood of defeating all three ($0.65 \times 0.75 \times 0.90 = 0.439$).

A lower SOS rating represents a lower likelihood of an elite team running the table, and thus a stronger schedule. For our calculations of FBS versus FCS games, with all due apologies to North Dakota State et al., the likelihood of victory is considered to be 100 percent.

Mean Wins and Win Probabilities: To project records for each team, we use Projected F/+ and PWE formulas to estimate the likelihood of victory for a given team in its individual games. The probabilities for winning each game are added together to represent the average number of wins the team is expected to tally over the course of its scheduled games. Potential conference championship games and bowl games are not included.

The projected records listed next to each team name in the conference chapters are rounded from the mean wins data listed in the team capsule. Mean Wins are not intended to represent projected outcomes of specific matchups; rather they are our most accurate forecast for the team's season as a whole. The correlation of mean projected wins to actual wins is 0.69 for all games, 0.61 for conference games.

The Win Probability tables that appear in each conference chapter are also based on the game-by-game PWE data for each team. The likelihood for each record is rounded to the nearest whole percent.

Team Preview Text by Chad Peltier

Statistics and Introduction by Bill Connelly and Brian Fremeau

NCAA Top 50

No. 1 Ohio State Buckeyes (11-1, 8-0)

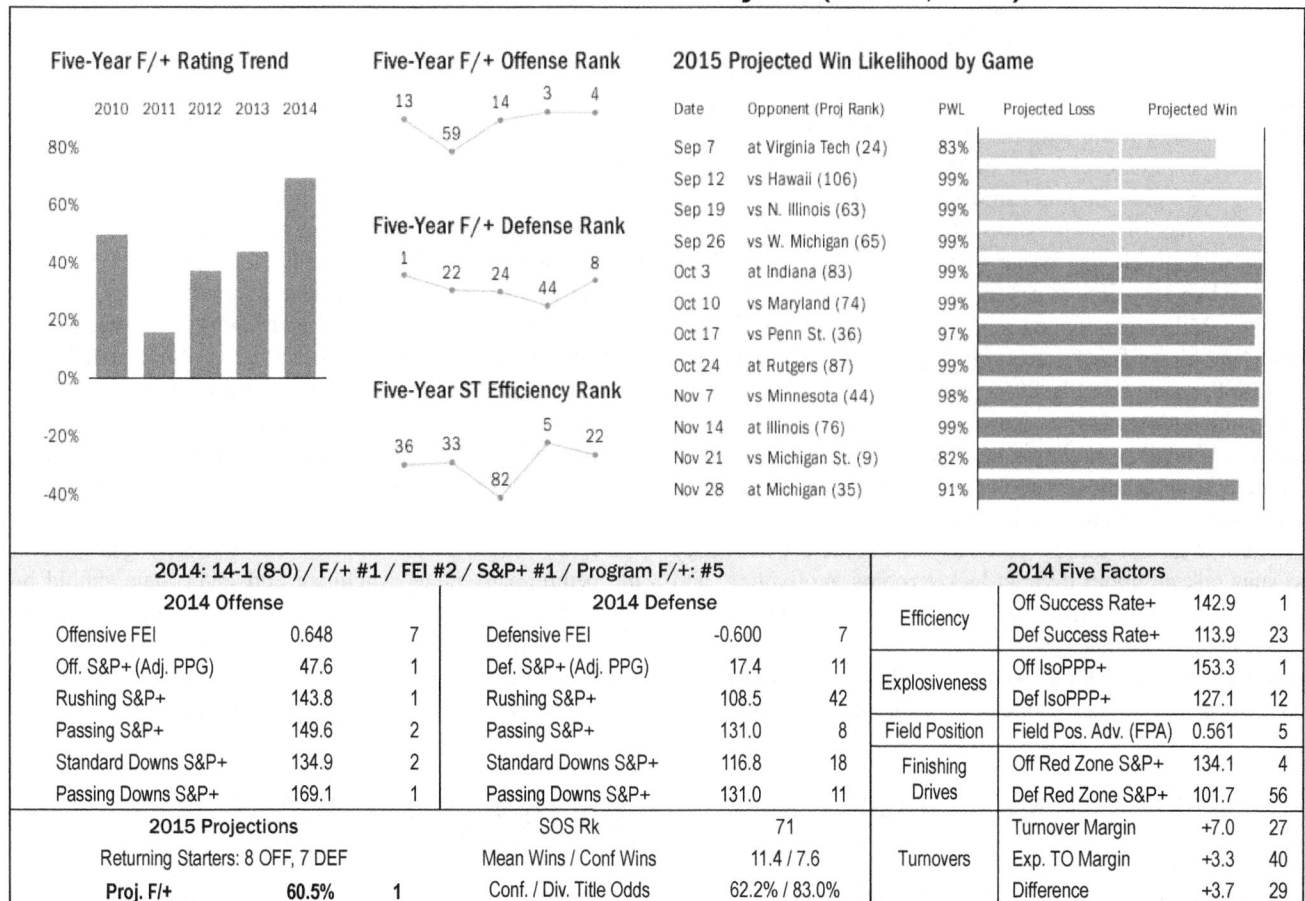

2014: 14-1 (8-0) / F/+ #1 / FEI #2 / S&P+ #1 / Program F/+: #5							2014 Five Factors			
2014 Offense			**2014 Defense**				Efficiency	Off Success Rate+	142.9	1
Offensive FEI	0.648	7	Defensive FEI	-0.600	7			Def Success Rate+	113.9	23
Off. S&P+ (Adj. PPG)	47.6	1	Def. S&P+ (Adj. PPG)	17.4	11		Explosiveness	Off IsoPPP+	153.3	1
Rushing S&P+	143.8	1	Rushing S&P+	108.5	42			Def IsoPPP+	127.1	12
Passing S&P+	149.6	2	Passing S&P+	131.0	8		Field Position	Field Pos. Adv. (FPA)	0.561	5
Standard Downs S&P+	134.9	2	Standard Downs S&P+	116.8	18		Finishing Drives	Off Red Zone S&P+	134.1	4
Passing Downs S&P+	169.1	1	Passing Downs S&P+	131.0	11			Def Red Zone S&P+	101.7	56
2015 Projections			SOS Rk		71		Turnovers	Turnover Margin	+7.0	27
Returning Starters: 8 OFF, 7 DEF			Mean Wins / Conf Wins		11.4 / 7.6			Exp. TO Margin	+3.3	40
Proj. F/+	**60.5%**	**1**	Conf. / Div. Title Odds		62.2% / 83.0%			Difference	+3.7	29

The reigning national champions return three starting quarterbacks; last season's top five rushers; the top two receiving threats; four members of an offensive line that ranked second overall in adjusted line yards and first in opportunity rate; and arguably the best defensive player in the Big Ten. Meanwhile, they only lose one starting linebacker and one starter from the nation's eighth-ranked secondary. Oh, and the Buckeyes pulled in another top-ten recruiting class. With almost every major contributor returning, it's hard not to project the Buckeyes in to another Playoff berth. So where, if anywhere, are the potential impediments to another Ohio State title run?

The biggest issues for the national champions last season, by far, were likely related: run defense (where they ranked 45th in rushing success rate) and red zone defense (56th in red zone S&P+). After allowing 370 rushing yards to Navy in the opener, they let Minnesota's David Cobb bully his way to 145, and Indiana's Tevin Coleman explode for 228. However, it was relatively easy for the Buckeyes defense to hide these deficiencies because opponents were often forced into an unbalanced, pass-heavy catch-up strategy. In fact, Ohio State's four-touchdown run in the middle of the Sugar Bowl against Alabama (putting the Tide down 13 points with three minutes

to go in the third) may have been the only reason Alabama turned away from running back Derrick Henry, who was having a phenomenally efficient game (averaging 7.3 yards per carry with a 50 percent opportunity rate) against the Buckeyes. Sometimes the best defense really is a good offense.

The defense was often able to do what it did best: create big defensive plays (20th in havoc rate) and help win the field-position battle (second in offensive FP+). Joey Bosa (whose 13.5 sacks were fourth-best in the county) is the star here, combining size, elite speed and short-area burst, but he's joined by Adolphus Washington and playmaking revelation Darron Lee, as well as a number of talented freshmen and sophomores. The line does lose Michael Bennett (14 tackles for loss and seven sacks) and Steve Miller, but don't expect any drop-off in ability to pressure the quarterback, as Miller's replacement will likely be Jalyn Holmes, Sam Hubbard, or Tyquan Lewis—all extremely high-ceiling edge rushers. The offense was usually able to mask the defense's relative inability to stop the run, but the solid secondary was also a big help. Vonn Bell is the playmaking safety (six interceptions and six pass breakups), while sophomore Eli Apple looks to continue Ohio State's legacy of shutdown cornerbacks.

It's hard to find much to criticize about an offense that ranked first or second in every offensive S&P+ category and seventh or better in all PPP+ stats, but it is unclear how touches will be distributed. Nowhere is that more important than quarterback. Between J.T. Barrett (second in the country in quarterback rating and led the second-most efficient passing offense most of the season) and Cardale Jones (who led the Buckeyes to wins over the 25th-, second-, and third-ranked F/+ teams to win the national championship), Urban Meyer has both an embarrassment of riches and a dilemma over playing time. How do you name one the starter while keeping the other championship-caliber athlete sidelined? Would the wrong pick divide the locker room? Urban's job got a little easier when two-time Big Ten Offensive Player of the Year Braxton Miller announced that he was moving to H-back, removing himself from the starting quarterback race (though he'll still spend roughly 20 percent of fall camp at quarterback) and adding another explosive weapon to the Ohio State offense. If the goal is simply to get the best starting eleven on the field in some way or another, then Braxton switching positions clearly accomplishes that goal. When you're looking for problem areas for the 2015 Buckeyes, it's almost necessary to start talking about divided locker rooms, motivation, and focus, because the offense returns almost everyone and has few statistical weaknesses.

But if we're nitpicking, two areas might be cause for (some) concern on the offensive side of the ball. First, as excellent as the offensive line was in run blocking, it was mediocre in pass protection (74th in adjusted sack rate), particularly on standard downs. While running quarterbacks tend to take more sacks (and that falls in line with the standard downs sack rating being much worse than the passing downs sack rating, 108th vs. 40th), neither ranking is necessarily elite. Second, most of the offense's second-best passing PPP+ ranking can be traced to receiver Devin Smith, who led the country in average yards per catch as the primary vertical threat in the play-action pass game. Smith had one responsibility: beat his man on deep play-action strikes precipitated by the efficient inside run game. Yes, he ended up catching nearly 69 percent of his passes, but his real value was in adding a vertical dimension to Tom Herman's offense. It's unclear who will play that role for the 2015 Buckeyes. Senior receiver Corey Smith has a shot, as does former high school quarterback Jalin Marshall, but the answer might be one of the seven freshmen or sophomore receivers the Buckeyes have stockpiled in the past two recruiting classes. Braxton Miller is likely deadlier in the short passing game, where he can make defenders miss instead of just outrunning them on play-action passes.

Besides Virginia Tech in week one and Michigan State in the penultimate game, Michigan and Penn State should be Ohio State's most competitive opponents (the Buckeyes miss Wisconsin this season). Michigan State looks to be the team most capable of dethroning the Buckeyes, but it's hard to bet against Ohio State with this much returning talent.

No. 2 Alabama Crimson Tide (10-2, 6-2)

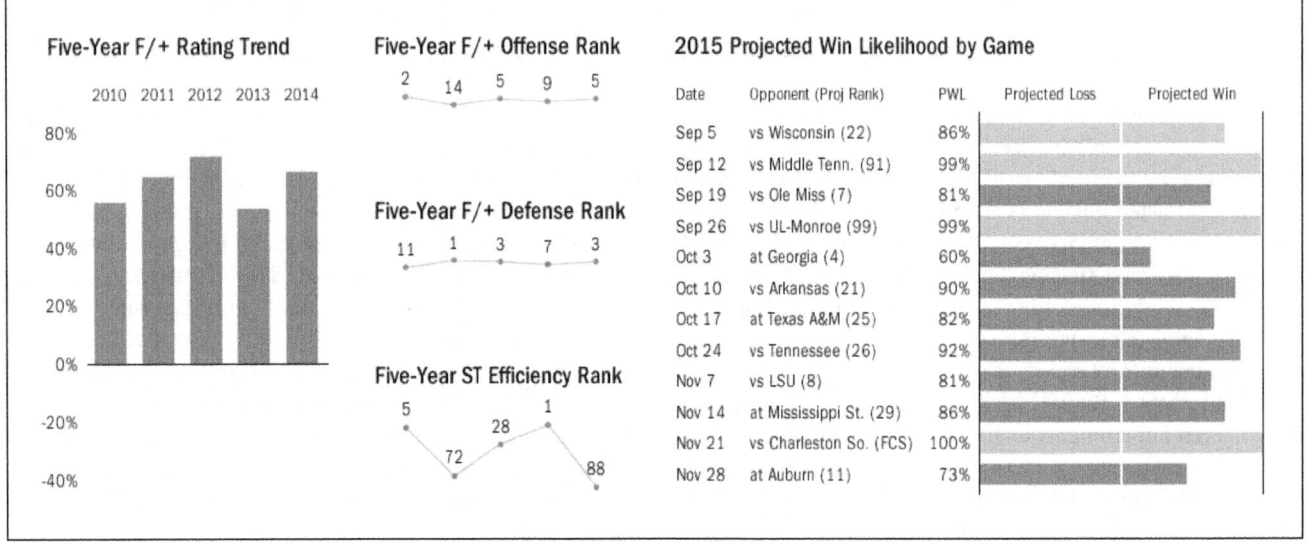

2014: 12-2 (7-1) / F/+ #2 / FEI #3 / S&P+ #2 / Program F/+: #1						2014 Five Factors			
2014 Offense			**2014 Defense**			Efficiency	Off Success Rate+	133.5	2
Offensive FEI	0.655	5	Defensive FEI	-0.599	8		Def Success Rate+	123.0	7
Off. S&P+ (Adj. PPG)	43.1	5	Def. S&P+ (Adj. PPG)	14.8	3	Explosiveness	Off IsoPPP+	140.9	5
Rushing S&P+	127.8	11	Rushing S&P+	146.8	1		Def IsoPPP+	133.7	6
Passing S&P+	146.2	3	Passing S&P+	119.9	17	Field Position	Field Pos. Adv. (FPA)	0.493	75
Standard Downs S&P+	131.7	3	Standard Downs S&P+	133.2	2	Finishing Drives	Off Red Zone S&P+	134.1	3
Passing Downs S&P+	137.3	7	Passing Downs S&P+	116.4	32		Def Red Zone S&P+	141.3	3
2015 Projections			SOS Rk	4		Turnovers	Turnover Margin	-2.0	73
Returning Starters: 4 OFF, 7 DEF			Mean Wins / Conf Wins	10.3 / 6.5			Exp. TO Margin	+7.2	13
Proj. F/+	**59.8%**	**2**	Conf. / Div. Title Odds	30.7% / 61.4%			Difference	-9.2	122

It's no secret that Alabama has amassed the most talent on either side of the ball in college football. With multiple top overall composite recruiting classes, Alabama will consistently compete for a Playoff berth. But despite advancing to the Sugar Bowl last season against Ohio State, Nick Saban and the Crimson Tide have now been upset in two straight bowl games (by the Buckeyes last year and Oklahoma the year before), leaving Tide fans hungry for their next crack at a championship. Last season's primary weakness was the secondary (which still ranked 16th in passing S&P+) that allowed Ohio State's Cardale Jones to pass for 243 yards and Auburn's Nick Marshall to throw for an astounding 456 yards. Alabama seemed to address most of those deficiencies in this year's signing class (as it typically does) and also hired Mel Tucker to coach the secondary. That secondary—and the Tide's third starting quarterback in three seasons—will determine whether the Tide can once again reach the top of the college football world.

Starting with the Tide's many strengths, the front seven might be the best in college football. The Tide had the top run defense (though they allowed Ezekiel Elliott to run for 230 yards in the Sugar Bowl) and the 27th-best havoc rate in the country, but looks to get even better this season. Jonathan Allen, Da'Shawn Hand, A'Shawn Robinson, and Daron Payne were all blue-chip recruits, while Reggie Ragland and Reuben Foster are the same at linebacker. While they struggled (relatively) with spread-to-run offenses like Auburn and Ohio State, the front seven has all of the talent in the world.

Similarly, the running backs and offensive line should once again be elite. The Tide's rushing stats were nearly as good on offense as they were on defense: eighth in rushing S&P+, sixth in adjusted line yards, second in opportunity rate, and sixth in adjusted sack rate. There was concern at running back with Altee Tenpenny transferred, Tyren Jones was dismissed, T.J. Yeldon off to the NFL, Jalston Foster graduated, freshman early enrollee DeSherrius Flowers ruled ineligible, and Bo Scarbrough tearing his ACL this spring. While that bad luck would decimate most teams, the Tide still have two top threats in Derrick Henry—who might have preserved the Tide's lead against Ohio State if they had stuck with the run in the second half—and change-of-pace explosive weapon Kenyan Drake.

Freshman Damien Harris was also the top composite running back in the country. Henry was a workhorse back who many thought would outgrow the position, and though his highlight yards per opportunity was fairly low (4.6) he has an outstanding opportunity rate (46.5 percent, ninth overall). Henry will keep the Tide running consistently, while Drake should perfectly complement him with explosive ability.

The passing game is still a question mark, however. Alabama must replace the top three receivers from last season and starting quarterback Blake Sims. Despite numerous former five-stars on the roster, Florida State transfer Jacob Coker looks to have the slight edge over David Cornwell, who will fight for the job he couldn't lock up over Sims last season. Coker and Cornwell had similar spring game numbers, likely because they were working with elite receivers like Chris Black, Robert Foster, and ArDarius Stewart. Only one receiver in the country was targeted more last year than Amari Cooper, who was both efficient (an absurd 72 percent catch rate) and explosive (averaging 13.9 yards per catch). Lane Kiffin fed most of the offense through short passes and screens to get Cooper in to space along the edge. There are plenty of options to replace Cooper on the roster, but it's likely no single receiver will repeat his production. Kiffin offenses tend to feature one or two elite receivers, and there are plenty of candidates for 2015, including five-star freshman Calvin Ridley, the nation's overall top receiver. With the talent around him, whoever wins the quarterback job doesn't need to be a superstar.

Finally, the Tide secondary is maybe the biggest area of concern, but freshman Ronnie Harrison already looks to make an impact at safety and Mel Tucker has Tony Brown, Marlon Humphrey, and Cyrus Jones at corner. The talent is here. There are five- and four-star athletes filling up all slots on the depth chart, and now Tucker can focus on technique and fixing the issues that led to the 29th IsoPPP defense last season. In short, Tide faithful can expect a quick turnaround here.

All in all, regardless of the starter at quarterback, the Tide have the talent and experience in position to contend for the Playoff again. While luck always plays some role in college football and the SEC West has challengers (Auburn in particular), you can expect the Tide to be Playoff or bust again in 2015.

No. 3 Oregon Ducks (10-2, 8-1)

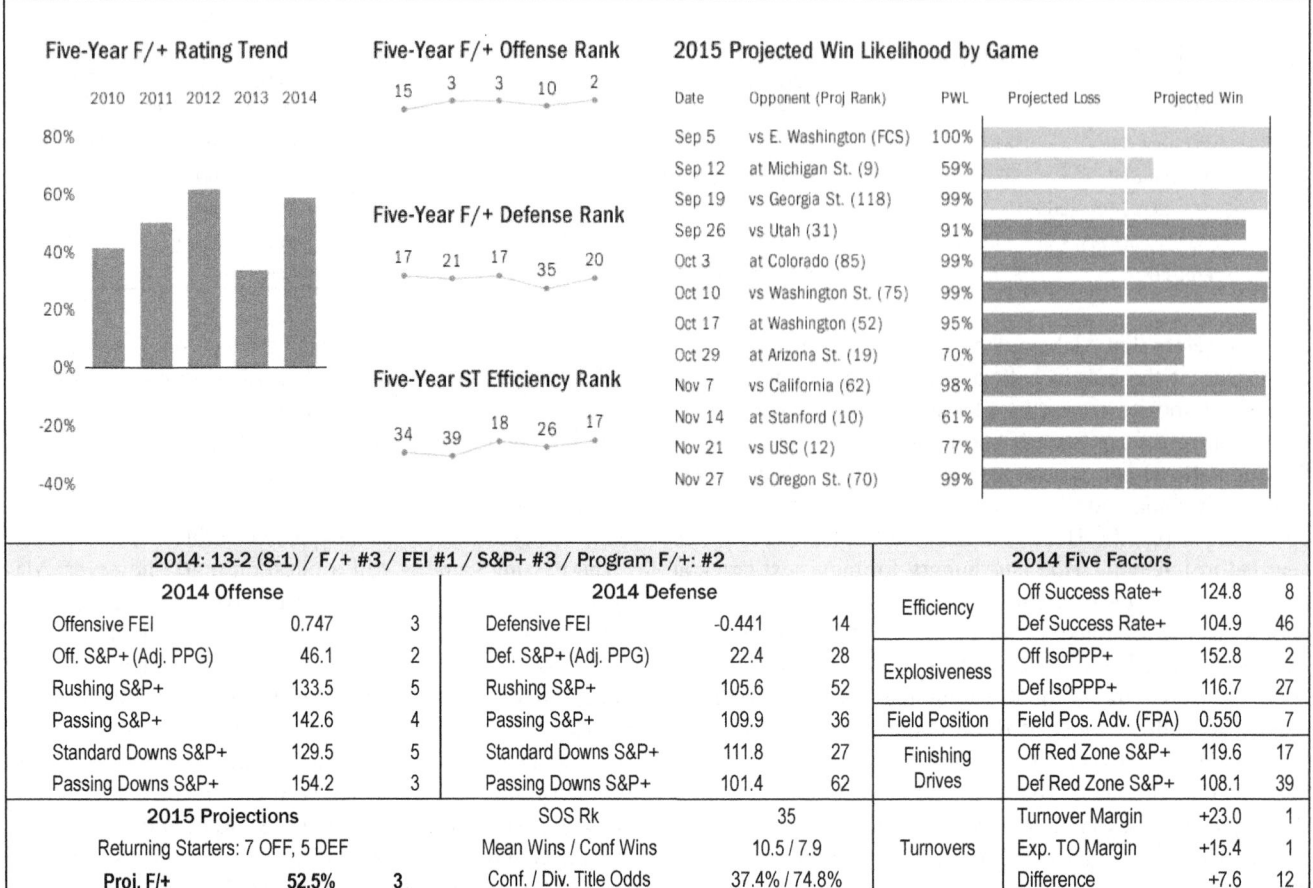

2014: 13-2 (8-1) / F/+ #3 / FEI #1 / S&P+ #3 / Program F/+: #2						2014 Five Factors		
2014 Offense			**2014 Defense**			Efficiency	Off Success Rate+	124.8	8
Offensive FEI	0.747	3	Defensive FEI	-0.441	14		Def Success Rate+	104.9	46
Off. S&P+ (Adj. PPG)	46.1	2	Def. S&P+ (Adj. PPG)	22.4	28	Explosiveness	Off IsoPPP+	152.8	2
Rushing S&P+	133.5	5	Rushing S&P+	105.6	52		Def IsoPPP+	116.7	27
Passing S&P+	142.6	4	Passing S&P+	109.9	36	Field Position	Field Pos. Adv. (FPA)	0.550	7
Standard Downs S&P+	129.5	5	Standard Downs S&P+	111.8	27	Finishing Drives	Off Red Zone S&P+	119.6	17
Passing Downs S&P+	154.2	3	Passing Downs S&P+	101.4	62		Def Red Zone S&P+	108.1	39
2015 Projections			SOS Rk	35		Turnovers	Turnover Margin	+23.0	1
Returning Starters: 7 OFF, 5 DEF			Mean Wins / Conf Wins	10.5 / 7.9			Exp. TO Margin	+15.4	1
Proj. F/+	**52.5%**	**3**	Conf. / Div. Title Odds	37.4% / 74.8%			Difference	+7.6	12

After years of stability under Marcus Mariota, it is a transition year in Eugene, but that doesn't mean expectations have been lowered at all. The Ducks reached the national championship game last season after blowing past the defending champion Seminoles, but couldn't capitalize on four Ohio State turnovers or stop the Buckeyes' run game. That has seemingly been the Ducks' ceiling since Chip Kelly arrived—talented enough to consistently win the Pac-12 and contend for a title, but unable to outlast the eventual champions. But two near-misses for the title don't necessarily make a long-term trend, nor does it deterministically limit the Ducks' chances in 2015 even though they lost the best quarterback (and likely best player) in school history. Instead, it's better to think of Oregon's recent history, and their likely future, as the establishment of a high floor rather than a limited ceiling. Yes, the Ducks have just the 23rd-ranked recruiting impact (by far the lowest of the Playoff contenders last season), but their scheme, their coaching, and the skill talent will seemingly always ensure a high level of play at Oregon.

It's hard not to concentrate on the battle for Mariota's replacement, likely between longtime backup Jeff Lockie and graduate transfer Vernon Adams. Adams has the hype and seemingly the momentum despite Lockie's excellent spring game performance (9-of-9 for 223 yards). Adams is small in stature but put up impressive numbers at Eastern Washington last season, completing 66 percent of his passes for 3,483

yards against only eight interceptions. Against Washington last season, Adams was 31-for-46 for 475 yards, seven touchdowns, and no interceptions. The depth of skill players around either quarterback ensures there won't be a significant drop-off in overall offensive productivity: the Royce Freeman and Thomas Tyner duo at running back is among the best in the country, while Bralon Addison, Byron Marshall, and Darren Carrington are all reliable and explosive receiving options.

However, the offensive line must replace three starters, including all-Pac-12 selections Jake Fisher and Hroniss Grasu. Last year's line excelled at zone blocking, finishing first in adjusted line yards and 12th in opportunity rate. The line may have lost two of its top members, but senior Tyler Crosby also returns after a season-ending injury last year. Last season's line was far less efficient in pass protection (41st in adjusted sack rate), particularly in obvious passing situations (97th, though the Ducks ran 42 percent of the time on passing downs, which was 19th-most in the country as Mariota often passed on early downs).

Here the offensive line, rather than the quarterback battle, is most deterministic of the Ducks' ceiling in 2015. The Ducks have already proved time and again that their run game is explosive enough (second in IsoPPP) to win the Pac-12 (though the Stanford run defense has been a consistent challenge), but the championship game illustrates how even the Ducks' rushing offense can be stymied by an athletic defense. Ohio State used its linebackers to match numbers on either side of center, accounting for all packaged run/pass options, while the defensive line could focus on the base inside run game. With this scheme and Ohio State's athletic front seven, Oregon's running back tandem combined for just 22 carries for 84 yards; Freeman was held to just 2.2 yards per rush with a single carry gaining more than 5 yards. The offensive line must not only replace its departed seniors, it has to improve its efficiency against elite defensive fronts.

Just as important to Oregon's 2015 campaign is the defensive line. Last year's group was average in run defense (62nd) and worse in pass defense (75th in adjusted sack rate and 55th in front seven havoc rate). Unfortunately the line loses pass rusher and first-round pick Arik Armstead and must develop a strong pass rush regardless. Last year's secondary was not only 28th in passing S&P+, but shut down explo-

sive plays (12th in IsoPPP). All-American Ifo Ekpre-Olomu was certainly one of the top corners in college football last season, but with former receiver Charles Nelson as a natural converted cornerback (he starred as a two-way player in the spring game), the Ducks have reason to expect a strong performance even from a rebuilt secondary. The pass defense was the strength of last year's team—the question is whether secondary coach John Neal can once again rebuild the unit as the run defense suffers fewer losses.

With a critical early-season matchup with the unforgiving Michigan State defense, the Ducks have their hands full this offseason replacing notable stars on both sides of the ball. But the middle of the schedule offers plenty of leeway for player development before later-season games against Arizona State, Stanford, and USC. The Ducks have every opportunity to make a repeat bid at the Playoff—and with that schedule, they will have earned it.

No. 4 Georgia Bulldogs (10-2, 6-2)

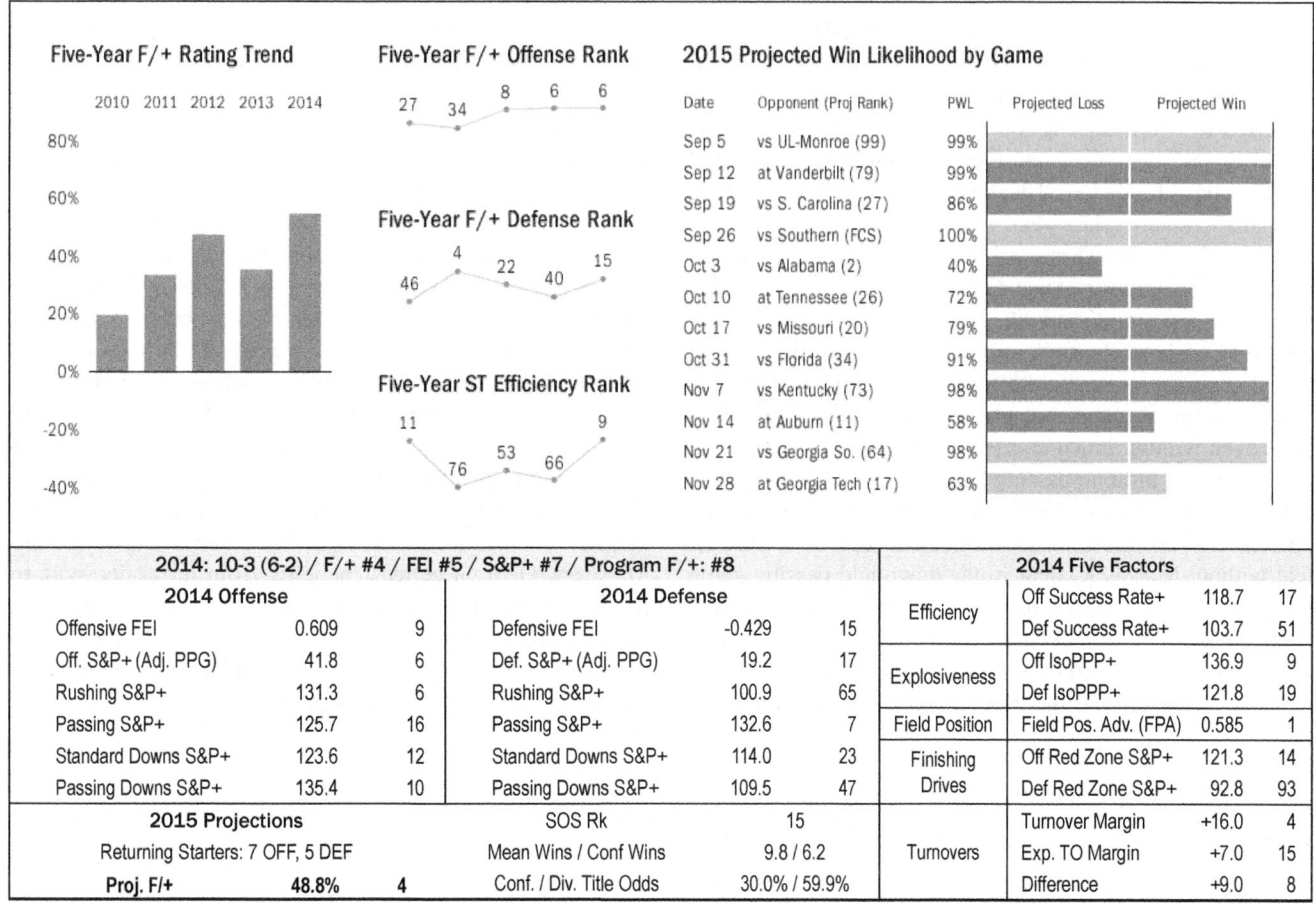

2014: 10-3 (6-2) / F/+ #4 / FEI #5 / S&P+ #7 / Program F/+: #8						2014 Five Factors			
2014 Offense			**2014 Defense**			Efficiency	Off Success Rate+	118.7	17
Offensive FEI	0.609	9	Defensive FEI	-0.429	15		Def Success Rate+	103.7	51
Off. S&P+ (Adj. PPG)	41.8	6	Def. S&P+ (Adj. PPG)	19.2	17	Explosiveness	Off IsoPPP+	136.9	9
Rushing S&P+	131.3	6	Rushing S&P+	100.9	65		Def IsoPPP+	121.8	19
Passing S&P+	125.7	16	Passing S&P+	132.6	7	Field Position	Field Pos. Adv. (FPA)	0.585	1
Standard Downs S&P+	123.6	12	Standard Downs S&P+	114.0	23	Finishing Drives	Off Red Zone S&P+	121.3	14
Passing Downs S&P+	135.4	10	Passing Downs S&P+	109.5	47		Def Red Zone S&P+	92.8	93
2015 Projections			SOS Rk	15			Turnover Margin	+16.0	4
Returning Starters: 7 OFF, 5 DEF			Mean Wins / Conf Wins	9.8 / 6.2		Turnovers	Exp. TO Margin	+7.0	15
Proj. F/+	**48.8%**	**4**	Conf. / Div. Title Odds	30.0% / 59.9%			Difference	+9.0	8

Like a lot of teams, the Bulldogs' ceiling may be determined by an ongoing quarterback battle. With four-year starter Aaron Murray gone, Hutson Mason was the fifth-year senior starter at quarterback in 2014, and now the Bulldogs must find their third starting quarterback in as many years. Presumed favorite Brice Ramsey will try to fend off Faton Bauta, and Virginia transfer Greyson Lambert. To add to the

transitions, longtime offensive coordinator Mike Bobo left for the head coaching job at Colorado State, meaning new OC Brian Schottenheimer will join now second-year defensive coordinator Jeremy Pruitt in a revamped coaching staff. Little is expected to change from a schematic standpoint as Georgia should rely heavily on sophomore running back Nick Chubb and a punishing ground game that also features four-star recruits Sony Michel, Keith Marshall, and A.J. Turman. To take the next step and improve on a string of consistently good-but-not-great seasons, it's likely that Georgia will have to find a quarterback who can confidently throw vertical play-action.

The Bulldogs must also improve their run defense in a year when running backs may define SEC play. Georgia will face Alabama's Derrick Henry and Kenyan Drake, Florida's Kelvin Taylor, Missouri's Russell Hansbrough, and Tennessee's Jalen Hurd, not to mention whoever wins Auburn's running back battle. That is a lot of talent for a Georgia run defense that ranked 58th in rushing S&P+ and 85th in front seven havoc rate last season. The line lacked a difference-maker at defensive tackle, a player who could consistently command double teams while occasionally making explosive negative plays of his own. While Pruitt had plenty of experienced linemen to substitute, most were relatively undersized, allowing opposing offensive lines a high opportunity rate. Look no further than the otherwise bewildering loss to Florida for evidence, as an offense that otherwise rated 67th in rushing S&P+ ran for 418 yards, including 197 from Kelvin Taylor and 192 from Matt Jones (all while staying truly one-dimensional—quarterback Treon Harris attempted only six passes!). The answer for the Bulldogs might be true freshman and No. 1 overall recruit for the 247 Composite Trent Thompson. Thompson is poised to win a starting job immediately, but he might be joined by early enrollees and fellow freshmen Natrez Patrick and Jonathan Ledbetter. The linebackers were some of the best in the country last year, with Jordan Jenkins, Leonard Floyd, and Lorenzo Carter all back and hoping to improve on last season's poor havoc rating. Last year's biggest improvement and Pruitt's private position group, the secondary, should be anchored by sophomore revelation Dominick Sanders. That group is maybe the thinnest in terms of depth and overall recruited talent, but played at an exceptionally high level even without much quarterback pressure from the front seven, ranking ninth in passing S&P+.

Mason was underrated in his one year as Georgia's starting quarterback, but the offense nonetheless took on a different feel without Murray's talent in the downfield passing game. For years, Bobo's Georgia offense relied on a steady run game complemented by an explosive play-action passing game. Georgia's offense churned out well-prepared pro-style quarterbacks and improved the play of countless wide receivers,

but the offense shifted with no effective vertical ability. That's not to say it wasn't effective: the tandem of Todd Gurley and Nick Chubb plowed ahead for the eighth overall offense and a 16th-ranked IsoPPP score, even though opponents often knew exactly what was coming. Georgia ran the ball on two-thirds of standard downs (29th) and 44.3 percent of passing downs (12th). But the two elite backs and Georgia's offensive line, which ranked fourth in adjusted line yards and returns all but center David Andrews, proved that a predictable offense can still be devastatingly effective.

The problem for 2015 is that it's unclear whether any of the three quarterbacks vying for Mason's old job can match his efficiency (21 touchdowns to just four interceptions) or improve on his deep passing ability (Georgia had only 34 passes of 20-plus yards last season). Spring practice and limited game film from last season suggest Ramsey has the arm talent but might have too much of a gunslinger mentality. Bauta is an effective runner and protects the ball well, but has a lower ceiling than Ramsey. Lambert is an interesting late addition to the team, joining via graduate transfer with two years of eligibility. While losing the starting job at Virginia, Lambert is recognized as a cerebral quarterback with a big arm that may have been mismatched in Virginia's quarterback-unfriendly system.

Regardless of who the starter turns out to be, just as important will be finding a solid group of receivers. Currently the unit is led by veteran Malcom Mitchell, out to prove that he's back to form after several leg injuries, and sophomore tight end Jeb Blazevich. But after those two it's anyone's guess, as depth is certainly a concern. Young talent will be available (blue-chip athlete Terry Godwin is expected to begin his career as a wide receiver), but it remains to be seen whether all of the moving pieces—including Schottenheimer's schematic variations, a new starting quarterback, and chemistry with a new group of receivers—will all amount to the record-setting offenses from the past two seasons. Though the overall schedule is stout, with Auburn and Alabama from the SEC West as well as upstart Tennessee and always-solid Missouri, Georgia at least benefits from an easier start to the season. Anything less than a trip to Atlanta would be a disappointment for a Bulldogs team that's projected to be third overall in the S&P+ and fifth in FEI, despite all of the transitions for the Georgia offense.

No. 5 UCLA Bruins (10-2, 7-2)

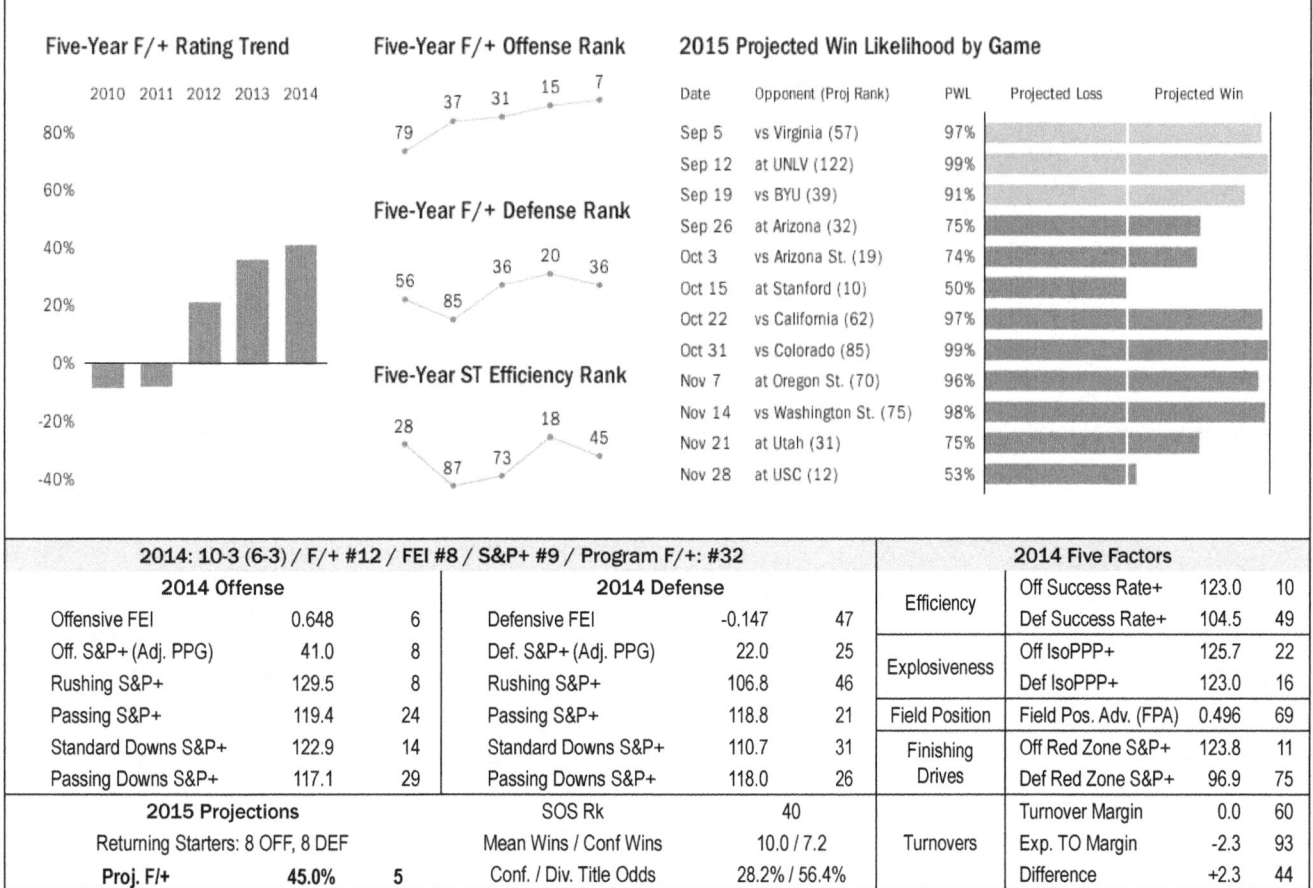

Five-Year F/+ Rating Trend

Five-Year F/+ Offense Rank

Five-Year F/+ Defense Rank

Five-Year ST Efficiency Rank

2015 Projected Win Likelihood by Game

Date	Opponent (Proj Rank)	PWL	Projected Loss	Projected Win
Sep 5	vs Virginia (57)	97%		
Sep 12	at UNLV (122)	99%		
Sep 19	vs BYU (39)	91%		
Sep 26	at Arizona (32)	75%		
Oct 3	vs Arizona St. (19)	74%		
Oct 15	at Stanford (10)	50%		
Oct 22	vs California (62)	97%		
Oct 31	vs Colorado (85)	99%		
Nov 7	at Oregon St. (70)	96%		
Nov 14	vs Washington St. (75)	98%		
Nov 21	at Utah (31)	75%		
Nov 28	at USC (12)	53%		

2014: 10-3 (6-3) / F/+ #12 / FEI #8 / S&P+ #9 / Program F/+: #32

2014 Offense

Offensive FEI	0.648	6
Off. S&P+ (Adj. PPG)	41.0	8
Rushing S&P+	129.5	8
Passing S&P+	119.4	24
Standard Downs S&P+	122.9	14
Passing Downs S&P+	117.1	29

2014 Defense

Defensive FEI	-0.147	47
Def. S&P+ (Adj. PPG)	22.0	25
Rushing S&P+	106.8	46
Passing S&P+	118.8	21
Standard Downs S&P+	110.7	31
Passing Downs S&P+	118.0	26

2015 Projections

Returning Starters: 8 OFF, 8 DEF		
Proj. F/+	45.0%	5

SOS Rk	40
Mean Wins / Conf Wins	10.0 / 7.2
Conf. / Div. Title Odds	28.2% / 56.4%

2014 Five Factors

Efficiency	Off Success Rate+	123.0	10
	Def Success Rate+	104.5	49
Explosiveness	Off IsoPPP+	125.7	22
	Def IsoPPP+	123.0	16
Field Position	Field Pos. Adv. (FPA)	0.496	69
Finishing Drives	Off Red Zone S&P+	123.8	11
	Def Red Zone S&P+	96.9	75
Turnovers	Turnover Margin	0.0	60
	Exp. TO Margin	-2.3	93
	Difference	+2.3	44

Jim Mora's three years at UCLA have been defined by good-but-not-great teams on the verge of contending for a national championship (just don't tell that to Lee Corso). Mora's teams have failed to reach the game's highest level despite Brett Hundley's play and a consistently high level of recruiting (fourth in recruiting impact). Although they lost Hundley to the NFL, few teams return more starters than the 2015 Bruins. Yes, there's a quarterback battle, the offensive line absolutely must improve its pass blocking, and the run defense needed some work, but with Oregon also in the middle of a quarterback battle and USC unproven under Steve Sarkisian, there is certainly opportunity yet again for a Mora-led Bruins squad to reach the next level.

Most eyes will be on the quarterback duel between all-world true freshman and early enrollee Josh Rosen, steady backup Jerry Neuheisel, and athletic redshirt freshman Asiantii Woulard. Hundley never quite reached Heisman expectations during his tenure, but he had a command of the offense and a solid combination of athletic ability and pure talent to lead the 26th passing offense in S&P+. Interestingly enough, despite Hundley's experience and explosive talent, the offense was geared towards efficiency, Paul Perkins, and the run game—and that is exactly what Bruins fans should expect this season as well.

The Hundley offense was efficient (27th in success rate), particularly in the run game (sixth in S&P+) but not ex-plosive (84th in IsoPPP). That reflects the offensive line's unique position as an elite run blocking unit (sixth in adjusted line yards), but like a slightly worse-off Ohio State offensive line, there was a huge disparity between its run blocking ability and its pass protection (115th in adjusted sack rate and *dead last* in passing downs sack rate). Hundley was likely at fault for some of those sacks, but it is truly a testament to his ability as a passer that the Bruins were 26th in passing offense despite such poor protection. This will be a make-or-break factor for the 2015 Bruins. With early off-season reports suggesting that Rosen has the upper hand in the quarterback race, the freshman will need all the help he can get in pass protection. His supporting cast is strong—the offense can lean on the Pac-12's leading rusher Paul Perkins (6.3 yards per carry) and the line's road grating ability, while Devin Fuller, Jordan Payton, and Thomas Duarte all return in the passing game. In short, as long as the very experienced line progresses in pass blocking, then the new quarterback will certainly have a strong enough supporting cast for the Bruins to achieve their offensive goals.

The Bruins defense is similarly full of star power like do-everything linebacker Myles Jack and stout defensive lineman Eddie Vanderdoes, but new defensive coordinator Tom Bradley (via Paterno-era Penn State) must improve a sometimes hesitant bend-don't-break unit that failed to generate big plays and had only average run defense. In UCLA's three losses last season, Utah, Oregon, and Stanford all rushed for more than 200 yards. The Bruins defensive line was mediocre (79th in adjusted line yards), especially in short-yardage situations where they were blown off the ball (127th in power success rate). The Bruins clamped down on explosive plays (21st), but the poor run defense kept opposing offenses on schedule (61st in success rate). Bruins fans also complained of the vanilla play calling, and there's evidence in the havoc statistics, where the Bruins ranked 91st and 111th in defensive back havoc rate. Given the mediocre efficiency numbers but excel-

lent explosive play defense, it is also possible that a vanilla scheme was simply a better alternative than a playmaking but leaky secondary. Regardless, Bradley has plenty of talent to work with and his resume speaks for itself.

Ultimately, UCLA is in a similar position as it was last year despite losing Hundley. They are once again in a position to win the Pac-12, but must win the annual battle with USC and take down a talented Stanford team. On the plus side, they will avoid Oregon until a potential matchup in the Pac-12 championship.

No. 6 Baylor Bears (10-2, 7-2)

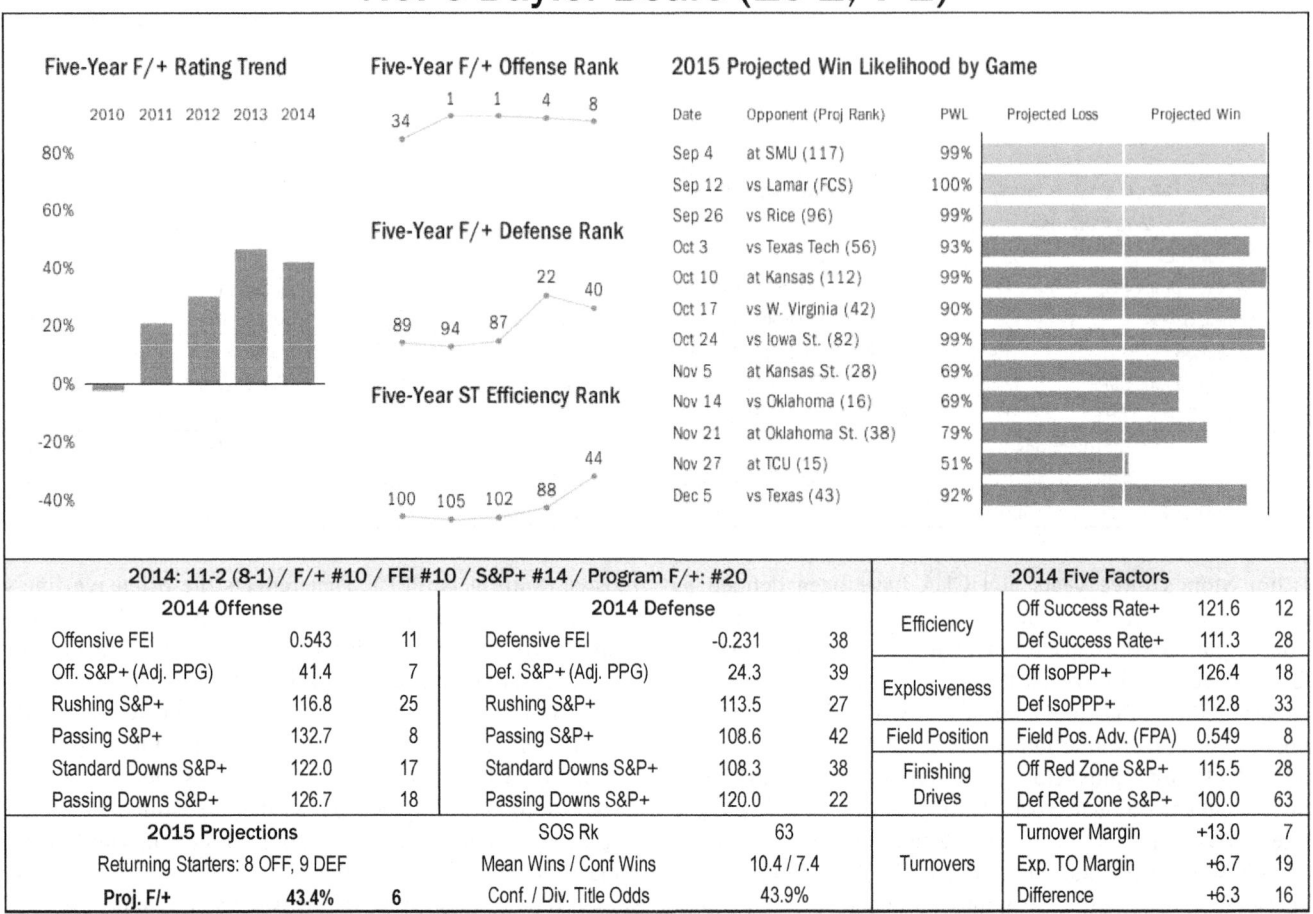

2014: 11-2 (8-1) / F/+ #10 / FEI #10 / S&P+ #14 / Program F/+: #20							2014 Five Factors			
2014 Offense			**2014 Defense**				Efficiency	Off Success Rate+	121.6	12
Offensive FEI	0.543	11	Defensive FEI	-0.231	38			Def Success Rate+	111.3	28
Off. S&P+ (Adj. PPG)	41.4	7	Def. S&P+ (Adj. PPG)	24.3	39		Explosiveness	Off IsoPPP+	126.4	18
Rushing S&P+	116.8	25	Rushing S&P+	113.5	27			Def IsoPPP+	112.8	33
Passing S&P+	132.7	8	Passing S&P+	108.6	42		Field Position	Field Pos. Adv. (FPA)	0.549	8
Standard Downs S&P+	122.0	17	Standard Downs S&P+	108.3	38		Finishing Drives	Off Red Zone S&P+	115.5	28
Passing Downs S&P+	126.7	18	Passing Downs S&P+	120.0	22			Def Red Zone S&P+	100.0	63
2015 Projections			SOS Rk		63			Turnover Margin	+13.0	7
Returning Starters: 8 OFF, 9 DEF			Mean Wins / Conf Wins		10.4 / 7.4		Turnovers	Exp. TO Margin	+6.7	19
Proj. F/+	**43.4%**	**6**	Conf. / Div. Title Odds		43.9%			Difference	+6.3	16

Baylor had just as much of a claim to the final spot in the inaugural College Football Playoff as TCU—the Bears topped the Horned Frogs head to head in a shootout match-up, and the two teams were ranked within five spots of one another in the final F/+ rankings for 2014. Art Briles' group allowed an improbable fourth-quarter comeback to Michigan State to close the season and lost quarterback Bryce Petty to the NFL, but nevertheless they are one of the most experienced teams in the country, returning 17 starters including four offensive linemen. With that much stability up front—including all four defensive linemen and All-American candidate Shawn Oakman—Baylor has the potential to be at the top of the Big 12 again and right back in contention for a Playoff spot.

Baylor is somewhat of a plug-and-play offense for quarter-backs. In 2012, after Robert Griffin's Heisman winning season, Baylor turned to Nick Florence, who guided the Bears to the 12th-ranked passing S&P+ offense. Then, after Florence's only season, Petty took the reins and the offense finished second in passing S&P+ offense. Both Florence and Petty were only three-star ranked 247 Composite quarterbacks. Both of RGIII's backups had the advantage of not only playing in a quarterback-friendly system that relies on many post-snap run/pass reads, but also playing behind a veteran player until they were experienced in Briles' system. Now junior Seth Russell will lead the Bears after serving as Petty's primary backup last season. Russell wasn't as accurate as Petty, but had a slightly higher average yards per attempt. Importantly, he also returns running back Shock Linwood, who was efficient (39.8 percent opportunity rate) if not explosive (only 4.21 highlight yards per carry). But the nation's fastest offense (first in adjusted pace) will rely on a trio of veteran receivers for more than enough explosiveness (Baylor was 19th in IsoPPP last season)—sophomore K.D. Cannon, junior Corey Coleman, and senior Jay Lee all averaged more than 15.4 yards per reception and caught at least 62 percent of their targets. Junior Lynx Hawthorne joins them as the fourth starting receiver, and figures to be a more high-percentage possession-style receiver with a 74 percent catch rate and 11.8 yards per catch average. That's all to say, don't expect the Baylor offense to skip a beat even with a new quarterback.

The defense made great strides last season, ranking tenth in defensive S&P+ and 38th in defensive FEI. Baylor struggled with explosive plays (54th in IsoPPP and 99th in explosive drive rating), but was solid against the run and generated a good amount of quarterback pressure, particularly from Oak-

man at defensive end. Baylor allowed three games to turn in to track meets: TCU, Texas Tech, and Michigan State. It was clear that Baylor's weakness was in the back end rather than the front seven, which was strong against the run (12th in adjusted line yards) and had a solid pass rush (15th in adjusted sack rate). Don't expect the defense to change significantly for 2015 with nine starters returning, though that experience should help limit breakdowns and confusion that resulted in big plays last season.

The Bears' schedule is entirely back-loaded. Outside of West Virginia visiting in mid-October, Baylor doesn't play a team that finished higher than 82nd in last season's F/+ rankings. However, Baylor ends the season with consecutive games against Kansas State, Oklahoma, Oklahoma State, TCU, and Texas, which just might be the most difficult stretch of games for anyone in the country. Expect Baylor to put up incredible numbers throughout the beginning of the season, but they won't truly be tested until November.

No. 7 Ole Miss Rebels (9-3, 5-3)

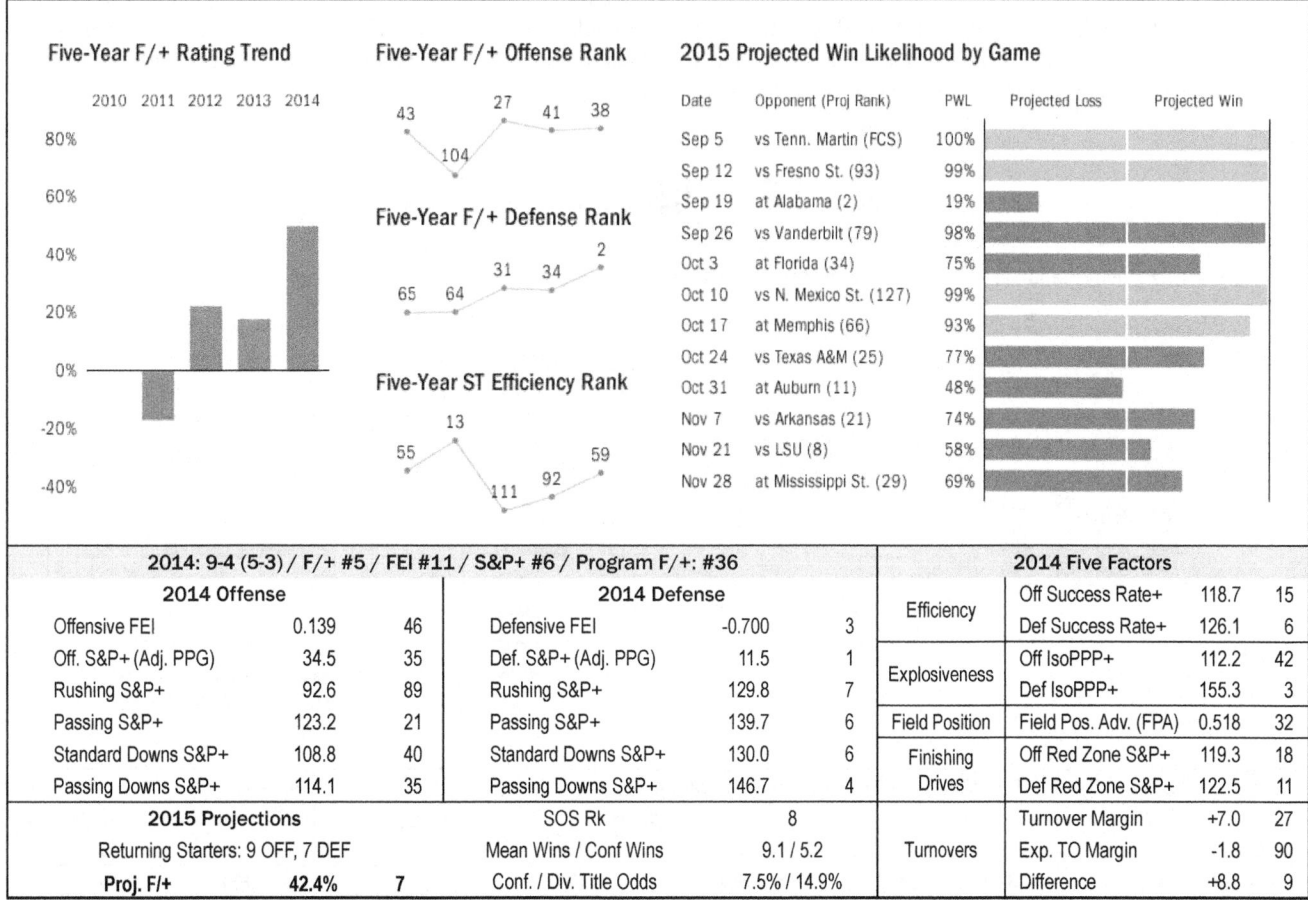

The Rebels were one of the big stories of 2014, with both Ole Miss and their archrival Bulldogs rising to national prominence, culminating in an ESPN GameDay hosting at the Grove and a win over Alabama. But things fell apart in the tail end of the season as the Rebels were shut out by Arkansas and then plastered by TCU in the bowl game. Once

known for Hugh Freeze's exciting offenses, Ole Miss won last year with its incredibly talented defense. The Rebels were the epitome of bend-don't-break, ranking seventh overall in defensive S&P+ and first in IsoPPP, but 49th in success rate. The Rebels allowed offenses to get their yards, but they generated unbelievable pressure on opposing quarterbacks and offensive lines (tenth in havoc rate) and stalled drives short of touchdowns (third in defensive FEI). Most of the team returns for 2015, though Ole Miss will have to find a new quarterback following Bo Wallace's graduation.

Despite the up-and-down nature of Wallace's performances, he was extremely productive as demonstrated by the team's tenth-best passing S&P+. The problem was that the offense was stop-and-start with little per-play efficiency (85th in success rate) and fairly predictable play calling (passing on almost 80 percent of passing downs). The run game wasn't ranked highly (49th) and the leading rusher, Jaylen Walton, totaled just 586 rushing yards on an average of only eight attempts per game. However, despite Walton's limited number of carries, he was very efficient with great explosiveness (7.1 highlight yards per opportunity) and a better efficiency than his team average (40.6 percent). If anything, Walton was underutilized, particularly after Laquon Treadwell's injury hurt receiver depth. Tight end Evan Engram has the highest yards per reception average for returning pass catchers, with other receivers hovering around the 10.0 to 12.0 yards per reception mark. But while a returning Treadwell, Engram, Damore'ea Stringfellow, and Quincy Adeboyejo give the passing game some options, it's completely unclear who will actually be doing the throwing next season. Freeze gave the slight nod to Ryan Buchanan over recent Clemson transfer Chad Kelly, but

Kelly has the clearly higher ceiling as a passer than either Buchanan or the run-first option, DeVante Kincade. Kelly gives Ole Miss their only real chance at a vertical passing game, as Kincade doesn't command much of a pocket presence and Buchanan struggled with pass placement. While the offensive line has serious depth issues, quarterback play will define Ole Miss's potential in the SEC West next season.

The Ole miss defense was really where you could see Freeze's recruiting impact translate to on-field production. The front seven did an excellent job limiting the run game, limiting plays even if they didn't account for as much havoc as you might expect (33rd) and allowed a fairly mediocre opportunity rate to opposing running backs (37.8 percent, 51st). The strength was in pass defense and limiting big passing plays, going so far as to limit Alabama's Blake Sims to no touchdowns and an interception in the Rebels' October victory last season. Robert Nkemdiche and sophomore pass rusher Marquis Haynes return in the front and Tee Shepard, Tony Bridges, and Tony Conner will challenge Florida for the top secondary in the conference. The Rebels defense can't carry the team by itself, particularly in what should be a run-heavy year for the SEC (Alabama, LSU, and Florida all have quarterback questions but excellent running backs), so the quarterback battle and development will be the most important thing to watch in Oxford.

No. 8 LSU Tigers (9-3, 5-3)

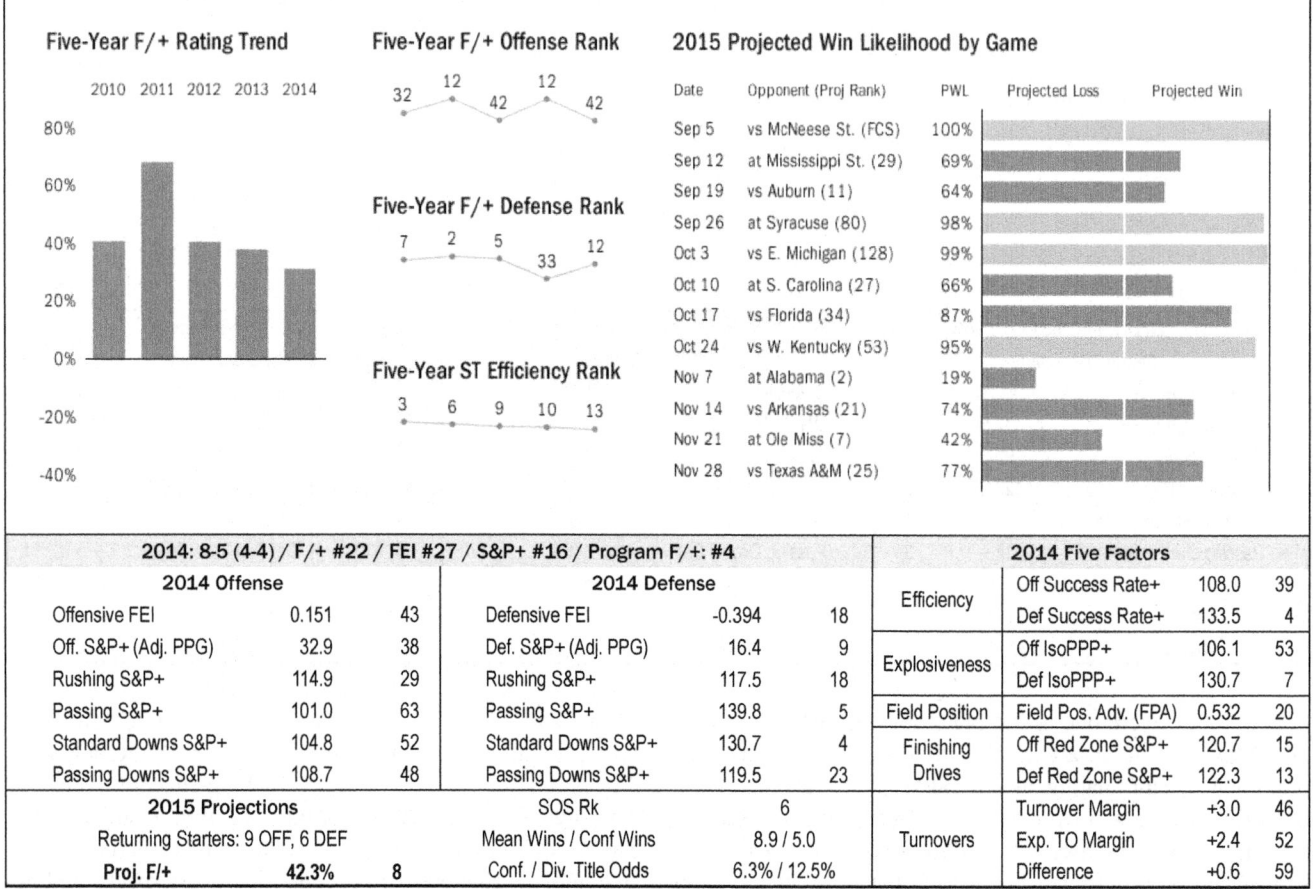

Five-Year F/+ Rating Trend

2010	2011	2012	2013	2014

Five-Year F/+ Offense Rank
32 — 12 — 42 — 12 — 42

Five-Year F/+ Defense Rank
7 — 2 — 5 — 33 — 12

Five-Year ST Efficiency Rank
3 — 6 — 9 — 10 — 13

2015 Projected Win Likelihood by Game

Date	Opponent (Proj Rank)	PWL
Sep 5	vs McNeese St. (FCS)	100%
Sep 12	at Mississippi St. (29)	69%
Sep 19	vs Auburn (11)	64%
Sep 26	at Syracuse (80)	98%
Oct 3	vs E. Michigan (128)	99%
Oct 10	at S. Carolina (27)	66%
Oct 17	vs Florida (34)	87%
Oct 24	vs W. Kentucky (53)	95%
Nov 7	at Alabama (2)	19%
Nov 14	vs Arkansas (21)	74%
Nov 21	at Ole Miss (7)	42%
Nov 28	vs Texas A&M (25)	77%

2014: 8-5 (4-4) / F/+ #22 / FEI #27 / S&P+ #16 / Program F/+: #4

2014 Offense			2014 Defense		
Offensive FEI	0.151	43	Defensive FEI	-0.394	18
Off. S&P+ (Adj. PPG)	32.9	38	Def. S&P+ (Adj. PPG)	16.4	9
Rushing S&P+	114.9	29	Rushing S&P+	117.5	18
Passing S&P+	101.0	63	Passing S&P+	139.8	5
Standard Downs S&P+	104.8	52	Standard Downs S&P+	130.7	4
Passing Downs S&P+	108.7	48	Passing Downs S&P+	119.5	23

2015 Projections		SOS Rk	6
Returning Starters: 9 OFF, 6 DEF		Mean Wins / Conf Wins	8.9 / 5.0
Proj. F/+	42.3%	8	Conf. / Div. Title Odds	6.3% / 12.5%

2014 Five Factors

Efficiency	Off Success Rate+	108.0	39
	Def Success Rate+	133.5	4
Explosiveness	Off IsoPPP+	106.1	53
	Def IsoPPP+	130.7	7
Field Position	Field Pos. Adv. (FPA)	0.532	20
Finishing Drives	Off Red Zone S&P+	120.7	15
	Def Red Zone S&P+	122.3	13
Turnovers	Turnover Margin	+3.0	46
	Exp. TO Margin	+2.4	52
	Difference	+0.6	59

LSU has been one of the most consistent teams year-to-year, ranking 22nd, 17th, and 11th over the last three years, but always seems to be hampered by quarterback play. Aside from Zach Mettenberger's senior season in 2013, quarterback play has been inconsistent at best, despite the typically incredible cast of receivers that flock to Baton Rouge in every recruiting class (including Odell Beckham Jr., Jarvis Landry, Rueben Randle, and current players like Travin Dural and Malachi Dupre). The passing game has ranked 51st, 8th, and 46th over the last three seasons. With an easier schedule last season that avoided both Georgia and Missouri from the East, 8-5 was a big disappointment.

So the question that will determine whether the Tigers can contend for championships again in 2015 is whether Anthony Jennings or Brandon Harris can be consistent enough to balance what should be a strong running game. Harris had more limited time as a freshman last season, but he outdid Jennings in both efficiency (55.6 percent completion rate to Jennings' 48.9 percent) and explosiveness (ten yards per attempt to Jennings' 7.1). Harris also seemed to have a better arm, making accurate touch throws even deep—and the play-action constraint is the primary responsibility for LSU quarterbacks. However, both quarterbacks looked solid in the spring game, thanks largely to explosive plays from their receivers.

The offensive line last season didn't do the quarterbacks any favors. Ranking 110th in adjusted sack rate, the line excelled in run blocking, but floundered in protecting the quarterback. Without adequate pass protection, either quarterback will struggle to get the ball to his wide receivers. Travin Dural—who was very explosive, averaging 20.5 yards per catch,

but had a poor catch rate at 45.1 percent—and Malachi Dupre are joined this year by yet another blue-chip recruit, five-star Tyron Johnson, again suggesting that the Tigers are just a quarterback away from an elite offense.

How did Les Miles convince four-star running backs in Derrius Guice and Nick Brossette to come to LSU despite last season's No.1 overall recruit, Leonard Fournette, entering only his sophomore season? Fournette had a good but not great freshman season, posting good efficiency numbers (40.1 percent opportunity rate) and average explosiveness (5.22 highlight yards per opportunity), but many think we rarely saw Fournette's true potential, especially since defenses could load the box against an ineffective passing attack.

LSU's defense once again should be championship-caliber after last season's 12th-overall defensive S&P+ performance. This season's group has the usual mix of excellent front seven performers, like Kendall Beckwith, and high-ceiling young secondary members, like Kevin Tolliver and Xavier Lewis. If last season's group had any room for improvement, it was that the front seven didn't apply as much pressure as they would have liked (46th in front seven havoc) and that they allowed too many explosive plays (64th in IsoPPP). But the biggest challenge will be replacing defensive coordinator John Chavis, who left for Texas A&M. He was the guiding force behind the Tigers' consistency, and it's fair to expect a little regression for this group. The SEC West is always formidable, with Alabama, Ole Miss, and Auburn, but the Tigers should nonetheless be in contention, assuming either Harris or Jennings can take hold of the quarterback position.

No. 9 Michigan State Spartans (10-2, 6-2)

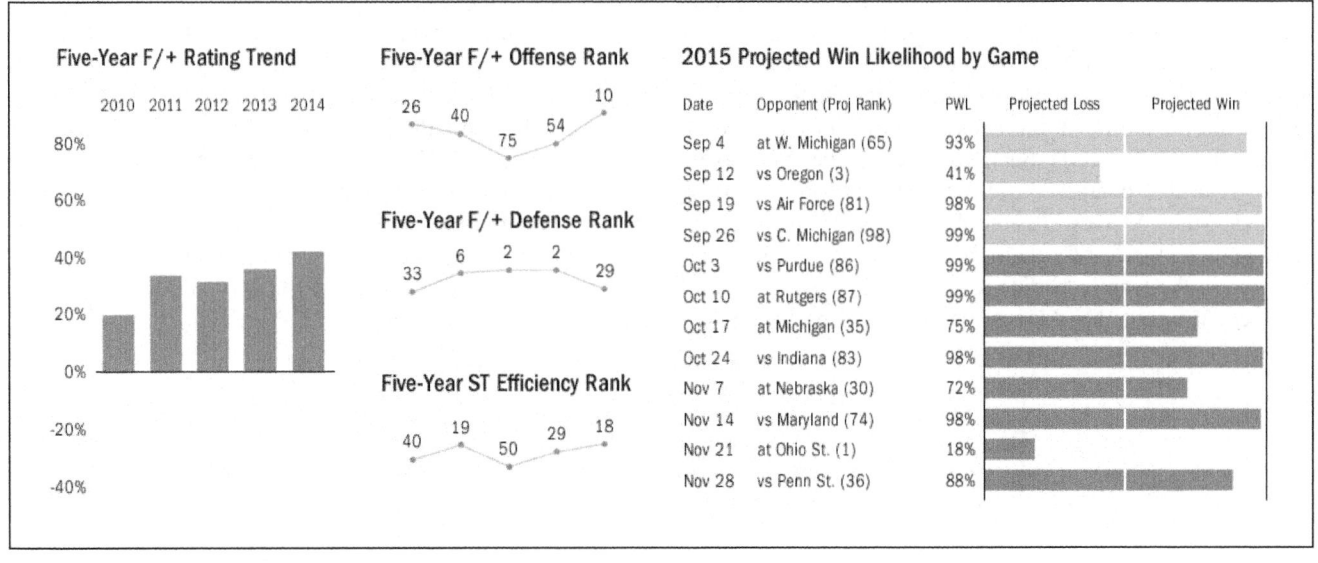

2014: 11-2 (7-1) / F/+ #11 / FEI #15 / S&P+ #11 / Program F/+: #15						2014 Five Factors		
2014 Offense			2014 Defense					
Offensive FEI	0.399	14	Defensive FEI	-0.212	40	Efficiency	Off Success Rate+	122.2	11
Off. S&P+ (Adj. PPG)	40.1	10	Def. S&P+ (Adj. PPG)	21.4	22		Def Success Rate+	138.2	3
Rushing S&P+	122.7	17	Rushing S&P+	123.7	13	Explosiveness	Off IsoPPP+	138.7	6
Passing S&P+	136.7	6	Passing S&P+	120.0	16		Def IsoPPP+	110.2	41
Standard Downs S&P+	123.1	13	Standard Downs S&P+	109.7	32	Field Position	Field Pos. Adv. (FPA)	0.545	10
Passing Downs S&P+	141.1	5	Passing Downs S&P+	142.7	5	Finishing Drives	Off Red Zone S&P+	118.6	23
2015 Projections			SOS Rk		19		Def Red Zone S&P+	108.6	37
Returning Starters: 7 OFF, 7 DEF			Mean Wins / Conf Wins		9.8 / 6.5	Turnovers	Turnover Margin	+19.0	2
							Exp. TO Margin	+8.8	6
Proj. F/+	42.0%	9	Conf. / Div. Title Odds		11.4% / 15.2%		Difference	+10.2	6

The consistency that Mark Dantonio has maintained at Michigan State has been among the most impressive coaching feats in the last decade of college football. Once a mediocre team, the Spartans are now a regular Big Ten contender whose only impediment is sharing a division with Urban Meyer's Buckeyes. Dantonio faces a few challenges in 2015—both Tony Lippett and Jeremy Langford are gone on offense, while the defense was prone to giving up big plays last season and loses stellar defensive coordinator Pat Narduzzi—but it's hard not to favor the Spartans in every game, except possibly the rematch with Oregon and the likely conference-deciding match with Ohio State.

First, let's dig in to the Narduzzi-less defense. Last year's defense lost some of its luster, though it was still among the best in the country (12th in S&P+, third in success rate), playing its own brand of aggressive, press cover-4 quarters. The Spartans are built around aggressiveness, as they were third in defensive adjusted line yards and 18th in adjusted sack rate while staying at ninth overall in havoc rate. But that normally elite defense survived a wild 42-41 shootout with Baylor, spotted Ohio State 49 points, and was sliced and diced by Marcus Mariota, as its personnel and aggressive coverages were hurt by play-action and complementary run games by all three teams. With Narduzzi headed to Pittsburgh, there might be some increased schematic diversity, but this is likely to stay one of the most aggressive defenses in the country. The good news is that the Spartans have an elite front seven, led by returning defensive end Shilique Calhoun, Lawrence Thomas, Malik McDowell, and plenty of other linemen who seem to move too fast for their size. The linebackers lose Taiwan Jones, the team's leading tackler in 2014, but return all other contributors. The biggest question will be in the sec-

ondary, where stalwart safety Kurtis Drummond is gone, as is the latest highly drafted Spartans corner, Trae Waynes. With a defensive scheme that relies so heavily on its corners, finding a replacement for Waynes will be critical.

Another issue will be finding some new skill players to complement veteran quarterback Connor Cook and an experienced offensive line. That offensive line deserves plenty of praise. Returning two All-Big Ten picks, including All-American center Jack Allen, it's a deep and talented group that ranked seventh in adjusted sack rate last season. Connor Cook should have plenty of protection as he attempts to connect with a receiver group that lost much of its explosiveness with Tony Lippett's graduation. The Spartans were surprisingly a top-ten explosive offense in 2014 (sixth in IsoPPP+), but their top returning wideouts are more high-percentage possession receivers than breakaway threats (Macgarrett Kings Jr. had a 66 percent catch rate last season, while junior R.J. Shelton caught 76 percent of his passes). Most of the returning receivers have been in the system for a while, so at least Cook can rely on experience. Cook is the constant here, and outside of Ohio State's three-headed monster and possibly Penn State's Christian Hackenberg, he's the best quarterback in the Big Ten. Cook was efficient and accurate as the Spartans ran a balanced, efficient, and explosive offense. Langford and Nick Hill were a nice one-two punch at running back, but now the job is likely up for grabs between a sophomore and four freshmen, including stud true freshman L.J. Scott. Scott certainly has the most upside, so his development this summer and fall will bear watching. Overall, Michigan State has one of the highest floors in the Big Ten and likely only needs a few skill players to fall into place to challenge for the Big Ten title.

No. 10 Stanford Cardinal (9-3, 7-2)

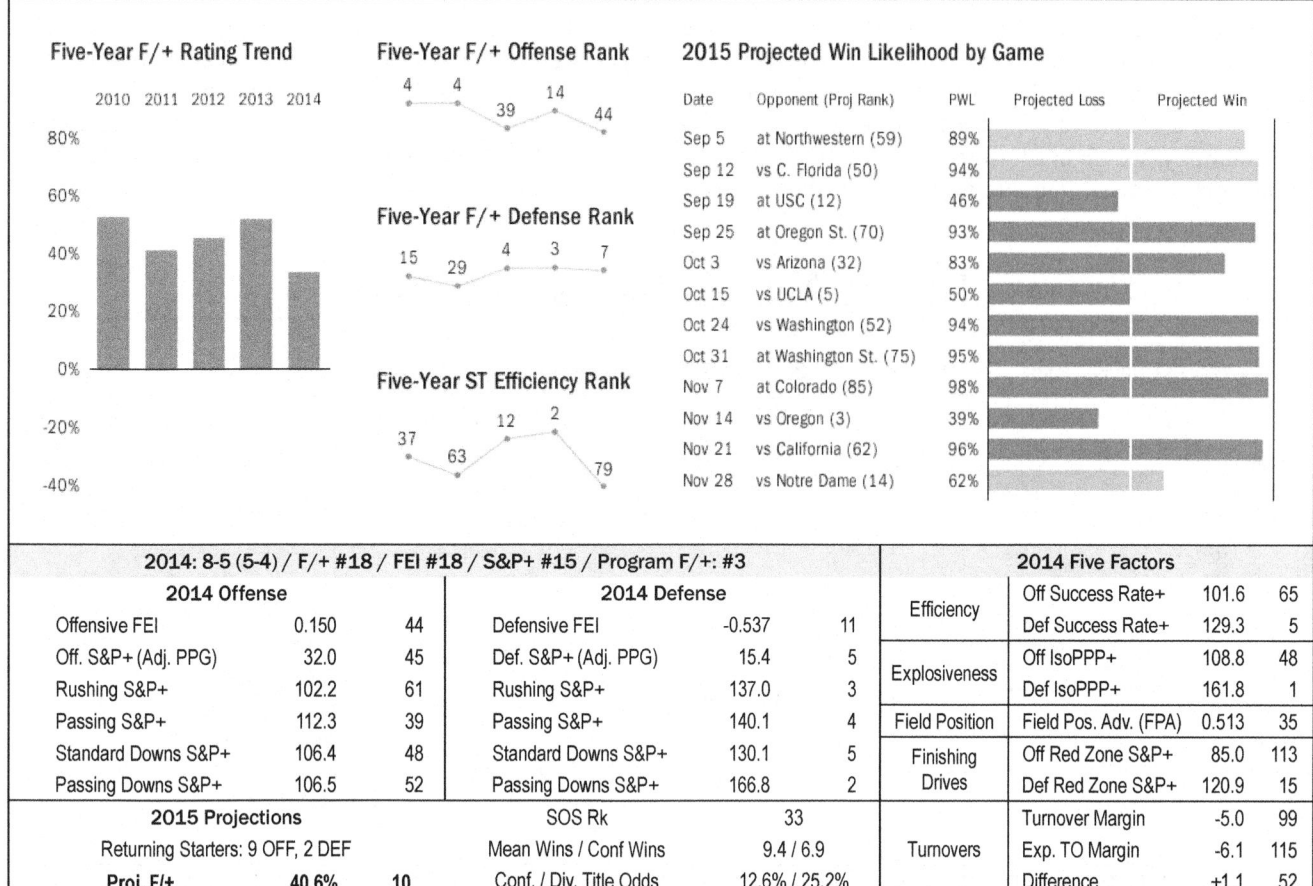

Five-Year F/+ Rating Trend
2010 2011 2012 2013 2014

Five-Year F/+ Offense Rank
4 4 39 14 44

Five-Year F/+ Defense Rank
15 29 4 3 7

Five-Year ST Efficiency Rank
37 63 12 2 79

2015 Projected Win Likelihood by Game

Date	Opponent (Proj Rank)	PWL	Projected Loss	Projected Win
Sep 5	at Northwestern (59)	89%		
Sep 12	vs C. Florida (50)	94%		
Sep 19	at USC (12)	46%		
Sep 25	at Oregon St. (70)	93%		
Oct 3	vs Arizona (32)	83%		
Oct 15	vs UCLA (5)	50%		
Oct 24	vs Washington (52)	94%		
Oct 31	at Washington St. (75)	95%		
Nov 7	at Colorado (85)	98%		
Nov 14	vs Oregon (3)	39%		
Nov 21	vs California (62)	96%		
Nov 28	vs Notre Dame (14)	62%		

2014: 8-5 (5-4) / F/+ #18 / FEI #18 / S&P+ #15 / Program F/+: #3

2014 Offense			2014 Defense		
Offensive FEI	0.150	44	Defensive FEI	-0.537	11
Off. S&P+ (Adj. PPG)	32.0	45	Def. S&P+ (Adj. PPG)	15.4	5
Rushing S&P+	102.2	61	Rushing S&P+	137.0	3
Passing S&P+	112.3	39	Passing S&P+	140.1	4
Standard Downs S&P+	106.4	48	Standard Downs S&P+	130.1	5
Passing Downs S&P+	106.5	52	Passing Downs S&P+	166.8	2

2015 Projections			SOS Rk	33	
Returning Starters: 9 OFF, 2 DEF			Mean Wins / Conf Wins	9.4 / 6.9	
Proj. F/+	40.6%	10	Conf. / Div. Title Odds	12.6% / 25.2%	

2014 Five Factors

Efficiency	Off Success Rate+	101.6	65
	Def Success Rate+	129.3	5
Explosiveness	Off IsoPPP+	108.8	48
	Def IsoPPP+	161.8	1
Field Position	Field Pos. Adv. (FPA)	0.513	35
Finishing Drives	Off Red Zone S&P+	85.0	113
	Def Red Zone S&P+	120.9	15
Turnovers	Turnover Margin	-5.0	99
	Exp. TO Margin	-6.1	115
	Difference	+1.1	52

The Cardinal will have plenty of turnover in 2015, as both senior running backs are gone, as are eight members of the sixth-overall defense (including four defenders taken in the first five rounds of the NFL draft). But despite the personnel losses, Stanford's defense under Lance Anderson has been nothing if not consistent, improving from eleventh in S&P+ in 2012 to ninth in 2013 and sixth last season. The Cardinal were strong against the run (fourth in S&P+) and the pass (sixth), and were efficient (ninth) while being even more effective against explosive plays (second in IsoPPP). In short, few units have played at a higher level more consistently than the Stanford defense.

The star of last season's recruiting class, Soloman Thomas, will return to lead the new-look defense. Thomas was a five-star defensive lineman who controls the point of attack with strength and an explosive first step, and he should help the Cardinal improve on their 23rd-ranked front seven havoc ranking from last season. But even if Thomas fails to get the explosive play on his own, he'll open the door for a play-making linebacker corps behind him, including Blake Martinez, one of the defense's few returning players, and underclassman star Joey Alfieri. With Martinez, Alfieri, and rising star Mike Tyler, Stanford has one of the top linebacking corps in the nation. Look for Stanford to be just as efficient, but potentially even more disruptive in the front seven.

The challenge for the Cardinal will likely be offense, where Kevin Hogan returns as the starter after fending off a challenge from highly recruited quarterback Keller Chryst in the spring. Chryst had a dismal showing in the spring game, completing just one pass, but he displayed the raw potential and athleticism that led to his four-star recruiting ranking. While there is some potential for either Chryst or backup Ryan Burns to unseat Hogan during fall camp, Hogan likely gives the Cardinal their best chance for a Pac-12 championship or better. Whoever starts at quarterback, he will lead an offense that lost Ty Montgomery to the NFL draft. While Montgomery's yards per catch average was down in 2014, he remained reliable (65 percent catch rate) and was the target on over a quarter of Hogan's passes. Though the Cardinal have identified a few potential receiver replacements, including fifth-year senior wideout Devon Cajuste and the latest in a seemingly endless string of top-flight tight ends in Austin Hooper and Dalton Schultz, the passing game likely won't have to carry the bulk of the load this season, as sophomore running back Christian McCaffrey has the potential to become a household name. McCaffrey, who rushed for 300 yards as a freshman, offers a different blend of open field explosiveness than powerful Stanford running backs in years past. After the senior duo of Remound Wright and Kelsey Young combined for only 931 yards on 201 carries last year (the run game was 71st in S&P+), a return to a run focus will take pressure off Hogan and the passing game.

To illustrate how much of an outlier last year's Stanford offense was, the Cardinal ran on less than 59 percent of standard downs (69th). The offensive line must become more efficient, despite losing Andrus Peat to the NFL. The Cardinal likely moved away from the run not only because they lacked a feature running back, but because the offensive line was just 59th in adjusted line yards. It's difficult to disentangle offensive line and running back performance, but given that the line's opportunity rate was just 35 percent (103rd), it is fair to expect more from the run-blocking in 2015. By all accounts from the spring game, the first string was cohesive and held its own, while depth appears to be an issue. If the Cardinal can develop offensive linemen—or use enough tight ends instead—then the run game and the whole offense will return to its balanced production from previous seasons.

No. 11 Auburn Tigers (8-4, 4-4)

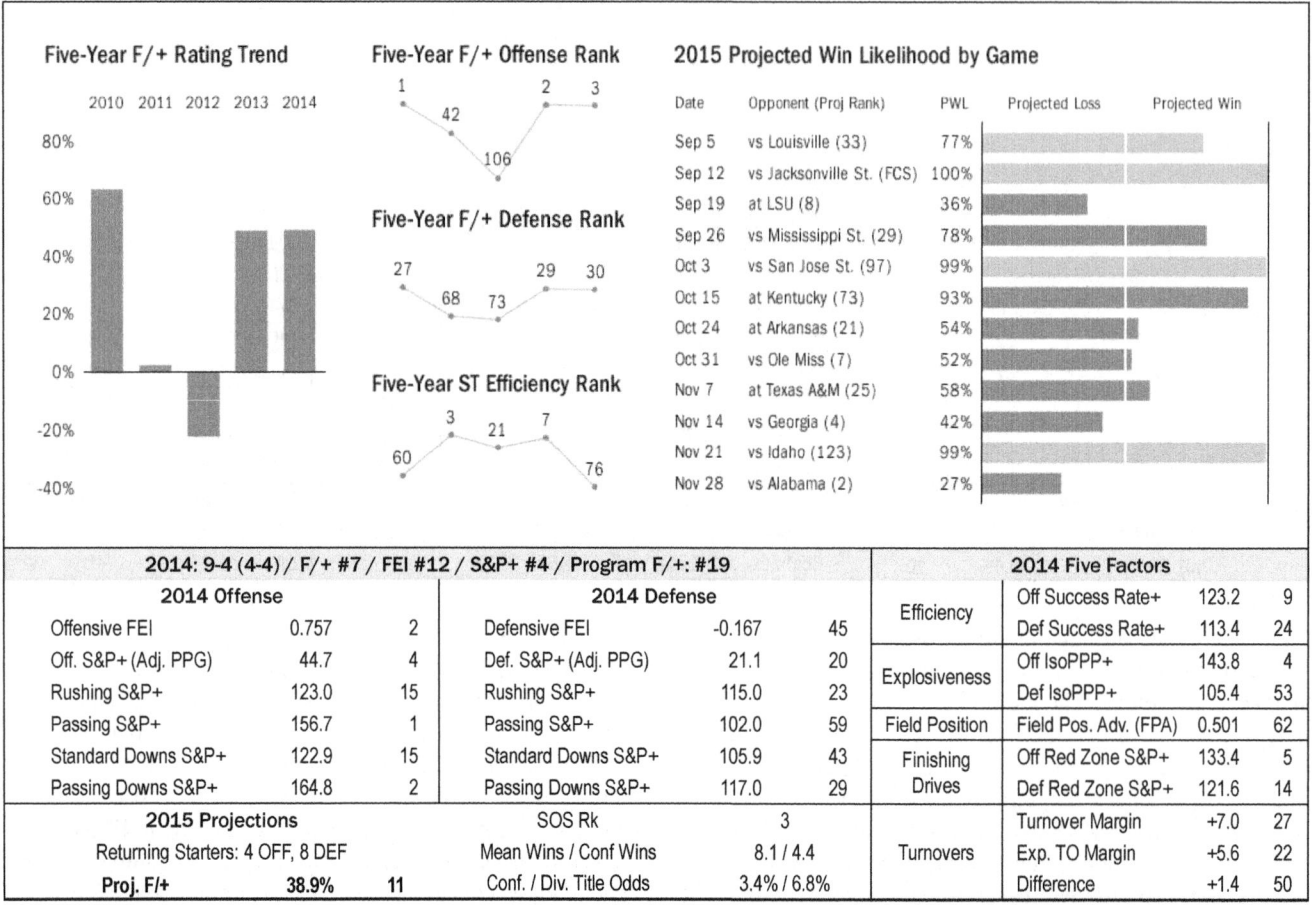

2014: 9-4 (4-4) / F/+ #7 / FEI #12 / S&P+ #4 / Program F/+: #19							2014 Five Factors			
2014 Offense			**2014 Defense**			Efficiency	Off Success Rate+	123.2	9
Offensive FEI	0.757	2	Defensive FEI	-0.167	45		Def Success Rate+	113.4	24
Off. S&P+ (Adj. PPG)	44.7	4	Def. S&P+ (Adj. PPG)	21.1	20	Explosiveness	Off IsoPPP+	143.8	4
Rushing S&P+	123.0	15	Rushing S&P+	115.0	23		Def IsoPPP+	105.4	53
Passing S&P+	156.7	1	Passing S&P+	102.0	59	Field Position	Field Pos. Adv. (FPA)	0.501	62
Standard Downs S&P+	122.9	15	Standard Downs S&P+	105.9	43	Finishing Drives	Off Red Zone S&P+	133.4	5
Passing Downs S&P+	164.8	2	Passing Downs S&P+	117.0	29		Def Red Zone S&P+	121.6	14
2015 Projections			SOS Rk	3		Turnovers	Turnover Margin	+7.0	27
Returning Starters: 4 OFF, 8 DEF			Mean Wins / Conf Wins	8.1 / 4.4			Exp. TO Margin	+5.6	22
Proj. F/+	**38.9%**	**11**	Conf. / Div. Title Odds	3.4% / 6.8%			Difference	+1.4	50

Just how good is new starting quarterback Jeremy Johnson? The junior and former four-star recruit has played sparingly behind Nick Marshall, but has demonstrated a strong arm and excellent accuracy in his two years of experience (71 percent completion rate in 2013 and 76 percent in 78 attempts in 2014). Johnson brings a different skill set to the position than the run-first Marshall. Though he's athletic enough to keep defenses honest in Gus Malzahn's scheme, Johnson is built more like a traditional pro-style quarterback and has far better accuracy and touch on deep passes. Named the starting quarterback following spring practices over highly touted underclassman Sean White, Johnson is the primary reason Auburn has become the trendy pick to win the SEC. But the defense, now led by defensive coordinator Will Muschamp, will likely be the determining factor in whether the Tigers can take the conference championship.

The Auburn offense will experience some turnover, with Marshall, several leading receivers, two offensive linemen, tight end C.J. Uzomah, and reliable running back Cameron Artis-Payne all leaving for the NFL or graduating. But the Tigers appear set to reload quickly. At 6-foot-0 and 230 pounds, No. 1 overall junior college running back Jovon Robinson Jr. is maybe the biggest back to ever play in a Malzahn offense. He brings not only power, but also the one-cut-and-go style that excels with inside zone running. His competition, sophomore Roc Thomas, ensures that Auburn shouldn't have any dip in production with their third starting running back in as many years. After all, with Artis-Payne last season and Tre Mason before that, the Tigers were 16th and second, respectively, in rushing S&P+. Artis-Payne was fairly efficient (41.9 percent opportunity rate to the team's overall 44.5 percent), but never very explosive (averaging 4.58 highlight yards per opportunity—and his offensive line, which ranked fifth in adjusted line yards, gave him plenty of opportunities). One of the newcomers should be a more than adequate replacement.

The hope with Johnson is that the Auburn passing game will rival its running game. That's not to say that the passing game was inefficient last season—it ranked first overall in passing S&P+. Instead, the Tigers offense simply hopes to improve its completion percentage and open up more difficult, mid-range routes and the vertical play-action game to complement the high-percentage short throws and explosive deep routes that were a staple of Marshall's game. Johnson won't have deep threat Sammie Coates (who averaged 21.8 yards per reception, but with a 45.3 percent catch rate), but he will have one of the top overall receivers in the conference in Duke Williams (66.2 percent catch rate while averaging 16.2 yards per reception) returning for his senior season, as well as senior Ricardo Louis and freshmen Darius Slayton and Ryan Davis. The offensive line, meanwhile, will return three starter's from a unit that was exemplary in pass protection, especially for having a mobile quarterback, ranking 28th in adjusted sack rate.

The defense will likely determine this team's ceiling. The unit was respectable last season after figuring in opponent adjustments (29th in S&P+, but 81st and 98th in unadjusted success rate and IsoPPP), but struggled in generating quarterback pressure and in the secondary (65th in front seven havoc, 96th

in adjusted sack rate, and 43rd in passing S&P+). Defensive coordinator Will Muschamp has repeatedly stressed how thin the secondary is, noting the lack of depth behind the excellent starting safeties and corners. Georgia transfer Tray Matthews looks to have locked down one of the starting safety spots, and there is plenty of incoming talent to join Montavius Adams and Carl Lawson on the defensive line, including consensus five-star defensive end Byron Cowart. Auburn has recruited extremely well on defense for the past few years (except for the lack of depth in the secondary), but the production hasn't matched the talent. Last season part of that could be attributed to losing Lawson for the year because of a spring practice ACL tear, but the team's sack leader nevertheless only had 3.5 sacks. What the team likely needed was a system upgrade, not a talent upgrade—and it might have found the answer in Muschamp. Auburn will find out a lot about its defense in the season opener against Louisville. The Cardinals may be trying to choose a quarterback and replace their offensive line and receiving corps, but they have plenty of talent, and they should give Auburn plenty of opportunity to show their defensive muscle from the beginning of the season. If the defense improves and Johnson plays as expected, there is no question that this is a Playoff-caliber team. Unfortunately for the Tigers, they play in a conference with several other Playoff-caliber teams.

No. 12 USC Trojans (9-3, 6-3)

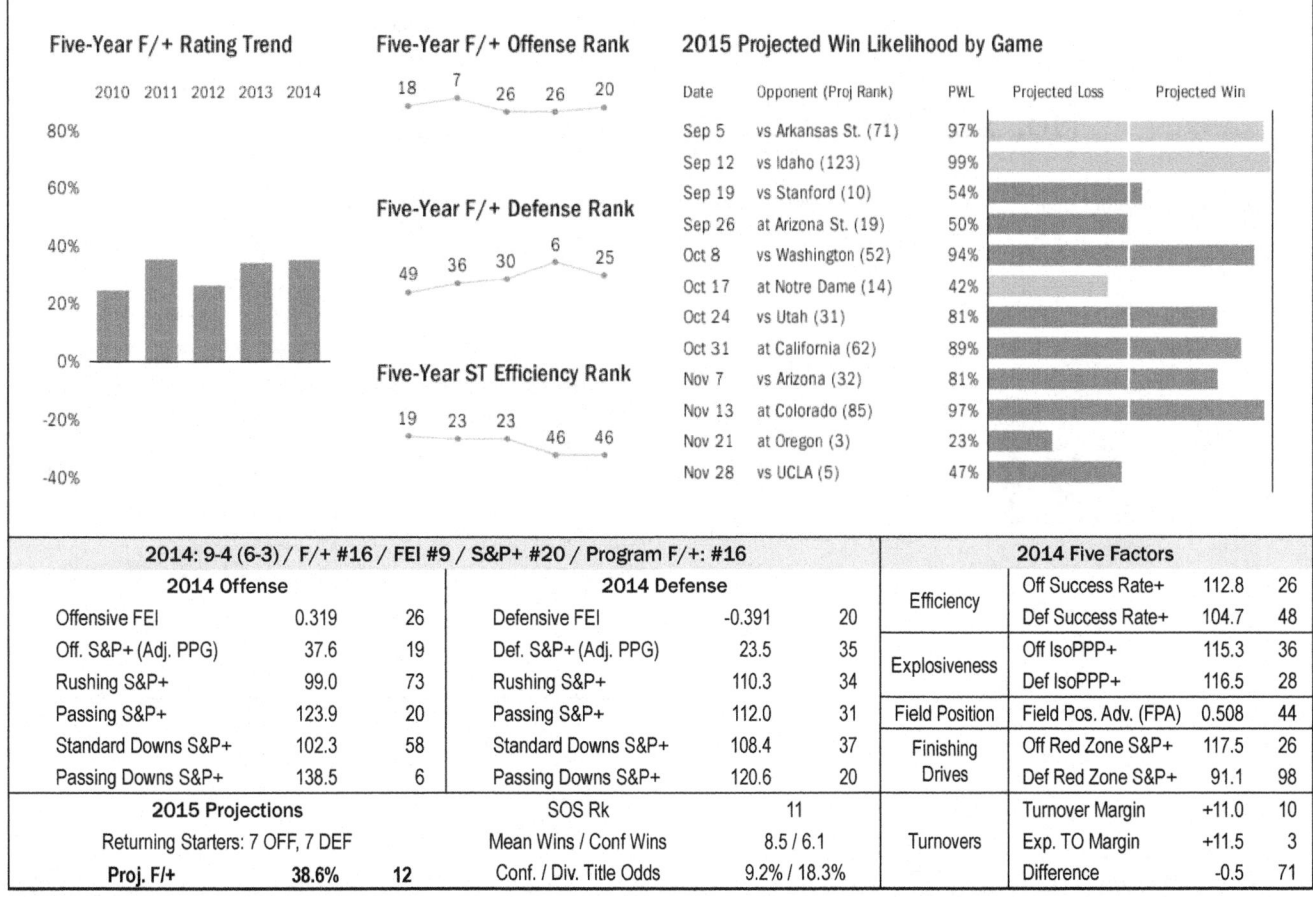

In coach Steve Sarkisian's second season at USC, nothing short of a Playoff berth will satisfy fan and media expectations. Quarterback Cody Kessler has grown from an underrated but extremely efficient signal caller to a Heisman contender who might be valuable enough to overcome the Trojans' flaws. While S&P+ projections rank USC 13th overall, three other Pac-12 teams are ahead of them (Oregon, UCLA, and Stanford), and all three are on the Trojans' conference schedule. But there is no denying that this team is talented: they have the second-ranked recruiting impact, and many of last year's primary contributors were young, including Adoree' Jackson and Juju Smith. But with a still-small roster, a depleted defensive line and a difficult schedule, the Trojans will have an uphill battle.

Kessler, Jackson, and Smith will lead an offense that ranked 20th in passing S&P+ in 2014. Few teams were better on passing downs (sixth in passing downs S&P+), even though the Trojans' offensive line did not play at an elite level in pass protection (56th in adjusted sack rate). The USC offense was strong overall (24th in S&P+), but it was neither particularly efficient (43rd in success rate) nor explosive (37th in IsoPPP+). But it is a veteran group with plenty of weapons. The key for the offense will likely be finding some balance in the run game. While the line had a poor run-blocking efficiency rate (38 percent opportunity rate, 76th overall), running back Buck Allen was effective and consistent. With Allen now in the NFL, the two primary contenders for his job are last season's backups, Justin Davis and Tre Madden, who both were out with injuries for parts of the last two seasons. Incoming freshman Ronald Jones II is an explosive back who could give the Trojans the home run threat they've missed. Look for the run game to improve beginning with the interior of the offensive line, featuring Max Tuerk, new starter Damien Mama, and Viane Talamaivao. Currently this is a good unit—to contend for a Playoff berth, or even a Pac-12 championship, it will need to be a great one.

Maybe the biggest impediment for the Trojans is depth in the defensive front seven. Many of the starters are either household names or soon will be, despite the loss of defensive end Leonard Williams to the NFL. From former safety Su'a Cravens at linebacker (who led the team in tackles for loss last season in run support) to tackle Delvon Simmons to end Claude Pelon, the talent is there. But many of the new faces have little production so far in their careers despite high recruiting rankings, including Scott Felix, Anthony Sarao, and Lamar Dawson. Last year the defense favored a bend-don't-break style, preventing explosive plays but being less efficient (64th in success rate), particularly against the run (40th). The Trojans' secondary was the defense's best unit, as despite little pressure from the front seven—even including Leonard Williams, who was often double-teamed, the front seven ranked only 80th in front seven havoc rate—the defensive backs ranked 18th in havoc rate and were 21st in passing downs S&P+. A chunk of that production came from the disruptive and rangy Cravens (who moved between linebacker and safety last season), though Jackson, a freshman All-American, made his mark early as well. The defense's challenges for 2015 will likely be the same as in 2014: can the front seven apply consistent pressure on standard downs? Will the defensive line depth be an issue against the run?

No. 13 Florida State Seminoles (10-2, 6-2)

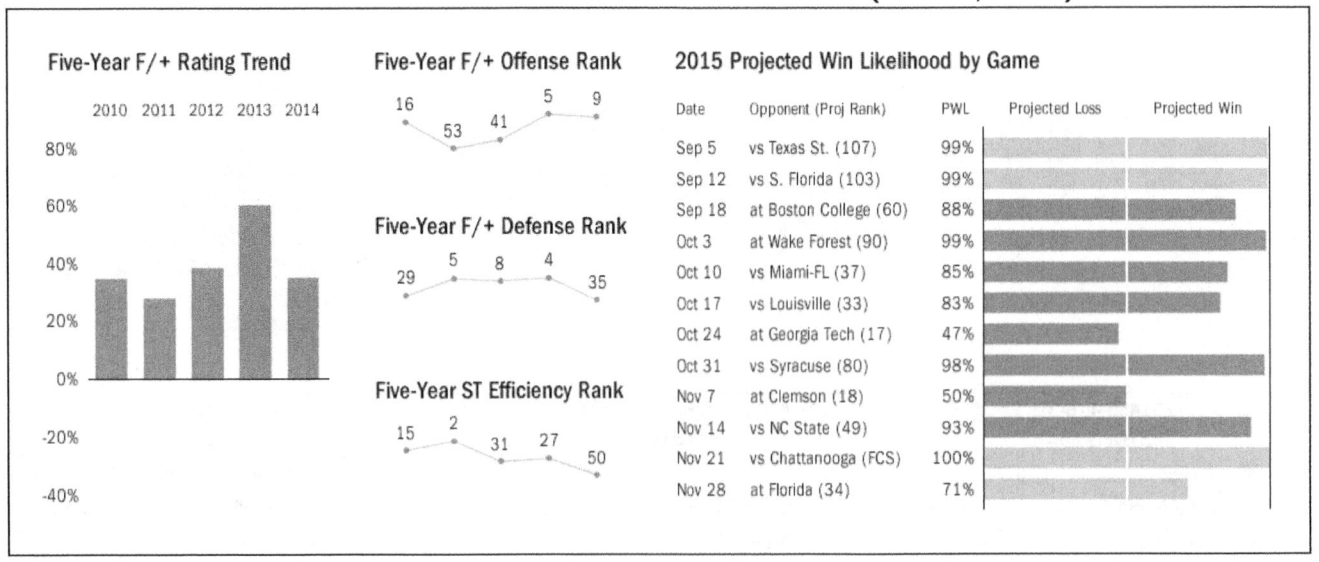

2014: 13-1 (8-0) / F/+ #15 / FEI #7 / S&P+ #22 / Program F/+: #7						2014 Five Factors			
2014 Offense			**2014 Defense**			Efficiency	Off Success Rate+	126.9	5
Offensive FEI	0.643	8	Defensive FEI	-0.301	28		Def Success Rate+	99.3	68
Off. S&P+ (Adj. PPG)	37.9	16	Def. S&P+ (Adj. PPG)	24.3	40	Explosiveness	Off IsoPPP+	131.4	13
Rushing S&P+	120.8	19	Rushing S&P+	105.7	50		Def IsoPPP+	112.6	36
Passing S&P+	135.1	7	Passing S&P+	105.0	50	Field Position	Field Pos. Adv. (FPA)	0.480	100
Standard Downs S&P+	128.6	7	Standard Downs S&P+	105.4	45	Finishing	Off Red Zone S&P+	126.1	8
Passing Downs S&P+	124.8	20	Passing Downs S&P+	110.0	43	Drives	Def Red Zone S&P+	103.4	50
2015 Projections			SOS Rk	66			Turnover Margin	-6.0	105
Returning Starters: 4 OFF, 7 DEF			Mean Wins / Conf Wins	10.1 / 6.4		Turnovers	Exp. TO Margin	-1.4	88
Proj. F/+	**38.5%**	**13**	Conf. / Div. Title Odds	25.8% / 51.7%			Difference	-4.6	103

The Seminoles took one undefeated national championship season and followed it up with an undefeated regular season, but the final game, a 59-20 Playoff loss to Oregon, left a bitter taste in many Florida State fans' mouths. The Seminoles played like a top-15 team in multiple narrow wins (37-31 over 75th F/+ ranked Oklahoma State, a four-point win over 34th Notre Dame, then four straight wins of five points or less beginning with Miami) for most of the year rather than the clear top team they were in Jameis Winston's Heisman-winning redshirt freshman season. Now Florida State enters a rebuilding season with lots of new faces on both lines and, crucially, a new starting quarterback.

After waiting patiently behind Winston, Sean Maguire was supposed to take over as Florida State's starting quarterback this fall. Sure, his debut against Clemson last season left a lot to be desired, but Clemson might have been the worst possible opponent for him to face in his first start. And he did lead the Seminoles to an overtime win. But then Notre Dame's Everett Golson became the latest in a line of high profile graduate quarterback transfers, moving to Florida State in hopes of grabbing the starting job and contending for a national title. Graduate transfers don't always start (see: Jeremiah Masoli) but sometimes a change of scenery and another year lead to Russell Wilson-at-Wisconsin type seasons. It's not clear whether Golson is the missing piece in Florida State's offensive puzzle. While Golson has a high ceiling, he also has a turnover-laden floor; in 2014, he threw 14 interceptions, fumbled 12 times, and was sacked 27 times. His sack rate is actually lower than Maguire's (5.9 percent to 10.9 percent), but whoever wins the job will need to respond well to pressure, as it's unclear how the new-look offensive line will fare.

Last year's line was built around protecting Winston (ninth in adjusted sack rate), rather than driving defenders back in the run game (45th adjusted line yards, but 79th in opportunity rate). But the 2015 group will need to replace four starters and a prominent backup. There is certainly talent in the wings, but it is mostly young, with six freshmen (four redshirted). Both quarterback and offensive line need only worry about efficiency, because the Seminoles have amassed potentially the most talented group of offensive skill players in the country. Mario Pender might begin the season as the starter at running back; He's not quite as explosive or efficient as the indefinitely suspended Dalvin Cook, but certainly capable. Incoming freshman Jacques Patrick could end up eventually taking over the job. He's a home run hitter that could replace Cook's explosiveness if his legal situation is unresolved before the beginning of the season. The receiving corps is even more loaded, with Travis Rudolph (reliable and balanced), Ermon Lane (a big, explosive target who averaged 20.5 yards per catch), and Kermit Whitfield (dynamic in the open field with a solid catch rate) as now-sophomores and four more freshmen four- or five-star receivers behind them. The offensive skill talent is almost unmatched across the FBS; the key will be whether there is a quarterback to put the ball in their hands or an offensive line to give them opportunities.

Offensive production remained at a high level in Winston's second season, but the team's defensive efficiency—particularly its disruptive ability—fell off significantly. Florida State was both inefficient against the run (85th in rushing success rate) and lacking in quarterback pressure (115th in adjusted sack rate, 94th in front seven havoc rate). It's a testament to the strong secondary that even though opposing offenses were not often pressured by the front seven, the defense as a whole wasn't worse on passing downs (43rd in passing downs S&P+). But a team with Mario Edwards Jr. and Eddie Goldman on the line should have had more production. Those two, along with fellow starter Desmond Hollin, are now gone, but the depth behind them is excellent, if unproven. The linebackers don't have the same problem, as all starters return as seasoned veterans. While many, like linebacker Matthew Thomas and incoming defensive end Josh Sweat, are recovering from injuries, the talent is there. So the secondary should once again carry the load on passing downs, especially if the run defense does not improve.

With questions and inexperience on both lines and at quarterback, it's fair to be bearish on the Seminoles' chances for a repeat Playoff appearance. But if players live up to their recruiting rankings, anything is possible.

No. 14 Notre Dame Fighting Irish (9-3, -)

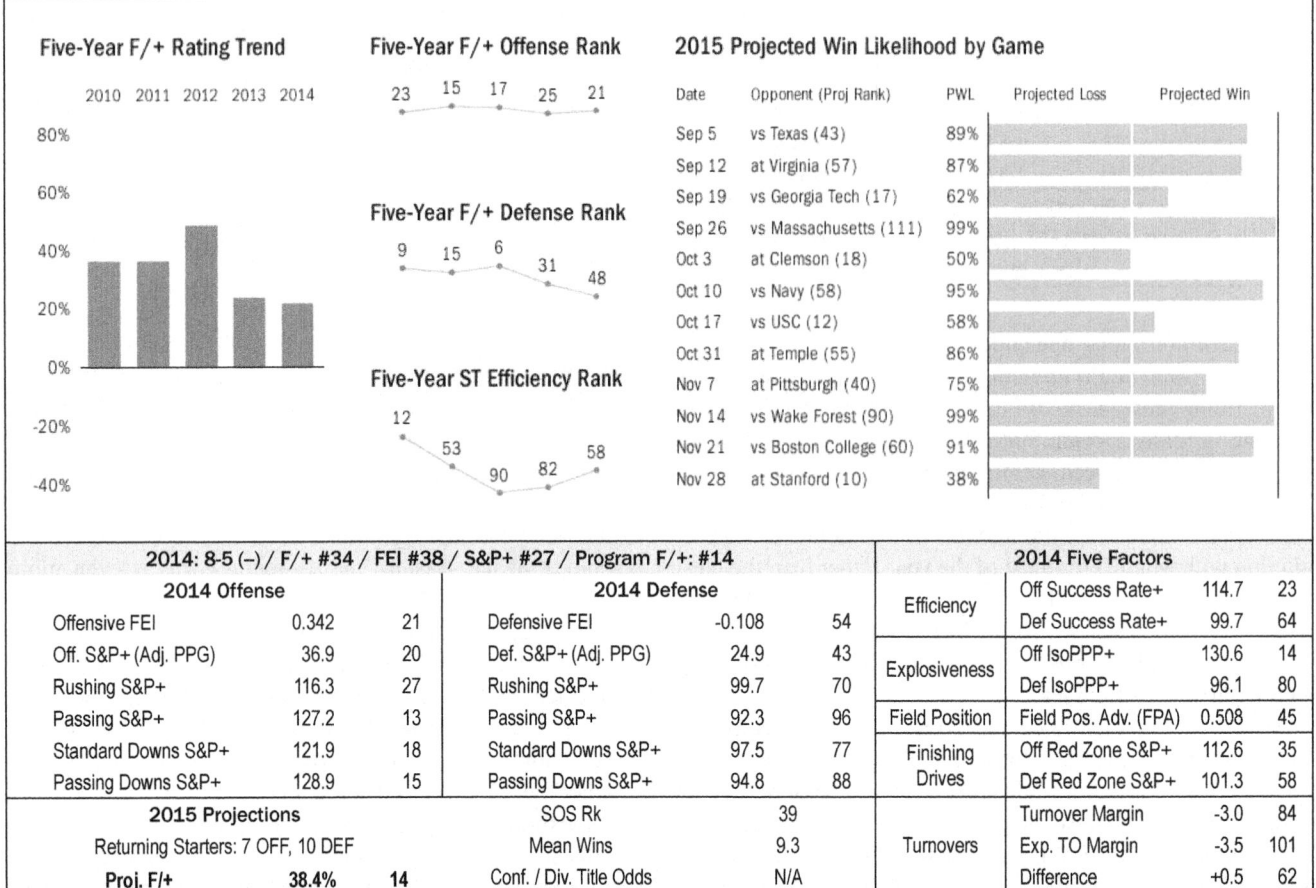

2014: 8-5 (–) / F/+ #34 / FEI #38 / S&P+ #27 / Program F/+: #14							2014 Five Factors		
2014 Offense			**2014 Defense**			Efficiency	Off Success Rate+	114.7	23
Offensive FEI	0.342	21	Defensive FEI	-0.108	54		Def Success Rate+	99.7	64
Off. S&P+ (Adj. PPG)	36.9	20	Def. S&P+ (Adj. PPG)	24.9	43	Explosiveness	Off IsoPPP+	130.6	14
Rushing S&P+	116.3	27	Rushing S&P+	99.7	70		Def IsoPPP+	96.1	80
Passing S&P+	127.2	13	Passing S&P+	92.3	96	Field Position	Field Pos. Adv. (FPA)	0.508	45
Standard Downs S&P+	121.9	18	Standard Downs S&P+	97.5	77	Finishing Drives	Off Red Zone S&P+	112.6	35
Passing Downs S&P+	128.9	15	Passing Downs S&P+	94.8	88		Def Red Zone S&P+	101.3	58
2015 Projections			SOS Rk		39	Turnovers	Turnover Margin	-3.0	84
Returning Starters: 7 OFF, 10 DEF			Mean Wins		9.3		Exp. TO Margin	-3.5	101
Proj. F/+	**38.4%**	**14**	Conf. / Div. Title Odds		N/A		Difference	+0.5	62

Notre Dame went 8-5 in 2014, finished the season ranked a disappointing 34th in the F/+ rankings, and lost former starting quarterback Everett Golson to transfer, but nonetheless is projected at eighth by FEI and 16th by S&P+. So where is the predicted improvement coming from? For one, Notre Dame has recruited extremely well, pulling in the No. 13 class for 2015 and the No. 11 class in 2014. For another, the team was fairly inconsistent week-to-week, taking down Stanford, shutting out Michigan, and slipping by LSU, but losing four in a row in one stretch, including two to Northwestern and Louisville. Much of the inconsistency had to do with turnovers by Golson, who had 12 fumbles and 14 interceptions. But the team as a whole was also unlucky, with a plus-four turnover difference between expected and actual turnovers. Beyond recruiting and a regression of bad luck to the mean, there's still a lot to like about Notre Dame's roster: three extremely high-ceiling quarterbacks, enough explosive skill players to go toe-to-toe with any Pac-12 or SEC school, and almost everyone returning on defense. So will 2015 look more like the accumulated talent and stats project it should, or are Irish faithful in for a 2014 repeat, given a schedule that includes top-20 projected F/+ teams Georgia Tech, Clemson, USC, and Stanford?

On the positive side, the offense is just a quarterback away from being one of the best of Brian Kelly's tenure—at least on paper. And when the coaches have to choose among three incredibly athletic dual-threat options in Malik Zaire, DeShone Kizer, and Brandon Wimbush, that isn't a major negative. What the group lacks is experience. Zaire appears to have the starting spot locked up, barring a major upset in preseason camp, but he only has 35 passes to his name as a college quarterback, and he struggled with accuracy, even at short range. If Zaire is the starter, expect the offense to mix his ability to execute power option runs with downfield play-action and on-the-run passing. But the quarterback shouldn't be tasked with too much beyond safely distributing the ball to his supporting cast. Tarean Folston and Greg Bryant are both solid options at running back, though neither broke off quite as many explosive plays as you'd like to see (solid opportunity rates at 43 percent and 52 percent respectively, but low highlight yards per opportunity at 3.5 and 3.3). All four starting receivers return, including emergent No. 1 threat Will Fuller, who balanced consistency (catching 66 percent of his targets) with a 14.4 yards per reception average. The rangy Corey Robinson and a deep group of tight ends will also contribute.

Notre Dame's 2015 trajectory will likely depend primarily on the improvement of the defense in defensive coordinator Brian VanGorder's second season implementing an aggressive 4-3. They certainly have a lot of work to do in the offseason. Despite being riddled with experienced talent, the defensive line wasn't as productive as past Notre Dame lines, settling for average to below average in both run defense (65th in adjusted line yards) and pass defense (78th in adjusted sack rate). The Irish were susceptible to explosive plays (80th in IsoPPP+), even though they ostensibly played a bend-don't-break defense. The key question for this defense is whether last year's mediocrity can be attributed to the schematic change, injuries, and academic suspensions, or whether individual defenders are not playing up to their recruiting rankings. One area for concern might be the secondary, which isn't deep at cornerback and lacks youth. It's an experienced group to be sure, so the first string shouldn't be a problem, but rotations and injuries might limit this unit's overall effectiveness.

No. 15 TCU Horned Frogs (10-2, 7-2)

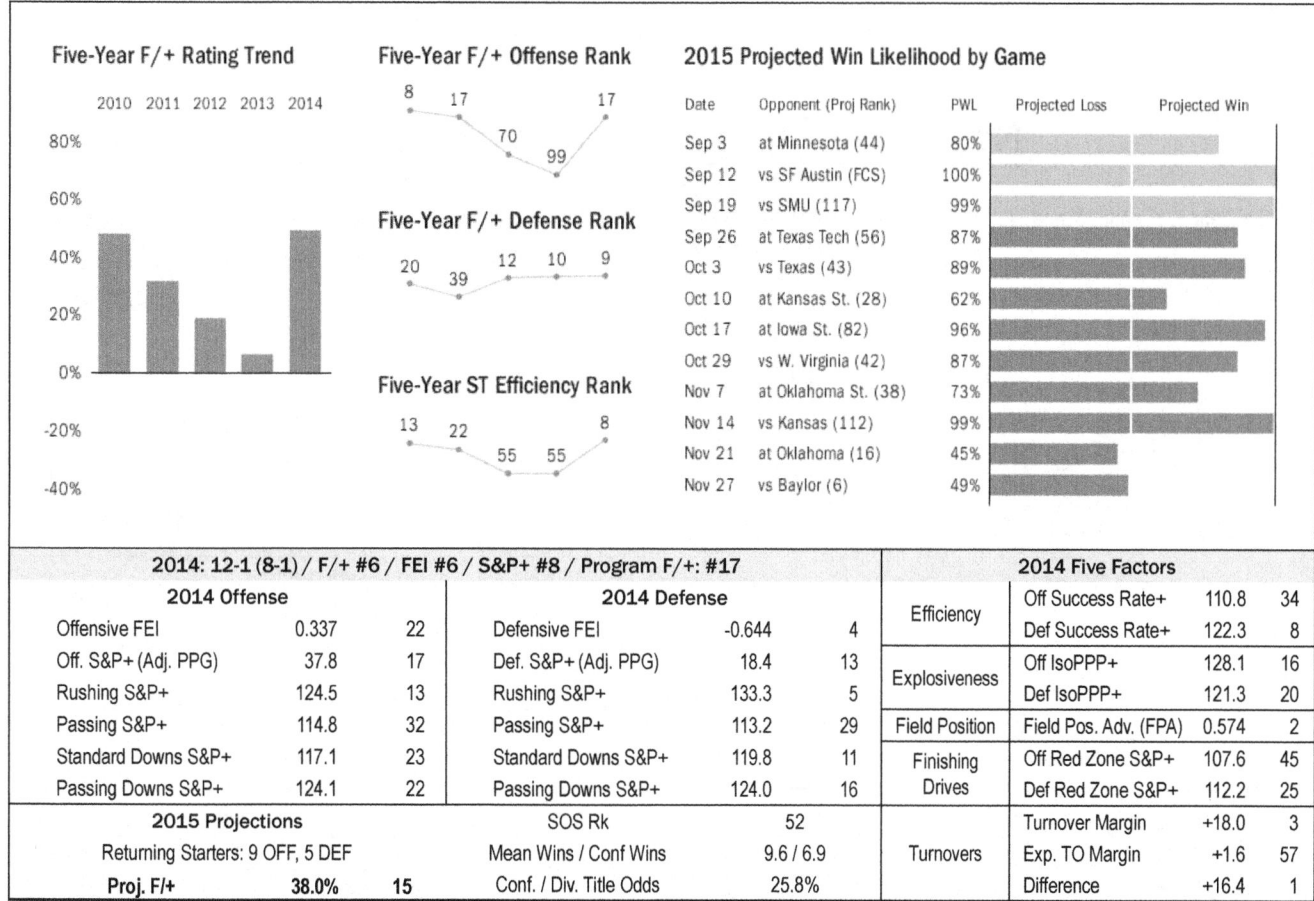

Five-Year F/+ Rating Trend

Five-Year F/+ Offense Rank

Five-Year F/+ Defense Rank

Five-Year ST Efficiency Rank

2015 Projected Win Likelihood by Game

Date	Opponent (Proj Rank)	PWL	Projected Loss	Projected Win
Sep 3	at Minnesota (44)	80%		
Sep 12	vs SF Austin (FCS)	100%		
Sep 19	vs SMU (117)	99%		
Sep 26	at Texas Tech (56)	87%		
Oct 3	vs Texas (43)	89%		
Oct 10	at Kansas St. (28)	62%		
Oct 17	at Iowa St. (82)	96%		
Oct 29	vs W. Virginia (42)	87%		
Nov 7	at Oklahoma St. (38)	73%		
Nov 14	vs Kansas (112)	99%		
Nov 21	at Oklahoma (16)	45%		
Nov 27	vs Baylor (6)	49%		

2014: 12-1 (8-1) / F/+ #6 / FEI #6 / S&P+ #8 / Program F/+: #17

2014 Offense			2014 Defense		
Offensive FEI	0.337	22	Defensive FEI	-0.644	4
Off. S&P+ (Adj. PPG)	37.8	17	Def. S&P+ (Adj. PPG)	18.4	13
Rushing S&P+	124.5	13	Rushing S&P+	133.3	5
Passing S&P+	114.8	32	Passing S&P+	113.2	29
Standard Downs S&P+	117.1	23	Standard Downs S&P+	119.8	11
Passing Downs S&P+	124.1	22	Passing Downs S&P+	124.0	16

2015 Projections			SOS Rk	52
Returning Starters: 9 OFF, 5 DEF			Mean Wins / Conf Wins	9.6 / 6.9
Proj. F/+	**38.0%**	**15**	Conf. / Div. Title Odds	25.8%

2014 Five Factors

Efficiency	Off Success Rate+	110.8	34
	Def Success Rate+	122.3	8
Explosiveness	Off IsoPPP+	128.1	16
	Def IsoPPP+	121.3	20
Field Position	Field Pos. Adv. (FPA)	0.574	2
Finishing Drives	Off Red Zone S&P+	107.6	45
	Def Red Zone S&P+	112.2	25
Turnovers	Turnover Margin	+18.0	3
	Exp. TO Margin	+1.6	57
	Difference	+16.4	1

Maybe no team has received more hype this offseason—and enjoyed a bigger improvement from 2013—than TCU. TCU went 4-8 in 2013 before moving to an air raid-style offense in 2014, giving quarterback Trevone Boykin a foundation for a breakout 2014 season. Boykin capped a 3,901-yard passing season (33rd passing S&P+, 16th in overall offensive S&P+) with a 42-3 demolition of Ole Miss in the Chick-fil-A Peach Bowl. Looking to make a statement after getting snubbed by the Playoff Selection Committee for the final Playoff spot, the Horned Frogs displayed a disruptive, efficient defense and an explosive offense against a hapless Rebels squad. Expectations are understandably high for 2015, as nine offensive starters return, including Boykin, a leading Heisman contender, but the defense must replace six starters from last year's fifth-ranked S&P+ squad.

The turnaround started with Boykin coming in to his own in the new offense. Boykin didn't have the highest average yards per attempt, nor was he among the top ten quarterback rushers in college football, but he was consistent, and he only had one game throwing more than one interception (the blowout win against Ole Miss). Boykin's offense threw early (104th in standard downs running percentage) and often, and he excelled as both a playmaker and a distributor for TCU's deep receivers unit. That group had four juniors or younger total more than 300 receiving yards, all averaging 10+ yards per catch. In fact, the two leading receivers, Josh Doctson (who broke his hand this spring) and Kolby Listenbee, had similar statistical profiles, with high average yards per catch (18.4 and 15.5, respectively) and low catch rates (in the 50s for both). Those two received more than a third of the team's overall targets. Even more crucially, TCU returns all but a single starting lineman from a group that was 37th in adjusted line yards and 39th in adjusted sack rate. The run game, meanwhile, was efficient and explosive thanks to Aaron Green. Green didn't put up prolific numbers by common measures, but he was extremely efficient in limited opportunities—he averaged 7.8 highlight yards per carry and beat his team's opportunity rate at 44.6 percent.

The defense will experience higher turnover, and losing senior linebacker Paul Dawson certainly hurts. Dawson had 20 tackles for loss and six sacks and was the most disruptive player on the team. The returning line isn't necessarily full of stars, but it is experienced, with Davion Pierson leading in the middle. As good as the TCU defense was—it held Minnesota to a touchdown and Ole Miss to a field goal—it had problems with big plays. Giving up 61 points to Baylor (where three receivers averaged over 18 yards per catch), 33 to Oklahoma (Sterling Shepard had seven catches for 215 yards), and 30 to

Kansas (Kansas!), the Horned Frogs were boom most of the time, and bust in several conference games. Hardly anyone was more disruptive up front (second in front seven havoc), but they were prone to breakdowns (70th in IsoPPP).

So can TCU take the next step and be one of the four Play-off teams this season? The schedule is solid but manageable, and the Horned Frogs may well be undefeated heading into the second-to-last game of the season versus Oklahoma. With season-ending games against the Sooners and Baylor, they will have to save their best for last.

No. 16 Oklahoma Sooners (9-3, 7-2)

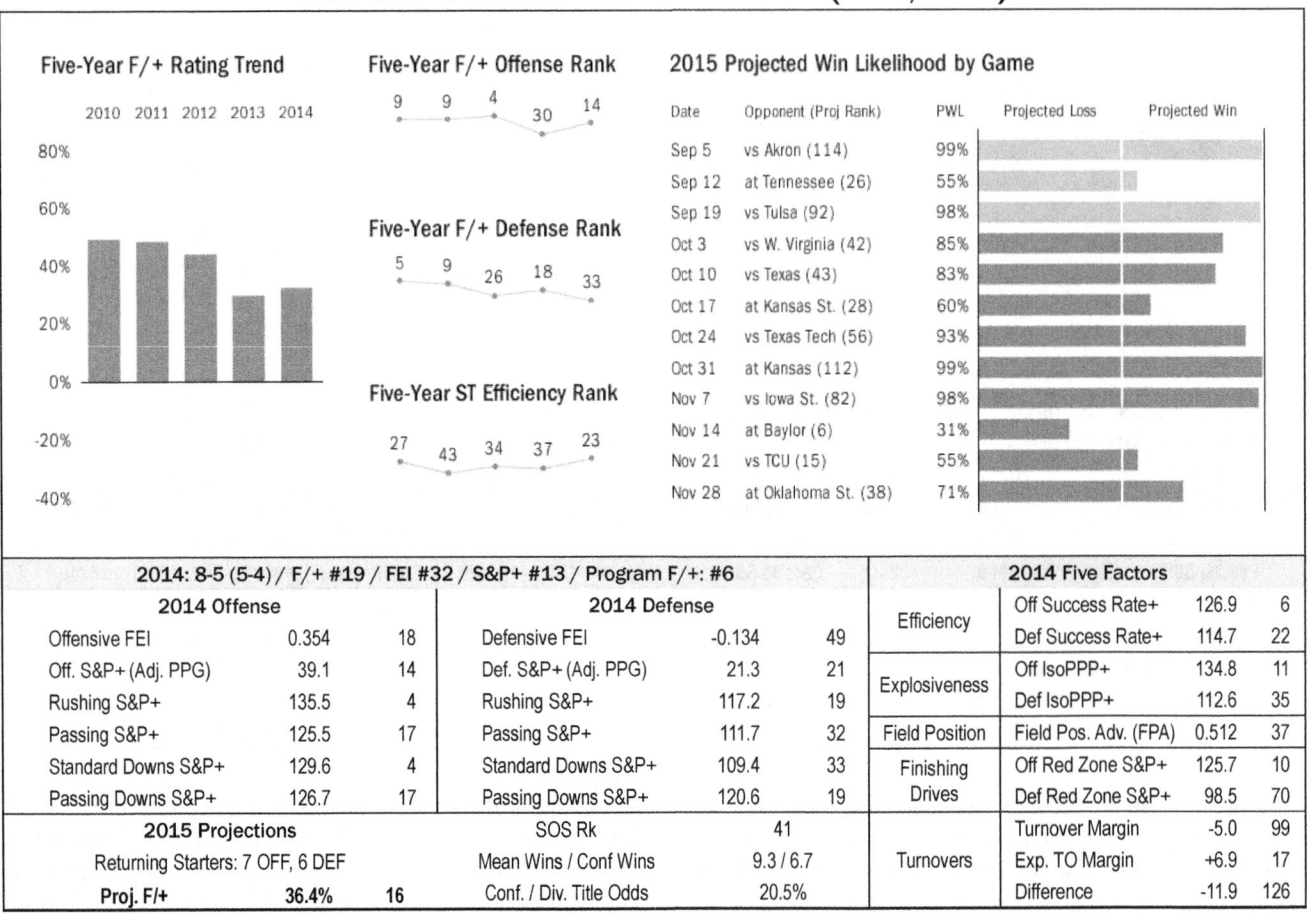

2014: 8-5 (5-4) / F/+ #19 / FEI #32 / S&P+ #13 / Program F/+: #6							2014 Five Factors		
2014 Offense			**2014 Defense**			Efficiency	Off Success Rate+	126.9	6
Offensive FEI	0.354	18	Defensive FEI	-0.134	49		Def Success Rate+	114.7	22
Off. S&P+ (Adj. PPG)	39.1	14	Def. S&P+ (Adj. PPG)	21.3	21	Explosiveness	Off IsoPPP+	134.8	11
Rushing S&P+	135.5	4	Rushing S&P+	117.2	19		Def IsoPPP+	112.6	35
Passing S&P+	125.5	17	Passing S&P+	111.7	32	Field Position	Field Pos. Adv. (FPA)	0.512	37
Standard Downs S&P+	129.6	4	Standard Downs S&P+	109.4	33	Finishing Drives	Off Red Zone S&P+	125.7	10
Passing Downs S&P+	126.7	17	Passing Downs S&P+	120.6	19		Def Red Zone S&P+	98.5	70
2015 Projections			SOS Rk		41	Turnovers	Turnover Margin	-5.0	99
Returning Starters: 7 OFF, 6 DEF			Mean Wins / Conf Wins		9.3 / 6.7		Exp. TO Margin	+6.9	17
Proj. F/+	**36.4%**	**16**	Conf. / Div. Title Odds		20.5%		Difference	-11.9	126

It's not very often that an offense finishes in the top ten of the offensive S&P+ and the top twenty of the offensive FEI and still replaces its coordinator. But that's what happened this offseason in Norman, Oklahoma, as Bob Stoops made the call to bring on East Carolina offensive coordinator Lincoln Riley to install a new offense for the Sooners. Riley is a descendant of the Mike Leach air raid school, and his offense at East Carolina put up big numbers (if not necessarily great explosiveness; see last year's 47th-ranked passing S&P+ offense) that Stoops hopes will take root in Norman. That offensive transition coincides with a spring quarterback race between incumbent Trevor Knight and three challengers, all of whom have had their moments in spring practice. All of this was necessitated by a dismal end to an 8-5 2014 season

(which followed a brilliant 11-2 2013 season that included an upset bowl win over Alabama), with back-to-back losses to rival Oklahoma State and Clemson, the latter of which was a 40-6 Russell Athletic Bowl blowout sparked by the Tigers' relentless defense.

While the offense will be in transition, the defense should be more stable. The top four tacklers and top three in tackles for loss all return, including pass rushing machine Eric Striker. The Sooners were excellent against the run and solid against the pass, but struggled with explosive plays and generating pressure outside of Striker's continuous presence in opposing backfields. The disparity between Oklahoma's success rate (22nd) and explosiveness prevention (83rd in IsoPPP) was striking; even more so is that it's not just a standard downs vs. passing downs division—the Sooners were actually more efficient on passing downs (26th) than standard downs (33rd), despite being consistently more efficient than solid at shutting down explosive plays. That suggests Oklahoma allowed explosive plays on standard downs. The poor havoc rates (84th in defensive back havoc rate, 61st overall) means that few outside of Striker were pressuring the quarterback consistently. With the second-, third-, and fourth-place players in team sacks leaving, the pressure is on young players to step up on defense. New signees Neville Gallimore and Ricky DeBerry provide immediate talent, while veterans Jordan Evans and Matt Romar are experienced members of the front seven that can step up to leadership roles. Meanwhile, the secondary has room to improve on the 31st overall passing defense and begin preventing explosive plays (Clemson's Artavis Scott and Mike Williams both averaged over 12 yards per catch, with longs of 65 and 31 yards, respectively).

Most eyes are on the quarterback race, since the offensive backfield is in capable hands with the trio of Samaje Perine, Alex Ross, and Joe Mixon. Perine was durable (263 carries as a freshman), explosive (averaging 7.17 highlight yards per opportunity), and efficient (with a 41.1 percent opportunity rate, higher than the offensive line's average). But both Ross and Mixon have incredible athletic ability and explosive potential. The offensive line set up them up for success, as it was one of the most consistent units in the country, ranking tenth in adjusted line yards and third in adjusted sack rate, even with a mobile quarterback in Trevor Knight. If the offensive line can replace left tackle Tyrus Thompson, potentially with Josiah St. John, and tackle Daryl William, then it will once again be hard to slow the Sooners' ground game. In addition to watching who wins the quarterback competition, keep an eye on the run/pass balance in the first year of the air raid—with this much talent in the Sooners backfield, it will be difficult to not call run after run.

While the Sooners have a talented roster, the transition in offensive philosophy, a potential change at quarterback, and secondary troubles with explosive plays might keep them from Playoff contention in 2015. But if Baker Mayfield, Trevor Knight, Cody Thomas, or Justice Hansen wins the quarterback job and begins to excel, then the sky is the limit. Mayfield had arguably the best spring, with the best completion percentage (77 percent) and average per pass (17.6) of the contenders, but he also threw two interceptions. Trevor Knight was a consistent runner (sixth among quarterbacks with a 61.3 percent opportunity rate), but he only averaged 7.3 yards per attempt, with a 57 percent completion percentage. Whoever wins the job, he will have the explosive Sterling Shepard (19 yards per reception) and Durron Neal (who had a surprisingly low catch rate at 52.5 percent) to help him.

No. 17 Georgia Tech Yellow Jackets (9-3, 6-2)

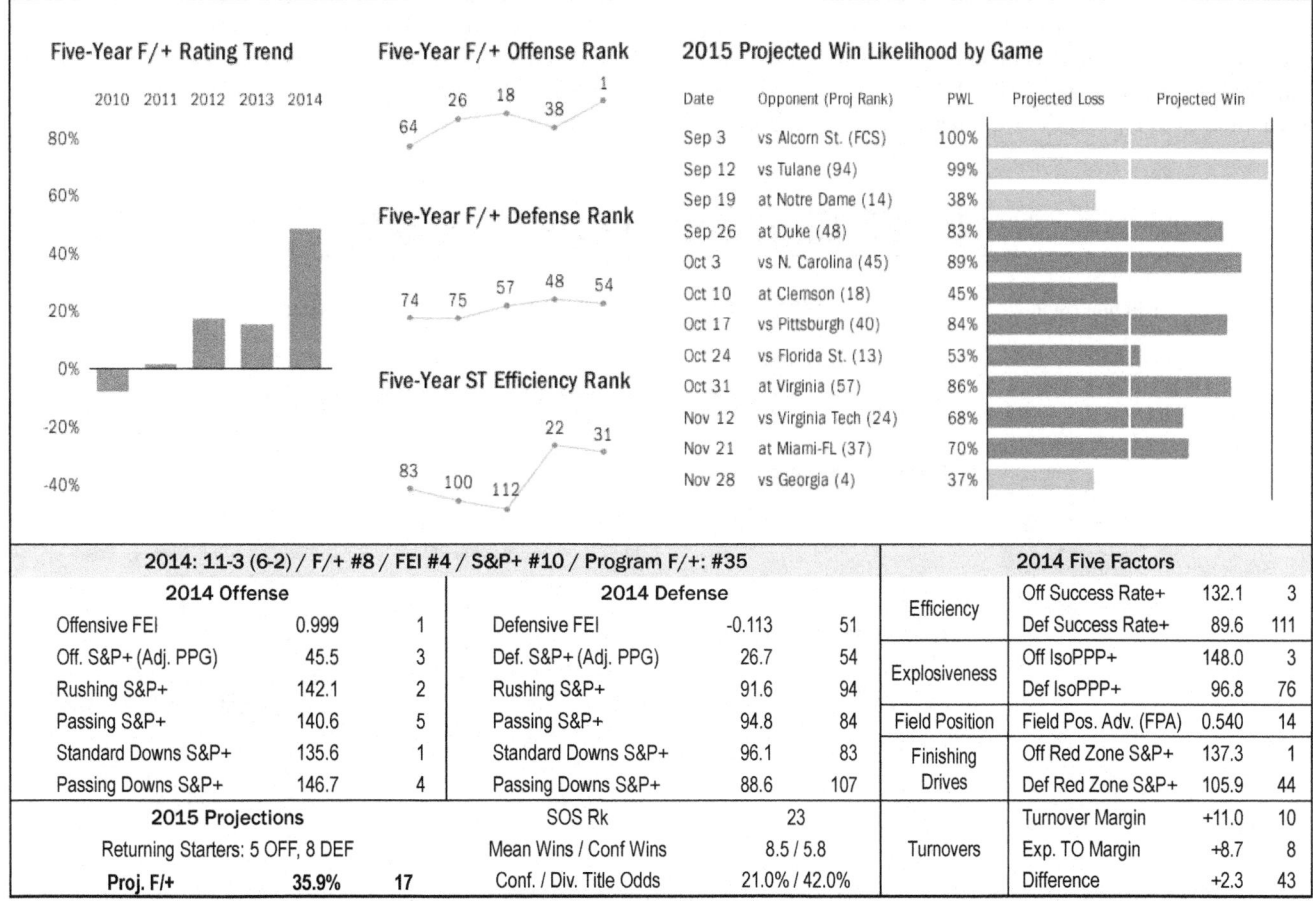

Date	Opponent (Proj Rank)	PWL
Sep 3	vs Alcorn St. (FCS)	100%
Sep 12	vs Tulane (94)	99%
Sep 19	at Notre Dame (14)	38%
Sep 26	at Duke (48)	83%
Oct 3	vs N. Carolina (45)	89%
Oct 10	at Clemson (18)	45%
Oct 17	vs Pittsburgh (40)	84%
Oct 24	vs Florida St. (13)	53%
Oct 31	at Virginia (57)	86%
Nov 12	vs Virginia Tech (24)	68%
Nov 21	at Miami-FL (37)	70%
Nov 28	vs Georgia (4)	37%

2014: 11-3 (6-2) / F/+ #8 / FEI #4 / S&P+ #10 / Program F/+: #35						2014 Five Factors		
2014 Offense			**2014 Defense**			Efficiency	Off Success Rate+	132.1	3
Offensive FEI	0.999	1	Defensive FEI	-0.113	51		Def Success Rate+	89.6	111
Off. S&P+ (Adj. PPG)	45.5	3	Def. S&P+ (Adj. PPG)	26.7	54	Explosiveness	Off IsoPPP+	148.0	3
Rushing S&P+	142.1	2	Rushing S&P+	91.6	94		Def IsoPPP+	96.8	76
Passing S&P+	140.6	5	Passing S&P+	94.8	84	Field Position	Field Pos. Adv. (FPA)	0.540	14
Standard Downs S&P+	135.6	1	Standard Downs S&P+	96.1	83	Finishing Drives	Off Red Zone S&P+	137.3	1
Passing Downs S&P+	146.7	4	Passing Downs S&P+	88.6	107		Def Red Zone S&P+	105.9	44
2015 Projections			SOS Rk	23		Turnovers	Turnover Margin	+11.0	10
Returning Starters: 5 OFF, 8 DEF			Mean Wins / Conf Wins	8.5 / 5.8			Exp. TO Margin	+8.7	8
Proj. F/+	**35.9%**	17	Conf. / Div. Title Odds	21.0% / 42.0%			Difference	+2.3	43

Five-Year F/+ Rating Trend

Five-Year F/+ Offense Rank: 64, 26, 18, 38, 1

Five-Year F/+ Defense Rank: 74, 75, 57, 48, 54

Five-Year ST Efficiency Rank: 83, 100, 112, 22, 31

Is the flexbone triple option still a gimmick if it produces results like it did in 2014? The No. 1 combined offense according to FEI and S&P+, Georgia Tech could run on everyone and found the ideal option quarterback in Justin Thomas. The former four-star recruit was the perfect mix of an explosive and efficient runner and an efficient-enough passer. While the offense was rarely slowed, the defense was far from efficient, but it leaned towards preventing explosive plays and was serviceable in that regard. The most important pieces of the Tech offense and defense return—Thomas and most of both lines—while the skill talent is fairly interchangeable in this scheme. But can the Yellow Jackets really suffer so many losses of offensive talent without improving much on defense and still hold up against a brutal schedule?

The Yellow Jackets offense is anything but balanced, with the passing game merely serving as an occasional constraint for the devastating rushing attack. The driving forces of the offense are the quarterback as a decision maker and option executor and the offensive line. In that regard, Georgia Tech should be optimistic for a repeat performance of their third-most explosive and efficient offense from 2014. However, the amount of skill player talent they lose is staggering. The top five A- and B-backs, as well as eight of the top nine receiving targets, are all gone. Returning receivers accounted for just 8.1 percent of the team's targets last season. The Georgia Tech passing game often doesn't ask for much more than straight line speed, excellent blocking, and/or jump ball proficiency, but that's still a lot of experience to replace. Synjyn Days was the most efficient B-back and Charles Perkins was arguably the most explosive A-back, but both are gone, leaving only Broderick Snoddy with decent game experience (and even he had just 28 carries in 2014). The Yellow Jackets have plenty of candidates to replace the eight departed running backs, in-

cluding eight freshmen. It's likely that at least a few will join the rotation with Snoddy and Stanford graduate transfer Patrick Skov. Again, at least the line only lost one member, even if it was All-American Shaquille Mason. Though there will be fresh faces throughout the running back and wide receiver rotations, don't expect much of a drop in production from the offense; Tech never recruits five-star players anyway (Thomas is easily the highest recruited player on the offense), so it's fair to predict similar results from this well-oiled machine.

The defense, however, enjoys a very high degree of continuity, though that might not be a good thing. An optimist might say that another year of experience could mean a cohesive and knowledgeable group, while a pessimist would suggest that it means a repeat of last season's leaky scheme. The problem with Tech's bend-don't-break scheme was that it certainly bent (111th in success rate+), but it also frequently broke (76th in IsoPPP+). The only area where the defense was solid (if unspectacular) was in the red zone, where the Jackets improved to 44th-most efficient. Tech has never been large on defense, particularly up front, but they also lacked the edge rushing ability to create havoc in the backfield (102nd in adjusted sack rate, 83rd in front seven havoc). Last year's team sacks leader, KeShun Freeman, is now a sophomore, and the Jackets return formerly suspended tackle Jabari Hunt-Days. The loss of athletic linebacker Quayshawn Nealy might hurt in pass defense, but overall the defense should benefit from more cohesion and experience.

The main obstacle to another ten-win season is the difficulty of Tech's schedule. Their out of conference lineup includes rival Georgia and Notre Dame, and their conference slate includes Clemson, Florida State, Miami, and Virginia. That's an extremely difficult lineup, especially with so much to replace on offense.

No. 18 Clemson Tigers (9-3, 6-2)

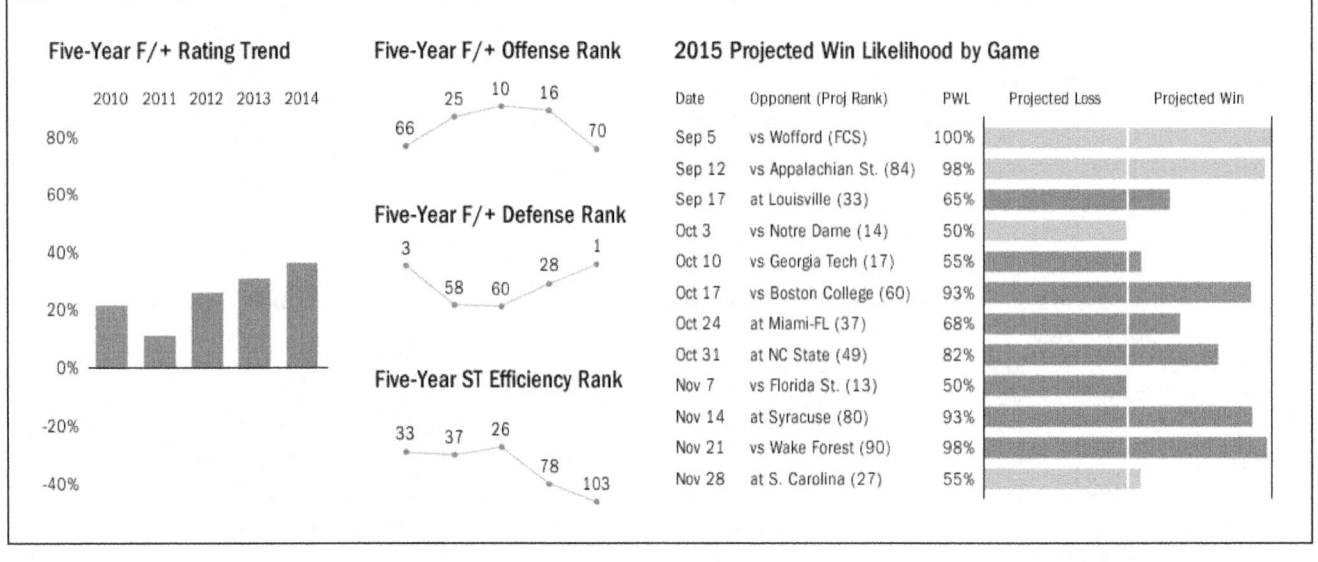

2014: 10-3 (6-2) / F/+ #14 / FEI #14 / S&P+ #17 / Program F/+: #22						2014 Five Factors			
2014 Offense			**2014 Defense**			Efficiency	Off Success Rate+	91.7	102
Offensive FEI	-0.005	61	Defensive FEI	-0.928	1		Def Success Rate+	144.0	1
Off. S&P+ (Adj. PPG)	27.7	73	Def. S&P+ (Adj. PPG)	12.2	2	Explosiveness	Off IsoPPP+	100.2	67
Rushing S&P+	88.0	107	Rushing S&P+	146.7	2		Def IsoPPP+	161.0	2
Passing S&P+	105.6	50	Passing S&P+	158.2	1	Field Position	Field Pos. Adv. (FPA)	0.507	47
Standard Downs S&P+	94.5	85	Standard Downs S&P+	141.8	1	Finishing Drives	Off Red Zone S&P+	92.7	86
Passing Downs S&P+	103.0	58	Passing Downs S&P+	167.7	1		Def Red Zone S&P+	157.5	1
2015 Projections			SOS Rk		50	Turnovers	Turnover Margin	+6.0	33
Returning Starters: 7 OFF, 4 DEF			Mean Wins / Conf Wins		9.1 / 6.0		Exp. TO Margin	+2.9	42
Proj. F/+	**34.0%**	**18**	Conf. / Div. Title Odds		17.4% / 34.8%		Difference	+3.1	34

Clemson has three priorities for 2015 to be an ACC challenger. In order of importance, they are: (1) keep Deshaun Watson healthy, (2) improve the run blocking, and (3) reload the defensive line. There are few players more critical to the success of their teams than Watson, who suffered multiple injuries last season. Clemson was simply a different team when Watson was on the field. Veteran Cole Stoudt was competent, but Watson was accurate, displayed excellent footwork, and opened up the downfield passing game despite little help from the run game. The offensive line has lost three starters, but there's plenty of potential with a group that includes (like most of Clemson's units) a glut of underclassmen blue-chip recruits ready for their opportunities. Finally, the defensive line needs to replace the most talent of any position group on the team, including NFL draftees Grady Jarrett and Vic Beasley (as well as four other linemen with multiple sacks from their rotation). But like the offensive line, the (first in the country in S&P+ and success rate+, second in IsoPPP+) is full of blue-chip replacements waiting in the wings. There are answers for all of these questions on the roster (well, except maybe Watson's health), but the range of possible outcomes for Clemson this season spans from ACC champ and national contender to middle-of-the-pack ACC team.

In his 2014 freshman season, Watson was one of the most electrifying passers in the country when he was healthy. Living up to his composite five-star recruiting ranking, the Georgia native only threw two interceptions and completed 68 percent of his passes for 9.7 yards per attempt in what turned out to be limited action despite winning the starting job. Given Watson's receivers in 2015, a full season would mean one of the most deadly offenses in the country, even without departed offensive coordinator Chad Morris. Not only does Watson return big play (and big target) receiver Mike Williams and reliable Artavis Scott (83 percent catch rate), but five-star freshmen Deon Cain and Ray Ray McCloud join a strong stable of wideouts.

The offensive line at least did its job in pass protection in 2014 (26th in adjusted sack rate), though they fared worse in obvious passing situations, likely because opposing defenses didn't fear Stoudt or the run game on passing downs. The right side of the line is now gone, but talented freshmen like Mitch Hyatt and Jake Fruhmorgen are ready to take over. The Tigers will need to improve their run blocking, as only a little more than a third of their running back carries were for more than five yards (95th). If the passing offense is going to reach its full potential—and if the Tigers hope to improve on their 86th-ranked red zone S&P+ offense—then the run game has to get better. It's not just the offensive line, but the running backs as well. Wayne Gallman was certainly not Andre Ellington, but he performed right at the line's level of efficiency and was the best option for explosiveness among the backs, averaging five highlight yards per carry. Sophomore Adam Choice was highly recruited, but wasn't a better option according to either explosiveness or efficiency measures. Fellow sophomore Tyshon Dye presents the best challenge to Gallman—he's a bigger back than Gallman and was more efficient, if less explosive. These three will likely need to shoulder the burden and at least take advantage of their opportunities for explosive run plays to relieve the pressure on Watson and the passing game.

It's difficult to emphasize properly how good the 2014 Clemson defense was. Written off by many following at 45-21 loss in the season opener against Georgia, the Tigers played the rest of the season with a vengeance. Clemson was either first or second against the run and the pass in terms of efficiency and explosiveness, and they were the best defense in the country in the red zone. The only hope opposing defenses had was in the fourth quarter, when they fell to 34th. The defensive line was one for the ages with Jarrett and Beasley, but those two and four other linemen are now gone in what will be an almost entirely different line. While it's a lot to ask of three new starters to replicate the departed group's production, a mix of veterans like Shaq Lawson and D.J. Reader, as well as blue-chip freshmen like Christian Wilkins and Albert Huggins, ensure raw talent is not in short supply. The question is whether the talent can be used as seamlessly as the veteran group from last year.

Clemson has a difficult schedule, and the Tigers are likely to feel the heat if Watson misses any time or the line doesn't manage to generate opportunities for the running backs. With top-32 projected S&P+ teams Louisville, Miami, Notre Dame, Georgia Tech, Florida State, and South Carolina on the docket, Clemson has little room for error. But given the sheer amount of talent Dabo Swinney has amassed, it's hard to discount the Tigers in any game on the schedule.

No. 19 Arizona State Sun Devils (9-3, 6-3)

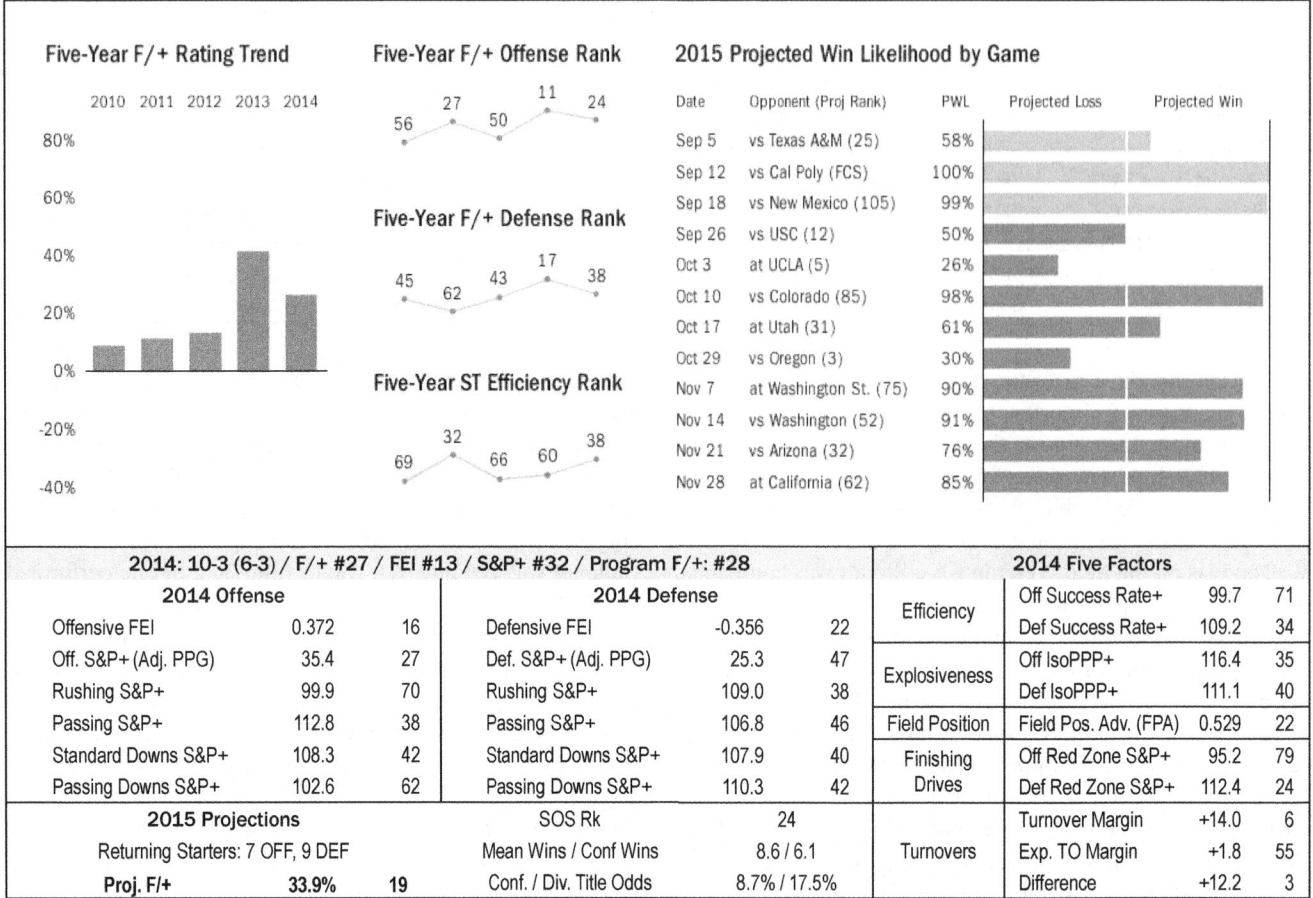

Five-Year F/+ Rating Trend

Five-Year F/+ Offense Rank

Five-Year F/+ Defense Rank

Five-Year ST Efficiency Rank

2015 Projected Win Likelihood by Game

Date	Opponent (Proj Rank)	PWL	Projected Loss	Projected Win
Sep 5	vs Texas A&M (25)	58%		
Sep 12	vs Cal Poly (FCS)	100%		
Sep 18	vs New Mexico (105)	99%		
Sep 26	vs USC (12)	50%		
Oct 3	at UCLA (5)	26%		
Oct 10	vs Colorado (85)	98%		
Oct 17	at Utah (31)	61%		
Oct 29	vs Oregon (3)	30%		
Nov 7	at Washington St. (75)	90%		
Nov 14	vs Washington (52)	91%		
Nov 21	vs Arizona (32)	76%		
Nov 28	at California (62)	85%		

2014: 10-3 (6-3) / F/+ #27 / FEI #13 / S&P+ #32 / Program F/+: #28

2014 Offense

Offensive FEI	0.372	16
Off. S&P+ (Adj. PPG)	35.4	27
Rushing S&P+	99.9	70
Passing S&P+	112.8	38
Standard Downs S&P+	108.3	42
Passing Downs S&P+	102.6	62

2014 Defense

Defensive FEI	-0.356	22
Def. S&P+ (Adj. PPG)	25.3	47
Rushing S&P+	109.0	38
Passing S&P+	106.8	46
Standard Downs S&P+	107.9	40
Passing Downs S&P+	110.3	42

2014 Five Factors

Efficiency	Off Success Rate+	99.7	71
	Def Success Rate+	109.2	34
Explosiveness	Off IsoPPP+	116.4	35
	Def IsoPPP+	111.1	40
Field Position	Field Pos. Adv. (FPA)	0.529	22
Finishing Drives	Off Red Zone S&P+	95.2	79
	Def Red Zone S&P+	112.4	24
Turnovers	Turnover Margin	+14.0	6
	Exp. TO Margin	+1.8	55
	Difference	+12.2	3

2015 Projections

Returning Starters: 7 OFF, 9 DEF		
Proj. F/+	33.9%	19

SOS Rk	24
Mean Wins / Conf Wins	8.6 / 6.1
Conf. / Div. Title Odds	8.7% / 17.5%

Arizona State returns 16 starters from last year's team that recorded double digit wins and a bowl victory over 9-4 Duke. The strong continuity should ensure that Todd Graham's Sun Devils are competitive in the Pac-12 South once again. Quarterback Taylor Kelly, a three-year starter, graduated, but likely starter Mike Bercovici filled in for Kelly in four games, bettering both Kelly's yards per attempt (7.8) and his completion percentage (61.8 percent), while only having a slightly higher interception rate (.022). Senior running back/wide receiver D.J. Foster returns as well, further boosting a passing game full of talent. The defense, which was consistently solid except for games against UCLA and Arizona, held similar rankings in the 30s and 40s across the board in defensive stats. So what is the Sun Devils' ceiling? With their Pac-12 schedule and season opener against Texas A&M, they have one of the toughest schedules in the country, which will make their path to contention difficult.

Despite losing Kelly to graduation and dynamic receiver Jaelen Strong to the NFL, the Sun Devils' passing game should be in excellent shape. Since last year's squad passed on 47 percent of standard downs, the depth at receiver should be one of the most important offseason considerations for offensive coordinator Mike Norvell. Losing Strong no doubt hurts—he was the seventh most-targeted receiver in the country, accounting for over a third of the Sun Devils' targets. Strong's catch rate was poor among elite receivers (53.9

percent), but his average yards per catch (14.2) made up for it. To help counteract his loss, former running back D.J. Foster was moved to receiver full time after ranking second on the team in targets and receiving yards last season. Foster should fill some of Strong's void nicely, with his higher (66.7 percent) catch rate despite a lower target rate (20.8 percent). Graham and Norvell are also excited about the prospects for De'Chavon Hayes as a transition slot receiver and running back, stretching the field while Ellis Jefferson and Fred Gammage offer options as high catch rate, lower yards per catch possession-receiver types. Bercovici had similar statistics to Kelly, and despite only attempting four passes prior to last season, was poised and consistent whenever his number was called. The run game was never the focus for the Sun Devils (73rd), but likely new starter Demario Richard compared favorably to Foster as a runner (5.69 yards per carry). Regardless of the emphasis on the run game, the Sun Devils could stand to be more efficient and consistent, whether by running or passing, as they ranked only 63rd in success rate compared to an explosive 20th in IsoPPP. Of course, with an offensive line that was 82nd in adjusted line yards and 116th in adjusted sack rate, that's easier said than done.

It's usually not good when defensive backs are the leading tacklers on the team, but Arizona State played at a fairly high level most of the season. The leading defensive lineman tackler was senior Marcus Hardison, at seventh on the team

(Hardison did lead the team in tackles for loss with 15 and in sacks with 10). The fact that Hardison was seventh on the team in tackles but led the team in tackles for loss and sacks suggests that the players doing the majority of the tackling were getting to ball carriers past the line of scrimmage. The front seven havoc rate supports this, ranking 61st despite decent numbers for efficiency (43rd) and preventing big plays (42nd). However, the defensive line-specific numbers tell a different story, as they ranked 21st in adjusted line yards and ninth in adjusted sack rate. They were particularly effective with pressure on standard downs, so the line was effective even if it wasn't piling on the tackles. Replacing Hardison's

explosive plays will be difficult for the defense. While there are several linebacker candidates, including Laiu Moeakiola and Salamo Fiso, the line will need early enrollee defensive tackle George Lea to play at a high level despite being relatively undersized for the position. But with Hardison and safety Damarius Randall the only major losses, it's easy to be bullish on the Sun Devils defensively. Overall, the Sun Devils have more returning than most of their Pac-12 rivals. While Arizona loses over half of their defense, USC has shaky defensive line depth, and Oregon must find a replacement for Marcus Mariota, the Sun Devils have an opportunity to win the Pac-12 South and potentially the conference.

No. 20 Missouri Tigers (9-3, 5-3)

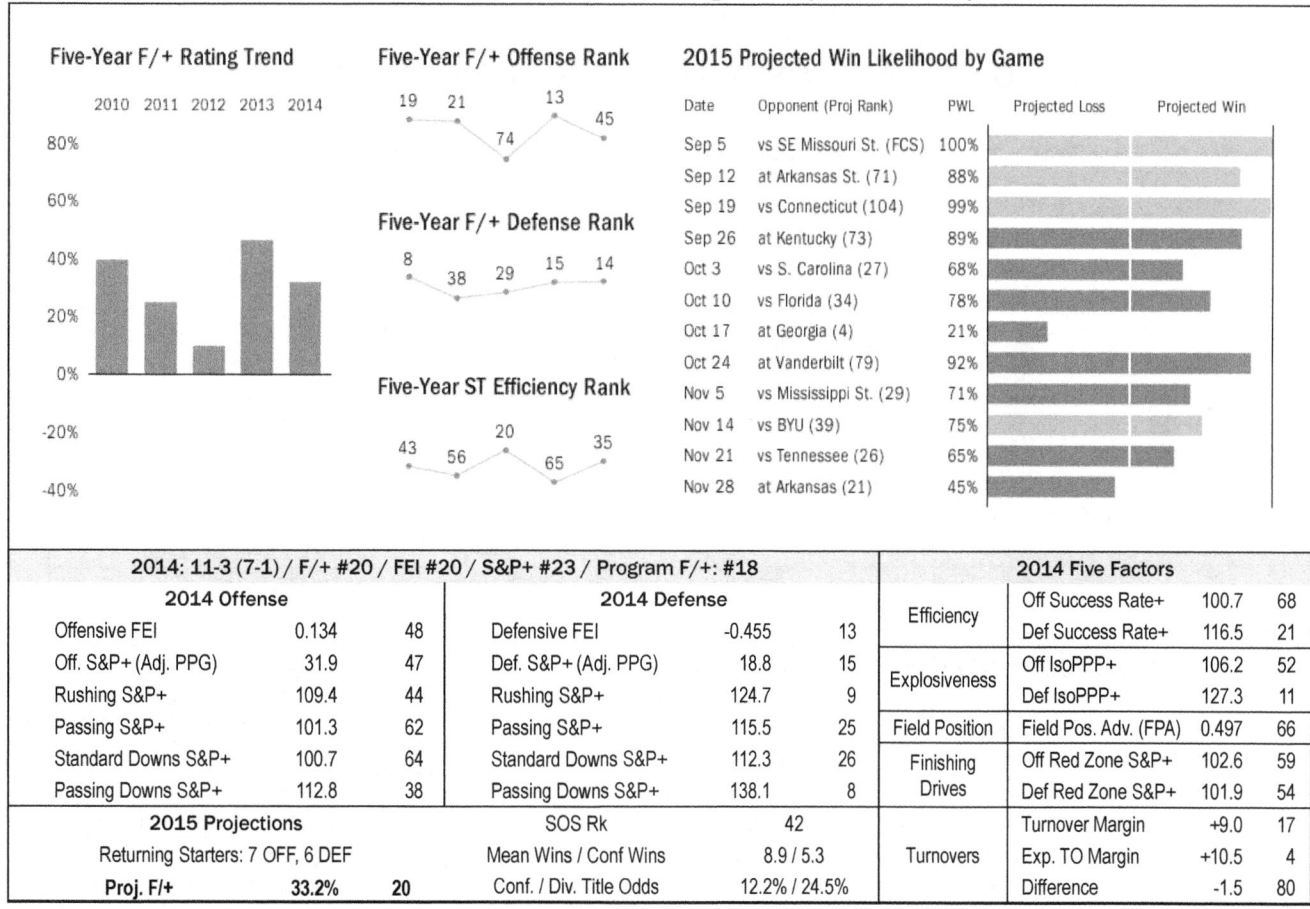

2014 Offense			2014 Defense		
Offensive FEI	0.134	48	Defensive FEI	-0.455	13
Off. S&P+ (Adj. PPG)	31.9	47	Def. S&P+ (Adj. PPG)	18.8	15
Rushing S&P+	109.4	44	Rushing S&P+	124.7	9
Passing S&P+	101.3	62	Passing S&P+	115.5	25
Standard Downs S&P+	100.7	64	Standard Downs S&P+	112.3	26
Passing Downs S&P+	112.8	38	Passing Downs S&P+	138.1	8

2014: 11-3 (7-1) / F/+ #20 / FEI #20 / S&P+ #23 / Program F/+: #18

2015 Projections		
Returning Starters: 7 OFF, 6 DEF		
Proj. F/+	33.2%	20

SOS Rk	42
Mean Wins / Conf Wins	8.9 / 5.3
Conf. / Div. Title Odds	12.2% / 24.5%

2014 Five Factors			
Efficiency	Off Success Rate+	100.7	68
	Def Success Rate+	116.5	21
Explosiveness	Off IsoPPP+	106.2	52
	Def IsoPPP+	127.3	11
Field Position	Field Pos. Adv. (FPA)	0.497	66
Finishing Drives	Off Red Zone S&P+	102.6	59
	Def Red Zone S&P+	101.9	54
Turnovers	Turnover Margin	+9.0	17
	Exp. TO Margin	+10.5	4
	Difference	-1.5	80

Maty Mauk is a lot like former Ole Miss quarterback Bo Wallace, with his good days and bad days. Mauk has plenty of upside—he set records for high school passing yards, completions, and touchdowns, and was recently voted to the SEC second team by conference SIDs—but he also had six games last season with a sub-50 percent completion percentage, including the Georgia game, in which he also threw four interceptions. But heading into 2015, Mauk, breakthrough senior running back Russell Hansbrough, and the offensive line will all be stabilizing forces for a Tigers team that loses half of its starting defense, including three defensive linemen.

The Tigers have had a consistently good and havoc-generating defense since their move to the SEC. While originally thought to be the worse of the two additions (compared to Texas A&M), the Tigers have won the SEC East twice, primarily on the back of an aggressive defense led by linemen like Shane Ray, Michael Sam, Markus Golden, and Sheldon Richardson (the Tigers were 22nd in overall havoc rate and eleventh in front seven havoc rate last season). This strong play up front made the Tigers devastating on passing downs (9th) and strong against both the run (12th) and the pass (27th). While they lose four of their top five most productive linemen to graduation or the NFL (including Ray and Golden), the Tigers have reloaded like a much higher-ranked recruiting defense (the Tigers had just three four- or five-star recruits in last season's class of 23). This year consensus five star defensive tackle Terry Beckner Jr. decided to stay in state and looks to become the next great Tigers defensive linemen. Barry Odom's defense will likely continue to be as solid and aggressive as we've come to expect, with experienced linemen filling in for now-departed seniors.

The offense benefits from continuity along the offensive line, which ranked 24th in adjusted line yards and 51st in adjusted sack rate. While his receiving corps didn't do him many favors this spring, recording a number of drops in scrimmages, Mauk looks to have developed a rapport with sophomore J'Mon Moore, who led all receivers in spring scrimmages.

The top four receiving options all graduated, including often targeted (32 percent) Bud Sasser, so replacing their production will be key for Mauk's consistency and to balance the ground game. Russell Hansbrough has emerged as Missouri's top running back, with strong explosiveness but less efficiency (6.74 highlight yards per carry and a 36.1 percent opportunity rate). Hansbrough disappeared against strong defenses, averaging 3.75 yards per carry against Georgia, 2.69 against Florida, and 1.62 against Alabama, but he exploded against Texas A&M (9.95 yards per carry) and Minnesota (7.6). If Mauk's skill players can be more consistent, then this offense can likely match the defense's production for another run at the SEC East. The biggest competition will likely come from Georgia, as it has for the past three years, but Tennessee is a rising power in the East as well.

No. 21 Arkansas Razorbacks (7-5, 3-5)

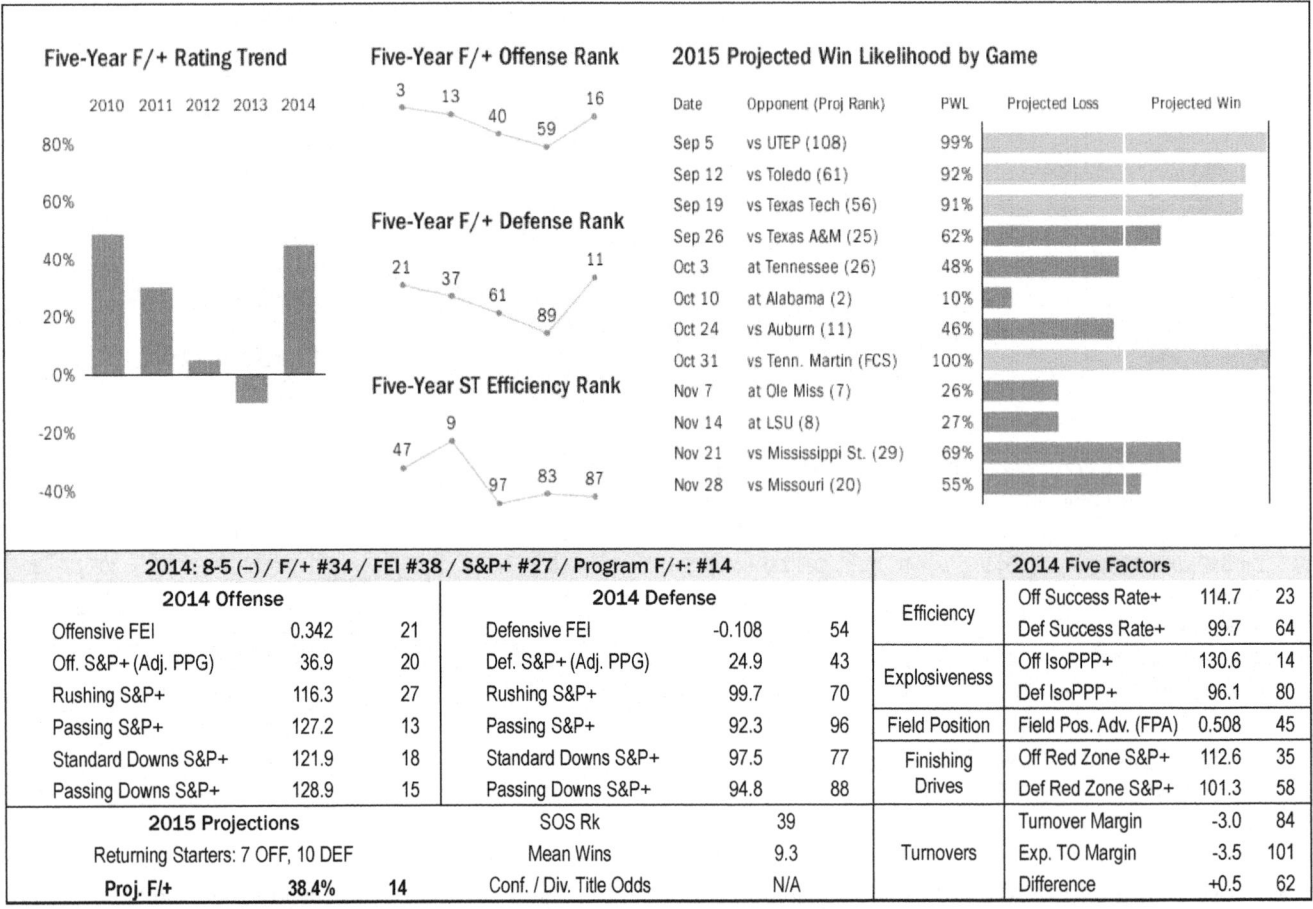

There might not have been a better team statistically that finished with a poorer record than Bret Bielema's Arkansas in 2014. The 7-6 Razorbacks finished the season ranked ninth in F/+ after scoring the first SEC win of Bielema's tenure over LSU (a 17-0 shut out, at that). Wins over Ole Miss and Texas further fueled the Razorbacks' momentum heading in to 2015. Bielema hasn't quite turned Arkansas into the rushing powerhouse that his Wisconsin teams were, but 26th in rushing S&P+ certainly isn't shabby. After their impressive season

statistically and momentum from the end of the season, Arkansas is one of the most hyped teams across national media this offseason. But can they live up to expectations?

The Arkansas offense was impressively efficient according to both rushing S&P+ (26th) and passing S&P+ (21st), but had poorer success rate and explosiveness rankings (48th and 60th respectively). This is likely because Arkansas's offensive performances were very impressive after making opponent adjustments, given the quality of the defenses they faced last season—Alabama (third in defensive S&P+), Georgia (17th), Mississippi State (16th), Ole Miss (7th), LSU (12th), Missouri (23rd), and Texas (20th). The offense is ostensibly led by the 1,000-yard rushing duo of Jonathan Williams and Alex Collins (Collins had slightly higher explosiveness, while Williams was slightly more consistent, according to opportunity rate), but Brandon Allen actually led the 21st-ranked passing S&P+ offense despite not having a receiver in the RYPR top 100 (though leading receiver Keon Hatcher and tight end Hunter Henry were close). Allen's base numbers were decent but unspectacular, but given the level of pass defenses he faced in the seven games mentioned above, his numbers were incredibly efficient. His biggest asset might be that he simply doesn't turn the ball over (a 1.5 percent interception rate) and excels on passing downs (where Arkansas was fifth in the country). Both Collins and Williams return on the ground, as do four starting offensive linemen, so it's fair to expect the offense to maintain its high level of play in Allen's senior season.

The Razorbacks' defense was underrated for most of the season, but was recognized for holding Alabama to 13 points and then shutting out LSU and Ole Miss in consecutive weeks. Defensive lineman Trey Flowers was an underrated edge rusher in a conference full of high quality defensive linemen, and his loss (as well as the departures of three other starting members of the front seven) certainly hurts, but the next five team leaders in sacks were all sophomores. The front seven loses a good bit for a unit ranked seventh in front seven havoc rate, but the likely replacements all frequently rotated in last season and are now mostly juniors or seniors. Bielema also has several high quality freshmen who could work their way in to the rotation, including Hjalte Froholdt, who enrolled early, early enrollee and juco transfer Jeremiah Ledbetter, and consensus four-star end Jamario Bell. While the defense must replace nearly half of last season's starters, the depth should be there for the Razorbacks to pick up where they left off last season. Whether that's enough to upend SEC West foes LSU, Auburn, Ole Miss, and Alabama again isn't clear, but they should be competitive every week.

No. 22 Wisconsin Badgers (10-2, 7-1)

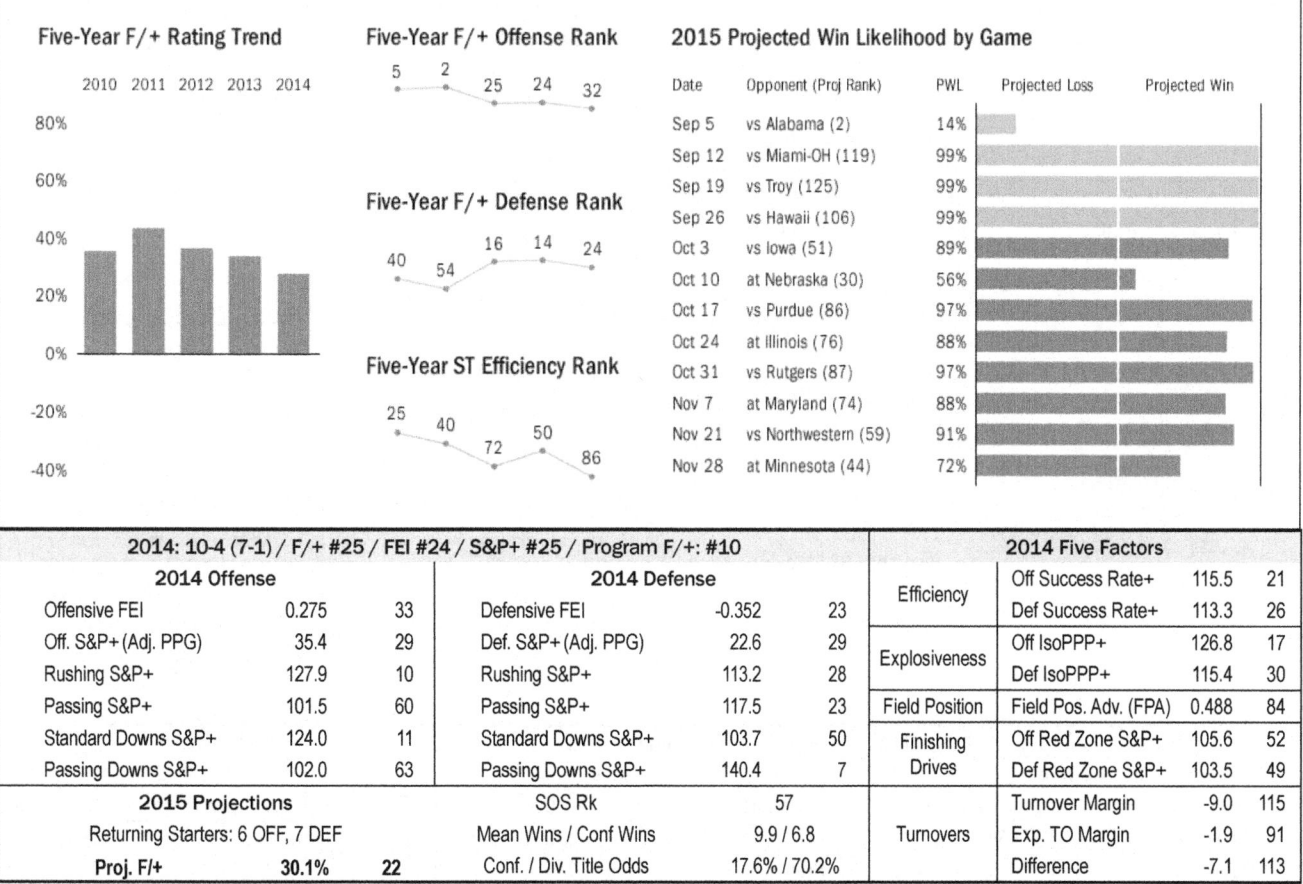

2014: 10-4 (7-1) / F/+ #25 / FEI #24 / S&P+ #25 / Program F/+: #10						2014 Five Factors			
2014 Offense			**2014 Defense**			Efficiency	Off Success Rate+	115.5	21
Offensive FEI	0.275	33	Defensive FEI	-0.352	23		Def Success Rate+	113.3	26
Off. S&P+ (Adj. PPG)	35.4	29	Def. S&P+ (Adj. PPG)	22.6	29	Explosiveness	Off IsoPPP+	126.8	17
Rushing S&P+	127.9	10	Rushing S&P+	113.2	28		Def IsoPPP+	115.4	30
Passing S&P+	101.5	60	Passing S&P+	117.5	23	Field Position	Field Pos. Adv. (FPA)	0.488	84
Standard Downs S&P+	124.0	11	Standard Downs S&P+	103.7	50	Finishing Drives	Off Red Zone S&P+	105.6	52
Passing Downs S&P+	102.0	63	Passing Downs S&P+	140.4	7		Def Red Zone S&P+	103.5	49
2015 Projections			SOS Rk	57			Turnover Margin	-9.0	115
Returning Starters: 6 OFF, 7 DEF			Mean Wins / Conf Wins	9.9 / 6.8		Turnovers	Exp. TO Margin	-1.9	91
Proj. F/+	**30.1%**	**22**	Conf. / Div. Title Odds	17.6% / 70.2%			Difference	-7.1	113

With the out-of-left-field news that Gary Andersen would be replacing Mike Riley at Oregon State, the Badgers find themselves with another new coach, though Paul Chryst is certainly no stranger to Madison. While it seemed almost predestined for Chryst to one day return as head coach for the

Badgers after both playing and coaching there previously, it's not clear whether it was a slam-dunk, no-brainer hire for athletic director Barry Alvarez. Christ undoubtedly inherited a sloppy Pitt program three years ago, but his teams have also only ranked in the 40s of the F/+ rankings while Chryst himself had the fourth-worst coaching effect of any coach in the last ten years (according to second-order wins).

One thing is clear for the Badgers every season: the running backs are going to run for a lot of yards. Whether it's John Clay, Montee Ball, James White, Melvin Gordon, or now Corey Clement, Madison has been a running back factory since Bret Bielema became head coach. Even after Clement, Chryst will have three four-star freshman backs to rotate in. An offensive line that ranked 12th in adjusted line yards lost two All-Americans and another two-year starter, but the rest of the roster is full of similarly-sized road-graters ready for their opportunity. In fact, the run game was so good that the offense completely lacked an identity in the passing game but was still a top-25 unit according to S&P+, PPP+, and yards per game. Sure, things got hairy on passing downs, but that was mostly not a problem. Only when the offensive line met two even bigger and more athletic defensive fronts did the run game suffer. Against LSU in the season opener and Ohio State in the Big Ten Championship, the Badgers running backs were funneled inside and gang tackled, limiting their highlight yard opportunities and keeping gains minimal. What makes the Badgers offense special is that they can often constrain defenses with just the run game, mixing the jet sweep with the inside zone to great effect. However, in those two losses, the lack of a passing game left the Badgers one-dimensional. Chryst has Joel Stave back next year, but he

had a negative touchdown-to-interception ratio and doesn't inspire much confidence despite keeping junior Bart Houston and redshirt freshman D.J. Gillins at bay during the spring.

The Badgers were unexpectedly a hot defensive team last season thanks to defensive coordinator Dave Aranda, who is likely to have his name come up for job openings next season if the Badgers continue their strong defensive play. Like the Badgers have traditionally done on offense, Aranda took a group of less-heralded players and forged a tough unit that was among the Big Ten's best. The Badgers defense was extremely efficient, strong on passing downs, and a sack-making machine (ranking fifth in adjusted sack rate). But if there was one area the Badgers defense could stand to improve, it was in the fourth quarter, where the Badgers dropped to 93rd from 13th. Regardless, little turnover outside of the linebackers means that a good defense in 2014 has the stability to become a great defense in 2015. The Badgers are one of the safest picks to make a conference championship, given their schedule. Outside of the season opener against Alabama, the Badgers only play one team in the Projected S&P+ top-30 (Nebraska, at 30th), and only one other team in the top 50 (Minnesota, at 42nd). Unless the Badgers inexplicably slip up like they did against Northwestern in 2014, they may not see another elite opponent until a likely matchup with Ohio State or Michigan State in the Big Ten Championship.

No. 23 Boise State Broncos (11-1, 7-1)

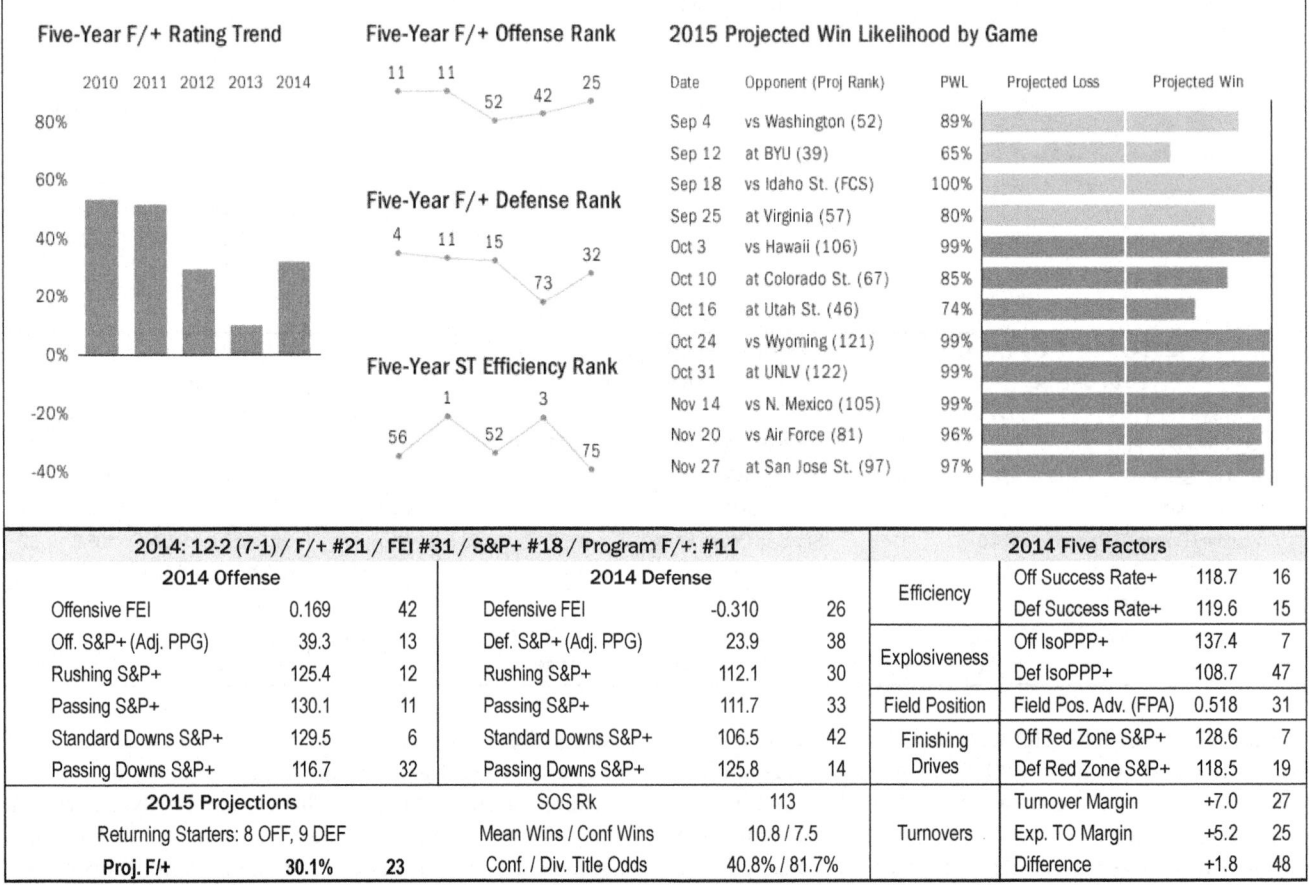

2014: 12-2 (7-1) / F/+ #21 / FEI #31 / S&P+ #18 / Program F/+: #11			2014 Five Factors			
2014 Offense			**2014 Defense**			

2014 Offense			2014 Defense			Efficiency	Off Success Rate+	118.7	16
Offensive FEI	0.169	42	Defensive FEI	-0.310	26	Efficiency	Def Success Rate+	119.6	15
Off. S&P+ (Adj. PPG)	39.3	13	Def. S&P+ (Adj. PPG)	23.9	38	Explosiveness	Off IsoPPP+	137.4	7
Rushing S&P+	125.4	12	Rushing S&P+	112.1	30	Explosiveness	Def IsoPPP+	108.7	47
Passing S&P+	130.1	11	Passing S&P+	111.7	33	Field Position	Field Pos. Adv. (FPA)	0.518	31
Standard Downs S&P+	129.5	6	Standard Downs S&P+	106.5	42	Finishing Drives	Off Red Zone S&P+	128.6	7
Passing Downs S&P+	116.7	32	Passing Downs S&P+	125.8	14	Finishing Drives	Def Red Zone S&P+	118.5	19
2015 Projections			SOS Rk	113			Turnover Margin	+7.0	27
Returning Starters: 8 OFF, 9 DEF			Mean Wins / Conf Wins	10.8 / 7.5		Turnovers	Exp. TO Margin	+5.2	25
Proj. F/+	30.1%	23	Conf. / Div. Title Odds	40.8% / 81.7%			Difference	+1.8	48

After last season's 12-2 record and top-25 F/+ finish, it's fair to predict that Boise State is on the way back to its former top-five F/+ glory from the Kellen Moore years. Now, in coach Bryan Harsin's second year, the Broncos return the vast majority of contributors outside of quarterback Grant Hedrick and running back Jay Ajayi. It's not necessarily plug-and-play at either of those positions (particularly at running back, where Ajayi carried the ball an average of 25 times per game), but there are quality options waiting in the wings, and Boise has a more than manageable schedule (77th in opponents' average F/+ rank) to make them a likely favorite in every game this season.

For all of the offensive pieces Boise State returns—and they have quite a few among the top three receivers and the entire offensive line—priority number one for the entire team will be finding Hedrick's replacement. It's not necessarily so simple as giving the job to last year's backup, Ryan Finley, as his 44 percent completion percentage last season flies in the face of what Boise State wants to do offensively (i.e., plenty of high-percentage horizontal passes on standard downs to keep the defense guessing). Finley was the leader coming out of the spring, but will need to fight off highly regarded true freshman Brett Rypien for the position, as Finley only has 27 more career passes than Rypien (and the other two potential starters, for that matter). Whichever quarterback wins the job, he will have two extremely efficient receiving options in Shane Williams-Rhodes and Thomas Sperbeck, who had catch rates of 89.5 percent and 72.9 percent, respectively. They were primarily tasked with horizontal routes and extended handoffs, but they played that part perfectly. At running back, however, the Broncos will need to replace Ajayi's extreme production.

While he wasn't the most efficient back (36.3 percent opportunity rate), the Broncos relied on him heavily in terms of sheer quantity of carries (he led the nation in run attempts last season). Backup Devan Demas is diminutive and only received a single game's worth of Ajayi's carries, but he was explosive at the second level (11.6 highlight yards per opportunity). If Demas, who averaged less than even Ajayi's pedestrian opportunity rate at 32 percent, is unable to be the workhorse back, the Broncos will likely give redshirt freshman Cory Young an opportunity.

The Boise State defense, meanwhile, not only returns most of the star talent from last year, but has an excellent mix of proven experience and raw talent that should stop opposing run games from even getting started. The defensive line was a top-20 unit in both run- and pass-defense and lost only Beau Martin from the starting unit, and the secondary is in a similar position after losing only Corey Bell. The core of the defense—star safety Darian Thompson, cornerback Donte Deayon, run-stopping linebacker Tanner Vallejo, and prototypical edge rusher Kamalei Correa—all return. Yes, the defense was a strange mix of break-don't-bend (ranking 47th in IsoPPP+ and 71st in rushing PPP+, versus 15th in Success Rate+ and 11th in rushing success rate), but beyond a few long runs, the defense controlled field position, locked down the red zone, and was extremely efficient on a per-play basis against the run. Assuming either Rypien or Finley locks down the job and comes close to Hedrick's completion percentage, it's difficult to pick out a loss from the 2015 schedule. BYU, Utah State, and Air Force could all give Boise State a run for their money, but don't be surprised if the Broncos complicate the Playoff picture in late November.

No. 24 Virginia Tech Hokies (9-3, 6-2)

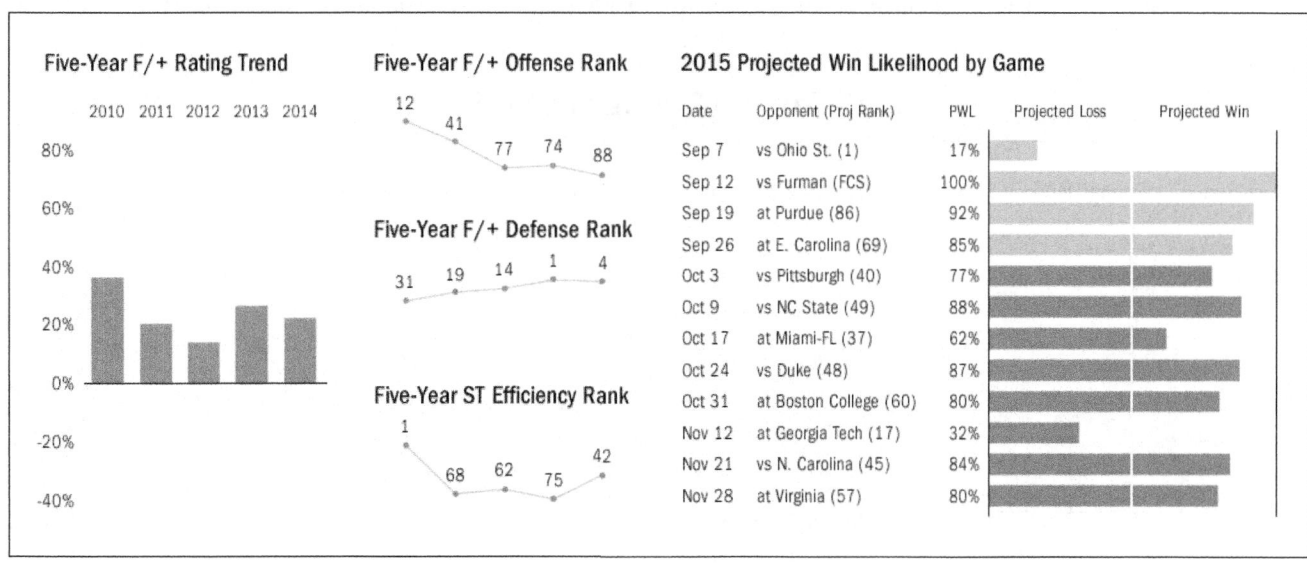

Five-Year F/+ Rating Trend
2010 2011 2012 2013 2014

Five-Year F/+ Offense Rank
12, 41, 77, 74, 88

Five-Year F/+ Defense Rank
31, 19, 14, 1, 4

Five-Year ST Efficiency Rank
1, 68, 62, 75, 42

2015 Projected Win Likelihood by Game

Date	Opponent (Proj Rank)	PWL	Projected Loss	Projected Win
Sep 7	vs Ohio St. (1)	17%		
Sep 12	vs Furman (FCS)	100%		
Sep 19	at Purdue (86)	92%		
Sep 26	at E. Carolina (69)	85%		
Oct 3	vs Pittsburgh (40)	77%		
Oct 9	vs NC State (49)	88%		
Oct 17	at Miami-FL (37)	62%		
Oct 24	vs Duke (48)	87%		
Oct 31	at Boston College (60)	80%		
Nov 12	at Georgia Tech (17)	32%		
Nov 21	vs N. Carolina (45)	84%		
Nov 28	at Virginia (57)	80%		

2014: 7-6 (3-5) / F/+ #33 / FEI #23 / S&P+ #37 / Program F/+: #24						2014 Five Factors			
2014 Offense			**2014 Defense**			Efficiency	Off Success Rate+	93.8	93
Offensive FEI	-0.246	93	Defensive FEI	-0.718	2		Def Success Rate+	143.3	2
Off. S&P+ (Adj. PPG)	25.8	85	Def. S&P+ (Adj. PPG)	16.9	10	Explosiveness	Off IsoPPP+	84.4	104
Rushing S&P+	88.0	108	Rushing S&P+	121.2	16		Def IsoPPP+	128.6	10
Passing S&P+	91.4	86	Passing S&P+	147.6	2	Field Position	Field Pos. Adv. (FPA)	0.493	76
Standard Downs S&P+	95.1	84	Standard Downs S&P+	131.9	3	Finishing Drives	Off Red Zone S&P+	93.6	83
Passing Downs S&P+	79.2	116	Passing Downs S&P+	131.9	10		Def Red Zone S&P+	145.2	2
2015 Projections			SOS Rk	45		Turnovers	Turnover Margin	-4.0	93
Returning Starters: 8 OFF, 8 DEF			Mean Wins / Conf Wins	8.8 / 5.9			Exp. TO Margin	-0.8	77
Proj. F/+	**29.1%**	**24**	Conf. / Div. Title Odds	19.6% / 39.1%			Difference	-3.2	94

Another year, another stellar defense and another poor offense that prevented the Hokies from doing even more. Expectations were high for new transfer quarterback Michael Brewer, but a sub-60 percent completion percentage, a 6.4 percent sack rate, and 15 interceptions crippled the passing game, while poor offensive line play crippled run game efficiency. Maligned offensive coordinator Scot Loeffler returns, as do Brewer, the top four receiving targets, and the top two tailbacks, so there's at least continuity and experience this year. And with that should come raised expectations; assuming the offense is merely competent, this could be a 10-win team in 2015.

Last season's offensive woes started with the line, which was 98th in adjusted line yards and 102nd in adjusted sack rate (including 113th in passing downs sack rate). Without a steady line, Virginia Tech's deep and talented stable of running backs had no room to run, as they only gained five or more yards on 36 percent of their carries. The receiving corps was similarly deep, albeit lacking a vertical threat, but in obvious passing situations (of which there were many, as the Hokies passed on roughly 74 percent of passing downs), Brewer was frequently harassed by edge rushers. Now three members of last year's starting offensive line are gone, with plenty of options to replace them. There are promising young linemen on the team, like true freshman tackle Austin Clark and sophomore guard Wyatt Teller, but it's an unproven group at best. Among skill players, what's remarkable is how young most of last season's primary contributors are. Leading receiver Isaiah Ford is now a sophomore (12 yards per catch, 62 percent catch rate), as are the other top two returning receivers and second-leading rusher Marshawn Williams.

The Hokies hang their hat on Bud Foster's impenetrable defense, which defines bend-don't-break: prevent big plays (tenth in IsoPPP+) and lock down the red zone (second in red zone S&P+). But the Hokies also excel on a per-play efficiency basis (second in success rate+). If the Virginia Tech defense had any weakness, it was that they sometimes allowed explosive run plays (41st in rushing PPP+, compared to sixth in rushing success rate). This year's unit returns almost everyone, including pass-rushing specialists Dadi Nicolas and Ken Ekanem, but loses the two starting safeties. That's not cause for concern, especially with the fierce pass rush, which had the top overall adjusted sack rate in the country, staying completely intact. Passing downs will be harrowing for all opposing offenses. Looking at the schedule, it's difficult to find a team besides Ohio State and Georgia Tech that has explosive running backs capable of finding holes in the Hokies' defense.

No. 25 Texas A&M Aggies (7-5, 4-4)

2014: 8-5 (3-5) / F/+ #42 / FEI #48 / S&P+ #30 / Program F/+: #13						2014 Five Factors			
2014 Offense			2014 Defense			Efficiency	Off Success Rate+	118.9	14
Offensive FEI	0.327	24	Defensive FEI	0.201	86		Def Success Rate+	95.3	87
Off. S&P+ (Adj. PPG)	37.6	18	Def. S&P+ (Adj. PPG)	27.3	58	Explosiveness	Off IsoPPP+	126.0	20
Rushing S&P+	116.5	26	Rushing S&P+	81.2	119		Def IsoPPP+	96.5	78
Passing S&P+	126.6	14	Passing S&P+	115.7	24	Field Position	Field Pos. Adv. (FPA)	0.490	79
Standard Downs S&P+	121.5	20	Standard Downs S&P+	93.0	90	Finishing Drives	Off Red Zone S&P+	112.8	33
Passing Downs S&P+	121.5	25	Passing Downs S&P+	106.5	50		Def Red Zone S&P+	109.6	33
2015 Projections			SOS Rk	2			Turnover Margin	-7.0	108
Returning Starters: 8 OFF, 7 DEF			Mean Wins / Conf Wins	6.9 / 3.6		Turnovers	Exp. TO Margin	-1.5	89
Proj. F/+	29.1%	25	Conf. / Div. Title Odds	1.0% / 2.1%			Difference	-5.5	106

The Aggies have been one of the most exciting additions to the SEC since their upset win over Alabama with Johnny Manziel. Last season's 8-5 record was a step back after they went 11-2 in 2012 and 9-4 in 2013, but an ongoing quarterback controversy between Kenny Hill and freshman Kyle Allen and the 73rd-ranked S&P+ defense were clearly to blame.

There is a huge disparity between the advanced efficiency metrics and the raw data for the Aggies' run game. You could look at the Aggies and see that no back gained more than 581 rushing yards, or that the yards per attempt declined from 5.2 to 4.6 after Manziel left, but the truth is that they were only slightly less efficient in 2014 than in years past (20th in rushing S&P+ last season, from fourth in 2013 and first in 2012). It went from a top-five unit to just a top-20 unit, but the rushing offense is far from a liability; it's simply not the focus of this modified air raid offense. Still, the drop-off in offensive line play (the 2014 unit was 17th in adjusted line yards and 20th in opportunity rate) after losing first-round NFL picks Luke Joeckel and Jake Matthews led to a reshuffling of the line and the hiring of new offensive line coach Dave Christensen. The line also lost Cedric Ogbuehi and Jarvis Harrison, but a mix of returning starters and junior college transfers Avery Gennesy and Jermaine Eluemunor should actually elevate the overall play of the line.

The Aggies' group of receivers will contend with Florida State for the nation's best receiving corps. In Speedy Noil, Josh Reynolds, Ricky Seals-Jones and new recruits Christian Kirk and Damion Ratley, either Allen or top overall composite quarterback Kyler Murray will have an excellent group of pass catchers. That group's mix of speed and size will cause plenty of mismatches, despite the excellent pass defenses in the SEC (the average pass defense in the SEC West last season ranked 17th in passing S&P+).

In order for the Aggies to be a surprise contender for the SEC West with Alabama and Auburn (and potentially Ole Miss), they will not only need consistent quarterback play, but also improved defensive play, especially in the secondary. The Aggies do have one of the top defensive end units in the country, led by Myles Garrett, who was second in the SEC with 12 sacks as a freshman in 2014. Garrett is joined by Daylon Mack, another five-star lineman, who boosts one of the weakest parts of the defense, the front and middle. Despite all of the talent, the defense simply didn't put very much pressure on quarterbacks last season, ranking 103rd in overall havoc rate and struggling with opposing run games, with the 110th rushing S&P+ defense. The new defensive line depth and talent should help, but the linebacking corps is still undecided and the secondary lacks significant depth. Even with all of the big name defensive signees, the biggest was former LSU defensive coordinator John Chavis. Chavis' units at LSU were known for their lockdown secondary play, strong and big defensive tackles, and bend-don't-break style of play that was extraordinarily consistent year-to-year. That is exactly what the Aggies need in order to take the next step in the SEC—but SEC West contention (and Playoff contention by extension) might still be a year away.

No. 26 Tennessee Volunteers (8-4, 4-4)

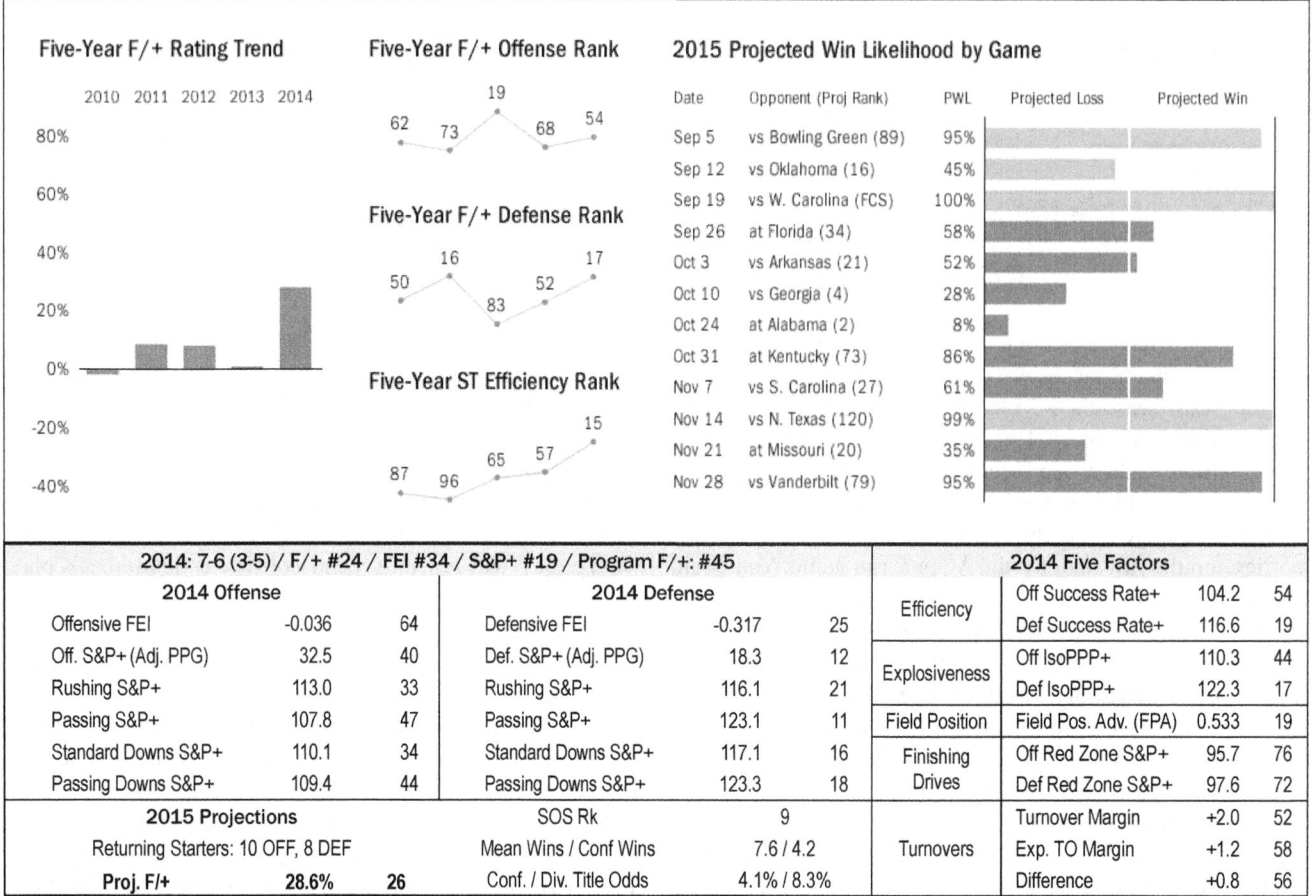

2014: 7-6 (3-5) / F/+ #24 / FEI #34 / S&P+ #19 / Program F/+: #45						2014 Five Factors			
2014 Offense			**2014 Defense**			Efficiency	Off Success Rate+	104.2	54
Offensive FEI	-0.036	64	Defensive FEI	-0.317	25		Def Success Rate+	116.6	19
Off. S&P+ (Adj. PPG)	32.5	40	Def. S&P+ (Adj. PPG)	18.3	12	Explosiveness	Off IsoPPP+	110.3	44
Rushing S&P+	113.0	33	Rushing S&P+	116.1	21		Def IsoPPP+	122.3	17
Passing S&P+	107.8	47	Passing S&P+	123.1	11	Field Position	Field Pos. Adv. (FPA)	0.533	19
Standard Downs S&P+	110.1	34	Standard Downs S&P+	117.1	16	Finishing	Off Red Zone S&P+	95.7	76
Passing Downs S&P+	109.4	44	Passing Downs S&P+	123.3	18	Drives	Def Red Zone S&P+	97.6	72
2015 Projections			SOS Rk	9			Turnover Margin	+2.0	52
Returning Starters: 10 OFF, 8 DEF			Mean Wins / Conf Wins	7.6 / 4.2		Turnovers	Exp. TO Margin	+1.2	58
Proj. F/+	**28.6%**	**26**	Conf. / Div. Title Odds	4.1% / 8.3%			Difference	+0.8	56

Along with USC, Tennessee has generated a substantial amount of preseason hype based on their recent recruiting. The Volunteers get the benefit of playing in an easier division than the Trojans' Pac-12 South, as the SEC East has its problems: Georgia is breaking in a new offensive coordinator, South Carolina has lost a great deal of its offense, and Florida is still without a quarterback and is now getting a new head coach. Butch Jones' Volunteers recruited the fourth, seventh, and 24th-best classes over the last three years according to the 247 Composite, and they seem to have found their long-term answer at quarterback in Josh Dobbs. They have young talent across the roster, from Dobbs to running back Jalen Hurd to Curt Maggitt and Derek Barnett on defense, and one of the most talented receiving corps in the country with Pig Howard, Josh Smith, Marquez North, Jason Croom, and Josh Malone. The offense was 47th in S&P+ and 64th in FEI, but with the last few recruiting classes cycling in, they should be much more explosive 2015, while the defense already played at a high level (24th) and didn't suffer many losses. In fact, Tennessee only loses a single lineman on offense and three defenders for one of the most up-and-coming teams in the country.

Butch Jones reinvigorated recruiting in Knoxville with his brand of hokey enthusiasm, and this might be the season it begins to pay dividends after last year's 7-6 record. Beating an overmatched Iowa team 45-28 in the postseason has car-

ried this momentum, but it was national signing day that gave Jones the biggest boost. Tennessee signed an impressive class that raised the overall talent level of the team, signed some immediate-impact players like Kahlil McKenzie and Preston Williams, and addressed a few depth concerns at offensive line. The offensive skill positions are all deep and talented. Hurd was one of the most highly recruited high school backs in his class, but he amassed a fairly pedestrian 899 rushing yards and 4.73 yards per carry average last season, but while he wasn't exactly explosive (3.91 highlight yards per carry), he was by far the best option and made the offensive line's numbers much better than they might have been otherwise. At 32nd in adjusted line yards and 52nd in opportunity rate (33.8 percent), the offensive line wasn't terrible, but Hurd's own opportunity rate was 38.9 percent. The line was much more of a liability in pass protection, ranking 118th in adjusted sack rate. That figure makes Dobbs' performance after he took over in the Alabama game even more impressive. But his insane group of receivers certainly makes his job easier. Howard became the reliable go-to guy (65.1 percent catch rate), but Jones has recruited extremely well at the position. Malone and North, two highly recruited receivers, have excellent athleticism and have already built a collection of highlight reel catches during their time in Knoxville, but they must improve their consistency above 50 percent catch rates. Overall, the priority remains the offensive line in pass protection, but the talent is certainly in place for the Volunteers to be one of the SEC's best offenses.

The defense gets somewhat of a head start compared to the offense, ranking 24th overall in S&P+ and playing a break-don't-bend (18th in success rate and 69th in IsoPPP) blend that applied decent pressure thanks to guys like Barnett and Maggitt. But the incoming front seven talent is likely to make an immediate mark. Shy Tuttle and McKenzie are two of the highest-rated defensive tackles in the country, while junior college transfer Justin Martin will help at defensive back. It's the secondary that likely needs the most help, as the mediocre IsoPPP score suggests. Sophomore defensive backs Evan Berry and Rashaan Gaulden could also be the answers for breakout stars in the secondary. Tennessee's schedule is front-loaded, with Oklahoma coming to visit in week two, then Florida, Arkansas, Georgia, and Alabama all in a row, so we'll likely know Tennessee's ceiling in the SEC East before October is over.

No. 27 South Carolina Gamecocks (7-5, 4-4)

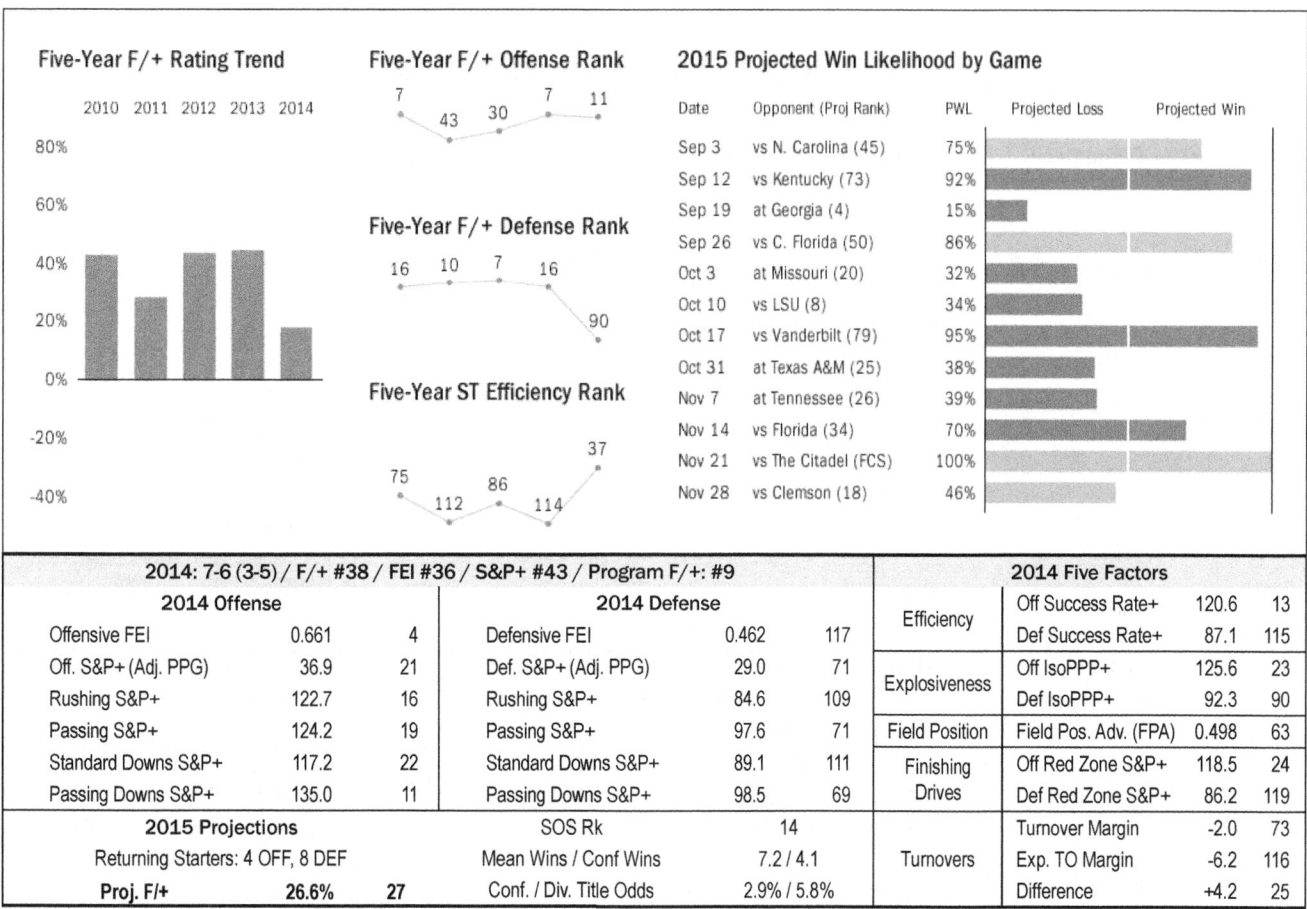

Five-Year F/+ Rating Trend

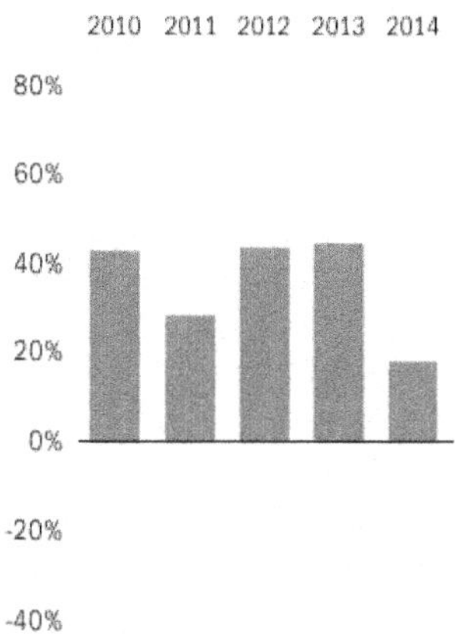

2010 2011 2012 2013 2014
80%
60%
40%
20%
0%
-20%
-40%

Five-Year F/+ Offense Rank

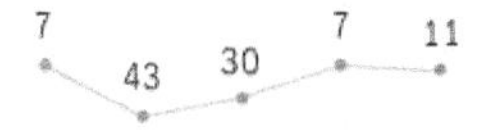

7
43
30
7
11

Five-Year F/+ Defense Rank

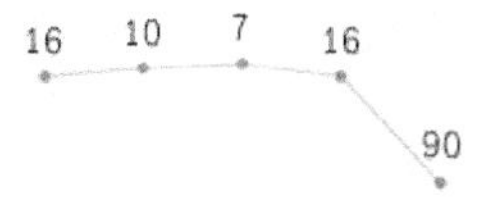

16
10
7
16
90

Five-Year ST Efficiency Rank

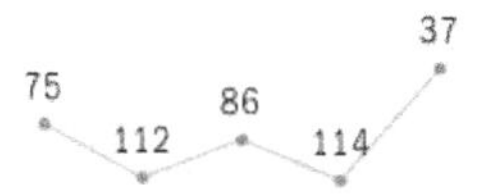

75
112
86
114
37

2015 Projected Win Likelihood by Game

Date	Opponent (Proj Rank)	PWL
Sep 3	vs N. Carolina (45)	75%
Sep 12	vs Kentucky (73)	92%
Sep 19	at Georgia (4)	15%
Sep 26	vs C. Florida (50)	86%
Oct 3	at Missouri (20)	32%
Oct 10	vs LSU (8)	34%
Oct 17	vs Vanderbilt (79)	95%
Oct 31	at Texas A&M (25)	38%
Nov 7	at Tennessee (26)	39%
Nov 14	vs Florida (34)	70%
Nov 21	vs The Citadel (FCS)	100%
Nov 28	vs Clemson (18)	46%

Projected Loss
Projected Win

2014: 7-6 (3-5) / F/+ #38 / FEI #36 / S&P+ #43 / Program F/+: #9						2014 Five Factors			
2014 Offense			2014 Defense						
Offensive FEI	0.661	4	Defensive FEI	0.462	117	Efficiency	Off Success Rate+	120.6	13
Off. S&P+ (Adj. PPG)	36.9	21	Def. S&P+ (Adj. PPG)	29.0	71	Efficiency	Def Success Rate+	87.1	115
Rushing S&P+	122.7	16	Rushing S&P+	84.6	109	Explosiveness	Off IsoPPP+	125.6	23
Passing S&P+	124.2	19	Passing S&P+	97.6	71	Explosiveness	Def IsoPPP+	92.3	90
Standard Downs S&P+	117.2	22	Standard Downs S&P+	89.1	111	Field Position	Field Pos. Adv. (FPA)	0.498	63
Passing Downs S&P+	135.0	11	Passing Downs S&P+	98.5	69	Finishing Drives	Off Red Zone S&P+	118.5	24
						Finishing Drives	Def Red Zone S&P+	86.2	119
2015 Projections			SOS Rk	14		Turnovers	Turnover Margin	-2.0	73
Returning Starters: 4 OFF, 8 DEF			Mean Wins / Conf Wins	7.2 / 4.1		Turnovers	Exp. TO Margin	-6.2	116
Proj. F/+	**26.6%**	**27**	Conf. / Div. Title Odds	2.9% / 5.8%		Turnovers	Difference	+4.2	25

After South Carolina went 7-6 last season following sky-high preseason expectations, most of the offseason conversation about the Gamecocks has them trending down and, potentially, Steve Spurrier's time as Old Ball Coach coming to an end in the next season or two. The defense certainly fell off from 2013 to 2014 (from 22nd in defensive S&P+ to 89th) because of heavy losses in the front seven (Kelcy Quarles and Jadeveon Clowney, notably), but is it premature for us to write off the Old Ball Coach and his Gamecocks from the SEC East race? After all, four of their six losses last season were by a touchdown or less, and they still beat Georgia and Miami.

The bad news is that last season's 23rd-ranked S&P+ offense loses seven starters, including several linemen, quarterback Dylan Thompson (who led the 17th-ranked passing S&P+ attack), and bruising running back Mike Davis. The good news, on the other hand, is that junior receiver Pharoh Cooper was reliable, explosive, versatile, and even underutilized. Not only did he catch 69 percent of his targets, but he led the team in yards per catch (16.5), averaged 7.41 yards per carry rushing, and was only targeted on slightly more than a fifth of the team's passes. Cooper will be joined by explosive redshirt freshman Deebo Samuel and Terry Googer in the passing game. Brandon Wilds will take over for Mike Davis at running back (Wilds actually had better explosiveness at 4.85 highlight yards per carry and better efficiency at 45.3 percent than Davis last season), but he'll have highly recruited back David Williams behind him as well. Quarterback Connor Mitch hasn't shown much in his time at South Carolina, completing two passes in six attempts, but his good spring suggests there might not be much of a dropoff from Thompson. It's fair to expect the offense to take a step back from last season's efficient but not explosive (61st in IsoPPP) group, but given Spurrier's ability to adapt his offense to his players, the dropoff won't be much.

In contrast with the offensive turnover, the defense returns all but three starters, though Gamecocks fans likely wish it were the other way around. Last season's unit was 117th in FEI and 89th in S&P+, generated little to no quarterback pressure (dead last in defensive back havoc and 122nd in overall havoc rate, with the team sack leader only recording two sacks) and had one of the worst per-play success rates in the country (118th). The Gamecocks were fairly bend-don't-break (118th in success

rate compared to 68th in IsoPPP), at least after the season opener against Texas A&M, where the confused secondary briefly turned Kenny Hill in to a superstar. But with another year of experience and little turnover, it's fair to be excited about the prospects for players like Kelsey Griffin, Skai Moore, Marquavius Lewis, and T.J. Gurley. There is plenty of talent on the roster, and with Spurrier's old colleague Jon Hoke joining Lorenzo Ward as co-defensive coordinator, it's reasonable to expect improvement from the defense. With the offensive personnel turnover and the state of the defense last season, it's tough to expect South Carolina to challenge for the SEC crown this season, but don't write them off if Mitch gets into a groove.

No. 28 Kansas State Wildcats (9-3, 6-3)

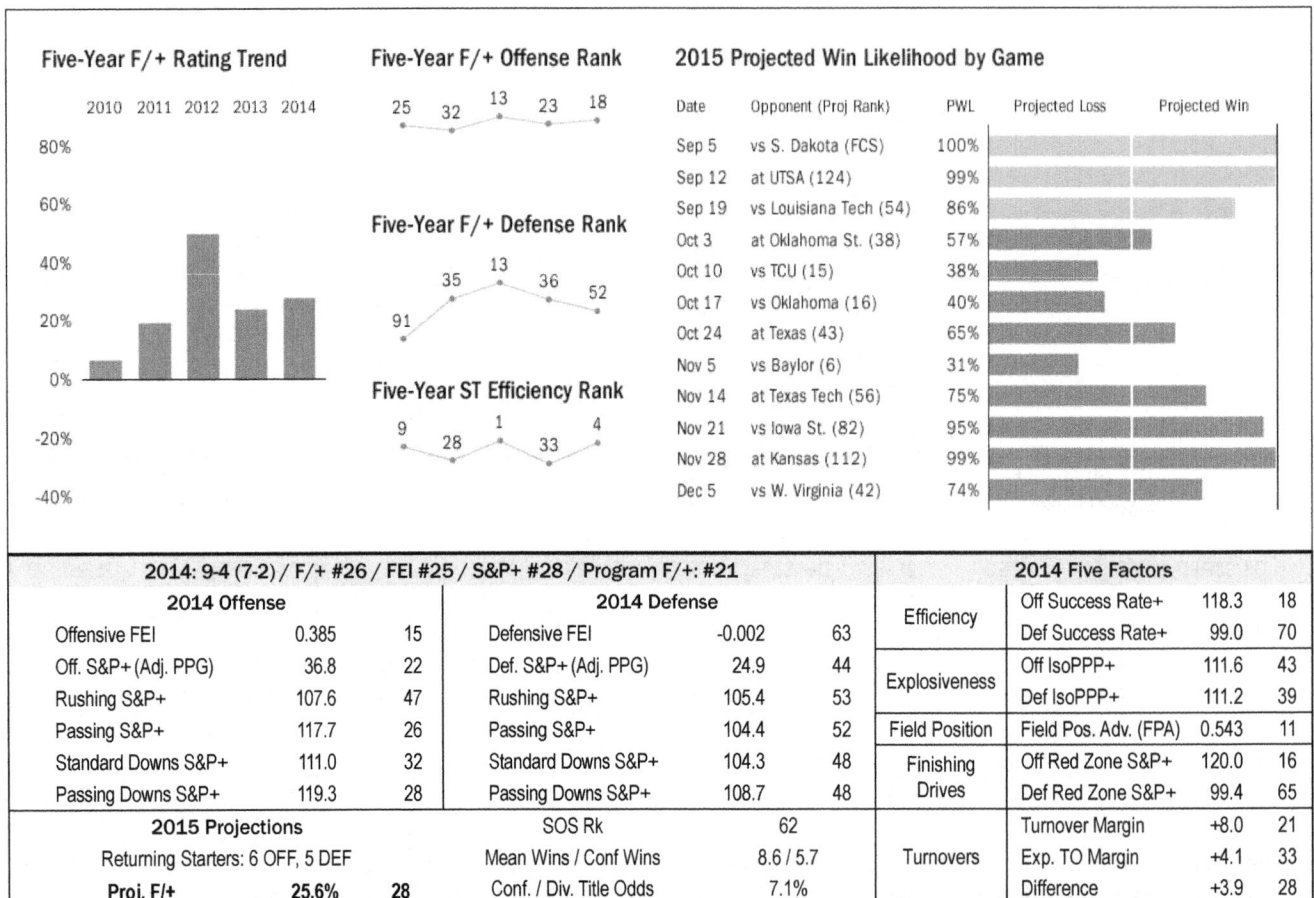

Five-Year F/+ Rating Trend

2010 2011 2012 2013 2014

Five-Year F/+ Offense Rank

25 32 13 23 18

Five-Year F/+ Defense Rank

91 35 13 36 52

Five-Year ST Efficiency Rank

9 28 1 33 4

2015 Projected Win Likelihood by Game

Date	Opponent (Proj Rank)	PWL	Projected Loss	Projected Win
Sep 5	vs S. Dakota (FCS)	100%		
Sep 12	at UTSA (124)	99%		
Sep 19	vs Louisiana Tech (54)	86%		
Oct 3	at Oklahoma St. (38)	57%		
Oct 10	vs TCU (15)	38%		
Oct 17	vs Oklahoma (16)	40%		
Oct 24	at Texas (43)	65%		
Nov 5	vs Baylor (6)	31%		
Nov 14	at Texas Tech (56)	75%		
Nov 21	vs Iowa St. (82)	95%		
Nov 28	at Kansas (112)	99%		
Dec 5	vs W. Virginia (42)	74%		

2014: 9-4 (7-2) / F/+ #26 / FEI #25 / S&P+ #28 / Program F/+: #21

2014 Offense			2014 Defense		
Offensive FEI	0.385	15	Defensive FEI	-0.002	63
Off. S&P+ (Adj. PPG)	36.8	22	Def. S&P+ (Adj. PPG)	24.9	44
Rushing S&P+	107.6	47	Rushing S&P+	105.4	53
Passing S&P+	117.7	26	Passing S&P+	104.4	52
Standard Downs S&P+	111.0	32	Standard Downs S&P+	104.3	48
Passing Downs S&P+	119.3	28	Passing Downs S&P+	108.7	48

2015 Projections			SOS Rk	62
Returning Starters: 6 OFF, 5 DEF			Mean Wins / Conf Wins	8.6 / 5.7
Proj. F/+	25.6%	28	Conf. / Div. Title Odds	7.1%

2014 Five Factors

Efficiency	Off Success Rate+	118.3	18
	Def Success Rate+	99.0	70
Explosiveness	Off IsoPPP+	111.6	43
	Def IsoPPP+	111.2	39
Field Position	Field Pos. Adv. (FPA)	0.543	11
Finishing Drives	Off Red Zone S&P+	120.0	16
	Def Red Zone S&P+	99.4	65
Turnovers	Turnover Margin	+8.0	21
	Exp. TO Margin	+4.1	33
	Difference	+3.9	28

Bill Snyder is a noted wizard, seemingly extracting all possible talent from a variety of under-recruited high school players and juco transfers alike. He'll have his work cut out for him in 2015, in large part because of the production he must replace at quarterback and wide receiver. Former juco transfer and surprisingly efficient and mobile Jake Waters has graduated, as have top two receivers Tyler Lockett and Curry Sexton. Lockett and Sexton were reliable (both had catch rates above 70 percent) and together combined for more than 54 percent of Waters' overall targets.

The number one priority for the Wildcats will be reinventing the passing game for 2015: finding a quarterback out of

former backup Joe Hubener, Jesse Ertz, Alex Delton, and post-spring practice transfer Jonathan Banks and identifying which receivers are reliable and explosive enough to fill the gap left by Lockett and Sexton. Last season's 1,000-yard receiving duo led the 25th overall passing S&P+ offense, which was efficient (24th in success rate) without being overly explosive (62nd). The leading returning receiver, senior Kody Cook, had just 20 receptions last season. There are young receivers on the roster, and a wide variety of running backs who have a reception or two to their names, but it is an understatement to say that this year's passing attack won't resemble that of the previous two seasons. None of the three quarterbacks on campus for spring ball impressed enough to seize the job outright, and Banks was brought in as a possible surprise dual-threat talent, but they're grouped closely together. Hubener probably has a slight advantage, considering he is the only one with game experience (53 percent completion percentage, an interception, and 235 yards on 17 attempts), but it's anyone's guess until fall camp. Banks certainly has the athletic ability, but the question is whether he can pick up the playbook and develop a rapport with the receivers in a small amount of time.

The defense was decidedly bend-don't-break, conceding steady progress to offenses (102nd in success rate) as long as it contained explosive plays (22nd). The secondary was to thank for much of that containment and playmaking ability, as they ranked 15th in havoc rate to the front seven's 96th and 73rd in adjusted sack rate. The front seven's ability to generate pressure should improve with the move of Elijah Lee to linebacker, where he was a disruptive force in the spring. Defensive backs Danzel McDaniel and Dante Barnett round out the other names to keep tabs on for the defense. Snyder is without a doubt facing his most daunting rebuilding project in years, but he consistently outperforms expectations based on the talent he's recruited and the schedule he's given. With a brutal four-game midyear stretch of TCU, Oklahoma, Texas, and Baylor, the Wildcats' ceiling should be identified by early November.

No. 29 Mississippi State Bulldogs (7-5, 3-5)

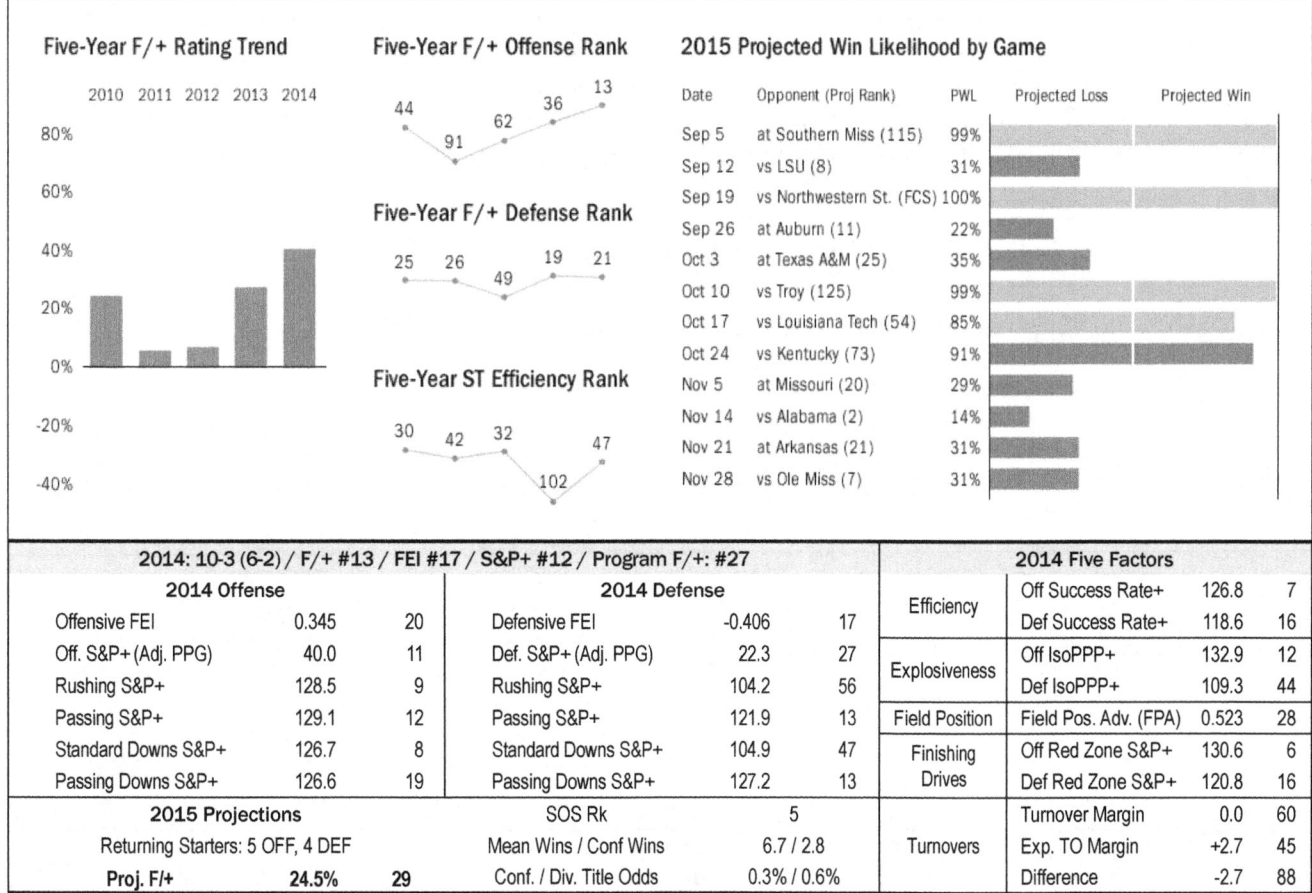

Few teams lost more 2014 starters than Mississippi State. All but four members of last season's 16th-ranked defense are new starters, while the offense must replace six members, including three offensive linemen from last year's 12th-ranked adjusted line yards unit. Heisman candidate quarterback Dak Prescott returns, as do his top two receivers, but it's unclear whether he can carry the team after the loss of so many experienced players. Mississippi State has never recruited at a high level relative to their SEC West peers (they're still great relative to the rest of the country, averaging 26th over the past three years in the 247 Composite, but they averaged 10th in the conference over that same span), so last season's success

relied heavily on a seasoned group of players. But does that mean we've already seen the Bulldogs' ceiling in the SEC West, or can they follow up with a repeat performance in 2015?

Despite the losses, the Bulldogs' replacements were actually much more heavily recruited than the players they are replacing. That's the case at running back, where Josh Robinson was a three-star recruit and the 59th overall running back, but his likely replacement, Ashton Shumpert, was a four-star recruit and the 19th-ranked running back in his class (and Aeris Williams was another four-star recruit and 16th in his class). On defense, meanwhile, the Bulldogs often frequently rotated starters in and out, giving underclassmen plenty of game experience. It's difficult to project a team with so many starting personnel gone, but that doesn't mean that the relative lack of experience is either a downgrade in talent or a death sentence for the team's hopes.

The Bulldogs' defense excelled against the pass relative to the run (42nd in rushing S&P+ and 15th in passing S&P+), and four of the team's top five in interceptions return. The Bulldogs were excellent on passing downs (eleventh) because of their havoc rate (17th overall), and though four of the top five team leaders in sacks are gone, the next four will all be juniors (and this group combined for nine sacks—the four players who won't return combined for 19). The point is that it's not all doom and gloom for the defense due to how deep last season's defense was. If those new starters on the defensive line can continue to generate as much pressure per play as they did in limited time last season, then don't expect much of a regression.

The Bulldogs' offense, meanwhile, was led by Prescott and the efficient and explosive (though his explosiveness was underrated at 6.28 highlight yards per opportunity) Robinson.

The Bulldogs were 10th and 13th in rushing and passing S&P+, respectively, and were far more efficient (sixth in success rate) than explosive (43rd). The offense shouldn't change much in 2015, as long as the offensive line can gel in time for their second game of the season against LSU. The top two receiving targets return, and there were numerous sophomore and freshmen contributors last season, as Prescott spread the ball around. In fact, leading receiver De'Runnya Wilson only accounted for 19.4 percent of Prescott's targets, despite averaging 14.5 yards per catch. As mentioned above, the two backs who replace Robinson are both more talented on paper than he was, and both impressed in limited opportunities in 2014 (Shumpert averaged 5.8 yards per carry). But the run game is likely to be aided even further by second-leading rusher Prescott, who averaged 4.7 yards per carry and had the second-most carries by a quarterback in the country. All in all, while it's true that Mississippi State lost a ton of experience last season and doesn't recruit at the same level as its SEC West peers, the Bulldogs might have the highest overall talent level the school has ever had this season, and they have much more talent than their reputation suggests.

No. 30 Nebraska Cornhuskers (9-3, 6-2)

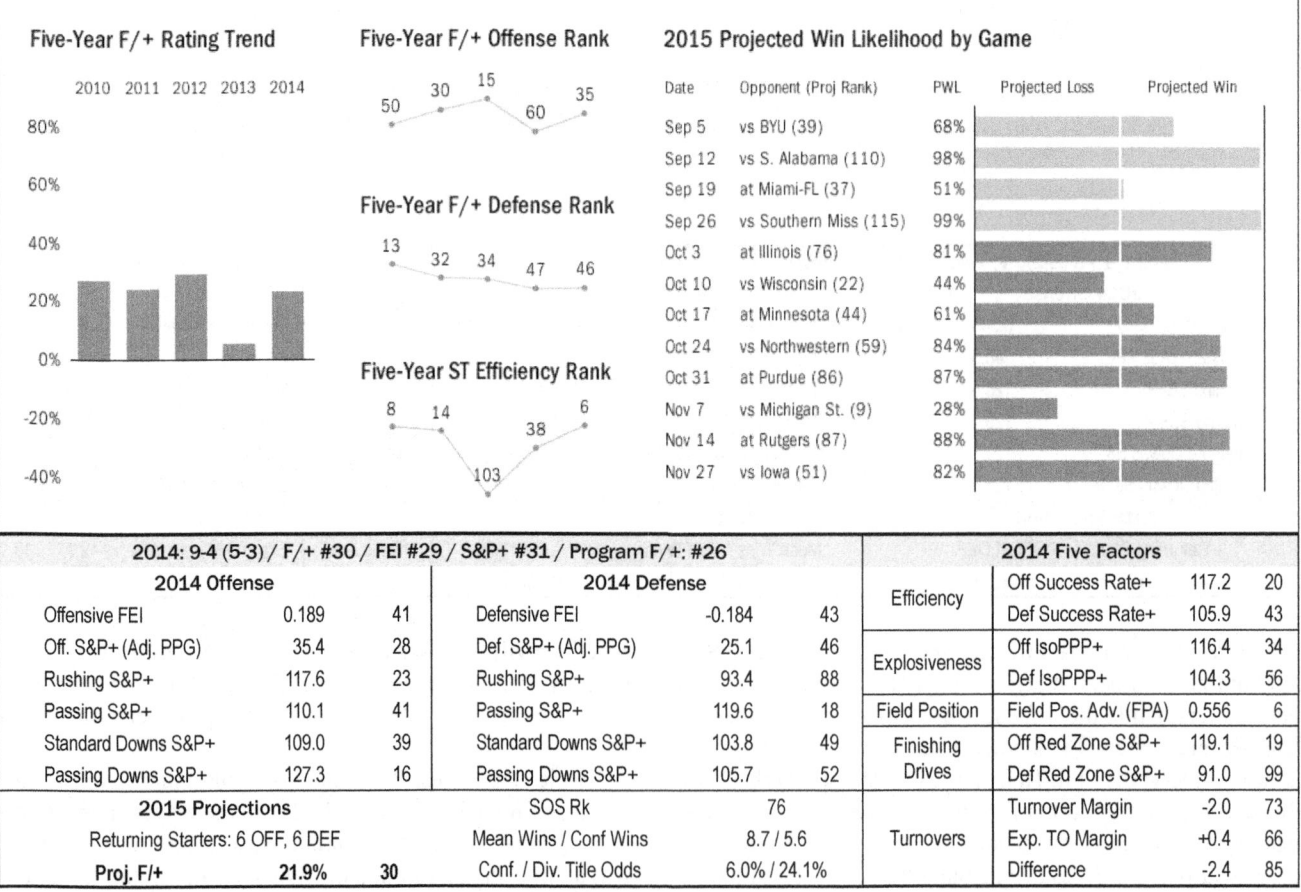

2014: 9-4 (5-3) / F/+ #30 / FEI #29 / S&P+ #31 / Program F/+: #26							2014 Five Factors		
2014 Offense			**2014 Defense**			Efficiency	Off Success Rate+	117.2	20
Offensive FEI	0.189	41	Defensive FEI	-0.184	43		Def Success Rate+	105.9	43
Off. S&P+ (Adj. PPG)	35.4	28	Def. S&P+ (Adj. PPG)	25.1	46	Explosiveness	Off IsoPPP+	116.4	34
Rushing S&P+	117.6	23	Rushing S&P+	93.4	88		Def IsoPPP+	104.3	56
Passing S&P+	110.1	41	Passing S&P+	119.6	18	Field Position	Field Pos. Adv. (FPA)	0.556	6
Standard Downs S&P+	109.0	39	Standard Downs S&P+	103.8	49	Finishing Drives	Off Red Zone S&P+	119.1	19
Passing Downs S&P+	127.3	16	Passing Downs S&P+	105.7	52		Def Red Zone S&P+	91.0	99
2015 Projections			SOS Rk	76		Turnovers	Turnover Margin	-2.0	73
Returning Starters: 6 OFF, 6 DEF			Mean Wins / Conf Wins	8.7 / 5.6			Exp. TO Margin	+0.4	66
Proj. F/+	**21.9%**	**30**	Conf. / Div. Title Odds	6.0% / 24.1%			Difference	-2.4	85

Following the 2014 season, Nebraska made one of the least surprising fires in getting rid of Bo Pelini and one of the most surprising hires in bringing in Mike Riley. The 2014 Corn-

huskers were a good team, but not a great team. And that was the problem for Pelini—he won a consistent eight or nine games a year, but fell short against elite teams and failed to elevate the Huskers to top-10 status. It's unclear whether Riley is the answer (he has a career winning rate of 54 percent, but is on the positive side of coaching impact using second-order wins), but it's unquestionable that Riley is a refreshingly nice guy for the job.

Nebraska had multiple identities in its wins and losses last season, but looked the part of a top-20 program overall. Led by running back Ameer Abdullah (who had the fifth-highest combination of explosiveness and efficiency in the country, looking at opportunity rate and highlight yards per opportunity), the Huskers had an explosive and efficient offense that excelled in finishing drives and winning the field-position battle, paired with a poor rush defense that excelled against the pass. That rush defense allowed Wisconsin's Melvin Gordon to break the single-game rushing record with 408 rushing yards. Riley's priorities this summer and fall are clear: find two new offensive stars to replace Abdullah and wide receiver Kenny Bell, improve an offensive line that gave up far too many sacks (91st in standard downs sack rate), and most importantly, tighten up the run defense.

Priority number one for Riley will be attempting to fix the run defense that put Gordon in the record books, ranked 93rd in opponent-adjusted points per play, and contributed to the 99th-ranked red zone S&P+ defense. Most of the defensive line returns, outside of edge rusher Randy Gregory, but there's turnover at two starting linebacker spots. The linebacker unit as a whole is talented, but fairly thin, with only six players who were rated by recruiting services in high school. Any injuries to the linebacker corps could be devastating. There is a glut of defensive linemen, but again, the line was poor against the run even with Gregory, and every other starter returns, so improvement might have to come from the seven freshmen defensive linemen on the roster or from development by the new coaching staff.

On the other side of the ball, the middle of the line is going to be all new. The line had a very poor standard down sack rate, but dual-threat quarterbacks like Tommy Armstrong Jr. tend to take far more sacks than their pro-style peers, and the difference between standard and passing down sack rates seems to support that theory. Of last year's two dynamic playmakers in Abdullah and Bell, Bell should be the easier player to replace, as Jordan Westerkamp was almost Bell's equal in terms of target rate and total yards, and was far more dependable (65.7 percent catch rate). De'Mornay Pierson-El, Alonzo Moore, and freshman Stanley Morgan all are promising as well. The bigger question will be replacing Abdullah's home run ability. He averaged an excellent 6.7 highlight yards per opportunity last season as the offensive line excelled in run blocking, ranking 11th in adjusted line yards. The line excelled at creating opportunities, while Abdullah excelled at maximizing those opportunities for explosive plays. The other backs on the roster haven't shown the same ability to generate explosive runs, but there are three relatively unproven former four-star backs waiting in the wings in Terrell Newby, Adam Taylor, and Mikale Wilbon. Riley's offenses typically require a high-efficiency horizontal passer, so the running backs and slot receivers will likely be tasked with upping their receiving contributions as well.

No. 31 Utah Utes (7-5, 5-4)

Five-Year F/+ Rating Trend

Five-Year F/+ Offense Rank
54, 108, 95, 37, 57

Five-Year F/+ Defense Rank
30, 17, 50, 24, 19

Five-Year ST Efficiency Rank
21, 25, 27, 39, 5

2015 Projected Win Likelihood by Game

Date	Opponent (Proj Rank)	PWL	Projected Loss	Projected Win
Sep 3	vs Michigan (35)	63%		
Sep 11	vs Utah St. (46)	77%		
Sep 19	at Fresno St. (93)	90%		
Sep 26	at Oregon (3)	9%		
Oct 10	vs California (62)	85%		
Oct 17	vs Arizona St. (19)	39%		
Oct 24	at USC (12)	20%		
Oct 31	vs Oregon St. (70)	89%		
Nov 7	at Washington (52)	69%		
Nov 14	at Arizona (32)	43%		
Nov 21	vs UCLA (5)	25%		
Nov 28	vs Colorado (85)	94%		

2014: 9-4 (5-4) / F/+ #29 / FEI #16 / S&P+ #41 / Program F/+: #41							2014 Five Factors			
2014 Offense			**2014 Defense**			Efficiency	Off Success Rate+	97.8	76
Offensive FEI	-0.056	69	Defensive FEI	-0.519	12		Def Success Rate+	108.8	36
Off. S&P+ (Adj. PPG)	30.7	54	Def. S&P+ (Adj. PPG)	22.7	30	Explosiveness	Off IsoPPP+	96.5	76
Rushing S&P+	98.0	79	Rushing S&P+	105.7	51		Def IsoPPP+	121.1	21
Passing S&P+	98.5	66	Passing S&P+	120.8	14	Field Position	Field Pos. Adv. (FPA)	0.541	12
Standard Downs S&P+	97.1	74	Standard Downs S&P+	116.0	20	Finishing Drives	Off Red Zone S&P+	103.2	57
Passing Downs S&P+	98.9	73	Passing Downs S&P+	111.3	41		Def Red Zone S&P+	122.9	9
2015 Projections			SOS Rk		16	Turnovers	Turnover Margin	+5.0	37
Returning Starters: 6 OFF, 7 DEF			Mean Wins / Conf Wins		7.0 / 4.7		Exp. TO Margin	+4.5	29
Proj. F/+	**21.8%**	**31**	Conf. / Div. Title Odds		1.5% / 3.0%		Difference	+0.5	63

The Utes return a great deal of last year's 9-4 team, including much of the stout pass defense, quarterback Travis Wilson, and workhorse running back Devontae Booker. The Utes made headlines for their upset wins over Michigan, UCLA, USC, and Stanford—all teams that the majority of the college football world thought would handle the Utes with ease. Two of Utah's losses, meanwhile (Washington State and Arizona State), were by a field goal or less. Their only blowout losses were to two teams that had strong spread-to-run offenses—Oregon and Arizona. The Utes achieved their remarkable string of upsets through a strong pass defense, an extremely disruptive front seven, and a battering ram running back in Booker. With the general team profile returning again in 2015, can the Utes solidify their pecking order in the Pac-12 and turn upsets into expected wins?

The Utes' offense was extremely reliant on Booker for their 66th overall S&P+ ranking because of the relative lack of a passing game. Only seven running backs received more touches than Booker last season. He was a standard bearer for durability despite a much smaller frame than other backs with a similar number of carries, like Pittsburgh's James Conner and Oklahoma's Samaje Perine. While Booker amassed 1,512 yards, it wasn't the most efficient performance, as he only had a 36.6 percent opportunity rate. The offensive line's adjusted line yards ranking (42nd) was solid if unspectacular, but it was clear that Booker's efficiency took a hit once defenses began to load the box, daring Wilson to beat them over the top. This was a largely successful strategy, as the offense was far from explosive (92nd in IsoPPP) and Utah was one of the most run-heavy teams in the country (21st in passing downs run percentage). Booker gets some help in juco transfer Joseph Williams, who is built similarly and can share some of the load. The question for the offense will be whether the offensive line can protect Wilson (94th in adjusted sack rate) and whether the lack of receiver depth will hurt an already inefficient passing game.

Departed senior Nate Orchard and the Utes' attacking defense were most responsible for the Utes successful 2014. Orchard was second in the country in sacks (18.5) and fifth in tackles for loss (21) as the front seven surged to the third overall adjusted sack rate and the 15th havoc rate. This made the secondary's job much easier, as they constantly harassed opposing passing quarterbacks (11th in passing S&P+) and shut down opposing pro-style offenses like Michigan, Stanford, and USC. Orchard is gone, but the proven depth behind him in players like Hunter Dimick (10 sacks and 14.5 tackles for loss) and Jason Fanaika (five sacks) mean that the defense isn't likely to see much of a drop-off. However, as impressive as the pass rush was, the run game suffered against spread-to-run offenses, allowing Oregon to rush for 269 yards and Arizona to hit 298 (6.34 yards per carry). With a similar schedule to last year, look for the Utes to continue to punch above their weight in 2015.

No. 32 Arizona Wildcats (8-4, 5-4)

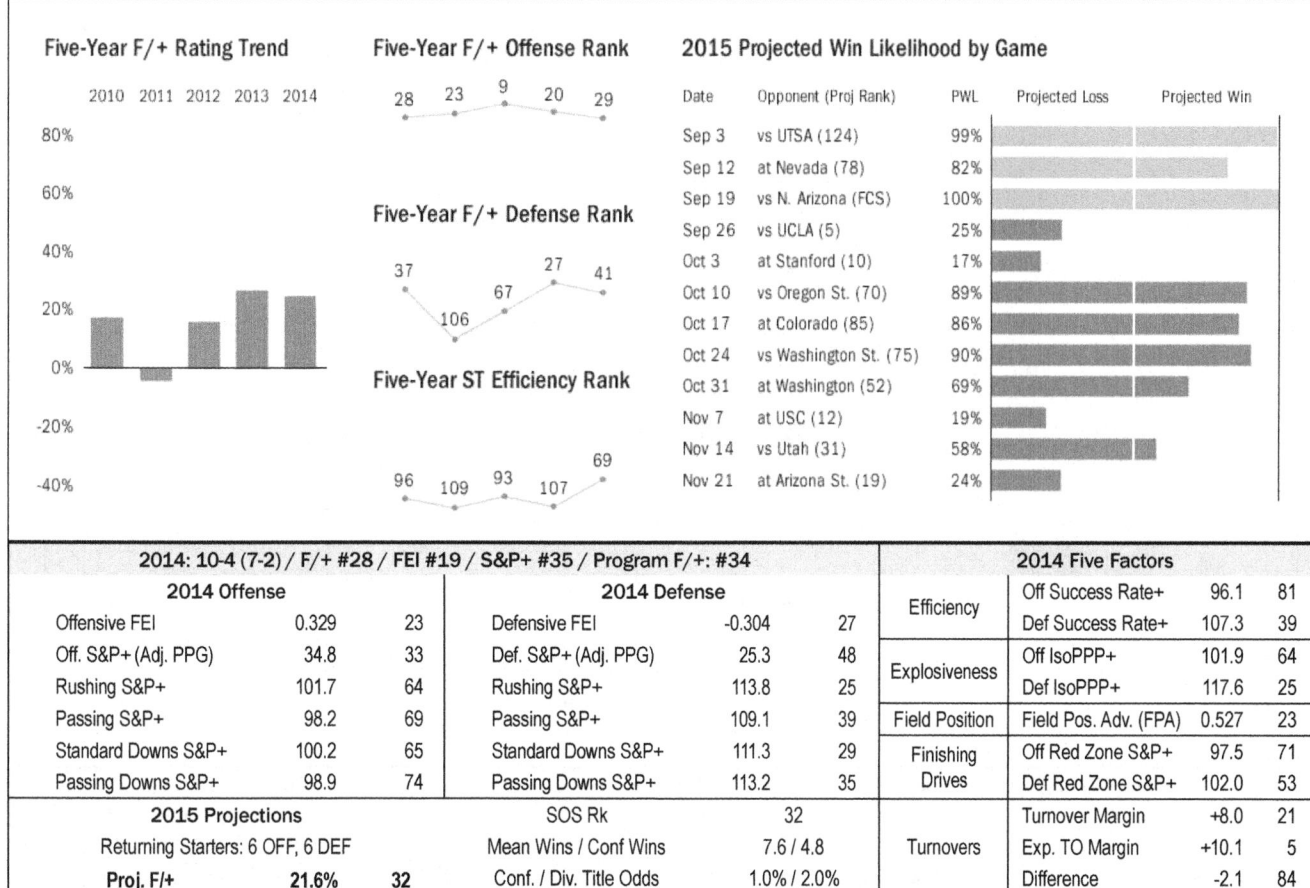

Five-Year F/+ Rating Trend

Five-Year F/+ Offense Rank

Five-Year F/+ Defense Rank

Five-Year ST Efficiency Rank

2015 Projected Win Likelihood by Game

Date	Opponent (Proj Rank)	PWL	Projected Loss	Projected Win
Sep 3	vs UTSA (124)	99%		
Sep 12	at Nevada (78)	82%		
Sep 19	vs N. Arizona (FCS)	100%		
Sep 26	vs UCLA (5)	25%		
Oct 3	at Stanford (10)	17%		
Oct 10	vs Oregon St. (70)	89%		
Oct 17	at Colorado (85)	86%		
Oct 24	vs Washington St. (75)	90%		
Oct 31	at Washington (52)	69%		
Nov 7	at USC (12)	19%		
Nov 14	vs Utah (31)	58%		
Nov 21	at Arizona St. (19)	24%		

2014: 10-4 (7-2) / F/+ #28 / FEI #19 / S&P+ #35 / Program F/+: #34

2014 Offense			2014 Defense		
Offensive FEI	0.329	23	Defensive FEI	-0.304	27
Off. S&P+ (Adj. PPG)	34.8	33	Def. S&P+ (Adj. PPG)	25.3	48
Rushing S&P+	101.7	64	Rushing S&P+	113.8	25
Passing S&P+	98.2	69	Passing S&P+	109.1	39
Standard Downs S&P+	100.2	65	Standard Downs S&P+	111.3	29
Passing Downs S&P+	98.9	74	Passing Downs S&P+	113.2	35

2015 Projections				
Returning Starters: 6 OFF, 6 DEF		SOS Rk	32	
		Mean Wins / Conf Wins	7.6 / 4.8	
Proj. F/+	21.6%	32	Conf. / Div. Title Odds	1.0% / 2.0%

2014 Five Factors

Efficiency	Off Success Rate+	96.1	81
	Def Success Rate+	107.3	39
Explosiveness	Off IsoPPP+	101.9	64
	Def IsoPPP+	117.6	25
Field Position	Field Pos. Adv. (FPA)	0.527	23
Finishing Drives	Off Red Zone S&P+	97.5	71
	Def Red Zone S&P+	102.0	53
Turnovers	Turnover Margin	+8.0	21
	Exp. TO Margin	+10.1	5
	Difference	-2.1	84

Rich Rodriguez has kept a relatively low profile since his move to Arizona in 2012, consistently delivering a solid on-field product while avoiding off-field issues and news—and any preseason hype that might coincide with increased coverage. The Wildcats finished 28th in the 2014 F/+ rankings, after ending 25th in 2013 and 38th in 2012. Last season, the Wildcats were picked for fourth in the Pac-12 South preseason polls, only to accept a Fiesta Bowl bid with a 10-4 record (which included wins over Oregon, Utah, and Arizona State). And all of this was with two freshmen leading the offensive attack in quarterback Anu Solomon and running back Nick Wilson. Of course, one of the top defensive players in college football, Scooby Wright III, provided a boost to the Wildcats' defense, and he returns for another season. The Wildcats did have a lot of turnover, particularly on defense, but this remains a dangerous team that should contest Arizona State, UCLA, and USC for the Pac-12 South title once again.

The Wildcats' offense managed to put up big numbers (Solomon passed for 3,793 yards, freshman running back Wilson totaled 1,375 on the ground, and the offense was 26th overall in average yards per game) without being terribly efficient or explosive. Arizona was only 79th in success rate, and its passing game was based mostly on quantity over quality, especially for a Rich Rodriguez offense that is usually based primarily on the ground game (passing on 45 percent of standard downs while ranking 71st in passing S&P+). Wilson shouldered a

huge load for a freshman (236 carries), but with low efficiency (31.4 percent opportunity rate), even though he made the most of his blocking for explosive plays (8.33 highlight yards per opportunity). What the Wildcats did exceptionally well was pick up value drives. The Wildcats were 23rd in offensive FEI and gained at least one first down on nearly 75 percent of their possessions. Arizona moved the ball well, even if it was from running a lot of plays very quickly (they were second in overall adjusted pace), rather than with high per-play efficiency. While the offensive line was only average (56th in adjusted line yards and 83rd in adjusted sack rate), the Wildcats managed to be decently consistent and return the bulk of their offensive production from last season. Most of their receiving corps, for instance, were sophomores last season, including the top two threats Cayleb Jones and Samajie Grant. The skill players are now uniformly experienced and explosive, so continued offensive development will hinge on the offensive line's performance.

The defense is and should be centered on Wright's explosive playmaking ability. One of the lasting images of the Wildcats' 2014 season was Wright's sack, strip, and recovery of Marcus Mariota in their first meeting to preserve the 31-24 win in the fourth quarter. Wright was third in the country in sacks (14), first in tackles for loss (29), and first in forced fumbles (six). Obviously it's dangerous to concentrate so much of the defense's production in the hands of a single player, but

Wright has unique playmaking ability. The defense was one of Rodriguez's best, at 23rd against the run and 32nd against the pass, featuring solid bend-don't-break principles (44th in IsoPPP to 69th in success rate). The Wildcats will be replacing several members of the defensive line and four of the top five

contributors at defensive back, however, so even more pressure will be on the front seven to generate havoc and contain the explosive offenses on the Wildcats' schedule. Moving Da-Vonte' Neal from wide receiver to cornerback, where he has a higher ceiling, should help elevate the play of the secondary.

No. 33 Louisville Cardinals (8-4, 5-3)

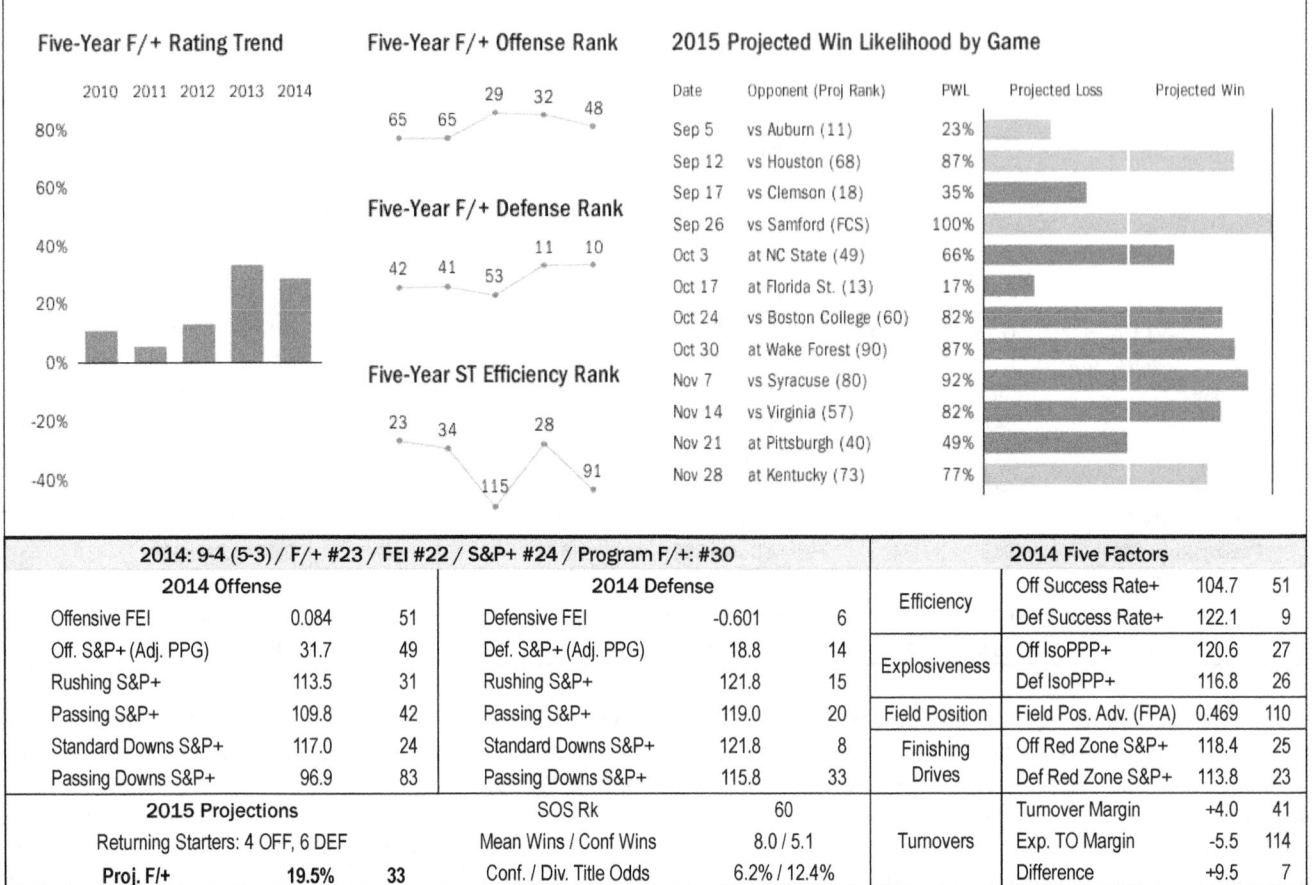

2015 Projected Win Likelihood by Game

Date	Opponent (Proj Rank)	PWL
Sep 5	vs Auburn (11)	23%
Sep 12	vs Houston (68)	87%
Sep 17	vs Clemson (18)	35%
Sep 26	vs Samford (FCS)	100%
Oct 3	at NC State (49)	66%
Oct 17	at Florida St. (13)	17%
Oct 24	vs Boston College (60)	82%
Oct 30	at Wake Forest (90)	87%
Nov 7	vs Syracuse (80)	92%
Nov 14	vs Virginia (57)	82%
Nov 21	at Pittsburgh (40)	49%
Nov 28	at Kentucky (73)	77%

2014: 9-4 (5-3) / F/+ #23 / FEI #22 / S&P+ #24 / Program F/+: #30

2014 Offense			2014 Defense		
Offensive FEI	0.084	51	Defensive FEI	-0.601	6
Off. S&P+ (Adj. PPG)	31.7	49	Def. S&P+ (Adj. PPG)	18.8	14
Rushing S&P+	113.5	31	Rushing S&P+	121.8	15
Passing S&P+	109.8	42	Passing S&P+	119.0	20
Standard Downs S&P+	117.0	24	Standard Downs S&P+	121.8	8
Passing Downs S&P+	96.9	83	Passing Downs S&P+	115.8	33

2015 Projections		
Returning Starters: 4 OFF, 6 DEF		
Proj. F/+	19.5%	33

	SOS Rk	60
Mean Wins / Conf Wins	8.0 / 5.1	
Conf. / Div. Title Odds	6.2% / 12.4%	

2014 Five Factors

Efficiency	Off Success Rate+	104.7	51
	Def Success Rate+	122.1	9
Explosiveness	Off IsoPPP+	120.6	27
	Def IsoPPP+	116.8	26
Field Position	Field Pos. Adv. (FPA)	0.469	110
Finishing Drives	Off Red Zone S&P+	118.4	25
	Def Red Zone S&P+	113.8	23
Turnovers	Turnover Margin	+4.0	41
	Exp. TO Margin	-5.5	114
	Difference	+9.5	7

Louisville's 2014 season went about as well as you might have hoped (or not hoped, depending on your opinion of Bobby Petrino): the Cardinals generally won the games they would have been expected to win, save the early Virginia upset, and lost to the best teams on their schedule in Clemson, Florida State, and Georgia. For most of the season, defensive coordinator Todd Grantham's unit was the most efficient in the country, before it finished 14th overall in S&P+ and second in success rate (defending explosive plays is another story). Even more impressive than that efficient defense was the fact that three young quarterbacks—one sophomore and two freshmen—played significant minutes for the Cardinals due to injury and the offense still ranked 32nd in S&P+, with the 38th-ranked passing offense. Bobby Petrino's reputation as a quarterback developer appears to be well-founded, as none of the three quarterbacks were high school blue-chippers, but all performed fairly well given their limited experience (Will Gardner had thrown 12 passes in relief of Teddy Bridgewater in 2013). For 2015, the challenge won't be at quarterback,

where all three experienced players return, nor will it likely be in the defensive front seven, where Grantham returns almost everyone. Instead, it will be in three position groups that will replace nearly everyone: the green receiving corps, an offensive line that only returns a single starter, and a totally new-look secondary.

The more things change for Grantham, the more they stay the same. Despite a seemingly inexplicable (at the time) move from Georgia to Louisville last season, Grantham's defense retained its attacking character (20th in adjusted sack rate and 12th on passing downs) and characteristically ball-hawking secondary, but it also was one of the most extreme examples of a break-don't-bend defense. At ninth in success rate+ and 15th and 20th against the run and the pass, respectively, the Louisville defense was amazingly efficient, but it had issues allowing big plays (107th in IsoPPP, but much better at 26th in opponent-adjusted IsoPPP+). Aggression and risk generally were rewarded for the Cardinals. But now the entire secondary is gone, including safety Gerod Holliman and his fourteen interceptions. Likely new starters include Shaq Wiggins and Josh Harvey-Clemons, both former Georgia players seeking a new start with their old defensive coordinator. While both are talented and experienced in Grantham's scheme, the core of the defense is an impressive front seven led by TCU transfer Devonte Fields and defensive end Sheldon Rankins. The front seven was equally impressive against the run (26th in adjusted line yards) and the pass (20th in adjusted sack rate) and should ease the burden on the rebuilt secondary. However, if last year's trends continue, the defense must improve its containment of explosive plays and its fourth-quarter play (the defense dropped from 10th and ninth in S&P+ in the first half to 75th in the fourth quarter).

As for the quarterbacks, an injury to Gardner gave Reggie Bonnafon and Kyle Bolin chances toward the end of the season, and all three have slightly different styles of play. Gardner was the most consistent in terms of interceptions and completion percentage, while Bolin had the highest average yards per completion, and Bonnafon offers a running ability that the other

two lack. Whichever one ends up starting, he will have experience behind him in running back Brandon Radcliff, who was consistent (42.4 percent opportunity rate), but not very explosive (four highlight yards per opportunity). Unfortunately, the other pieces of the offense are far more worrisome. The receiving corps loses star DeVante Parker, as well as four of the top five other receiving options (the consistent Kai De La Cruz and the often-targeted Eli Rogers particularly hurt). James Quick returns as the likely No. 1 receiving option, but the other starters are up in the air. At least they won't be short on options, including incoming 6-foot-6 target Devonte Peete and Texas A&M transfer JaQuay Williams. The bigger issue is the offensive line, which replaces everyone but center Tobijah Hughley. Those four departed linemen were long-time starters, and their absences will certainly be noticed, as it's unclear whether any of their replacements are upgrades. The play of the line—and the rebuilt secondary—will go a long way in determining whether Louisville can challenge Clemson, Florida State, and Georgia Tech for the ACC crown.

No. 34 Florida Gators (6-6, 3-5)

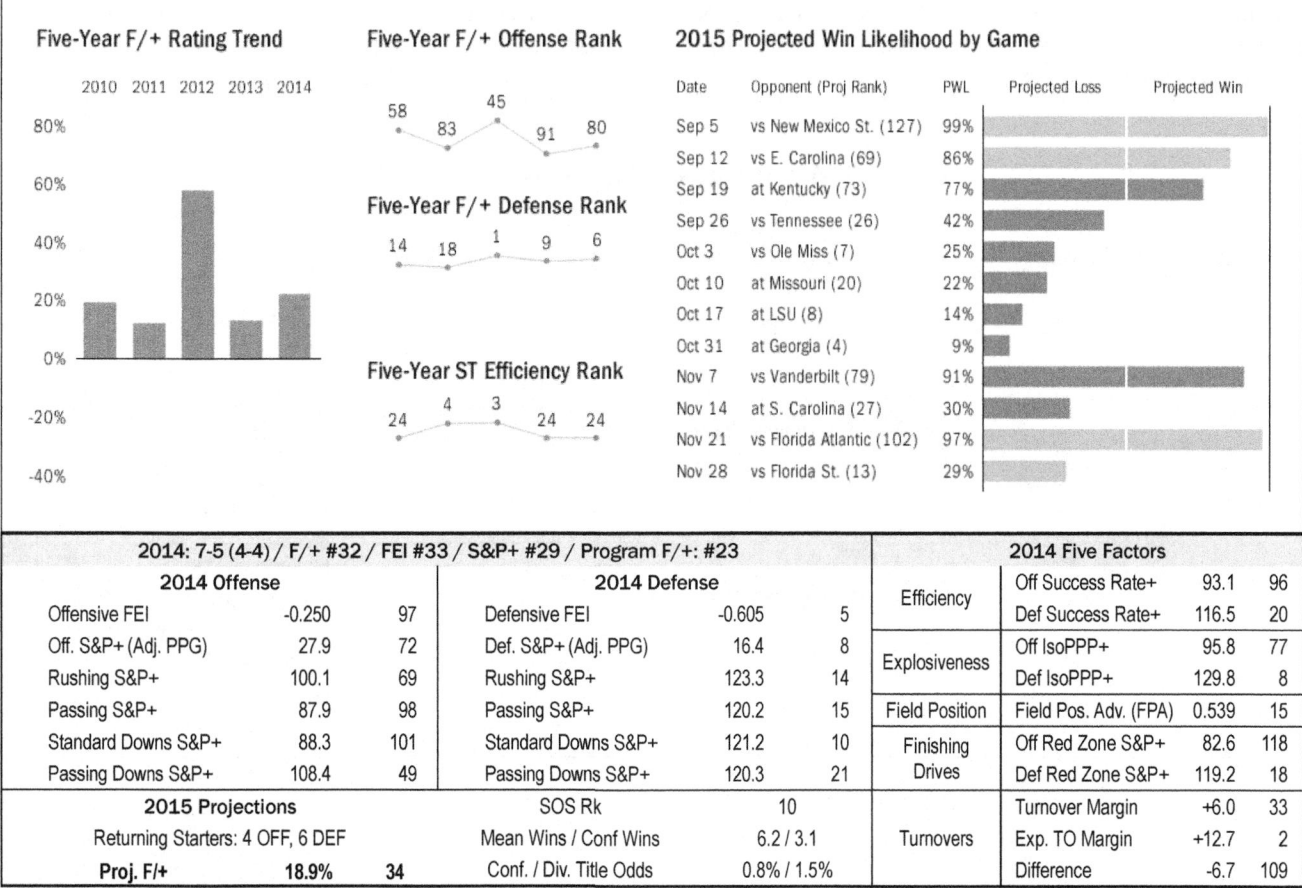

2014: 7-5 (4-4) / F/+ #32 / FEI #33 / S&P+ #29 / Program F/+: #23						2014 Five Factors			
2014 Offense			**2014 Defense**			Efficiency	Off Success Rate+	93.1	96
Offensive FEI	-0.250	97	Defensive FEI	-0.605	5		Def Success Rate+	116.5	20
Off. S&P+ (Adj. PPG)	27.9	72	Def. S&P+ (Adj. PPG)	16.4	8	Explosiveness	Off IsoPPP+	95.8	77
Rushing S&P+	100.1	69	Rushing S&P+	123.3	14		Def IsoPPP+	129.8	8
Passing S&P+	87.9	98	Passing S&P+	120.2	15	Field Position	Field Pos. Adv. (FPA)	0.539	15
Standard Downs S&P+	88.3	101	Standard Downs S&P+	121.2	10	Finishing Drives	Off Red Zone S&P+	82.6	118
Passing Downs S&P+	108.4	49	Passing Downs S&P+	120.3	21		Def Red Zone S&P+	119.2	18
2015 Projections			SOS Rk	10		Turnovers	Turnover Margin	+6.0	33
Returning Starters: 4 OFF, 6 DEF			Mean Wins / Conf Wins	6.2 / 3.1			Exp. TO Margin	+12.7	2
Proj. F/+	**18.9%**	**34**	Conf. / Div. Title Odds	0.8% / 1.5%			Difference	-6.7	109

It's fair to say that success in Jim McElwain's first season at Florida will hinge on the play of the offensive line. The Gators' defense was consistent throughout Will Muschamp's tenure—ranking 21st, 15th, fourth, and 35th—but the offense was plagued by poor offensive line and quarterback play. The

Gators have fertile recruiting grounds to stockpile Sunshine State talent, but offensive coordinator turnover (three during the Muschamp era) certainly contributed to the streak of underdeveloped quarterbacks that played behind shoddy and often-injured offensive lines. The big question for the beginning of the McElwain era is whether the offensive line will be able to protect a rebuilt unit of talented skill players.

The Gators' offensive line was mediocre in 2014, at 74th in adjusted line yards and 48th in adjusted sack rate. Unfortunately, they lost starting right tackle Rod Johnson to a career-ending injury, and Chaz Green, D.J. Humphries, and Max Garcia all left for the NFL. That kind of turnover is exactly what the Gators don't need, as they continue to search for their first quality starting quarterback since Tim Tebow. The spring game put the shaky offensive line depth on display, as the Gators could only put a single scholarship lineman on the Blue team. Will Grier looks to have the edge at quarterback over last season's frequent starter Treon Harris, and consistency at quarterback and offensive coordinator would go a long way toward not only elevating the offense, but also simply picking up some slack from the defense. Grier was sharp at the spring game (7-of-9 passing for 130 mostly meaningless yards), but he clearly has the higher ceiling as a passer (second overall pro style passer in the 247 Composite last season). Freshman tackle Martez Ivey should be an instant upgrade on the line, but this is still the most critical and the most underdeveloped position group on the team right now. Without an adequate offensive line, Florida's highly recruited running backs were held to inefficient totals (Kelvin Taylor averaged a 33.6 percent opportunity rate as Florida ran on a predictable 69 percent of standard downs).

The defense has been the Gators' calling card going back to Urban Meyer's days at Florida, and it is likely to be strong once again despite turnover in the front seven. Dante Fowler Jr., the Gators' main edge rushing threat, is gone, as is linebacker Michael Taylor. But with Jonathan Bullard and Antonio Morrison opting to return, the 39th-best havoc generating front seven should have some senior leadership to go along with an infusion of young talent. Between Gerald Willis III, Thomas Holley (who tore his labrum before last season), and CeCe Jefferson, the front seven is full of highly recruited playmakers who should be plug-and-play, ready to match last season's fifth overall havoc ranking while playing exemplary bend-don't-break defense (24th in success rate and fourth in IsoPPP). But the Gators shine at defensive back, where it's no stretch to say Jalen Tarbor and Vernon Hargreaves III form the best shutdown corner duo in college football. These two helped form the 12th-overall passing S&P+ defense last season, even as Tarbor was just a freshman.

Even with the turnover on defense, that was never going to be McElwain's biggest problem in year one—the offensive line and finding a quarterback are far more critical issues in the rebuilding process. The talent is in place at most spots on the Gators' roster. The offensive line depth is thin, but recruitment has been steady regardless of the on-field product in all but last season's class. Whenever the passing game improves, the Gators will be right back in contention for the SEC.

No. 35 Michigan Wolverines (8-4, 5-3)

2014: 5-7 (3-5) / F/+ #54 / FEI #67 / S&P+ #45 / Program F/+: #29						2014 Five Factors			
2014 Offense			**2014 Defense**			Efficiency	Off Success Rate+	108.5	36
Offensive FEI	-0.135	82	Defensive FEI	-0.193	41		Def Success Rate+	108.9	35
Off. S&P+ (Adj. PPG)	26.3	82	Def. S&P+ (Adj. PPG)	19.6	18	Explosiveness	Off IsoPPP+	89.0	97
Rushing S&P+	101.8	62	Rushing S&P+	127.5	8		Def IsoPPP+	124.5	13
Passing S&P+	92.5	84	Passing S&P+	107.2	45	Field Position	Field Pos. Adv. (FPA)	0.488	82
Standard Downs S&P+	102.8	57	Standard Downs S&P+	114.9	22	Finishing Drives	Off Red Zone S&P+	104.2	56
Passing Downs S&P+	82.8	111	Passing Downs S&P+	113.3	34		Def Red Zone S&P+	110.9	28
2015 Projections			SOS Rk		38	Turnovers	Turnover Margin	-16.0	125
Returning Starters: 8 OFF, 7 DEF			Mean Wins / Conf Wins		7.6 / 4.7		Exp. TO Margin	-10.5	126
Proj. F/+	**18.6%**	**35**	Conf. / Div. Title Odds		0.8% / 1.1%		Difference	-5.5	107

Jim Harbaugh is a good football coach. He built Stanford into a national brand and perennial Pac-12 contender, took San Francisco to the Super Bowl, and is now back as the promised savior for Michigan football. Michigan got its second Michigan Man in a row, but this time there's no question about his coaching pedigree. Expectations are high, and deservedly so.

But the rebuilding process will not necessarily be instantaneous. Brady Hoke and staff recruited fairly well, ranking 14th in recruiting impact and bringing in three top-20 classes in a row according to the 247 Composite team rankings. There's talent in the program, but there are several immediate needs that need to be addressed before Michigan can start to play like Michigan fans expect. First and foremost, Michigan needs an answer at quarterback. Ranking 84th in S&P+ and 99th in PPP+, the passing game was inconsistent in 2014 and now turns to a new starter after Devin Gardner's graduation. Harbaugh has a reputation as a quarterback whisperer, with Andrew Luck and Colin Kaepernick as former pupils. In former blue-chip quarterback Shane Morris and Iowa transfer Jake Rudock, along with two four-star recuirts, Harbaugh has plenty to work with. But none of them is a sure thing. Morris has had a largely disappointing career so far after sky-high expectations, completing just 14 passes to three interceptions last season, but he compares to Christian Hackenberg in terms of raw arm talent. Rudock is a one-year mercenary option, with plenty of experience, but perhaps a lower ceiling and less of a long-term future than Morris.

What's certain is that Michigan has plenty of skill players for its supporting cast. With veterans like tight end Jake Butt and wide receiver Amara Darboh and young receivers like highly-hyped Drake Harris, whichever quarterback wins the job should have someone to throw to. Of course, the real strength of the offense will be at running back, where there are two former five-star players in Derrick Green and USC transfer Ty Isaac who can carry the load. Green is recovering from a broken clavicle that knocked him out of most of last season, while Isaac is eligible to play after sitting out last season due to NCAA transfer rules. This is one of the most potentially fearsome, if unproven, backfields in the country. Based on limited data, Green has the slightly better average highlight yards per opportunity, while Isaac looks to be more consistent with a 42.5 percent opportunity rate while at USC as a freshman (though it's certainly apples to oranges due to two different offensive lines).

Of course, the run game hinges on another one of Harbaugh's priorities: the continued improvement of the offense line. Despite some impressive recruiting efforts by Hoke, the offensive line was perhaps the team's primary liability during his tenure. 2014 saw a marked improvement to 50th in adjusted line yards and 72nd in adjusted sack rate, though those are hardly championship-caliber levels. Again, like many other position groups, there is significant talent in place for the run game to take off immediately.

Priority number three will be a defense that played well for most of the season under Greg Mattison (who stays on the staff as line coach with D. J. Durkin coming in as defensive coordinator), and in particular improving a pass defense that ranked 59th in success rate. The defensive line was excellent at applying pressure in obvious passing situations, but was inconsistent and without a single world-class unblockable lineman. The linebackers are all experienced and talented, so there's little to be concerned about in the front seven. There's likely even more talent in the secondary, with all-world safety Jabrill Peppers making his true debut after injuries took away his freshman year. The staff is also excited about the addition of Stanford transfer Wayne Lyons, who will have a year to make a run at a Big Ten Championship. That starting four could go toe-to-toe with the most athletic wide receivers in the country, but they'll need to make more explosive plays than last year, when they ranked 125th in defensive back havoc rate. With the talent on the roster and the coaching staff that Harbaugh has assembled, it's tempting to look at the Wolverines as one of the programs most primed for a turnaround, but Michigan may nonetheless be a year away from serious Playoff contention.

No. 36 Penn State Nittany Lions (8-4, 5-3)

Five-Year F/+ Rating Trend

2010 2011 2012 2013 2014

80%

60%

40%

20%

0%

-20%

-40%

Five-Year F/+ Offense Rank

63   63   51   63

106

Five-Year F/+ Defense Rank

3   18   5

44   42

Five-Year ST Efficiency Rank

16

66

94   112   116

2015 Projected Win Likelihood by Game

Date	Opponent (Proj Rank)	PWL	Projected Loss	Projected Win
Sep 5	at Temple (55)	64%		
Sep 12	vs Buffalo (113)	98%		
Sep 19	vs Rutgers (87)	92%		
Sep 26	vs San Diego St. (72)	86%		
Oct 3	vs Army (126)	99%		
Oct 10	vs Indiana (83)	91%		
Oct 17	at Ohio St. (1)	3%		
Oct 24	vs Maryland (74)	82%		
Oct 31	vs Illinois (76)	87%		
Nov 7	at Northwestern (59)	67%		
Nov 21	vs Michigan (35)	55%		
Nov 28	at Michigan St. (9)	12%		

2014: 7-6 (2-6) / F/+ #45 / FEI #46 / S&P+ #46 / Program F/+: #40

2014 Offense			2014 Defense		
Offensive FEI	-0.295	101	Defensive FEI	-0.560	9
Off. S&P+ (Adj. PPG)	21.3	109	Def. S&P+ (Adj. PPG)	15.1	4
Rushing S&P+	83.8	115	Rushing S&P+	135.5	4
Passing S&P+	91.8	85	Passing S&P+	127.3	10
Standard Downs S&P+	85.4	115	Standard Downs S&P+	121.2	9
Passing Downs S&P+	97.5	80	Passing Downs S&P+	157.7	3

2015 Projections					
Returning Starters: 8 OFF, 7 DEF			SOS Rk	28	
			Mean Wins / Conf Wins	8.4 / 4.9	
Proj. F/+	17.1%	36	Conf. / Div. Title Odds	0.5% / 0.7%	

2014 Five Factors

Efficiency	Off Success Rate+	95.8	84
	Def Success Rate+	121.9	10
Explosiveness	Off IsoPPP+	81.2	111
	Def IsoPPP+	141.8	4
Field Position	Field Pos. Adv. (FPA)	0.483	97
Finishing Drives	Off Red Zone S&P+	88.4	103
	Def Red Zone S&P+	110.3	29
Turnovers	Turnover Margin	-5.0	99
	Exp. TO Margin	-1.0	82
	Difference	-4.0	100

The Nittany Lions are full of potential in James Franklin's second year as coach, but a double-digit win total depends on the improvement of the offensive line and the supporting offensive skill players.

Two things that are definite: quarterback Christian Hackenberg looks and acts the part for Penn State and is now in his second year in Franklin's offensive system, and the defense is full of havoc-creating playmakers, particularly along the defensive line. Hackenberg took an undue amount of heat for his underwhelming sophomore campaign (as quarterbacks tend to), but the general retrospective consensus is that the poor offensive performance (111th in explosiveness, 103rd finishing drives, 115th in rushing S&P+) was due to his supporting cast, rather than Hackenberg himself. Fans also complained that James Franklin's offensive system was a poor match for the pro-style quarterback. And whether it was simply due to fatigue or to poor offensive coaching adaptations, the team's offensive efficiency dropped from 69th in the first quarter to 115th in the second and from 78th in the third to 108th in the fourth.

At least in terms of the skill positions, the answer seems to be in the young talent. Franklin hasn't had any problem recruiting blue-chip players to State College (ranking 20th in recruiting impact) and brought in the 12th-ranked class according to 247's Composite team rankings. The Nittany Lions return DaeSean Hamilton, who received nearly a third

of Hackenberg's targets last season, Geno Lewis, and Chris Godwin, and they also have six other former four-star freshman and sophomore wide receivers. There isn't as much star power in the backfield to boost the anemic ground game (Akeel Lynch is the veteran, while incoming freshman Saquon Barkley may be the most explosive back on the roster already), but the run game's top priority will be boosting an offensive line that ranked 111th in adjusted line yards and 105th in adjusted sack rate. Having a veteran line isn't always a good thing, but Penn State at least returns all but their left tackle after replacing four starters last season. Without the balance from a respectable run game (not to mention adequate pass protection), the offense lost explosive potential (111th in IsoPPP+) and was not as effective in the passing game as it might have been otherwise. But a more veteran offensive line and six freshman or redshirt freshman linemen justify the optimism in Happy Valley.

But in all likelihood the strength of the 2015 Nittany Lions will be the defense, which completely shut down opponents' explosive plays (4th in IsoPPP+) while creating plenty of explosive plays of their own. Anthony Zettel is the name to know here, as he led the team with 17 tackles for loss and eight sacks as a defensive tackle last season, but the entire front seven excelled at both stopping the run (10th in adjusted line yards) and applying quarterback pressure. The secondary is led by newly moved safety Jordan Lucas, who led the way with nine pass breakups last season. Penn State's ceiling in 2015 is as high as its offensive line will let it be. Especially with a schedule that includes only three teams

ranked ahead of their 37th-place spot in our F/+ projections, the Nittany Lions should be favored in at least nine games this season.

No. 37 Miami Hurricanes (7-5, 4-4)

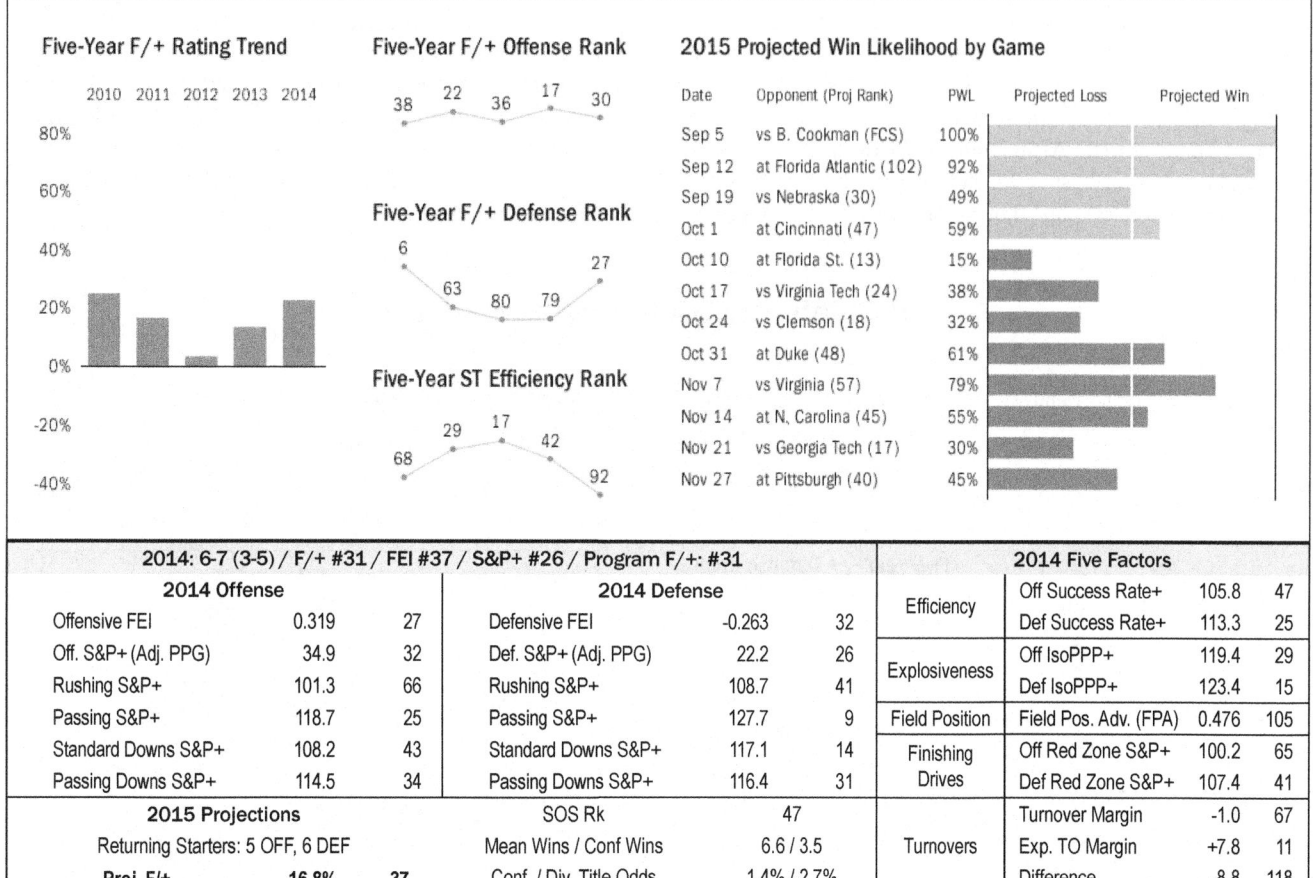

Five-Year F/+ Rating Trend

Five-Year F/+ Offense Rank

38 22 36 17 30

Five-Year F/+ Defense Rank

6 63 80 79 27

Five-Year ST Efficiency Rank

68 29 17 42 92

2015 Projected Win Likelihood by Game

Date	Opponent (Proj Rank)	PWL	Projected Loss / Projected Win
Sep 5	vs B. Cookman (FCS)	100%	
Sep 12	at Florida Atlantic (102)	92%	
Sep 19	vs Nebraska (30)	49%	
Oct 1	at Cincinnati (47)	59%	
Oct 10	at Florida St. (13)	15%	
Oct 17	vs Virginia Tech (24)	38%	
Oct 24	vs Clemson (18)	32%	
Oct 31	at Duke (48)	61%	
Nov 7	vs Virginia (57)	79%	
Nov 14	at N. Carolina (45)	55%	
Nov 21	vs Georgia Tech (17)	30%	
Nov 27	at Pittsburgh (40)	45%	

2014: 6-7 (3-5) / F/+ #31 / FEI #37 / S&P+ #26 / Program F/+: #31

2014 Offense			2014 Defense		
Offensive FEI	0.319	27	Defensive FEI	-0.263	32
Off. S&P+ (Adj. PPG)	34.9	32	Def. S&P+ (Adj. PPG)	22.2	26
Rushing S&P+	101.3	66	Rushing S&P+	108.7	41
Passing S&P+	118.7	25	Passing S&P+	127.7	9
Standard Downs S&P+	108.2	43	Standard Downs S&P+	117.1	14
Passing Downs S&P+	114.5	34	Passing Downs S&P+	116.4	31

2015 Projections			SOS Rk	47
Returning Starters: 5 OFF, 6 DEF			Mean Wins / Conf Wins	6.6 / 3.5
Proj. F/+	16.8%	37	Conf. / Div. Title Odds	1.4% / 2.7%

2014 Five Factors

Efficiency	Off Success Rate+	105.8	47
	Def Success Rate+	113.3	25
Explosiveness	Off IsoPPP+	119.4	29
	Def IsoPPP+	123.4	15
Field Position	Field Pos. Adv. (FPA)	0.476	105
Finishing Drives	Off Red Zone S&P+	100.2	65
	Def Red Zone S&P+	107.4	41
Turnovers	Turnover Margin	-1.0	67
	Exp. TO Margin	+7.8	11
	Difference	-8.8	118

Miami fans would never have believed that their stadium would seldom be even half full 15 years after they appeared in back-to-back national championship games, but that is where the Hurricanes find themselves heading into Al Golden's fifth year as coach. You can make a compelling case that, given the state's high level of high school talent and their top-20 recruiting impact ranking, the Hurricanes haven't recovered quickly enough from NCAA- and self-imposed sanctions. Many will argue that a 6-7 record is unacceptable, given that Miami had six players taken in the first five rounds of the 2015 draft. However, with stellar offensive skill talent, a seasoned secondary that rarely gave up big plays, and a manageable schedule, 2015 may be the year for the Hurricanes to take the next step on the long road back to national relevance.

That return will begin with quarterback Brad Kaaya. Kaaya won the job in preseason camp last year as a true freshman, edging transfer quarterback Jake Heaps, and went on to complete 59 percent of his passes for 8.5 yards per attempt (16th overall) in the 25th-ranked passing S&P+ offense. In fact, Kaaya's passing offense became both more reliable and more explosive than the run game led by veteran Duke Johnson.

Despite Johnson's explosiveness (7.1 highlight yards per opportunity) and relatively high efficiency (44.2 percent), the run game was just the 66th-ranked unit in the country, in large part because of the offensive line (52nd in adjusted line yards). The run game will be almost entirely different in 2015, as the Hurricanes must replace not only Johnson, but the entire left side of the offensive line, including two All-ACC members. The run game arguably has a higher ceiling now, but certainly a lower floor with so many first-time starters. Sophomore Joseph Yearby will likely take over as the starting running back. Yearby was just as efficient but less explosive than Johnson, and freshman Mark Walton and sophomore Trayone Gray provide some insurance behind Yearby. Having a consistent run game will be crucial for the Hurricanes to take the next step and close out both games and individual drives, as Miami struggled both in the red zone (65th, compared to 39th overall) and late in games (getting worse quarter-to-quarter from 17th in the first to 76th in the fourth). But with an offense that relied so heavily on the passing game last season, the biggest concern will be replacing Kaaya's top three receiving targets (roughly 50 percent of his overall targets) in Phillip

Dorsett, Duke Johnson, and tight end Clive Walford. Walford and Johnson were Kaaya's high-efficiency targets, catching a combined 72 percent of their targets, while Dorsett had the country's second-highest yards per catch average (24 yards per reception). It's unclear who will move in to Dorsett's role as the explosive receiving option.

The Hurricanes' defense might have been the biggest revelation last season. They excelled at preventing explosive plays (15th overall) and had one of the top pass defenses in the country (ninth in passing S&P+). The secondary is the highlight of the team, led by senior safety Deon Bush and entrenched junior corners Artie Burns and Corn Elder. The pass rush was average at best (70th in adjusted sack rate), which makes the secondary play that much more impressive. Opposing offenses quickly learned that they needed to run on the Hurricanes, as they were less efficient (32nd in success rate) and allowed more explosive runs (44th in PPP+). This led to less efficiency in the red zone (41st), as offenses could outmuscle the defensive line in short yardage situations (50th in power success rate). The line loses anchor Anthony Chickillo and has no proven replacement, but there are plenty of options as Miami has at least recruited well along the defensive line. Ultimately Miami's season—which is particularly stout in the middle with games against Nebraska, Virginia Tech, Clemson, and Florida State in a six-week stretch—will hinge on the development of the front seven against the run and how quickly the offensive skill players can make up for the losses of Johnson and Dorsett.

No. 38 Oklahoma State Cowboys (8-4, 5-4)

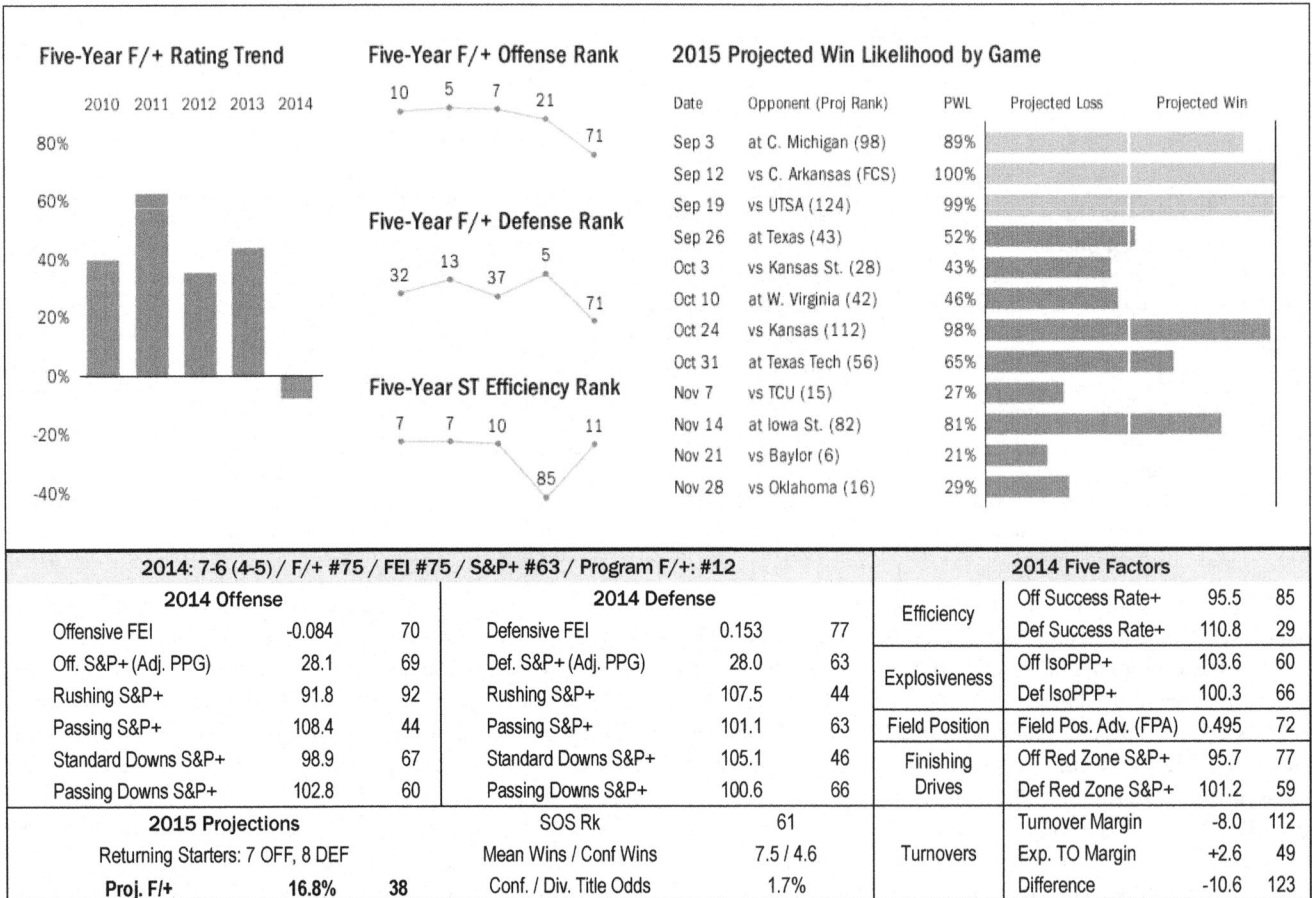

Mike Gundy's Cowboys had their worst year since 2007 last season, dropping six games as they struggled to find an answer at quarterback. Since Brandon Weeden, the Cowboys have been marked by inconsistent quarterback play, with varying levels of success (10-3 in 2013 despite playing two quarterbacks). Hopes are high that sophomore Mason Rudolph, who didn't play until the eleventh game in 2014 but went 2-1 as a starter, wasn't a temporary answer, but a long-term and program-building player for the Cowboys.

Starting for the first time in a losing effort against Baylor,

Rudolph was explosive (averaging 9.9 yards per passing attempt in 86 passes) and only seemed to get better. Rudolph had a fairly low completion percentage, but that too improved from 52 percent in his first start to 65.4 percent in the bowl game. With a spring and summer for Rudolph to build rapport with his receivers, it's not far-fetched to expect a higher level of play from the 44th-ranked passing offense in 2014.

Rudolph's play and continued development is central to the Cowboys getting back on track in a fairly open Big 12 race, but he isn't the only hope in Stillwater. The biggest issue with the passing offense was the offensive line's play, as only four teams in the country had a worse adjusted sack rate; that might explain why, despite a relatively mediocre run game (66th in adjusted line yards, 97th opportunity rate, and 89th rushing S&P+), the Cowboys had one of the highest passing downs run percentages in the nation (42 percent, 18th-highest). The offensive coordinator couldn't trust the line to protect former starter J.W. Walsh. That should change both with the more experienced offensive line and the high level of wide receiver talent, starting with James Washington and Jhajuan Seales. There's a lot of optimism around the offensive line, which returns five players with experience, received two transfers, added three new freshman, and hired former NFL offensive line coach Greg Adkins. The tepid running game, meanwhile, had as much to do with the running backs as the offensive line, and it's unclear who will take the mantle in 2015. Rennie

Childs looks like the obvious choice to replace Desmond Roland and Tyreek Hill, but he averaged just 3.77 yards per carry last season and looked more like a change of pace back than a feature back. A lot of the run game's hopes rest on juco transfer Chris Carson out of Butler Community College (originally a Georgia commit).

The strength of the team is in the defensive line, which includes All-American candidate Emmanuel Ogbah (eleven sacks and 17 tackles for loss last season as a sophomore). Ogbah was a big part of the reason why the Cowboys ranked 26th in adjusted sack rate. But the Cowboys' defense also allowed a number of explosive plays (96th IsoPPP) and was far less effective in the secondary than the front seven (96th in defensive back havoc rate). It was boom or bust as far as the defense went, but now there is at least continuity in the secondary to go along with an explosive defensive front.

No. 39 BYU Cougars (7-5, -)

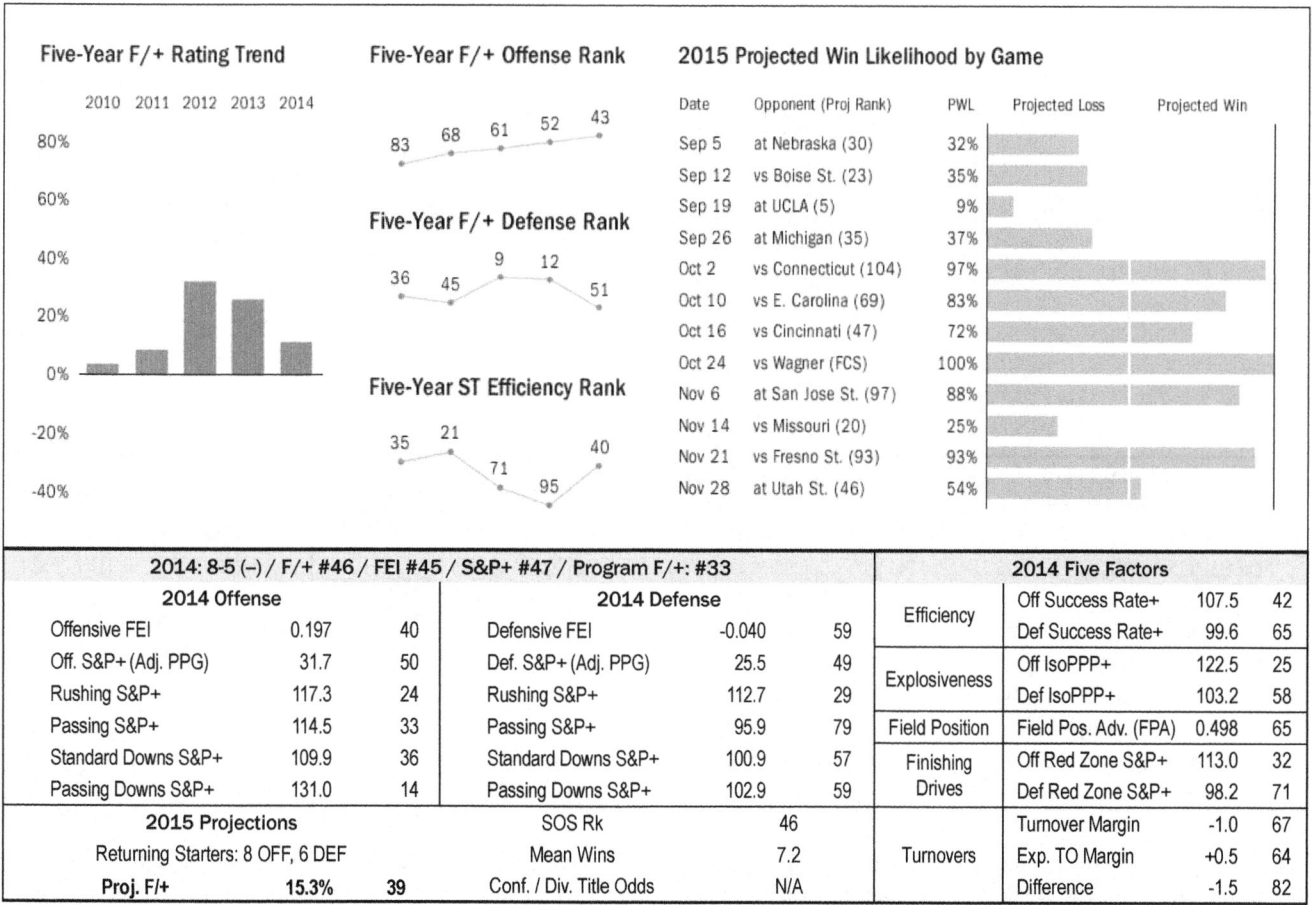

2014: 8-5 (–) / F/+ #46 / FEI #45 / S&P+ #47 / Program F/+: #33						2014 Five Factors			
2014 Offense			**2014 Defense**			Efficiency	Off Success Rate+	107.5	42
Offensive FEI	0.197	40	Defensive FEI	-0.040	59		Def Success Rate+	99.6	65
Off. S&P+ (Adj. PPG)	31.7	50	Def. S&P+ (Adj. PPG)	25.5	49	Explosiveness	Off IsoPPP+	122.5	25
Rushing S&P+	117.3	24	Rushing S&P+	112.7	29		Def IsoPPP+	103.2	58
Passing S&P+	114.5	33	Passing S&P+	95.9	79	Field Position	Field Pos. Adv. (FPA)	0.498	65
Standard Downs S&P+	109.9	36	Standard Downs S&P+	100.9	57	Finishing Drives	Off Red Zone S&P+	113.0	32
Passing Downs S&P+	131.0	14	Passing Downs S&P+	102.9	59		Def Red Zone S&P+	98.2	71
2015 Projections			SOS Rk		46		Turnover Margin	-1.0	67
Returning Starters: 8 OFF, 6 DEF			Mean Wins		7.2	Turnovers	Exp. TO Margin	+0.5	64
Proj. F/+	**15.3%**	**39**	Conf. / Div. Title Odds		N/A		Difference	-1.5	82

The Cougars return quarterback Taysom Hill, which completely changes what we can expect from the BYU offense in 2015. Hill fractured his leg against Utah State last season, but led a ground-heavy charge as the team's leading and most-efficient rusher at the time of his injury. In those few games, Hill averaged a 68 percent opportunity rate, meaning that he gained at least five yards on over two-thirds of his carries last year—far outpacing his offensive line's season average of

43.7 percent (which was still 22nd in the country). On the other side of the ball, the defense must improve its pass rush and replace the three top tacklers in the secondary to better last season's 79th-ranked pass defense.

Though Hill, with a 66.7 percent completion percentage, was a more efficient passer than his replacement, Christian Stewart (57.2 percent), BYU stands to gain the most in the run game. No running back on the roster was nearly as efficient as

Hill—leading rusher Jamaal Williams averaged 4.6 yards per carry, but only a 36.6 percent opportunity rate. Only senior backup Adam Hine beat Hill's explosiveness, with 4.8 highlight yards per opportunity to Hill's four. The Cougars will have a number of new starting linemen, as they lose four players who started at least nine games, but they were in a similar situation last year before producing one of the most consistent and efficient rushing offenses in the country. As long as star left tackle Ryker Mathews is healthy, look for the Cougars' offense to be as efficient as ever on the ground.

However, the defense is in search of both a new secondary and a missing pass rush. Last year's 99th-ranked adjusted sack rate put a now-graduated secondary on its heels. The secondary will feature an almost entirely new two-deep, with five of the top seven tacklers from last season gone. On the defensive line, senior Bronson Kaufusi (seven sacks and 11.5 tackles for loss in 2014) is set to lead the way, but he'll need some help from a line that didn't have any other player record more than 1.5 sacks or six tackles for loss last season. At least the linebackers should be stout, and young Sione Takitaki shined with his playing time as a true freshman last season. With an interesting schedule that brings Nebraska, Boise State, UCLA, and Michigan at the start of the season, we should have a good idea of BYU's potential by game five. If the Cougars can emerge with two or three wins out of those first four, then don't count out a ten-win season for BYU.

No. 40 Pittsburgh Panthers (7-5, 4-4)

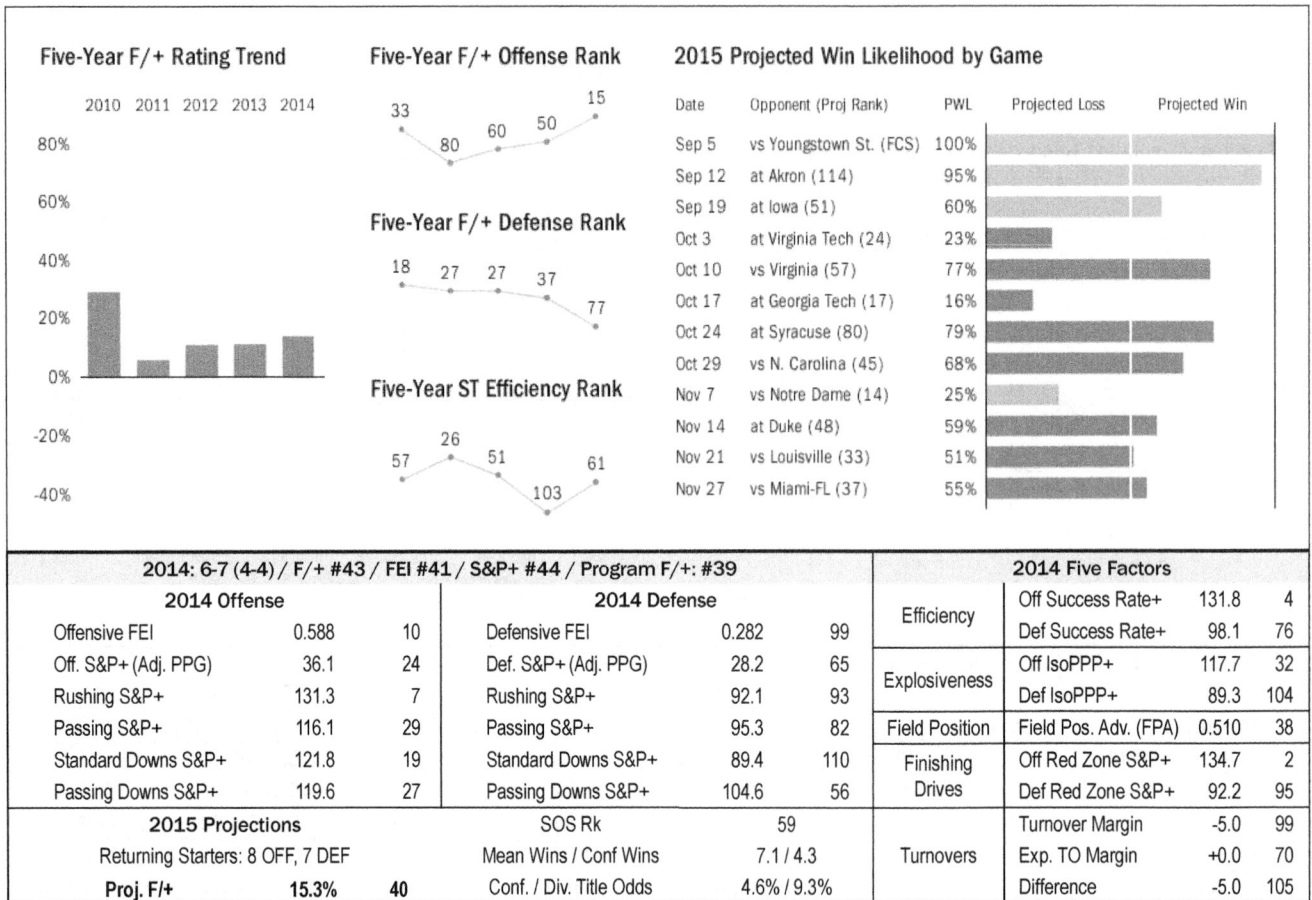

2014: 6-7 (4-4) / F/+ #43 / FEI #41 / S&P+ #44 / Program F/+: #39						2014 Five Factors			
2014 Offense			**2014 Defense**			Efficiency	Off Success Rate+	131.8	4
Offensive FEI	0.588	10	Defensive FEI	0.282	99		Def Success Rate+	98.1	76
Off. S&P+ (Adj. PPG)	36.1	24	Def. S&P+ (Adj. PPG)	28.2	65	Explosiveness	Off IsoPPP+	117.7	32
Rushing S&P+	131.3	7	Rushing S&P+	92.1	93		Def IsoPPP+	89.3	104
Passing S&P+	116.1	29	Passing S&P+	95.3	82	Field Position	Field Pos. Adv. (FPA)	0.510	38
Standard Downs S&P+	121.8	19	Standard Downs S&P+	89.4	110	Finishing Drives	Off Red Zone S&P+	134.7	2
Passing Downs S&P+	119.6	27	Passing Downs S&P+	104.6	56		Def Red Zone S&P+	92.2	95
2015 Projections			SOS Rk	59		Turnovers	Turnover Margin	-5.0	99
Returning Starters: 8 OFF, 7 DEF			Mean Wins / Conf Wins	7.1 / 4.3			Exp. TO Margin	+0.0	70
Proj. F/+	15.3%	40	Conf. / Div. Title Odds	4.6% / 9.3%			Difference	-5.0	105

Pittsburgh had a losing record last season despite having one of the most efficient rushers in the country in James Conner (who averaged a 46 percent opportunity rate on his way to 1,765 total rushing yards), a solid quarterback in Chad Voytik (who contributed 6.9 yards per carry and a 53.4 percent opportunity rate of his own), and one of the best receivers in the country in Tyler Boyd. This trio returns for 2015, along with new coach Pat Narduzzi. Narduzzi has had incredible success as a defensive coordinator for Michigan State, and he was instrumental in building that formerly mediocre program into a consistent conference contender. Not all excellent coordinators have immediate success as first-time coaches, but Narduzzi walks into a very positive situation where his offense is filled with veterans and the defense he inherits has room for him to leave his mark.

Pittsburgh fans can be most bullish about the state of the offense. The Panthers ran with absurd efficiency thanks to an offensive line that churned out a five yard gain on nearly every other down (48.4 percent opportunity rate) and returns leading big man James Conner and his backup Chris James, along with Voytik for the occasional explosive run (he actually led the team in highlight yards per opportunity with 5.9).

The line does lose its two best players in All-ACC selections T.J. Clemmings and Matt Rotheram on the right side, but there is young, if inexperienced, talent waiting in the wings. Nearly as big a concern as the new right side of the line will be finding other receiving options besides Boyd. Boyd was targeted on an absurd 42 percent of passes last year, and Pitt lost its second option, Manasseh Garner, so the new receiving corps will have little to no experience.

The 2014 Panthers defense had the unfortunate combination of being both lackluster on standard downs (110th) and poor against big plays (104th in IsoPPP+). Normally defenses that struggle on standard downs have an efficiency problem and/or a run defense problem. While the Panthers certainly weren't stellar in either of those categories (76th and 93rd, respectively), they combined that mediocrity with an inability to create big plays and a tendency to allow them instead. There was little to no pass rush from the front seven (103rd in adjusted sack rate). However, all hope isn't lost for 2015. While the Panthers replace two linebackers and one defensive end, everyone else returns, and defensive end Rori Blair looks like a lightweight edge rushing machine. In only 12.5 tackles last season as a freshman, Blair had five sacks and 5.5 tackles for loss. The hope is that Narduzzi's influence can instill a previously unknown aggressiveness, particularly against the run. It certainly helps that almost the entire secondary returns, including both starting corners, for a defense that is so reliant on competent cornerback play.

No. 41 Marshall Thundering Herd (11-1, 7-1)

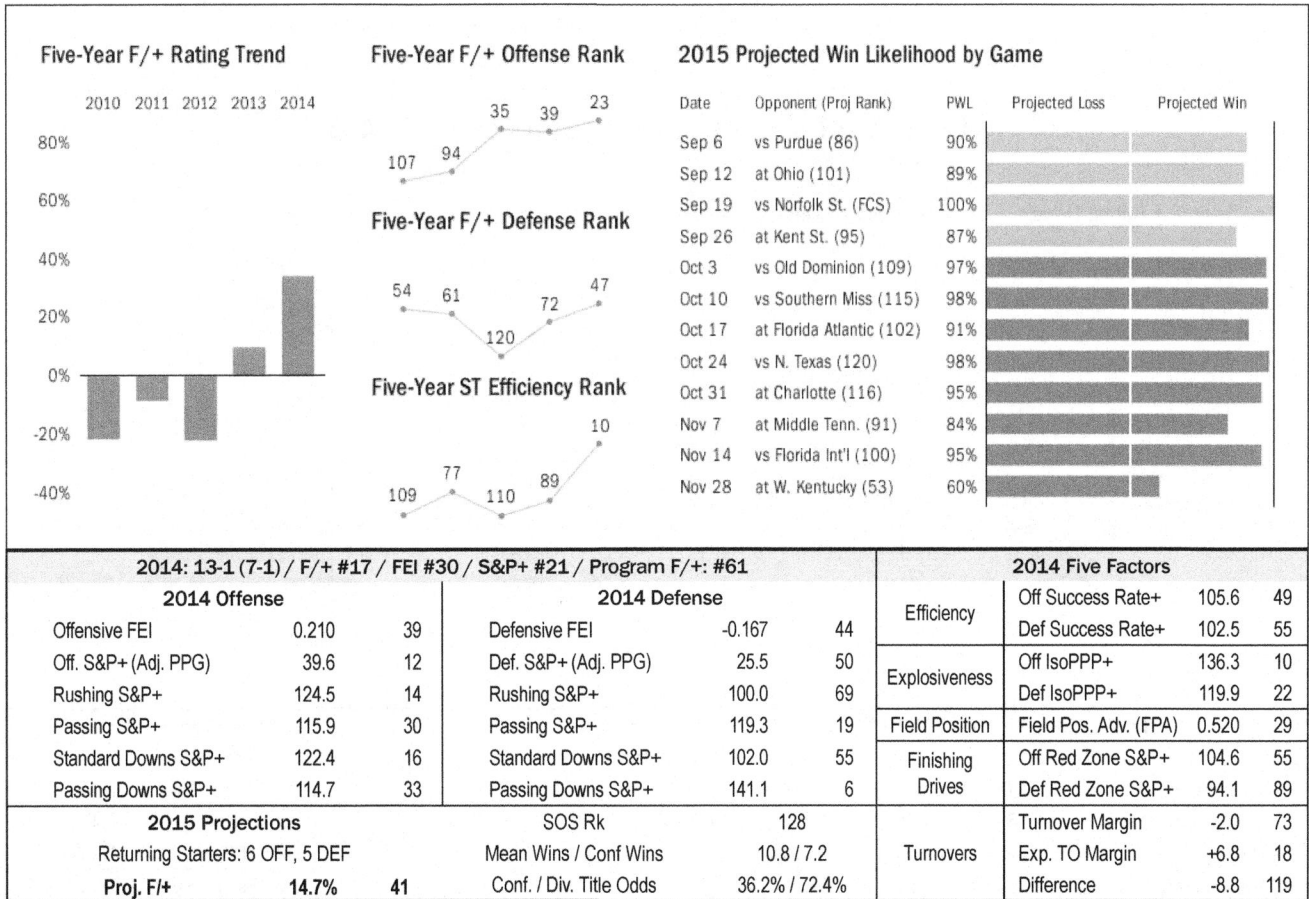

2014: 13-1 (7-1) / F/+ #17 / FEI #30 / S&P+ #21 / Program F/+: #61							2014 Five Factors			
2014 Offense			**2014 Defense**			Efficiency	Off Success Rate+	105.6	49
Offensive FEI	0.210	39	Defensive FEI	-0.167	44		Def Success Rate+	102.5	55
Off. S&P+ (Adj. PPG)	39.6	12	Def. S&P+ (Adj. PPG)	25.5	50	Explosiveness	Off IsoPPP+	136.3	10
Rushing S&P+	124.5	14	Rushing S&P+	100.0	69		Def IsoPPP+	119.9	22
Passing S&P+	115.9	30	Passing S&P+	119.3	19	Field Position	Field Pos. Adv. (FPA)	0.520	29
Standard Downs S&P+	122.4	16	Standard Downs S&P+	102.0	55	Finishing Drives	Off Red Zone S&P+	104.6	55
Passing Downs S&P+	114.7	33	Passing Downs S&P+	141.1	6		Def Red Zone S&P+	94.1	89
2015 Projections			SOS Rk	128		Turnovers	Turnover Margin	-2.0	73
Returning Starters: 6 OFF, 5 DEF			Mean Wins / Conf Wins	10.8 / 7.2			Exp. TO Margin	+6.8	18
Proj. F/+	**14.7%**	**41**	Conf. / Div. Title Odds	36.2% / 72.4%			Difference	-8.8	119

Rakeem Cato almost led Marshall to an undefeated season in 2014, as well as a storm of controversy about conference parity, scheduling, and brands in the College Football Playoff's first year. On November 27th, the eventual 13-1, 17th F/+-ranked Thundering Herd were not only undefeated, but had blown out every opponent they had faced. They had ten games in a row with win expectancies of either 99 percent or 100 percent, and only one of the eleven games they had played was even within two touchdowns. At the center was Cato, who not only passed for 3,900 yards, but also ran for 609 (averaging 8.3 yards per carry with a 60 percent opportunity rate).

But their schedule was not up to the Selection Committee's standards—the best team they had faced to that point finished the season 79th in F/+. But they had won convincingly even after opponent statistical adjustments. The Herd eventually suffered a heartbreaking 67-66 loss to Western Kentucky, but Marshall nonetheless had a breakthrough 2014—and is set up for more success in 2015.

In 2015, it will be an extreme disappointment if Marshall loses a game before their end-of-season matchup with Western Kentucky. In fact, the Herd only play one team all season that was ranked higher than 84th in the F/+ rankings last season—and that's the Hilltoppers (50th). Otherwise, Marshall's schedule includes just three opponents who are even ranked in the top 100.

Marshall must replace Cato, but it has several options. Most likely Cato's understudy, Gunnar Holcombe, will hold onto the job, but James Madison transfer Michael Birdsong is another solid option. Holcombe had limited opportunities in 2014 (21 attempts), but has been in the system for two years already. And he'll be supported by an explosive group of running backs and receivers. Senior running back Devon Johnson returns to ease the new starting quarterback in. He averaged over 7.5 yards per carry and over eight highlight yards per opportunity, but he's also consistent, with a 51 percent opportunity rate. The run game was geared towards big plays over efficiency (62nd in rushing success rate and second in rushing PPP+). Of course, when your line churns out the 14th-ranked adjusted line yard average and gains five yards on 47 percent of plays (9th), your life as a running back is much easier. The line loses All-Confer-

ence USA center Chris Jasperse, but returns three other starters and has a large group of sophomores and redshirt freshmen to challenge for the open spots. Yes, the line struggled with sacks in obvious passing situations (102nd in passing downs sack rate), but the line performed well overall. Finally, No. 1 receiving threat Tommy Shuler (30 percent target rate and 1,138 total receiving yards) is gone, but sophomore Hyleck Foster had similar production in limited opportunities.

On defense there is plenty of turnover for a unit that bent but rarely broke, controlling big plays (22nd in IsoPPP+) while being relatively weak up front against the run (69th in rushing S&P+ and 91st in adjusted line yards). The front seven loses five starters, including stud pass rusher Arnold Blackmon, but that turnover at least offers opportunity for improvement for a weak run defense. Even though cornerback Darryl Roberts is the only starter from the secondary to move on, the pass defense will certainly miss his 18 passes defensed—but expect this unit to be fine due to excellent depth.

No. 42 West Virginia Mountaineers (7-5, 4-5)

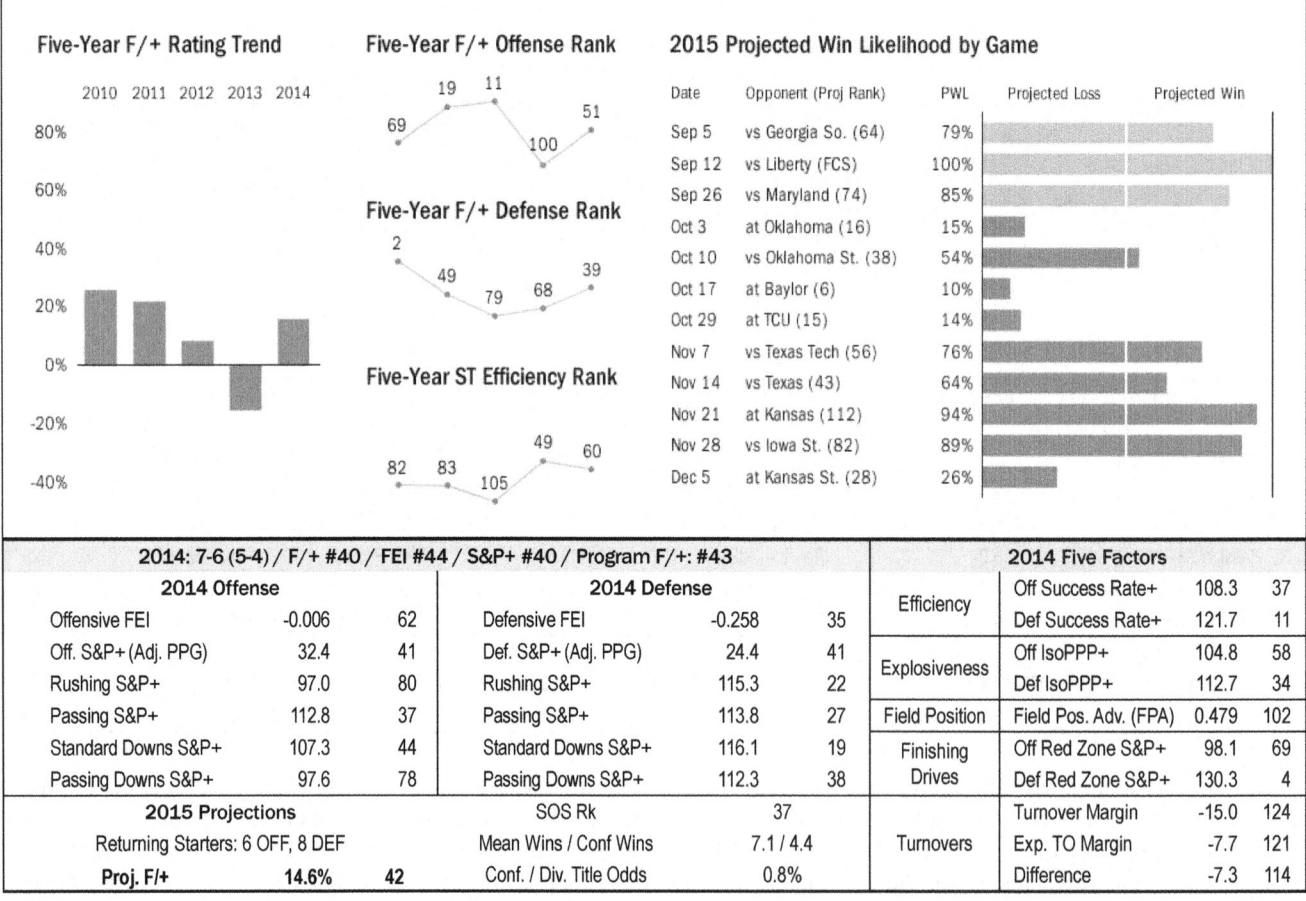

2014: 7-6 (5-4) / F/+ #40 / FEI #44 / S&P+ #40 / Program F/+: #43						2014 Five Factors			
2014 Offense			**2014 Defense**			Efficiency	Off Success Rate+	108.3	37
Offensive FEI	-0.006	62	Defensive FEI	-0.258	35		Def Success Rate+	121.7	11
Off. S&P+ (Adj. PPG)	32.4	41	Def. S&P+ (Adj. PPG)	24.4	41	Explosiveness	Off IsoPPP+	104.8	58
Rushing S&P+	97.0	80	Rushing S&P+	115.3	22		Def IsoPPP+	112.7	34
Passing S&P+	112.8	37	Passing S&P+	113.8	27	Field Position	Field Pos. Adv. (FPA)	0.479	102
Standard Downs S&P+	107.3	44	Standard Downs S&P+	116.1	19	Finishing Drives	Off Red Zone S&P+	98.1	69
Passing Downs S&P+	97.6	78	Passing Downs S&P+	112.3	38		Def Red Zone S&P+	130.3	4
2015 Projections			SOS Rk	37			Turnover Margin	-15.0	124
Returning Starters: 6 OFF, 8 DEF			Mean Wins / Conf Wins	7.1 / 4.4		Turnovers	Exp. TO Margin	-7.7	121
Proj. F/+	**14.6%**	**42**	Conf. / Div. Title Odds	0.8%			Difference	-7.3	114

West Virginia coach Dana Holgorsen has appeared on many hot-seat lists this offseason due to the Mountaineers' 7-6 record in 2014, but it's far from cut-and-dry whether that's deserved. Yes, the Mountaineers barely broke .500 in his fourth year and must now replace both quarterback Clint Trickett and star wide receiver Kevin White, but the biggest indignation for Mountain-

eers fans might be that the offense regressed last season despite Holgorsen's reputation and a veteran group of skill players.

Holgorsen, one of the new-wave air raid gurus, has always relied on innovative and explosive offenses that compensate for undermanned defenses. But the script was flipped last season, as West Virginia was 25th in defensive S&P+ and 40th in offensive S&P+. The senior-led offense wasn't explosive (72nd in IsoPPP), despite moving at lightning speed (sixth-fastest in adjusted pace). Kevin White tripled his receiving yards and fellow senior Mario Alford doubled his as the offense improved from ranking 97th in 2013, but these were historic lows for Holgorsen's normally high-flying offenses. The offensive line was middle-of-the-road in terms of sack prevention, allowing a sack on 7.3 percent of passing downs (65th), but the biggest disappoint was in the run game, which ranked 79th. Theoretically, the Holgorsen air raid is built on run-pass options and allows for balance and unpredictability in the distribution between rushing and passing. But the offense hasn't actually functioned that way for the past few years, despite highly hyped running back Rushel Shell receiving the bulk of

the carries last season. The running back rotation will also feature redshirt freshman Donte Thomas-Williams. Junior Skyler Howard is the clear frontrunner in the race to replace Trickett at quarterback.

The West Virginia defense was a pleasant surprise last season, as it was particularly strong against the run (17th) and efficient on standard downs. It was break-don't-bend, however, ranking 89th in IsoPPP and failing to put much pressure on opposing quarterbacks (81st in overall havoc rate). The biggest issue for the defense in 2015 will be whether they can generate more turnovers and big defensive plays, especially with most of their already-low sack production leaving—the top three defenders in sacks and two of the top three defenders in tackles for loss were all seniors.

No. 43 Texas Longhorns (6-6, 4-5)

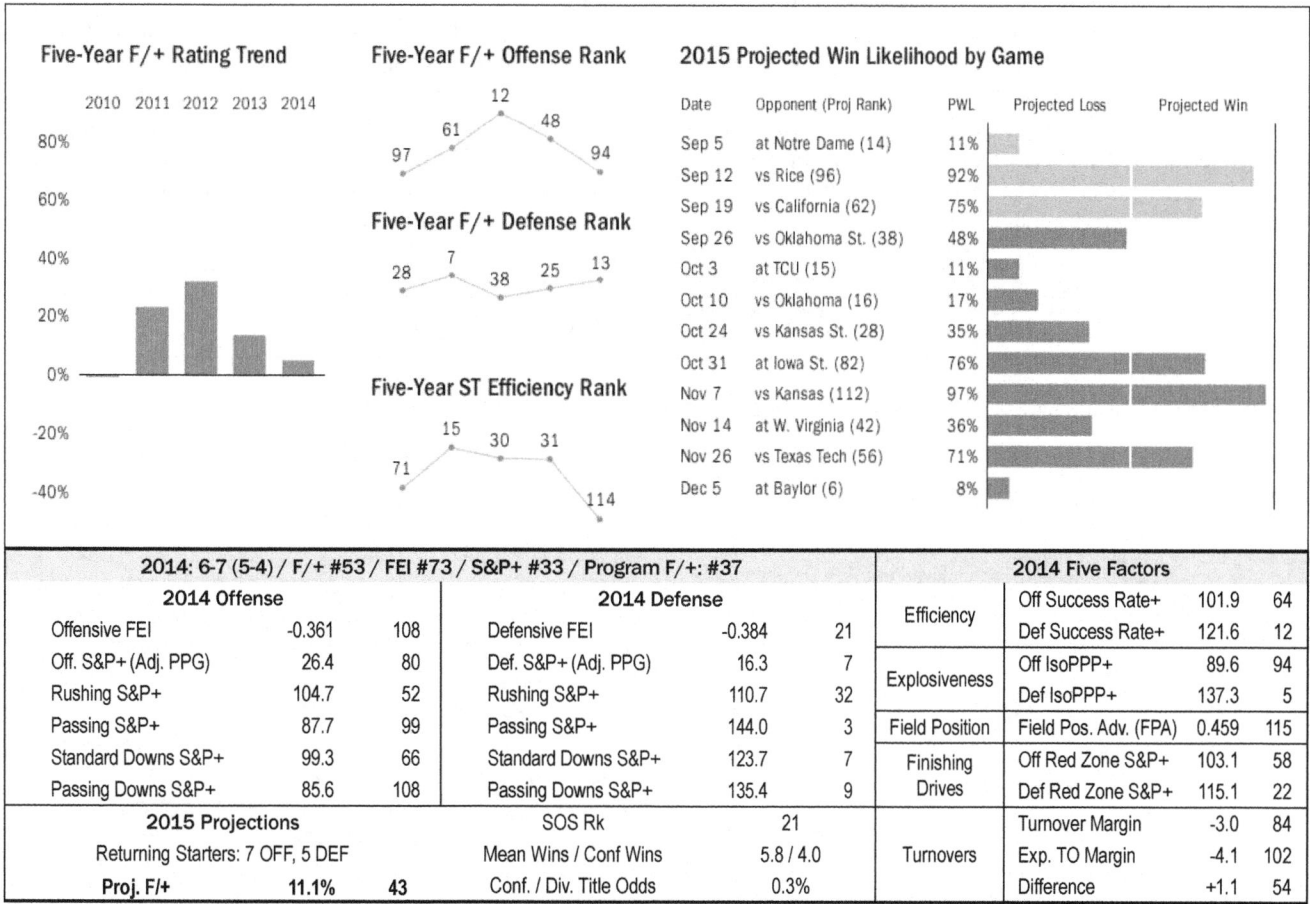

2014: 6-7 (5-4) / F/+ #53 / FEI #73 / S&P+ #33 / Program F/+: #37						2014 Five Factors			
2014 Offense			**2014 Defense**			Efficiency	Off Success Rate+	101.9	64
Offensive FEI	-0.361	108	Defensive FEI	-0.384	21		Def Success Rate+	121.6	12
Off. S&P+ (Adj. PPG)	26.4	80	Def. S&P+ (Adj. PPG)	16.3	7	Explosiveness	Off IsoPPP+	89.6	94
Rushing S&P+	104.7	52	Rushing S&P+	110.7	32		Def IsoPPP+	137.3	5
Passing S&P+	87.7	99	Passing S&P+	144.0	3	Field Position	Field Pos. Adv. (FPA)	0.459	115
Standard Downs S&P+	99.3	66	Standard Downs S&P+	123.7	7	Finishing Drives	Off Red Zone S&P+	103.1	58
Passing Downs S&P+	85.6	108	Passing Downs S&P+	135.4	9		Def Red Zone S&P+	115.1	22
2015 Projections			SOS Rk	21			Turnover Margin	-3.0	84
Returning Starters: 7 OFF, 5 DEF			Mean Wins / Conf Wins	5.8 / 4.0		Turnovers	Exp. TO Margin	-4.1	102
Proj. F/+	**11.1%**	**43**	Conf. / Div. Title Odds	0.3%			Difference	+1.1	54

It is now going on six seasons since Texas won 10 games (2009, with Colt McCoy and the national championship appearance against Alabama), and some are restless at the beginning of Charlie Strong's second season as coach. Much like post-Urban Meyer Florida, the Longhorns have recruited fairly well and have played well defensively, but haven't had a reliable quarterback since McCoy went down in the first quarter against Alabama. The search for a quarterback will continue to be the primary storyline in Austin, unless either Tyrone Swoopes or Jerrod Heard proves capable of being the

long-term solution. But this Texas team has other issues as well—namely, how to replace more than half of last year's starting defense that ranked 20th in defensive S&P+.

Heard and Swoopes are similar options athletically with slightly different strengths. Heard offers a little more explosive playmaking ability with his legs based on practice observations so far, while Swoopes is more developed as a passer. Both are big dual-threat quarterbacks who have struggled with accuracy issues and going through reads and progressions (Swoopes completed 58 percent of his passes last season), but have high ceilings depending on the offense and the play calling. It's unlikely that Heard will win the job over Swoopes as a pure passer; if he wins the battle it will be because of the flexibility his running brings to the table and because he stops locking on to his first target. A more veteran offensive line should help whoever lands the job. After Strong cleaned house on the line last season and injuries seemed to constantly reshuffle the starting five, this year's group is more experienced and has younger depth behind them, so there's optimism that the Longhorns will improve on a 76th ranking in both adjusted line yards and sack rate. The Longhorns have had no shortage of top tier running backs, but without elite line play for the past five years, much of that talent has gone wasted. Senior Johnathan Gray was the No. 1 overall running back in his recruiting class, but he hasn't yet lived up to expectations. Assuming the line can improve on its 31.6 percent opportunity rate last season (Gray averaged 34.2 percent, bettering his line's average), Gray might be able to show the hard downhill running style he often displayed in high school. Unfortunately, with the run game's growth dependent on the offensive line's consistency, an unsettled quarterback battle, and the receivers' frequent drops this spring (neither of the two projected veteran starters had above a 55 percent catch rate last season, and sophomore projected starter Dorain Leonard only caught one pass), it's too early to predict the Longhorns to return to their 2009 levels of offensive production.

The defense, meanwhile, must replace six starters from last season's efficient group that ranked fourth in passing S&P+, 19th in success rate, and 10th in preventing explosive plays. The group had a few deficiencies—the run defense could have been stouter, and they could have pressured the quarterback more—but overall it performed up to expectations, particularly considering that it was Strong's first season. Strong seemed to bring a toughness to the unit that was absent in Mack Brown's final seasons, but now he's already forced to reload. Five-star recruit and early enrollee linebacker Malik Jefferson should threaten for a starting job almost immediately. Secondary depth is limited and is a concern even with the high overall talent level on defense. However, the key will be whether the front seven can not only replace their losses (defensive tackle Malcom Brown, for instance), but improve their disruptiveness (78th in havoc rate) as the defense gains game experience and becomes more comfortable in Strong's second season.

With so much defensive turnover, it's unclear whether the Texas defense can pick up the offense's slack for another season. The future is bright in the Strong regime thanks to the refreshed and hardened attitude he's brought to the program and the high level of recruiting he's maintained, but Longhorn faithful may need to wait another year for the team to meet expectations for competition with the national elite.

No. 44 Minnesota Golden Gophers (6-6, 4-4)

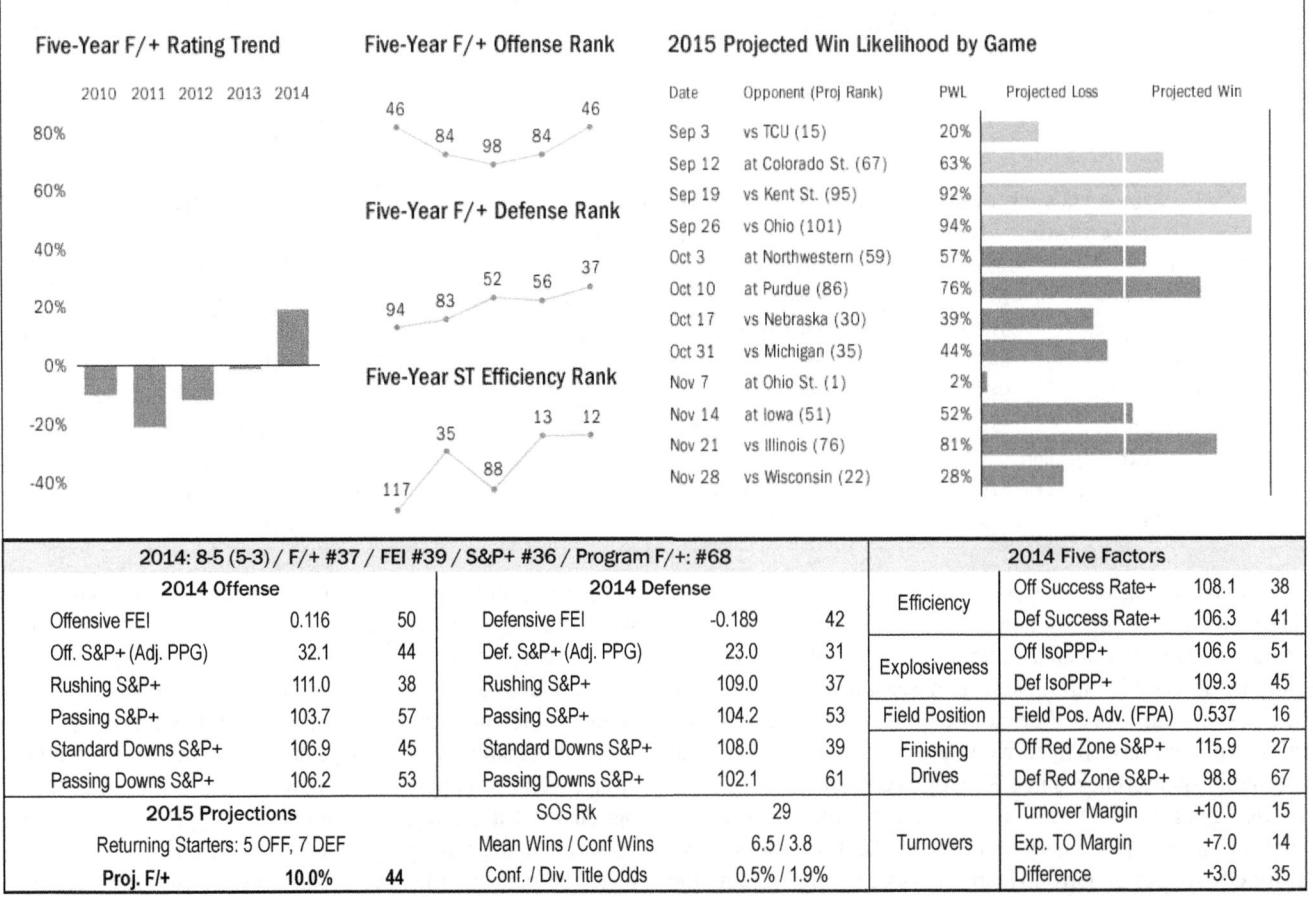

2014: 8-5 (5-3) / F/+ #37 / FEI #39 / S&P+ #36 / Program F/+: #68						2014 Five Factors			
2014 Offense			**2014 Defense**			Efficiency	Off Success Rate+	108.1	38
Offensive FEI	0.116	50	Defensive FEI	-0.189	42		Def Success Rate+	106.3	41
Off. S&P+ (Adj. PPG)	32.1	44	Def. S&P+ (Adj. PPG)	23.0	31	Explosiveness	Off IsoPPP+	106.6	51
Rushing S&P+	111.0	38	Rushing S&P+	109.0	37		Def IsoPPP+	109.3	45
Passing S&P+	103.7	57	Passing S&P+	104.2	53	Field Position	Field Pos. Adv. (FPA)	0.537	16
Standard Downs S&P+	106.9	45	Standard Downs S&P+	108.0	39	Finishing Drives	Off Red Zone S&P+	115.9	27
Passing Downs S&P+	106.2	53	Passing Downs S&P+	102.1	61		Def Red Zone S&P+	98.8	67
2015 Projections			SOS Rk	29		Turnovers	Turnover Margin	+10.0	15
Returning Starters: 5 OFF, 7 DEF			Mean Wins / Conf Wins	6.5 / 3.8			Exp. TO Margin	+7.0	14
Proj. F/+	**10.0%**	**44**	Conf. / Div. Title Odds	0.5% / 1.9%			Difference	+3.0	35

Coach Jerry Kill has certainly earned his pay at Minnesota, engineering an impressive three-year improvement in F/+ and an 8-5 record in 2014. Kill sparked the turnaround by running the ball early and often (ranking eighth in adjusted run-pass ratio), throwing to athletic freak tight end Maxx Williams (taken by the Ravens in the second round of the NFL Draft), and playing solid field position football (ranking seventh in defensive FP+). Sounds like a prototypical Big Ten champion, doesn't it? But without workhorse running back David Cobb, can the Golden Gophers sustain their success with a challenging schedule? Minnesota has a chance to set the tone for 2015 almost immediately with out of conference games against Heisman contender Trevone Boykin and TCU, followed by new coach Mike Bobo's Colorado State Rams. The schedule eases up until mid-October, when Nebraska and Michigan come to town, followed by a trip to Ohio State.

David Cobb was the definition of a workhorse Big Ten running back, and only Heisman finalist Melvin Gordon and Boise State running back Jay Ajayi had more attempts than Cobb's 315 last season. Cobb wasn't the most efficient back in the country, averaging just under a 40 percent opportunity rate, nor was he flashy, with just 4.6 highlight yards per opportunity, but he was consistent and dependable. The question for 2015 is whether the Gophers will distribute carries to the seven scholarship running backs on the roster or if one can seize the majority of the carries. Junior Rodrick Williams Jr. looks to be the safe choice (averaging 4.1 highlight yards per opportunity in limited action last season), but can highly-recruited redshirt freshman Jeff Jones or one of the three six-foot-plus freshman running backs take the job away mid-season? Despite Cobb's graduation, the number of potential replacement backs should

give Gopher faithful some confidence that the run game will be consistent yet again. A much bigger issue is certainly the turnover at wide receiver, where the leading returning receiver has just 16 catches. Williams was the most-targeted player in the passing game (26.6 percent target rate), so the entire unit is fairly green—but it is full of big bodies. Drew Wolitarsky (6-foot-3), Brandon Lingen (6-foot-5), Nate Wozniak (6-foot-10), Duke Anyanwu (6-foot-4), and four other first-year players stand above six feet tall as potential red zone targets in the passing game. The offense was slightly better than average overall in 2014 (44th in S&P+, 51st in PPP+), but the red zone offense was more efficient, likely due to Williams; height and Cobb's tenacity. The game plan will likely stay the same with Mitch Leidner back at quarterback (Leidner was an underrated runner himself, averaging 5.6 yards per carry and rushing over 100 times).

Like the offense, the defense excelled the most in winning the field-position battle, but struggled at the margins—on passing downs (64th), in the red zone (67th), and in the fourth quarter (67th). The defense, and particularly the defensive line, was excellent at stopping the run (27th in adjusted line yards), but failed to generate a significant pass rush from the front seven (87th in adjusted sack rate, despite ranking 23rd overall in havoc rate), which might explain some of the issues on passing downs. The thing that stands out about the secondary and the defense overall is that it is fairly deep, but very experienced. The secondary boasts four seniors and seven players with game experience. With a schedule that includes five teams in the top 36 of the F/+ projections, consistency and depth will likely be the most important assets in the Gophers' efforts to secure another New Year's Day bowl bid.

No. 45 North Carolina Tar Heels (7-5, 4-4)

2014: 6-7 (4-4) / F/+ #70 / FEI #71 / S&P+ #55 / Program F/+: #51							2014 Five Factors			
2014 Offense			**2014 Defense**				Efficiency	Off Success Rate+	114.0	25
Offensive FEI	0.304	30	Defensive FEI	0.439	114			Def Success Rate+	95.6	85
Off. S&P+ (Adj. PPG)	35.7	25	Def. S&P+ (Adj. PPG)	33.6	99		Explosiveness	Off IsoPPP+	108.9	47
Rushing S&P+	109.5	42	Rushing S&P+	89.2	101			Def IsoPPP+	84.4	111
Passing S&P+	115.0	31	Passing S&P+	87.3	108		Field Position	Field Pos. Adv. (FPA)	0.513	34
Standard Downs S&P+	109.6	37	Standard Downs S&P+	94.0	88		Finishing Drives	Off Red Zone S&P+	123.2	12
Passing Downs S&P+	113.8	37	Passing Downs S&P+	76.9	120			Def Red Zone S&P+	89.5	108
2015 Projections			SOS Rk		64		Turnovers	Turnover Margin	0.0	60
Returning Starters: 10 OFF, 7 DEF			Mean Wins / Conf Wins		6.8 / 3.8			Exp. TO Margin	-4.1	104
Proj. F/+	**9.0%**	**45**	Conf. / Div. Title Odds		1.9% / 3.8%			Difference	+4.1	27

The Tar Heels were amazingly inconsistent in 2014, losing to Rutgers and allowing 70 points to East Carolina, but outshooting a very good Georgia Tech team. Coach Larry Fedora enters his third year (with a minus-.3 difference between actual and second-order wins), but the typically excellent pass defense completely went out the window last season as the Tar Heels' identity shifted. Speaking of inconsistency, quarterback Marquise Williams led a passing renaissance as the offense ranked 31st in passing S&P+, but had too many head scratching bouts of inaccuracy that directly contributed to losses against East Carolina and NC State.

But the bigger priority for the Tar Heels will be fixing a pass defense that was 108th in passing S&P+ (to be fair, the run defense was 101st). They allowed far too many explosive plays (111th in IsoPPP+) and were abysmal in red zone defense (108th). Enter journeyman Gene Chizik, the Tar Heels' new defensive coordinator. While it's true that it's been a while since Chizik was a coordinator, he is widely respected for his defensive coaching at Auburn and Texas, and he has

high expectations at North Carolina—as indicated by his salary. Chizik will have most of last season's secondary to work with, but will need to find a new group of linebackers behind senior leader Jeff Schoettmer. That might start with finding a way to apply more pressure, as the Tar Heels ranked 116th in defensive back havoc rate and 124th in defending passing downs (by PPP+).

A lower level priority, but certainly one that would take some pressure off Marquise Williams, is finding a bell cow running back. Following Gio Bernard's departure, the Tar Heels' leading rusher in 2014 was actually Williams, who averaged a full yard per carry more and had a higher opportunity rate (49.1 percent to 42 percent) than the leading tailback on the roster, T.J. Logan. Former blue-chipper Elijah Hood is now a sophomore and has a chance to take more advantage of highlight opportunities (he averaged just 3.3 yards per opportunity last season) and to be more consistent overall (31 percent opportunity rate in 2014). Either Hood or Logan will need to step up to make it more than a one-man show for Williams.

No. 46 Utah State Aggies (8-4, 6-2)

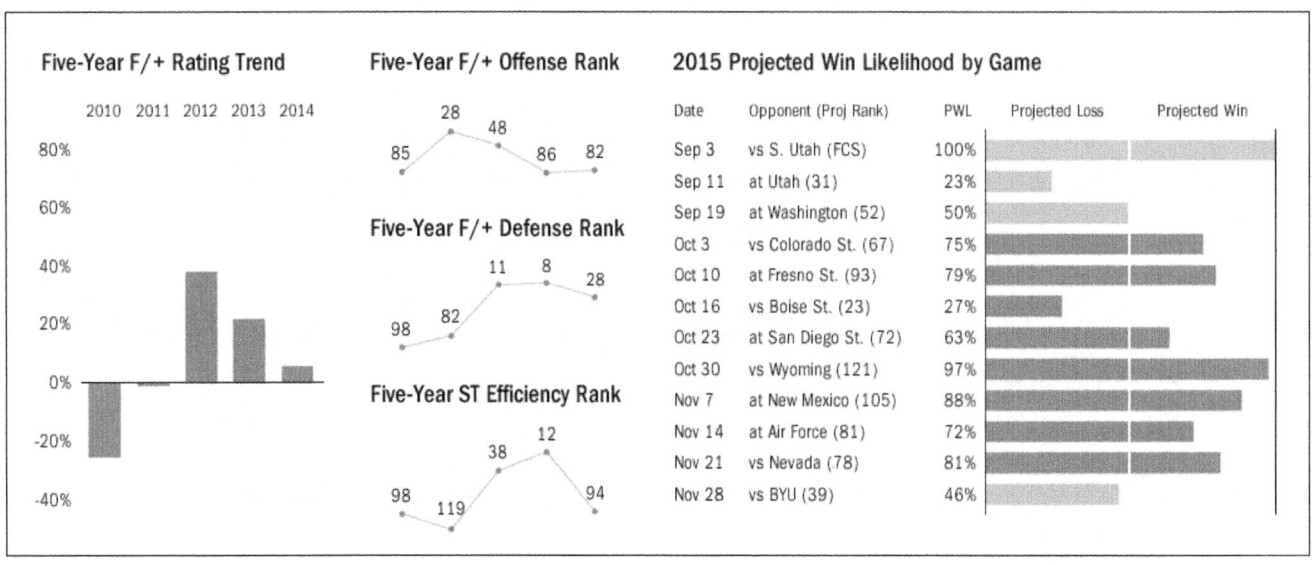

2014: 10-4 (6-2) / F/+ #52 / FEI #60 / S&P+ #52 / Program F/+: #49						2014 Five Factors			
2014 Offense			**2014 Defense**			Efficiency	Off Success Rate+	92.4	99
Offensive FEI	-0.225	90	Defensive FEI	-0.324	24		Def Success Rate+	107.6	37
Off. S&P+ (Adj. PPG)	26.8	77	Def. S&P+ (Adj. PPG)	23.1	32	Explosiveness	Off IsoPPP+	101.0	66
Rushing S&P+	101.8	63	Rushing S&P+	116.3	20		Def IsoPPP+	129.1	9
Passing S&P+	93.8	79	Passing S&P+	122.5	12	Field Position	Field Pos. Adv. (FPA)	0.507	46
Standard Downs S&P+	96.5	79	Standard Downs S&P+	116.0	21	Finishing Drives	Off Red Zone S&P+	88.3	104
Passing Downs S&P+	100.4	67	Passing Downs S&P+	124.1	15		Def Red Zone S&P+	117.0	20
2015 Projections			SOS Rk	101		Turnovers	Turnover Margin	+9.0	17
Returning Starters: 8 OFF, 7 DEF			Mean Wins / Conf Wins	8.0 / 5.8			Exp. TO Margin	+4.1	34
Proj. F/+	**8.3%**	**46**	Conf. / Div. Title Odds	6.7% / 13.3%			Difference	+4.9	20

Despite high-profile losses to Tennessee and Boise State at the beginning and end of the 2014 season, and despite losing quarterback Chuckie Keeton for the season (again), Utah State reached double-digit wins. 2015 brings two new coordinators and Keeton's return, along with a host of new starters at running back and on defense. There aren't any obvious deficiencies on this team—there are starting positions that need to be won, but this is mostly an experienced team modeled after the past few seasons' successes.

The big question will be whether Keeton's knees hold up this time. The backup quarterbacks got plenty of work in his absence, but Keeton was one of the most efficient signal callers in the country when healthy. He'll also have an experienced option at receiver in junior Hunter Sharp, a deep threat who catches roughly two-thirds of his targets. The passing game is set to be a highly efficient unit, which is needed considering last year's offense was 99th in success rate+ and 110th in passing success rate. The Aggies were locked in to the committee running back setup in 2014, as six players received 40 or more carries. Most of the true running backs have similar statistical profiles (low 30s in opportunity rate, five or so highlight yards per opportunity). If an efficient

running back emerged to complement the duo of Sharp and Keeton, then the offense would be far more complete. It's not clear whether there's a back on the roster that is up to the challenge, but redshirt freshman Justen Hervey is a new hat in the ring. Of course, this all starts with the offensive line, which was 106th in adjusted line yards and 60th in opportunity rate; with the line's best player, left tackle Kevin Whimpey, moving on, it may be a long shot to hope for the unit to improve.

Utah State's defense has been consistently excellent over the last few years, playing a bend-don't-break style (9th in IsoPPP+) that was particularly solid at preventing big runs. The defensive line was content at allowing steady gains (69th in adjusted line yards), but the defense locked down in the red zone (20th). The linebackers are the stars of the show here, and Nick Vigil is the likely leader after his brother Zach's graduation. Behind the front seven's stability, the secondary faces a degree of turnover, losing two safeties and a corner—but the depth chart is filled with upper class and experienced players, so don't expect the defense to drop off. The schedule is manageable for this unit, but watch out for the Boise State, BYU, and Air Force games as true tests for the defense.

No. 47 Cincinnati Bearcats (8-4, 6-2)

Date	Opponent (Proj Rank)	PWL
Sep 5	vs Alabama A&M (FCS)	100%
Sep 12	vs Temple (55)	63%
Sep 19	at Miami-OH (119)	92%
Sep 24	at Memphis (66)	57%
Oct 1	vs Miami-FL (37)	41%
Oct 16	at BYU (39)	28%
Oct 24	vs Connecticut (104)	94%
Oct 31	vs C. Florida (50)	62%
Nov 7	at Houston (68)	59%
Nov 14	vs Tulsa (92)	87%
Nov 20	at S. Florida (103)	85%
Nov 28	at E. Carolina (69)	59%

2014: 9-4 (7-1) / F/+ #47 / FEI #61 / S&P+ #38 / Program F/+: #47						2014 Five Factors			
2014 Offense			**2014 Defense**			Efficiency	Off Success Rate+	110.2	35
Offensive FEI	0.314	29	Defensive FEI	0.202	87		Def Success Rate+	91.4	103
Off. S&P+ (Adj. PPG)	35.1	31	Def. S&P+ (Adj. PPG)	26.4	52	Explosiveness	Off IsoPPP+	130.0	15
Rushing S&P+	108.0	46	Rushing S&P+	92.4	92		Def IsoPPP+	97.2	74
Passing S&P+	130.9	10	Passing S&P+	94.4	87	Field Position	Field Pos. Adv. (FPA)	0.484	96
Standard Downs S&P+	115.4	25	Standard Downs S&P+	98.2	75	Finishing Drives	Off Red Zone S&P+	109.2	43
Passing Downs S&P+	134.6	12	Passing Downs S&P+	85.2	109		Def Red Zone S&P+	100.4	62
2015 Projections			SOS Rk	116		Turnovers	Turnover Margin	+2.0	52
Returning Starters: 8 OFF, 4 DEF			Mean Wins / Conf Wins	8.3 / 5.7			Exp. TO Margin	+2.6	46
Proj. F/+	**6.2%**	**47**	Conf. / Div. Title Odds	17.6% / 35.1%			Difference	-0.6	73

The Bearcats had an up-and-down 2014 due to injuries and a few tough matchups, but one thing is clear in 2015: this team is all about Gunner Kiel's arm. The junior quarterback was a gunslinger, leading one of the most explosive offenses in the country (15th in IsoPPP+) and a top-ten passing attack despite an inconsistent ground game. Returning every major contributor at wide receiver—including five seniors who had over 400 receiving yards apiece—the offense looks to be just as downfield and deadly as last season. But can a more consistent ground game under sophomore Mike Boone (who led the team with 650 total rushing yards and 6.7 highlight yards per opportunity) and an even average defense push the Bearcats to the top of the AAC at the very least?

Over the course of the entire season, the Bearcats were simply not very good on defense. At 103rd in opponent-adjusted success rate and 109th on passing downs, the Bearcats were prone to big plays and long drives. Even a mediocre defensive performance could have the Bearcats looking beyond just the AAC Championship game for 2015. The schedule is very manageable, despite a tough three-game stretch at Memphis, against Miami, and at BYU. The problem is that those three teams are likely to be very stout offensively, and even with Cincinnati's likely prolific offense, they will need some semblance of a run defense to keep up. Someone on the defensive line must step up to replace defensive end Terrell Hartsfield, who graduated after posting twelve tackles for loss and nine sacks, and middle linebacker Jeff Luc, who had the most tackles on the team, along with nine tackles for loss and 6.5 sacks. The defensive coaching staff said repeatedly during the spring that the Bearcats would be more aggressive and blitz more often due to more trust in the secondary's coverage abilities. As long as the defense doesn't regress after losing arguably its top two playmakers from last season, another year of Kiel and a veteran receiver group should be enough for a crack at a ten-win season.

No. 48 Duke Blue Devils (7-5, 3-5)

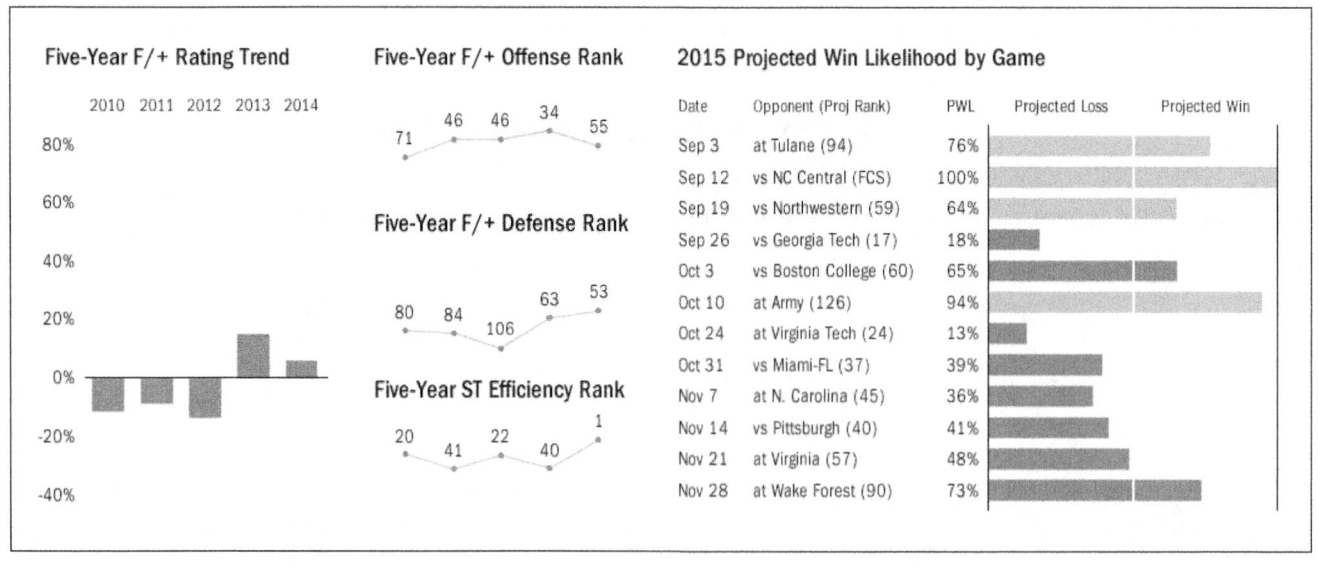

2014: 9-4 (5-3) / F/+ #51 / FEI #26 / S&P+ #73 / Program F/+: #66						2014 Five Factors			
2014 Offense			**2014 Defense**			Efficiency	Off Success Rate+	104.1	55
Offensive FEI	0.212	37	Defensive FEI	-0.261	33		Def Success Rate+	86.0	117
Off. S&P+ (Adj. PPG)	27.6	76	Def. S&P+ (Adj. PPG)	28.6	68	Explosiveness	Off IsoPPP+	98.6	72
Rushing S&P+	109.5	43	Rushing S&P+	83.3	112		Def IsoPPP+	100.6	64
Passing S&P+	93.9	78	Passing S&P+	102.4	57	Field Position	Field Pos. Adv. (FPA)	0.546	9
Standard Downs S&P+	103.5	55	Standard Downs S&P+	92.5	98	Finishing Drives	Off Red Zone S&P+	118.8	21
Passing Downs S&P+	95.4	85	Passing Downs S&P+	93.5	92		Def Red Zone S&P+	97.6	73
2015 Projections			SOS Rk	77		Turnovers	Turnover Margin	+6.0	33
Returning Starters: 6 OFF, 8 DEF			Mean Wins / Conf Wins	6.7 / 3.3			Exp. TO Margin	-0.8	78
Proj. F/+	**5.1%**	**48**	Conf. / Div. Title Odds	1.3% / 2.5%			Difference	+6.8	14

The Blue Devils have been steadily trending up since 2005, despite slight regression every three or so years, but the breakthrough season, where they first beat their conference average, was in 2013. They didn't manage that in 2014, but two of their four losses—to Virginia Tech (33rd in F/+) and Arizona State (27th)—were by a combined six points. This year, Duke loses starting quarterback Anthony Boone, who regressed slightly last season with poorer efficiency numbers as the passing offense dropped to 78th in the S&P+ after hitting 30th in 2013. Without efficient passing, this pass-happy offense was also less explosive than before in offensive coordinator Scottie Montgomery's first season. This year, the Blue Devils must replace their quarterback, their top two receivers, an All-American right guard, and a multi-year starting left tackle, all while trying to improve one of the worst run defenses in the country.

While there are three quarterbacks with experience on the roster, including last season's backup, Thomas Sirk (who was 10-of-14 passing with three touchdowns last season), finding a new receiving corps will be difficult. Jamison Crowder had almost a third of the team's targets and a 60 percent catch rate and recorded 1,085 receiving yards, and the team also loses Issac Blakeney, who was the second-most targeted receiver behind Crowder. Sirk brings not just experience, but also explosive rushing ability to the table as a quarterback, as he had the second-highest highlight yards per opportunity average of any back last season (8.4, though that's paired with just a 27 percent opportunity rate). The most explosive rushing threat, Shaun Wilson, was just a third-string freshman, but he led the team in both opportunity rate (44.9 percent) and highlight yards per opportunity (8.6) in limited overall opportunities (78 total carries, despite being just 20 yards from matching

starter Shaquille Powell's team-leading 618 rushing yards). Montgomery has options at running back; his work will likely need to be with the group of young receivers. However, if the offensive line can manage to absorb the blow of losing its two best linemen, then one of the country's most underrated lines (15th in adjusted line yards and fourth in adjusted sack rate) will certainly ease the burden on the new starting quarterback.

Duke was one of the most bend-don't-break defenses in the country, but that was mainly due to a poor run defense (125th in rushing S&P+) and consequently low success rate (117th). The Blue Devils also did their fair share of breaking—they ranked 73rd in red zone S&P+. But there were two shining spots for the Duke defense last season that should carry over to 2015: both starting safeties are playmaking ball hawks, and the defense consistently improved in the second halves of games (ranking 111th in the first half and 46th in the second). Both DeVon Edwards and Jeremy Cash return for 2015, and the pair combined for 194.5 tackles, 10 sacks, three interceptions, 16 pass breakups, and nine forced fumbles last season. In some ways the defense was all backwards, as the leaky sieve of a defensive line was 123rd in adjusted line yards, allowing opponents a 46.8 percent opportunity rate. When they were unable to stop the run up front, Edwards and Cash had to fly in from the secondary in run support. With a lot of new personnel along a defensive line that lost five contributors from last season, Duke's defense will likely be a success if Cash and Edwards actually have worse numbers than last season. With tough matchups with Georgia Tech, Virginia Tech, and Miami on the docket, the Blue Devils will have to take a few from the winnable-but-difficult group of games, including Northwestern, Boston College, North Carolina, and Virginia.

No. 49 N.C. State Wolfpack (7-5, 3-5)

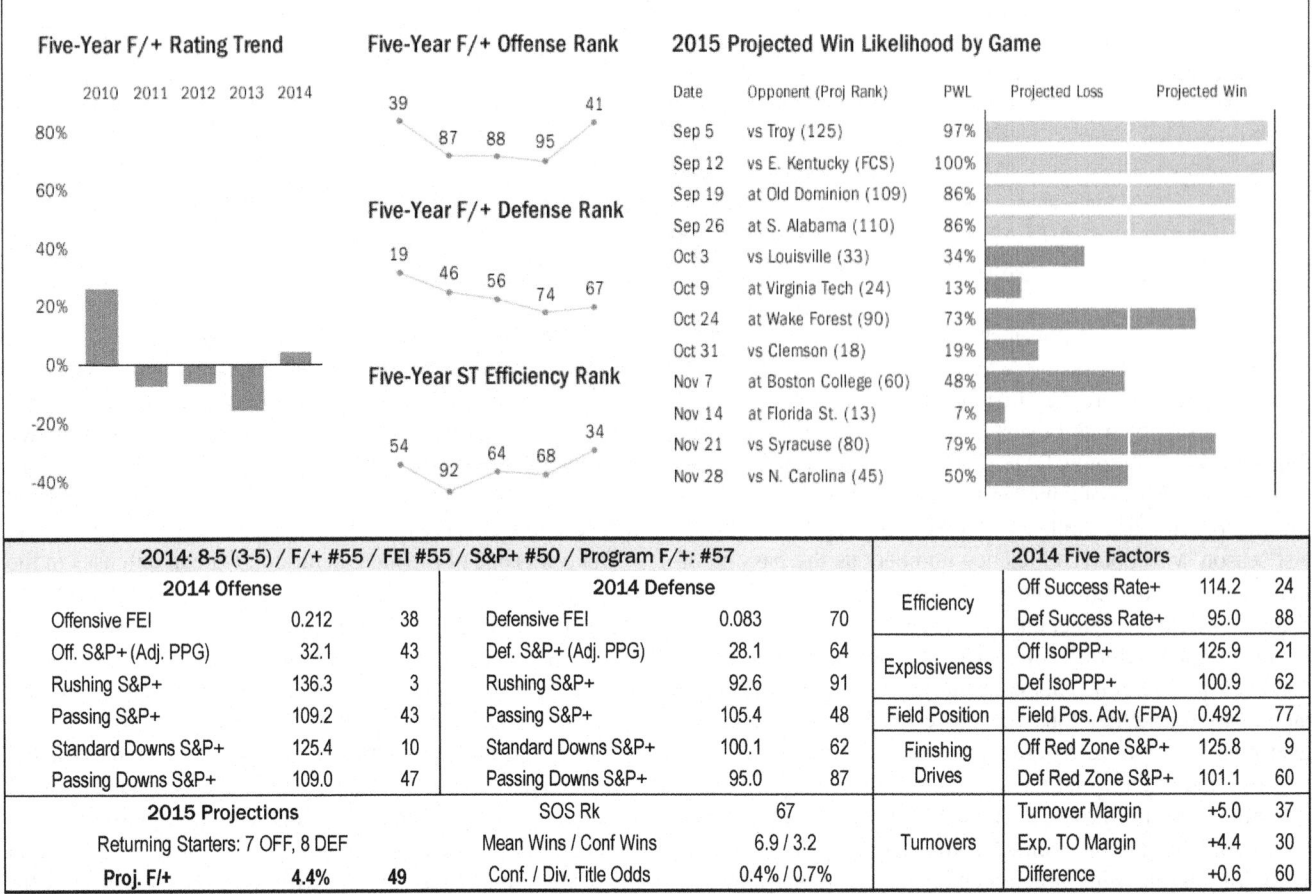

2014: 8-5 (3-5) / F/+ #55 / FEI #55 / S&P+ #50 / Program F/+: #57							2014 Five Factors		
2014 Offense			**2014 Defense**			Efficiency	Off Success Rate+	114.2	24
Offensive FEI	0.212	38	Defensive FEI	0.083	70		Def Success Rate+	95.0	88
Off. S&P+ (Adj. PPG)	32.1	43	Def. S&P+ (Adj. PPG)	28.1	64	Explosiveness	Off IsoPPP+	125.9	21
Rushing S&P+	136.3	3	Rushing S&P+	92.6	91		Def IsoPPP+	100.9	62
Passing S&P+	109.2	43	Passing S&P+	105.4	48	Field Position	Field Pos. Adv. (FPA)	0.492	77
Standard Downs S&P+	125.4	10	Standard Downs S&P+	100.1	62	Finishing	Off Red Zone S&P+	125.8	9
Passing Downs S&P+	109.0	47	Passing Downs S&P+	95.0	87	Drives	Def Red Zone S&P+	101.1	60
2015 Projections			SOS Rk	67			Turnover Margin	+5.0	37
Returning Starters: 7 OFF, 8 DEF			Mean Wins / Conf Wins	6.9 / 3.2		Turnovers	Exp. TO Margin	+4.4	30
Proj. F/+	4.4%	49	Conf. / Div. Title Odds	0.4% / 0.7%			Difference	+0.6	60

The Wolfpack were built on two things during their 8-5 2014 season: quarterback Jacoby Brissett and one of the best run-blocking offensive lines in the country. There is reason for optimism for 2015, as Brissett and three starting offensive linemen return and the defense doesn't look like it will take many steps back. Offensive coordinator Matt Canada has developed a reputation for his work with offensive lines, but it was Florida transfer Brissett and his running that revolutionized the offense last season. Brissett paced the third-most efficient and eighth-most explosive rushing attack (24th in overall offensive efficiency), even though he only averaged 7.4 rushes per game.

Just as important was the offensive line, which got a consistent push (to the extent that 47.9 percent of rushes were for at least five yards) and returns its three interior players. While the new left tackle will likely be fairly inexperienced, presumptive right tackle Alex Barr certainly has the size (6-foot-8) and has already started 18 games. It's fair to say that outside of Brissett's obvious contributions (he averaged 7.7 yards per carry and six highlight yards per carry, more than leading rusher Shadrach Thornton's 5.5 and 4.2, respectively), the offensive line was the biggest reason for the success of the run game. Getting those two new tackles up to speed should be priority number one for this offense, especially as

the three leading rushers return (though the future is certainly bright for the run game with three true freshman four-star running back recruits).

The offense should put up big numbers, assuming the passing game can overcome the loss of its top two wide receivers from last season. While the offense relies heavily on high-percentage short passes and many non-receivers are involved as pass catchers, Bo Hines in particular was a legitimate threat who decided to transfer in the offseason. There are options at receiver, but they are mostly unproven.

The Wolfpack's defense was unremarkable in 2014, ranking in the middle of the pack in nearly every statistical category. The biggest deficiency was in run defense, where they ranked 91st in S&P+ and 85th in PPP+, while the defensive line was 94th in adjusted line yards. Put simply, the front seven were getting outmanned, allowing five-yard gains on 39 percent of opponent runs. There was a lot of turnover, especially in the middle of the front seven, where three of the top five linemen and two of the top three linebackers are gone, so there is certainly opportunity. The line will be very young this season, with eight freshmen expected to contribute, while all of the secondary returns. With Louisville, Virginia Tech, Clemson, and Florida State on the schedule, the run defense will have to improve for the Wolfpack to rise above last season's effort.

No. 50 Central Florida Golden Knights (8-4, 6-2)

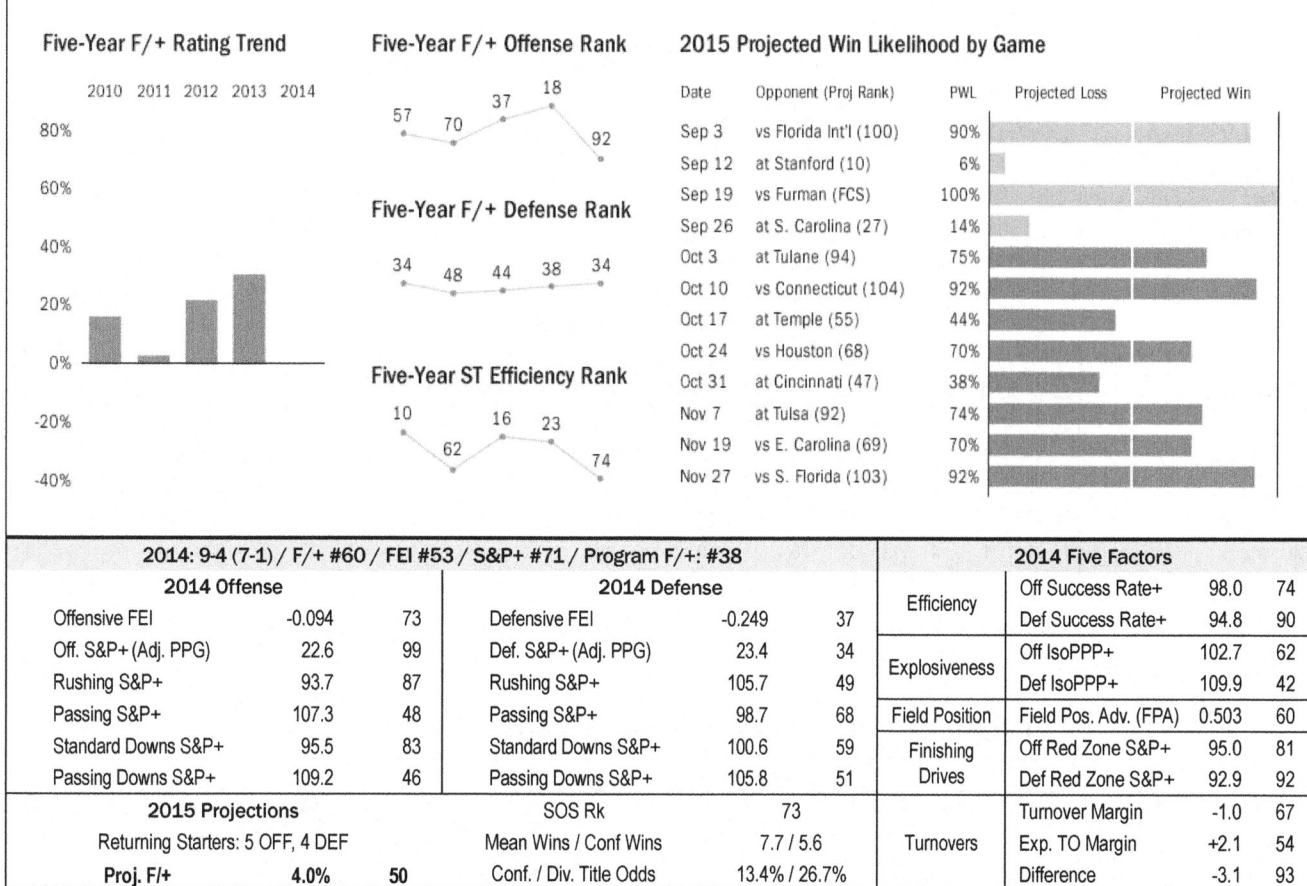

Five-Year F/+ Rating Trend

2010 2011 2012 2013 2014

Five-Year F/+ Offense Rank

57 70 37 18 92

Five-Year F/+ Defense Rank

34 48 44 38 34

Five-Year ST Efficiency Rank

10 62 16 23 74

2015 Projected Win Likelihood by Game

Date	Opponent (Proj Rank)	PWL	Projected Loss	Projected Win
Sep 3	vs Florida Int'l (100)	90%		
Sep 12	at Stanford (10)	6%		
Sep 19	vs Furman (FCS)	100%		
Sep 26	at S. Carolina (27)	14%		
Oct 3	at Tulane (94)	75%		
Oct 10	vs Connecticut (104)	92%		
Oct 17	at Temple (55)	44%		
Oct 24	vs Houston (68)	70%		
Oct 31	at Cincinnati (47)	38%		
Nov 7	at Tulsa (92)	74%		
Nov 19	vs E. Carolina (69)	70%		
Nov 27	vs S. Florida (103)	92%		

2014: 9-4 (7-1) / F/+ #60 / FEI #53 / S&P+ #71 / Program F/+: #38

2014 Offense			2014 Defense		
Offensive FEI	-0.094	73	Defensive FEI	-0.249	37
Off. S&P+ (Adj. PPG)	22.6	99	Def. S&P+ (Adj. PPG)	23.4	34
Rushing S&P+	93.7	87	Rushing S&P+	105.7	49
Passing S&P+	107.3	48	Passing S&P+	98.7	68
Standard Downs S&P+	95.5	83	Standard Downs S&P+	100.6	59
Passing Downs S&P+	109.2	46	Passing Downs S&P+	105.8	51

2015 Projections			SOS Rk	73
Returning Starters: 5 OFF, 4 DEF			Mean Wins / Conf Wins	7.7 / 5.6
Proj. F/+	**4.0%**	**50**	Conf. / Div. Title Odds	13.4% / 26.7%

2014 Five Factors

Efficiency	Off Success Rate+	98.0	74
	Def Success Rate+	94.8	90
Explosiveness	Off IsoPPP+	102.7	62
	Def IsoPPP+	109.9	42
Field Position	Field Pos. Adv. (FPA)	0.503	60
Finishing Drives	Off Red Zone S&P+	95.0	81
	Def Red Zone S&P+	92.9	92
Turnovers	Turnover Margin	-1.0	67
	Exp. TO Margin	+2.1	54
	Difference	-3.1	93

The AAC race will likely be one of the most underrated in the country, with Central Florida, Memphis, Navy, and Cincinnati all likely vying for the title. For Central Florida, the primary question is whether the Knights can turn around an anemic rushing offense after losing Storm Johnson to the NFL. Of course, the bigger loss in the NFL's eyes was quarterback Blake Bortles, but new starter Justin Holman was solid, if unspectacular (2,952 passing yards, 14 picks, 56.9 percent completion percentage). With the loss of those two stars, it was expected that the Knights' offense would regress in 2014 (it went from ninth to 75th in offensive S&P+), but the question was whether there was, and is now, enough offensive infrastructure around to mitigate the loss of two superstars.

Unfortunately for Holman, he loses his top four receivers, which equates to approximately 80 percent of his targets last season. The leading receiver among returning players, sophomore Jordan Akins, had just 12 catches for 135 yards last season. There is young talent, with six freshman or redshirt freshman receivers on the roster, including blue-chip signee Tristan Payton. Even with all of the departures at receiver, the offensive line and run game remain the primary offensive question marks, as the line ranked 111th in adjusted line yards and the top three running backs (all returning juniors), averaged 3.7 yards per carry and under a 36 percent opportunity rate. With eight returning and experienced linemen and two young running backs, there is some hope for the unit, but they will need to be consistent to relieve some pressure on Holman and his dearth of proven receivers.

The defense, meanwhile, returns most of last season's primary contributors, including senior defensive end Thomas Niles (7.5 sacks), and the strength is undoubtedly up front. The defensive line ranked 22nd and 28th in adjusted line yards and sack rate, respectively, and is likely the best position group on the team. As experienced as the front seven is, the Knights are very green in the secondary, replacing all four starters. With Central Florida essentially replacing two entire position groups, the Knights are likely to be highly volatile in 2015.

NCAA Win Projections

Projected Win Probabilities For ACC Teams

ACC Atlantic	12-0	11-1	10-2	9-3	8-4	7-5	6-6	5-7	4-8	3-9	2-10	1-11	0-12	8-0	7-1	6-2	5-3	4-4	3-5	2-6	1-7	0-8
Boston College	-	-	-	1	5	16	29	29	16	4	-	-	-	-	-	1	7	20	34	27	10	1
Clemson	2	11	25	30	21	9	2	-	-	-	-	-	-	8	27	35	22	7	1	-	-	-
Florida State	9	29	35	20	6	1	-	-	-	-	-	-	-	13	36	34	14	3	-	-	-	-
Louisville	-	2	10	23	29	22	10	3	1	-	-	-	-	1	9	27	34	21	7	1	-	-
NC State	-	-	2	9	22	31	24	10	2	-	-	-	-	-	-	2	11	27	32	21	6	1
Syracuse	-	-	-	-	1	3	13	27	30	19	6	1	-	-	-	-	1	6	20	35	30	8
Wake Forest	-	-	-	-	-	1	5	17	30	30	15	2	-	-	-	-	-	2	10	28	39	21

ACC Coastal	12-0	11-1	10-2	9-3	8-4	7-5	6-6	5-7	4-8	3-9	2-10	1-11	0-12	8-0	7-1	6-2	5-3	4-4	3-5	2-6	1-7	0-8
Duke	-	-	2	8	18	27	25	14	5	1	-	-	-	-	1	4	13	26	30	19	6	1
Georgia Tech	1	6	17	28	26	15	6	1	-	-	-	-	-	6	22	33	25	11	3	-	-	-
Miami-FL	-	-	2	7	17	25	25	16	6	2	-	-	-	-	1	5	16	28	28	16	5	1
North Carolina	-	-	2	8	20	28	25	12	4	1	-	-	-	-	1	6	20	31	27	12	3	-
Pittsburgh	-	1	4	12	22	26	21	10	3	1	-	-	-	-	3	13	27	30	19	7	1	-
Virginia	-	-	-	-	-	2	8	20	30	26	12	2	-	-	-	1	5	15	29	31	16	3
Virginia Tech	1	7	23	31	23	11	3	1	-	-	-	-	-	6	25	35	23	9	2	-	-	-

Projected Win Probabilities For American Teams

American East	12-0	11-1	10-2	9-3	8-4	7-5	6-6	5-7	4-8	3-9	2-10	1-11	0-12	8-0	7-1	6-2	5-3	4-4	3-5	2-6	1-7	0-8
Central Florida	-	1	6	19	30	26	13	4	1	-	-	-	-	4	18	31	28	14	4	1	-	-
Cincinnati	1	4	14	25	28	18	8	2	-	-	-	-	-	5	20	31	26	13	4	1	-	-
Connecticut	-	-	-	-	-	1	4	15	30	31	16	3	-	-	-	-	1	5	17	33	32	12
East Carolina	-	-	1	4	13	24	28	20	8	2	-	-	-	1	6	20	32	26	12	3	-	-
South Florida	-	-	-	-	-	1	5	14	27	31	18	4	-	-	-	-	1	7	22	36	27	7
Temple	-	2	9	21	28	23	12	4	1	-	-	-	-	4	19	33	28	13	3	-	-	-

American West	12-0	11-1	10-2	9-3	8-4	7-5	6-6	5-7	4-8	3-9	2-10	1-11	0-12	8-0	7-1	6-2	5-3	4-4	3-5	2-6	1-7	0-8
Houston	-	1	6	16	26	26	16	7	2	-	-	-	-	1	7	20	31	25	13	3	-	-
Memphis	-	1	5	16	26	26	17	7	2	-	-	-	-	1	8	22	31	24	11	3	-	-
Navy	-	6	20	30	26	13	4	1	-	-	-	-	-	7	24	33	24	10	2	-	-	-
SMU	-	-	-	-	-	-	2	9	23	34	25	7	-	-	-	-	-	3	12	29	37	19
Tulane	-	-	-	1	3	10	22	30	22	10	2	-	-	-	-	2	9	23	32	24	9	1
Tulsa	-	-	-	1	3	9	18	26	23	14	5	1	-	-	-	1	7	18	29	28	14	3

Projected Win Probabilities For Big 12 Teams

Big 12	12-0	11-1	10-2	9-3	8-4	7-5	6-6	5-7	4-8	3-9	2-10	1-11	0-12	9-0	8-1	7-2	6-3	5-4	4-5	3-6	2-7	1-8	0-9
							Overall Wins																
Baylor	14	34	32	15	4	1	-	-	-	-	-	-	-	14	35	32	15	4	-	-	-	-	-
Iowa State	-	-	-	-	-	-	3	11	26	35	22	3	-	-	-	-	-	-	3	15	37	39	6
Kansas	-	-	-	-	-	-	-	-	3	16	40	41	-	-	-	-	-	-	-	1	6	32	61
Kansas State	1	6	18	28	26	15	5	1	-	-	-	-	-	1	7	20	31	26	12	3	-	-	-
Oklahoma	2	13	28	31	19	6	1	-	-	-	-	-	-	5	21	34	27	11	2	-	-	-	-
Oklahoma State	-	1	6	16	27	27	16	6	1	-	-	-	-	-	1	6	17	29	28	15	4	-	-
TCU	5	20	31	26	13	4	1	-	-	-	-	-	-	6	23	34	25	10	2	-	-	-	-
Texas	-	-	-	2	8	19	28	25	13	4	1	-	-	-	-	2	8	23	33	24	9	1	-
Texas Tech	-	-	-	-	2	9	23	33	24	8	1	-	-	-	-	-	2	8	23	34	25	7	1
West Virginia	-	-	2	10	24	31	22	9	2	-	-	-	-	-	-	3	13	30	33	17	4	-	-

Projected Win Probabilities For Big 10 Teams

Overall Wins

Big Ten East	12-0	11-1	10-2	9-3	8-4	7-5	6-6	5-7	4-8	3-9	2-10	1-11	0-12	8-0	7-1	6-2	5-3	4-4	3-5	2-6	1-7	0-8
Indiana	-	-	-	-	1	6	17	27	27	16	5	1		-	-	-	1	7	23	36	26	7
Maryland	-	-	-	-	1	7	19	31	27	12	3	-		-	-	-	1	7	24	37	25	6
Michigan	-	1	6	17	28	27	15	5	1	-		-		-	4	19	35	29	11	2	-	-
Michigan State	3	21	39	27	9	1	-	-	-	-	-	-		8	44	36	11	1	-	-	-	-
Ohio State	53	36	10	1	-	-	-	-	-	-	-	-		68	28	4	-	-	-	-	-	-
Penn State	-	2	15	31	30	16	5	1	-	-	-			-	3	25	40	24	7	1	-	-
Rutgers	-	-	-	-	-	2	10	26	34	21	6	1		-	-	-	-	1	6	25	43	25
Big Ten West	12-0	11-1	10-2	9-3	8-4	7-5	6-6	5-7	4-8	3-9	2-10	1-11	0-12	8-0	7-1	6-2	5-3	4-4	3-5	2-6	1-7	0-8
Illinois	-	-	-	-	1	5	15	27	29	17	5	1		-	-	-	1	5	18	34	31	11
Iowa	-	1	4	14	25	27	19	8	2	-	-	-		-	2	12	27	32	19	7	1	-
Minnesota	-	-	1	6	16	27	26	16	6	2	-	-		-	1	7	20	31	26	12	3	-
Nebraska	1	7	20	30	24	13	4	1	-	-	-	-		3	17	33	29	13	4	1	-	-
Northwestern	-	-	-	1	5	14	25	26	19	8	2	-		-	-	2	11	25	32	22	7	1
Purdue	-	-	-	-	-	1	6	17	29	29	15	3		-	-	-	1	6	19	35	30	9
Wisconsin	3	24	38	25	8	2	-	-	-	-	-	-		23	42	26	8	1	-	-	-	-

Projected Win Probabilities For Conference USA Teams

Overall Wins

Conf USA East	12-0	11-1	10-2	9-3	8-4	7-5	6-6	5-7	4-8	3-9	2-10	1-11	0-12	8-0	7-1	6-2	5-3	4-4	3-5	2-6	1-7	0-8
Charlotte	-	-	-	-	2	6	16	26	26	17	6	1		-	-	1	7	20	31	27	12	2
Florida Atlantic	-	-	-	-	1	5	13	23	25	20	10	3		-	-	3	11	24	30	22	9	1
Florida International	-	-	-	1	3	11	24	29	21	9	2	-		-	-	2	11	27	33	20	6	1
Marshall	27	41	24	7	1	-	-	-	-	-	-	-		39	44	15	2	-	-	-	-	-
Middle Tennessee	-	-	-	2	9	21	30	24	11	3	-	-		-	1	9	27	35	21	6	1	-
Old Dominion	-	-	-	2	7	16	26	26	16	6	1	-		-	-	3	13	27	30	19	7	1
Western Kentucky	-	4	17	28	27	16	6	2	-	-	-	-		9	29	34	20	7	1	-	-	-
Conf USA West	12-0	11-1	10-2	9-3	8-4	7-5	6-6	5-7	4-8	3-9	2-10	1-11	0-12	8-0	7-1	6-2	5-3	4-4	3-5	2-6	1-7	0-8
Louisiana Tech	-	4	20	36	26	11	3	-	-	-	-	-		17	41	30	10	2	-	-	-	-
North Texas	-	-	-	-	-	1	5	16	29	30	16	3		-	-	-	2	9	25	35	23	6
Rice	-	-	1	5	16	27	27	17	6	1	-	-		-	4	16	30	28	16	5	1	-
Southern Miss	-	-	-	-	1	5	16	28	28	16	5	1		-	-	2	11	26	32	21	7	1
UTEP	-	-	-	1	5	14	24	27	19	8	2	-		-	1	6	17	27	27	16	5	1
UTSA	-	-	-	-	-	-	1	4	13	25	30	21	6	-	-	1	3	11	24	31	23	7

Projected Win Probabilities For Independent Teams

Independents	12-0	11-1	10-2	9-3	8-4	7-5	6-6	5-7	4-8	3-9	2-10	1-11	0-12
						Overall Wins							
Army	-	-	-	-	-	1	7	20	35	29	8	-	-
BYU	-	-	3	13	25	31	20	7	1	-	-	-	-
Notre Dame	3	14	28	28	18	7	2	-	-	-	-	-	-

Projected Win Probabilities For MAC Teams

MAC East	12-0	11-1	10-2	9-3	8-4	7-5	6-6	5-7	4-8	3-9	2-10	1-11	0-12	8-0	7-1	6-2	5-3	4-4	3-5	2-6	1-7	0-8
							Overall Wins															
Akron	-	-	-	-	3	9	20	27	24	13	4	-	-	-	1	7	17	27	27	15	5	1
Bowling Green	-	-	-	2	6	15	24	25	18	8	2	-	-	-	3	14	27	31	18	6	1	-
Buffalo	-	-	-	-	2	7	15	25	26	17	7	1	-	-	-	2	9	21	29	25	12	2
Kent State	-	-	-	3	10	21	28	23	11	3	1	-	-	-	5	17	29	27	16	5	1	-
Massachusetts	-	-	-	-	1	4	11	22	27	22	10	3	-	-	-	3	13	27	31	19	6	1
Miami-OH	-	-	-	-	-	2	9	22	32	25	9	1	-	-	-	1	7	20	33	27	11	1
Ohio	-	-	-	1	5	13	24	26	20	9	2	-	-	-	1	4	15	27	28	18	6	1
MAC West	**12-0**	**11-1**	**10-2**	**9-3**	**8-4**	**7-5**	**6-6**	**5-7**	**4-8**	**3-9**	**2-10**	**1-11**	**0-12**	**8-0**	**7-1**	**6-2**	**5-3**	**4-4**	**3-5**	**2-6**	**1-7**	**0-8**
Ball State	-	1	4	14	26	29	18	7	1	-	-	-	-	1	10	26	32	22	8	1	-	
Central Michigan	-	-	-	-	3	9	21	31	24	10	2	-	-	-	1	5	16	30	30	15	3	-
Eastern Michigan	-	-	-	-	-	-	1	4	14	30	34	17		-	-	-	-	-	3	15	41	41
Northern Illinois	-	3	15	29	29	17	6	1	-	-	-	-	-	8	27	34	22	8	1	-	-	-
Toledo	-	5	16	27	27	16	7	2	-	-	-	-	-	7	24	33	24	10	2	-	-	-
Western Michigan	-	-	2	12	26	32	20	7	1	-	-	-	-	4	20	35	28	11	2	-	-	-

Projected Win Probabilities For MWC Teams

MWC Mountain	12-0	11-1	10-2	9-3	8-4	7-5	6-6	5-7	4-8	3-9	2-10	1-11	0-12	8-0	7-1	6-2	5-3	4-4	3-5	2-6	1-7	0-8
							Overall Wins															
Air Force	-	-	1	4	16	29	28	16	5	1	-	-	-	-	2	13	29	32	18	5	1	-
Boise State	25	41	25	8	1	-	-	-	-	-	-	-	-	54	37	8	1	-	-	-	-	-
Colorado State	-	2	9	22	28	23	11	4	1	-	-	-	-	1	7	25	34	23	8	2	-	-
New Mexico	-	-	-	-	1	5	15	27	27	18	6	1	-	-	-	-	3	11	27	33	21	5
Utah State	-	3	11	23	28	21	10	3	1	-	-	-	-	5	23	35	25	10	2	-	-	-
Wyoming	-	-	-	-	-	1	5	16	31	32	13	2	-	-	-	-	-	3	14	35	36	12
MWC West	**12-0**	**11-1**	**10-2**	**9-3**	**8-4**	**7-5**	**6-6**	**5-7**	**4-8**	**3-9**	**2-10**	**1-11**	**0-12**	**8-0**	**7-1**	**6-2**	**5-3**	**4-4**	**3-5**	**2-6**	**1-7**	**0-8**
Fresno State	-	-	-	-	1	6	16	28	28	16	5	-	-	-	1	4	14	27	29	18	6	1
Hawaii*	-	-	-	-	-	1	6	15	25	27	18	7	1	-	-	1	5	16	29	29	16	4
Nevada	-	-	3	14	28	30	18	6	1	-	-	-	-	2	13	31	31	17	5	1	-	-
San Diego State	-	2	8	20	28	24	13	4	1	-	-	-	-	3	15	30	30	16	5	1	-	-
San Jose State	-	-	-	-	1	6	17	28	27	15	5	1	-	-	-	3	13	27	31	19	6	1
UNLV	-	-	-	-	-	1	5	16	32	33	13	-	-	-	-	-	1	4	15	32	34	14

*Hawaii will play 13 regular season games; for projected overall records, 12-0 means 13-0, 11-1 means 12-1, etc.

Projected Win Probabilities For Pac-12 Teams

Pac 12 North	Overall Wins																						
	12-0	11-1	10-2	9-3	8-4	7-5	6-6	5-7	4-8	3-9	2-10	1-11	0-12	9-0	8-1	7-2	6-3	5-4	4-5	3-6	2-7	1-8	0-9
California	-	-	-	-	-	2	10	24	32	23	8	1	-	-	-	-	-	1	8	26	39	22	4
Oregon	15	36	32	14	3	-	-	-	-	-	-	-	-	27	42	24	6	1	-	-	-	-	-
Oregon State	-	-	-	-	-	3	12	26	31	21	6	1	-	-	-	-	-	2	11	28	35	20	4
Stanford	3	15	30	30	16	5	1	-	-	-	-	-	-	6	24	37	25	7	1	-	-	-	-
Washington	-	-	-	-	1	5	15	27	29	17	5	1	-	-	-	-	1	6	20	34	28	10	1
Washington State	-	-	-	-	1	4	16	31	30	15	3	-	-	-	-	-	-	1	8	24	36	25	6
Pac 12 South	12-0	11-1	10-2	9-3	8-4	7-5	6-6	5-7	4-8	3-9	2-10	1-11	0-12	9-0	8-1	7-2	6-3	5-4	4-5	3-6	2-7	1-8	0-9
Arizona	-	1	5	17	30	28	14	4	1	-	-	-	-	-	1	6	19	34	27	11	2	-	-
Arizona State	1	6	19	29	26	14	4	1	-	-	-	-	-	1	9	26	34	22	7	1	-	-	-
Colorado*	-	-	-	-	-	-	1	5	18	34	30	11	1	-	-	-	-	-	-	4	18	43	35
UCLA	9	27	35	21	7	1	-	-	-	-	-	-	-	10	30	34	19	6	1	-	-	-	-
USC	1	5	17	29	27	15	5	1	-	-	-	-	-	2	11	27	32	20	7	1	-	-	-
Utah	-	-	3	11	23	28	22	10	3	-	-	-	-	-	1	5	19	33	28	12	2	-	-

*Colorado will play 13 regular season games; for projected overall records, 12-0 means 13-0, 11-1 means 12-1, etc.

Projected Win Probabilities For SEC Teams

SEC East	Overall Wins																					
	12-0	11-1	10-2	9-3	8-4	7-5	6-6	5-7	4-8	3-9	2-10	1-11	0-12	8-0	7-1	6-2	5-3	4-4	3-5	2-6	1-7	0-8
Florida	-	-	-	3	11	24	32	22	7	1	-	-	-	-	-	2	9	24	35	24	6	-
Georgia	6	23	34	25	10	2	-	-	-	-	-	-	-	10	32	35	18	4	1	-	-	-
Kentucky	-	-	-	-	-	2	9	23	35	24	7	-	-	-	-	-	-	1	8	26	43	22
Missouri	1	9	23	31	22	10	3	1	-	-	-	-	-	2	13	30	30	18	6	1	-	-
South Carolina	-	1	4	13	24	28	20	8	2	-	-	-	-	-	2	10	25	33	22	7	1	-
Tennessee	-	1	6	18	29	27	14	4	1	-	-	-	-	-	2	12	27	32	20	6	1	-
Vanderbilt	-	-	-	-	-	-	2	9	24	34	24	7	-	-	-	-	-	-	3	17	47	33
SEC West	12-0	11-1	10-2	9-3	8-4	7-5	6-6	5-7	4-8	3-9	2-10	1-11	0-12	8-0	7-1	6-2	5-3	4-4	3-5	2-6	1-7	0-8
Alabama	13	32	31	17	6	1	-	-	-	-	-	-	-	17	34	30	14	4	1	-	-	-
Arkansas	-	1	4	13	25	28	19	8	2	-	-	-	-	-	1	5	15	27	28	17	6	1
Auburn	-	3	12	24	29	21	9	2	-	-	-	-	-	-	4	15	27	30	17	6	1	-
LSU	1	8	22	31	23	11	3	1	-	-	-	-	-	1	9	25	32	22	9	2	-	-
Mississippi State	-	-	1	6	17	29	29	15	3	-	-	-	-	-	-	1	7	19	32	28	12	1
Ole Miss	1	10	26	32	21	8	2	-	-	-	-	-	-	2	12	28	30	20	7	1	-	-
Texas A&M	-	-	2	9	21	30	24	11	3	-	-	-	-	-	1	5	17	30	29	15	3	-

Projected Win Probabilities For Sun Belt Teams

Sun Belt	Overall Wins																					
	12-0	11-1	10-2	9-3	8-4	7-5	6-6	5-7	4-8	3-9	2-10	1-11	0-12	8-0	7-1	6-2	5-3	4-4	3-5	2-6	1-7	0-8
Appalachian State	-	2	9	21	27	23	13	4	1	-	-	-	-	2	12	26	30	20	8	2	-	-
Arkansas State	-	1	8	23	32	23	10	3	-	-	-	-	-	15	34	31	15	4	1	-	-	-
Georgia Southern	-	4	21	34	27	11	3	-	-	-	-	-	-	28	41	23	7	1	-	-	-	-
Georgia State	-	-	-	-	1	5	14	25	28	19	7	1	-	-	-	1	5	17	31	29	14	3
Idaho	-	-	-	-	-	2	8	18	28	27	14	3	-	-	-	1	4	13	27	30	20	5
New Mexico State	-	-	-	-	-	-	3	9	20	30	25	11	2	-	-	2	11	27	34	21	5	-
South Alabama	-	-	-	-	1	6	15	26	28	17	6	1	-	-	-	3	12	25	31	21	7	1
Texas State	-	-	-	1	4	14	26	27	19	7	2	-	-	-	1	4	16	31	29	15	4	-
Troy	-	-	-	-	-	1	4	13	27	30	20	5	-	-	-	3	12	26	33	21	5	-
UL-Lafayette	-	1	7	18	29	25	14	5	1	-	-	-	-	2	14	30	31	17	5	1	-	-
UL-Monroe*	-	-	-	1	3	9	19	26	23	13	5	1	-	-	2	9	21	31	24	11	2	-

*UL-Monroe will play 13 regular season games; for projected overall records, 12-0 means 13-0, 11-1 means 12-1, etc.

NCAA F/+ Projections

NCAA Teams, No. 1 to No. 128

Rk	Team	Conf	Proj F/+	TMW	Rec	Conf	SOS	Rk	Play	Rk	Team	Conf	Proj F/+	TMW	Rec	Conf	SOS	Rk	Play
1	Ohio State	Big Ten	60.5%	11.4	11-1	8-0	0.343	71	57.6	51	Iowa	Big Ten	4.0%	7.2	7-5	4-4	0.459	87	0.3
2	Alabama	SEC	59.8%	10.3	10-2	6-2	0.038	4	43.7	52	Washington	Pac 12	4.0%	4.5	4-8	3-6	0.066	13	0.0
3	Oregon	Pac 12	52.5%	10.5	10-2	8-1	0.125	35	40.0	53	W. Kentucky	CUSA	3.8%	8.4	8-4	6-2	0.458	86	0.0
4	Georgia	SEC	48.8%	9.8	10-2	6-2	0.072	15	24.1	54	Louisiana Tech	CUSA	3.4%	8.7	9-3	7-1	0.512	95	0.0
5	UCLA	Pac 12	45.0%	10.0	10-2	7-2	0.153	40	25.5	55	Temple	American	2.9%	7.8	8-4	6-2	0.564	104	0.0
6	Baylor	Big 12	43.4%	10.4	10-2	7-2	0.252	63	29.7	56	Texas Tech	Big 12	2.2%	5.1	5-7	3-6	0.122	30	0.0
7	Ole Miss	SEC	42.4%	9.1	9-3	5-3	0.048	8	9.5	57	Virginia	ACC	1.5%	3.9	4-8	3-5	0.108	26	0.0
8	LSU	SEC	42.3%	8.9	9-3	5-3	0.039	6	7.5	58	Navy	American	1.1%	8.6	9-3	6-2	0.532	100	0.0
9	Michigan State	Big Ten	42.0%	9.8	10-2	6-2	0.080	19	17.8	59	Northwestern	Big Ten	1.1%	5.3	5-7	3-5	0.266	65	0.0
10	Stanford	Pac 12	40.6%	9.4	9-3	7-2	0.123	33	12.8	60	Boston College	ACC	0.9%	5.6	6-6	3-5	0.203	51	0.0
11	Auburn	SEC	38.9%	8.1	8-4	4-4	0.036	3	3.0	61	Toledo	MAC	0.3%	8.4	8-4	6-2	0.614	111	0.0
12	USC	Pac 12	38.6%	8.5	9-3	6-3	0.054	11	4.6	62	California	Pac 12	-0.3%	4.1	4-8	2-7	0.042	7	0.0
13	Florida State	ACC	38.5%	10.1	10-2	6-2	0.268	66	21.4	63	Northern Illinois	MAC	-0.6%	8.4	8-4	6-2	0.223	58	0.0
14	Notre Dame	Ind-ND	38.4%	9.3	9-3	-	0.151	39	11.4	64	Ga. Southern	Sun Belt	-1.1%	8.7	9-3	7-1	0.345	72	0.0
15	TCU	Big 12	38.0%	9.6	10-2	7-2	0.207	52	15.1	65	W. Michigan	MAC	-2.4%	7.2	7-5	6-2	0.156	43	0.0
16	Oklahoma	Big 12	36.4%	9.3	9-3	7-2	0.154	41	10.4	66	Memphis	American	-2.8%	7.4	7-5	5-3	0.574	105	0.0
17	Georgia Tech	ACC	35.9%	8.5	9-3	6-2	0.102	23	4.9	67	Colorado State	MWC	-3.4%	7.9	8-4	5-3	0.667	114	0.0
18	Clemson	ACC	34.0%	9.1	9-3	6-2	0.201	50	8.2	68	Houston	American	-4.0%	7.4	7-5	5-3	0.674	115	0.0
19	Arizona State	Pac 12	33.9%	8.6	9-3	6-3	0.104	24	4.6	69	East Carolina	American	-4.0%	6.2	6-6	5-3	0.485	91	0.0
20	Missouri	SEC	33.2%	8.9	9-3	5-3	0.155	42	6.6	70	Oregon State	Pac 12	-4.8%	4.2	4-8	2-7	0.087	20	0.0
21	Arkansas	SEC	31.8%	7.3	7-5	3-5	0.025	1	0.5	71	Arkansas State	Sun Belt	-4.9%	7.9	8-4	6-2	0.431	83	0.0
22	Wisconsin	Big Ten	30.1%	9.9	10-2	7-1	0.221	57	15.3	72	San Diego St.	MWC	-5.1%	7.8	8-4	5-3	0.710	120	0.0
23	Boise State	MWC	30.1%	10.8	11-1	7-1	0.663	113	2.8	73	Kentucky	SEC	-5.7%	4.1	4-8	1-7	0.106	25	0.0
24	Virginia Tech	ACC	29.1%	8.8	9-3	6-2	0.165	45	5.1	74	Maryland	Big Ten	-7.0%	4.8	5-7	2-6	0.078	18	0.0
25	Texas A&M	SEC	29.1%	6.9	7-5	4-4	0.035	2	0.3	75	Washington St.	Pac 12	-7.0%	4.5	5-7	2-7	0.076	17	0.0
26	Tennessee	SEC	28.6%	7.6	8-4	4-4	0.048	9	0.8	76	Illinois	Big Ten	-7.5%	4.5	4-8	2-6	0.184	48	0.0
27	South Carolina	SEC	26.6%	7.2	7-5	4-4	0.072	14	0.5	77	Ball State	MAC	-7.8%	7.3	7-5	5-3	0.598	110	0.0
28	Kansas State	Big 12	25.6%	8.6	9-3	6-3	0.250	62	3.5	78	Nevada	MWC	-8.8%	7.3	7-5	5-3	0.546	103	0.0
29	Mississippi St.	SEC	24.5%	6.7	7-5	3-5	0.039	5	0.1	79	Vanderbilt	SEC	-10.7%	3.1	3-9	1-7	0.095	22	0.0
30	Nebraska	Big Ten	21.9%	8.7	9-3	6-2	0.376	76	3.8	80	Syracuse	ACC	-11.2%	4.3	4-8	2-6	0.218	56	0.0
31	Utah	Pac 12	21.8%	7.0	7-5	5-4	0.076	16	0.2	81	Air Force	MWC	-11.8%	6.5	6-6	4-4	0.334	70	0.0
32	Arizona	Pac 12	21.6%	7.6	8-4	5-4	0.122	32	0.5	82	Iowa State	Big 12	-12.5%	3.3	3-9	2-7	0.130	36	0.0
33	Louisville	ACC	19.5%	8.0	8-4	5-3	0.237	60	1.2	83	Indiana	Big Ten	-12.5%	4.6	5-7	2-6	0.158	44	0.0
34	Florida	SEC	18.9%	6.2	6-6	3-5	0.051	10	0.0	84	Appalachian St.	Sun Belt	-13.2%	7.8	8-4	5-3	0.594	109	0.0
35	Michigan	Big Ten	18.6%	7.6	8-4	5-3	0.150	38	0.6	85	Colorado	Pac 12	-13.3%	3.8	4-9	1-8	0.066	12	0.0
36	Penn State	Big Ten	17.1%	8.4	8-4	5-3	0.113	28	1.2	86	Purdue	Big Ten	-13.8%	3.7	4-8	2-6	0.214	54	0.0
37	Miami-FL	ACC	16.8%	6.6	7-5	4-4	0.183	47	0.2	87	Rutgers	Big Ten	-15.1%	4.2	4-8	1-7	0.122	31	0.0
38	Oklahoma St.	Big 12	16.8%	7.5	8-4	5-4	0.242	61	0.6	88	UL-Lafayette	Sun Belt	-15.2%	7.6	8-4	5-3	0.843	127	0.0
39	BYU	Ind-BYU	15.3%	7.2	7-5	-	0.175	46	0.3	89	Bowling Green	MAC	-16.4%	5.4	5-7	4-4	0.682	117	0.0
40	Pittsburgh	ACC	15.3%	7.1	7-5	4-4	0.236	59	0.3	90	Wake Forest	ACC	-16.6%	3.6	4-8	1-7	0.218	55	0.0
41	Marshall	CUSA	14.7%	10.8	11-1	7-1	0.848	128	2.5	91	Mid. Tennessee	CUSA	-17.5%	5.9	6-6	4-4	0.212	53	0.0
42	West Virginia	Big 12	14.6%	7.1	7-5	4-5	0.131	37	0.1	92	Tulsa	American	-18.0%	4.8	5-7	3-5	0.503	93	0.0
43	Texas	Big 12	11.1%	5.8	6-6	4-5	0.091	21	0.0	93	Fresno State	MWC	-19.0%	4.6	5-7	3-5	0.375	75	0.0
44	Minnesota	Big Ten	10.0%	6.5	6-6	4-4	0.116	29	0.1	94	Tulane	American	-19.3%	5.0	5-7	3-5	0.502	92	0.0
45	North Carolina	ACC	9.0%	6.8	7-5	4-4	0.260	64	0.1	95	Kent State	MAC	-21.0%	6.0	6-6	5-3	0.744	123	0.0
46	Utah State	MWC	8.3%	8.0	8-4	6-2	0.540	101	0.0	96	Rice	CUSA	-21.1%	6.4	6-6	4-4	0.419	80	0.0
47	Cincinnati	American	6.2%	8.3	8-4	6-2	0.679	116	0.1	97	San Jose State	MWC	-22.1%	4.6	5-7	3-5	0.429	82	0.0
48	Duke	ACC	5.1%	6.7	7-5	3-5	0.391	77	0.1	98	C. Michigan	MAC	-22.1%	5.0	5-7	4-4	0.452	85	0.0
49	NC State	ACC	4.4%	6.9	7-5	3-5	0.279	67	0.1	99	UL-Monroe	Sun Belt	-24.5%	5.8	6-7	4-4	0.108	27	0.0
50	Central Florida	American	4.0%	7.7	8-4	6-2	0.347	73	0.0	100	Florida Intl.	CUSA	-24.5%	5.1	5-7	3-5	0.688	119	0.0

Rk	Team	Conf	Proj F/+	TMW	Rec	Conf	SOS	Rk	Play	Rk	Team	Conf	Proj F/+	TMW	Rec	Conf	SOS	Rk	Play
101	Ohio	MAC	-24.6%	5.2	5-7	3-5	0.742	122	0.0	115	Southern Miss	CUSA	-33.6%	4.5	5-7	3-5	0.532	99	0.0
102	Florida Atlantic	CUSA	-27.1%	4.2	4-8	3-5	0.623	112	0.0	116	Charlotte	CUSA	-34.3%	4.5	5-7	3-5	0.833	126	0.0
103	South Florida	American	-27.8%	3.5	3-9	2-6	0.473	90	0.0	117	SMU	American	-35.6%	3.1	3-9	1-7	0.351	74	0.0
104	Connecticut	American	-28.5%	3.5	4-8	2-6	0.434	84	0.0	118	Georgia State	Sun Belt	-36.6%	4.3	4-8	3-5	0.333	69	0.0
105	New Mexico	MWC	-29.4%	4.4	4-8	2-6	0.421	81	0.0	119	Miami-OH	MAC	-37.0%	4.0	4-8	3-5	0.582	106	0.0
106	Hawaii	MWC	-29.9%	4.4	4-9	3-5	0.123	34	0.0	120	North Texas	CUSA	-37.2%	3.6	4-8	2-6	0.508	94	0.0
107	Texas State	Sun Belt	-30.2%	5.3	5-7	4-4	0.527	96	0.0	121	Wyoming	MWC	-37.8%	3.6	4-8	2-6	0.587	107	0.0
108	UTEP	CUSA	-30.8%	5.3	5-7	4-4	0.591	108	0.0	122	UNLV	MWC	-39.0%	2.7	3-9	2-6	0.403	79	0.0
109	Old Dominion	CUSA	-30.9%	5.5	6-6	3-5	0.753	124	0.0	123	Idaho	Sun Belt	-39.9%	3.7	4-8	2-6	0.328	68	0.0
110	South Alabama	Sun Belt	-30.9%	4.5	4-8	3-5	0.686	118	0.0	124	UTSA	CUSA	-41.7%	2.3	2-10	2-6	0.529	97	0.0
111	Massachusetts	MAC	-32.5%	4.1	4-8	3-5	0.530	98	0.0	125	Troy	Sun Belt	-42.2%	3.3	3-9	2-6	0.473	89	0.0
112	Kansas	Big 12	-32.6%	1.8	2-10	0-9	0.187	49	0.0	126	Army	Ind-Army	-42.3%	3.9	4-8	-	0.736	121	0.0
113	Buffalo	MAC	-33.1%	4.5	4-8	3-5	0.755	125	0.0	127	New Mexico St.	Sun Belt	-42.7%	2.9	3-9	2-6	0.398	78	0.0
114	Akron	MAC	-33.4%	4.9	5-7	4-4	0.543	102	0.0	128	E. Michigan	MAC	-57.2%	1.5	2-10	1-7	0.459	88	0.0

Developing QBASE and How It Works

Making projections with stats is a little like cooking at home.

You have your questions of cereal-level difficulty, simple and straightforward: What will the ocean temperature be in six months? Will the Raiders make the playoffs? (No.)

Then you have your chicken marsala-level questions, ones that used to be hard to answer until better information and tools made them pretty easy: Weeks before an election, who will be the next president? What will the weather be in three days?

Finally, even now, there are still the Baked Alaska-level questions, ones that remain difficult even with all the data that's out there: When will the next recession hit? How will Jameis Winston and Marcus Mariota do in the NFL?

The noisiness in projecting college quarterbacks jumps off the list of the last five years of draft picks. Teams remain mostly clueless about which quarterbacks will be future stars. First-round quarterbacks include Blaine Gabbert, Jake Locker, Christian Ponder, Brandon Weeden, EJ Manuel, and Johnny Manziel. Only one first-rounder (Luck) has outperformed Russell Wilson, who went in the third round in 2012. From 2010 to 2014, NFL teams selected 23 quarterbacks with higher picks than the 75th selection that Seattle used to take Wilson.

Wilson is a case of the stats trumping the scouts. Our original projection system, known as the Lewin Career Forecast, loved Wilson at the time. Our new Quarterback Adjusted Stats and Experience (QBASE) system also puts Wilson among the top five prospects since 1997. Moreover, QBASE sees red flags in the resumes of players such as Gabbert (low yards per attempt) and Locker (low completion percentage) that almost certainly should have kept those players out of the top ten. But, like the scouts, QBASE also makes mistakes. It would have given Matt Ryan a small chance of succeeding, for example, and it really liked Cade McNown.

One of the most important things we wanted to incorporate into QBASE was information about how much doubt there is when projecting college quarterbacks. Our model thus simulates each player's career 50,000 times, generating a range of possible outcomes. Consider, for example, our projection of the No. 1 pick, where DYAR refers to Defense-adjusted Yards Above Replacement:

Jameis Winston (Florida State, No. 1 pick)	
Mean Projection in Years 3-5:	378 DYAR
Bust (< 500 DYAR)	61.3 percent
Adequate Starter (500-1499 DYAR)	25.8 percent
Upper Tier (1500-2500 DYAR)	9.5 percent
Elite (>2500 DYAR)	3.3 percent

QBASE is pretty down on Winston, but it still gives him a 12.8 percent chance altogether of being upper tier or elite. If Winston fails, it will not be conclusive evidence that QBASE worked. And if Winston succeeds, it will not be conclusive evidence that QBASE failed. A weather forecast of a 20 percent chance of rain is not wrong when it rains. Forecasts work if, over the long run, it rains one out of five days when Brick Tamland gives it a 20 percent chance of raining. The same logic applies to QBASE.

To predict NFL success for this year's quarterback class, QBASE looks at a range of statistics that have been particularly useful for predicting success for college quarterbacks over the last 20 years. We limited the number of ingredients that go into the model to avoid overfitting. The ingredients are multi-layered; for example, the statistics account for the opposing defenses that each quarterback faced and the quality of his offensive teammates. In predictive modeling, it is usually better to include just a few multi-layered variables than lots of very specific ones, making the model as parsimonious as possible without missing something important. We designed QBASE with Winston Churchill's speech-length rule in mind: enough variables to cover the subject, few enough to keep it simple.

It's also important to note that QBASE is designed to project quarterbacks into the NFL as passers, not runners. That's important when looking at the forecasts for players such as Michael Vick, Cam Newton, and even Marcus Mariota.

QBASE's ingredients

Each prospect's QBASE projection of passing performance in Years 3-5 is based on three main ingredients:

1) College performance, adjusted for opposition and teammates: The strongest predictor of NFL success. To account for a changing college game, we look across three aspects of performance: A) completion percentage, B) adjusted yards per attempt, which means yards per attempt with adjustments for touchdowns and interceptions, and C) team passing efficiency from Football Outsiders' S&P ratings. The best prospects succeed across all three of these areas, so we take the minimum performance across the three areas. A quarterback who has an inflated completion percentage because of a screen-heavy offense (e.g. Brandon Weeden) thus can get caught here by his lower adjusted yards per attempt.

We make adjustments for team passing efficiency for 2005-14, the years for which the passing efficiency data are available. Most importantly, team passing efficiency is the model component that adjusts for a quarterback's propensity for taking sacks; sack avoidance is an important part of an efficient passing game. While the official college football statistics treat sacks as running plays, the S&P ratings correctly view these plays as passes. We scale the adjustment to account for quarterbacks who didn't play a full season.

QBASE makes two particularly important adjustments to the raw numbers by accounting for the strength of opposing defenses and the quality of a quarterback's teammates. The first of these corrections makes our measure more accurate for a player such as Josh Freeman, whose strength of schedule in his final college season ranked 99th. The strength of opposing defenses back to 1995 was measured in the same way as Pro Football Reference's Simple Rating System.

The second correction gives more credit to players such as Philip Rivers, who succeeded in college without great surrounding talent, as opposed to a player such as Matt Leinart, who played for an NFL finishing school. We measured teammate quality based on the draft-pick value of offensive teammates in both the player's draft year and the following year. For this year's prospects, these measures are based on both the 2015 draft and mock drafts for 2016.

2) College experience, adjusted for quality: Our previous measure of total games started has been replaced with a measure that counts seasons with at least 150 attempts, with adjustments to count poor seasons less than good ones. Experience counts, but successful experience counts more. This variable can capture the better quality of players who get more starts and more opportunities to improve, as well as the underappreciated idea that players who succeed in a smaller sample may not live up to that short-term success. Mark Sanchez could have gotten lucky to do so well in his one season as a starter. Four-year starter Russell Wilson? Not so much.

3) Projected draft slot: Based in large part on scouts' ratings of quarterbacks' intangibles, accuracy, and other attributes for recent years, the draft slot accounts for how scouting information predicts players' NFL success. These projections are now updated for the 2015 class to reflect their actual draft position rather than their projected draft slot. The model is only designed to project top 100 picks, so the projections for Bryce Petty and particularly Brett Hundley have even a little more uncertainty. And Hundley's projection is, of course, much lower than when we originally published it online because he fell to the fifth round. In fact, QBASE now likes Hundley even less than Jameis Winston (Table 1).

QBASE's all-time favorites are Philip Rivers and Carson Palmer. Each was a four-year starter who excelled across the board statistically as a senior. Donovan McNabb and Russell Wilson also fit that bill. Robert Griffin III projected more as the first-year player he was in the NFL than the one we have seen for the last two seasons. If QBASE was the GM of a quarterback-hungry team, it would probably be trying to steal Griffin now for a mid-round pick.

Table 1. QBASE Projections for Top 100 Picks, 1997-2014

Player	Team	Pick	Year	Predicted DYAR Years 3-5	Actual DYAR Years 3-5	Player	Team	Pick	Year	Predicted DYAR Years 3-5	Actual DYAR Years 3-5
Philip Rivers	SD	4	2004	2317	2679	Brian Brohm	GB	56	2008	853	0
Carson Palmer	CIN	1	2003	2266	2268	Tim Tebow	DEN	25	2010	849	-9
Donovan McNabb	PHI	2	1999	1946	1075	Geno Smith	NYJ	39	2013	839	--***
Russell Wilson	SEA	75	2012	1561	503*	Kevin Kolb	PHI	36	2007	830	33
Robert Griffin	WAS	2	2012	1519	-374*	Kellen Clemens	NYJ	49	2006	800	-92
Peyton Manning	IND	1	1998	1463	3922	Jake Plummer	ARI	42	1997	790	266
Byron Leftwich	JAC	7	2003	1200	369	Cam Newton	CAR	1	2011	781	316**
Aaron Rodgers	GB	24	2005	1198	1891	Alex Smith	SF	1	2005	771	-763
Ben Roethlisberger	PIT	11	2004	1193	1381	Drew Brees	SD	32	2001	737	1822
John Beck	MIA	40	2007	1151	-143	Vince Young	TEN	3	2006	690	616
Matthew Stafford	DET	1	2009	1125	3021	Derek Carr	OAK	36	2014	641	--***
Andrew Luck	IND	1	2012	1076	879*	Sam Bradford	STL	1	2010	617	692
Chad Pennington	NYJ	18	2000	1069	2631	Colt McCoy	CLE	85	2010	610	-19
Christian Ponder	MIN	12	2011	1061	-188**	Andrew Walter	OAK	69	2005	583	-227
Daunte Culpepper	MIN	11	1999	1061	1620	JaMarcus Russell	OAK	1	2007	535	-834
Cade McNown	CHI	12	1999	972	0	Johnny Manziel	CLE	22	2014	486	--***
Teddy Bridgewater	MIN	32	2014	945	--***	Blake Bortles	JAC	3	2014	471	--***
Jay Cutler	DEN	11	2006	936	831	Matt Schaub	ATL	90	2004	437	1181
Danny Wuerffel	NO	99	1997	928	-160	David Greene	SEA	85	2005	432	0
Matt Leinart	ARI	10	2006	915	-56	Tim Couch	CLE	1	1999	428	-366
Eli Manning	NYG	1	2004	892	1179	Nick Foles	PHI	88	2012	392	264*
Jason Campbell	WAS	25	2005	891	666	Charlie Frye	CLE	67	2005	368	-271

Year 3 only
**Years 3 and 4 only*
***Not yet reached Year 3*

Peyton Manning shows the importance of the opponent adjustments. As a senior, Manning faced the strongest schedule of opposing defenses in Division I. Accounting for that strength of schedule pushes his projection to the sixth-highest one.

For its successes in capturing past quarterbacks, QBASE also has some notable misses. Included among the quarterbacks with projections over 1000 DYAR are notable failures John Beck and Christian Ponder. Beck was one of three quarterbacks in the data to be 25 or older by the end of the draft year. Jim Druckenmiller and Brandon Weeden were also failures, as was Chris Weinke, who narrowly misses being part of the dataset at pick 106. So we considered adding a variable for age to get a lower prediction for Beck. But since the effect of the age variable cannot be estimated with precision, it is better to keep the model simple and leave that variable out. We will consider including it in future versions of QBASE if more data increase precision.

On the low end, QBASE's clearest miss is Matt Ryan. While QBASE beats the scouts in cases such as Russell Wilson and David Carr, the scouts may have seen something in Ryan that QBASE missed. In the historical table, Ryan falls right in the middle of a long run of quarterbacks like Joey Harrington and Blaine Gabbert who were just as terrible as their adjusted stats and experience predicted. But only Peyton Manning's DYAR eclipses Matt Ryan's among

all the top 100-drafted quarterbacks since 1995. It is possible according to QBASE's projections that Ryan would be that good. We would have expected about one of the bottom 50 quarterbacks on the list to be elite, and Ryan appears to be that one surprising outlier.

Another player QBASE seems to have missed on is Ryan Tannehill, though QBASE didn't miss quite as much as we thought when we originally introduced the system online. At one point, we had Tannehill listed with the third-lowest projection of any quarterback since 1997. This turned out to be an error where we were only giving him credit for one season as the starter at Texas A&M; he actually had enough pass attempts in his junior year, when he took over for Jerrod Johnson at midseason, to qualify with two seasons. That has increased Tannehill's QBASE projection to the point where he now seems reasonably underrated, but not absurdly so.

Finally, there is the case of Brian Griese. This outlier seems to be more about an inconsistent player whose best seasons happened to fall right in the period being projected by QBASE, rather than any problem with the system itself. Griese's two best years—and only two of the three seasons where he had positive DVOA—happened to fall in 2000 and 2002, his third and fifth seasons. Overall, his NFL reputation matches his QBASE projection more than it does the 2004 DYAR he happened to put up in Years 3-5.

Table 1. QBASE Projections for Top 100 Picks, 1997-2014

Player	Team	Pick	Year	Predicted DYAR Years 3-5	Actual DYAR Years 3-5	Player	Team	Pick	Year	Predicted DYAR Years 3-5	Actual DYAR Years 3-5
David Carr	HOU	1	2002	365	-215	Chris Redman	BAL	75	2000	-45	-67
Brandon Weeden	CLE	22	2012	325	21*	Rex Grossman	CHI	22	2003	-82	-175
Brady Quinn	CLE	22	2007	262	-207	Dave Ragone	HOU	88	2003	-114	0
Drew Stanton	DET	43	2007	257	174	Pat White	MIA	44	2009	-155	0
Quincy Carter	DAL	53	2001	248	263	Brian Griese	DEN	91	1998	-172	2004
Chad Henne	MIA	57	2008	220	183	Mark Sanchez	NYJ	5	2009	-184	-649
Matt Barkley	PHI	98	2013	208	--***	J.P. Losman	BUF	22	2004	-192	-310
Akili Smith	CIN	3	1999	198	-55	Josh Freeman	TB	17	2009	-194	-154
Shaun King	TB	50	1999	183	-102	Kyle Boller	BAL	19	2003	-222	56
Joey Harrington	DET	3	2002	178	-149	Brodie Croyle	KC	85	2006	-226	-62
EJ Manuel	BUF	16	2013	170	--***	Patrick Ramsey	WAS	32	2002	-234	-169
Ryan Mallett	NE	74	2011	168	120*	Chris Simms	TB	97	2003	-318	-166
Matt Ryan	ATL	3	2008	158	3438	Marques Tuiasosopo	OAK	59	2001	-348	-49
Jimmy Clausen	CAR	48	2010	153	-5	Charlie Whitehurst	SD	81	2006	-358	-141
Brock Huard	SEA	77	1999	139	-8	Michael Vick	ATL	1	2001	-446	-518
Andy Dalton	CIN	35	2011	138	778**	Mike Glennon	TB	73	2013	-486	--***
Ryan Leaf	SD	2	1998	105	-727	Kevin O'Connell	NE	94	2008	-499	0
Jim Druckenmiller	SF	26	1997	54	0	Charlie Batch	DET	60	1998	-530	59
Colin Kaepernick	SF	36	2011	22	882**	Trent Edwards	BUF	92	2007	-647	-564
Ryan Tannehill	MIA	8	2012	15	630*	Brock Osweiler	DEN	57	2012	-791	-5*
Blaine Gabbert	JAC	10	2011	14	-429**	Josh McCown	ARI	81	2002	-1304	-102
Jake Locker	TEN	8	2011	2	-102**						

* Year 3 only
** Years 3 and 4 only
*** Not yet reached Year 3

Projections for 2015 Draft Class

Below are QBASE's projections for the 2015 draft class. QBASE gives only one quarterback a better than even-money chance of avoiding NFL bustdom. The No. 1 pick is not that guy.

Jameis Winston (Florida State, No. 1 pick)	
Mean Projection in Years 3-5:	378 DYAR
Bust (< 500 DYAR)	61.3 percent
Adequate Starter (500-1499 DYAR)	25.8 percent
Upper Tier (1500-2500 DYAR)	9.5 percent
Elite (>2500 DYAR)	3.3 percent

Winston faces long odds of becoming a successful NFL quarterback. QBASE gives Winston a 61.3 percent chance of being a bust (less than 500 DYAR in Years 3-5) and just a 12.8 percent chance of being at least an upper-tier quarterback. His projection here is higher than it would be if the stats did not correct for his tough schedule of opposing defenses. Florida State only faced the tenth-toughest schedule overall according to our numbers, but it faced the nation's toughest set of defenses in 2014.

QBASE gives Winston the third-lowest projection among the 13 No. 1 overall quarterbacks since 1996. David Carr and Michael Vick are the only two top selections who rank lower. Tim Couch is just a little higher.

QBASE finds fault with Winston for the same reasons it dislikes Couch and Carr. All three quarterbacks started for only two college seasons. Also, all three had good-not-great stats in their last college season. QBASE wants to see high levels of performance across all passing statistics and Winston has the same weakness as Couch: an adjusted yards per attempt figure that is not as good as his completion percentage. QBASE also docks Winston a little for having some elite teammates.

Note that the projection does not account for the hard-to-quantify potential concerns surrounding Winston's off-field issues or his weight. Any adjustment for those issues could push Winston's bust potential even higher. Winston does not look good like a first pick should.

Marcus Mariota (Oregon, No. 2 pick)	
Mean Projection in Years 3-5:	1275 DYAR
Bust (< 500 DYAR)	22.8 percent
Adequate Starter (500-1499 DYAR)	40.5 percent
Upper Tier (1500-2500 DYAR)	24.1 percent
Elite (>2500 DYAR)	12.6 percent

Mariota has the highest projection since 2012. Since 1995, only six quarterbacks—Philip Rivers, Carson Palmer, Donovan McNabb, Russell Wilson, Robert Griffin III, and Peyton Manning—had better projections. QBASE sees Mariota as a three-year starter who posted huge numbers without any weak point. Adjusting for opposition and teammates, Mariota's adjusted yards per attempt relative to other Division I quarterbacks in his last college season trails only Wilson and Griffin. Also, QBASE likes that Mariota's completion percentage is high relative to his peers.

But are Mariota's numbers a product of the talent that surrounded him and the system in which he played? Mariota's projection accounts for Oregon having two tackles and a center projected to go in the early rounds of the 2015 and 2016 drafts, but makes no adjustments for Oregon's unusual pace of play. Questions about Mariota's ability to adapt to a more standard NFL offense do lend a note of caution to his projection. At the same time, the model also ignores Mariota's potential off-field strengths. And the two other quarterbacks with top-ten projections who got the most questions about their college production translating to the NFL—Wilson and Aaron Rodgers—both turned out well, although the concerns with Wilson and Rodgers were different from those with Mariota.

There has not been a quarterback in the last three drafts with Mariota's chances of being an upper-tier to elite-level quarterback.

Garrett Grayson (Colorado State, No. 75 pick)	
Mean Projection in Years 3-5:	-274 DYAR
Bust (< 500 DYAR)	80.6 percent
Adequate Starter (500-1499 DYAR)	13.2 percent
Upper Tier (1500-2500 DYAR)	5.3 percent
Elite (>2500 DYAR)	0.9 percent

Grayson projects poorly in large part because Colorado State's offensive strength of schedule ranked just 73rd last season. Only eleven quarterbacks taken in top 100 picks since 1997 projected worse than Grayson. The Saints seemed to be moving towards more sensible personnel moves this offseason but QBASE is pretty down on them using a third-round pick on Grayson.

Sean Mannion (Oregon State, No. 89 pick)	
Mean Projection in Years 3-5:	203 DYAR
Bust (< 500 DYAR)	64.9 percent
Adequate Starter (500-1499 DYAR)	23.2 percent
Upper Tier (1500-2500 DYAR)	8.9 percent
Elite (>2500 DYAR)	3.0 percent

Mannion, like most middle-round quarterbacks, is a likely bust. His bust potential is even higher now given the final adjustment to account for Oregon State's passing offense ranking just 80th in 2014. But Mannion has the highest chance of NFL success outside the top three prospects. With a 12.9 percent chance of being an upper-tier quarterback or elite quarterback, the odds against Mannion succeeding are at least shorter than those facing Grayson and Bryce Petty.

Bryce Petty (Baylor, No. 103 pick)	
Mean Projection in Years 3-5:	-309 DYAR
Bust (< 500 DYAR)	80.7 percent
Adequate Starter (500-1499 DYAR)	13.3 percent
Upper Tier (1500-2500 DYAR)	5.1 percent
Elite (>2500 DYAR)	0.9 percent

Brett Hundley (UCLA, No. 147 pick)	
Mean Projection in Years 3-5:	330 DYAR
Bust (< 500 DYAR)	59.2 percent
Adequate Starter (500-1499 DYAR)	26.1 percent
Upper Tier (1500-2500 DYAR)	10.5 percent
Elite (>2500 DYAR)	4.2 percent

Like Grayson, Petty projects to be substantially worse than replacement level because QBASE questions the opposition that he faced in 2014. Petty accumulated his college stats against a slate of opposing defenses that ranked 70th in college football. His six percent chance of developing into an upper-tier quarterback makes Petty barely more likely than Geno Smith or Richard Todd to end the Jets' quarterback drought.

The adjustment to include 2014 team passing efficiency knocks down Hundley's projection by 144 DYAR. His projection now penalizes him for his worrying tendency to take sacks. While not as highly-ranked as his completion percentage, Hundley's adjusted yards per attempt is more impressive than it seems at first glance. Hundley faced the third-toughest set of opposing defenses in Division I last year. (As noted earlier, Florida State had the toughest schedule; Alabama was No. 2.) He also had fewer future early-round offensive teammates than either Mariota or Winston. But Hundley's projection falls dramatically due to his fall into the fifth round. If scouts are that scared of Hundley's alarming sack rate, QBASE is, too. Hundley's projection ends up 600 DYAR lower than when we originally published it online due to his cliff dive deep into Day 3.

by Andrew Healy

Rookie Projections

Over the years, Football Outsiders has developed a number of methods for forecasting the NFL success of highly-drafted players at various positions. Now that you've read about the new QBASE system, here is a rundown of the other three methods and what they say about the NFL's Class of 2015.

Running Backs: Speed Score

Speed Score was created by Bill Barnwell and introduced in *Pro Football Prospectus 2008*. The basic theory is simple: not all 40-yard dash times are created equal. A fast time means more from a bigger running back, and the range of 40 times for backs is so small that even a miniscule difference can be meaningful. The formula for Speed Score is:

(Weight x 200) / 40 time ^4

In general, you want a back chosen in the first couple rounds to be above 100. There's been some indication that Speed Score can be improved by also considering a couple of other things such as the three-cone drill; we hope to introduce an improved version soon.

Here are the Speed Scores for all backs chosen in the first three rounds, as well as the top five Speed Scores for backs chosen in the final four rounds. Note that Todd Gurley and Tevin Coleman did not run at the combine and therefore do not have official Speed Scores. Unlike in 2014, no player with a Speed Score above 100 went undrafted in 2015.

Name	College	Team	Rnd	Pick	40 time	Weight	Speed Score
Melvin Gordon	Wisconsin	SD	1	15	4.52	215	103.0
T.J. Yeldon	Alabama	JAC	2	36	4.61	226	100.1
Ameer Abdullah	Nebraska	DET	2	54	4.60	205	91.6
David Johnson	Northern Iowa	ARI	3	86	4.50	224	109.3
Matt Jones	Florida	WAS	3	95	4.61	231	102.3
Duke Johnson	Miami	CLE	3	77	4.54	207	97.4
Jeremy Langford	Michigan St.	CHI	4	106	4.42	208	109.0
Javorius Allen	USC	BAL	4	125	4.53	221	105.0
Karlos Williams	Florida St.	BUF	5	155	4.48	230	114.2
Jay Ajayi	Boise St.	MIA	5	149	4.57	221	101.3
Cameron Artis-Payne	Auburn	CAR	5	174	4.53	212	100.7

Edge Rushers: SackSEER

SackSEER is a method that projects sacks for edge rushers, including both 3-4 outside linebackers and 3-4 defensive ends, using the following criteria:

• An "explosion index" that measures the prospect's scores in the forty-yard dash, the vertical jump, and the broad jump in pre-draft workouts.
• Sacks per game, adjusted for factors such as early entry in the NFL Draft and position switches during college.
• Passes defensed per game.
• Missed games of NCAA eligibility due to academic problems, injuries, benchings, suspensions, or attendance at junior college.

SackSEER outputs two numbers. The first, SackSEER Rating, solely measures how high the prospect scores compared to players of the past. The second, SackSEER Projection, represents a forecast of sacks for the player's first five years in the NFL. It synthesizes metrics with conventional wisdom by adjusting based on the player's expected draft position (interestingly, not his actual draft position) based on pre-draft analysis at the site NFLDraftScout.com.

Here are the SackSEER numbers for players drafted in the first three rounds of the 2015 draft, along with later-round picks (and one UDFA) with a high SackSEER Rating. Defensive ends drafted by 3-4 teams are not included. Linebackers drafted by 4-3 teams who will sometimes rush the passer (i.e. "Von Miller types") are included with an asterisk.

Name	College	Team	Rnd	Pick	SackSEER Projection	SackSEER Rating
Vic Beasley*	Clemson	ATL	1	8	33.7	95.2%
Bud Dupree	Kentucky	PIT	1	22	28.8	94.0%
Dante Fowler*	Florida	JAC	1	3	21.3	39.3%
Shane Ray	Missouri	DEN	1	23	20.0	14.2%
Randy Gregory	Nebraska	DAL	2	60	31.8	88.3%
Preston Smith	Mississippi St.	WAS	2	38	21.8	70.7%
Nate Orchard	Utah	CLE	2	51	16.8	35.3%
Hau'oli Kikaha	Washington	NO	2	44	9.8	20.2%
Frank Clark	Michigan	SEA	2	63	4.5	61.5%
Markus Golden	Missouri	ARI	2	58	3.7	8.3%
Eli Harold	Virginia	SF	3	79	24.5	63.8%
Danielle Hunter	LSU	MIN	3	88	19.8	43.0%
O. Odighizuwa	UCLA	NYG	3	74	14.9	42.7%
Lorenzo Mauldin	Louisville	NYJ	3	82	10.3	25.6%
Henry Anderson	Stanford	IND	3	93	6.0	31.9%
Davis Tull	Chattanooga	NO	5	148	17.4	90.9%
Trey Flowers	Arkansas	NE	4	101	16.8	67.0%
Lynden Trail	Norfolk St.	HOU	UDFA	--	12.3	80.6%

SackSEER was created by Nathan Forster.

Wide Receivers: Playmaker Score

Playmaker Score projects success for NFL wide receivers using the following criteria:

• The wide receiver's peak season for receiving yards per team attempt and receiving touchdowns per team attempt.
• Differences between this prospect's peak season and most recent season, to adjust for players who declined in their final college year.
• College career yards per reception.
• Rushing attempts per game.
• Vertical jump from pre-draft workouts.
• A binary variable that rewards players who enter the draft as underclassmen.

Like SackSEER, Playmaker Score outputs two numbers. The first, Playmaker Rating, solely measures how high the prospect scores compared to players of the past. The second, Playmaker Projection, represents a forecast of average receiving yards per year in the player's first five seasons, synthesizing metrics with conventional wisdom by adjusting based on the player's expected draft position.

2014 was a historic year for wide receiver prospects, with 14 different players drafted with Playmaker Rating above 80 percent. This year's draft was more standard, with seven such players. Here are the Playmaker Score numbers for players drafted in the first three rounds of the 2015 draft, along with later-round picks (and one UDFA) with a high Playmaker Rating.

Name	College	Team	Rnd	Pick	Playmaker Projection	Playmaker Rating
Amari Cooper	Alabama	OAK	1	4	643	95.2%
Kevin White	West Virginia	CHI	1	7	406	36.5%
DeVante Parker	Louisville	MIA	1	14	404	42.6%
Nelson Agholor	USC	PHI	1	20	454	86.4%
Breshad Perriman	UCF	BAL	1	26	491	86.4%
Phillip Dorsett	Miami	IND	1	29	309	58.9%
Devin Smith	Ohio St.	NYJ	2	37	381	76.5%
D. Green-Beckham	Missouri	TEN	2	40	438	56.5%
Devin Funchess	Michigan	CAR	2	41	356	73.2%
Tyler Lockett	Kansas St.	SEA	3	69	387	77.8%
Jaelen Strong	Arizona St.	HOU	3	70	514	86.4%
Chris Conley	Georgia	KC	3	76	207	71.9%
Sammie Coates	Auburn	PIT	3	87	507	94.1%
Ty Montgomery	Stanford	GB	3	94	190	68.6%
Stefon Diggs	Maryland	MIN	5	146	305	87.5%
DeAndre Smelter	Georgia Tech	SF	4	132	235	84.6%
Titus Davis	Central Mich.	SD	UDFA	--	306	79.3%
Darren Waller	Georgia Tech	BAL	6	204	235	67.7%
Tony Lippett	Michigan St.	MIA	5	156	278	64.0%
Tre McBride	Wm. & Mary	TEN	7	245	273	61.5%

Playmaker Score was originally created by Vincent Verhei and then further developed by Nathan Forster.

Top 25 Prospects

This is Football Outsiders' ninth annual list of under-the-radar, lower-drafted prospects who could have a big impact on the NFL in the coming seasons. In the past, Rotoworld has referred to our Top 25 Prospects list as "an all-star team of waiver pickups" after we used it to promote young players such as Miles Austin, Jamaal Charles, and Arian Foster. We've also picked out defensive players who went on to have a big impact: our first list included Elvis Dumervil and Cortland Finnegan, while more recent lists have introduced readers to future stars such as Geno Atkins and Lardarius Webb. Of course we can't get them all right, but a lot of these are names you're going to want to know over the next few seasons.

For the uninitiated, this list is not like the prospect lists you read about in the world of baseball. Because the top prospects in college football are stars on national television before they get taken in the first round of the NFL Draft, there's not much utility in listing them here. Everyone knows who Marcus Mariota and Todd Gurley are by this point. Instead, we use a combination of statistics, scouting, measurables, context, and expected role to compile a list of under-the-radar players whom we expect to make an impact in the NFL, both in 2015 and beyond. To focus on these players, we limit the pool to guys who fit the following criteria:

- Drafted in the third round or later, or signed as an undrafted free agent
- Entered the NFL between 2012 and 2014
- Fewer than five career games started
- Have not signed a contract extension (however, players who were cut and picked up elsewhere still qualify for the list)
- Age 26 or younger in 2015

This year's list had a lot of candidates, and even cutting players from the honorable mention list was tough. The players between No. 2 and No. 25 moved around a lot during the process of compiling and finalizing our list. The player at No. 1 was glaringly obvious from the get-go.

1 Martavis Bryant, WR, Steelers

Bryant is a 6-foot-4 receiver who ran a 4.42-second 40 and averaged 22 yards per reception in college. How on earth did he last until the fourth round? Bryant scored an excellent 85.2 percent Playmaker Score, and even that might have been artificially low because Bryant had to share the field at Clemson with Sammy Watkins. Bryant has pretty much everything you want from a star receiver: speed, athleticism, size, and the ability to win at the catch point. Last year, Bryant was only the second rookie receiver since 1995 to gain over 20 yards per reception with at least 25 receptions. (Kenny Stills in 2013 was the other.) An offseason elbow procedure may put Bryant a bit behind Markus Wheaton in Steelers training camp, which could keep him from becoming a starter until late this season or perhaps next season. But in all truth, the only thing standing between Bryant and stardom may be a little waiting time.

2 T.J. Carrie, CB, Raiders

One year after Oakland took him out of Ohio University in the seventh round, Travis "T.J." Carrie may already be the Raiders' best cornerback. Carrie was already playing 80 percent of defensive snaps in Week 1 of his rookie season, and with four games started he just barely qualifies for our Top Prospects list. He had a strong 53 percent success rate in coverage according to Football Outsiders game charting, and his 7.1 adjusted yards per pass was the best figure on the team last year. Carrie has good hands, good instincts, and he can go up to compete with physical receivers: he's six feet tall and his 41-inch vertical jump ranked third among corners at the 2014 combine. Carrie is a local kid out of Catholic high school powerhouse De La Salle, which you may remember from the recent film "When the Game Stands Tall." Now he's one of the numerous young talents finally giving Raiders fans hope for the future.

3 Jordan Hill, DT, Seahawks

Seattle chose Hill out of Penn State in the third-round of the 2013 draft. He only played in four games as a rookie, but last year he became an important part of the Seahawks' defensive tackle rotation and ended up with 10 defeats and 5.5 sacks in only 360 snaps. That's more sacks on a per-snap basis than Cameron Wake, Marcell Dareus, DeMarcus Ware, Aaron Donald, or Robert Quinn. Hill missed last year's playoffs with a calf injury, but he'll play a major role for the Seahawks in 2015. Tony McDaniel's release right before we went to press will likely make Hill a starter this season. The big question about Hill will be just how many snaps he can play as a starter, because his lack of bulk (6-foot-1, 303 pounds) led to him wearing down against the run in college.

4 Aaron Lynch, OLB, 49ers

Last year, this fifth-round rookie tied for the 49ers' team lead with six sacks despite playing only half the defensive snaps. He also led the 49ers with 21 hurries and 11 quarterback hits. Our SackSEER projection system liked Lynch's potential more than his past: he had a 50.8 percent SackSEER rating because of a strong explosion index, but only had 10.5 sacks in his two seasons of college ball. (Lynch had to sit out the 2012 season after transferring from Notre Dame to South Florida.) Lynch will rotate with Aldon Smith and Ahmad Brooks this year, and is essentially the 31-year-old Brooks' heir apparent because the 49ers may need to cut Brooks for cap reasons after 2015. The tough part for Lynch will be stepping into Brooks' shoes as an all-around linebacker, but he's probably already the better pass-rusher.

5 Latavius Murray, RB, Raiders

One tool Football Outsiders uses to scout running back prospects is Speed Score, which adjusts the back's 40 time for his weight. A good running back has a Speed Score of 100. Murray ran his pro day 40 in 4.38 seconds at 223 pounds, for a Speed Score of 121.2—with an asterisk. Normally, we only consider Speed Score when players run at the combine because players tend to run faster on their home tracks at pro days. But even if there is a little bit of home cooking in that pro day time, it doesn't change the fact that Latavius Murray is big and fast. He's also now the Raiders' starting running back, two years after they took him out of Central Florida in the sixth round of the 2013 draft. Murray lost his rookie season to an ankle injury and then barely played in the first half of last year. But he made some big plays once Oakland got him on the field in November, especially the 90-yard touchdown that he scored against Kansas City in Oakland's first win of the season in Week 11.

The question with Murray is whether he can use that size to challenge defenders. We charted him with only three broken tackles in 99 touches last season, and ESPN Stats & Information only tracked him with just 1.0 yards after contact, the lowest average for any back with at least 40 runs in 2014.

6 Jeremy Lane, CB, Seahawks

Lane presented a bit of a dilemma when we were debating this list among the Football Outsiders staff writers. Does a player who may not play this year count as a prospect for 2015? We eventually decided to include Lane because he should have a strong future as a starting NFL cornerback even though he's likely to start 2015 on the PUP list (or even go on injured reserve) because of the arm and knee injuries he suffered in last year's Super Bowl. Lane only was healthy for seven games last year, but he was excellent, with a 71 percent success rate and 3.7 adjusted yards per pass allowed. In three seasons, we've charted him with 54 passes, which would be just enough for him to be ranked on our cornerback leaderboards. Combine those three years, and you get a 57 percent success rate and 6.3 adjusted yards per pass. Both numbers would have ranked Lane among last year's top 20 cornerbacks. Plus, he's one of four men who can say they've intercepted Tom Brady in a Super Bowl.

7 Ryan Davis, DE, Jaguars

Last season saw a number of undrafted veterans suddenly explode with big sack numbers, but there's a big difference with Davis. While Jacquies Smith and George Johnson of Tampa Bay had bounced around multiple organizations, Davis has been developed solely by the Jaguars since they brought him up I-95 from Bethune-Cookman in 2012. Gus Bradley used Davis in a number of ways: as a traditional end, a standing "Leo" end, and a pass-rushing defensive tackle. If you read the Jacksonville chapter, you know that the Jaguars built their high sack count last year with coverage sacks or blitzes, but that's not where Davis got his sacks. Six of Davis' 6.5 sacks were marked as blown blocks, and four of those six came with a standard four pass-rushers. Davis was also second on the Jaguars with 11.5 hurries and 6 quarterback hits.

8 Donte Moncrief, WR, Colts

Moncrief was one of the 14 different wide receivers with a Playmaker Score over 80 percent last year, and they couldn't all go in the first two rounds. We're sure he was fine lasting until the Colts at No. 90, because that plugged him into a powerful offense with the best young quarterback in the game. Like Martavis Bryant, Moncrief combines size (6-foot-2, 221 pounds) with speed (4.40-second 40), and he just turned 22 in August. The Patriots respected Moncrief enough to put Darrelle Revis on him for most of the AFC Championship Game. The problem for Moncrief now is that the Colts' decision to draft Philip Dorsett really confused his place on the depth chart. Moncrief should get more playing time this season, especially early on, but what happens if Dorsett surpasses him? NFL teams do not throw a lot to their No. 4 receivers, no matter how much the offense loves to throw the ball overall.

9 Joseph Randle, RB, Cowboys

Randle has both ability and opportunity, but let's be honest—the latter outweighs the former right now. Having the first crack at a starting job behind the best offensive line in football is a pretty nice ticket to stardom. Randle certainly looked like a future star last year, gaining 343 yards on 51 carries for a remarkable 6.7 yards per carry. But you don't want to put more stock into that than you do into the 3.0 yards per carry he put up with 54 carries the year before. The worry about Randle coming out of Oklahoma State was that he didn't have the burst or power to get more than what the line blocked for him. It might be hard to tell if that's still the case if the Cowboys' line blocks as well as it did last year.

10 Malcolm Butler, CB, Patriots

How unknown was the hero of Super Bowl XLIX before he got his hands on that final pass to end Seattle's dreams of a repeat? As of late July, Butler was still listed on the NFL's website as a strong safety. The three passes Butler got his hand on during Seattle's last drive showed an upside that makes you wonder how he came within a whisker of not even getting an NFL shot. (Playing college ball at Division II West Alabama was part of it.) On the other hand, Butler was just mediocre in his overall regular-season performance and got beat deep a couple times, leading to a 51 percent adjusted success rate (fairly average) and 10.5 adjusted yards allowed per pass (not good). He'll need more consistency to become a long-time NFL starter and not the Timmy Smith of defensive backs.

By the way, the other Super Bowl hero, Chris Matthews, is ineligible for our list because he's been a professional too long. He was one of Cleveland's last cuts as an undrafted rookie in 2011, then went to Arena Football and the CFL before returning to the NFL with Seattle last year. As we saw in the Super Bowl, he definitely has potential for a nice (but late-starting) NFL career.

11 Pierre Desir, CB, Browns

The undrafted K'Wuan Williams played more than Desir as a rookie, but Desir is the more talented player in the long run. The Browns knew Desir would require some development time when they took him in the fourth-round out of Division II Lindenwood, and knee problems in the preseason of his rookie year didn't help. Like Antonio Cromartie, Desir is a long, boundary cornerback who has natural ball skills but needs to stay outside to be effective. Unlike Cromartie, he is a mature individual of high character who already had a wife and two kids by the time the Browns drafted him at age 24.

12 Isaiah Crowell, RB, Browns

Crowell and Desir make a strange pair: same team, other side of the ball, completely opposite story. Once upon a time, Crowell was an elite five-star running back recruit. Then he got kicked out of the University of Georgia for a felony weapons arrest and finished his college career at FCS Alabama State. The Browns signed Crowell as an undrafted free agent; he hasn't caused any off-field problems, and the talent was clearly still there. Crowell still has excellent balance and vision to move through his blockers. His combine 40 time of 4.57 seconds is more impressive when you consider that he weighed in at 224 pounds, giving him a 102.7 Speed Score. By the end of his rookie year, Crowell moved past third-round pick Terrence West on the Cleveland depth chart, and he'll probably be the Cleveland starter in 2015. He's not much of a receiver, so rookie Duke Johnson will fill the role of third-down back.

13 Shawn Williams, FS, Bengals

Williams is clearly being groomed as replacement for Reggie Nelson—unless George Iloka gets a huge free-agent offer and leaves instead. He has hardly played on defense since the Bengals took him in the third round of the 2013 draft, but that's because the starters have been so good and the Bengals don't use three safeties. He's been excellent on special teams, with 18 special-teams tackles over his first two seasons. Williams is a good tackler with excellent range, though he needs to further his ball skills. Plus, he's a Georgia Bulldog, and we all know what that means in Cincinnati these days.

14 John Urschel, G, Ravens

Our favorite math wizard won't get into the lineup ahead of Marshal Yanda or Kelechi Osemele, but he's the top reserve and in line to take over when one of the two starters leaves via free agency next year. As you might expect from a guy who won the Campbell Trophy, a.k.a. the "Academic Heisman," Urschel is considered technically sound but athletically limited. However, his play as a rookie was anything but limited. When injuries forced him to start three games as a rookie, we charted him with no sacks allowed and just one blown block leading to a run for loss. Urschel can also play center, and is Baltimore's top backup there as well.

15 Jonathan Newsome, OLB, Colts

Jonathan Newsome has already had some pretty big days in his one year as a member of the Indianapolis Colts. He had his first NFL start in Week 17 last year and won the AFC Defensive Player of the Week award with two sacks, a forced fumble, and eight tackles. Then he strip-sacked Peyton Manning in the AFC playoffs. For the regular season as a whole, Newsome had 6.5 sacks and 13.8 hurries in just 390 snaps, basically the same rate of pressure as Aaron Lynch.

Newsome's NFL success was a bit surprising, since he had a very poor SackSEER rating of 15.4 percent. Part of that rating is that passes defensed are a strong sign of a versatile pass rusher, and Newsome had just two in college. But his rating is also depressed by the two years he spent as a benchwarmer with no sacks at Ohio State before transferring to Ball State for his final two seasons. There's a real question as to whether Newsome will even get a chance to build on the success of his rookie year. His path to playing time seems blocked by the return of Robert Mathis, the free-agent signing of Trent Cole, and the continued employment of Erik Walden.

16 Antone Exum, FS, Vikings

Harrison Smith is a great young safety for the Minnesota Vikings, but who will play next to him? The Vikings seem lukewarm on Robert Blanton, and they may want to go with more of a centerfielder so Smith can play closer to the line of scrimmage and make big plays. Enter 2014 sixth-round pick Antone Exum out of Virginia Tech, a converted college cornerback who played primarily on special teams as he learned a new position last season. Exum is a fluid mover with ball skills, though he sometimes took poor angles to tackle in college.

17 Devonta Freeman, RB, Falcons

Atlanta's fourth-round pick last year is a 5-foot-8 scatback with a lot of short-area quickness. He didn't have great numbers as a rookie—3.8 yards per carry with -22.9% DVOA—but he wasn't exactly running behind great blocking either. Freeman did have a nice rookie year as a receiver, though, catching 30 passes for 225 yards, and he had an impressive 15 broken tackles on less than 100 touches. Freeman may start the year as the Atlanta starter, but will likely lose the job by the end of the year to rookie Tevin Coleman. But even as a backup, he'll have a lot of value to Atlanta on third downs.

18 Brandon Thomas, G, 49ers

Thomas is one of the 49ers' recent "redshirt" draft picks. The Clemson product tore his ACL at a pre-draft workout with New Orleans, which enabled the 49ers to snap him up with the last third-round pick in last year's draft. Now he's healthy and ready to compete for Mike Iupati's old spot at left guard. Thomas has a strong initial punch and above-average quickness to get to the second level. He should fit in well with San Francisco's run-heavy offensive scheme.

19 Aaron Colvin, CB, Jaguars

Mr. Thomas, Aaron Colvin will take your ACL torn at a pre-draft workout and raise you one ACL torn at the Senior Bowl. That injury dropped the Oklahoma product down to the Jaguars in the fourth round, but it actually didn't cause him to miss his entire rookie season. Colvin was activated in Week 12 and played at least 50 percent of the snaps in each of Jacksonville's last six games. Colvin had unimpressive charting metrics, but it still takes time for players to recover and get their full speed back after returning from ACL surgery. Colvin (5-foot-11, 177 pounds) doesn't quite have the size associated with the Seahawks/Jaguars defensive scheme, but the Jaguars' coaching staff love his instincts, work ethic, and physical play in zone coverage.

20 Josh Huff, WR, Eagles

Look, it's a shifty YAC-producing slot receiver who went to the University of Oregon. You wouldn't be able to find space for a guy like that in the Philadelphia Eagles offense, would you? In his second season, Huff will likely be the Eagles' main slot receiver. He's fast, but he'll need more route-running work before he can play outside regularly. It's a nice added bonus that he's also a strong run-blocker.

21 Caraun Reid, DT, Lions

Hey, somebody has to get snaps at defensive tackle besides Haloti Ngata. Reid was probably a little underdrafted as a fifth-round pick last year; yes, he comes out of Princeton, but he impressed against stronger competition at the Senior Bowl. He's more of a pass-rusher than a run-stopper, and scouting reports suggested he could be good as a 4-3 "tilted" nose tackle or as an end in one-gapping 3-4 schemes. The Lions are talking about incorporating more of the latter into their defense this season, making Reid a challenger to Tyrunn Walker for pass-rushing snaps.

22 Dontae Johnson, CB, 49ers

A fourth-round rookie from North Carolina State, Johnson gradually took over last year as San Francisco's nickelback and was a full-time player by Week 15. He started and played 97 percent of defensive snaps in the last three games of the year. As befits a nickelback, Johnson did an excellent job of preventing yardage (6.7 adjusted yards per pass) but was not quite as strong at preventing first downs (49 percent success rate). But those numbers are a little more impressive given that Johnson was seen on draft day as a raw athlete with questionable college film. Johnson was supposed to require development, but the original baseline was supposed to be "not ready to play in the NFL." Instead, it looks like his development is already starting with a baseline of "reasonable," which means there's a better chance that the end-point of Johnson's potential is going to be "very good."

23 DaQuan Jones, DE, Titans

Our No. 23 prospect actually played alongside our No. 3 prospect Jordan Hill as a junior at Penn State. Most draft analysts expected him to go in the second round, but he ended up falling to the fourth, where Tennessee snagged him to play as a 5-technique in their 3-4 defense. Jones didn't play much last year until he started the final game of the season, but the Titans are ready to put him in the starting lineup for this year. Jones has good size at 6-foot-4 and 322 pounds, and he has outstanding upper body strength with a great, violent rip move. Unlike his old teammate Hill, he's not going to be a gap-shooting pass-rusher who shows up in the highlights taking down the quarterback. He's more of a run-stuffer to complement Jurrell Casey on the other side, and may come off the field when the Titans go to a 4-2-5 nickel.

24 Billy Turner, G, Dolphins

Miami's new right guard has strong bloodlines, as his father Maurice played five years in the NFL as a running back. The Dolphins made him the highest drafted player from North Dakota State since 2002 when they took him in last year's third round. Turner was a two-time All-American at the FCS level and like Caraun Reid, he impressed against bigger-school competition at the 2014 Senior Bowl. Unlike most college tackles who move inside at the pro level, Turner is considered a better pass blocker than run blocker.

25 Barrett Jones, C, Rams

Jones poses an interesting question about trying to translate college linemen to the pros: just how meaningful are the awards that a player wins in college? As a junior left tackle, Jones won the Outland Trophy as the best lineman in college football. As a senior, he switched to center to fill a hole on the Alabama depth chart and won the Rimington Trophy as the best center in college football. Despite all these accolades, Jones fell to the fourth round because he's only considered an average athlete. Then he lost his first two NFL seasons, missing his rookie year with a Lisfranc foot injury and his second year with back problems. Jones is penciled in as the Rams' starting center this season.

HONORABLE MENTION

Carl Bradford, ILB, Packers
Jay Bromley, DT, Giants
Jaron Brown, WR, Cardinals
Jackson Jeffcoat, OLB, Redskins
Patrick Lewis, C, Seahawks
A.J. McCarron, QB, Bengals
Kevin Pamphile, G/T, Buccaneers
James White, RB, Patriots
Damien Williams, RB, Dolphins
Albert Wilson, WR, Chiefs

Fantasy Projections

Here are the top 280 players according to the KUBIAK projection system, ranked by projected fantasy value (**FANT**) in 2015. We've used the following generic scoring system:

- 1 point for each 10 yards rushing, 10 yards receiving, or 20 yards passing
- 6 points for each rushing or receiving TD, 4 points for each passing TD
- -2 points for each interception or fumble lost
- 1 point for each extra point, 3 points for each field goal
- Team defense: 2 points for a fumble recovery, interception, or safety, 1 point for a sack, and 6 points for a touchdown.

These totals are then adjusted based on each player's listed **Risk** for 2015:

- Green: Standard risk, no change
- Yellow: Higher than normal risk, value dropped by five percent
- Red: Highest risk, value dropped by 10 percent
- Blue: Significantly lower than normal risk, value increased by five percent

Note that fantasy totals may not exactly equal these calculations, because each touchdown projection is not necessarily a round number. (For example, a quarterback listed with 2 rushing touchdowns may actually be projected with 2.4 rushing touchdowns, which will add 14 fantasy points to the player's total rather than 12.) Fantasy value does not include adjustments for week-to-week consistency,

Players are ranked in order based on marginal value of each player, the idea that you draft based on how many more points a player will score compared to the worst starting player at that position, not how many points a player scores overall. We've ranked players by value in a 12-team league working with three sets of rules:

- Flex Rk: starts 1 QB, 2 RB, 2 WR, 1 FLEX (RB/WR), 1 TE, 1 K, and 1 D.
- 3WR Rk: starts 1 QB, 2 RB, 3 WR, 1 TE, 1 K, and 1 D.
- PPR Rk: starts 1 QB, 2 RB, 2 WR, 1 FLEX (RB/WR), 1 TE, 1 K, and 1 D. Also adds one point per reception to scoring.

The rankings also include half value for the first running back on the bench, and reduce the value of kickers and defenses to reflect the general drafting habits of fantasy football players. We urge you to draft using common sense, not a strict reading of these rankings.

A customizable spreadsheet featuring these projections is also available at FootballOutsiders.com for a $20 fee. This spreadsheet is updated based on injuries and changing forecasts of playing time during the preseason, and also has a version which includes individual defensive players.

Please note that projections for Le'Veon Bell, Antonio Gates, and LeGarrette Blount are reduced due to suspensions. Tom Brady's projection is not reduced by suspension, but he does have a Red Risk factor dropping his value because of the possibility he will serve some or all of his suspension.

Player	Team	Bye	Pos	Age	PaYd	PaTD	INT	Ru	RuYd	RuTD	Rec	RcYd	RcTD	FL	XP	FG	Fant	Risk	Flex Rk	3WR Rk	PPR Rk
Marshawn Lynch	SEA	9	RB	29	0	0	0	275	1270	12	33	267	2	4	0	0	233	Green	1	1	13
Eddie Lacy	GB	7	RB	25	0	0	0	274	1275	10	39	317	2	3	0	0	229	Green	2	2	12
Le'Veon Bell	PIT	11	RB	23	0	0	0	249	1122	9	60	536	2	2	0	0	218	Yellow	3	3	7
Jamaal Charles	KC	9	RB	29	0	0	0	229	1121	10	57	419	2	3	0	0	217	Green	4	4	8
Dez Bryant	DAL	6	WR	27	0	0	0	2	9	0	95	1336	14	0	0	0	216	Green	5	5	2
Antonio Brown	PIT	11	WR	27	0	0	0	5	30	0	112	1481	10	0	0	0	211	Green	6	6	1
C.J. Anderson	DEN	7	RB	24	0	0	0	254	1105	10	48	433	2	2	0	0	211	Yellow	7	7	16
Arian Foster	HOU	9	RB	29	0	0	0	301	1383	9	36	274	3	3	0	0	210	Red	8	8	23
Aaron Rodgers	GB	7	QB	32	4625	38	12	38	160	2	0	0	0	0	0	0	375	Green	9	9	15
Andrew Luck	IND	10	QB	26	4788	35	16	62	246	2	0	0	0	0	0	0	373	Green	10	12	17
Adrian Peterson	MIN	5	RB	30	0	0	0	290	1320	11	38	303	1	3	0	0	205	Red	11	10	24
Demaryius Thomas	DEN	7	WR	28	0	0	0	0	0	0	107	1474	11	0	0	0	204	Yellow	12	11	3
Matt Forte	CHI	7	RB	30	0	0	0	246	999	7	70	591	2	1	0	0	204	Green	13	13	9
Jeremy Hill	CIN	7	RB	23	0	0	0	274	1250	10	32	208	1	3	0	0	203	Green	14	14	26
Calvin Johnson	DET	9	WR	30	0	0	0	0	0	0	98	1487	12	0	0	0	198	Red	15	15	5
DeMarco Murray	PHI	8	RB	27	0	0	0	270	1208	9	45	360	3	2	0	0	198	Red	16	16	25
Rob Gronkowski	NE	4	TE	26	0	0	0	0	0	0	85	1106	11	0	0	0	165	Yellow	17	19	10
Julio Jones	ATL	10	WR	26	0	0	0	2	10	0	100	1403	9	0	0	0	192	Green	18	17	4
Odell Beckham	NYG	11	WR	23	0	0	0	7	41	0	92	1235	11	0	0	0	191	Green	19	18	6
LeSean McCoy	BUF	8	RB	27	0	0	0	302	1252	7	28	180	0	3	0	0	185	Green	20	20	36
Jordy Nelson	GB	7	WR	30	0	0	0	0	0	0	88	1239	10	0	0	0	183	Green	21	21	11
Justin Forsett	BAL	9	RB	30	0	0	0	234	1120	7	50	352	1	3	0	0	179	Yellow	22	22	31

Player	Team	Bye	Pos	Age	PaYd	PaTD	INT	Ru	RuYd	RuTD	Rec	RcYd	RcTD	FL	XP	FG	Fant	Risk	Flex Rk	3WR Rk	PPR Rk
Lamar Miller	MIA	5	RB	24	0	0	0	218	1024	7	39	312	1	2	0	0	179	Green	23	23	33
Randall Cobb	GB	7	WR	25	0	0	0	8	37	0	87	1227	8	0	0	0	175	Green	24	24	14
A.J. Green	CIN	7	WR	27	0	0	0	0	0	0	84	1187	9	0	0	0	171	Green	25	25	18
Alshon Jeffery	CHI	7	WR	25	0	0	0	4	18	0	85	1169	9	0	0	0	170	Green	26	26	19
DeAndre Hopkins	HOU	9	WR	23	0	0	0	2	9	0	83	1269	7	0	0	0	167	Green	27	27	20
T.Y. Hilton	IND	10	WR	26	0	0	0	3	16	0	80	1178	6	0	0	0	166	Green	28	28	22
Emmanuel Sanders	DEN	7	WR	28	0	0	0	6	29	0	85	1142	8	0	0	0	164	Green	29	29	21
Jimmy Graham	SEA	9	TE	29	0	0	0	0	0	0	74	889	9	0	0	0	133	Yellow	30	33	28
Melvin Gordon	SD	10	RB	22	0	0	0	223	946	7	27	220	1	2	0	0	162	Green	31	30	61
Mike Evans	TB	6	WR	22	0	0	0	2	9	0	77	1230	9	0	0	0	161	Red	32	31	30
Alfred Morris	WAS	8	RB	27	0	0	0	274	1129	7	22	170	0	2	0	0	161	Yellow	33	32	69
Drew Brees	NO	11	QB	36	4612	36	15	26	45	0	0	0	0	0	0	0	324	Yellow	34	34	40
Russell Wilson	SEA	9	QB	27	3562	25	11	98	508	5	0	0	0	0	0	0	323	Green	35	35	42
Greg Olsen	CAR	5	TE	30	0	0	0	0	0	0	77	926	6	0	0	0	126	Green	36	37	29
Kelvin Benjamin	CAR	5	WR	24	0	0	0	0	0	0	74	1082	9	0	0	0	152	Yellow	37	36	32
Mark Ingram	NO	11	RB	26	0	0	0	214	962	4	42	313	1	2	0	0	150	Green	38	38	57
Frank Gore	IND	10	RB	32	0	0	0	220	944	8	28	201	1	1	0	0	147	Red	39	39	80
Peyton Manning	DEN	7	QB	39	4396	34	12	23	31	1	0	0	0	0	0	0	312	Yellow	40	40	53
Cam Newton	CAR	5	QB	26	3617	24	12	106	512	5	0	0	0	0	0	0	309	Yellow	41	44	55
Travis Kelce	KC	9	TE	26	0	0	0	0	0	0	74	826	5	0	0	0	113	Green	42	46	35
Devonta Freeman	ATL	10	RB	23	0	0	0	178	740	6	42	307	2	1	0	0	142	Yellow	43	41	70
Matt Ryan	ATL	10	QB	30	4303	28	14	33	111	0	0	0	0	0	0	0	306	Green	44	50	58
Ben Roethlisberger	PIT	11	QB	33	4597	29	13	41	66	1	0	0	0	0	0	0	306	Yellow	45	51	59
Tony Romo	DAL	6	QB	35	4067	33	15	30	77	0	0	0	0	0	0	0	306	Green	46	52	60
Brandin Cooks	NO	11	WR	22	0	0	0	11	49	0	70	926	7	0	0	0	140	Green	47	42	38
DeSean Jackson	WAS	8	WR	29	0	0	0	3	16	0	58	1019	6	0	0	0	140	Yellow	48	43	46
Jordan Matthews	PHI	8	WR	23	0	0	0	0	0	0	75	1001	8	0	0	0	139	Yellow	49	45	39
Joseph Randle	DAL	6	RB	24	0	0	0	225	1003	7	20	139	1	1	0	0	139	Red	50	47	118
Sammy Watkins	BUF	8	WR	22	0	0	0	5	24	0	61	927	9	0	0	0	138	Yellow	51	48	52
Matthew Stafford	DET	9	QB	27	4192	29	16	36	96	1	0	0	0	0	0	0	303	Green	52	56	63
Golden Tate	DET	9	WR	27	0	0	0	4	20	0	80	1007	6	0	0	0	137	Green	53	49	34
Jonathan Stewart	CAR	5	RB	28	0	0	0	192	876	5	37	262	0	1	0	0	136	Yellow	54	53	86
Carlos Hyde	SF	10	RB	24	0	0	0	214	834	6	20	163	1	1	0	0	136	Green	55	54	123
Rashad Jennings	NYG	11	RB	30	0	0	0	207	819	6	33	248	1	1	0	0	136	Yellow	56	55	94
Zach Ertz	PHI	8	TE	25	0	0	0	0	0	0	63	801	4	0	0	0	106	Green	57	59	50
LeGarrette Blount	NE	4	RB	29	0	0	0	157	789	7	24	168	1	2	0	0	133	Yellow	58	57	129
Martellus Bennett	CHI	7	TE	28	0	0	0	0	0	0	66	750	5	0	0	0	103	Green	59	63	51
Julian Edelman	NE	4	WR	29	0	0	0	8	51	0	99	1005	5	0	0	0	132	Green	60	58	27
Andre Ellington	ARI	9	RB	26	0	0	0	178	709	4	46	399	1	0	0	0	132	Yellow	61	60	78
Jason Witten	DAL	6	TE	33	0	0	0	0	0	0	71	804	5	0	0	0	102	Yellow	62	65	48
T.J. Yeldon	JAC	8	RB	22	0	0	0	200	818	6	25	219	1	1	0	0	131	Yellow	63	69	136
Latavius Murray	OAK	6	RB	24	0	0	0	203	896	5	30	227	1	1	0	0	131	Yellow	64	70	111
Amari Cooper	OAK	6	WR	21	0	0	0	4	26	0	74	991	7	0	0	0	130	Red	65	61	49
Pierre Garcon	WAS	8	WR	29	0	0	0	2	9	0	81	1024	6	0	0	0	130	Yellow	66	62	41
Jordan Cameron	MIA	5	TE	27	0	0	0	0	0	0	57	710	7	0	0	0	100	Red	67	68	72
Bishop Sankey	TEN	4	RB	23	0	0	0	197	856	3	34	256	1	1	0	0	129	Green	68	74	99
Julius Thomas	JAC	8	TE	27	0	0	0	0	0	0	61	715	7	0	0	0	99	Red	69	73	71
Anquan Boldin	SF	10	WR	35	0	0	0	0	0	0	82	1029	6	0	0	0	128	Yellow	70	64	43
Mike Wallace	MIN	5	WR	29	0	0	0	3	14	0	69	958	6	0	0	0	127	Yellow	71	66	56
Stephen Gostkowski	NE	4	K	31	0	0	0	0	0	0	0	0	0	0	44	31	135	Green	72	75	81
Roddy White	ATL	10	WR	34	0	0	0	0	0	0	80	943	7	0	0	0	126	Yellow	73	67	44
Todd Gurley	STL	6	RB	21	0	0	0	191	801	7	22	158	1	2	0	0	126	Red	74	76	159
Vincent Jackson	TB	6	WR	32	0	0	0	0	0	0	62	935	7	0	0	0	125	Yellow	75	71	67
Jeremy Maclin	KC	9	WR	27	0	0	0	0	0	0	70	921	6	0	0	0	125	Green	76	72	54
Jared Cook	STL	6	TE	28	0	0	0	0	0	0	51	647	5	0	0	0	95	Green	77	81	79
Delanie Walker	TEN	4	TE	31	0	0	0	0	0	0	60	717	5	0	0	0	94	Yellow	78	83	73
Ryan Tannehill	MIA	5	QB	27	4089	27	15	50	220	1	0	0	0	0	0	0	288	Yellow	79	87	82
Colin Kaepernick	SF	10	QB	28	3452	22	13	96	544	2	0	0	0	0	0	0	288	Green	80	88	83
Keenan Allen	SD	10	WR	23	0	0	0	4	38	0	78	911	5	0	0	0	122	Green	81	77	45
Jarvis Landry	MIA	5	WR	23	0	0	0	4	31	0	89	861	6	0	0	0	122	Green	82	78	37
Andre Johnson	IND	10	WR	34	0	0	0	0	0	0	76	868	6	0	0	0	122	Green	83	79	47
Joique Bell	DET	9	RB	29	0	0	0	182	748	6	29	184	1	1	0	0	122	Yellow	84	80	149
Coby Fleener	IND	10	TE	27	0	0	0	0	0	0	49	602	5	0	0	0	92	Green	85	93	90
Martavis Bryant	PIT	11	WR	24	0	0	0	2	13	0	55	923	7	0	0	0	120	Red	86	82	88
Philip Rivers	SD	10	QB	34	4238	27	11	36	87	0	0	0	0	0	0	0	285	Yellow	87	101	91
Eli Manning	NYG	11	QB	34	4194	29	14	20	41	0	0	0	0	0	0	0	285	Yellow	88	102	92

Player	Team	Bye	Pos	Age	PaYd	PaTD	INT	Ru	RuYd	RuTD	Rec	RcYd	RcTD	FL	XP	FG	Fant	Risk	Flex Rk	3WR Rk	PPR Rk
Adam Vinatieri	IND	10	K	43	0	0	0	0	0	0	0	0	0	0	41	29	128	Green	89	96	97
Eric Decker	NYJ	5	WR	28	0	0	0	0	0	0	66	838	6	0	0	0	119	Green	90	84	64
Kendall Wright	TEN	4	WR	26	0	0	0	4	19	0	68	835	6	0	0	0	119	Green	91	85	62
C.J. Spiller	NO	11	RB	28	0	0	0	117	510	3	62	492	3	0	0	0	119	Yellow	92	86	75
Seahawks D	SEA	9	D	--	0	0	0	0	0	0	0	0	0	0	0	0	108	Yellow	93	100	98
John Brown	ARI	9	WR	25	0	0	0	3	14	0	64	930	6	0	0	0	118	Red	94	89	77
Michael Floyd	ARI	9	WR	26	0	0	0	2	11	0	66	974	6	0	0	0	118	Red	95	90	74
Brandon Marshall	NYJ	5	WR	31	0	0	0	0	0	0	74	898	7	0	0	0	118	Red	96	91	65
Blair Walsh	MIN	5	K	25	0	0	0	0	0	0	0	0	0	0	38	30	126	Green	97	104	101
Matt Bryant	ATL	10	K	40	0	0	0	0	0	0	0	0	0	0	39	29	126	Green	98	105	102
Steve Smith	BAL	9	WR	36	0	0	0	0	0	0	71	867	6	0	0	0	117	Yellow	99	94	66
Bills D	BUF	8	D	--	0	0	0	0	0	0	0	0	0	0	0	0	106	Yellow	100	106	103
Owen Daniels	DEN	7	TE	33	0	0	0	0	0	0	56	601	5	0	0	0	87	Green	101	109	87
Tom Brady	NE	4	QB	38	4198	31	11	32	67	1	0	0	0	0	0	0	282	Red	102	110	96
Mason Crosby	GB	7	K	31	0	0	0	0	0	0	0	0	0	0	51	28	125	Yellow	103	107	105
Brandon LaFell	NE	4	WR	29	0	0	0	2	10	0	69	896	6	0	0	0	116	Yellow	104	97	68
Mike Nugent	CIN	7	K	33	0	0	0	0	0	0	0	0	0	0	38	31	124	Yellow	105	111	106
Marques Colston	NO	11	WR	32	0	0	0	0	0	0	55	755	7	0	0	0	115	Green	106	103	89
Isaiah Crowell	CLE	11	RB	22	0	0	0	169	676	6	18	133	0	1	0	0	115	Green	107	92	182
Chiefs D	KC	9	D	--	0	0	0	0	0	0	0	0	0	0	0	0	104	Yellow	108	113	107
Eric Ebron	DET	9	TE	22	0	0	0	0	0	0	46	565	6	0	0	0	85	Yellow	109	118	119
Austin Seferian-Jenkins	TB	6	TE	23	0	0	0	0	0	0	48	591	5	0	0	0	85	Yellow	110	119	113
Eagles D	PHI	8	D	--	0	0	0	0	0	0	0	0	0	0	0	0	103	Green	111	112	109
Broncos D	DEN	7	D	--	0	0	0	0	0	0	0	0	0	0	0	0	103	Yellow	112	114	110
Steven Hauschka	SEA	9	K	30	0	0	0	0	0	0	0	0	0	0	43	27	122	Green	113	120	114
Chris Ivory	NYJ	5	RB	27	0	0	0	187	759	5	23	158	0	1	0	0	113	Yellow	114	95	180
Patriots D	NE	4	D	--	0	0	0	0	0	0	0	0	0	0	0	0	102	Yellow	115	116	115
Ameer Abdullah	DET	9	RB	22	0	0	0	146	608	4	30	280	1	0	0	0	112	Yellow	116	98	163
Rams D	STL	6	D	--	0	0	0	0	0	0	0	0	0	0	0	0	101	Yellow	117	125	117
Allen Robinson	JAC	8	WR	22	0	0	0	2	8	0	70	870	5	0	0	0	111	Yellow	118	115	76
Tevin Coleman	ATL	10	RB	22	0	0	0	160	641	5	33	191	1	1	0	0	111	Yellow	119	99	161
Josh Hill	NO	11	TE	25	0	0	0	0	0	0	52	639	5	0	0	0	81	Red	120	137	130
Justin Tucker	BAL	9	K	26	0	0	0	0	0	0	0	0	0	0	35	28	119	Green	121	132	124
Josh Brown	NYG	11	K	36	0	0	0	0	0	0	0	0	0	0	39	27	119	Green	122	133	125
Torrey Smith	SF	10	WR	26	0	0	0	2	9	0	49	810	6	0	0	0	110	Yellow	123	121	121
Texans D	HOU	9	D	--	0	0	0	0	0	0	0	0	0	0	0	0	99	Green	124	134	126
Heath Miller	PIT	11	TE	33	0	0	0	0	0	0	55	605	3	0	0	0	80	Green	125	145	100
Kyle Rudolph	MIN	5	TE	26	0	0	0	0	0	0	58	579	5	0	0	0	80	Red	126	146	108
Greg Zuerlein	STL	6	K	28	0	0	0	0	0	0	0	0	0	0	34	31	118	Yellow	127	138	131
Davante Adams	GB	7	WR	23	0	0	0	2	7	0	58	803	7	0	0	0	109	Red	128	123	104
Larry Fitzgerald	ARI	9	WR	32	0	0	0	0	0	0	65	812	6	0	0	0	109	Yellow	129	124	84
Cardinals D	ARI	9	D	--	0	0	0	0	0	0	0	0	0	0	0	0	98	Green	130	141	132
Packers D	GB	7	D	--	0	0	0	0	0	0	0	0	0	0	0	0	98	Yellow	131	142	133
Jordan Reed	WAS	8	TE	25	0	0	0	0	0	0	62	631	4	0	0	0	79	Yellow	132	153	95
Connor Barth	DEN	7	K	29	0	0	0	0	0	0	0	0	0	0	46	29	117	Red	133	147	138
Randy Bullock	HOU	9	K	26	0	0	0	0	0	0	0	0	0	0	32	33	117	Red	134	148	139
Matt Prater	DET	9	K	31	0	0	0	0	0	0	0	0	0	0	37	27	117	Green	135	149	140
Shaun Suisham	PIT	11	K	34	0	0	0	0	0	0	0	0	0	0	42	25	117	Green	136	150	141
Terrance Williams	DAL	6	WR	26	0	0	0	2	8	0	48	755	6	0	0	0	108	Green	137	127	122
Victor Cruz	NYG	11	WR	29	0	0	0	0	0	0	70	872	6	0	0	0	108	Red	138	128	85
Ravens D	BAL	9	D	--	0	0	0	0	0	0	0	0	0	0	0	0	97	Red	139	143	142
Dolphins D	MIA	5	D	--	0	0	0	0	0	0	0	0	0	0	0	0	97	Yellow	140	151	143
Tyler Eifert	CIN	7	TE	25	0	0	0	0	0	0	48	526	5	0	0	0	78	Yellow	141	154	146
Robert Griffin	WAS	8	QB	25	4059	24	16	87	406	2	0	0	0	0	0	0	273	Red	142	155	120
Andy Dalton	CIN	7	QB	28	3665	25	17	41	187	2	0	0	0	0	0	0	272	Green	143	157	127
Doug Baldwin	SEA	9	WR	27	0	0	0	3	16	0	62	834	4	0	0	0	106	Green	144	139	93
Breshad Perriman	BAL	9	WR	22	0	0	0	2	14	0	53	882	5	0	0	0	106	Red	145	140	145
Duke Johnson	CLE	11	RB	22	0	0	0	120	535	6	23	161	1	0	0	0	106	Green	146	108	188
Jace Amaro	NYJ	5	TE	23	0	0	0	0	0	0	50	571	4	0	0	0	76	Yellow	147	160	148
Jay Cutler	CHI	7	QB	32	3986	27	15	39	157	1	0	0	0	0	0	0	271	Yellow	148	161	134
Carson Palmer	ARI	9	QB	36	4193	23	15	22	63	0	0	0	0	0	0	0	271	Green	149	162	135
Marcus Mariota	TEN	4	QB	22	3476	23	15	108	493	5	0	0	0	0	0	0	270	Red	150	164	144
Mychal Rivera	OAK	6	TE	25	0	0	0	0	0	0	55	586	3	0	0	0	74	Yellow	151	165	137
Dwayne Allen	IND	10	TE	25	0	0	0	0	0	0	37	458	5	0	0	0	74	Green	152	166	164
Antonio Gates	SD	10	TE	35	0	0	0	0	0	0	50	529	5	0	0	0	73	Red	153	168	155
Charles Clay	BUF	8	TE	26	0	0	0	0	0	0	49	608	4	0	0	0	73	Red	154	169	156

Player	Team	Bye	Pos	Age	PaYd	PaTD	INT	Ru	RuYd	RuTD	Rec	RcYd	RcTD	FL	XP	FG	Fant	Risk	Flex Rk	3WR Rk	PPR Rk
Teddy Bridgewater	MIN	5	QB	23	3670	24	13	56	254	2	0	0	0	0	0	0	268	Yellow	155	170	147
Kenny Stills	MIA	5	WR	23	0	0	0	2	14	0	57	762	4	0	0	0	101	Green	156	163	116
James White	NE	4	RB	23	0	0	0	109	435	4	47	324	2	0	0	0	101	Yellow	157	117	153
Vernon Davis	SF	10	TE	31	0	0	0	0	0	0	44	529	5	0	0	0	71	Red	158	175	168
Giovani Bernard	CIN	7	RB	24	0	0	0	108	475	1	60	457	1	0	0	0	99	Green	159	122	112
Maxx Williams	BAL	9	TE	21	0	0	0	0	0	0	46	521	4	0	0	0	69	Red	160	180	169
Alex Smith	KC	9	QB	31	3375	22	12	59	281	2	0	0	0	0	0	0	264	Green	161	182	151
Brian Quick	STL	6	WR	26	0	0	0	0	0	0	56	787	5	0	0	0	98	Red	162	171	150
Joe Flacco	BAL	9	QB	30	3937	25	14	26	82	1	0	0	0	0	0	0	263	Yellow	163	188	152
Knile Davis	KC	9	RB	24	0	0	0	104	448	6	24	182	0	0	0	0	97	Green	164	126	211
Rob Housler	CLE	11	TE	27	0	0	0	0	0	0	39	454	4	0	0	0	67	Green	165	189	181
Sam Bradford	PHI	8	QB	28	4173	26	19	52	107	2	0	0	0	0	0	0	261	Red	166	192	157
Kevin White	CHI	7	WR	23	0	0	0	0	0	0	53	714	5	0	0	0	95	Yellow	167	178	154
Andre Williams	NYG	11	RB	23	0	0	0	135	523	5	22	155	0	0	0	0	95	Green	168	129	225
Danny Woodhead	SD	10	RB	30	0	0	0	86	350	2	54	509	2	0	0	0	95	Red	169	130	160
DeAngelo Williams	PIT	11	RB	32	0	0	0	110	474	4	32	283	2	0	0	0	95	Red	170	131	202
Larry Donnell	NYG	11	TE	27	0	0	0	0	0	0	48	506	3	0	0	0	65	Yellow	171	194	165
Nelson Agholor	PHI	8	WR	22	0	0	0	0	0	0	55	789	5	0	0	0	94	Red	172	183	158
Dwayne Bowe	CLE	11	WR	31	0	0	0	0	0	0	61	724	4	0	0	0	94	Green	173	184	128
Charles Sims	TB	6	RB	25	0	0	0	133	561	2	39	313	0	0	0	0	93	Yellow	174	135	186
Tre Mason	STL	6	RB	22	0	0	0	140	602	2	26	189	0	1	0	0	93	Blue	175	136	216
Dan Bailey	DAL	6	K	27	0	0	0	0	0	0	0	0	0	0	44	27	116	Yellow	176	196	173
Cody Parkey	PHI	8	K	23	0	0	0	0	0	0	0	0	0	0	43	29	116	Red	177	197	174
Cowboys D	DAL	6	D	--	0	0	0	0	0	0	0	0	0	0	0	0	96	Green	178	198	175
Jets D	NYJ	5	D	--	0	0	0	0	0	0	0	0	0	0	0	0	96	Red	179	199	176
Charles Johnson	MIN	5	WR	26	0	0	0	2	11	0	47	690	5	0	0	0	92	Yellow	180	191	170
Darren McFadden	DAL	6	RB	28	0	0	0	126	564	4	23	178	1	0	0	0	92	Yellow	181	144	232
Donte Moncrief	IND	10	WR	22	0	0	0	2	10	0	50	672	5	0	0	0	91	Yellow	182	193	167
Sebastian Janikowski	OAK	6	K	37	0	0	0	0	0	0	0	0	0	0	33	30	115	Yellow	183	202	183
Panthers D	CAR	5	D	--	0	0	0	0	0	0	0	0	0	0	0	0	95	Green	184	203	184
Derek Carr	OAK	6	QB	24	3869	21	16	36	124	1	0	0	0	0	0	0	255	Green	185	207	166
Kenny Britt	STL	6	WR	27	0	0	0	0	0	0	45	590	5	0	0	0	89	Green	186	201	177
Doug Martin	TB	6	RB	26	0	0	0	181	664	3	12	84	0	1	0	0	89	Green	187	152	251
Lions D	DET	9	D	--	0	0	0	0	0	0	0	0	0	0	0	0	94	Red	188	204	185
Ladarius Green	SD	10	TE	24	0	0	0	0	0	0	36	439	3	0	0	0	57	Yellow	189	218	215
Bucs D	TB	6	D	--	0	0	0	0	0	0	0	0	0	0	0	0	93	Green	190	214	189
Vikings D	MIN	5	D	--	0	0	0	0	0	0	0	0	0	0	0	0	93	Red	191	215	190
Falcons D	ATL	10	D	--	0	0	0	0	0	0	0	0	0	0	0	0	93	Yellow	192	221	191
Malcom Floyd	SD	10	WR	34	0	0	0	0	0	0	41	642	5	0	0	0	86	Yellow	193	205	197
Reggie Bush	SF	10	RB	30	0	0	0	121	473	2	32	258	1	0	0	0	86	Green	194	156	222
Niles Paul	WAS	8	TE	26	0	0	0	0	0	0	44	434	2	0	0	0	56	Green	195	222	193
Andrew Hawkins	CLE	11	WR	29	0	0	0	4	18	0	59	724	3	0	0	0	85	Yellow	196	208	162
Steve Johnson	SD	10	WR	29	0	0	0	0	0	0	56	694	4	0	0	0	85	Red	197	209	171
Richard Rodgers	GB	7	TE	23	0	0	0	0	0	0	28	336	4	0	0	0	55	Yellow	198	225	239
Nick Folk	NYJ	5	K	31	0	0	0	0	0	0	0	0	0	0	34	27	112	Green	199	219	195
49ers D	SF	10	D	--	0	0	0	0	0	0	0	0	0	0	0	0	92	Yellow	200	213	196
Darren Sproles	PHI	8	RB	32	0	0	0	42	212	2	51	414	2	0	0	0	84	Green	201	158	172
Rueben Randle	NYG	11	WR	24	0	0	0	2	12	0	46	595	4	0	0	0	83	Green	202	217	187
Roy Helu	OAK	6	RB	27	0	0	0	79	338	2	45	343	1	0	0	0	83	Green	203	159	192
Benjamin Watson	NO	11	TE	35	0	0	0	0	0	0	31	334	4	0	0	0	53	Yellow	204	227	237
Bengals D	CIN	7	D	--	0	0	0	0	0	0	0	0	0	0	0	0	91	Yellow	205	220	200
Garrett Graham	HOU	9	TE	29	0	0	0	0	0	0	48	487	1	0	0	0	52	Yellow	206	230	199
Scott Chandler	NE	4	TE	30	0	0	0	0	0	0	26	310	4	0	0	0	52	Yellow	207	231	249
Michael Crabtree	OAK	6	WR	28	0	0	0	2	8	0	53	628	3	0	0	0	81	Green	208	223	178
Allen Hurns	JAC	8	WR	24	0	0	0	0	0	0	56	653	4	0	0	0	81	Yellow	209	224	179
Luke Willson	SEA	9	TE	25	0	0	0	0	0	0	28	343	3	0	0	0	51	Green	210	235	242
Giants D	NYG	11	D	--	0	0	0	0	0	0	0	0	0	0	0	0	90	Red	211	228	206
Titans D	TEN	4	D	--	0	0	0	0	0	0	0	0	0	0	0	0	90	Yellow	212	238	207
Phillip Dorsett	IND	10	WR	22	0	0	0	0	0	0	38	621	4	0	0	0	80	Yellow	213	226	229
Caleb Sturgis	MIA	5	K	26	0	0	0	0	0	0	0	0	0	0	38	29	109	Red	214	236	212
Graham Gano	CAR	5	K	28	0	0	0	0	0	0	0	0	0	0	39	26	109	Yellow	215	237	213
Dorial Green-Beckham	TEN	4	WR	22	0	0	0	6	34	0	41	582	4	0	0	0	78	Yellow	216	229	223
Marvin Jones	CIN	7	WR	25	0	0	0	2	9	0	47	558	4	0	0	0	77	Green	217	232	201
Mohamed Sanu	CIN	7	WR	26	50	1	0	6	33	0	41	519	3	0	0	0	77	Green	218	233	221
Harry Douglas	TEN	4	WR	31	0	0	0	0	0	0	50	585	4	0	0	0	77	Green	219	234	194
David Johnson	ARI	9	RB	24	0	0	0	111	447	3	23	179	1	0	0	0	77	Yellow	220	167	256

Player	Team	Bye	Pos	Age	PaYd	PaTD	INT	Ru	RuYd	RuTD	Rec	RcYd	RcTD	FL	XP	FG	Fant	Risk	Flex Rk	3WR Rk	PPR Rk
Phil Dawson	SF	10	K	40	0	0	0	0	0	0	0	0	0	0	35	27	108	Yellow	221	242	217
Browns D	CLE	11	D	--	0	0	0	0	0	0	0	0	0	0	0	0	88	Green	222	243	218
Steelers D	PIT	11	D	--	0	0	0	0	0	0	0	0	0	0	0	0	88	Yellow	223	244	219
Jaguars D	JAC	8	D	--	0	0	0	0	0	0	0	0	0	0	0	0	88	Yellow	224	247	220
Marqise Lee	JAC	8	WR	24	0	0	0	3	11	0	49	617	3	0	0	0	76	Yellow	225	239	209
Robert Woods	BUF	8	WR	23	0	0	0	0	0	0	45	543	4	0	0	0	75	Green	226	240	214
Rod Streater	OAK	6	WR	27	0	0	0	0	0	0	42	571	3	0	0	0	75	Green	227	241	224
Jacob Tamme	ATL	10	TE	30	0	0	0	0	0	0	31	294	4	0	0	0	45	Red	228	249	254
Blake Bortles	JAC	8	QB	24	3611	22	14	61	333	1	0	0	0	0	0	0	240	Red	229	250	203
Nick Foles	STL	6	QB	26	3499	23	15	29	74	1	0	0	0	0	0	0	240	Green	230	251	204
Colts D	IND	10	D	--	0	0	0	0	0	0	0	0	0	0	0	0	87	Yellow	231	246	227
Saints D	NO	11	D	--	0	0	0	0	0	0	0	0	0	0	0	0	87	Red	232	253	228
Percy Harvin	BUF	8	WR	27	0	0	0	29	132	1	48	473	2	0	0	0	74	Green	233	245	210
David Cobb	TEN	4	RB	22	0	0	0	119	431	3	22	164	1	0	0	0	74	Yellow	234	172	261
Shane Vereen	NYG	11	RB	26	0	0	0	55	227	2	43	343	1	0	0	0	74	Green	235	173	226
Geno Smith	NYJ	5	QB	25	3271	22	15	64	280	2	0	0	0	0	0	0	239	Yellow	236	255	208
Ryan Mathews	PHI	8	RB	28	0	0	0	109	480	3	17	108	0	0	0	0	73	Green	237	174	265
Chandler Catanzaro	ARI	9	K	24	0	0	0	0	0	0	0	0	0	0	32	28	106	Yellow	238	252	230
Redskins D	WAS	8	D	--	0	0	0	0	0	0	0	0	0	0	0	0	86	Yellow	239	254	231
James Starks	GB	7	RB	29	0	0	0	82	348	3	19	170	1	0	0	0	72	Green	240	176	263
Benny Cunningham	STL	6	RB	25	0	0	0	65	251	1	50	347	1	0	0	0	72	Blue	241	177	205
Marlon Brown	BAL	9	WR	24	0	0	0	0	0	0	57	566	3	0	0	0	71	Yellow	242	248	198
Nick Novak	SD	10	K	34	0	0	0	0	0	0	0	0	0	0	40	24	105	Yellow	243	256	234
Cairo Santos	KC	9	K	24	0	0	0	0	0	0	0	0	0	0	37	25	105	Yellow	244	257	235
Bilal Powell	NYJ	5	RB	27	0	0	0	97	371	1	35	252	1	0	0	0	70	Green	245	179	244
Lance Dunbar	DAL	6	RB	25	0	0	0	71	320	1	30	275	1	0	0	0	69	Green	246	181	257
Dan Carpenter	BUF	8	K	30	0	0	0	0	0	0	0	0	0	0	30	28	104	Yellow	247	260	236
Denard Robinson	JAC	8	RB	25	0	0	0	86	328	3	36	214	0	0	0	0	68	Green	248	185	248
Dan Herron	IND	10	RB	26	0	0	0	71	297	1	32	319	1	0	0	0	68	Yellow	249	186	259
Marcedes Lewis	JAC	8	TE	31	0	0	0	0	0	0	26	268	3	0	0	0	38	Yellow	250	266	264
Jermaine Gresham	ARI	9	TE	27	0	0	0	0	0	0	32	300	2	0	0	0	38	Red	251	267	262
DeVante Parker	MIA	5	WR	22	0	0	0	2	14	0	36	556	3	0	0	0	67	Red	252	258	255
Cecil Shorts	HOU	9	WR	28	0	0	0	0	0	0	44	564	3	0	0	0	67	Red	253	259	240
Mike Tolbert	CAR	5	RB	30	0	0	0	89	369	3	24	202	1	0	0	0	67	Red	254	187	266
Gavin Escobar	DAL	6	TE	24	0	0	0	0	0	0	21	225	3	0	0	0	37	Green	255	270	269
Bears D	CHI	7	D	--	0	0	0	0	0	0	0	0	0	0	0	0	83	Green	256	263	238
Markus Wheaton	PIT	11	WR	24	0	0	0	3	14	0	40	518	2	0	0	0	66	Green	257	261	243
Cody Latimer	DEN	7	WR	23	0	0	0	2	13	0	35	526	4	0	0	0	66	Red	258	262	258
Lorenzo Taliaferro	BAL	9	RB	23	0	0	0	95	370	2	21	192	1	0	0	0	65	Yellow	259	190	270
Chargers D	SD	10	D	--	0	0	0	0	0	0	0	0	0	0	0	0	82	Yellow	260	271	241
Cole Beasley	DAL	6	WR	26	0	0	0	2	9	0	49	521	2	0	0	0	64	Green	261	264	233
Devin Funchess	CAR	5	WR	21	0	0	0	4	23	0	36	425	3	0	0	0	64	Green	262	265	252
Riley Cooper	PHI	8	WR	28	0	0	0	0	0	0	35	477	3	0	0	0	63	Yellow	263	268	260
Tavon Austin	STL	6	WR	24	0	0	0	31	160	1	37	396	1	0	0	0	63	Green	264	269	253
Ryan Succop	TEN	4	K	29	0	0	0	0	0	0	0	0	0	0	34	23	101	Green	265	273	245
Dustin Hopkins	NO	11	K	25	0	0	0	0	0	0	0	0	0	0	44	24	101	Red	266	274	246
Josh Harris	PIT	11	RB	24	0	0	0	42	177	3	23	198	2	0	0	0	62	Green	267	195	250
Greg Jennings	MIA	5	WR	32	0	0	0	0	0	0	41	428	3	0	0	0	61	Green	268	272	250
Ronnie Hillman	DEN	7	RB	24	0	0	0	56	234	2	29	219	1	0	0	0	59	Green	269	200	267
Chris Conley	KC	9	WR	23	0	0	0	2	12	0	32	441	3	0	0	0	58	Red	270	275	268
Kai Forbath	WAS	8	K	28	0	0	0	0	0	0	0	0	0	0	32	27	98	Red	271	276	271
Jameis Winston	TB	6	QB	21	3763	23	22	49	106	2	0	0	0	0	0	0	221	Red	272	278	247
Robbie Gould	CHI	7	K	33	0	0	0	0	0	0	0	0	0	0	34	24	97	Yellow	273	277	273
Fred Jackson	BUF	8	RB	34	0	0	0	45	196	0	33	263	1	0	0	0	51	Green	274	206	274
Stedman Bailey	STL	6	WR	25	0	0	0	2	10	0	29	398	2	0	0	0	50	Green	275	279	275
Robert Turbin	SEA	9	RB	26	0	0	0	86	347	2	13	106	0	0	0	0	50	Green	276	210	277
Tyler Lockett	SEA	9	WR	23	0	0	0	0	0	0	30	414	2	0	0	0	49	Red	277	280	276
Montee Ball	DEN	7	RB	25	0	0	0	81	337	2	11	88	0	0	0	0	49	Green	278	211	278
Jerick McKinnon	MIN	5	RB	23	0	0	0	73	336	1	15	109	1	0	0	0	49	Blue	279	212	279
Damien Williams	MIA	5	RB	23	0	0	0	63	236	2	23	149	0	0	0	0	48	Green	280	216	280

Statistical Appendix

Broken Tackles by Team, Offense

Rk	Team	Plays	Plays w/ BTkl	Pct	Total BTkl
1	SEA	1036	126	12.2%	156
2	IND	1116	106	9.5%	121
3	DAL	1018	89	8.7%	102
4	TEN	925	78	8.4%	87
5	GB	1003	84	8.4%	103
6	SF	1019	85	8.3%	98
7	PIT	1064	88	8.3%	108
8	WAS	1033	83	8.0%	98
9	CIN	1027	77	7.5%	84
10	NYG	1107	81	7.3%	99
11	KC	970	70	7.2%	84
12	NYJ	1066	75	7.0%	82
13	MIA	1052	74	7.0%	83
14	CHI	1028	72	7.0%	80
15	HOU	1066	72	6.8%	86
16	PHI	1134	75	6.6%	86
17	BUF	1028	67	6.5%	74
18	ATL	1045	68	6.5%	77
19	DEN	1070	69	6.4%	86
20	DET	1042	66	6.3%	74
21	NE	1081	67	6.2%	77
22	NO	1101	68	6.2%	85
23	BAL	1029	63	6.1%	70
24	CAR	1073	65	6.1%	74
25	STL	975	59	6.1%	66
26	SD	1019	60	5.9%	70
27	MIN	988	57	5.8%	63
28	JAC	1001	57	5.7%	65
29	CLE	1027	51	5.0%	58
30	TB	957	47	4.9%	51
31	ARI	1013	49	4.8%	54
32	OAK	1011	36	3.6%	43

Play total includes Defensive Pass Interference.

Broken Tackles by Team, Defense

Rk	Team	Plays	Plays w/ BTkl	Pct	Total BTkl
1	NE	1046	50	4.8%	52
2	CHI	1016	54	5.3%	63
3	TB	1072	57	5.3%	69
4	DEN	1050	57	5.4%	64
5	BAL	1058	63	6.0%	70
6	MIN	1037	62	6.0%	64
7	WAS	997	60	6.0%	72
8	SF	999	62	6.2%	69
9	SEA	927	58	6.3%	68
10	SD	1006	63	6.3%	68
11	PHI	1134	72	6.3%	81
12	CIN	1081	70	6.5%	80
13	BUF	1049	70	6.7%	79
14	DET	1002	67	6.7%	73
15	OAK	1060	71	6.7%	90
16	NYJ	978	66	6.7%	76
17	DAL	1000	68	6.8%	80
18	CAR	1007	70	7.0%	78
19	TEN	1109	78	7.0%	83
20	MIA	1027	73	7.1%	81
21	CLE	1125	81	7.2%	98
22	STL	1014	74	7.3%	81
23	PIT	953	70	7.3%	83
24	ATL	1041	77	7.4%	89
25	HOU	1080	83	7.7%	91
26	NO	1029	80	7.8%	95
27	NYG	1005	79	7.9%	96
28	ARI	1024	83	8.1%	106
29	KC	1035	88	8.5%	108
30	IND	1016	88	8.7%	111
31	GB	1062	93	8.8%	105
32	JAC	1085	97	8.9%	121

Play total includes Defensive Pass Interference.

Top 20 Defenders, Broken Tackles

Rk	Player	Team	BTkl	Rk	Player	Team	BTkl
1	J.Evans	JAC	22	10	M.Burnett	GB	14
2	C.Woodson	OAK	21	10	L.Foote	ARI	14
3	R.Parker	KC	20	10	R.McLeod	STL	14
4	J.Cyprien	JAC	17	14	D.Hawthorne	NO	13
4	M.Griffin	TEN	17	14	D.Jackson	IND	13
4	R.Johnson	ARI	17	14	J.Jenkins	STL	13
7	R.Clark	WAS	16	14	D.Levy	DET	13
8	G.Toler	IND	15	14	K.Lewis	HOU	13
8	P.Worrilow	ATL	15	14	A.Ogletree	STL	13
10	M.Adams	IND	14	20	9 tied with		12

Top 20 Defenders, Broken Tackle Rate

Rk	Player	Team	BTkl	Tkl	Rate
1	J.Bostic	CHI	0	63	0.0%
1	F.Cox	PHI	0	53	0.0%
1	M.Foster	TB	0	41	0.0%
1	C.Heyward	PIT	0	45	0.0%
5	J.McCourty	TEN	1	82	1.2%
6	L.David	TB	2	110	1.8%
7	B.Logan	PHI	1	49	2.0%
8	D.Searcy	BUF	1	47	2.1%
9	D.Revis	NE	1	44	2.2%
9	M.Wilkerson	NYJ	1	44	2.2%
11	J.Mayo	NE	1	43	2.3%
12	C.Thornton	PHI	1	42	2.3%
13	P.Amukamara	NYG	1	42	2.4%
14	D.Lansanah	TB	2	69	2.8%
15	D.Hightower	NE	2	64	3.0%
16	T.McDonald	STL	3	92	3.2%
17	E.Weddle	SD	3	86	3.4%
18	J.Laurinaitis	STL	3	85	3.4%
19	J.Casey	TEN	2	55	3.5%
20	A.Cason	2TM	2	53	3.6%

Broken Tackles divided by Broken Tackles + Solo Tackles.
Special teams not included; min. 40 Solo Tackles

Bottom 20 Defenders, Broken Tackle Rate

Rk	Player	Team	BTkl	Tkl	Rate
1	J.Evans	JAC	22	70	24.2%
2	G.Toler	IND	15	54	22.1%
3	D.Butler	IND	11	41	21.2%
4	R.Maualuga	CIN	11	43	20.4%
5	J.Jenkins	STL	13	54	20.0%
6	C.Sensabaugh	TEN	10	43	20.0%
7	J.Wilson	MIA	12	52	19.4%
8	K.Jackson	HOU	12	51	19.0%
9	A.Cromartie	ARI	10	45	18.9%
10	C.Woodson	OAK	21	92	18.8%
11	R.Parker	KC	20	88	18.5%
12	R.Johnson	ARI	17	79	18.5%
13	D.Hawthorne	NO	13	62	17.6%
13	R.McLeod	STL	14	64	18.4%
15	L.Foote	ARI	14	68	17.3%
15	K.Lewis	HOU	13	65	17.3%
17	R.Clark	WAS	16	78	17.0%
18	D.J.Swearinger	HOU	12	61	16.9%
18	D.Walls	NYJ	8	40	17.0%
20	P.Kruger	CLE	9	45	16.7%

Broken Tackles divided by Broken Tackles + Solo Tackles.
Special teams not included; min. 40 Solo Tackles

Most Broken Tackles, Running Backs

Rk	Player	Team	BTkl
1	M.Lynch	SEA	88
2	L.Bell	PIT	59
3	E.Lacy	GB	51
3	D.Murray	DAL	51
5	C.J.Anderson	DEN	46
6	A.Foster	HOU	43
7	L.McCoy	PHI	40
8	A.Bradshaw	IND	33
8	C.Ivory	NYJ	33
10	T.Richardson	IND	32
10	J.Stewart	CAR	32
12	J.Charles	KC	30
12	M.Forte	CHI	30
12	M.Ingram	NO	30
15	B.Oliver	SD	29
16	A.Morris	WAS	28
17	J.Hill	CIN	26
17	R.Jennings	NYG	26
19	J.Forsett	BAL	25
19	F.Jackson	BUF	25

Most Broken Tackles, WR/TE

Rk	Player	Team	BTkl
1	R.Gronkowski	NE	24
2	M.Bennett	CHI	19
3	A.Brown	PIT	18
3	D.Bryant	DAL	18
3	G.Tate	DET	18
6	O.Beckham	NYG	14
6	J.Jones	ATL	14
6	D.Walker	TEN	14
6	K.Wright	TEN	14
10	S.Smith	BAL	13
11	A.Boldin	SF	12
11	J.Gresham	CIN	12
11	T.Kelce	KC	12
14	J.Nelson	GB	11
15	R.Cobb	GB	10
15	P.Harvin	2TM	10
15	J.Landry	MIA	10
15	J.Reed	WAS	10
15	M.Wallace	MIA	10
20	6 tied with		9

Most Broken Tackles, Quarterbacks

Rk	Player	Team	Behind LOS	Beyond LOS	BTkl		Rk	Player	Team	Behind LOS	Beyond LOS	BTkl
1	C.Kaepernick	SF	21	6	27		6	A.Luck	IND	6	3	9
2	R.Wilson	SEA	18	7	25		7	R.Griffin	WAS	7	1	8
3	C.Newton	CAR	10	4	14		7	B.Roethlisberger	PIT	8	0	8
4	R.Fitzpatrick	HOU	11	0	11		7	G.Smith	NYJ	7	1	8
5	B.Bortles	JAC	9	1	10		7	M.Vick	NYJ	3	5	8

Best Broken Tackle Rate, Offensive Players (min. 80 touches)

Rk	Player	Team	BTkl	Touch	Rate		Rk	Player	Team	BTkl	Touch	Rate
1	R.Gronkowski	NE	24	82	29.3%		11	P.Thomas	NO	16	90	17.8%
2	M.Lynch	SEA	88	317	27.8%		12	E.Lacy	GB	51	288	17.7%
3	A.Bradshaw	IND	33	128	25.8%		13	G.Tate	DET	18	104	17.3%
4	R.Helu	WAS	21	82	25.6%		14	T.Richardson	IND	32	186	17.2%
5	C.Hyde	SF	21	95	22.1%		15	J.Stewart	CAR	32	200	16.0%
6	C.Anderson	DEN	46	213	21.6%		16	L.Bell	PIT	59	373	15.8%
7	M.Bennett	CHI	19	90	21.1%		17	D.Freeman	ATL	15	95	15.8%
8	D.Bryant	DAL	18	88	20.5%		18	C.Ivory	NYJ	33	216	15.3%
9	K.Robinson	NO	16	84	19.0%		19	B.Oliver	SD	29	196	14.8%
10	D.Sproles	PHI	18	97	18.6%		20	A.Foster	HOU	43	298	14.4%

(Min. 80 touches)

Top 20 Defenders, Passes Defensed

Rk	Player	Team	PD
1	B.Fletcher	PHI	22
2	V.Davis	IND	18
2	J.Haden	CLE	18
2	X.Rhodes	MIN	18
5	C.Graham	BUF	17
6	P.Cox	SF	16
6	D.Slay	DET	16
6	D.Trufant	ATL	16
9	R.Nelson	CIN	15
9	B.Skrine	CLE	15
9	S.Smith	KC	15
9	A.Talib	DEN	15
13	E.J.Gaines	STL	14
13	M.Jenkins	PHI	14
13	K.Lewis	NO	14
13	J.Norman	CAR	14
17	B.Breeland	WAS	13
17	C.Culliver	SF	13
17	C.Harris	DEN	13
17	T.Newman	CIN	13
17	D.Revis	NE	13
17	B.Roby	DEN	13

Note: Based on the definition given in the Statistical Toolbox, not NFL totals.

Top 20 Defenders, Defeats

Rk	Player	Team	PD
1	J.J.Watt	HOU	43
2	L.David	TB	42
3	D.Levy	DET	35
4	J.Houston	KC	33
5	C.Mosley	BAL	30
6	L.Kuechly	CAR	29
7	C.Barwin	PHI	28
8	C.Dunlap	CIN	27
8	J.Pierre-Paul	NYG	27
8	L.Timmons	PIT	27
11	N.Suh	DET	26
12	A.Donald	STL	25
12	K.Mack	OAK	25
12	M.Williams	BUF	25
15	E.Ansah	DET	24
15	T.Davis	CAR	24
15	E.Griffen	MIN	24
15	V.Miller	DEN	24
19	S.Marks	JAC	23
19	C.Matthews	GB	23
19	J.Peppers	GB	23
19	H.Smith	MIN	23
19	T.Smith	JAC	23
19	M.Wilkerson	NYJ	23

Top 20 Defenders, Run Tackles for Loss

Rk	Player	Team	Dfts
1	J.J.Watt	HOU	17
2	L.David	TB	14
2	K.Mack	OAK	14
4	M.Bennett	SEA	12
4	C.Liuget	SD	12
6	A.Donald	STL	11
6	N.Suh	DET	11
6	M.Wilkerson	NYJ	11
9	D.Lansanah	TB	10
9	S.Marks	JAC	10
11	C.Borland	SF	9
11	C.Campbell	ARI	9
11	G.Hayes	JAC	9
11	L.Kuechly	CAR	9
11	D.Levy	DET	9
16	14 tied with		8

Top 20 Defenders, Quarterback Hits

Rk	Player	Team	Hits
1	J.J.Watt	HOU	35
2	E.Ansah	DET	19
2	C.Dunlap	CIN	19
2	P.McPhee	BAL	19
5	J.Worilds	PIT	16
6	J.Allen	CHI	15
6	E.Griffen	MIN	15
8	C.Avril	SEA	14
9	M.Bennett	SEA	13
9	J.Casey	TEN	13
9	T.Crawford	DAL	13
9	W.Gilberry	CIN	13
9	C.Johnson	CAR	13
9	E.Walden	IND	13
9	M.Wilkerson	NYJ	13
16	J.Jones	DET	12
16	V.Miller	DEN	12
16	C.Redding	IND	12
16	S.Richardson	NYJ	12
16	C.Wake	MIA	12

Top 20 Defenders, QB Knockdowns (Sacks + Hits)

Rk	Defender	Team	KD
1	J.J.Watt	HOU	54
2	E.Dumervil	BAL	31
3	C.Dunlap	CIN	28
3	V.Miller	DEN	28
5	E.Ansah	DET	27
5	E.Griffen	MIN	27
7	P.McPhee	BAL	26
8	J.Houston	KC	25
9	C.Matthews	GB	24
9	J.Worilds	PIT	24
11	C.Wake	MIA	23
12	C.Barwin	PHI	22
12	J.Pierre-Paul	NYG	22
12	M.Wilkerson	NYJ	22
15	M.Bennett	SEA	21
15	J.Hughes	BUF	21
15	R.Quinn	STL	21
15	S.Richardson	NYJ	21
15	T.Suggs	BAL	21
15	N.Suh	DET	21
15	E.Walden	IND	21
15	D.Ware	DEN	21

Full credit for whole and half sacks; includes sacks cancelled by penalty.
Does not include strip sacks.

Top 20 Defenders, Hurries

Rk	Defender	Team	Hur
1	J.J.Watt	HOU	54.0
2	V.Miller	DEN	43.0
3	J.Houston	KC	32.8
4	J.Galette	NO	32.5
5	J.Hughes	BUF	32.0
6	K.Mack	OAK	30.5
7	R.Kerrigan	WAS	30.0
8	E.Ansah	DET	29.5
8	C.Johnson	CAR	29.5
10	M.Bennett	SEA	28.5
11	J.Allen	CHI	27.5
12	C.Dunlap	CIN	26.0
12	B.Robison	MIN	26.0
12	D.Ware	DEN	26.0
15	D.Freeney	SD	25.5
15	C.Wake	MIA	25.5
17	C.Barwin	PHI	24.5
17	J.Peppers	GB	24.5
19	R.Ninkovich	NE	24.0
20	J.Pierre-Paul	NYG	24.0

Top 20 Defenders, Drawing Offensive Holding Flags

Rk	Player	Team	Total	Pass/ Scramble	Run/ Screen
1	J.Pierre-Paul	NYG	9	6	3
2	S.Floyd	MIN	8	3	5
2	J.Hughes	BUF	8	5	3
2	K.Mack	OAK	8	3	5
2	R.Quinn	STL	8	4	4
6	M.Bennett	SEA	7	2	5
6	R.Kerrigan	WAS	7	5	2
6	S.Richardson	NYJ	7	3	4
6	J.J.Watt	HOU	7	4	3
10	J.Galette	NO	6	5	1
11	J.Allen	CHI	5	4	1
11	E.Ansah	DET	5	3	2
11	T.Cole	PHI	5	4	1
11	V.Curry	PHI	5	4	1
11	W.Gilberry	CIN	5	4	1
11	N.Suh	DET	5	4	1
11	C.Wake	MIA	5	4	1
18	14 tied with		4		

Top 20 Quarterbacks, QB Hits

Rk	Player	Team	Hits
1	A.Luck	IND	91
2	M.Ryan	ATL	65
3	T.Brady	NE	61
3	R.Tannehill	MIA	61
5	J.McCown	TB	59
6	D.Brees	NO	56
6	R.Wilson	SEA	56
8	M.Stafford	DET	51
9	E.Manning	NYG	44
9	P.Rivers	SD	44
11	R.Griffin	WAS	43
12	R.Fitzpatrick	HOU	42
12	J.Flacco	BAL	42
12	B.Hoyer	CLE	42
15	G.Smith	NYJ	40
15	D.Stanton	ARI	40
17	B.Bortles	JAC	39
17	J.Cutler	CHI	39
19	A.Rodgers	GB	36
20	N.Foles	PHI	34

Top 20 Quarterbacks, QB Knockdowns (Sacks + Hits)

Rk	Player	Team	Adj KD
1	A.Luck	IND	115
2	R.Tannehill	MIA	106
3	M.Ryan	ATL	98
4	R.Wilson	SEA	96
5	M.Stafford	DET	95
6	J.McCown	TB	94
7	B.Bortles	JAC	92
8	D.Brees	NO	85
9	T.Brady	NE	80
10	P.Rivers	SD	79
11	R.Griffin	WAS	78
12	J.Cutler	CHI	77
13	A.Smith	KC	74
14	C.Kaepernick	SF	71
15	T.Bridgewater	MIN	70
15	E.Manning	NYG	70
17	B.Hoyer	CLE	65
18	C.Newton	CAR	64
18	B.Roethlisberger	PIT	64
18	G.Smith	NYJ	64

Includes sacks cancelled by penalties
Does not include strip sacks or "self sacks" with no defender listed.

Top 10 Quarterbacks, Knockdowns per Pass

Rk	Player	Team	KD	Pct
1	R.Griffin	WAS	78	29.5%
2	J.McCown	TB	94	24.9%
3	Z.Mettenberger	TEN	39	18.7%
4	D.Stanton	ARI	52	18.6%
5	R.Wilson	SEA	96	18.5%
6	C.Whitehurst	TEN	38	17.9%
7	A.Davis	STL	57	17.3%
8	R.Fitzpatrick	HOU	61	17.0%
9	A.Luck	IND	115	16.9%
10	M.Glennon	TB	40	16.7%

Min. 200 passes; includes passes cancelled by penalty

Bottom 10 Quarterbacks in Knockdowns per Pass

Rk	Player	Team	KD	Pct
1	P.Manning	DEN	43	6.6%
2	D.Carr	OAK	52	8.0%
2	K.Cousins	WAS	16	7.1%
4	M.Sanchez	PHI	33	9.5%
5	B.Roethlisberger	PIT	64	9.6%
6	A.Dalton	CIN	52	9.7%
7	J.Flacco	BAL	60	9.8%
8	E.Manning	NYG	70	10.6%
9	T.Romo	DAL	52	10.6%
10	A.Rodgers	GB	63	10.8%

Min. 200 passes; includes passes cancelled by penalty

Top 10 Most Passes Tipped at Line, Quarterbacks

Rk	Player	Team	Total
1	R.Tannehill	MIA	20
2	B.Bortles	JAC	19
3	A.Smith	KC	17
4	D.Brees	NO	16
5	D.Carr	OAK	15
5	J.Cutler	CHI	15
7	A.Luck	IND	14
8	T.Brady	NE	12
8	B.Hoyer	CLE	12
8	P.Manning	DEN	12

Top 10 Tipped at the Line, Defenders

Rk	Player	Team	Total
1	J.J.Watt	HOU	9
2	A.Ogletree	STL	7
3	C.Barwin	PHI	6
3	J.Peppers	GB	6
5	J.Crick	HOU	5
5	J.Houston	KC	5
5	C.Jordan	NO	5
5	C.Matthews	GB	5
5	H.Ngata	BAL	5
5	J.Odrick	MIA	5
5	M.Wilkerson	NYJ	5

2014 Quarterbacks with and without Pass Pressure

Rank	Player	Team	Plays	Pct Pressure	DVOA with Pressure	Yds with Pressure	DVOA w/o Pressure	Yds w/o Pressure	DVOA Dif	Rank
1	P.Manning	DEN	624	13.1%	-89.6%	2.5	62.9%	8.4	-152.5%	32
2	B.Roethlisberger	PIT	648	17.4%	-0.9%	5.5	58.4%	8.2	-59.3%	2
3	K.Cousins	WAS	216	17.6%	-75.2%	3.4	35.6%	8.7	-110.9%	11
4	K.Orton	BUF	485	19.0%	-110.4%	1.7	26.7%	6.9	-137.1%	27
5	A.Dalton	CIN	525	19.6%	-92.5%	4.7	31.1%	7.0	-123.6%	19
6	A.Rodgers	GB	583	20.2%	-47.0%	3.7	81.0%	9.0	-128.0%	20
7	M.Stafford	DET	669	20.8%	-96.8%	2.4	38.4%	7.3	-135.2%	24
8	D.Brees	NO	704	21.0%	-72.2%	3.5	48.7%	8.0	-120.9%	17
9	T.Romo	DAL	477	21.2%	-87.1%	3.9	77.8%	8.7	-164.9%	35
10	P.Rivers	SD	634	21.6%	-27.5%	4.6	49.1%	7.5	-76.6%	4
11	C.Newton	CAR	519	22.0%	-100.1%	1.5	30.5%	7.2	-130.6%	22
12	J.Cutler	CHI	629	22.1%	-69.4%	3.6	40.7%	7.1	-110.1%	10
13	T.Brady	NE	622	22.5%	-67.3%	3.3	65.9%	7.7	-133.3%	23
14	J.Flacco	BAL	591	23.0%	-73.1%	4.0	62.5%	8.0	-135.5%	26
15	A.Luck	IND	688	23.4%	-70.6%	4.0	49.1%	8.3	-119.7%	16
16	E.Manning	NYG	644	23.4%	-46.6%	4.3	36.3%	7.7	-82.9%	7
17	D.Stanton	ARI	267	24.0%	-11.9%	5.2	18.5%	7.4	-30.4%	1
18	D.Carr	OAK	635	24.1%	-84.5%	1.8	26.9%	6.2	-111.4%	12
19	M.Sanchez	PHI	348	24.4%	-83.7%	3.4	44.5%	7.9	-128.1%	21
20	B.Hoyer	CLE	477	24.7%	-101.4%	2.8	51.6%	8.1	-152.9%	33
21	B.Bortles	JAC	555	24.9%	-128.9%	1.4	6.5%	6.4	-135.4%	25
22	R.Tannehill	MIA	651	26.1%	-89.7%	2.3	56.6%	7.2	-146.3%	29
23	M.Ryan	ATL	681	26.4%	-30.9%	4.6	44.8%	7.7	-75.7%	3
24	C.Palmer	ARI	243	26.7%	-47.7%	4.8	31.8%	7.7	-79.5%	5
25	S.Hill	STL	252	27.8%	-118.3%	2.1	28.8%	8.2	-147.1%	30
26	A.Smith	KC	547	27.8%	-72.8%	2.7	49.6%	7.3	-122.4%	18
27	R.Fitzpatrick	HOU	368	28.3%	-50.4%	4.6	49.9%	8.3	-100.3%	8
28	T.Bridgewater	MIN	470	28.3%	-102.8%	1.8	45.3%	7.8	-148.1%	31
29	N.Foles	PHI	333	29.1%	-46.4%	5.3	34.8%	7.4	-81.2%	6
30	G.Smith	NYJ	428	29.4%	-74.6%	3.3	38.0%	7.2	-112.7%	14
31	R.Griffin	WAS	267	29.6%	-155.0%	1.2	33.3%	7.9	-188.3%	36
32	M.Glennon	TB	226	29.6%	-71.3%	3.3	30.3%	7.4	-101.6%	9
33	C.Whitehurst	TEN	213	30.5%	-98.6%	2.0	56.0%	7.9	-154.5%	34
34	C.Kaepernick	SF	585	30.9%	-65.2%	3.9	46.9%	7.3	-112.1%	13
35	J.McCown	TB	380	33.7%	-155.6%	2.8	32.8%	7.1	-188.4%	37
36	A.Davis	STL	319	34.5%	-91.7%	2.0	51.0%	8.1	-142.6%	28
37	R.Wilson	SEA	547	39.1%	-44.5%	4.1	75.3%	8.8	-119.7%	15

Includes scrambles and Defensive Pass Interference. Does not include aborted snaps.
Minimum: 200 passes.

Top 20 Players, Passes Dropped

Rk	Player	Team	Total
1	J.Edelman	NE	10
2	M.Bennett	CHI	8
2	D.Thomas	DEN	8
2	R.Wayne	IND	8
5	K.Benjamin	CAR	7
5	A.Boldin	SF	7
5	D.Bowe	KC	7
5	M.Rivera	OAK	7
9	J.Amaro	NYJ	6
9	M.Asiata	MIN	6
9	J.Charles	KC	6
9	M.Colston	NO	6
9	V.Cruz	NYG	6
9	A.Johnson	HOU	6
9	D.Johnson	HOU	6
9	L.Miller	MIA	6
9	M.Reece	OAK	6
9	M.Sanu	CIN	6
19	21 tied with		5

Top 20 Players, Pct. Passes Dropped

Rk	Player	Team	Drops	Passes	Pct
1	J.Jones	BAL	4	18	22.2%
2	A.Morris	WAS	4	26	15.4%
3	V.Cruz	NYG	6	41	14.6%
4	D.Johnson	HOU	6	49	12.2%
5	R.Jennings	NYG	5	41	12.2%
6	L.Miller	MIA	6	52	11.5%
7	J.Amaro	NYJ	6	53	11.3%
8	J.Todman	JAC	4	37	10.8%
9	A.Bradshaw	IND	5	47	10.6%
10	M.Reece	OAK	6	59	10.2%
11	J.Charles	KC	6	60	10.0%
12	L.Willson	SEA	4	40	10.0%
13	M.Asiata	MIN	6	63	9.5%
14	D.Brown	SD	4	42	9.5%
15	J.Carlson	ARI	5	55	9.1%
16	C.J.Anderson	DEN	4	44	9.1%
17	L.Murphy	TB	5	56	8.9%
18	E.Ebron	DET	4	47	8.5%
19	J.Cumberland	NYJ	4	47	8.5%
20	D.Allen	IND	4	50	8.0%

Min. four drops

Top 10 Teams, Pct Passes Dropped

Rk	Team	Drops	Passes	Pct
1	DAL	12	456	2.6%
2	SD	15	540	2.8%
3	WAS	15	518	2.9%
4	TEN	15	474	3.2%
5	ATL	21	597	3.5%
6	DET	20	563	3.6%
7	BUF	20	547	3.7%
8	PHI	22	595	3.7%
9	TB	18	486	3.7%
10	DEN	22	589	3.7%

Top 20 Intended Receivers on Interceptions

Rk	Player	Team	Total
1	K.Allen	SD	7
1	D.Hopkins	HOU	7
1	J.Maclin	PHI	7
1	D.Walker	TEN	7
5	M.Evans	TB	6
5	A.Green	CIN	6
5	V.Jackson	TB	6
5	A.Roberts	WAS	6
5	T.Smith	BAL	6
5	D.Thomas	DEN	6
11	M.Bennett	CHI	5
11	K.Britt	STL	5
11	D.Bryant	DAL	5
11	R.Cooper	PHI	5
11	B.Marshall	CHI	5
11	C.Patterson	MIN	5
11	R.Randle	NYG	5
11	R.Wayne	IND	5
19	16 tied with		4

Bottom 10 Teams, Pct Passes Dropped

Rk	Team	Drops	Passes	Pct
23	MIA	26	555	4.7%
24	JAC	25	521	4.8%
25	MIN	23	479	4.8%
26	HOU	22	458	4.8%
27	OAK	28	577	4.9%
28	NE	28	573	4.9%
29	CHI	29	579	5.0%
30	IND	34	619	5.5%
31	NYJ	25	443	5.6%
32	KC	31	455	6.8%

Top 10 Plus/Minus for Running Backs

Rk	Player	Team	Pass	+/-
1	M.Forte	CHI	131	+6.2
2	R.Helu	WAS	47	+6.1
3	B.Cunningham	STL	53	+6.1
4	D.Murray	DAL	64	+5.5
5	L.Bell	PIT	105	+4.5
6	M.Ingram	NO	36	+3.6
7	P.Thomas	NO	55	+3.4
8	T.Cadet	NO	51	+2.8
9	M.Lynch	SEA	48	+2.4
10	D.Freeman	ATL	37	+2.3

Min. 25 passes; plus/minus adjusted for passes tipped/thrown away.

Bottom 10 Plus/Minus for Running Backs

Rk	Player	Team	Pass	+/-
1	D.Sproles	PHI	63	-7.0
2	M.Reece	OAK	59	-5.4
3	M.Asiata	MIN	63	-5.4
4	J.Bell	DET	52	-5.2
5	J.McKinnon	MIN	41	-5.0
6	F.Jackson	BUF	90	-4.8
7	A.Williams	NYG	37	-4.7
8	J.Todman	JAC	37	-4.5
9	R.Hillman	DEN	34	-4.4
10	A.Morris	WAS	26	-4.3

Min. 25 passes; plus/minus adjusted for passes tipped/thrown away.

Top 10 Plus/Minus for Wide Receivers

Rk	Player	Team	Pass	+/-
1	A.Brown	PIT	181	+16.5
2	E.Sanders	DEN	141	+16.3
3	K.Stills	NO	84	+15.5
4	T.Y.Hilton	IND	131	+11.9
5	J.Nelson	GB	151	+11.6
6	O.Beckham	NYG	130	+11.1
7	B.Cooks	NO	69	+9.7
8	J.Landry	MIA	112	+8.7
9	R.Cobb	GB	127	+8.4
10	M.Floyd	SD	91	+7.2

Min. 50 passes; plus/minus adjusted for passes tipped/thrown away.

Bottom 10 Plus/Minus for Wide Receivers

Rk	Player	Team	Pass	+/-
1	C.Shorts	JAC	110	-13.2
2	J.Hunter	TEN	67	-8.7
3	S.Watkins	BUF	128	-8.5
4	K.Benjamin	CAR	145	-7.8
5	V.Jackson	TB	142	-7.8
6	Jo.Brown	ARI	103	-7.3
7	A.Roberts	WAS	73	-7.0
8	A.Johnson	HOU	147	-6.9
9	A.Hurns	JAC	97	-6.8
10	M.Sanu	CIN	98	-6.7

Min. 50 passes; plus/minus adjusted for passes tipped/thrown away.

Top 10 Plus/Minus for Tight Ends

Rk	Player	Team	Pass	+/-
1	T.Kelce	KC	87	+9.9
2	A.Gates	SD	98	+7.8
3	J.Witten	DAL	90	+6.0
4	H.Miller	PIT	91	+5.9
5	J.Gresham	CIN	79	+5.2
6	G.Olsen	CAR	123	+5.1
7	T.Wright	NE	33	+4.6
8	J.Thomas	DEN	62	+4.3
9	L.Donnell	NYG	92	+4.2
10	J.Graham	NO	124	+3.7

Min. 25 passes; plus/minus adjusted for passes tipped/thrown away.

Bottom 10 Plus/Minus for Tight Ends

Rk	Player	Team	Pass	+/-
1	J.Cook	STL	99	-8.1
2	J.Cameron	CLE	48	-5.0
3	L.Toilolo	ATL	53	-4.9
4	J.Cumberland	NYJ	47	-4.8
5	E.Ebron	DET	47	-4.0
6	J.Tamme	DEN	28	-3.9
7	C.Fleener	IND	92	-3.6
8	V.Davis	SF	51	-3.5
9	G.Barnidge	CLE	25	-2.8
10	J.Carlson	ARI	55	-2.8

Min. 25 passes; plus/minus adjusted for passes tipped/thrown away.

Top 10 Quarterbacks, Yards Gained on Defensive Pass Interference

Rk	Player	Team	Pen	Yds
1	J.Flacco	BAL	14	283
2	J.Cutler	CHI	9	192
3	T.Brady	NE	11	182
4	A.Rodgers	GB	7	173
5	E.Manning	NYG	10	165
6	A.Luck	IND	8	158
6	P.Manning	DEN	10	158
8	B.Roethlisberger	PIT	8	156
9	T.Romo	DAL	6	147
10	D.Brees	NO	8	145
10	P.Rivers	SD	8	145

Top 10 Receivers, Yards Gained on Defensive Pass Interference

Rk	Player	Team	Pen	Yds
1	T.Smith	BAL	11	229
2	J.Nelson	GB	6	129
3	A.Jeffery	CHI	4	125
4	A.Brown	PIT	5	97
5	Jo.Brown	ARI	3	96
6	M.Crabtree	SF	4	88
6	D.Jackson	WAS	5	88
8	M.Floyd	ARI	3	87
9	M.Wallace	MIA	4	77
10	R.Cooper	PHI	2	76

Top 10 Defenders, Yards Allowed on Defensive Pass Interference

Rk	Player	Team	Pen	Yds
1	S.Wright	SD	8	115
2	D.Slay	DET	5	106
3	B.Wreh-Wilson	TEN	7	102
4	B.Fletcher	PHI	4	101
5	B.Skrine	CLE	7	100
6	T.Jennings	CHI	2	99
7	R.Alford	ATL	4	95
8	B.Breeland	WAS	4	93
9	A.Cason	CAR	4	80
10	V.Davis	IND	3	76

Top 20 First Downs/Touchdowns Allowed, Coverage

Rk	Player	Team	Grand Total
1	J.McCourty	TEN	53
2	K.Fuller	CHI	48
3	B.Fletcher	PHI	47
4	D.Trufant	ATL	43
5	G.Toler	IND	42
6	J.Haden	CLE	40
7	B.Grimes	MIA	38
7	B.Skrine	CLE	38
9	B.Breeland	WAS	37
9	K.Lewis	NO	37
9	C.Williams	PHI	37
12	J.Banks	TB	36
12	D.Slay	DET	36
14	A.Cason	CAR	35
14	A.Verner	TB	35
16	W.Gay	PIT	34
16	B.Roby	DEN	34
16	A.Talib	DEN	34
19	T.Jennings	CHI	33
19	D.Walls	NYJ	33

Includes Defensive Pass Interference.

Top 20 Passing Yards Allowed, Coverage

Rk	Player	Team	Yards
1	B.Fletcher	PHI	1123
2	J.McCourty	TEN	976
3	K.Fuller	CHI	953
4	C.Williams	PHI	874
5	B.Skrine	CLE	860
6	J.Haden	CLE	840
7	D.Walls	NYJ	839
8	G.Toler	IND	798
9	D.Slay	DET	794
10	B.Carr	DAL	768
11	B.Breeland	WAS	767
12	W.Gay	PIT	747
13	A.Verner	TB	730
14	A.Cromartie	ARI	720
15	B.Wreh-Wilson	TEN	718
16	P.Peterson	ARI	694
17	D.Gratz	JAC	690
18	P.Cox	SF	689
19	T.Jennings	CHI	687
20	L.Webb	BAL	672

Includes Defensive Pass Interference.

Fewest Yards After Catch Allowed, Coverage by Cornerbacks

Rk	Player	Team	YAC
1	C.Graham	BUF	1.6
2	R.Mathis	DET	1.8
3	D.Amerson	WAS	1.8
4	J.Robinson	MIN	1.9
5	J.McCourty	TEN	2.1
6	M.Williams	NYJ	2.1
7	C.Culliver	SF	2.2
8	R.Sherman	SEA	2.2
9	D.McCray	JAC	2.2
10	S.Smith	KC	2.2
11	T.Newman	CIN	2.3
12	B.Browner	NE	2.3
13	V.Davis	IND	2.3
14	B.Maxwell	SEA	2.5
15	B.Breeland	WAS	2.5
16	J.Joseph	HOU	2.6
17	J.Haden	CLE	2.6
18	C.Harris	DEN	2.6
19	S.Gilmore	BUF	2.7
20	B.Grimes	MIA	2.7

Min. 50 passes or 8 games started.

Most Yards After Catch Allowed, Coverage by Cornerbacks

Rk	Player	Team	YAC
1	B.Carr	DAL	6.4
2	A.Cromartie	ARI	6.3
3	B.Wreh-Wilson	TEN	6.0
4	B.Flowers	SD	5.6
5	B.Fletcher	PHI	5.5
6	J.Jenkins	STL	5.0
7	K.Jackson	HOU	5.0
8	D.Gratz	JAC	5.0
9	R.Alford	ATL	5.0
10	O.Scandrick	DAL	4.9
11	C.Finnegan	MIA	4.8
12	J.Powers	ARI	4.7
13	K.Lewis	NO	4.7
14	D.Walls	NYJ	4.6
15	L.Webb	BAL	4.6
16	C.White	NO	4.5
17	C.Munnerlyn	MIN	4.5
18	D.Revis	NE	4.4
19	J.Banks	TB	4.3
20	W.Gay	PIT	4.3

Min. 50 passes or 8 games started.

Most Dropped Interceptions, 2014

Rk	Player	Team	Drops
1	P.Cox	SF	4
2	J.Haden	CLE	3
2	M.Jenkins	PHI	3
2	K.Lewis	HOU	3
5	17 tied with		2

Most Dropped Interceptions, 2012-2014

Rk	Player	Team	Drops
1	D.House	GB	7
2	A.Cromartie	ARI	6
2	J.Haden	CLE	6
2	T.Williams	GB	6
5	J.McCourty	TEN	5
5	O.Scandrick	DAL	5
5	D.Smith	BAL	5
8	P.Amukamara	NYG	4
8	P.Cox	SF	4
8	C.Hayward	GB	4
8	K.Lewis	KC/HOU	4
8	P.Robinson	NO	4
8	C.Rogers	SF/OAK	4
8	J.Sanford	MIN/NO	4
8	A.Verner	TEN/TB	4
8	C.Woodson	GB/OAK	4

Fewest Avg Yards on Run Tackle, Defensive Line or Edge Rusher

Rk	Player	Team	Tkl	Avg
1	A.Donald	STL	32	0.0
2	M.Bennett	SEA	29	0.6
3	J.J.Watt	HOU	53	0.8
4	M.Wilkerson	NYJ	43	0.9
5	S.Marks	JAC	25	0.9
6	G.Atkins	CIN	26	0.9
7	N.Suh	DET	40	1.0
8	T.Crawford	DAL	25	1.0
9	E.Mitchell	MIA	29	1.0
10	P.Soliai	ATL	25	1.1
11	K.Williams	BUF	31	1.1
12	T.Knighton	DEN	25	1.2
13	C.Liuget	SD	46	1.3
14	B.Logan	PHI	55	1.3
15	M.Jackson	DEN	32	1.3
16	A.Woods	TEN	25	1.4
17	M.Dareus	BUF	35	1.4
18	W.Hayes	STL	33	1.5
19	Q.Coples	NYJ	25	1.6
20	C.Campbell	ARI	48	1.6

Min. 25 run tackles

Fewest Avg Yards on Run Tackle, LB

Rk	Player	Team	Tkl	Avg
1	G.Hayes	JAC	33	1.4
2	B.Spikes	BUF	38	1.7
3	K.Mack	OAK	60	1.9
4	J.Johnson	KC	31	2.0
5	V.Miller	DEN	31	2.0
6	J.Durant	DAL	28	2.2
7	R.McClain	DAL	48	2.3
8	J.Trusnik	MIA	29	2.4
9	D.Lansanah	TB	42	2.5
10	B.Wagner	SEA	62	2.7
11	L.David	TB	85	2.7
12	C.Robertson	CLE	70	2.7
13	R.Maualuga	CIN	39	2.7
14	D.Kennard	NYG	31	2.8
15	P.Wheeler	MIA	33	2.8
16	D.Hawthorne	NO	57	2.8
17	A.Williamson	TEN	53	2.8
18	C.Borland	SF	69	2.8
19	B.Irvin	SEA	26	2.8
20	A.Hitchens	DAL	50	3.0

Min. 25 run tackles

Fewest Avg Yards on Run Tackle, DB

Rk	Player	Team	Tkl	Avg
1	W.Hill	BAL	20	2.8
2	T.J.Ward	DEN	29	3.3
3	T.McDonald	STL	56	3.8
4	B.Meriweather	WAS	30	3.8
5	E.J.Gaines	STL	21	4.2
6	B.McDougald	TB	21	4.3
7	D.Bucannon	ARI	26	4.3
8	A.Verner	TB	23	4.4
9	P.Chung	NE	52	4.5
10	T.Branch	OAK	20	4.7
11	R.Mundy	CHI	52	4.8
12	J.Ihedigbo	DET	28	4.8
13	L.Hall	CIN	22	4.8
14	M.Burnett	GB	76	4.8
15	S.Wright	SD	22	4.9
16	A.Bethea	SF	45	5.0
17	G.Wilson	TEN	50	5.0
18	T.Jefferson	ARI	38	5.1
19	J.Jarrett	NYJ	21	5.2
20	R.Harper	CAR	34	5.2

Min. 20 run tackles

Top 20 Offensive Tackles, Blown Blocks

Rk	Player	Pos	Team	Sacks	All Pass	All Run	Total
1	J.Britt	RT	SEA	5.5	30.0	8.5	38.5
2	D.J.Fluker	RT	SD	6.0	29.3	7.5	36.8
3	N.Solder	LT	NE	5.5	28.5	8.0	36.5
4	J.James	RT	MIA	6.0	25.5	10.5	36.0
5	S.Henderson	RT	BUF	7.5	29.5	6.0	35.5
6	G.Cherilus	RT	IND	5.5	29.3	6.0	35.3
7	M.Kalil	LT	MIN	12.5	27.8	5.5	33.3
8	B.Bell	LT	CAR	9.0	22.5	9.0	31.5
8	B.Giacomini	RT	NYJ	3.5	26.5	5.0	31.5
10	M.Schwartz	RT	CLE	6.5	23.5	7.0	30.5
11	J.Staley	LT	SF	5.0	23.0	7.0	30.0
12	J.Peters	LT	PHI	6.5	24.0	4.5	28.5
13	D.Newton	RT	HOU	3.0	22.0	5.0	27.0
13	R.Okung	LT	SEA	2.5	18.0	9.0	27.0
15	W.Beatty	LT	NYG	4.0	19.8	7.0	26.8
15	J.Matthews	LT	ATL	4.0	21.0	5.8	26.8
17	J.Barksdale	RT	STL	7.5	25.5	1.0	26.5
18	A.Castonzo	LT	IND	4.0	18.0	7.5	25.5
18	D.Ferguson	LT	NYJ	4.0	20.0	5.5	25.5
20	L.Joeckel	LT	JAC	8.5	21.3	4.0	25.3

Top 20 Offensive Tackles in Snaps per Blown Block

Rk	Player	Pos	Team	Sacks	All Pass	All Run	Total	Snaps	Snaps per BB
1	L.Waddle	RT	DET	2.0	5.0	1.0	8.0	550	91.7
2	A.Whitworth	LT	CIN	0.5	7.5	4.0	12.0	1029	89.5
3	R.Reiff	LT	DET	2.5	9.0	3.0	14.5	941	78.4
4	B.Bulaga	RT	GB	3.5	10.0	2.0	15.5	926	77.2
5	Z.Strief	RT	NO	3.0	10.0	4.0	17.0	1059	75.6
6	K.Dunlap	LT	SD	2.5	14.3	0.5	17.3	1058	71.3
7	L.Vasquez	RT/RG	DEN	3.0	12.0	5.0	20.0	1120	65.9
8	R.Schraeder	RT	ATL	2.5	7.0	3.0	12.5	646	64.6
8	T.Smith	LT	DAL	3.0	12.0	4.5	19.5	1059	64.2
10	T.Williams	LT	WAS	7.0	12.0	2.0	21.0	877	62.6
11	A.Smith	RT	CIN	4.0	7.0	1.0	12.0	482	60.3
12	J.Thomas	LT	CLE	4.5	15.0	2.5	22.0	1050	60.0
13	D.Dotson	RT	TB	4.5	13.0	4.0	21.5	979	57.6
14	B.Albert	LT	MIA	2.0	5.5	4.0	11.5	543	57.2
15	R.Clady	LT	DEN	2.0	13.5	5.0	20.5	1052	56.9
16	R.Wagner	RT	BAL	1.0	9.5	8.0	18.5	971	55.5
17	D.Free	RT	DAL	2.0	10.0	3.0	15.0	699	53.8
18	C.Lucas	OT	DET	4.5	7.5	1.0	13.0	448	52.7
19	J.Bushrod	LT	CHI	3.5	16.0	1.5	21.0	921	52.6
20	D.Brown	LT	HOU	1.5	14.5	6.5	22.5	1099	52.3

Minimum: 400 snaps

Top 20 Interior Linemen, Blown Blocks

Rk	Player	Pos	Team	Sacks	All Pass	All Run	Total
1	B.Jones	LG	HOU	1.5	17.0	10.0	27.0
2	P.Omameh	RG	TB	7.5	18.0	8.0	26.0
3	M.Iupati	LG	SF	6.0	20.0	5.5	25.5
4	C.Rinehart	LG	SD	3.0	18.0	7.0	25.0
5	A.Gardner	RG	PHI	5.0	18.0	6.0	24.0
5	D.Joseph	RG	STL	4.5	17.5	6.5	24.0
5	T.Larsen	LG	ARI	3.0	20.5	3.5	24.0
8	M.Ola	LG	CHI	6.0	15.0	8.0	23.0
8	S.Satele	C	MIA	3.5	14.5	8.5	23.0
10	J.Jerry	RG	NYG	2.0	16.3	6.5	22.8
11	A.Howard	RG	OAK	5.5	18.8	3.8	22.7
12	J.R.Sweezy	RG	SEA	4.0	15.5	7.0	22.5
13	J.Mewhort	LG	IND	1.5	17.3	5.0	22.3
14	J.Harrison	C	IND	2.0	14.5	7.0	21.5
14	W.Richburg	LG	NYG	2.0	16.5	5.0	21.5
16	M.Ramirez	C	DEN	1.0	9.0	12.0	21.0
17	M.McGlynn	LG	KC	5.0	17.0	3.8	20.8
18	Z.Fulton	RG	KC	2.5	16.5	4.0	20.5
18	J.D.Walton	C	NYG	1.0	8.5	12.0	20.5
20	C.Boling	LG	CIN	2.5	17.5	2.0	19.5

Top 20 Interior Linemen in Snaps per Blown Block

Rk	Player	Pos	Team	Sacks	All Pass	All Run	Total	Snaps	Snaps per BB
1	M.Pollak	RG	CIN	0.0	0.3	1.0	1.3	442	332.3
2	W.Montgomery	C	DEN	0.5	0.5	2.5	3.5	581	193.7
3	J.Sitton	LG	GB	0.0	0.0	5.3	5.3	995	186.7
4	R.Hudson	C	KC	2.0	3.0	3.3	8.3	1007	159.1
5	G.Jackson	LG	OAK	1.0	2.0	3.3	6.3	809	151.8
6	D.DeCastro	RG	PIT	0.0	5.5	2.0	7.5	1111	148.1
7	M.Pouncey	C	PIT	1.0	6.0	1.5	8.5	1104	147.2
8	N.Mangold	C	NYJ	1.0	7.5	0.5	9.0	979	122.4
9	R.Saffold	LG	STL	0.5	5.5	2.0	8.0	916	122.1
10	J.Sullivan	C	MIN	0.0	7.0	1.0	8.0	972	121.5
11	B.Linder	RG	JAC	4.5	6.5	1.0	12.0	901	120.1
12	R.Garza	C	CHI	1.0	4.5	2.0	7.5	746	114.8
13	R.Foster	LG	PIT	1.0	6.5	2.0	9.5	963	113.3
14	C.Linsley	C	GB	1.0	4.0	5.5	10.5	1050	110.5
15	K.Zeitler	RG	CIN	0.0	3.5	3.5	7.0	736	105.1
16	J.Asamoah	RG	ATL	1.5	5.5	3.5	10.5	945	105.0
17	E.Wood	C	BUF	3.5	6.5	4.0	14.0	1059	100.9
18	Z.Martin	RG	DAL	1.0	6.0	4.5	11.5	1053	100.3
19	K.Long	RG	CHI	0.5	5.5	5.0	11.0	994	94.7
20	T.Turner	RG	CAR	0.0	3.0	4.0	7.0	660	94.3

Minimum: 400 snaps

Top 20 Non-Offensive Linemen, Blown Blocks

Rk	Player	Pos	Team	Sacks	All Pass	All Run	Total
1	J.Cumberland	TE	NYJ	3.0	6.5	10.0	16.5
2	M.Forte	RB	CHI	7.0	13.0	0.0	13.0
3	C.J.Fiedorowicz	TE	HOU	1.0	4.0	7.0	11.0
4	H.Miller	TE	PIT	1.5	5.5	5.0	10.5
5	R.Rodgers	TE	GB	2.0	3.0	7.0	10.0
6	J.Cameron	TE	CLE	2.0	3.0	6.5	9.5
6	J.Carlson	TE	ARI	1.0	4.0	5.5	9.5
6	B.Celek	TE	PHI	1.0	6.0	3.5	9.5
6	R.Ellison	TE	MIN	1.5	5.5	4.0	9.5
10	B.Pettigrew	TE	DET	1.0	3.0	6.0	9.0
10	V.Davis	TE	SF	0.0	2.0	7.0	9.0
12	L.Donnell	TE	NYG	0.0	1.5	6.5	8.0
12	A.Fasano	TE	KC	2.0	3.0	5.0	8.0
12	C.Ivory	RB	NYJ	1.0	8.0	0.0	8.0
12	G.Olsen	TE	CAR	0.0	0.0	8.0	8.0
16	G.Graham	TE	HOU	0.0	4.0	3.5	7.5
17	D.Allen	TE	IND	0.0	1.0	6.0	7.0
17	B.Cunningham	RB	STL	1.0	7.0	0.0	7.0
17	J.Dray	TE	CLE	1.0	3.0	4.0	7.0
17	C.Fleener	TE	IND	0.0	4.0	3.0	7.0
17	D.Martin	RB	TB	2.0	7.0	0.0	7.0
17	N.Paul	TE	WAS	0.0	1.0	6.0	7.0

Most Penalties, Offense

Rk	Player	Team	Pen	Yds
1	D.Dotson	TB	16	127
1	W.Colon	NYJ	14	87
3	J.Peters	PHI	12	90
3	J.Staley	SF	12	65
3	T.Williams	WAS	12	86
6	M.Kalil	MIN	11	80
6	T.Larsen	ARI	11	59
6	J.Matthews	ATL	11	75
6	G.Robinson	STL	11	95
10	D.Carr	OAK	10	65
10	A.Collins	TB	10	70
10	O.Franklin	DEN	10	75
10	J.James	MIA	10	70
10	A.Levitre	TEN	10	65
10	R.Okung	SEA	10	49
10	J.Thomas	CLE	10	45
17	11 tied with		9	

Includes declined and offsetting, but not special teams or penalties on turnover returns.

Most False Starts, Offense

Rk	Player	Team	Pen
1	W.Colon	NYJ	7
2	J.Barksdale	STL	6
2	D.J.Fluker	SD	6
2	T.Larsen	ARI	6
2	R.Okung	SEA	6
6	J.Bushrod	CHI	5
6	E.Fisher	KC	5
6	O.Franklin	DEN	5
6	B.Giacomini	NYJ	5
6	A.Levitre	TEN	5
6	J.Mills	CHI	5
6	G.Olsen	CAR	5
6	J.Peters	PHI	5
6	J.Pugh	NYG	5
6	T.Smith	DAL	5
16	16 tied with		4

Most Penalties, Defense

Rk	Player	Team	Pen	Yds
1	B.Browner	NE	15	118
1	B.Skrine	CLE	15	135
3	M.Bennett	SEA	13	79
3	B.Breeland	WAS	13	153
5	J.Hughes	BUF	12	84
5	P.Peterson	ARI	12	98
7	A.J.Bouye	HOU	11	107
7	E.Griffen	MIN	11	45
7	J.Haden	CLE	11	69
7	X.Rhodes	MIN	11	63
7	G.Toler	IND	11	53
7	S.Wright	SD	11	123
13	B.Carr	DAL	10	56
13	K.Vaccaro	NO	10	62
13	B.Wreh-Wilson	TEN	10	112
16	C.Allen	PIT	9	66
16	S.Gilmore	BUF	9	74
16	B.Maxwell	SEA	9	105
16	G.McCoy	TB	9	40
16	T.Newman	CIN	9	70
16	T.Suggs	BAL	9	45

Includes declined and offsetting, but not special teams or penalties on turnover returns.

Top 10 Kickers, Gross Kickoff Value over Average

Rk	Player	Team	Kick Pts+	Net Pts+	Kicks
1	J.Tucker	BAL	+7.3	+8.3	86
2	G.Gano	CAR	+5.8	-2.2	79
3	S.Hauschka	SEA	+4.1	+4.0	84
4	T.Morstead	NO	+4.0	-2.5	77
5	B.Cundiff	CLE	+4.0	+9.7	62
6	S.Janikowski	OAK	+4.0	-5.4	55
7	P.McAfee	IND	+3.3	+4.9	96
8	C.Catanzaro	ARI	+3.1	+2.0	75
9	J.Gay	BUF	+3.0	+7.4	80
10	M.Nugent	CIN	+2.9	+0.3	79

Min. 20 kickoffs; squibs and onside not included

Bottom 10 Kickers, Gross Kickoff Value over Average

Rk	Player	Team	Kick Pts+	Net Pts+	Kicks
1	N.Novak	SD	-15.8	-8.3	73
2	C.Santos	KC	-5.4	-3.2	77
3	S.Suisham	PIT	-4.1	-2.6	86
4	P.Dawson	SF	-3.8	+0.7	71
5	R.Gould	CHI	-3.4	+2.0	48
6	N.Folk	NYJ	-2.9	+5.3	66
7	J.Brown	NYG	-2.1	+7.0	77
8	M.Bosher	ATL	-1.8	-6.2	77
9	C.Sturgis	MIA	-1.7	-12.6	83
10	M.Crosby	GB	-1.4	-6.1	96

Min. 20 kickoffs; squibs and onside not included

Top 10 Punters, Gross Punt Value over Average

Rk	Player	Team	Punt Pts+	Net Pts+	Punts
1	S.Koch	BAL	+11.8	+17.9	60
2	J.Hekker	STL	+7.8	+11.3	81
3	K.Huber	CIN	+7.6	+12.1	73
4	S.Martin	DET	+6.8	-0.6	68
5	P.McAfee	IND	+6.2	+11.2	69
6	T.Morstead	NO	+6.1	+13.4	58
7	D.Colquitt	KC	+5.7	+11.6	71
8	M.Bosher	ATL	+5.6	+5.2	67
9	B.Kern	TEN	+5.0	+2.7	89
10	M.King	OAK	+4.2	+2.7	109

Min. 20 punts

Bottom 10 Punters, Gross Punt Value over Average

Rk	Player	Team	Punt Pts+	Net Pts+	Punts
1	M.Koenen	TB	-12.1	-0.6	79
2	D.Butler	ARI	-11.9	-8.3	81
3	T.Masthay	GB	-9.7	-9.4	51
4	P.O'Donnell	CHI	-8.3	-6.9	73
5	C.Schmidt	BUF	-7.5	+2.2	86
6	J.Locke	MIN	-6.9	+3.4	76
7	A.Lee	SF	-3.7	-8.3	73
8	B.Anger	JAC	-3.3	-13.2	96
9	J.Ryan	SEA	-2.7	-4.0	63
10	B.Colquitt	DEN	-2.5	-7.7	69

Min. 20 punts

Top 10 Kick Returners, Value over Average

Rk	Player	Team	Pts+	Returns
1	A.Jones	CIN	+9.3	27
2	J.Jones	BAL	+8.7	32
3	O.Bolden	DEN	+7.6	12
4	K.Davis	KC	+7.5	28
5	J.Huff	PHI	+6.7	14
6	C.Polk	PHI	+6.6	11
7	C.J.Spiller	BUF	+5.7	10
8	D.Thomas	KC	+3.9	13
9	M.Mariani	CHI	+2.7	21
10	C.Williams	CHI	+2.5	24

Min. eight returns

Bottom 10 Kick Returners, Value over Average

Rk	Player	Team	Pts+	Returns
1	P.Harvin	2TM	-6.5	32
2	T.Ginn	ARI	-6.2	21
3	B.Tate	CIN	-5.1	18
4	D.Manning	HOU	-4.8	12
5	G.Atkinson	OAK	-4.5	8
6	P.Richardson	SEA	-3.9	16
7	A.Roberts	WAS	-3.8	30
8	D.Archer	PIT	-3.6	9
9	T.Benjamin	CLE	-3.6	12
10	Q.Demps	NYG	-3.5	12

Min. eight returns

Top 10 Punt Returners, Value over Average

Rk	Player	Team	Pts+	Returns
1	D.Sproles	PHI	+13.8	39
2	M.Hyde	GB	+12.6	14
3	D.Thomas	KC	+9.5	34
4	D.Hester	ATL	+7.7	18
5	J.Edelman	NE	+7.6	25
6	M.Thigpen	2TM	+6.5	16
7	A.Brown	PIT	+5.6	30
8	F.Hammond	KC	+5.3	15
9	A.Jones	CIN	+5.3	22
10	T.Austin	STL	+5.1	35

Min. eight returns

Bottom 10 Punt Returners, Value over Average

Rk	Player	Team	Pts+	Returns
1	A.Sanders	JAC	-6.0	32
2	I.Burse	DEN	-5.2	29
3	J.Landry	MIA	-4.8	25
4	G.Whalen	IND	-4.6	26
5	K.Martin	HOU	-4.1	25
6	B.Cooks	NO	-4.1	10
7	J.Cribbs	IND	-3.9	19
8	P.Cox	SF	-3.7	10
9	A.Roberts	WAS	-3.7	28
10	B.Bersin	CAR	-3.5	14

Min. eight returns

Top 20 Special Teams Plays

Rk	Player	Team	Plays	Rk	Player	Team	Plays
1	J.Bethel	ARI	17	8	T.Robinson	WAS	14
2	D.Stuckey	SD	16	8	R.Shepard	TB	14
3	S.Ajirotutu	SD	15	14	A.Gachkar	SD	13
3	T.Garvin	PIT	15	14	Z.Sudfeld	NYJ	13
3	C.Reynolds	STL	15	16	J.Bademosi	CLE	12
3	M.Slater	NE	15	16	O.Bolden	DEN	12
3	V.Williams	PIT	15	16	D.Harris	DAL	12
8	C.Anderson	IND	14	16	C.Maragos	PHI	12
8	N.Bellore	NYJ	14	16	A.McClellan	BAL	12
8	K.Conner	SD	14	16	A.Sherman	KC	12
8	C.Peerman	CIN	14	16	E.Weems	ATL	12

lays = tackles + assists; does not include onside or end-half squib kicks.

Top 10 Offenses, 3-and-out per drive

Rk	Team	Pct
1	MIA	13.5%
2	GB	14.1%
3	NO	16.5%
4	DAL	16.5%
5	PIT	16.7%
6	BAL	17.0%
7	SEA	17.6%
8	PHI	18.4%
9	MIN	18.7%
10	SF	19.4%

Top 10 Defenses, 3-and-out per drive

Rk	Team	Pct
1	DEN	31.8%
2	IND	29.5%
3	NYJ	29.2%
4	DET	27.0%
5	CAR	25.1%
6	BAL	24.6%
7	BUF	24.4%
8	SEA	24.2%
9	PIT	23.7%
10	SF	23.5%

Top 10 Offenses, Yards per drive

Rk	Team	Yds/Dr
1	PIT	39.38
2	NO	38.98
3	GB	38.39
4	DAL	35.94
5	DEN	34.73
6	BAL	34.44
7	SEA	34.08
8	IND	33.89
9	ATL	33.83
10	NE	33.56

Top 10 Defenses, Yards per drive

Rk	Team	Yds/Dr
1	DEN	25.76
2	BUF	26.12
3	SEA	26.90
4	DET	27.17
5	HOU	29.09
6	IND	29.27
7	PHI	29.34
8	SF	29.44
9	OAK	29.66
10	NYJ	29.74

Bottom 10 Offenses, 3-and-out per drive

Rk	Team	Pct
23	SD	23.1%
24	HOU	24.5%
25	ARI	25.0%
26	JAC	25.9%
27	TB	26.1%
28	BUF	26.2%
29	NYJ	26.2%
30	TEN	28.2%
31	CLE	28.6%
32	OAK	36.8%

Bottom 10 Defenses, 3-and-out per drive

Rk	Team	Pct
23	NE	19.3%
24	CLE	19.0%
24	TEN	18.9%
26	GB	18.2%
27	TB	18.1%
27	MIA	17.7%
29	JAC	16.8%
30	CHI	15.6%
31	ATL	15.2%
32	NO	13.9%

Bottom 10 Offenses, Yards per drive

Rk	Team	Yds/Dr
23	HOU	29.76
24	MIN	29.06
25	NYJ	27.72
26	CLE	27.48
27	STL	26.97
28	BUF	25.96
29	TEN	25.70
30	TB	24.91
31	JAC	24.60
32	OAK	22.63

Bottom 10 Defenses, Yards per drive

Rk	Team	Yds/Dr
23	NE	32.20
24	STL	32.22
25	TEN	32.36
26	GB	32.39
27	DAL	32.45
28	TB	32.93
29	PIT	33.36
30	CHI	35.78
31	NO	36.58
32	ATL	37.70

Top 10 Offenses, avg LOS to start drive

Rk	Team	LOS
1	MIA	31.1
2	NE	30.3
3	BUF	30.2
4	SEA	30.2
5	PHI	30.0
6	DET	30.0
7	CIN	29.9
8	KC	28.8
9	DEN	28.7
10	BAL	28.6

Top 10 Defenses, avg LOS to start drive

Rk	Team	LOS
1	SEA	25.3
2	NE	25.3
3	STL	25.4
4	IND	25.4
5	NO	25.6
6	ARI	25.6
7	SF	26.0
8	CIN	26.1
9	DET	26.3
10	PHI	26.3

Top 10 Offenses, Points per drive

Rk	Team	Pts/Dr
1	GB	2.73
2	DAL	2.62
3	NE	2.49
4	DEN	2.48
5	NO	2.35
6	PIT	2.31
7	IND	2.27
8	BAL	2.20
9	SEA	2.19
10	MIA	2.11

Top 10 Defenses, Points per drive

Rk	Team	Pts/Dr
1	BUF	1.41
2	SEA	1.44
3	DET	1.52
4	HOU	1.53
5	ARI	1.60
6	STL	1.63
7	KC	1.64
8	NE	1.69
9	CLE	1.70
10	BAL	1.71

Bottom 10 Offenses, avg LOS to start drive

Rk	Team	LOS
23	ARI	26.5
24	SF	26.4
25	ATL	26.3
26	CHI	26.1
27	TEN	25.8
28	NO	25.5
29	JAC	25.3
30	PIT	25.3
31	WAS	24.8
32	OAK	24.1

Bottom 10 Defenses, avg LOS to start drive

Rk	Team	LOS
23	MIN	28.3
24	DEN	28.4
25	NYJ	28.7
26	JAC	29.3
27	TEN	29.6
28	WAS	29.7
29	MIA	29.9
30	TB	31.0
31	OAK	32.4
32	CHI	32.5

Bottom 10 Offenses, Points per drive

Rk	Team	Pts/Dr
23	BUF	1.63
24	WAS	1.62
25	STL	1.61
26	ARI	1.57
27	NYJ	1.56
28	CLE	1.47
29	TB	1.42
30	TEN	1.32
31	OAK	1.24
32	JAC	1.18

Bottom 10 Defenses, Points per drive

Rk	Team	Pts/Dr
23	MIA	2.05
24	NYJ	2.09
25	PIT	2.15
26	WAS	2.18
27	TB	2.19
28	TEN	2.24
29	OAK	2.25
30	ATL	2.30
31	NO	2.37
32	CHI	2.52

Top 10 Offenses, Better DVOA with Shotgun

Rk	Team	% Plays Shotgun	DVOA Shot	DVOA Not	Yd/Play Shot	Yd/Play Not	DVOA Dif
1	SD	77%	17.8%	-22.5%	6.2	3.5	40.4%
2	DEN	73%	29.1%	-1.5%	6.6	5.4	30.6%
3	DAL	48%	33.3%	3.7%	7.0	5.5	29.7%
4	PHI	86%	5.3%	-22.9%	6.1	4.3	28.2%
5	MIN	66%	2.9%	-24.3%	5.6	4.6	27.2%
6	BAL	24%	30.8%	4.0%	6.5	5.9	26.8%
7	HOU	50%	5.3%	-17.2%	6.3	4.3	22.5%
8	DET	56%	4.7%	-12.5%	5.9	4.7	17.2%
9	NE	47%	23.3%	6.4%	6.0	5.4	16.9%
10	GB	64%	30.0%	16.3%	6.6	6.1	13.7%

Top 10 Offenses, Better DVOA with Play-Action

Rk	Team	% PA	DVOA PA	DVOA No PA	Yd/Play PA	Yd/Play No PA	DVOA Dif
1	WAS	22%	55.1%	-23.0%	10.2	5.7	78.2%
2	SD	8%	90.3%	26.7%	9.6	6.6	63.6%
3	PHI	33%	41.3%	-2.4%	8.1	6.2	43.7%
4	OAK	21%	25.2%	-15.1%	5.0	5.1	40.3%
5	CLE	31%	32.7%	-6.9%	8.8	5.4	39.6%
6	KC	30%	39.5%	0.6%	7.7	5.2	38.9%
7	TEN	16%	25.4%	-11.4%	8.6	5.7	36.8%
8	CHI	21%	34.9%	10.7%	6.5	6.0	24.2%
9	NYG	23%	35.4%	11.3%	7.8	6.6	24.1%
10	IND	19%	38.9%	16.8%	7.9	7.1	22.1%

Bottom 10 Offenses, Better DVOA with Shotgun

Rk	Team	% Plays Shotgun	DVOA Shot	DVOA Not	Yd/Play Shot	Yd/Play Not	DVOA Dif
23	SEA	69%	18.3%	13.7%	6.3	5.6	4.7%
24	STL	48%	-8.9%	-12.8%	6.0	4.8	3.9%
25	TEN	69%	-16.7%	-15.8%	5.5	5.1	-0.9%
26	OAK	65%	-20.2%	-18.2%	4.9	4.1	-2.0%
27	CLE	41%	-11.5%	-9.5%	5.1	5.2	-2.1%
28	NYJ	73%	-12.2%	-9.1%	5.1	4.8	-3.1%
29	JAC	70%	-25.6%	-22.0%	5.0	4.1	-3.7%
30	BUF	68%	-12.7%	-8.5%	5.5	4.2	-4.1%
31	KC	57%	1.1%	9.5%	5.5	5.2	-8.4%
32	WAS	65%	-15.1%	-6.5%	5.8	5.8	-8.5%

Bottom 10 Offenses, Better DVOA with Play-Action

Rk	Team	% PA	DVOA PA	DVOA No PA	Yd/Play PA	Yd/Play No PA	DVOA Dif
23	DAL	17%	38.6%	39.1%	9.7	7.3	-0.5%
24	BAL	18%	30.3%	33.4%	8.5	6.7	-3.1%
25	DET	19%	5.2%	12.0%	6.7	6.2	-6.8%
26	DEN	23%	33.9%	45.0%	10.3	6.8	-11.2%
27	ATL	17%	15.1%	27.4%	7.4	6.8	-12.3%
28	SF	20%	-1.4%	18.7%	5.3	6.5	-20.1%
29	MIA	26%	-4.0%	27.9%	6.0	5.9	-31.8%
30	MIN	23%	-28.6%	4.9%	5.4	6.0	-33.6%
31	CIN	23%	-25.3%	16.7%	7.1	6.3	-42.1%
32	TB	11%	-55.9%	-9.1%	4.1	6.1	-46.8%

Top 10 Defenses, Better DVOA vs. Shotgun

Rk	Team	% Plays Shotgun	DVOA Shot	DVOA Not	Yd/Play Shot	Yd/Play Not	DVOA Dif
1	NE	78%	-3.5%	9.1%	5.5	5.4	-12.6%
2	MIN	69%	2.9%	7.9%	5.5	5.3	-5.0%
3	CIN	68%	-3.3%	-0.5%	5.4	5.2	-2.8%
4	TEN	65%	9.0%	11.5%	5.6	5.4	-2.5%
5	SEA	73%	-16.8%	-14.9%	4.9	4.5	-1.9%
6	KC	73%	0.9%	2.7%	5.3	4.7	-1.8%
7	CLE	67%	-2.6%	-1.5%	5.5	5.2	-1.1%
8	BUF	73%	-15.8%	-16.4%	5.0	4.8	0.6%
9	STL	73%	-4.3%	-5.5%	5.8	5.4	1.2%
10	SD	72%	4.5%	3.0%	5.7	5.5	1.5%

Top 10 Defenses, Better DVOA vs. Play-Action

Rk	Team	% PA	DVOA PA	DVOA No PA	Yd/Play PA	Yd/Play No PA	DVOA Dif
1	SF	20%	-23.4%	-1.8%	6.5	6.0	-21.6%
2	NYJ	19%	2.1%	21.2%	6.9	6.5	-19.1%
3	KC	16%	-12.3%	6.3%	5.2	5.6	-18.7%
4	TB	25%	5.0%	18.8%	7.4	6.6	-13.8%
5	CAR	20%	-6.7%	6.9%	6.4	6.3	-13.6%
6	IND	20%	-6.1%	4.6%	7.3	6.3	-10.7%
7	ATL	23%	19.6%	30.2%	8.3	7.8	-10.6%
8	PHI	19%	2.2%	12.2%	6.5	6.9	-10.0%
9	DAL	23%	6.2%	12.5%	7.2	6.8	-6.3%
10	MIN	23%	6.1%	11.6%	7.0	6.2	-5.4%

Bottom 10 Defenses, Better DVOA vs. Shotgun

Rk	Team	% Plays Shotgun	DVOA Shot	DVOA Not	Yd/Play Shot	Yd/Play Not	DVOA Dif
23	NYG	71%	4.0%	-4.4%	6.2	5.6	8.4%
24	IND	65%	0.8%	-8.4%	5.8	5.0	9.2%
25	SF	72%	-10.2%	-20.0%	5.3	4.4	9.9%
26	NO	69%	14.1%	3.1%	6.2	5.2	11.0%
27	PHI	68%	-2.8%	-14.4%	5.7	4.5	11.6%
28	NYJ	71%	4.2%	-9.7%	5.6	4.4	13.9%
29	DEN	78%	-12.8%	-28.8%	4.8	3.8	16.0%
30	OAK	74%	7.8%	-10.2%	5.8	4.1	18.0%
31	DET	78%	-14.3%	-32.7%	5.0	3.7	18.4%
32	WAS	71%	10.5%	-8.2%	6.1	5.0	18.7%

Bottom 10 Defenses, Better DVOA vs. Play-Action

Rk	Team	% PA	DVOA PA	DVOA No PA	Yd/Play PA	Yd/Play No PA	DVOA Dif
23	HOU	20%	14.6%	-9.8%	8.0	5.5	24.4%
24	NYG	27%	27.9%	2.8%	8.1	6.6	25.1%
25	CIN	21%	18.4%	-8.4%	8.2	5.8	26.8%
26	MIA	22%	28.4%	-1.0%	8.3	5.5	29.4%
27	WAS	24%	52.6%	21.8%	8.4	7.0	30.8%
28	ARI	23%	29.8%	-1.9%	8.9	6.4	31.7%
29	PIT	23%	49.0%	17.3%	9.4	6.4	31.7%
30	JAC	28%	32.4%	-0.8%	8.2	6.1	33.2%
31	STL	19%	44.1%	-0.3%	8.5	6.6	44.5%
32	TEN	22%	55.1%	9.6%	8.9	6.0	45.6%

2014 Defenses with and without Pass Pressure

Rank	Team	Plays	Pct Pressure	DVOA with Pressure	Yds with Pressure	DVOA w/o Pressure	Yds w/o Pressure	DVOA Dif	Rank
1	PHI	675	29.6%	-71.6%	3.5	43.6%	8.2	-115.2%	13
2	NYG	596	29.4%	-69.2%	4.5	43.7%	8.0	-112.9%	15
3	ARI	649	29.1%	-73.2%	3.4	38.4%	8.4	-111.6%	16
4	HOU	683	27.2%	-75.3%	3.4	21.4%	7.0	-96.7%	23
5	DEN	716	26.8%	-45.3%	4.3	8.3%	5.9	-53.5%	32
6	NYJ	600	26.7%	-65.6%	3.7	44.9%	7.7	-110.5%	18
7	BUF	644	26.4%	-98.0%	1.9	12.7%	7.0	-110.8%	17
8	STL	603	26.2%	-97.8%	3.3	47.3%	8.2	-145.2%	5
9	SF	607	26.0%	-82.2%	3.4	18.0%	7.1	-100.2%	22
10	DET	656	25.9%	-83.2%	2.3	27.0%	7.3	-110.2%	19
11	SD	589	25.8%	-69.8%	3.8	46.4%	7.6	-116.2%	12
12	WAS	590	25.8%	-84.3%	3.0	69.7%	8.9	-154.0%	3
13	SEA	567	25.4%	-69.4%	2.8	8.7%	6.7	-78.1%	27
14	GB	639	25.2%	-78.2%	2.3	30.3%	7.3	-108.4%	20
15	BAL	668	25.1%	-113.7%	1.7	42.9%	7.7	-156.5%	2
16	NO	606	25.1%	-32.0%	4.1	38.6%	8.1	-70.6%	30
17	CAR	627	25.0%	-88.6%	2.6	34.1%	7.5	-122.7%	10
18	CHI	614	24.4%	-55.7%	4.6	48.7%	8.4	-104.4%	21
19	OAK	586	24.4%	-45.0%	4.2	42.7%	7.9	-87.7%	26
20	MIA	602	24.1%	-101.1%	2.4	38.7%	7.3	-139.9%	7
21	PIT	600	24.0%	-82.7%	3.2	57.7%	8.3	-140.4%	6
22	KC	621	23.3%	-85.3%	2.0	29.3%	6.7	-114.7%	14
23	MIN	602	22.9%	-84.5%	2.5	37.8%	7.6	-122.2%	11
24	IND	608	22.7%	-70.2%	3.3	24.3%	7.5	-94.5%	24
25	NE	648	22.5%	-119.0%	1.0	38.8%	8.0	-157.8%	1
26	ATL	609	22.2%	-29.5%	6.0	44.2%	8.4	-73.7%	28
27	DAL	610	22.1%	-46.3%	3.7	26.5%	7.9	-72.9%	29
28	TB	613	21.9%	-91.5%	3.2	45.6%	7.9	-137.0%	8
29	TEN	616	20.8%	-53.0%	3.0	39.7%	7.6	-92.8%	25
30	CLE	643	20.5%	-108.7%	2.9	16.9%	6.9	-125.5%	9
31	JAC	603	20.1%	-112.4%	2.2	37.3%	7.9	-149.7%	4
32	CIN	652	19.3%	-53.4%	3.9	8.8%	6.9	-62.2%	31
NFL AVERAGE			24.6%	-76.0%	3.2	34.4%	7.6	-110.4%	

Includes scrambles and Defensive Pass Interference. Does not include aborted snaps.

Author Bios

Editor-in-Chief and NFL Statistician

Aaron Schatz is the creator of FootballOutsiders.com and the proprietary NFL statistics within *Football Outsiders Almanac*, including DVOA, DYAR, adjusted line yards, and the KUBIAK fantasy football projections. He writes regularly for ESPN.com and *ESPN the Magazine*, and he has done custom research for a number of NFL teams. *The New York Times Magazine* has referred to him as "the Bill James of football." Before creating Football Outsiders, he was a radio disc jockey and spent three years tracking search trends online as the writer and producer of the Internet column "The Lycos 50." He has a B.A. in Economics from Brown University and lives in Framingham, Massachusetts. He promises that someday Bill Belichick will retire, the Patriots will be awful, and he will write very mean and nasty things about them.

Layout and Design

Vincent Verhei has been a writer and editor for Football Outsiders since 2007. In addition to writing for *Football Outsiders Almanac 2015*, he did all layout and design on the book. During the season, he writes the "Quick Reads" column covering the best and worst players of each week according to Football Outsiders metrics. His writings have also appeared in *ESPN the Magazine* and in Maple Street Press publications, and he has done layout on a number of other books for Football Outsiders and for Prospectus Entertainment Ventures. His other night job is as a writer and podcast host for pro wrestling/MMA website Figurefouronline.com. He is a graduate of Western Washington University.

College Football Statisticians

Bill Connelly analyzes the ins and outs of college football play-by-play data in the weekly Football Outsiders column, "Varsity Numbers." He is also the College Sports Editor and Analytics Director for SB Nation, where he runs the college football blog Football Study Hall. His first book, *Study Hall: College Football, Its Stats and Its Stories*, was published in July 2013. He grew up a numbers and sports nerd in western Oklahoma, but now lives in Missouri with his wife, pets, and young daughter.

Brian Fremeau joined Football Outsiders in 2006 and is a regular contributor to ESPN Insider and *Blue & Gold Illustrated*. He spends every home football Saturday cheering for his beloved Fighting Irish in the south end zone of Notre Dame Stadium. He lives in South Bend, Indiana with his wife and two daughters, each of whom prefers HGTV over college football.

Contributors

It was a single moment that brought **Cian Fahey** to the NFL when he was 12 years old. Like many fans, it came at the behest of a family member. Unlike most fans, it came at 1am on Christmas Eve in Ireland. His uncle Dex had implored him to watch on as Brett Favre threw one of his many game-winning touchdown passes. The excitement of that moment began a journey that would stretch over the next decade and more. A journey that led him to become a New England Patriots beat writer during his college days before moving on to more in-depth analysis writing for Bleacher Report, *The Guardian*, Football Outsiders, Football Guys and Rotoworld amongst others. Cian owes his career to his grandfather, Eddie Brennan, who constantly inspires and pushes every member of his family towards their goals.

Tom Gower joined the writing staff in 2009 after serving three seasons as a game charter. He has co-written our "Scramble for the Ball" column for the past six seasons and in 2014 wrote a weekly Sunday Night Football preview column for NBC Sports. His work has also appeared on ESPN.com and *ESPN The Magazine*. He has degrees from Georgetown University and the University of Chicago, whose football programs have combined for an Orange Bowl appearance and seven Big Ten Titles but are still trying to find success after Pearl Harbor. When not practicing law in the Chicago area or writing for FO, he keeps an eye on Tennessee for the blog Total Titans.

Andrew Healy looks forward to the day when teams go for two after a fourth-quarter touchdown cuts into a 14-point deficit. A professor of economics at Loyola Marymount University, his research on voting behavior has appeared in indispensable-to-a-football-fan outlets such as the *American Political Science Review* and the *Proceedings of the National Academy of Sciences*, and has been highlighted in *The New Yorker*, *The New York Times*, and on *CBS Sunday Morning*. In addition to FO, his football writing has appeared or is forthcoming at ESPN.com, *ESPN The Magazine*, Football Perspective, and *Maxim*.

Scott Kacsmar proves that leaving thoughtful comments on the Internet can actually lead to a career. He was a frequent commenter on the Pro Football Reference blog, but when Doug Drinen asked him about the research he had on quarterback games started, he discovered you can actually make money by selling NFL data. He wrote his first article for the PFR blog in August 2009, proving that the Denver Broncos inflated John Elway's fourth-quarter comeback total and that Dan Marino was the true "Comeback King." He has created the first standardized database of fourth-quarter comebacks and game-winning drives: two statistics that are now a growing part of NFL coverage. This work touches on some of Scott's main interests: drive stats, late-game strategies and making sure those damn "clutch" quarterback narratives are built on facts. His work has appeared on various outlets, including SI.com, Bleacher Report, ESPN Insider and NFL Network. He joined Football Outsiders as assistant editor in August 2013 and will be covering his fifth NFL season in 2015. He has an Industrial Engineering degree from the University of Pittsburgh, and recommends that major for anyone interested in becoming an NFL analyst.

Rivers McCown is a freelance writer whose work has appeared on ESPN.com, Bleacher Report, USA Today, and Deadspin, among other places. He lives in Houston, Texas, and hopes to one day root for a team that has an actual quarterback.

Chad Peltier was raised to be an Ohio State fan, but four years of "Run the damn ball, Bobo!" at the University of Georgia and living in Athens have made him a Bulldawg fan as well. In addition to writing two columns on college football at Football Outsiders, Chad also contributes to the SB Nation blogs Land Grant Holy Land and Football Study Hall. He currently lives in New Haven, Connecticut, working in aerospace and defense, but misses SEC country.

Since 2009, avowed 3-cone fetishist and bow tie advocate **Christopher Price** has covered the NFL for WEEI.com, while also working as a co-host for WEEI's "NFL Sunday" and the "It Is What It Is" podcast. He's also authored three books, including *The Blueprint: How the New England Patriots Beat the System to Create the Last Great NFL Superpower*, which was named one of the five sports books of 2007 by *Sports Illustrated*. He's also written *Baseball by the Beach*, the definitive history of the Cape Cod Baseball League, as well as *New England Patriots: The Complete Illustrated History*. His work has appeared at ESPN.com, SI.com and Baseball America, as well as the *Boston Globe*, the *Washington Post*, and the *Cape Cod Times*. He lives outside of Boston with his wife and son.

This is **Mike Tanier**'s 11th *Football Outsiders Almanac* or *Almanac*-like publication. He has been with us since the days of individual kicker comments and publisher-mandated May deadlines, since before NFL Game Rewind made verifying plays or scouting an unknown player a breeze, since before social networking as we now know it, and since before any of us could ever get a press credential, let alone sometimes chew the ear of an actual player/coach/GM. Tanier has gone from *The New York Times* to Sports on Earth to NFL lead writer at Bleacher Report, another thing that didn't exist when we starting writing annuals. Tanier no longer teaches high-school math, but he still lives with his wife and two sons just one minute from the base of the Walt Whitman Bridge in South Jersey, making him a first responder whenever the Chip Signal (it's shaped like a duck in flight) shines across the night sky.

Robert Weintraub is the author of the *New York Times* bestseller *No Better Friend: One Man, One Dog, and their Extraordinary Story of Courage and Survival in WWII*, as well as *The Victory Season* and *The House That Ruth Built*. He is also a regular contributor to Sports on Earth, Grantland, Slate, *Columbia Journalism Review*, and *The New York Times*.

Sterling Xie grew up in the Division II football hotbed of West Virginia, where the Shepherd Rams' annual playoff letdowns have allowed him to sympathize with residents of Kansas City and Cincinnati. Sterling joined the Football Outsiders staff in 2015 after interning during the 2014 season, and his work has previously appeared at Advanced Football Analytics, Bleacher Report and ESPN.com. He is currently working towards his degree in English Literature at Hamilton College, which he plans on using to publish Danny Woodhead fan fiction. His last name is pronounced "Z" but he is no relation to Jay.

Acknowledgements

We want to thank all the Football Outsiders readers, all the people in the media who have helped to spread the word about our website and books, and all the people in the NFL who have shown interest in our work. A few specific acknowledgements:

• FO techmaster Steven Steinman, who is *still* working hard on the long-awaited FootballOutsiders.com back-end technical upgrade. (We swear this will not be a thing in next year's book.)
• J.J. Cooper for sack timing data.
• Mike Harris for help with the season simulation.
• Premium programmer Sean McCall, Excel macro master John Argentiero, and drive stats guru Jim Armstrong.
• FO writers who did not write for the book, including Mike Kurtz, Ben Muth, and Matt Waldman.
• Nathan Forster, creator of SackSEER and current curator of Playmaker Score.
• Jason McKinley, creator of Offensive Line Continuity Score.

• Jeremy Snyder, our incredibly prolific transcriber of old play-by-play gamebooks. (Stay tuned to FootballOutsiders.com for the unveiling of DVOA from the 1986-1988 seasons very soon.)

• Roland Beech of the Dallas Mavericks, formerly of Two-MinuteWarning.com, who came up with the original ideas behind our individual defensive stats.

• Our editors at ESPN.com and *ESPN the Magazine*, including Daniel Kaufman, Jeffrey Dooley, Scott Miller, and Chris Sprow.

• Everybody at ESPN Stats & Information, for all the charting data and for listening to us when we suggested endless revisions to all the charting data. Special props to our brothers in model-building: Ben Alamar, Brian Burke, and Jeff Bennett.

• Rory Hickey for compiling The Week in Quotes during the NFL season, The Month in Quotes in the offseason, and the Year in Quotes. for *FOA 2015*.

• Bill Simmons, for constantly promoting us on his podcast, and Peter King, for lots of promotion on The MMQB.

• Chris Hoeltge and Michael Katzenoff at the NFL, for responding to our endless questions about specific items in the official play-by-play, and for collecting old gamebooks and making them available to us.

• All the friends we've made on coaching staffs and in front offices across the National Football League, who generally don't want to be mentioned by name. You know who you are.

• Our comrades in the revolution: Doug Drinen (creator of the indispensable Pro Football Reference), Bill Barnwell (our long lost brother), Neil Paine, Robert Mays, and K.C. Joyner, plus the kids at Numberfire, the football guys from footballguys.com, and our friends at Prospectus Entertainment Ventures.

• Also, our scouting buddies, including Greg Bedard, Andy Benoit, Chris Brown, Greg Cosell, Doug Farrar, and Russ Lande.

• Joe Alread and William Schautz, who handle the special Football Outsiders cards in Madden Ultimate Team, and the other folks at EA Sports who make FO a part of the Madden universe.

• Sharon Farnell, winner of our cover art contest, who made our book so pretty to look at.

• Interns who helped prepare data over the past year or for this book specifically, including Zach Binney, Luke McKenna, Andrew Potter, Joe Treutlein, and Carl Yedor.

• All those who have volunteered their time and effort for the Football Outsiders game charting project, particularly those people who have been consistently charting for multiple seasons. Our regular charters last year included: Aimal Arsalla, Matthew Baumann, Casey Boguslaw, Michael Bonner, David Cavallaro, Kevin Clay, John DeVol, Jason Dooley, Michael Dunn, Dave DuPlantis, Robert Grebel, Ben Gundy (who also helped with proofreading for *FOA 2015*), Willy Hu, Bo Hurley, Ajit Kirpekar, Bin Lee, Aaron Lindsey, Aaron McCurrie, Seth McDonald, Nate Richards, Michael Rutter, Augie Salick, Harley Sherman, Ben St. Clair, Rob Stewart, Ben Swartz, Abe vander Bent, David Vesel, Matthew Weston, and Mark Wierichs. Weekly data collection was handled by Peter Koski.

We would also like to thank our family and friends for their support, this year even more than in past years. This year's book is late because of a family crisis, but there wouldn't even be a book this year without the incredible assistance and dedication of Mallory Brooks in helping me make it through that crisis. Thanks for everything, love. I couldn't have pulled this off without you. I hope Uncle Bill and our friends in Wellesley will forgive you for cavorting with the enemy.

— Aaron Schatz

Follow Football Outsiders on Twitter

Follow the official account announcing new Football Outsiders articles at **@fboutsiders**. You can follow other FO and *FOA 2015* writers at these Twitter addresses:

Bill Connelly: **@SBN_BillC**
Cian Fahey: **@cianaf**
Brian Fremeau: **@bcfremeau**
Tom Gower: **@ThomasGower**
Andrew Healy: **@AndHealy**
Scott Kacsmar: **@FO_ScottKacsmar**
Rivers McCown: **@RiversMcCown**
Ben Muth: **@FO_WordofMuth**
Chad Peltier: **@cgpeltier**
Christopher Price: **@CPriceNFL**
Aaron Schatz: **@FO_ASchatz**
Mike Tanier: **@MikeTanier**
Vince Verhei: **@FO_VVerhei**
Robert Weintraub: **@robwein**
Sterling Xie: **@SterlingXie**

CPSIA information can be obtained at www.ICGtesting.com
Printed in the USA
LVOW03s0857290815

452044LV00027B/780/P